edmunds.com
where smart car buyers start

USED CARS & TRUCKS

PRICES

"WHERE SMART CAR BUYERS START"

Cover photo:
'97 Ford F-150

ISBN: 0-87759-678-6
ISSN: 1523-8024

USED CARS & TRUCKS

TABLE OF CONTENTS

SPRING/SUMMER 2002   **VOL. U3601-0001**

Publisher
Peter Steinlauf
Vice President, Web Site Development
Matthew Kumin
Editor-in-Chief
Karl Brauer
Executive Director, Automotive Data
Garth Nalleweg
Director, Creative Services
Guy Schackman
Senior Editor
Chris Wardlaw
Director of Data Analysis
Jane Liu

Senior Road Test Editor
Brent Romans
Managing Editor
Bryn MacKinnon
Road Test Coordinator
Neil Chirico
Photography Editor
Scott Jacobs
Road Test Editors
Liz Kim
Edward Hellwig
John DiPietro
Consumer Advice Editor
Phil Reed
Contributing Editor
Erin Riches
Manager, Web Site Data for EDS
Charlie Schiavone

New Car Team Leader
Richard Milenkovich
New Truck Team Leader
Doug Snyder
New & Used Vehicle Data Editor
Wandi Kunene
New Vehicle Data Editors
Dianne Hassan
Ken Brown
Trevor Reed
Robert Cosetta
Hudd Giles
Valorie Gerow
Incentives Coordinator
Brian Moody
Maintenance Data Editors
Jose Luis Munoz
KJ Jones

Dan Orosco
Photo Archivist:
Letitia Poteet
Manager, Data Management
Neil Lieberman
Used Car Pricing Manager
Jeff Huang
Chief Statistician
Ray Zhou
Senior Layout & Design Artist
Dori Merifield
Layout & Design Artists
Jeff Zugale
Sara Flemming
Nadia Potiyenok

Printed in U.S.A.

INTRODUCTION

Thanks for consulting Edmunds Used Cars & Trucks Prices! You've made a wise purchase, because the values contained in this publication are the most accurate values available for the U.S. used car market. Unlike other pricing sources, who publish values based on suggested prices (in effect, starting prices for negotiation), our True Market Value^{SM} (TMV®) prices are the estimates of actual median (i.e. "average") transaction prices. The values are, in essence, what you would expect to pay or receive for your vehicle given current market conditions.

Explanation of TMV Prices

There are actually three values (trade-in, private party and dealer retail) that exist in the used vehicle market; however, most other pricing sources provide only two values. In our efforts to provide you with as much useful and accurate information as possible, Edmunds provides True Market Values for all three of these transactions.

Trade-in:

This is how much you can expect to receive from a dealer for your used vehicle as a trade-in. To determine the amount a dealer is willing to pay for your vehicle, the dealer considers how much preparation is needed to sell the vehicle (fixing what needs repaired, cleaning it inside and out), while still making a profit. Most dealers won't give a customer wholesale value (the price a dealer could expect to receive at an auction) on a trade-in. This is because the dealer must assume the customer's risk. If the trade-in has a problem, the dealer must fix it. If the car is only in fair condition, the dealer must recondition it. If the car won't pass an emission inspection, the dealer must repair it. And there is no guarantee that the car will sell on the dealer's lot. Therefore, the dealer must presume the car will be a wholesale unit, which will be sold to a wholesaler or taken to an auction house

Private Party:

This price represents how much buyers are willing to pay private sellers for similar vehicles — or how much you could expect to receive if you sell your vehicle to someone other than a dealer.

Dealer Retail:

This price represents what customers are willing to pay a used car dealer for this vehicle. This value will be higher than the Private Party price due, in part, to the inspection, reconditioning and other costs a dealer must incur before selling the vehicle.

TMV Components

Now that you understand what TMV is, you'll need to understand the components that go into making it the most accurate method for valuing a used vehicle.

Base Prices:

The base vehicle price is the value for a base vehicle with standard equipment for the specified trim level. This price represents the average national value for the vehicle, with average miles for a vehicle of its age, and in clean condition. The price does not include any vehicle-specific pricing adjustments.

Optional Equipment:

Optional equipment adds value to your vehicle. The value of each option must be added to the base vehicle value to arrive at an accurate value for the specific vehicle.

Mileage Adjustment:

A vehicle's mileage suggests the amount of wear and tear the vehicle has experienced. Another way to look at it is that mileage is a good indicator of how much of the vehicle's life has been used up. The published price is for a vehicle with normal mileage for a vehicle of its age. The appropriate amount for mileage below or above the normal range should be added to or subtracted from the vehicle's value. This can be accomplished by using the Mileage Adjustment Table at the back of this book or by using the TMV Used Vehicle Appraiser at www.usedtmv.com.

Condition Adjustment:

The condition of a vehicle — Outstanding, Clean, Average, Rough and Damaged — affects its value. These classifications generally refer to the way the vehicle had been maintained. The published price is the value of a vehicle in Clean condition. If a vehicle is not in clean condition, an adjustment to the value of the vehicle should be made by using the TMV Used Vehicle Appraiser at www.usedtmv.com .

Regional and Seasonal Adjustments:

Vehicles sell for different prices in different parts of the country, and seasonal fluctuations in price exist. The published price represents the national average value of the vehicle as of November 2001. Adjustments to the value of the vehicle should be made for regional and seasonal differences. This can be accomplished by using the TMV Used Vehicle Appraiser at www.usedtmv.com .

Color Adjustment:

Edmunds' TMV prices as determined by the TMV Used Vehicle Appraiser take into account variations in value attributable to a vehicle's color. However, no such adjustment is reflected for the values published in this book.

We believe that this pricing book is the most accurate and easy-to-understand publication available. If you have questions, comments, suggestions or complaints, please write to us at the following address:

Automotive Editors
Edmunds.com
2401 Colorado Avenue, Suite 250
Santa Monica, CA 90404

Or you can send us e-mail to manager@edmunds.com. We look forward to your feedback!

HOW TO USE THIS GUIDE

Understanding the Layout

Finding the Right Model

We've listed all makes and models in alphabetical order, from Acura to Volvo. To find the make and model you want to value, look at the title bar at the top of each page. The title bar defines each section of the book by listing the *Automobile Make* and *Model Year* covered on each page. When the proper section has been found, you can find the right model by looking at the gray shaded title bars that begin each model listing. In this gray bar, you will find the *Model Name* and *Model Year*. To distinguish cars from trucks, we've printed truck data over a gray background.

Mileage Categories

Each vehicle in this guide has been assigned to a specific mileage category, which contains other vehicles with similar characteristics. For example, Category C contains mid-sized American cars like the Ford Contour. Category E contains economy cars like the Toyota Tercel. And, Category G contains compact pickups, compact SUVs, and minivans like the Chevrolet S-10, the Nissan Pathfinder, and the Dodge Caravan. The mileage adjustment table is keyed to each vehicle by category. Sometimes, different versions of the same model may fall into different categories. In this event, versions belonging to different categories will be listed separately within the individual model listing section.

Data Presentations

The first column of data contains a *Model Description* for each individual model that has pricing data. The number of doors, trim level, drive system (if something other than two-wheel drive), and body style are described here. The next column is the baseline Trade-in TMV. The third column is the baseline Private Party TMV. And the last column is the Dealer TMV. Beneath the pricing data for each individual model you might find values for *Optional Equipment*. Conveniently located on the last page of this book is a *Mileage Adjustment Table*.

Pricing a Vehicle

Options and Packages

Below the baseline pricing data for most vehicles are lists of optional equipment that require price adjustments. If the vehicle you're valuing is equipped with any of these items, you must add the appropriate value to the baseline values. Also listed with the options are expensive option packages. For example, a BMW might be equipped with a Luxury Package that includes power leather seats, cruise control, an onboard computer, wood trim, special aluminum wheels, and special trim. Some of these items might be found separately in the equipment list, and some might not. The published package price includes the intrinsic value for those items that are not otherwise listed as options. Most private sellers will be able to tell you if a vehicle is equipped with a certain package, but don't expect a dealer to know much about a used car except the price. Do your homework!

Transmissions

Our values include the standard transmission

on that model, whether manual shift or automatic. Keep in mind that sometimes manufacturers would install a 3-speed automatic transmission as standard equipment, but would offer an upgraded 4-speed automatic transmission as an option. Newer Chevrolet Cavalier LS sedans provide an excellent example of this practice; the 3-speed automatic is standard, and the 4-speed automatic is optional. Don't assume that a listing for an optional automatic transmission means that the basic vehicle came with a stick shift.

The Mileage Table

There are five basic engine types: gasoline; diesel; supercharged gasoline; turbocharged gasoline and turbocharged diesel. Some engines appear in the optional equipment listings. Each vehicle record is listed including the standard gasoline engine. Similarly, models with standard turbocharged or supercharged engines are listed individually. The only engines contained in the optional equipment lists are optional gasoline- or diesel-powered powerplants. Make sure you find out what engine is under the hood of the vehicle you're valuing. If the vehicle you're buying or selling has an optional engine, look for the value in the optional equipment list.

Engines

Once the proper adjusted value has been determined, you must further modify the price of the vehicle using the Mileage Table on the last page of this book. Edmunds links mileage adjustments directly to each vehicle category and presents the data in a single table. The table features an average mileage range for each category and model year, and provides an exact value to be added or subtracted **per mile** over or under the average mileage range. No other value guide provides such detailed, or realistic, mileage adjustments. Because the

acceptable mileage range is based on an actual average mileage of all vehicles within a given category, an exotic car like the Acura NSX will be valued according to a substantially lower and tighter average mileage range than a mid-sized import like the Honda Accord. If the vehicle you're valuing has excessively high or low mileage, you should not add or subtract value in excess of half of the vehicle's adjusted trade-in value.

The Disclaimer

That's all there is to valuing a used car with Edmunds.com. Now you've got accurate ballpark values for trade-in value and market value. *Keep the following in mind, however. Regional price differences, seasonal price differences, seasonal demand, vehicle condition, and the economic laws of supply and demand all help determine the actual worth of a used car. The values calculated using this guide are designed to represent average values nationwide for a used car in average condition, and should be used only as a guide to set an acceptable price range for selling or purchasing. None of the values published herein are intended to represent absolute values.*

Pricing Examples

	Trade-in TMV	Private-Party TMV	Dealer TMV
1. 1996 Ford Explorer XLT 4WD			
	$6,843	**$7,867**	**$9,282**
Automatic Transmission	409	409	409
AM/FM Stereo Tape	139	139	139
Dual Power Seats	217	217	217
JBL Sound System	239	239	239
Leather Seats	271	271	271
Value before Mileage Adjustment	$8,118	$9,142	$10,557
74,500 miles (Category G)	-0	-0	-0
	---------	---------	---------
TOTAL ADJUSTED VALUE:	**$8,118**	**$9,142**	**$10,557**
2. 1993 Nissan Altima GXE			
	$2,554	**$2,978**	**$3,685**
Automatic Transmission	224	224	224
Air Conditioning	140	140	140
Value before Mileage Adjustment	$2,918	$3,342	$4,049
117,200 miles (Category D)	-316	-316	-316
	---------	---------	---------
TOTAL ADJUSTED VALUE:	**$2,602**	**$3,026**	**$3,733**
3. 1994 BMW 325i 4 Dr Sedan			
	$9,609	**$10,738**	**$12,619**
Compact Disc Changer	193	193	193
Value before Mileage Adjustment	$9,802	$10,931	$12,812
67,250© miles (Category D)	+1023	+1023	+1023
	---------	---------	---------
TOTAL ADJUSTED VALUE:	**$10,825**	**$11,954**	**$13,835**

CAR BUYING AND SELLING TIPS

Buying a Used Car

- Visually inspect the car in daylight. If buying from a dealer, request that any items that are broken or damaged be repaired. If buying from a private seller, devalue the vehicle for broken or damaged items. Signs of paint overspray may indicate a history of bodywork.

- Have the car thoroughly inspected by a mechanic. If mechanical repair is necessary, devalue the vehicle accordingly.

- Have the car looked at by a body shop technician for signs of accident repair. Inspect the title, too. If the car has been wrecked and repaired, but has a clear title, chances are good that the vehicle is still in sound condition. If the vehicle is saddled with a salvage title, you should steer clear of it. This means it has been damaged so badly that the insurance company totaled it, and an enterprising person has repaired the vehicle for sale.

- Do a VIN search to help determine if the car has a clear title. Visit our website at www.edmunds.com to run a CarFax VIN report on any used car you're considering.

- Pay for the car with a cashier's check.

- Prepare a bill of sale. The bill of sale can be written in crayon on the back of a paper towel as long as a notary public witnesses the signatures of both parties. If the owner of the car has a lien against it, the bill of sale, when properly notarized, will serve as proof of purchase until the owner's loan is paid and you receive the title.

Selling a Used Car

- Clean the vehicle thoroughly, and make sure it is in good operating condition.

- Make sure all paperwork related to the vehicle is in order, particularly the title and registration.

- Advertise, advertise, advertise in major newspapers and used car magazine classifieds. If possible, park the car in high-traffic areas with For Sale signs in the windows and flyers tucked under the wiper blade that explain why someone would want your car. However, beware of local ordinances prohibiting the display of vehicles for sale.

- Realize that Japanese cars are generally in more demand than most American and European cars on the used car market.

Trading a Used Car

- Clean the vehicle thoroughly, and make sure it is in good operating condition.

- Make sure all paperwork related to the vehicle is in order, particularly the title and registration.

- Expect the dealer to offer far less than the car is worth. Negotiate as close to Trade-in Value as possible.

- Make sure the trade-in value doesn't get lost in the purchase or lease contract. Keep your eye on the ball.

4A	4 speed automatic	GAWR	gross axle weight rating	PIO	Port Installed Option
5A	5 speed automatic	GVW	gross vehicle weight	Pkg.	package
6A	6 speed automatic			PRNDL	Park, Reverse, Neutral, Drive, Low
2dr	2 door	GVWR	gross vehicle weight rating		
4dr	4 door			RBL	raised black-letter
5M	5 speed manual	GPS	global positioning satellite	Reg.	regular
6M	6 speed manual			RH	right hand
8V	8-valve	Hbk.	hatchback	r/l	right and left
12V	12-valve	HD	heavy duty	rpm	revolutions per minute
16V	16-valve	Hp	horsepower		
24V	24-valve	HUD	heads-up display	RWD	rear-wheel drive
2WD	two-wheel drive	HVAC	heating, ventilation and air conditioning	SAE	Society of Automotive Engineers
4WD	four-wheel drive				
ABS	antilock braking system				
A/C	air conditioning	I-4	inline four	SB	shortbed
ALR	automatic locking retractor	I-5	inline five	SBR	steel-belted radial
		I-6	inline six	Sdn	sedan
Amp	ampere	ISRV	inside rearview mirror	SFI	sequential fuel injection
A/S	all-season				
ASR	automatic slip regulation	KW	kilowatt	SLA	short/long arm
		L	liter	SMPI	sequential multi-port injection
AT	automatic	LB	longbed		
Auto	automatic	lb(s).	pound(s)	SOHC	single overhead cam
AWD	all-wheel drive	LCD	liquid crystal display		
BSW	black sidewall			SPI	sequential port injection
Cass.	cassette	LED	light emitting diode		
CC	cubic centimeter	LEV	low emission vehicle	SRW	single rear wheels
CD	compact disc			Std.	standard
CFC	chloroflourocarbon	LH	left hand	SULEV	super ultra low emission vehicle
Conv.	convertible	LWB	long wheelbase		
Cpe	coupe	mm	millimeter	SUV	sport utility vehicle
Cu. Ft.	cubic foot (feet)	mpg	miles per gallon	SWB	short wheelbase
Cyl.	cylinder	mph	miles per hour	TDI	turbocharged direct injection
DOHC	dual overhead cam	MPI	multi-port injection		
		MSRP	manufacturer's suggested retail price	TMV[sm]	Edmunds.com's True Market Value[sm]
DRL	daytime running light(s)				
DRW	dual rear wheels	N/A	not available OR not applicable	TOD	torque on demand
DSC	dynamic stability control			ULEV	ultra low emission vehicle
		NC	no charge		
DVD	digital video disc	NHTSA	National Highway and Traffic Safety Administration	V6	V-type six
EDL	electronic differential lock			V8	V-type eight
				V10	V-type ten
EFI	electronic fuel injection	NLEV	National Low Emission Vehicle	V12	V-type twelve
				VR	v-rated
EPA	Environmental Protection Agency	Nm	Newton meters	VSC	vehicle skid control
		NVH	noise, vibration and harshness	VTEC	variable valve timing and lift electronic control
ETR	electronically-tuned radio				
		OD	overdrive		
Ext.	extended	OHC	overhead cam	VVT-i	variable valve timing, intelligence
ft-lbs.	foot-pounds (measurement of torque)	OHV	overhead valve		
		Opt.	option OR optional	Wgn.	wagon
		OSRV	outside rearview mirror	WOL	white outline-letter
				WS	work series
FWD	front-wheel drive	OWL	outline white-letter	WSW	white sidewall
Gal.	gallon(s)	Pass.	passenger	W/T	work truck
				X-Cab	extended cab

FORD F-150

JUSTIFIED POPULARITY

B. GRANT WHITMORE

Pickup trucks are supposed to be big and bad, conjuring images of the Wild West and Marlboro men. Pickup trucks are supposed to be no-nonsense workhorses capable of hauling, towing, pushing, pulling and plowing darn near anything a regular Joe could want. Pickup trucks are supposed to be great for off-road adventures like camping and weekend hunting trips. Pickup trucks are supposed to be practical for commuters who need reliable, comfortable transportation at an affordable price with lots of standard equipment and safety features. I threw that last one in to see if you were paying attention. Pickups are many things, but until recently have not made a very sensible argument for the around-town duties generally served by the family sedan. Over the last 5 to 10 years, however, more and more people have been choosing full-size pickups to do the job that was formerly relegated to cars like the Buick Century. Call it rugged individualism; call it the shrinking nuclear family; but please call it something, because there is a growing number of Americans who are willing to put up with the poor handling, dismal gas mileage and uncomfortable ride that is a part of the pickup truck ownership experience.

Living in Arizona gives one the opportunity to experience a wide variety of pickups; as ubiquitous as BMWs on the Santa Monica freeway, full-size pickups are a way of life in my neck of the woods. As a fan of small, quick sport sedans and coupes, I have never been thrilled with pickups. They are typically slow-turning, slow-accelerating, impossible to see around and generally annoying to those of us trying to get some place in a hurry. Oh sure, they were essential in moving me from apartment to apartment in my college days, and they are great for trips to the lake, river and mountains. They are even OK for giving drooly dogs a place to ride on trips to the groomer. But the attraction of driving a cumbersome, unwieldy, traffic-hogging pickup has always escaped me. Until about two years ago, that is.

Cars receive major makeovers every 4 to 10 years, depending on the manufacturer. Honda, for example, gives its models a four-year run before it dramatically alter their styling, equipment content and dimensions. Truck technology traditionally changes very little. Over the last 15 to 20 years, a few bells and whistles have been added to the various full-size pickups on the market, but this was a thin disguise for vehicles that were essentially the same as when I was a kid. The previous-generation Ford F-Series had a 15-year run without any major revisions. Fifteen years. Could you imagine if Ford hadn't changed the design of its Mustang since 1982? There would be mass hysteria and possibly riots! Car enthusiasts would never put up with such laziness on the part of the builders. Thankfully, Dodge upped the pickup truck ante in 1994 by dramatically redesigning its full-sized line. The new Ram sported aggressive styling, more cab space and, dare I say, interior ergonomics. Needless to say, Dodge Ram sales skyrocketed and their competitors trembled.

With the writing on the wall, Ford scurried to the design studios to update its aging offerings. After five million miles of testing and about a gazillion dollars in research, the new F-series was ready. Taking cues from the success of the Ram pickups, the 1997 F-150 looks aggressive: a formidable grille, powerful curves and standard 16-inch wheels are the order of the day. Fortunately Ford's makeover was more than skin deep. A totally redesigned interior takes a page out of the passenger-car book of ergonomics. Backlit power door and window buttons, steering wheel-mounted cruise control and an instrument control panel that has easy-to-find and -use stereo and climate controls are just a few of the things that make driving this truck easier. Supportive seats and the most headroom in its class give the F-150 a distinct advantage over competitors on long-distance trips. The exceptional seating and dashboard materials are far superior to the hose-down interior that my father's work truck has, but they still impart a feeling of durability. Regular cab models have usable storage space behind the split-fold seats that is big enough to hold the week's groceries for two or the weekend's mall purchases. All in all, the cab of this truck isn't such a bad place to spend time.

Especially if you consider the joy you will get piloting this vehicle around town. That's right, around town. Ford redesigned its full-size pickup to be as livable in the city as it is in the country. This is important since Ford projects a full 90 percent of its new truck buyers will be using the F-150 as a personal-use vehicle. In order to do that, the 1997 F-150

has increased rigidity due to a cross-truck beam and a fully boxed frame. This results in a body that doesn't flex and twist over bumps and is rattle-free over expansion joints and railroad tracks. Ford has also replaced the F-150's aging Twin I-Beam suspension with a new unequal-length control-arm suspension, giving way to improved on-road handling and better visibility due to a lower hoodline allowed by the less bulky system. Smooth, powerful acceleration sets the stage for the driving experience. Rear wheels stay planted on wet surfaces, even without a full payload. Steering is light and precise, hardly the adjectives usually associated with driving a full-size pickup. The optional antilock braking system provides sure-footed, straight stopping without much nose dive. Standard driver and passenger airbags, an industry first, have a passenger-side defeat switch that can accommodate rear-facing child seats. Side-impact protection on the 1997 F-150 already meets 1999 government standards for light trucks. We find these safety features particularly shrewd considering the number of families that are likely to be shopping for full-size pickups in the coming years. Visibility is good out of the large windows and interior noise is kept to a minimum by the inclusion of such niceties as aerodynamic sideview mirrors.

I surprised myself by preferring the V6 engine/manual transmission arrangement over the larger engine combinations. Overhead cam technology replaces the pushrod arrangement found in earlier F-150s, allowing cleaner-burning engines and a smaller displacement without sacrificing power. Horsepower figures are nearly equal for the 4.2-liter V6 and the 4.6-liter V8 but the V6 gets better gas mileage. Additionally, the V6's lower torque rating isn't readily apparent. Overall, the F-150 handles with an aplomb that is typified by midsize sedans rather than full-size trucks.

The 1997 F-150 is bigger than the model it replaces. Regular-cab shortbeds are 5.1 inches longer than their 1996 brethren; longbed models are 7.5 inches longer. SuperCab trucks are also stretched by 1.7 inches and 4.1 inches, respectively. This extended length improves the ride of the F-150 without unduly increasing the turning radius of the truck. Ford has thoughtfully installed a locking tailgate to deter theft, a growing problem with the increased popularity of these vehicles.

The full-size pickup market is in overdrive these days. Upscale pickups that were once the vehicle of choice among wealthy weekend ranchers are now finding their way into upper-class suburban neighborhoods. With this increased visibility and status, expect to see the same sort of refinement that has become the standard in the sport-utility market. In other words, expect to see more trucks that sports car-like features, styling and handling. Ford has done a great job of improving truck-friendliness without sacrificing truck-toughness; I imagine that they will continue along this track, offering better and better models more and more frequently. The days of cinder block-shaped, 15-year-old bodystyles are over. Who knows, if they keep improving at this rate, I may even want one.

NISSAN FRONTIER

Dogs May Love This Truck, But Will People?

C̲HRISTIAN W̲ARDLAW

Two years ago, we drove a nearly identical truck to the one pictured here. That 1996 Nissan Truck 4WD King Cab was painted dark red with a gray interior, just like the one in the picture. A 2.4-liter four-cylinder engine mated to a five-speed manual transmission powered it, just like the powertrain in the truck pictured. It was loaded with comfort and convenience features, as is the one in the picture. The price was right, just as the price of the truck in the picture is right. We liked it, both for its inherent value and its capable off-road demeanor. We also thought it a very attractive chunk of metal, glass and plastic. Our only complaints revolved around interior space, certain styling elements and the weak powertrain. We also like the truck in the picture, but our complaints haven't changed.

The truck in the picture, in case you're wondering, is the redesigned 1998 Nissan Frontier. You may need to squint to see the differences between this pickup and the one Nissan dealers have peddled for more than a decade, particularly if viewing the Frontier from behind. The major differences between the old truck and the new one include fresh styling inside and out, more power and torque from the standard 2.4-liter four-cylinder engine, shift-on-the-fly four-wheel drive and a 100-watt audio system that comes standard on the SE model we drove. Oh, and there's the small matter of ride comfort. The old Nissan truck rode like a buckboard around town, and a crash helmet was almost necessary when the pavement ended. The new Frontier rides as well as most popular sport-utes, though traversing drainage channels with an unloaded bed might still cause whiplash to the unprepared.

We drove the Frontier for a week of errand running. It was used to help a new staff member change residences, buy a Christmas tree, pick up new furniture and for a brief tear down a muddy road; you know, all those things trucks get used for. While none of the staff members who drove the truck cared for it right off the bat, the Frontier grew on those able to spend more time behind the wheel.

First and foremost, the Frontier has more power and torque than the old Nissan Truck. In fact, no compact truck makes as much horsepower with a four, but the Toyota Tacoma's 2.4-liter quad-pot does provide more torque. With 143 horsepower made at 5,200 rpm and 154 lb-ft of torque available at 4,000 rpm, it takes a few revs to get the Frontier launched. But once underway, the truck doesn't ever really feel underpowered. It takes minor grades easily and cruises effortlessly at speed on the Interstate. With a load in the bed and on steeper hills, the Frontier's engine would likely be taxed, but most of the time it's able to stay out of its own way. We're guessing that lighter 2WD Frontiers are actually entertaining with this motor under the hood.

The softer ride of the Frontier was a pleasant surprise, though you're not going to mistake cruising in this truck for a spin in a Lincoln Town Car. On the road, the truck absorbs most irregularities with ease. Off the pavement, the truck bounds and sways a bit, but never feels uncontrollable. Sharp bumps and severe dips taken with an empty bed still result in a skittish tail, but this is not unexpected in any pickup.

Antilock brakes come standard on all Frontiers, but our test truck exhibited a frightening degree of brake fade. We had to make a panic stop, or so we thought at first. We mashed the pedal to avoid a car that appeared to be pulling out of a strip mall into our lane. The car paused, so we let up on the brake pedal. Then the car pulled out, so we stomped on the brake pedal again. At first the brakes grabbed nicely, and then they faded away completely. The pedal felt as though the power boost to the system had been totally cut off. Once to a safe area, we tested the brakes, duplicating what we had done when the idiot shopper pulled out in front of us. Each time, the brakes faded during the second hard application. Perhaps our test truck was a pre-production unit. We'll try panic-braking in another Frontier when offered an opportunity.

The interior has been completely reworked, placing the climate and radio controls higher on the dash for ease of use. Materials inside the Frontier appear to be durable and are tastefully executed. Controls are easy to find and operate. We must take issue, however, with the seats. Not uncomfortable, they simply don't slide far enough rearward to accommodate the long-legged. Realistically, no one but extras from *Willy Wonka and the Chocolate Factory* will even attempt to climb into the rear quarters of the King Cab, and even if they did, the fold-out jump seats are totally inadequate. C'mon, design the front

chairs to slide further back already. Also, we find it almost inexcusable that Nissan didn't design a third-door option for the Frontier. The point of a King Cab is to provide interior shelter for belongings that shouldn't be exposed to the elements. With no third door, loading such belongings behind the front seats is a real pain in the butt. Furthermore, the front passenger seat doesn't return to its original position after wrestling goods into the Frontier's cab. Aggravating? You betcha. But on the plus side, there are no irritating rattles like those found inside GM's third-door compacts. When driving the Frontier, you get the impression that the truck will last a good long time.

And thanks to those huge exterior mud guards and fender flares, the paint will hold up nicely, too. We drove around on wet roads, both paved and unpaved, for a week, and the Frontier barely got dirty. Now that the blistered fenders of the old truck are history, the gray plastic appendages that kept water and dirt off our test Frontier are necessary to give this truck some character. While generally attractive, from some forward angles, the Frontier is downright ugly. Anybody see the *Seinfeld* episode where Jerry is dating a "two-face," according to George? Under certain lighting conditions, his beautiful girlfriend looks like death warmed over. The

Frontier is like Jerry's girlfriend. A stunner from most views, but look at it from the wrong perspective and, well, Mom always said if you can't say something nice...

In some ways, the 1998 Frontier is rather anachronistic. Take the emergency brake handle, for example. Located under the dash to the right of the driver's leg, setting the brake requires a yank of the handle toward the driver. To release, the driver must pull, twist and push it back into place. I believe my grandfather's 1972 Ford F-150 Explorer had the same kind of setup. But there are modern conveniences on the Frontier that weren't on the old truck. In terms of sound quality and ergonomic function, the 100-watt sound system with CD player is a huge improvement over the stereo in the 1996 pickup we drove. Also, there is a new shift-on-the-fly 4WD system that came in handy more than once. The night we went to pick up a Christmas tree, roads had iced over where puddles had formed from melting snow. Pulling out of the tree lot in 2WD, the Frontier made little headway as the rear tires spun crazily on the ice. A pull of the floor-mounted transfer case lever engaged the 4WD system, and the Frontier regained its composure instantly. When dry pavement loomed, we switched back into 2WD and continued on our merry way. Fa-la-la-la-la, la-la la-la. In the old truck, we would have had to stop the truck, get out, manually lock the front hubs and then reverse the process when the street offered traction.

Overall, the Frontier made a favorable impression. What really helped was the low price tag. A fully loaded 4WD extended cab pickup for a little more than $20,000? That's a bargain in our book. That's also why the Frontier might not seem as refined as others in this class. Frugal buyers looking for V6 power will have to wait for the 1999 Frontier, when the torquey 3.3-liter six from the Pathfinder becomes available. In the meantime, dog owners looking for cheap pick-'em-up wheels will want to investigate the Frontier. Your pooch will probably love it, and we think you'll at least like it.

1999
SUBARU LEGACY OUTBACK

Subaru's Rapidly Aging Outback Still a Staff Favorite

CHRISTIAN WARDLAW

When cash-strapped family types ask us what roomy, reliable but inexpensive SUV we recommend, we almost always respond, "Subaru Legacy Outback." The reasons are simple. This jacked-up all-wheel-drive station wagon meets the needs of most Americans most of the time. Plus, it boasts an impressive reliability record and decent crash-test scores. And though our fully loaded test example topped $27,000, going easy on the options and some shrewd negotiating should net a purchase price not much over 20 grand.

What makes the Outback special? Chutzpah, primarily. Who would have thought that by dressing a dowdy wagon in what approximates Ford's Eddie Bauer garb, lifting the suspension an inch or two, and slapping the outdoorsy Outback nameplate on the liftgate, that Subaru could not only reverse dwindling fortunes in the U.S. but also carve what has become one of the hottest niches in automotive history? Not us. Back in 1996, when the Outback was unveiled, we thought it didn't make much sense. Nor did we enjoy the Crocodile Dundee ad campaign, starring has-been Paul Hogan. Good thing we're auto writers and not product planners or advertising executives.

But time spent with the Outback proved that the formula worked, not only for us but for thousands of would-be SUV buyers who wanted the active-lifestyle look and security of foul-weather drivability but not the truck-like ride and handling mix nor the lousy fuel economy most sport-utility vehicles deliver.

Subaru loaned us this Winestone Pearl Legacy Outback Limited 30th Anniversary Edition with Dual Sunroofs. Equipped with nearly every option, our test vehicle was quite comfortable and agreeable enough to drive, but the interior is aging quicker than a ripe banana left in the sun. Controls are small and

difficult to use, and the cupholders block access to the center stack, where the climate and stereo systems are housed. Plastic interior trim looks cheap, thanks to a glossy appearance and brittle feel. Nobody will confuse the sparse fake-wood accents in the Limited with real timber. We also take extreme issue with the hard center-console cover that supposedly serves as an armrest.

The exterior of our test car was brash in the Outback tradition, with huge foglights, white-letter tires and two-tone paint. In 30th Anniversary trim, the lower body is painted Sandstone metallic rather than traditional gray. Mated to bright aluminum wheels with gold accents, this two-tone paint scheme lends a more classy appearance to the car. Equipped with dual sunroofs, our test vehicle provided rear-seat riders with an unobstructed view of the sky, but front-seat passengers contented themselves with only a tilting vent-style pane of glass. Due to the raised roofline of the Outback, a sliding sunroof for front-seat passengers is not possible.

Cargo capacity is generous, with the rear seats erect or folded. Room in the back seat is prodigious enough for 6-footers to ride in comfort, though we felt the front-seat tracks needed an inch or two more travel for optimal front-passenger positioning. With 7.3 inches of ground clearance and standard all-wheel drive, the Outback is capable of light off-roading and effortlessly dispenses with moderate snowfall.

The 2.5-liter horizontally opposed four-cylinder engine makes 165 horsepower and 162 pound-feet of torque, but peak power is available high in the rev range, meaning the Outback lacks oomph off the line. When the car is equipped with a stick shift, the driver can make better use of available power. Still, this engine is charged with moving 3,250 pounds of metal. More grunt would be appreciated.

Because of its competence in every way, we still recommend the Outback to friends looking for a roomy, reliable, inexpensive SUV that can carry the kids and the dog with confidence.

Model Description	Trade-in TMV	Private TMV	Dealer TMV	Model Description	Trade-in TMV	Private TMV	Dealer TMV

ACURA   Japan

1997 Acura TL

2001 ACURA

CL   2001

Acura's CL undergoes a major makeover to gain headway in the luxury coupe market. New from the ground up, the CL receives upgraded 3.2-liter V6 engines making up to 260 horsepower (in Type S form), a five-speed automatic transmission with sequential SportShift, and a full load of standard equipment for a bargain-basement price. A new sport-tuned Type S is worth the extra money if you value performance over ride comfort.

Category H

| 2 Dr 3.2 Type S Cpe | 22132 | 23157 | 24867 |
| 2 Dr 3.2 Cpe | 20406 | 21352 | 22928 |

OPTIONS FOR CL
Navigation System +1451

INTEGRA   2001

Carpeted floor mats are newly standard, and an emergency trunk release is added to the inside of the sedan's cargo area. Four new colors round out the changes for 2001, Integra's final year before an all-new model debuts for 2002. By the way, this is your last chance for an Integra Sedan — the new car will be offered only as a three-door hatchback.

Category E

2 Dr GS Hbk	13808	14679	16131
4 Dr GS Sdn	14168	15061	16551
2 Dr GS-R Hbk	14626	15548	17086
4 Dr GS-R Sdn	14820	15755	17313
2 Dr LS Hbk	12731	13534	14873
4 Dr LS Sdn	13253	14089	15482

| 2 Dr Type R Hbk | 16029 | 17040 | 18725 |

OPTIONS FOR INTEGRA
Automatic 4-Speed Transmission +580

MDX   2001

Acura brings a new sport-utility vehicle to the marketplace, combining great on-road performance, class-leading fuel economy and outstanding all-weather handling with seven-passenger seating and cavernous cargo capacity.

Category O

| 4 Dr Touring 4WD Wgn | 31886 | 33215 | 35429 |
| 4 Dr STD 4WD Wgn | 29878 | 31123 | 33198 |

OPTIONS FOR MDX
Navigation System +1451

NSX   2001

Acura's decade-old, aluminum-bodied, mid-engined supercar carries over for 2001 with no major changes.

Category R

| 2 Dr NSX-T Cpe | 72068 | 74259 | 77911 |
| 2 Dr STD Cpe | 69233 | 71338 | 74846 |

RL   2001

Acura decides dinging luxury car buyers for floor mats is a bad idea, and so makes them standard for 2001, leaving the DVD-based navigation system alone on the factory option list. Also new is an emergency trunk release located on the inside of the cargo area.

Category I

| 4 Dr STD Sdn | 27984 | 29347 | 31620 |

OPTIONS FOR RL
Navigation System +1451

TL   2001

Standard equipment now includes floor mats and an emergency trunk release. No other changes have been made to the hot-selling TL, now in its third model year.

Category H

| 4 Dr 3.2 Sdn | 21646 | 22649 | 24321 |

OPTIONS FOR TL
Navigation System +1451

2000 ACURA

INTEGRA   2000

The Type R is baaack, thankfully, and it arrives with two more color choices. The four-speed automatic transmission has been enhanced for better shift quality, and all Integras now have a tune-up interval of 100,000 miles.

Don't forget to refer to the Mileage Adjustment Table at the back of this book!

Model Description	Trade-in TMV	Private TMV	Dealer TMV
Category E			
2 Dr GS Hbk	12868	14067	15174
4 Dr GS Sdn	13203	14434	15570
2 Dr GS-R Hbk	13632	14902	16075
4 Dr GS-R Sdn	13813	15101	16289
2 Dr LS Hbk	11861	12967	13987
4 Dr LS Sdn	12349	13500	14562
2 Dr Type R Hbk	14944	16337	17623

OPTIONS FOR INTEGRA
Automatic 4-Speed Transmission +580
Fog Lights +127
Gold Package +182
Keyless Entry System +123

NSX   2000

For 2000 the NSX gets improvements to its six-speed manual transmission, an upgraded, perforated leather interior, and a cleaner engine that now qualifies it as a low-emission vehicle.

Category R			
2 Dr NSX-T Cpe	60768	63903	66797
2 Dr STD Cpe	58902	61940	64745

RL-SERIES   2000

A new Vehicle Stability Assist system keeps the RL pointed straight, a new navigation system offers a larger screen and more information, and the 3.5-liter V6 now meets low-emission vehicle standards.

Category I			
4 Dr STD Sdn	26679	28665	30497

OPTIONS FOR RL-SERIES
AM/FM Stereo/CD/Tape +272
Navigation System +1452

TL-SERIES   2000

The real scoop is that the 2000 TL gets a bit faster, thanks to a new five-speed sequential SportShift automatic transmission and free-flowing intake manifold. A side-airbag system becomes standard as does a dual-stage inflator for the front-passenger airbag. The optional navigation system now features a DVD database.

Category H			
4 Dr 3.2 Sdn	20399	21860	23208

OPTIONS FOR TL-SERIES
Navigation System +1452

1999 ACURA

CL-SERIES   1999

The previously optional Premium package, consisting of leather seats, is now standard.

Model Description	Trade-in TMV	Private TMV	Dealer TMV
Category H			
2 Dr 2.3 Cpe	14425	15740	17054
2 Dr 3.0 Cpe	16375	17867	19359

OPTIONS FOR CL-SERIES
Automatic 4-Speed Transmission[Std on 3.0] +470
Rear Spoiler +265

INTEGRA   1999

In a small step up-market, Acura has decided to kill the Integra's entry-level RS trim. The LS gets leather accents and 15-inch wheels, and the sporty GS-R now comes with leather seats. Type R will return in limited numbers later in the year.

Category E			
2 Dr GS Hbk	11597	12796	13995
4 Dr GS Sdn	11901	13132	14362
2 Dr GS-R Hbk	12286	13557	14827
4 Dr GS-R Sdn	12450	13738	15025
2 Dr LS Hbk	10690	11796	12901
4 Dr LS Sdn	11130	12280	13431

OPTIONS FOR INTEGRA
Alarm System +198
Automatic 4-Speed Transmission +470
Compact Disc Changer +293
Fog Lights +103
Keyless Entry System +100

NSX   1999

An Alex Zanardi Edition of the NSX is new this year, but get your orders in early: only 50 will be made for sale in North America. The special edition car features a fixed roof, lighter rear spoiler and manual steering in its quest to shed nearly 150 pounds. For flair, the Zanardi Edition adds BBS alloy wheels, a titanium shifter and softer red-stitched leather seats. And it wouldn't be a tribute to the CART champion without a stiffer suspension and lower height. Hang on for the ride.

Category R			
2 Dr STD Cpe	54140	57174	60207
2 Dr NSX-T Cpe	54919	57996	61073

RL-SERIES   1999

There are more than 300 changes to the RL this year, so we'll just touch on the important ones: the suspension has been revised for better handling and a firmer ride, brake rotors have added mass, side air bags are standard, styling is more aggressive, the Premium features have been incorporated into one trim level, and, best of all, the price has been slashed.

Category I			
4 Dr STD Sdn	24414	26271	28129

OPTIONS FOR RL-SERIES
AM/FM Stereo/CD/Tape +220

Don't forget to refer to the Mileage Adjustment Table at the back of this book!

Model Description	Trade-in TMV	Private TMV	Dealer TMV
Navigation System +939			

SLX — 1999

The SLX is carried over unchanged from a year ago.

Category O

Model Description	Trade-in TMV	Private TMV	Dealer TMV
4 Dr STD 4WD Wgn	14948	16368	17787

TL-SERIES — 1999

The TL has been redesigned for 1999, with everything just getting better. The 2.5-liter engine is gone, making way for an all-new 3.2-liter V6. The transmission has been refined, the interior design makes better use of space, and the exterior is updated with a less stodgy appearance.

Category H

Model Description	Trade-in TMV	Private TMV	Dealer TMV
4 Dr 3.2 Sdn	18106	19756	21406

OPTIONS FOR TL-SERIES

Chrome Wheels +660
Compact Disc Changer +381
Gold Package +173
Navigation System +939
Rear Spoiler +205

1998 ACURA

CL-SERIES — 1998

A new 2.3L engine replaces last year's 2.2L unit. All CL models get a revised grille and new alloy wheels.

Category H

Model Description	Trade-in TMV	Private TMV	Dealer TMV
2 Dr 2.3 Cpe	11729	12811	13982
2 Dr 2.3 Premium Cpe	12691	13861	15128
2 Dr 3.0 Cpe	13460	14701	16045
2 Dr 3.0 Premium Cpe	14037	15331	16733

OPTIONS FOR CL-SERIES

Automatic 4-Speed Transmission[Opt on 2.3, 2.3 Premium] +403
Gold Package +163
Rear Spoiler +227

INTEGRA — 1998

A slight nose job, designed for a more aerodynamic approach, is added this year. LS, GS and GS-R models get a little more comfortable with a tilt- and height-adjustable driver's seat and new alloy wheels appear on the LS and GS-R. The performance edition Type R is available again this year.

Category E

Model Description	Trade-in TMV	Private TMV	Dealer TMV
2 Dr GS Hbk	10427	11627	12926
4 Dr GS Sdn	11118	12396	13782
2 Dr GS-R Hbk	11047	12318	13695
4 Dr GS-R Sdn	11194	12482	13877
2 Dr LS Hbk	9612	10718	11916
4 Dr LS Sdn	10007	11158	12405
2 Dr RS Hbk	8799	9811	10908
2 Dr Type R Hbk	12111	13504	15013

OPTIONS FOR INTEGRA

AM/FM Stereo Tape +126
Air Conditioning[Opt on RS, Type R] +365
Alarm System +168
Aluminum/Alloy Wheels[Opt on RS] +126
Automatic 4-Speed Transmission +403
Leather Seats[Std on GS] +327
Rear Spoiler +126

NSX — 1998

No changes for 1998.

Category R

Model Description	Trade-in TMV	Private TMV	Dealer TMV
2 Dr STD Cpe	44321	47128	50169
2 Dr NSX-T Cpe	45466	48346	51465

RL-SERIES — 1998

Slight suspension enhancements provide more sporty handling without sacrificing the ride.

Category I

Model Description	Trade-in TMV	Private TMV	Dealer TMV
4 Dr STD Sdn	21455	23277	25251
4 Dr Premium Sdn	22767	24701	26795
4 Dr Special Edition Sdn	22084	23959	25991

OPTIONS FOR RL-SERIES

AM/FM Stereo/CD/Tape +188
Compact Disc Changer[Opt on STD] +277
Navigation System +805

SLX — 1998

Acura's rebadged Isuzu Trooper gets more power and torque, a trick new 4WD system and revised styling for 1998.

Category O

Model Description	Trade-in TMV	Private TMV	Dealer TMV
4 Dr STD 4WD Wgn	12713	14082	15566

TL-SERIES — 1998

The premium level is gone, but the TL-Series gets more standard equipment.

Category H

Model Description	Trade-in TMV	Private TMV	Dealer TMV
4 Dr 2.5 Sdn	14880	16252	17738
4 Dr 3.2 Sdn	17185	18769	20485

OPTIONS FOR TL-SERIES

Rear Spoiler +176

1997 ACURA

CL-SERIES — 1997

Introduced as a 1997 model, the CL is supposed to compete in the growing personal coupe segment. Like many Acura products, the CL is based on a Honda

ACURA 97-96

Model Description	Trade-in TMV	Private TMV	Dealer TMV	Model Description	Trade-in TMV	Private TMV	Dealer TMV

platform, in this case the Honda Accord. The CL's sights are aimed squarely at BMW's 3-Series coupes.

Category H

2 Dr 2.2 Cpe	9275	10235	11408
2 Dr 2.2 Premium Cpe	10017	11053	12320
2 Dr 3.0 Cpe	10945	12077	13461
2 Dr 3.0 Premium Cpe	11502	12692	14146

OPTIONS FOR CL-SERIES

AM/FM Stereo/CD/Tape +131
Automatic 4-Speed Transmission[Opt on 2.2CL] +350
Rear Spoiler +197

INTEGRA   1997

No major changes to what may be the last Acura Integra. The good news is that prices for Special Edition (now called GS), LS and RS models remain the same as last year.

Category E

2 Dr GS Hbk	9477	10619	12015
4 Dr GS Sdn	10066	11279	12762
2 Dr GS-R Hbk	9913	11107	12567
4 Dr GS-R Sdn	10174	11400	12898
2 Dr LS Hbk	8736	9788	11075
4 Dr LS Sdn	9095	10191	11530
2 Dr RS Hbk	7881	8830	9991
2 Dr Type R Hbk	10017	11225	12700

OPTIONS FOR INTEGRA

AM/FM Stereo Tape[Std on LS] +109
AM/FM Stereo/CD/Tape +165
Air Conditioning[Opt on RS, Type R] +317
Alarm System +147
Aluminum/Alloy Wheels[Opt on LS] +109
Automatic 4-Speed Transmission +350
Leather Seats[Std on GS] +285
Rear Spoiler +109

NSX   1997

The six-speed NSX comes to us this year with a larger, 3.2-liter V6 engine that makes 290- ponies. Automatic NSXs continue with the 3.0-liter, 252-horse V6.

Category R

2 Dr STD Cpe	36841	39492	42733
2 Dr NSX-T Cpe	38052	40791	44138

RL-SERIES   1997

No changes for the 1997 3.5RL.

Category I

4 Dr STD Sdn	17156	18819	20851
4 Dr Premium Sdn	17993	19737	21868

OPTIONS FOR RL-SERIES

AM/FM Stereo/CD/Tape +165
Alarm System +109
Compact Disc Changer[Opt on STD] +241

Navigation System +700

SLX   1997

No changes to Acura's upscale Isuzu Trooper twin.

Category O

4 Dr STD 4WD Wgn	10524	11748	13244
4 Dr Premium 4WD Wgn	11501	12839	14474

TL-SERIES   1997

The TL is unchanged for 1997.

Category H

4 Dr 2.5 Sdn	11567	12764	14227
4 Dr 3.2 Sdn	13678	15093	16823
4 Dr 2.5 Premium Sdn	12826	14153	15775
4 Dr 3.2 Premium Sdn	15220	16794	18719

1996 ACURA

INTEGRA   1996

All Integras get new wheel cover and alloy wheel designs this year, as well as green tinted glass. LS models receive body-colored moldings. Three new colors can be applied to the 1996 Integra: pearls in red, green or black.

Category E

2 Dr GS-R Hbk	8786	9899	11436
4 Dr GS-R Sdn	8909	10038	11596
2 Dr LS Hbk	7712	8689	10038
4 Dr LS Sdn	8031	9048	10453
2 Dr RS Hbk	6745	7599	8779
4 Dr RS Sdn	7055	7949	9183
2 Dr Special Edition Hbk			
	8583	9670	11171
4 Dr Special Edition Sdn			
	8809	9924	11465

OPTIONS FOR INTEGRA

AM/FM Compact Disc Player +137
AM/FM Stereo/CD/Tape +158
Air Conditioning[Opt on RS] +304
Alarm System +141
Aluminum/Alloy Wheels[Opt on LS] +105
Automatic 4-Speed Transmission +336
Compact Disc Changer +210
Leather Seats[Opt on GS-R] +273

NSX   1996

The hardtop NSX is reintroduced to the Acura lineup.

Category R

2 Dr STD Cpe	35082	37662	41226
2 Dr NSX-T Cpe	36290	38960	42646

OPTIONS FOR NSX

Model Description	Trade-in TMV	Private TMV	Dealer TMV	Model Description	Trade-in TMV	Private TMV	Dealer TMV

Automatic 4-Speed Transmission +1286

RL-SERIES 1996

The replacement for the Legend arrives wearing Acura's new alphanumeric naming system: the 3.5 RL. The 3.5 refers to the Acura's engine size. Detractors claim that the RL stands for little more than "Revised Legend." While the 3.5 RL is definitely luxurious, we think that many will miss the Legend's sporty feel. The front wheels of the 3.5 RL are powered by a torquey V6 engine mated to an electronic four-speed automatic transmission. Other changes include 101 ways to isolate bumps, vibrations and road noise. Acura's new flagship promises to be about as noisy as a sensory-deprivation chamber.

Category I

4 Dr 3.5 Sdn	14596	15976	17881
4 Dr 3.5 Premium Sdn	14929	16340	18288

OPTIONS FOR RL-SERIES
AM/FM Compact Disc Player +137
Compact Disc Changer[Opt on 3.5] +231
Navigation System +672

SLX 1996

In typical Acura form, the SLX is one of the first luxury-badged sport-utes to be released in this country. Based on the successful Isuzu Trooper, the SLX is very similar to its twin.

Category O

4 Dr STD 4WD Wgn	7718	8694	10041

OPTIONS FOR SLX
Dual Power Seats +227
Leather Seats +416
Limited Slip Differential +137
Power Moonroof +462
Premium Package +840

TL-SERIES 1996

Vigor replacement designed to do battle with new Infiniti I30 and the Lexus ES300 in the near-luxury segment. Cleanly styled with room for four, the new TL-Series comes with either a 2.5-liter, inline five- cylinder, or a smooth, 3.2-liter V6.

Category H

4 Dr 2.5 Sdn	9909	10903	12275
4 Dr 2.5 Premium Sdn	10864	11953	13457
4 Dr 3.2 Sdn	11283	12414	13976
4 Dr 3.2 Premium Sdn	12578	13839	15581

OPTIONS FOR TL-SERIES
Compact Disc Changer +273
Gold Package +124
Rear Spoiler +148

1995 ACURA

INTEGRA 1995

A Special Edition model debuts, sporting leather interior, spoiler and larger tires. All LS models receive a sunroof.

Category E

2 Dr GS-R Hbk	7528	8453	9995
4 Dr GS-R Sdn	7647	8587	10153
2 Dr LS Hbk	6726	7553	8931
4 Dr LS Sdn	7016	7879	9316
2 Dr RS Hbk	5756	6463	7642
4 Dr RS Sdn	6030	6771	8006
2 Dr Special Edition Hbk			
	7361	8265	9773
4 Dr Special Edition Sdn			
	7560	8489	10038

OPTIONS FOR INTEGRA
AM/FM Compact Disc Player +117
AM/FM Stereo/CD/Tape +136
Air Conditioning[Opt on RS] +261
Alarm System +121
Aluminum/Alloy Wheels[Opt on LS,RS] +90
Automatic 4-Speed Transmission +289
Leather Seats[Opt on GS-R] +234
Rear Spoiler +90

LEGEND 1995

Last year for the Acura flagship, the 1996 model will bear Acura's new alphanumeric nomenclature. No changes for this year's model.

Category H

4 Dr GS Sdn	12007	13180	15134
2 Dr L Cpe	10251	11252	12921
4 Dr L Sdn	9590	10526	12087
2 Dr LS Cpe	12930	14193	16297
4 Dr LS Sdn	10808	11864	13623
4 Dr SE Sdn	10646	11685	13418

OPTIONS FOR LEGEND
Automatic 4-Speed Transmission[Opt on GS,L,Cpe] +289
Compact Disc Changer[Opt on L] +217
Gold Package +103
Leather Seats[Opt on L Sdn] +307

NSX 1995

Acura finally offers an open top version of the NSX, called the NSX-T. The "T" stands for targa (removeable) top. Other than the pop-top, the NSX-T is identical to the standard NSX.

Category R

2 Dr NSX-T Cpe	31304	33620	37479

OPTIONS FOR NSX

Model Description	Trade-in TMV	Private TMV	Dealer TMV
AM/FM Stereo/CD/Tape +160			
Automatic 4-Speed Transmission +1052			

TL-SERIES 1995

Category H

Model Description	Trade-in TMV	Private TMV	Dealer TMV
4 Dr 2.5 Sdn	7776	8535	9801
4 Dr 2.5 Premium Sdn	8861	9726	11168

OPTIONS FOR TL-SERIES
Gold Package +107
Rear Spoiler +127

1994 ACURA

INTEGRA 1994

Redesigned for 1994, the Integra sports a distinctive four-headlight front end. All models receive four-wheel disc brakes to aid stopping; LS and GS-R models get antilock brakes. GS-Rs get a 10-horsepower boost over last year to improve performance. Dual airbags finally replace the annoying motorized seat belts as the passive restraint system on the Integra.

Category E

Model Description	Trade-in TMV	Private TMV	Dealer TMV
2 Dr GS-R Hbk	5908	6814	8325
4 Dr GS-R Sdn	6416	7400	9041
2 Dr LS Hbk	5266	6074	7421
4 Dr LS Sdn	5207	6006	7338
2 Dr RS Hbk	4486	5174	6321
4 Dr RS Sdn	4662	5377	6569

OPTIONS FOR INTEGRA
AM/FM Stereo/CD/Tape +122
Air Conditioning[Opt on RS] +235
Alarm System +109
Aluminum/Alloy Wheels +81
Automatic 4-Speed Transmission +260
Compact Disc Changer +162
Leather Seats +211
Rear Spoiler +81

LEGEND 1994

The base Legend is dropped from the lineup and a GS sedan is added. The new sedan offers the same 230-horsepower engine found in the coupe as well as traction control and a sport-tuned suspension. A new grille and bumpers find their way to all Legends and the LS coupe gets a new chin-spoiler. An automatically tilting steering wheel raises as soon as the key is removed from the ignition. Further improvements include a steering wheel position memory that is incorporated into the seat memory feature.

Category H

Model Description	Trade-in TMV	Private TMV	Dealer TMV
4 Dr GS Sdn	10098	11260	13198
2 Dr L Cpe	9924	11067	12971
4 Dr L Sdn	8397	9364	10975
2 Dr LS Cpe	10459	11663	13670
4 Dr LS Sdn	10021	11174	13097

OPTIONS FOR LEGEND
AM/FM Stereo/CD/Tape +122
Automatic 4-Speed Transmission[Opt on GS,L,Cpe] +260
Compact Disc Changer +195
Leather Seats[Std on GS,LS,Cpe] +276

NSX 1994

Still no changes for the four-year-old NSX.

Category R

Model Description	Trade-in TMV	Private TMV	Dealer TMV
2 Dr STD Cpe	27839	30137	33967

OPTIONS FOR NSX
Automatic 4-Speed Transmission +947

VIGOR 1994

Dual airbags are now standard on all Vigors. Burled walnut trim replaces the Zebrano wood trim and GS models get a standard CD player. This is the final year for the Vigor.

Category H

Model Description	Trade-in TMV	Private TMV	Dealer TMV
4 Dr GS Sdn	7562	8433	9884
4 Dr LS Sdn	6722	7496	8786

OPTIONS FOR VIGOR
AM/FM Stereo/CD/Tape[Opt on GS] +122
Automatic 4-Speed Transmission +260

1993 ACURA

INTEGRA 1993

An LS Special model is introduced to the Integra line-up. Standard leather upholstery, rear spoiler and bigger tires make this midlevel Integra attractive to luxury-oriented buyers. An improved warranty boosts coverage to four years/45,000 miles.

Category E

Model Description	Trade-in TMV	Private TMV	Dealer TMV
2 Dr GS Hbk	4266	4969	6141
2 Dr GS Sdn	4401	5126	6335
2 Dr GS-R Hbk	4575	5329	6586
2 Dr LS Hbk	3734	4349	5375
4 Dr LS Sdn	3919	4565	5641
2 Dr LS Special Hbk	4102	4778	5905
2 Dr RS Hbk	3266	3805	4702
4 Dr RS Sdn	3495	4071	5031

OPTIONS FOR INTEGRA
AM/FM Stereo/CD/Tape +111
Air Conditioning +213
Alarm System +99
Automatic 4-Speed Transmission +236
Compact Disc Changer +147

Don't forget to refer to the Mileage Adjustment Table at the back of this book!

Model Description	Trade-in TMV	Private TMV	Dealer TMV	Model Description	Trade-in TMV	Private TMV	Dealer TMV
				2 Dr GS-R Hbk	4041	4769	5982
				2 Dr LS Hbk	3283	3874	4860
				4 Dr LS Sdn	3448	4070	5105
				2 Dr RS Hbk	2861	3377	4236
				4 Dr RS Sdn	3066	3618	4539

Leather Seats[Opt on GS] +192

LEGEND   1993

Thirty more horsepower and a six-speed manual transmission make the Legend coupe a viable luxury-performance contender. A passenger airbag is now standard on the base Legend. Upgraded stereos are standard on the L and LS models. Warranty coverage is extended to four years/45,000 miles.

Category H

	Trade-in	Private	Dealer
4 Dr STD Sdn	7170	8147	9776
2 Dr L Cpe	7767	8826	10591
4 Dr L Sdn	7236	8223	9867
2 Dr LS Cpe	8535	9699	11638
4 Dr LS Sdn	8646	9825	11789

OPTIONS FOR LEGEND
AM/FM Compact Disc Player[Opt on LS Sdn] +95
AM/FM Stereo/CD/Tape +111
Automatic 4-Speed Transmission +236
Compact Disc Changer +177
Dual Power Seats[Opt on L Sdn] +177
Leather Seats[Opt on L] +251

NSX   1993

A passenger airbag is introduced this year, as is a cupholder for the center console. Warranty coverage is improved from three years/36,000 miles to four years/45,000 miles.

Category R

	Trade-in	Private	Dealer
2 Dr STD Cpe	23536	25715	29347

OPTIONS FOR NSX
Automatic 4-Speed Transmission +860

VIGOR   1993

A passenger airbag debuts on the up-level GS Vigor. Restyled front grille and sound insulation mark the other changes to this car. Warranty coverage increases to four years/45,000 miles.

Category H

	Trade-in	Private	Dealer
4 Dr GS Sdn	6264	7118	8541
4 Dr LS Sdn	5461	6205	7446

OPTIONS FOR VIGOR
Automatic 4-Speed Transmission +236

1992 ACURA

INTEGRA   1992

A minor facelift and more horsepower are the only changes for the '92 Integra. A GS-R performance model is introduced with a 160 horsepower VTEC engine.

Category E

	Trade-in	Private	Dealer
2 Dr GS Hbk	3763	4441	5571
4 Dr GS Sdn	3883	4583	5749

OPTIONS FOR INTEGRA
AM/FM Stereo/CD/Tape +101
Air Conditioning +195
Automatic 4-Speed Transmission +217
Leather Seats +175

LEGEND   1992

A passenger airbag joins the standard equipment list on LS models. Cupholders are finally available to front-seat passengers. LS models are now available with heated front seats.

Category H

	Trade-in	Private	Dealer
4 Dr STD Sdn	5796	6681	8155
2 Dr L Cpe	7303	8417	10275
4 Dr L Sdn	6286	7246	8845
2 Dr LS Cpe	7814	9006	10994
4 Dr LS Sdn	7568	8723	10648

OPTIONS FOR LEGEND
Automatic 4-Speed Transmission +217
Compact Disc Changer +162
Gold Package +77
Leather Seats[Opt on L] +229

NSX   1992

No changes for the sweetest looking car since the Ferrari 308.

Category R

	Trade-in	Private	Dealer
2 Dr STD Cpe	19900	22174	25963

OPTIONS FOR NSX
Automatic 4-Speed Transmission +788

VIGOR   1992

The Vigor is introduced to broaden Acura's market. It is a midsized near-luxury sedan based on the Honda Accord. Offered in two trim levels, the Vigor can be had with an automatic or manual transmission. Power comes via an inline five-cylinder engine. Antilock brakes, power everything and a security system are standard on the Vigor.

Category H

	Trade-in	Private	Dealer
4 Dr GS Sdn	4669	5381	6569
4 Dr LS Sdn	4202	4843	5912

OPTIONS FOR VIGOR
Automatic 4-Speed Transmission +217

Don't forget to refer to the Mileage Adjustment Table at the back of this book!

Model Description	Trade-in TMV	Private TMV	Dealer TMV	Model Description	Trade-in TMV	Private TMV	Dealer TMV

AUDI 01

AUDI

Germany

1997 Audi A8

2001 AUDI

A4 — 2001

The entire Audi lineup receives a new 4-year/50,000-mile limited warranty and no-charge scheduled maintenance, a 12-year limited warranty against corrosion perforation, and 24-hour Roadside Assistance for 4 years. All A4s are now equipped with head protection airbags, have lengthier oil change intervals, and an optional Electronic Stability Program (ESP). The 1.8T engine gets a horsepower boost from 150 to a racy 170 and meets ULEV standards.

Category H

Model Description	Trade-in TMV	Private TMV	Dealer TMV
4 Dr Avant Quattro Turbo AWD Wgn			
	21316	22458	24361
4 Dr Quattro 1.8T AWD Sdn			
	20913	22033	23900
4 Dr STD 1.8T Sdn	18375	19359	21000
4 Dr Avant Quattro 2.8 AWD Wgn			
	24500	25813	28000
4 Dr Quattro 2.8 AWD Sdn			
	23625	24891	27000
4 Dr STD 2.8 Sdn	22313	23508	25500

OPTIONS FOR A4
Automatic 5-Speed Transmission[Std on 2.8 STD] +772
Automatic Stability Control +386
Bose Sound System +456
Compact Disc Changer +386
Heated Front Seats +183
Leather Seats +926
Metallic Paint +316
Navigation System +898
Power Moonroof +666
Ski Sack +167

Sport Seats +351
Sport Suspension +300
Sport Wheels +175
Xenon Headlamps +351

A6 — 2001

All 2001 Audis receive a new 4-year/50,000-mile limited warranty and no-charge scheduled maintenance, a 12-year limited warranty against corrosion perforation and 24-hour Roadside Assistance for four years. All A6s are now equipped with the high-tech Immobilizer III security system, side-curtain airbags, a 12-millimeter increase in the headrest height adjustment and an optional multifunction steering wheel.

Category I

Model Description	Trade-in TMV	Private TMV	Dealer TMV
4 Dr Quattro 2.7 Turbo AWD Sdn			
	30555	32222	35000
4 Dr 2.8 Quattro AWD Sdn			
	27063	28539	31000
4 Dr Avant Quattro 2.8 AWD Wgn			
	27936	29460	32000
4 Dr STD 2.8 Sdn	24881	26238	28500
4 Dr Quattro 4.2 AWD Sdn			
	35793	37746	41000

OPTIONS FOR A6
Automatic Stability Control[Opt on 2.8] +386
Compact Disc Changer +386
Forged Alloy Wheels +701
Heated Seats +233
Leather Seats[Std on 4.2 Quattro] +1087
Navigation System +898
Park Distance Control +290
Pearlescent White Paint +842
Power Moonroof[Std on 4.2 Quattro] +666
Rear Side Air Bags +246
Ski Sack[Std on 4.2 Quattro,Avant] +167
Sport Seats +333
Sport Suspension +300
Third Seat +526
Xenon Headlamps +333

A8 — 2001

The Electronic Stabilization Program (ESP) now comes standard, as does a multifunctional steering wheel with audio, telephone and Tiptronic controls. Audi adds an oil level sensor to the A8 and an Office Package consisting of an electrically folding desk and minibar/cold storage for the rear seat is added to the options list.

Category I

Model Description	Trade-in TMV	Private TMV	Dealer TMV
4 Dr L Quattro AWD Sdn			
	46505	49042	53270
4 Dr Quattro AWD Sdn	46269	48793	53000

Don't forget to refer to the Mileage Adjustment Table at the back of this book!

AUDI 01-00

OPTIONS FOR A8

Alcantara & Leather Package +2455
Forged Alloy Wheels +701
Heated Seats[Opt on Quattro] +316
Navigation System[Std on L Quattro] +898
Park Distance Control +491
Pearlescent White Paint +842
Power Sunroof[Std on L Quattro] +596
Ski Sack +167
Xenon Headlamps +333

ALLROAD QUATTRO   2001

Based on the A6 platform, the height-adjustable allroad debuts this year to fill a slot left in Audi's lineup by the lack of an SUV. This luxury-station-wagon-turned-SUV is powered by the A6's 250-horsepower 2.7-liter V6 engine and features Audi's legendary quattro all-wheel-drive system. Audi blends these features in a distinctive vehicle that can handle a wide range of transportation needs.

Category I

Model	Trade-in	Private	Dealer
4 Dr STD AWD Wgn	33611	35444	38500

OPTIONS FOR ALLROAD QUATTRO

Automatic 5-Speed Transmission +701
Compact Disc Changer +386
Heated Seats +316
Navigation System +898
Park Distance Control +290
Power Moonroof +701
Rear Side Air Bags +246
Solar Sun Roof +1192
Steering Wheel Radio Controls +140
Third Seat +526
Xenon Headlamps +333

S4   2001

The Electronic Stabilization Program is made standard on the S4 Sedan. The S4 Avant debuts for 2001, allowing for more cargo space and family-hauling capabilities. Casablanca White is made available as an exterior color, as are aluminum mirror housings in combination with the Pearl Napa/Alcantara sets and aluminum trim. A new four-year warranty concept is introduced this year.

Category F

Model	Trade-in	Private	Dealer
4 Dr Avant Quattro Turbo AWD Wgn			
	32746	34342	37001
4 Dr Quattro Turbo AWD Sdn			
	32321	33896	36521

OPTIONS FOR S4

Alcantara & Leather Package +316
Bose Sound System +456
Compact Disc Changer +386

Heated Front Seats +167
Navigation System +898
Pearlescent White Paint +842
Power Moonroof +666
Ski Sack +167

S8   2001

The S8 is Audi's new high-performance version of the flagship A8. It's armed with more horsepower, a stiffer suspension and more powerful brakes. As with other 2001 A8s, the 2001 S8 has the Electronic Stabilization Program (ESP) and the new multifunctional steering wheel as standard equipment.

Category I

Model	Trade-in	Private	Dealer
4 Dr Quattro AWD Sdn	58055	61222	66500

OPTIONS FOR S8

Alcantara & Leather Package +2455
Navigation System +898
Park Distance Control +536
Pearlescent White Paint +842
Power Sunroof +596
Ski Sack +167

TT   2001

For 2001 Audi introduces the TT Roadster, which retains the same interior and chassis as the coupe. Makes sense, as the coupe was designed with the roadster version in mind. There's also a 225-horsepower quattro version for both the coupe and convertible. The entire Audi lineup receives a new 4-year/50,000-mile limited warranty and no-charge scheduled maintenance, a 12-year limited warranty against corrosion perforation and 24-hour Roadside Assistance for 4 years.

Category F

Model	Trade-in	Private	Dealer
2 Dr Quattro Turbo AWD Conv			
	29674	31120	33530
2 Dr Quattro Turbo AWD Cpe			
	26993	28308	30500
2 Dr STD Turbo Conv	27141	28464	30668
2 Dr STD Turbo Cpe	25665	26916	29000

OPTIONS FOR TT

6-Speed Transmission +631
Bose Sound System +433
Compact Disc Changer +367
Heated Front Seats +167
Navigation System +898
Power Convertible Top +561
Xenon Headlamps +281

2000 AUDI

A4   2000

All A4 models receive minor updates to the interior,

Don't forget to refer to the Mileage Adjustment Table at the back of this book!

AUDI 00

Model Description	Trade-in TMV	Private TMV	Dealer TMV	Model Description	Trade-in TMV	Private TMV	Dealer TMV

exterior and chassis. The front styling has been changed with new headlights, a new grille, new door handles, and new mirror housings. Inside, there's a revised instrument cluster and center console, along with other minor interior changes. The rear seats have been modified to improve comfort. There are now optional head airbags and xenon headlights. The chassis has been reworked for improved ride comfort and responsiveness.

Category H

Model Description	Trade-in TMV	Private TMV	Dealer TMV
4 Dr Avant Quattro 1.8T AWD Wgn			
	18566	20092	21500
4 Dr Avant Quattro 2.8 AWD Wgn			
	20293	21961	23500
4 Dr STD 1.8T Sdn	15354	16615	17780
4 Dr STD 2.8 Sdn	19094	20663	22111
4 Dr Quattro 1.8T AWD Sdn			
	18048	19531	20900
4 Dr Quattro 2.8 AWD Sdn			
	19492	21093	22572

OPTIONS FOR A4

Auto-Manual Transmission +717
Automatic Dimming Mirror +100
Bose Sound System +433
Compact Disc Changer +367
Head Protection Air Bag +200
Heated Front Seats +183
Leather Seats +730
Navigation System +853
Power Moonroof +666
Ski Sack[Std on Avant Quattro] +167
Special Factory Paint +316
Spoke Wheels +233
Sport Seats +333
Sport Suspension +300
Steering Wheel Radio Controls +100
Xenon Headlamps +333

A6　　　　2000

There are two new models joining the A6 2.8 and A6 2.8 Avant. The first is the A6 2.7T powered by a turbocharged V6 engine. The second model is the A6 4.2 powered by a powerful V8.

Category I

Model Description	Trade-in TMV	Private TMV	Dealer TMV
4 Dr Quattro 2.7T AWD Sdn			
	28314	30646	32800
4 Dr Quattro 4.2 AWD Sdn			
	31853	34477	36900
4 Dr Avant 2.8 AWD Wgn			
	25033	27096	29000
4 Dr STD 2.8 Sdn	22444	24293	26000
4 Dr 2.8 Quattro AWD Sdn			
	24602	26629	28500

OPTIONS FOR A6

Automatic Dimming Mirror[Std on 4.2 Quattro] +123
Bose Sound System[Std on 4.2 Quattro] +440
Compact Disc Changer +383
Head Protection Air Bag[Std on 4.2 Quattro] +200
Heated Seats +233
Leather Seats[Std on 4.2 Quattro] +833
Metallic Paint +650
Navigation System +853
Power Moonroof[Std on 4.2 Quattro] +666
Rear Side Air Bags +133
Ski Sack[Std on 4.2 Quattro, Avant] +167
Spoke Wheels +500
Sport Seats +333
Sport Suspension +300
Third Seat +466
Warm Weather Package +533
Xenon Headlamps +333

A8　　　　2000

Updated styling in the form of a revised grille, enlarged headlights, added chrome and aluminum trim and reshaped bumpers provides a subtle new look. Inside, new interior surfaces and standard Valcona leather intensify an already richly appointed cabin. Revised switchgear makes it easier to pilot the A8, and a new navigation system is available. A new 4.2-liter, 40-valve V8 resides under the hood, and aluminum suspension components reduce unsprung weight and enhance handling. A long wheelbase version (A8L) is now available for increased comfort of rear passengers, and comes standard with an electronic stability control system and GPS.

Category I

Model Description	Trade-in TMV	Private TMV	Dealer TMV
4 Dr L Quattro AWD Sdn			
	41434	44849	48000
4 Dr Quattro AWD Sdn	38413	41578	44500

OPTIONS FOR A8

10-Spoke Polishied Wheels[Opt on L Quattro] +666
Alcantara & Leather Package +2216
Heated Seats[Opt on Quattro] +233
Navigation System +853
Polished Alloy Wheels +666
Premium Comfort Package +1000
Ski Sack +167
Solar Sun Roof +666
Warm Weather Package +631
Xenon Headlamps +333

S4　　　　2000

The Audi S4 is a new sport sedan based off the excellent A4 platform. Highlights include a turbocharged, 250-horsepower engine, all-wheel drive and improved handling and braking.

Category F

Don't forget to refer to the Mileage Adjustment Table at the back of this book!

Model Description	Trade-in TMV	Private TMV	Dealer TMV	Model Description	Trade-in TMV	Private TMV	Dealer TMV
4 Dr Quattro Turbo AWD Sdn	27499	29839	32000	Spoke Wheels +187			
				Sport Seats +267			
				Sport Suspension +241			
				Trip Computer +134			

OPTIONS FOR S4
Automatic Dimming Mirror +100
Bose Sound System +433
Compact Disc Changer +367
Heated Front Seats +167
Navigation System +853
Power Moonroof +666
Ski Sack +133

TT   2000

Audi introduces the funky-looking TT Coupe for the 2000 model year. A turbocharged, 1.8-liter engine squeezes out 180-horsepower for this avant-garde sports car.

Category F

	Trade-in	Private	Dealer
2 Dr STD Turbo Cpe	21483	23312	25000
2 Dr Quattro Turbo AWD Coupe	24062	26110	28000

OPTIONS FOR TT
Bose Sound System +433
Compact Disc Changer +367
Heated Front Seats +167
Performance Package +421
Trip Computer +133
Xenon Headlamps +281

1999 AUDI

A4   1999

Audi introduces the 1.8T Avant wagon to its lineup, while other A4 models gain standard equipment and new options.

Category H

	Trade-in	Private	Dealer
4 Dr Avant Quattro 1.8T AWD Wgn	17400	19000	20600
4 Dr Avant Quattro 2.8 AWD Wgn	20694	22597	24500
4 Dr STD 1.8T Sdn	13838	15110	16383
4 Dr STD 2.8 Sdn	18178	19849	21521
4 Dr Quattro 1.8T AWD Sdn	16893	18447	20000
4 Dr Quattro 2.8 AWD Sdn	19849	21675	23500

OPTIONS FOR A4
Auto-Manual Transmission +576
Compact Disc Changer +295
Heated Front Seats +147
Leather Seats +586
Power Moonroof +535
Ski Sack[Std on Avant Quattro] +134
Special Factory Paint +282

A6   1999

The A6 continues basically unchanged after last year's redesign.

Category I

	Trade-in	Private	Dealer
4 Dr Avant AWD Wgn	23304	25402	27500
4 Dr STD Sdn	18220	19860	21500
4 Dr Quattro AWD Sdn	21186	23093	25000

OPTIONS FOR A6
Automatic Dimming Mirror +99
Bose Sound System +354
Cast Alloy Wheels +120
Compact Disc Changer +308
Enhanced Security Package +508
Heated Seats +187
Leather Seats +668
Metallic Paint +305
Power Moonroof +535
Ski Sack[Std on Avant] +134
Third Seat +375
Warm Weather Package +429

A8   1999

The A8's warm weather package is modified to improve electronic accessory performance, while dual pane laminated glass replaces insulated glass. Standard on the A8 is a larger right outside mirror, a first aid kit and a CD changer. A premium leather/alcantra trim package and a new volcano black exterior paint color are optional. A8 prices will remain unchanged from 1998.

Category I

	Trade-in	Private	Dealer
4 Dr STD Sdn	26298	28666	31033
4 Dr Quattro AWD Sdn	30202	32920	35639

OPTIONS FOR A8
Alcantara & Leather Package +1779
Bose Sound System[Opt on STD] +455
Electronics Package +751
Heated Seats +187
Metallic Paint +305
Polished Alloy Wheels +535
Ski Sack +134
Warm Weather Package +751

1998 AUDI

A4   1998

The 2.8 sedan gets a valve job resulting in 18 more horsepower and additional torque. Side-impact airbags are standard, as is traction control. Opt for the automatic and you'll get the same Tiptronic technology

AUDI 98-97

Model Description	Trade-in TMV	Private TMV	Dealer TMV	Model Description	Trade-in TMV	Private TMV	Dealer TMV

that allows Biff to manually shift Buffy's 911 Cabriolet. A new station wagon called Avant debuts, while the A4 1.8T gets new wheels, a sport package and an ambient temperature gauge. New colors and stereo improvements round out the changes for 1998.

Category H

Model Description	Trade-in TMV	Private TMV	Dealer TMV
4 Dr Avant 2.8 AWD Wgn	17249	18810	20500
4 Dr Avant 2.8 Wgn	15020	16379	17851
4 Dr STD 1.8T Sdn	12394	13515	14730
4 Dr Quattro 1.8T AWD Sdn	12573	13710	14942
4 Dr Quattro 2.8 AWD Sdn	14702	16031	17472
4 Dr STD 2.8 Sdn	14308	15602	17004

OPTIONS FOR A4
Auto-Manual Transmission +493
Bose Sound System +302
Compact Disc Changer +252
Heated Front Seats +126
Leather Seats +501
Metallic Paint +210
Power Moonroof +458
Ski Sack[Std on Avant] +114
Special Factory Paint +241
Spoke Wheels +161
Sport Seats +229
Sport Suspension +206
Trip Computer +114

A6 1998

Stretch an A4 platform, add rounded styling with plenty of edges for character, toss in a sumptuously comfortable interior available in several "atmosphere" styles, blend it all with traditional Germanic handling, and what do you get? The excellent new Audi A6 sedan. Our only quibble is the with the dorky taillights, which appear to have been inspired by the Chevrolet S-10 pickup. The wagon is carried over from 1997.

Category I

Model Description	Trade-in TMV	Private TMV	Dealer TMV
4 Dr STD Sdn	13832	15087	16448
4 Dr STD Wgn	16537	18038	19665
4 Dr Quattro AWD Sdn	16827	18355	20010
4 Dr Quattro AWD Wgn	18119	19764	21546

OPTIONS FOR A6
Bose Sound System +302
Compact Disc Changer +263
Dual Power Seats +252
Enhanced Security Package +435
Heated Front Seats +161
Keyless Entry System +92
Leather Seats +572

Metallic Paint +261
Power Moonroof +458
Ski Sack +114
Warm Weather Package +824

A8 1998

Tiptronic automanual gear shifting is standard, as is a glass sunroof, dual-pane laminated window glass, an improved stereo and an upgraded antilock braking system.

Category I

Model Description	Trade-in TMV	Private TMV	Dealer TMV
4 Dr STD Sdn	22681	24740	26971
4 Dr Quattro AWD Sdn	28320	30891	33677

OPTIONS FOR A8
Bose Sound System[Opt on STD] +389
Compact Disc Changer +247
Heated Seats +161
Metallic Paint +261
Polished Alloy Wheels +458
Ski Sack +114
Sunscreen Glass +134
Warm Weather Package +642

CABRIOLET 1998

Here's an argument for euthanasia. Based on the ancient 80/90 platform from the late 80s, the Cabriolet soldiers on with minimal change. A new steering wheel design is standard, and the Audi logo disappears from the side moldings.

Category H

Model Description	Trade-in TMV	Private TMV	Dealer TMV
2 Dr STD Conv	14308	15602	17004

OPTIONS FOR CABRIOLET
Heated Front Seats +161
Keyless Entry System +161
Leather Seats +588
Metallic Paint +210
Power Convertible Top +535
Special Factory Paint +210
Sport Seats +206

1997 AUDI

A4 1997

A cheaper Audi A4 1.8T debuts, featuring a 150-horsepower, 20-valve, turbocharged inline four-cylinder engine and a base price in the low 20s. The 2.8 gains a revised decklid and expanded central locking features. All models have new cloth upholstery, and the console and armrests are trimmed with the same fabric as the seats. Three new colors debut for 1997.

Category H

Model Description	Trade-in TMV	Private TMV	Dealer TMV
4 Dr STD 1.8T Sdn	10665	11734	13041
4 Dr STD 2.8 Sdn	11793	12976	14421

Don't forget to refer to the Mileage Adjustment Table at the back of this book!

Model Description	Trade-in TMV	Private TMV	Dealer TMV
4 Dr Quattro 1.8T AWD Sdn	11063	12172	13528
4 Dr Quattro 2.8 AWD Sdn	12379	13621	15138

OPTIONS FOR A4

Automatic 5-Speed Transmission +354
Bose Sound System +251
Heated Front Seats +105
Leather Seats +418
Metallic Paint +176
Power Moonroof +381
Ski Sack +95
Special Factory Paint +201
Sport Seats +180
Trip Computer +95

A6 1997

A new Quattro Value Package is available with a power glass sunroof, larger alloy wheels, bigger tires, and, of course, the quattro all-wheel drive system. Selective unlocking capability expands to the remote keyless entry fob, and the alarm system now features interior monitoring. Jacquard cloth upholstery is new, and three new colors debut: Tornado Red, Volcano Black metallic and Byzantine metallic.

Category I

Model Description	Trade-in TMV	Private TMV	Dealer TMV
4 Dr STD Sdn	11080	12119	13389
4 Dr STD Wgn	12919	14130	15611
4 Dr Quattro AWD Sdn	12639	13824	15272
4 Dr Quattro AWD Wgn	14384	15733	17381

OPTIONS FOR A6

Bose Sound System +251
Dual Power Seats +209
Heated Front Seats +133
Leather Seats +477
Metallic Paint +217
Power Moonroof +381

A8 1997

Audi revolutionizes luxury sedan construction with the Audi Space Frame, which employs seven new aircraft-grade aluminum alloys to lighten weight and provide a tighter, more crashworthy structure. The new A8 is also the first passenger car equipped with six airbags. The usual accouterments associated with a premium German sedan are all in place.

Category I

Model Description	Trade-in TMV	Private TMV	Dealer TMV
4 Dr STD Sdn	15616	17080	18870
4 Dr Quattro AWD Sdn	22330	24424	26983

OPTIONS FOR A8

Bose Sound System[Opt on STD] +305
Heated Seats +222
Metallic Paint +217
Polished Alloy Wheels +381

Ski Sack +134
Sunscreen Glass +111
Warm Weather Package +535

CABRIOLET 1997

Base price drops a couple grand, but at the expense of the power top, burled walnut wood trim, and leather seats. Opt for the Premium Equipment Package, and these items magically reappear. Casablanca White and Cactus Green join the list of paint colors, and three new top colors debut. Leather seats can be had in two new shades, too.

Category H

Model Description	Trade-in TMV	Private TMV	Dealer TMV
2 Dr STD Conv	12457	13706	15233

OPTIONS FOR CABRIOLET

Bucket Seats +454
Heated Front Seats +133
Keyless Entry System +134
Leather Seats +491
Metallic Paint +176
Power Convertible Top +446
Special Factory Paint +176
Sport Seats +172

1996 AUDI

A4 1996

All-new, the A4 replaces the compact 90. This car performs better than the lackluster 90, and features a full load of standard features. Plus, it's drop-dead gorgeous. For the first time, a five-speed automatic transmission is available with the optional Quattro all-whee-drive system.

Category H

Model Description	Trade-in TMV	Private TMV	Dealer TMV
4 Dr STD 2.8 Sdn	8961	9929	11266
4 Dr Quattro 2.8 AWD Sdn	10383	11505	13054

OPTIONS FOR A4

Automatic 5-Speed Transmission +336
Bose Sound System +231
Heated Front Seats +100
Leather Seats +397
Metallic Paint +199
Power Moonroof +358
Ski Sack +90

A6 1996

Traction control systems have been improved this year. Fans of the manual transmission will mourn the loss of it; all 1996 A6 models are saddled with an automatic shifter.

Category I

Model Description	Trade-in TMV	Private TMV	Dealer TMV
4 Dr STD Sdn	8744	9733	11099

Don't forget to refer to the Mileage Adjustment Table at the back of this book!

Model Description	Trade-in TMV	Private TMV	Dealer TMV
4 Dr STD Wgn	9988	11118	12678
4 Dr Quattro AWD Sdn	9904	11025	12572
4 Dr Quattro AWD Wgn	11473	12771	14563

OPTIONS FOR A6
Bose Sound System +231
Dual Power Seats +199
Heated Front Seats +127
Leather Seats +452
Metallic Paint +206
Power Moonroof +354

CABRIOLET   1996
Better acceleration, a new radio, a new color and revised alloy wheels are the only changes.
Category H

	Trade-in	Private	Dealer
2 Dr STD Conv	11377	12606	14304

OPTIONS FOR CABRIOLET
Bucket Seats +416
Heated Front Seats +127
Metallic Paint +166

90   1995
Sport 90 model introduced, featuring lowered suspension.
Category H

	Trade-in	Private	Dealer
4 Dr STD Sdn	5337	5961	7000
4 Dr Quattro AWD Sdn	6382	7127	8370
4 Dr Sport Sdn	5718	6386	7500

OPTIONS FOR 90
Automatic 4-Speed Transmission +240
Heated Front Seats +90
Leather Seats +262
Power Drivers Seat +90
Power Sunroof +225

A6   1995
Subtle restyle of last year's 100 brings new name. Sedan or wagon available in either front- or all-wheel drive. Wagon comes only with an automatic transmission.
Category I

	Trade-in	Private	Dealer
4 Dr STD Sdn	6873	7671	9000
4 Dr STD Wgn	8553	9546	11200
4 Dr Quattro AWD Sdn	8479	9462	11102
4 Dr Quattro AWD Wgn	8596	9594	11256

OPTIONS FOR A6
AM/FM Compact Disc Player +90
Automatic 4-Speed Transmission[Std on Wgn] +240
Bose Sound System +191
Dual Power Seats +149
Heated Front Seats +105

Leather Seats +374
Power Moonroof +293

CABRIOLET   1995
No changes.
Category H

	Trade-in	Private	Dealer
2 Dr STD Conv	9802	10947	12856

OPTIONS FOR CABRIOLET
Heated Front Seats +105

S6   1995
Category F

	Trade-in	Private	Dealer
4 Dr STD Turbo AWD Sdn	14224	15714	18197

OPTIONS FOR S6
Compact Disc Changer +194

100   1994
Base sedan dropped. CS sedan gets standard automatic transmission. Rear ashtrays and cigarette lighters disappear from all models.
Category H

	Trade-in	Private	Dealer
4 Dr CS Sdn	7424	8355	9906
4 Dr CS Quattro AWD Sdn	7714	8681	10293
4 Dr CS Quattro AWD Wgn	8089	9103	10794
4 Dr S Sdn	6710	7551	8953
4 Dr S Wgn	7212	8116	9623

OPTIONS FOR 100
Automatic 4-Speed Transmission[Std on CS,Wgn] +181
Bose Sound System[Opt on S Sdn] +136
Compact Disc Changer +136
Leather Seats +198

90   1994
Passenger airbag newly standard. S model can be equipped with leather and a power sunroof.
Category H

	Trade-in	Private	Dealer
4 Dr CS Sdn	5475	6162	7306
4 Dr CS Quattro AWD Sdn	5701	6416	7607
4 Dr S Sdn	4911	5527	6553

OPTIONS FOR 90
Automatic 4-Speed Transmission +181
Power Sunroof[Opt on S] +170

CABRIOLET   1994
Based on 90 platform. Features dual airbags, ABS and 2.8-liter V6 engine. No manual transmission available.

Model Description	Trade-in TMV	Private TMV	Dealer TMV
Rear window is plastic.			
Category H			
2 Dr STD Conv	8547	9619	11405

OPTIONS FOR CABRIOLET
Heated Front Seats +80
Special Factory Paint +104

S4   1994

Category F

Model Description	Trade-in TMV	Private TMV	Dealer TMV
4 Dr STD Turbo AWD Sdn	11672	13078	15420

OPTIONS FOR S4
Compact Disc Changer +136

V8   1994

Category I

Model Description	Trade-in TMV	Private TMV	Dealer TMV
4 Dr Quattro AWD Sdn	10545	11750	13759

1993 AUDI

100   1993

Passenger airbag standard.
Category H

Model Description	Trade-in TMV	Private TMV	Dealer TMV
4 Dr STD Sdn	4259	4870	5889
4 Dr CS Sdn	5311	6074	7345
4 Dr CS Quattro AWD Sdn	6635	7587	9175
4 Dr CS Quattro AWD Wgn	7082	8099	9794
4 Dr S Sdn	5297	6058	7325

OPTIONS FOR 100
Automatic 4-Speed Transmission[Std on CS,Wgn] +153
Compact Disc Changer +114
Leather Seats[Opt on S] +167

90   1993

All-new 90 model debuts, with 2.8-liter V6 under the hood. ABS and driver airbag standard. Quattro AWD system still available.
Category H

Model Description	Trade-in TMV	Private TMV	Dealer TMV
4 Dr CS Sdn	4032	4610	5575
4 Dr CS Quattro AWD Sdn	4848	5544	6704
4 Dr S Sdn	3533	4040	4885

OPTIONS FOR 90
Automatic 4-Speed Transmission +153
Power Sunroof +144

S4   1993

Passenger airbag standard.
Category F

Model Description	Trade-in TMV	Private TMV	Dealer TMV
4 Dr STD Turbo AWD Sdn	10119	11438	13635

V8   1993

Category I

Model Description	Trade-in TMV	Private TMV	Dealer TMV
4 Dr Quattro AWD Sdn	7917	8951	10674

1992 AUDI

100   1992

Sheetmetal redesigned, and 2.8-liter V6 replaces five-cylinder motor. Quattro models available with automatic transmission. Driver airbag and ABS standard. All wagons are Quattro-equipped.
Category H

Model Description	Trade-in TMV	Private TMV	Dealer TMV
4 Dr STD Sdn	3467	4038	4991
4 Dr CS Sdn	4736	5517	6818
4 Dr CS Quattro AWD Sdn	5447	6345	7842
4 Dr CS Quattro AWD Wgn	5799	6755	8348
4 Dr S Sdn	4116	4794	5925

OPTIONS FOR 100
Automatic 4-Speed Transmission[Std on Wgn] +136
Compact Disc Changer +102
Leather Seats[Std on Wgn] +149

80   1992

90 model discontinued. Coupe Quattro disappears. Antilock brakes made standard on 80, and optional power sunroof replaces last year's manual one.
Category H

Model Description	Trade-in TMV	Private TMV	Dealer TMV
4 Dr STD Sdn	2706	3152	3895
4 Dr Quattro AWD Sdn	3293	3836	4741

OPTIONS FOR 80
Automatic 4-Speed Transmission +136
Compact Disc Changer +102
Power Sunroof +128

S4   1992

200 designation dropped in favor of S4. Driver airbag and ABS standard.
Category F

Model Description	Trade-in TMV	Private TMV	Dealer TMV
4 Dr STD Turbo AWD Sdn	5852	6714	8151

V8   1992

Category I

Model Description	Trade-in TMV	Private TMV	Dealer TMV
4 Dr Quattro AWD Sdn	5958	6836	8300

Don't forget to refer to the Mileage Adjustment Table at the back of this book!

Model Description	Trade-in TMV	Private TMV	Dealer TMV	Model Description	Trade-in TMV	Private TMV	Dealer TMV

BMW 01

BMW — Germany

2000 BMW 528i Sedan

2001 BMW

3-SERIES 2001

A boost in engine displacement and technology, plus an available all-wheel-drive system, keeps BMW's venerable 3 Series at the top of its game in the competitive entry-level luxury market. Larger wheels and brakes are part of the engine upgrade. Addressing concerns that their cars are low on feature content, BMW adds automatic climate control, foglights, heated mirrors and cruise control as standard equipment for all 325 models. The 330s get power seats and a premium audio package at no extra cost.

Category H

	Trade-in	Private	Dealer
2 Dr 325Ci Conv	29983	31302	33500
2 Dr 325Ci Cpe	24363	25435	27221
4 Dr 325i Sdn	21928	22892	24500
4 Dr 325iT Wgn	24673	25759	27568
4 Dr 325xi AWD Sdn	24165	25228	27000
4 Dr 325xiT AWD Wgn	25508	26630	28500
2 Dr 330Ci Conv	34681	36207	38750
2 Dr 330Ci Cpe	28416	29666	31750
4 Dr 330i Sdn	27298	28498	30500
4 Dr 330xi AWD Sdn	28640	29900	32000

OPTIONS FOR 3-SERIES

AM/FM Compact Disc Player +153
Automatic 5-Speed Transmission +972
Dual Power Seats +721
Hardtop Roof +1750
Harman Kardon Sound System +515
Heated Front Seats +381
Leather Seats +818
Metallic Paint +362
Navigation System +1373

Onboard Computer[Std on 330, 325Ci] +229
Park Distance Control +267
Power Convertible Top[Opt on 325i Conv] +572
Power Moonroof +801
Rear Side Air Bags +294
Ski Sack +201
Sport Package +458
Xenon Headlamps +381

5-SERIES 2001

The former base 2.8-liter engine gets bumped up to 3.0 liters, with an expected horsepower and torque increase to go along with the larger displacement. A new 2.5-liter engine premieres this year, as do rear seat head airbags and a slightly freshened exterior. BMW also improved some of the optional equipment, including Park Distance Control for both the front and rear of the vehicle, a bigger LCD screen for the navigation system, and an optional single-disc in-dash CD player.

Category I

	Trade-in	Private	Dealer
4 Dr 525i Sdn	29640	30713	32500
4 Dr 525iT Wgn	31099	32225	34100
4 Dr 530i Sdn	33060	34256	36250
4 Dr 540i Sdn	44916	46541	49250
4 Dr 540iT Wgn	44232	45833	48500

OPTIONS FOR 5-SERIES

AM/FM Compact Disc Player +153
Automatic 5-Speed Transmission[Opt on 525i,525iT,530i] +972
Automatic Dimming Mirror[Std on 540i,540iT] +140
Automatic Load Leveling[Opt on 525iT] +580
Comfort Seats +915
Dual Power Seats[Opt on 540iT] +362
Heated Front Seats +229
Leather Seats[Std on 540i,540iT] +1106
Navigation System +1373
Park Distance Control +534
Power Moonroof[Std on 540i,540iT] +801
Power Passenger Seat[Opt on 525i,525iT,530i] +305
Rear Side Air Bags +294
Ski Sack[Opt on 528i,540i] +362
Sport Package +1144
Xenon Headlamps[Std on 540i,540iT] +381

7-SERIES 2001

All 7 Series models receive an integrated Motorola StarTAC cell phone with BMW's Mayday function. Body-colored rocker panels and lower-bumper valances, as well as white turn signal lenses, enhance the 7 Series exterior look. Sport Packages are now available on the 740iL and 750iL models.

Category I

	Trade-in	Private	Dealer
4 Dr 740i Sdn	46284	47959	50750
4 Dr 740iL Protection Sdn			

Model Description	Trade-in TMV	Private TMV	Dealer TMV
	70224	72765	77000
4 Dr 740iL Sdn	49157	50936	53900
4 Dr 750iL Protection Sdn			
	81168	84105	89000
4 Dr 750iL Sdn	65573	67946	71900

OPTIONS FOR 7-SERIES
Active Comfort Seats[Opt on 740i] +381
Automatic Load Leveling[Std on 750iL,750iL Protection] +580
Electronic Damping Control Suspension[Std on 750iL,750iL Protection] +763
Heated Front Seats[Std on 750iL,750iL Protection] +381
Park Distance Control +686
Rear Side Air Bags +419
Security Sun Roof[Std on Protection] +1983
Ski Sack[Std on 750iL] +229
Sport Package +1373

M   2001

BMW's performance sport coupe and roadster are powered by a new inline six-cylinder engine capable of generating 315 horses. Complementing the increase in power is a more tautly sprung suspension. Standard equipment Dynamic Stability Control keeps overenthusiastic drivers in check, and a new tire pressure monitoring system alerts you of underinflated rubber.

Category F			
2 Dr M Conv	37993	39402	41750
2 Dr M Cpe	34125	35391	37500

OPTIONS FOR M
AM/FM Compact Disc Player +153
Hardtop Roof[Opt on Conv] +1449
Power Moonroof[Opt on Cpe] +229

M3   2001

The Teutons finally release their grip on the magnificent M3s, and they land on American shores with the proper fanfare. Powered by a 333-horsepower inline six, the athletic coupe and convertible have the appeal, functionality and performance to have every luxury sport car enthusiast's salivary glands working overtime.

Category F			
2 Dr M3 Conv	41405	42941	45500
2 Dr M3 Cpe	35945	37278	39500

OPTIONS FOR M3
AM/FM Compact Disc Player +153
Dual Power Seats[Std on Conv] +439
Hardtop Roof +1750
Harman Kardon Sound System +515
Heated Front Seats +201
Metallic Paint +362
Navigation System +1373
Park Distance Control +267
Power Moonroof +801

Rear Side Air Bags +294
Ski Sack +201
Xenon Headlamps +381

M5   2001

BMW's top performance sedan, the 394-horsepower M5, gets subtle exterior tweaks and a new head-protection airbag system for rear seat passengers.

Category F			
4 Dr M5 Sdn	66885	69366	73500

X5   2001

A lower-priced X5, with a standard 3.0-liter inline six, is offered for 2001. Other newsworthy items include available sunshades for the back doors, as well as optional heated rear seats. The Sport package includes a sport steering wheel, and 16-way power front seats can be purchased. All X5s come with a self-leveling rear suspension as standard equipment.

Category O			
4 Dr 3.0i AWD Wgn	32510	33864	36122
4 Dr 4.4i AWD Wgn	39375	41016	43750

OPTIONS FOR X5
AM/FM Compact Disc Player +153
Automatic 5-Speed Transmission[Std on 4.4i] +972
Automatic Dimming Mirror +229
Automatic Load Leveling +580
Cast Alloy Wheels +686
Climate Control for AC[Std on 4.4i] +229
Comfort Seats +915
Dual Air Conditioning[Std on 4.4i] +572
Dual Power Seats +362
Heated Front Seats +352
Leather Seats[Std on 4.4i] +1106
Navigation System +1517
Onboard Computer +229
Park Distance Control +267
Power Moonroof +801
Premium Sound System +915
Privacy Glass +210
Rear Side Air Bags +419
Ski Sack +148
Sport Seats +362
Sport Suspension +518
Xenon Headlamps +381

Z3   2001

Engine displacement in the 2.8 Roadster and Coupe is bumped from 2.8 liters to 3.0 liters. Horsepower and torque have been increased to 225 and 214 foot-pounds, respectively. Bigger brakes and larger 17-inch wheels and tires accompany the new engine. The base 2.5-liter engine also sees a 14 horsepower increase, and will appropriately be called the Z3 2.5i. An optional

Model Description	Trade-in TMV	Private TMV	Dealer TMV	Model Description	Trade-in TMV	Private TMV	Dealer TMV

five-speed automatic with manual shifting capability replaces last year's four-speed automatic transmission.

Category H

Model Description	Trade-in TMV	Private TMV	Dealer TMV
2 Dr 2.5i Conv	23270	24294	26000
2 Dr 3.0i Conv	26180	27331	29251
2 Dr 3.0i Cpe	25977	27120	29025

OPTIONS FOR Z3

AM/FM Compact Disc Player +153
Automatic 5-Speed Transmission +972
Cross-Spoke Wheels[Opt on 3.0 Cpe] +229
Dual Power Seats +439
Hardtop Roof[Opt on Conv] +1449
Harman Kardon Sound System[Opt on 2.5 Conv] +515
Heated Power Mirrors +133
Heated Seats +248
Leather Seats[Opt on 2.5 Conv] +693
Metallic Paint +362
Onboard Computer +229
Power Convertible Top +572
Power Moonroof +229
Sport Package +458
Sport Seats[Opt on Conv] +305

Z8   2001

BMW has created an all-new sports car with philosophical and styling elements gleaned from its original 1955 507 roadster.

Category R

Model Description	Trade-in TMV	Private TMV	Dealer TMV
2 Dr STD Conv	126900	129938	135000

2000 BMW

3-SERIES   2000

3-Series coupes, convertibles and wagons are all-new for 2000; the hatchback has been discontinued. After last year's complete redesign, 2000 sedans see only minor improvements.

Category H

Model Description	Trade-in TMV	Private TMV	Dealer TMV
2 Dr 323Ci Cpe	20836	22319	23687
2 Dr 323Ci Conv	26103	27960	29674
4 Dr 323i Sdn	19301	20674	21942
4 Dr 323iT Wgn	22525	24128	25607
2 Dr 328Ci Cpe	24757	26518	28144
4 Dr 328i Sdn	24040	25750	27329

OPTIONS FOR 3-SERIES

AM/FM Compact Disc Player +166
AM/FM Stereo/CD/Tape +384
Automatic 5-Speed Transmission +801
Automatic Dimming Mirror +101
Compact Disc Changer +390
Cruise Control[Opt on 323i,323iT] +185
Dual Power Seats[Std on 328Ci,328i,Conv] +439
Fog Lights[Opt on 323i,323iT] +174
Hardtop Roof +1379
Harman Kardon Sound System +451

Heated Front Seats +201
Heated Power Mirrors[Opt on 323i,323iT] +101
Leather Seats +818
Metallic Paint +317
Navigation System +1202
Onboard Computer[Opt on 323i,323iT] +176
Power Moonroof +701
Premium Package +843
Rear Side Air Bags +258
Ski Sack[Std on 323Ci] +201
Split Folding Rear Seat[Opt on 323i,328i] +317
Spoke Wheels +333
Sport Seats +333
Sport Suspension[Std on 323Ci,328Ci] +250
Xenon Headlamps +333

5-SERIES   2000

The 5-Series cars carryover from last year with small changes and no price increase.

Category I

Model Description	Trade-in TMV	Private TMV	Dealer TMV
4 Dr 528i Sdn	29376	30997	32494
4 Dr 528iT Wgn	30215	31882	33422
4 Dr 540i Sdn	38988	41140	43127
4 Dr 540iT Wgn	39541	41724	43739

OPTIONS FOR 5-SERIES

6-Speed Transmission +1809
Automatic 5-Speed Transmission[Opt on 528i,528iT] +686
Automatic Dimming Mirror[Std on 540i,540iT] +140
Automatic Load Leveling[Std on 540iT] +534
Comfort Seats +843
Compact Disc Changer +352
Heated Front Seats +229
Leather Seats[Std on 540i,540iT] +1035
Metallic Paint +334
Navigation System +1266
Power Moonroof[Std on 540i,540iT] +737
Premium Hi-Fi Sound System +843
Premium Package +2070
Rear Jump Seats +334
Rear Side Air Bags +271
Rear Spoiler +281
Ski Sack[Opt on 528i,540i] +263
Spoke Wheels +555
Sport Package +1109
Sport Seats +334
Sport Suspension +527
Xenon Headlamps[Std on 540i,540iT] +352

7-SERIES   2000

The Premium Package is standard on the 740i and 740iL and the Cold Weather Package now includes heated rear seats. Two new "Protection" trim levels are also available that provide light armor, bullet-resistant glass and run-flat tires.

Category I

Model Description	Trade-in TMV	Private TMV	Dealer TMV
4 Dr 740iA Sdn	41454	43743	45855
4 Dr 740iL Protection Sdn			

Model Description	Trade-in TMV	Private TMV	Dealer TMV
	69312	73138	76670
4 Dr 740iL Sdn	43660	46070	48295
4 Dr 750iL Protection Sdn			
	82308	86852	91046
4 Dr 750iL Sdn	53362	56308	59027

OPTIONS FOR 7-SERIES
AM/FM Stereo/CD/Tape[Opt on 740iL Protection] +444
Active Comfort Seats[Opt on 740iA] +370
Adaptive Ride Package +1335
Heated Front Seats[Std on 750iL,750iL Protection] +352
Metallic Paint +140
Park Distance Control +632
Power Sunroof +1036
Rear Side Air Bags +271
Security Glass[Std on Protection] +1827
Ski Sack[Std on 750iL] +229
Spoke Wheels +592
Sport Package +444
Sport Seats +370
Sport Suspension +518

M — 2000

The M cars carry over for 2000, save for two new exterior colors. Prices remain unchanged.
Category F

2 Dr M Conv	31291	33323	35199
2 Dr M Cpe	28789	30658	32384

OPTIONS FOR M
AM/FM Compact Disc Player +158
Hardtop Roof[Opt on Conv] +1201
Power Moonroof[Opt on Cpe] +695

M5 — 2000

The M5 is a powerful (400-horsepower), all-new sport sedan based on the 540i.
Category F

4 Dr M5 Sdn	57159	60872	64298

OPTIONS FOR M5
Ski Sack +106

X5 — 2000

BMW joins the SUV craze with its all-new X5 SAV (sport activity vehicle), powered by the same superb V8 fitted to the 540i.
Category O

4 Dr STD AWD Wgn	36721	38976	41058

OPTIONS FOR X5
AM/FM Compact Disc Player +148
AM/FM Stereo/CD/Tape +404
Automatic Dimming Mirror +106
Compact Disc Changer +422
Heated Front Seats +352
Navigation System +1398
Power Moonroof +737

Premium Audio System +628
Privacy Glass +196
Rear Side Air Bags +270
Ski Sack +148
Sport Package +703
Sport Seats +370
Sport Suspension +518
Xenon Headlamps +352

Z3 — 2000

Dynamic Stability Control is now standard on all Z3s. The cars also receive freshened exterior and interior appointments.
Category H

2 Dr 2.3 Conv	20730	22205	23566
2 Dr 2.8 Conv	23020	24658	26170
2 Dr 2.8 Cpe	22123	23697	25150

OPTIONS FOR Z3
AM/FM Compact Disc Player +175
Automatic 4-Speed Transmission +686
Chrome Trim +106
Chrome Wheels[Opt on 2.3 Conv] +598
Cross-Spoke Wheels[Opt on 2.8 Conv] +352
Cruise Control[Opt on 2.3 Conv] +208
Fog Lights[Opt on 2.3 Conv] +183
Hardtop Roof[Opt on Conv] +1335
Harman Kardon Sound System[Opt on 2.3 Conv] +474
Heated Front Seats +246
Heated Power Mirrors +123
Leather Seats[Opt on 2.3 Conv] +693
Metallic Paint +334
Onboard Computer +246
Power Convertible Top[Opt on Conv] +527
Power Moonroof[Opt on 2.8 Cpe] +703
Radial Alloy Wheels[Opt on 2.8 Cpe] +791
Spoke Wheels[Opt on 2.3 Conv] +791
Sport Seats[Opt on Conv] +281

1999 BMW

3-SERIES — 1999

3-Series sedans redesigned for 1999, offering 5-Series style along with more room for rear seat passengers.
Category H

2 Dr 318ti Hbk	13909	15069	16229
2 Dr 323i Conv	22703	24597	26490
4 Dr 323i Sdn	17328	18773	20218
2 Dr 323is Cpe	18707	20267	21827
2 Dr 328i Conv	27229	29500	31771
4 Dr 328i Sdn	22322	24183	26045
2 Dr 328is Cpe	22294	24154	26013

OPTIONS FOR 3-SERIES
AM/FM Compact Disc Player +132
AM/FM Stereo/CD/Tape +304
Alarm System[Opt on 323] +172

Model Description	Trade-in TMV	Private TMV	Dealer TMV	Model Description	Trade-in TMV	Private TMV	Dealer TMV

BMW 99

Automatic 4-Speed Transmission +516
Automatic 5-Speed Transmission[Opt on Sdns] +635
Compact Disc Changer +343
Cruise Control[Opt on 318ti,323i Sdn] +146
Dual Power Seats[Opt on 323i] +387
Fog Lights[Opt on 323i, 323is] +124
Hardtop Roof +1214
Harman Kardon Sound System +358
Heated Front Seats +159
Keyless Entry System[Std on Sdn] +132
Leather Seats +648
Metallic Paint +252
Navigation System +761
Onboard Computer[Std on 328i Sdn] +154
Power Convertible Top +714
Power Moonroof +555
Rear Side Air Bags +203
Ski Sack +159
Sport Package +371
Sport Seats +154
Sport Suspension[Std on 318ti] +199
Xenon Headlamps[Opt on Sdns] +265

5-SERIES   1999

This fall, new 528i and 540i sport wagons debut, all 5-Series models achieve Low Emission Vehicle (LEV) status, and consumers will find extensive new standard and optional equipment on the cars.
Category I

Model	Trade-in	Private	Dealer
4 Dr 528i Sdn	26186	27912	29637
4 Dr 528iT Wgn	28201	30059	31917
4 Dr 540i Sdn	30120	32105	34089
4 Dr 540iT Wgn	33438	35641	37844

OPTIONS FOR 5-SERIES
6-Speed Transmission +1434
Automatic 4-Speed Transmission +543
Automatic Dimming Mirror[Std on 540i,540iT] +111
Automatic Load Leveling[Std on 540iT] +423
Compact Disc Changer +279
Heated Front Seats +181
Leather Seats[Std on 540i,540iT] +766
Metallic Paint +265
Navigation System +802
Power Moonroof[Std on 540i,540iT] +585
Premium Package +1639
Rear Jump Seats +265
Rear Side Air Bags +213
Rear Spoiler +223
Ski Sack[Std on Wgn] +209
Spoke Wheels +489
Sport Package +1275
Sport Seats +265
Sport Suspension +418
Xenon Headlamps +279

7-SERIES   1999

All 7-Series engines achieve LEV (Low Emission Vehicle) status. Revised standard and optional equipment add to the cars' appeal.
Category I

Model	Trade-in	Private	Dealer
4 Dr 740i Sdn	35856	38219	40581
4 Dr 740iL Sdn	36283	38674	41064
4 Dr 750iL Sdn	41618	44360	47102

OPTIONS FOR 7-SERIES
AM/FM Stereo/CD/Tape[Std on 750iL] +391
Automatic Load Leveling[Std on 750iL] +446
Compact Disc Changer[Std on 750iL] +361
Electronic Damping Control[Std on 750iL] +1057
Heated Front Seats[Std on 750iL] +279
Metallic Paint +111
Navigation System +1247
Park Distance Control[Std on 750iL] +501
Power Sunroof +912
Rear Side Air Bags +213
Ski Sack[Std on 750iL] +181
Sport Package +521
Sport Seats +326
Sport Suspension +456
Xenon Headlamps +334

M   1999

These high-performance versions of the Z3 roadster and coupe make 240 M-power ponies.
Category F

Model	Trade-in	Private	Dealer
2 Dr M Conv	26888	28663	30437
2 Dr M Cpe	25569	27257	28944

OPTIONS FOR M
AM/FM Compact Disc Player +140
Hardtop Roof[Opt on Conv] +1057
Power Moonroof[Opt on Cpe] +612

M3   1999

Production of M3 four-door sedans ends this year as BMW concentrates on selling the M3 coupe and recently introduced M3 convertible. These models go unchanged for 1999.
Category F

Model	Trade-in	Private	Dealer
2 Dr M3 Conv	32212	34337	36463
2 Dr M3 Cpe	27699	29527	31355

OPTIONS FOR M3
AM/FM Compact Disc Player +140
AM/FM Stereo/CD/Tape +377
Automatic 5-Speed Transmission +668
Compact Disc Changer +307
Cruise Control +140
Dual Power Seats +526
Forged Alloy Wheels +521
Hardtop Roof +1278
Harman Kardon Sound System +377
Heated Front Seats +279
Onboard Computer +205
Power Moonroof +529
Rear Spoiler +195

Don't forget to refer to the Mileage Adjustment Table at the back of this book!

BMW 99-98

Z3 — 1999

The Z3 Coupe 2.8 is new, side airbags are now standard on all models, and a 2.5-liter inline six replaces the 1.9-liter four-cylinder engine on the entry-level roadster.

Category H

Model Description	Trade-in TMV	Private TMV	Dealer TMV
2 Dr 2.3 Conv	18061	19568	21074
2 Dr 2.8 Conv	20458	22165	23871
2 Dr 2.8 Cpe	19661	21300	22940

OPTIONS FOR Z3

AM/FM Compact Disc Player +140
Automatic 4-Speed Transmission +543
Chrome Wheels +473
Cruise Control[Opt on 2.3 Conv] +164
Fog Lights[Opt on 2.3 Conv] +144
Hardtop Roof +1057
Harman Kardon Sound System[Opt on 2.3 Conv] +377
Heated Front Seats +195
Leather Seats[Opt on 2.3 Conv] +610
Metallic Paint +265
Onboard Computer +195
Power Convertible Top +418
Power Moonroof +557
Spoke Wheels +626
Sport Seats[Opt on Conv] +223

1998 BMW

3-SERIES — 1998

BMW adds a 2.5-liter inline-six engine to their entry-level coupe and convertible, making them the cheapest six-cylinder BMWs in years. Also new are standard side-impact airbags for front seat passengers in all models except the 318ti, in which they're optional.

Category H

Model Description	Trade-in TMV	Private TMV	Dealer TMV
4 Dr 318i Sdn	14549	15886	17334
2 Dr 318ti Hbk	11967	13066	14257
2 Dr 323i Conv	19510	21302	23244
2 Dr 323is Cpe	16272	17767	19386
2 Dr 328i Conv	23925	26123	28504
4 Dr 328i Sdn	18301	19983	21804
2 Dr 328is Cpe	18358	20045	21872

Category F

Model Description	Trade-in TMV	Private TMV	Dealer TMV
2 Dr M3 Conv	27653	29674	31864
2 Dr M3 Cpe	23224	24922	26761
4 Dr M3 Sdn	23659	25389	27262

OPTIONS FOR 3-SERIES

AM/FM Compact Disc Player +118
AM/FM Stereo/CD/Tape[Std on M3] +271
Alarm System[Opt on 318i,318ti] +153
Aluminum/Alloy Wheels[Opt on 318i,318ti] +282
Automatic 4-Speed Transmission +458
Automatic 5-Speed Transmission[Opt on M3] +564
Compact Disc Changer +305
Cruise Control[Opt on 318ti,M3] +130
Dual Power Seats[Opt on M3] +344
Fog Lights[Opt on 318i,318ti] +122
Hardtop Roof +1079
Heated Front Seats +141
Keyless Entry System +118
Leather Seats[Std on M3] +575
Limited Slip Differential[Std on M3] +165
Metallic Paint +224
Onboard Computer +138
Power Convertible Top +635
Power Sunroof +447
Rear Spoiler +165
Rollover Protection System +682
Side Air Bag Restraints[Opt on 318ti] +181
Ski Sack +141
Sport Package +330
Sport Suspension +177

5-SERIES — 1998

Side-impact airbags are now available for rear-seat passengers, as is break-resistant glass for the windows and moonroof.

Category I

Model Description	Trade-in TMV	Private TMV	Dealer TMV
4 Dr 528i Sdn	23896	25712	27678
4 Dr 540i Sdn	29871	32140	34598

OPTIONS FOR 5-SERIES

6-Speed Transmission[Opt on 540i] +1275
Automatic 4-Speed Transmission +483
Heated Front Seats +161
Leather Seats[Opt on 528i] +811
Metallic Paint +236
Navigation System +990
Power Moonroof[Opt on 528i] +520
Rear Side Air Bags +190
Rear Spoiler +198
Ski Sack +186
Spoke Wheels +435
Sport Package +627
Sport Seats +236
Sport Suspension +290

7-SERIES — 1998

BMW introduces Dynamic Stability Control (DSC) to the big Bimmer. DSC is designed to automatically correct the yaw on all 7-Series cars, preventing plowing and fishtailing. Guess this means no more smoky burnouts in the Beverly Hilton's parking lot.

Category I

Model Description	Trade-in TMV	Private TMV	Dealer TMV
4 Dr 740i Sdn	29126	31338	33735
4 Dr 740iL Sdn	30593	32916	35434
4 Dr 750iL Sdn	40438	43510	46838

OPTIONS FOR 7-SERIES

AM/FM Stereo/CD/Tape[Std on 750iL] +347
Automatic Load Leveling[Opt on 740iL] +396

Don't forget to refer to the Mileage Adjustment Table at the back of this book!

Model Description	Trade-in TMV	Private TMV	Dealer TMV
Comfort Seats[Opt on 740i] +593			
Compact Disc Changer +322			
Electronic Damping Control[Opt on 740i,740iL] +990			
Heated Front Seats[Std on 750iL] +247			
Metallic Paint +99			
Navigation System +1109			
Park Distance Control[Opt on 740iL] +446			
Power Sunroof +811			
Rear Side Air Bags +190			
Ski Sack[Std on 750iL] +161			

Z3   1998

The M Roadster, a 240-horsepower version of the Z3 convertible, arrives for 1998. An electric top also becomes available this year.

Category H			
2 Dr 1.9 Conv	16098	17577	19179
2 Dr 2.8 Conv	17644	19265	21021
Category F			
2 Dr M Conv	24599	26397	28345

OPTIONS FOR Z3
AM/FM Compact Disc Player[Opt on 1.9] +124
Automatic 4-Speed Transmission +483
Heated Front Seats[Std on M] +174
Leather Seats[Opt on 1.9] +543
Metallic Paint[Std on M] +236
Onboard Computer +174
Power Convertible Top[Std on M] +371
Side Air Bag Restraints +124
Special Factory Paint +236
Sport Seats +198
Theft Deterrent System +174

1997 BMW

3-SERIES   1997

An M3 sedan has arrived at a store near you. Those of you claiming to want power and practicality no longer have an excuse for driving that old jalopy currently parked in your driveway. Buy one now. Also, All-Season Traction is now standard on all models.

Category H			
2 Dr 318i Conv	16149	17562	19289
4 Dr 318i Sdn	12687	13797	15154
2 Dr 318is Cpe	13690	14888	16352
2 Dr 318ti Hbk	10843	11792	12951
2 Dr 328i Conv	22675	24658	27083
4 Dr 328i Sdn	16126	17537	19261
2 Dr 328is Cpe	16141	17553	19279
Category F			
2 Dr M3 Cpe	20121	21704	23639
4 Dr M3 Sdn	19838	21399	23307

OPTIONS FOR 3-SERIES
AM/FM Compact Disc Player +111
AM/FM Stereo/CD/Tape +257

Model Description	Trade-in TMV	Private TMV	Dealer TMV
Alarm System +145			
Aluminum/Alloy Wheels[Opt on 318i,318ti] +268			
Automatic 4-Speed Transmission +436			
Automatic 5-Speed Transmission +536			
Compact Disc Changer +290			
Cruise Control[Opt on 318ti,M3] +123			
Dual Power Seats[Opt on M3] +327			
Fog Lights[Opt on 318ti,318i Sdn] +116			
Hardtop Roof +1026			
Heated Front Seats +134			
Leather Seats[Std on M3,328i Conv] +525			
Limited Slip Differential[Std on M3] +156			
Luxury Package +627			
Metallic Paint +212			
Onboard Computer +131			
Power Sunroof +424			
Rear Spoiler +156			
Rollover Protection System +647			
Side Air Bag Restraints +172			
Ski Sack +134			
Sport Seats +89			
Sport Suspension +168			
Sports Package +313			

5-SERIES   1997

The 5-Series is redesigned and introduced midway through 1996 as a 1997 model. Bearing a strong resemblance to its 3- and 7-Series siblings, the 5-Series offers a lot of car for a lot of money. The Touring wagons are no longer available, and the 3.0-liter V8 is history. New 5-Series models can be had as a six-cylinder 528i or a V8 540i. Both models feature new engines, all-aluminum suspensions, improved brakes and available side impact airbag protection.

Category I			
4 Dr 528i Sdn	21701	23488	25672
4 Dr 540i Sdn	24829	26874	29373

OPTIONS FOR 5-SERIES
6-Speed Transmission[Opt on 540i] +1095
AM/FM Stereo/CD/Tape +224
Automatic 4-Speed Transmission +436
Comfort Seats +536
Compact Disc Changer +224
Heated Front Seats +145
Leather Seats[Opt on 528i] +615
Metallic Paint +212
Navigation System +1001
Power Moonroof[Opt on 528i] +451
Premium Package +706
Rear Spoiler +179
Ski Sack +168
Sport Suspension +335

7-SERIES   1997

BMW reintroduces the regular length 740i after the uproar caused over its cancellation for the 1996 model

BMW 97-96

Model Description	Trade-in TMV	Private TMV	Dealer TMV	Model Description	Trade-in TMV	Private TMV	Dealer TMV

year. Like the rest of the 7-Series, the 740i has a standard equipment list that will leave the Sultan of Brunei drooling with desire.

Category I

4 Dr 740i Sdn	24251	26248	28689
4 Dr 740iL Sdn	24862	26910	29412
4 Dr 750iL Sdn	35232	38133	41679

OPTIONS FOR 7-SERIES

AM/FM Compact Disc Player +190
Automatic Load Leveling[Opt on 740iL] +358
Electronic Damping Control[Std on 750iL] +849
Heated Front Seats[Std on 750iL] +224
Metallic Paint +89
Navigation System +947
Park Distance Control[Opt on 740iL] +402
Ski Sack[Std on 750iL] +145

8-SERIES   1997

Engine displacement is bumped, making the 1997 840Ci and 850Ci a bit stronger than last year's models. BMW's five-speed Steptronic is now standard on both models.

Category I

2 Dr 840Ci Cpe	32696	35388	38679
2 Dr 850Ci Cpe	38170	41313	45155

OPTIONS FOR 8-SERIES

Forged Alloy Wheels +418
Metallic Paint +89

Z3   1997

Hooray, the market for sports cars is alive and kicking. Despite the ever-increasing number of minivans and sport-utes on our clogged highways, there are still enough of us that like to drive to support this wonderful little car. As a reward for keeping the segment alive, BMW makes its 190-horsepower six-cylinder engine available in the Z3 2.8.

Category H

2 Dr 1.9 Conv	14261	15509	17034
2 Dr 2.8 Conv	15892	17283	18982

OPTIONS FOR Z3

Automatic 4-Speed Transmission +436
Compact Disc Changer +246
Heated Front Seats +156
Leather Seats[Opt on 1.9] +490
Metallic Paint +212
Onboard Computer +156
Special Factory Paint +212
Special Wheels +335
Traction Control System[Opt on 1.9] +358

1996 BMW

3-SERIES   1996

BMW's highly acclaimed 3-series receives new engines across the board. The 318 remains a 318 despite an increase in displacement to 1.9 liters. The six-cylinder model becomes the 328 with an improved engine that increases torque by a whopping 14 percent. Vented rear disc brakes aid the 328's stopping power by reducing brake fade. Automatic climate control is standard, except in the 318ti, and improved sound systems are optional on all models.

Category H

2 Dr 318i Conv	13162	14488	16319
4 Dr 318i Sdn	10449	11501	12955
2 Dr 318is Cpe	10729	11809	13302
2 Dr 318ti Hbk	8949	9850	11095
2 Dr 328i Conv	16954	18662	21021
4 Dr 328i Sdn	13335	14679	16534
2 Dr 328is Cpe	13412	14763	16629

Category F

2 Dr M3 Cpe	17407	18796	20714

OPTIONS FOR 3-SERIES

AM/FM Compact Disc Player +107
AM/FM Stereo/CD/Tape +246
Air Conditioning[Opt on 318ti] +344
Aluminum/Alloy Wheels[Opt on 318ti,318i Sdn] +256
Automatic 4-Speed Transmission +417
Cruise Control[Opt on 318ti,M3] +118
Dual Power Seats[Opt on M3] +297
Fog Lights[Opt on 318ti,318i Sdn] +111
Hardtop Roof +981
Heated Front Seats +128
Keyless Entry System +107
Leather Seats[Std on M3,328i Conv] +502
Limited Slip Differential[Std on M3] +150
Metallic Paint +203
Onboard Computer +150
Power Sunroof[Opt on 318ti,M3] +406
Rear Spoiler +150
Rollover Protection System +620
Ski Sack +128
Sport Suspension +161
Sports Package +308
Traction Control System +139

7-SERIES   1996

BMW's flagship gets stretched; the only 7-Series models available for 1996 are long wheelbase models. The 740iL receives a larger V8 that substantially increases torque. BMW's killer 440-watt sound system is now standard on the 750iL and optional on the 740iL. A sophisticated interior-motion theft-deterrent system is now available.

Don't forget to refer to the Mileage Adjustment Table at the back of this book!

Model Description	Trade-in TMV	Private TMV	Dealer TMV
Category I			
4 Dr 740iL Sdn	20828	22622	25100
4 Dr 750iL Sdn	28061	30478	33816

OPTIONS FOR 7-SERIES
Automatic Load Leveling[Std on 750iL] +325
Comfort Seats[Std on 750iL] +513
Park Distance Control[Std on 750iL] +385
Ski Sack[Std on 750iL] +139

8-SERIES   1996

Model Description	Trade-in TMV	Private TMV	Dealer TMV
Category I			
2 Dr 840Ci Cpe	25160	27327	30320
Category F			
2 Dr 850CSi Cpe	37804	40820	44986
Category I			
2 Dr 850Ci Cpe	31998	34754	38560

OPTIONS FOR 8-SERIES
Aluminum/Alloy Wheels +534
Forged Alloy Wheels +380

Z3   1996

BMW follows Mazda's lead and introduces a roadster. This dreamy two-seater made its debut in the James Bond movie, "Golden Eye", and has had enthusiasts across the country drooling over its smart styling and impressive refinement. Featured as the perfect Christmas gift in the 1995 Neiman Marcus Christmas catalog, BMW sold out of Z3s before the first one was released to the public.

Model Description	Trade-in TMV	Private TMV	Dealer TMV
Category I			
2 Dr STD Conv	12826	14118	15902

OPTIONS FOR Z3
Automatic 4-Speed Transmission +417
Heated Front Seats +150
Leather Seats +468
Metallic Paint +203
Onboard Computer +150
Special Factory Paint +203
Traction Control System +342

1995 BMW

3-SERIES   1995

A new M3 coupe debuts with blistering performance and exceptional grace. Available only as a five-speed manual, the M3 has 240 horsepower, a limited-slip differential and 17-inch wheels. The 318 series gains a convertible and a hatchback (318ti). Two new packages debut that allow a driver to choose between a sports or luxury orientation.

Model Description	Trade-in TMV	Private TMV	Dealer TMV
Category H			
2 Dr 318i Conv	9866	10925	12690
4 Dr 318i Sdn	8570	9490	11023
2 Dr 318is Cpe	9186	10172	11816
2 Dr 318ti Hbk	7732	8562	9945
2 Dr 325i Conv	14348	15889	18456
4 Dr 325i Sdn	10915	12087	14040
2 Dr 325is Cpe	11207	12410	14415
Category F			
2 Dr M3 Cpe	14822	16083	18186

OPTIONS FOR 3-SERIES
AM/FM Compact Disc Player +109
AM/FM Stereo/CD/Tape +208
Alarm System +117
Aluminum/Alloy Wheels[Opt on 318i Sdn] +217
Automatic 4-Speed Transmission +353
Automatic 5-Speed Transmission +433
Compact Disc Changer +223
Dual Power Seats[Opt on M3] +251
Leather Seats[Opt on 318i,318is,318ti] +425
Limited Slip Differential +126
Luxury Package +482
Metallic Paint +117
Onboard Computer +126
Power Sunroof[Opt on 318ti,M3] +343
Rollover Protection System +523
Sport Suspension +136
Sports Package +260
Traction Control System +117

5-SERIES   1995

BMW sports up its 540i by making a six-speed manual transmission available. That option includes 12-way power sport seats, a sport suspension and beefy anti-roll bars. Unfortunately, all models lose their V-rated tires in favor of wimpy H-rated tires in an attempt to improve fuel economy.

Model Description	Trade-in TMV	Private TMV	Dealer TMV
Category I			
4 Dr 525i Sdn	12471	13528	15291
4 Dr 525i Touring Wgn	12858	13948	15765
4 Dr 530i Sdn	13617	14772	16696
4 Dr 530i Touring Wgn	14154	15355	17355
4 Dr 540i Sdn	14945	16212	18324

OPTIONS FOR 5-SERIES
6-Speed Transmission +885
AM/FM Compact Disc Player +126
Alarm System[Opt on 525i] +117
Automatic 4-Speed Transmission[Std on Touring] +353
Compact Disc Changer +181
Dual Sunroofs +506
Heated Front Seats +117
Leather Seats[Opt on 525i] +497
Metallic Paint +172
Onboard Computer[Opt on 525i] +126
Premium Package +482
Traction Control System +181

7-SERIES   1995

The big Bimmer is totally redesigned for 1995. The flagship sedan now features sleek styling and a

Model Description	Trade-in TMV	Private TMV	Dealer TMV

lengthened wheelbase. Three models are available for 1995, including a new 740i regular-wheelbase model. The V12 engine found in the 750iL gains 27 horsepower and 30 foot-pounds of torque. New interior refinements include a residual heat system which will continue to heat the car after the power has been turned off, and 14-way power seats.

Category I

Model Description	Trade-in TMV	Private TMV	Dealer TMV
4 Dr 740i Sdn	15539	16857	19053
4 Dr 740iL Sdn	16130	17497	19777
4 Dr 750iL Sdn	20959	22736	25698

OPTIONS FOR 7-SERIES
Compact Disc Changer[Std on 750iL] +235
Heated Front Seats[Std on 750iL] +136
Park Distance Control[Std on 750iL] +325
Ski Sack[Std on 750iL] +117
Traction Control System[Std on 750iL] +117

8-SERIES   1995

No changes for the 8-Series.
Category I

Model Description	Trade-in TMV	Private TMV	Dealer TMV
2 Dr 840Ci Cpe	19549	21207	23970

Category F

Model Description	Trade-in TMV	Private TMV	Dealer TMV
2 Dr 850CSi Cpe	33501	36353	41105

Category I

Model Description	Trade-in TMV	Private TMV	Dealer TMV
2 Dr 850Ci Cpe	24873	26982	30497

OPTIONS FOR 8-SERIES
Aluminum/Alloy Wheels +144
Electronic Damping Control +506
Forged Alloy Wheels +321

1994 BMW

3-SERIES   1994

Dual airbags appear on all 3-series models. A new six-cylinder convertible joins the stable and traction control becomes optional for all cars.

Category H

Model Description	Trade-in TMV	Private TMV	Dealer TMV
2 Dr 318i Conv	8442	9433	11086
4 Dr 318i Sdn	7265	8119	9541
2 Dr 318is Cpe	7706	8611	10120
2 Dr 325i Conv	11730	13108	15404
4 Dr 325i Sdn	9609	10738	12619
2 Dr 325is Cpe	9838	10993	12919

OPTIONS FOR 3-SERIES
AM/FM Compact Disc Player +94
AM/FM Stereo/CD/Tape +180
Alarm System +101
Automatic 4-Speed Transmission +305
Compact Disc Changer +193
Cruise Control[Opt on 318i,318is] +87
Fog Lights[Opt on 318] +82
Leather Seats[Opt on 318is,Sdn] +367

Limited Slip Differential +109
Metallic Paint +101
Onboard Computer +109
Rollover Protection System +454
Sport Suspension +118
Traction Control System +101

5-SERIES   1994

A passenger airbag debuts on all models and two new V8s join the lineup. The 535i and M5 are dropped. BMW's traction control system becomes standard on the 530i Touring and optional on other models. Both 525i models gain a premium sound system.

Category I

Model Description	Trade-in TMV	Private TMV	Dealer TMV
4 Dr 525i Sdn	10977	12045	13825
4 Dr 525i Touring Wgn	11211	12301	14119
4 Dr 530i Sdn	11284	12382	14211
4 Dr 530i Touring Wgn	11748	12890	14795
4 Dr 540i Sdn	12019	13188	15137

OPTIONS FOR 5-SERIES
AM/FM Compact Disc Player +109
AM/FM Stereo/CD/Tape +156
Automatic 4-Speed Transmission[Std on Touring] +305
Automatic 5-Speed Transmission +313
Dual Sunroofs +438
Heated Front Seats +101
Onboard Computer[Std on 540i] +109
Ski Sack +118
Traction Control System[Opt on 525i,540i] +156

7-SERIES   1994

No changes for the 7-Series.
Category I

Model Description	Trade-in TMV	Private TMV	Dealer TMV
4 Dr 740i Sdn	11783	12930	14840
4 Dr 740iL Sdn	12544	13764	15798
4 Dr 750iL Sdn	15887	17432	20008

OPTIONS FOR 7-SERIES
Electronic Damping Control[Std on 750iL] +438
Heated Front Seats[Std on 750iL] +118
Ski Sack[Std on 750iL] +101
Traction Control System[Std on 750iL] +101

8-SERIES   1994

Two new models are introduced to the 8-Series: the 840Ci and the 850CSi. The 840Ci has the same V8 power found in the 740 and 540. The 850CSi gets an increased displacement V12 that offers a whopping 372-horsepower. The CSi comes standard with a sports suspension and a six-speed manual transmission. Unfortunately, the introduction of the CSi takes away from the sportiness of the 850Ci, which is now saddled with a four-speed automatic as the only transmission choice.
Category I

Don't forget to refer to the Mileage Adjustment Table at the back of this book!

Model Description	Trade-in TMV	Private TMV	Dealer TMV
2 Dr 840Ci Cpe	15373	16869	19361
Category F			
2 Dr 850CSi Cpe	28991	31637	36047
Category I			
2 Dr 850Ci Cpe	22454	24639	28279

OPTIONS FOR 8-SERIES
Electronic Damping Control +438
Forged Alloy Wheels +278

1993 BMW

3-SERIES   1993

Four-bangers can now be equipped with an automatic transmission. Six-cylinder models get a variable valve timing system that improves low-end torque.

Category H

Model Description	Trade-in TMV	Private TMV	Dealer TMV
4 Dr 318i Sdn	5798	6554	7814
2 Dr 318is Cpe	6189	6996	8341
2 Dr 325i Conv	10293	11636	13873
4 Dr 325i Sdn	7761	8773	10460
2 Dr 325is Cpe	8114	9172	10936

OPTIONS FOR 3-SERIES
AM/FM Compact Disc Player[Opt on 325i Sdn] +83
Aluminum/Alloy Wheels[Opt on 318i] +166
Automatic 4-Speed Transmission +271
Gold Package +97
Heated Front Seats +83
Leather Seats[Opt on Sdn] +326
Limited Slip Differential +97
Metallic Paint +90
Onboard Computer[Std on Conv] +97
Sport Suspension +104
Sport Wheels +139

5-SERIES   1993

Bad news for trees and cows: wood trim and leather upholstery are now standard on the 525i. The 525i gets a variable valve timing system that improves low-end torque. The M5 gets new wheels for 1993.

Category I

Model Description	Trade-in TMV	Private TMV	Dealer TMV
4 Dr 525i Sdn	8918	9931	11620
4 Dr 525i Touring Wgn	9466	10542	12334
4 Dr 535i Sdn	10500	11693	13681
Category F			
4 Dr M5 Sdn	16895	18734	21800

OPTIONS FOR 5-SERIES
Alarm System +90
Automatic 4-Speed Transmission[Std on Touring] +271
Automatic Stability Control +319
Leather Seats[Opt on Touring] +381
Limited Slip Differential[Std on M5] +97
Onboard Computer[Opt on 525i] +97

7-SERIES   1993

The 7-Series' cheapest model swaps I-6 for V8 power. The entry-level 7-Series is now called the 740 to denote this change. The new engine has 282-horsepower that is mated to a five-speed automatic transmission. More wood for the interior, Z-rated tires, and an upgraded stereo round out the changes for the 1993 7-Series.

Category I

Model Description	Trade-in TMV	Private TMV	Dealer TMV
4 Dr 740i Sdn	9647	10743	12570
4 Dr 740iL Sdn	10593	11796	13802
4 Dr 750iL Sdn	11319	12605	14748

OPTIONS FOR 7-SERIES
AM/FM Compact Disc Player +117
Electronic Damping Control[Std on 750iL] +388
Ski Sack[Std on 750iL] +90
Traction Control System[Std on 750iL] +90

8-SERIES   1993

The 850i is now called the 850Ci. A passenger airbag is added to the standard equipment list, as is a split-fold rear seat. All interior materials have been upgraded over previous models.

Category I

Model Description	Trade-in TMV	Private TMV	Dealer TMV
2 Dr 850Ci Cpe	18456	20553	24047

OPTIONS FOR 8-SERIES
Automatic 4-Speed Transmission +235
Forged Alloy Wheels +246

1992 BMW

3-SERIES   1992

New sheetmetal for the 3-series; all the corners are rounded and the wheelbase is stretched. Interior space is marginally greater than previous models. A driver airbag is added to the equipment list. Buyers can choose between a sports or luxury package, depending on their predilections.

Category H

Model Description	Trade-in TMV	Private TMV	Dealer TMV
2 Dr 318i Conv	6592	7519	9065
4 Dr 318i Sdn	4789	5463	6586
2 Dr 318is Cpe	5274	6016	7252
2 Dr 325i Conv	9209	10505	12664
4 Dr 325i Sdn	6353	7247	8736
2 Dr 325is Cpe	7302	8329	10041

OPTIONS FOR 3-SERIES
AM/FM Stereo/CD/Tape +146
Aluminum/Alloy Wheels[Opt on 318i] +152
Appearance Package +140
Automatic 4-Speed Transmission +247
Leather Seats[Opt on Sdn] +252
Limited Slip Differential +89
Metallic Paint +82

Don't forget to refer to the Mileage Adjustment Table at the back of this book!

Model Description	Trade-in TMV	Private TMV	Dealer TMV	Model Description	Trade-in TMV	Private TMV	Dealer TMV

5-SERIES 1992

The 525 loses some luxury items from its standard equipment list; the steering wheel is now wrapped in leatherette instead of leather and the spare tire is shod with a steel wheel instead of an alloy. The 535 gains options like a nifty on-board computer and a power-adjustable steering wheel with a position memory. A security system is now standard. A Touring model is introduced as a wagon body style.

Category I

Model	Trade-in	Private	Dealer
4 Dr 525i Sdn	7836	8857	10559
4 Dr 525i Touring Wgn	7995	9037	10773
4 Dr 535i Sdn	8946	10111	12054

OPTIONS FOR 5-SERIES
Automatic 4-Speed Transmission[Std on 535i, Touring] +247
Automatic Stability Control +291
Compact Disc Changer +127
Heated Front Seats +82
Leather Seats[Opt on 525i] +348
Limited Slip Differential +89
Wood & Leather Package +215

7-SERIES 1992

7-Series cars equipped with an automatic transmission now have a shift interlock that prevents the car from being shifted out of park without simultaneously applying the brake. The one-touch-down power window feature now applies to all windows, not just the driver's. The 750iL model receives double-paned windows to improve noise reduction. All 1992 7-Series cars get a new Infinity stereo.

Category I

Model	Trade-in	Private	Dealer
4 Dr 735i Sdn	7228	8170	9740
4 Dr 735iL Sdn	8790	9935	11844
4 Dr 750iL Sdn	9250	10455	12464

OPTIONS FOR 7-SERIES
Automatic Stability Control[Std on 750iL] +291
Compact Disc Changer[Opt on 735i] +165
Electronic Damping Control +354
Heated Front Seats[Std on 750iL] +82
Limited Slip Differential[Std on 750iL] +89
Ski Sack[Std on 750iL] +82

8-SERIES 1992

BMW's most expensive coupe gets a few tweaks for 1992. Models equipped with an automatic transmission now have a shift interlock to prevent the car from unintentionally being shifted out of "park". BMW's Electronic Damping System is improved for 1992 as well, offering greater diversity between the sports and comfort settings.

Category I

Model	Trade-in	Private	Dealer
2 Dr 850i Cpe	15560	17587	20966

OPTIONS FOR 8-SERIES
Automatic Stability Control +291
Electronic Damping Control +354
Forged Alloy Wheels +225

M5 1992

The M5 gets better power steering and a higher final-drive ratio.

Category F

Model	Trade-in	Private	Dealer
4 Dr STD Sdn	14933	16796	19900

OPTIONS FOR M5
Heated Front Seats +76

Don't forget to refer to the Mileage Adjustment Table at the back of this book!

Model Description	Trade-in TMV	Private TMV	Dealer TMV	Model Description	Trade-in TMV	Private TMV	Dealer TMV

BUICK 01

BUICK   USA

1995 Buick Riviera

2001 BUICK

CENTURY   2001

Buick's midsize Century remains relatively unchanged for 2001. New rear-wheel house liners promise a quieter ride on wet roads, a special appearance package is offered and OnStar in-vehicle safety, security and information service is now standard on Limited models.

Category D

	Trade-in	Private	Dealer
4 Dr Custom Sdn	11690	12556	14000
4 Dr Limited Sdn	13360	14350	16000

OPTIONS FOR CENTURY
Aluminum/Alloy Wheels +214
Dual Power Seats +349
OnStar Telematic System[Std on Limited] +272
Power Drivers Seat +174
Power Passenger Seat +189
Power Sunroof +398
Premium Sound System +129

LESABRE   2001

The best-selling U.S. full-size car for eight straight years, Buick's LeSabre has been mildly updated after being totally redesigned last year. Changes include dual-stage airbags, standard OnStar in-vehicle safety, security and information service, and the engine oil change interval has been increased to 10,000 miles.

Category G

	Trade-in	Private	Dealer
4 Dr Custom Sdn	15412	16345	17900
4 Dr Limited Sdn	18512	19632	21500

OPTIONS FOR LESABRE
AM/FM Stereo/CD/Tape +200
Aluminum/Alloy Wheels[Opt on Custom] +186
Automatic Stability Control +283
Compact Disc Changer +340
Heated Front Seats[Opt on Limited] +169
Leather Seats +446
OnStar Telematic System[Std on Limited] +272
Power Passenger Seat[Std on Limited] +189
Power Sunroof +515

PARK AVENUE   2001

Enjoying mild sales success since its 1997 redesign, Buick's full-size Park Avenue gets only minor refinements in the areas of safety, convenience and colors for 2001. The biggest news is the addition of the Ultrasonic Rear Park Assist system, improving safety while backing up.

Category H

	Trade-in	Private	Dealer
4 Dr Ultra Sprchgd Sdn	21800	23000	25000
4 Dr STD Sdn	18748	19780	21500

OPTIONS FOR PARK AVENUE
AM/FM Stereo/CD/Tape +123
Automatic Stability Control +283
Chrome Wheels +435
Compact Disc Changer +340
Dual Power Seats +349
Heated Seats[Std on Ultra] +169
Park Distance Control +169
Power Sunroof +626
Special Factory Paint +257

REGAL   2001

For the 2001 model year, the "Car for the Supercharged Family" gets new rear-wheel house liners for a quieter ride, a standard trunk entrapment release and two new colors, Graphite Metallic and "White". An Olympic appearance package is now available and OnStar in-vehicle safety, security and information service is standard on GS models.

Category D

	Trade-in	Private	Dealer
4 Dr GS Sprchgd Sdn	15197	16323	18200
4 Dr LS Sdn	13360	14350	16000

OPTIONS FOR REGAL
Aluminum/Alloy Wheels[Std on GS] +192
Chrome Wheels +226
Head Air Bag Restraint[Opt on LS] +143
Heated Seats +169
Leather Seats[Std on GS] +315
Monsoon Sound System +169
OnStar Telematic System[Opt on LS] +272
Power Moonroof +398
Power Passenger Seat +189
Side Air Bag Restraints[Std on GS] +143

Don't forget to refer to the Mileage Adjustment Table at the back of this book!

BUICK 00-99

Model Description	Trade-in TMV	Private TMV	Dealer TMV	Model Description	Trade-in TMV	Private TMV	Dealer TMV

2000 BUICK

CENTURY   2000

Buick's midsize Century heads into the new millennium with a Special Edition model commemorating the turn of the century and more horsepower in all three models from a revised 3.1-liter 3100 V6.

Category D

	Trade-in	Private	Dealer
4 Dr Custom Sdn	9565	10623	11600
4 Dr Limited Sdn	10637	11814	12900

OPTIONS FOR CENTURY

AM/FM Stereo Tape +112
AM/FM Stereo/CD/Tape +240
Aluminum/Alloy Wheels +214
Climate Control for AC +100
Cruise Control +109
Dual Power Seats +349
Power Drivers Seat +174
Power Moonroof +398

LESABRE   2000

The best-selling U.S. full-size car for seven straight years, Buick's LeSabre has been totally redesigned for the 2000 model year. Though it looks a lot like a '99, this car has undergone a remarkable transformation, riding on a new platform with mildly tweaked sheetmetal and an entirely reworked cabin. Better ride, steering and seats, plus side airbags and integrated seatbelts, make it an even better value than before.

Category G

	Trade-in	Private	Dealer
4 Dr Custom Sdn	12955	14174	15300
4 Dr Limited Sdn	15326	16769	18100

OPTIONS FOR LESABRE

AM/FM Compact Disc Player[Opt on Custom] +143
AM/FM Stereo Tape[Opt on Custom] +94
AM/FM Stereo/CD/Tape +143
Alarm System[Opt on Custom] +100
Aluminum/Alloy Wheels[Opt on Custom] +186
Compact Disc Changer +340
Dual Power Seats[Opt on Custom] +349
Heated Front Seats[Opt on Limited] +128
Leather Seats +569
Power Drivers Seat[Opt on Custom] +174
Power Moonroof +569
Traction Control System +100

PARK AVENUE   2000

Enjoying mild sales success since its 1997 redesign, Buick's full-size Park Avenue gets only minor refinements in the areas of safety, stability and comfort for 2000. The biggest news is the addition of StabiliTrak, GM's advanced vehicle stability control system.

Category H

	Trade-in	Private	Dealer
4 Dr STD Sdn	14749	16023	17200
4 Dr Ultra Sprchgd Sdn	17579	19098	20500

OPTIONS FOR PARK AVENUE

AM/FM Compact Disc Player[Opt on STD] +143
AM/FM Stereo/CD/Tape +143
Bucket Seats +106
Chrome Wheels +398
Compact Disc Changer +340
Heated Front Seats[Opt on STD] +128
Heated Power Mirrors[Opt on STD] +103
Leather Seats[Opt on STD] +430
Power Moonroof +626
Special Factory Paint +226
Traction Control System[Opt on STD] +100
Trip Computer[Opt on STD] +114

REGAL   2000

For the 2000 model year, the "Official Car of the Supercharged Family" gets new alloy wheels, a standard body-colored grille on the GS and two new colors, Gold Metallic and Sterling Silver. Inside, there's now a split-folding rear seat and an optional side airbag for the driver on leather-lined Regals.

Category D

	Trade-in	Private	Dealer
4 Dr GS Sprchgd Sdn	12203	13554	14800
4 Dr LS Sdn	10967	12180	13300
4 Dr LSE Sdn Sdn	11214	12455	13600

OPTIONS FOR REGAL

AM/FM Stereo/CD/Tape +114
Aluminum/Alloy Wheels[Std on GS] +192
Chrome Wheels +226
Climate Control for AC +100
Compact Disc Changer +314
Dual Power Seats +349
Heated Front Seats +128
Leather Seats[Std on GS] +372
Monsoon Sound System +169
Power Drivers Seat[Opt on LS] +188
Power Moonroof +398
Side Air Bag Restraints[Std on GS] +143

1999 BUICK

CENTURY   1999

After a complete redesign in 1997 put the Century into carryover status last year, 1999 brings a host of safety feature improvements, many of them standard. Additionally, the suspension has been retuned for less body roll, the sound systems have been upgraded and one new paint color, called Auburn Nightmist, has been added.

Category D

	Trade-in	Private	Dealer
4 Dr Custom Sdn	7800	8750	9700
4 Dr Limited Sdn	9328	10464	11600

Don't forget to refer to the Mileage Adjustment Table at the back of this book!

Model Description	Trade-in TMV	Private TMV	Dealer TMV	Model Description	Trade-in TMV	Private TMV	Dealer TMV

OPTIONS FOR CENTURY
AM/FM Stereo/CD/Tape +192
Aluminum/Alloy Wheels +171
Dual Power Seats +278
Leather Seats +285
Power Drivers Seat +138
Power Moonroof +317

LESABRE 1999

Buick's LeSabre celebrates its 40th year in the marketplace as a carryover model for 1999. Perhaps deciding there's no need to mess with success (more than 6 million LeSabres have been sold since the nameplate's 1959 introduction), Buick has merely made some emissions system improvements for '99, and added two exterior metallic paint choices, Sterling Silver and Dark Bronzemist.

Category G

4 Dr Custom Sdn	9944	10972	12000
4 Dr Limited Sdn	11684	12892	14100

OPTIONS FOR LESABRE
AM/FM Compact Disc Player +114
AM/FM Stereo/CD/Tape +114
Aluminum/Alloy Wheels[Opt on Custom] +147
Dual Power Seats[Opt on Custom] +278
Leather Seats +336
Power Drivers Seat +138

PARK AVENUE 1999

Riding a wave of sales success since its 1997 redesign, Buick didn't feel like fiddling much with its Park Avenue recipe for 1999. One noticeable change is a revision of the Park Avenue's taillamps, which are now similar to those found on the upscale Ultra model. Also new this year is an enhanced eight-speaker audio system dubbed Concert Sound III, a new hood-to-fender seal for improved appearance, an adjustable rubber bumper for the decklid, and four new exterior colors.

Category H

4 Dr STD Sdn	12564	13832	15100
4 Dr Ultra Sprchgd Sdn	15061	16580	18100

OPTIONS FOR PARK AVENUE
AM/FM Compact Disc Player[Opt on STD] +114
AM/FM Stereo/CD/Tape +114
Chrome Wheels +317
Compact Disc Changer +271
Heated Front Seats[Opt on STD] +114
Leather Seats[Opt on STD] +342
Power Moonroof +500
Special Factory Paint +180

REGAL 1999

Performance-oriented changes, such as more power, sporty tweaks to the steering and suspension, firmer motor mounts and the addition of a strut tower brace underhood, lead the news for the '99 Regal. Other changes include enhancements to the ABS and traction control systems, as well as the addition of a tire inflation monitor, perimeter lighting and the Concert Sound II audio system to Regal's already long list of standard equipment. New options include a self-dimming electrochromic outside rearview mirror, redesigned 15-inch alloy wheels and the eight-speaker, 220-watt Monsoon audio system. And that's all in addition to a new exterior paint color, Auburn Nightmist.

Category D

4 Dr GS Sprchgd Sdn	10534	11817	13100
4 Dr LS Sdn	8926	10013	11100

OPTIONS FOR REGAL
AM/FM Stereo/CD/Tape +91
Aluminum/Alloy Wheels[Std on GS] +153
Chrome Wheels +180
Compact Disc Changer +250
Dual Power Seats +278
Heated Front Seats +102
LSE Package +1139
Leather Seats[Std on GS] +296
Monsoon Sound System +134
Power Drivers Seat[Std on GS] +150
Power Moonroof +317

RIVIERA 1999

We were going to mention that traction control is now standard on the Riviera and that this year brings the choice of four new paint colors (Sterling Silver, Titanium Blue, Gold Firemist and Dark Bronzemist), but that was before Buick decided to pull the plug on the big coupe soon after production began. Now you also need to know that only approximately 2,000 Riveras will be built for the 1999 model year, along with a special run of 200 special edition models dubbed Silver Arrow."

Category H

2 Dr STD Sprchgd Cpe	14312	15756	17200

OPTIONS FOR RIVIERA
Chrome Wheels +317
Heated Front Seats +134
Power Moonroof +500
Special Factory Paint +180

1998 BUICK

CENTURY 1998

The addition of second-generation airbags, three new exterior colors, one new interior color and the availability of OnStar mobile communications are this year's changes.

Category D

4 Dr Custom Sdn	6592	7460	8400

Don't forget to refer to the Mileage Adjustment Table at the back of this book!

Model Description	Trade-in TMV	Private TMV	Dealer TMV	Model Description	Trade-in TMV	Private TMV	Dealer TMV
4 Dr Limited Sdn	7377	8348	9400	4 Dr GS Sprchgd Sdn	9025	10213	11500
				4 Dr LS Sdn	7691	8703	9800

OPTIONS FOR CENTURY
AM/FM Stereo/CD/Tape +174
Aluminum/Alloy Wheels +156
Dual Power Seats +253
Leather Seats[Opt on Limited] +227
Power Drivers Seat +127
Power Moonroof +288

OPTIONS FOR REGAL
AM/FM Stereo/CD/Tape[Opt on GS,LS] +104
Chrome Wheels[Opt on GS,LS] +163
Compact Disc Changer +227
Dual Power Seats +253
Leather Seats[Opt on LS] +249
Power Drivers Seat +127
Power Moonroof +288

LESABRE 1998

Cruise control is standard on base models, OnStar Mobile Communications is a dealer-installed option, Limited models get a couple of electrochromic mirrors, and new colors are on tap inside and out. Second-generation airbags are made standard.

Category G

	Trade-in	Private	Dealer
4 Dr Custom Sdn	8341	9282	10300
4 Dr Limited Sdn	9799	10904	12100

OPTIONS FOR LESABRE
AM/FM Stereo/CD/Tape +104
Aluminum/Alloy Wheels[Opt on Custom] +134
Dual Power Seats[Opt on Custom] +253
Leather Seats +227
Power Drivers Seat +127

PARK AVENUE 1998

Exterior mirrors can be folded away, a new optional feature tilts the exterior mirrors down for curb viewing during reversing, dealers can install an OnStar Communications system and new colors are available inside and out. Second-generation airbags are made standard.

Category H

	Trade-in	Private	Dealer
4 Dr STD Sdn	10197	11302	12500
4 Dr Ultra Sprchgd Sdn	12399	13744	15200

OPTIONS FOR PARK AVENUE
AM/FM Compact Disc Player[Opt on STD] +104
AM/FM Stereo/CD/Tape +104
Chrome Wheels +288
Compact Disc Changer +247
Heated Front Seats[Opt on STD] +104
Leather Seats[Opt on STD] +249
Power Moonroof +412

REGAL 1998

Regal LS gets a new standard four-speed automatic transmission, and three new exterior colors are available. Dealers will install an OnStar Mobile Communications system if the buyer desires, and second-generation airbags are added.

Category D

	Trade-in	Private	Dealer
4 Dr 25TH Anniversary Sdn	9103	10302	11600

RIVIERA 1998

Supercharged power is standard, OnStar satellite communications system is a new option and de-powered airbags debut. Four exterior colors are new, suspension and steering have been massaged and a heated passenger seat with lumbar support has been added to the options list.

Category H

	Trade-in	Private	Dealer
2 Dr STD Sprchgd Cpe	13052	14467	16000

OPTIONS FOR RIVIERA
Chrome Wheels +288
Heated Front Seats +122
Power Moonroof +412
Special Factory Paint +163

SKYLARK 1998

Skylark was sold strictly to fleets for 1998. If you're buying one used, chances are good that it was once a rental car.

Category C

	Trade-in	Private	Dealer
4 Dr Custom Sdn	5378	6109	6900

OPTIONS FOR SKYLARK
6 cyl 3.1 L Engine +163
Power Windows +121

1997 BUICK

CENTURY 1997

After a decade and a half, Buick finally redesigns its bread-and-butter mid-size sedan, dropping the wagon variant in the process. A spunky 3.1-liter V6 engine, roomier interior, larger trunk and traditional Buick styling cues should convince Grandpa to trade the old warhorse in on a new one.

Category D

	Trade-in	Private	Dealer
4 Dr Custom Sdn	5468	6337	7400
4 Dr Limited Sdn	6133	7108	8300

OPTIONS FOR CENTURY
AM/FM Stereo/CD/Tape +148
Aluminum/Alloy Wheels +115
Dual Power Seats +216
Leather Seats +194

Don't forget to refer to the Mileage Adjustment Table at the back of this book!

Model Description	Trade-in TMV	Private TMV	Dealer TMV

Power Drivers Seat +108
Power Moonroof +246

LESABRE 1997

Buick freshens the somewhat stale LeSabre with new front and rear styling. Redesigned wheel selections, new seats on Custom models, and walnut instrument panel appliques round out the visual changes. Structurally, the LeSabre now meets side-impact standards.

Category G

Model Description	Trade-in TMV	Private TMV	Dealer TMV
4 Dr Custom Sdn	6661	7534	8600
4 Dr Limited Sdn	7746	8760	10000

OPTIONS FOR LESABRE
Aluminum/Alloy Wheels[Opt on Custom] +115
Dual Power Seats[Opt on Custom] +216
Leather Seats +194
Power Drivers Seat +108

PARK AVENUE 1997

Buick engineers substantially improve the Park Avenue for 1997 by strengthening the body structure, improving interior ergonomics, and introducing a sleek new look. Powertrains are carried over, and two models are available: base and Ultra. Prices have risen, but the Park Avenue represents real value in comparison to other traditional luxury sedans.

Category H

Model Description	Trade-in TMV	Private TMV	Dealer TMV
4 Dr STD Sdn	7961	8923	10100
4 Dr Ultra Sprchgd Sdn	9695	10867	12300

OPTIONS FOR PARK AVENUE
Chrome Wheels +246
Compact Disc Changer +211
Leather Seats[Opt on STD] +213
Power Moonroof +352

REGAL 1997

Long overdue, the complete redesign of the Regal means Buick finally has a viable entry in the midsized sedan marketplace. The standard equipment list is a mile long, including ABS, traction control, dual-zone climate controls, heated exterior mirrors, retained accessory power and battery rundown protection.

Category D

Model Description	Trade-in TMV	Private TMV	Dealer TMV
4 Dr GS Sprchgd Sdn	6872	7964	9300
4 Dr LS Sdn	6207	7194	8400

OPTIONS FOR REGAL
AM/FM Stereo/CD/Tape +104
Aluminum/Alloy Wheels[Opt on LS] +118
Chrome Wheels +140
Dual Power Seats +216
Leather Seats[Opt on LS] +213
Power Drivers Seat +108

Power Moonroof +246

RIVIERA 1997

Upgraded transmissions, several new colors inside and out, additional standard equipment and new options summarize minimal changes to the Riviera.

Category H

Model Description	Trade-in TMV	Private TMV	Dealer TMV
2 Dr STD Cpe	9222	10337	11700
2 Dr STD Sprchgd Cpe	10167	11397	12900

OPTIONS FOR RIVIERA
Chrome Wheels +246
Heated Front Seats +104
Leather Seats +265
Power Moonroof +387
Special Factory Paint +140

SKYLARK 1997

Skylark gets minimal revisions this year. The standard equipment list is expanded.

Category C

Model Description	Trade-in TMV	Private TMV	Dealer TMV
2 Dr Custom Cpe	4003	4677	5500
4 Dr Custom Sdn	4076	4762	5600
2 Dr Gran Sport Cpe	5022	5867	6900
4 Dr Gran Sport Sdn	4804	5612	6600

OPTIONS FOR SKYLARK
6 cyl 3.1 L Engine[Opt on Custom] +140
AM/FM Stereo/CD/Tape +148
Leather Seats +219
Power Moonroof +217
Power Windows[Opt on Custom] +103

1996 BUICK

CENTURY 1996

In many states, this design is just a decade away from antique car status. Wagons get the V6 as standard equipment. Power windows, cassette player, rear window defogger and a remote trunk release make the standard equipment list as this ancient A-body rolls into its final year of production.

Category D

Model Description	Trade-in TMV	Private TMV	Dealer TMV
4 Dr STD Sdn	3536	4193	5100
4 Dr STD Wgn	3882	4604	5600

OPTIONS FOR CENTURY
6 cyl 3.1 L Engine[Opt on Custom] +194
Leather Seats +174

LESABRE 1996

Finally, the Series II engine is standard on LeSabre. Order the Gran Touring suspension, and get the same magnetic variable effort steering found on the Park Avenue Ultra. Now standard on the Custom is an electric rear window defogger and storage armrest.

Don't forget to refer to the Mileage Adjustment Table at the back of this book!

BUICK 96

Model Description	Trade-in TMV	Private TMV	Dealer TMV	Model Description	Trade-in TMV	Private TMV	Dealer TMV

Limited trim levels get Twilight Sentinel, dual automatic ComforTemp climate controls, and a rear seat center armrest.

Category G

4 Dr Custom Sdn	4872	5640	6700
4 Dr Limited Sdn	6035	6987	8300

OPTIONS FOR LESABRE

AM/FM Stereo/CD/Tape +111
Aluminum/Alloy Wheels[Opt on Custom] +102
Leather Seats +174
Prestige Package +193

PARK AVENUE   1996

Ultra gets new Series II supercharged engine as standard equipment, as well as magnetic variable effort steering gear. Colors and trim are revised, battery rundown protection is added, and long-life engine components keep the Park going longer between maintenance stops.

Category H

4 Dr STD Sdn	5952	6854	8100
4 Dr Ultra Sprchgd Sdn	7349	8462	10000

OPTIONS FOR PARK AVENUE

Dual Power Seats[Opt on STD] +194
Leather Seats[Opt on STD] +190
Luxury Package +531
Power Moonroof +315
Prestige Package +464

REGAL   1996

The Series II 3.8-liter V6 is standard on Limited and Gran Sport, optional on base Custom models. Standard equipment now includes dual ComforTemp climate controls and a cassette player. Revised wheels, available in chrome, are standard on the Gran Sport. Base V6 is upgraded, and both engines feature long-life engine components.

Category D

2 Dr Custom Cpe	3744	4439	5400
4 Dr Custom Sdn	3813	4521	5500
2 Dr Gran Sport Cpe	4414	5234	6367
4 Dr Gran Sport Sdn	4460	5288	6433
4 Dr Limited Sdn	4258	5049	6142
4 Dr Olympic Gold Sdn	4200	4980	6058

OPTIONS FOR REGAL

6 cyl 3.8 L Engine[Opt on STD] +125
Aluminum/Alloy Wheels +102
Chrome Wheels +125
Dual Power Seats +184
Leather Seats +174
Power Moonroof +221

RIVIERA   1996

Series II supercharged engine gives top-of-the-line Riv 240 horsepower. There are new colors inside and out, real wood on the dash, and revised climate and radio controls. Chrome wheels are optional.

Category H

2 Dr STD Cpe	7055	8124	9600
2 Dr STD Sprchgd Cpe	7275	8378	9900

OPTIONS FOR RIVIERA

Chrome Wheels +221
Leather Seats +222
Power Moonroof +315
Prestige Package +364
Special Factory Paint +125

ROADMASTER   1996

Last year for 260 hp land yacht. All models are designated Collector's Editions.

Category G

4 Dr STD Sdn	7344	8502	10100
4 Dr Estate Wgn	8435	9764	11600
4 Dr Limited Sdn	8362	9680	11500

OPTIONS FOR ROADMASTER

Aluminum/Alloy Wheels[Opt on Sdn] +102
Camper/Towing Package +119
Heated Front Seats +125
Heated Seats +125
Landau/Half Vinyl Roof +221
Leather Seats +246
Limited Package +611
Prestige Package +409

SKYLARK   1996

Styling changes inside and out make the Skylark far more marketable, and credible. Dual airbags are new, as are three-point seatbelts mounted to the B-pillar where they should be. A new twin-cam engine replaces the 2.3-liter Quad 4, and automatic transmissions include traction control. Air conditioning, a rear window defroster, and a tilt wheel are now standard. Long-life engine components round out the long list of improvements to Buick's lame duck.

Category C

2 Dr Custom Cpe	2981	3577	4400
4 Dr Custom Sdn	2913	3495	4300
4 Dr Olympic Gold Sdn	3116	3739	4600

OPTIONS FOR SKYLARK

6 cyl 3.1 L Engine +125
AM/FM Compact Disc Player +102
AM/FM Stereo/CD/Tape +133
Gran Sport Package +699
Leather Seats +196
Power Moonroof +188

Don't forget to refer to the Mileage Adjustment Table at the back of this book!

Model Description	Trade-in TMV	Private TMV	Dealer TMV		Model Description	Trade-in TMV	Private TMV	Dealer TMV

1995 BUICK

CENTURY 1995

Instruments newly backlit, and seats are revised.
Category D

4 Dr Custom Sdn	2361	2804	3542
4 Dr Limited Sdn	2732	3245	4100
4 Dr Special Sdn	2199	2612	3300
4 Dr Special Wgn	2305	2737	3458

OPTIONS FOR CENTURY
6 cyl 3.1 L Engine[Opt on Special] +155
Aluminum/Alloy Wheels +75
Leather Seats[Std on Limited] +140
Power Drivers Seat +77
Styled Steel Wheels[Opt on Sdn] +75

LESABRE 1995

New climate controls and radios are major changes.
Category G

4 Dr Custom Sdn	3637	4223	5200
4 Dr Limited Sdn	4267	4954	6100

OPTIONS FOR LESABRE
AM/FM Stereo/CD/Tape +76
Aluminum/Alloy Wheels[Opt on Custom] +83
Leather Seats +140
Power Drivers Seat[Opt on Custom] +77
Power Passenger Seat +77

PARK AVENUE 1995

Base engine upgraded to 3800 Series II status; makes 35 more horsepower than previous year. Base models get styling tweaks front and rear. New climate controls and radios are added.
Category H

4 Dr STD Sdn	4825	5566	6800
4 Dr Ultra Sprchgd Sdn			
	5819	6712	8200

OPTIONS FOR PARK AVENUE
Alarm System +76
Leather Seats[Opt on STD] +152
Luxury Package +427
Power Moonroof +253
Premium Sound System +165
Prestige Package[Opt on STD] +372

REGAL 1995

New interior has dual airbags housed in revised instrument panel. Gauges are actually legible. Seats are new, too. Fake wood has been chopped from door panels. Exterior styling is updated.
Category D

2 Dr Custom Cpe	2866	3404	4300

4 Dr Custom Sdn	3066	3641	4600
4 Dr Custom Select Sdn			
	2799	3324	4200
2 Dr Gran Sport Cpe	3466	4116	5200
4 Dr Gran Sport Sdn	3399	4037	5100
4 Dr Limited Sdn	3199	3799	4800

OPTIONS FOR REGAL
6 cyl 3.8 L Engine[Opt on Custom] +101
AM/FM Compact Disc Player +89
AM/FM Stereo/CD/Tape +75
Aluminum/Alloy Wheels[Std on Gran Sport] +83
Chrome Wheels[Opt on Gran Sport] +89
Dual Power Seats +147
Leather Seats +140
Power Moonroof +176

RIVIERA 1995

All-new Riv debuts with controversial styling. Dual airbags and ABS are standard. Base engine is 3800 Series II V6; optional is a supercharged 3.8-liter. Traction control is optional.
Category H

2 Dr STD Cpe	5393	6221	7600
2 Dr STD Sprchgd Cpe	6173	7121	8700

OPTIONS FOR RIVIERA
AM/FM Compact Disc Player +89
AM/FM Stereo/CD/Tape +127
Heated Front Seats +75
Leather Seats +178
Power Moonroof +253

ROADMASTER 1995

New radios and larger rearview mirrors are added. Cassette player is made standard. Wagon gets standard alloy wheels. New options are heated front seats and memory feature for power driver's seat.
Category G

4 Dr STD Sdn	5316	6172	7600
4 Dr Estate Wgn	5875	6822	8400
4 Dr Limited Sdn	6085	7066	8700

OPTIONS FOR ROADMASTER
Aluminum/Alloy Wheels[Opt on Sdn] +83
Camper/Towing Package +95
Dual Power Seats +140
Full Vinyl Top +127
Heated Front Seats +101
Leather Seats +197
Limited Wagon Package +330
Power Drivers Seat +77
Power Passenger Seat +77

SKYLARK 1995

Rear suspension is revised. New base engine is 150-horsepower Quad 4, packing 35 more ponies than

Don't forget to refer to the Mileage Adjustment Table at the back of this book!

BUICK 95-94

Model Description	Trade-in TMV	Private TMV	Dealer TMV	Model Description	Trade-in TMV	Private TMV	Dealer TMV

previous base engine. GS gets 3.1-liter V6 standard. Power sunroof is a new option.

Category C

2 Dr Custom Cpe	2258	2711	3465
4 Dr Custom Sdn	2304	2766	3535
2 Dr Gran Sport Cpe	2542	3051	3900
4 Dr Gran Sport Sdn	2542	3051	3900

OPTIONS FOR SKYLARK

6 cyl 3.1 L Engine[Opt on Custom] +101
AM/FM Compact Disc Player[Opt on Custom] +81
Air Conditioning[Opt on Custom] +140
Leather Seats +126
Power Moonroof +151
Power Windows[Opt on Custom] +74

1994 BUICK

CENTURY 1994

A driver airbag and ABS are standard on all models. This marks the first time ABS is offered on the Century. Coupe trimmed from lineup. The 2.2-liter engine gains 10 horsepower, and the optional 3.3-liter V6 is replaced by a 3.1-liter unit. When transmission is shifted into "Park," automatic door locks unlock themselves. Defeat this feature by removing a fuse. Tilt steering is standard on Special. New gauges debut.

Category D

4 Dr Custom Sdn	2083	2560	3355
4 Dr Special Sdn	1899	2334	3059
4 Dr Special Wgn	1987	2442	3200

OPTIONS FOR CENTURY

6 cyl 3.1 L Engine +128
Leather Seats +115

LESABRE 1994

Passenger airbag installed. Traction control system now cuts engine power to slipping wheels in addition to applying brake. Front seat travel increased one inch.

Category G

| 4 Dr Custom Sdn | 2743 | 3252 | 4100 |
| 4 Dr Limited Sdn | 3211 | 3807 | 4800 |

OPTIONS FOR LESABRE

Leather Seats +115

PARK AVENUE 1994

Passenger airbag debuts, and Ultra model gets 20 more horsepower. Traction control system now cuts engine power to slipping wheels in addition to applying brake, and can be turned off if desired. Remote keyless entry, power trunk pull-down and auto dimming rearview mirror added to Ultra standard equipment list. Front seat travel increased one inch. Heated front seats are newly optional.

Category H

4 Dr STD Sdn	3369	3981	5000
4 Dr Ultra Sprchgd Sdn			
	4178	4936	6200

OPTIONS FOR PARK AVENUE

Astro Roof +199
Delco/Bose Stereo System +105
Leather Seats[Opt on STD] +126
Prestige Package +307

REGAL 1994

Driver airbag and ABS standard on all Regals. 3.1-liter V6 gets 20 more horsepower. Power windows standard across the board, and automatic door locks automatically unlock when car is shifted into "Park." Defeat this feature by removing a fuse.

Category D

2 Dr Custom Cpe	2174	2671	3501
4 Dr Custom Sdn	2173	2670	3499
2 Dr Gran Sport Cpe	2295	2821	3697
4 Dr Gran Sport Sdn	2312	2841	3723
4 Dr Limited Sdn	2284	2807	3679

OPTIONS FOR REGAL

6 cyl 3.8 L Engine[Opt on Custom] +83
AM/FM Compact Disc Player +73
Leather Seats +115
Power Moonroof +146
Power Sunroof +199

ROADMASTER 1994

Detuned Corvette engine transplanted into big Buick, giving Roadmaster 80 additional horsepower. Dual airbags housed in redesigned dashboard with new gauges.

Category G

4 Dr STD Sdn	3679	4362	5500
4 Dr Estate Wgn	4014	4759	6000
4 Dr Limited Sdn	4482	5314	6700

OPTIONS FOR ROADMASTER

AM/FM Compact Disc Player +73
Camper/Towing Package +78
Full Vinyl Top +105
Leather Seats +163

SKYLARK 1994

Driver airbag added to all models. New 3.1-liter V6 replaces 3.3-liter V6 from 1993. Automatic transmission gets overdrive gear. Gran Sport and Limited gain standard equipment including air conditioning, power windows, cruise control and tilt steering wheel. Automatic door locks automatically unlock when car is put in "Park." Defeat this feature by removing a fuse.

Category C

Don't forget to refer to the Mileage Adjustment Table at the back of this book!

Model Description	Trade-in TMV	Private TMV	Dealer TMV	Model Description	Trade-in TMV	Private TMV	Dealer TMV
2 Dr Custom Cpe	1925	2403	3200	4 Dr STD Sdn	2396	2923	3800
4 Dr Custom Sdn	1804	2253	3000	4 Dr Ultra Sprchgd Sdn			
2 Dr Gran Sport Cpe	2285	2853	3800		2837	3461	4500
4 Dr Gran Sport Sdn	2225	2778	3700				
4 Dr Limited Sdn	2045	2553	3400				

OPTIONS FOR SKYLARK
6 cyl 3.1 L Engine[Opt on Custom,Limited Sdn] +83
Air Conditioning[Opt on Custom] +115

OPTIONS FOR PARK AVENUE
Astro Roof[Opt on STD] +171
Bose Sound System +99
Leather Seats[Opt on STD] +108
Luxury Package +301
Power Sunroof +171
Prestige Package +263

1993 BUICK

CENTURY 1993

Driver airbag standard on Custom and Limited; optional on Special. New 2.2-liter four-cylinder replaces old 2.5-liter unit with no loss of power. Fuel tank capacity increased.
Category D

	Trade-in	Private	Dealer
2 Dr Custom Cpe	1387	1825	2555
4 Dr Custom Sdn	1465	1928	2699
4 Dr Custom Wgn	1683	2214	3100
4 Dr Limited Sdn	1520	2000	2800
4 Dr Special Sdn	1326	1745	2443
4 Dr Special Wgn	1359	1788	2503

OPTIONS FOR CENTURY
6 cyl 3.3 L Engine +128
Air Bag Restraint[Opt on Special] +90
Leather Seats +99
Premium Package +126
Prestige Package +291

LESABRE 1993

Engine gets more torque, and both ABS and power door locks standard on all models. Limited offers variable-assist steering.
Category G
4 Dr 90th Anniversary Sdn

	Trade-in	Private	Dealer
	2180	2660	3460
4 Dr Custom Sdn	2230	2721	3540
4 Dr Limited Sdn	2394	2921	3800

OPTIONS FOR LESABRE
Dual Power Seats +110
Leather Seats[Opt on Limited] +99
Luxury Package +180
Premium Sound System +90
Prestige Package +110

PARK AVENUE 1993

Base V6 gains power. Revisions made to grilles and taillights. An automatic ride control system adjusts the suspension between three different modes ranging from soft to firm.
Category H

REGAL 1993

A new transmission, grille and taillights debut. The 3.8-liter V6 gains torque. 15-inch wheels replace 14-inch wheels. Optional on Limited and Gran Sport is a steering wheel with radio controls.
Category D

	Trade-in	Private	Dealer
2 Dr Custom Cpe	1460	1921	2690
4 Dr Custom Sdn	1471	1936	2710
2 Dr Gran Sport Cpe	1641	2160	3024
4 Dr Gran Sport Sdn	1683	2214	3100
2 Dr Limited Cpe	1574	2071	2900
4 Dr Limited Sdn	1615	2126	2976

OPTIONS FOR REGAL
6 cyl 3.8 L Engine[Opt on Custom,Limited] +71
Anti-Lock Brakes[Opt on Custom] +90
Dual Power Seats +104
Leather Seats +99
Power Sunroof +171

RIVIERA 1993

Gran Touring model gets larger wheels and tires from defunct Reatta.
Category H

	Trade-in	Private	Dealer
2 Dr STD Cpe	2585	3153	4100

OPTIONS FOR RIVIERA
Full Vinyl Top +90
Leather Seats +117
Power Sunroof +171
Premium Sound System +117
Special Factory Paint +71

ROADMASTER 1993

Wagons get Solar-Ray tinted windshield. Both models receive power window lockout switch and more sound deadening.
Category G

	Trade-in	Private	Dealer
4 Dr STD Sdn	2898	3536	4600
4 Dr Estate Wgn	2961	3613	4700
4 Dr Limited Sdn	3402	4151	5400

OPTIONS FOR ROADMASTER
Dual Power Seats[Opt on STD] +99
Full Vinyl Top +90

Don't forget to refer to the Mileage Adjustment Table at the back of this book!

Model Description	Trade-in TMV	Private TMV	Dealer TMV	Model Description	Trade-in TMV	Private TMV	Dealer TMV

Leather Seats +139
Prestige Package +231

SKYLARK   1993

New entry-level Custom model debuts. Base engine
loses five horsepower. Split-folding rear seat optional
on Limited; not available on Custom. Adjustable Ride
Control moves to GS options list from standard
equipment roster.

Category C

	Trade-in	Private	Dealer
2 Dr Custom Cpe	1422	1901	2700
4 Dr Custom Sdn	1369	1831	2600
2 Dr Gran Sport Cpe	1843	2465	3500
4 Dr Gran Sport Sdn	1843	2465	3500
2 Dr Limited Cpe	1527	2042	2900
4 Dr Limited Sdn	1475	1972	2800

OPTIONS FOR SKYLARK
6 cyl 3.3 L Engine[Std on Gran Sport] +128
Air Conditioning +99
Premium Sound System +72

1992 BUICK

CENTURY   1992

Power door locks made standard.

Category D

	Trade-in	Private	Dealer
2 Dr Custom Cpe	1090	1506	2200
4 Dr Custom Sdn	1122	1551	2266
4 Dr Custom Wgn	1238	1711	2499
4 Dr Limited Sdn	1239	1712	2501
4 Dr Limited Wgn	1288	1780	2600
4 Dr Special Sdn	1023	1414	2066

OPTIONS FOR CENTURY
6 cyl 3.3 L Engine +105
Leather Seats +81

LESABRE   1992

All-new car debuts based on 1991 Park Avenue
redesign. ABS is standard on Limited, optional on
Custom. Driver airbag is standard. Coupe dropped;
all LeSabres are sedans. 3.8-liter V6 gets more power.
Theft-deterrent system, power windows, and child-
proof rear door locks are standard.

Category G

	Trade-in	Private	Dealer
4 Dr Custom Sdn	1750	2219	3000
4 Dr Limited Sdn	1867	2367	3200

OPTIONS FOR LESABRE
Anti-Lock Brakes[Opt on Custom] +74
Full Vinyl Top +74
Leather Seats[Opt on Limited] +81
Premium Sound System +74

PARK AVENUE   1992

Ultra gets 205-horsepower supercharged V6. Traction
control is a new option. Variable-effort power steering
and dual cupholders are new for all Park Avenues.

Category H

	Trade-in	Private	Dealer
4 Dr STD Sdn	1660	2088	2800
4 Dr Ultra Sprchgd Sdn			
	2075	2609	3500

OPTIONS FOR PARK AVENUE
Astro Roof +140
Bose Sound System +81
Leather Seats[Opt on STD] +89
Premium Package +140
Premium Sound System +96
Prestige Package +216

REGAL   1992

Gran Sport no longer an option package; becomes a
full-fledged model designation. ABS newly standard
on Gran Sport and Limited. Power door locks made
standard on all Regals. Power front passenger seat is
new option.

Category D

	Trade-in	Private	Dealer
2 Dr Custom Cpe	987	1364	1993
4 Dr Custom Sdn	994	1374	2007
2 Dr Gran Sport Cpe	1337	1848	2700
4 Dr Gran Sport Sdn	1486	2054	3000
2 Dr Limited Cpe	1040	1438	2100
4 Dr Limited Sdn	1189	1643	2400

OPTIONS FOR REGAL
Anti-Lock Brakes[Opt on Custom] +74
Leather Seats +81
Power Sunroof +140

RIVIERA   1992

Solar-control glass is standard. Brake system gets
larger rotors and calipers.

Category H

	Trade-in	Private	Dealer
2 Dr STD Cpe	2253	2833	3800

OPTIONS FOR RIVIERA
AM/FM Stereo/CD/Tape +74
Astro Roof +118
Bose Sound System +81
Delco/Bose Stereo System +74
Leather Seats +96
Padded Vinyl Roof +88

ROADMASTER   1992

Wagon gets 5.7-liter engine. Sedan debuts.

Category G

	Trade-in	Private	Dealer
4 Dr STD Sdn	2042	2588	3500

Model Description	Trade-in TMV	Private TMV	Dealer TMV	Model Description	Trade-in TMV	Private TMV	Dealer TMV
4 Dr Estate Wgn	2158	2736	3700				
4 Dr Limited Sdn	2625	3328	4500				

OPTIONS FOR ROADMASTER
Landau/Half Vinyl Roof +102
Leather Seats +114
Premium Sound System +85

SKYLARK   1992

Redesign meant to bring younger buyers into showrooms backfires. Choice of four- or six-cylinder engines available. Automatic transmission, ABS, power door locks and split-folding rear seat are standard. Still has door-mounted seatbelts. Adjustable Ride Control, standard on GS and optional on other Skylarks, allows driver to select one of three suspension settings.
Category C

Model	Trade-in	Private	Dealer
2 Dr STD Cpe	912	1283	1900
4 Dr STD Sdn	1008	1418	2100
2 Dr Gran Sport Cpe	1249	1755	2600
4 Dr Gran Sport Sdn	1297	1823	2700

OPTIONS FOR SKYLARK
6 cyl 3.3 L Engine[Opt on STD] +105
Air Conditioning +81

Don't forget to refer to the Mileage Adjustment Table at the back of this book!

CADILLAC 01

Model Description	Trade-in TMV	Private TMV	Dealer TMV	Model Description	Trade-in TMV	Private TMV	Dealer TMV

CADILLAC   USA

1997 Cadillac DeVille

2001 CADILLAC

CATERA   2001

After mildly successful front and rear styling enhancements and a revised interior last year, the 2001 model year brings forth few changes for the Catera. OnStar 2.6 in-vehicle safety, security and information service, vented rear disc brakes and the Solar Protect windshield are now standard on all models. The Catera Sport receives new seats and projector beam headlamps are now standard on the base Catera.

Category H

4 Dr STD Sdn	18102	19189	21000

OPTIONS FOR CATERA

Bose Sound System +584
Chrome Wheels +477
Dual Power Seats +288
Heated Front Seats +255
Power Sunroof +598
Rear Spoiler +120
Xenon Headlamps +300

DEVILLE   2001

After a complete redesign last year, changes for 2001 are minimal at best. A tire pressure monitoring system is available, Graphite replaces Parisian Blue and Polo Green paint schemes, Dark Gray is added as an interior color and all Devilles are now certified throughout the U.S. as low-emissions vehicles.

Category I

4 Dr DHS Sdn	28128	29580	32000
4 Dr DTS Sdn	29007	30504	33000
4 Dr STD Sdn	23733	24958	27000

OPTIONS FOR DEVILLE

AM/FM Stereo/CD/Tape[Opt on STD] +732
Adaptive Front Seats +598
Automatic Stability Control[Std on DTS] +297
Chrome Wheels +477
Compact Disc Changer +357
Heated Seats[Std on DHS] +211
Leather Seats[Opt on STD] +471
Navigation System +1198
Night Vision +1351
Park Distance Control +177
Power Sunroof +931
Rear Side Air Bags +177
Special Factory Paint +390

ELDORADO   2001

Only three minor changes grace the Eldorado for 2001: Sequoia is added for an exterior color, Dark Gray is added for the interior and the Bose sound system with mini-disc player goes away.

Category I

2 Dr ESC Cpe	24612	25883	28000
2 Dr ETC Cpe	27249	28656	31000

OPTIONS FOR ELDORADO

Automatic Stability Control[Std on ETC] +297
Bose Sound System[Std on ETC] +732
Chrome Wheels +477
Compact Disc Changer +357
Power Sunroof +931
Special Factory Paint +390

SEVILLE   2001

Tire pressure monitoring is now available on the STS, as well as an e-mail-capable Infotainment radio, a hands-free integrated cellular phone, 17-inch chrome wheels and high-intensity discharge headlamps. OnStar in-vehicle safety, security and information service is now standard fare on the STS and available on the SLS. Two new SLS and three STS packages round out the changes.

Category I

4 Dr SLS Sdn	26370	27731	30000
4 Dr STS Sdn	29886	31429	34000

OPTIONS FOR SEVILLE

Adaptive Front Seats +598
Bose Sound System[Std on STS] +571
Chrome Wheels +477
Compact Disc Changer +330
Heated Seats +136
Park Distance Control +177
Power Sunroof +931
Premium Sound System +571
Special Factory Paint +390
Xenon Headlamps +300

Don't forget to refer to the Mileage Adjustment Table at the back of this book!

Model Description	Trade-in TMV	Private TMV	Dealer TMV	Model Description	Trade-in TMV	Private TMV	Dealer TMV

CADILLAC 00-99

2000 CADILLAC

CATERA   2000

Mildly successful front and rear styling enhancements and a revised interior update Catera for 2000. Side airbags are standard on all models, and an optional sport package finally arrives with 17-inch wheels, heated sport seats, a spoiler, rocker panel extensions, xenon HID headlights and brushed-aluminum interior trim. Electronic drive-by-wire throttle control and a revised torque converter improve oomph off the line. Revised suspension tuning better controls ride motions and body roll, while tightened steering improves road feel. Two new colors round out the changes.

Category H

4 Dr STD Sdn	15966	17440	18800
4 Dr Sport Sdn Sdn	16136	17625	19000

OPTIONS FOR CATERA
AM/FM Stereo/CD/Tape +211
Alarm System[Opt on STD] +120
Bose Sound System +262
Chrome Wheels +477
Compact Disc Changer +270
Dual Power Seats[Opt on STD] +288
Heated Front Seats[Opt on STD] +255
Power Moonroof +597

DEVILLE   2000

The 2000 DeVille is all-new inside and out and showcases new automotive technologies such as Night Vision, Ultrasonic Rear Parking Assist and the newest generation of GM's StabiliTrak traction-control system. It also boasts improvements to the Northstar V8 that not only improve fuel economy, but make this engine operate even smoother than before.

Category I

4 Dr STD Sdn	19473	20995	22400
4 Dr DHS Sdn	24689	26619	28400
4 Dr DTS Sdn	25819	27837	29700

OPTIONS FOR DEVILLE
AM/FM Stereo/CD/Tape[Opt on STD] +180
Chrome Wheels[Std on DHS] +477
Compact Disc Changer +330
Heated Seats[Std on DHS] +211
Leather Seats[Opt on STD] +471
Navigation System +1198
Night Vision +1198
Power Moonroof +932
Rear Side Air Bags +177
Safety/Security Package +450
Special Factory Paint +390

ELDORADO   2000

The Northstar V8s have been improved, and the standard Eldorado gets a new logo, ESC (for Eldorado Sport Coupe). The racy Eldorado Touring Coupe (ETC) lands exterior enhancements such as body-color fascia moldings and side inserts (replacing chrome), new seven-spoke wheels with Cadillac logos in the center caps, and a new ETC decklid logo.

Category I

2 Dr ESC Cpe	22168	23900	25500
2 Dr ETC Cpe	23819	25681	27400

OPTIONS FOR ELDORADO
AM/FM Stereo/CD/Tape[Std on ETC] +180
Bose Sound System[Std on ETC] +361
Compact Disc Changer +330
Heated Front Seats[Std on ETC] +136
Power Moonroof +932
Special Factory Paint +300

ESCALADE   2000

The big change for 2000 is the availability of vertical-split rear cargo doors in addition to the standard split-tailgate rear-hatch design.

Category O

4 Dr STD 4WD Wgn	28442	30812	33000

SEVILLE   2000

The Northstar V8s have been improved, and all models get a new airbag suppression system and the revised version of GM's StabiliTrak. A new ultrasonic rear parking assist feature and an advanced navigation system is optional on both STS and SLS. There are also two new exterior colors, Midnight Blue and Bronzemist.

Category I

4 Dr SLS Sdn	25558	27556	29400
4 Dr STS Sdn	27123	29243	31200

OPTIONS FOR SEVILLE
Bose Sound System[Std on STS] +571
Chrome Wheels +477
Compact Disc Changer +330
Heated Seats +136
Navigation System +1198
Personalization Package +1020
Power Moonroof +932
Special Factory Paint +390

1999 CADILLAC

CATERA   1999

Catera's "black chrome" grille will be darkened this year, while new electronics and emissions systems make the '99 Catera the first Cadillac to meet the federal Low Emissions Vehicle (LEV) standards. There's also a redesigned fuel cap and tether with an instrument

CADILLAC 99

Model Description	Trade-in TMV	Private TMV	Dealer TMV	Model Description	Trade-in TMV	Private TMV	Dealer TMV

cluster telltale to indicate a loose fuel cap. Up to four remote entry key fobs can now be programmed for separate memory settings, all with enhanced automatic door lock/unlock functions. Cadillac is rumored to be working on a special Sport Edition planned for later in the model year.

Category H

4 Dr STD Sdn	13594	15047	16500

OPTIONS FOR CATERA

AM/FM Stereo/CD/Tape +163
Chrome Wheels +369
Compact Disc Changer +209
Delco/Bose Stereo System +183
Heated Seats +163
Power Moonroof +461
Rear Spoiler +137

DEVILLE   1999

Comfort is big with Cadillac, so who else would offer massaging lumbar seats? Sure enough, this industry-first option is available on '99 d'Elegance and Concours models. All DeVilles get an electrochromic inside rearview mirror with compass added to the standard equipment list, in addition to an audible theft deterrent system. There are three new exterior colors this year, and one different shade of leather inside. As if that weren't enough, side airbag deployment now communicates with the optional OnStar communications system, so the outside world will know when you've taken a broadside hit. Comforting, indeed. Look for a limited run of about 2000 specially badged and optioned Golden Anniversary Edition DeVilles, painted White Diamond with gold trim, to celebrate the nameplate's 50th anniversary.

Category I

4 Dr STD Sdn	16365	17883	19400
4 Dr Concours Sdn	18980	20740	22500
4 Dr D'elegance Sdn	18559	20279	22000

OPTIONS FOR DEVILLE

AM/FM Stereo/CD/Tape[Opt on STD] +232
Chrome Wheels[Std on D'Elegance] +369
Compact Disc Changer +255
Leather Seats[Opt on STD] +364
Power Moonroof +719
Special Factory Paint +301

ELDORADO   1999

Colors are big each year with Cadillac, and 1999 is no different. Cashmere, Parisian Blue and Sterling Silver replace Frost Beige, Baltic Blue Silver Mist and Shale on Eldorado's exterior color chart. Oatmeal leather replaces Cappuccino Cream as an interior color, while Pewter cloth has been deleted, leaving only Shale and Blue cloth available. In the hardware department, an

electrochromic inside rearview mirror with compass and an audible theft deterrent system are now standard equipment. The Eldorado Touring Coupe (ETC) also gets the Bose four-speaker AM/FM cassette/single-slot CD and Weather Band audio system standard, with the option of adding massaging lumbar seats that provide a gentle back rub as you drive.

Category I

2 Dr STD Cpe	16365	17883	19400
2 Dr Touring Cpe	18812	20556	22300

OPTIONS FOR ELDORADO

Chrome Wheels +369
Compact Disc Changer +255
Delco/Bose Stereo System[Opt on STD] +565
Leather Seats[Opt on STD] +364
Power Moonroof +719
Special Factory Paint +232

ESCALADE   1999

The new Cadillac Escalade is really more a 1999 GMC Yukon Denali than it is a Cadillac. (And GMC's Yukon Denali is really more Yukon than anything else-except, perhaps, a Chevrolet Tahoe, but that's another story) Regardless of its origins, think of the Escalade as a big, four-wheel-drive Cadillac limo for well-heeled, outdoorsy types. Loaded with luxury touches and every possible convenience (even GM's OnStar mobile communications system), Escalade comes in four special colors and lacks only one thing: an options list. Why? It's got it all.

Category O

4 Dr STD 4WD Wgn	25333	27666	30000

SEVILLE   1999

The Seville sees only minor changes after its successful redesign in 1998. Cadillac's new massaging lumbar seats are offered as an option on the STS. Heated seats become part of the adaptive seat package, which is now available on both SLS and STS trim levels. And the optional OnStar mobile communications system will automatically notify the OnStar customer assistance center in the case of any airbag deployment, front or side, so that the center can dispatch emergency services to the scene. Previously, notification occurred only with a front airbag deployment. There are also three new exterior colors, Cashmere, Parisian Blue and Sterling Silver, and one new interior shade called Oatmeal.

Category I

4 Dr SLS Sdn	21258	23229	25200
4 Dr STS Sdn	23620	25810	28000

OPTIONS FOR SEVILLE

Chrome Wheels +369

Don't forget to refer to the Mileage Adjustment Table at the back of this book!

Model Description	Trade-in TMV	Private TMV	Dealer TMV

Compact Disc Changer +255
Delco/Bose Stereo System[Opt on STD] +382
Personalization Package +787
Power Moonroof +719
Special Factory Paint +301

1998 CADILLAC

CATERA   1998

New radios are available across the board, and a new option is a power rear sunshade. Second-generation airbags arrived during the middle of the model year.
Category H

| 4 Dr STD Sdn | 11187 | 12537 | 14000 |

OPTIONS FOR CATERA
Alarm System +146
Chrome Wheels +330
Delco/Bose Stereo System +312
Dual Power Seats +127
Heated Seats +146
Leather Seats +624
Power Moonroof +414

DEVILLE   1998

StabiliTrak, an integrated chassis control system that corrects four-wheel lateral skids, is available on base and d'Elegance. New radio systems debut, and door lock programmability is enhanced. An idiot light is added to warn about loose fuel caps, and new colors are available inside and out. Heated seats are added to the d'Elegance and Concours while the Concours also gets a much-needed alloy wheel redesign. Second-generation airbags debut as standard equipment.
Category I

4 Dr STD Sdn	14899	16436	18100
4 Dr Concours Sdn	16463	18161	20000
4 Dr D'elegance Sdn	15640	17253	19000

OPTIONS FOR DEVILLE
AM/FM Stereo/CD/Tape[Opt on STD] +208
Alarm System +146
Chrome Wheels[Std on D'Elegance] +330
Compact Disc Changer +229
Gold Package +118
Leather Seats[Opt on STD] +326
Power Moonroof +645
Special Factory Paint +208

ELDORADO   1998

New radios, a revised interior electrochromic mirror, enhanced programmable features, second-generation airbags and the addition of StabiliTrak to the base model's option list are the major improvements for 1998.
Category I

| 2 Dr STD Cpe | 16545 | 18252 | 20100 |
| 2 Dr Touring Cpe | 17122 | 18887 | 20800 |

OPTIONS FOR ELDORADO
AM/FM Stereo/CD/Tape[Opt on STD] +208
Alarm System[Opt on STD] +123
Chrome Wheels +330
Compact Disc Changer +229
Delco/Bose Stereo System[Opt on STD] +507
Leather Seats[Opt on STD] +326
Power Moonroof +645
Special Factory Paint +208

SEVILLE   1998

Cadillac redefines the American luxury car by debuting an athletic sedan that boasts the performance, style, refinement and technological innovation necessary to play ball on a global level.
Category I

| 4 Dr SLS Sdn | 16134 | 17798 | 19600 |
| 4 Dr STS Sdn | 18109 | 19977 | 22000 |

OPTIONS FOR SEVILLE
Chrome Wheels +330
Compact Disc Changer +229
Delco/Bose Stereo System[Opt on SLS] +343
Personalization Package +706
Power Moonroof +645
Special Factory Paint +208

1997 CADILLAC

CATERA   1997

Cadillac leaps into the near luxury segment of the market with a stylish, German-engineered sedan that features a 200-horsepower V6, an impressive load of standard equipment, and proper rear-wheel drive.
Category H

| 4 Dr STD Sdn | 8529 | 9641 | 11000 |

OPTIONS FOR CATERA
AM/FM Stereo/CD/Tape +123
Alarm System +123
Chrome Wheels +279
Compact Disc Changer +158
Delco/Bose Stereo System +139
Dual Power Seats +107
Heated Seats +123
Leather Seats +525
Power Moonroof +349
Spoke Wheels +125

DEVILLE   1997

DeVille undergoes a substantial revamp for 1997, including revised styling, the addition of standard side-impact airbags, and a fresh interior that is actually functional. Concours receives stability enhancement and road texture detection as part of its Integrated

Model Description	Trade-in TMV	Private TMV	Dealer TMV	Model Description	Trade-in TMV	Private TMV	Dealer TMV

Chassis Control System (ICCS), while a new D'elegance model picks up where the defunct Fleetwood left off. Finally, the OnStar Services package provides DeVille owners with security and convenience features that will pinpoint the car's location at any given time or allow you to book a flight to Paris from the comfort of your driver's seat.

Category I

Model	Trade-in	Private	Dealer
4 Dr STD Sdn	12150	13567	15300
4 Dr Concours Sdn	13499	15075	17000
4 Dr D'elegance Sdn	13102	14631	16500

OPTIONS FOR DEVILLE
AM/FM Stereo/CD/Tape +175
Alarm System +123
Chrome Wheels +279
Compact Disc Changer +192
Gold Package +100
Leather Seats[Opt on STD] +275
Power Moonroof +543
Special Factory Paint +175

ELDORADO   1997

Structural, suspension, and brake system enhancements are made across the board. Base models get MagnaSteer variable effort steering, while the Eldorado Touring Coupe (ETC) receives a new Integrated Chassis Control System (ICCS) that includes stability enhancement and road texture detection. All Eldos have slightly revised stereo and climate controls, and the OnStar services package is a slick new option that can notify emergency personnel where your disabled car is located or can allow you to book dinner reservations from the driver's seat.

Category I

Model	Trade-in	Private	Dealer
2 Dr STD Cpe	12229	13656	15400
2 Dr Touring Cpe	13499	15075	17000

OPTIONS FOR ELDORADO
Alarm System[Opt on STD] +104
Chrome Wheels +279
Compact Disc Changer +192
Delco/Bose Stereo System +427
Leather Seats[Opt on STD] +275
Power Moonroof +543
Special Factory Paint +175

SEVILLE   1997

All Sevilles receive body structure, suspension, brake system, and interior enhancements. STS models get a new stability enhancement feature designed to correct lateral skids, and road texture detection, which helps modulate the ABS more effectively on rough roads. Enhanced, programmable memory systems are new to both models, as is a revised rear seatback and the availability of OnStar, a vehicle information and communications service. SLS models get MagnaSteer variable-effort steering.

Category I

Model	Trade-in	Private	Dealer
4 Dr SLS Sdn	11514	12858	14500
4 Dr STS Sdn	13102	14631	16500

OPTIONS FOR SEVILLE
Alarm System[Opt on SLS] +104
Chrome Wheels +279
Compact Disc Changer +192
Delco/Bose Stereo System +289
Leather Seats[Opt on SLS] +275
Power Moonroof +543
Special Factory Paint +175

1996 CADILLAC

DEVILLE   1996

Northstar V8 is installed in base DeVille, along with a new transmission, Integrated Chassis Control System, and Road-Sensing Suspension. Concours gets 25 horsepower boost to 300, along with a higher final-drive ratio for quicker pickup and an improved continuously-variable Road-Sensing Suspension. Automatic windshield wipers and new variable-effort steering are standard on the Concours. Daytime running lights debut on both of these monsters.

Category I

Model	Trade-in	Private	Dealer
4 Dr STD Sdn	8956	10108	11700
4 Dr Concours Sdn	9951	11231	13000

OPTIONS FOR DEVILLE
Carriage Roof +218
Chrome Wheels +232
Compact Disc Changer +161
Leather Seats[Opt on STD] +229
Power Moonroof +451
Special Factory Paint +145

ELDORADO   1996

Sea Mist Green is a new interior and exterior color, and daytime running lights are standard. Eldorado gets new seats and revised audio systems. Touring Coupe interior is revised, with a center-stack console, bigger gauges, and seamless passenger airbag. Rainsense, an automatic windshield wiper system, is standard on the ETC, as is an updated continuously-variable Road-Sensing Suspension.

Category I

Model	Trade-in	Private	Dealer
2 Dr STD Cpe	8879	10022	11600
2 Dr Touring Cpe	9568	10799	12500

OPTIONS FOR ELDORADO
AM/FM Stereo/CD/Tape +145
Chrome Wheels +232
Compact Disc Changer +161
Delco/Bose Stereo System +210
Leather Seats[Opt on STD] +229
Power Moonroof +451

Don't forget to refer to the Mileage Adjustment Table at the back of this book!

Model Description	Trade-in TMV	Private TMV	Dealer TMV	Model Description	Trade-in TMV	Private TMV	Dealer TMV

Special Factory Paint +145

FLEETWOOD 1996

Final year for the longest production car sold in the U.S. Updates are limited to a new audio system, revised center storage armrest, and pre-wiring for Cadillac's Dual Mode cellular phone.

Category I

4 Dr STD Sdn	9032	10195	11800

OPTIONS FOR FLEETWOOD
Alarm System +105
Chrome Wheels +348
Leather Seats +229
Padded Vinyl Roof +269
Power Moonroof +451

SEVILLE 1996

All Sevilles get new seats and seat trim, redesigned sound systems, an (optional) integrated voice-activated cellular phone, daytime running lights, and programmable door lock functions and seating positions. The STS also receives an updated instrument panel with big gauges and a new center console, the Cadillac-exclusive Rainsense Wiper System (which detects rainfall and turns the wipers on automatically) and a newly improved continuously-variable Road-Sensing Suspension. Magnasteer variable-assist steering replaces the old speed-sensitive gear on last year's STS.

Category I

4 Dr SLS Sdn	8879	10022	11600
4 Dr STS Sdn	9721	10972	12700

OPTIONS FOR SEVILLE
Chrome Wheels +232
Compact Disc Changer +161
Delco/Bose Stereo System +218
Leather Seats +229
Power Moonroof +451
Special Factory Paint +145

1995 CADILLAC

DEVILLE 1995

Traction control (which can be shut off) is standard on base DeVille. Headlights come on automatically when windshield wipers are activated. Chrome wheels can be ordered on Concours. Garage door opener is optional on DeVille; standard on Concours.

Category I

4 Dr STD Sdn	6857	7773	9300
4 Dr Concours Sdn	7373	8358	10000

OPTIONS FOR DEVILLE
AM/FM Stereo/CD/Tape +119
Chrome Wheels +190

Leather Seats[Opt on STD] +187
Power Moonroof +370
Special Factory Paint +119

ELDORADO 1995

Northstar V8 power is increased. Electronic chassis controls now evaluate steering angle when deciding what to do with the Road Sensing Suspension, traction control, and ABS. Styling is slightly revised front and rear. Headlights come on automatically when windshield wipers are activated.

Category I

2 Dr STD Cpe	6710	7606	9100
2 Dr Touring Cpe	7373	8358	10000

OPTIONS FOR ELDORADO
AM/FM Stereo/CD/Tape +119
Chrome Wheels +190
Delco/Bose Stereo System +173
Leather Seats[Opt on STD] +187
Power Moonroof +370
Special Factory Paint +119

FLEETWOOD 1995

Traction control gets on/off switch. Platinum-tipped spark plugs are added, allowing tune-ups to occur every 100,000 miles. Anti-lockout feature added. Remote keyless entry, central unlocking, and fold-away outside mirrors are added. Garage door opener is new option.

Category I

4 Dr STD Sdn	6415	7272	8700

OPTIONS FOR FLEETWOOD
Alarm System +86
Chrome Wheels +285
Coachbuilder Limo Package +238
Leather Seats +187
Padded Vinyl Roof +220
Power Moonroof +370

SEVILLE 1995

Northstar V8 power is increased. Electronic chassis controls now evaluate steering angle when deciding what to do with the Road Sensing Suspension, traction control, and ABS. Headlights come on automatically when windshield wipers are activated. Chrome wheels are new option.

Category I

4 Dr SLS Sdn	6562	7439	8900
4 Dr STS Sdn	7078	8024	9600

OPTIONS FOR SEVILLE
AM/FM Stereo/CD/Tape +119
Chrome Wheels +190
Leather Seats[Opt on SLS] +187
Power Moonroof +370
Special Factory Paint +119

Don't forget to refer to the Mileage Adjustment Table at the back of this book!

Model Description	Trade-in TMV	Private TMV	Dealer TMV

1994 CADILLAC

DEVILLE 1994

Redesigned with dual airbags, height-adjustable seat belts, and side-impact protection meeting 1997 standards. Base and Concours models available, with Concours replacing Touring Sedan. Concours comes with Northstar V8 and Road Sensing Suspension. Coupe DeVille and Sixty Special are retired. Base DeVille powered by 1993's 4.9-liter V8. Remote keyless entry is standard.

Category I

	Trade-in	Private	Dealer
4 Dr STD Sdn	4346	4966	6000
4 Dr Concours Sdn	5360	6125	7400

OPTIONS FOR DEVILLE
AM/FM Stereo/CD/Tape +96
Astro Roof +220
Chrome Wheels +152
Leather Seats[Opt on STD] +150
Special Factory Paint +96

ELDORADO 1994

Base model gets Northstar V8, Road Sensing Suspension, and traction control. Remote keyless entry and automatic door locks are made standard.

Category I

	Trade-in	Private	Dealer
2 Dr STD Cpe	5650	6456	7800
2 Dr Touring Cpe	6085	6953	8400

OPTIONS FOR ELDORADO
AM/FM Stereo/CD/Tape +96
Astro Roof +220
Chrome Wheels +152
Leather Seats[Opt on STD] +150
Special Factory Paint +96

FLEETWOOD 1994

Detuned Corvette 5.7-liter engine makes its way under Fleetwood's gargantuan hood. Performance is much improved. New transmission comes with new engine. Brougham package includes padded vinyl roof and alloy wheels. Flash-to-pass is a new feature, and a battery saver is installed.

Category I

	Trade-in	Private	Dealer
4 Dr STD Sdn	4926	5629	6800

OPTIONS FOR FLEETWOOD
Astro Roof +220
Chrome Wheels +228
Cloth Brougham Package +181
Leather Brougham Package +181
Leather Seats +150
Padded Vinyl Roof +176

SEVILLE 1994

Base model now called SLS. SLS gets Northstar V8, traction control, and Road Sensing Suspension. Remote keyless entry is standard this year.

Category I

	Trade-in	Private	Dealer
4 Dr STD Sdn	5505	6291	7600
4 Dr STS Sdn	5578	6373	7700

OPTIONS FOR SEVILLE
AM/FM Stereo/CD/Tape +96
Astro Roof +220
Chrome Wheels +152
Delco/Bose Stereo System +143
Leather Seats[Opt on STD] +150
Special Factory Paint +96

1993 CADILLAC

60 SPECIAL 1993

Speed-sensitive steering debuts. Speed Sensitive Suspension is standard on all models. Grille is revised.

Category I

	Trade-in	Private	Dealer
4 Dr STD Sdn	3715	4384	5500

OPTIONS FOR 60 SPECIAL
Astro Roof +177
Leather Seats +150
Ultra Seating Package +76

ALLANTE 1993

Final year for ill-fated convertible, and this is the year to buy. Why? This is the only Allante with Northstar V8 engine. Along with the superb engine, Allante gets a new transmission, new traction control system, and a Road Sensing Suspension. Rear suspension is redesigned, and tires are rated to 155 mph. Audio system is revised, dual cupholders are added, alloy wheels are restyled, and seats are all-new. Buy one. Store it.

Category I

	Trade-in	Private	Dealer
2 Dr STD Conv	12360	14588	18300

DEVILLE 1993

Fleetwood tag moved to big new rear-drive sedan. Speed-sensitive steering debuts. Speed Sensitive Suspension is standard on all models. Grille is revised. Special Edition option packages include really cool stuff like gold trim and Phaeton roof.

Category I

	Trade-in	Private	Dealer
2 Dr STD Cpe	3782	4464	5600
4 Dr STD Sdn	3580	4225	5300
4 Dr Touring Sdn	4188	4942	6200

OPTIONS FOR DEVILLE
Astro Roof +203
Bose Sound System +102
Cabriolet Roof +142
Carriage Roof +133
Chrome Wheels +141

Don't forget to refer to the Mileage Adjustment Table at the back of this book!

Model Description	Trade-in TMV	Private TMV	Dealer TMV	Model Description	Trade-in TMV	Private TMV	Dealer TMV

Delco/Bose Stereo System +102
Leather Seats[Opt on STD] +139
Option Package C +148
Special Factory Paint +89

ELDORADO 1993

Touring Coupe gets stellar Northstar V8, Road Sensing Suspension, and traction control. Passenger airbag debuts. Rear suspension redesigned. Speed-sensitive steering made standard. Base Eldo gets Speed Sensitive Suspension standard. Sport Performance package is a blend of base model and TC with detuned Northstar. Sport Appearance package gives look of Sport Performance package with 4.9-liter V8 from base coupe. Got that?

Category I

	Trade-in	Private	Dealer
2 Dr STD Cpe	3985	4703	5900
2 Dr Touring Cpe	4660	5500	6900

OPTIONS FOR ELDORADO
8 cyl 4.6 L Engine[Opt on STD] +97
AM/FM Stereo/CD/Tape +89
Astro Roof +203
Chrome Wheels +141
Leather Seats +139
Special Factory Paint +89
Sport Appearance Package +452
Traction Control System[Opt on STD] +88

FLEETWOOD 1993

Dual airbags and rounded styling characterize this Brougham replacement, which is based on stretched Chevy Caprice chassis. Length is up 4.1 inches. Yowza! Traction control and ABS are standard. Optional trailer tow group gives car a 7,000-lb. towing capacity. Goofy digital dashboard standard.

Category I

	Trade-in	Private	Dealer
4 Dr STD Sdn	3918	4623	5800

OPTIONS FOR FLEETWOOD
Astro Roof +203
Leather Seats +139
Padded Vinyl Roof +163

SEVILLE 1993

STS gets Northstar V8, Road Sensing Suspension, and traction control. Passenger airbag added to all Sevilles. Base Seville gets Speed Sensitive Suspension. Bigger fuel tank is added, rear suspension is redesigned, and a cupholder is added to center console. ABS and speed-sensitive steering standard on all Sevilles.

Category I

	Trade-in	Private	Dealer
4 Dr STD Sdn	3985	4703	5900
4 Dr STS Sdn	4323	5102	6400

OPTIONS FOR SEVILLE
AM/FM Stereo/CD/Tape +89

Astro Roof +203
Bose Sound System +102
Carriage Roof +142
Chrome Wheels +141
Leather Seats[Opt on STD] +139
Special Factory Paint +89

1992 CADILLAC

ALLANTE 1992

No changes.
Category I

	Trade-in	Private	Dealer
2 Dr STD Conv	9988	12205	15900

OPTIONS FOR ALLANTE
Hardtop Roof +417

BROUGHAM 1992

5.7-liter V8 escapes gas-guzzler tax. Towing capacity increased 2,000 lbs. Final edition.
Category I

	Trade-in	Private	Dealer
4 Dr STD Sdn	2827	3454	4500

OPTIONS FOR BROUGHAM
AM/FM Stereo/CD/Tape +84
Astro Roof +169
D'Elegance Package +227
Leather Seats +125

DEVILLE 1992

Traction control optional on base DeVille; standard on all others. Platinum-tipped spark plugs mean tune-ups happen every 100,000 miles. Power passenger seat made standard on DeVille. Electrochromic rearview mirror made standard on all models.
Category I

	Trade-in	Private	Dealer
2 Dr STD Cpe	2073	2533	3300
4 Dr STD Sdn	2638	3224	4200
4 Dr Touring Sdn	3078	3761	4900

OPTIONS FOR DEVILLE
Astro Roof +169
Bose Sound System +84
Leather Seats +115
Special Factory Paint +73

ELDORADO 1992

Complete makeover results in distinctly European-flavored coupe. Powertrains are carried over from 1991. ABS and driver airbag are standard. Sport interior option includes analog gauges rather than digital gauges.
Category I

	Trade-in	Private	Dealer
2 Dr STD Cpe	2827	3454	4500

OPTIONS FOR ELDORADO
AM/FM Stereo/CD/Tape +73
Astro Roof +169

Don't forget to refer to the Mileage Adjustment Table at the back of this book!

Model Description	Trade-in TMV	Private TMV	Dealer TMV	Model Description	Trade-in TMV	Private TMV	Dealer TMV

Delco/Bose Stereo System +106
Leather Seats +115
Special Factory Paint +73
Touring Package +125

FLEETWOOD 1992

Traction control standard. Platinum-tipped spark plugs mean tune-ups happen every 100,000 miles. Electrochromatic rearview mirror made standard on all models.

Category I

Model	Trade-in	Private	Dealer
2 Dr STD Cpe	2701	3301	4300
4 Dr STD Sdn	2701	3301	4300
4 Dr Sixty Special Sdn	3015	3684	4800

OPTIONS FOR FLEETWOOD
Astro Roof +169
Bose Sound System +84

Leather Seats +115

SEVILLE 1992

Complete makeover results in distinctly European-flavored sedan. Powertrains are carried over from 1991. ABS and driver airbag are standard. Sport interior option includes analog gauges rather than digital gauges. Leather upholstery and analog gauges are standard on STS.

Category I

Model	Trade-in	Private	Dealer
4 Dr STD Sdn	2827	3454	4500
4 Dr STS Sdn	3455	4222	5500

OPTIONS FOR SEVILLE
AM/FM Stereo/CD/Tape +73
Astro Roof +169
Bose Sound System +84
Leather Seats[Opt on STD] +115
Padded Vinyl Roof +117
Special Factory Paint +73

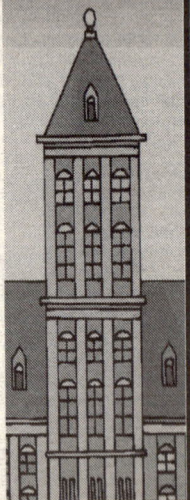

Don't forget to refer to the Mileage Adjustment Table at the back of this book!

Model Description	Trade-in TMV	Private TMV	Dealer TMV

CHEVROLET USA

1995 Chevrolet Suburban

2001 CHEVROLET

ASTRO 2001

Performance from Astro's Vortec 4300 V6 is enhanced, compliments of a new powertrain control module. Also new is a low-emission-vehicle (LEV) version. Color choices are expanded to include Light Pewter Metallic and Dark Carmine Red Metallic.

Category P

Model Description	Trade-in TMV	Private TMV	Dealer TMV
2 Dr STD AWD Pass. Van Ext			
	16900	18063	20000
2 Dr STD Pass. Van Ext			
	14365	15353	17000

OPTIONS FOR ASTRO
AM/FM Stereo/CD/Tape +238
Aluminum/Alloy Wheels +241
Dual Air Conditioning +528
Leather Seats +627
Locking Differential +166
Power Drivers Seat +158
Rear Heater +135
Running Boards +264
Trailer Hitch +204

BLAZER 2001

Now that the new TrailBlazer has arrived, the aging Blazer platform soldiers on as a low-cost alternative. As such, Blazer buyers this year make do with slap-dash add-ons such as standard OnStar on high-level models. Xtreme, a new trim level on the two-door, two-wheel-drive model that includes a low-riding sport suspension lowered by 2.5 inches, body cladding and special wheels, is now available.

Category M

Model Description	Trade-in TMV	Private TMV	Dealer TMV
2 Dr LS 4WD Utility	14705	15678	17300
2 Dr LS Utility	12410	13231	14600
4 Dr LS 4WD Wgn	18445	19666	21700
4 Dr LS Wgn	16745	17853	19700
4 Dr LT 4WD Wgn	20315	21659	23900
4 Dr LT Wgn	18530	19756	21800
4 Dr TrailBlazer 4WD Wgn			
	22525	24016	26500
4 Dr TrailBlazer Wgn	20910	22294	24600
2 Dr Xtreme Utility	13940	14863	16400

OPTIONS FOR BLAZER
AM/FM Stereo/CD/Tape +132
Automatic 4-Speed Transmission[Opt on Utility] +660
Bose Sound System +327
Compact Disc Changer +261
Cruise Control[Opt on LS] +128
Dual Power Seats +317
Heated Front Seats +165
Heated Power Mirrors[Opt on LS] +115
Leather Seats[Opt on LT] +561
Locking Differential +219
Power Door Locks[Opt on LS] +132
Power Drivers Seat[Std on LT] +158
Power Sunroof +528
Power Windows[Opt on LS] +172
Privacy Glass[Opt on LS] +132
Tilt Steering Wheel[Opt on LS] +115
Wide Stance Suspension +1320

CAMARO 2001

More horsepower is on tap for the Z28 and SS models, while newly styled chrome 16-inch wheels are a new option for base and Z28 models and Sunset Orange Metallic is added to the list of colors.

Category E

Model Description	Trade-in TMV	Private TMV	Dealer TMV
2 Dr Z28 Conv	20315	21659	23900
2 Dr Z28 Cpe	14535	15497	17100
2 Dr STD Conv	16830	17944	19800
2 Dr STD Cpe	10965	11691	12900

OPTIONS FOR CAMARO
8 cyl 5.7 L w/Ram Air Engine +2606
Aluminum/Alloy Wheels[Opt on STD] +181
Automatic 4-Speed Transmission[Opt on STD] +538
Chrome Wheels +478
Compact Disc Changer +393
Cruise Control[Opt on Cpe] +122
Glass Panel T-Tops +657
Leather Seats +330
Limited Slip Differential[Opt on STD] +297
Monsoon Sound System +231
Power Door Locks[Opt on STD, Cpe] +145
Power Drivers Seat[Opt on STD, Cpe] +178
Power Windows[Opt on STD, Cpe] +172
Traction Control System +165

Don't forget to refer to the Mileage Adjustment Table at the back of this book!

Model Description	Trade-in TMV	Private TMV	Dealer TMV

CAVALIER 2001

Indigo Blue is added to the exterior palette. A CD player is made standard on the LS Sedan and Z24 Coupe. The Z24 Convertible has vanished from the lineup.

Category B

Model Description	Trade-in TMV	Private TMV	Dealer TMV
4 Dr LS Sdn	8811	9632	11000
2 Dr Z24 Cpe	9932	10858	12400
2 Dr STD Cpe	7529	8231	9400
4 Dr STD Sdn	7610	8318	9500

OPTIONS FOR CAVALIER

4 cyl 2.4 L Engine[Opt on LS] +297
AM/FM Compact Disc Player +211
Aluminum/Alloy Wheels[Std on Z24] +195
Automatic 3-Speed Transmission +462
Automatic 4-Speed Transmission[Std on LS] +515
Cruise Control[Opt on STD] +115
Flex Fuel Option +3916
Power Door Locks[Std on Z24] +139
Power Mirrors[Std on Z24] +125
Power Sunroof +393
Power Windows[Std on Z24] +174
Tilt Steering Wheel[Opt on STD Cpe] +122

CORVETTE 2001

The entire Corvette lineup receives a dose of additional horsepower and torque. The exceptional Z06 model joins the lineup, and Active Handling is now standard on all Corvettes.

Category F

Model Description	Trade-in TMV	Private TMV	Dealer TMV
2 Dr Z06 Cpe	38915	40447	43000
2 Dr STD Conv	37829	39318	41800
2 Dr STD Cpe	33485	34803	37000

OPTIONS FOR CORVETTE

6-Speed Transmission +538
Adaptive Damping System +1118
Compact Disc Changer +396
Dual Air Conditioning +429
Dual Power Seats +201
Magnesium Wheels +1320
Metallic Paint +396
Removable Panorama Roof +495
Solid & Glass Targa Tops +626
Special Factory Paint +396
Sport Seats +412

EXPRESS 2001

A new LT trim level with leather and an on-board entertainment system, and a more powerful V8 are the only major changes. Two new exterior colors and upgraded radios and alternators round out the updates for 2001.

Category Q

Model Description	Trade-in TMV	Private TMV	Dealer TMV
2 Dr G1500 LT Pass. Van	20760	21975	24000
2 Dr G1500 Pass. Van	14705	15566	17000
2 Dr G2500 Pass. Van	17041	18038	19700
2 Dr G3500 Pass. Van	17214	18221	19900
2 Dr G2500 Pass. Van Ext	17733	18770	20500
2 Dr G3500 Pass. Van Ext	17992	19045	20800

OPTIONS FOR EXPRESS

15 Passenger Seating +245
8 cyl 5.0 L Engine +327
8 cyl 5.7 L Engine[Std on G3500, G3500 Ext] +788
8 cyl 6.5 L Turbodiesel Engine +1887
AM/FM Compact Disc Player +358
AM/FM Stereo/CD/Tape[Std on LT] +424
Aluminum/Alloy Wheels +165
Compact Disc Changer +195
Cruise Control +122
Dual Air Conditioning +530
Leather Seats[Std on LT] +858
Locking Differential[Std on LT] +166
Power Door Locks +148
Power Drivers Seat +158
Power Passenger Seat[Std on LT] +158
Power Windows +158
Privacy Glass +257
Rear Air Conditioning w/Rear Heater +567
Tilt Steering Wheel +115
Trailer Hitch +205

IMPALA 2001

GM resurrected the Impala nameplate last year (a staple in Chevy's lineup from 1959 to the early '80s and then again briefly from 1994 to '96) and put it on an all-new full-size sedan body that rides on the Lumina front-drive platform. Although the Lumina itself is still with us for the 2001 model year, the Impala will eventually replace it as Chevy's large-car entry to battle the likes of Ford's Crown Victoria, Buick's LeSabre and Chrysler's LH cars.

Category G

Model Description	Trade-in TMV	Private TMV	Dealer TMV
4 Dr LS Sdn	14157	15036	16500
4 Dr STD Sdn	11583	12302	13500

OPTIONS FOR IMPALA

6 cyl 3.8 L Engine[Std on LS] +651
AM/FM Stereo/CD/Tape +147
Aluminum/Alloy Wheels[Std on LS] +198
Anti-Lock Brakes[Std on LS] +396
Climate Control for AC[Std on LS] +115
Cruise Control[Std on LS] +158
Heated Front Seats +165
Leather Seats +412
OnStar Telematic System[Std on LS] +313
Power Drivers Seat +201
Power Passenger Seat +201
Power Sunroof +525
Side Air Bag Restraints[Std on LS] +165

Don't forget to refer to the Mileage Adjustment Table at the back of this book!

CHEVROLET 01

| Model Description | Trade-in TMV | Private TMV | Dealer TMV | Model Description | Trade-in TMV | Private TMV | Dealer TMV |

Trip Computer +181

MALIBU 2001

Base models receive black rocker moldings, black molded-in-color outside rearview mirrors and a rear window defogger. LS models get front seatback map pockets. Both models receive auto headlamp on/off, new stereos and new cloth interiors.

Category C

4 Dr LS Sdn	10837	11723	13200
4 Dr STD Sdn	9277	10036	11300

OPTIONS FOR MALIBU

AM/FM Stereo/CD/Tape[Std on LS] +132
Aluminum/Alloy Wheels[Std on LS] +205
Cruise Control[Std on LS] +148
Leather Seats +393
Power Mirrors[Std on LS] +128
Power Sunroof +429
Power Windows[Std on LS] +172
Rear Spoiler +115

MONTE CARLO 2001

Chevy's large personal-luxury coupe receives optional sport appearance packages, a standard driver's side-impact airbag and traction control and OnStar comes with the SS model.

Category D

2 Dr LS Cpe	11926	12816	14300
2 Dr SS Cpe	13844	14878	16600

OPTIONS FOR MONTE CARLO

AM/FM Stereo/CD/Tape +147
Aero Kit[Opt on SS] +495
Aluminum/Alloy Wheels[Std on SS] +198
Cruise Control[Std on SS] +158
Keyless Entry System[Std on SS] +119
Leather Seats +412
OnStar Telematic System[Opt on LS] +313
Power Drivers Seat +201
Power Passenger Seat +201
Power Sunroof +525
Rear Spoiler[Opt on LS] +115
Sport Package +1386

PRIZM 2001

The Prizm remains relatively unchanged for 2001. An emergency trunk release becomes standard issue and Medium Red Metallic is added to the color palette.

Category B

4 Dr LSi Sdn	8891	9719	11100
4 Dr STD Sdn	7930	8669	9900

OPTIONS FOR PRIZM

AM/FM Stereo Tape[Std on LSi] +366
Aluminum/Alloy Wheels +187
Anti-Lock Brakes +426

Automatic 3-Speed Transmission +327
Automatic 4-Speed Transmission +528
Cruise Control[Std on LSi] +122
Power Door Locks[Std on LSi] +145
Power Sunroof +432
Power Windows[Std on LSi] +198
Side Air Bag Restraints +195

S-10 2001

A new four-door crew cab 4WD version is offered, ostensibly with enough room for five passengers. Chevy's compact truck now offers a national low-emission vehicle (NLEV) option.

Category J

2 Dr LS Std Cab LB	9018	9686	10800
2 Dr LS 4WD Ext Cab SB			
	13778	14798	16500
2 Dr LS Ext Cab SB	10521	11301	12600
2 Dr LS Std Cab SB	8768	9417	10500
4 Dr LS 4WD Crew Cab SB			
	16366	17579	19600
2 Dr STD Std Cab LB	8517	9148	10200
2 Dr STD 4WD Ext Cab SB			
	13277	14260	15900
2 Dr STD Ext Cab SB	10354	11121	12400
2 Dr STD Std Cab SB	8350	8969	10000

OPTIONS FOR S-10

6 cyl 4.3 L Vortec Engine[Opt on 2WD] +854
AM/FM Compact Disc Player +199
AM/FM Stereo/CD/Tape +265
Air Conditioning[Opt on STD,LS,2WD Reg Cab LB] +531
Aluminum/Alloy Wheels[Opt on STD,LS,2WD Reg Cab LB] +185
Automatic 4-Speed Transmission +722
Bucket Seats +225
Cruise Control +122
Heated Power Mirrors[Std on LS Wide Stance 4WD Ext Cab SB] +155
Locking Differential +153
Power Door Locks[Std on LS Wide Stance 4WD Ext Cab SB] +148
Power Mirrors +115
Power Windows[Std on LS Wide Stance 4WD Ext Cab SB] +168
Sport Suspension[Std on LS Xtreme] +459
Tilt Steering Wheel +115
Wide Stance Suspension +2670

SILVERADO 1500 2001

A 1500HD crew cab makes its debut in 2001 featuring the 6.0-liter Vortec V8. An available PRO TEC composite truck box and optional traction control are also added to the Silverado this year along with new colors and the OnStar vehicle assistance system.

Category K

Model Description	Trade-in TMV	Private TMV	Dealer TMV
2 Dr LS 4WD Std Cab LB			
	15570	16481	18000
2 Dr LS Std Cab LB	13840	14650	16000
4 Dr LS 4WD Ext Cab LB			
	19636	20785	22700
4 Dr LS Ext Cab LB	17733	18770	20500
2 Dr LS 4WD Std Cab SB			
	15311	16207	17700
2 Dr LS Std Cab SB	13754	14558	15900
4 Dr LS 4WD Ext Cab SB			
	19354	20486	22374
4 Dr LS Ext Cab SB	16176	17122	18700
4 Dr LT 4WD Ext Cab LB			
	21366	22616	24700
4 Dr LT Ext Cab LB	19882	21046	22985
4 Dr LT 4WD Ext Cab SB			
	21193	22433	24500
4 Dr LT Ext Cab SB	19732	20887	22812
2 Dr STD 4WD Std Cab LB			
	13148	13918	15200
2 Dr STD Std Cab LB	10553	11171	12200
4 Dr STD 4WD Ext Cab LB			
	17906	18953	20700
4 Dr STD Ext Cab LB	15224	16115	17600
2 Dr STD 4WD Std Cab SB			
	12456	13185	14400
2 Dr STD Std Cab SB	10380	10988	12000
4 Dr STD 4WD Ext Cab SB			
	17560	18587	20300
4 Dr STD Ext Cab SB	14186	15016	16400

OPTIONS FOR SILVERADO 1500
8 cyl 4.8 L Engine +459
8 cyl 5.3 L Engine[Opt on LS,STD] +528
Air Conditioning +544
Automatic 4-Speed Transmission +722
Automatic Dimming Mirror[Opt on LS] +115
Cruise Control +158
Dual Power Seats +317
Electronic Ride Selection +214
Leather Seats[Opt on LS] +845
Locking Differential +188
Off-Road Package +261
OnStar Telematic System +313
Tonneau Cover +158
Traction Control System +148
Trailer Hitch +188
Tutone Paint +165

SILVERADO 1500HD 2001

A 1500HD crew cab makes its debut in 2001 featuring the 6.0-liter Vortec V8. An available PRO TEC composite truck box and optional traction control are also added to the Silverado this year along with new colors and the OnStar vehicle assistance system.

Model Description	Trade-in TMV	Private TMV	Dealer TMV
Category K			
4 Dr LS 4WD Crew Cab SB HD			
	21106	22341	24400
4 Dr LS Crew Cab SB HD			
	18771	19869	21700
4 Dr LT 4WD Crew Cab SB HD			
	23269	24630	26900
4 Dr LT Crew Cab SB HD			
	20933	22158	24200

OPTIONS FOR SILVERADO 1500HD
Automatic Dimming Mirror[Std on LT] +115
Dual Power Seats[Std on LT] +317
Leather Seats[Std on LT] +891
Locking Differential[Std on LT] +188
Privacy Glass[Std on LT] +119
Tonneau Cover +158
Trailer Hitch +125

SILVERADO 2500 2001

Both light- and heavy-duty 2500s sport new torsion bar front suspensions. Light-duty models get an 8,600 lb. Gross Vehicle Weight Rating in addition to optional traction control and standard child safety-seat tether hooks. Heavy-duty models are completely redesigned for 2001 offering two new engines and transmissions, bigger interiors, and numerous other improvements aimed at securing Chevrolet's place in the booming heavy-duty truck market.

Model Description	Trade-in TMV	Private TMV	Dealer TMV
Category K			
2 Dr LS Std Cab LB	16435	17397	19000
4 Dr LS 4WD Ext Cab SB			
	19463	20602	22500
4 Dr LT 4WD Ext Cab SB			
	22058	23348	25500
2 Dr STD Std Cab LB	13927	14742	16100
4 Dr STD 4WD Ext Cab SB			
	17300	18313	20000

OPTIONS FOR SILVERADO 2500
AM/FM Stereo/CD/Tape +119
Air Conditioning +544
Automatic 4-Speed Transmission +722
Automatic Dimming Mirror[Opt on LS] +115
Cruise Control +158
Dual Power Seats +317
Leather Seats[Opt on LS] +845
Locking Differential +188
OnStar Telematic System +313
Tonneau Cover +158
Trailer Hitch +125
Tutone Paint +165

SILVERADO 2500HD 2001

Both light- and heavy-duty 2500s sport new torsion bar front suspensions. Light-duty models get an 8,600 lb. Gross Vehicle Weight Rating in addition to optional traction control and standard child safety-seat tether hooks. Heavy-duty models are completely redesigned for 2001 offering two new engines and transmissions, bigger interiors, and numerous other improvements aimed at securing Chevrolet's place in the booming heavy-duty truck market.

Category K

Model Description	Trade-in TMV	Private TMV	Dealer TMV
2 Dr LS 4WD Std Cab LB HD			
	18596	19684	21498
2 Dr LS Std Cab LB HD	16009	16946	18508
4 Dr LS 4WD Crew Cab LB			
	21193	22433	24500
4 Dr LS 4WD Ext Cab LB HD			
	20328	21517	23500
4 Dr LS Crew Cab LB	19216	20341	22215
4 Dr LS Ext Cab LB HD	18566	19653	21464
4 Dr LS 4WD Crew Cab SB			
	20760	21975	24000
4 Dr LS 4WD Ext Cab SB HD			
	19636	20785	22700
4 Dr LS Crew Cab SB	19030	20144	22000
4 Dr LS Ext Cab SB HD	17819	18862	20600
4 Dr LT 4WD Crew Cab LB			
	24307	25729	28100
4 Dr LT 4WD Ext Cab LB HD			
	22923	24264	26500
4 Dr LT Crew Cab LB	22058	23348	25500
4 Dr LT Ext Cab LB HD	20674	21883	23900
4 Dr LT 4WD Crew Cab SB			
	24134	25546	27900
4 Dr LT 4WD Ext Cab SB HD			
	22663	23989	26200
4 Dr LT Crew Cab SB	21885	23165	25300
4 Dr LT Ext Cab SB HD	20414	21609	23600
2 Dr STD 4WD Std Cab LB HD			
	16435	17397	19000
2 Dr STD Std Cab LB HD			
	13927	14742	16100
4 Dr STD 4WD Crew Cab LB			
	19290	20418	22300
4 Dr STD 4WD Ext Cab LB HD			
	18630	19721	21538
4 Dr STD Crew Cab LB	17486	18509	20215
4 Dr STD Ext Cab LB HD			
	16042	16981	18546
4 Dr STD 4WD Crew Cab SB			
	19152	20273	22141
4 Dr STD 4WD Ext Cab SB HD			
	18165	19228	21000
4 Dr STD Crew Cab SB	17300	18313	20000
4 Dr STD Ext Cab SB HD			
	15955	16889	18445

OPTIONS FOR SILVERADO 2500HD
AM/FM Stereo/CD/Tape[Opt on LS] +119
Air Conditioning[Opt on STD] +544
Automatic 4-Speed Transmission[Std on LT] +722
Automatic 5-Speed Transmission +792
Automatic Dimming Mirror[Std on LT] +115
Cruise Control[Opt on STD] +158
Dual Power Seats[Std on LT] +317
Leather Seats[Std on LT] +845
Locking Differential[Std on LT] +188
Tonneau Cover +158
Trailer Hitch +125

SILVERADO 3500   2001

Chevrolet's heavy-duty pickups get a complete redesign for 2001 including two new engines and transmissions, new exterior styling, and numerous other improvements aimed at restoring GM's heavy-duty market share.

Category K

Model Description	Trade-in TMV	Private TMV	Dealer TMV
2 Dr LS 4WD Std Cab LB DRW			
	20241	21426	23400
4 Dr LS 4WD Crew Cab LB DRW			
	23269	24630	26900
4 Dr LS 4WD Ext Cab LB DRW			
	22144	23440	25600
4 Dr LS Crew Cab LB DRW			
	21020	22250	24300
4 Dr LS Ext Cab LB DRW			
	19895	21059	23000
4 Dr LT 4WD Crew Cab LB DRW			
	24912	26370	28800
4 Dr LT 4WD Ext Cab LB DRW			
	23788	25180	27500
4 Dr LT Crew Cab LB DRW			
	23354	24721	26999
4 Dr LT Ext Cab LB DRW			
	22489	23805	25999
2 Dr STD 4WD Std Cab LB DRW			
	18165	19228	21000
4 Dr STD 4WD Crew Cab LB DRW			
	21133	22370	24431
4 Dr STD 4WD Ext Cab LB DRW			
	20328	21517	23500
4 Dr STD Crew Cab LB DRW			
	18598	19686	21500
4 Dr STD Ext Cab LB DRW			
	17560	18587	20300

OPTIONS FOR SILVERADO 3500
AM/FM Stereo/CD/Tape[Opt on LS] +119
Air Conditioning[Opt on STD] +544
Automatic 4-Speed Transmission[Std on LT] +722
Automatic 5-Speed Transmission +792
Automatic Dimming Mirror[Std on LT] +115

Model Description	Trade-in TMV	Private TMV	Dealer TMV
Cruise Control[Opt on STD] +158			
Dual Power Seats[Std on LT] +317			
Leather Seats[Std on LT] +845			
Locking Differential +188			
Power Door Locks[Opt on STD] +151			
Trailer Hitch +125			

SUBURBAN   2001

The self-proclaimed "king of the full-size sport-utility segment" was completely redesigned last year, yet 2001 still sees improvements to the powertrain. Chevy has upped the horsepower rating of the Vortec 6000 to 320, and 360 foot-pounds of torque is now made at 4,000 revs. A new 8.1-liter engine cranks out 340 horsepower at 4,200 rpm and 455 foot-pounds of torque at 3,200 rpm. You can maintain a relationship with your mechanic on a less intimate level, thanks to an increase in the recommended oil change interval from 7,500 miles to 10,000 miles.

Category N

Model Description	Trade-in TMV	Private TMV	Dealer TMV
4 Dr C1500 LS Wgn	22575	23784	25800
4 Dr C2500 LS Wgn	23800	25075	27200
4 Dr K1500 LS 4WD Wgn	24588	25905	28100
4 Dr K2500 LS 4WD Wgn	25900	27288	29600
4 Dr C1500 LT Wgn	26163	27564	29900
4 Dr C2500 LT Wgn	27125	28578	31000
4 Dr K1500 LT 4WD Wgn	28263	29777	32300
4 Dr K2500 LT 4WD Wgn	29138	30698	33300
4 Dr C1500 Wgn	17325	18253	19800
4 Dr C2500 Wgn	18638	19636	21300
4 Dr K1500 4WD Wgn	19425	20466	22200
4 Dr K2500 4WD Wgn	20825	21941	23800

OPTIONS FOR SUBURBAN

60/40 Bench Seat[Std on LS,LT] +416			
Air Conditioning[Std on LS,LT] +533			
Autoride Suspension Package +462			
Camper/Towing Package +134			
Cruise Control +121			
Dual Power Seats +317			
Leather Seats +627			
Locking Differential[Std on LS,LT] +166			
Off-Road Package +2240			
OnStar Telematic System[Std on LT] +344			
Power Moonroof +623			
Privacy Glass +191			
Side Steps +204			
Third Seat +812			
Traction Control System +304			

TAHOE   2001

Two new exterior colors and OnStar availability are the only changes for 2001.

Category N

Model Description	Trade-in TMV	Private TMV	Dealer TMV
4 Dr LS 4WD Wgn	23100	24338	26400
4 Dr LS Wgn	21000	22125	24000
4 Dr LT 4WD Wgn	26950	28394	30800
4 Dr LT Wgn	24588	25905	28100
4 Dr STD 4WD Wgn	18725	19728	21400
4 Dr STD Wgn	16538	17423	18900

OPTIONS FOR TAHOE

Air Conditioning[Opt on STD] +533			
Autoride Suspension Package +462			
Camper/Towing Package +179			
Dual Power Seats[Opt on LS] +301			
Leather Seats[Opt on LS] +825			
Locking Differential +166			
Luggage Rack[Opt on STD] +188			
Off-Road Package +2240			
OnStar Telematic System[Opt on LS] +344			
Power Moonroof +552			
Privacy Glass[Opt on STD] +213			
Rear Heater[Opt on LS] +141			
Running Boards[Opt on LS] +261			
Third Seat +470			
Traction Control System +157			

TRACKER   2001

Now into its third year of the current body style, the Tracker gets two new trim packages (LT and ZR2) and a new V6 on four-door models. Air conditioning, AM/FM cassette stereo and child-seat tether anchors are now standard on all models. The base 1.6-liter engine has been dropped in favor of the more powerful 127-horsepower 2.0-liter that is now standard on all two-door and base four-door models.

Category L

Model Description	Trade-in TMV	Private TMV	Dealer TMV
4 Dr LT 4WD Wgn	12180	13050	14500
4 Dr LT Wgn	11592	12420	13800
2 Dr ZR2 4WD Conv	10416	11160	12400
4 Dr ZR2 4WD Wgn	11760	12600	14000
2 Dr STD 4WD Conv	9156	9810	10900
2 Dr STD Conv	8484	9090	10100
4 Dr STD 4WD Wgn	9660	10350	11500
4 Dr STD Wgn	8904	9540	10600

OPTIONS FOR TRACKER

Aluminum/Alloy Wheels +241			
Anti-Lock Brakes +393			
Automatic 4-Speed Transmission +660			
Cruise Control +115			
Leather Seats +393			
Power Door Locks +139			
Power Windows +158			

VENTURE   2001

A new grille and front fascia give the 2001 Venture an updated look, while a rear parking aid system helps keep extended wheelbase drivers from inadvertently updating the tail. OnStar is now standard on all models except the Value Van; a six-disc CD changer and fold-flat captain's chairs are available options on passenger models.

Don't forget to refer to the Mileage Adjustment Table at the back of this book!

Model Description	Trade-in TMV	Private TMV	Dealer TMV
Category P			
4 Dr LS Pass. Van	15548	16618	18400
4 Dr LS Pass. Van Ext	16393	17521	19400
4 Dr LT Pass. Van Ext	17999	19237	21300
4 Dr Plus Pass. Van	15126	16166	17900
4 Dr Plus Pass. Van Ext			
	15633	16708	18500
4 Dr Value Pass. Van	12760	13637	15100
4 Dr Warner Bros. Ed. Pass. Van Ext			
	18506	19778	21900

OPTIONS FOR VENTURE
8 Passenger Seating +191
Aluminum/Alloy Wheels[Opt on Plus] +195
Automatic Load Leveling[Std on LT] +267
Compact Disc Changer +261
Dual Air Conditioning[Opt on LS,Plus] +313
Leather Seats[Opt on LT] +412
Luggage Rack[Opt on LS,Plus] +148
Park Distance Control[Opt on LS] +129
Power Sliding Door[Opt on LS,Plus] +475
Traction Control System[Std on LT] +128

2000 CHEVROLET

ASTRO   2000

Retained accessory power and additional warning chimes are added to this ancient van for 2000. Also new are automatic headlights with a flash-to-pass feature, remote keyless entry, battery rundown protection, lockout protection, and a tow/haul trailering mode for the transmission. The ABS, engine and exhaust have been improved, and a plastic 27-gallon fuel tank is standard.

Model Description	Trade-in TMV	Private TMV	Dealer TMV
Category P			
2 Dr STD AWD Pass. Van Ext			
	12895	14301	15600
2 Dr STD Pass. Van Ext			
	11242	12468	13600
2 Dr LS AWD Pass. Van Ext			
	13721	15218	16600
2 Dr LS Pass. Van Ext	12399	13751	15000
2 Dr LT AWD Pass. Van Ext			
	16532	18335	20000
2 Dr LT Pass. Van Ext	15209	16868	18400

OPTIONS FOR ASTRO
7 Passenger Seating +396
AM/FM Compact Disc Player +269
AM/FM Stereo/CD/Tape[Std on LT] +334
Aluminum/Alloy Wheels[Std on LT] +241
Camper/Towing Package +204
Chrome Wheels[Std on LS] +224
Cruise Control[Opt on STD] +122
Dual Air Conditioning[Std on LT] +346
Dual Power Seats +317

Keyless Entry System[Opt on STD] +98
Leather Seats +626
Limited Slip Differential +167
Overhead Console[Opt on STD] +105
Power Door Locks[Opt on STD] +147
Power Drivers Seat[Std on LT] +158
Power Windows[Opt on STD] +174
Privacy Glass[Std on LT,LS] +191
Rear Heater[Std on LT] +135
Running Boards +263
Tilt Steering Wheel[Opt on STD] +122
Trailer Hitch +204
Tutone Paint +98

BLAZER   2000

Base models are dropped as Chevy learns SUV buyers prioritize goodies and a luxury image rather than rugged go-anywhere capability. The engine, exhaust and ABS are refined for increased durability, and exterior trim on some models is modified. Two new colors are available.

Model Description	Trade-in TMV	Private TMV	Dealer TMV
Category M			
2 Dr LS 4WD Utility	12015	13255	14400
2 Dr LS Utility	9178	10125	11000
4 Dr LS 4WD Wgn	14518	16017	17400
4 Dr LS Wgn	12515	13807	15000
4 Dr LT 4WD Wgn	14935	16477	17900
4 Dr LT Wgn	13850	15280	16600
4 Dr Trailblazer 4WD Wgn			
	17104	18870	20500
4 Dr Trailblazer Wgn	15185	16753	18200

OPTIONS FOR BLAZER
AM/FM Compact Disc Player[Opt on LS] +217
AM/FM Stereo/CD/Tape +132
Automatic 4-Speed Transmission[Opt on Utility] +660
Bose Sound System +327
Camper/Towing Package +139
Compact Disc Changer +263
Cruise Control[Opt on LS] +128
Dual Power Seats +317
Heated Front Seats +165
Heated Power Mirrors[Opt on LS] +115
Keyless Entry System[Opt on LS] +113
Leather Seats[Opt on LT] +561
Limited Slip Differential +178
Power Door Locks[Opt on LS] +132
Power Drivers Seat[Std on LT] +158
Power Sunroof +495
Power Windows[Opt on LS] +172
Privacy Glass[Opt on LS] +132
Tilt Steering Wheel[Opt on LS] +115
Trip Computer +98
Tutone Paint +98
ZR2 Suspension Package +1221

C/K 2500   2000

Literally, one new paint color. The C/K is a dead duck after this model year.

Model Description	Trade-in TMV	Private TMV	Dealer TMV	Model Description	Trade-in TMV	Private TMV	Dealer TMV
Category K				4 Dr STD Crew Cab LB	15336	16669	17900
2 Dr STD 4WD Ext Cab LB				4 Dr STD 4WD Crew Cab SB			
	15850	17228	18500		18934	20580	22100
2 Dr STD 4WD Std Cab LB				4 Dr STD Crew Cab SB	16706	18159	19500
	14136	15365	16500	2 Dr LS 4WD Ext Cab LB			
2 Dr STD Ext Cab LB	12851	13968	15000		19876	21605	23200
2 Dr STD Std Cab LB	11994	13037	14000	2 Dr LS 4WD Std Cab LB			
2 Dr STD 4WD Ext Cab SB					17306	18811	20200
	15847	17225	18497	2 Dr LS Ext Cab LB	17820	19370	20800
4 Dr STD 4WD Crew Cab SB				2 Dr LS Standard Cab LB			
	17400	18913	20310		14736	16017	17200
4 Dr STD Crew Cab SB	15681	17044	18303	2 Dr LS 4WD Crew Cab LB			
2 Dr LS 4WD Ext Cab LB 4WD Ext Cab LB HD					20990	22815	24500
	17392	18904	20300	4 Dr LS Crew Cab LB	18677	20301	21800
2 Dr LS 4WD Std Cab LB HD				4 Dr LS 4WD Crew Cab SB			
	15935	17321	18600		22189	24119	25900
2 Dr LS Ext Cab SB HD	15421	16762	18000	4 Dr LS Crew Cab SB	19705	21418	23000
2 Dr LS Std Cab LB	14050	15272	16400				
2 Dr LS 4WD Ext Cab SB HD							
	16792	18252	19600				
4 Dr LS 4WD Crew Cab SB							
	18934	20580	22100				
4 Dr LS Crew Cab SB	17554	19081	20490				

OPTIONS FOR C/K 3500
8 cyl 6.5 L Turbodiesel Engine +1793
8 cyl 7.4 L Engine +396
AM/FM Compact Disc Player +158
AM/FM Stereo/CD/Tape +191
Air Conditioning +531
Automatic 4-Speed Transmission +656
Automatic Dimming Mirror +96
Bed Liner +148
Bucket Seats +178
Camper/Towing Package +108
Chrome Step Bumper[Opt on STD] +151
Cruise Control[Opt on STD] +128
Dual Rear Wheels +565
Keyless Entry System +98
Leather Seats +660
Limited Slip Differential +189
Locking Differential +189
Overhead Console +98
Power Door Locks[Opt on STD] +103
Power Drivers Seat +158
Tilt Steering Wheel[Opt on STD] +128
Trailer Hitch +108

OPTIONS FOR C/K 2500
8 cyl 6.5 L Turbodiesel Engine +1793
8 cyl 7.4 L Engine +396
AM/FM Compact Disc Player +125
AM/FM Stereo/CD/Tape +191
Air Conditioning +531
Automatic 4-Speed Transmission +722
Automatic Dimming Mirror +96
Bed Liner +148
Bucket Seats +178
Camper/Towing Package +108
Cruise Control[Opt on STD] +127
Keyless Entry System +98
Leather Seats +660
Limited Slip Differential +189
Power Door Locks[Opt on STD] +103
Power Drivers Seat +158
Tilt Steering Wheel[Opt on STD] +113

C/K 3500   2000

Literally, one new paint color. The C/K is a dead duck after this model year.

Model Description	Trade-in TMV	Private TMV	Dealer TMV
Category K			
2 Dr STD 4WD Ext Cab LB			
	18077	19649	21100
2 Dr STD 4WD Std Cab LB			
	15250	16576	17800
2 Dr STD Ext Cab LB	15421	16762	18000
2 Dr STD Std Cab LB	13108	14248	15300
4 Dr STD 4WD Crew Cab LB			
	18334	19928	21400

CAMARO   2000

New interior colors and fabrics, redundant steering-wheel radio controls, new alloy wheels, and a new exterior color spruce up the aging Camaro. V6 and V8 engines meet California's Low-Emission Vehicle (LEV) standards.

Model Description	Trade-in TMV	Private TMV	Dealer TMV
Category E			
2 Dr STD Conv	13423	14763	16000
2 Dr STD Cpe	9480	10426	11300
2 Dr Z28 Conv	16778	18454	20000
2 Dr Z28 Cpe	12248	13471	14600
2 Dr Z28 SS Conv	19715	21683	23500
2 Dr Z28 SS Cpe	15101	16608	18000

OPTIONS FOR CAMARO

Model Description	Trade-in TMV	Private TMV	Dealer TMV
AM/FM Compact Disc Player +208			
Aluminum/Alloy Wheels[Opt on STD] +181			
Automatic 4-Speed Transmission[Opt on STD] +538			
Compact Disc Changer +393			
Cruise Control[Opt on Cpe] +122			
Fog Lights[Opt on Cpe] +98			
Glass Panel T-tops +656			
Leather Seats +297			
Lighted Entry System[Opt on Cpe] +102			
Limited Slip Differential[Opt on STD] +297			
Monsoon Sound System +231			
Power Door Locks[Opt on STD,Cpe] +145			
Power Drivers Seat[Opt on STD,Cpe] +178			
Power Mirrors[Opt on Cpe] +119			
Power Windows[Opt on STD,Cpe] +172			
Sport Appearance Package +889			

CAVALIER 2000

Still available as a coupe, sedan or convertible, Chevy's best-selling car gets several subtle changes for 2000. Outside it has new body-colored front and rear fascias, new headlamp/taillamp assemblies, new badging and restyled wheel covers/alloy wheels. Inside, the instrument panel now features an electronic odometer and tripmeter, a revamped center console with three front cupholders and an improved storage area. Functionally, it gets a better-shifting five-speed manual transaxle, smoother-operating ABS, Passlock II security system and standard air-conditioning.

Category B			
2 Dr STD Cpe	6475	7372	8200
4 Dr STD Sdn	6554	7462	8300
4 Dr LS Sdn	6949	7912	8800
2 Dr Z24 Conv	9634	10968	12200
2 Dr Z24 Cpe	7502	8541	9500

OPTIONS FOR CAVALIER
4 cyl 2.4 L Engine[Opt on LS] +297
AM/FM Compact Disc Player +211
AM/FM Stereo/CD/Tape[Opt on STD LS,Z24] +152
Alarm System +165
Aluminum/Alloy Wheels[Std on Z24] +195
Automatic 3-Speed Transmission +396
Automatic 4-Speed Transmission[Std on LS] +515
Cruise Control[Opt on STD] +115
Gold Package +98
Keyless Entry System[Std on Z24] +98
Power Door Locks[Std on Z24] +139
Power Mirrors[Std on Z24] +125
Power Moonroof[Opt on Cpe] +393
Power Windows[Std on Z24] +174
Rear Spoiler[Std on Z24] +98
Tilt Steering Wheel[Opt on STD Cpe] +122
Traction Control System[Std on LS] +132

CORVETTE 2000

Minor refinements improve the Corvette for 2000. The Z51 performance-handling package has larger front and rear stabilizer bars for improved handling, while new, thin-spoke alloy wheels with optional high-polish finish subtly change the outward appearance. Two new colors are available on coupe and convertible: extra-cost Millennium Yellow and no-cost Dark Bowling Green Metallic. A garish Torch Red interior can be ordered, the stupendous LS1 5.7-liter V8 engine meets LEV regulations in California, the remote keyless-entry system has been upgraded, and the passenger door-lock cylinder has been deleted.

Category F			
2 Dr STD Conv	34044	36257	38300
2 Dr STD Cpe	31289	33323	35200
2 Dr STD Hardtop	30755	32755	34600

OPTIONS FOR CORVETTE
Bose Sound System[Opt on Hardtop] +541
Climate Control for AC +241
Compact Disc Changer +396
Dual Power Seats +201
Glass Targa Top +626
Magnesium Wheels +591
Power Drivers Seat[Opt on Hardtop] +201
Solid & Glass Targa Tops +626
Special Factory Paint +330
Sport Seats +412
Telescopic Steering Wheel +231

EXPRESS 2000

Chevy updates the basic V6 for quieter operation, enhanced durability and reduced emissions. New exterior colors and side striping debut, and a new rear defogger for models with fixed rear glass and swing-out vent windows improves visibility.

Category Q			
2 Dr G1500 Cargo Van	10471	11422	12300
2 Dr G2500 Cargo Van	10727	11701	12600
2 Dr G2500 Cargo Van Ext	11238	12258	13200
2 Dr G3500 Cargo Van	11834	12908	13900
2 Dr G3500 Cargo Van Ext	12089	13187	14200

OPTIONS FOR EXPRESS
8 cyl 5.0 L Engine +327
8 cyl 5.7 L Engine[Std on G3500,G3500 Ext] +637
8 cyl 6.5 L Turbodiesel Engine +1793
8 cyl 7.4 L Engine +396
AM/FM Stereo Tape +97
Air Conditioning +307
Camper/Towing Package +204
Cruise Control +135
Dual Air Conditioning +567
Heated Power Mirrors +98
Limited Slip Differential +167
Power Door Locks +148
Power Drivers Seat +158
Power Windows +174

CHEVROLET 00

Model Description	Trade-in TMV	Private TMV	Dealer TMV	Model Description	Trade-in TMV	Private TMV	Dealer TMV

Privacy Glass +257
Rear Heater +135
Tilt Steering Wheel +115
Trailer Hitch +204

EXPRESS PASSENGER 2000

Chevy updates the basic V6 for quieter operation, enhanced durability and reduced emissions. New exterior colors and side striping debut, and a new rear defogger for models with fixed rear glass and swing-out vent windows improves visibility.

Category Q

Model	Trade-in	Private	Dealer
2 Dr G1500 Pass. Van	11748	12815	13800
2 Dr G2500 Pass. Van	12770	13930	15000
2 Dr G2500 Pass. Van Ext	13025	14208	15300
2 Dr G3500 Pass. Van	12855	14022	15100
2 Dr G3500 Pass. Van Ext	13570	14803	15940
2 Dr G1500 LS Pass. Van	12430	13558	14600
2 Dr G2500 LS Pass. Van	13672	14914	16060
2 Dr G2500 LS Pass. Van Ext	14132	15415	16600
2 Dr G3500 LS Pass. Van	13707	14951	16100
2 Dr G3500 LS Pass. Van Ext	14388	15694	16900

OPTIONS FOR EXPRESS PASSENGER
15 Passenger Seating +245
8 cyl 5.0 L Engine +327
8 cyl 5.7 L Engine[Opt on G1500, G1500 LS] +788
8 cyl 6.5 L Turbodiesel Engine +1793
8 cyl 7.4 L Engine +396
AM/FM Compact Disc Player +358
AM/FM Stereo/CD/Tape +424
Aluminum/Alloy Wheels +165
Camper/Towing Package +204
Chrome Wheels +204
Cruise Control[Opt on STD] +132
Dual Air Conditioning[Opt on G1500] +346
Dual Power Seats +317
Keyless Entry System[Opt on LS] +98
Limited Slip Differential +167
Power Door Locks[Opt on STD] +148
Power Drivers Seat +158
Power Windows[Opt on STD] +174
Privacy Glass +191
Rear Heater[Opt on G1500] +135
Tilt Steering Wheel[Opt on STD] +122
Trailer Hitch +204

IMPALA 2000

GM has resurrected the Impala nameplate (a staple in Chevy's lineup from 1959 to the early '80s and then briefly from 1994 to '96) and put it on an all-new, full-sized sedan body that rides on the Lumina front-drive platform. Although the Lumina itself is back for the 2000-model year, Impala will eventually replace it as Chevy's large-car entry to battle the likes of Ford's Crown Victoria, Buick's LeSabre and Chrysler's LH cars.

Category G

Model	Trade-in	Private	Dealer
4 Dr STD Sdn	9566	10467	11300
4 Dr LS Sdn	12105	13246	14300

OPTIONS FOR IMPALA
6 cyl 3.8 L Engine[Std on LS] +651
AM/FM Compact Disc Player +267
AM/FM Stereo/CD/Tape +333
Alarm System +98
Aluminum/Alloy Wheels[Std on LS] +198
Anti-Lock Brakes[Std on LS] +396
Automatic Dimming Mirror[Opt on STD] +98
Cruise Control[Std on LS] +158
Dual Power Seats[Std on LS] +201
Heated Front Seats +165
Heated Power Mirrors[Std on LS] +109
Leather Seats +412
Power Drivers Seat +201
Power Sunroof +462
Rear Spoiler[Std on LS] +115
Side Air Bag Restraints[Std on LS] +165
Steering Wheel Radio Controls[Std on LS] +113

LUMINA 2000

Base models receive additional standard equipment, while the standard 3.1-liter V6 gets more power and torque. The sporty LTZ and upscale LS models are dropped. This is the final year for the Lumina.

Category D

Model	Trade-in	Private	Dealer
4 Dr STD Sdn	8410	9341	10200

OPTIONS FOR LUMINA
AM/FM Compact Disc Player +214
Aluminum/Alloy Wheels +198
Anti-Lock Brakes +379
Keyless Entry System +145
Power Drivers Seat +201

MALIBU 2000

Revised front styling ties Malibu to Impala, while the 1999's perfectly good brushed-aluminum wheels have been redesigned to look like Prizm hubcaps. The 3.1-liter V6 engine is standard this year, and has been improved to offer more horsepower while meeting low-emission vehicle (LEV) standards. And hold on to your hats - a spoiler and a gold package are available. Yikes! Where are the landau roof and whitewall tires, Chevy?

Category C

Model	Trade-in	Private	Dealer
4 Dr STD Sdn	7417	8292	9100
4 Dr LS Sdn	9210	10297	11300

OPTIONS FOR MALIBU

Model Description	Trade-in TMV	Private TMV	Dealer TMV
AM/FM Compact Disc Player +211			
AM/FM Stereo/CD/Tape[Std on LS] +278			
Aluminum/Alloy Wheels[Std on LS] +204			
Cruise Control[Std on LS] +148			
Keyless Entry System[Opt on STD] +98			
Leather Seats +393			
Power Door Locks[Std on LS] +155			
Power Drivers Seat[Std on LS] +204			
Power Mirrors[Std on LS] +128			
Power Sunroof +430			
Power Windows[Std on LS] +172			
Rear Spoiler +115			

METRO — 2000

Two new colors help buyers differentiate between 1999 and 2000 Metros.

Category A

Model	Trade-in	Private	Dealer
2 Dr STD Hbk	3850	4448	5000
2 Dr LSi Hbk	4312	4982	5600
4 Dr LSi Sdn	4543	5248	5900

OPTIONS FOR METRO

AM/FM Compact Disc Player +297	
AM/FM Stereo Tape +363	
Air Conditioning +518	
Anti-Lock Brakes +373	
Automatic 3-Speed Transmission +393	
Power Door Locks +393	
Power Steering +191	

MONTE CARLO — 2000

Chevy's large personal-luxury coupe is all-new for 2000, based on the Impala platform and sporting distinctive, heritage styling cues.

Category D

Model	Trade-in	Private	Dealer
2 Dr LS Cpe	10142	11264	12300
2 Dr SS Cpe	11708	13004	14200

OPTIONS FOR MONTE CARLO

AM/FM Stereo/CD/Tape +147	
Alarm System +98	
Aluminum/Alloy Wheels[Std on SS] +198	
Cruise Control[Std on SS] +158	
Dual Power Seats +402	
Heated Power Mirrors +98	
Keyless Entry System[Std on SS] +145	
Leather Seats +426	
Power Drivers Seat +201	
Power Moonroof +462	

PRIZM — 2000

New standard features improve the Prizm's value quotient, and variable valve timing boosts power and torque. The tweaked engine now meets low-emission vehicle status in California, and three new colors freshen the exterior.

Category B

Model	Trade-in	Private	Dealer
4 Dr STD Sdn	6317	7192	8000
4 Dr LSi Sdn	7186	8181	9100

OPTIONS FOR PRIZM

AM/FM Compact Disc Player +432	
AM/FM Stereo Tape[Std on Lsi] +366	
Aluminum/Alloy Wheels +221	
Anti-Lock Brakes +426	
Automatic 3-Speed Transmission +327	
Automatic 4-Speed Transmission +528	
Cruise Control[Std on LSi] +122	
Power Door Locks[Std on LSi] +145	
Power Sunroof +445	
Power Windows[Std on LSi] +198	
Side Air Bag Restraints +195	

S-10 — 2000

Performance and durability enhancements have been made to the engine, exhaust system, manual transmission, and antilock braking system, but they don't result in more horsepower. Trucks equipped with the ZR2 package get a new axle ratio designed to improve acceleration. Extended cabs are available in Base trim this year, and LS models have revised exterior moldings.

Category J

Model	Trade-in	Private	Dealer
2 Dr STD Std Cab LB	6942	7700	8400
2 Dr STD 4WD Ext Cab SB	11570	12834	14000
2 Dr STD 4WD Std Cab SB	9504	10542	11500
2 Dr STD Ext Cab SB	8677	9625	10500
2 Dr STD Std Cab SB	6859	7608	8300
2 Dr LS Std Cab LB	7603	8433	9200
2 Dr LS 4WD Ext Cab SB	12148	13475	14700
2 Dr LS 4WD Std Cab SB	10826	12009	13100
2 Dr LS Ext Cab SB	8843	9808	10700
2 Dr LS Std Cab SB	7272	8067	8800
2 Dr LS Wide Stance 4WD Ext Cab SB	15206	16867	18400
2 Dr LS Xtreme Ext Cab SB	10909	12100	13200
2 Dr LS Xtreme Std Cab SB	8925	9900	10800
2 Dr LS 4WD Ext Cab Stepside SB	12314	13659	14900
2 Dr LS 4WD Std Cab Stepside SB	10991	12192	13300
2 Dr LS Ext Cab Stepside SB	9339	10358	11300
2 Dr LS Std Cab Stepside SB	7686	8525	9300
2 Dr LS Xtreme Ext Cab Stepside SB	11074	12284	13400

Don't forget to refer to the Mileage Adjustment Table at the back of this book!

OPTIONS FOR S-10

6 cyl 4.3 L Engine[Std on 4WD] +719
AM/FM Compact Disc Player +199
AM/FM Stereo/CD/Tape +265
Air Conditioning[Opt on STD,LS,2WD Reg Cab LB] +531
Aluminum/Alloy Wheels[Opt on STD,LS,2WD Reg Cab LB] +185
Automatic 4-Speed Transmission +722
Bucket Seats +192
Cruise Control +122
Fog Lights[Opt on LS] +98
Heated Power Mirrors[Std on LS Wide Stance 4WD Ext Cab SB] +155
Hinged Third Door[Std on LS Wide Stance 4WD Ext Cab SB] +195
Keyless Entry System +102
Limited Slip Differential[Std on LS Wide Stance 4WD Ext Cab SB] +178
Locking Differential +178
Power Door Locks[Std on LS Wide Stance 4WD Ext Cab SB] +148
Power Windows[Std on LS Wide Stance 4WD Ext Cab SB] +168
Sport Suspension[Std on LS Xtreme] +459
Tilt Steering Wheel +122

SILVERADO 1500   2000

After a complete redesign last year, few changes make news for 2000. Most substantial is the addition of an optional fourth access door to extended cab models. The already potent Vortec 4800 and 5300 V8 engines make more power, and programmable door locks can be instructed to unlock automatically when the Silverado is shut off, solving an irritating problem on 1999 trucks. A Sportside cargo box is available on 1500 LT models, and 1500 4WD trucks can be equipped with wheel flares this year. LS and LT trucks get a standard electrochromic self-dimming rearview mirror with compass and exterior temperature display, and a soft tonneau cover is available from the factory.

Category K

Model Description	Trade-in TMV	Private TMV	Dealer TMV
2 Dr STD 4WD Ext Cab LB			
	15706	17072	18333
2 Dr STD 4WD Std Cab LB			
	11395	12385	13300
2 Dr STD Ext Cab LB	13209	14358	15418
2 Dr STD Std Cab LB	9338	10150	10900
2 Dr STD 4WD Ext Cab SB			
	15340	16674	17905
2 Dr STD 4WD Std Cab SB			
	11138	12106	13000
2 Dr STD Ext Cab SB	12080	13130	14100
2 Dr STD Std Cab SB	9167	9964	10700
2 Dr STD 4WD Ext Cab Stepside SB			
	15850	17228	18500
2 Dr STD 4WD Std Cab Stepside SB			
	11994	13037	14000
2 Dr STD Ext Cab Stepside SB			
	13178	14324	15382
2 Dr STD Std Cab Stepside SB			
	9852	10709	11500
2 Dr LS 4WD Ext Cab LB			
	17220	18718	20100
2 Dr LS 4WD Std Cab LB			
	13622	14807	15900
2 Dr LS Ext Cab LB	15331	16664	17895
2 Dr LS Std Cab LB	12337	13410	14400
2 Dr LS 4WD Ext Cab SB			
	17135	18625	20000
2 Dr LS 4WD Std Cab SB			
	13365	14527	15600
2 Dr LS Ext Cab SB	13279	14434	15500
2 Dr LS Std Cab SB	12251	13317	14300
2 Dr LS 4WD Ext Cab Stepside SB			
	17306	18811	20200
2 Dr LS 4WD Std Cab Stepside SB			
	15650	17011	18267
2 Dr LS Ext Cab Stepside SB			
	15250	16576	17800
2 Dr LS Std Cab Stepside SB			
	12937	14062	15100
2 Dr LT 4WD Ext Cab LB			
	19105	20766	22300
2 Dr LT Ext Cab LB	17477	18997	20400
2 Dr LT 4WD Ext Cab SB			
	18934	20580	22100
2 Dr LT Ext Cab SB	17392	18904	20300
2 Dr LT 4WD Ext Cab Stepside SB			
	21333	23188	24900
2 Dr LT Ext Cab Stepside SB			
	18591	20208	21700

OPTIONS FOR SILVERADO 1500

8 cyl 4.8 L Engine +459
8 cyl 5.3 L Engine[Opt on LS,STD] +528
AM/FM Compact Disc Player +132
Air Conditioning +544
Automatic 4-Speed Transmission +656
Automatic Dimming Mirror[Opt on LS] +109
Bucket Seats +248
Camper/Towing Package +189
Cruise Control +158
Dual Power Seats +317
Fog Lights[Opt on LS] +92
Hinged Fourth Door +218
Leather Seats[Opt on LS] +757
Limited Slip Differential +189
Power Door Locks[Opt on STD] +108
Tonneau Cover +158

Don't forget to refer to the Mileage Adjustment Table at the back of this book!

Model Description	Trade-in TMV	Private TMV	Dealer TMV

Trailer Hitch +96
Tutone Paint +98

SILVERADO 2500　　　2000

After a complete redesign last year, few changes make news for 2000. Most substantial is the addition of a fourth access door to extended cab models, but it's optional, unlike the standard quad-portal arrangement on the Ford F-150. The already potent Vortec 4800 and 5300 V8 engines make more power, and programmable door locks can be instructed to unlock automatically when the Silverado is shut off, solving an irritating problem on 1999 trucks. A Sportside cargo box is available on 1500 LT models, and 1500 4WD trucks can be equipped with wheel flares this year. LS and LT trucks get a standard electrochromic self-dimming rearview mirror with compass and exterior temperature display, and a soft tonneau cover is available from the factory.

Category K

Model Description	Trade-in TMV	Private TMV	Dealer TMV
2 Dr STD 4WD Ext Cab LB HD	16278	17693	19000
2 Dr STD 4WD Std Cab LB HD	15079	16390	17600
2 Dr STD Extended Cab LB HD	13708	14900	16000
2 Dr STD Std Cab LB	11823	12851	13800
2 Dr STD Std Cab LB	12594	13689	14700
2 Dr STD 4WD Ext Cab SB HD	15850	17228	18500
2 Dr STD Ext Cab SB	13793	14993	16100
2 Dr LS 4WD Ext Cab LB HD	17991	19556	21000
2 Dr LS 4WD Std Cab LB HD	14993	16297	17500
2 Dr LS Extended Cab LB HD	15764	17135	18400
2 Dr LS Std Cab LB	14307	15552	16700
2 Dr LS Std Cab LB	15250	16576	17800
2 Dr LS 4WD Ext Cab SB HD	17820	19370	20800
2 Dr LS Ext Cab SB	16192	17600	18900
2 Dr LT 4WD Ext Cab LB HD	20904	22722	24400
2 Dr LT Ext Cab LB HD	18248	19835	21300
2 Dr LT 4WD Ext Cab SB HD	20647	22443	24100
2 Dr LT Ext Cab SB	17906	19463	20900

OPTIONS FOR SILVERADO 2500
8 cyl 6.0 L Engine +234
Air Conditioning +544
Automatic 4-Speed Transmission +656
Automatic Dimming Mirror[Opt on LS] +109

Bucket Seats +248
Camper/Towing Package +189
Cruise Control +158
Dual Power Seats +317
Fog Lights[Opt on LS] +92
Heated Power Mirrors[Opt on LS] +98
Hinged Fourth Door +218
Leather Seats[Opt on LS] +977
Limited Slip Differential +189
Power Door Locks[Opt on STD] +108
Tonneau Cover +278
Trailer Hitch +189
Tutone Paint +98

SUBURBAN　　　2000

The 2000 Chevrolet Suburban is completely redesigned. It's roomier, safer, more comfortable and a more powerful ride.

Category N

Model Description	Trade-in TMV	Private TMV	Dealer TMV
4 Dr C1500 Wgn	15719	17165	18500
4 Dr C2500 Wgn	16993	18557	20000
4 Dr K1500 4WD Wgn	17673	19299	20800
4 Dr K2500 4WD Wgn	18947	20691	22300
4 Dr C1500 LS Wgn	20562	22454	24200
4 Dr C2500 LS Wgn	21751	23753	25600
4 Dr K1500 LS 4WD Wgn	22431	24495	26400
4 Dr K2500 LS 4WD Wgn	23705	25887	27900
4 Dr C1500 LT Wgn	23620	25794	27800
4 Dr C2500 LT Wgn	24980	27278	29400
4 Dr K1500 LT 4WD Wgn	25575	27928	30100
4 Dr K2500 LT 4WD Wgn	26339	28763	31000

OPTIONS FOR SUBURBAN
AM/FM Compact Disc Player +189
AM/FM Stereo/CD/Tape +252
Automatic Load Leveling +439
Bucket Seats +169
Camper/Towing Package +134
Center & Rear Bench Seat[Std on LS,LT] +686
Cruise Control +121
Dual Air Conditioning +874
Dual Power Seats +301
Leather Seats +627
Limited Slip Differential +158
Luggage Rack[Std on LS,LT] +94
Power Moonroof +623
Privacy Glass +191
Side Steps +204
Skid Plates +141
Traction Control System +304
Tutone Paint +94

TAHOE　　　2000

The engineers at Chevy redesigned the Tahoe from top to bottom, making it safer, more powerful and a more pleasurable vehicle to drive.

Category N

Model Description	Trade-in TMV	Private TMV	Dealer TMV
4 Dr STD 4WD Wgn	17163	18742	20200

Don't forget to refer to the Mileage Adjustment Table at the back of this book!

Model Description	Trade-in TMV	Private TMV	Dealer TMV
4 Dr STD Wgn	15039	16423	17700
4 Dr LS 4WD Wgn	21156	23103	24900
4 Dr LS Wgn	19202	20969	22600
4 Dr LT 4WD Wgn	24555	26814	28900
4 Dr LT Wgn	22261	24309	26200

OPTIONS FOR TAHOE
8 cyl 5.3 L Engine +439
Air Conditioning +533
Aluminum/Alloy Wheels +157
Automatic Load Leveling +230
Bucket Seats +235
Camper/Towing Package +179
Dual Power Seats +301
Leather Seats +564
Limited Slip Differential +158
Locking Differential +158
Luggage Rack +188
OnStar Telematic System +344
Power Moonroof +552
Privacy Glass +213
Rear Heater +141
Running Boards +204
Third Seat +470
Traction Control System +157
Tutone Paint +125

TAHOE LIMITED/Z71   2000

All old-style Tahoes are dropped, except these two four-door special editions. The rugged 4WD Z71 is for the rock-hopping weekend warrior set, while the swanky 2WD Limited appeals to those who'd otherwise have a truck reworked by Earl Sheib and Tirerack.com.

Category N

	Trade-in	Private	Dealer
4 Dr Limited Wgn	19712	21526	23200
4 Dr Z71 4WD Wgn	22006	24031	25900

OPTIONS FOR TAHOE LIMITED/Z71
Heated Front Seats +198
Heated Power Mirrors +115
Power Passenger Seat +158

TRACKER   2000

After a complete redesign in 1999, new colors sum up the changes for 2000.

Category L

	Trade-in	Private	Dealer
2 Dr STD 4WD Conv	7355	8158	8900
2 Dr STD Conv	6777	7517	8200
4 Dr STD 4WD Wgn	8182	9075	9900
4 Dr STD Wgn	7438	8250	9000

OPTIONS FOR TRACKER
4 cyl 2.0 L Engine[Std on Wgn] +263
AM/FM Compact Disc Player +211
AM/FM Stereo Tape +145
Air Conditioning +617
Aluminum/Alloy Wheels +241
Anti-Lock Brakes +393

Automatic 4-Speed Transmission +660
Cruise Control +115
Keyless Entry System +98
Power Door Locks +139
Power Windows +158
Tilt Steering Wheel +96

VENTURE   2000

Chevy adds two new models on either end of the price spectrum for 2000. On the low end, a new Value Van includes basic equipment for a low price, while on the high end, a Warner Bros. Edition provides leather and a video entertainment system. New radios include RDS (radio data system) on uplevel versions. Three-door models die this year, while remaining models get new interior fabric patterns and a redesigned gauge cluster with a scratch-resistant lens. Smokey Carmel is a new paint color.

Category P

	Trade-in	Private	Dealer
4 Dr STD Pass. Van	12151	13476	14700
4 Dr STD Cargo Van Ext.	11737	13018	14200
4 Dr LS Pass. Van	13308	14760	16100
4 Dr LS Pass. Van Ext	14217	15768	17200
4 Dr LT Pass. Van Ext	15209	16868	18400
4 Dr Plus Pass. Van	12977	14393	15700
4 Dr Plus Pass. Van Ext	13308	14760	16100
4 Dr Value Pass. Van	10911	12101	13200
4 Dr Warner Bros. Ed. Pass. Van Ext	15953	17693	19300

OPTIONS FOR VENTURE
8 Passenger Seating +185
AM/FM Compact Disc Player +178
AM/FM Stereo/CD/Tape[Opt on LS,Plus,STD] +244
Aluminum/Alloy Wheels[Opt on Plus] +195
Automatic Load Leveling[Std on LT] +99
Camper/Towing Package +98
Captain Chairs (4)[Std on LT] +185
Child Seats (2) +148
Cruise Control[Opt on Cargo] +112
Dual Air Conditioning[Opt on LS,Plus] +313
Keyless Entry System[Opt on Cargo] +112
Leather Seats[Opt on LT] +591
Luggage Rack[Opt on LS,Plus] +132
Power Drivers Seat +178
Power Sliding Door[Opt on LS,Plus] +297
Power Windows[Opt on Cargo] +165
Privacy Glass[Opt on Cargo] +181
Rear Heater[Opt on Cargo] +165
Traction Control System[Std on LT] +128

Don't forget to refer to the Mileage Adjustment Table at the back of this book!

CHEVROLET 99

Model Description	Trade-in TMV	Private TMV	Dealer TMV	Model Description	Trade-in TMV	Private TMV	Dealer TMV

1999 CHEVROLET

ASTRO 1999

A new, all-wheel-drive active transfer case replaces the previous AWD system, and includes a new control module and service light. There are two new interior roof consoles: one with storage is optional on base model, another with trip computer is standard on LS and LT trim. A new LT stripe design comes in three new colors. Dealer-installed running boards are available, as are new optional aluminum wheels. Three exterior paint colors are added for '99, while depowered airbags finally arrive this year. Finally, the outside mirrors are redesigned, available heated and with or without electrochromatic glare reduction.

Category P

Model Description	Trade-in	Private	Dealer
2 Dr STD AWD Cargo Van Ext	10056	11278	12500
2 Dr STD AWD Pass. Van Ext	11263	12632	14000
2 Dr STD Cargo Van Ext	9091	10195	11300
2 Dr STD Pass. Van Ext	9171	10286	11400
2 Dr LS AWD Pass. Van Ext	11826	13263	14700
2 Dr LS Pass. Van Ext	10700	12000	13300
2 Dr LT AWD Pass. Van Ext	13274	14887	16500
2 Dr LT Pass. Van Ext	12229	13714	15200

OPTIONS FOR ASTRO
7 Passenger Seating +324
AM/FM Compact Disc Player +219
AM/FM Stereo/CD/Tape +274
Aluminum/Alloy Wheels[Std on LT] +197
Camper/Towing Package +166
Chrome Wheels[Std on LS] +184
Cruise Control[Opt on STD] +100
Dual Air Conditioning +283
Dual Power Seats +259
Leather Seats +513
Locking Differential +136
Power Door Locks[Opt on STD] +121
Power Drivers Seat[Std on LT] +130
Power Windows[Opt on STD] +143
Privacy Glass[Opt on STD] +157
Rear Heater +110
Running Boards +216
Tilt Steering Wheel[Opt on STD] +100

BLAZER 1999

Blazer gets automatic transmission improvements, new exterior colors and larger outside mirrors, while four-wheel-drive versions can be equipped with GM's AutoTrac active transfer case. Inside, there're new power-seating features, upgraded sound system options and available redundant radio controls in the steering wheel. On the safety side, the '99 Blazer now offers a vehicle content theft alarm, flash-to-pass headlamp feature, and a liftgate ajar warning lamp. What's more, a new TrailBlazer trim package is available on four-door versions, featuring monochrome paint with gold accents, unique aluminum wheels, touring suspension and leather-lined interior.

Category M

Model Description	Trade-in	Private	Dealer
2 Dr STD 4WD Utility	10262	11431	12600
2 Dr STD Utility	7900	8800	9700
4 Dr STD 4WD Wgn	11969	13333	14696
4 Dr STD Wgn	10425	11613	12800
2 Dr LS 4WD Utility	11487	12796	14104
2 Dr LS Utility	8796	9798	10800
4 Dr LS 4WD Wgn	13683	15241	16800
4 Dr LS Wgn	12204	13594	14984
4 Dr LT 4WD Wgn	15312	17056	18800
4 Dr LT Wgn	13764	15332	16900
4 Dr Trailblazer 4WD Wgn	15475	17237	19000
4 Dr Trailblazer Wgn	13846	15423	17000

OPTIONS FOR BLAZER
AM/FM Compact Disc Player[Std on Utility] +178
AM/FM Stereo/CD/Tape +109
Aluminum/Alloy Wheels[Std on LS,LT,Trailblazer,Utility] +146
Camper/Towing Package +113
Compact Disc Changer +216
Cruise Control[Opt on STD] +106
Delco/Bose Stereo System +268
Dual Power Seats[Opt on LS] +259
Heated Front Seats +135
Heated Power Mirrors[Opt on STD] +94
Keyless Entry System[Opt on LS] +92
Locking Differential +146
Power Door Locks[Opt on STD] +109
Power Drivers Seat[Opt on Wgn] +130
Power Sunroof[Opt on LS] +405
Power Windows[Opt on STD] +140
Tilt Steering Wheel[Opt on STD] +94
ZR2 Suspension Package +999

C/K 1500 SERIES 1999

A few new colors are added to Chevrolet's popular pickup in anticipation of the all-new Silverado.

Category K

Model Description	Trade-in	Private	Dealer
2 Dr LS 4WD Ext Cab SB	15192	16646	18100
2 Dr LS Ext Cab SB	13178	14439	15700

OPTIONS FOR C/K 1500 SERIES
8 cyl 5.7 L Engine +378
AM/FM Compact Disc Player +135
AM/FM Stereo/CD/Tape +157

CHEVROLET 99

Model Description	Trade-in TMV	Private TMV	Dealer TMV	Model Description	Trade-in TMV	Private TMV	Dealer TMV

Alarm System +135
Aluminum/Alloy Wheels +184
Bed Liner +121
Bucket Seats +146
Chrome Wheels +135
Leather Seats +540
Locking Differential +136
Power Drivers Seat +130

Leather Seats +634
Locking Differential +136
Power Drivers Seat[Opt on LS] +130
Split Front Bench Seat[Opt on LS Std Cab] +94
Tilt Steering Wheel[Opt on STD] +106
Velour/Cloth Seats[Opt on STD] +109

C/K 2500 SERIES   1999

Model consolidation is taking place in anticipation of the all-new Silverado. Trim levels have been changed from three to two (Base and LS) and two new Crew Cab Short Box models (C/K2500 and C/K3500 series) are offered. Additionally, the C/K1500 will be available only as an LS Extended Cab Short Box with the third door. Mechanical upgrades include new internal components and seals for automatic transmissions, improved cooling system and starter motor durability, and three new exterior paint colors.

Category K

Model	Trade-in	Private	Dealer
2 Dr STD 4WD Ext Cab LB HD	13849	15175	16500
2 Dr STD 4WD Std Cab LB HD	12674	13887	15100
2 Dr STD Ext Cab LB HD	11499	12600	13700
2 Dr STD Std Cab LB HD	10492	11496	12500
2 Dr STD 4WD Ext Cab SB HD	13765	15083	16400
4 Dr STD 4WD Crew Cab SB	15533	17020	18506
4 Dr STD Crew Cab SB	13010	14255	15500
2 Dr LS 4WD Ext Cab LB HD	15523	17009	18494
2 Dr LS 4WD Std Cab LB HD	14353	15726	17100
2 Dr LS Ext Cab LB HD	12926	14163	15400
2 Dr LS Std Cab LB HD	11751	12875	14000
2 Dr LS 4WD Ext Cab SB HD	15444	16922	18400
4 Dr LS 4WD Crew Cab SB	18046	19773	21500

OPTIONS FOR C/K 2500 SERIES
8 cyl 6.5 L Turbodiesel Engine +1468
8 cyl 7.4 L Engine +324
AM/FM Compact Disc Player +102
AM/FM Stereo/CD/Tape +157
Air Conditioning +435
Automatic 4-Speed Transmission +538
Bed Liner +121
Bucket Seats[Opt on LS] +146
Chrome Step Bumper[Opt on STD,LS Std Cab] +124
Cruise Control[Opt on STD] +104

C/K 3500 SERIES   1999

Model consolidation is taking place in anticipation of the all-new Silverado. Trim levels have been changed from three to two (Base and LS) and two new Crew Cab Short Box models (C/K2500 and C/K3500 series) are offered. Additionally, the C/K1500 will be available only as an LS Extended Cab Short Box with the third door. Mechanical upgrades include new internal components and seals for automatic transmissions, improved cooling system and starter motor durability, and three new exterior paint colors.

Category K

Model	Trade-in	Private	Dealer
2 Dr STD 4WD Ext Cab LB	14857	16278	17700
2 Dr STD 4WD Std Cab LB	12926	14163	15400
2 Dr STD Ext Cab LB	13262	14531	15800
2 Dr STD Std Cab LB	10912	11956	13000
4 Dr STD 4WD Crew Cab LB	14941	16370	17800
4 Dr STD Crew Cab LB	13178	14439	15700
4 Dr STD 4WD Crew Cab SB	15780	17290	18800
4 Dr STD Crew Cab SB	14017	15359	16700
2 Dr LS 4WD Ext Cab LB	17337	18996	20655
2 Dr LS 4WD Std Cab LB	14185	15543	16900
2 Dr LS Ext Cab LB	14689	16094	17500
2 Dr LS Std Cab LB	12590	13795	15000
4 Dr LS 4WD Crew Cab LB	17626	19313	21000
4 Dr LS Crew Cab LB	15612	17106	18600
4 Dr LS 4WD Crew Cab SB	18466	20233	22000
4 Dr LS Crew Cab SB	17291	18945	20600

OPTIONS FOR C/K 3500 SERIES
8 cyl 6.5 L Turbodiesel Engine +1468
8 cyl 7.4 L Engine +324
AM/FM Compact Disc Player +130
AM/FM Stereo/CD/Tape +157
Air Conditioning +435
Automatic 4-Speed Transmission +538
Bed Liner +121
Bucket Seats[Opt on LS] +146
Chrome Step Bumper[Opt on STD] +124

Don't forget to refer to the Mileage Adjustment Table at the back of this book!

Model Description	Trade-in TMV	Private TMV	Dealer TMV
Cruise Control[Opt on STD] +106			
Dual Rear Wheels +463			
Leather Seats +634			
Locking Differential +154			
Power Drivers Seat[Opt on LS] +130			
Tilt Steering Wheel[Opt on STD] +106			

CAMARO 1999

Traction control (Acceleration Slip Regulation in Chevrolet parlance) is available on all models in 1999, and on the Z28 ASR allows for some tire slip before killing the power to the rear wheels. Electronic throttle control is newly standard on V6 models, a new engine oil-life monitor tracks specific driving conditions to determine when the next change should occur and a Zexel Torsen differential is employed in the limited-slip rear axle.

Category E

Model	Trade-in	Private	Dealer
2 Dr STD Conv	11816	13158	14500
2 Dr STD Cpe	7497	8349	9200
2 Dr Z28 Conv	14995	16697	18400
2 Dr Z28 Cpe	10757	11978	13200
2 Dr Z28 SS Conv	18173	20236	22300
2 Dr Z28 SS Cpe	13446	14973	16500

OPTIONS FOR CAMARO
AM/FM Compact Disc Player +171
Aluminum/Alloy Wheels[Opt on STD] +149
Automatic 4-Speed Transmission[Opt on STD] +441
Chrome Wheels +271
Compact Disc Changer +322
Cruise Control +100
Glass Panel T-tops +538
Leather Seats +243
Limited Slip Differential[Opt on STD] +243
Performance Package +648
Power Door Locks[Opt on STD,Cpe] +119
Power Drivers Seat[Opt on STD,Cpe] +146
Power Mirrors[Opt on STD,Cpe] +97
Power Windows[Opt on STD,Cpe] +140
Sport Appearance Package +728

CAVALIER 1999

Chevrolet changes little on this slow-selling compact for 1999. The 2.4 twin cam engine benefits from reliability, emissions and fuel economy enhancements, and new front brake linings increase pad life. Minor interior and exterior revisions have been made, and Fern Green Metallic and Sandrift Metallic replace Bright Aqua and Deep Purple on the paint chart.

Category B

Model	Trade-in	Private	Dealer
2 Dr STD Cpe	5194	5947	6700
4 Dr STD Sdn	5272	6036	6800
4 Dr LS Sdn	6357	7279	8200
2 Dr RS Cpe	5737	6568	7400
2 Dr Z24 Conv	8295	9498	10700
2 Dr Z24 Cpe	6745	7722	8700

OPTIONS FOR CAVALIER
4 cyl 2.4 L Engine[Opt on LS] +243
AM/FM Compact Disc Player +172
AM/FM Stereo Tape[Std on LS,Z24] +119
Air Conditioning[Std on LS,Z24] +430
Alarm System +135
Aluminum/Alloy Wheels[Std on Z24] +160
Automatic 3-Speed Transmission +324
Automatic 4-Speed Transmission[Std on LS] +421
Cruise Control[Opt on STD] +94
Power Door Locks[Std on Z24] +113
Power Mirrors[Std on Z24] +102
Power Sunroof +322
Power Windows[Std on Z24] +143
Tilt Steering Wheel[Opt on STD] +100
Traction Control System[Std on LS] +109

CORVETTE 1999

A hardtop model aimed at enthusiasts is introduced, and it's options list is short. Other Corvettes can be equipped with numerous options including a new heads-up display and a power tilt/telescope steering wheel.

Category F

Model	Trade-in	Private	Dealer
2 Dr STD Conv	32467	34834	37200
2 Dr STD Cpe	28103	30152	32200
2 Dr STD Hardtop	27929	29964	32000

OPTIONS FOR CORVETTE
Climate Control for AC +197
Compact Disc Changer +324
Damping Suspension +915
Delco/Bose Stereo System[Opt on Hardtop] +443
Dual Power Seats +164
Glass Targa Top +513
Power Drivers Seat[Opt on Hardtop] +164
Solid & Glass Targa Tops +513
Sport Magnesium Wheels +1540
Sport Seats +337
Telescopic Steering Wheel +189

EXPRESS 1999

The Chevy Express line of full-size vans now include both the Passenger Van version and the newly renamed Cargo Van, in a variety of configurations, including the G1500 (1/2-ton), G2500 (3/4-ton) and G3500 (1-ton) series. Two wheelbases (135-inches and 155-inches) are available on 2500 and 3500 models. For '99, all Express vans get automatic transmission enhancements to increase durability and improve sealing, plus de-powered dual front airbags. There are also two new exterior paint colors and one new interior shade for the 1999 model year.

Category Q

Model	Trade-in	Private	Dealer
2 Dr G1500 Cargo Van	8976	9838	10700

Don't forget to refer to the Mileage Adjustment Table at the back of this book!

Model Description	Trade-in TMV	Private TMV	Dealer TMV
2 Dr G1500 Pass. Van	10822	11861	12900
2 Dr G2500 Cargo Van	9144	10022	10900
2 Dr G2500 Cargo Van Ext	9480	10390	11300
2 Dr G2500 Pass. Van	11745	12872	14000
2 Dr G2500 Pass. Van Ext	12416	13608	14800
2 Dr G3500 Cargo Van	10235	11217	12200
2 Dr G3500 Cargo Van Ext	10738	11769	12800
2 Dr G3500 Pass. Van	12080	13240	14400
2 Dr G3500 Pass. Van Ext	12500	13700	14900
2 Dr G1500 LS Pass. Van	11493	12597	13700
2 Dr G2500 LS Pass. Van	12751	13976	15200
2 Dr G2500 LS Pass. Van Ext	13003	14252	15500
2 Dr G3500 LS Pass. Van	12835	14068	15300
2 Dr G3500 LS Pass. Van Ext	13087	14343	15600

OPTIONS FOR EXPRESS
15 Passenger Seating +200
8 cyl 5.0 L Engine +268
8 cyl 5.7 L Engine[Opt on G15,G25] +521
8 cyl 6.5 L Turbodiesel Engine +1468
8 cyl 7.4 L Engine +324
AM/FM Compact Disc Player +293
AM/FM Stereo/CD/Tape +347
Air Conditioning[Opt on Cargo,Cargo Ext] +250
Aluminum/Alloy Wheels +135
Camper/Towing Package +167
Chrome Wheels +135
Cruise Control[Std on LS] +110
Dual Air Conditioning +465
Dual Power Seats +259
Locking Differential +136
Power Door Locks[Std on LS] +121
Power Drivers Seat +130
Power Windows[Std on LS] +143
Privacy Glass +211
Rear Heater +110
Tilt Steering Wheel[Std on LS] +94

LUMINA   1999

Chevrolet adds standard equipment to the LTZ and introduces Auburn Nightmist Medium Metallic to the base and LS models.

Category D

	Trade-in	Private	Dealer
4 Dr STD Sdn	6911	7805	8700
4 Dr LS Sdn	7705	8703	9700
4 Dr LTZ Sdn	7785	8792	9800

OPTIONS FOR LUMINA
AM/FM Compact Disc Player +175
AM/FM Stereo Tape[Opt on STD] +125
Aluminum/Alloy Wheels[Opt on STD] +162
Anti-Lock Brakes[Opt on STD] +312
Keyless Entry System +119
Leather Seats +349
Power Drivers Seat +164
Power Mirrors[Opt on STD] +106
Power Moonroof +378

MALIBU   1999

The 1999 Malibu is identical to the 1998 model, unless you consider the addition of Medium Bronzemist Metallic to the paint chart big news.

Category C

	Trade-in	Private	Dealer
4 Dr STD Sdn	6637	7468	8300
4 Dr LS Sdn	7756	8728	9700

OPTIONS FOR MALIBU
6 cyl 3.1 L Engine[Std on LS] +322
AM/FM Stereo Tape[Std on LS] +119
AM/FM Stereo/CD/Tape +109
Aluminum/Alloy Wheels[Std on LS] +167
Cruise Control[Std on LS] +121
Leather Seats +322
Power Door Locks[Std on LS] +127
Power Drivers Seat[Std on LS] +167
Power Mirrors[Opt on STD] +106
Power Sunroof +351
Power Windows[Std on LS] +140
Rear Spoiler +94

METRO   1999

After getting a makeover last year to mark its move from the old Geo nameplate to the Chevrolet model family, the Metro is a carryover product for 1999, save for the addition of two new exterior colors: Dark Green Metallic and Silver Metallic.

Category A

	Trade-in	Private	Dealer
2 Dr STD Hbk	3325	3863	4400
2 Dr LSi Hbk	3703	4301	4900
4 Dr LSi Sdn	4081	4740	5400

OPTIONS FOR METRO
AM/FM Compact Disc Player +243
AM/FM Stereo Tape +297
Air Conditioning +424
Anti-Lock Brakes +305
Automatic 3-Speed Transmission +322
Power Door Locks +119
Power Steering +157

MONTE CARLO   1999

Deep Purple is gone. No, we're not talking about '70s rock bands here, just metallic paint. Meaning that, except for Medium Auburn Nightmist replacing Deep Purple on Chevy's color availability chart (we could

Model Description	Trade-in TMV	Private TMV	Dealer TMV

guess what Deep Purple looked like, but Medium Auburn Nightmist?), the Monte Carlo is a carryover model. Unless, of course, you count the availability of the optional OnStar communications system, a 24-hour roadside assistance network that is accessed through a dealer-installed cellular phone.

Category D

Model Description	Trade-in TMV	Private TMV	Dealer TMV
2 Dr LS Cpe	6911	7805	8700
2 Dr Z34 Cpe	8102	9151	10200

OPTIONS FOR MONTE CARLO

Aluminum/Alloy Wheels[Opt on LS] +162
Bucket Seats[Opt on LS] +109
Keyless Entry System[Opt on LS] +119
Leather Seats +349
Power Drivers Seat +164
Power Moonroof +378
Rear Spoiler +94

PRIZM   1999

After a thorough revision last year, the only changes for 1999 are four new paint colors.

Category B

Model Description	Trade-in TMV	Private TMV	Dealer TMV
4 Dr STD Sdn	4962	5681	6400
4 Dr LSi Sdn	6125	7012	7900

OPTIONS FOR PRIZM

AM/FM Compact Disc Player +354
AM/FM Stereo Tape[Std on LSI] +300
Air Conditioning[Std on LSI] +424
Aluminum/Alloy Wheels +181
Anti-Lock Brakes +349
Automatic 3-Speed Transmission +268
Automatic 4-Speed Transmission +432
Cruise Control[Std on LSI] +100
Power Door Locks[Std on LSI] +119
Power Sunroof +365
Power Windows +162
Side Air Bag Restraints +160

S-10   1999

An all-new sport package called the Xtreme replaces the old SS model. All S-10s get automatic transmission enhancements to improve sealing and durability and larger outside mirrors with an optional power heated mirror. Other changes for '99 include a content theft alarm, headlamp flash-to-pass feature, three new exterior paint choices and the availability of GM's AutoTrac electronic push-button transfer case on select four-wheel-drive models.

Category J

Model Description	Trade-in TMV	Private TMV	Dealer TMV
2 Dr STD 4WD Std Cab LB			
	8933	10016	11100
2 Dr STD Std Cab LB	6196	6948	7700
2 Dr STD 4WD Std Cab SB			
	8450	9475	10500
2 Dr STD Std Cab SB	6036	6768	7500
2 Dr LS 4WD Std Cab LB			
	9496	10648	11800
2 Dr LS Std Cab LB	6679	7490	8300
2 Dr LS 4WD Ext Cab SB			
	9979	11189	12400
2 Dr LS 4WD Std Cab SB			
	9335	10467	11600
2 Dr LS Ext Cab SB	7082	7941	8800
2 Dr LS Std Cab SB	6277	7038	7800
2 Dr LS Wide Stance 4WD Ext Cab SB			
	13037	14618	16200
2 Dr LS Wide Stance 4WD Std Cab SB			
	11669	13084	14500
2 Dr LS Xtreme Ext Cab SB			
	9013	10107	11200
2 Dr LS Xtreme Std Cab SB			
	7565	8482	9400
2 Dr LS 4WD Ext Cab Stepside SB			
	10542	11821	13100
2 Dr LS 4WD Std Cab Stepside SB			
	9737	10919	12100
2 Dr LS Ext Cab Stepside SB			
	7645	8572	9500
2 Dr LS Std Cab Stepside SB			
	6357	7129	7900
2 Dr LS Xtreme Ext Cab Stepside SB			
	9415	10558	11700

OPTIONS FOR S-10

6 cyl 4.3 L Engine[Std on 4WD] +589
6 cyl 4.3 L Vortec Engine[Std on LS Wide Stance] +140
AM/FM Compact Disc Player +163
AM/FM Stereo/CD/Tape +218
Air Conditioning[Std on ZR2] +435
Aluminum/Alloy Wheels[Std on ZR2] +151
Automatic 4-Speed Transmission +592
Bucket Seats +157
Cruise Control +100
Heated Power Mirrors +127
Hinged Third Door[Opt on LS,LS Xtreme] +160
Locking Differential[Std on LS Wide Stance] +146
Power Door Locks[Opt on LS,LS Xtreme] +121
Power Mirrors +110
Power Windows[Opt on LS,LS Xtreme] +138
Sport Suspension +375
Tilt Steering Wheel +100

SILVERADO 1500   1999

Chevrolet has redesigned the decade-old C/K pickup and given the truck an actual name. Major structural, power, braking and interior enhancements characterize the new Silverado. Styling is evolutionary rather than revolutionary, inside and out.

Category K

2 Dr STD 4WD Ext Cab LB

Model Description	Trade-in TMV	Private TMV	Dealer TMV
	13598	14899	16200
2 Dr STD 4WD Std Cab LB			
	10072	11036	12000
2 Dr STD Ext Cab LB	11835	12967	14100
2 Dr STD Std Cab LB	8226	9013	9800
2 Dr STD 4WD Ext Cab SB			
	13346	14623	15900
2 Dr STD 4WD Std Cab SB			
	9988	10944	11900
2 Dr STD Ext Cab SB	10744	11772	12800
2 Dr STD Std Cab SB	8142	8921	9700
2 Dr STD 4WD Ext Cab Stepside SB			
	14017	15359	16700
2 Dr STD 4WD Std Cab Stepside SB			
	10492	11496	12500
2 Dr STD Ext Cab Stepside SB			
	11583	12692	13800
2 Dr STD Std Cab Stepside SB			
	8561	9381	10200
2 Dr LS 4WD Ext Cab LB			
	15360	16830	18300
2 Dr LS 4WD Std Cab LB			
	12850	14079	15309
2 Dr LS Ext Cab LB	12926	14163	15400
2 Dr LS Std Cab LB	10996	12048	13100
2 Dr LS 4WD Ext Cab SB			
	15192	16646	18100
2 Dr LS 4WD Std Cab SB			
	12590	13795	15000
2 Dr LS Ext Cab SB	12506	13703	14900
2 Dr LS Std Cab SB	10576	11588	12600
2 Dr LS 4WD Ext Cab Stepside SB			
	15528	17014	18500
2 Dr LS 4WD Std Cab Stepside SB			
	13262	14531	15800
2 Dr LS Ext Cab Stepside SB			
	12835	14063	15291
2 Dr LS Std Cab Stepside SB			
	11499	12600	13700
2 Dr LT 4WD Ext Cab LB			
	17207	18853	20500
2 Dr LT Ext Cab LB	15948	17474	19000
2 Dr LT 4WD Ext Cab SB			
	17039	18669	20300
2 Dr LT Ext Cab SB	15612	17106	18600

OPTIONS FOR SILVERADO 1500
8 cyl 4.8 L Engine +375
8 cyl 5.3 L Engine +432
Air Conditioning[Opt on STD] +445
Automatic 4-Speed Transmission +538
Bucket Seats +203
Camper/Towing Package +154
Cruise Control[Opt on STD] +130
Dual Power Seats +259
Leather Seats +620
Locking Differential +154
Rear Window Defroster[Opt on LS,STD] +94

SILVERADO 2500   1999

Chevrolet has redesigned the decade-old C/K pickup and given the truck an actual name. Major structural, power, braking and interior enhancements characterize the new Silverado. Styling is evolutionary rather than revolutionary, inside and out.

Category K

Model Description	Trade-in TMV	Private TMV	Dealer TMV
2 Dr STD 4WD Ext Cab LB HD			
	16451	18026	19600
2 Dr STD Ext Cab LB HD			
	13178	14439	15700
2 Dr STD Std Cab LB	11080	12140	13200
2 Dr STD 4WD Ext Cab SB HD			
	15696	17198	18700
2 Dr STD 4WD Std Cab LB HD			
	13346	14623	15900
2 Dr STD Ext Cab SB	12506	13703	14900
2 Dr STD Std Cab LB HD			
	9317	10208	11100
2 Dr LS 4WD Ext Cab LB HD			
	17710	19405	21100
2 Dr LS 4WD Std Cab LB HD			
	16367	17934	19500
2 Dr LS Ext Cab LB HD	15276	16738	18200
2 Dr LS Std Cab LB	12588	13792	14997
2 Dr LS Std Cab LB HD	12593	13798	15003
2 Dr LS 4WD Ext Cab SB HD			
	17291	18945	20600
2 Dr LS Ext Cab SB	14269	15635	17000
2 Dr LT 4WD Ext Cab LB HD			
	18802	20601	22400
2 Dr LT 4WD Ext Cab SB HD			
	18634	20417	22200
2 Dr LT Ext Cab LB HD	17878	19589	21300
2 Dr LT Ext Cab SB	17039	18669	20300

OPTIONS FOR SILVERADO 2500
8 cyl 6.0 L Engine +193
Air Conditioning[Opt on STD] +445
Bucket Seats +203
Camper/Towing Package +154
Cruise Control[Opt on STD] +130
Dual Power Seats +259
Leather Seats +800
Rear Window Defroster[Opt on LS,STD] +94

SUBURBAN   1999

A couple of new colors are the only modifications to the Suburban as Chevrolet prepares a redesigned model for 2000.

Model Description	Trade-in TMV	Private TMV	Dealer TMV
Category N			
4 Dr C1500 Wgn	14312	15656	17000
4 Dr C2500 Wgn	15407	16853	18300
4 Dr K1500 4WD Wgn	16080	17590	19100
4 Dr K2500 4WD Wgn	17259	18880	20500

OPTIONS FOR SUBURBAN

8 cyl 6.5 L Turbodiesel Engine +1468
8 cyl 7.4 L Engine +308
AM/FM Compact Disc Player +155
AM/FM Stereo Tape +108
AM/FM Stereo/CD/Tape +207
Air Conditioning +433
Aluminum/Alloy Wheels +159
Bucket Seats +139
Camper/Towing Package +110
Center & Rear Bench Seat +563
Center Bench Seat +325
Cruise Control[Std on LS,LT] +100
Dual Air Conditioning +717
Dual Power Seats +246
Heated Front Seats +179
LS Package +1574
LT Package +2382
Leather Seats +570
Locking Differential +130
Power Drivers Seat +124
Power Windows +136
Privacy Glass +156
Rear Heater +104
Running Boards +166
Skid Plates +115
Tilt Steering Wheel[Std on LS,LT] +95

TAHOE   1999

The standard cargo net is deleted, and new colors are added as Tahoe cruises into final model year in current guise.

Model Description	Trade-in TMV	Private TMV	Dealer TMV
Category N			
2 Dr STD 4WD Utility	14397	15748	17100
2 Dr STD Utility	11955	13078	14200
2 Dr LS 4WD Utility	17091	18695	20300
2 Dr LS Utility	15070	16485	17900
4 Dr LS 4WD Wgn	18522	20261	22000
4 Dr LS Wgn	16417	17959	19500
2 Dr LT 4WD Utility	18438	20169	21900
2 Dr LT Utility	15407	16853	18300
4 Dr LT 4WD Wgn	18943	20721	22500
4 Dr LT Wgn	17680	19340	21000

OPTIONS FOR TAHOE

8 cyl 6.5 L Turbodiesel Engine +1468
AM/FM Stereo/CD/Tape[Std on LT] +103
Air Conditioning[Opt on STD] +433
Aluminum/Alloy Wheels[Opt on STD] +159
Bucket Seats +121
Camper/Towing Package +110
Cruise Control[Opt on STD] +97

Dual Air Conditioning +282
Dual Power Seats +246
Heated Front Seats +166
Heated Power Mirrors +104
Locking Differential +130
Privacy Glass[Opt on STD] +110
Running Boards +166
Side Steps +115
Special Z-71 Package +1357
Tilt Steering Wheel[Opt on STD] +97

TRACKER   1999

The redesigned-for-1999 Tracker, available in either two-door convertible or four-door hardtop versions and in two- or four-wheel drive, features sporty new looks, more power, improved ride and handling and a roomier, more comfortable interior.

Model Description	Trade-in TMV	Private TMV	Dealer TMV
Category L			
2 Dr STD 4WD Conv	6666	7483	8300
2 Dr STD Conv	6344	7122	7900
4 Dr STD 4WD Wgn	7308	8204	9100
4 Dr STD Wgn	6746	7573	8400

OPTIONS FOR TRACKER

4 cyl 2.0 L Engine[Std on Wgn] +216
AM/FM Compact Disc Player +172
AM/FM Stereo Tape +119
Air Conditioning +505
Aluminum/Alloy Wheels +197
Anti-Lock Brakes +322
Automatic 4-Speed Transmission +540
Cruise Control +94
Power Door Locks +113
Power Windows +130

VENTURE   1999

Venture gets some performance and safety enhancements. Other changes include additional seating choices, four new exterior and two new interior colors, as well as fatter standard tires. What's more, there's a newly badged LT model that packages an upgraded audio system with a touring suspension, traction control and captain's seats with available leather.

Model Description	Trade-in TMV	Private TMV	Dealer TMV
Category P			
2 Dr STD Pass. Van	9654	10827	12000
4 Dr STD Pass. Van	10298	11549	12800
4 Dr STD Pass. Van Ext			
	11022	12361	13700
4 Dr STD Cargo Van Ext.			
	9895	11098	12300
4 Dr LS Pass. Van	11263	12632	14000
4 Dr LS Pass. Van Ext	12068	13534	15000
4 Dr LT Pass. Van Ext	13033	14617	16200

OPTIONS FOR VENTURE

Don't forget to refer to the Mileage Adjustment Table at the back of this book!

Model Description	Trade-in TMV	Private TMV	Dealer TMV	Model Description	Trade-in TMV	Private TMV	Dealer TMV
8 Passenger Seating +151				Power Drivers Seat[Std on LT] +116			
AM/FM Compact Disc Player +200				Power Windows[Opt on STD] +129			
AM/FM Stereo/CD/Tape[Std on LT] +254				Privacy Glass[Opt on STD] +140			
Aluminum/Alloy Wheels[Opt on STD] +160				Rear Heater +99			
Captain Chairs (4)[Std on LT] +151							

BLAZER   1998

Blazer gets a nose job and an interior redesign. New standard equipment includes a theft deterrent system, automatic headlight control, four-wheel disc brakes and dual airbags incorporating second-generation technology to reduce the bags' inflation force. New radios, colors, and a column-mounted automatic shift selector round out the major changes.

Child Seats (2) +121
Cruise Control[Opt on STD] +100
Dual Air Conditioning[Std on LT] +257
Leather Seats +484
Luggage Rack[Opt on STD] +94
Power Drivers Seat +146
Power Sliding Door[Std on LT] +243
Power Windows[Opt on STD] +149
Privacy Glass[Opt on STD] +149
Rear Heater[Opt on Cargo] +150
Traction Control System[Opt on Cargo,LS] +106

1998 CHEVROLET

ASTRO   1998

New colors, improved clearcoating, a standard theft deterrent system (like anybody wants to steal one of these) and the addition of composite headlights and an uplevel grille to base models are all that's different on this year's Astro. Full-power airbags continue for 1998.

Category P	Trade-in	Private	Dealer
2 Dr STD AWD Cargo Van Ext	8256	9285	10400
2 Dr STD AWD Pass. Van Ext	8336	9375	10500
2 Dr STD Cargo Van Ext	6986	7857	8800
2 Dr STD Pass. Van Ext	7304	8214	9200
2 Dr LS AWD Pass. Van Ext	10241	11517	12900
2 Dr LS Pass. Van Ext	8971	10089	11300
2 Dr LT AWD Pass. Van Ext	10717	12053	13500
2 Dr LT Pass. Van Ext	9844	11071	12400

OPTIONS FOR ASTRO
7 Passenger Seating +290
8 Passenger Seating[Opt on STD] +192
AM/FM Compact Disc Player +197
AM/FM Stereo Tape +148
AM/FM Stereo/CD/Tape +246
Aluminum/Alloy Wheels[Std on LT] +148
Camper/Towing Package +150
Child Seats (2) +116
Chrome Wheels +143
Dual Air Conditioning +253
Dual Power Seats +232
Leather Seats +460
Locking Differential +123
Power Door Locks[Opt on STD] +108

Category M	Trade-in	Private	Dealer
2 Dr STD 4WD Utility	9565	10734	12000
2 Dr STD Utility	8210	9213	10300
4 Dr STD 4WD Wgn	10442	11718	13100
4 Dr STD Wgn	8854	9936	11108
2 Dr LS 4WD Utility	10283	11539	12900
2 Dr LS Utility	8841	9922	11092
4 Dr LS 4WD Wgn	11080	12433	13900
4 Dr LS Wgn	10522	11807	13200
4 Dr LT 4WD Wgn	12355	13865	15500
4 Dr LT Wgn	11159	12523	14000

OPTIONS FOR BLAZER
AM/FM Compact Disc Player +159
AM/FM Stereo/CD/Tape +97
Aluminum/Alloy Wheels[Opt on STD] +130
Camper/Towing Package +102
Cruise Control[Opt on STD] +95
Heated Front Seats +120
Locking Differential +123
Power Door Locks[Opt on STD] +97
Power Drivers Seat[Opt on LS] +116
Power Sunroof +336
Power Windows[Opt on STD] +126
Sport Suspension +315
Theft Deterrent System +97
Wide Stance Suspension +895

C/K 1500 SERIES   1998

This year's big news is a standard theft-deterrent system, revised color choices and fresh tailgate lettering. The Sport package has been dropped from the option list. Second-generation airbags are standard on models under 8,600 GVWR.

Category K	Trade-in	Private	Dealer
2 Dr C1500 Cheyenne Ext Cab LB	9644	10665	11770
2 Dr C1500 Cheyenne Std Cab LB	8112	8970	9900
2 Dr K1500 Cheyenne 4WD Ext Cab LB	11881	13138	14500
2 Dr K1500 Cheyenne 4WD Std Cab LB	9751	10782	11900

Don't forget to refer to the Mileage Adjustment Table at the back of this book!

Model Description	Trade-in TMV	Private TMV	Dealer TMV
2 Dr C1500 Cheyenne Ext Cab SB	9095	10057	11100
2 Dr C1500 Cheyenne Std Cab SB	7948	8789	9700
2 Dr K1500 Cheyenne 4WD Ext Cab SB	11307	12504	13800
2 Dr K1500 Cheyenne 4WD Std Cab SB	9693	10719	11830
2 Dr C1500 Cheyenne Std Cab Stepside SB	8194	9061	10000
2 Dr K1500 Cheyenne 4WD Std Cab Stepside SB	9833	10873	12000
2 Dr C1500 Silverado Ext Cab LB	11062	12232	13500
2 Dr C1500 Silverado Std Cab LB	9155	10124	11173
2 Dr K1500 Silverado 4WD Ext Cab LB	12700	14044	15500
2 Dr K1500 Silverado 4WD Std Cab LB	11389	12595	13900
2 Dr C1500 Silverado Ext Cab SB	10570	11688	12900
2 Dr C1500 Silverado Std Cab SB	8849	9786	10800
2 Dr K1500 Silverado 4WD Ext Cab SB	12455	13772	15200
2 Dr K1500 Silverado 4WD Std Cab SB	11226	12413	13700
2 Dr C1500 Silverado Ext Cab Stepside SB	12373	13682	15100
2 Dr C1500 Silverado Std Cab Stepside SB	9259	10239	11300
2 Dr K1500 Silverado 4WD Ext Cab Stepside SB	13930	15403	17000
2 Dr K1500 Silverado 4WD Std Cab Stepside SB	11471	12685	14000
2 Dr C1500 WT Std Cab LB	7211	7974	8800
2 Dr K1500 WT 4WD Std Cab LB	9423	10420	11500
2 Dr C1500 WT Std Cab SB	7047	7792	8600
2 Dr K1500 WT 4WD Std Cab SB	9199	10173	11227

OPTIONS FOR C/K 1500 SERIES
8 cyl 5.0 L Engine +240
8 cyl 5.7 L Engine +339
8 cyl 6.5 L Turbodiesel Engine +1637
AM/FM Compact Disc Player +120
AM/FM Stereo/CD/Tape +140
Air Conditioning[Std on Silverado] +389
Automatic 4-Speed Transmission +470
Bed Liner +109

Bucket Seats +187
Chrome Wheels +165
Cruise Control[Std on Silverado] +99
Hinged Third Door +204
Leather Seats +483
Locking Differential +123
Power Drivers Seat +116
Tilt Steering Wheel[Std on Silverado] +91

C/K 2500 SERIES 1998

This year's big news is a standard theft deterrent system, revised color choices, and fresh tailgate lettering. The Sport package has been dropped from the option list. Second generation airbags are standard on models under 8,600 GVWR.

Category K

Model Description	Trade-in TMV	Private TMV	Dealer TMV
2 Dr C2500 Cheyenne Std Cab LB	7456	8245	9100
2 Dr C2500 HD Cheyenne Ext Cab LB	10242	11326	12500
2 Dr C2500 HD Cheyenne Std Cab LB	9259	10239	11300
2 Dr K2500 HD Cheyenne 4WD Ext Cab LB	12694	14037	15492
2 Dr K2500 HD Cheyenne 4WD Std Cab LB	11062	12232	13500
2 Dr C2500 Cheyenne Ext Cab SB	10078	11145	12300
2 Dr K2500 HD Cheyenne 4WD Ext Cab SB	12661	14001	15452
2 Dr C2500 HD Silverado Ext Cab LB	12050	13325	14706
2 Dr C2500 HD Silverado Std Cab LB	10980	12141	13400
2 Dr C2500 Silverado Std Cab LB	9833	10873	12000
2 Dr K2500 HD Silverado 4WD Ext Cab LB	13766	15222	16800
2 Dr K2500 HD Silverado 4WD Std Cab LB	12746	14095	15556
2 Dr C2500 Silverado Ext Cab SB	12040	13314	14694
2 Dr K2500 HD Silverado 4WD Ext Cab SB	13520	14950	16500

OPTIONS FOR C/K 2500 SERIES
8 cyl 5.7 L Engine[Std on HD] +339
8 cyl 6.5 L Turbodiesel Engine +1315
8 cyl 7.4 L Engine +290
AM/FM Compact Disc Player +91
AM/FM Stereo/CD/Tape +140
Air Conditioning[Std on Silverado] +389
Automatic 4-Speed Transmission +470
Bed Liner +109
Bucket Seats +187

Don't forget to refer to the Mileage Adjustment Table at the back of this book!

CHEVROLET 98

Model Description	Trade-in TMV	Private TMV	Dealer TMV	Model Description	Trade-in TMV	Private TMV	Dealer TMV

Chrome Step Bumper[Std on Silverado] +110
Cruise Control[Std on Silverado] +93
Leather Seats +483
Locking Differential +123
Power Drivers Seat +116
Tilt Steering Wheel[Std on Silverado] +95

C/K 3500 SERIES   1998

Category K
2 Dr C3500 Cheyenne Ext Cab LB

| | 11717 | 12957 | 14300 |

2 Dr C3500 Cheyenne Std Cab LB

| | 9751 | 10782 | 11900 |

2 Dr K3500 Cheyenne 4WD Ext Cab LB

| | 13438 | 14860 | 16400 |

2 Dr K3500 Cheyenne 4WD Std Cab LB

| | 11389 | 12595 | 13900 |

4 Dr C3500 Cheyenne Crew Cab LB

| | 11471 | 12685 | 14000 |

4 Dr K3500 Cheyenne 4WD Crew Cab LB

| | 13520 | 14950 | 16500 |

2 Dr C3500 Silverado Ext Cab LB

| | 12700 | 14044 | 15500 |

2 Dr C3500 Silverado Std Cab LB

| | 11062 | 12232 | 13500 |

2 Dr K3500 Silverado 4WD Ext Cab LB

| | 14749 | 16309 | 18000 |

2 Dr K3500 Silverado 4WD Std Cab LB

| | 12291 | 13591 | 15000 |

4 Dr C3500 Silverado Crew Cab LB

| | 13930 | 15403 | 17000 |

4 Dr K3500 Silverado 4WD Crew Cab LB

| | 15896 | 17578 | 19400 |

OPTIONS FOR C/K 3500 SERIES
8 cyl 6.5 L Turbodiesel Engine +1315
8 cyl 7.4 L Engine +290
AM/FM Compact Disc Player +116
AM/FM Stereo/CD/Tape +140
Air Conditioning[Std on Silverado] +389
Automatic 4-Speed Transmission +470
Bed Liner +109
Bucket Seats +187
Chrome Step Bumper[Std on Silverado] +110
Cruise Control[Std on Silverado] +95
Dual Rear Wheels +414
Leather Seats +483
Locking Differential +123
Power Drivers Seat +116
Tilt Steering Wheel[Std on Silverado] +95

CAMARO   1998

Chevrolet dumps a 305-horsepower version of the Corvette's V8 engine under a new front end, adds standard four-wheel disc brakes on all models, adds a couple of new colors, makes second generation airbags standard, and revises trim levels. The midyear SS package makes 320 horsepower. Uh, why were you considering that Mustang again?

Category E

	Trade-in	Private	Dealer
2 Dr STD Conv	10112	11258	12500
2 Dr STD Cpe	6795	7566	8400
2 Dr Z28 Conv	12863	14321	15900
2 Dr Z28 Cpe	9061	10088	11200
2 Dr Z28 SS Conv	15613	17383	19300
2 Dr Z28 SS Cpe	11326	12609	14000

OPTIONS FOR CAMARO
AM/FM Compact Disc Player +152
AM/FM Stereo/CD/Tape[Opt on STD Cpe] +217
Aluminum/Alloy Wheels[Opt on STD] +133
Automatic 4-Speed Transmission[Opt on STD] +395
Chrome Wheels +242
Compact Disc Changer +288
Glass Panel T-tops +482
Leather Seats +217
Limited Slip Differential[Opt on STD] +217
Performance Package +569
Power Door Locks[Opt on STD,Cpe] +106
Power Drivers Seat[Opt on STD,Cpe] +131
Power Windows[Opt on STD,Cpe,Z28] +124
Sport Appearance Package +716

CAVALIER   1998

A Z24 convertible is introduced, cruise control is standard on all but base models, power windows and remote keyless entry are no longer available on base cars, and...hold on to your seats, buyers can no longer delete the AM/FM radio. Second-generation airbags debut on all models.

Category B

	Trade-in	Private	Dealer
2 Dr STD Cpe	4305	5022	5800
4 Dr STD Sdn	4379	5109	5900
4 Dr LS Sdn	5344	6235	7200
2 Dr RS Cpe	4898	5715	6600
2 Dr Z24 Conv	6754	7880	9100
2 Dr Z24 Cpe	6011	7014	8100

OPTIONS FOR CAVALIER
4 cyl 2.4 L Engine[Opt on LS] +217
AM/FM Compact Disc Player +155
AM/FM Stereo Tape[Opt on RS,STD] +106
Air Conditioning[Opt on RS,STD] +385
Alarm System +120
Aluminum/Alloy Wheels[Std on Z24] +143
Automatic 3-Speed Transmission +290
Automatic 4-Speed Transmission[Std on LS] +377
Power Door Locks[Std on Z24] +102
Power Mirrors[Std on Z24] +91
Power Sunroof +288
Power Windows[Std on Z24] +129
Traction Control System +97

Don't forget to refer to the Mileage Adjustment Table at the back of this book!

CHEVROLET 98

Model Description	Trade-in TMV	Private TMV	Dealer TMV	Model Description	Trade-in TMV	Private TMV	Dealer TMV

CORVETTE 1998

Two fresh colors are available, but the new convertible model steals the show. Equipped with a manual folding top, a hard tonneau that extends along the rear wall of the passenger compartment and a real live trunk that holds golf bags, this new drop top should prove quite popular. Lower-powered airbags are not available on the Corvette.

Category F

	Trade-in	Private	Dealer
2 Dr STD Conv	29293	31648	34200
2 Dr STD Cpe	24325	26281	28400

OPTIONS FOR CORVETTE
Climate Control for AC +176
Compact Disc Changer +290
Dual Power Seats +147
Glass Targa Top +315
Selective Damping System +821
Solid & Glass Targa Tops +460
Sport Magnesium Wheels +1379
Sport Seats +302

EXPRESS 1998

All vans equipped with airbags switch to mini-module bag designs for the driver, but they still deploy with more force than second-generation types. A theft-deterrent system is standard, and three new colors debut.

Category Q

	Trade-in	Private	Dealer
2 Dr G1500 Express Van	8379	9301	10300
2 Dr G2500 Express Van	9111	10114	11200
2 Dr G2500 Express Van Ext	9436	10475	11600
2 Dr G3500 Express Van	9192	10204	11300
2 Dr G3500 Express Van Ext	9518	10565	11700
2 Dr G1500 LS Express Van	9029	10023	11100
2 Dr G2500 LS Express Van	10006	11107	12300
2 Dr G2500 LS Express Van Ext	10250	11378	12600
2 Dr G3500 LS Express Van	10087	11197	12400
2 Dr G3500 LS Express Van Ext	10331	11468	12700

OPTIONS FOR EXPRESS
15 Passenger Seating +180
8 cyl 5.0 L Engine[Opt on 1500] +240
8 cyl 5.7 L Engine[Opt on 1500] +466
8 cyl 6.5 L Turbodiesel Engine +1315
8 cyl 7.4 L Engine +290
AM/FM Compact Disc Player +263
AM/FM Stereo/CD/Tape +311
Aluminum/Alloy Wheels[Opt on 1500] +120
Camper/Towing Package +150
Chrome Wheels[Opt on 1500] +120
Cruise Control[Std on LS] +99
Dual Air Conditioning +416
Dual Power Seats +232
Locking Differential +123
Power Door Locks[Std on LS] +109
Power Drivers Seat +116
Power Windows[Std on LS] +129
Privacy Glass +189
Rear Heater +99

LUMINA 1998

Last year's aborted LTZ sport sedan comes on strong for 1998, with a 200-horsepower 3800 V6 engine and machine-faced aluminum wheels. Four new exterior colors and one new interior color are also available on all Lumina models. To help give Lumina a more upscale image than Malibu, an OnStar Mobile Communications system is a dealer-installed option. Second-generation airbags are standard equipment.

Category D

	Trade-in	Private	Dealer
4 Dr STD Sdn	6341	7185	8100
4 Dr LS Sdn	7046	7984	9000
4 Dr LTZ Sdn	7124	8072	9100

OPTIONS FOR LUMINA
6 cyl 3.8 L Engine[Opt on LTZ] +217
AM/FM Compact Disc Player +156
AM/FM Stereo Tape[Opt on STD] +112
Aluminum/Alloy Wheels[Opt on STD] +146
Anti-Lock Brakes[Opt on STD] +278
Cruise Control +105
Keyless Entry System +106
Leather Seats +311
Power Drivers Seat +147
Power Mirrors[Opt on STD] +95
Power Moonroof +339
Power Windows[Opt on STD] +129

MALIBU 1998

Leather trim is newly optional on LS models, aluminum wheels are revised, a sunroof can be ordered and Base models can be equipped with Medium Oak colored interior. Second-generation airbags debut.

Category C

	Trade-in	Private	Dealer
4 Dr STD Sdn	6040	6837	7700
4 Dr LS Sdn	6824	7724	8700

OPTIONS FOR MALIBU
6 cyl 3.1 L Engine[Std on LS] +240
AM/FM Stereo Tape[Std on LS] +106
AM/FM Stereo/CD/Tape +97
Aluminum/Alloy Wheels[Std on LS] +150

Don't forget to refer to the Mileage Adjustment Table at the back of this book!

Model Description	Trade-in TMV	Private TMV	Dealer TMV	Model Description	Trade-in TMV	Private TMV	Dealer TMV

Cruise Control[Std on LS] +109
Leather Seats +230
Power Door Locks[Std on LS] +114
Power Drivers Seat[Std on LS] +150
Power Mirrors[Opt on STD] +95
Power Sunroof +288
Power Windows[Std on LS] +126

METRO   1998

The Geo badge is replaced with a Chevy bowtie. Styling is updated front and rear. The LSi's four-cylinder engine gets four valves per cylinder for more power and better acceleration. Second-generation airbags are standard equipment. Wheel covers are revised, new radios, new interior fabrics, and the addition of California Gold Metallic to the paint palette round out the changes.

Category A

Model	Trade-in	Private	Dealer
2 Dr STD Hbk	2522	2992	3500
2 Dr LSi Hbk	2738	3248	3800
4 Dr LSi Sdn	3099	3675	4300

OPTIONS FOR METRO

AM/FM Compact Disc Player +217
AM/FM Stereo Tape +266
Air Conditioning +380
Anti-Lock Brakes +273
Automatic 3-Speed Transmission +288
Power Door Locks +106
Power Steering +140

MONTE CARLO   1998

The Z34 model gets a different engine and fresh wheels. Second-generation airbags are added. New paint colors and one new interior hue round out the changes.

Category D

Model	Trade-in	Private	Dealer
2 Dr LS Cpe	6341	7185	8100
2 Dr Z34 Cpe	7124	8072	9100

OPTIONS FOR MONTE CARLO

AM/FM Stereo/CD/Tape +120
Aluminum/Alloy Wheels[Opt on LS] +146
Bucket Seats +97
Cruise Control[Opt on LS] +105
Keyless Entry System[Opt on LS] +106
Leather Seats +311
Power Drivers Seat +147
Power Moonroof +339

PRIZM   1998

Chevy replaces the Geo badge with their own on the completely redesigned Prizm. Among the improvements are a larger standard engine, optional side airbags, an optional handling package for LSi models and new colors inside and out. Front airbags are of the de-powered variety.

Category B

Model	Trade-in	Private	Dealer
4 Dr STD Sdn	4453	5196	6000
4 Dr LSi Sdn	5566	6494	7500

OPTIONS FOR PRIZM

AM/FM Compact Disc Player +317
AM/FM Stereo Tape +269
Air Conditioning +380
Aluminum/Alloy Wheels +162
Anti-Lock Brakes +311
Automatic 3-Speed Transmission +240
Automatic 4-Speed Transmission +387
Power Door Locks[Opt on STD] +106
Power Sunroof +327
Power Windows +146
Side Air Bag Restraints +143

S-10   1998

The S-10 gets a sheetmetal makeover and a new interior with dual airbags that incorporate second-generation technology for reduced force deployments. The basic four-cylinder engine benefits from Vortec technology this year, while 4WD models now have four-wheel disc brakes and a more refined transfer case on trucks with an automatic transmission. New radios, automatic headlight control, and a standard theft-deterrent system sum up the changes.

Category J

Model	Trade-in	Private	Dealer
2 Dr STD 4WD Std Cab LB	7095	7961	8900
2 Dr STD Std Cab LB	5819	6530	7300
2 Dr STD 4WD Std Cab SB	6935	7782	8700
2 Dr STD Std Cab SB	5740	6441	7200
2 Dr LS 4WD Std Cab LB	8131	9124	10200
2 Dr LS Std Cab LB	6377	7156	8000
2 Dr LS 4WD Ext Cab SB	9088	10198	11400
2 Dr LS 4WD Std Cab SB	7732	8677	9700
2 Dr LS Ext Cab SB	6537	7335	8200
2 Dr LS Std Cab SB	5899	6619	7400
2 Dr LS 4WD Ext Cab Stepside SB	9167	10287	11500
2 Dr LS 4WD Std Cab Stepside SB	8211	9214	10300
2 Dr LS Ext Cab Stepside SB	6616	7425	8300
2 Dr LS Std Cab Stepside SB	6457	7246	8100
2 Dr ZR2 4WD Ext Cab SB	11559	12971	14500
2 Dr ZR2 4WD Std Cab SB	10762	12076	13500

Don't forget to refer to the Mileage Adjustment Table at the back of this book!

Model Description	Trade-in TMV	Private TMV	Dealer TMV	Model Description	Trade-in TMV	Private TMV	Dealer TMV

OPTIONS FOR S-10

6 cyl 4.3 L Engine[Opt on 2WD] +527
6 cyl 4.3 L Vortec Engine[Std on ZR2] +125
AM/FM Compact Disc Player +146
AM/FM Stereo/CD/Tape +194
Air Conditioning[Std on ZR2] +389
Aluminum/Alloy Wheels[Opt on LS] +135
Automatic 4-Speed Transmission[Std on ZR2] +518
Bucket Seats +116
Hinged Third Door +143
Locking Differential[Std on ZR2] +131
Power Door Locks[Opt on LS] +109
Power Mirrors[Opt on LS] +99
Power Windows[Opt on LS] +124
Sport Suspension +336

SUBURBAN   1998

New colors, a standard theft deterrent system, optional heated seats, second generation airbags, and an automatic 4WD system improve the 1998 Suburban.

Category N

Model	Trade-in	Private	Dealer
4 Dr C1500 Wgn	12900	14196	15600
4 Dr C2500 Wgn	13975	15379	16900
4 Dr K1500 4WD Wgn	14554	16016	17600
4 Dr K2500 4WD Wgn	15546	17108	18800

OPTIONS FOR SUBURBAN

8 cyl 6.5 L Turbodiesel Engine[Opt on 2500] +1315
8 cyl 7.4 L Engine[Opt on 2500] +276
AM/FM Compact Disc Player +139
AM/FM Stereo/CD/Tape +92
Air Conditioning +389
Aluminum/Alloy Wheels +142
Bucket Seats +125
Camper/Towing Package +98
Center & Rear Bench Seat +504
Center Bench Seat +291
Dual Air Conditioning +641
Dual Power Seats +220
Heated Front Seats +161
LS Package +1763
LT Package +2135
Leather Seats +511
Locking Differential +117
Power Drivers Seat +110
Power Windows +122
Privacy Glass +140
Rear Heater +95
Running Boards +148
Skid Plates +108

TAHOE   1998

Autotrac is a new optional automatic four-wheel drive system that switches from 2WD to 4WD automatically as conditions warrant. A new option package includes heated seats and heated exterior mirrors. Second generation airbags deploy with less force than last year. A theft deterrent system is standard, and color selections are modified.

Category N

Model	Trade-in	Private	Dealer
2 Dr STD 4WD Utility	11246	12376	13600
2 Dr STD Utility	9427	10374	11400
2 Dr LS 4WD Utility	13810	15197	16700
2 Dr LS Utility	12239	13468	14800
4 Dr LS 4WD Wgn	15215	16744	18400
4 Dr LS Wgn	13727	15106	16600
2 Dr LT 4WD Utility	15133	16653	18300
2 Dr LT Utility	13148	14469	15900
4 Dr LT 4WD Wgn	15464	17017	18700
4 Dr LT Wgn	14058	15470	17000

OPTIONS FOR TAHOE

8 cyl 6.5 L Turbodiesel Engine[Opt on 2DOOR] +1315
AM/FM Stereo/CD/Tape[Opt on LS] +92
Air Conditioning[Opt on STD] +389
Aluminum/Alloy Wheels[Opt on STD] +142
Bucket Seats +109
Camper/Towing Package +204
Dual Air Conditioning +253
Dual Power Seats +220
Heated Front Seats +148
Heated Power Mirrors +95
Locking Differential +117
Privacy Glass[Opt on STD] +99
Running Boards +127

TRACKER   1998

Geo is gone, so all Trackers are now badged as Chevrolets. The LSi models are dropped, though an LSi equipment package is available on Base models. Two new colors are available. Second-generation airbags are standard.

Category L

Model	Trade-in	Private	Dealer
2 Dr STD 4WD Conv	5809	6573	7400
2 Dr STD Conv	5259	5951	6700
4 Dr STD 4WD Wgn	6358	7194	8100
4 Dr STD Wgn	6044	6839	7700

OPTIONS FOR TRACKER

AM/FM Compact Disc Player +254
AM/FM Stereo Tape +254
Air Conditioning +453
Aluminum/Alloy Wheels +176
Anti-Lock Brakes +288
Automatic 3-Speed Transmission +302
Automatic 4-Speed Transmission +483
Automatic Locking Hubs (4WD) +97
Power Door Locks[Opt on Wgn] +102
Power Steering[Std on Wgn, 4WD] +140
Power Windows +116

VENTURE   1998

Venture is the first minivan to get side-impact airbags.

Model Description	Trade-in TMV	Private TMV	Dealer TMV

Other changes include the availability of a cargo van edition, a wider variety of dual door models, and an optional power sliding door on regular wheelbase vans. Power rear window vents are also added for 1998. Front airbags deploy with less force thanks to second-generation technology.

Category P

Model Description	Trade-in TMV	Private TMV	Dealer TMV
2 Dr STD Cargo Van Ext	6430	7232	8100
2 Dr STD Pass. Van	8733	9821	11000
2 Dr STD Pass. Van Ext	9288	10446	11700
2 Dr LS Pass. Van	9368	10535	11800
2 Dr LS Pass. Van Ext	9844	11071	12400

OPTIONS FOR VENTURE
AM/FM Compact Disc Player +179
AM/FM Stereo/CD/Tape +227
Aluminum/Alloy Wheels +143
Automatic Load Leveling[Opt on STD] +104
Captain Chairs (2) +129
Child Seats (2) +109
Dual Air Conditioning +217
Overhead Console[Opt on LS] +131
Power Drivers Seat +131
Power Sliding Door +211
Power Windows[Std on LS] +133
Privacy Glass +133
Rear Heater +134
Sliding Driver Side Door +134
Traction Control System +95

1997 CHEVROLET

ASTRO   1997

Daytime running lights debut, and LT models can be equipped with leather upholstery. Also optional this year is a HomeLink three-channel transmitter. Delayed entry/exit lighting is now standard on all Astro passenger vans. Transmission refinements mean smoother shifts, and electronic variable orifice steering eases steering effort at low speeds.

Category P

Model Description	Trade-in TMV	Private TMV	Dealer TMV
2 Dr STD AWD Cargo Van Ext	7122	8102	9300
2 Dr STD AWD Pass. Van Ext	7352	8364	9600
2 Dr STD Cargo Van Ext	5208	5924	6800
2 Dr STD Pass. Van Ext	6280	7144	8200
2 Dr LS AWD Pass. Van Ext	7965	9061	10400
2 Dr LS Pass. Van Ext	7275	8276	9500

Model Description	Trade-in TMV	Private TMV	Dealer TMV
2 Dr LT AWD Pass. Van Ext	8884	10106	11600
2 Dr LT Pass. Van Ext	8041	9148	10500

OPTIONS FOR ASTRO
7 Passenger Seating +263
8 Passenger Seating[Opt on STD] +173
AM/FM Compact Disc Player +178
AM/FM Stereo Tape +135
AM/FM Stereo/CD/Tape +222
Aluminum/Alloy Wheels[Std on LT] +135
Camper/Towing Package +135
Child Seats (2) +105
Chrome Wheels +130
Dual Air Conditioning +230
Dual Power Seats +211
Leather Seats +417
Locking Differential +111
Power Door Locks[Opt on STD] +98
Power Drivers Seat[Std on LT] +105
Power Windows[Opt on STD] +116
Privacy Glass[Opt on STD] +127
Rear Heater +90

BLAZER   1997

Those who prefer a liftgate over a tailgate have that option on 1997 four-door Blazers. A power sunroof is a new option for all Blazers, and models equipped with LT decor are equipped with a HomeLink transmitter that will open your garage, among other things. All-wheel drive Blazers get four-wheel disc brakes, and automatic transmissions are revised for smoother shifting. Early production 4WD two-door Blazers could be ordered with a ZR2 suspension package, but by the time we got pricing, Chevrolet had cancelled the option. Base Blazers get a chrome grille, while LT four-door models have body-color grilles in six exterior colors. Two new paint colors round out the changes.

Category M

Model Description	Trade-in TMV	Private TMV	Dealer TMV
2 Dr STD 4WD Utility	7753	8764	10000
2 Dr STD Utility	6668	7537	8600
4 Dr STD 4WD Wgn	8519	9630	10988
4 Dr STD Wgn	7133	8063	9200
2 Dr LS 4WD Utility	8451	9553	10900
2 Dr LS Utility	7211	8151	9300
4 Dr LS 4WD Wgn	9226	10430	11900
4 Dr LS Wgn	8538	9651	11012
4 Dr LT 4WD Wgn	10002	11306	12900
4 Dr LT Wgn	9304	10517	12000

OPTIONS FOR BLAZER
AM/FM Compact Disc Player +145
Aluminum/Alloy Wheels[Opt on STD] +117
Camper/Towing Package +93
Locking Differential +111
Power Drivers Seat[Opt on LS] +105
Power Sunroof +305

Don't forget to refer to the Mileage Adjustment Table at the back of this book!

Model Description	Trade-in TMV	Private TMV	Dealer TMV

Power Windows[Opt on STD] +115
Wide Stance Suspension +812

C/K 1500 SERIES   1997

Order a truck under 8,600 lbs. GVWR, and you'll get a passenger airbag. The airbag can be deactivated when a rear-facing child safety seat is installed. Low-speed steering effort is reduced this year, and a refined transmission fluid pump results in smoother shifts. An alternative fuel version of the Vortec 5700 is available, but only on a specific model. K1500's get a tighter turning radius, and three new colors debut. The third door option will be more widely available, because it is now a required option on all C/K 1500 shortbed extended cab trucks.

Category K

Model Description	Trade-in TMV	Private TMV	Dealer TMV
2 Dr C1500 Cheyenne Ext Cab LB			
	8028	8961	10100
2 Dr C1500 Cheyenne Std Cab LB			
	6598	7364	8300
2 Dr K1500 Cheyenne 4WD Ext Cab LB			
	10152	11331	12772
2 Dr K1500 Cheyenne 4WD Std Cab LB			
	8267	9227	10400
2 Dr C1500 Cheyenne Ext Cab SB			
	7472	8340	9400
2 Dr C1500 Cheyenne Std Cab SB			
	6518	7275	8200
2 Dr K1500 Cheyenne 4WD Ext Cab SB			
	9459	10558	11900
2 Dr K1500 Cheyenne 4WD Std Cab SB			
	7949	8872	10000
2 Dr C1500 Cheyenne Ext Cab Stepside SB			
	7869	8783	9900
2 Dr C1500 Cheyenne Std Cab Stepside SB			
	6757	7541	8500
2 Dr K1500 Cheyenne 4WD Ext Cab Stepside SB			
	9857	11001	12400
2 Dr K1500 Cheyenne 4WD Std Cab Stepside SB			
	8664	9670	10900
2 Dr C1500 Silverado Ext Cab LB			
	9618	10735	12100
2 Dr C1500 Silverado Std Cab LB			
	7551	8428	9500
2 Dr K1500 Silverado 4WD Ext Cab LB			
	10731	11977	13500
2 Dr K1500 Silverado 4WD Std Cab LB			
	9777	10912	12300
2 Dr C1500 Silverado Ext Cab SB			
	8744	9759	11000
2 Dr C1500 Silverado Std Cab SB			
	7313	8162	9200
2 Dr K1500 Silverado 4WD Ext Cab SB			
	10356	11558	13028
2 Dr K1500 Silverado 4WD Std Cab SB			
	9539	10646	12000
2 Dr C1500 Silverado Ext Cab Stepside SB			
	9141	10203	11500
2 Dr C1500 Silverado Std Cab Stepside SB			
	7778	8681	9785
2 Dr K1500 Silverado 4WD Ext Cab Stepside SB			
	10692	11934	13451
2 Dr K1500 Silverado 4WD Std Cab Stepside SB			
	9936	11090	12500
2 Dr C1500 WT Std Cab LB			
	6200	6920	7800
2 Dr K1500 WT 4WD Std Cab LB			
	7802	8708	9815
2 Dr C1500 WT Std Cab SB			
	6121	6831	7700
2 Dr K1500 WT 4WD Std Cab SB			
	7710	8606	9700

OPTIONS FOR C/K 1500 SERIES

8 cyl 5.0 L Engine +218
8 cyl 5.7 L Engine +307
8 cyl 6.5 L Turbodiesel Engine +1483
AM/FM Compact Disc Player +109
AM/FM Stereo/CD/Tape +127
Air Conditioning[Std on Silverado] +353
Aluminum/Alloy Wheels +109
Automatic 4-Speed Transmission +425
Bed Liner +98
Bucket Seats +118
Chrome Step Bumper[Std on Silverado] +100
Chrome Wheels +109
Cruise Control[Std on Silverado] +90
Hinged Third Door +184
Leather Seats +439
Locking Differential +111
Power Drivers Seat +105

C/K 2500 SERIES   1997

Order a truck under 8,600 lbs. GVWR, and you'll get a passenger airbag. The airbag can be deactivated when a rear-facing child safety seat is installed. Low-speed steering effort is reduced this year, and a refined transmission fluid pump results in smoother shifts. An alternative fuel version of the Vortec 5700 is available, but only on a specific model. K1500's get a tighter turning radius, and three new colors debut. The third door option will be more widely available.

Category K

Model Description	Trade-in TMV	Private TMV	Dealer TMV
2 Dr C2500 Cheyenne Std Cab LB			
	6757	7541	8500
2 Dr C2500 HD Cheyenne Ext Cab LB			
	8346	9315	10500

Don't forget to refer to the Mileage Adjustment Table at the back of this book!

Model Description	Trade-in TMV	Private TMV	Dealer TMV
2 Dr C2500 HD Cheyenne Std Cab LB	7472	8340	9400
2 Dr K2500 HD Cheyenne 4WD Ext Cab LB	10095	11267	12700
2 Dr K2500 HD Cheyenne 4WD Std Cab LB	8982	10025	11300
2 Dr C2500 Cheyenne Ext Cab SB	8585	9582	10800
2 Dr K2500 HD Cheyenne 4WD Ext Cab SB	9936	11090	12500
2 Dr C2500 HD Silverado Ext Cab LB	9221	10291	11600
2 Dr C2500 HD Silverado Std Cab LB	8823	9848	11100
2 Dr C2500 Silverado Std Cab LB	8028	8961	10100
2 Dr K2500 HD Silverado 4WD Ext Cab LB	11128	12421	14000
2 Dr K2500 HD Silverado 4WD Std Cab LB	10175	11356	12800
2 Dr C2500 Silverado Ext Cab SB	9857	11001	12400
2 Dr K2500 HD Silverado 4WD Ext Cab SB	11049	12332	13900

OPTIONS FOR C/K 2500 SERIES

8 cyl 5.7 L Engine[Std on HD] +307
8 cyl 6.5 L Turbodiesel Engine +1192
8 cyl 7.4 L Engine +263
AM/FM Stereo/CD/Tape +127
Air Conditioning[Std on Silverado] +353
Automatic 4-Speed Transmission +437
Bed Liner +98
Chrome Step Bumper[Std on Silverado] +100
Leather Seats +515
Locking Differential +111
Power Drivers Seat +105

C/K 3500 SERIES   1997

Order a truck under 8,600 lbs. GVWR, and you'll get a passenger airbag. The airbag can be deactivated when a rear-facing child safety seat is installed. Low-speed steering effort is reduced this year, and a refined transmission fluid pump results in smoother shifts. An alternative fuel version of the Vortec 5700 is available, but only on a specific model. K1500's get a tighter turning radius, and three new colors debut. The third door option will be more widely available.

Category K

Model Description	Trade-in TMV	Private TMV	Dealer TMV
2 Dr C3500 Cheyenne Ext Cab LB	9380	10469	11800
2 Dr C3500 Cheyenne Std Cab LB	7869	8783	9900
2 Dr K3500 Cheyenne 4WD Ext Cab LB	10890	12155	13700
2 Dr K3500 Cheyenne 4WD Std Cab LB	9141	10203	11500
4 Dr C3500 Cheyenne Crew Cab LB	9300	10380	11700
4 Dr K3500 Cheyenne 4WD Crew Cab LB	10969	12243	13800
2 Dr C3500 Silverado Ext Cab LB	10334	11533	13000
2 Dr C3500 Silverado Std Cab LB	8744	9759	11000
2 Dr K3500 Silverado 4WD Ext Cab LB	11526	12864	14500
2 Dr K3500 Silverado 4WD Std Cab LB	10254	11445	12900
4 Dr C3500 Silverado Crew Cab LB	11128	12421	14000
4 Dr K3500 Silverado 4WD Crew Cab LB	13116	14639	16500

OPTIONS FOR C/K 3500 SERIES

8 cyl 6.5 L Turbodiesel Engine +1192
8 cyl 7.4 L Engine +263
AM/FM Compact Disc Player +105
AM/FM Stereo/CD/Tape +127
Air Conditioning[Std on Silverado] +353
Automatic 4-Speed Transmission +425
Bed Liner +98
Bucket Seats +118
Chrome Step Bumper[Std on Silverado] +100
Dual Rear Wheels +376
Leather Seats +439
Locking Differential +124
Power Drivers Seat +105

CAMARO   1997

Chevrolet celebrates the Camaro's 30th Anniversary with a special-edition Z28 that emulates the appearance of the 1969 SS Indy Pace Car with white paint, Hugger Orange stripes, and black-and-white houndstooth seat inserts. Interior revisions to seats, center console and dashboard freshen the look inside for 1997. Two new shades of gray are available for interiors, while exteriors get new green and purple hues. Tri-color taillamps debut, and new five-spoke alloy wheels are optional. On the safety front, daytime running lights are standard and side-impact regulations are met.

Category E

Model Description	Trade-in TMV	Private TMV	Dealer TMV
2 Dr STD Conv	8058	9112	10400
2 Dr STD Cpe	6353	7184	8200
2 Dr RS Conv	8600	9725	11100
2 Dr RS Cpe	7051	7973	9100
2 Dr Z28 Conv	9917	11215	12800
2 Dr Z28 Cpe	7515	8498	9700
2 Dr Z28 SS Conv	12009	13580	15500

Don't forget to refer to the Mileage Adjustment Table at the back of this book!

Model Description	Trade-in TMV	Private TMV	Dealer TMV
2 Dr Z28 SS Cpe	9065	10251	11700

OPTIONS FOR CAMARO
AM/FM Compact Disc Player +139
Additional 'SS' Wheels +154
Aluminum/Alloy Wheels[Opt on STD] +121
Automatic 4-Speed Transmission[Std on Z28,SS] +358
Chrome Wheels +340
Compact Disc Changer +261
Glass Panel T-tops +437
Leather Seats +197
Limited Slip Differential[Opt on RS,STD] +197
Performance Package +526
Power Door Locks +96
Power Drivers Seat +118
Power Windows +112
Sport Suspension Package +175
Torsen Torque Sensing Axle +132

CAVALIER 1997

The historically on-again off-again Rally Sport (RS) trim level is evidently on-again, attached for 1997 to the coupe and slotted between base and Z24 editions of the Cavalier. RS trim nets buyers the rear spoiler from the Z24, 15-inch tires, AM/FM stereo, tachometer, interior and exterior trim goodies, and a really cool (yeah, right) 3D rear quarter panel decal. Base coupes have new wheel covers and safety belt guide loops. All 1997 Cavaliers meet federal side-impact standards for the first time. One new interior color and three new exterior colors freshen the lineup.
Category B

Model Description	Trade-in TMV	Private TMV	Dealer TMV
2 Dr STD Cpe	3301	3931	4700
4 Dr STD Sdn	3301	3931	4700
2 Dr LS Conv	5619	6690	8000
4 Dr LS Sdn	4144	4934	5900
2 Dr RS Cpe	3863	4600	5500
2 Dr Z24 Cpe	4495	5352	6400

OPTIONS FOR CAVALIER
4 cyl 2.4 L Engine[Opt on LS,Z24] +173
AM/FM Compact Disc Player +140
AM/FM Stereo Tape +96
Air Conditioning[Opt on RS,STD] +349
Aluminum/Alloy Wheels[Std on Z24] +130
Automatic 3-Speed Transmission[Std on LS] +241
Automatic 4-Speed Transmission +349
Power Door Locks +93
Power Sunroof +294
Power Windows +116

CORVETTE 1997

Fifth-generation Corvette debuts 44 years after the original, and is better than ever with world-class build quality and performance at a bargain price.
Category F

Model Description	Trade-in TMV	Private TMV	Dealer TMV
2 Dr STD Cpe	20870	22818	25200

OPTIONS FOR CORVETTE
Climate Control for AC +160
Compact Disc Changer +263
Dual Power Seats +134
Glass Targa Top +285
Selective Damping System +744
Solid & Glass Targa Tops +417
Sport Seats +274

EXPRESS 1997

Dual airbags appear on the G3500 model, while daytime running lights and three fresh exterior colors make this van easier to see. (Editor's Note: If you can't see this monster van without DRL's, perhaps you should consider surrendering your driver's license.) Electronic variable orifice steering reduces effort at low speeds for easier parking, and automatic transmissions shift more smoothly.
Category Q

Model Description	Trade-in TMV	Private TMV	Dealer TMV
2 Dr G1500 Express Van	6951	7828	8900
2 Dr G2500 Express Van	7341	8268	9400
2 Dr G2500 Express Van Ext	7732	8707	9900
2 Dr G3500 Express Van	7654	8619	9800
2 Dr G3500 Express Van Ext	7810	8795	10000
2 Dr G1500 LS Express Van	7185	8092	9200
2 Dr G2500 LS Express Van	8044	9059	10300
2 Dr G2500 LS Express Van Ext	8435	9499	10800
2 Dr G3500 LS Express Van	8278	9323	10600
2 Dr G3500 LS Express Van Ext	8513	9587	10900

OPTIONS FOR EXPRESS
15 Passenger Seating[Opt on 3500] +163
8 cyl 5.0 L Engine[Opt on 1500] +218
8 cyl 5.7 L Engine[Opt on 1500] +423
8 cyl 6.5 L Turbodiesel Engine[Opt on 2500,3500] +1192
8 cyl 7.4 L Engine[Opt on 2500,3500] +263
AM/FM Compact Disc Player +238
AM/FM Stereo/CD/Tape +282
Aluminum/Alloy Wheels[Opt on 1500] +109
Camper/Towing Package +136
Chrome Wheels[Opt on 1500] +109
Cruise Control[Std on LS] +90
Dual Air Conditioning +377
Dual Power Seats +211
Locking Differential +111
Power Door Locks[Std on LS] +98

Don't forget to refer to the Mileage Adjustment Table at the back of this book!

Model Description	Trade-in TMV	Private TMV	Dealer TMV
Power Drivers Seat +105			
Power Windows[Std on LS] +116			
Privacy Glass +172			
Rear Heater +90			

LUMINA 1997

Performance-oriented Lumina LTZ debuts, though a spoiler, special front and rear styling, graphics, and alloy wheels don't amount to performance in our book. Daytime running lamps are standard on all Luminas, and the power sunroof expected last year finally arrives. New colors and an oil life monitor round out changes to Lumina for 1997.

Category D

	Trade-in	Private	Dealer
4 Dr STD Sdn	5157	6032	7100
4 Dr LS Sdn	5811	6796	8000
4 Dr LTZ Sdn	5884	6881	8100

OPTIONS FOR LUMINA
6 cyl 3.4 L Engine +405
AM/FM Compact Disc Player +142
AM/FM Stereo Tape[Opt on STD] +102
Aluminum/Alloy Wheels[Opt on STD] +132
Anti-Lock Brakes[Opt on STD] +252
Cruise Control +95
Keyless Entry System +96
Leather Seats +282
Power Drivers Seat +134
Power Moonroof +307
Power Windows[Opt on STD] +116

MALIBU 1997

Malibu returns after consumer clinics tell Chevrolet they want a tight, solid, roomy, fun-to-drive midsize sedan. Guess what? Chevrolet delivers.

Category C

	Trade-in	Private	Dealer
4 Dr STD Sdn	4760	5588	6600
4 Dr LS Sdn	5842	6858	8100

OPTIONS FOR MALIBU
6 cyl 3.1 L Engine[Std on LS] +173
AM/FM Stereo Tape[Std on LS] +96
Aluminum/Alloy Wheels[Std on LS] +130
Cruise Control[Std on LS] +98
Power Door Locks[Std on LS] +103
Power Drivers Seat[Std on LS] +134
Power Windows[Std on LS] +115

MONTE CARLO 1997

Hot-rod Z34 gets a new transmission, while all models have daytime running lights. Newly optional is a power sunroof. Two new colors freshen the rather dull sheetmetal.

Category D

	Trade-in	Private	Dealer
2 Dr LS Cpe	5157	6032	7100
2 Dr Z34 Cpe	5521	6456	7600

OPTIONS FOR MONTE CARLO

Model Description	Trade-in TMV	Private TMV	Dealer TMV
Aluminum/Alloy Wheels[Opt on LS] +132			
Cruise Control[Opt on LS] +95			
Keyless Entry System[Opt on LS] +96			
Leather Seats +282			
Power Drivers Seat +132			
Power Sunroof +307			

S-10 1997

Chevy strengthens the 2WD S-10 frame by using tougher components. Refinements to the automatic transmission result in improved efficiency and smoother shifts. Four-wheel drive models have lighter-weight plug-in half shafts. Two new colors are available.

Category J

	Trade-in	Private	Dealer
2 Dr STD 4WD Std Cab LB	6549	7427	8500
2 Dr STD Std Cab LB	4700	5330	6100
2 Dr STD 4WD Std Cab SB	6395	7252	8300
2 Dr STD Std Cab SB	4315	4893	5600
2 Dr LS 4WD Std Cab LB	6857	7776	8900
2 Dr LS Std Cab LB	5085	5767	6600
2 Dr LS 4WD Ext Cab SB	7474	8475	9700
2 Dr LS 4WD Std Cab SB	6703	7602	8700
2 Dr LS Ext Cab SB	5701	6466	7400
2 Dr LS Std Cab SB	5008	5679	6500
2 Dr LS 4WD Ext Cab Stepside SB	7705	8738	10000
2 Dr LS 4WD Std Cab Stepside SB	6934	7864	9000
2 Dr LS Ext Cab Stepside SB	5779	6553	7500
2 Dr LS Std Cab Stepside SB	5162	5854	6700

OPTIONS FOR S-10
6 cyl 4.3 L Engine[Opt on 2WD] +478
6 cyl 4.3 L Vortec Engine +114
AM/FM Compact Disc Player +133
AM/FM Stereo Tape +89
Air Conditioning +353
Aluminum/Alloy Wheels +123
Automatic 4-Speed Transmission +469
Bucket Seats +106
Hinged Third Door +130
Locking Differential +118
Power Door Locks +98
Power Mirrors[Opt on LS] +90
Power Windows +112
Wide Stance Suspension +765

SUBURBAN 1997

Dual airbags debut, and a cargo area power lock switch

CHEVROLET 97-96

| Model Description | Trade-in TMV | Private TMV | Dealer TMV | Model Description | Trade-in TMV | Private TMV | Dealer TMV |

makes locking up the vehicle after unloading cargo more convenient. Electronic Variable Orifice power steering lightens low-speed steering effort, and automatic transmissions are improved. Two new exterior colors are added to the paint roster.

Category N

	Trade-in	Private	Dealer
4 Dr C1500 Wgn	11124	12418	14000
4 Dr C2500 Wgn	11680	13039	14700
4 Dr K1500 4WD Wgn	12316	13749	15500
4 Dr K2500 4WD Wgn	12713	14192	16000

OPTIONS FOR SUBURBAN

8 cyl 6.5 L Turbodiesel Engine +690
8 cyl 7.4 L Engine +250
AM/FM Compact Disc Player +126
AM/FM Stereo/CD/Tape +168
Air Conditioning +352
Aluminum/Alloy Wheels +129
Bucket Seats +109
Camper/Towing Package +89
Captain Chairs (2) +104
Center Bench Seat +264
Dual Air Conditioning +540
LS Package +1598
LT Package +1934
Leather Seats +463
Locking Differential +106
Power Drivers Seat +100
Power Windows +110
Privacy Glass +127
Running Boards +135
Skid Plates +94

TAHOE   1997

A passenger-side airbag is added, and the automatic transmission is improved. Electronic Variable Orifice steering debuts, and cargo areas have a power door lock switch. A new center console comes with high-back bucket seats, and two new paint colors are available.

Category N

	Trade-in	Private	Dealer
2 Dr STD 4WD Utility	9217	10289	11600
2 Dr STD Utility	8422	9402	10600
2 Dr LS 4WD Utility	12713	14192	16000
2 Dr LS Utility	10011	11176	12600
4 Dr LS 4WD Wgn	13110	14636	16500
4 Dr LS Wgn	11521	12862	14500
2 Dr LT 4WD Utility	13507	15079	17000
2 Dr LT Utility	11680	13039	14700
4 Dr LT 4WD Wgn	14222	15877	17900
4 Dr LT Wgn	12872	14369	16200

OPTIONS FOR TAHOE

8 cyl 6.5 L Turbodiesel Engine +1192
AM/FM Stereo/CD/Tape +125
Air Conditioning[Opt on STD] +352
Aluminum/Alloy Wheels[Opt on STD] +129

Bucket Seats +99
Camper/Towing Package +126
Dual Air Conditioning +229
Locking Differential +106
Power Drivers Seat[Opt on LS] +100
Privacy Glass[Opt on STD] +90
Running Boards +135

VENTURE   1997

Complete redesign of Chevy's minivan results in a new name, a left-side sliding door, optional traction control, a powerful standard engine, and a fun-to-drive demeanor. Nice van, except for the big chrome grille.

Category P

	Trade-in	Private	Dealer
2 Dr STD Pass. Van	6816	7754	8900
2 Dr STD Pass. Van Ext	7582	8625	9900
2 Dr LS Pass. Van	7658	8712	10000
2 Dr LS Pass. Van Ext	7888	8973	10300

OPTIONS FOR VENTURE

AM/FM Compact Disc Player +162
AM/FM Stereo/CD/Tape +206
Aluminum/Alloy Wheels +130
Automatic Load Leveling[Opt on LS] +95
Bucket Seats[Opt on LS] +197
Child Seats (2) +98
Dual Air Conditioning +197
Power Drivers Seat +118
Power Sliding Door +197
Power Windows +121
Privacy Glass +121
Sliding Driver Side Door +169

1996 CHEVROLET

ASTRO   1996

A new interior with dual airbags, new radio systems, an improved V6, and three new paint colors are the changes for this year.

Category P

	Trade-in	Private	Dealer
2 Dr STD AWD Cargo Van Ext	5467	6321	7500
2 Dr STD AWD Pass. Van Ext	6195	7163	8500
2 Dr STD Cargo Van Ext	4592	5309	6300
2 Dr STD Pass. Van Ext	4956	5731	6800
2 Dr LS AWD Pass. Van Ext	6851	7922	9400
2 Dr LS Pass. Van Ext	5612	6489	7700
2 Dr LT AWD Pass. Van Ext	7070	8175	9700
2 Dr LT Pass. Van Ext	6924	8006	9500

Don't forget to refer to the Mileage Adjustment Table at the back of this book!

Model Description	Trade-in TMV	Private TMV	Dealer TMV

OPTIONS FOR ASTRO

7 Passenger Seating +222
8 Passenger Seating[Opt on STD] +167
AM/FM Compact Disc Player +167
AM/FM Stereo Tape +167
AM/FM Stereo/CD/Tape +215
Aluminum/Alloy Wheels[Std on LT] +105
Camper/Towing Package +131
Chrome Wheels +125
Dual Air Conditioning +222
Locking Differential +107
Power Drivers Seat[Std on LT] +101
Power Passenger Seat +101
Power Windows[Opt on STD] +109
Privacy Glass[Opt on STD] +123

BERETTA   1996

Final year for Beretta. Only change is the addition of long-life coolant to the engine.

Category C

Model Description	Trade-in TMV	Private TMV	Dealer TMV
2 Dr STD Cpe	3013	3722	4700
2 Dr Z26 Cpe	3590	4434	5600

OPTIONS FOR BERETTA

6 cyl 3.1 L Engine[Opt on STD] +539
AM/FM Compact Disc Player +116
Automatic 3-Speed Transmission +235
Automatic 4-Speed Transmission[Opt on STD] +362
Power Windows +116
Sunroof +212

BLAZER   1996

More power, available all-wheel drive, and five new colors improve the 1996 Blazer. A five-speed manual transmission is optional on two-door models.

Category M

Model Description	Trade-in TMV	Private TMV	Dealer TMV
2 Dr STD 4WD Utility	5824	6696	7900
2 Dr STD Utility	5234	6018	7100
4 Dr STD 4WD Wgn	6810	7829	9237
4 Dr STD Wgn	5677	6526	7700
2 Dr LS 4WD Utility	6930	7967	9400
2 Dr LS Utility	5972	6865	8100
4 Dr LS 4WD Wgn	7299	8391	9900
4 Dr LS Wgn	6903	7936	9363
4 Dr LT 4WD Wgn	8036	9239	10900
4 Dr LT Wgn	7667	8815	10400

OPTIONS FOR BLAZER

AM/FM Compact Disc Player +139
Aluminum/Alloy Wheels[Opt on STD] +105
Locking Differential +103
Power Drivers Seat[Std on LT] +101
Power Windows[Opt on STD] +109

C/K 1500 SERIES   1996

Category K

Model Description	Trade-in TMV	Private TMV	Dealer TMV
2 Dr C1500 Cheyenne Ext Cab LB	7057	7915	9100
2 Dr C1500 Cheyenne Std Cab LB	5894	6610	7600
2 Dr K1500 Cheyenne 4WD Ext Cab LB	8453	9481	10900
2 Dr K1500 Cheyenne 4WD Std Cab LB	7134	8002	9200
2 Dr C1500 Cheyenne Ext Cab SB	6204	6958	8000
2 Dr C1500 Cheyenne Std Cab SB	6049	6784	7800
2 Dr K1500 Cheyenne 4WD Ext Cab SB	8030	9007	10355
2 Dr K1500 Cheyenne 4WD Std Cab SB	6979	7828	9000
2 Dr C1500 Cheyenne Ext Cab Stepside SB	6514	7306	8400
2 Dr C1500 Cheyenne Std Cab Stepside SB	5816	6523	7500
2 Dr K1500 Cheyenne 4WD Ext Cab Stepside SB	8132	9120	10486
2 Dr K1500 Cheyenne 4WD Std Cab Stepside SB	7212	8089	9300
2 Dr C1500 Silverado Ext Cab LB	8092	9076	10435
2 Dr C1500 Silverado Std Cab LB	6599	7401	8509
2 Dr K1500 Silverado 4WD Ext Cab LB	9228	10350	11900
2 Dr K1500 Silverado 4WD Std Cab LB	8153	9145	10514
2 Dr C1500 Silverado Ext Cab SB	7367	8263	9500
2 Dr C1500 Silverado Std Cab SB	6126	6871	7900
2 Dr K1500 Silverado 4WD Ext Cab SB	9306	10437	12000
2 Dr K1500 Silverado 4WD Std Cab SB	8073	9054	10410
2 Dr C1500 Silverado Ext Cab Stepside SB	7600	8524	9800
2 Dr C1500 Silverado Std Cab Stepside SB	6585	7385	8491
2 Dr K1500 Silverado 4WD Ext Cab Stepside SB	9693	10872	12500
2 Dr K1500 Silverado 4WD Std Cab Stepside SB	8375	9394	10800
2 Dr C1500 WT Std Cab LB	5428	6088	7000
2 Dr K1500 WT 4WD Std Cab LB	6359	7132	8200
2 Dr C1500 WT Std Cab SB			

Model Description	Trade-in TMV	Private TMV	Dealer TMV
	5273	5914	6800
2 Dr K1500 WT 4WD Std Cab SB			
	6281	7045	8100

OPTIONS FOR C/K 1500 SERIES
8 cyl 5.0 L Engine +209
8 cyl 5.7 L Engine +296
8 cyl 6.5 L Turbodiesel Engine +1429
AM/FM Compact Disc Player +106
Air Conditioning[Std on Silverado] +340
Aluminum/Alloy Wheels +106
Automatic 4-Speed Transmission +410
Chrome Step Bumper[Std on Silverado] +97
Chrome Wheels +106
Hinged Third Door +178
Leather Seats +423
Locking Differential +107
Power Drivers Seat +101

C/K 2500 SERIES   1996

Category K

Model Description	Trade-in TMV	Private TMV	Dealer TMV
2 Dr C2500 Cheyenne Std Cab LB			
	6436	7219	8300
2 Dr C2500 HD Cheyenne Ext Cab LB			
	7910	8872	10200
2 Dr K2500 Cheyenne 4WD Ext Cab LB			
	9306	10437	12000
2 Dr K2500 Cheyenne 4WD Std Cab LB			
	8220	9220	10600
2 Dr C2500 Cheyenne Ext Cab SB			
	7600	8524	9800
2 Dr K2500 Cheyenne 4WD Ext Cab SB			
	8918	10002	11500
2 Dr C2500 HD Silverado Ext Cab LB			
	8840	9915	11400
2 Dr C2500 Silverado Std Cab LB			
	6747	7567	8700
2 Dr K2500 Silverado 4WD Ext Cab LB			
	10469	11742	13500
2 Dr K2500 Silverado 4WD Std Cab LB			
	9616	10785	12400
2 Dr K2500 Silverado 4WD Ext Cab SB			
	10391	11655	13400
2 Dr Silverado Ext Cab SB			
	8685	9741	11200

OPTIONS FOR C/K 2500 SERIES
8 cyl 5.0 L Engine[Opt on Cheyenne Std Cab] +296
8 cyl 5.7 L Engine[Std on HD] +296
8 cyl 6.5 L Turbodiesel Engine +1148
8 cyl 7.4 L Engine +254
AM/FM Stereo/CD/Tape +123
Air Conditioning[Std on Silverado] +340
Automatic 4-Speed Transmission +410
Chrome Bumpers[Std on Silverado] +108
Leather Seats +423
Locking Differential +107

Power Drivers Seat[Opt on Silverado] +101

C/K 3500 SERIES   1996

Category K

Model Description	Trade-in TMV	Private TMV	Dealer TMV
2 Dr C3500 Cheyenne Ext Cab LB			
	8530	9568	11000
2 Dr C3500 Cheyenne Std Cab LB			
	6979	7828	9000
2 Dr K3500 Cheyenne 4WD Ext Cab LB			
	10081	11307	13000
2 Dr K3500 Cheyenne 4WD Std Cab LB			
	8298	9307	10700
4 Dr C3500 Cheyenne Crew Cab LB			
	8375	9394	10800
4 Dr K3500 Cheyenne 4WD Crew Cab LB			
	10159	11394	13100
2 Dr C3500 Silverado Ext Cab LB			
	9461	10611	12200
2 Dr C3500 Silverado Std Cab LB			
	7910	8872	10200
2 Dr K3500 Silverado 4WD Ext Cab LB			
	10469	11742	13500
2 Dr K3500 Silverado 4WD Std Cab LB			
	9306	10437	12000
4 Dr C3500 Silverado Crew Cab LB			
	10236	11481	13200
4 Dr K3500 Silverado 4WD Crew Cab LB			
	12020	13482	15500

OPTIONS FOR C/K 3500 SERIES
8 cyl 6.5 L Turbodiesel Engine +1148
8 cyl 7.4 L Engine +254
AM/FM Compact Disc Player +101
AM/FM Stereo/CD/Tape +123
Air Conditioning[Std on Silverado] +340
Automatic 4-Speed Transmission +410
Bucket Seats +114
Chrome Step Bumper[Std on Silverado] +97
Dual Rear Wheels +363
Leather Seats +423
Locking Differential +107

CAMARO   1996

Hot, new, 200 hp base V6 whumps the Mustang. Z28's 285 hp, LT1 V8 (with 10 more horsepower this year), whumps the Mustang GT. SLP Engineering provides a 305-horse Z28 SS, which ties the new Mustang Cobra for horsepower. The RS trim level returns, and chrome aluminum wheels are optional.

Category E

Model Description	Trade-in TMV	Private TMV	Dealer TMV
2 Dr STD Conv	6683	7614	8900
2 Dr STD Cpe	5256	5989	7000
2 Dr RS Conv	7134	8127	9500
2 Dr RS Cpe	6007	6844	8000

Don't forget to refer to the Mileage Adjustment Table at the back of this book!

Model Description	Trade-in TMV	Private TMV	Dealer TMV
2 Dr Z28 Conv	8110	9240	10800
2 Dr Z28 Cpe	6383	7272	8500
2 Dr Z28 SS Conv	9687	11036	12900
2 Dr Z28 SS Cpe	7359	8384	9800

OPTIONS FOR CAMARO
AM/FM Compact Disc Player +134
Air Conditioning[Opt on STD,Cpe] +378
Aluminum/Alloy Wheels[Opt on STD] +116
Automatic 4-Speed Transmission +334
Chrome Wheels +212
Compact Disc Changer +252
Delco/Bose Stereo System +256
Glass Panel T-tops +410
Leather Seats +190
Limited Slip Differential[Opt on RS,STD] +190
Performance Package +497
Power Drivers Seat +114
Power Windows +108
R1 Wheels/Tires Package +212
Suspension Package +497
Torque Sensing Axle +106

CAPRICE   1996

Zero changes as Caprice enters final year of production.

Category G

Model Description	Trade-in TMV	Private TMV	Dealer TMV
4 Dr STD Sdn	6075	7009	8300
4 Dr STD Wgn	7100	8192	9700

OPTIONS FOR CAPRICE
8 cyl 5.7 L Engine[Opt on Sdn] +232
AM/FM Compact Disc Player +167
AM/FM Stereo/CD/Tape +116
Dual Power Seats +245
Leather Seats +327
Power Windows[Opt on Wgn] +108
Sport Suspension +215

CAVALIER   1996

The 2.3-liter Quad 4 is replaced after just one year by a 2.4-liter twin-cam engine. Four-speed automatic transmission includes traction control. Daytime running lights debut, remote keyless entry is optional on LS and Z24, and base models get new interior fabrics and an Appearance Package.

Category B

Model Description	Trade-in TMV	Private TMV	Dealer TMV
2 Dr STD Cpe	2291	2799	3500
4 Dr STD Sdn	2422	2959	3700
2 Dr LS Conv	4189	5117	6400
4 Dr LS Sdn	3011	3678	4600
2 Dr Z24 Cpe	3403	4158	5200

OPTIONS FOR CAVALIER
4 cyl 2.4 L Engine[Opt on LS] +167
AM/FM Compact Disc Player +135
Air Conditioning[Opt on STD] +336
Aluminum/Alloy Wheels +125
Automatic 3-Speed Transmission[Std on LS] +232

Automatic 4-Speed Transmission +336
Power Sunroof +284
Power Windows +112

CORSICA   1996

Chevy's fleet favorite rolls into the sunset with long-life coolant.

Category C

Model Description	Trade-in TMV	Private TMV	Dealer TMV
4 Dr STD Sdn	2693	3326	4200

OPTIONS FOR CORSICA
6 cyl 3.1 L Engine +304
AM/FM Compact Disc Player +167
Power Windows +144

CORVETTE   1996

New 330-horsepower LT4 engine debuts on all manually shifted Corvettes. Two special editions are available, the Collector Edition and the Grand Sport, to send the fourth-generation Vette off in style. Next year, an all-new Corvette debuts. Other additions for 1996 include a Selective Real Time Damping system for the shock absorbers, and a tooth-jarring Z51 suspension setup.

Category F

Model Description	Trade-in TMV	Private TMV	Dealer TMV
2 Dr STD Conv	17605	19577	22300
2 Dr STD Cpe	15473	17206	19600
2 Dr Grand Sport Conv	18710	20806	23700
2 Dr Grand Sport Cpe	16894	18787	21400

OPTIONS FOR CORVETTE
8 cyl 5.7 L Engine +613
Climate Control for AC +154
Delco/Bose Stereo System +167
Dual Power Seats +257
Electronic Suspension +148
Glass Targa Top +275
Hardtop Roof +843
Power Drivers Seat +128
Solid & Glass Targa Tops +275
Sport Seats[Opt on STD] +264
Sport Suspension +148

EXPRESS VAN   1996

Category Q

Model Description	Trade-in TMV	Private TMV	Dealer TMV
2 Dr G1500 Express Van	5915	6748	7900
2 Dr G2500 Express Van	6289	7176	8400
2 Dr G2500 Express Van Ext	6663	7603	8900
2 Dr G3500 Express Van	6364	7261	8500
2 Dr G3500 Express Van Ext	6813	7773	9100

OPTIONS FOR EXPRESS VAN

Don't forget to refer to the Mileage Adjustment Table at the back of this book!

Model Description	Trade-in TMV	Private TMV	Dealer TMV
15 Passenger Seating [Opt on 3500] +157			
8 cyl 5.0 L Engine [Opt on 1500] +209			
8 cyl 5.7 L Engine [Opt on 1500] +209			
8 cyl 6.5 L Turbodiesel Engine +1148			
8 cyl 7.4 L Engine +254			
AM/FM Compact Disc Player +229			
AM/FM Stereo/CD/Tape +272			
Camper/Towing Package +131			
Dual Air Conditioning +343			
Locking Differential +107			
Power Door Locks +100			
Power Drivers Seat +101			
Power Passenger Seat +101			
Power Windows +112			
Privacy Glass +161			

IMPALA 1996

Big surprise. The car is finally correct with the addition of a tachometer and floor shifter, and General Motors kills it. Take note collectors: the 1996 Impala SS should be on your list.

Category G

Model Description	Trade-in TMV	Private TMV	Dealer TMV
4 Dr SS Sdn	9515	10979	13000

OPTIONS FOR IMPALA
Power Passenger Seat +128

LUMINA 1996

The ultimate family sedan is now available with an integrated child safety seat. Driver and passenger get their own climate controls. LS models offer available leather, and four-wheel disc brakes when equipped with the 3.4-liter V6.

Category D

Model Description	Trade-in TMV	Private TMV	Dealer TMV
4 Dr STD Sdn	3833	4575	5600
4 Dr LS Sdn	4175	4983	6100

OPTIONS FOR LUMINA
6 cyl 3.4 L Engine +390
AM/FM Compact Disc Player +137
AM/FM Stereo Tape [Std on LS] +98
Aluminum/Alloy Wheels +126
Anti-Lock Brakes [Std on LS] +243
Leather Seats +273
Power Drivers Seat +126
Power Windows [Std on LS] +112

LUMINA MINIVAN 1996

Last year for sloped-nose, plastic-bodied van. A 3.4-liter V6 good for 180 horsepower replaces standard and optional V6 engines from last year. Air conditioning, seven-passenger seating, and an electronically controlled four-speed automatic transmission are standard.

Category P

Model Description	Trade-in TMV	Private TMV	Dealer TMV
2 Dr STD Cargo Van	4082	4719	5600
2 Dr STD Pass. Van	4227	4888	5800

OPTIONS FOR LUMINA MINIVAN
AM/FM Compact Disc Player +167
Aluminum/Alloy Wheels +116
Camper/Towing Package +135
Dual Air Bag Restraints +106
Dual Air Conditioning +190
Power Door Locks +126
Power Drivers Seat +114
Power Sliding Door +148
Power Windows +116

MONTE CARLO 1996

Dual-zone climate controls reduce marital spats. The 3.4-liter V6 makes more power this year, and four-wheel disc brakes, standard on the Z34, are optional on the LS.

Category D

Model Description	Trade-in TMV	Private TMV	Dealer TMV
2 Dr LS Cpe	3833	4575	5600
2 Dr Z34 Cpe	4517	5392	6600

OPTIONS FOR MONTE CARLO
Aluminum/Alloy Wheels +126
Leather Seats +273
Power Drivers Seat +126
Power Sunroof +296

S10 PICKUP 1996

Improved V6 engines make more power and torque this year. A new five-speed manual gives four-cylinder models better acceleration, and four-bangers also get four-wheel antilock brakes. Extended-cab models get third-door access panel on the driver's side to make loading cargo and passengers easier. A new sport suspension turns the S-10 into a competent sports truck, and the new Sportside cargo box allows the S-Series to go head-to-head with the Ford Ranger Splash.

Category J

Model Description	Trade-in TMV	Private TMV	Dealer TMV
2 Dr STD 4WD Std Cab LB	5381	6187	7300
2 Dr STD Std Cab LB	3538	4068	4800
2 Dr STD 4WD Std Cab SB	5308	6102	7200
2 Dr STD Std Cab SB	3465	3984	4700
2 Dr LS 4WD Std Cab LB	6045	6950	8200
2 Dr LS Std Cab LB	3907	4492	5300
2 Dr LS 4WD Ext Cab SB	6192	7119	8400
2 Dr LS 4WD Std Cab SB	5897	6780	8000
2 Dr LS Ext Cab SB	4423	5085	6000
2 Dr LS Std Cab SB	3833	4407	5200
2 Dr LS 4WD Ext Cab Stepside SB	6266	7204	8500
2 Dr LS 4WD Std Cab Stepside SB			

Model Description	Trade-in TMV	Private TMV	Dealer TMV
	5971	6865	8100
2 Dr LS Ext Cab Stepside SB			
	4865	5594	6600
2 Dr LS Std Cab Stepside SB			
	4054	4662	5500

OPTIONS FOR S10 PICKUP

6 cyl 4.3 L Engine[Opt on 2WD] +418
6 cyl 4.3 L Vortec Engine +105
AM/FM Compact Disc Player +171
AM/FM Stereo Tape +147
Air Conditioning +340
Aluminum/Alloy Wheels +144
Anti-Lock Brakes[Opt on 2WD] +254
Automatic 4-Speed Transmission +452
Hinged Third Door +146
Limited Slip Differential +107
Locking Differential +107
Wide Stance Suspension +728

SPORTVAN   1996

Category Q

Model Description	Trade-in TMV	Private TMV	Dealer TMV
2 Dr G30 Sportvan	6663	7603	8900
2 Dr G30 Sportvan Ext	7038	8030	9400
2 Dr G30 Beauville Sportvan			
	7187	8201	9600
2 Dr G30 Beauville Sportvan Ext			
	7337	8371	9800

OPTIONS FOR SPORTVAN

15 Passenger Seating +157
8 cyl 6.5 L Diesel Engine +700
8 cyl 7.4 L Engine +256
AM/FM Compact Disc Player +116
Air Conditioning[Std on Beauville] +413
Bucket Seats +170
Camper/Towing Package +131
Dual Air Conditioning +666
Locking Differential +107
Privacy Glass +161

SUBURBAN   1996

Improved engines generate lots of horsepower and torque. Four-wheel-drive models get an optional electronic shift transfer case. Daytime running lights, rear seat heating ducts, and two new paint colors summarize the changes to Chevy's Texas Cadillac.

Category N

Model Description	Trade-in TMV	Private TMV	Dealer TMV
4 Dr C1500 Wgn	9302	10435	12000
4 Dr C2500 Wgn	9922	11131	12800
4 Dr K1500 4WD Wgn	10542	11827	13600
4 Dr K2500 4WD Wgn	10775	12088	13900

OPTIONS FOR SUBURBAN

8 cyl 6.5 L Turbodiesel Engine +665
8 cyl 7.4 L Engine +243
AM/FM Compact Disc Player +121
AM/FM Stereo/CD/Tape +161

Air Conditioning +339
Aluminum/Alloy Wheels +124
Bucket Seats +104
Camper/Towing Package +120
Captain Chairs (2) +100
Center Bench Seat +254
Dual Air Conditioning +520
LS Package +1539
LS Preferred Equipment Package +1539
LS Preferred Package +1425
LT Package +1864
LT Preferred Equipment Package +1864
LT Preferred Package +1750
Leather Seats +401
Locking Differential +101
Power Drivers Seat +96
Power Windows +107
Privacy Glass +122
Running Boards +130

TAHOE   1996

For 1996, Tahoe gets 50 additional horsepower and more torque out of a new 5700 V8. Other improvements include rear seat heating ducts, quieter-riding P-metric tires, improved automatic transmissions, and extended interval service schedules. Daytime running lights are new for 1996.

Category N

Model Description	Trade-in TMV	Private TMV	Dealer TMV
2 Dr STD 4WD Utility	8139	9131	10500
2 Dr STD Utility	6279	7044	8100
2 Dr LS 4WD Utility	10000	11218	12900
2 Dr LS Utility	8294	9305	10700
4 Dr LS 4WD Wgn	10310	11566	13300
4 Dr LS Wgn	9380	10522	12100
2 Dr LT 4WD Utility	10077	11305	13000
2 Dr LT Utility	9070	10174	11700
4 Dr LT 4WD Wgn	10542	11827	13600
4 Dr LT Wgn	9922	11131	12800

OPTIONS FOR TAHOE

8 cyl 6.5 L Turbodiesel Engine +1148
AM/FM Compact Disc Player +121
AM/FM Stereo/CD/Tape +161
Air Conditioning[Opt on STD] +339
Aluminum/Alloy Wheels[Opt on STD] +124
Bucket Seats +153
Camper/Towing Package +120
Locking Differential +101
Power Drivers Seat[Std on LT] +96
Running Boards +111

1995 CHEVROLET

ASTRO   1995

Front sheetmetal is restyled. Regular-length versions are dropped from the lineup, leaving only the extended-length model. Multi-leaf steel springs replace single-

---

Don't forget to refer to the Mileage Adjustment Table at the back of this book!

Model Description	Trade-in TMV	Private TMV	Dealer TMV

leaf plastic springs. One engine is available, the 190-horsepower, 4.3-liter V6. Air conditioning is newly standard, and remote keyless entry is a new option.

Category P

Model	Trade-in	Private	Dealer
2 Dr STD AWD Cargo Van			
	4578	5322	6561
2 Dr STD AWD Pass. Van Ext			
	4633	5385	6639
2 Dr STD Cargo Van	3945	4586	5654
2 Dr STD Pass. Van Ext			
	4009	4661	5746
2 Dr CL AWD Pass. Van Ext			
	5164	6002	7400
2 Dr CL Pass. Van Ext	4466	5191	6400
2 Dr CS AWD Pass. Van Ext			
	4675	5434	6700
2 Dr CS Pass. Van Ext	4047	4704	5800
2 Dr LT AWD Pass. Van Ext			
	5303	6164	7600
2 Dr LT Pass. Van Ext	5233	6083	7500

OPTIONS FOR ASTRO

7 Passenger Seating +200
8 Passenger Seating[Std on CL,LT] +132
AM/FM Compact Disc Player +151
AM/FM Stereo Tape +105
Aluminum/Alloy Wheels[Std on LT] +94
Camper/Towing Package +118
Dual Air Conditioning +199
Locking Differential +96
Power Door Locks[Opt on CS,STD] +85
Power Drivers Seat +92
Power Windows[Std on LT] +100
Privacy Glass[Std on LT] +111
Rear Heater +78

BERETTA   1995

Daytime running lights are newly standard. 170-horse Quad 4 engine is dropped, and 3.1-liter V6 loses five horsepower. Platinum-tipped spark plugs are standard on both engines.

Category C

2 Dr STD Cpe	2258	2799	3700
2 Dr Z26 Cpe	2868	3555	4700

OPTIONS FOR BERETTA

6 cyl 3.1 L Engine[Opt on STD] +486
AM/FM Compact Disc Player +105
AM/FM Stereo Tape[Opt on STD] +76
Automatic 3-Speed Transmission +212
Automatic 4-Speed Transmission[Opt on STD] +326
Cruise Control +86
Power Windows +105
Sunroof +191

BLAZER   1995

All-new SUV appears based on revamped S10. S10 nomenclature is dropped, and full-size Blazer becomes Tahoe. Four-wheel-drive models have electronic transfer case as standard equipment. Spare tire on four-door model is mounted beneath cargo bay instead of in it. Five different suspension packages are available. One engine, a 195-horsepower 4.3-liter V6, is available. All-wheel drive is optional. Driver airbag and air conditioning are standard equipment.

Category M

2 Dr STD 4WD Utility	4712	5420	6600
2 Dr STD Utility	4498	5174	6300
4 Dr STD 4WD Wgn	5282	6076	7399
4 Dr STD Wgn	4783	5502	6700
2 Dr LS 4WD Utility	5354	6159	7500
2 Dr LS Utility	4997	5748	7000
4 Dr LS 4WD Wgn	5711	6570	8000
4 Dr LS Wgn	5284	6078	7401
4 Dr LT 4WD Wgn	6354	7309	8900
4 Dr LT Wgn	5854	6734	8200

OPTIONS FOR BLAZER

AM/FM Compact Disc Player +125
AM/FM Stereo Tape[Opt on STD] +95
Aluminum/Alloy Wheels[Opt on STD] +94
Camper/Towing Package +81
Cruise Control[Opt on STD] +75
Locking Differential +93
Power Drivers Seat[Std on LT] +92
Power Windows[Opt on STD] +100

C/K 1500 SERIES   1995

Category K

2 Dr C1500 Cheyenne Ext Cab LB			
	5619	6404	7713
2 Dr C1500 Cheyenne Std Cab LB			
	4735	5397	6500
2 Dr K1500 Cheyenne 4WD Ext Cab LB			
	6192	7058	8500
2 Dr K1500 Cheyenne 4WD Std Cab LB			
	5602	6385	7690
2 Dr C1500 Cheyenne Ext Cab SB			
	5320	6064	7303
2 Dr C1500 Cheyenne Std Cab SB			
	4517	5148	6200
2 Dr K1500 Cheyenne 4WD Ext Cab SB			
	5974	6808	8200
2 Dr K1500 Cheyenne 4WD Std Cab SB			
	5534	6308	7597
2 Dr C1500 Cheyenne Ext Cab Stepside SB			
	5539	6313	7603
2 Dr C1500 Cheyenne Std Cab Stepside SB			
	4954	5646	6800
2 Dr K1500 Cheyenne 4WD Ext Cab Stepside SB			

Don't forget to refer to the Mileage Adjustment Table at the back of this book!

Model Description	Trade-in TMV	Private TMV	Dealer TMV
	6112	6966	8390
2 Dr K1500 Cheyenne 4WD Std Cab Stepside SB			
	5682	6476	7800
2 Dr C1500 Silverado Ext Cab LB			
	6123	6979	8405
2 Dr C1500 Silverado Std Cab LB			
	5464	6227	7500
2 Dr K1500 Silverado 4WD Ext Cab LB			
	7431	8469	10200
2 Dr K1500 Silverado 4WD Std Cab LB			
	6059	6906	8317
2 Dr C1500 Silverado Ext Cab SB			
	5755	6559	7900
2 Dr C1500 Silverado Std Cab SB			
	5391	6144	7400
2 Dr K1500 Silverado 4WD Ext Cab SB			
	7066	8054	9700
2 Dr K1500 Silverado 4WD Std Cab SB			
	5828	6642	8000
2 Dr C1500 Silverado Ext Cab Stepside SB			
	6034	6877	8283
2 Dr C1500 Silverado Std Cab Stepside SB			
	5607	6391	7697
2 Dr K1500 Silverado 4WD Ext Cab Stepside SB			
	7285	8303	10000
2 Dr K1500 Silverado 4WD Std Cab Stepside SB			
	6123	6979	8405
2 Dr C1500 WT Std Cab LB			
	4371	4982	6000
2 Dr K1500 WT 4WD Std Cab LB			
	5316	6059	7297
2 Dr C1500 WT Std Cab SB			
	4298	4899	5900
2 Dr K1500 WT 4WD Std Cab SB			
	5245	5978	7200

OPTIONS FOR C/K 1500 SERIES
8 cyl 5.0 L Engine +189
8 cyl 5.7 L Engine +267
8 cyl 6.5 L Diesel Engine +1041
8 cyl 6.5 L Turbodiesel Engine +1291
8 cyl 7.4 L Engine +322
AM/FM Compact Disc Player +95
AM/FM Stereo/CD/Tape +111
Air Conditioning[Std on Silverado] +307
Aluminum/Alloy Wheels +76
Automatic 4-Speed Transmission +370
Bed Liner +86
Captain Chairs (2) +103
Chrome Wheels +95
Cruise Control[Std on Silverado] +73
Leather Seats +381
Locking Differential +96
Power Drivers Seat +92

C/K 2500 SERIES   1995
Category K

Model Description	Trade-in TMV	Private TMV	Dealer TMV
2 Dr C2500 Cheyenne Ext Cab LB			
	6046	6892	8300
2 Dr C2500 Cheyenne Std Cab LB			
	5099	5812	7000
2 Dr K2500 Cheyenne 4WD Ext Cab LB			
	7285	8303	10000
2 Dr K2500 Cheyenne 4WD Std Cab LB			
	5901	6725	8100
2 Dr C2500 Cheyenne Ext Cab SB			
	5974	6808	8200
2 Dr K2500 Cheyenne 4WD Ext Cab SB			
	6556	7473	9000
2 Dr C2500 Silverado Ext Cab LB			
	6775	7722	9300
2 Dr C2500 Silverado Std Cab LB			
	5755	6559	7900
2 Dr K2500 Silverado 4WD Ext Cab LB			
	8013	9133	11000
2 Dr K2500 Silverado 4WD Std Cab LB			
	6484	7390	8900
2 Dr C2500 Silverado Ext Cab SB			
	6702	7639	9200
2 Dr K2500 Silverado 4WD Ext Cab SB			
	7795	8884	10700

OPTIONS FOR C/K 2500 SERIES
8 cyl 5.0 L Engine +267
8 cyl 5.7 L Engine +267
8 cyl 6.5 L Diesel Engine +1041
8 cyl 6.5 L Turbodiesel Engine +1037
8 cyl 7.4 L Engine +228
AM/FM Stereo/CD/Tape +111
Air Bag Restraint[Opt on Std Cab] +134
Air Conditioning[Std on Silverado] +307
Aluminum/Alloy Wheels[Opt on Std Cab] +95
Automatic 4-Speed Transmission +370
Bed Liner +86
Chrome Step Bumper[Std on Silverado] +88
Leather Seats +381
Locking Differential +96
Power Drivers Seat +92

C/K 3500 SERIES   1995
Category K

Model Description	Trade-in TMV	Private TMV	Dealer TMV
2 Dr C3500 Cheyenne Ext Cab LB			
	6775	7722	9300
2 Dr C3500 Cheyenne Std Cab LB			
	5974	6808	8200
2 Dr K3500 Cheyenne 4WD Ext Cab LB			
	7649	8718	10500
2 Dr K3500 Cheyenne 4WD Std Cab LB			
	6688	7623	9181
4 Dr C3500 Cheyenne Crew Cab LB			

Don't forget to refer to the Mileage Adjustment Table at the back of this book!

Model Description	Trade-in TMV	Private TMV	Dealer TMV
	6716	7655	9219
4 Dr K3500 Cheyenne 4WD Crew Cab LB			
	7868	8967	10800
2 Dr C3500 Silverado Ext Cab LB			
	7795	8884	10700
2 Dr C3500 Silverado Std Cab LB			
	6629	7556	9100
2 Dr K3500 Silverado 4WD Ext Cab LB			
	8815	10047	12100
2 Dr K3500 Silverado 4WD Std Cab LB			
	7503	8552	10300
4 Dr C3500 Silverado Crew Cab LB			
	8232	9382	11300
4 Dr K3500 Silverado 4WD Crew Cab LB			
	9543	10877	13100

OPTIONS FOR C/K 3500 SERIES
8 cyl 6.5 L Turbodiesel Engine +1037
8 cyl 7.4 L Engine +228
AM/FM Compact Disc Player +92
AM/FM Stereo/CD/Tape +111
Air Conditioning[Std on Silverado] +307
Automatic 4-Speed Transmission +370
Bed Liner +86
Bucket Seats +103
Chrome Step Bumper +88
Dual Rear Wheels +305
Leather Seats +381
Locking Differential +96
Power Drivers Seat +92

CAMARO 1995

Z28 gets optional traction control. Z28 can now be ordered with body-color roof and side mirrors (standard color is gloss black). Chrome-plated alloys are newly optional.

Category E

Model Description	Trade-in TMV	Private TMV	Dealer TMV
2 Dr STD Conv	5599	6500	8000
2 Dr STD Cpe	4269	4956	6100
2 Dr Z28 Conv	6789	7881	9700
2 Dr Z28 Cpe	5249	6093	7500

OPTIONS FOR CAMARO
8 cyl 5.7 L Engine +307
AM/FM Compact Disc Player +121
Air Conditioning +342
Aluminum/Alloy Wheels[Opt on STD] +105
Automatic 4-Speed Transmission +267
Delco/Bose Stereo System +231
Glass Panel T-tops +370
Leather Seats +172
Power Door Locks +84
Power Drivers Seat +103
Power Windows +98

CAPRICE 1995

Impala SS styling treatment for C-pillar is carried over to more mainstream sedan. New seats and radios debut. Outside mirrors can be folded in, and a new option is a radio with speed-compensated volume control.

Category G

Model Description	Trade-in TMV	Private TMV	Dealer TMV
4 Dr STD Sdn	4617	5360	6600
4 Dr STD Wgn	4896	5685	7000

OPTIONS FOR CAPRICE
8 cyl 5.7 L Engine[Std on Wgn] +210
AM/FM Compact Disc Player +151
AM/FM Stereo Tape[Opt on Sdn] +100
Automatic Load Leveling[Opt on Wgn] +76
Dual Power Seats[Opt on Sdn] +221
Leather Seats +296
Limited Slip Differential +82
Power Drivers Seat +103
Power Passenger Seat +103
Power Windows +98
Preferred Equipment Group 2 +275
Sport Suspension +194

CAVALIER 1995

First redesign since 1982 debut. Sedan, coupe and convertible are available. Wagon is dropped. Sedan comes in base and LS trim. Coupe comes in base and Z24 trim. Convertible is available as LS only. Dual airbags and ABS are standard. Base engine is a 2.2-liter, 120-horsepower four-cylinder engine. Optional on LS sedan and convertible is the Z24's standard powerplant; a 2.3-liter, DOHC four-cylinder making 150 horsepower.

Category B

Model Description	Trade-in TMV	Private TMV	Dealer TMV
2 Dr STD Cpe	1814	2254	2986
4 Dr STD Sdn	1831	2275	3014
2 Dr LS Conv	3159	3924	5200
4 Dr LS Sdn	2187	2717	3600
2 Dr Z24 Cpe	2552	3170	4200

OPTIONS FOR CAVALIER
4 cyl 2.3 L Engine[Opt on STD] +105
4 cyl 2.3 L Quad 4 Engine[Opt on LS] +151
AM/FM Compact Disc Player +151
AM/FM Stereo Tape +84
Air Conditioning[Opt on STD] +304
Aluminum/Alloy Wheels +112
Automatic 3-Speed Transmission[Std on LS] +210
Automatic 4-Speed Transmission +298
Power Door Locks +81
Power Sunroof +228
Power Windows +100

CORSICA 1995

Daytime running lights debut. Rear suspension is revised, and larger tires are standard.

Category C

Model Description	Trade-in TMV	Private TMV	Dealer TMV
4 Dr STD Sdn	2563	3177	4200

OPTIONS FOR CORSICA
6 cyl 3.1 L Engine +274

Model Description	Trade-in TMV	Private TMV	Dealer TMV

AM/FM Compact Disc Player +151
Automatic 4-Speed Transmission +267
Cruise Control +86
Power Windows +130

CORVETTE 1995

ZR-1's brakes trickle down to base models. Front fenders get revised gills. Only 448 ZR-1s were produced in 1995.

Category F

	Trade-in	Private	Dealer
2 Dr STD Conv	15208	16817	19500
2 Dr STD Cpe	13726	15179	17600
2 Dr ZR1 Cpe	25424	28115	32600

OPTIONS FOR CORVETTE

AM/FM Stereo/CD/Tape[Opt on STD] +228
Automatic 4-Speed Transmission +305
Climate Control for AC[Opt on STD] +139
Delco/Bose Stereo System[Opt on STD] +151
Glass Targa Top +248
Handling Package +648
Hardtop Roof +761
Metallic Paint[Opt on STD] +76
Power Drivers Seat[Opt on STD] +116
Power Passenger Seat[Opt on STD] +103
Ride/Handling Suspension[Opt on Conv] +667
Selective Ride Suspension[Opt on STD] +630
Solid & Glass Targa Tops +248
Sport Seats +239

IMPALA 1995

Dark Cherry and Green Gray paint colors join basic black. New seats and radios debut. Outside mirrors can be folded in, and a new option is a radio with speed-compensated volume control.

Category G

	Trade-in	Private	Dealer
4 Dr SS Sdn	7275	8447	10400

OPTIONS FOR IMPALA

Power Passenger Seat +116
Premium Sound System +191

LUMINA 1995

Midsize sedan is redesigned; features dual airbags. Base and LS trim levels are available. ABS is optional on base model; standard on LS. Standard powerplant is a 160-horsepower, 3.1-liter V6. Optional on LS is a 210-horsepower, 3.4-liter V6. Air conditioning is standard.

Category D

	Trade-in	Private	Dealer
4 Dr STD Sdn	2871	3444	4400
4 Dr LS Sdn	3262	3914	5000

OPTIONS FOR LUMINA

6 cyl 3.4 L Engine +353
AM/FM Compact Disc Player +123
AM/FM Stereo/CD/Tape +193
Aluminum/Alloy Wheels +114

Anti-Lock Brakes[Std on LS] +220
Cruise Control +82
Keyless Entry System +84
Power Drivers Seat +114
Power Windows[Std on LS] +100

LUMINA MINIVAN 1995

Transmission gets brake/shift interlock.

Category P

	Trade-in	Private	Dealer
2 Dr STD Cargo Van	2791	3244	4000
2 Dr STD Pass. Van	3140	3650	4500

OPTIONS FOR LUMINA MINIVAN

6 cyl 3.8 L Engine +235
7 Passenger Seating +210
AM/FM Compact Disc Player +151
Air Conditioning +305
Aluminum/Alloy Wheels +105
Automatic 4-Speed Transmission +305
Automatic Load Leveling +78
Camper/Towing Package +123
Child Seats (2) +86
Cruise Control +86
Dual Air Conditioning +172
Power Door Locks +114
Power Drivers Seat +103
Power Mirrors +75
Power Sliding Door +134
Power Windows +105
Sunroof +191
Traction Control System +95

MONTE CARLO 1995

Chevy slaps revered moniker on coupe version of Lumina. Available in LS or Z34 trim levels. Dual airbags and ABS are standard. LS comes with 160-horsepower, 3.1-liter V6, while Z34 is powered by 3.4-liter, twin-cam V6 good for 210 horsepower. All Monte Carlos have automatic transmissions. Air conditioning is standard.

Category D

	Trade-in	Private	Dealer
2 Dr LS Cpe	3001	3601	4600
2 Dr Z34 Cpe	3458	4149	5300

OPTIONS FOR MONTE CARLO

AM/FM Stereo/CD/Tape +95
Aluminum/Alloy Wheels +114
Cruise Control[Opt on LS] +82
Keyless Entry System[Opt on LS] +84
Leather Seats +246
Power Drivers Seat +114

S10 PICKUP 1995

Driver airbag is added, and daytime running lights are standard. ZR2 off-road package can be ordered on the extended-cab. Power window and lock buttons are illuminated at night. Remote keyless entry is a new option. A single key operates both the door locks and the ignition. A manual transmission can now be

Model Description	Trade-in TMV	Private TMV	Dealer TMV

ordered with the 191-horsepower, 4.3-liter V6.

Category J

Model Description	Trade-in TMV	Private TMV	Dealer TMV
2 Dr STD 4WD Std Cab LB			
	4440	5138	6300
2 Dr STD Std Cab LB	2960	3425	4200
2 Dr STD 4WD Std Cab SB			
	3806	4404	5400
2 Dr STD Std Cab SB	2890	3343	4100
2 Dr LS 4WD Std Cab LB			
	4933	5708	7000
2 Dr LS Std Cab LB	3453	3996	4900
2 Dr LS 4WD Ext Cab SB			
	5145	5953	7300
2 Dr LS 4WD Std Cab SB			
	4652	5382	6600
2 Dr LS Ext Cab SB	3594	4159	5100
2 Dr LS Std Cab SB	3383	3914	4800

OPTIONS FOR S10 PICKUP

6 cyl 4.3 L CPI Engine +213
6 cyl 4.3 L Engine[Opt on 2WD] +378
AM/FM Compact Disc Player +154
AM/FM Stereo Tape +133
Air Conditioning +307
Aluminum/Alloy Wheels +130
Anti-Lock Brakes[Opt on 2WD] +228
Automatic 4-Speed Transmission +409
Bucket Seats +73
Cruise Control +75
Limited Slip Differential +96
Power Door Locks +81
Power Mirrors +75
Power Windows +86
Tilt Steering Wheel +75
Wide Stance Suspension +658

SPORTVAN   1995

Category Q

Model Description	Trade-in TMV	Private TMV	Dealer TMV
2 Dr G20 Sportvan	4877	5598	6800
2 Dr G30 Sportvan	5092	5845	7100
2 Dr G30 Sportvan Ext	5308	6092	7400
2 Dr G20 Beauville Sportvan			
	5236	6010	7300
2 Dr G30 Beauville Sportvan			
	5451	6257	7600
2 Dr G30 Beauville Sportvan Ext			
	5523	6339	7700

OPTIONS FOR SPORTVAN

16 Passenger Seating +153
8 cyl 5.0 L Engine[Opt on G20] +220
8 cyl 5.7 L Engine[Opt on G20] +322
8 cyl 6.5 L Diesel Engine +632
8 cyl 7.4 L Engine +230
AM/FM Compact Disc Player[Opt on Beauville] +105
AM/FM Stereo Tape[Std on Beauville] +81

Air Conditioning[Std on Beauville] +372
Aluminum/Alloy Wheels[Opt on G20] +95
Bucket Seats +153
Camper/Towing Package +118
Cruise Control[Std on Beauville] +73
Dual Air Conditioning +601
Locking Differential +96
Power Door Locks[Std on Beauville] +85
Privacy Glass +145
Rear Heater +78

SUBURBAN   1995

New interior with driver airbag debuts. New dashboard features modular design with controls that are much easier to read and use. 1500 models can now be ordered with turbodiesel engine. Brake/transmission shift interlock is added to automatic transmission. Seats and door panels are revised. New console on models with bucket seats features pivoting writing surface, along with rear cupholders and storage drawer. Uplevel radios come with automatic volume controls that raise or lower the volume depending on vehicle speed.

Category N

Model Description	Trade-in TMV	Private TMV	Dealer TMV
4 Dr C1500 Wgn	6920	7887	9500
4 Dr C2500 Wgn	7648	8718	10500
4 Dr K1500 4WD Wgn	8013	9133	11000
4 Dr K2500 4WD Wgn	8304	9465	11400

OPTIONS FOR SUBURBAN

8 cyl 6.5 L Turbodiesel Engine +600
8 cyl 7.4 L Engine +217
AM/FM Compact Disc Player +109
Air Conditioning +306
Aluminum/Alloy Wheels +112
Bucket Seats +95
Camper/Towing Package +77
Captain Chairs (2) +90
Center Bench Seat +229
Dual Air Conditioning +470
LS Package +1390
LS Preferred Equipment Package +1390
LS Preferred Package +1287
LT Package +1683
LT Preferred Equipment Package +1683
LT Preferred Package +1580
Leather Seats +362
Locking Differential +91
Power Door Locks +82
Power Drivers Seat +87
Power Windows +95
Privacy Glass +110
Rear Heater +74
Skid Plates +82

TAHOE   1995

Full-size SUV gets a new name as S10-based model takes Blazer moniker. New interior with driver airbag debuts. New dashboard features modular design with

Model Description	Trade-in TMV	Private TMV	Dealer TMV

controls that are much easier to read and use. New five-door model is added midyear, nicely sized between Blazer and Suburban. New model is offered only in LS or LT trim with a 5.7-liter V8 and an automatic transmission in either 2WD or 4WD. Brake/transmission shift interlock is added to automatic transmission. New console on models with bucket seats features pivoting writing surface, along with rear cupholders and storage drawer.

Category N

Model Description	Trade-in TMV	Private TMV	Dealer TMV
2 Dr STD 4WD Utility	6483	7389	8900
2 Dr LS 4WD Utility	8158	9299	11200
4 Dr LS 4WD Wgn	9178	10461	12600
4 Dr LS Wgn	8304	9465	11400
2 Dr LT 4WD Utility	9032	10295	12400
4 Dr LT 4WD Wgn	9251	10544	12700
4 Dr LT Wgn	9105	10378	12500

OPTIONS FOR TAHOE

8 cyl 6.5 L Turbodiesel Engine +1037
Air Conditioning[Opt on STD] +306
Aluminum/Alloy Wheels +112
Automatic 4-Speed Transmission[Std on 4 Dr] +290
Bucket Seats[Opt on LS] +83
Locking Differential +91
Power Door Locks[Opt on STD] +78
Power Drivers Seat[Opt on LS] +87
Privacy Glass[Opt on STD] +78
Running Boards +100

1994 CHEVROLET

ASTRO   1994

Driver airbag is made standard. Side-door guard beams are stronger, and air conditioners use CFC-free refrigerant. A high-mount center brake light is added. Analog gauges get new graphics, and carpet is treated with Scotchgard.

Category P

Model Description	Trade-in TMV	Private TMV	Dealer TMV
2 Dr STD AWD Cargo Van			
	3237	3860	4900
2 Dr STD AWD Cargo Van Ext			
	3369	4018	5100
2 Dr STD AWD Pass. Van			
	3475	4145	5261
2 Dr STD AWD Pass. Van Ext			
	3502	4177	5302
2 Dr STD Cargo Van	2114	2521	3200
2 Dr STD Cargo Van Ext			
	2642	3151	4000
2 Dr STD Pass. Van	2906	3466	4400
2 Dr STD Pass. Van Ext			
	2972	3545	4500
2 Dr CL AWD Pass. Van	3699	4412	5600
2 Dr CL AWD Pass. Van Ext			
	3831	4569	5800
2 Dr CL Pass. Van	3104	3703	4700
2 Dr CL Pass. Van Ext	3170	3782	4800
2 Dr LT AWD Pass. Van	4095	4884	6200
2 Dr LT AWD Pass. Van Ext			
	4161	4963	6300
2 Dr LT Pass. Van	3526	4205	5338
2 Dr LT Pass. Van Ext	3567	4254	5400

OPTIONS FOR ASTRO

6 cyl 4.3 L CPI Engine[Opt on 2WD] +170
7 Passenger Seating +160
8 Passenger Seating +117
AM/FM Compact Disc Player +134
AM/FM Stereo Tape +94
Air Conditioning +272
Aluminum/Alloy Wheels +84
Camper/Towing Package +104
Captain Chairs (2) +102
Chrome Bumpers +80
Dual Air Conditioning +178
Limited Slip Differential +84
Power Door Locks +76
Power Drivers Seat +82
Power Windows +88
Privacy Glass[Std on LT] +98

BERETTA   1994

GT and GTZ are dropped in favor of Z26 model, which offers a standard 170-horsepower Quad 4 engine. Base models get 10 more horsepower, and the 3.1-liter V6 makes an additional 20 horsepower, up to 160. Automatic transmission is unavailable with Quad 4; manual transmission is unavailable with V6. Door-mounted seat belts are added. Automatic door locks lock doors once Beretta is underway, and unlock car is stopped. Disable this feature by yanking a fuse. Interior lights shut off after 10 minutes to save battery. Warning chime reminds driver that turn signal has been left on.

Category C

Model Description	Trade-in TMV	Private TMV	Dealer TMV
2 Dr STD Cpe	1881	2413	3300
2 Dr Z26 Cpe	2109	2706	3700

OPTIONS FOR BERETTA

6 cyl 3.1 L Engine +433
AM/FM Compact Disc Player +94
Automatic 3-Speed Transmission +189
Automatic 4-Speed Transmission +290
Cruise Control +76
Power Windows +94
Sunroof +170

BLAZER   1994

Air conditioning receives CFC-free coolant. Side-door guard beams are added. A new grille appears, and models equipped with a decor package get composite

Model Description	Trade-in TMV	Private TMV	Dealer TMV

headlamps. A turbocharged diesel is newly optional. Third brake light is added.

Category N

Model Description	Trade-in TMV	Private TMV	Dealer TMV
2 Dr STD 4WD Utility	4672	5432	6700
2 Dr Silverado 4WD Utility			
	6834	7946	9800
2 Dr Sport 4WD Utility			
	7322	8514	10500

OPTIONS FOR BLAZER
8 cyl 6.5 L Turbodiesel Engine +963
AM/FM Stereo Tape +84
Air Conditioning[Opt on STD] +272
Aluminum/Alloy Wheels +84
Automatic 4-Speed Transmission +238
Limited Slip Differential +84
Power Drivers Seat[Std on Sport] +82
Power Windows[Std on Sport] +88

C/K 1500 SERIES   1994

Category K

Model Description	Trade-in TMV	Private TMV	Dealer TMV
2 Dr C1500 Cheyenne Ext Cab LB			
	4665	5426	6693
2 Dr C1500 Cheyenne Std Cab LB			
	3973	4621	5700
2 Dr K1500 Cheyenne 4WD Ext Cab LB			
	5507	6404	7900
2 Dr K1500 Cheyenne 4WD Std Cab LB			
	4675	5437	6707
2 Dr C1500 Cheyenne Ext Cab SB			
	4461	5188	6400
2 Dr C1500 Cheyenne Std Cab SB			
	3834	4459	5500
2 Dr K1500 Cheyenne 4WD Ext Cab SB			
	5360	6233	7689
2 Dr K1500 Cheyenne 4WD Std Cab SB			
	4322	5026	6200
2 Dr C1500 Cheyenne Ext Cab Stepside SB			
	4601	5350	6600
2 Dr C1500 Cheyenne Std Cab Stepside SB			
	4043	4702	5800
2 Dr K1500 Cheyenne 4WD Ext Cab Stepside SB			
	5437	6323	7800
2 Dr K1500 Cheyenne 4WD Std Cab Stepside SB			
	4740	5513	6800
2 Dr C1500 Silverado Ext Cab LB			
	5293	6155	7593
2 Dr C1500 Silverado Std Cab LB			
	4178	4858	5993
2 Dr K1500 Silverado 4WD Ext Cab LB			
	5786	6729	8300
2 Dr K1500 Silverado 4WD Std Cab LB			
	5303	6167	7607
2 Dr C1500 Silverado Ext Cab SB			
	4991	5804	7160
2 Dr C1500 Silverado Std Cab SB			
	4103	4772	5886
2 Dr K1500 Silverado 4WD Ext Cab SB			
	5646	6566	8100
2 Dr K1500 Silverado 4WD Std Cab SB			
	5089	5918	7300
2 Dr C1500 Silverado Ext Cab Stepside SB			
	5047	5869	7240
2 Dr C1500 Silverado Std Cab Stepside SB			
	4531	5269	6500
2 Dr K1500 Silverado 4WD Ext Cab Stepside SB			
	5731	6664	8221
2 Dr K1500 Silverado 4WD Std Cab Stepside SB			
	5375	6251	7711
2 Dr K1500 Sport 4WD Std Cab Stepside SB			
	5701	6630	8179
2 Dr C1500 Work Truck Std Cab LB			
	3067	3567	4400
2 Dr K1500 Work Truck 4WD Std Cab LB			
	4187	4870	6007
2 Dr C1500 Work Truck Std Cab SB			
	2997	3486	4300
2 Dr K1500 Work Truck 4WD Std Cab SB			
	4122	4794	5914

OPTIONS FOR C/K 1500 SERIES
8 cyl 5.0 L Engine +168
8 cyl 5.7 L Engine +238
8 cyl 6.5 L Diesel Engine +926
8 cyl 6.5 L Turbodiesel Engine +1148
Air Conditioning[Std on Silverado] +273
Automatic 4-Speed Transmission +329
Bed Liner +76
Captain Chairs (2) +92
Chrome Wheels +84
LT Package +575
Leather Seats +339
Limited Slip Differential +84
Power Drivers Seat +82
Power Windows +83

C/K 2500 SERIES   1994

Category K

Model Description	Trade-in TMV	Private TMV	Dealer TMV
2 Dr C2500 Cheyenne Ext Cab LB			
	5367	6242	7700
2 Dr C2500 Cheyenne Std Cab LB			
	4182	4864	6000
2 Dr K2500 Cheyenne 4WD Ext Cab LB			
	5925	6891	8500
2 Dr K2500 Cheyenne 4WD Std Cab LB			
	5089	5918	7300
2 Dr C2500 Cheyenne Ext Cab SB			
	5158	5999	7400

Model Description	Trade-in TMV	Private TMV	Dealer TMV
2 Dr K2500 Cheyenne 4WD Ext Cab SB	5507	6404	7900
2 Dr C2500 Silverado Ext Cab LB	5577	6485	8000
2 Dr C2500 Silverado Std Cab LB	4392	5107	6300
2 Dr K2500 Silverado 4WD Ext Cab LB	6413	7458	9200
2 Dr K2500 Silverado 4WD Std Cab LB	5396	6275	7741
2 Dr C2500 Silverado Ext Cab SB	5478	6371	7859
2 Dr K2500 Silverado 4WD Ext Cab SB	5855	6810	8400

OPTIONS FOR C/K 2500 SERIES
8 cyl 5.0 L Engine +238
8 cyl 5.7 L Engine +238
8 cyl 6.5 L Diesel Engine +926
8 cyl 6.5 L Turbodiesel Engine +922
8 cyl 7.4 L Engine +204
Air Conditioning[Std on Silverado] +273
Automatic 4-Speed Transmission +329
Bed Liner +76
Captain Chairs (2) +102
Chrome Step Bumper +78
Limited Slip Differential +84
Power Drivers Seat +82
Power Windows +83

C/K 3500 SERIES   1994

Category K

Model Description	Trade-in TMV	Private TMV	Dealer TMV
4 Dr K3500 4WD Crew Cab LB	6552	7620	9400
2 Dr C3500 Cheyenne Ext Cab LB	5786	6729	8300
2 Dr C3500 Cheyenne Std Cab LB	5089	5918	7300
2 Dr K3500 Cheyenne 4WD Ext Cab LB	6413	7458	9200
2 Dr K3500 Cheyenne 4WD Std Cab LB	5577	6485	8000
4 Dr C3500 Cheyenne Crew Cab LB	5716	6647	8200
2 Dr C3500 Silverado Ext Cab LB	6343	7377	9100
2 Dr C3500 Silverado Std Cab LB	5507	6404	7900
2 Dr K3500 Silverado 4WD Ext Cab LB	7110	8269	10200
2 Dr K3500 Silverado 4WD Std Cab LB	6204	7215	8900
4 Dr C3500 Silverado Crew Cab LB	6274	7296	9000
4 Dr K3500 Silverado 4WD Crew Cab LB	7459	8674	10700

OPTIONS FOR C/K 3500 SERIES
8 cyl 6.5 L Turbodiesel Engine +922
8 cyl 7.4 L Engine +204
Air Conditioning[Std on Silverado] +273
Automatic 4-Speed Transmission +329
Bed Liner +76
Bucket Seats +92
Captain Chairs (2) +102
Chrome Step Bumper +78
Dual Rear Wheels +272
Limited Slip Differential +84
Power Windows +83

CAMARO   1994

Convertible returns in base and Z28 trim. First-to-fourth shift pattern added to six-speed manual transmission to meet fuel economy regulations. Z28 with manual transmission gets revised gearing for better acceleration.

Category E

Model Description	Trade-in TMV	Private TMV	Dealer TMV
2 Dr STD Conv	4915	5884	7500
2 Dr STD Cpe	3080	3688	4700
2 Dr Z28 Conv	5439	6512	8300
2 Dr Z28 Cpe	3998	4786	6100

OPTIONS FOR CAMARO
AM/FM Compact Disc Player +107
AM/FM Stereo/CD/Tape +180
Air Conditioning +304
Aluminum/Alloy Wheels[Opt on STD Cpe] +94
Automatic 4-Speed Transmission +204
Bose Sound System +118
Glass Panel T-tops +329
Leather Seats +152
Power Door Locks +74
Power Drivers Seat +92
Power Windows +87

CAPRICE   1994

Passenger airbag added. New base engine for sedan is a 200-horsepower, 4.3-liter V8. Optional on sedan and standard on wagon is a more powerful 260-horsepower, 5.7-liter V8. Automatic transmissions get electronic controls. Pass-Key II is a standard theft-deterrent system, and CFC-free refrigerant is added to air conditioning systems.

Category G

Model Description	Trade-in TMV	Private TMV	Dealer TMV
4 Dr STD Sdn	3167	3779	4800
4 Dr STD Wgn	3628	4330	5500
4 Dr LS Sdn	3694	4409	5600

OPTIONS FOR CAPRICE
8 cyl 5.7 L Engine[Std on Wgn] +186
AM/FM Compact Disc Player +134
AM/FM Stereo Tape[Opt on STD Sdn] +90

Don't forget to refer to the Mileage Adjustment Table at the back of this book!

CHEVROLET 94

Model Description	Trade-in TMV	Private TMV	Dealer TMV	Model Description	Trade-in TMV	Private TMV	Dealer TMV

Bose Sound System +118
Leather Seats +263
Power Drivers Seat[Std on LS] +92
Power Passenger Seat +92
Power Windows[Std on LS] +87
Sport Suspension +172

CAVALIER   1994

Wagon is sold without trim designation. Base engine is up 10 horsepower to 120. Automatic door locks unlock when ignition is turned off. Feature is defeated by yanking a fuse.

Category B

4 Dr STD Wgn	1726	2237	3088
2 Dr RS Conv	2292	2970	4100
2 Dr RS Cpe	1686	2185	3016
4 Dr RS Sdn	1708	2213	3055
2 Dr VL Cpe	1565	2028	2800
4 Dr VL Sdn	1596	2068	2855
2 Dr Z24 Conv	2515	3260	4500
2 Dr Z24 Cpe	1733	2245	3100

OPTIONS FOR CAVALIER
6 cyl 3.1 L Engine[Std on Z24] +232
AM/FM Compact Disc Player +134
AM/FM Stereo Tape +74
Air Conditioning[Opt on VL] +270
Aluminum/Alloy Wheels[Opt on RS Cpe] +100
Automatic 3-Speed Transmission[Opt on VL,Z24,RS Cpe] +186
Power Windows +90
Sunroof +170

CORSICA   1994

Door mounted seatbelts are added. Engines gain power; the 2.2-liter unit is up to 120 horsepower, and the optional, 3.1-liter V6 now makes 160 horsepower. Sport Handling Package dropped from options list. Manual transmission dropped. Automatic door locks now unlock when car is shut off. This feature can be disabled by pulling a fuse. Interior lights will shut off automatically after 10 minutes to save the battery. Warning chime sounds if turn signal is left on.

Category C

4 Dr STD Sdn	1482	1901	2600

OPTIONS FOR CORSICA
6 cyl 3.1 L Engine +244
AM/FM Compact Disc Player +134
Automatic 4-Speed Transmission +238
Cruise Control +76
Power Windows +116

CORVETTE   1994

Passenger airbag is added. Traction control is standard. A new steering wheel and redesigned seats are added inside. Leather upholstery is standard.

Automatic transmission gets electronic shift controls and brake/transmission shift interlock. Convertible gets glass rear window with defogger. ZR-1 has new five-spoke alloys. Power windows gain express-down feature for driver's side. Selective Ride Control system has softer springs.

Category F

2 Dr STD Conv	12564	14002	16400
2 Dr STD Cpe	11031	12295	14400
2 Dr ZR1 Cpe	21833	24333	28500

OPTIONS FOR CORVETTE
AM/FM Stereo/CD/Tape +204
Adjustable Handling Package +696
Climate Control for AC[Opt on STD] +124
Delco/Bose Stereo System[Opt on STD] +134
Glass Targa Top +220
Hardtop Roof +677
Power Drivers Seat[Opt on STD] +104
Power Passenger Seat[Opt on STD] +92
Selective Ride & Handling +560
Solid & Glass Targa Tops +220
Sport Seats +212

IMPALA   1994

Caprice-based sedan powered by 260-horsepower, 5.7-liter V8 and sporting monochromatic black paint debuts to critical acclaim. Has four-wheel disc brakes, dual airbags, ABS, five-spoke alloys, and restyled C-pillars.

Category G

4 Dr SS Sdn	6003	7165	9100

OPTIONS FOR IMPALA
Power Passenger Seat +104

LUMINA   1994

Base coupe is dropped from lineup. Manual transmission disappears.

Category D

4 Dr STD Sdn	2147	2655	3500
2 Dr Euro Cpe	2454	3034	4000
4 Dr Euro Sdn	2209	2730	3600
2 Dr Z34 Cpe	2761	3413	4500

OPTIONS FOR LUMINA
6 cyl 3.4 L Engine[Std on Z34] +314
AM/FM Compact Disc Player +110
Anti-Lock Brakes[Opt on STD] +195
Bose Sound System +127
Power Drivers Seat[Opt on Sdn] +102
Power Windows[Opt on Sdn] +90
Sport Suspension[Std on Z34] +127

LUMINA MINIVAN   1994

APV designation dropped in favor of more descriptive "Minivan" nomenclature. Front styling is revised;

Don't forget to refer to the Mileage Adjustment Table at the back of this book!

CHEVROLET 94

Model Description	Trade-in TMV	Private TMV	Dealer TMV	Model Description	Trade-in TMV	Private TMV	Dealer TMV

overall length drops three inches. Driver airbag is standard. Integrated child seats and remote keyless entry are newly optional. Midyear, traction control becomes available on LS model.

Category P

2 Dr STD Cargo Van	2510	2994	3800
2 Dr STD Pass. Van	2774	3309	4200

OPTIONS FOR LUMINA MINIVAN

6 cyl 3.8 L Engine +210
7 Passenger Seating +186
AM/FM Compact Disc Player +134
Air Conditioning +272
Aluminum/Alloy Wheels +94
Automatic 4-Speed Transmission +272
Camper/Towing Package +108
Child Seats (2) +76
Cruise Control +76
Dual Air Conditioning +152
Power Door Locks +102
Power Drivers Seat +92
Power Sliding Door +118
Power Windows +94
Sunroof +170
Traction Control System +84

S10 BLAZER   1994

Side-door guard beams and a high-mount center brake light are added. Front bench seat is now standard on four-door models.

Category M

2 Dr STD 4WD Utility	3171	3744	4700
2 Dr STD Utility	2968	3505	4400
4 Dr STD 4WD Wgn	3507	4142	5199
4 Dr STD Wgn	3070	3625	4551
2 Dr Tahoe 4WD Utility			
	3509	4143	5201
2 Dr Tahoe Utility	3113	3676	4614
4 Dr Tahoe 4WD Wgn	3575	4222	5300
4 Dr Tahoe Wgn	3127	3692	4635
2 Dr Tahoe LT 4WD Utility			
	3845	4541	5700
2 Dr Tahoe LT Utility	3643	4302	5400
4 Dr Tahoe LT 4WD Wgn	4182	4939	6200
4 Dr Tahoe LT Wgn	3710	4381	5500

OPTIONS FOR S10 BLAZER

6 cyl 4.3 L CPI Engine +136
AM/FM Compact Disc Player +118
AM/FM Stereo Tape[Std on Tahoe LT] +88
Air Conditioning[Std on Tahoe LT] +272
Aluminum/Alloy Wheels[Std on Tahoe LT] +84
Automatic 4-Speed Transmission +272
Captain Chairs (2) +102
Limited Slip Differential +84
Power Drivers Seat[Std on Tahoe LT] +88
Power Windows[Std on Tahoe LT] +88

S10 PICKUP   1994

All-new truck debuts with more powerful engines and available four-wheel ABS. Side-door guard beams are standard. Rear ABS is standard on four cylinder models; V6 trucks get the new, four-wheel ABS system that works in both two- and four-wheel drive. ZR2 package is for serious off-roaders. Available only on regular-cab shortbed models, the ZR2 package includes four-inch wider track, three-inch height increase, off-road suspension and tires, wheel flares and thick skid plates. Base engine is 118-horse, 2.2-liter four cylinder. Standard on 4WD models is a 165-horsepower 4.3-liter V6. Optional on all models is a 195-horsepower, high-output 4.3-liter V6. SS package available with high-output engine, sport suspension and alloy wheels.

Category J

2 Dr STD 4WD Std Cab LB			
	3750	4444	5600
2 Dr STD Std Cab LB	2477	2936	3700
2 Dr STD 4WD Std Cab SB			
	3683	4364	5500
2 Dr STD Std Cab SB	2277	2698	3400
2 Dr LS 4WD Std Cab LB			
	3951	4682	5900
2 Dr LS Std Cab LB	2745	3253	4100
2 Dr LS 4WD Ext Cab SB			
	4151	4920	6200
2 Dr LS 4WD Std Cab SB			
	3884	4602	5800
2 Dr LS Ext Cab SB	2879	3412	4300
2 Dr LS Std Cab SB	2544	3015	3800

OPTIONS FOR S10 PICKUP

6 cyl 4.3 L CPI Engine +190
6 cyl 4.3 L Engine[Opt on 2WD] +336
AM/FM Compact Disc Player +138
AM/FM Stereo Tape +118
Air Conditioning +273
Aluminum/Alloy Wheels +116
Anti-Lock Brakes[Opt on 2WD] +204
Automatic 4-Speed Transmission +363
Chrome Step Bumper[Opt on STD Std Cab] +80
Limited Slip Differential +85
Power Windows +76
Wide Stance Package +322

SPORTVAN   1994

Category Q

2 Dr G20 Sportvan	3758	4411	5500
2 Dr G30 Sportvan	4168	4892	6100
2 Dr G30 Sportvan Ext	4441	5213	6500
2 Dr G20 Beauville Sportvan			
	4236	4972	6200

Don't forget to refer to the Mileage Adjustment Table at the back of this book!

Model Description	Trade-in TMV	Private TMV	Dealer TMV
2 Dr G30 Beauville Sportvan			
	4509	5293	6600
2 Dr G30 Beauville Sportvan Ext			
	4646	5454	6800

OPTIONS FOR SPORTVAN
15 Passenger Seating +126
8 cyl 5.0 L Engine[Opt on G20] +195
8 cyl 5.7 L Engine[Opt on G20] +286
8 cyl 6.5 L Diesel Engine +528
8 cyl 7.4 L Engine +206
AM/FM Compact Disc Player +94
Air Conditioning[Std on Beauville] +331
Camper/Towing Package +106
Captain Chairs (2) +102
Dual Air Conditioning +534
Limited Slip Differential +84
Power Door Locks[Std on Beauville] +76
Power Windows[Std on Beauville] +83
Privacy Glass +129

SUBURBAN   1994

Side-door guard beams are added, as well as a high-mounted center brake light. A turbocharged diesel is newly optional on 2500 models. A new grille appears.

Category N

Model Description	Trade-in TMV	Private TMV	Dealer TMV
4 Dr C1500 Wgn	5509	6405	7900
4 Dr C2500 Wgn	5788	6730	8300
4 Dr K1500 4WD Wgn	5927	6892	8500
4 Dr K2500 4WD Wgn	6206	7216	8900

OPTIONS FOR SUBURBAN
8 cyl 6.5 L Turbodiesel Engine +534
8 cyl 7.4 L Engine +193
Air Conditioning +272
Aluminum/Alloy Wheels +100
Center & Rear Bench Seat +353
Dual Air Conditioning +418
Leather Seats +304
Limited Slip Differential +80
Power Drivers Seat +78
Power Windows +85
Privacy Glass +98
Silverado Package +372

1993 CHEVROLET

APV   1993

Category P

Model Description	Trade-in TMV	Private TMV	Dealer TMV
2 Dr STD Cargo Van	2181	2675	3500

OPTIONS FOR APV
AM/FM Stereo Tape +79
Air Conditioning +241

ASTRO   1993

Base 4.3-liter V6 gets 15 additional horsepower. Automatic transmission gets electronic shift controls

and second-gear start feature. New speedometer reads to 100 mph. Driver airbag is offered as an option midyear.

Category P

Model Description	Trade-in TMV	Private TMV	Dealer TMV
2 Dr STD AWD Cargo Van			
	2310	2834	3708
2 Dr STD AWD Cargo Van Ext			
	2356	2890	3781
2 Dr STD AWD Pass. Van			
	2504	3072	4019
2 Dr STD Cargo Van	2056	2523	3300
2 Dr STD Cargo Van Ext			
	2118	2599	3400
2 Dr STD Pass. Van	2056	2523	3300
2 Dr STD Pass. Van Ext			
	2181	2675	3500
2 Dr CL AWD Pass. Van	2379	2919	3819
2 Dr CL AWD Pass. Van Ext			
	2430	2981	3900
2 Dr CL Pass. Van	2290	2809	3675
2 Dr CL Pass. Van Ext	2316	2841	3717
2 Dr LT AWD Pass. Van	2991	3669	4800
2 Dr LT AWD Pass. Van Ext			
	3053	3746	4900
2 Dr LT Pass. Van	2480	3043	3981
2 Dr LT Pass. Van Ext	2554	3134	4100

OPTIONS FOR ASTRO
6 cyl 4.3 L CPI Engine[Opt on CL,Pass Van Ext,2WD] +151
7 Passenger Seating +142
8 Passenger Seating +96
AM/FM Compact Disc Player +120
AM/FM Stereo Tape +83
Air Bag Restraint[Opt on CL,LT,Pass Van Ext,2WD] +121
Air Conditioning +241
Aluminum/Alloy Wheels +75
Camper/Towing Package +93
Dual Air Conditioning +158
Limited Slip Differential +75
Power Windows +79
Privacy Glass[Std on LT] +87

BERETTA   1993

Standard engine on the GT is now a ridiculous 110-horsepower four-cylinder from the base car. The V6 is optional. GTZ's Quad 4 engine loses five horsepower to emissions regulations. A brake/shift interlock has been added to automatic transmissions. Manuals get an improved clutch.

Category C

Model Description	Trade-in TMV	Private TMV	Dealer TMV
2 Dr STD Cpe	1401	1930	2811
2 Dr GT Cpe	1490	2052	2989
2 Dr GTZ Cpe	1695	2334	3400

OPTIONS FOR BERETTA
6 cyl 3.1 L Engine +385

Don't forget to refer to the Mileage Adjustment Table at the back of this book!

AM/FM Compact Disc Player +83
Air Conditioning[Std on GTZ] +241
Automatic 3-Speed Transmission +168
Power Windows +83
Sunroof +151

BLAZER   1993

No changes.
Category N

Model Description	Trade-in TMV	Private TMV	Dealer TMV
2 Dr STD 4WD Utility	4068	4830	6100
2 Dr Silverado 4WD Utility	5335	6335	8000
2 Dr Sport 4WD Utility	5669	6731	8500

OPTIONS FOR BLAZER

AM/FM Stereo Tape +75
Air Conditioning[Opt on Sport,STD] +241
Aluminum/Alloy Wheels +75
Automatic 4-Speed Transmission +212
Power Windows +79

C/K 1500 SERIES   1993

Category K

Model Description	Trade-in TMV	Private TMV	Dealer TMV
2 Dr C1500 454SS Std Cab SB	5601	6651	8400
2 Dr C1500 Cheyenne Ext Cab LB	3725	4423	5586
2 Dr C1500 Cheyenne Std Cab LB	2911	3457	4366
2 Dr K1500 Cheyenne 4WD Ext Cab LB	4401	5226	6600
2 Dr K1500 Cheyenne 4WD Std Cab LB	3818	4533	5725
2 Dr C1500 Cheyenne Ext Cab SB	3534	4196	5299
2 Dr C1500 Cheyenne Std Cab SB	2902	3446	4352
2 Dr K1500 Cheyenne 4WD Ext Cab SB	4334	5147	6500
2 Dr K1500 Cheyenne 4WD Std Cab SB	3784	4493	5675
2 Dr C1500 Cheyenne Ext Cab Stepside SB	3741	4442	5610
2 Dr C1500 Cheyenne Std Cab Stepside SB	2934	3484	4400
2 Dr K1500 Cheyenne 4WD Ext Cab Stepside SB	4468	5305	6700
2 Dr K1500 Cheyenne 4WD Std Cab Stepside SB	3870	4595	5803
2 Dr C1500 Indy Pace Std Cab SB	4001	4751	6000
2 Dr C1500 Silverado Ext Cab LB	3939	4677	5907
2 Dr C1500 Silverado Std Cab LB	3535	4197	5301
2 Dr K1500 Silverado 4WD Ext Cab LB	4819	5722	7227
2 Dr K1500 Silverado 4WD Std Cab LB	4334	5147	6500
2 Dr C1500 Silverado Ext Cab SB	3910	4642	5863
2 Dr C1500 Silverado Std Cab SB	3468	4117	5200
2 Dr K1500 Silverado 4WD Ext Cab SB	4783	5679	7173
2 Dr K1500 Silverado 4WD Std Cab SB	4268	5067	6400
2 Dr C1500 Silverado Ext Cab Stepside SB	3955	4696	5931
2 Dr C1500 Silverado Std Cab Stepside SB	3601	4276	5400
2 Dr K1500 Silverado 4WD Ext Cab Stepside SB	4868	5780	7300
2 Dr K1500 Silverado 4WD Std Cab Stepside SB	3737	4437	5604
2 Dr C1500 Sport Std Cab Stepside SB	3866	4590	5797
2 Dr C1500 Work Truck Std Cab LB	2699	3205	4048
2 Dr K1500 Work Truck 4WD Std Cab LB	3334	3959	5000

OPTIONS FOR C/K 1500 SERIES

8 cyl 5.0 L Engine +149
8 cyl 5.7 L Engine +212
8 cyl 6.2 L Diesel Engine +724
AM/FM Compact Disc Player +75
Air Conditioning[Std on Silverado] +243
Automatic 4-Speed Transmission +293
Captain Chairs (2) +81
Chrome Wheels +75
Locking Differential +76

C/K 2500 SERIES   1993

Category K

Model Description	Trade-in TMV	Private TMV	Dealer TMV
2 Dr C2500 Cheyenne Ext Cab LB	4068	4830	6100
2 Dr C2500 Cheyenne Std Cab LB	3534	4196	5300
2 Dr K2500 Cheyenne 4WD Ext Cab LB	4735	5622	7100
2 Dr K2500 Cheyenne 4WD Std Cab LB	4201	4988	6300
2 Dr C2500 Cheyenne Ext Cab SB	4004	4755	6005
2 Dr K2500 Cheyenne 4WD Ext Cab SB	4671	5546	7005

Don't forget to refer to the Mileage Adjustment Table at the back of this book!

Model Description	Trade-in TMV	Private TMV	Dealer TMV
2 Dr C2500 Silverado Ext Cab LB			
	4665	5538	6995
2 Dr C2500 Silverado Std Cab LB			
	3998	4747	5995
2 Dr K2500 Silverado 4WD Ext Cab LB			
	5201	6176	7800
2 Dr K2500 Silverado 4WD Std Cab LB			
	4605	5467	6905
2 Dr C2500 Silverado Ext Cab SB			
	4598	5459	6895
2 Dr K2500 Silverado 4WD Ext Cab SB			
	5135	6097	7700

OPTIONS FOR C/K 2500 SERIES
8 cyl 5.0 L Engine +212
8 cyl 5.7 L Engine +212
8 cyl 6.2 L Diesel Engine +724
8 cyl 6.5 L Turbodiesel Engine +819
8 cyl 7.4 L Engine +181
Air Conditioning[Std on Silverado] +243
Automatic 4-Speed Transmission +293
Locking Differential +76

C/K 3500 SERIES   1993

Category K

Model Description	Trade-in TMV	Private TMV	Dealer TMV
2 Dr C3500 Ext Cab LB	5068	6018	7600
4 Dr C3500 Crew Cab LB			
	5135	6097	7700
4 Dr K3500 4WD Crew Cab LB			
	5735	6809	8600
2 Dr C3500 Cheyenne Std Cab LB			
	4801	5701	7200
2 Dr K3500 Cheyenne 4WD Ext Cab LB			
	5668	6730	8500
2 Dr K3500 Cheyenne 4WD Std Cab LB			
	5401	6413	8100
2 Dr C3500 Silverado Ext Cab LB			
	5535	6572	8300
2 Dr C3500 Silverado Std Cab LB			
	5201	6176	7800
2 Dr K3500 Silverado 4WD Ext Cab LB			
	6002	7126	9000
2 Dr K3500 Silverado 4WD Std Cab LB			
	5637	6693	8453
4 Dr C3500 Silverado Crew Cab LB			
	5566	6609	8347
4 Dr K3500 Silverado 4WD Crew Cab LB			
	6135	7284	9200

OPTIONS FOR C/K 3500 SERIES
8 cyl 6.2 L Diesel Engine +508
8 cyl 6.5 L Turbodiesel Engine +819
8 cyl 7.4 L Engine +181
Air Conditioning[Std on Silverado] +243
Automatic 4-Speed Transmission +293

Bucket Seats +81
Dual Rear Wheels +241
Locking Differential +76

CAMARO   1993

All-new sports coupe is redesigned for the first time in 12 years. Dual airbags and ABS are standard. Convertible disappears for one year. Available in base and Z28 trim. Base model powered by 3.4-liter V6; Z28 gets 5.7-liter V8 rated at 275 horsepower (115 more than base Camaro). Z28 has a six-speed manual transmission standard.

Category E

Model Description	Trade-in TMV	Private TMV	Dealer TMV
2 Dr STD Cpe	2648	3230	4200
2 Dr Z28 Cpe	3216	3922	5100

OPTIONS FOR CAMARO
AM/FM Compact Disc Player +96
Air Conditioning +270
Aluminum/Alloy Wheels +83
Automatic 4-Speed Transmission +212
Bose Sound System +106
Glass Panel T-tops +293
Power Drivers Seat +81
Power Windows +77

CAPRICE   1993

Rear styling is revised, and rear wheel wells are opened up. Rear track is increased 1.6 inches. LTZ gets a 180-horsepower 5.7-liter V8 standard. Acoustical package added to reduce noise. LS trim level gets gold accents on wheels and trim.

Category G

Model Description	Trade-in TMV	Private TMV	Dealer TMV
4 Dr STD Sdn	2143	2614	3400
4 Dr STD Wgn	2206	2691	3500
4 Dr LS Sdn	2521	3075	4000
4 Dr LTZ Sdn	3025	3691	4800

OPTIONS FOR CAPRICE
8 cyl 5.7 L Engine +166
AM/FM Compact Disc Player +120
AM/FM Stereo Tape +80
Bose Sound System +106
Leather Seats +234
Power Drivers Seat +81
Power Passenger Seat +81
Power Windows[Std on LTZ] +77
Third Seat +121

CAVALIER   1993

Convertible gets glass rear window, and RS coupes and sedans can be equipped with the Z24's 3.1-liter V6. A CD player is a new option on VL models. RS gets Z24 interior trimmings.

Category B

Model Description	Trade-in TMV	Private TMV	Dealer TMV
2 Dr RS Conv	1634	2259	3300

Don't forget to refer to the Mileage Adjustment Table at the back of this book!

Model Description	Trade-in TMV	Private TMV	Dealer TMV
2 Dr RS Cpe	1186	1639	2394
4 Dr RS Sdn	1191	1647	2406
4 Dr RS Wgn	1387	1917	2800
2 Dr VL Cpe	1040	1437	2100
4 Dr VL Sdn	1139	1574	2300
4 Dr VL Wgn	1238	1711	2500
2 Dr Z24 Conv	1882	2601	3800
2 Dr Z24 Cpe	1486	2054	3000

OPTIONS FOR CAVALIER

6 cyl 3.1 L Engine[Opt on RS] +207
AM/FM Compact Disc Player +120
Air Conditioning +240
Automatic 3-Speed Transmission +166
Power Windows +80
Sunroof +151

CORSICA   1993

Wow. A brake/transmission shift interlock is added. Larger muffler is supposed to make Corsica quieter.

Category C

	Trade-in TMV	Private TMV	Dealer TMV
4 Dr LT Sdn	1296	1785	2600

OPTIONS FOR CORSICA

6 cyl 3.1 L Engine +217
AM/FM Compact Disc Player +120
Air Conditioning +241
Aluminum/Alloy Wheels +75
Automatic 3-Speed Transmission +166
Power Drivers Seat +81
Power Windows +103
Sport Suspension +113

CORVETTE   1993

Base model gets narrower front tires and wider rear tires. LT1 V8 gets additional torque. ZR-1 horsepower is up to 405 this year. All models can be ordered in 40th Anniversary trim, consisting of Ruby Red paint and badging. Passive Keyless Entry is newly optional, and locks or unlocks the doors simply by having the key fob close to the car.

Category F

	Trade-in TMV	Private TMV	Dealer TMV
2 Dr STD Conv	11463	13052	15700
2 Dr STD Cpe	9053	10308	12400
2 Dr ZR1 Cpe	16281	18538	22300

OPTIONS FOR CORVETTE

AM/FM Stereo/CD/Tape[Opt on STD] +181
Adjustable Handling Package +618
Bose Sound System[Opt on STD] +106
Climate Control for AC[Opt on STD] +110
Glass Targa Top +196
Hardtop Roof +602
Leather Seats[Opt on STD] +301
Power Drivers Seat[Opt on STD] +92
Power Passenger Seat +81
Selective Ride & Handling[Opt on STD] +498
Solid & Glass Targa Tops +196

Sport Seats +188

LUMINA   1993

Base sedans get five more horsepower this year, and base coupes now have standard V6 power. Doors lock automatically when vehicle reaches eight mph.

Category D

	Trade-in TMV	Private TMV	Dealer TMV
2 Dr STD Cpe	1703	2247	3154
4 Dr STD Sdn	1620	2138	3000
2 Dr Euro Cpe	1753	2313	3246
4 Dr Euro Sdn	1782	2351	3300
2 Dr Z34 Cpe	2268	2993	4200

OPTIONS FOR LUMINA

6 cyl 3.1 L Engine[Std on EURO,Cpe] +207
6 cyl 3.4 L Engine[Std on Z34] +279
AM/FM Compact Disc Player +98
Air Conditioning[Opt on STD Sdn] +241
Anti-Lock Brakes[Opt on STD] +173
Automatic 4-Speed Transmission +241
Bose Sound System[Opt on Euro] +113
Euro Package +377
Power Drivers Seat +91
Power Windows +80
Sport Seats +75

LUMINA MINIVAN   1993

Uplevel trim switches from CL to LS designation. Sunroof joins options list this year. Center console is redesigned to include dual cupholders.

Category P

	Trade-in TMV	Private TMV	Dealer TMV
2 Dr STD Pass. Van	2118	2599	3400
2 Dr LS Pass. Van	2430	2981	3900

OPTIONS FOR LUMINA MINIVAN

6 cyl 3.8 L Engine +186
7 Passenger Seating +166
AM/FM Compact Disc Player +120
Air Conditioning[Std on LS] +241
Aluminum/Alloy Wheels +83
Automatic 4-Speed Transmission +241
Camper/Towing Package +97
Dual Air Conditioning +135
Power Door Locks +91
Power Drivers Seat +81
Power Windows +83
Sunroof +151

S10 BLAZER   1993

Two-door model available in LT trim. All models get two-tone paint scheme in LT trim. V6 engines get internal balance shaft designed to reduce vibration. Automatic transmission receives electronic shift controls and second-gear start feature. Manual lumbar adjusters are newly standard on front seats.

Category M

	Trade-in TMV	Private TMV	Dealer TMV
2 Dr STD 4WD Utility	2567	3142	4100

Don't forget to refer to the Mileage Adjustment Table at the back of this book!

Model Description	Trade-in TMV	Private TMV	Dealer TMV
2 Dr STD Utility	2316	2835	3700
4 Dr STD 4WD Wgn	2754	3371	4400
4 Dr STD Wgn	2374	2906	3792
2 Dr Tahoe 4WD Utility			
	2692	3295	4300
2 Dr Tahoe Utility	2384	2918	3808
4 Dr Tahoe 4WD Wgn	2942	3601	4700
4 Dr Tahoe Wgn	2504	3065	4000
2 Dr Tahoe LT 4WD Utility			
	3318	4061	5300
2 Dr Tahoe LT Utility	3005	3678	4800
4 Dr Tahoe LT 4WD Wgn	3380	4138	5400
4 Dr Tahoe LT Wgn	3067	3755	4900

OPTIONS FOR S10 BLAZER

6 cyl 4.3 L CPI Engine +121
AM/FM Compact Disc Player +106
AM/FM Stereo Tape[Std on Tahoe LT] +79
Air Conditioning[Std on Tahoe LT] +241
Aluminum/Alloy Wheels +75
Automatic 4-Speed Transmission +241
Leather Seats +181
Locking Differential +80
Power Drivers Seat[Std on Tahoe LT] +79
Power Windows[Std on Tahoe LT] +79

S10 PICKUP — 1993

V6 engines get internal balance shaft designed to reduce vibration. Automatic transmission gets electronic shift controls.

Category J

Model Description	Trade-in TMV	Private TMV	Dealer TMV
2 Dr STD 4WD Std Cab LB			
	2349	2875	3751
2 Dr STD Std Cab LB	1873	2292	2990
2 Dr STD 4WD Ext Cab SB			
	2693	3296	4300
2 Dr STD 4WD Std Cab SB			
	2349	2875	3751
2 Dr STD Ext Cab SB	2067	2529	3300
2 Dr STD Std Cab SB	1873	2292	2990
2 Dr EL 4WD Std Cab SB			
	2289	2801	3655
2 Dr EL Std Cab SB	1816	2223	2900
2 Dr Tahoe 4WD Std Cab LB			
	2380	2913	3800
2 Dr Tahoe Std Cab LB	1891	2314	3019
2 Dr Tahoe 4WD Ext Cab SB			
	2944	3602	4700
2 Dr Tahoe 4WD Std Cab SB			
	2505	3066	4000
2 Dr Tahoe Ext Cab SB	2255	2759	3600
2 Dr Tahoe Std Cab SB	1942	2376	3100

OPTIONS FOR S10 PICKUP

6 cyl 2.8 L Engine +159

6 cyl 4.3 L Engine[Opt on 2WD] +299
AM/FM Compact Disc Player +122
AM/FM Stereo Tape +105
Air Conditioning +243
Aluminum/Alloy Wheels +103
Automatic 4-Speed Transmission +323
Locking Differential +76

SPORTVAN — 1993

Category Q

Model Description	Trade-in TMV	Private TMV	Dealer TMV
2 Dr G10 Sportvan	2638	3186	4100
2 Dr G10 Sportvan Ext	2767	3342	4300
2 Dr G20 Sportvan Ext	2831	3419	4400
2 Dr G30 Sportvan	3145	3799	4888
2 Dr G30 Sportvan Ext	3160	3817	4912
2 Dr G10 Beauville Sportvan			
	2960	3575	4600
2 Dr G10 Beauville Sportvan Ext			
	3217	3886	5000
2 Dr G20 Beauville Sportvan Ext			
	3024	3653	4700
2 Dr G30 Beauville Sportvan			
	3667	4430	5700
2 Dr G30 Beauville Sportvan Ext			
	3796	4585	5900

OPTIONS FOR SPORTVAN

12 Passenger Seating[Opt on Beauville,G30] +113
8 Passenger Seating +75
8 cyl 5.0 L Engine[Opt on G10, G20] +173
8 cyl 5.7 L Engine[Opt on G10, G20] +255
8 cyl 6.2 L Diesel Engine +469
8 cyl 7.4 L Engine +183
AM/FM Compact Disc Player +82
Air Conditioning +294
Aluminum/Alloy Wheels +75
Bucket Seats +121
Camper/Towing Package +94
Dual Air Conditioning +475
Locking Differential +76
Premium Sound System +151
Privacy Glass +115

SUBURBAN — 1993

No changes.

Category N

Model Description	Trade-in TMV	Private TMV	Dealer TMV
4 Dr C1500 Wgn	4402	5226	6600
4 Dr C2500 Wgn	4735	5622	7100
4 Dr K1500 4WD Wgn	5069	6018	7600
4 Dr K2500 4WD Wgn	5202	6176	7800

OPTIONS FOR SUBURBAN

8 cyl 7.4 L Engine +172
Air Conditioning +242
Aluminum/Alloy Wheels +89
Bucket Seats +75
Center & Rear Bench Seat +314

Don't forget to refer to the Mileage Adjustment Table at the back of this book!

Model Description	Trade-in TMV	Private TMV	Dealer TMV

Center Bench Seat +182
Dual Air Conditioning +372
Leather Seats +322
Power Windows +76
Premium Sound System +143
Privacy Glass +87
Silverado Package +331
Suburban Silverado Package 1 +1021
Suburban Silverado Package 2 +1123

1992 CHEVROLET

ASTRO   1992

Dutch rear door treatment is available. With Dutch doors, a rear washer/wiper and rear defogger can be ordered. All-wheel-drive models get high-output, 200-horsepower, V6 standard. Engine is optional on 2WD models.

Category P

Model Description	Trade-in TMV	Private TMV	Dealer TMV
2 Dr STD AWD Cargo Van	1894	2438	3345
2 Dr STD AWD Cargo Van Ext	1930	2485	3409
2 Dr STD AWD Pass. Van	1945	2503	3434
2 Dr STD AWD Pass. Van Ext	1971	2537	3480
2 Dr STD Cargo Van	1680	2163	2967
2 Dr STD Cargo Van Ext	1717	2211	3033
2 Dr STD Pass. Van	1793	2308	3167
2 Dr STD Pass. Van Ext	1831	2357	3233
2 Dr CL AWD Pass. Van	1993	2566	3520
2 Dr CL AWD Pass. Van Ext	2095	2697	3700
2 Dr CL Pass. Van	1868	2405	3299
2 Dr CL Pass. Van Ext	1928	2482	3405
2 Dr LT AWD Pass. Van	2039	2624	3600
2 Dr LT AWD Pass. Van Ext	2265	2916	4000
2 Dr LT Pass. Van	1869	2406	3301
2 Dr LT Pass. Van Ext	1929	2483	3407

OPTIONS FOR ASTRO
6 cyl 4.3 L CPI Engine +134
7 Passenger Seating +126
8 Passenger Seating +86
AM/FM Compact Disc Player +107
Air Conditioning +215
Camper/Towing Package +83
Dual Air Conditioning +141
Privacy Glass +78

BERETTA   1992

ABS is standard. Base engine gains 15 horsepower. GTZ gets revised gearing for better off-the-line acceleration. Base V6 models get gearing change designed to save fuel. Order a GTZ with the V6, and you'll get touring tires instead of high-performance rubber. Front brakes are slightly larger on all models.

Category C

Model Description	Trade-in TMV	Private TMV	Dealer TMV
2 Dr STD Cpe	1104	1553	2300
2 Dr GT Cpe	1248	1755	2600
2 Dr GTZ Cpe	1536	2160	3200

OPTIONS FOR BERETTA
6 cyl 3.1 L Engine +343
Air Conditioning[Std on GT] +215
Automatic 3-Speed Transmission +149
Sunroof +134

BLAZER   1992

Totally redesigned and based on same platform and sheetmetal as C/K pickup. Six-passenger seating is standard. Cargo area gets fixed metal roof rather than fiberglass shell. Four-wheel ABS is standard and works in 4WD. New Sport appearance package includes two-tone paint and wheelwell flares. Diesel option is dropped. Five-speed manual is standard transmission. An automatic is optional. Shift-on-the-fly 4WD is standard.

Category N

Model Description	Trade-in TMV	Private TMV	Dealer TMV
2 Dr STD 4WD Utility	3298	4086	5400
2 Dr Silverado 4WD Utility	3725	4616	6100
2 Dr Sport 4WD Utility	3786	4691	6200

OPTIONS FOR BLAZER
Air Conditioning +215
Automatic 4-Speed Transmission +188

C/K 1500 SERIES   1992

Category K

Model Description	Trade-in TMV	Private TMV	Dealer TMV
2 Dr C1500 454SS Std Cab SB	4032	4995	6600
2 Dr C1500 Ext Cab LB	2627	3254	4300
2 Dr C1500 Std Cab LB	2396	2968	3921
2 Dr K1500 4WD Ext Cab LB	3058	3788	5005
2 Dr K1500 4WD Std Cab LB	2933	3633	4800
2 Dr C1500 Ext Cab SB	2570	3183	4206
2 Dr C1500 Std Cab SB	2370	2936	3879
2 Dr K1500 4WD Ext Cab SB	3010	3728	4926
2 Dr K1500 4WD Std Cab SB	2871	3557	4700
2 Dr C1500 Ext Cab Stepside SB			

C/K 1500 SERIES

Model Description	Trade-in TMV	Private TMV	Dealer TMV
2 Dr C1500 Std Cab Stepside SB	2636	3265	4314
2 Dr K1500 4WD Ext Cab Stepside SB	2439	3021	3992
2 Dr K1500 4WD Std Cab Stepside SB	3066	3799	5019
2 Dr C1500 Scottsdale Ext Cab LB	2961	3668	4846
2 Dr C1500 Scottsdale Std Cab LB	2740	3394	4485
2 Dr K1500 Scottsdale 4WD Ext Cab LB	2572	3186	4210
2 Dr K1500 Scottsdale 4WD Std Cab LB	3171	3928	5190
2 Dr C1500 Scottsdale Ext Cab SB	3012	3731	4930
2 Dr C1500 Scottsdale Std Cab SB	2678	3318	4384
2 Dr K1500 Scottsdale 4WD Ext Cab SB	2546	3155	4168
2 Dr K1500 Scottsdale 4WD Std Cab SB	3171	3928	5190
2 Dr C1500 Scottsdale Ext Cab Stepside SB	2986	3699	4887
2 Dr C1500 Scottsdale Std Cab Stepside SB	2749	3405	4499
2 Dr K1500 Scottsdale 4WD Ext Cab Stepside SB	2581	3198	4225
2 Dr K1500 Scottsdale 4WD Std Cab Stepside SB	3234	4006	5293
2 Dr C1500 Silverado Ext Cab LB	3043	3769	4980
2 Dr C1500 Silverado Std Cab LB	2759	3418	4516
2 Dr K1500 Silverado 4WD Ext Cab LB	2619	3245	4287
2 Dr K1500 Silverado 4WD Std Cab LB	3242	4017	5307
2 Dr C1500 Silverado Ext Cab SB	3049	3777	4990
2 Dr C1500 Silverado Std Cab SB	2698	3342	4416
2 Dr K1500 Silverado 4WD Ext Cab SB	2561	3173	4192
2 Dr K1500 Silverado 4WD Std Cab SB	3189	3950	5219
2 Dr C1500 Silverado Ext Cab Stepside SB	3000	3717	4911
2 Dr C1500 Silverado Std Cab Stepside SB	2810	3481	4600
2 Dr K1500 Silverado 4WD Ext Cab Stepside SB	2627	3254	4300
2 Dr K1500 Silverado 4WD Std Cab Stepside SB	3360	4163	5500
2 Dr C1500 Work Truck Std Cab LB	3058	3788	5005
2 Dr K1500 Work Truck 4WD Std Cab LB	2016	2498	3300
	2449	3033	4008

OPTIONS FOR C/K 1500 SERIES
8 cyl 5.0 L Engine +133
8 cyl 5.7 L Engine +188
8 cyl 6.2 L Diesel Engine +644
Air Conditioning[Std on Silverado] +216
Automatic 4-Speed Transmission +261

C/K 2500 SERIES 1992

Category K

Model Description	Trade-in TMV	Private TMV	Dealer TMV
2 Dr C2500 Ext Cab LB	2739	3393	4483
2 Dr C2500 Std Cab LB	2505	3103	4100
2 Dr K2500 4WD Ext Cab LB	3175	3933	5197
2 Dr K2500 4WD Std Cab LB	2810	3481	4600
2 Dr C2500 Ext Cab SB	2694	3338	4410
2 Dr K2500 4WD Ext Cab SB	3116	3860	5100
2 Dr C2500 Scottsdale Ext Cab LB	2767	3428	4529
2 Dr C2500 Scottsdale Std Cab LB	2627	3254	4300
2 Dr K2500 Scottsdale 4WD Ext Cab LB	3238	4011	5300
2 Dr K2500 Scottsdale 4WD Std Cab LB	2994	3709	4900
2 Dr C2500 Scottsdale Ext Cab SB	2742	3397	4488
2 Dr K2500 Scottsdale 4WD Ext Cab SB	3179	3938	5203
2 Dr C2500 Silverado Ext Cab LB	2933	3633	4800
2 Dr C2500 Silverado Std Cab LB	2682	3323	4390
2 Dr K2500 Silverado 4WD Ext Cab LB	3360	4163	5500
2 Dr K2500 Silverado 4WD Std Cab LB	3055	3784	5000
2 Dr C2500 Silverado Ext Cab SB	2871	3557	4700
2 Dr K2500 Silverado 4WD Ext Cab SB	3299	4087	5400

OPTIONS FOR C/K 2500 SERIES
8 cyl 5.0 L Engine +188
8 cyl 5.7 L Engine +188

Don't forget to refer to the Mileage Adjustment Table at the back of this book!

CHEVROLET 92

Model Description	Trade-in TMV	Private TMV	Dealer TMV
8 cyl 6.2 L Diesel Engine +644			
8 cyl 6.5 L Turbodiesel Engine +730			
8 cyl 7.4 L Engine +161			
Air Conditioning[Std on Silverado] +216			
Automatic 4-Speed Transmission +261			

C/K 3500 SERIES — 1992

Model Description	Trade-in TMV	Private TMV	Dealer TMV
Category K			
2 Dr C3500 Ext Cab LB	3116	3860	5100
2 Dr C3500 Std Cab LB	2810	3481	4600
2 Dr K3500 4WD Ext Cab LB	3514	4353	5752
2 Dr K3500 4WD Std Cab LB	3248	4024	5317
4 Dr C3500 Crew Cab LB	3203	3968	5243
4 Dr K3500 4WD Crew Cab LB	3849	4768	6300
2 Dr C3500 Scottsdale Ext Cab LB	3187	3948	5216
2 Dr C3500 Scottsdale Std Cab LB	2871	3557	4700
2 Dr K3500 Scottsdale 4WD Ext Cab LB	3666	4541	6000
2 Dr K3500 Scottsdale 4WD Std Cab LB	3451	4275	5648
2 Dr C3500 Silverado Ext Cab LB	3228	3998	5283
2 Dr C3500 Silverado Std Cab LB	3141	3891	5141
2 Dr K3500 Silverado 4WD Ext Cab LB	3788	4692	6200
2 Dr K3500 Silverado 4WD Std Cab LB	3544	4390	5800
4 Dr Silverado Crew Cab LB	3727	4617	6100

OPTIONS FOR C/K 3500 SERIES
8 cyl 6.2 L Diesel Engine +452			
8 cyl 6.5 L Turbodiesel Engine +730			
8 cyl 7.4 L Engine +161			
Air Conditioning[Std on Silverado] +216			
Automatic 4-Speed Transmission +261			
Dual Rear Wheels +215			

CAMARO — 1992

Heritage Appearance option, essentially a couple of sport stripes and a dashboard plaque, commemorates Camaro's 25th anniversary. Z28 models get quicker steering and an improved suspension.

Model Description	Trade-in TMV	Private TMV	Dealer TMV
Category E			
2 Dr RS Conv	2864	3703	5100
2 Dr RS Cpe	1853	2396	3300
2 Dr Z28 Conv	3594	4646	6400
2 Dr Z28 Cpe	2359	3049	4200

OPTIONS FOR CAMARO
8 cyl 5.0 L Engine[Opt on RS] +94			
8 cyl 5.7 L Engine +216			
AM/FM Compact Disc Player +107			
Air Conditioning +241			
Automatic 4-Speed Transmission +174			
Bose Sound System[Opt on Cpe] +94			
Glass Panel T-tops +261			
Leather Seats +121			
T-Tops (Solid/Colored) +161			

CAPRICE — 1992

Station wagon gets more powerful V8 option. Speedometer now reads to 100 mph, tilt steering is standard, and wagon's quarter vent windows are power operated.

Model Description	Trade-in TMV	Private TMV	Dealer TMV
Category G			
4 Dr STD Sdn	1723	2202	3000
4 Dr STD Wgn	1953	2496	3400
4 Dr Classic Sdn	2183	2789	3800

OPTIONS FOR CAPRICE
8 cyl 5.7 L Engine +148			
AM/FM Compact Disc Player +107			
Bose Sound System +94			
Dual Power Seats +156			
Leather Seats +209			

CAVALIER — 1992

ABS is standard, and base engines are bumped 15 horsepower to 110. RS and Z24 convertibles are back after two-year hiatus. Automatic door locks are added. VL and RS models get new wheelcovers. Z24 trades performance tires for touring.

Model Description	Trade-in TMV	Private TMV	Dealer TMV
Category B			
2 Dr RS Conv	1459	2037	3000
2 Dr RS Cpe	1021	1426	2100
4 Dr RS Sdn	1119	1562	2300
4 Dr RS Wgn	1313	1833	2700
2 Dr VL Cpe	924	1290	1900
4 Dr VL Sdn	973	1358	2000
4 Dr VL Wgn	1070	1494	2200
2 Dr Z24 Conv	1702	2377	3500
2 Dr Z24 Cpe	1411	1969	2900

OPTIONS FOR CAVALIER
6 cyl 3.1 L Engine[Opt on RS] +184			
AM/FM Compact Disc Player +107			
Air Conditioning +213			
Automatic 3-Speed Transmission[Std on Wgn] +148			
Sunroof +134			

CORSICA — 1992

Five-door hatchback is dropped. ABS is standard, and base engine makes more power. Manual transmission cannot be ordered with V6 this year. V6 models get more fuel-efficient gearing. Front brakes are larger,

Model Description	Trade-in TMV	Private TMV	Dealer TMV

and optional CD player gets theft-deterrent system. Outside mirrors are body-color.

Category C

	Trade-in	Private	Dealer
4 Dr LT Sdn	1008	1418	2100

OPTIONS FOR CORSICA

6 cyl 3.1 L Engine +193
AM/FM Compact Disc Player +107
Air Conditioning +215
Automatic 3-Speed Transmission +148
Power Windows +91

CORVETTE 1992

New base V8 is the LT1 engine, making 300 horsepower. ZR-1 gets fender badging to distinguish itself from lesser Corvettes. All Corvettes get traction control standard. Speedometer swaps spots with the fuel gauge for better readability. A Quiet Car option adds weather-stripping and sound insulation.

Category F

	Trade-in	Private	Dealer
2 Dr STD Conv	9690	11456	14400
2 Dr STD Cpe	7402	8751	11000
2 Dr ZR1 Cpe	14199	16787	21100

OPTIONS FOR CORVETTE

AM/FM Stereo/CD/Tape[Opt on STD] +161
Bose Sound System[Opt on STD] +94
Climate Control for AC[Opt on STD] +98
Glass Targa Top +174
Handling Package +457
Hardtop Roof +536
Leather Seats[Opt on STD] +268
Power Drivers Seat[Opt on STD] +82
Selective Suspension[Opt on STD] +443
Solid & Glass Targa Tops +174
Sport Seats +168

LUMINA 1992

Euro sedan can be equipped with 3.4-liter twin-cam engine. Base engine loses five horsepower. ABS is standard on Z34 and Euro; optional on base models. A CD player joins the options sheet.

Category D

	Trade-in	Private	Dealer
2 Dr STD Cpe	1325	1878	2800
4 Dr STD Sdn	1231	1744	2600
2 Dr Euro Cpe	1416	2006	2991
4 Dr Euro Sdn	1424	2018	3009
2 Dr Z34 Cpe	1562	2214	3300

OPTIONS FOR LUMINA

6 cyl 3.1 L Engine[Opt on STD] +184
6 cyl 3.4 L Engine[Std on Z34] +249
AM/FM Compact Disc Player +88
Air Conditioning[Opt on STD] +215
Anti-Lock Brakes[Opt on STD] +154
Automatic 4-Speed Transmission +215
Bose Sound System +101

Euro 3.4 Package +506
Power Drivers Seat +81

LUMINA MINIVAN 1992

An optional 165-horsepower, 3.8-liter V6 with a four-speed automatic is newly available. Wheels and tires are larger this year. Power mirrors and a four-way manual seat adjuster for the driver are new options.

Category P

	Trade-in	Private	Dealer
2 Dr STD Cargo Van	1812	2333	3200
2 Dr STD Pass. Van	1925	2478	3400
2 Dr CL Pass. Van	1982	2551	3500

OPTIONS FOR LUMINA MINIVAN

6 cyl 3.8 L Engine +166
7 Passenger Seating +148
AM/FM Compact Disc Player +107
Air Conditioning[Std on CL] +215
Automatic 4-Speed Transmission +215
Camper/Towing Package +86
Dual Air Conditioning +121
Power Door Locks +81

S10 BLAZER 1992

Four-wheel ABS is standard on all models. Electronic-shift transfer case is added to options list of 4WD models. A high-performance 4.3-liter V6 debuts with 40 additional horsepower, bringing total output to 200 ponies. Bucket seats are redesigned, a new speedometer is installed, and a four-spoke steering wheel is added.

Category M

	Trade-in	Private	Dealer
2 Dr STD 4WD Utility	2278	2886	3900
2 Dr STD Utility	2044	2590	3500
4 Dr STD Wgn	2097	2657	3590
2 Dr Tahoe 4WD Utility	2336	2960	4000
2 Dr Tahoe Utility	2090	2648	3578
4 Dr Tahoe 4WD Wgn	2394	3034	4100
4 Dr Tahoe Wgn	2121	2688	3632

OPTIONS FOR S10 BLAZER

6 cyl 4.3 L CPI Engine +94
AM/FM Compact Disc Player +94
Air Conditioning +215
Automatic 4-Speed Transmission +215
LT Package +731
Leather Seats +161
Premium Sound System +94

S10 PICKUP 1992

Base EL model can be equipped with four-wheel drive. Baja package dropped. Front bucket seats are redesigned, integral head restraints are added, and Extended Cabs can be equipped with leather seats. New speedometer and four-spoke steering wheel are

Model Description	Trade-in TMV	Private TMV	Dealer TMV

installed. Premium sound system with CD player is added to options list. Four-wheel-drive models can be equipped with an electronic-shift transfer case.

Category J

Model Description	Trade-in TMV	Private TMV	Dealer TMV
2 Dr STD 4WD Std Cab LB	1901	2408	3254
2 Dr STD Std Cab LB	1636	2072	2800
2 Dr STD 4WD Ext Cab SB	2103	2665	3600
2 Dr STD 4WD Std Cab SB	1928	2443	3300
2 Dr STD Ext Cab SB	1778	2252	3043
2 Dr STD Std Cab SB	1636	2072	2800
2 Dr EL 4WD Std Cab SB	1845	2337	3157
2 Dr EL Std Cab SB	1577	1998	2700
2 Dr Tahoe 4WD Std Cab LB	2045	2591	3500
2 Dr Tahoe Std Cab LB	1694	2146	2900
2 Dr Tahoe 4WD Ext Cab SB	2220	2813	3800
2 Dr Tahoe 4WD Std Cab SB	2045	2591	3500
2 Dr Tahoe Ext Cab SB	1851	2345	3168
2 Dr Tahoe Std Cab SB	1753	2220	3000

Model Description	Trade-in TMV	Private TMV	Dealer TMV	Model Description	Trade-in TMV	Private TMV	Dealer TMV

CHRYSLER 01

CHRYSLER   USA

1995 Chrysler Sebring

2001 CHRYSLER

300M   2001

DaimlerChrysler ups the feature content for the 300M by including standard steering wheel controls for the stereo, offering the option of side airbags and adding a luxury group package that includes real wood trim and an overhead console-mounted vehicle information center. The rear end gets a makeover in the form of clear-lens taillamps and chrome dual exhaust outlets while new 17-inch wheels and anodized aluminum window trim dresses up the 300M's profile. There's now a three-point shoulder/lap belt for the central rear seat passenger and an internal emergency trunk release. Additional luxury package features include an auto dimming rearview mirror and exterior mirrors that tilt down automatically when the vehicle is placed in reverse. Two new exterior colors, Black and Deep Sapphire Blue, plus three new interior colors, Sandstone, Dark Slate Grey and Taupe, round out the changes for 2001.
Category H

4 Dr STD Sdn	20429	21656	23700

OPTIONS FOR 300M
Chrome Wheels +453
Infinity Sound System +311
Power Moonroof +541
Side Air Bag Restraints +236
Sport Package +338

CONCORDE   2001

Supplemental side airbags are a new option for the year, and an internal trunk release and center shoulder belt for the rear seat are standard. A center console

power outlet exists for those models equipped with bucket seats, and all models get steering wheel-mounted audio controls. Two new exterior colors and three new interior colors are available this year, and both engines now meet LEV standards for all 50 states.
Category G

4 Dr LX Sdn	14569	15518	17100
4 Dr LXi Sdn	17040	18150	20000

OPTIONS FOR CONCORDE
AM/FM Stereo/CD/Tape[Opt on LX] +136
Aluminum/Alloy Wheels[Opt on LX] +221
Anti-Lock Brakes[Opt on LX] +362
Chrome Wheels +362
Dual Power Seats[Opt on LX] +230
Leather Seats[Opt on LX] +453
Power Sunroof +541
Premium Sound System[Opt on LX] +347
Side Air Bag Restraints +236
Special Factory Paint +121

LHS   2001

An optional luxury package includes automatic adjusting side mirrors, electrochromic driver's side mirror, walnut wood trim and an overhead console-mounted vehicle information display. There's an additional electrical power outlet in the center console, an overhead console with a driver information display, standard steering wheel-mounted stereo controls, and three new interior colors. The LHS' 17-inch wheels now come in a Sparkle Silver finish while aluminum replaces the chrome window molding trim and two new exterior colors, Black and Deep Sapphire Blue Pearl Coat, further dress up this upscale sedan. For safety's sake, an internal trunk release and a center shoulder belt for the rear seat comes standard while side airbags are now optional for front passengers.
Category H

4 Dr STD Sdn	18878	20011	21900

OPTIONS FOR LHS
Infinity Sound System +311
Power Sunroof +541
Side Air Bag Restraints +236

PROWLER   2001

In January, the Plymouth brand was dropped from the Prowler name, and it became a Chrysler. To mark the change, a new "Mulholland Edition" was introduced in a dark blue with white pinstriping. Also new this year, Chrysler is offering two new paint schemes for its over-the-top Prowler. A two-tone version (the top of the car will be black and the sides will be silver), called the "Black Tie Edition," will make a grand entry this year. It also includes a silver instrument cluster bezel and silver floormats. And, later in 2001, a new color, Prowler

Don't forget to refer to the Mileage Adjustment Table at the back of this book!

CHRYSLER 01

Model Description	Trade-in TMV	Private TMV	Dealer TMV	Model Description	Trade-in TMV	Private TMV	Dealer TMV

Orange, will also be available. Silver will still be offered, but red, yellow, black and purple are discontinued.

Category F

2 Dr STD Conv	37968	39480	42000

OPTIONS FOR PROWLER
Special Factory Paint +1208

PT CRUISER   2001

Classic styling and modern utility were the guiding forces behind Chrysler's all-new PT Cruiser. Based loosely on the Neon platform, this small van offers a flexible interior, head-turning looks and, sadly, only 150 horsepower. But feature content is high and a more powerful engine is reportedly in the works for 2002.

Category L

4 Dr Limited Edition Wgn

	15084	16122	17851
4 Dr STD Wgn	11704	12509	13851

OPTIONS FOR PT CRUISER
AM/FM Stereo/CD/Tape +136
Alarm System[Opt on STD] +136
Anti-Lock Brakes +359
Automatic 4-Speed Transmission +498
Chrome Wheels[Opt on STD] +242
Cruise Control[Opt on STD] +142
Power Door Locks[Opt on STD] +136
Power Moonroof[Opt on STD] +362
Privacy Glass[Opt on STD] +166
Side Air Bag Restraints[Opt on STD] +211
Special Factory Paint +121

SEBRING   2001

The Sebring sedan debuts for 2001 along with redesigned versions of the coupe and convertible. A new, more powerful V6 joins the enlarged 4 cylinder, with a manual 5 speed available in the coupe. The Autostick manu-matic is still an option for those who can't decide where they stand on the shift issue, but only on upscale LXi models with the V6. An Infinity premium sound system with an in-dash CD changer is also new this year.

Category D

2 Dr LX Conv	14613	15695	17500
4 Dr LX Sdn	11273	12108	13500

Category E

2 Dr LX Cpe	12506	13366	14800

Category D

2 Dr LXi Conv	16700	17938	20000
4 Dr LXi Sdn	12837	13789	15374

Category E

2 Dr LXi Cpe	13204	14112	15626

Category D

2 Dr Limited Conv	18120	19462	21700

OPTIONS FOR SEBRING
6 cyl 2.7 L Engine[Opt on LX Sdn] +483
6 cyl 3.0 L Engine[Opt on LX Cpe] +574
AM/FM Stereo/CD/Tape[Std on LXi Cpe] +151
Alarm System[Std on LXi] +184
Aluminum/Alloy Wheels[Opt on LX] +196
Anti-Lock Brakes[Std on Limited] +341
Automatic 4-Speed Transmission[Opt on LXi Cpe] +498
Chrome Wheels[Opt on LXi Sdn] +332
Compact Disc Changer +227
Infinity Sound System[Opt on LX Conv] +287
Leather Seats[Opt on LXi Cpe] +514
Power Drivers Seat[Std on Conv,LXi Sdn] +124
Power Sunroof +414
Side Air Bag Restraints +236
Special Factory Paint +121

TOWN AND COUNTRY   2001

Chrysler's top-of-the-line minivans are all new for the 2001 model year, with new gewgaws such as a power liftgate and a removable center console with three power outlets.

Category P

4 Dr EX Pass. Van Ext	17000	18125	20000
4 Dr LX AWD Pass. Van Ext			
	20315	21659	23900
4 Dr LX Pass. Van Ext	15725	16766	18500
4 Dr LXi AWD Pass. Van Ext			
	21250	22656	25000
4 Dr LXi Pass. Van Ext			
	18700	19938	22000
4 Dr Limited AWD Pass. Van Ext			
	24225	25828	28500
4 Dr Limited Pass. Van Ext			
	22440	23925	26400

OPTIONS FOR TOWN AND COUNTRY
6 cyl 3.8 L Engine[Opt on LXi FWD] +278
AM/FM Stereo/CD/Tape[Opt on LX,LXi] +238
Alarm System[Opt on LX] +118
Aluminum/Alloy Wheels +251
Automatic Load Leveling[Std on Limited,4WD] +175
Dual Air Conditioning[Opt on LX,LXi] +272
Dual Power Seats[Opt on LXi] +278
Heated Front Seats[Opt on LXi] +151
Infinity Sound System[Opt on LX] +299
Leather Seats[Opt on LXi] +538
Luggage Rack[Opt on LX,LXi] +151
Power Drivers Seat[Opt on LX FWD] +224
Power Sliding Door[Opt on LX FWD] +233
Rear Air Conditioning w/Rear Heater[Opt on LX FWD] +332
Side Air Bag Restraints +236
Special Factory Paint +121

VOYAGER   2001

Chrysler's low-end minivan receives an available 3.3-liter V6 engine that's been massaged to put forth more

---

Don't forget to refer to the Mileage Adjustment Table at the back of this book!

Model Description	Trade-in TMV	Private TMV	Dealer TMV

power, an improved suspension and drivetrain to increase ride comfort and reduce vibrations, upgraded brakes, standard dual sliding doors, and available side airbags, all under new, sleek sheet metal.

Category P

Model Description	Trade-in TMV	Private TMV	Dealer TMV
4 Dr LX Pass. Van	14365	15316	16900
4 Dr STD Pass. Van	11900	12688	14000

OPTIONS FOR VOYAGER

6 cyl 3.3 L Engine[Opt on STD] +586
AM/FM Stereo/CD/Tape +136
Alarm System +118
Anti-Lock Brakes[Opt on STD] +341
Automatic 4-Speed Transmission[Opt on STD] +121
Automatic Load Leveling +175
Child Seats (2) +136
Compact Disc Changer +420
Dual Air Conditioning +363
Infinity Sound System +299
Luggage Rack +151
Power Door Locks[Opt on STD] +136
Power Drivers Seat +224
Power Sliding Door +233
Power Windows[Opt on STD] +159
Side Air Bag Restraints +236

2000 CHRYSLER

300M   2000

There are five new colors, interior upgrades such as rear-seat cupholders and color-keyed switches, and a four-disc in-dash CD player. The rear suspension has been improved for less noise, vibration and harshness. The 2000 has the brake-shift interlock safety feature, which won't allow the driver to shift out of "park" unless his foot is on the brake.

Category H

Model Description	Trade-in TMV	Private TMV	Dealer TMV
4 Dr STD Sdn	18003	19666	21200

OPTIONS FOR 300M

Chrome Wheels +423
Compact Disc Changer +311
Metallic Paint +121
Power Moonroof +480

CIRRUS   2000

With a redesigned Cirrus modeled after the exceptionally attractive Concorde due in showrooms for 2001, the 2000 model is essentially a carryover model. Child-seat tethers have been added behind the back seat, four new colors debut, and an entry level LX arrives.

Category C

Model Description	Trade-in TMV	Private TMV	Dealer TMV
4 Dr LX Sdn	8772	9827	10800
4 Dr LXi Sdn	9747	10918	12000

OPTIONS FOR CIRRUS

AM/FM Compact Disc Player +205

Aluminum/Alloy Wheels[Opt on LX] +178
Anti-Lock Brakes[Opt on LX] +341
Automatic 4-Speed Transmission[Opt on LX] +635
Chrome Wheels +212
Compact Disc Changer +230
Power Drivers Seat[Opt on LX] +196
Power Moonroof +127
Power Windows[Opt on LX] +151

CONCORDE   2000

All models are given a more refined touring suspension, and variable-assist, speed-proportional steering is standard on LXi. Five new colors come aboard, and the instrument panel has been freshened.

Category G

Model Description	Trade-in TMV	Private TMV	Dealer TMV
4 Dr LX Sdn	11407	12547	13600
4 Dr LXi Sdn	13084	14392	15600

OPTIONS FOR CONCORDE

AM/FM Stereo/CD/Tape[Opt on LX] +224
Aluminum/Alloy Wheels[Opt on LX] +221
Anti-Lock Brakes[Opt on LX] +363
Chrome Wheels +363
Compact Disc Changer +212
Dual Power Seats[Opt on LX] +230
Infinity Sound System +224
Leather Seats[Opt on LX] +601
Metallic Paint +121
Power Moonroof +480

LHS   2000

Nothing dramatically changes for 2000. There are interior upgrades, including a four-disc in-dash CD changer, and a modified rear suspension for less noise, vibration and harshness. An automatic transaxle brake-shift interlock is now standard, and there are four more color choices.

Category H

Model Description	Trade-in TMV	Private TMV	Dealer TMV
4 Dr STD Sdn	16220	17718	19100

OPTIONS FOR LHS

Chrome Wheels +423
Compact Disc Changer +311
Power Moonroof +480

SEBRING CONVERTIBLE   2000

This year's rear suspension has been re-tuned for improved ride quality and reduced noise. Four colors have been added.

Category D

Model Description	Trade-in TMV	Private TMV	Dealer TMV
2 Dr JX Conv	11956	13279	14500
2 Dr JXi Conv	14100	15660	17100
2 Dr JXi Limited Conv	14759	16392	17900

OPTIONS FOR SEBRING CONVERTIBLE

AM/FM Stereo/CD/Tape[Std on JXi, JXi Limited] +97
Alarm System[Std on JXi, JXi Limited] +106
Aluminum/Alloy Wheels[Std on JXi, JXi Limited] +166

Don't forget to refer to the Mileage Adjustment Table at the back of this book!

CHRYSLER 00-99

Model Description	Trade-in TMV	Private TMV	Dealer TMV	Model Description	Trade-in TMV	Private TMV	Dealer TMV

Chrome Wheels[Opt on JXi] +212
Compact Disc Changer[Opt on JXi] +302
Traction Control System[Opt on JXi] +242

SEBRING COUPE   2000

For 2000, the standard-equipment list has increased. Also, Ice Silver is the newest color, and the LX trim fabric has been updated.

Category E

	Trade-in	Private	Dealer
2 Dr LX Cpe	10031	11159	12200
2 Dr LXi Cpe	11182	12439	13600

OPTIONS FOR SEBRING COUPE
AM/FM Stereo/CD/Tape[Std on LXi] +263
Alarm System[Std on LXi] +184
Aluminum/Alloy Wheels[Std on LXi] +121
Anti-Lock Brakes +363
Infinity Sound System +196
Power Drivers Seat[Std on LXi] +124
Power Sunroof +414

TOWN AND COUNTRY   2000

The model lineup changes this year, and telling the difference between the LX and LXi will be easier to the untrained eye, thanks to distinctive exterior and interior modifications. New colors for 2000 are Shale Green, Bright White, Patriot Blue, Bright Silver and Inferno Red.

Category P

	Trade-in	Private	Dealer
4 Dr LX AWD Pass. Van Ext	16345	18090	19700
4 Dr LX Pass. Van Ext	14520	16070	17500
4 Dr LXi AWD Pass. Van Ext	17756	19651	21400
4 Dr LXi Pass. Van Ext	15930	17631	19200
4 Dr Limited AWD Pass. Van Ext	19747	21855	23800
4 Dr Limited Pass. Van Ext	18088	20018	21800

OPTIONS FOR TOWN AND COUNTRY
6 cyl 3.8 L Engine[Opt on Lxi FWD] +278
AM/FM Stereo/CD/Tape[Opt on LX,LXi] +238
Aluminum/Alloy Wheels +251
Automatic Load Leveling[Std on Limited,4WD] +175
Camper/Towing Package +172
Compact Disc Changer +332
Dual Air Conditioning[Opt on LX,LXi] +272
Dual Power Seats[Opt on LXi] +278
Heated Front Seats[Opt on LXi] +151
Infinity Sound System[Opt on LX] +212
Leather Seats[Opt on LXi] +538
Luggage Rack[Opt on LX,LXi] +117
Special Factory Paint +121

VOYAGER   2000

With Plymouth's impending death, the Voyager turns into a Chrysler this year, but it is otherwise unchanged. Four new colors and a new Value-Plus option package that includes a V6 and power goodies for about $20,000 are new this year.

Category P

	Trade-in	Private	Dealer
2 Dr STD Pass. Van	9293	10285	11200
4 Dr Grand Pass. Van	10952	12121	13200
4 Dr Grand SE Pass. Van	11782	13039	14200
4 Dr SE Pass. Van	11367	12580	13700

OPTIONS FOR VOYAGER
6 cyl 3.0 L Engine[Opt on STD] +484
6 cyl 3.3 L Flex Fuel Engine[Opt on STD] +586
7 Passenger Seating[Opt on STD] +227
AM/FM Stereo/CD/Tape +181
Air Conditioning[Opt on STD] +520
Aluminum/Alloy Wheels +251
Anti-Lock Brakes[Opt on Grand,STD] +341
Automatic 4-Speed Transmission[Opt on STD] +121
Automatic Load Leveling +175
Camper/Towing Package +263
Captain Chairs (4) +420
Child Seats (2) +136
Dual Air Conditioning +363
Infinity Sound System +253
Luggage Rack +130
Power Door Locks[Std on Grand SE,SE] +136
Power Drivers Seat[Opt on Grand SE,SE] +145
Power Windows[Std on Grand SE,SE] +159
Sliding Driver Side Door[Opt on STD] +359
Sunscreen Glass +181

1999 CHRYSLER

300M   1999

This all-new car from Chrysler will try to win some international recognition for the marque.

Category H

	Trade-in	Private	Dealer
4 Dr STD Sdn	15547	17223	18900

OPTIONS FOR 300M
Chrome Wheels +357
Metallic Paint +101
Power Moonroof +405

CIRRUS   1999

A slightly revised suspension gives the Cirrus a softer ride, and the interior improvements include a new instrument cluster and lower NVH levels. Outside, 15-inch chrome wheel covers are standard, and a winged Chrysler badge now decorates the front grille.

Category C

	Trade-in	Private	Dealer
4 Dr LXi Sdn	8028	9014	10000

OPTIONS FOR CIRRUS

Model Description	Trade-in TMV	Private TMV	Dealer TMV

Aluminum/Alloy Wheels +150
Compact Disc Changer +280
Gold Package +254
Leather Seats +509
Power Drivers Seat +165
Power Moonroof +296

CONCORDE 1999

Bigger sway bar links and tubular rear trailing arms will be phased in during the model year, two changes that Chrysler promises will provide more road isolation for a more luxurious ride. Premium carpeting is added to the interior, and the LXi leather is improved.

Category G

Model Description	Trade-in TMV	Private TMV	Dealer TMV
4 Dr LX Sdn	9944	10972	12000
4 Dr LXi Sdn	11435	12618	13800

OPTIONS FOR CONCORDE
AM/FM Compact Disc Player[Opt on LX] +153
AM/FM Stereo/CD/Tape[Opt on LXi] +188
Aluminum/Alloy Wheels[Opt on LX] +186
Anti-Lock Brakes[Opt on LX] +306
Dual Power Seats[Opt on LX] +194
Infinity Sound System +188
Leather Seats[Opt on LX] +507
Metallic Paint +101
Power Moonroof +405

LHS 1999

What a difference two years can make. The luxury-tuned LHS has been completely redesigned for 1999. In fact, it's such a new car, we're kinda' disappointed that they kept the name.

Category H

Model Description	Trade-in TMV	Private TMV	Dealer TMV
4 Dr STD Sdn	14971	16585	18200

OPTIONS FOR LHS
Chrome Wheels +357
Power Moonroof +405

SEBRING 1999

Body-colored mirrors lend the Sebring LXi a more elegant style.

Category E

Model Description	Trade-in TMV	Private TMV	Dealer TMV
2 Dr LX Cpe	8855	9928	11000
2 Dr LXi Cpe	10707	12003	13300

OPTIONS FOR SEBRING
6 cyl 2.5 L Engine[Opt on LX] +389
AM/FM Stereo/CD/Tape[Opt on Conv,LX] +354
Anti-Lock Brakes[Opt on Cpe] +288
Automatic 4-Speed Transmission[Opt on LX] +354
Cruise Control[Opt on LX] +97
Leather Seats[Opt on Lxi] +383
Power Door Locks[Opt on LX] +100
Power Drivers Seat[Opt on Cpe] +104
Power Sunroof +326
Power Windows[Opt on LX] +122

SEBRING CONVERTIBLE 1999

Chrysler's "winged" badge makes its way across the model line, hitting the Sebring square on the nose.

Category D

Model Description	Trade-in TMV	Private TMV	Dealer TMV
2 Dr JX Conv	10693	11996	13300
2 Dr JXi Conv	12301	13800	15300

OPTIONS FOR SEBRING CONVERTIBLE
Aluminum/Alloy Wheels[Opt on JX,LX] +140
Chrome Wheels +178
Compact Disc Changer[Opt on Conv] +254
Traction Control System +204

TOWN AND COUNTRY 1999

The top-of-the-line trim level is now called "Limited," and it offers more standard equipment (hence less options) than any other Chrysler minivan. Leather upgrades, steering wheel mounted stereo controls, and a center armrest in the rear bench are new this year, and the exterior features such details as 16-inch 15-spoke chrome wheels and chrome door handles.

Category P

Model Description	Trade-in TMV	Private TMV	Dealer TMV
4 Dr LX AWD Pass. Van Ext	14690	16257	17825
4 Dr LX Pass. Van Ext	13927	15413	16899
4 Dr LXi AWD Pass. Van Ext	17504	19372	21240
4 Dr LXi Pass. Van Ext	14813	16394	17975
4 Dr Limited AWD Pass. Van Ext	17933	19846	21760
4 Dr Limited Pass. Van Ext	17059	18880	20700
4 Dr SX Pass. Van	13598	15049	16500

OPTIONS FOR TOWN AND COUNTRY
6 cyl 3.8 L Engine[Opt on SX,LX FWD] +234
AM/FM Stereo/CD/Tape[Opt on LX,SX] +201
Aluminum/Alloy Wheels[Opt on LX] +212
Automatic Load Leveling[Std on Limited,4WD] +148
Camper/Towing Package +145
Compact Disc Changer +280
Dual Air Conditioning[Opt on LX] +230
Heated Front Seats[Opt on LXi] +127
Leather Seats[Opt on LX,SX] +453
Sunscreen Glass[Opt on LX,SX] +192

1998 CHRYSLER

CIRRUS 1998

There's just one model to choose from this year, as Chrysler says "goodbye" to the base LX, and "hello" to a higher price. That means that leather seats, a powered driver's seat, a 2.5-liter V6 engine, a tilt wheel, and power windows, locks, and mirrors are now

CHRYSLER 98-97

Model Description	Trade-in TMV	Private TMV	Dealer TMV	Model Description	Trade-in TMV	Private TMV	Dealer TMV

standard equipment. The LXi also comes in five new colors and as with all other Chrysler products, depowered airbags are standard.

Category C

4 Dr LXi Sdn	6928	7826	8800

OPTIONS FOR CIRRUS
Chrome Wheels +156
Compact Disc Changer +244
Gold Package +111
Leather Seats +444
Power Drivers Seat +144
Power Moonroof +257

CONCORDE   1998

The Concorde is all-new for 1998. The only thing they didn't change is the name.

Category G

4 Dr LX Sdn	8569	9544	10600
4 Dr LXi Sdn	9781	10894	12100

OPTIONS FOR CONCORDE
AM/FM Stereo/CD/Tape +133
Aluminum/Alloy Wheels[Opt on LX] +162
Anti-Lock Brakes[Opt on LX] +266
Dual Power Seats[Opt on LX] +169
Leather Seats +442
Power Moonroof +353

SEBRING   1998

Evolutionary, mostly aesthetic changes enhance the Sebrings this year. The Sebring Coupe LX and LXi now offer a black and gray interior, and the exterior color of the day is "Caffe Latte" (not to be confused with Macchiato or Cappuccino).

Category D

2 Dr JX Conv	8597	9703	10900
2 Dr JXi Conv	10254	11572	13000

Category E

2 Dr LX Cpe	7184	8104	9100
2 Dr LXi Cpe	8842	9974	11200

OPTIONS FOR SEBRING
AM/FM Compact Disc Player +197
AM/FM Stereo/CD/Tape[Std on Lxi] +151
Aluminum/Alloy Wheels[Opt on JX,LX] +217
Anti-Lock Brakes[Opt on JX,LX] +250
Automatic 4-Speed Transmission[Opt on LX] +309
Compact Disc Changer +222
Leather Seats[Opt on Lxi] +333
Power Sunroof +284
Power Windows[Opt on LX] +107

TOWN AND COUNTRY   1998

Chrysler's luxury minivans get a few improvements this year, with the addition of a new Chrysler-signature grille, more powerful 3.8-liter V6, high-performance

headlights, and three fancy new colors.

Category P

4 Dr LX AWD Pass. Van Ext	11965	13326	14800
4 Dr LX Pass. Van Ext	10995	12245	13600
4 Dr LXi AWD Pass. Van Ext	13663	15217	16900
4 Dr LXi Pass. Van Ext	12612	14046	15600
4 Dr SX Pass. Van	10267	11435	12700

OPTIONS FOR TOWN AND COUNTRY
6 cyl 3.8 L Engine[Std on Lxi,4WD] +204
AM/FM Stereo/CD/Tape[Std on Lxi] +175
Automatic Load Leveling[Std on Lxi,4WD] +129
Camper/Towing Package +120
Compact Disc Changer +244
Dual Air Conditioning[Opt on LX] +200
Heated Front Seats +111
Leather Seats[Std on Lxi] +394
Power Drivers Seat +111
Special Wheels +208
Sunscreen Glass[Std on Lxi] +167

1997 CHRYSLER

CIRRUS   1997

New wheels for everyone; the LXi trim level gets chrome wheels and the LX gets optional aluminum wheels. The Gold Package is also available on the LX, for any driver who wants to be mistaken for Slick Jimmy, your friendly, neighborhood pimp. On a more positive note, an in-dash CD changer is now available on LX and LXi models, as is a trip computer.

Category C

4 Dr LX Sdn	5133	6018	7100
4 Dr LXi Sdn	5494	6442	7600

OPTIONS FOR CIRRUS
6 cyl 2.5 L Engine +298
AM/FM Compact Disc Player +112
Aluminum/Alloy Wheels +119
Compact Disc Changer +205
Gold Package +186
Power Drivers Seat[Opt on LX] +121

CONCORDE   1997

The 3.5-liter engine is now standard on the LX trim level. An upgraded stereo debuts along with hood-mounted windshield-washer nozzles. The automatic transmission receives refinements.

Category G

4 Dr LX Sdn	6082	6945	8000
4 Dr LXi Sdn	6842	7813	9000

OPTIONS FOR CONCORDE

Don't forget to refer to the Mileage Adjustment Table at the back of this book!

Model Description	Trade-in TMV	Private TMV	Dealer TMV

AM/FM Stereo/CD/Tape +223
Aluminum/Alloy Wheels[Std on Lxi] +136
Anti-Lock Brakes[Std on Lxi] +223
Dual Power Seats +142
Leather Seats[Opt on LX] +370
Power Moonroof +268

LHS 1997

What's new for 1997? Deep Amethyst Pearl Paint. Oh yeah, the automatic transmission receives some fine-tuning.
Category H

	Trade-in	Private	Dealer
4 Dr STD Sdn	7812	8886	10200

OPTIONS FOR LHS
AM/FM Stereo/CD/Tape +112
Power Moonroof +296

SEBRING 1997

After just one year in production, the Sebring Convertible receives a rash of changes. The most significant are a quieter intake manifold for the 2.4-liter engine and the availability of Chrysler's AutoStick transmission. Other changes include the addition of new colors, auto-dimming mirror, trip computer, enhanced vehicle theft system, and damage resistant power antenna to the options list.
Category D

	Trade-in	Private	Dealer
2 Dr JX Conv	7428	8541	9900
2 Dr JXi Conv	8929	10266	11900
Category E			
2 Dr LX Cpe	5303	6157	7200
2 Dr LXi Cpe	7734	8979	10500

OPTIONS FOR SEBRING
AM/FM Compact Disc Player +165
AM/FM Stereo/CD/Tape +127
Aluminum/Alloy Wheels[Opt on JX,LX] +183
Anti-Lock Brakes[Opt on JX,LX] +210
Automatic 4-Speed Transmission[Opt on LX] +258
Compact Disc Changer +186
Leather Seats[Opt on Lxi] +279
Power Sunroof +239

TOWN AND COUNTRY 1997

Chrysler's luxury minivans get a few improvements this year, as AWD extended length models are added to the lineup. Also new this year is a sporty SX model, which replaces last year's LX as the regular length Town and Country. Families with kids will love the standard left side sliding door on this vehicle.
Category P

	Trade-in	Private	Dealer
4 Dr LX AWD Pass. Van Ext			
	9050	10197	11600
4 Dr LX Pass. Van Ext	8426	9494	10800
4 Dr LXi AWD Pass. Van Ext			
	10532	11868	13500
4 Dr LXi Pass. Van Ext			
	10142	11428	13000
4 Dr SX Pass. Van	8348	9406	10700

OPTIONS FOR TOWN AND COUNTRY
6 cyl 3.8 L Engine[Std on Lxi,LX 4WD] +171
AM/FM Stereo/CD/Tape[Std on Lxi] +148
Automatic Load Leveling[Std on Lxi,LX 4WD] +108
Dual Air Conditioning[Std on Lxi] +167
Leather Seats[Std on Lxi] +331
Sunscreen Glass +140

1996 CHRYSLER

CIRRUS 1996

Base LX model gets a four-cylinder engine in a cost-cutting move. Uplevel LXi gets revised torque converter for better V6 response. A power sunroof, chrome-plated aluminum wheels, and new colors are available for 1996.
Category C

	Trade-in	Private	Dealer
4 Dr LX Sdn	4104	4942	6100
4 Dr LXi Sdn	4440	5347	6600

OPTIONS FOR CIRRUS
6 cyl 2.5 L Engine[Opt on LX] +272
Chrome Wheels +119
Compact Disc Changer +187
Power Drivers Seat[Opt on LX] +110
Power Sunroof +197

CONCORDE 1996

Improved headlight illumination, a revised exterior appearance, a quieter interior and new colors bow on all Concorde models. Base cars get standard 16-inch wheels. LXi models get gold accented wheels and trim.
Category G

	Trade-in	Private	Dealer
4 Dr LX Sdn	4277	5001	6000
4 Dr LXi Sdn	5133	6001	7200

OPTIONS FOR CONCORDE
6 cyl 3.5 L Engine +246
AM/FM Stereo/CD/Tape +204
Aluminum/Alloy Wheels +124
Dual Power Seats +129
Leather Seats[Opt on LX] +338
Power Moonroof +245

LHS 1996

A quieter interior and new colors entice buyers for 1996. Revised sound systems and a HomeLink Universal transmitter that opens your garage door for you when you pull in the driveway debut.
Category H

	Trade-in	Private	Dealer
4 Dr STD Sdn	6373	7435	8900

OPTIONS FOR LHS

Model Description	Trade-in TMV	Private TMV	Dealer TMV	Model Description	Trade-in TMV	Private TMV	Dealer TMV
AM/FM Compact Disc Player +102					7799	9017	10700
AM/FM Stereo/CD/Tape +102							
Infinity Sound System +102							
Power Moonroof +270							

NEW YORKER — 1996

Gets same changes as LHS, plus added standard equipment over last year's New Yorker. After a short 1996 production run, the New Yorker is axed from the lineup in favor of the more popular LHS.

Category H

4 Dr STD Sdn	5800	6766	8100

OPTIONS FOR NEW YORKER
Compact Disc Changer +204
Leather Seats +367
Power Moonroof +270
Power Passenger Seat +129

SEBRING — 1996

Remote keyless entry system gets a panic feature, and a HomeLink Universal Transmitter debuts on this suave sport coupe. Three new paint colors are also available. Chrysler dumps its final K-Car variant this year in favor of the fine looking Sebring Convertible. Based on the Cirrus platform and drivetrains, this drop top shares only the name of the Sebring coupe.

Category D

2 Dr JX Conv	4993	5878	7100
2 Dr JXi Conv	6962	8196	9900

Category E

2 Dr LX Cpe	3984	4704	5700
2 Dr LXi Cpe	5381	6355	7700

OPTIONS FOR SEBRING
6 cyl 2.5 L Engine[Opt on JX,LX] +259
AM/FM Stereo/CD/Tape +236
Anti-Lock Brakes[Opt on JX] +191
Automatic 4-Speed Transmission[Opt on LX] +236
Cast Alloy Wheels +161
Compact Disc Changer +170
Leather Seats[Opt on Lxi] +255
Power Sunroof +218

TOWN AND COUNTRY — 1996

Totally redesigned for 1996, the TandC raises the bar for luxury minivans. In a departure from last year, the TandC is offered in a short wheelbase version, and is available in two trim levels: LX and LXi. New innovations include a driver's side passenger door, dual-zone temperature controls, and a one-hand latch system on the integrated child safety seats.

Category P

2 Dr STD Pass. Van Ext			
	6560	7585	9000
2 Dr LX Pass. Van	6414	7416	8800
4 Dr LXi Pass. Van Ext			

OPTIONS FOR TOWN AND COUNTRY
6 cyl 3.8 L Engine[Std on Lxi] +156
AM/FM Stereo/CD/Tape[Std on Lxi] +135
Aluminum/Alloy Wheels +139
Captain Chairs (4)[Std on Lxi] +212
Dual Air Conditioning[Opt on STD] +152
Infinity Sound System +135
Leather Seats[Std on Lxi] +303
Sliding Driver Side Door[Std on Lxi] +137
Sunscreen Glass[Std on Lxi] +127

1995 CHRYSLER

CIRRUS — 1995

The Cirrus is replacing the LeBaron sedan. A cab-forward design, a 164-horsepower V6 coupled with an automatic transmission, dual airbags, antilock brakes, air conditioning, power door locks, and power windows are just a few of the improvements this car has over the LeBaron.

Category C

4 Dr LX Sdn	3241	3900	5000
4 Dr LXi Sdn	3629	4368	5600

OPTIONS FOR CIRRUS
4 cyl 2.4 L Engine +151
AM/FM Compact Disc Player +82
Power Drivers Seat[Opt on LX] +89

CONCORDE — 1995

No significant changes for the 1995 Concorde.

Category G

4 Dr STD Sdn	3464	4002	4900

OPTIONS FOR CONCORDE
6 cyl 3.5 L Engine +199
AM/FM Compact Disc Player +82
Aluminum/Alloy Wheels +100
Infinity Sound System +102
Leather Seats +274
Power Moonroof +198
Power Passenger Seat +78

LE BARON — 1995

The last of the K-cars, the LeBaron convertible rides into the sunset in GTC trim.

Category C

2 Dr GTC Conv	2722	3276	4200

OPTIONS FOR LE BARON
AM/FM Compact Disc Player +96
Anti-Lock Brakes +206
Leather Seats +206
Premium Sound System +138
Quick Order Package 2 +303

Don't forget to refer to the Mileage Adjustment Table at the back of this book!

LHS — 1995

No changes to the highly acclaimed LHS.

Category H

Model Description	Trade-in TMV	Private TMV	Dealer TMV
4 Dr STD Sdn	4768	5567	6900

OPTIONS FOR LHS
AM/FM Compact Disc Player +82
Power Moonroof +219

NEW YORKER — 1995

No changes to the highly acclaimed New Yorker.

Category H

	Trade-in	Private	Dealer
4 Dr STD Sdn	4146	4841	6000

OPTIONS FOR NEW YORKER
Infinity Sound System +179
Leather Seats +297
Power Moonroof +219
Power Passenger Seat +105

SEBRING — 1995

Chrysler's sporty replacement for the LeBaron coupe is the Sebring. Based on the Dodge Avenger, the Sebring offers more luxury than its corporate cousin. The Sebring is available as a four-cylinder LX or an upscale 2.5-liter V6 LXi; both come standard with an automatic transmission.

Category E

	Trade-in	Private	Dealer
2 Dr LX Cpe	3827	4529	5700
2 Dr LXi Cpe	4364	5165	6500

OPTIONS FOR SEBRING
6 cyl 2.5 L Engine[Opt on LX] +210
AM/FM Compact Disc Player +122
Aluminum/Alloy Wheels +135
Automatic 4-Speed Transmission[Opt on LX] +191
Leather Seats +206
Power Sunroof +176

TOWN AND COUNTRY — 1995

There are no changes for the 1995 Town and Country.

Category P

	Trade-in	Private	Dealer
2 Dr STD AWD Pass. Van	5443	6327	7800
2 Dr STD Pass. Van	4885	5678	7000

OPTIONS FOR TOWN AND COUNTRY
AM/FM Compact Disc Player +108

1994 CHRYSLER

CONCORDE — 1994

The base 3.3-liter engine is upped to 161 horsepower. A flexible-fuel version of the Concorde is available that will allow the car to run on alternative fuels such as methanol. Variable-assist power steering and a touring suspension are also added to the standard equipment list.

Category G

	Trade-in	Private	Dealer
4 Dr STD Sdn	2501	3026	3900

OPTIONS FOR CONCORDE
6 cyl 3.5 L Engine +144
Leather Seats +198
Power Moonroof +144

LE BARON — 1994

The two-door coupe is cancelled, leaving the convertible and sedan in place. The 100-horsepower four-cylinder engine is dropped, leaving the 141-horsepower V6 as the sole powerplant.

Category C

	Trade-in	Private	Dealer
2 Dr GTC Conv	1934	2447	3300
4 Dr LE Sdn	1641	2076	2800
4 Dr Landau Sdn	2227	2817	3800

OPTIONS FOR LE BARON
Air Conditioning[Opt on LE] +159
Anti-Lock Brakes +149
Automatic 4-Speed Transmission[Opt on LE] +159
Infinity Sound System +129
Leather Seats +149

LHS — 1994

The de-chromed LHS model is the sporty edition of the New Yorker.

Category H

	Trade-in	Private	Dealer
4 Dr STD Sdn	3749	4518	5800

OPTIONS FOR LHS
Power Moonroof +159

NEW YORKER — 1994

An all-new New Yorker replaces the stodgy car of yesteryear. Improved handling, styling and luxury mark a significant change in direction for the once-ailing Chrysler corporation.

Category H

	Trade-in	Private	Dealer
4 Dr STD Sdn	2650	3194	4100

OPTIONS FOR NEW YORKER
AM/FM Compact Disc Player +100
Leather Seats +215
Power Moonroof +159
Premium Sound System +100

TOWN AND COUNTRY — 1994

A passenger airbag joins the standard equipment list of the Chrysler Town and Country, once again pushing the envelope of the growing minivan segment. A larger engine is also available in the 1994 Town and Country.

Category P

	Trade-in	Private	Dealer
2 Dr STD AWD Pass. Van	4024	4803	6100

Don't forget to refer to the Mileage Adjustment Table at the back of this book!

Model Description	Trade-in TMV	Private TMV	Dealer TMV	Model Description	Trade-in TMV	Private TMV	Dealer TMV
2 Dr STD Pass. Van	3892	4645	5900	Category C			
				2 Dr STD Conv	1305	1790	2598
				2 Dr STD Cpe	955	1309	1900
				2 Dr GTC Conv	1484	2035	2953
				2 Dr GTC Cpe	1307	1793	2602
				4 Dr LE Sdn	982	1347	1955
				2 Dr LX Conv	1531	2099	3047
				2 Dr LX Cpe	1206	1654	2400
				4 Dr Landau Sdn	1356	1860	2700

OPTIONS FOR TOWN AND COUNTRY
AM/FM Compact Disc Player +79

OPTIONS FOR LE BARON
6 cyl 3.0 L Engine[Opt on LE,STD] +103
Air Conditioning[Opt on LE,STD] +127
Anti-Lock Brakes +119
Automatic 4-Speed Transmission[Std on Landau,LX] +127
Leather Seats[Std on LX Conv] +119

1993 CHRYSLER

CONCORDE   1993

Chrysler's new near-luxury sedan is designed to compete with cars like the Acura Vigor and the Lexus ES 300. Standard antilock brakes, dual airbags, an optional integrated child-seat, and optional traction control are some of the Concorde's available safety features. Cab-forward design and a long wheelbase insure good passenger space and a comfortable ride for all occupants. A 3.5-liter V6 engine that produces 214 horsepower is available instead of the standard 3.3-liter V6 that produces 153 horsepower.

Category G

	Trade-in	Private	Dealer
4 Dr STD Sdn	1962	2426	3200

OPTIONS FOR CONCORDE
6 cyl 3.5 L Engine +115
Leather Seats +158

FIFTH AVENUE   1993

A new stereo is available on the Fifth Avenue; buyers can now choose between a CD player or a cassette player for their listening pleasure. A tamper-resistant odometer is also added.

Category H

	Trade-in	Private	Dealer
4 Dr STD Sdn	1671	2132	2900

OPTIONS FOR FIFTH AVENUE
AM/FM Compact Disc Player +79
Anti-Lock Brakes +119
Infinity Sound System +103
Leather Seats +135
Premium Sound System +79

IMPERIAL   1993

A new stereo is available on the Imperial. Buyers can choose between a CD player or a cassette player. A tamper-resistant odometer is also added; this means that the miles displayed should be true.

Category H

	Trade-in	Private	Dealer
4 Dr STD Sdn	2132	2720	3700

OPTIONS FOR IMPERIAL
AM/FM Compact Disc Player +79
Dual Power Seats +98
Infinity Sound System +103
Leather Seats +127

LE BARON   1993

The turbocharged engine is dropped and a new grille is added.

NEW YORKER   1993

This is the last model year for the New Yorker in its current form. Interior changes include a six-way power seat and an upgraded stereo.

Category H

	Trade-in	Private	Dealer
4 Dr Salon Sdn	1729	2205	3000

OPTIONS FOR NEW YORKER
Anti-Lock Brakes +119
Infinity Sound System +103
Leather Seats +171
Premium Sound System +79

TOWN AND COUNTRY   1993

A stainless-steel exhaust system, new wheels and adjustable front shoulder belts are the main changes for the 1993 Town and Country.

Category P

	Trade-in	Private	Dealer
2 Dr STD AWD Pass. Van	2929	3593	4700
2 Dr STD Pass. Van	2555	3134	4100

OPTIONS FOR TOWN AND COUNTRY
Dual Air Conditioning[Opt on STD 2WD] +72
Leather Seats +141

1992 CHRYSLER

FIFTH AVENUE   1992

The Fifth Avenue gets revised front-end styling that includes a new hood, grille and headlights.

Category H

	Trade-in	Private	Dealer
4 Dr STD Sdn	1440	1913	2700

OPTIONS FOR FIFTH AVENUE
Anti-Lock Brakes +106
Infinity Sound System +91
Leather Seats +120
Power Sunroof +120

Don't forget to refer to the Mileage Adjustment Table at the back of this book!

Model Description	Trade-in TMV	Private TMV	Dealer TMV

IMPERIAL 1992

No changes for 1992.
Category H

Model Description	Trade-in TMV	Private TMV	Dealer TMV
4 Dr STD Sdn	1600	2125	3000

OPTIONS FOR IMPERIAL
Infinity Sound System +91
Leather Seats +113

LE BARON 1992

Antilock brakes become an available option on the 1992 LeBaron. A transmission interlock also joins the list of safety equipment. Designed to keep the car from being started while in gear, the interlock requires that the clutch be fully depressed before the car will start. This year there are three trim levels available for the LeBaron, including a Landau and base model that have a 100-horsepower four-cylinder engine.
Category C

Model Description	Trade-in TMV	Private TMV	Dealer TMV
2 Dr STD Conv	1033	1497	2272
2 Dr STD Cpe	773	1120	1700
2 Dr STD Turbo Conv	1036	1503	2280
2 Dr STD Turbo Cpe	848	1230	1867
4 Dr STD Sdn	818	1186	1800
2 Dr GTC Conv	1120	1625	2465
2 Dr GTC Cpe	1017	1474	2237
2 Dr GTC Turbo Conv	1096	1589	2411
2 Dr GTC Turbo Cpe	1001	1451	2202
2 Dr LX Conv	1152	1671	2535
2 Dr LX Cpe	999	1449	2198
4 Dr LX Sdn	878	1274	1933
4 Dr Landau Sdn	909	1318	2000

OPTIONS FOR LE BARON
6 cyl 3.0 L Engine[Opt on Landau,STD] +91
Air Conditioning[Opt on STD,LX Sdn] +113
Anti-Lock Brakes +106
Automatic 4-Speed Transmission[Std on LX] +113
Leather Seats[Std on LX Conv] +106

NEW YORKER 1992

Revised styling results in rounded front and rear corners on Chrysler's midsized luxury cars. The landau top is reintroduced and an electromagnetic mirror is added to the options list.
Category H

Model Description	Trade-in TMV	Private TMV	Dealer TMV
4 Dr Salon Sdn	1494	1983	2800

OPTIONS FOR NEW YORKER
Anti-Lock Brakes +106
Dual Power Seats +87
Infinity Sound System +91
Leather Seats +152
Power Sunroof +120

TOWN AND COUNTRY 1992

The Town and Country can finally be ordered without the awful wood paneling that has "graced" previous year's models.
Category P

Model Description	Trade-in TMV	Private TMV	Dealer TMV
2 Dr STD AWD Pass. Van	2217	2811	3800
2 Dr STD Pass. Van	1751	2219	3000

OPTIONS FOR TOWN AND COUNTRY
Leather Seats +126

Model Description	Trade-in TMV	Private TMV	Dealer TMV	Model Description	Trade-in TMV	Private TMV	Dealer TMV
				4 Dr CDX Sdn	11199	12249	13999
				4 Dr SE Sdn	8472	9266	10590
				4 Dr SX Sdn	10152	11104	12690

DAEWOO   S. Korea

1999 Daewoo Leganza

OPTIONS FOR LEGANZA
AM/FM Stereo/CD/Tape[Opt on SE] +123
Alarm System[Opt on SE] +123
Aluminum/Alloy Wheels[Std on CDX] +308
Automatic 4-Speed Transmission[Opt on SE] +493
Compact Disc Changer +277
Power Moonroof[Opt on SX] +400

NUBIRA   2001

You can now pick up a Daewoo Nubira with Diamond Blue Metallic paint. The sedan gets a new 14-inch standard wheel cover and the wagon has a fresh rear tail lamp design.

Category B

	Trade-in	Private	Dealer
4 Dr CDX Sdn	8381	9182	10516
4 Dr CDX Wgn	8957	9812	11238
4 Dr SE Sdn	7085	7761	8889

OPTIONS FOR NUBIRA
Air Conditioning[Opt on SE] +524
Automatic 4-Speed Transmission +493
Leather Seats +400
Power Door Locks[Opt on SE] +123
Power Moonroof +308

2001 DAEWOO

LANOS   2001

Daewoo adds the new Sport Hatchback model to the Lanos lineup for 2001, but discontinues the SE Hatchback and SX Sedan. Pacific Blue Mica and Red Rock Mica are added to the palette for the sedan and hatchback, while Super Red and Granada Black Mica are available exclusively on the Sport. The new premium package available on the S models includes power windows, power door locks, power passenger rearview mirror, tilt steering wheel, AM/FM/cassette/CD stereo, digital clock and variable intermittent wipers.

Category A

	Trade-in	Private	Dealer
2 Dr S Hbk	5374	5875	6709
4 Dr S Sdn	6144	6717	7671
2 Dr Sport Hbk	7812	8540	9753

OPTIONS FOR LANOS
Air Conditioning[Std on Sport] +462
Aluminum/Alloy Wheels[Std on Sport] +246
Automatic 4-Speed Transmission +493
Power Door Locks[Std on Sport] +123

LEGANZA   2001

Scarlet Mica and Harbor Mist Mica are the new exterior colors. Outside rearview mirrors get a blue tint and a new audio head unit is added for improved sound quality. A new option package for the SE includes front and rear power windows, power door locks, AM/FM/cassette/CD stereo with six speakers, dual body-color heated power rearview mirrors, anti-theft alarm with remote keyless entry, tilt steering wheel and front foglamps.

Category C

2000 DAEWOO

LANOS   2000

The three-door SX disappears, as does the SE Sedan. Daewoo picks up the tab for all scheduled maintenance during the warranty period and has added ownership peace of mind with 24-hour roadside assistance for three years or 36,000 miles.

Category A

	Trade-in	Private	Dealer
2 Dr S Hbk	4485	5183	5828
4 Dr S Sdn	5235	6050	6803
2 Dr SE Hbk	5385	6223	6997
4 Dr SX Sdn	6374	7367	8283

OPTIONS FOR LANOS
Air Conditioning[Std on SX] +432
Anti-Lock Brakes +308
Automatic 4-Speed Transmission +493
Power Moonroof +308

LEGANZA   2000

Content is pulled from the base SE model, but all Leganzas have new grilles and larger stereo knobs. New seat fabric on SE models, revised alloy wheels and a more convenient remote keyless-entry design debut, and buyers now get 24-hour roadside assistance and free scheduled maintenance for the

Model Description	Trade-in TMV	Private TMV	Dealer TMV
duration of the basic warranty period. New colors round out the changes.			

Category C

Model Description	Trade-in TMV	Private TMV	Dealer TMV
4 Dr CDX Sdn	10319	11772	13114
4 Dr SE Sdn	7613	8685	9675
4 Dr SX Sdn	8973	10237	11404

OPTIONS FOR LEGANZA
AM/FM Stereo/CD/Tape[Opt on SE] +123
Aluminum/Alloy Wheels[Std on CDX] +185
Automatic 4-Speed Transmission[Opt on SE] +493
Compact Disc Changer +320
Power Moonroof[Opt on SX] +524

NUBIRA 2000

Nubira, already the most appealing choice from the Daewoo buffet, is restyled inside and out and becomes even more attractive to cash-strapped buyers. Firmer springs and a new rear stabilizer bar tighten handling, and the new SE trim level replaces last year's SX model. The five-door hatchback is dropped, but four new colors debut. Scheduled maintenance for the duration of the basic warranty, and three-year/36,000-mile 24-hour roadside assistance is standard.

Category B

	Trade-in	Private	Dealer
4 Dr CDX Sdn	7352	8435	9434
4 Dr CDX Wgn	7676	8806	9849
4 Dr SE Sdn	6176	7085	7924

OPTIONS FOR NUBIRA
Air Conditioning[Opt on SE] +432
Automatic 4-Speed Transmission +493
Leather Seats +308
Power Door Locks[Opt on SE] +123
Power Moonroof +308

1999 DAEWOO

LANOS 1999

This entry into the subcompact class is Daewoo's attack on the Honda Civic.

Category A

	Trade-in	Private	Dealer
2 Dr S Hbk	3749	4423	5097
4 Dr S Sdn	4033	4758	5483
2 Dr SE Hbk	4409	5202	5994
4 Dr SE Sdn	4759	5614	6469
2 Dr SX Hbk	5259	6204	7149
4 Dr SX Sdn	5339	6299	7258

OPTIONS FOR LANOS
Air Conditioning[Std on SX] +344
Anti-Lock Brakes +246
Automatic 4-Speed Transmission +393
Power Moonroof +246

LEGANZA 1999

The whole car is new to the United States, as is the motor company that makes it.

Category C

	Trade-in	Private	Dealer
4 Dr CDX Sdn	8289	9564	10838
4 Dr SE Sdn	6820	7869	8917
4 Dr SX Sdn	7886	9099	10311

OPTIONS FOR LEGANZA
Aluminum/Alloy Wheels[Std on CDX] +148
Automatic 4-Speed Transmission[Opt on SE] +393
Compact Disc Changer +256
Power Drivers Seat +148
Power Moonroof[Opt on SX] +417

NUBIRA 1999

In an attempt to lure consumer's away from the likes of Honda and Toyota, the new Korean upstart fields their loaded-with-features Nubira. A/C, power windows, keyless entry, four-wheel disc brakes, 129 horsepower and a funny name all come as standard equipment.

Category B

	Trade-in	Private	Dealer
4 Dr CDX Hbk	6539	7598	8657
4 Dr CDX Sdn	6539	7598	8657
4 Dr CDX Wgn	6698	7783	8868
4 Dr SX Hbk	5930	6890	7851
4 Dr SX Sdn	5930	6890	7851
4 Dr SX Wgn	6095	7083	8070

OPTIONS FOR NUBIRA
Anti-Lock Brakes[Opt on SX] +246
Automatic 4-Speed Transmission +393
Leather Seats +246
Power Moonroof +246

DODGE 01

Model Description	Trade-in TMV	Private TMV	Dealer TMV	Model Description	Trade-in TMV	Private TMV	Dealer TMV

DODGE   USA

1994 Dodge Ram 1500 2WD

2001 DODGE

CARAVAN   2001

America's best-selling minivan has been revised for 2001 and boasts new sheet metal, boosted horsepower, a refined suspension, upgraded brakes, improved safety features and plenty of additional gadgets. Third-row seats are now easier to remove and install, but still don't fold flat.

Category P

Model Description	Trade-in TMV	Private TMV	Dealer TMV
4 Dr SE Pass. Van	11928	12705	14000
4 Dr Sport Pass. Van	14910	15881	17500

OPTIONS FOR CARAVAN
AM/FM Compact Disc Player +115
AM/FM Stereo/CD/Tape +148
Alarm System +128
Aluminum/Alloy Wheels +447
Anti-Lock Brakes[Opt on SE] +371
Automatic Load Leveling +191
Child Seats (2) +148
Compact Disc Changer +457
Cruise Control[Opt on SE] +122
Dual Air Conditioning +394
Infinity Sound System +325
Luggage Rack +164
Power Door Locks[Opt on SE] +207
Power Drivers Seat +243
Power Mirrors[Opt on SE] +115
Power Sliding Door[Opt on Sport] +263
Power Windows[Opt on SE] +171
Side Air Bag Restraints +256
Special Factory Paint +131
Tilt Steering Wheel[Opt on SE] +122

DAKOTA   2001

The Dakota gets a redesigned interior with upgraded audio components, optional steering wheel controls, larger exterior mirrors and a redesigned front fascia on the Sport models. Four-wheel-drive models get a dash-mounted, electronically controlled transfer case. New 15x7-inch cast aluminum wheels are standard on Sport and SLT models, and a leather interior is now available in Quad Cab models. Quad Cabs also benefit from front seatbelt pre-tensioners, Club Cabs have added rear window defrost as an option, and Sentry Key Engine Immobilizer technology is now part of the optional security alarm system. Finally, the 3.9-liter V6, 4.7-liter V8 and 5.9-liter V8 engines meet low-emission-vehicle standards for 2001.

Category J

Model Description	Trade-in TMV	Private TMV	Dealer TMV
2 Dr SLT 4WD Ext Cab SB	14467	15417	17000
2 Dr SLT 4WD Std Cab SB	14042	14963	16500
2 Dr SLT Ext Cab SB	11914	12696	14000
2 Dr SLT Std Cab SB	10723	11427	12600
4 Dr SLT 4WD Crew Cab SB	15744	16777	18500
4 Dr SLT Crew Cab SB	13616	14510	16000
2 Dr Sport 4WD Ext Cab SB	13616	14510	16000
2 Dr Sport 4WD Std Cab SB	12340	13150	14500
2 Dr Sport Ext Cab SB	11063	11789	13000
2 Dr Sport Std Cab SB	10127	10792	11900
4 Dr Sport 4WD Crew Cab SB	14637	15598	17200
4 Dr Sport Crew Cab SB	13105	13966	15400
2 Dr STD Ext Cab SB	11063	11789	13000
2 Dr STD 4WD Ext Cab SB	13871	14782	16300
2 Dr STD 4WD Std Cab SB	11318	12061	13300
2 Dr STD Std Cab SB	9276	9885	10900

OPTIONS FOR DAKOTA
8 cyl 4.7 L Engine +388
8 cyl 5.9 L Engine +739
AM/FM Compact Disc Player +315
AM/FM Stereo/CD/Tape +434
Air Conditioning +526
Alarm System +148
Anti-Lock Brakes +325
Automatic 4-Speed Transmission +641
Bed Liner +161
Camper/Towing Package +181

Don't forget to refer to the Mileage Adjustment Table at the back of this book!

Model Description	Trade-in TMV	Private TMV	Dealer TMV	Model Description	Trade-in TMV	Private TMV	Dealer TMV

Cruise Control +115
Leather Seats[Opt on Crew Cab] +381
Limited Slip Differential +187
Power Drivers Seat +210
Power Windows +131
Tutone Paint +128

DURANGO   2001

Dodge's brute of a mid-sized ute receives numerous improvements for 2001. An electronic transfer case for its four-wheel drive system is now standard on 4WD models. A new instrument panel, center console w/ cupholders, interior trim and upgraded stereo has been added, and a tilt steering column is now standard on all Durangos. The 5.2-liter V8 engine is dropped, leaving the more efficient 4.7-liter V8 as standard equipment in both 4x2 and 4x4 Durangos. A variable-delay intermittent rear wiper is offered, and auto-dimming, heated outside power mirrors can be had on in SLT trim. A new appearance option group for the SLT includes 16-inch aluminum wheels, along with special body side moldings, running boards and lower panels. New 15-inch Sparkle Silver aluminum wheels are standard across the Durango lineup.

Category M

4 Dr SLT 4WD Wgn	20124	21353	23400
4 Dr SLT Wgn	17886	18978	20798
4 Dr Sport 4WD Wgn	18234	19347	21202
4 Dr Sport Wgn	16340	17338	19000

OPTIONS FOR DURANGO

8 cyl 5.9 L Engine[Opt on SLT] +390
AM/FM Stereo/CD/Tape +197
Anti-Lock Brakes +325
Camper/Towing Package +181
Dual Power Seats[Opt on SLT] +296
Heated Front Seats[Opt on SLT] +181
Infinity Sound System +141
Leather Seats +394
Limited Slip Differential +187
Rear Air Conditioning w/Rear Heater +361
Third Seat +329

GRAND CARAVAN   2001

America's best-selling minivan is all new for 2001, with many industry-first features including a power rear tailgate, a power sliding door obstacle detection system, a removable and powered center console and a pop-up rear cargo organizer, all residing under sleek new sheet metal.

Category P

4 Dr ES AWD Pass. Van	20022	21326	23500
4 Dr ES Pass. Van	18574	19784	21800
4 Dr EX Pass. Van	17040	18150	20000
4 Dr SE Pass. Van	14058	14974	16500
4 Dr Sport AWD Pass. Van	19170	20419	22500
4 Dr Sport Pass. Van	15762	16789	18500

OPTIONS FOR GRAND CARAVAN

AM/FM Compact Disc Player +115
AM/FM Stereo/CD/Tape +148
Alarm System +128
Aluminum/Alloy Wheels +447
Automatic Dimming Mirror[Opt on ES] +115
Automatic Load Leveling +191
Child Seats (2) +148
Chrome Wheels +447
Cruise Control[Opt on SE] +122
Dual Air Conditioning[Opt on Sport] +394
Heated Front Seats[Opt on ES] +164
Infinity Sound System[Opt on Sport] +325
Leather Seats[Opt on ES] +821
Luggage Rack +164
Power Door Locks[Opt on SE] +207
Power Drivers Seat[Opt on Sport] +243
Power Sliding Door[Opt on Sport] +253
Power Windows[Opt on SE] +171
Rear Air Conditioning w/Rear Heater[Opt on Sport] +361
Side Air Bag Restraints +256
Special Factory Paint +131
Tilt Steering Wheel[Opt on SE] +122
Traction Control System[Opt on ES] +115

INTREPID   2001

Changes to this family sedan for the 2001 model year include optional side airbags, a shoulder belt for the central rear passenger, an internal trunk release, three new interior colors, two additional exterior colors and an additional power outlet in the center console if you get a model with bucket seats. For those cars equipped with the Infinity sound system, you'll receive steering wheel-mounted controls and a four-disc in-dash CD player. SE is now the base Intrepid designation (previously it was the mid-level model), and it includes higher grade fabric this year. All engine choices meet LEV standards, and all models receive thicker side glass and upgraded windshield moldings for a quieter ride.

Category G

4 Dr ES Sdn	15264	16290	18000
4 Dr R/T Sdn	16536	17648	19500
4 Dr STD Sdn	13144	14028	15500

OPTIONS FOR INTREPID

6 cyl 3.2 L Engine +329
AM/FM Stereo/CD/Tape[Std on R/T] +378
Aluminum/Alloy Wheels[Opt on STD] +256
Anti-Lock Brakes[Std on R/T] +394
Compact Disc Changer +231
Dual Power Seats +499
Leather Seats +575
Power Drivers Seat[Std on ES] +158

Don't forget to refer to the Mileage Adjustment Table at the back of this book!

Model Description	Trade-in TMV	Private TMV	Dealer TMV
Power Sunroof +588			
Rear Spoiler +131			
Side Air Bag Restraints +256			
Special Factory Paint +131			

NEON   2001

The Neon R/T and Neon ACR, both models sporting a 2.0-liter 150-horsepower engine, make their much-anticipated return this year. Side-impact airbags and leather seats are now available in Dodge's economy car, as is a new interior color and four new exterior colors. An internal trunk release keeps young and old from being trapped in the Neon's cargo hold, and four new option packages, one of which includes a four-disc in-dash CD player, further widen its appeal to buyers seeking an American-made economy car.

Category B

Model Description	Trade-in TMV	Private TMV	Dealer TMV
4 Dr Highline ACR Sdn	9223	10077	11500
4 Dr Highline ES Sdn	8822	9639	11000
4 Dr Highline R/T Sdn	10266	11216	12800
4 Dr Highline SE Sdn	7619	8324	9500

OPTIONS FOR NEON
AM/FM Compact Disc Player +260
Air Conditioning[Opt on ES] +550
Aluminum/Alloy Wheels +269
Anti-Lock Brakes +391
Automatic 3-Speed Transmission +394
Compact Disc Changer +246
Cruise Control[Std on ES] +154
Leather Seats +434
Power Sunroof +390
Power Windows[Std on ES] +168
Rear Spoiler +131
Side Air Bag Restraints +230

RAM PICKUP 2500   2001

Electronic cruise control is now offered for the Cummings turbodiesel models with a manual transmission, improved braking systems with standard ABS come on all 2500 and 3500 Rams, two new exterior colors debut and child-seat anchors are mounted on the rear of the cab. A high-output Cummings turbodiesel model, with a six-speed transmission, 245 horsepower and 505 foot-pounds of torque, is offered in addition to a slightly improved 235-horsepower/460-ft-lbs version, available with a manual or automatic tranny.

Category K

Model Description	Trade-in TMV	Private TMV	Dealer TMV
2 Dr SLT 4WD Std Cab LB			
	17698	18814	20675
2 Dr SLT Std Cab LB	15004	15950	17528
4 Dr SLT 4WD Ext Cab LB			
	19313	20531	22562
4 Dr SLT Ext Cab LB	16368	17401	19122
4 Dr SLT 4WD Ext Cab SB			
	18832	20020	22000
4 Dr SLT Ext Cab SB	16264	17290	19000
4 Dr SLT Plus 4WD Ext Cab LB			
	20544	21840	24000
4 Dr SLT Plus Ext Cab LB			
	18318	19474	21400
4 Dr SLT Plus 4WD Ext Cab SB			
	20373	21658	23800
4 Dr SLT Plus Ext Cab SB			
	18233	19383	21300
2 Dr ST 4WD Std Cab LB			
	15237	16198	17800
2 Dr ST Std Cab LB	13268	14105	15500
4 Dr ST 4WD Ext Cab LB			
	17150	18232	20035
4 Dr ST Ext Cab LB	14956	15900	17472
4 Dr ST 4WD Ext Cab SB			
	17090	18168	19965
4 Dr ST Ext Cab SB	14552	15470	17000

OPTIONS FOR RAM PICKUP 2500
10 cyl 8.0 L Engine +309
6 cyl 5.9 L Turbodiesel Engine +3433
6-Speed Transmission +263
AM/FM Stereo/CD/Tape[Opt on SLT] +453
Air Conditioning[Opt on ST] +529
Automatic 4-Speed Transmission +641
Automatic Dimming Mirror[Opt on SLT] +115
Bed Liner +161
Camper/Towing Package +181
Cruise Control[Opt on ST] +128
Infinity Sound System[Opt on SLT] +335
Keyless Entry System[Opt on SLT] +125
Leather Seats[Opt on SLT] +822
Limited Slip Differential +187
Power Drivers Seat[Opt on SLT] +210
Tilt Steering Wheel[Opt on ST] +128
Tutone Paint +148

RAM PICKUP 3500   2001

Electronic cruise control is now offered for the Cummings turbodiesel models with a manual transmission, improved braking systems with standard ABS come on all 2500 and 3500 Rams, two new exterior colors debut and child-seat anchors are mounted on the rear of the cab. A high-output Cummings turbodiesel model, with a six-speed transmission, 245 horsepower and 505 foot-pounds of torque, is offered in addition to a slightly improved 235-horsepower/460-ft-lbs version, available with a manual or automatic tranny.

Category K

Model Description	Trade-in TMV	Private TMV	Dealer TMV
2 Dr SLT 4WD Std Cab LB			
	18304	19459	21383
2 Dr SLT Std Cab LB	15408	16380	18000

Don't forget to refer to the Mileage Adjustment Table at the back of this book!

Model Description	Trade-in TMV	Private TMV	Dealer TMV
4 Dr SLT 4WD Ext Cab LB			
	19688	20930	23000
4 Dr SLT Ext Cab LB	18231	19381	21298
4 Dr SLT Plus 4WD Ext Cab LB			
	20972	22295	24500
4 Dr SLT Plus Ext Cab LB			
	18832	20020	22000
2 Dr ST 4WD Std Cab LB			
	16692	17745	19500
2 Dr ST Std Cab LB	14552	15470	17000
4 Dr ST 4WD Ext Cab LB			
	18677	19855	21819
4 Dr ST Ext Cab LB	15836	16835	18500

OPTIONS FOR RAM PICKUP 3500
10 cyl 8.0 L Engine +309
6 cyl 5.9 L Turbodiesel Engine +3433
6-Speed Transmission +263
AM/FM Compact Disc Player[Opt on SLT] +335
AM/FM Stereo/CD/Tape[Opt on SLT] +453
Air Conditioning[Opt on ST] +529
Automatic 4-Speed Transmission +641
Automatic Dimming Mirror[Opt on SLT] +115
Bed Liner +161
Camper/Towing Package +181
Cruise Control[Opt on ST] +128
Keyless Entry System[Opt on SLT] +125
Leather Seats[Opt on SLT] +822
Limited Slip Differential +187
Power Drivers Seat[Opt on SLT] +210
Tilt Steering Wheel[Opt on ST] +128

RAM WAGON 2001

Minor changes come with the 2001 model year, with a new trailer tow package and a Class IV receiver hitch. The tilt steering wheel comes with three new positions to find that perfect driving position.
Category Q

Model Description	Trade-in TMV	Private TMV	Dealer TMV
2 Dr 1500 STD Pass. Van	13808	14630	16000
2 Dr 2500 STD Pass. Van Ext	14671	15544	17000
2 Dr 3500 Maxi Pass. Van Ext	16742	17739	19400

OPTIONS FOR RAM WAGON
8 cyl 5.2 L Engine[Opt on 1500] +388
8 cyl 5.9 L Engine +388
AM/FM Stereo/CD/Tape +148
Anti-Lock Brakes +286
Automatic 4-Speed Transmission[Opt on 1500] +197
Camper/Towing Package +148
Cruise Control +168
Infinity Sound System +299
Limited Slip Differential +187
Power Door Locks +141

Power Drivers Seat +197
Power Windows +173
Privacy Glass +269
Rear Air Conditioning w/Rear Heater +509

STRATUS 2001

The Avenger nameplate has been dropped from the Dodge lineup, replaced by the all-new Stratus Coupe. The Stratus Sedan continues with a full redesign but retains much of its predecessor's look and feel. A new engine debuts along with additional safety features that make the Stratus a family sedan in the truest sense. Last year, we marveled at the list of standard options on this moderately priced sedan; this year we're rechecking our numbers once again as more features debut for 2001.

Model Description	Trade-in TMV	Private TMV	Dealer TMV
Category C			
4 Dr ES Sdn	12151	13144	14800
Category E			
2 Dr R/T Cpe	13335	14260	15800
Category C			
4 Dr SE Sdn	11207	12124	13651
Category E			
2 Dr SE Cpe	11225	12003	13300

OPTIONS FOR STRATUS
6 cyl 3.0 L 24V Engine[Opt on SE Cpe] +558
AM/FM Compact Disc Player +131
AM/FM Stereo/CD/Tape +164
Aluminum/Alloy Wheels +230
Anti-Lock Brakes +371
Automatic 4-Speed Transmission[Opt on Cpe] +542
Chrome Wheels[Opt on SE Sdn] +394
Keyless Entry System +125
Leather Seats +381
Power Drivers Seat +249
Power Sunroof +450
Premium Sound System +230
Side Air Bag Restraints +256
Special Factory Paint +131

VIPER 2001

Slightly refining the snake's venomous bite are standard four-wheel disc ABS, an ACR option group with air conditioning and a CD player, and an internal trunk release, useful if you get trapped in the belly of the beast. If your Viper's aural impact on the environment isn't enough, choose the new Race Yellow or Deep Sapphire Blue exterior hues to visually assault those around you.
Category R

Model Description	Trade-in TMV	Private TMV	Dealer TMV
2 Dr ACR Competition Cpe	68250	70781	75000
2 Dr GTS Cpe	59150	61344	65000
2 Dr RT/10 Conv	57330	59456	63000

OPTIONS FOR VIPER

Don't forget to refer to the Mileage Adjustment Table at the back of this book!

Model Description	Trade-in TMV	Private TMV	Dealer TMV
AM/FM Compact Disc Player[Std on GTS,R/T 10] +362			
Hardtop Roof +1643			
Tonneau Cover +164			

2000 DODGE

AVENGER 2000

Base Avengers get new standard equipment, including the 2.5-liter V6 and automatic transmission from the uplevel ES, new cloth fabric on the seats and standard 16-inch wheels with luxury wheelcovers. A sport package is newly optional. A power leather-trimmed driver's seat is included with ES trim for 2000. Two key fobs come with the remote keyless-entry system this year, and two new colors are available. The Avenger will be completely redesigned for 2001.

Category E

Model Description	Trade-in TMV	Private TMV	Dealer TMV
2 Dr STD Cpe	9947	11067	12100
2 Dr ES Cpe	11016	12256	13400

OPTIONS FOR AVENGER

AM/FM Stereo/CD/Tape[Std on ES] +286
Alarm System[Std on ES] +200
Anti-Lock Brakes +394
Infinity Sound System +214
Power Moonroof +420

CARAVAN 2000

New colors, more standard equipment, and an AWD Sport model keep Chrysler's best-selling minivans up to date until the redesigned 2001 model arrives.

Category P

Model Description	Trade-in TMV	Private TMV	Dealer TMV
2 Dr STD Pass. Van	9409	10393	11300
4 Dr Grand Pass. Van	11408	12600	13700
4 Dr Grand ES AWD Pass. Van	16347	18055	19632
4 Dr Grand ES Pass. Van	15405	17014	18500
4 Dr Grand LE AWD Pass. Van	15821	17474	19000
4 Dr Grand LE Pass. Van	14406	15911	17300
4 Dr Grand SE Pass. Van	12990	14347	15600
4 Dr SE Pass. Van	11908	13152	14300
4 Dr Grand Sport AWD Pass. Van	14739	16279	17700

OPTIONS FOR CARAVAN

6 cyl 3.0 L Engine[Opt on SE,STD] +526
6 cyl 3.3 L Engine +637
6 cyl 3.3 L Flex Fuel Engine +637
6 cyl 3.8 L Engine +335
AM/FM Stereo/CD/Tape +204
Alarm System +131

Model Description	Trade-in TMV	Private TMV	Dealer TMV
Aluminum/Alloy Wheels +173			
Anti-Lock Brakes[Opt on Grand,STD] +371			
Automatic 4-Speed Transmission[Opt on STD] +131			
Automatic Load Leveling +191			
Camper/Towing Package +118			
Captain Chairs (4) +392			
Child Seats (2) +148			
Compact Disc Changer +263			
Cruise Control[Opt on Grand,STD] +112			
Dual Air Conditioning +394			
Dual Power Seats[Opt on Grand ES] +315			
Fog Lights[Opt on SE] +99			
Infinity Sound System +296			
Keyless Entry System +115			
Leather Seats +522			
Luggage Rack +128			
Power Door Locks[Opt on Grand,STD] +148			
Power Drivers Seat +158			
Power Windows[Opt on Grand,STD] +155			
Rear Heater +135			
Special Factory Paint +131			
Sunscreen Glass +231			
Tilt Steering Wheel[Opt on Grand,STD] +115			

DAKOTA 2000

The biggest change this year is design oriented - the Dakota is now available with four full-size doors, and with that, a family name: Quad Cab. A 4.7-liter V8 has been added, but the 8-foot bed is gone. You can select from five more colors as well.

Category J

Model Description	Trade-in TMV	Private TMV	Dealer TMV
2 Dr SLT Plus 4WD Std Cab SB	12849	14148	15348
2 Dr SLT Plus Std Cab SB	10799	11892	12900
2 Dr STD 4WD Ext Cab SB	12700	13984	15170
2 Dr STD 4WD Std Cab SB	10632	11707	12700
2 Dr STD Ext Cab SB	10213	11246	12200
2 Dr STD Std Cab SB	8455	9311	10100
2 Dr R/T Sport Ext Cab SB	13813	15210	16500
2 Dr R/T Sport Std Cab SB	11636	12814	13900
2 Dr SLT 4WD Ext Cab SB	12936	14244	15452
2 Dr SLT 4WD Std Cab SB	12474	13735	14900
2 Dr SLT Ext Cab SB	10883	11984	13000
2 Dr SLT Std Cab SB	9878	10878	11800
4 Dr SLT 4WD Crew Cab SB	14818	16316	17700
4 Dr SLT Crew Cab SB	12737	14025	15214

Model Description	Trade-in TMV	Private TMV	Dealer TMV
2 Dr SLT Plus 4WD Ext Cab SB	14148	15579	16900
2 Dr SLT Plus Ext Cab SB	11971	13182	14300
4 Dr SLT Plus 4WD Crew Cab SB	15655	17238	18700
4 Dr SLT Plus Crew Cab SB	13060	14381	15600
2 Dr Sport 4WD Ext Cab SB	13379	14732	15981
2 Dr Sport 4WD Std Cab SB	11472	12633	13704
2 Dr Sport Ext Cab SB	10967	12076	13100
2 Dr Sport Std Cab SB	9125	10048	10900
2 Dr Sport Plus 4WD Ext Cab SB	13410	14767	16019
2 Dr Sport Plus 4WD Std Cab SB	12306	13551	14700
2 Dr Sport Plus Ext Cab SB	11466	12625	13696
2 Dr Sport Plus Std Cab SB	9795	10785	11700
4 Dr Sport Plus 4WD Crew Cab SB	14650	16132	17500
4 Dr Sport Plus Crew Cab SB	12738	14027	15216

OPTIONS FOR DAKOTA

6 cyl 3.9 L Engine[Opt on Std Cab] +368
8 cyl 4.7 L Engine +348
8 cyl 5.9 L Engine[Std on R/T Sport] +739
AM/FM Compact Disc Player +184
AM/FM Stereo/CD/Tape +237
Air Conditioning +526
Alarm System +99
Anti-Lock Brakes +231
Automatic 4-Speed Transmission[Std on R/T Sport Ext Cab SB,R/T Sport Std Cab SB] +641
Bed Liner +154
Bucket Seats[Std on R/T Sport Ext Cab SB,R/T Sport Std Cab SB] +99
Camper/Towing Package +115
Compact Disc Changer +263
Cruise Control +115
Heated Power Mirrors +99
Keyless Entry System +99
Limited Slip Differential[Std on R/T Sport Ext Cab SB,R/T Sport Std Cab SB] +187
Power Door Locks +128
Power Drivers Seat +210
Power Windows +155
Tutone Paint +99

DURANGO   2000

The next-generation 4.7-liter V8 is now available on four-wheel-drive models and is linked to an all-new automatic transmission. Rack-and-pinion steering becomes standard for both two- and four-wheel-drives. A performance-oriented R/T model has been added to the lineup that already includes the SLT and the decked-out SLT Plus.

Category M

Model Description	Trade-in TMV	Private TMV	Dealer TMV
4 Dr STD 4WD Wgn	17511	19221	20800
4 Dr STD Wgn	14986	16449	17800
4 Dr R/T 4WD Wgn	21047	23103	25000
4 Dr SLT 4WD Wgn	17680	19406	21000
4 Dr SLT Wgn	15322	16819	18200
4 Dr SLT Plus 4WD Wgn	19532	21439	23200
4 Dr SLT Plus Wgn	18269	20053	21700

OPTIONS FOR DURANGO

8 cyl 5.9 L Engine[Std on R/T 4WD Wgn] +390
AM/FM Stereo/CD/Tape[Std on R/T 4WD Wgn] +197
Alarm System[Std on R/T 4WD Wgn] +99
Anti-Lock Brakes +260
Automatic Dimming Mirror[Opt on SLT] +99
Camper/Towing Package +181
Dual Air Conditioning +283
Infinity Sound System[Std on R/T 4WD Wgn] +217
Limited Slip Differential +187
Running Boards[Opt on SLT] +260
Third Seat +361
Trailer Hitch +181

INTREPID   2000

A performance R/T model is onboard for 2000. Intrepids get five new colors, new seat fabric in Base models, and added horsepower and torque to ES models powered by the 2.7-liter V6. AutoStick is newly available with that engine, and ES buyers can order an in-dash CD changer. Tether-ready child-seat anchors have been added behind the rear seat, and cars sold in California meet LEV standards.

Category G

Model Description	Trade-in TMV	Private TMV	Dealer TMV
4 Dr STD Sdn	10590	11687	12700
4 Dr ES Sdn	11424	12607	13700
4 Dr R/T Sdn	12758	14080	15300

OPTIONS FOR INTREPID

6 cyl 3.2 L Engine +329
AM/FM Compact Disc Player +214
AM/FM Stereo/CD/Tape[Std on R/T] +378
Alarm System +99
Anti-Lock Brakes[Std on R/T] +394
Automatic Dimming Mirror +99
Climate Control for AC +108
Compact Disc Changer +231
Dual Power Seats +499
Infinity Sound System +378
Keyless Entry System +99
Leather Seats +575

Model Description	Trade-in TMV	Private TMV	Dealer TMV

Lighted Entry System[Std on ES] +99
Power Drivers Seat[Std on ES] +158
Power Sunroof +522
Special Factory Paint +131
Traction Control System[Opt on ES] +165
Trip Computer[Opt on ES] +99

NEON 2000

Everything's new inside and out, as the second-generation Neon grows up, not old. A totally redesigned suspension and steering system, low-speed traction control, and a complete exterior redesign head up the notable changes.

Category B

Model Description	Trade-in TMV	Private TMV	Dealer TMV
4 Dr ES Sdn	6871	7822	8700
4 Dr Highline Sdn	6397	7282	8100

OPTIONS FOR NEON

AM/FM Compact Disc Player +260
Air Conditioning[Opt on ES] +657
Alarm System[Opt on ES] +112
Aluminum/Alloy Wheels +233
Anti-Lock Brakes +390
Automatic 3-Speed Transmission +394
Compact Disc Changer +329
Cruise Control[Std on ES Sdn] +141
Power Door Locks[Std on ES Sdn] +112
Power Moonroof +390
Power Windows[Std on ES Sdn] +168
Rear Spoiler +131
Tilt Steering Wheel[Std on ES Sdn] +115
Traction Control System +115

RAM 1500 2000

The 1500 Club Cab models with the 8-foot bed have been discontinued; also eliminated for 2000 are the 2500 Club Cabs. All Rams receive a new front suspension and steering system to improve ride quality and steering precision, and 2500s and 3500s have a revised rear suspension for a better ride when loaded. An off-road package is now available for the short-wheelbase four-wheel-drive 1500.

Category K

Model Description	Trade-in TMV	Private TMV	Dealer TMV
2 Dr SLT 4WD Std Cab LB	13787	15073	16261
2 Dr SLT Std Cab LB	11107	12143	13100
4 Dr SLT 4WD Ext Cab LB	15261	16685	18000
4 Dr SLT Ext Cab LB	13736	15018	16201
2 Dr SLT 4WD Ext Cab SB	14583	15944	17200
2 Dr SLT 4WD Std Cab SB	13725	15006	16188
2 Dr SLT Ext Cab SB	12802	13997	15100
2 Dr SLT Std Cab SB	10852	11865	12800
4 Dr SLT 4WD Ext Cab SB	15176	16593	17900
4 Dr SLT Ext Cab SB	13480	14739	15900
2 Dr ST 4WD Std Cab LB	12633	13812	14900
2 Dr ST Std Cab LB	9750	10660	11500
4 Dr ST 4WD Ext Cab LB	14413	15758	17000
4 Dr ST Ext Cab LB	12063	13189	14228
2 Dr ST 4WD Ext Cab SB	13683	14960	16139
2 Dr ST 4WD Std Cab SB	12015	13137	14172
2 Dr ST Ext Cab SB	11446	12514	13500
2 Dr ST Std Cab SB	9326	10197	11000
4 Dr ST 4WD Ext Cab SB	14159	15480	16700
4 Dr ST Ext Cab SB	11530	12607	13600
2 Dr WS Std Cab LB	8685	9496	10244
2 Dr WS Std Cab SB	8611	9414	10156

OPTIONS FOR RAM 1500

8 cyl 5.2 L Engine +388
8 cyl 5.9 L Engine +390
AM/FM Compact Disc Player +279
AM/FM Stereo/CD/Tape +453
Air Conditioning +529
Alarm System +99
Anti-Lock Brakes +329
Automatic 4-Speed Transmission +641
Automatic Dimming Mirror +115
Bed Liner +155
Camper/Towing Package +181
Chrome Wheels +99
Cruise Control +122
Heated Power Mirrors[Opt on ST] +99
Infinity Sound System[Opt on SLT] +299
Keyless Entry System[Opt on SLT] +125
Leather Seats +822
Limited Slip Differential +187
Off-Road Group +575
Overhead Console +122
Power Drivers Seat +211
Tilt Steering Wheel[Opt on ST,WS] +128
Trailer Hitch +181
Tutone Paint +99

RAM 2500 2000

The 1500 Club Cab models with the 8-foot bed box have been discontinued; also eliminated for 2000 are the 2500 Club Cabs. All Rams receive a new front suspension and steering system to improve ride quality and steering precision, and 2500s and 3500s have a revised rear suspension for a better ride when loaded. An off-road package is now available for the short-

Model Description	Trade-in TMV	Private TMV	Dealer TMV
wheelbase four-wheel-drive 1500.			
Category K			
2 Dr SLT 4WD Std Cab LB			
	15939	17427	18800
2 Dr SLT Std Cab LB	13396	14646	15800
4 Dr SLT 4WD Ext Cab LB			
	17041	18632	20100
4 Dr SLT Ext Cab LB	14498	15851	17100
4 Dr SLT 4WD Ext Cab SB			
	16957	18539	20000
4 Dr SLT Ext Cab SB	14413	15758	17000
2 Dr ST 4WD Std Cab LB			
	14244	15573	16800
2 Dr ST Std Cab LB	12378	13534	14600
4 Dr ST 4WD Ext Cab LB			
	15770	17241	18600
4 Dr ST Ext Cab LB	13311	14553	15700
4 Dr ST 4WD Ext Cab SB			
	15430	16871	18200
4 Dr ST Ext Cab SB	12972	14182	15300

OPTIONS FOR RAM 2500
10 cyl 8.0 L Engine +309
6 cyl 5.9 L Turbodiesel Engine +3261
AM/FM Compact Disc Player +279
AM/FM Stereo/CD/Tape +453
Air Conditioning +529
Alarm System +99
Anti-Lock Brakes +329
Automatic 4-Speed Transmission +641
Automatic Dimming Mirror +115
Bed Liner +155
Camper/Towing Package +181
Chrome Wheels +214
Cruise Control +128
Heated Power Mirrors[Opt on ST] +95
Keyless Entry System +125
Leather Seats +822
Limited Slip Differential +187
Overhead Console +122
Power Drivers Seat +211
Tilt Steering Wheel[Opt on ST] +128
Trailer Hitch +181
Tutone Paint +99

RAM 3500   2000

The 1500 Club Cab models with the 8-foot bed box have been discontinued; also eliminated for 2000 are the 2500 Club Cabs. All Rams receive a new front suspension and steering system to improve ride quality and steering precision, and 2500s and 3500s have a revised rear suspension for a better ride when loaded. An off-road package is now available for the short-wheelbase four-wheel-drive 1500.
Category K

Model Description	Trade-in TMV	Private TMV	Dealer TMV
2 Dr SLT 4WD Std Cab LB			
	15091	16500	17800
2 Dr SLT Std Cab LB	12717	13904	15000
4 Dr SLT 4WD Ext Cab LB			
	15854	17334	18700
4 Dr SLT Ext Cab LB Ext Cab LB			
	14595	15957	17214
2 Dr ST 4WD Std Cab LB			
	14232	15560	16786
2 Dr ST Std Cab LB	11785	12885	13900
4 Dr ST 4WD Ext Cab LB			
	15430	16871	18200
4 Dr ST Ext Cab LB	13311	14553	15700

OPTIONS FOR RAM 3500
10 cyl 8.0 L Engine +309
6 cyl 5.9 L Turbodiesel Engine +3261
6-Speed Transmission +263
AM/FM Compact Disc Player +335
AM/FM Stereo/CD/Tape +453
Air Conditioning +529
Alarm System +99
Automatic 4-Speed Transmission +641
Automatic Dimming Mirror +115
Bed Liner +155
Camper/Towing Package +181
Cruise Control +128
Keyless Entry System +125
Leather Seats +822
Limited Slip Differential +187
Overhead Console +122
Power Drivers Seat +211
Tilt Steering Wheel[Opt on ST] +128
Trailer Hitch +181

RAM WAGON   2000

Minor changes come with the 2000 model year, including hood-mounted windshield-washer nozzles and chrome-clad wheels. Sealing has been improved to reduce noise and keep out the weather, and Ram Wagons get a six-speaker audio system as standard equipment.
Category Q

Model Description	Trade-in TMV	Private TMV	Dealer TMV
2 Dr 1500 STD Pass. Van			
	10862	11922	12900
2 Dr 2500 STD Pass. Van Ext			
	11873	13031	14100
2 Dr 3500 Maxi Pass. Van Ext			
	13557	14879	16100

OPTIONS FOR RAM WAGON
12 Passenger Seating +187
8 cyl 5.2 L Engine[Opt on 1500] +388
8 cyl 5.9 L Engine +388
AM/FM Stereo/CD/Tape +148
Alarm System +99

Don't forget to refer to the Mileage Adjustment Table at the back of this book!

Model Description	Trade-in TMV	Private TMV	Dealer TMV

Anti-Lock Brakes +325
Automatic 4-Speed Transmission[Opt on 1500] +197
Camper/Towing Package +148
Chrome Wheels +99
Cruise Control +168
Dual Air Conditioning +555
Infinity Sound System +299
Keyless Entry System +99
Lighted Entry System +112
Limited Slip Differential +187
Power Door Locks +141
Power Drivers Seat +197
Power Mirrors +105
Power Windows +173
Rear Heater +99
Sunscreen Glass +283

STRATUS 2000

A new entry-level SE replaces last year's Base model and comes with so much standard equipment and free optional equipment that you'll have a whole new kind of sticker shock! The upper-level ES steps up to a 2.5-liter V6, and new colors also debut.

Category C

Model Description	Trade-in TMV	Private TMV	Dealer TMV
4 Dr ES Sdn	9083	10184	11200
4 Dr SE Sdn	7380	8274	9100

OPTIONS FOR STRATUS

4 cyl 2.4 L Engine +296
AM/FM Compact Disc Player +131
AM/FM Stereo/CD/Tape +223
Alarm System +99
Aluminum/Alloy Wheels +131
Anti-Lock Brakes[Std on ES] +371
Automatic 4-Speed Transmission[Std on ES] +691
Compact Disc Changer +362
Cruise Control[Std on ES] +112
Heated Power Mirrors[Std on ES] +115
Keyless Entry System +125
Lighted Entry System +102
Power Door Locks[Opt on SE] +155
Power Drivers Seat +249
Power Sunroof +456
Power Windows[Std on ES] +171
Special Factory Paint +131

VIPER 2000

The 2000 Viper is available in a new Steel Gray color and the ACR version has been revised to further poison the snake's venomous bite.

Category R

Model Description	Trade-in TMV	Private TMV	Dealer TMV
2 Dr ACR Competition Cpe	63334	66800	70000
2 Dr GTS Cpe	55643	58689	61500
2 Dr RT/10 Conv	52929	55826	58500

OPTIONS FOR VIPER

AM/FM Compact Disc Player[Std on GTS,R/T 10] +362
Hardtop Roof +1643
Tonneau Cover +165

1999 DODGE

AVENGER 1999

One new color for the exterior: Shark Blue (replaces Silver Mist).

Category E

Model Description	Trade-in TMV	Private TMV	Dealer TMV
2 Dr STD Cpe	8453	9476	10500
2 Dr ES Cpe	9339	10469	11600

OPTIONS FOR AVENGER

6 cyl 2.5 L Engine +337
AM/FM Stereo/CD/Tape +179
Air Conditioning[Std on ES] +436
Alarm System +167
Aluminum/Alloy Wheels[Std on ES] +270
Anti-Lock Brakes +330
Automatic 4-Speed Transmission +381
Cruise Control[Opt on STD] +110
Infinity Sound System[Opt on STD] +179
Leather Seats +233
Power Door Locks +123
Power Drivers Seat[Std on ES] +113
Power Moonroof +353
Power Windows +140
Rear Spoiler[Std on ES] +165

CARAVAN 1999

A revised front fascia is common to all models.

Category P

Model Description	Trade-in TMV	Private TMV	Dealer TMV
2 Dr STD Pass. Van	7718	8559	9400
4 Dr LE Pass. Van	12151	13476	14800
4 Dr SE Pass. Van	10099	11199	12300

OPTIONS FOR CARAVAN

6 cyl 3.0 L Engine +441
6 cyl 3.3 L Engine +535
6 cyl 3.8 L Engine +207
7 Passenger Seating +207
AM/FM Compact Disc Player[Opt on STD] +179
AM/FM Stereo/CD/Tape +218
Air Conditioning +475
Alarm System +138
Aluminum/Alloy Wheels +146
Anti-Lock Brakes +312
Automatic 4-Speed Transmission[Opt on STD] +110
Automatic Load Leveling +161
Captain Chairs (4) +328
Child Seats (2)[Std on LE] +123
Heated Power Mirrors[Opt on STD] +138
Infinity Sound System[Opt on SE] +397
Leather Seats[Opt on LE] +439
Luggage Rack +108
Metallic Paint +110
Power Door Locks[Std on LE] +184
Power Drivers Seat +154

Don't forget to refer to the Mileage Adjustment Table at the back of this book!

Model Description	Trade-in TMV	Private TMV	Dealer TMV	Model Description	Trade-in TMV	Private TMV	Dealer TMV

Power Windows +143
Sliding Driver Side Door[Opt on STD] +328
Sunscreen Glass[Std on LE] +249
Tilt Steering Wheel[Opt on STD] +102
Traction Control System +97

DAKOTA   1999

Solar Yellow paint is now available for those who want their pickups to get noticed. Other un-pickup-like refinements include an express down feature for the driver's window, extra storage space for cassettes or CDs, and remote radio controls on the steering wheel.

Category J

Model	Trade-in	Private	Dealer
2 Dr STD Std Cab LB	7720	8560	9400
2 Dr STD 4WD Ext Cab SB	10943	12134	13325
2 Dr STD 4WD Std Cab SB	9205	10207	11209
2 Dr STD Ext Cab SB	9125	10118	11111
2 Dr STD Std Cab SB	7227	8014	8800
2 Dr R/T Sport Ext Cab SB	11990	13295	14600
2 Dr R/T Sport Std Cab SB	10184	11292	12400
2 Dr SLT Std Cab LB	8870	9835	10800
2 Dr SLT 4WD Ext Cab SB	11251	12476	13700
2 Dr SLT 4WD Std Cab SB	10676	11838	13000
2 Dr SLT Ext Cab SB	9273	10282	11291
2 Dr SLT Std Cab SB	8705	9653	10600
2 Dr Sport Std Cab LB	8130	9015	9900
2 Dr Sport 4WD Ext Cab SB	10902	12089	13275
2 Dr Sport 4WD Std Cab SB	9691	10745	11800
2 Dr Sport Ext Cab SB	9117	10109	11101
2 Dr Sport Std Cab SB	7966	8833	9700

OPTIONS FOR DAKOTA
8 cyl 5.2 L Engine +293
8 cyl 5.9 L Engine[Std on R/T Sport] +928
AM/FM Compact Disc Player +265
AM/FM Stereo/CD/Tape +364
Air Conditioning[Std on SLT] +441
Alarm System +138
Anti-Lock Brakes +193
Automatic 4-Speed Transmission[Std on R/T Sport] +537
Bed Liner +130
Bucket Seats +110
Camper/Towing Package +152
Compact Disc Changer +414
Cruise Control[Opt on Sport, STD] +108
Limited Slip Differential[Std on R/T Sport] +157

Power Door Locks +121
Power Drivers Seat +176
Power Windows +130

DURANGO   1999

Two-wheel drive models finally show up for true flatlander use, and all Durangos gain a rear power outlet. Also available are steering wheel-mounted radio controls, heated mirrors, and two new colors: Bright Platinum Metallic and Patriot Blue.

Category M

Model	Trade-in	Private	Dealer
4 Dr SLT 4WD Wgn	14791	16346	17900
4 Dr SLT Wgn	14213	15706	17200

OPTIONS FOR DURANGO
8 cyl 5.9 L Engine +328
AM/FM Stereo/CD/Tape +152
Anti-Lock Brakes +218
Camper/Towing Package +152
Dual Air Conditioning +237
Infinity Sound System +182
Leather Seats +369
Limited Slip Differential +157
Power Drivers Seat +176
Third Seat +303

GRAND CARAVAN   1999

A revised front fascia is common to all models. The Grand Caravan ES gets an AutoStick transmission, 17-inch wheels and tires, and steering wheel-mounted radio controls.

Category P

Model	Trade-in	Private	Dealer
4 Dr Grand Pass. Van	9934	11017	12100
4 Dr Grand ES AWD Pass. Van	14614	16207	17800
4 Dr Grand ES Pass. Van	13629	15115	16600
4 Dr Grand LE AWD Pass. Van	14450	16025	17600
4 Dr Grand LE Pass. Van	12233	13567	14900
4 Dr Grand SE AWD Pass. Van	12069	13385	14700
4 Dr Grand SE Pass. Van	10509	11655	12800

OPTIONS FOR GRAND CARAVAN
6 cyl 3.0 L Engine +441
6 cyl 3.3 L Engine +535
6 cyl 3.8 L Engine +254
AM/FM Compact Disc Player[Opt on Grand] +179
AM/FM Stereo/CD/Tape +179
Air Conditioning +276
Alarm System +138
Aluminum/Alloy Wheels +229
Anti-Lock Brakes +312

Don't forget to refer to the Mileage Adjustment Table at the back of this book!

Model Description	Trade-in TMV	Private TMV	Dealer TMV	Model Description	Trade-in TMV	Private TMV	Dealer TMV

Automatic Load Leveling[Opt on STD 4WD] +161
Camper/Towing Package +232
Captain Chairs (4) +369
Child Seats (2) +123
Compact Disc Changer +249
Dual Air Conditioning +381
Dual Power Seats[Opt on ES] +196
Infinity Sound System[Opt on SE] +397
Leather Seats +491
Luggage Rack +108
Metallic Paint +110
Power Drivers Seat +132
Power Windows +140
Rear Heater +119
Rear Spoiler +119
Sunscreen Glass[Opt on Grand,SE] +249

INTREPID · 1999

Minor appearance tweaks such as chrome badging and improved floor carpeting debut for 1999. A new engine immobilizer is now available on the ES.

Category G

	Trade-in	Private	Dealer
4 Dr STD Sdn	9252	10176	11100
4 Dr ES Sdn	10586	11643	12700

OPTIONS FOR INTREPID

AM/FM Compact Disc Player +179
AM/FM Stereo/CD/Tape +273
Anti-Lock Brakes[Std on ES] +330
Compact Disc Changer +193
Dual Power Seats +419
Leather Seats +483
Metallic Paint +110
Power Drivers Seat[Std on ES] +132
Power Sunroof +439
Traction Control System +138

NEON · 1999

One new color is available for the Neon Style Package: Inferno Red. Disco, anyone?

Category B

	Trade-in	Private	Dealer
2 Dr Competition Cpe	5350	6125	6900
4 Dr Competition Sdn	5660	6480	7300
2 Dr Highline Cpe	5805	6646	7487
4 Dr Highline Sdn	5825	6669	7513
2 Dr R/T Cpe	6047	6924	7800
4 Dr R/T Sdn	6125	7012	7900
2 Dr Sport Cpe	5970	6835	7700
4 Dr Sport Sdn	5892	6746	7600

OPTIONS FOR NEON

AM/FM Compact Disc Player +218
AM/FM Stereo Tape[Std on R/T] +143
Air Conditioning[Std on R/T,Sport] +551
Aluminum/Alloy Wheels[Std on R/T] +196
Anti-Lock Brakes +328
Automatic 3-Speed Transmission +330
Compact Disc Changer +276

Competition Package +1135
Cruise Control +119
Power Moonroof +328
Power Windows +140

RAM 1500 · 1999

The Sport model gets a new front bumper, fascia, grille, headlamps, graphics, and Solar Yellow exterior color just to make sure it won't go unnoticed in traffic. All Rams get an express down feature for the power windows, a new headlamp switch, and four-wheel ABS is standard on vehicles over 10,000-lb. GVW.

Category K

	Trade-in	Private	Dealer
2 Dr Laramie SLT 4WD Ext Cab LB	13273	14636	16000
2 Dr Laramie SLT 4WD Std Cab LB	12464	13744	15025
2 Dr Laramie SLT Ext Cab LB	11598	12789	13981
2 Dr Laramie SLT Std Cab LB	9789	10794	11800
4 Dr Laramie SLT 4WD Ext Cab LB	14019	15460	16900
4 Dr Laramie SLT Ext Cab LB	12323	13589	14855
2 Dr Laramie SLT 4WD Ext Cab SB	13107	14453	15800
2 Dr Laramie SLT 4WD Std Cab SB	12213	13467	14722
2 Dr Laramie SLT Ext Cab SB	11448	12624	13800
2 Dr Laramie SLT Std Cab SB	9457	10428	11400
4 Dr Laramie SLT 4WD Ext Cab SB	13687	15094	16500
4 Dr Laramie SLT Ext Cab SB	12176	13427	14678
2 Dr ST 4WD Ext Cab LB	12360	13630	14900
2 Dr ST 4WD Std Cab LB	11199	12349	13500
2 Dr ST Ext Cab LB	10120	11160	12200
2 Dr ST Std Cab LB	8793	9697	10600
4 Dr ST 4WD Ext Cab LB	12775	14087	15400
4 Dr ST Ext Cab LB	10631	11723	12815
2 Dr ST 4WD Ext Cab SB	12278	13540	14801
2 Dr ST 4WD Std Cab SB	10535	11618	12700
2 Dr ST Ext Cab SB	10037	11069	12100
2 Dr ST Standard Cab SB			

Don't forget to refer to the Mileage Adjustment Table at the back of this book!

Model Description	Trade-in TMV	Private TMV	Dealer TMV
	8544	9422	10300
4 Dr ST 4WD Ext Cab SB			
	12588	13882	15175
4 Dr ST Ext Cab SB	10286	11343	12400
2 Dr WS Std Cab LB	8130	8965	9800
2 Dr WS Std Cab SB	7881	8690	9500

OPTIONS FOR RAM 1500
8 cyl 5.2 L Engine[Opt on Laramie SLT Std Cab, ST Std Cab] +325
8 cyl 5.9 L Engine +218
AM/FM Compact Disc Player +234
AM/FM Stereo/CD/Tape +303
Air Conditioning[Opt on ST,WS] +444
Anti-Lock Brakes +276
Automatic 4-Speed Transmission +537
Bed Liner +130
Camper/Towing Package +152
Leather Seats +689
Limited Slip Differential +157
Power Drivers Seat +176
Tilt Steering Wheel[Opt on ST,WS] +108

RAM 2500   1999

The Sport model gets a new front bumper, fascia, grille, headlamps, graphics, and Solar Yellow exterior color just to make sure it won't go unnoticed in traffic. All Rams get an express down feature for the power windows, a new headlamp switch, and four-wheel ABS is standard on vehicles over 10,000-lb. GVW.

Category K

Model Description	Trade-in TMV	Private TMV	Dealer TMV
2 Dr Laramie SLT 4WD Ext Cab LB			
	14932	16466	18000
2 Dr Laramie SLT 4WD Std Cab LB			
	14102	15551	17000
2 Dr Laramie SLT Ext Cab LB			
	12775	14087	15400
2 Dr Laramie SLT Std Cab LB			
	12301	13565	14829
4 Dr Laramie SLT 4WD Ext Cab LB			
	15512	17106	18700
4 Dr Laramie SLT Ext Cab LB			
	13439	14819	16200
2 Dr Laramie SLT 4WD Ext Cab SB			
	14766	16283	17800
2 Dr Laramie SLT Ext Cab SB			
	12526	13813	15100
4 Dr Laramie SLT 4WD Ext Cab SB			
	15264	16832	18400
4 Dr Laramie SLT Ext Cab SB			
	13190	14545	15900
2 Dr ST 4WD Ext Cab LB			
	13936	15368	16800
2 Dr ST 4WD Std Cab LB			

Model Description	Trade-in TMV	Private TMV	Dealer TMV
	12443	13722	15000
2 Dr ST Ext Cab LB	11697	12898	14100
2 Dr ST Std Cab LB	10535	11618	12700
4 Dr ST 4WD Ext Cab LB			
	14609	16110	17611
4 Dr ST Ext Cab LB	12360	13630	14900
2 Dr ST 4WD Ext Cab SB			
	13356	14728	16100
2 Dr ST Ext Cab SB	10950	12075	13200
4 Dr ST 4WD Ext Cab SB			
	14268	15734	17200
4 Dr ST Ext Cab SB	12253	13512	14771

OPTIONS FOR RAM 2500
10 cyl 8.0 L Engine +259
6 cyl 5.9 L Turbodiesel Engine +2423
AM/FM Compact Disc Player +234
AM/FM Stereo/CD/Tape +381
Air Conditioning[Opt on ST] +444
Anti-Lock Brakes +276
Automatic 4-Speed Transmission +537
Bed Liner +130
Camper/Towing Package +135
Chrome Wheels[Opt on ST] +179
Cruise Control[Opt on ST] +108
Leather Seats +689
Limited Slip Differential +157
Power Drivers Seat +176
Tilt Steering Wheel[Opt on ST] +108

RAM 3500   1999

The Sport model gets a new front bumper, fascia, grille, headlamps, graphics, and Solar Yellow exterior color just to make sure it won't go unnoticed in traffic. All Rams get an express down feature for the power windows, a new headlamp switch, and four-wheel ABS is standard on vehicles over 10,000-lb. GVW.

Category K

Model Description	Trade-in TMV	Private TMV	Dealer TMV
2 Dr Laramie SLT 4WD Std Cab LB			
	14936	16470	18005
2 Dr Laramie SLT Std Cab LB			
	13273	14636	16000
4 Dr Laramie SLT 4WD Ext Cab LB			
	16591	18295	20000
4 Dr Laramie SLT Ext Cab LB			
	14928	16461	17995
2 Dr ST 4WD Std Cab LB			
	13936	15368	16800
2 Dr ST Std Cab LB	12443	13722	15000
4 Dr ST 4WD Ext Cab LB			
	15595	17198	18800
4 Dr ST Ext Cab LB	13853	15277	16700

OPTIONS FOR RAM 3500

Model Description	Trade-in TMV	Private TMV	Dealer TMV	Model Description	Trade-in TMV	Private TMV	Dealer TMV

10 cyl 8.0 L Engine +259
6 cyl 5.9 L Turbodiesel Engine +2423
AM/FM Compact Disc Player +281
AM/FM Stereo/CD/Tape +381
Air Conditioning[Opt on ST] +444
Automatic 4-Speed Transmission +537
Bed Liner +130
Camper/Towing Package +152
Cruise Control[Opt on ST] +108
Leather Seats +689
Limited Slip Differential +130
Power Drivers Seat +176
Tilt Steering Wheel[Opt on ST] +108

STRATUS   1999

The instrument panel gauges are now white-faced, wheels are better looking, and some work has been done to reduce the interior noise levels.

Category C

4 Dr STD Sdn	6676	7538	8400
4 Dr ES Sdn	7471	8435	9400

OPTIONS FOR STRATUS

4 cyl 2.4 L Engine +249
AM/FM Compact Disc Player[Opt on STD] +110
AM/FM Stereo/CD/Tape +303
Anti-Lock Brakes[Std on ES] +312
Automatic 4-Speed Transmission[Std on ES] +579
Compact Disc Changer +303
Leather Seats +344
Power Door Locks[Std on ES] +130
Power Drivers Seat +210
Power Sunroof +320
Power Windows[Std on ES] +143
Special Factory Paint +110

VIPER   1999

Goodies for the '99 Viper include power mirrors, Connolly leather for various interior surfaces, a new shift knob, aluminum interior accents, and a remote release for the glass hatch on the GTS. Black is again an exterior color choice, available with or without silver stripes. New 18-inch aluminum wheels with the Viper logo on the caps round out the changes.

Category R

2 Dr GTS Cpe	48320	51160	54000
2 Dr RT/10 Conv	46978	49739	52500

OPTIONS FOR VIPER

AM/FM Compact Disc Player[Opt on GTS] +303
Hardtop Roof +1379
Tonneau Cover +138

WAGON   1999

Seat track travel has increased substantially, and the remote keyless entry has been improved. For fleet customers, the Ram vans and wagons have an available 5.2-liter Compressed Natural Gas V8 engine.

Category Q

2 Dr 1500 STD Pass. Van			
	9818	10809	11800
2 Dr 2500 STD Pass. Van Ext			
	10900	12000	13100
2 Dr 3500 Maxi Pass. Van Ext			
	11732	12916	14100

OPTIONS FOR WAGON

8 cyl 5.2 L Engine[Opt on 1500] +325
8 cyl 5.9 L Engine +218
AM/FM Compact Disc Player +268
AM/FM Stereo/CD/Tape +366
Anti-Lock Brakes +193
Automatic 4-Speed Transmission[Opt on 1500] +138
Camper/Towing Package +123
Chrome Wheels +138
Dual Air Conditioning +466
Limited Slip Differential +157
Power Door Locks +123
Power Drivers Seat +165
Power Windows +146
Sunscreen Glass +226

1998 DODGE

AVENGER   1998

Interior fabrics are new, as is a black and gray color scheme. The ES model gets a new Sport package that affects appearance, not performance. Also available for the ES are new 16-inch aluminum wheels and a rear sway bar that improves handling.

Category E

2 Dr STD Cpe	7026	7926	8900
2 Dr ES Cpe	8289	9350	10500

OPTIONS FOR AVENGER

6 cyl 2.5 L Engine +304
AM/FM Stereo/CD/Tape +162
Air Conditioning[Std on ES] +394
Aluminum/Alloy Wheels[Std on ES] +245
Anti-Lock Brakes +300
Automatic 4-Speed Transmission +347
Leather Seats +212
Power Door Locks +112
Power Sunroof +319
Power Windows +127
Rear Spoiler[Std on ES] +149

CARAVAN   1998

Available this year is a 3.8-liter V6 that puts out 180 horsepower and 240 foot-pounds of torque. And for convenience, Caravans come with rear-seat mounted grocery bag hooks, and driver's-side easy-entry Quad seating. All Chrysler products are equipped with "Next Generation" depowered airbags.

Category P

Don't forget to refer to the Mileage Adjustment Table at the back of this book!

Model Description	Trade-in TMV	Private TMV	Dealer TMV
2 Dr STD Pass. Van	6654	7444	8300
4 Dr Grand Pass. Van	8738	9776	10900
4 Dr Grand ES AWD Pass. Van	12586	14081	15700
4 Dr Grand ES Pass. Van	11464	12825	14300
4 Dr Grand LE AWD Pass. Van	12426	13901	15500
4 Dr Grand LE Pass. Van	11143	12466	13900
4 Dr LE Pass. Van	9860	11031	12300
4 Dr Grand SE AWD Pass. Van	11063	12377	13800
4 Dr Grand SE Pass. Van	9379	10493	11700
4 Dr SE Pass. Van	9059	10135	11300

OPTIONS FOR CARAVAN

6 cyl 3.0 L Engine[Std on Grand,SE] +384
6 cyl 3.8 L Engine[Std on 4WD] +187
7 Passenger Seating[Opt on STD] +174
AM/FM Compact Disc Player +162
AM/FM Stereo/CD/Tape +197
Air Conditioning[Std on Grand ES,Grand LE,LE,4WD] +430
Alarm System +125
Aluminum/Alloy Wheels[Std on Grand ES] +131
Anti-Lock Brakes[Opt on Grand,STD] +282
Automatic 4-Speed Transmission[Opt on Grand,STD] +125
Automatic Load Leveling[Std on 4WD] +145
Captain Chairs (4) +334
Child Seats (2) +112
Dual Air Conditioning +444
Heated Power Mirrors[Std on LE] +125
Infinity Sound System[Opt on Grand SE] +197
Leather Seats +397
Power Door Locks[Std on LE] +167
Power Drivers Seat +140
Power Windows[Opt on Grand SE,SE] +130
Sliding Driver Side Door[Opt on STD] +297
Sunscreen Glass[Std on LE] +149

DAKOTA 1998

The Dakota R/T, featuring a 250-horsepower V8, is available for those seeking a performance pickup. The passenger airbag can now be deactivated in all Dakotas, so a rear-facing child seat is perfectly safe. The Dakota is also available in three new colors.

Category J

Model Description	Trade-in TMV	Private TMV	Dealer TMV
2 Dr STD Std Cab LB	6568	7303	8100
2 Dr STD 4WD Ext Cab SB	9649	10729	11900
2 Dr STD 4WD Std Cab SB	8420	9363	10385
2 Dr STD Ext Cab SB	7784	8656	9600
2 Dr STD Std Cab SB	6162	6852	7600
2 Dr R/T Sport Ext Cab SB	10071	11199	12421
2 Dr R/T Sport Std Cab SB	8398	9338	10357
2 Dr SLT Std Cab LB	7297	8115	9000
2 Dr SLT 4WD Ext Cab SB	10199	11341	12579
2 Dr SLT 4WD Std Cab SB	9000	10008	11100
2 Dr SLT Ext Cab SB	8433	9378	10401
2 Dr SLT Std Cab SB	7054	7844	8700
2 Dr Sport Std Cab LB	6973	7754	8600
2 Dr Sport 4WD Ext Cab SB	10297	11451	12700
2 Dr Sport 4WD Std Cab SB	8676	9647	10700
2 Dr Sport Ext Cab SB	8479	9429	10458
2 Dr Sport Std Cab SB	6677	7425	8235

OPTIONS FOR DAKOTA

8 cyl 5.2 L Engine +294
8 cyl 5.9 L Engine[Std on R/T Sport] +841
AM/FM Compact Disc Player +240
AM/FM Stereo/CD/Tape +329
Air Conditioning[Std on SLT] +399
Anti-Lock Brakes +250
Automatic 4-Speed Transmission[Std on R/T Sport] +474
Bed Liner +118
Camper/Towing Package +122
Cruise Control +98
Limited Slip Differential[Std on R/T Sport] +143
Power Door Locks +109
Power Drivers Seat +160
Power Windows +118

DURANGO 1998

As the most recent addition to the Dodge truck lineup, the Durango makes quite an entry. Offering the most cargo space in its class, along with eight-passenger seating and three-and-a-half tons of towing capacity, the Durango is the most versatile sport-utility on the market.

Category M

Model Description	Trade-in TMV	Private TMV	Dealer TMV
4 Dr STD 4WD Wgn	13451	14963	16600
4 Dr SLT 4WD Wgn	14099	15684	17400

OPTIONS FOR DURANGO

8 cyl 5.9 L Engine +197
AM/FM Stereo/CD/Tape +149
Anti-Lock Brakes +282
Camper/Towing Package +122
Dual Air Conditioning +215
Infinity Sound System[Opt on SLT] +165
Leather Seats +334
Limited Slip Differential +143
Power Drivers Seat +160

Don't forget to refer to the Mileage Adjustment Table at the back of this book!

Model Description	Trade-in TMV	Private TMV	Dealer TMV	Model Description	Trade-in TMV	Private TMV	Dealer TMV

Third Seat +275

INTREPID 1998

Completely redesigned for 1998, the Intrepid is a sedan that has the graceful styling of a coupe, thanks to a continuation of Chrysler's cab-forward design. Dodge's trademark cross hair grille dominates the front end along with two large, sparkling headlights. And the new Intrepid is powered by your choice of two new V6 engines.

Category G

Model	Trade-in	Private	Dealer
4 Dr STD Sdn	7256	8093	9000
4 Dr ES Sdn	8546	9532	10600

OPTIONS FOR INTREPID

AM/FM Compact Disc Player +162
AM/FM Stereo/CD/Tape +247
Anti-Lock Brakes[Std on ES] +300
Compact Disc Changer +174
Dual Power Seats +379
Leather Seats +437
Power Drivers Seat[Std on ES] +120
Power Moonroof +397
Traction Control System +125

NEON 1998

An R/T appearance package makes people think you're driving a Viper! Improved option packages, LEV emissions and next-generation airbags round out the changes.

Category B

Model	Trade-in	Private	Dealer
2 Dr Competition Cpe	4237	4987	5800
4 Dr Competition Sdn	4310	5073	5900
2 Dr Highline Cpe	4383	5159	6000
4 Dr Highline Sdn	4456	5245	6100
2 Dr R/T Cpe	4675	5503	6400
4 Dr R/T Sdn	4748	5589	6500
2 Dr Sport Cpe	4535	5338	6208
4 Dr Sport Sdn	4613	5430	6315

OPTIONS FOR NEON

AM/FM Compact Disc Player +185
AM/FM Stereo Tape[Std on R/T] +130
Air Conditioning[Std on R/T,Sport] +499
Aluminum/Alloy Wheels[Std on R/T] +177
Anti-Lock Brakes +297
Automatic 3-Speed Transmission +300
Compact Disc Changer +250
Competition Package +1028
Cruise Control +108
Power Moonroof +297
Power Windows +127

RAM 1500 1998

The Ram Quad Cab, as in four doors, becomes the first pickup on the market with two rear access doors. And for convenience, the front seat belts are now integrated into the front seats, making for obstruction-free rear access. All Rams get a totally redesigned interior, standard passenger-side airbag with cutoff switch, and all airbags are "depowered" for safety.

Category K

Model	Trade-in	Private	Dealer
2 Dr Laramie SLT 4WD Ext Cab LB			
	11974	13282	14700
2 Dr Laramie SLT 4WD Std Cab LB			
	11334	12573	13915
2 Dr Laramie SLT Ext Cab LB			
	10752	11927	13200
2 Dr Laramie SLT Std Cab LB			
	8823	9787	10832
4 Dr Laramie SLT 4WD Ext Cab LB			
	12299	13644	15100
4 Dr Laramie SLT Ext Cab LB			
	11184	12406	13730
2 Dr Laramie SLT 4WD Ext Cab SB			
	11729	13011	14400
2 Dr Laramie SLT 4WD Std Cab SB			
	11135	12352	13670
2 Dr Laramie SLT Ext Cab SB			
	10670	11837	13100
2 Dr Laramie SLT Std Cab SB			
	8634	9578	10600
4 Dr Laramie SLT 4WD Ext Cab SB			
	12218	13553	15000
4 Dr Laramie SLT Ext Cab SB			
	10915	12108	13400
2 Dr SS/T Std Cab SB	10589	11746	13000
2 Dr ST 4WD Ext Cab LB			
	11280	12513	13849
2 Dr ST 4WD Std Cab LB			
	9693	10752	11900
2 Dr ST Ext Cab LB	8961	9941	11002
2 Dr ST Std Cab LB	8282	9187	10168
4 Dr ST 4WD Ext Cab LB			
	11566	12831	14200
4 Dr ST Ext Cab LB	9596	10645	11781
2 Dr ST 4WD Ext Cab SB			
	11119	12334	13651
2 Dr ST 4WD Std Cab SB			
	9300	10317	11418
2 Dr ST Ext Cab SB	8891	9862	10915
2 Dr ST Std Cab SB	7982	8855	9800
4 Dr ST 4WD Ext Cab SB			
	11374	12617	13964
4 Dr ST Ext Cab SB	9164	10166	11251
2 Dr WS Std Cab LB	7657	8493	9400

Don't forget to refer to the Mileage Adjustment Table at the back of this book!

Model Description	Trade-in TMV	Private TMV	Dealer TMV
2 Dr WS Std Cab SB	7494	8313	9200

OPTIONS FOR RAM 1500

8 cyl 5.2 L Engine[Opt on Laramie SLT Std Cab,ST Std Cab] +294
8 cyl 5.9 L Engine +148
AM/FM Compact Disc Player +212
AM/FM Stereo/CD/Tape +275
Air Conditioning[Opt on ST,WS] +401
Anti-Lock Brakes +250
Automatic 4-Speed Transmission[Std on SS/T] +474
Bed Liner +118
Camper/Towing Package +122
Chrome Wheels +148
Leather Seats +623
Limited Slip Differential +143
Power Drivers Seat +160

RAM 2500   1998

Available as a sedan! The Ram Quad Cab, as in four doors, becomes the first pickup on the market with two rear access doors. And for convenience, the front seat belts are now integrated into the front seats, making for obstruction-free rear access. All Rams get a totally redesigned interior, standard passenger-side airbag with cutoff switch, and all airbags are "depowered" for safety.

Category K

Model Description	Trade-in TMV	Private TMV	Dealer TMV
2 Dr Laramie SLT 4WD Ext Cab LB	13684	15180	16800
2 Dr Laramie SLT 4WD Std Cab LB	12218	13553	15000
2 Dr Laramie SLT Ext Cab LB	11943	13248	14662
2 Dr Laramie SLT Std Cab LB	10833	12017	13300
4 Dr Laramie SLT 4WD Ext Cab LB	13928	15451	17100
4 Dr Laramie SLT Ext Cab LB	12134	13460	14897
2 Dr Laramie SLT 4WD Ext Cab SB	13668	15162	16780
2 Dr Laramie SLT Ext Cab SB	11806	13096	14494
4 Dr Laramie SLT 4WD Ext Cab SB	13863	15379	17020
4 Dr Laramie SLT Ext Cab SB	12088	13410	14841
2 Dr ST 4WD Ext Cab LB	12149	13477	14915
2 Dr ST 4WD Std Cab LB	11653	12926	14306
2 Dr ST Ext Cab LB	10752	11927	13200
2 Dr ST Std Cab LB	9774	10843	12000
4 Dr ST 4WD Ext Cab LB	12967	14384	15919
4 Dr ST Ext Cab LB	11159	12379	13700
2 Dr ST 4WD Ext Cab SB	12722	14113	15619
2 Dr ST Ext Cab SB	10589	11746	13000
4 Dr ST 4WD Ext Cab SB	12919	14331	15861
4 Dr ST Ext Cab SB	10996	12198	13500

OPTIONS FOR RAM 2500

10 cyl 8.0 L Engine +486
6 cyl 5.9 L Turbodiesel Engine +2193
AM/FM Compact Disc Player +212
AM/FM Stereo/CD/Tape +344
Air Conditioning[Opt on ST] +401
Anti-Lock Brakes +250
Automatic 4-Speed Transmission +474
Bed Liner +118
Camper/Towing Package +122
Chrome Wheels +148
Leather Seats +623
Limited Slip Differential +143
Power Drivers Seat +160

RAM 3500   1998

All Rams get a totally redesigned interior, standard passenger-side airbag with cutoff switch, and all airbags are "depowered" for safety.

Category K

Model Description	Trade-in TMV	Private TMV	Dealer TMV
2 Dr Laramie SLT 4WD Std Cab LB	14064	15601	17266
2 Dr Laramie SLT Std Cab LB	11485	12740	14100
4 Dr Laramie SLT 4WD Ext Cab LB	15476	17168	19000
4 Dr Laramie SLT Ext Cab LB	14345	15913	17611
2 Dr ST 4WD Std Cab LB	13033	14457	16000
2 Dr ST Std Cab LB	10752	11927	13200
4 Dr ST 4WD Ext Cab LB	14499	16083	17800
4 Dr ST Ext Cab LB	13630	15120	16734

OPTIONS FOR RAM 3500

10 cyl 8.0 L Engine +486
6 cyl 5.9 L Turbodiesel Engine +2193
AM/FM Compact Disc Player +255
AM/FM Stereo/CD/Tape +344
Air Conditioning[Opt on ST] +401
Anti-Lock Brakes +250
Automatic 4-Speed Transmission +474
Bed Liner +118
Camper/Towing Package +122
Leather Seats +623

Don't forget to refer to the Mileage Adjustment Table at the back of this book!

Model Description	Trade-in TMV	Private TMV	Dealer TMV
Limited Slip Differential +143			
Power Drivers Seat +160			
Tilt Steering Wheel[Opt on ST] +98			

STRATUS — 1998

The 2.4-liter engine with automatic transmission is now standard on the ES. New colors are available this year and numerous refinements were made to reduce noise and vibration.

Category C

Model Description	Trade-in TMV	Private TMV	Dealer TMV
4 Dr STD Sdn	5500	6268	7100
4 Dr ES Sdn	6507	7416	8400

OPTIONS FOR STRATUS
4 cyl 2.4 L Engine[Std on ES] +224
6 cyl 2.5 L Engine +474
AM/FM Stereo/CD/Tape +275
Anti-Lock Brakes +282
Automatic 4-Speed Transmission[Std on ES] +524
Compact Disc Changer +275
Leather Seats +311
Power Door Locks[Std on ES] +118
Power Drivers Seat +190
Power Sunroof +289
Power Windows +130

VIPER — 1998

Tubular, stainless steel exhaust manifolds help reduce emissions and weight. Silver Metallic paint is a new option and the powerful Dodge gets a passenger airbag cutoff switch and second-generation depowered airbags.

Category R

Model Description	Trade-in TMV	Private TMV	Dealer TMV
2 Dr GTS Cpe	41266	44258	47500
2 Dr RT/10 Conv	40136	43047	46200

OPTIONS FOR VIPER
Hardtop Roof +1248
Tonneau Cover +125

WAGON — 1998

A minor redesign this year includes better build quality, so we're told. Of note are the appearance of dual airbags in the revised dash and upgrades to the brakes, front doors and sound system. The V8 engines have also been relocated forward to reduce the size of that annoying "doghouse."

Category Q

Model Description	Trade-in TMV	Private TMV	Dealer TMV
2 Dr 1500 Ram Wagon	7924	8825	9800
2 Dr 1500 SLT Ram Wagon	8167	9095	10100
2 Dr 2500 Ram Wagon Ext	8652	9635	10700
2 Dr 2500 SLT Ram Wagon Ext	8975	9995	11100
2 Dr 3500 Maxi Ram Wagon Ext	9542	10626	11800
2 Dr 3500 SLT Maxi Ram Wagon Ext	9703	10806	12000

OPTIONS FOR WAGON
12 Passenger Seating[Opt on 2500] +143
8 cyl 5.2 L Engine[Opt on 1500] +294
8 cyl 5.9 L Engine +197
AM/FM Compact Disc Player +242
AM/FM Stereo/CD/Tape +332
Anti-Lock Brakes +250
Automatic 4-Speed Transmission[Opt on 1500] +125
Camper/Towing Package +112
Chrome Wheels +125
Dual Air Conditioning +439
Limited Slip Differential +143
Power Door Locks +112
Power Drivers Seat +149
Power Windows +131
Premium Sound System +275
Sunscreen Glass +205

1997 DODGE

AVENGER — 1997

Front and rear styling is updated, while ES models lose the standard V6 engine. The V6 is available on base and ES models, and includes 17-inch wheels and tires on the ES. New colors inside and out and two additional speakers with cassette stereos further broaden the appeal of this roomy coupe.

Category E

Model Description	Trade-in TMV	Private TMV	Dealer TMV
2 Dr STD Cpe	5704	6512	7500
2 Dr ES Cpe	6844	7814	9000

OPTIONS FOR AVENGER
6 cyl 2.5 L Engine +266
AM/FM Compact Disc Player[Opt on STD] +190
AM/FM Stereo/CD/Tape +190
Air Conditioning[Std on ES] +344
Alarm System +125
Aluminum/Alloy Wheels[Std on ES] +213
Anti-Lock Brakes[Std on ES] +261
Automatic 4-Speed Transmission +297
Compact Disc Changer +196
Infinity Sound System +141
Leather Seats +185
Power Sunroof +279
Power Windows +112
Rear Spoiler +131

CARAVAN — 1997

Traction control is a new option, so long as you get LE or ES trim, and an enhanced accident response system will automatically unlock the doors and illuminate the interior when an airbag deploys. Appearance and equipment refinements complete the modest changes

DODGE 97

Model Description	Trade-in TMV	Private TMV	Dealer TMV	Model Description	Trade-in TMV	Private TMV	Dealer TMV

to this best-in-class minivan.

Category P

Model Description	Trade-in TMV	Private TMV	Dealer TMV
2 Dr Grand Pass. Van	6830	7716	8800
2 Dr STD Pass. Van	5666	6401	7300
4 Dr ES Pass. Van	8994	10162	11589
4 Dr Grand ES AWD Pass. Van	10212	11538	13158
4 Dr Grand ES Pass. Van	9236	10435	11900
4 Dr Grand LE AWD Pass. Van	10122	11436	13042
4 Dr Grand LE Pass. Van	9011	10181	11611
4 Dr LE Pass. Van	8227	9295	10600
2 Dr Grand SE AWD Pass. Van	8732	9866	11251
2 Dr Grand SE Pass. Van	7451	8418	9600
2 Dr SE Pass. Van	7218	8155	9300

OPTIONS FOR CARAVAN
6 cyl 3.0 L Engine +113
6 cyl 3.8 L Engine[Opt on ES,LE] +163
7 Passenger Seating[Opt on STD] +152
AM/FM Stereo/CD/Tape +172
Air Conditioning[Opt on Grand,Grand SE,SE,STD] +375
Alarm System +109
Aluminum/Alloy Wheels[Std on ES,Grand ES] +115
Anti-Lock Brakes[Opt on Grand,STD] +246
Automatic Load Leveling +126
Captain Chairs (4) +260
Compact Disc Changer +240
Dual Air Conditioning +388
Infinity Sound System[Opt on Grand ES] +146
Leather Seats +347
Power Door Locks[Opt on Grand,Grand SE,SE,STD] +146
Power Drivers Seat +122
Power Windows[Opt on Grand SE,SE] +113
Sliding Driver Side Door[Opt on Grand,Grand SE,STD] +260
Sport Package +540
Sunscreen Glass +196

DAKOTA   1997

What's new? Almost the entire truck, that's what. Powertrains are carried over, but everything else is new. Distinctions? Tightest turning circle in class, roomiest cabs and dual airbags are standard. Faux pas? No third door option, and the passenger airbag cannot be deactivated, so a rear-facing child seat is out of the question unless you cram it into the rear of the Club Cab.

Category J

Model Description	Trade-in TMV	Private TMV	Dealer TMV
2 Dr STD Std Cab LB	5343	6018	6843
2 Dr STD 4WD Ext Cab SB	8257	9300	10575
2 Dr STD 4WD Std Cab SB	6871	7739	8800
2 Dr STD Ext Cab SB	6637	7475	8500
2 Dr STD Std Cab SB	5310	5980	6800
2 Dr SLT Std Cab LB	6169	6948	7900
2 Dr SLT 4WD Ext Cab SB	8745	9850	11200
2 Dr SLT 4WD Std Cab SB	7808	8795	10000
2 Dr SLT Ext Cab SB	6949	7827	8900
2 Dr SLT Std Cab SB	6072	6840	7777
2 Dr Sport Std Cab LB	5952	6704	7623
2 Dr Sport 4WD Ext Cab SB	8296	9344	10625
2 Dr Sport 4WD Std Cab SB	7496	8443	9600
2 Dr Sport Ext Cab SB	6793	7651	8700
2 Dr Sport Std Cab SB	5432	6118	6957

OPTIONS FOR DAKOTA
6 cyl 3.9 L Engine +217
8 cyl 5.2 L Engine +257
AM/FM Compact Disc Player +209
AM/FM Stereo/CD/Tape +287
Air Conditioning[Std on SLT] +348
Anti-Lock Brakes +217
Automatic 4-Speed Transmission +425
Camper/Towing Package +121
Limited Slip Differential +124

INTREPID   1997

Few changes as first-generation Intrepid enters final year of production. A Sport Group including the 3.5-liter V6 engine is optional on base models, which also get an upgraded cassette stereo standard. Bolt-on wheel covers debut, and a new exterior color is introduced. Automatic transmissions get new software.

Category G

Model Description	Trade-in TMV	Private TMV	Dealer TMV
4 Dr STD Sdn	5474	6251	7200
4 Dr ES Sdn	6234	7119	8200

OPTIONS FOR INTREPID
6 cyl 3.5 L Engine[Std on ES] +316
AM/FM Stereo/CD/Tape +216
Anti-Lock Brakes[Std on ES] +262
Compact Disc Changer +152
Dual Power Seats +331
Leather Seats +382
Power Drivers Seat[Opt on STD] +105
Power Moonroof +347
Premium Sound System +305
Traction Control System +109

NEON   1997

Sport trim level disappears in favor of Sport Package

Model Description	Trade-in TMV	Private TMV	Dealer TMV	Model Description	Trade-in TMV	Private TMV	Dealer TMV

for Highline models. Twin-cam engine is now optional on Highline models. Federal side-impact standards are met for the first time. More work has been done to quiet the Neon's boisterous demeanor.

Category B

Model	Trade-in	Private	Dealer
2 Dr STD Cpe	3272	3915	4700
4 Dr STD Sdn	3333	3988	4788
2 Dr Highline Cpe	3439	4115	4940
4 Dr Highline Sdn	3480	4164	4999
2 Dr Sport Cpe	3481	4165	5000
4 Dr Sport Sdn	3760	4498	5400

OPTIONS FOR NEON

AM/FM Compact Disc Player +161
AM/FM Stereo Tape +113
Air Conditioning[Opt on STD] +436
Aluminum/Alloy Wheels +155
Anti-Lock Brakes +260
Automatic 3-Speed Transmission +262
Compact Disc Changer +217
Competition Package +898
Power Moonroof +260
Power Windows +112

RAM 1500   1997

No major changes to this popular truck for 1997. Refinements include available leather seating and woodgrain trim on SLT models, optional remote keyless entry, and standard deep-tinted quarter glass on Club Cab models. Newly available is a combination CD/cassette stereo. Items from the 1996 Indy 500 Special Edition are available in a new Sport Package upgrade. Fresh interior and exterior colors sum up the changes this year.

Category K

Model	Trade-in	Private	Dealer
2 Dr LT 4WD Std Cab LB	7853	8819	10000
2 Dr LT Std Cab LB	6596	7408	8400
2 Dr LT 4WD Std Cab SB	7696	8643	9800
2 Dr LT Std Cab SB	6361	7143	8100
2 Dr Laramie SLT 4WD Ext Cab LB	10142	11390	12915
2 Dr Laramie SLT 4WD Std Cab LB	9474	10639	12064
2 Dr Laramie SLT Ext Cab LB	8089	9084	10300
2 Dr Laramie SLT Std Cab LB	7146	8025	9100
2 Dr Laramie SLT 4WD Ext Cab SB	10130	11377	12900
2 Dr Laramie SLT 4WD Std Cab SB	8717	9789	11100

Model	Trade-in	Private	Dealer
2 Dr Laramie SLT Ext Cab SB	7931	8907	10100
2 Dr Laramie SLT Std Cab SB	6911	7761	8800
2 Dr SS/T Std Cab SB	7892	8863	10050
2 Dr ST 4WD Ext Cab LB	9530	10703	12136
2 Dr ST Ext Cab LB	7487	8408	9534
2 Dr ST 4WD Ext Cab SB	9424	10584	12001
2 Dr ST Ext Cab SB	7434	8348	9466
2 Dr WS Std Cab LB	5968	6703	7600
2 Dr WS Std Cab SB	5419	6085	6900

OPTIONS FOR RAM 1500

8 cyl 5.2 L Engine[Opt on Laramie SLT Std Cab,LT Std Cab] +257
8 cyl 5.9 L Engine +172
AM/FM Compact Disc Player +185
AM/FM Stereo/CD/Tape +240
Air Conditioning[Opt on LT,ST,WS] +351
Anti-Lock Brakes +217
Automatic 4-Speed Transmission +414
Camper/Towing Package +121
Chrome Wheels +129
Leather Seats +544
Limited Slip Differential +124
Power Drivers Seat +140
Premium Sound System +135

RAM 2500   1997

No major changes to this popular truck for 1997. Refinements include available leather seating and woodgrain trim on SLT models, optional remote keyless entry, and standard deep-tinted quarter glass on Club Cab models. Newly available is a combination CD/cassette stereo. Items from the 1996 Indy 500 Special Edition are available in a new Sport Package upgrade. Fresh interior and exterior colors sum up the changes this year.

Category K

Model	Trade-in	Private	Dealer
2 Dr LT 4WD Std Cab LB	9031	10142	11500
2 Dr LT Std Cab LB	7382	8290	9400
2 Dr Laramie SLT 4WD Ext Cab LB	10758	12082	13700
2 Dr Laramie SLT 4WD Std Cab LB	10130	11377	12900
2 Dr Laramie SLT Ext Cab LB	9277	10419	11814
2 Dr Laramie SLT Std Cab LB	8638	9701	11000
2 Dr Laramie SLT 4WD Ext Cab SB	10680	11994	13600

Don't forget to refer to the Mileage Adjustment Table at the back of this book!

Model Description	Trade-in TMV	Private TMV	Dealer TMV	Model Description	Trade-in TMV	Private TMV	Dealer TMV
2 Dr Laramie SLT Ext Cab SB				2 Dr ST Std Cab LB	9031	10142	11500
	9266	10407	11800				
2 Dr ST 4WD Ext Cab LB							
	10052	11288	12800				
2 Dr ST 4WD Std Cab LB							
	9098	10218	11586				
2 Dr ST Ext Cab LB	8324	9348	10600				
2 Dr ST Std Cab LB	7696	8643	9800				
2 Dr ST 4WD Ext Cab SB							
	9895	11112	12600				
2 Dr ST Ext Cab SB	8246	9260	10500				

OPTIONS FOR RAM 3500
10 cyl 8.0 L Engine +425
6 cyl 5.9 L Turbodiesel Engine +1915
AM/FM Compact Disc Player +222
AM/FM Stereo/CD/Tape +301
Air Conditioning[Opt on LT,ST] +351
Anti-Lock Brakes +217
Automatic 4-Speed Transmission +425
Camper/Towing Package +121
Leather Seats +544
Limited Slip Differential +124
Power Drivers Seat +140
Premium Sound System +135

OPTIONS FOR RAM 2500
10 cyl 8.0 L Engine +425
6 cyl 5.9 L Turbodiesel Engine +1915
AM/FM Compact Disc Player +185
AM/FM Stereo/CD/Tape +301
Air Conditioning[Opt on LT,ST] +351
Anti-Lock Brakes +217
Automatic 4-Speed Transmission +425
Camper/Towing Package +107
Chrome Wheels[Opt on LT,ST] +129
Leather Seats +544
Limited Slip Differential +124
Power Drivers Seat +140
Premium Sound System +185

STRATUS — 1997

Subtle styling revisions are the most obvious change to the Stratus for 1997. Sound systems have been improved, rear seat heat ducts benefit from improved flow, and the optional 2.4-liter engine runs quieter. New colors and a revised console round out changes.
Category C

Model Description	Trade-in TMV	Private TMV	Dealer TMV
4 Dr STD Sdn	4439	5186	6100
4 Dr ES Sdn	4875	5696	6700

OPTIONS FOR STRATUS
4 cyl 2.4 L Engine +196
6 cyl 2.5 L Engine +414
AM/FM Stereo/CD/Tape +240
Anti-Lock Brakes[Std on ES] +246
Automatic 4-Speed Transmission +359
Compact Disc Changer +240
Leather Seats +272
Power Door Locks +102
Power Drivers Seat +166
Power Windows[Std on ES] +113

RAM 3500 — 1997

No major changes to this popular truck for 1997. Refinements include available leather seating and woodgrain trim on SLT models, optional remote keyless entry, and standard deep-tinted quarter glass on Club Cab models. Newly available is a combination CD/cassette stereo. Items from the 1996 Indy 500 Special Edition are available in a new Sport Package upgrade. Fresh interior and exterior colors sum up the changes this year.
Category K

Model Description	Trade-in TMV	Private TMV	Dealer TMV
2 Dr LT 4WD Std Cab LB			
	10523	11818	13400
2 Dr LT Std Cab LB	8560	9613	10900
2 Dr Laramie SLT 4WD Ext Cab LB			
	12486	14022	15900
2 Dr Laramie SLT 4WD Std Cab LB			
	12172	13670	15500
2 Dr Laramie SLT Ext Cab LB			
	10837	12170	13800
2 Dr Laramie SLT Std Cab LB			
	10052	11288	12800
2 Dr ST 4WD Ext Cab LB			
	12093	13581	15400
2 Dr ST 4WD Std Cab LB			
	10758	12082	13700
2 Dr ST Ext Cab LB	9895	11112	12600

VIPER — 1997

One new color, flame red, with or without white stripes, is available for 1997. Silver, sparkle gold or yellow gold wheels come with red Vipers. The original blue with white stripes paint scheme is available as an option, as are last year's standard polished aluminum wheels. The RT/10 roadster is set to return later this year, with dual airbags, power windows and door locks, and the 450-horsepower V10 from the GTS. Also set to debut on the revamped drop top are the four-wheel independent suspension and adjustable pedals from the GTS.
Category R

Model Description	Trade-in TMV	Private TMV	Dealer TMV
2 Dr GTS Cpe	38601	41840	45800
2 Dr RT/10 Conv	37505	40653	44500

OPTIONS FOR VIPER
Hardtop Roof +1090

Don't forget to refer to the Mileage Adjustment Table at the back of this book!

Model Description	Trade-in TMV	Private TMV	Dealer TMV

WAGON   1997

New this year are wider cargo doors, upgraded stereo systems, and an improved ignition switch with anti-theft protection. Front quarter vent windows disappear for 1997, and underhood service points feature colored identification.

Category Q

Model Description	Trade-in TMV	Private TMV	Dealer TMV
2 Dr 1500 Ram Wagon	6638	7476	8500
2 Dr 2500 Ram Wagon Ext	7029	7916	9000
2 Dr 3500 Ram Wagon Ext	7263	8180	9300
2 Dr 3500 Maxi Ram Wagon Ext	7575	8531	9700
2 Dr 1500 SLT Ram Wagon	7185	8092	9200
2 Dr 2500 SLT Ram Wagon Ext	7497	8443	9600
2 Dr 3500 SLT Maxi Ram Wagon Ext	8747	9851	11200
2 Dr 3500 SLT Ram Wagon Ext	7653	8619	9800

OPTIONS FOR WAGON

8 cyl 5.2 L Engine[Opt on 1500,2500] +257
8 cyl 5.9 L Engine +172
AM/FM Compact Disc Player +211
Anti-Lock Brakes +217
Automatic 4-Speed Transmission[Opt on 1500] +109
Chrome Wheels +109
Dual Air Conditioning[Opt on 1500] +384
Limited Slip Differential +124
Power Drivers Seat +131
Power Windows +115
Premium Sound System +240
Sunscreen Glass +179

1996 DODGE

AVENGER   1996

Dodge's sporty coupe gets a panic mode for the remote keyless entry system and a HomeLink transmitter that will open your garage door. ES models get new seat fabric, and three new colors are on the roster.

Category E

Model Description	Trade-in TMV	Private TMV	Dealer TMV
2 Dr STD Cpe	4788	5507	6500
2 Dr ES Cpe	5820	6693	7900

OPTIONS FOR AVENGER

AM/FM Stereo/CD/Tape +350
Air Conditioning[Std on ES] +328
Alarm System +114
Aluminum/Alloy Wheels +193
Anti-Lock Brakes[Std on ES] +249

Automatic 4-Speed Transmission[Std on ES] +284
Leather Seats +176
Power Sunroof +266
Premium Sound System +228

CARAVAN   1996

A complete redesign yields a cavernous interior, best-in-class driveability, and new innovations such as the optional driver's side passenger door. And although the all-wheel drive version is discontinued for now, Caravan dethrones the Ford Windstar and once again reigns as king of the minivans.

Category P

Model Description	Trade-in TMV	Private TMV	Dealer TMV
2 Dr Grand Pass. Van	5525	6397	7600
2 Dr STD Pass. Van	4362	5050	6000
2 Dr ES Pass. Van	6656	7705	9155
2 Dr Grand ES Pass. Van	6907	7996	9500
2 Dr Grand LE Pass. Van	6625	7670	9113
2 Dr LE Pass. Van	6576	7613	9045
2 Dr Grand SE Pass. Van	5961	6902	8200
2 Dr SE Pass. Van	5889	6818	8100

OPTIONS FOR CARAVAN

6 cyl 3.0 L Engine +320
6 cyl 3.3 L CNG Engine +364
6 cyl 3.3 L Engine[Opt on Grand SE,SE] +370
6 cyl 3.8 L Engine[Opt on LE,ES] +156
7 Passenger Seating[Opt on STD] +145
AM/FM Stereo/CD/Tape +164
Air Conditioning[Opt on Grand,Grand SE,SE,STD] +358
Aluminum/Alloy Wheels +110
Anti-Lock Brakes[Opt on SE,STD] +235
Automatic Load Leveling[Opt on Grand LE] +120
Captain Chairs (4) +260
Dual Air Conditioning +370
Infinity Sound System +140
Leather Seats +331
Power Door Locks[Opt on Grand,Grand SE,SE,STD] +131
Power Drivers Seat +110
Power Windows[Opt on Grand SE,SE] +108
Sliding Driver Side Door +248
Sunscreen Glass +187

DAKOTA   1996

America's first midsized pickup gets a more powerful standard four-cylinder engine, revised sound system, and three new colors.

Category J

Model Description	Trade-in TMV	Private TMV	Dealer TMV
2 Dr STD 4WD Std Cab LB	5490	6353	7545
2 Dr STD Std Cab LB	3494	4043	4801
2 Dr STD 4WD Ext Cab SB			

Model Description	Trade-in TMV	Private TMV	Dealer TMV
	5894	6821	8100
2 Dr STD 4WD Std Cab SB			
	5239	6063	7200
2 Dr STD Ext Cab SB	5005	5792	6878
2 Dr STD Std Cab SB	4075	4715	5600
2 Dr SLT 4WD Std Cab LB			
	5749	6652	7900
2 Dr SLT Std Cab LB	4439	5136	6100
2 Dr SLT 4WD Ext Cab SB			
	6040	6989	8300
2 Dr SLT 4WD Std Cab SB			
	5570	6446	7655
2 Dr SLT Ext Cab SB	5037	5829	6922
2 Dr SLT Std Cab SB	4220	4884	5800
2 Dr Sport 4WD Ext Cab SB			
	5676	6568	7800
2 Dr Sport 4WD Std Cab SB			
	5103	5905	7013
2 Dr Sport Ext Cab SB	4730	5473	6500
2 Dr Sport Std Cab SB	3566	4126	4900
2 Dr WS 4WD Std Cab LB			
	5084	5883	6987
2 Dr WS Std Cab LB	3492	4041	4799
2 Dr WS 4WD Std Cab SB			
	4875	5642	6700
2 Dr WS Std Cab SB	3202	3705	4400

OPTIONS FOR DAKOTA

6 cyl 3.9 L Engine +291
8 cyl 5.2 L Engine +244
AM/FM Compact Disc Player +199
Air Conditioning[Std on SLT] +331
Anti-Lock Brakes +208
Automatic 4-Speed Transmission +385

INTREPID 1996

ES carries over, but the base model gets several improvements to remain competitive with the new Ford Taurus. ES styling cues and 16-inch wheels come standard on the base Intrepid. New colors and seat fabrics update this full-size sedan, and all Intrepids get noise, vibration and harshness improvements.

Category G

Model Description	Trade-in TMV	Private TMV	Dealer TMV
4 Dr STD Sdn	4278	5001	6000
4 Dr ES Sdn	4849	5668	6800

OPTIONS FOR INTREPID

AM/FM Compact Disc Player +135
Anti-Lock Brakes[Std on Sport] +249
Leather Seats +364
Power Moonroof +331

NEON 1996

A raft of improvements make the sprightly Neon even more attractive to compact buyers. Base models get more equipment, and the ugly gray bumpers are history. A base coupe is newly available. Interior noise levels are supposedly subdued this year. ABS is available across the board this year.

Category B

Model Description	Trade-in TMV	Private TMV	Dealer TMV
2 Dr STD Cpe	2341	2934	3754
4 Dr STD Sdn	2398	3006	3846
2 Dr Highline Cpe	2494	3127	4000
4 Dr Highline Sdn	2681	3361	4300
2 Dr Sport Cpe	2913	3652	4672
4 Dr Sport Sdn	2823	3539	4528

OPTIONS FOR NEON

AM/FM Compact Disc Player +200
Air Conditioning +416
Aluminum/Alloy Wheels +140
Anti-Lock Brakes +235
Automatic 3-Speed Transmission +249
Compact Disc Changer +208
Power Moonroof +248
Power Windows +106
Rear Spoiler +103

RAM 1500 1996

Category K

Model Description	Trade-in TMV	Private TMV	Dealer TMV
2 Dr LT 4WD Std Cab LB			
	7098	8009	9266
2 Dr LT Std Cab LB	5439	6136	7100
2 Dr LT 4WD Std Cab SB			
	7047	7952	9200
2 Dr LT Std Cab SB	5362	6050	7000
2 Dr Laramie SLT 4WD Ext Cab LB			
	8361	9434	10915
2 Dr Laramie SLT 4WD Std Cab LB			
	7813	8816	10200
2 Dr Laramie SLT Ext Cab LB			
	7704	8692	10057
2 Dr Laramie SLT Std Cab LB			
	6741	7606	8800
2 Dr Laramie SLT 4WD Ext Cab SB			
	8273	9334	10800
2 Dr Laramie SLT 4WD Std Cab SB			
	7737	8729	10100
2 Dr Laramie SLT Ext Cab SB			
	7303	8240	9534
2 Dr Laramie SLT Std Cab SB			
	5975	6741	7800
2 Dr ST 4WD Ext Cab LB			
	7664	8647	10005
2 Dr ST Ext Cab LB	6783	7653	8855
2 Dr ST 4WD Ext Cab SB			
	7617	8594	9943

Model Description	Trade-in TMV	Private TMV	Dealer TMV
2 Dr ST Ext Cab SB	6639	7491	8667
2 Dr WS Std Cab LB	5233	5905	6832
2 Dr WS Std Cab SB	5184	5850	6768

OPTIONS FOR RAM 1500

8 cyl 5.2 L Engine[Opt on Laramie SLT Std Cab,LT Std Cab] +244
8 cyl 5.9 L Engine +164
AM/FM Compact Disc Player +176
AM/FM Stereo Tape[Std on Laramie SLT] +133
Air Conditioning[Std on Laramie SLT] +331
Anti-Lock Brakes +208
Automatic 4-Speed Transmission +385
Chrome Wheels +123
Compact Disc Changer +228
Infinity Sound System +138
Leather Seats +582
Power Drivers Seat +123
Premium Sound System +128

RAM 2500   1996

Category K

Model Description	Trade-in TMV	Private TMV	Dealer TMV
2 Dr LT 4WD Std Cab LB	7623	8601	9952
2 Dr LT Std Cab LB	6128	6914	8000
2 Dr Laramie SLT 4WD Ext Cab LB	9652	10890	12600
2 Dr Laramie SLT 4WD Std Cab LB	7890	8902	10300
2 Dr Laramie SLT Ext Cab LB	8426	9507	11000
2 Dr Laramie SLT Std Cab LB	6741	7606	8800
2 Dr Laramie SLT 4WD Ext Cab SB	9729	10977	12700
2 Dr Laramie SLT Ext Cab SB	8043	9075	10500
2 Dr ST 4WD Ext Cab LB	9422	10631	12300
2 Dr ST 4WD Std Cab LB	7697	8684	10048
2 Dr ST Ext Cab LB	7833	8837	10225
2 Dr ST Std Cab LB	6205	7001	8100
2 Dr ST 4WD Ext Cab SB	9039	10199	11800
2 Dr ST Ext Cab SB	7794	8794	10175

OPTIONS FOR RAM 2500

10 cyl 8.0 L Engine +195
6 cyl 5.9 L Turbodiesel Engine +1637
8 cyl 5.9 L Engine[Opt on Std Cab] +112
AM/FM Compact Disc Player +176
Air Conditioning[Opt on LT,ST] +331
Anti-Lock Brakes +208
Automatic 4-Speed Transmission +385
Compact Disc Changer +281

Infinity Sound System +212
Power Drivers Seat +123
Premium Sound System +176

RAM 3500   1996

Category K

Model Description	Trade-in TMV	Private TMV	Dealer TMV
2 Dr LT 4WD Std Cab LB	9039	10199	11800
2 Dr LT Std Cab LB	7430	8384	9700
2 Dr Laramie SLT 4WD Ext Cab LB	10341	11668	13500
2 Dr Laramie SLT 4WD Std Cab LB	9958	11236	13000
2 Dr Laramie SLT Ext Cab LB	9346	10544	12200
2 Dr Laramie SLT Std Cab LB	8426	9507	11000
2 Dr ST 4WD Ext Cab LB	9805	11063	12800
2 Dr ST 4WD Std Cab LB	9269	10458	12100
2 Dr ST Ext Cab LB	8273	9334	10800
2 Dr ST Std Cab LB	7660	8643	10000

OPTIONS FOR RAM 3500

10 cyl 8.0 L Engine +195
6 cyl 5.9 L Turbodiesel Engine +1637
AM/FM Compact Disc Player +212
Air Conditioning[Opt on LT,ST] +331
Anti-Lock Brakes +208
Automatic 4-Speed Transmission +385
Camper/Towing Package +101
Infinity Sound System +138
Power Drivers Seat +123
Premium Sound System +128

RAM WAGON   1996

Category Q

Model Description	Trade-in TMV	Private TMV	Dealer TMV
2 Dr 1500 Ram Wagon	5091	5809	6800
2 Dr 2500 Ram Wagon Ext	5840	6663	7800
2 Dr 3500 Ram Wagon Ext	6214	7090	8300
2 Dr 3500 Maxi Ram Wagon Ext	6513	7432	8700
2 Dr 1500 SLT Ram Wagon	6139	7005	8200
2 Dr 2500 SLT Ram Wagon Ext	6364	7261	8500
2 Dr 3500 SLT Maxi Ram Wagon Ext	7037	8030	9400
2 Dr 3500 SLT Ram Wagon Ext	6588	7517	8800

OPTIONS FOR RAM WAGON

Don't forget to refer to the Mileage Adjustment Table at the back of this book!

Model Description	Trade-in TMV	Private TMV	Dealer TMV
8 cyl 5.2 L Engine[Opt on 1500,2500] +244			
8 cyl 5.9 L Engine +164			
AM/FM Compact Disc Player +128			
Air Conditioning +277			
Anti-Lock Brakes +208			
Automatic 4-Speed Transmission[Opt on 1500,2500] +203			
Dual Air Conditioning +277			
Power Door Locks +130			
Power Drivers Seat +123			
Power Windows +130			
Sunscreen Glass +170			

STEALTH 1996

Final year for slow-selling Japanese-built sports car. A new rear spoiler and body-color roof mark the 1996 model. A chrome 18-inch wheel package is available with Pirelli P-Zero tires and base models get an optional Infinity sound system.

Model Description	Trade-in TMV	Private TMV	Dealer TMV
Category E			
2 Dr STD Hbk	7809	8981	10600
Category F			
2 Dr R/T Hbk	9513	10935	12900
2 Dr R/T Turbo AWD Hbk	12168	13987	16500

OPTIONS FOR STEALTH
AM/FM Compact Disc Player +128
Anti-Lock Brakes +332
Automatic 4-Speed Transmission +367
Chrome Wheels +379
Compact Disc Changer +225
Leather Seats +350
Power Sunroof +263

STRATUS 1996

Excellent midsized sedan gets a more responsive torque converter when equipped with the 2.5-liter V6. New colors and a power sunroof are also new for 1996.

Model Description	Trade-in TMV	Private TMV	Dealer TMV
Category C			
4 Dr STD Sdn	3434	4092	5000
4 Dr ES Sdn	3571	4255	5200

OPTIONS FOR STRATUS
4 cyl 2.4 L Engine +187
6 cyl 2.5 L Engine +395
AM/FM Compact Disc Player +206
Anti-Lock Brakes[Std on ES] +235
Automatic 4-Speed Transmission +343
Leather Seats +260
Power Drivers Seat +145
Power Sunroof +241
Premium Sound System +153

VIPER 1996

Final year for Viper in current form. More power is eked from the V10 engine via a low-restriction rear outlet exhaust system, and an optional hardtop with sliding side curtains is available. Five-spoke aluminum wheels and three exterior styling themes replace the trim on the 1995 Viper. GTS coupe begins production when convertibles have completed their run. Scheduled to pace the 1996 Indianapolis 500, the GTS will arrive in showrooms with dual airbags and air conditioning.

Model Description	Trade-in TMV	Private TMV	Dealer TMV
Category R			
2 Dr GTS Cpe	34544	37676	42000
2 Dr RT/10 Conv	31419	34267	38200

OPTIONS FOR VIPER
Air Conditioning[Std on GTS] +499
Hardtop Roof +1040

1995 DODGE

AVENGER 1995

New coupe is late replacement for Daytona. Based on a Mitsubishi Galant platform, the Avenger is about the size of a Camry coupe. Base and ES models are available. Base cars have a 2.0-liter, 140-horsepower four-cylinder engine underhood. ES gets a Mitsubishi-built 2.5-liter V6 making 155 horsepower. An automatic is the only transmission available on the ES. ABS is optional on base models; standard on ES. All Avengers have dual airbags, height-adjustable driver's seat, split-folding rear seat, rear defroster, and tilt steering wheel.

Model Description	Trade-in TMV	Private TMV	Dealer TMV
Category E			
2 Dr ES Cpe	4195	4872	6000
2 Dr Highline Cpe	3636	4222	5200

OPTIONS FOR AVENGER
AM/FM Compact Disc Player +160
Air Conditioning[Std on ES] +290
Anti-Lock Brakes[Std on ES] +219
Automatic 4-Speed Transmission[Std on ES] +250
Infinity Sound System +118
Leather Seats +155
Power Door Locks +82
Power Drivers Seat +75
Power Sunroof +234
Power Windows +94
Premium Sound System +201

CARAVAN 1995

Newly optional is a 3.3-liter V6 engine designed to operate on compressed natural gas. Sport and SE decor packages are available this year. The five-speed manual transmission, available only with the four-cylinder engine, has been canceled.

Model Description	Trade-in TMV	Private TMV	Dealer TMV
Category P			
2 Dr Grand Pass. Van	3882	4526	5600
2 Dr STD Cargo Van	3327	3879	4800
2 Dr STD Cargo Van Ext	3535	4122	5100
2 Dr STD Pass. Van	3407	3972	4915

Don't forget to refer to the Mileage Adjustment Table at the back of this book!

DODGE 95

Model Description	Trade-in TMV	Private TMV	Dealer TMV
2 Dr ES Pass. Van	4906	5720	7078
2 Dr Grand ES AWD Pass. Van	5129	5981	7400
2 Dr Grand ES Pass. Van	4936	5756	7122
2 Dr Grand LE AWD Pass. Van	4991	5819	7200
2 Dr Grand LE Pass. Van	4699	5480	6780
2 Dr LE Pass. Van	4670	5446	6738
2 Dr Grand SE AWD Pass. Van	4563	5320	6583
2 Dr Grand SE Pass. Van	4320	5038	6233
2 Dr SE Pass. Van	4228	4930	6100

OPTIONS FOR CARAVAN

6 cyl 3.0 L Engine[Opt on STD] +95
6 cyl 3.3 L CNG Engine +321
6 cyl 3.8 L Engine +137
7 Passenger Seating[Opt on STD] +128
AM/FM Compact Disc Player +118
Air Conditioning[Opt on Grand,Grand SE,SE,STD] +315
Aluminum/Alloy Wheels +97
Anti-Lock Brakes +207
Captain Chairs (4) +218
Child Seats (2) +82
Dual Air Conditioning +255
Infinity Sound System[Opt on ES,SE] +123
Leather Seats +292
Power Door Locks[Opt on Grand,Grand SE,SE,STD] +116
Power Drivers Seat +97
Power Windows +95
Premium Sound System +123
Sunscreen Glass +110

Model Description	Trade-in TMV	Private TMV	Dealer TMV
	4723	5464	6701
2 Dr SLT Ext Cab SB	4088	4730	5800
2 Dr SLT Std Cab SB	3422	3959	4855
2 Dr Sport 4WD Ext Cab SB	4762	5510	6757
2 Dr Sport 4WD Std Cab SB	4510	5219	6400
2 Dr Sport Ext Cab SB	3806	4404	5400
2 Dr Sport Std Cab SB	3101	3588	4400
2 Dr WS 4WD Std Cab LB	4534	5246	6433
2 Dr WS Std Cab LB	3312	3833	4700
2 Dr WS 4WD Std Cab SB	4017	4648	5700
2 Dr WS Std Cab SB	2890	3343	4100

OPTIONS FOR DAKOTA

4 cyl 2.5 L Engine +165
6 cyl 3.9 L Engine +118
8 cyl 5.2 L Engine +216
AM/FM Compact Disc Player +176
AM/FM Stereo Tape[Opt on STD,WS] +77
Air Conditioning[Std on SLT] +292
Anti-Lock Brakes +128
Automatic 4-Speed Transmission +340
Camper/Towing Package +88
Limited Slip Differential +94
Power Door Locks +75
Power Windows +82

INTREPID   1995

ABS is now standard on ES. Traction control is a new ES option.

Category G

Model Description	Trade-in TMV	Private TMV	Dealer TMV
4 Dr STD Sdn	3520	4113	5100
4 Dr ES Sdn	3658	4274	5300

OPTIONS FOR INTREPID

6 cyl 3.3 L Flex Fuel Engine[Opt on STD] +110
6 cyl 3.5 L Engine +266
AM/FM Compact Disc Player +118
Anti-Lock Brakes[Std on ES] +220
Dual Power Seats +279
Infinity Sound System +220
Leather Seats +321
Power Door Locks[Opt on STD] +77
Power Drivers Seat +88
Power Moonroof +292
Power Windows[Opt on STD] +101
Quick Order Package 2 +642
Traction Control System[Opt on ES] +91

NEON   1995

This spunky Shadow replacement is cleverly designed, adequately powered, and cute to boot. Base, Highline and Sport models are available. Coupe and sedan

DAKOTA   1995

A 2WD Club Cab Sport is added to the model mix.

Category J

Model Description	Trade-in TMV	Private TMV	Dealer TMV
2 Dr STD 4WD Std Cab LB	4682	5417	6643
2 Dr STD Std Cab LB	3530	4085	5009
2 Dr STD 4WD Ext Cab SB	5074	5871	7200
2 Dr STD 4WD Std Cab SB	4580	5300	6499
2 Dr STD Ext Cab SB	4019	4651	5703
2 Dr STD Std Cab SB	3376	3907	4791
2 Dr SLT 4WD Std Cab LB	4792	5545	6800
2 Dr SLT Std Cab LB	3874	4483	5497
2 Dr SLT 4WD Ext Cab SB	5145	5953	7300
2 Dr SLT 4WD Std Cab SB			

Model Description	Trade-in TMV	Private TMV	Dealer TMV

body styles are offered. All except Sport Coupe have a 132-horsepower, 2.0-liter four-cylinder engine. Sport Coupe gets a 150-horsepower twin-cam edition of the base motor. Dual airbags are standard on all models; ABS is standard on Sport and optional on others. Integrated child seats are optional.

Category B

Model	Trade-in	Private	Dealer
4 Dr STD Sdn	1777	2236	3000
2 Dr Highline Cpe	2073	2608	3500
4 Dr Highline Sdn	2014	2534	3400
2 Dr Sport Cpe	2306	2902	3894
4 Dr Sport Sdn	2195	2762	3706

OPTIONS FOR NEON
AM/FM Compact Disc Player +154
AM/FM Stereo Tape +95
Air Conditioning +366
Aluminum/Alloy Wheels +123
Anti-Lock Brakes +207
Automatic 3-Speed Transmission +220
Cruise Control +75
Power Windows +94
Premium Sound System +184
Rear Spoiler +91

RAM 1500   1995

Category K

Model	Trade-in	Private	Dealer
2 Dr LT 4WD Std Cab LB			
	5863	6702	8100
2 Dr LT Std Cab LB	4508	5153	6228
2 Dr LT 4WD Std Cab SB			
	5501	6288	7600
2 Dr LT Std Cab SB	4467	5107	6172
2 Dr Laramie SLT 4WD Ext Cab LB			
	6887	7873	9515
2 Dr Laramie SLT 4WD Std Cab LB			
	6659	7612	9200
2 Dr Laramie SLT Ext Cab LB			
	6153	7033	8500
2 Dr Laramie SLT Std Cab LB			
	4922	5626	6800
2 Dr Laramie SLT 4WD Ext Cab SB			
	6866	7848	9485
2 Dr Laramie SLT 4WD Std Cab SB			
	6596	7540	9113
2 Dr Laramie SLT Ext Cab SB			
	5935	6785	8200
2 Dr Laramie SLT Std Cab SB			
	4850	5544	6700
2 Dr ST 4WD Ext Cab LB			
	6635	7584	9166
2 Dr ST Ext Cab LB	5250	6001	7253
2 Dr ST 4WD Ext Cab SB			
	6577	7519	9087
2 Dr ST Ext Cab SB	5067	5792	7000
2 Dr WS Std Cab LB	3933	4495	5433
2 Dr WS Std Cab SB	3909	4468	5400

OPTIONS FOR RAM 1500
8 cyl 5.2 L Engine[Opt on Laramie SLT Std Cab,LT Std Cab] +215
8 cyl 5.9 L Engine +99
AM/FM Compact Disc Player +155
AM/FM Stereo Tape +118
Air Conditioning[Std on Laramie SLT] +292
Anti-Lock Brakes +184
Automatic 4-Speed Transmission +340
Camper/Towing Package +88
Infinity Sound System +121
Limited Slip Differential +94
Power Door Locks +85
Power Drivers Seat +108
Power Windows +94

RAM 2500   1995

Category K

Model	Trade-in	Private	Dealer
2 Dr LT 4WD Std Cab LB			
	6008	6867	8300
2 Dr LT Std Cab LB	4922	5626	6800
2 Dr Laramie SLT 4WD Ext Cab LB			
	7962	9101	11000
2 Dr Laramie SLT 4WD Std Cab LB			
	6774	7743	9358
2 Dr Laramie SLT Ext Cab LB			
	6926	7917	9569
2 Dr Laramie SLT Std Cab LB			
	6297	7198	8700
2 Dr Laramie SLT 4WD Ext Cab SB			
	7890	9019	10900
2 Dr ST 4WD Ext Cab LB			
	7238	8274	10000
2 Dr ST 4WD Std Cab LB			
	6370	7281	8800
2 Dr ST Ext Cab LB	6531	7466	9023
2 Dr ST Std Cab LB	5067	5792	7000
2 Dr ST 4WD Ext Cab SB			
	7094	8108	9800
2 Dr ST Ext Cab SB	6498	7428	8977
2 Dr Sport 4WD Ext Cab SB			
	7383	8439	10200
2 Dr Sport Ext Cab SB	6682	7638	9231

OPTIONS FOR RAM 2500
10 cyl 8.0 L Engine +172
6 cyl 5.9 L Turbodiesel Engine +1547
8 cyl 5.9 L Engine[Opt on Std Cab] +99
AM/FM Compact Disc Player +155
AM/FM Stereo Tape[Opt on LT,Sport,ST] +77
Air Conditioning[Opt on LT,Sport,ST] +292

Don't forget to refer to the Mileage Adjustment Table at the back of this book!

Model Description	Trade-in TMV	Private TMV	Dealer TMV	Model Description	Trade-in TMV	Private TMV	Dealer TMV
Anti-Lock Brakes +184					5630	6481	7900
Automatic 4-Speed Transmission +340				2 Dr 3500 SLT Ram Wagon Ext			
Camper/Towing Package +88					5844	6727	8200
Infinity Sound System +187							
Limited Slip Differential +94							
Power Door Locks +85							
Power Drivers Seat +108							

OPTIONS FOR RAM WAGON

- 12 Passenger Seating +229
- 15 Passenger Seating +312
- 5 Passenger Seating[Opt on 2500] +91
- 8 Passenger Seating +220
- 8 cyl 5.2 L Engine[Opt on 1500,2500] +215
- 8 cyl 5.9 L Engine +145
- AM/FM Compact Disc Player +113
- Air Conditioning +245
- Automatic 4-Speed Transmission +180
- Camper/Towing Package +82
- Dual Air Conditioning +245
- Limited Slip Differential +94
- Power Drivers Seat +108
- Sunscreen Glass +149

RAM 3500 — 1995

Model Description	Trade-in TMV	Private TMV	Dealer TMV
Category K			
2 Dr LT 4WD Std Cab LB			
	7238	8274	10000
2 Dr LT Std Cab LB	5646	6454	7800
2 Dr Laramie SLT 4WD Ext Cab LB			
	8614	9846	11900
2 Dr Laramie SLT 4WD Std Cab LB			
	8324	9515	11500
2 Dr Laramie SLT Ext Cab LB			
	7600	8688	10500
2 Dr Laramie SLT Std Cab LB			
	6876	7860	9500
2 Dr ST 4WD Ext Cab LB			
	8252	9432	11400
2 Dr ST Ext Cab LB	6732	7695	9300
2 Dr ST Std Cab LB	6370	7281	8800

OPTIONS FOR RAM 3500

- 10 cyl 8.0 L Engine +172
- 6 cyl 5.9 L Turbodiesel Engine +1547
- AM/FM Compact Disc Player +187
- AM/FM Stereo Tape[Std on Laramie SLT] +77
- Air Conditioning[Opt on LT,ST] +292
- Anti-Lock Brakes +184
- Automatic 4-Speed Transmission +340
- Camper/Towing Package +88
- Infinity Sound System +121
- Limited Slip Differential +87
- Power Drivers Seat +108

RAM WAGON — 1995

Model Description	Trade-in TMV	Private TMV	Dealer TMV
Category Q			
2 Dr 1500 Ram Wagon	4134	4758	5800
2 Dr 2500 Ram Wagon	4775	5497	6700
2 Dr 3500 Ram Wagon	4885	5624	6855
2 Dr 3500 Ram Wagon Ext			
	5274	6071	7400
2 Dr 2500 Maxi Ram Wagon Ext			
	4917	5661	6900
2 Dr 1500 SLT Ram Wagon			
	4561	5251	6400
2 Dr 2500 SLT Ram Wagon			
	5392	6207	7566
2 Dr 2500 SLT Ram Wagon Ext			
	5416	6235	7600
2 Dr 3500 SLT Ram Wagon			

SPIRIT — 1995

Flexible fuel model and optional four-speed automatic transmission are dropped. A three-speed automatic continues as standard equipment.

Model Description	Trade-in TMV	Private TMV	Dealer TMV
Category C			
4 Dr STD Sdn	2314	2796	3600

OPTIONS FOR SPIRIT

- 6 cyl 3.0 L Engine +254
- Aluminum/Alloy Wheels +82
- Power Drivers Seat +91
- Power Windows +95

STEALTH — 1995

Chromed 18-inch aluminum wheels are available on R/T Turbo.

Model Description	Trade-in TMV	Private TMV	Dealer TMV
Category E			
2 Dr STD Hbk	6083	7064	8700
Category F			
2 Dr R/T Hbk	7240	8350	10200
2 Dr R/T Turbo AWD Hbk			
	9654	11134	13600

OPTIONS FOR STEALTH

- Anti-Lock Brakes[Std on R/T Turbo] +293
- Automatic 4-Speed Transmission +324
- Chrome Wheels +334
- Compact Disc Changer +199
- Leather Seats +309
- Power Door Locks[Std on R/T Turbo] +87
- Power Sunroof +233
- Power Windows[Std on R/T Turbo] +97

STRATUS — 1995

Spirit replacement features cutting-edge styling and class-leading accommodations. Dual airbags and ABS are standard. Base and ES models are available. Base

---

Don't forget to refer to the Mileage Adjustment Table at the back of this book!

Model Description	Trade-in TMV	Private TMV	Dealer TMV

model has 2.0-liter, four-cylinder engine making 132 horsepower and a five-speed manual transmission. ES is powered by 155-horsepower, Mitsubishi 2.5-liter V6. A credit option on the ES is the Neon's 2.0-liter four hooked to a five-speed manual transmission.

Category C

Model Description	Trade-in TMV	Private TMV	Dealer TMV
4 Dr STD Sdn	2635	3185	4100
4 Dr ES Sdn	2957	3573	4600

OPTIONS FOR STRATUS
4 cyl 2.4 L Engine +165
Anti-Lock Brakes[Std on ES] +207
Automatic 4-Speed Transmission[Std on ES] +302
Leather Seats +229
Power Door Locks[Opt on STD] +87
Power Drivers Seat +128
Power Windows[Opt on STD] +95
Premium Sound System +136

VIPER   1995

No changes.

Category R

Model Description	Trade-in TMV	Private TMV	Dealer TMV
2 Dr RT/10 Conv	29291	31995	36500

OPTIONS FOR VIPER
AM/FM Compact Disc Player +201
Air Conditioning +439

1994 DODGE

CARAVAN   1994

A passenger airbag is added to a redesigned dashboard, and new side-door guard beams meet 1997 passenger car safety standards. All-wheel drive is no longer available on regular-length models. Bumpers are restyled, and seats with integrated child seats can be reclined for the first time.

Category P

Model Description	Trade-in TMV	Private TMV	Dealer TMV
2 Dr Grand Pass. Van	3291	3933	5003
2 Dr STD Cargo Van	2697	3223	4100
2 Dr STD Cargo Van Ext	3092	3695	4700
2 Dr STD Pass. Van	2763	3302	4200
2 Dr ES Pass. Van	3574	4271	5433
2 Dr Grand ES AWD Pass. Van	3882	4638	5900
2 Dr Grand ES Pass. Van	3685	4403	5601
2 Dr Grand LE AWD Pass. Van	3695	4416	5617
2 Dr Grand LE Pass. Van	3655	4367	5555
2 Dr LE Pass. Van	3421	4088	5200
2 Dr Grand SE AWD Pass. Van	3487	4167	5300
2 Dr Grand SE Pass. Van	3370	4027	5122
2 Dr SE Pass. Van	3287	3929	4997

OPTIONS FOR CARAVAN
6 cyl 3.0 L Engine[Opt on STD] +83
6 cyl 3.8 L Engine +120
7 Passenger Seating[Opt on Grand,SE,STD] +112
AM/FM Compact Disc Player +104
AM/FM Stereo/CD/Tape +126
Air Conditioning[Std on Grand LE,LE] +275
Aluminum/Alloy Wheels +85
Anti-Lock Brakes +180
Captain Chairs (4) +191
Dual Air Conditioning +223
Infinity Sound System +107
Leather Seats +255
Power Door Locks[Std on LE] +101
Power Drivers Seat +85
Power Windows +83
Sunscreen Glass +96

COLT   1994

A driver airbag debuts. ES trim replaces GL nomenclature. Order ABS on an ES sedan and you'll get rear discs instead of drums. The optional 1.8-liter engine is available on the coupe this year, but only with ES trim. Sedans gain standard power steering. Air conditioners use CFC-free refrigerant.

Category B

Model Description	Trade-in TMV	Private TMV	Dealer TMV
2 Dr STD Sdn	1081	1426	2000
4 Dr STD Sdn	1189	1568	2200
2 Dr ES Sdn	1135	1497	2100
4 Dr ES Sdn	1243	1640	2300

OPTIONS FOR COLT
4 cyl 1.8 L Engine[Opt on ES] +111
AM/FM Stereo Tape +83
Air Conditioning +224
Anti-Lock Brakes +192
Automatic 3-Speed Transmission +175
Automatic 4-Speed Transmission +248
Option Package 2 +185
Power Windows +82

DAKOTA   1994

Driver airbag is added, along with side-door guard beams. LE trim level now called SLT. A strengthened roof now meets passenger car crush standards. The 5.2-liter V8 loses horsepower but gains torque.

Category J

Model Description	Trade-in TMV	Private TMV	Dealer TMV
2 Dr STD 4WD Std Cab LB	3720	4400	5533
2 Dr STD Std Cab LB	2757	3260	4100
2 Dr STD 4WD Ext Cab SB	4067	4810	6049

Don't forget to refer to the Mileage Adjustment Table at the back of this book!

Model Description	Trade-in TMV	Private TMV	Dealer TMV
2 Dr STD 4WD Std Cab SB			
	3563	4215	5300
2 Dr STD Ext Cab SB	3227	3817	4800
2 Dr STD Std Cab SB	2646	3130	3936
2 Dr SLT 4WD Std Cab LB			
	3871	4579	5758
2 Dr SLT Std Cab LB	2958	3499	4400
2 Dr SLT 4WD Ext Cab SB			
	4236	5010	6300
2 Dr SLT 4WD Std Cab SB			
	3832	4533	5700
2 Dr SLT Ext Cab SB	3445	4075	5124
2 Dr SLT Std Cab SB	2732	3232	4064
2 Dr Sport 4WD Ext Cab SB			
	3900	4612	5800
2 Dr Sport 4WD Std Cab SB			
	3530	4176	5251
2 Dr Sport Ext Cab SB	3170	3749	4715
2 Dr Sport Std Cab SB	2555	3022	3800
2 Dr WS 4WD Std Cab LB			
	3413	4036	5076
2 Dr WS Std Cab LB	2622	3101	3900
2 Dr WS 4WD Std Cab SB			
	3362	3976	5000
2 Dr WS Std Cab SB	2151	2545	3200

OPTIONS FOR DAKOTA

8 cyl 5.2 L Engine +184
Air Bag Restraint +128
Air Conditioning[Opt on Sport,STD,WS] +255
Anti-Lock Brakes +112
Automatic 4-Speed Transmission +296
Camper/Towing Package +77
Limited Slip Differential +82
Power Steering[Opt on STD,WS] +80

INTREPID   1994

Base engine is upgraded with eight more horsepower. A flexible-fuel model is introduced to all states except California. Standard equipment now includes air conditioning and a touring suspension. ES models gain variable-assist power steering, which is optional on base models with the Wheel and Handling Group. New options include a power sunroof, security alarm and power passenger seat.

Category G

	Trade-in	Private	Dealer
4 Dr STD Sdn	2501	3026	3900
4 Dr ES Sdn	2822	3414	4400

OPTIONS FOR INTREPID

6 cyl 3.5 L Engine +231
AM/FM Stereo Tape[Opt on STD] +78
AM/FM Stereo/CD/Tape +158
Anti-Lock Brakes +192

Dual Power Seats +243
Infinity Sound System +192
Leather Seats +279
Power Drivers Seat +77
Power Moonroof +255
Power Windows +88
Traction Control System +80

RAM 1500   1994

Category K

Model Description	Trade-in TMV	Private TMV	Dealer TMV
2 Dr LT 4WD Std Cab LB			
	4761	5537	6830
2 Dr LT Std Cab LB	3695	4297	5300
2 Dr LT 4WD Std Cab SB			
	4719	5488	6770
2 Dr LT Std Cab SB	3366	3914	4828
2 Dr Laramie SLT 4WD Std Cab LB			
	5437	6323	7800
2 Dr Laramie SLT Std Cab LB			
	4144	4819	5944
2 Dr Laramie SLT 4WD Std Cab SB			
	5368	6242	7700
2 Dr Laramie SLT Std Cab SB			
	4046	4705	5804
2 Dr ST 4WD Std Cab LB			
	5089	5918	7300
2 Dr ST Std Cab LB	3901	4537	5596
2 Dr ST 4WD Std Cab SB			
	4740	5512	6799
2 Dr ST Std Cab SB	3834	4459	5500
2 Dr WS Std Cab LB	3187	3706	4572
2 Dr WS Std Cab SB	3137	3648	4500

OPTIONS FOR RAM 1500

8 cyl 5.2 L Engine[Opt on 2WD Std Cab] +188
8 cyl 5.9 L Engine +87
AM/FM Stereo Tape +102
AM/FM Stereo/CD/Tape +175
Air Conditioning[Std on Laramie SLT] +255
Anti-Lock Brakes +160
Automatic 4-Speed Transmission +296
Camper/Towing Package +77
Chrome Wheels +80
Limited Slip Differential +82
Power Drivers Seat +94

RAM 2500   1994

Category K

Model Description	Trade-in TMV	Private TMV	Dealer TMV
2 Dr LT 4WD Std Cab LB			
	5437	6323	7800
2 Dr LT Std Cab LB	4019	4674	5765
2 Dr Laramie SLT 4WD Std Cab LB			
	5925	6891	8500
2 Dr Laramie SLT Std Cab LB			
	4392	5107	6300

Don't forget to refer to the Mileage Adjustment Table at the back of this book!

Model Description	Trade-in TMV	Private TMV	Dealer TMV
2 Dr ST 4WD Std Cab LB			
	5577	6486	8000
2 Dr ST Std Cab LB	4068	4730	5835

OPTIONS FOR RAM 2500
10 cyl 8.0 L Engine +150
6 cyl 5.9 L Turbodiesel Engine +1349
8 cyl 5.9 L Engine +87
Air Conditioning[Std on Laramie SLT] +255
Anti-Lock Brakes +160
Automatic 4-Speed Transmission +296
Camper/Towing Package +77
Chrome Wheels +80
Limited Slip Differential +82
Power Drivers Seat +94

RAM 3500 1994

Category K

Model Description	Trade-in TMV	Private TMV	Dealer TMV
2 Dr LT 4WD Std Cab LB			
	6204	7215	8900
2 Dr LT Std Cab LB	5228	6080	7500
2 Dr Laramie SLT 4WD Std Cab LB			
	7115	8274	10206
2 Dr Laramie SLT Std Cab LB			
	6762	7864	9700
2 Dr ST 4WD Std Cab LB			
	6827	7940	9794
2 Dr ST Std Cab LB	5507	6404	7900

OPTIONS FOR RAM 3500
10 cyl 8.0 L Engine +150
6 cyl 5.9 L Turbodiesel Engine +1349
Air Conditioning[Std on Laramie SLT] +255
Automatic 4-Speed Transmission +296
Camper/Towing Package +77
Power Drivers Seat +94

RAM WAGON 1994

Category Q

Model Description	Trade-in TMV	Private TMV	Dealer TMV
2 Dr B150 Ram Wagon	2869	3368	4200
2 Dr B250 Ram Wagon	3553	4170	5200
2 Dr B350 Ram Wagon	4167	4892	6100
2 Dr B350 Ram Wagon Ext			
	4272	5015	6253
2 Dr B150 LE Ram Wagon			
	2938	3449	4300
2 Dr B250 LE Ram Wagon			
	4304	5053	6300
2 Dr B350 LE Ram Wagon			
	4919	5774	7200
2 Dr B350 LE Ram Wagon Ext			
	4987	5854	7300
2 Dr B250 Maxi Ram Wagon			
	3962	4652	5800

OPTIONS FOR RAM WAGON

12 Passenger Seating +200
15 Passenger Seating +272
8 Passenger Seating +192
8 cyl 5.2 L Engine[Opt on 1500,2500] +188
8 cyl 5.9 L Engine +126
Air Conditioning +213
Anti-Lock Brakes +160
Automatic 4-Speed Transmission +156
Dual Air Conditioning +213
Limited Slip Differential +82
Power Door Locks +100
Power Windows +100
Sunscreen Glass +131

SHADOW 1994

Four-door hatchback production stops midyear. Front passengers are now restrained by the dreaded motorized seatbelt to comply with federal regulations. Air conditioning runs on CFC-free coolant this year.

Category B

Model Description	Trade-in TMV	Private TMV	Dealer TMV
2 Dr STD Hbk	1337	1764	2474
4 Dr STD Hbk	1365	1801	2526
2 Dr ES Hbk	1405	1853	2600
4 Dr ES Hbk	1676	2210	3100

OPTIONS FOR SHADOW
4 cyl 2.5 L Engine[Std on ES] +143
6 cyl 3.0 L Engine +222
AM/FM Compact Disc Player +112
AM/FM Stereo Tape +78
Air Conditioning +240
Anti-Lock Brakes +192
Automatic 3-Speed Transmission +175
Automatic 4-Speed Transmission +240
Power Drivers Seat +83
Power Windows +83
Sunroof +112

SPIRIT 1994

Motorized seatbelt is introduced for front passengers. Highline and ES trim designations are retired in favor of ... well, nothing. All 1994 Spirits come equipped one way, with various option packages available.

Category C

Model Description	Trade-in TMV	Private TMV	Dealer TMV
4 Dr STD Sdn	1609	2056	2800

OPTIONS FOR SPIRIT
4 cyl 2.5 L Flex Fuel Engine +178
6 cyl 3.0 L Engine +222
AM/FM Stereo Tape +78
Anti-Lock Brakes +192
Automatic 3-Speed Transmission +175
Automatic 4-Speed Transmission +240
Power Drivers Seat +80
Power Windows +83

STEALTH 1994

Passenger airbag is added. R/T Turbo gains 20

Don't forget to refer to the Mileage Adjustment Table at the back of this book!

Model Description	Trade-in TMV	Private TMV	Dealer TMV

horsepower and a six-speed transmission. ES trim level is dropped. Styling is slightly revised front and rear, revealing the addition of projector-beam headlamps in place of the hidden lights used previously. CFC-free refrigerant is used in the air conditioning system, and R/T models can be painted a really bright shade of yellow.

Category E

Model Description	Trade-in TMV	Private TMV	Dealer TMV
2 Dr STD Hbk	4488	5355	6800

Category F

2 Dr R/T Hbk	4822	5751	7300
2 Dr R/T Turbo AWD Hbk			
	6473	7721	9800
2 Dr R/T Luxury Hbk	5681	6775	8600

OPTIONS FOR STEALTH

AM/FM Stereo Tape[Opt on R/T] +78
Air Conditioning[Std on R/T,R/T Turbo] +224
Anti-Lock Brakes[Std on R/T Turbo] +255
Automatic 4-Speed Transmission +282
Chrome Wheels +291
Compact Disc Changer +174
Leather Seats +270
Power Sunroof[Std on R/T Turbo] +202
Power Windows[Std on R/T Turbo] +85
Premium Sound System[Std on R/T Turbo] +160

VIPER   1994

Air conditioning with CFC-free refrigerant can be installed at the factory when the appropriate option box is checked. Green and yellow are added to the color chart. Green cars get a new black-and-tan interior.

Category R

2 Dr RT/10 Cpe	26634	29584	34500

1993 DODGE

CARAVAN   1993

No changes.

Category P

2 Dr Grand Pass. Van	2313	2899	3876
2 Dr STD Cargo Van	1996	2501	3344
2 Dr STD Cargo Van Ext			
	2222	2785	3724
2 Dr STD Pass. Van	1910	2394	3200
2 Dr ES AWD Pass. Van	2685	3366	4500
2 Dr ES Pass. Van	2466	3091	4132
2 Dr Grand ES AWD Pass. Van			
	2761	3460	4626
2 Dr Grand ES Pass. Van			
	2598	3257	4354
2 Dr Grand LE AWD Pass. Van			
	2730	3421	4574
2 Dr Grand LE Pass. Van			

Model Description	Trade-in TMV	Private TMV	Dealer TMV
	2486	3115	4165
2 Dr LE AWD Pass. Van	2653	3326	4446
2 Dr LE Pass. Van	2431	3047	4074
2 Dr Grand SE AWD Pass. Van			
	2389	2994	4003
2 Dr Grand SE Pass. Van			
	2327	2917	3900
2 Dr SE AWD Pass. Van	2343	2937	3926
2 Dr SE Pass. Van	2029	2543	3400

OPTIONS FOR CARAVAN

7 Passenger Seating +93
AM/FM Compact Disc Player +87
Air Conditioning[Std on ES,Grand ES,Grand LE,LE] +228
Anti-Lock Brakes +149
Captain Chairs (4) +158
Dual Air Conditioning +184
Leather Seats +211
Power Door Locks[Std on LE] +84
Sunscreen Glass +80

COLT   1993

Complete redesign results in two- and four-door notchback models; the hatchback is dropped. Coupes and sedans come in base or GL trim. Coupe and base sedan are powered by same 1.5-liter engine from last year. GL has a stronger 113-horsepower, 1.8-liter engine; this powerplant is optional on base sedan. GL sedan is only Colt that can be equipped with optional ABS.

Category B

2 Dr STD Sdn	763	1077	1600
4 Dr STD Sdn	859	1212	1800
2 Dr GL Sdn	811	1144	1700
4 Dr GL Sdn	907	1279	1900

OPTIONS FOR COLT

4 cyl 1.8 L Engine[Opt on STD] +91
Air Conditioning +185
Anti-Lock Brakes +159
Automatic 3-Speed Transmission +146
Automatic 4-Speed Transmission +206

DAKOTA   1993

Sport model gets new graphics.

Category J

2 Dr STD 4WD Std Cab LB			
	2696	3335	4400
2 Dr STD Std Cab LB	2145	2653	3500
2 Dr STD 4WD Ext Cab SB			
	2800	3464	4570
2 Dr STD 4WD Std Cab SB			
	2635	3259	4300
2 Dr STD Ext Cab SB	2344	2899	3825

Don't forget to refer to the Mileage Adjustment Table at the back of this book!

Model Description	Trade-in TMV	Private TMV	Dealer TMV
2 Dr STD Std Cab SB	2083	2577	3400
2 Dr LE 4WD Std Cab LB			
	2669	3301	4355
2 Dr LE Std Cab LB	2267	2805	3700
2 Dr LE 4WD Ext Cab SB			
	2941	3638	4800
2 Dr LE 4WD Std Cab SB			
	2696	3334	4399
2 Dr LE Ext Cab SB	2436	3013	3975
2 Dr LE Std Cab SB	2329	2880	3800
2 Dr S Std Cab SB	1654	2047	2700
2 Dr Sport 4WD Std Cab SB			
	2451	3032	4000
2 Dr Sport Std Cab SB	1838	2274	3000

OPTIONS FOR DAKOTA
8 cyl 5.2 L Engine +152
Air Conditioning[Std on LE] +212
Anti-Lock Brakes +93
Automatic 4-Speed Transmission +246

DAYTONA 1993

ABS is now available on base model. IROC loses turbocharged engine, though the limited-edition IROC R/T continues with turbo power.
Category E

2 Dr STD Hbk	1090	1394	1900
2 Dr ES Hbk	1262	1614	2200
2 Dr IROC Hbk	1836	2347	3200
2 Dr IROC R/T Turbo Hbk			
	2065	2641	3600

OPTIONS FOR DAYTONA
6 cyl 3.0 L Engine[Std on IROC] +184
AM/FM Compact Disc Player +93
Air Conditioning[Std on IROC R/T] +185
Anti-Lock Brakes[Opt on ES] +159
Automatic 3-Speed Transmission +146
Automatic 4-Speed Transmission +219
Leather Seats +226

DYNASTY 1993

Audio system is upgraded, a tamper-resistant odometer is added, and a stainless steel exhaust system is installed.
Category D

4 Dr STD Sdn	1199	1612	2300
4 Dr LE Sdn	1303	1752	2500

OPTIONS FOR DYNASTY
6 cyl 3.0 L Engine[Std on LE] +184
6 cyl 3.3 L Engine +184
Air Conditioning +159
Anti-Lock Brakes +172
Automatic 4-Speed Transmission[Std on LE] +219
Dual Power Seats +138

Leather Seats +199

INTREPID 1993

This midsized car represents the beginning of a revolution at Chrysler. Introducing cab-forward styling, Intrepid is powered by one of two V6 engines and comes in base or ES trim. ES model has four-wheel disc brakes. ABS is optional on base and ES. All Intrepids are equipped with dual airbags and height-adjustable seatbelts, while an integrated child seat is optional.
Category G

4 Dr STD Sdn	1828	2305	3100
4 Dr ES Sdn	2004	2528	3400

OPTIONS FOR INTREPID
6 cyl 3.5 L Engine +192
AM/FM Compact Disc Player +87
AM/FM Stereo/CD/Tape +132
Air Conditioning +159
Anti-Lock Brakes +159
Dual Power Seats +201
Infinity Sound System +159
Leather Seats +232

RAM 150 1993

Category K

Model Description	Trade-in TMV	Private TMV	Dealer TMV
2 Dr STD 4WD Ext Cab LB			
	3983	4744	6013
2 Dr STD 4WD Std Cab LB			
	3591	4278	5422
2 Dr STD Ext Cab LB	3311	3944	4999
2 Dr STD Std Cab LB	2992	3564	4517
2 Dr STD 4WD Std Cab SB			
	3577	4260	5400
2 Dr STD Ext Cab SB	3444	4103	5200
2 Dr STD Std Cab SB	2969	3537	4483
2 Dr LE 4WD Ext Cab LB			
	4098	4881	6187
2 Dr LE 4WD Std Cab LB			
	3775	4497	5700
2 Dr LE Ext Cab LB	3643	4339	5500
2 Dr LE Std Cab LB	3257	3879	4917
2 Dr LE 4WD Std Cab SB			
	3842	4576	5800
2 Dr LE Ext Cab SB	3709	4418	5600
2 Dr LE Std Cab SB	3120	3717	4711

OPTIONS FOR RAM 150
8 cyl 5.2 L Engine[Opt on Std Cab] +152
8 cyl 5.9 L Engine +232
Air Conditioning[Opt on STD] +213
Automatic 3-Speed Transmission[Opt on Std Cab 2WD] +146
Automatic 4-Speed Transmission +226

Don't forget to refer to the Mileage Adjustment Table at the back of this book!

Model Description	Trade-in TMV	Private TMV	Dealer TMV

RAM 250　　　　1993

Category K

2 Dr STD 4WD Ext Cab LB

	4301	5124	6494

2 Dr STD 4WD Std Cab LB

	3775	4497	5700

| 2 Dr STD Ext Cab LB | 3693 | 4399 | 5576 |
| 2 Dr STD Std Cab LB | 3577 | 4260 | 5400 |

2 Dr LE 4WD Ext Cab LB

	4442	5291	6706

2 Dr LE 4WD Std Cab LB

	4040	4813	6100

| 2 Dr LE Std Cab LB | 3593 | 4279 | 5424 |

2 Dr LE Turbodsl Ext Cab LB

	4637	5523	7000

OPTIONS FOR RAM 250
6 cyl 5.9 L Turbodiesel Engine +1008
8 cyl 5.9 L Engine +232
Air Conditioning[Opt on STD] +213
Automatic 4-Speed Transmission +226

RAM 350　　　　1993

Category K

2 Dr STD 4WD Std Cab LB

	4703	5602	7100

| 2 Dr STD Std Cab LB | 4504 | 5365 | 6800 |

2 Dr STD Turbodsl 4WD Ext Cab LB

	6359	7574	9600

2 Dr STD Turbodsl Ext Cab LB

	5829	6943	8800

2 Dr LE 4WD Std Cab LB

	5498	6549	8300

| 2 Dr LE Std Cab LB | 4570 | 5444 | 6900 |

2 Dr LE Turbodsl 4WD Ext Cab LB

	6624	7890	10000

2 Dr LE Turbodsl Ext Cab LB

	6094	7259	9200

OPTIONS FOR RAM 350
6 cyl 5.9 L Turbodiesel Engine +1008
Air Conditioning[Opt on STD] +213
Automatic 4-Speed Transmission +226
Dual Rear Wheels +172

RAM 50 PICKUP　　　1993

Rear-wheel ABS reappears as standard equipment on all models.

Category J

2 Dr STD Std Cab LB	1716	2122	2800

2 Dr STD 4WD Std Cab SB

	2022	2501	3300

| 2 Dr STD Std Cab SB | 1845 | 2282 | 3011 |
| 2 Dr SE Std Cab SB | 1954 | 2417 | 3189 |

OPTIONS FOR RAM 50 PICKUP
Air Conditioning +213
Automatic 4-Speed Transmission +199

RAM WAGON　　　　1993

Category Q

2 Dr B150 Ram Wagon	2310	2794	3600

2 Dr B150 Ram Wagon Ext

	2459	2974	3833

2 Dr B250 Ram Wagon Ext

	2540	3071	3958

| 2 Dr B350 Ram Wagon | 3034 | 3669 | 4728 |

2 Dr B350 Ram Wagon Ext

	3102	3751	4834

2 Dr B150 LE Ram Wagon

	3064	3705	4775

2 Dr B150 LE Ram Wagon Ext

	3179	3845	4955

2 Dr B250 LE Maxi Ram Wagon Ext

	3336	4035	5200

2 Dr B250 LE Ram Wagon Ext

	3208	3880	5000

2 Dr B350 LE Ram Wagon

	3401	4113	5300

2 Dr B350 LE Ram Wagon Ext

	3465	4190	5400

2 Dr B250 Maxi Ram Wagon Ext

	3034	3669	4728

2 Dr B150 Value Ram Wagon

	2508	3033	3909

2 Dr B150 Value Ram Wagon Ext

	2759	3337	4300

2 Dr B250 Value Maxi Ram Wagon Ext

	3118	3771	4860

2 Dr B250 Value Ram Wagon Ext

	2951	3570	4600

2 Dr B350 Value Ram Wagon

	3144	3802	4900

2 Dr B350 Value Ram Wagon Ext

	3272	3958	5100

OPTIONS FOR RAM WAGON
12 Passenger Seating +166
15 Passenger Seating +226
8 Passenger Seating +159
8 cyl 5.2 L Engine[Opt on 1500,2500] +155
8 cyl 5.9 L Engine +105
Air Conditioning +177
Automatic 4-Speed Transmission +130
Dual Air Conditioning +177
Power Door Locks +84
Power Windows +84

Don't forget to refer to the Mileage Adjustment Table at the back of this book!

Model Description	Trade-in TMV	Private TMV	Dealer TMV

Sunscreen Glass +108

RAMCHARGER — 1993

The optional 5.9-liter V8 is upgraded.

Category N

Model Description	Trade-in TMV	Private TMV	Dealer TMV
2 Dr STD 4WD Utility	3758	4491	5712
2 Dr STD Utility	3355	4010	5100
2 Dr Canyon Sport 4WD Utility	4013	4796	6100
2 Dr Canyon Sport Utility	3816	4560	5800
2 Dr LE 4WD Utility	3882	4639	5900
2 Dr LE Utility	3742	4472	5688
2 Dr S 4WD Utility	3684	4403	5600
2 Dr S Utility	3158	3774	4800

OPTIONS FOR RAMCHARGER
8 cyl 5.9 L Engine +232
Air Conditioning[Std on LE] +185
Ramcharger Snow Plow Package +185

SHADOW — 1993

America model is dropped. Convertible disappears midyear. ABS is newly optional.

Category B

Model Description	Trade-in TMV	Private TMV	Dealer TMV
2 Dr STD Hbk	811	1144	1700
4 Dr STD Hbk	907	1279	1900
2 Dr ES Conv	1575	2222	3300
2 Dr ES Hbk	954	1346	2000
4 Dr ES Hbk	1002	1414	2100
2 Dr Highline Conv	1527	2154	3200

OPTIONS FOR SHADOW
4 cyl 2.5 L Engine[Opt on STD] +119
6 cyl 3.0 L Engine +184
AM/FM Compact Disc Player +93
Air Conditioning +199
Anti-Lock Brakes +159
Automatic 3-Speed Transmission +146
Automatic 4-Speed Transmission +199
Sunroof +93

SPIRIT — 1993

LE and R/T models are dropped from lineup. Turbocharged engines are banished. Four thousand flexible-fuel models are produced. Grille is now color keyed. CD player is added to options list. Rear styling is revised.

Category C

Model Description	Trade-in TMV	Private TMV	Dealer TMV
4 Dr ES Sdn	1409	1931	2800
4 Dr Highline Sdn	1107	1517	2200

OPTIONS FOR SPIRIT
4 cyl 2.5 L Flex Fuel Engine +147
6 cyl 3.0 L Engine +184
AM/FM Compact Disc Player +93

Air Conditioning +185
Anti-Lock Brakes +159
Automatic 3-Speed Transmission +146
Automatic 4-Speed Transmission +199

STEALTH — 1993

Base model gets ES sill moldings, while R/T's spoiler is optional across the line. R/T Turbo can be ordered with chrome wheels. Remote keyless entry and a CD changer are new options.

Category E

Model Description	Trade-in TMV	Private TMV	Dealer TMV
2 Dr STD Hbk	2811	3594	4900
Category F			
2 Dr ES Hbk	3248	4018	5300
2 Dr R/T Hbk	4290	5307	7000
2 Dr R/T Turbo AWD Hbk	4842	5989	7900

OPTIONS FOR STEALTH
Air Conditioning[Std on R/T] +185
Anti-Lock Brakes[Std on R/T] +212
Automatic 4-Speed Transmission +234
Chrome Wheels +242
Compact Disc Changer +144
Leather Seats +224
Power Sunroof +168

VIPER — 1993

Black is added to the paint palette. Production slowed due to problems with resin-transfer molded hood, keeping production level to a low 1500 units.

Category R

Model Description	Trade-in TMV	Private TMV	Dealer TMV
2 Dr RT/10 Cpe	23229	26143	31000

1992 DODGE

CARAVAN — 1992

Integrated child seats are a new option. Exterior door handles are flush-mounted, and new wheels debut.

Category P

Model Description	Trade-in TMV	Private TMV	Dealer TMV
2 Dr Grand Pass. Van	1925	2478	3400
2 Dr STD AWD Cargo Van	1851	2382	3268
2 Dr STD AWD Cargo Van Ext	1869	2406	3300
2 Dr STD Cargo Van	1586	2041	2800
2 Dr STD Cargo Van Ext	1786	2298	3153
2 Dr STD Pass. Van	1699	2187	3000
2 Dr ES AWD Pass. Van	2367	3046	4179
2 Dr ES Pass. Van	2190	2819	3867
2 Dr Grand ES AWD Pass. Van	2397	3086	4233

Don't forget to refer to the Mileage Adjustment Table at the back of this book!

Model Description	Trade-in TMV	Private TMV	Dealer TMV	Model Description	Trade-in TMV	Private TMV	Dealer TMV
2 Dr Grand ES Pass. Van				2 Dr LE Std Cab LB	1813	2333	3200
	2266	2917	4001	2 Dr LE 4WD Ext Cab SB			
2 Dr Grand LE AWD Pass. Van					2376	3058	4194
	2372	3053	4188	2 Dr LE 4WD Std Cab SB			
2 Dr Grand LE Pass. Van					2147	2763	3790
	2227	2867	3933	2 Dr LE Ext Cab SB	1983	2552	3500
2 Dr LE AWD Pass. Van	2322	2989	4100	2 Dr LE Std Cab SB	1759	2263	3104
2 Dr LE Pass. Van	2136	2750	3772	2 Dr S Std Cab SB	1190	1531	2100
2 Dr Grand SE AWD Pass. Van				2 Dr Sport 4WD Ext Cab SB			
	2099	2701	3706		2096	2698	3700
2 Dr Grand SE Pass. Van				2 Dr Sport 4WD Std Cab SB			
	1982	2551	3500		2040	2625	3600
2 Dr SE AWD Pass. Van	2051	2640	3622	2 Dr Sport Ext Cab SB	1754	2257	3096
2 Dr SE Pass. Van	1800	2317	3179	2 Dr Sport Std Cab SB	1416	1823	2500

OPTIONS FOR CARAVAN
7 Passenger Seating[Opt on STD] +82
Air Conditioning[Opt on Grand,Grand SE,SE,STD] +202
Anti-Lock Brakes +132
Captain Chairs (4) +140
Dual Air Conditioning +163
Infinity Sound System +78
Leather Seats +186

COLT   1992

GL models can be equipped with a digital clock, but all Colts lose options such as factory floor mats, intermittent wipers, wheel trim rings, and alloy wheels.
Category B

Model	Trade-in	Private	Dealer
2 Dr STD Hbk	701	1038	1600
2 Dr GL Hbk	745	1103	1700

OPTIONS FOR COLT
Air Conditioning +164
Automatic 3-Speed Transmission +128

DAKOTA   1992

V6 and V8 engines get more power. The V6 is up considerably, from 125 to 180 horsepower. V8 models add a whopping 65 horsepower and 30 foot-pounds of torque. Four-wheel drive models can be equipped with an optional Off-Road Appearance package.
Category J

Model	Trade-in	Private	Dealer
2 Dr STD 4WD Std Cab LB			
	2163	2783	3817
2 Dr STD Std Cab LB	1586	2041	2800
2 Dr STD 4WD Ext Cab SB			
	2270	2921	4006
2 Dr STD 4WD Std Cab SB			
	2139	2752	3775
2 Dr STD Ext Cab SB	1700	2187	3000
2 Dr STD Std Cab SB	1530	1969	2700
2 Dr LE 4WD Std Cab LB			
	2163	2783	3817

OPTIONS FOR DAKOTA
6 cyl 3.9 L Engine +135
8 cyl 5.2 L Engine +135
Air Conditioning +186
Automatic 4-Speed Transmission +217

DAYTONA   1992

Front and rear styling is revised, unsuccessfully. ABS is a new option. Shelby model is replaced midyear by IROC R/T model, powered by a 224-horsepower, 2.2-liter turbocharged engine and limited to a production run of 800 units.
Category E

Model	Trade-in	Private	Dealer
2 Dr STD Hbk	925	1253	1800
2 Dr ES Hbk	1028	1392	2000
2 Dr IROC Hbk	1325	1795	2578
2 Dr IROC R/T Turbo Hbk			
	1553	2104	3022

OPTIONS FOR DAYTONA
6 cyl 3.0 L Engine[Std on IROC] +162
AM/FM Compact Disc Player +82
Air Conditioning +164
Anti-Lock Brakes +162
Automatic 4-Speed Transmission +193
Leather Seats +199
Sunroof +82

DYNASTY   1992

Child-proof door locks are added, and options include an overhead console with storage bin and console with cassette storage.
Category D

Model	Trade-in	Private	Dealer
4 Dr STD Sdn	828	1192	1800
4 Dr LE Sdn	920	1325	2000

OPTIONS FOR DYNASTY
6 cyl 3.0 L Engine[Std on LE] +162
6 cyl 3.3 L Engine +163
Air Conditioning +140
Anti-Lock Brakes +152

Don't forget to refer to the Mileage Adjustment Table at the back of this book!

Model Description	Trade-in TMV	Private TMV	Dealer TMV
Automatic 4-Speed Transmission[Opt on STD] +193			
Dual Power Seats +122			
Infinity Sound System +140			
Leather Seats +176			
Power Sunroof +164			

MONACO 1992

No changes.
Category D

Model Description	Trade-in TMV	Private TMV	Dealer TMV
4 Dr ES Sdn	966	1391	2100
4 Dr LE Sdn	920	1325	2000

OPTIONS FOR MONACO
Air Conditioning[Opt on LE] +140
Anti-Lock Brakes +152
Leather Seats +176

RAM 150 1992

Category K

Model Description	Trade-in TMV	Private TMV	Dealer TMV
2 Dr STD 4WD Ext Cab LB			
	3048	3818	5100
2 Dr STD 4WD Std Cab LB			
	2535	3175	4242
2 Dr STD Ext Cab LB	2506	3139	4193
2 Dr STD Std Cab LB	1972	2470	3300
2 Dr STD 4WD Std Cab SB			
	2528	3166	4229
2 Dr STD Ext Cab SB	2339	2929	3913
2 Dr STD Std Cab SB	2092	2620	3500
2 Dr LE 4WD Ext Cab LB			
	3168	3967	5300
2 Dr LE 4WD Std Cab LB			
	2809	3518	4700
2 Dr LE Ext Cab LB	2612	3272	4371
2 Dr LE Std Cab LB	2489	3118	4165
2 Dr LE 4WD Std Cab SB			
	2809	3518	4700
2 Dr LE Ext Cab SB	2690	3368	4500
2 Dr LE Std Cab SB	2323	2910	3887

OPTIONS FOR RAM 150
8 cyl 5.2 L Engine[Opt on Std Cab] +135
Air Conditioning[Opt on STD] +187
Automatic 4-Speed Transmission +199

RAM 250 1992

Category K

Model Description	Trade-in TMV	Private TMV	Dealer TMV
2 Dr STD 4WD Ext Cab LB			
	3320	4158	5555
2 Dr STD 4WD Std Cab LB			
	3108	3892	5200
2 Dr STD Ext Cab LB	2696	3377	4511
2 Dr STD Std Cab LB	2451	3069	4100
2 Dr LE 4WD Ext Cab LB			
	3526	4416	5900
2 Dr LE 4WD Std Cab LB			
	3347	4192	5600
2 Dr LE Ext Cab LB	3228	4042	5400
2 Dr LE Std Cab LB	2630	3294	4400

OPTIONS FOR RAM 250
6 cyl 5.9 L Turbodiesel Engine +889
8 cyl 5.2 L Engine +137
8 cyl 5.9 L Engine +204
Air Conditioning[Opt on STD] +187
Automatic 4-Speed Transmission +199

RAM 350 1992

Category K

Model Description	Trade-in TMV	Private TMV	Dealer TMV
2 Dr STD 4WD Std Cab LB			
	3168	3967	5300
2 Dr STD Std Cab LB	2570	3219	4300
2 Dr STD Turbodsl 4WD Ext Cab LB			
	3646	4566	6100
2 Dr STD Turbodsl Ext Cab LB			
	3228	4042	5400
2 Dr LE 4WD Std Cab LB			
	3207	4017	5366
2 Dr LE Std Cab LB	2690	3368	4500
2 Dr LE Turbodsl 4WD Ext Cab LB			
	3765	4716	6300
2 Dr LE Turbodsl Ext Cab LB			
	3467	4342	5800

OPTIONS FOR RAM 350
6 cyl 5.9 L Turbodiesel Engine +889
Air Conditioning[Opt on STD] +187
Automatic 4-Speed Transmission +199
Dual Rear Wheels +152

RAM 50 PICKUP 1992

The V6 engine, rear ABS, and extended-cab models are dropped from the lineup. Left are regular-cab trucks in 2WD or 4WD in base or SE trim.
Category J

Model Description	Trade-in TMV	Private TMV	Dealer TMV
2 Dr STD Std Cab LB	1416	1823	2500
2 Dr STD 4WD Std Cab SB			
	1700	2187	3000
2 Dr STD Std Cab SB	1416	1823	2500
2 Dr SE Std Cab LB	1586	2041	2800
2 Dr SE Std Cab SB	1586	2041	2800

OPTIONS FOR RAM 50 PICKUP
Air Conditioning +187
Automatic 4-Speed Transmission +176

RAM WAGON 1992

Category Q

Model Description	Trade-in TMV	Private TMV	Dealer TMV
2 Dr B150 Ram Wagon	1726	2204	3000
2 Dr B250 Ram Wagon Ext			

Don't forget to refer to the Mileage Adjustment Table at the back of this book!

DODGE 92

Model Description	Trade-in TMV	Private TMV	Dealer TMV
	1841	2351	3200
2 Dr B350 Ram Wagon Ext			
	2071	2644	3600
2 Dr B150 LE Ram Wagon			
	2014	2571	3500
2 Dr B250 LE Maxi Ram Wagon Ext			
	2186	2791	3800
2 Dr B250 LE Ram Wagon Ext			
	2108	2691	3664
2 Dr B350 LE Ram Wagon Ext			
	2359	3012	4100
2 Dr B250 Maxi Ram Wagon Ext			
	2244	2865	3900
2 Dr B350 Maxi Ram Wagon Ext			
	2149	2744	3736

OPTIONS FOR RAM WAGON

12 Passenger Seating +146
15 Passenger Seating +199
8 Passenger Seating +140
8 cyl 5.2 L Engine[Opt on 1500,2500] +137
8 cyl 5.9 L Engine +92
Air Conditioning +156
Automatic 4-Speed Transmission +115
Dual Air Conditioning +156
Sunscreen Glass +95

RAMCHARGER   1992

The 5.2-liter engine gains 50 horsepower, and manual transmissions have five speeds rather than four. A Canyon Sport trim level is available this year.

Category N

Model Description	Trade-in TMV	Private TMV	Dealer TMV
2 Dr STD 4WD Utility	2748	3405	4500
2 Dr STD Utility	2565	3178	4200
2 Dr Canyon Sport 4WD Utility			
	2992	3708	4900
2 Dr Canyon Sport Utility			
	2870	3556	4700
2 Dr LE 4WD Utility	2837	3516	4646
2 Dr LE Utility	2781	3446	4554
2 Dr S 4WD Utility	2504	3102	4100
2 Dr S Utility	2443	3027	4000

OPTIONS FOR RAMCHARGER

8 cyl 5.9 L Engine +204
Air Conditioning +164
Automatic 4-Speed Transmission[Opt on 4WD] +199

SHADOW   1992

ES model gets body-color bumpers. Midyear, the turbo engine found in the ES is swapped for a 3.0-liter V6.

Category B

Model Description	Trade-in TMV	Private TMV	Dealer TMV
2 Dr America Hbk	650	962	1483
4 Dr America Hbk	665	984	1517
2 Dr ES Conv	1402	2076	3200
2 Dr ES Hbk	820	1214	1871
2 Dr ES Turbo Conv	1446	2141	3300
2 Dr ES Turbo Hbk	845	1252	1929
4 Dr ES Hbk	832	1232	1899
4 Dr ES Turbo Hbk	1008	1492	2300
2 Dr Highline Conv	1271	1882	2900
2 Dr Highline Hbk	745	1103	1700
2 Dr Highline Turbo Conv			
	1314	1946	3000
4 Dr Highline Hbk	767	1135	1750

OPTIONS FOR SHADOW

4 cyl 2.5 L Engine[Opt on Highline] +105
6 cyl 3.0 L Engine +162
Air Conditioning +176
Automatic 3-Speed Transmission +128
Automatic 4-Speed Transmission +176

SPIRIT   1992

R/T gets revised gear ratios to make it accelerate faster, and revised suspension tuning to make it handle better. V6 models can be equipped with either a three-speed automatic or a four-speed unit. Alloy wheels are restyled.

Category C

Model Description	Trade-in TMV	Private TMV	Dealer TMV
4 Dr STD Sdn	713	1046	1600
4 Dr ES Sdn	1026	1503	2300
4 Dr ES Turbo Sdn	1070	1569	2400
4 Dr LE Sdn	925	1356	2074
4 Dr LE Turbo Sdn	948	1390	2126
4 Dr R/T Turbo Sdn	1248	1830	2800

OPTIONS FOR SPIRIT

6 cyl 3.0 L Engine[Std on ES] +162
Air Conditioning +164
Anti-Lock Brakes +140
Automatic 3-Speed Transmission[Std on LE] +128
Automatic 4-Speed Transmission +176

STEALTH   1992

A tilt/removable glass sunroof becomes available midyear.

Category E

Model Description	Trade-in TMV	Private TMV	Dealer TMV
2 Dr STD Hbk	2364	3203	4600

Category F

Model Description	Trade-in TMV	Private TMV	Dealer TMV
2 Dr ES Hbk	2946	3791	5200
2 Dr R/T Hbk	3683	4739	6500
2 Dr R/T Turbo AWD Hbk			
	4476	5760	7900

OPTIONS FOR STEALTH

AM/FM Stereo/CD/Tape +158
Air Conditioning[Std on R/T] +164
Anti-Lock Brakes[Std on R/T] +187
Automatic 4-Speed Transmission +206

Don't forget to refer to the Mileage Adjustment Table at the back of this book!

Model Description	Trade-in TMV	Private TMV	Dealer TMV	Model Description	Trade-in TMV	Private TMV	Dealer TMV
Compact Disc Changer +126							
Leather Seats +197							
Sunroof +82							

VIPER 1992

Monstrous V10 power, cartoonish styling, and red paint characterized Dodge's new mega-buck icon. Two hundred 1992 models were produced.

Category R

Model Description	Trade-in	Private	Dealer
2 Dr RT/10 Cpe	20578	23474	28300

EAGLE 98-96

Model Description	Trade-in TMV	Private TMV	Dealer TMV	Model Description	Trade-in TMV	Private TMV	Dealer TMV

EAGLE   USA

1998 Eagle Talon TSi

1998 EAGLE

TALON   1998

New silver exterior badging and a new black and gray interior mark the Eagle in its final year of production. A new four-speaker CD/cassette player is now optional on the ESi, and all Talons benefit from Chrysler's next generation depowered airbags.

Category E

Model Description	Trade-in	Private	Dealer
2 Dr STD Hbk	5288	5966	6700
2 Dr ESi Hbk	5445	6144	6900
2 Dr TSi Turbo AWD Hbk	7182	8102	9100
2 Dr TSi Turbo Hbk	6629	7479	8400

OPTIONS FOR TALON
AM/FM Compact Disc Player +172
AM/FM Stereo/CD/Tape +172
Air Conditioning +365
Alarm System +142
Aluminum/Alloy Wheels[Opt on ESi] +216
Anti-Lock Brakes +276
Automatic 4-Speed Transmission +316
Infinity Sound System +338
Leather Seats +195
Limited Slip Differential +112
Power Drivers Seat +135
Power Sunroof +309
Power Windows[Std on 4WD] +103

1997 EAGLE

TALON   1997

Eagle's sporty Talon sees a host of changes as Chrysler Corp. seeks to rescue this endangered species. New front and rear fascias, bodyside cladding, bright new paint colors and "sparkle" wheels and wheel covers are guaranteed to attract attention to this overshadowed model. A bargain-basement Talon is introduced with minimal standard equipment to serve as a value leader for the model.

Category E

Model Description	Trade-in	Private	Dealer
2 Dr STD Hbk	4309	4935	5700
2 Dr ESi Hbk	4536	5195	6000
2 Dr TSi Turbo AWD Hbk	6048	6926	8000
2 Dr TSi Turbo Hbk	5594	6407	7400

OPTIONS FOR TALON
AM/FM Compact Disc Player +131
AM/FM Stereo Tape[Std on TSi] +162
AM/FM Stereo/CD/Tape +127
Air Conditioning +278
Alarm System +108
Aluminum/Alloy Wheels[Opt on ESi] +164
Anti-Lock Brakes +210
Automatic 4-Speed Transmission +291
Leather Seats +148
Power Drivers Seat +107
Power Sunroof +236
Premium Sound System +239

VISION   1997

The 3.5-liter engine formerly exclusive to the TSi is now available on the ESi. Automatic transmission refinements are intended to improve shifting. Eagle Vision ESis gets an improved stereo. A new color, Deep Amethyst Pearl, is now available.

Category G

Model Description	Trade-in	Private	Dealer
4 Dr ESi Sdn	3131	3612	4200
4 Dr TSi Sdn	3579	4128	4800

OPTIONS FOR VISION
AM/FM Stereo/CD/Tape +194
Anti-Lock Brakes[Opt on ESi] +194
Compact Disc Changer[Opt on ESi] +226
Infinity Sound System +183
Leather Seats +200
Power Drivers Seat +123
Power Moonroof +233

1996 EAGLE

SUMMIT   1996

Nothing new for the Mitsubishi-built Summit except a new choice of paint colors. The Summit wagon, a funky cross between a sedan and a minivan, gets new colors and seat fabrics.

Category B

Model Description	Trade-in	Private	Dealer
4 Dr STD 4WD Wgn	3217	3924	4900
2 Dr DL Cpe	1904	2322	2900
4 Dr DL Wgn	2691	3283	4100
2 Dr ESi Cpe	2101	2562	3200

Don't forget to refer to the Mileage Adjustment Table at the back of this book!

Model Description	Trade-in TMV	Private TMV	Dealer TMV
4 Dr ESi Sdn	2560	3123	3900
4 Dr LX Sdn	2429	2963	3700
4 Dr LX Wgn	2954	3603	4500

OPTIONS FOR SUMMIT
Air Conditioning +257
Anti-Lock Brakes +212
Automatic 3-Speed Transmission +159
Automatic 4-Speed Transmission +225

TALON 1996

Based on Mitsubishi mechanicals, Talon receives minor upgrades for 1996, including revised sound systems, a panic alarm, a HomeLink transmitter, and two new colors. ESi trim level gets standard 16-inch wheels.
Category E

Model	Trade-in	Private	Dealer
2 Dr STD Hbk	3416	3955	4700
2 Dr ESi Hbk	3562	4124	4900
2 Dr TSi Turbo AWD Hbk	4434	5134	6100
2 Dr TSi Turbo Hbk	4070	4713	5600

OPTIONS FOR TALON
AM/FM Stereo Tape[Std on TSi] +151
AM/FM Stereo/CD/Tape +240
Air Conditioning +260
Aluminum/Alloy Wheels +147
Anti-Lock Brakes +196
Automatic 4-Speed Transmission +270
Leather Seats +138
Power Sunroof +221

VISION 1996

An automanual transmission called AutoStick gives the 1996 Vision a feature to distinguish it as Chrysler's premier sport sedan. Interiors have been quieted down, and the ESi gets standard 16-inch wheels. Headlight illumination has been improved, new colors and seat fabrics are on board, and improved sound systems debut; all in the hope that some interest can be sparked in this slow-selling Eagle.
Category G

Model	Trade-in	Private	Dealer
4 Dr ESi Sdn	3053	3577	4300
4 Dr TSi Sdn	3905	4575	5500

OPTIONS FOR VISION
AM/FM Stereo/CD/Tape +181
Anti-Lock Brakes[Opt on ESi] +181
Leather Seats +187
Power Drivers Seat +115
Power Moonroof +218

1995 EAGLE

SUMMIT 1995

Dual airbags for the slow-selling Eagle Summit are the only change for 1995.

Category B

Model	Trade-in	Private	Dealer
4 Dr STD 4WD Wgn	2263	2764	3600
2 Dr DL Cpe	1508	1843	2400
4 Dr DL Wgn	2011	2457	3200
2 Dr ESi Cpe	1760	2150	2800
4 Dr ESi Sdn	1948	2380	3100
4 Dr LX Sdn	1885	2303	3000
4 Dr LX Wgn	2200	2687	3500

OPTIONS FOR SUMMIT
Air Conditioning +211
Anti-Lock Brakes +174
Automatic 3-Speed Transmission +131
Automatic 4-Speed Transmission +186

TALON 1995

The Talon is redesigned for 1995. The new model features gorgeous curves and more power. Base engine creeps up to 140 horsepower, the turbo to 210 horsepower. Dual airbags replace the antiquated motorized seatbelts on the previous edition, and the Talon now meets 1997 federal side-impact standards.
Category E

Model	Trade-in	Private	Dealer
2 Dr ESi Hbk	2754	3259	4100
2 Dr TSi Turbo AWD Hbk	3493	4133	5200
2 Dr TSi Turbo Hbk	3090	3656	4600

OPTIONS FOR TALON
Air Conditioning +214
Anti-Lock Brakes +161
Automatic 4-Speed Transmission +186
Power Sunroof +182

VISION 1995

No changes to the Vision.
Category G

Model	Trade-in	Private	Dealer
4 Dr ESi Sdn	2451	2882	3600
4 Dr TSi Sdn	2723	3202	4000

OPTIONS FOR VISION
6 cyl 3.5 L Engine[Opt on ESi] +168
AM/FM Compact Disc Player +130
Anti-Lock Brakes[Opt on ESi] +149
Leather Seats +155
Power Moonroof +179

1994 EAGLE

SUMMIT 1994

A driver airbag is added to the standard equipment list of the Eagle Summit. CFC-free air conditioning is now standard on all models equipped with air conditioning. Power steering is standard on all sedan models.
Category B

Model	Trade-in	Private	Dealer
4 Dr STD 4WD Wgn	1724	2215	3034

Don't forget to refer to the Mileage Adjustment Table at the back of this book!

Model Description	Trade-in TMV	Private TMV	Dealer TMV
2 Dr DL Cpe	909	1168	1600
4 Dr DL Wgn	1421	1826	2500
2 Dr ES Cpe	1080	1387	1900
4 Dr ES Sdn	1364	1753	2400
2 Dr ESi Cpe	1194	1533	2100
4 Dr ESi Sdn	1535	1972	2700
4 Dr LX Sdn	1250	1606	2200
4 Dr LX Wgn	1686	2166	2966

OPTIONS FOR SUMMIT
Air Conditioning +173
Anti-Lock Brakes +143
Automatic 4-Speed Transmission +151

TALON   1994

No changes for the Talon.
Category E

Model Description	Trade-in TMV	Private TMV	Dealer TMV
2 Dr DL Hbk	1633	2033	2700
2 Dr ES Hbk	1875	2335	3100
2 Dr TSi Turbo AWD Hbk	2420	3012	4000
2 Dr TSi Turbo Hbk	2057	2561	3400

OPTIONS FOR TALON
Air Conditioning +175
Aluminum/Alloy Wheels +100
Anti-Lock Brakes +132
Automatic 4-Speed Transmission +151
Leather Seats +93
Sunroof +132

VISION   1994

ESi models restyled to resemble their TSi stablemates by adding body cladding and a similar front fascia. The ESi's engine gains an increase in horsepower for 1994 as well. A flexible fuel version of the Vision is released in all states but California.
Category G

Model Description	Trade-in TMV	Private TMV	Dealer TMV
4 Dr ESi Sdn	2088	2505	3200
4 Dr TSi Sdn	2218	2661	3400

OPTIONS FOR VISION
Anti-Lock Brakes[Opt on ESi] +122
Leather Seats +127
Power Moonroof +147

1993 EAGLE

SUMMIT   1993

The Eagle Summit is redesigned and in the process loses its hatchback. Offered as a coupe or sedan, the new Summit is longer than the one it replaces, which translates into more interior room for passengers. The Summit is now available as a base DL or upscale ES. Fortunately, the 113-horsepower engine can be had on both models. Antilock brakes are a thoughtful option

on the ES models and wagons. The minivan/station wagon hybrid is positioned to take advantage of those consumers who want the convenience of a minivan and the driveability of a car. There is seating for five in the Summit Wagon, which is available as a DL, LX or all-wheel-drive model.
Category B

Model Description	Trade-in TMV	Private TMV	Dealer TMV
4 Dr STD 4WD Wgn	1243	1639	2300
2 Dr DL Cpe	703	927	1300
4 Dr DL Sdn	865	1140	1600
4 Dr DL Wgn	1081	1426	2000
2 Dr ES Cpe	757	998	1400
4 Dr ES Sdn	973	1283	1800
4 Dr LX Wgn	1135	1497	2100

OPTIONS FOR SUMMIT
Air Conditioning +146
Anti-Lock Brakes +120
Automatic 4-Speed Transmission +128

TALON   1993

The Talon gets a new base model to attract bargain shoppers. The new Talon DL comes standard with a disappointing 92-horsepower engine. Geez, that's just a little more than the base Summit. The former base model is renamed the ES.
Category E

Model Description	Trade-in TMV	Private TMV	Dealer TMV
2 Dr DL Hbk	1258	1611	2200
2 Dr ES Hbk	1430	1831	2500
2 Dr TSi Turbo AWD Hbk	1887	2417	3300
2 Dr TSi Turbo Hbk	1601	2051	2800

OPTIONS FOR TALON
Air Conditioning +148
Anti-Lock Brakes +132
Automatic 4-Speed Transmission +128
Sunroof +111

VISION   1993

Eagle receives its version of the Chrysler LH sedan in the form of the Vision. Available as an ESi or TSi, the Vision features cab-forward styling, dual airbags, V6 power, and available antilock brakes. TSi models are the sportier of the two, it comes equipped with a touring suspension, standard antilock brakes, a 214-horsepower engine, and sixteen-inch wheels.
Category G

Model Description	Trade-in TMV	Private TMV	Dealer TMV
4 Dr ESi Sdn	1242	1526	2000
4 Dr TSi Sdn	1614	1984	2600

OPTIONS FOR VISION
AM/FM Compact Disc Player +90
Anti-Lock Brakes +103
Dual Power Seats +94
Leather Seats +107

Don't forget to refer to the Mileage Adjustment Table at the back of this book!

Model Description	Trade-in TMV	Private TMV	Dealer TMV

1992 EAGLE

PREMIER 1992

Exterior tweaks to the Premier include a new grille, tail lights and new paint.
Category D

Model Description	Trade-in TMV	Private TMV	Dealer TMV
4 Dr ES Sdn	761	1097	1655
4 Dr ES Limited Sdn	803	1156	1745
4 Dr LX Sdn	690	994	1500

OPTIONS FOR PREMIER
Anti-Lock Brakes[Opt on LX,ES] +92
Leather Seats[Opt on ES] +106

SUMMIT 1992

Cloth seats are now optional on base models for those who don't like the adhesive quality imparted by vinyl seats in the summer.
Category B

Model Description	Trade-in TMV	Private TMV	Dealer TMV
2 Dr STD Hbk	531	782	1200
4 Dr STD 4WD Wgn	885	1303	2000
4 Dr STD Sdn	604	889	1365
4 Dr DL Wgn	741	1092	1676
2 Dr ES Hbk	575	847	1300
4 Dr ES Sdn	635	935	1435
4 Dr LX Wgn	763	1123	1724

OPTIONS FOR SUMMIT
Air Conditioning +120
Anti-Lock Brakes +99
Automatic 4-Speed Transmission +105

TALON 1992

The Talon is redesigned for 1992, getting a new grille, headlights, taillights and sheetmetal.
Category E

Model Description	Trade-in TMV	Private TMV	Dealer TMV
2 Dr STD Hbk	1024	1390	2000
2 Dr TSi Turbo AWD Hbk	1331	1807	2600
2 Dr TSi Turbo Hbk	1228	1668	2400

OPTIONS FOR TALON
Air Conditioning +122
Anti-Lock Brakes +92
Automatic 4-Speed Transmission +105
Sunroof +92

Don't forget to refer to the Mileage Adjustment Table at the back of this book!

FORD 01

Model Description	Trade-in TMV	Private TMV	Dealer TMV	Model Description	Trade-in TMV	Private TMV	Dealer TMV

FORD   USA

1997 Ford F-150

2001 FORD

CROWN VICTORIA   2001

Power from the V8 engine is increased. The interior gets minor improvements and an optional adjustable pedal assembly. Safety has been improved via a crash severity sensor, safety belt pretensioners, dual-stage airbags and seat-position sensors.

Category G

4 Dr LX Sdn	14688	15653	17260
4 Dr STD Sdn	13446	14329	15800

OPTIONS FOR CROWN VICTORIA
Air Suspension System +182
Aluminum/Alloy Wheels +287
Anti-Lock Brakes +169
Automatic Dimming Mirror +118
Climate Control for AC +118
Compact Disc Changer +236
Keyless Entry System[Opt on STD] +162
Leather Seats +497
Power Drivers Seat +243
Power Passenger Seat +236
Traction Control System +169

ECONOLINE WAGON   2001

2001 Econoline Wagons are virtually the same as last year, with a deluxe engine cover console, dual illuminated sunvisors and a heavy-duty battery now standard on all models. One interesting new option is the Traveling Package for the E-150 XLT. This package features seven-passenger leather seating, a video cassette player with two 6-inch headliner mounted LCD screens, a electronic AM/FM/clock/cassette/CD sound system, a leather wrapped steering wheel and a unique two-tone paint combination.

Category Q

2 Dr E-150 XL Pass. Van	14716	15600	17072
2 Dr E-350 XL Pass. Van	16579	17574	19233
2 Dr E-350 XL Pass. Van Ext	17413	18459	20201
2 Dr E-150 XLT Pass. Van	16544	17537	19192
2 Dr E-350 XLT Pass. Van	18299	19398	21229
2 Dr E-350 XLT Pass. Van Ext	18623	19741	21604

OPTIONS FOR ECONOLINE WAGON
10 cyl 6.8 L Engine +473
7 Passenger Seating +220
8 cyl 4.6 L Engine +507
8 cyl 5.4 L Engine[Std on E350] +1047
8 cyl 7.3 L Turbodiesel Engine +3372
AM/FM Stereo/CD/Tape +186
Aluminum/Alloy Wheels[Opt on XLT] +209
Camper/Towing Package +176
Cruise Control[Opt on XL] +125
Dual Air Conditioning[Opt on XL] +557
Entertainment System +875
Keyless Entry System +135
Leather Seats +845
Limited Slip Differential +182
Power Door Locks[Opt on XL] +152
Power Drivers Seat +264
Power Windows[Std on XLT] +169
Privacy Glass +311
Rear Air Conditioning w/Rear Heater[Std on XLT] +541
Running Boards +216
Tilt Steering Wheel[Opt on XL] +118

ESCAPE   2001

The Escape is Ford's new SUV. Smaller in size than the Explorer (and dwarfed by an Excursion), the Escape competes in the same class as the Honda CR-V and Toyota RAV4. Its main calling cards are an optional V6 engine and a large interior.

Category L

4 Dr XLS 4WD Wgn	11906	12757	14174
4 Dr XLS Wgn	10952	11734	13038
4 Dr XLT 4WD Wgn	12800	13714	15238
4 Dr XLT Wgn	11854	12701	14112

OPTIONS FOR ESCAPE
6 cyl 3.0 L Engine +473
Aluminum/Alloy Wheels[Std on XLT] +253
Anti-Lock Brakes[Std on XLT] +389
Automatic 4-Speed Transmission +473
Compact Disc Changer +395
Cruise Control[Std on XLT] +152
Leather Seats +439

Don't forget to refer to the Mileage Adjustment Table at the back of this book!

Model Description	Trade-in TMV	Private TMV	Dealer TMV	Model Description	Trade-in TMV	Private TMV	Dealer TMV

Power Drivers Seat +162
Power Moonroof +395
Privacy Glass +186
Running Boards +186
Side Air Bag Restraints +233
Trailer Hitch +236

ESCORT 2001

Other than a couple of new exterior colors, the Escort ZX2 is unchanged for 2001. The high-performance S/R Package is no longer available.

Category B

Model Description	Trade-in TMV	Private TMV	Dealer TMV
2 Dr ZX2 Cpe	7666	8375	9558

OPTIONS FOR ESCORT
Air Conditioning +537
Anti-Lock Brakes +270
Automatic 4-Speed Transmission +551
Chrome Wheels +402
Leather Seats +267
Power Moonroof +402
Power Windows +155
Tilt Steering Wheel +118

EXCURSION 2001

Performance is beefed up to 250 horsepower on the 7.3-liter Power Stroke turbodiesel V8 and all engines are now LEV compliant. For your listening pleasure, a six-disc, in-dash CD player is made available. The Excursion XLT gets dolled up with platinum cladding and standard chrome steel wheels, and the Limited offers standard power signal aero mirrors, fog lamps and an optional rear seat entertainment system.

Category N

Model Description	Trade-in TMV	Private TMV	Dealer TMV
4 Dr Limited 4WD Utility			
	25832	27254	29624
4 Dr Limited Utility	23941	25259	27455
4 Dr XLT 4WD Utility	23580	24878	27041
4 Dr XLT Utility	21476	22658	24628

OPTIONS FOR EXCURSION
10 cyl 6.8 L Engine[Std on 4WD] +402
8 cyl 7.3 L Turbodiesel Engine +2747
Aluminum/Alloy Wheels[Opt on XLT] +209
Captain Chairs (2)[Opt on XLT] +135
Compact Disc Changer +172
Entertainment System +1030
Leather Seats[Opt on XLT] +716
Limited Slip Differential +169
Power Drivers Seat[Opt on XLT] +162

EXPEDITION 2001

Ford's second-largest SUV changes little for 2001 XLT models get privacy glass as standard equipment, while the upscale Eddie Bauer trim level now comes with HomeLink and a class IV trailer towing package (4x4 models only). Eddie Bauers also get second-row

leather captain's chairs and rear-seat entertainment system as optional equipment. A new "No Boundaries" option package includes a monochromatic black exterior, side body cladding, 17-inch wheels, illuminated running boards and special front seats.

Category N

Model Description	Trade-in TMV	Private TMV	Dealer TMV
4 Dr Eddie Bauer 4WD Utility			
	24560	25912	28165
4 Dr Eddie Bauer Utility			
	22561	23803	25873
4 Dr XLT 4WD Utility	20502	21631	23512
4 Dr XLT Utility	18459	19475	21169

OPTIONS FOR EXPEDITION
8 cyl 5.4 L Engine[Opt on XLT, 2WD] +470
Automatic Load Leveling +551
Camper/Towing Package +264
Captain Chairs (2)[Opt on XLT] +135
Entertainment System +909
Heated Front Seats +199
Leather Seats[Opt on XLT] +716
Limited Slip Differential +172
Park Distance Control +135
Power Drivers Seat[Opt on XLT] +162
Power Moonroof +541
Premium Sound System[Opt on XLT] +334
Rear Air Conditioning w/Rear Heater[Opt on XLT] +510
Running Boards[Opt on XLT] +293
Side Air Bag Restraints +267

EXPLORER 2001

A complete redesign is planned for 2002, so the Explorer changes little in 2001. The SOHC V6 is standard on all models, and the 4.0-liter OHV V6 and manual transmission are no longer available. Additional child safety-seat tether anchors have been added to the second-row seats.

Category M

Model Description	Trade-in TMV	Private TMV	Dealer TMV
4 Dr Eddie Bauer 4WD Utility			
	20459	21760	23929
4 Dr Eddie Bauer AWD Utility			
	20995	22330	24555
4 Dr Eddie Bauer Utility			
	18810	20006	22000
4 Dr Limited 4WD Utility			
	20886	22214	24428
4 Dr Limited AWD Utility			
	21009	22345	24572
4 Dr Limited Utility	19257	20482	22523
4 Dr XLS 4WD Utility	16241	17274	18995
4 Dr XLS Utility	14535	15459	17000
4 Dr XLT 4WD Utility	16915	17991	19784
4 Dr XLT AWD Utility	16929	18006	19800
4 Dr XLT Utility	16429	17474	19215

FORD 01

Model Description	Trade-in TMV	Private TMV	Dealer TMV	Model Description	Trade-in TMV	Private TMV	Dealer TMV

OPTIONS FOR EXPLORER

8 cyl 5.0 L Engine +284
Automatic Dimming Mirror[Opt on Sport,XLT] +125
Automatic Load Leveling +236
Camper/Towing Package +240
Captain Chairs (2)[Opt on XL] +135
Chrome Wheels +115
Compact Disc Changer +267
Cruise Control[Opt on XLS] +130
Heated Front Seats[Std on Limited] +172
Keyless Entry System[Opt on Sport,XLS] +125
Leather Seats[Opt on Sport,XLT] +642
Park Distance Control +172
Power Moonroof +541
Privacy Glass +135
Running Boards[Opt on XLS,XLT] +267
Side Air Bag Restraints +267
Tilt Steering Wheel[Opt on XLS] +130

EXPLORER SPORT   2001

The 2001 Ford Explorer Sport receives styling changes as well as minor mechanical and interior improvements.

Category M

Model Description	Trade-in TMV	Private TMV	Dealer TMV
2 Dr Sport 4WD Utility	14246	15152	16662
2 Dr Sport Utility	12469	13262	14584

OPTIONS FOR EXPLORER SPORT

Automatic 5-Speed Transmission +740
Bucket Seats +190
Compact Disc Changer +345
Cruise Control +130
Keyless Entry System +125
Leather Seats +642
Limited Slip Differential +240
Overhead Console +257
Power Drivers Seat +176
Power Moonroof +541
Premium Sound System +345
Running Boards +267
Side Air Bag Restraints +264
Tilt Steering Wheel +130

EXPLORER SPORT TRAC   2001

The Sport Trac is a combination of a pickup and an SUV. Basically, Ford has grafted a small cargo bed to the back of an updated Ford Explorer.

Category J

Model Description	Trade-in TMV	Private TMV	Dealer TMV
4 Dr STD 4WD Crew Cab	16222	17486	19592
4 Dr STD Crew Cab	14449	15575	17451

OPTIONS FOR EXPLORER SPORT TRAC

Automatic 5-Speed Transmission +740
Cruise Control +130
Keyless Entry System +125
Leather Seats +642
Limited Slip Differential +240

Overhead Console +257
Power Drivers Seat +176
Power Moonroof +541
Premium Sound System +345
Running Boards +267
Tilt Steering Wheel +130
Tonneau Cover +399

F-150   2001

Besides the introduction of the four-door SuperCrew and limited-edition Harley Davidson and King Ranch models, America's most popular truck receives only minor changes in 2001. Power adjustable accelerator and brake pedals are now standard on all F-150 Lariat models and optional on XL and XLT trucks. The Work Series model is no longer available, but there is a newly created Work Truck option group that deletes certain equipment from the XL model. Child safety-seat anchors and four-wheel ABS are now standard equipment on all trucks. XL and XLT trucks have upgraded standard-equipment radios.

Category K

Model Description	Trade-in TMV	Private TMV	Dealer TMV
4 Dr Harley-Davidson Crew Cab SB	25484	27066	29702
4 Dr King Ranch 4WD Crew Cab SB	25925	27534	30216
4 Dr King Ranch Crew Cab SB	23324	24771	27184
4 Dr Lariat 4WD Ext Cab LB	20591	21869	23999
4 Dr Lariat Ext Cab LB	18022	19141	21005
4 Dr Lariat 4WD Crew Cab SB	21629	22972	25209
4 Dr Lariat 4WD Ext Cab SB	19969	21208	23274
4 Dr Lariat Crew Cab SB	19381	20584	22589
4 Dr Lariat Ext Cab SB	17786	18890	20730
4 Dr Lariat 4WD Ext Cab Stepside SB	23434	24888	27312
4 Dr Lariat Ext Cab Stepside SB	18438	19582	21489
2 Dr XL 4WD Std Cab LB	14028	14899	16350
2 Dr XL Std Cab LB	11745	12474	13689
4 Dr XL 4WD Ext Cab LB	16152	17154	18825
4 Dr XL Ext Cab LB	13560	14401	15804
2 Dr XL 4WD Std Cab SB	13836	14695	16126

Model Description	Trade-in TMV	Private TMV	Dealer TMV
2 Dr XL Std Cab SB	11602	12322	13522
4 Dr XL 4WD Ext Cab SB			
	15911	16898	18544
4 Dr XL Ext Cab SB	13369	14199	15582
2 Dr XL 4WD Std Cab Stepside SB			
	14484	15383	16881
2 Dr XL Std Cab Stepside SB			
	12245	13004	14271
4 Dr XL 4WD Ext Cab Stepside SB			
	16611	17642	19360
4 Dr XL Ext Cab Stepside SB			
	14081	14955	16412
2 Dr XLT 4WD Std Cab LB			
	16037	17032	18691
2 Dr XLT Std Cab LB	13775	14630	16055
2 Dr XLT 4WD Ext Cab LB			
	18107	19231	21104
4 Dr XLT Ext Cab LB	15658	16629	18249
2 Dr XLT 4WD Std Cab SB			
	15847	16831	18470
2 Dr XLT Std Cab SB	13634	14481	15891
4 Dr XLT 4WD Crew Cab SB			
	20499	21772	23892
4 Dr XLT 4WD Ext Cab SB			
	18017	19135	20999
4 Dr XLT Crew Cab SB	17922	19034	20888
4 Dr XLT Ext Cab SB	15470	16430	18030
2 Dr XLT 4WD Std Cab Stepside SB			
	16495	17519	19225
2 Dr XLT Std Cab Stepside SB			
	14288	15175	16653
4 Dr XLT 4WD Ext Cab Stepside SB			
	18585	19739	21661
4 Dr XLT Ext Cab Stepside SB			
	16173	17177	18850

OPTIONS FOR F-150
60/40 Bench Seat[Opt on XL] +270
8 cyl 4.6 L Engine +507
8 cyl 5.4 L Engine +541
AM/FM Compact Disc Player[Opt on XL,XLT] +128
Air Conditioning +544
Aluminum/Alloy Wheels +135
Automatic 4-Speed Transmission +740
Bed Liner +220
Camper/Towing Package +201
Captain Chairs (2) +331
Cruise Control[Opt on XL] +118
Entertainment System +875
Flex Fuel Option +4051
Limited Slip Differential +193
Off-Road Package +304
Power Drivers Seat[Opt on XLT] +243
Power Moonroof +547

Running Boards +169
Tilt Steering Wheel[Opt on XL] +118

F-150 SVT LIGHTNING   2001

Ford's bad-boy pickup receives a few changes in 2001. Acceleration times should be even faster thanks to an increase in power and a shorter final drive ratio. The front turn signals and taillights have unique clear lenses. Styling of the 18x9.5-inch wheels is new. A six-disc CD changer is now standard.

Category K

Model Description	Trade-in TMV	Private TMV	Dealer TMV
2 Dr SVT Lightning Sprchgd Std Cab Stepside SB			
	22580	23981	26317

F-250 SUPER DUTY   2001

A trailer tow package is standard on all models, as is four-wheel ABS. XLT and Lariat models can be equipped with an ultrasonic reverse vehicle-aid sensor, an in-dash six-disc CD changer and chrome tubular cab steps. Heated seats are available on Lariat models. Rounding out the 2001 changes are minor interior updates and a horsepower upgrade for the 7.3-liter Power Stroke turbodiesel engine.

Category K

Model Description	Trade-in TMV	Private TMV	Dealer TMV
4 Dr Lariat 4WD Crew Cab LB			
	23093	24526	26915
4 Dr Lariat 4WD Ext Cab LB			
	24150	25649	28147
4 Dr Lariat Crew Cab LB			
	21879	23237	25500
4 Dr Lariat Ext Cab LB			
	20592	21870	24000
4 Dr Lariat 4WD Crew Cab SB			
	22867	24286	26651
4 Dr Lariat 4WD Ext Cab SB			
	23755	25230	27687
4 Dr Lariat Crew Cab SB			
	21725	23073	25320
4 Dr Lariat Ext Cab SB			
	20494	21766	23886
2 Dr XL 4WD Std Cab LB			
	16735	17774	19505
2 Dr XL Std Cab LB	14614	15521	17033
4 Dr XL 4WD Crew Cab LB			
	20262	21519	23615
4 Dr XL 4WD Ext Cab LB			
	19435	20641	22651
4 Dr XL Crew Cab LB	17166	18231	20007
4 Dr XL Ext Cab LB	16275	17286	18969
4 Dr XL 4WD Crew Cab SB			
	20072	21318	23394
4 Dr XL 4WD Ext Cab SB			

Model Description	Trade-in TMV	Private TMV	Dealer TMV
	19229	20422	22411
4 Dr XL Crew Cab SB	17005	18060	19819
4 Dr XL Ext Cab SB	16114	17114	18781
2 Dr XLT 4WD Std Cab LB			
	19606	20823	22851
2 Dr XLT Std Cab LB	16667	17701	19425
4 Dr XLT 4WD Crew Cab LB			
	22715	24124	26474
4 Dr XLT 4WD Ext Cab LB			
	21468	22800	25021
4 Dr XLT Crew Cab LB	20443	21711	23826
4 Dr XLT Ext Cab LB	19143	20331	22311
4 Dr XLT 4WD Crew Cab SB			
	22553	23953	26286
4 Dr XLT 4WD Ext Cab SB			
	21253	22572	24770
4 Dr XLT Crew Cab SB	20238	21494	23587
4 Dr XLT Ext Cab SB	18982	20160	22123

OPTIONS FOR F-250 SUPER DUTY

10 cyl 6.8 L Engine +405
8 cyl 7.3 L Turbodiesel Engine +3189
Air Conditioning[Opt on XL] +544
Aluminum/Alloy Wheels[Opt on XLT] +125
Automatic 4-Speed Transmission +740
Bucket Seats[Opt on XL] +135
Cruise Control[Opt on XL] +125
Heated Seats[Opt on Lariat] +149
Heavy Duty Suspension +118
Keyless Entry System[Opt on XLT] +115
Limited Slip Differential +193
Park Distance Control +166
Power Drivers Seat[Opt on XLT] +196
Premium Sound System +142
Tilt Steering Wheel[Opt on XL] +118
Tutone Paint +152

F-350 SUPER DUTY   2001

The Trailer Tow package is standard on all models, as is four-wheel ABS. XLT and Lariat models can be equipped with an ultrasonic reverse vehicle-aid sensor, an in-dash six-disc CD changer and chrome tubular cab steps. Heated seats are available on Lariat models. Rounding out the 2001 changes are minor interior updates and a horsepower upgrade to the 7.3-liter diesel engine.

Category K

Model Description	Trade-in TMV	Private TMV	Dealer TMV
4 Dr Lariat 4WD Crew Cab LB			
	23463	24919	27346
4 Dr Lariat 4WD Ext Cab LB			
	22917	24339	26710
4 Dr Lariat Crew Cab LB			
	21564	22902	25133
4 Dr Lariat Ext Cab LB			
	20557	21833	23959
4 Dr Lariat 4WD Crew Cab SB			
	23354	24803	27219
4 Dr Lariat 4WD Ext Cab SB			
	22635	24040	26381
4 Dr Lariat Crew Cab SB			
	21540	22877	25105
4 Dr Lariat Ext Cab SB			
	20449	21718	23833
2 Dr XL 4WD Std Cab LB			
	17010	18066	19825
2 Dr XL Std Cab LB	14827	15747	17281
4 Dr XL 4WD Crew Cab LB			
	19821	21051	23101
4 Dr XL 4WD Ext Cab LB			
	19447	20654	22666
4 Dr XL Crew Cab LB	17436	18518	20322
4 Dr XL Ext Cab LB	16686	17721	19447
4 Dr XL 4WD Crew Cab SB			
	19500	20710	22727
4 Dr XL 4WD Ext Cab SB			
	19066	20249	22221
4 Dr XL Crew Cab SB	17327	18403	20195
4 Dr XL Ext Cab SB	16525	17551	19260
2 Dr XLT 4WD Std Cab LB			
	19481	20690	22705
2 Dr XLT Std Cab LB	17085	18146	19913
4 Dr XLT 4WD Crew Cab LB			
	22311	23696	26004
4 Dr XLT 4WD Ext Cab LB			
	21482	22815	25037
4 Dr XLT Crew Cab LB	20396	21662	23772
4 Dr XLT Ext Cab LB	19473	20682	22696
4 Dr XLT 4WD Crew Cab SB			
	22206	23584	25881
4 Dr XLT 4WD Ext Cab SB			
	21320	22644	24849
4 Dr XLT Crew Cab SB	20156	21407	23492
4 Dr XLT Ext Cab SB	19418	20623	22632

OPTIONS FOR F-350 SUPER DUTY

10 cyl 6.8 L Engine +405
8 cyl 7.3 L Turbodiesel Engine +2953
Air Conditioning[Opt on XL] +544
Aluminum/Alloy Wheels[Opt on XLT] +125
Automatic 4-Speed Transmission +740
Bucket Seats[Opt on XL] +135
Cruise Control[Opt on XL] +125
Dual Rear Wheels +574
Heated Front Seats[Opt on Lariat] +149
Heavy Duty Suspension +118
Keyless Entry System[Opt on XLT] +115
Limited Slip Differential +193

FORD 01

Model Description	Trade-in TMV	Private TMV	Dealer TMV	Model Description	Trade-in TMV	Private TMV	Dealer TMV

Park Distance Control +166
Power Drivers Seat[Opt on XLT] +196
Premium Sound System +142
Tilt Steering Wheel[Opt on XL] +118
Tutone Paint +152

FOCUS 2001

Raising the bar for compact vehicles, Ford is offering its stability system — called AdvanceTrac — on ZTS Sedans and ZX3 Hatchbacks. Ford has also made previously optional features standard equipment. Highlights include a driver's armrest on every model except LX and power windows on SE Sedans and Wagons. SE Wagons also get the Zetec engine as standard and can be ordered with a manual transmission. A new manual moonroof is offered on the ZX3 and new 16-inch wheels are standard on ZTS Sedans and optional on ZX3 Coupes.

Category B

Model	Trade-in	Private	Dealer
4 Dr LX Sdn	8354	9128	10417
4 Dr SE Sdn	9553	10438	11912
4 Dr SE Wgn	10756	11752	13412
4 Dr Street Sdn	8775	9588	10942
4 Dr Street Wgn	10756	11752	13412
4 Dr ZTS Sdn	10496	11467	13087
2 Dr ZX3 Hbk	8147	8901	10158

OPTIONS FOR FOCUS
4 cyl 2.0 L Zetec Engine[Opt on SE] +200
Air Conditioning[Opt on LX, SE] +537
Anti-Lock Brakes[Std on ZTS] +270
Automatic 4-Speed Transmission[Std on Wgn] +551
Compact Disc Changer +236
Cruise Control[Std on ZTS] +145
Leather Seats +470
Moonroof +334
Power Door Locks[Opt on LX,ZX3] +131
Power Windows[Std on ZTS] +151
Side Air Bag Restraints +236
Traction Control System +828

MUSTANG 2001

GT models get unique hood and side scoops, so that you can tell 'em apart from V6 models. They also receive standard 17-inch wheels, and V6 Convertibles get 16-inch wheels as standard. All cars have a revised center console and blacked-out headlights and spoilers. The Mach 460 stereo system comes with an in-dash six-disc CD changer. A new "premium" trim line is created for both V6 and V8 models. After a one-year hiatus, the Ford SVT Mustang Cobra returns for 2001.

Category E

Model	Trade-in	Private	Dealer
2 Dr GT Bullitt Cpe	19858	21223	23500
2 Dr Deluxe Conv	15899	16992	18815
2 Dr GT Deluxe Conv	20154	21540	23851
2 Dr GT Deluxe Cpe	15936	17032	18859
2 Dr Cobra Conv	24937	26652	29511
2 Dr Cobra Cpe	21125	22578	25000
2 Dr STD Cpe	11581	12377	13705

OPTIONS FOR MUSTANG
Anti-Lock Brakes[Opt on STD] +338
Automatic 4-Speed Transmission +551
Compact Disc Changer +236
Leather Seats[Std on Cobra] +318
Power Drivers Seat[Std on Cobra] +135
Premium Sound System +135
Traction Control System[Std on Cobra] +169

RANGER 2001

Most notable for the '01 Ranger is the availability of the Explorer's 207-horsepower, 4.0-liter SOHC V6. In other engine news, the flexible-fuel feature on the 3.0-liter V6 has been dropped and there is a new base 2.3-liter four-cylinder. ABS is now standard on all models. A new Edge trim level has a monochromatic appearance, which includes color-keyed bumpers and wheel lip moldings. Exterior changes are numerous. All models get a new grille, bumpers, and headlamps, while the XLT 4x4 and Edge get a new hood and wheel lip moldings. Four colors are new as well as an optional in-dash, six-disc CD changer.

Category J

Model	Trade-in	Private	Dealer
2 Dr Edge Ext Cab SB	11317	12199	13668
2 Dr Edge Std Cab SB	9774	10535	11804
4 Dr Edge 4WD Ext Cab SB	13535	14590	16347
2 Dr Edge Plus 4WD Std Cab SB	13079	14098	15796
2 Dr Edge Plus Ext Cab SB	12470	13441	15060
4 Dr Edge Plus 4WD Ext Cab Stepside SB	15502	16709	18722
2 Dr Edge Plus 4WD Std Cab Stepside SB	13561	14617	16378
2 Dr Edge Plus Ext Cab Stepside SB	12773	13768	15426
2 Dr Edge Plus Std Cab Stepside SB	10597	11422	12798
4 Dr Edge Plus 4WD Ext Cab SB	15779	17008	19057
2 Dr XL Std Cab LB	8657	9331	10455
2 Dr XL Ext Cab SB	10748	11586	12981
2 Dr XL Std Cab SB	8036	8662	9705
2 Dr XLT Std Cab LB	10834	11677	13084
2 Dr XLT Ext Cab SB	11019	11877	13308
2 Dr XLT Std Cab SB	9279	10001	11206

Don't forget to refer to the Mileage Adjustment Table at the back of this book!

Model Description	Trade-in TMV	Private TMV	Dealer TMV
4 Dr XLT 4WD Ext Cab SB			
	14325	15441	17301
2 Dr XLT Std Cab Stepside SB			
	9590	10337	11582
4 Dr XLT 4WD Ext Cab Stepside SB			
	14772	15923	17841
2 Dr XLT Ext Cab Stepside SB			
	13738	14808	16592

OPTIONS FOR RANGER

6 cyl 3.0 L Engine +297
6 cyl 4.0 L Engine +372
AM/FM Compact Disc Player[Opt on XL] +162
Air Conditioning +439
Appearance Package +220
Automatic 4-Speed Transmission +676
Automatic 5-Speed Transmission +676
Bed Extender +132
Bed Liner +203
Cruise Control +125
Hinged Fourth Door +449
Limited Slip Differential +199
Off-Road Package[Opt on XLT] +497
Power Door Locks +162
Power Windows +186
Tilt Steering Wheel +118
Tonneau Cover +270
Trailer Hitch +145

TAURUS   2001

After the 2000 redesign, updates are minor. A Lower Anchor and Tether for Children (LATCH) is now standard on all models. LATCH is an anchoring system for child safety seats. Also new is Spruce Green Clearcoat Metallic, an increase in fuel tank capacity to 18 gallons, a six-disc CD changer is standard on SES models, power locks are standard on LX and an optional rear spoiler can give your Taurus that extra bit of attitude.

Category D

Model Description	Trade-in TMV	Private TMV	Dealer TMV
4 Dr LX Sdn	11065	11903	13299
4 Dr SE Sdn	11503	12374	13826
4 Dr SE Wgn	12216	13141	14683
4 Dr SEL Sdn	12948	13928	15562
4 Dr SES Sdn	12132	13051	14582

OPTIONS FOR TAURUS

Anti-Lock Brakes[Opt on LX,SE] +405
Leather Seats[Opt on LX] +605
Power Drivers Seat[Opt on LX,SE] +236
Power Moonroof +601
Power Passenger Seat +236
Premium Sound System +216
Rear Spoiler +155
Side Air Bag Restraints +264
Third Seat +135
Traction Control System +118

WINDSTAR   2001

There are several model/series changes for Windstar this year, as well as updates to the exterior, interior and powertrain. Ford says a new transmission has improved shift quality and the 3.8-liter V6 is standard on all Windstars. The base model is now called the Windstar LX three-door. The SE Sport is a new trim level and it includes driving lights, painted bumpers and body-side molding, a rear lift gate spoiler, second-row bucket/console seats, a roof rack with brushed aluminum crossbars, black rocker cladding, and different wheels and tires.

Category P

Model Description	Trade-in TMV	Private TMV	Dealer TMV
2 Dr LX Pass. Van	14066	15055	16705
4 Dr LX Pass. Van	15667	16770	18607
4 Dr Limited Pass. Van			
	21131	22618	25096
4 Dr SE Pass. Van	17610	18850	20915
4 Dr SE Sport Pass. Van			
	17150	18357	20368
4 Dr SEL Pass. Van	19182	20532	22782

OPTIONS FOR WINDSTAR

AM/FM Stereo/CD/Tape[Opt on LX,SE] +169
Aluminum/Alloy Wheels[Opt on LX] +280
Camper/Towing Package[Std on Limited] +301
Cruise Control[Opt on LX] +125
Entertainment System +672
Leather Seats[Opt on SE] +584
Luggage Rack[Opt on LX] +166
Power Drivers Seat[Opt on LX] +220
Power Dual Sliding Doors[Opt on SE] +608
Power Sliding Door[Opt on LX,SE] +608
Privacy Glass[Opt on LX,STD] +280
Rear Air Conditioning w/Rear Heater +338
Side Air Bag Restraints[Std on Limited] +264
Tilt Steering Wheel[Opt on STD] +125
Traction Control System[Std on Limited] +267

2000 FORD

CARGO VAN   2000

The 5.4-liter V8 and the 6.8-liter V10 gas engines generate more horsepower and torque. Four-wheel antilock brakes are now standard on all models. The Light Convenience Group, including courtesy lights, a rear cargo light, a chime warning module, a "headlamps on" alert, and illuminated courtesy door lights, is now standard on all models. The handling package has been made standard on all Econolines. The towing package is standard on all wagons. The instrument panel has been simplified. Remote keyless entry and power sail-mount mirrors are standard on recreational vans.

Don't forget to refer to the Mileage Adjustment Table at the back of this book!

Category Q

Model Description	Trade-in TMV	Private TMV	Dealer TMV
2 Dr E-150 STD Cargo Van	11449	12537	13542
2 Dr E-250 STD Cargo Van	12184	13343	14412
2 Dr E-250 STD Cargo Van Ext	12511	13701	14799
2 Dr E-350 STD Cargo Van	13575	14866	16057
2 Dr E-350 STD Cargo Van Ext	14147	15492	16734

OPTIONS FOR CARGO VAN

10 cyl 6.8 L Engine +474
8 cyl 4.6 L Engine +943
8 cyl 5.4 L Engine[Std on E350] +1482
8 cyl 7.3 L Turbodiesel Engine +3055
AM/FM Stereo Tape +105
Chrome Step Bumper +108
Cruise Control +130
Dual Air Bag Restraints[Std on E150] +166
Dual Air Conditioning +557
Keyless Entry System +118
Limited Slip Differential +182
Power Door Locks +169
Power Mirrors +108
Power Windows +220
Privacy Glass +284
Tilt Steering Wheel +118

CONTOUR 2000

The Contour LX is dropped, leaving either the Contour SE Sport or SVT Contour to pick from. New colors are offered and an emergency trunk-release handle is standard.

Category C

Model Description	Trade-in TMV	Private TMV	Dealer TMV
4 Dr SE Sdn	7175	8061	8880
4 Dr SE Sport Sdn	7198	8088	8909

Category E

4 Dr SVT Sdn	11655	12903	14055

OPTIONS FOR CONTOUR

6 cyl 2.5 L Engine[Opt on SE] +334
AM/FM Compact Disc Player +186
AM/FM Stereo/CD/Tape +186
Aluminum/Alloy Wheels[Opt on SE] +287
Anti-Lock Brakes[Std on SVT] +338
Keyless Entry System[Opt on SE] +128
Power Drivers Seat[Std on SVT] +236
Power Moonroof +402
Traction Control System[Std on SVT] +159

CROWN VICTORIA 2000

New safety items have been added, including an emergency trunk release, child seat-anchor brackets, and the Belt Minder system. The rear-axle ratio for Crown Victorias with the handling package changes from 3.27 to 3.55, for quicker acceleration. Two new shades of green are offered—Tropical Green and Dark Green Satin.

Category G

Model Description	Trade-in TMV	Private TMV	Dealer TMV
4 Dr STD Sdn	11326	12475	13535
4 Dr LX Sdn	12377	13632	14791

OPTIONS FOR CROWN VICTORIA

Aluminum/Alloy Wheels +287
Automatic Dimming Mirror +118
Climate Control for AC +118
Compact Disc Changer +236
Dual Power Seats +459
Keyless Entry System[Std on LX] +162
Leather Seats +497
Power Drivers Seat[Std on LX] +243
Traction Control System +118

ECONOLINE WAGON 2000

The 5.4-liter V8 and the 6.8-liter V10 gas engines generate more horsepower and torque. Four-wheel antilock brakes are now standard on all models. The Light Convenience Group, including courtesy lights, a rear cargo light, a chime warning module, a "headlamps on" alert, and illuminated courtesy door lights, is now standard on all models. The handling package has been made standard on all Econolines. The towing package is standard on all wagons. The instrument panel has been simplified. Remote keyless entry and power sail-mount mirrors are standard on recreational vans.

Category Q

Model Description	Trade-in TMV	Private TMV	Dealer TMV
2 Dr E-150 Chateau Pass. Van	14229	15582	16831
2 Dr E-350 Chateau Pass. Van	15619	17104	18475
2 Dr E-150 XL Pass. Van	12593	13791	14896
2 Dr E-350 XL Pass. Van	14065	15403	16637
2 Dr E-350 XL Pass. Van Ext	14883	16298	17604
2 Dr E-150 XLT Pass. Van	14310	15671	16927
2 Dr E-350 XLT Pass. Van	15701	17194	18572
2 Dr E-350 XLT Pass. Van Ext	15946	17462	18862

OPTIONS FOR ECONOLINE WAGON

10 cyl 6.8 L Engine +474
8 Passenger Seating[Opt on E350 SD XL Wgn] +128
8 cyl 4.6 L Engine +507
8 cyl 5.4 L Engine[Std on E350] +1047
8 cyl 7.3 L Turbodiesel Engine +3203

FORD 00

Model Description	Trade-in TMV	Private TMV	Dealer TMV	Model Description	Trade-in TMV	Private TMV	Dealer TMV

AM/FM Stereo/CD/Tape +186
Aluminum/Alloy Wheels[Opt on XLT] +210
Camper/Towing Package +176
Captain Chairs (2) +182
Cruise Control[Opt on XL] +130
Dual Air Conditioning[Opt on E150 XL Wgn, E350 SD XL Wgn] +557
Keyless Entry System +135
Limited Slip Differential +182
Power Door Locks[Opt on XL] +169
Power Drivers Seat +264
Power Windows[Std on Chateau, XLT] +220
Privacy Glass +311
Tilt Steering Wheel[Opt on XL] +118

ESCORT 2000

The 2000 Escort line has been simplified. The station wagon is discontinued, and there is now only one trim level for the sedan and coupe models.

Category B

	Trade-in	Private	Dealer
4 Dr STD Sdn	6467	7416	8292
2 Dr ZX2 Cpe	6392	7330	8196

OPTIONS FOR ESCORT

AM/FM Stereo/CD/Tape +199
Air Conditioning +537
Aluminum/Alloy Wheels[Std on ZX2] +179
Anti-Lock Brakes +271
Automatic 4-Speed Transmission +551
Chrome Wheels +402
Compact Disc Changer +199
Cruise Control +111
Keyless Entry System +111
Leather Seats +267
Power Door Locks +135
Power Moonroof +402
Power Windows +155
S/R Package +1010
Tilt Steering Wheel +118

EXCURSION 2000

The Excursion is an entirely new SUV based on Ford's F-250 Super Duty truck platform. It is the largest vehicle of its type, outgunning even the Chevy Suburban in terms of overall size and interior space.

Category N

	Trade-in	Private	Dealer
4 Dr Limited 4WDUtility	21491	23484	25323
4 Dr Limited Utility	19908	21754	23458
4 Dr XLT 4WD Utility	19325	21117	22771
4 Dr XLT Utility	17493	19115	20612

OPTIONS FOR EXCURSION

10 cyl 6.8 L Engine[Std on 4WD] +402
8 cyl 7.3 L Turbodiesel Engine +2953
Captain Chairs (2)[Opt on XLT] +135
Chrome Wheels +210
Compact Disc Changer +334

Heated Front Seats +196
Leather Seats[Opt on XLT] +743
Limited Slip Differential +169
Power Drivers Seat[Opt on XLT] +162

EXPEDITION 2000

The Expedition receives power-adjustable foot pedals, a rear sonar system for when the vehicle is backing up, optional side airbags, a revised center console and restyled wheels.

Category N

	Trade-in	Private	Dealer
4 Dr Eddie Bauer 4WD Utility	19742	21572	23262
4 Dr Eddie Bauer Utility	18576	20298	21888
4 Dr XLT 4WD Utility	16993	18569	20023
4 Dr XLT Utility	15078	16476	17766

OPTIONS FOR EXPEDITION

8 cyl 5.4 L Engine[Opt on XLT, 2WD] +470
AM/FM Stereo/CD/Tape +240
Alarm System +135
Aluminum/Alloy Wheels +210
Automatic Load Leveling +551
Camper/Towing Package +594
Captain Chairs (2)[Opt on XLT] +190
Captain Chairs (4) +537
Chrome Wheels[Opt on XLT] +115
Compact Disc Changer[Opt on XLT] +321
Dual Air Conditioning[Opt on XLT] +476
Heated Front Seats +196
Leather Seats[Opt on XLT] +675
Limited Slip Differential +172
Power Moonroof +541
Running Boards[Opt on XLT] +293
Side Air Bag Restraints +267

EXPLORER 2000

The recently introduced Reverse Sensing System continues to be an option. A color-keyed, two-spoke leather-wrapped steering wheel (with auxiliary audio, climate and speed control) is now standard on Eddie Bauer models. XLT Sport/Eddie Bauer/Limited models with 5.0-liter V8s receive a trailer-towing package as standard equipment. The XL is available only for fleet sales, and the XLS replaces the XL Appearance as the base retail model.

Category M

	Trade-in	Private	Dealer
4 Dr Eddie Bauer 4WD Utility	16421	18177	19798
4 Dr Eddie Bauer AWD Utility	16681	18465	20112
4 Dr Eddie Bauer Utility	15464	17117	18644

Don't forget to refer to the Mileage Adjustment Table at the back of this book!

Model Description	Trade-in TMV	Private TMV	Dealer TMV
4 Dr Limited 4WD Utility			
	16592	18366	20004
4 Dr Limited AWD Utility			
	16793	18589	20247
4 Dr Limited Utility	15625	17296	18839
2 Dr Sport 4WD Utility			
	11920	13195	14372
2 Dr Sport Utility	10310	11412	12430
4 Dr XL 4WD Utility	12565	13909	15149
4 Dr XL Utility	10712	11857	12915
4 Dr XLS 4WD Utility	12887	14265	15537
4 Dr XLS Utility	12081	13373	14566
4 Dr XLT 4WD Utility	14175	15692	17091
4 Dr XLT AWD Utility	14403	15943	17365
4 Dr XLT Utility	13370	14800	16120

OPTIONS FOR EXPLORER

6 cyl 4.0 L SOHC Engine[Std on Eddie Bauer,Limited] +365
8 cyl 5.0 L Engine +284
AM/FM Stereo/CD/Tape[Std on Eddie Bauer,Limited] +155
Alarm System[Opt on Sport] +145
Automatic 5-Speed Transmission[Std on Eddie Bauer,Limited,XLT] +740
Automatic Dimming Mirror[Opt on Sport,XLT] +125
Automatic Load Leveling +236
Bucket Seats[Opt on XLT] +190
Camper/Towing Package +240
Captain Chairs (2)[Opt on XL] +190
Chrome Wheels +115
Compact Disc Changer +251
Cruise Control[Std on Eddie Bauer,Limited,XLT] +130
Dual Power Seats[Opt on Sport,XLT] +348
Fog Lights[Opt on Sport] +111
Heated Front Seats[Std on Limited] +166
Keyless Entry System[Opt on Sport,XLS] +125
Leather Seats[Opt on Sport,XLT] +642
Limited Slip Differential +190
Overhead Console[Opt on Sport] +257
Power Drivers Seat[Std on XLT] +176
Power Moonroof +541
Privacy Glass +135
Running Boards[Std on Eddid Bauer,Limited] +267
Side Air Bag Restraints +264
Side Steps +199
Tilt Steering Wheel[Std on Eddie Bauer,Limited,XLT] +130

F-150   2000

The F-150 SuperCrew, a crew-cab truck with full-sized doors and a larger rear-passenger compartment, will bow in the first quarter of 2000 as a 2001 model. A limited-edition Harley-Davidson F-150 is available for 2000. The under 8,500-pound GVW F-250 has been discontinued and replaced by the F-150 7700 Payload Group. A new overhead console and left- and right-side visor vanity mirrors are optional on XL models and standard on XLT and Lariat F-150 pickups. A driver's-side keypad entry system is available on Lariat models. Chromed steel wheels and 17-inch tires are now available on 4x2 models. A comfort-enhancing flip-up 40/60 rear seat has been added to the F-150 SuperCab.

Category K

Model Description	Trade-in TMV	Private TMV	Dealer TMV
4 Dr Harley-Davidson Ext Cab Stepside SB			
	19948	21838	23583
4 Dr Lariat 4WD Ext Cab LB			
	17486	19142	20672
4 Dr Lariat Ext Cab LB			
	15512	16982	18339
4 Dr Lariat 4WD Ext Cab SB			
	17321	18963	20478
4 Dr Lariat Ext Cab SB			
	15348	16802	18145
4 Dr Lariat 4WD Ext Cab Stepside SB			
	17896	19592	21157
4 Dr Lariat Ext Cab Stepside SB			
	15926	17435	18828
2 Dr Work 4WD Std Cab LB			
	11329	12402	13393
2 Dr Work Std Cab LB	9359	10245	11064
4 Dr Work 4WD Ext Cab LB			
	13216	14469	15625
4 Dr Work Ext Cab LB	10918	11953	12908
2 Dr Work 4WD Std Cab SB			
	11164	12222	13199
2 Dr Work Std Cab SB	9194	10066	10870
4 Dr Work 4WD Ext Cab SB			
	13052	14289	15431
4 Dr Work Ext Cab SB	10754	11773	12714
2 Dr XL 4WD Std Cab LB			
	11977	13112	14160
2 Dr XL Std Cab LB	9939	10881	11750
4 Dr XL 4WD Ext Cab LB			
	13956	15278	16499
4 Dr XL Ext Cab LB	11579	12676	13689
2 Dr XL 4WD Std Cab SB			
	11821	12941	13975
2 Dr XL Std Cab SB	9927	10868	11736
4 Dr XL 4WD Ext Cab SB			
	13710	15009	16208
4 Dr XL Ext Cab SB	11411	12492	13490
2 Dr XL 4WD Std Cab Stepside SB			
	12396	13571	14655
2 Dr XL Std Cab Stepside SB			
	10343	11323	12228
4 Dr XL 4WD Ext Cab Stepside SB			
	14366	15727	16984

Model Description	Trade-in TMV	Private TMV	Dealer TMV
4 Dr XL Ext Cab Stepside SB	11993	13130	14179
2 Dr XLT 4WD Std Cab LB	13789	15096	16302
2 Dr XLT Std Cab LB	11739	12851	13878
4 Dr XLT 4WD Ext Cab LB	15519	16990	18347
4 Dr XLT Ext Cab LB	13381	14649	15819
2 Dr XLT 4WD Std Cab SB	13627	14918	16110
2 Dr XLT Std Cab SB	11570	12667	13679
4 Dr XLT 4WD Ext Cab SB	15354	16809	18152
4 Dr XLT Ext Cab SB	13463	14738	15916
2 Dr XLT 4WD Std Cab Stepside SB	14202	15548	16790
2 Dr XLT Std Cab Stepside SB	12232	13391	14461
4 Dr XLT 4WD Ext Cab Stepside SB	16008	17525	18925
4 Dr XLT Ext Cab Stepside SB	13793	15100	16307

OPTIONS FOR F-150
8 cyl 4.6 L Engine +507
8 cyl 5.4 L Engine +541
AM/FM Compact Disc Player[Opt on XL,XLT] +216
AM/FM Stereo/CD/Tape +142
Air Conditioning +544
Aluminum/Alloy Wheels +216
Anti-Lock Brakes +203
Automatic 4-Speed Transmission +740
Bed Liner +220
Camper/Towing Package +201
Captain Chairs (2) +332
Compact Disc Changer +271
Cruise Control[Opt on XL,Work] +130
Limited Slip Differential +182
Off-Road Equipment Group +419
Power Drivers Seat[Opt on XLT] +243
Running Boards +169
Tilt Steering Wheel[Opt on XL,Work] +131
Tonneau Cover +135

F-150 SVT — 2000

Completely new in 1999, the 2000 Lightning is the same, except for a new Silver Clearcoat exterior color.
Category K

Model Description	Trade-in TMV	Private TMV	Dealer TMV
2 Dr SVT Lightning Sprchgd Std Cab Stepside SB	18881	20670	22322

OPTIONS FOR F-150 SVT
Tonneau Cover +135

F-250 — 2000

Four-wheel antilock brakes are now standard on F-250 and F-350 trucks with Lariat trim levels. XL trim level trucks now have optional bucket seats. Clean fuel (LEV) gasoline engines are standard on all Super Duty trucks. Power windows and locks are now standard on XLT trim levels. The trailer/tow mirrors now telescope manually. Rear bumpers are standard on all F-250 and F-350 pickups. All Super Duty trucks get new interior and exterior colors.
Category K

Model Description	Trade-in TMV	Private TMV	Dealer TMV
2 Dr Lariat 4WD Std Cab LB	18717	20491	22128
2 Dr Lariat Std Cab LB	16664	18243	19701
4 Dr Lariat 4WD Crew Cab LB	20625	22580	24384
4 Dr Lariat 4WD Ext Cab LB	20359	22288	24069
4 Dr Lariat Crew Cab LB	19456	21299	23001
4 Dr Lariat Ext Cab LB	18086	19800	21382
4 Dr Lariat 4WD Crew Cab SB	20522	22467	24262
4 Dr Lariat 4WD Ext Cab SB	19866	21748	23486
4 Dr Lariat Crew Cab SB	19302	21131	22819
4 Dr Lariat Ext Cab SB	18019	19727	21303
2 Dr XL 4WD Std Cab LB	14694	16087	17372
2 Dr XL Std Cab LB	12724	13930	15043
4 Dr XL 4WD Crew Cab LB	18553	20311	21934
4 Dr XL 4WD Ext Cab LB	17158	18784	20285
4 Dr XL Crew Cab LB	15104	16536	17857
4 Dr XL Ext Cab LB	14284	15638	16887
4 Dr XL 4WD Crew Cab SB	18388	20131	21739
4 Dr XL 4WD Ext Cab SB	16994	18604	20091
4 Dr XL Crew Cab SB	14940	16356	17663
4 Dr XL Ext Cab SB	14120	15458	16693
2 Dr XLT 4WD Std Cab LB	17244	18878	20386
2 Dr XLT Std Cab LB	14530	15907	17178
4 Dr XLT 4WD Crew Cab LB	20441	22378	24166
4 Dr XLT 4WD Ext Cab LB			

Model Description	Trade-in TMV	Private TMV	Dealer TMV
	19127	20940	22613
4 Dr XLT Crew Cab LB	18306	20041	21642
4 Dr XLT Ext Cab LB	16911	18514	19993
4 Dr XLT 4WD Crew Cab SB			
	20277	22198	23972
4 Dr XLT 4WD Ext Cab SB			
	18881	20670	22322
4 Dr XLT Crew Cab SB	18075	19788	21369
4 Dr XLT Ext Cab SB	16746	18333	19798

OPTIONS FOR F-250
10 cyl 6.8 L Engine +405
8 cyl 7.3 L Turbodiesel Engine +2953
AM/FM Stereo Tape[Opt on XL] +151
AM/FM Stereo/CD/Tape +128
Air Conditioning +544
Aluminum/Alloy Wheels +257
Anti-Lock Brakes +253
Automatic 4-Speed Transmission +740
Automatic Locking Hubs (4WD) +108
Bucket Seats[Opt on XL] +135
Camper/Towing Package +271
Captain Chairs (2) +332
Cruise Control[Opt on XL] +135
Keyless Entry System[Opt on XLT] +115
Limited Slip Differential +192
Power Drivers Seat[Opt on XLT] +243
Power Mirrors[Opt on XLT] +118
Side Steps[Opt on XL,XLT] +199
Tilt Steering Wheel[Opt on XL] +131

F-350 2000

Four-wheel antilock brakes are now standard on F-250 and F-350 trucks with Lariat trim levels. XL trim level trucks now have optional bucket seats. Clean fuel (LEV) gasoline engines are standard on all Super Duty trucks. Power windows and locks are now standard on XLT trim levels. The trailer/tow mirrors now telescope manually. Rear bumpers are standard on all F-250 and F-350 pickups. All Super Duty trucks get new interior and exterior colors.

Category K

Model Description	Trade-in TMV	Private TMV	Dealer TMV
2 Dr Lariat 4WD Std Cab LB			
	18734	20509	22148
2 Dr Lariat Std Cab LB			
	17157	18783	20284
4 Dr Lariat 4WD Crew Cab LB			
	20851	22827	24651
4 Dr Lariat 4WD Ext Cab LB			
	20482	22423	24215
4 Dr Lariat Crew Cab LB			
	19127	20940	22613
4 Dr Lariat Ext Cab LB			
	18142	19861	21448
4 Dr Lariat 4WD Crew Cab SB			
	20769	22737	24554
4 Dr Lariat 4WD Ext Cab SB			
	20130	22037	23798
4 Dr Lariat Crew Cab SB			
	19045	20850	22516
4 Dr Lariat Ext Cab SB			
	18060	19771	21351
2 Dr XL 4WD Std Cab LB			
	15205	16646	17976
2 Dr XL Std Cab LB	13134	14379	15528
4 Dr XL 4WD Crew Cab LB			
	17905	19602	21168
4 Dr XL 4WD Ext Cab LB			
	17387	19035	20556
4 Dr XL Crew Cab LB	15516	16986	18343
4 Dr XL Ext Cab LB	14858	16266	17566
4 Dr XL 4WD Crew Cab SB			
	17486	19143	20673
4 Dr XL 4WD Ext Cab SB			
	17330	18972	20488
4 Dr XL Crew Cab SB	15433	16896	18246
4 Dr XL Ext Cab SB	14694	16087	17372
2 Dr XLT 4WD Std Cab LB			
	17445	19098	20624
2 Dr XLT Std Cab LB	15104	16536	17857
4 Dr XLT 4WD Crew Cab LB			
	19784	21658	23389
4 Dr XLT 4WD Ext Cab LB			
	18963	20760	22419
4 Dr XLT Crew Cab LB	18101	19817	21400
4 Dr XLT Ext Cab LB	17239	18873	20381
4 Dr XLT 4WD Crew Cab SB			
	19706	21573	23297
4 Dr XLT 4WD Ext Cab SB			
	18799	20581	22225
4 Dr XLT Crew Cab SB	17814	19502	21060
4 Dr XLT Ext Cab SB	17239	18872	20380

OPTIONS FOR F-350
10 cyl 6.8 L Engine +405
8 cyl 7.3 L Turbodiesel Engine +2953
AM/FM Stereo Tape[Opt on XL] +151
AM/FM Stereo/CD/Tape +128
Air Conditioning +544
Aluminum/Alloy Wheels +135
Anti-Lock Brakes +338
Automatic 4-Speed Transmission +740
Automatic Locking Hubs (4WD) +101
Bucket Seats[Opt on XL] +135
Camper/Towing Package +232
Cruise Control[Opt on XL] +130
Dual Rear Wheels +393

Don't forget to refer to the Mileage Adjustment Table at the back of this book!

FORD 00

Model Description	Trade-in TMV	Private TMV	Dealer TMV	Model Description	Trade-in TMV	Private TMV	Dealer TMV

Limited Slip Differential +192
Power Drivers Seat +196
Side Steps[Opt on XL,XLT] +199
Tilt Steering Wheel[Opt on XL] +131

FOCUS 2000

This is Ford's all-new "world car" that will be sold concurrently with the Escort. Everything from interior room to performance has been addressed to make this European-engineered compact a winner in the small-car segment.

Category B

4 Dr LX Sdn	7284	8353	9340
4 Dr SE Sdn	8250	9461	10579
4 Dr SE Wgn	9439	10825	12104
4 Dr Sony Limited Sdn	9290	10654	11913
4 Dr ZTS Sdn	9403	10783	12057
2 Dr ZX3 Hbk	7135	8182	9149

OPTIONS FOR FOCUS

4 cyl 2.0 L Zetec Engine[Opt on SE] +135
Air Conditioning[Opt on LX,SE] +537
Alarm System[Opt on ZX3] +101
Aluminum/Alloy Wheels[Opt on LX] +243
Anti-Lock Brakes[Std on ZTS] +271
Automatic 4-Speed Transmission[Std on Wgn] +551
Cruise Control[Std on ZTS] +145
Keyless Entry System[Opt on LX,ZX3] +98
Kona Mountain Bike Package +1010
Leather Seats +470
Power Door Locks[Opt on LX,ZX3] +131
Power Mirrors[Opt on ZX3] +101
Power Windows[Std on ZTS] +151
Side Air Bag Restraints +236

MUSTANG 2000

The Mustang has three updated colors: Performance Red, Amazon Green and Sunburst Gold. A child-safety-seat anchoring system is standard on both the coupe and convertible. New 16-inch wheels and tires are offered as an option on appearance package-equipped V6 Mustangs. The 2000 Mustang also features a tri-color bar emblem on the sides of the front fenders.

Category E

2 Dr STD Conv	14175	15692	17093
2 Dr STD Cpe	10317	11421	12441
2 Dr Cobra Conv	20004	22145	24122
2 Dr Cobra Cpe	17011	18832	20513
2 Dr GT Conv	16696	18483	20133
2 Dr GT Cpe	13860	15344	16714

OPTIONS FOR MUSTANG

AM/FM Stereo Tape +267
Anti-Lock Brakes[Opt on STD] +338
Automatic 4-Speed Transmission +551
Cruise Control[Std on Cobra] +115

Gold Package +101
Leather Seats[Std on Cobra] +338
Power Drivers Seat[Std on Cobra] +162
Rear Spoiler[Std on GT] +131
Traction Control System[Std on Cobra] +155

RANGER 2000

For 2000, the 2WD can be had with a "Trailhead" off-road style suspension package complete with larger tires and wheels, giving it the tough look of its 4WD cousin. All Ranger models have new wheel designs, and the XLT 4WD Off-Road Group receives a stainless steel front-suspension skid plate.

Category J

2 Dr XL 4WD Std Cab LB	9441	10594	11658
2 Dr XL Std Cab LB	6923	7769	8549
2 Dr XL 4WD Ext Cab SB	10071	11301	12436
2 Dr XL 4WD Std Cab SB	9205	10329	11367
2 Dr XL Ext Cab SB	8658	9715	10691
2 Dr XL Std Cab SB	6687	7504	8258
2 Dr XL 4WD Ext Cab Stepside SB	8651	9708	10683
2 Dr XL Std Cab Stepside SB	6844	7680	8452
2 Dr XLT 4WD Std Cab LB	10714	12022	13230
2 Dr XLT Std Cab LB	8182	9182	10104
2 Dr XLT 4WD Ext Cab SB	11408	12801	14087
2 Dr XLT 4WD Std Cab SB	10463	11741	12921
2 Dr XLT Ext Cab SB	9130	10245	11274
2 Dr XLT Std Cab SB	7867	8828	9715
2 Dr XLT 4WD Ext Cab Stepside SB	11329	12713	13990
2 Dr XLT 4WD Std Cab Stepside SB	10685	11990	13195
2 Dr XLT Ext Cab Stepside SB	9123	10237	11266
2 Dr XLT Std Cab Stepside SB	8104	9093	10007

OPTIONS FOR RANGER

6 cyl 3.0 L EFF Engine[Opt on XL,XLT] +267
6 cyl 4.0 L Engine +470
AM/FM Compact Disc Player[Opt on XL,XL Ext Cab Step SB,XL Std Cab Step SB] +196
AM/FM Stereo Tape +145
AM/FM Stereo/CD/Tape +162
Air Conditioning +544
Aluminum/Alloy Wheels +135

Don't forget to refer to the Mileage Adjustment Table at the back of this book!

FORD 00-99

Model Description	Trade-in TMV	Private TMV	Dealer TMV	Model Description	Trade-in TMV	Private TMV	Dealer TMV

Anti-Lock Brakes +203
Automatic 4-Speed Transmission +740
Automatic 5-Speed Transmission +774
Bed Liner +159
Bucket Seats +243
Chrome Wheels +135
Compact Disc Changer +338
Cruise Control +125
Fog Lights +125
Hinged Fourth Door +389
Keyless Entry System +108
Limited Slip Differential +232
Power Door Locks +162
Power Windows +186
Tilt Steering Wheel +125
Trailer Hitch +145

TAURUS   2000

Many changes are in store for the 2000 Taurus. Styling is the most obvious, with a new look for both the front and rear. Improved safety comes from a new airbag-deployment system, adjustable pedals, seatbelt pretensioners and child safety-seat anchors. The ride has been made more comfortable and the powertrain has been updated for more power and less noise. The V8-powered SHO has been dropped from the lineup.

Category D

	Trade-in	Private	Dealer
4 Dr LX Sdn	8934	9970	10926
4 Dr SE Sdn	9566	10676	11700
4 Dr SE Wgn	10199	11381	12473
4 Dr SEL Sdn	10673	11910	13053
4 Dr SES Sdn	10041	11205	12280

OPTIONS FOR TAURUS

6 cyl 3.0 L DOHC Engine +470
6 cyl 3.0 L EFF Engine +787
AM/FM Stereo Tape[Opt on LX] +125
Alarm System[Opt on LX] +118
Aluminum/Alloy Wheels[Opt on LX] +212
Anti-Lock Brakes[Opt on LX,SE] +405
Compact Disc Changer +236
Cruise Control[Opt on LX] +128
Dual Power Seats +236
Keyless Entry System[Opt on LX] +118
Leather Seats[Opt on LX] +605
Power Door Locks[Opt on LX] +179
Power Drivers Seat[Opt on LX,SE] +236
Power Moonroof +500
Rear Spoiler +169
Side Air Bag Restraints +264
Third Seat +135
Traction Control System +118

WINDSTAR   2000

The Windstar now has standard power-adjustable pedals and an optional rear-seat video entertainment center. There's also a new trim level called the Limited.

Available mid-year 2000, it will contain more standard features than the previously top-line SEL.

Category P

	Trade-in	Private	Dealer
2 Dr STD Pass. Van	11456	12696	13840
2 Dr STD Cargo Van	10903	12083	13172
2 Dr LX Pass. Van	12799	14184	15463
4 Dr Limited Pass. Van	17856	19788	21572
4 Dr SE Pass. Van	13510	14972	16322
4 Dr SEL Pass. Van	15960	17687	19281

OPTIONS FOR WINDSTAR

6 cyl 3.8 L Engine[Opt on STD] +463
AM/FM Stereo Tape[Opt on STD] +115
AM/FM Stereo/CD/Tape[Opt on LX,SE] +203
Aluminum/Alloy Wheels[Opt on LX] +280
Bucket Seats[Opt on Cargo] +331
Camper/Towing Package[Std on Limited] +293
Captain Chairs (4)[Std on SE] +483
Compact Disc Changer[Opt on LX] +271
Cruise Control[Opt on STD] +115
Dual Air Conditioning[Opt on LX] +321
Entertainment System +876
Keyless Entry System[Opt on LX,STD] +118
Leather Seats[Opt on SE] +584
Luggage Rack[Opt on LX] +166
Power Drivers Seat[Opt on LX] +220
Power Dual Sliding Doors[Opt on SE] +608
Power Sliding Door[Opt on LX,SE] +338
Privacy Glass[Opt on LX,STD] +280
Side Air Bag Restraints[Std on Limited] +264
Sliding Driver Side Door[Opt on LX,STD] +236
Spoke Wheels +115
Tilt Steering Wheel[Opt on STD] +122
Traction Control System[Std on Limited] +267

1999 FORD

CONTOUR   1999

All-speed traction control is a new option on V6 models equipped with ABS. Tropic Green and Medium Steel Blue replace Dark Green Satin, Light Denim Blue and Pacific Green on the color chart. The integrated child seat is dropped from the optional equipment list, as are the 15-inch wheel covers. The instrument panel receives a mild revision and the 10-way power seats become 6-way power seats thanks to the deletion of the power lumbar and recline adjustments. Ford increases rear seat room in the Contour for the third year in a row, desperately trying to shed this sedan's cramped car image.

Category C

	Trade-in	Private	Dealer
4 Dr LX Sdn	6066	6849	7632
4 Dr SE Sdn	6521	7363	8205

Category E

	Trade-in	Private	Dealer
4 Dr SVT Sdn	11393	12633	13874

Don't forget to refer to the Mileage Adjustment Table at the back of this book!

Model Description	Trade-in TMV	Private TMV	Dealer TMV

OPTIONS FOR CONTOUR

6 cyl 2.5 L Engine[Std on SE] +274
AM/FM Compact Disc Player +152
AM/FM Stereo/CD/Tape +138
Aluminum/Alloy Wheels[Std on SVT] +234
Anti-Lock Brakes[Std on SVT] +275
Automatic 4-Speed Transmission +450
Cruise Control[Opt on LX] +119
Leather Seats[Opt on SE] +494
Power Drivers Seat[Std on SVT] +194
Power Moonroof +328
Power Windows[Opt on LX] +196
Rear Spoiler[Std on SVT] +146
Traction Control System[Opt on SE] +129

CROWN VICTORIA   1999

Antilock brakes are now standard on Base and LX models. A stereo with cassette player is also newly standard on the Base model. Deep Wedgewood Blue, Light Blue and Harvest Gold are new exterior colors. Medium Wedgewood Blue, Light Denim Blue and Light Prairie Tan are no longer available.

Category G

	Trade-in	Private	Dealer
4 Dr STD Sdn	9935	10998	12061
4 Dr LX Sdn	10809	11965	13122

OPTIONS FOR CROWN VICTORIA

Aluminum/Alloy Wheels +234
Compact Disc Changer +194
Dual Power Seats +375
Keyless Entry System[Std on LX] +132
Leather Seats +406
Power Drivers Seat[Std on LX] +199

E-150   1999

An all-new alphanumeric vehicle badging system has been applied to Ford's Econoline Wagon models. These replace the past Club Wagon badges. Four-wheel disc brakes with ABS are now standard on all E350 Super Duty vans. The 4R70W electronic four-speed automatic is now standard on all E-150 models. Improved "fail-safe" cooling is now a feature on all Econoline gasoline engines.

Category Q

	Trade-in	Private	Dealer
2 Dr STD Econoline	9339	10336	11332

OPTIONS FOR E-150

8 cyl 4.6 L Engine +384
8 cyl 5.4 L Engine +623
AM/FM Stereo Tape +166
AM/FM Stereo/CD/Tape +148
Air Conditioning +455
Anti-Lock Brakes +337
Camper/Towing Package +113
Cruise Control +106
Dual Air Conditioning +455
Keyless Entry System +97

Limited Slip Differential +148
Power Door Locks +138
Power Windows +180
Privacy Glass +163
Tilt Steering Wheel +97

E-150 WAGON   1999

An all-new alphanumeric vehicle badging system is being applied to all Econoline Van and Club Wagon models. This will replace the past Club Wagon and Econoline badges. Four-wheel disc brakes with ABS are now standard on all E350 Super Duty vans. The 4R70W electronic four-speed automatic is now standard on all E-150/250 models. Improved fail-safe cooling is now a feature on all Econoline gasoline engines.

Category Q

	Trade-in	Private	Dealer
2 Dr Chateau Club Wagon	11575	12809	14044
2 Dr XL Pass. Van	10457	11573	12688
2 Dr XLT Pass. Van	11416	12633	13851

OPTIONS FOR E-150 WAGON

8 cyl 4.6 L Engine +384
8 cyl 5.4 L Engine +769
AM/FM Stereo/CD/Tape +152
Aluminum/Alloy Wheels +171
Camper/Towing Package +127
Captain Chairs (2)[Opt on XLT] +148
Cruise Control +106
Dual Air Conditioning +455
Keyless Entry System +110
Limited Slip Differential +148
Power Door Locks[Opt on XL] +138
Power Drivers Seat +215
Power Windows[Opt on XL] +180
Privacy Glass +254

E-250   1999

An all-new alphanumeric vehicle badging system has been applied to Ford's Econoline Wagon models. These replace the past Club Wagon badges. Four-wheel disc brakes with ABS are now standard on all E350 Super Duty vans. The 4R70W electronic four-speed automatic is now standard on all E-150 models. Improved "fail-safe" cooling is now a feature on all Econoline gasoline engines.

Category Q

	Trade-in	Private	Dealer
2 Dr STD Cargo Van	9579	10601	11623
2 Dr STD Cargo Van Ext	9978	11043	12107

OPTIONS FOR E-250

8 cyl 5.4 L Engine +623
AM/FM Stereo Tape +104
AM/FM Stereo/CD/Tape +165
Air Conditioning +538

Don't forget to refer to the Mileage Adjustment Table at the back of this book!

FORD 99

Model Description	Trade-in TMV	Private TMV	Dealer TMV	Model Description	Trade-in TMV	Private TMV	Dealer TMV

Anti-Lock Brakes +337				8 cyl 7.3 L Turbodiesel Engine +2573			
Camper/Towing Package +110				AM/FM Stereo/CD/Tape +152			
Cruise Control +106				Cruise Control +106			
Dual Air Conditioning +538				Dual Air Conditioning +455			
Limited Slip Differential +138				Keyless Entry System +110			
Power Door Locks +138				Limited Slip Differential +175			
Power Windows +180				Power Door Locks +138			
Privacy Glass +160				Power Drivers Seat +215			
Rear Heater +114				Power Windows +180			
				Privacy Glass +254			
				Rear Heater +113			

E-350 SUPER DUTY — 1999

An all-new alphanumeric vehicle badging system has been applied to Ford's Econoline Wagon models. These replace the past Club Wagon badges. Four-wheel disc brakes with ABS are now standard on all E350 Super Duty vans. The 4R70W electronic four-speed automatic is now standard on all E-150 models. Improved "fail-safe" cooling is now a feature on all Econoline gasoline engines.

Category Q

	Trade-in	Private	Dealer
2 Dr STD Cargo Van	11176	12368	13560
2 Dr STD Cargo Van Ext	11974	13252	14529

OPTIONS FOR E-350 SUPER DUTY
10 cyl 6.8 L Engine +333
8 cyl 7.3 L Turbodiesel Engine +2452
Air Conditioning +538
Anti-Lock Brakes +337
Dual Air Conditioning +455
Limited Slip Differential +148
Power Door Locks +138
Power Windows +180
Privacy Glass +163

E-350 SUPER DUTY WAGON

An all-new alphanumeric vehicle badging system is being applied to all Econoline Van and Club Wagon models. This will replace the past Club Wagon and Econoline badges. Four-wheel disc brakes with ABS are now standard on all E350 Super Duty vans. The 4R70W electronic four-speed automatic is now standard on all E-150/250 models. Improved fail-safe cooling is now a feature on all Econoline gasoline engines.

Category Q

	Trade-in	Private	Dealer
2 Dr E-350 Chateau Pass. Van	13251	14664	16078
2 Dr XL Pass. Van	12053	13339	14625
2 Dr XL Pass. Van Ext	12759	14120	15481
2 Dr XLT Pass. Van	12786	14150	15514
2 Dr XLT Pass. Van Ext	13341	14764	16187

OPTIONS FOR E-350 SUPER DUTY WAGON
10 cyl 6.8 L Engine +333

ESCORT — 1999

Ford's entry-level car gets new colors, new interior fabrics, and revised options. An AM/FM stereo with cassette is now standard on the Escort SE. An interior trunk release is now standard on all models. The sedans and wagon get all-door remote keyless entry added to their standard equipment lists. An integrated child seat is no longer available.

Category B

	Trade-in	Private	Dealer
4 Dr LX Sdn	5328	6144	6960
4 Dr SE Sdn	6005	6924	7844
4 Dr SE Wgn	6591	7600	8610
2 Dr ZX2 Cool Cpe	5363	6185	7006
2 Dr ZX2 Hot Cpe	6152	7094	8036

OPTIONS FOR ESCORT
Air Conditioning[Std on SE,ZX2 Hot] +439
Alarm System +138
Aluminum/Alloy Wheels +146
Anti-Lock Brakes +220
Automatic 4-Speed Transmission +450
Compact Disc Changer +163
Power Door Locks +110
Power Moonroof +328
Power Windows +127
Rear Spoiler +108

EXPEDITION — 1999

Power output is improved for both Triton V8 engines on Ford's full-size sport-ute. Package content is added for both XLT and Eddie Bauer trim levels. Power adjustable accelerator and brake pedals have been added to the option list to make it easier for the vertically challenged to reach the stop and go pedals. An updated Command Trac four-wheel drive system allows automatic four-wheel drive operation when required. Spruce Green, Harvest Gold, Tropic Green and Deep Wedgewood Blue replace Light Prairie Tan, Vermont Green, Light Denim Blue and Pacific Green on the color chart.

Category N

	Trade-in	Private	Dealer
4 Dr Eddie Bauer 4WD Utility	17241	18896	20551

Don't forget to refer to the Mileage Adjustment Table at the back of this book!

Model Description	Trade-in TMV	Private TMV	Dealer TMV
4 Dr Eddie Bauer Utility			
	15270	16736	18202
4 Dr XLT 4WD Utility	14614	16017	17420
4 Dr XLT Utility	13054	14307	15560

OPTIONS FOR EXPEDITION

8 cyl 5.4 L Engine[Opt on XLT,2WD] +366
AM/FM Stereo/CD/Tape +196
Air Conditioning[Opt on XLT] +275
Alarm System[Opt on XLT] +110
Automatic Load Leveling +450
Camper/Towing Package +215
Captain Chairs (2)[Opt on XLT] +154
Compact Disc Changer +262
Dual Air Conditioning[Opt on XLT] +389
Heated Front Seats +160
Leather Seats[Opt on XLT] +552
Limited Slip Differential +152
Power Moonroof +441
Running Boards[Opt on XLT] +240
Third Seat[Opt on XLT] +353

EXPLORER   1999

The Explorer gets exterior revisions including new fog lamps, rocker panel moldings, wheel moldings, running boards and wheels. Harvest Gold, Chestnut, Deep Wedgewood, Spruce Green and Tropic Green replaces Light Prairie Tan, Desert Violet, Light Denim Blue, Pacific Green and Evergreen Frost on the color chart. New options include a reverse sensing system and rear load leveling. Side impact airbags are also newly available.

Category M

Model Description	Trade-in TMV	Private TMV	Dealer TMV
4 Dr Eddie Bauer 4WD Utility			
	14529	16184	17839
4 Dr Eddie Bauer AWD Utility			
	14657	16327	17997
4 Dr Eddie Bauer Utility			
	13740	15305	16870
4 Dr Limited 4WD Utility			
	14880	16575	18270
4 Dr Limited AWD Utility			
	14969	16674	18379
4 Dr Limited Utility	14453	16099	17746
2 Dr Sport 4WD Utility			
	10739	11963	13186
2 Dr Sport Utility	9318	10379	11441
4 Dr XL 4WD Utility	11133	12402	13670
4 Dr XL Utility	9633	10731	11828
4 Dr XLS 4WD Utility	11449	12754	14058
4 Dr XLS Utility	11388	12686	13983
4 Dr XLT 4WD Utility	12634	14074	15513
4 Dr XLT AWD Utility	12713	14162	15610
4 Dr XLT Utility	11607	12930	14252

OPTIONS FOR EXPLORER

6 cyl 4.0 L SOHC Engine[Opt on Sport,XL,XLS,XLT] +298
8 cyl 5.0 L Engine +237
AM/FM Stereo/CD/Tape[Opt on Sport,XL,XLS,XLT] +176
Alarm System[Opt on Sport] +119
Aluminum/Alloy Wheels[Opt on XL] +97
Automatic 4-Speed Transmission +521
Automatic 5-Speed Transmission[Opt on Sport,XL,XLS] +587
Automatic Load Leveling +194
Bucket Seats +154
Camper/Towing Package +196
Captain Chairs (2)[Opt on XL] +154
Compact Disc Changer +204
Cruise Control[Opt on Sport,XL,XLS] +106
Dual Power Seats[Opt on XLT] +284
Heated Front Seats[Std on Limited] +135
Keyless Entry System[Opt on Sport,XL,XLS] +102
Leather Seats[Std on Eddie Bauer,Limited] +524
Limited Slip Differential +171
Overhead Console[Opt on Sport] +210
Power Door Locks[Opt on XL] +110
Power Drivers Seat[Opt on Sport,XLT] +143
Power Moonroof +441
Power Windows[Opt on XL] +146
Privacy Glass[Opt on XL,XLS] +110
Running Boards[Std on Eddie Bauer,Limited] +218
Side Air Bag Restraints +215
Side Steps[Opt on Sport] +163
Tilt Steering Wheel[Opt on XL,XLS] +106

F-150   1999

The Standard trim level is replaced by the Work trim level. XLT and Lariat models get standard four-wheel antilock brakes, and the XLT gets standard air conditioning. All SuperCab models get a fourth door and horsepower is improved for engines across the board. Option content is shuffled and simplified as Ford reduces the number of optional features.

Category K

Model Description	Trade-in TMV	Private TMV	Dealer TMV
2 Dr Lariat 4WD Std Cab LB			
	14573	16123	17673
2 Dr Lariat Std Cab LB			
	12251	13554	14857
4 Dr Lariat 4WD Ext Cab LB			
	15374	17009	18644
4 Dr Lariat Ext Cab LB			
	13600	15046	16492
2 Dr Lariat 4WD Std Cab SB			
	14408	15940	17472
2 Dr Lariat Std Cab SB			
	12150	13442	14734
4 Dr Lariat 4WD Ext Cab SB			
	15133	16743	18352
4 Dr Lariat Ext Cab SB			
	13452	14882	16313

Model Description	Trade-in TMV	Private TMV	Dealer TMV
2 Dr Lariat 4WD Std Cab Stepside SB			
	14973	16566	18158
2 Dr Lariat Std Cab Stepside SB			
	13052	14440	15828
4 Dr Lariat 4WD Ext Cab Stepside SB			
	15854	17540	19226
4 Dr Lariat Ext Cab Stepside SB			
	14493	16034	17575
2 Dr Work 4WD Std Cab LB			
	10089	11162	12235
2 Dr Work Std Cab LB	8328	9213	10099
4 Dr Work 4WD Ext Cab LB			
	11917	13184	14451
4 Dr Work Ext Cab LB	9768	10807	11846
2 Dr Work 4WD Std Cab SB			
	9929	10985	12041
2 Dr Work Std Cab SB	8167	9035	9904
4 Dr Work 4WD Ext Cab SB			
	11611	12845	14080
4 Dr Work Ext Cab SB	9608	10630	11652
2 Dr XL 4WD Std Cab LB			
	10650	11782	12915
2 Dr XL Std Cab LB	8808	9744	10681
4 Dr XL 4WD Ext Cab LB			
	12491	13820	15148
4 Dr XL Ext Cab LB	10329	11428	12526
2 Dr XL 4WD Std Cab SB			
	10489	11605	12720
2 Dr XL Std Cab SB	8648	9567	10487
4 Dr XL 4WD Ext Cab SB			
	12326	13636	14947
4 Dr XL Ext Cab SB	10169	11251	12332
2 Dr XL 4WD Std Cab Stepside SB			
	11050	12225	13400
2 Dr XL Std Cab Stepside SB			
	9208	10188	11167
4 Dr XL 4WD Ext Cab Stepside SB			
	13256	14665	16075
4 Dr XL Ext Cab Stepside SB			
	10730	11871	13012
2 Dr XLT 4WD Std Cab LB			
	12331	13643	14954
2 Dr XLT Std Cab LB	10409	11516	12623
4 Dr XLT 4WD Ext Cab LB			
	14418	15951	17484
4 Dr XLT Ext Cab LB	11931	13199	14468
2 Dr XLT 4WD Std Cab SB			
	12192	13488	14785
2 Dr XLT Std Cab SB	10249	11339	12429
4 Dr XLT 4WD Ext Cab SB			

Model Description	Trade-in TMV	Private TMV	Dealer TMV
	13625	15074	16523
4 Dr XLT Ext Cab SB	11851	13111	14371
2 Dr XLT 4WD Std Cab Stepside SB			
	13132	14529	15925
2 Dr XLT Std Cab Stepside SB			
	10810	11959	13109
4 Dr XLT 4WD Ext Cab Stepside SB			
	14893	16477	18061
4 Dr XLT Ext Cab Stepside SB			
	12336	13648	14960

OPTIONS FOR F-150
8 cyl 4.6 L Engine[Std on Lariat] +414
8 cyl 5.4 L Engine +366
AM/FM Compact Disc Player[Opt on XL,XLT] +176
AM/FM Stereo Tape[Opt on XL,Work] +143
Air Conditioning[Opt on XL,Work] +444
Aluminum/Alloy Wheels[Opt on XL] +176
Anti-Lock Brakes[Opt on XL,Work] +166
Automatic 4-Speed Transmission[Std on Lariat] +549
Camper/Towing Package +163
Captain Chairs (2)[Opt on XLT] +270
Chrome Wheels +110
Compact Disc Changer +220
Cruise Control[Opt on XL,Work] +106
Limited Slip Differential +148
Power Drivers Seat[Opt on XLT] +199
Side Steps +163
Tilt Steering Wheel[Opt on XL,Work] +108
Tonneau Cover +110

F-150 SVT — 1999

Ford has revived its F-150-based performance truck with all-new features like an Eaton supercharger, performance suspension and Z-rated Goodyear tires. Only 4,000 units will be built, and with their $30,000 price tag, they should go quick.
Category K

Model Description	Trade-in TMV	Private TMV	Dealer TMV
2 Dr Lightning Std Cab Stepside SB			
	16976	18781	20586

OPTIONS FOR F-150 SVT
Compact Disc Changer +116
Side Steps +163
Tonneau Cover +110

F-250 — 1999

The Standard trim level is replaced by the Work trim level. XLT and Lariat models get standard four-wheel antilock brakes, and the XLT gets standard air conditioning. All SuperCab models get a fourth door and horsepower is improved for engines across the board. Option content is shuffled and simplified as Ford reduces the number of optional features to a mere 78.
Category K
2 Dr Lariat 4WD Std Cab LB

Model Description	Trade-in TMV	Private TMV	Dealer TMV
	14813	16388	17963
2 Dr Lariat Std Cab LB			
	12891	14262	15633
4 Dr Lariat 4WD Ext Cab SB			
	16255	17983	19712
4 Dr Lariat Ext Cab SB			
	14333	15857	17381
2 Dr Work 4WD Std Cab LB			
	11050	12225	13400
2 Dr Work Std Cab LB	9448	10453	11458
4 Dr Work 4WD Ext Cab SB			
	12411	13731	15051
4 Dr Work Ext Cab SB	10810	11959	13109
2 Dr XL 4WD Std Cab LB			
	11611	12845	14080
2 Dr XL Std Cab LB	9929	10985	12041
4 Dr XL 4WD Ext Cab SB			
	13212	14617	16022
4 Dr XL Ext Cab SB	11451	12668	13886
2 Dr XLT 4WD Std Cab LB			
	13372	14794	16216
2 Dr XLT Std Cab LB	11531	12757	13983
4 Dr XLT 4WD Ext Cab SB			
	14814	16390	17965
4 Dr XLT Ext Cab SB	13132	14529	15925

OPTIONS FOR F-250

8 cyl 5.4 L Engine +366
AM/FM Compact Disc Player[Opt on XL] +166
AM/FM Stereo Tape[Opt on XL, Work] +123
Air Conditioning[Opt on XL, Work] +444
Anti-Lock Brakes[Opt on XL, Work] +207
Automatic 4-Speed Transmission[Opt on XL, XLT, Work] +549
Automatic Load Leveling +270
Camper/Towing Package +163
Captain Chairs (2)[Opt on XLT] +270
Chrome Wheels +110
Compact Disc Changer +116
Cruise Control[Opt on XL, Work] +110
Limited Slip Differential +148
Power Drivers Seat[Opt on XLT] +199
Side Steps +163
Tilt Steering Wheel[Opt on XL, Work] +108
Tonneau Cover +110

F-250 SUPER DUTY — 1999

The all-new Super Duty F-Series is a full-size truck developed and built on a separate platform from the under-8,500lb GVWR F150 and F250. For '99 the Super Duty is available in Regular Cab, four-door Super Cab or Crew Cab models, as well as in a class A Motor Home Chassis model.

Category K
2 Dr Lariat 4WD Std Cab LB

Model Description	Trade-in TMV	Private TMV	Dealer TMV
	15128	16736	18345
2 Dr Lariat Std Cab LB			
	13126	14522	15918
4 Dr Lariat 4WD Crew Cab LB			
	17375	19223	21071
4 Dr Lariat 4WD Ext Cab LB			
	16173	17893	19613
4 Dr Lariat Crew Cab LB			
	15454	17098	18741
4 Dr Lariat Ext Cab LB			
	14173	15680	17187
4 Dr Lariat 4WD Crew Cab SB			
	17216	19046	20877
4 Dr Lariat 4WD Ext Cab SB			
	16176	17896	19616
4 Dr Lariat Crew Cab SB			
	15374	17009	18644
4 Dr Lariat Ext Cab SB			
	14079	15576	17073
2 Dr XL 4WD Std Cab LB			
	12967	14346	15725
2 Dr XL Std Cab LB	11050	12225	13400
4 Dr XL 4WD Crew Cab LB			
	15293	16920	18546
4 Dr XL 4WD Ext Cab LB			
	14099	15599	17098
4 Dr XL Crew Cab LB	13292	14705	16119
4 Dr XL Ext Cab LB	12251	13554	14857
4 Dr XL 4WD Crew Cab SB			
	15139	16749	18359
4 Dr XL 4WD Ext Cab SB			
	14413	15945	17478
4 Dr XL Crew Cab SB	13137	14534	15931
4 Dr XL Ext Cab SB	12171	13465	14759
2 Dr XLT 4WD Std Cab LB			
	13772	15236	16701
2 Dr XLT Std Cab LB	11931	13199	14468
4 Dr XLT 4WD Crew Cab LB			
	16094	17806	19517
4 Dr XLT 4WD Ext Cab LB			
	15053	16654	18255
4 Dr XLT Crew Cab LB	14101	15600	17100
4 Dr XLT Ext Cab LB	13052	14440	15828
4 Dr XLT 4WD Crew Cab SB			
	16014	17717	19420
4 Dr XLT 4WD Ext Cab SB			
	14813	16389	17964
4 Dr XLT Crew Cab SB	14013	15503	16993
4 Dr XLT Ext Cab SB	12976	14356	15736

Don't forget to refer to the Mileage Adjustment Table at the back of this book!

OPTIONS FOR F-250 SUPER DUTY

10 cyl 6.8 L Engine +194
8 cyl 7.3 L Turbodiesel Engine +2384
AM/FM Compact Disc Player[Opt on Crew Cab] +104
AM/FM Stereo/CD/Tape +179
Air Conditioning +444
Aluminum/Alloy Wheels +176
Anti-Lock Brakes +275
Automatic 4-Speed Transmission +549
Camper/Towing Package +163
Chrome Wheels +110
Cruise Control +110
Leather Seats +201
Limited Slip Differential +176
Power Drivers Seat +160
Side Steps[Opt on XL,XLT] +163
Skid Plates +163
Tilt Steering Wheel +108

F-350   1999

The all-new Super Duty F-Series is a full-size truck developed and built on a separate platform from the under-8,500lb GVWR F150 and F250. For '99 the Super Duty is available in Regular Cab, four-door SuperCab or Crew Cab models.

Category K

Model Description	Trade-in TMV	Private TMV	Dealer TMV
2 Dr Lariat 4WD Std Cab LB			
	15534	17186	18838
2 Dr Lariat Std Cab LB			
	13601	15048	16494
4 Dr Lariat 4WD Crew Cab LB			
	17776	19667	21557
4 Dr Lariat 4WD Ext Cab LB			
	16976	18781	20586
4 Dr Lariat Crew Cab LB			
	16014	17717	19420
4 Dr Lariat Ext Cab LB			
	15053	16654	18255
4 Dr Lariat 4WD Crew Cab SB			
	17615	19489	21362
4 Dr Lariat 4WD Ext Cab SB			
	16815	18603	20391
4 Dr Lariat Crew Cab SB			
	15934	17629	19323
4 Dr Lariat Ext Cab SB			
	14973	16566	18158
2 Dr XL 4WD Std Cab LB			
	13292	14705	16119
2 Dr XL Std Cab LB			
	11451	12668	13886
4 Dr XL 4WD Crew Cab LB			
	15617	17278	18939
4 Dr XL 4WD Ext Cab LB			
	14653	16212	17770
4 Dr XL Crew Cab LB	13758	15221	16684
4 Dr XL Ext Cab LB	12811	14174	15536
4 Dr XL 4WD Crew Cab SB			
	15454	17098	18741
4 Dr XL 4WD Ext Cab SB			
	14573	16123	17673
4 Dr XL Crew Cab SB	13623	15072	16521
4 Dr XL Ext Cab SB	12731	14085	15439
2 Dr XLT 4WD Std Cab LB			
	14173	15680	17187
2 Dr XLT Std Cab LB	12491	13820	15148
4 Dr XLT 4WD Crew Cab LB			
	16495	18249	20003
4 Dr XLT 4WD Ext Cab LB			
	15694	17363	19032
4 Dr XLT Crew Cab LB	14813	16389	17964
4 Dr XLT Ext Cab LB	13808	15277	16745
4 Dr XLT 4WD Crew Cab SB			
	16415	18160	19906
4 Dr XLT 4WD Ext Cab SB			
	15611	17271	18931
4 Dr XLT Crew Cab SB	14733	16300	17867
4 Dr XLT Ext Cab SB	13750	15213	16675

OPTIONS FOR F-350

10 cyl 6.8 L Engine +194
8 cyl 7.3 L Turbodiesel Engine +2384
AM/FM Stereo Tape[Opt on XL] +123
AM/FM Stereo/CD/Tape +179
Air Conditioning +444
Aluminum/Alloy Wheels +110
Anti-Lock Brakes +275
Automatic 4-Speed Transmission +549
Camper/Towing Package +163
Cruise Control +106
Dual Rear Wheels +319
Leather Seats +201
Limited Slip Differential +148
Power Door Locks[Opt on XLT] +101
Power Drivers Seat +160
Power Windows[Opt on XLT] +101
Side Steps +163
Tilt Steering Wheel +108

MUSTANG   1999

Following on the heels of the '98 Camaro update, Ford gives its sports car fresh styling and more motor. The 3.8-liter V6 engine makes 190 horsepower and 220 foot-pounds of torque, putting it within spitting distance of the V6 Camaro. The SOHC V8 found in GT models gets an 16-percent increase in horsepower, and a new SVT Cobra model boasts 320 ponies and an independent rear suspension. Improvements to the V6 and GT suspension and steering gear, as well as a

---

Don't forget to refer to the Mileage Adjustment Table at the back of this book!

Model Description	Trade-in TMV	Private TMV	Dealer TMV

styling update, insure that this car will maintain its lead in the pony car wars.

Category E

Model Description	Trade-in TMV	Private TMV	Dealer TMV
2 Dr STD Conv	12847	14246	15645
2 Dr STD Cpe	9350	10368	11386
2 Dr Cobra Conv	18936	20998	23060
2 Dr Cobra Cpe	15400	17077	18754
2 Dr GT Conv	14693	16293	17893
2 Dr GT Cpe	12729	14115	15501

OPTIONS FOR MUSTANG

AM/FM Stereo Tape +218
Anti-Lock Brakes[Opt on STD] +275
Automatic 4-Speed Transmission +450
Bucket Seats +275
Compact Disc Changer[Opt on STD] +248
Power Drivers Seat[Opt on STD] +132
Rear Spoiler[Std on GT] +108
Spoke Wheels +275
Sport Seats +110
Traction Control System[Std on Cobra] +127

RANGER   1999

The Ranger is "Built Ford Tough" according to its ads and we tend to agree. This year's changes include standard 15-inch silver styled wheels, a class III frame-mounted hitch receiver for V6 applications, and a spare tire access lock. All models get dual front cup holders and Dark Graphite has been added to the interior colors option list while Willow Green and Denim Blue have been removed as interior choices. Too bad for you folks who liked the splashy "Splash" model, it has been discontinued. Finally, a 3.0-liter V6 flexible fuel engine is available that is designed specifically for ethanol/gasoline fuel blends.

Category J

Model Description	Trade-in TMV	Private TMV	Dealer TMV
2 Dr XL 4WD Std Cab LB			
	8297	9367	10437
2 Dr XL Std Cab LB	6300	7112	7925
2 Dr XL 4WD Ext Cab SB			
	8911	10061	11210
2 Dr XL 4WD Std Cab SB			
	7986	9016	10046
2 Dr XL Ext Cab SB	7682	8673	9664
2 Dr XL Std Cab SB	5915	6678	7441
2 Dr XL 4WD Ext Cab Stepside SB			
	9149	10329	11509
2 Dr XL 4WD Std Cab Stepside SB			
	8220	9281	10341
2 Dr XL Ext Cab Stepside SB			
	7993	9024	10055
2 Dr XL Std Cab Stepside SB			
	6223	7025	7828
2 Dr XLT 4WD Std Cab LB			
	9464	10685	11906
2 Dr XLT Std Cab LB	7298	8240	9181
2 Dr XLT 4WD Ext Cab SB			
	9987	11275	12563
2 Dr XLT 4WD Std Cab SB			
	9135	10314	11492
2 Dr XLT Ext Cab SB	8143	9194	10244
2 Dr XLT Std Cab SB	7068	7979	8891
2 Dr XLT 4WD Ext Cab Stepside SB			
	10217	11535	12853
2 Dr XLT 4WD Std Cab Stepside SB			
	9433	10650	11867
2 Dr XLT Ext Cab Stepside SB			
	8374	9454	10534
2 Dr XLT Std Cab Stepside SB			
	7375	8327	9278

OPTIONS FOR RANGER

6 cyl 3.0 L Engine[Std on 4WD] +287
6 cyl 4.0 L Engine +372
AM/FM Compact Disc Player +160
AM/FM Stereo Tape[Opt on XL] +119
AM/FM Stereo/CD/Tape +127
Air Conditioning +444
Aluminum/Alloy Wheels[Std on XLT 4WD] +110
Anti-Lock Brakes[Std on XLT 4WD] +166
Automatic 4-Speed Transmission +604
Automatic 5-Speed Transmission +623
Bed Liner +129
Bucket Seats +199
Chrome Wheels +110
Compact Disc Changer +275
Hinged Fourth Door[Opt on XLT] +426
Limited Slip Differential +148
Power Door Locks +132
Power Windows +152
Tilt Steering Wheel[Opt on XLT] +102
Trailer Hitch +119

TAURUS   1999

Against all odds, the Taurus SHO pulls through for another model year. The light group and speed control are now optional on LX level cars. Chrome wheels on the SE models have been replaced with five-spoke aluminum wheels.

Category D

Model Description	Trade-in TMV	Private TMV	Dealer TMV
4 Dr LX Sdn	7829	8812	9795
4 Dr SE Sdn	7922	8916	9911
4 Dr SE Wgn	8188	9217	10245
4 Dr SHO Sdn	13469	15161	16852

OPTIONS FOR TAURUS

6 cyl 3.0 L DOHC Engine +274
6 cyl 3.0 L EFF Engine +642
AM/FM Stereo Tape[Opt on LX] +102
Alarm System[Opt on LX,SE] +97

Don't forget to refer to the Mileage Adjustment Table at the back of this book!

Model Description	Trade-in TMV	Private TMV	Dealer TMV
Aluminum/Alloy Wheels +175			
Anti-Lock Brakes[Std on SHO] +331			
Chrome Wheels[Opt on SE] +274			
Climate Control for AC[Opt on SE] +116			
Compact Disc Changer[Opt on SE] +194			
Cruise Control[Opt on LX] +104			
Dual Power Seats[Opt on SE] +194			
Keyless Entry System[Opt on LX] +97			
Leather Seats[Opt on SE] +494			
Power Door Locks[Opt on LX] +146			
Power Drivers Seat +194			
Power Moonroof[Opt on SE] +408			
Rear Spoiler[Opt on SE] +138			
Spoke Wheels +319			
Third Seat +110			

WINDSTAR — 1999

Ford continues to battle it out with GM and Chrysler in the hotly contested minivan segment. This year the Windstar has been totally redesigned in yet another attempt to dethrone the top pentastar prospects. The biggest news for '99, in addition to the completely new exterior and interior styling, is a left-hand sliding door. The second and third row seats are now on rollers for easier adjustment/interchangeability and the instrument panel has been redesigned for improved ergonomics. There's also a more powerful and cleaner-burning 3.8-liter V6 plus upgraded suspension, transmission, brakes and air conditioning components. Hot new options include side airbags and a trick reverse sensing system to keep you from banging into those short gas station poles.

Category P			
2 Dr STD Cargo Van	9236	10315	11393
2 Dr STD Pass. Van	9543	10658	11772
2 Dr LX Pass. Van	11160	12463	13766
4 Dr SE Pass. Van	12006	13408	14810
4 Dr SEL Pass. Van	13161	14698	16235

OPTIONS FOR WINDSTAR

6 cyl 3.8 L Engine[Opt on STD] +378
AM/FM Stereo/CD/Tape[Std on SEL] +166
Air Conditioning[Opt on STD] +471
Aluminum/Alloy Wheels[Opt on LX] +229
Bucket Seats +270
Camper/Towing Package +240
Captain Chairs (4)[Opt on LX] +395
Compact Disc Changer +220
Cruise Control[Opt on STD] +102
Dual Air Conditioning[Opt on LX] +262
Keyless Entry System[Opt on LX, STD] +97
Leather Seats[Opt on SE] +477
Luggage Rack[Opt on LX] +135
Power Door Locks[Opt on STD] +110
Power Drivers Seat[Std on SE, SEL] +179
Power Dual Sliding Doors[Opt on SE] +441

Power Mirrors[Opt on STD] +110
Power Sliding Door +275
Power Windows[Opt on STD] +154
Privacy Glass[Std on SE, SEL] +229
Side Air Bag Restraints +215
Sliding Driver Side Door[Opt on LX, STD] +194
Tilt Steering Wheel[Opt on STD] +102
Traction Control System +218

1998 FORD

CONTOUR — 1998

A redesigned face gives this Ford more character, but the new taillight treatment is almost identical to the Contour's sibling, the Mercury Mystique. New alloy wheels and a slightly more commodious rear seat debut. The outstanding SVT model provides the performance of a BMW 328i at the price of a Buick Century. Mid-year changes included a model consolidation, the addition of de-powered airbags, as well as improved handling and new wheels for the SVT.

Category C			
4 Dr STD Sdn	4515	5163	5866
4 Dr LX Sdn	5096	5829	6622
4 Dr SE Sdn	5388	6162	7001
Category E			
4 Dr SVT Sdn	9630	10756	11976

OPTIONS FOR CONTOUR

6 cyl 2.5 L Engine[Std on SE, SVT] +249
AM/FM Compact Disc Player +139
AM/FM Stereo/CD/Tape +126
Air Conditioning[Std on SVT] +406
Alarm System[Opt on LX] +126
Aluminum/Alloy Wheels +214
Anti-Lock Brakes[Std on SVT] +252
Automatic 4-Speed Transmission +411
Compact Disc Changer +227
Cruise Control[Std on SVT] +109
Leather Seats[Std on SVT] +450
Power Drivers Seat[Std on SVT] +177
Power Moonroof +299
Power Windows[Std on SVT] +180
Rear Spoiler[Opt on GL, LX] +133
Traction Control System[Opt on SE] +119

CROWN VICTORIA — 1998

A formal roofline graces this favorite of police officers and taxi drivers. To further add to the Crown Victoria's driving excitement, the power steering and suspension have been improved.

Category G			
4 Dr STD Sdn	7750	8621	9564
4 Dr LX Sdn	8680	9655	10711

OPTIONS FOR CROWN VICTORIA

Don't forget to refer to the Mileage Adjustment Table at the back of this book!

Model Description	Trade-in TMV	Private TMV	Dealer TMV
AM/FM Compact Disc Player[Opt on LX] +181			
Aluminum/Alloy Wheels +214			
Anti-Lock Brakes +302			
Dual Power Seats +297			
Keyless Entry System[Std on LX] +121			
Leather Seats +370			
Power Drivers Seat[Std on LX] +181			
Premium Sound System[Opt on LX] +181			

E-150   1998

Category Q

Model Description	Trade-in TMV	Private TMV	Dealer TMV
2 Dr STD Econoline	7618	8503	9463
2 Dr Chateau Club Wagon			
	9328	10413	11588
2 Dr XL Club Wagon	8940	9979	11105
2 Dr XLT Club Wagon	9095	10152	11298

OPTIONS FOR E-150
8 cyl 4.6 L Engine +362
8 cyl 5.4 L Engine +569
AM/FM Stereo Tape +151
Air Conditioning[Opt on STD] +415
Aluminum/Alloy Wheels[Opt on XLT] +156
Anti-Lock Brakes[Opt on STD] +307
Camper/Towing Package +101
Dual Air Conditioning +415
Limited Slip Differential +131
Power Door Locks[Opt on STD,XL] +126
Power Drivers Seat +181
Power Windows +164
Privacy Glass +151
Rear Heater +104

E-250   1998

Category Q

Model Description	Trade-in TMV	Private TMV	Dealer TMV
2 Dr STD Econoline	7618	8503	9463
2 Dr STD Econoline Ext			
	7851	8764	9753

OPTIONS FOR E-250
8 cyl 5.4 L Engine +569
Air Conditioning +491
Anti-Lock Brakes +307
Camper/Towing Package +101
Dual Air Bag Restraints +126
Dual Air Conditioning +491
Limited Slip Differential +131
Power Door Locks +126
Power Windows +164
Privacy Glass +151
Rear Heater +104

E-350   1998

Category Q

Model Description	Trade-in TMV	Private TMV	Dealer TMV
2 Dr STD Econoline	8473	9459	10526
2 Dr STD Econoline Ext			
	8784	9806	10912
2 Dr Chateau Club Wagon			
	10339	11542	12844
2 Dr XL Club Wagon	9328	10413	11588
2 Dr XL Club Wagon Ext			
	9726	10857	12082
2 Dr XLT Club Wagon	10028	11194	12457
2 Dr XLT Club Wagon Ext			
	10338	11540	12842

OPTIONS FOR E-350
10 cyl 6.8 L Engine +280
8 cyl 7.3 L Turbodiesel Engine +2371
Air Conditioning +491
Anti-Lock Brakes +307
Camper/Towing Package +101
Dual Air Bag Restraints +126
Dual Air Conditioning +415
Limited Slip Differential +131
Power Door Locks[Opt on XL,STD] +126
Power Drivers Seat +196
Power Windows +164
Privacy Glass +151
Rear Heater +104

ESCORT   1998

Packages are reshuffled on Ford's entry-level cars. Available this year as sedans, wagons or stylish coupes, the Ford Escort now qualifies as a low emissions vehicle, thanks to the car's split-port induction 2.0-liter four-cylinder engine.

Category B

Model Description	Trade-in TMV	Private TMV	Dealer TMV
4 Dr LX Sdn	4259	5014	5831
4 Dr SE Sdn	4740	5580	6490
4 Dr SE Wgn	5221	6146	7148
2 Dr ZX2 Cool Cpe	4672	5499	6396
2 Dr ZX2 Hot Cpe	4946	5823	6772

OPTIONS FOR ESCORT
AM/FM Compact Disc Player[Opt on SE Sdn] +260
AM/FM Stereo/CD/Tape[Opt on ZX2] +260
Air Conditioning +400
Alarm System +126
Aluminum/Alloy Wheels +133
Anti-Lock Brakes +201
Automatic 4-Speed Transmission +411
Compact Disc Changer +148
Power Door Locks +101
Power Moonroof +299
Power Windows +116

EXPEDITION   1998

After an insanely successful first year, the Ford Expedition pounds its way into 1998 without changes.

Category N

Model Description	Trade-in TMV	Private TMV	Dealer TMV
4 Dr Eddie Bauer 4WD Utility			
	13195	14640	16205
4 Dr Eddie Bauer Utility			

Model Description	Trade-in TMV	Private TMV	Dealer TMV
	12638	14022	15521
4 Dr XLT 4WD Utility	12241	13581	15033
4 Dr XLT Utility	11923	13229	14643

OPTIONS FOR EXPEDITION
8 cyl 5.4 L Engine +335
AM/FM Stereo/CD/Tape +180
Automatic Load Leveling +411
Camper/Towing Package +252
Captain Chairs (2) +142
Compact Disc Changer +239
Cruise Control[Opt on XLT] +119
Dual Air Conditioning +355
Heated Front Seats +146
Leather Seats[Opt on XLT] +504
Limited Slip Differential +129
Power Drivers Seat[Opt on XLT] +151
Power Moonroof +403
Running Boards +219
Third Seat +302

EXPLORER   1998

The Ford Explorer gets a restyled tailgate for 1998.
Category M

Model Description	Trade-in TMV	Private TMV	Dealer TMV
4 Dr Eddie Bauer 4WD Utility			
	12012	13462	15033
4 Dr Eddie Bauer AWD Utility			
	11396	12772	14262
4 Dr Eddie Bauer Utility			
	11165	12513	13973
4 Dr Limited 4WD Utility			
	13090	14670	16382
4 Dr Limited AWD Utility			
	12628	14152	15804
4 Dr Limited Utility	12243	13721	15322
2 Dr Sport 4WD Utility			
	8855	9924	11082
2 Dr Sport Utility	7699	8629	9636
4 Dr XL 4WD Utility	9393	10527	11756
4 Dr XL Utility	8624	9665	10793
4 Dr XLT 4WD Utility	10318	11564	12913
4 Dr XLT AWD Utility	9933	11132	12431
4 Dr XLT Utility	9471	10614	11853

OPTIONS FOR EXPLORER
6 cyl 4.0 L SOHC Engine[Opt on Sport,XLT] +272
8 cyl 5.0 L Engine +302
AM/FM Compact Disc Player[Std on Eddie Bauer] +139
AM/FM Stereo/CD/Tape[Std on Limited] +161
Alarm System[Std on Limited] +109
Automatic 4-Speed Transmission +475
Automatic 5-Speed Transmission[Std on Eddie Bauer] +536
Bucket Seats[Opt on Sport,XLT,4WD] +142
Camper/Towing Package +180
Captain Chairs (2)[Opt on Sport,XL] +142

Compact Disc Changer +186
Dual Power Seats[Std on Limited] +260
Leather Seats[Std on Limited] +331
Limited Slip Differential +156
Overhead Console[Std on Limited] +192
Power Drivers Seat[Opt on Sport,XLT] +131
Power Moonroof +403
Power Windows +133
Running Boards[Std on Limited] +199
Side Steps[Opt on Sport] +148

F-150   1998

The 1998 F-150 gets a 50th Anniversary decal affixed to the lower left corner of the windshield. Other changes include making the locking tailgate standard on XLT and Lariat trims, optional on XL and Standard models. Fog lights become optional this year on all four-wheel drive models except for the Lariat, which gets them standard. An STX package featuring 17-inch tires, aluminum wheels, and color-keyed grille debuts as an option for the XLT 2WD. The Lariat receives a color-keyed steering column, leather-wrapped steering wheel, and outside power signal mirrors. Silver Metallic paint replaces Silver Frost paint, and Light Denim Blue replaces Portofino Blue.
Category K

Model Description	Trade-in TMV	Private TMV	Dealer TMV
2 Dr STD 4WD Ext Cab LB			
	11097	12389	13789
2 Dr STD 4WD Std Cab LB			
	9971	11132	12390
2 Dr STD Ext Cab LB	9144	10208	11362
2 Dr STD Std Cab LB	7737	8638	9614
2 Dr STD 4WD Ext Cab SB			
	10941	12215	13595
2 Dr STD 4WD Std Cab SB			
	9925	11081	12333
2 Dr STD Ext Cab SB	8949	9991	11120
2 Dr STD Std Cab SB	7502	8376	9322
2 Dr Lariat 4WD Ext Cab LB			
	14419	16098	17917
2 Dr Lariat 4WD Std Cab LB			
	12973	14483	16120
2 Dr Lariat Ext Cab LB			
	12503	13960	15537
2 Dr Lariat Std Cab LB			
	11254	12564	13984
2 Dr Lariat 4WD Ext Cab SB			
	14340	16010	17819
2 Dr Lariat 4WD Std Cab SB			
	12817	14309	15926
2 Dr Lariat Ext Cab SB			
	12425	13872	15440
2 Dr Lariat Std Cab SB			

Don't forget to refer to the Mileage Adjustment Table at the back of this book!

Model Description	Trade-in TMV	Private TMV	Dealer TMV
	11019	12302	13692
2 Dr Lariat 4WD Ext Cab Stepside SB			
	14457	16141	17965
2 Dr Lariat 4WD Std Cab Stepside SB			
	13129	14658	16314
2 Dr Lariat Ext Cab Stepside SB			
	13091	14615	16267
2 Dr Lariat Std Cab Stepside SB			
	11948	13340	14847
2 Dr XL 4WD Ext Cab LB			
	12310	13743	15296
2 Dr XL 4WD Std Cab LB			
	10506	11730	13055
2 Dr XL Ext Cab LB	10089	11264	12537
2 Dr XL Std Cab LB	8440	9423	10488
2 Dr XL 4WD Ext Cab SB			
	12051	13455	14975
2 Dr XL 4WD Std Cab SB			
	10461	11679	12999
2 Dr XL Ext Cab SB	10012	11178	12441
2 Dr XL Std Cab SB	8362	9336	10391
2 Dr XL 4WD Ext Cab Stepside SB			
	12347	13785	15343
2 Dr XL 4WD Std Cab Stepside SB			
	10550	11779	13110
2 Dr XL Ext Cab Stepside SB			
	10393	11604	12915
2 Dr XL Std Cab Stepside SB			
	8831	9859	10973
2 Dr XLT 4WD Ext Cab LB			
	13598	15181	16897
2 Dr XLT 4WD Std Cab LB			
	11956	13349	14857
2 Dr XLT Ext Cab LB	11606	12958	14422
2 Dr XLT Std Cab LB	10315	11517	12818
2 Dr XLT 4WD Ext Cab SB			
	13364	14920	16606
2 Dr XLT 4WD Std Cab SB			
	11800	13174	14663
2 Dr XLT Ext Cab SB	11566	12913	14372
2 Dr XLT Std Cab SB	10042	11211	12478
2 Dr XLT 4WD Ext Cab Stepside SB			
	13676	15269	16994
2 Dr XLT 4WD Std Cab Stepside SB			
	12269	13698	15246
2 Dr XLT Ext Cab Stepside SB			
	11966	13359	14869
2 Dr XLT Std Cab Stepside SB			
	10472	11692	13013

OPTIONS FOR F-150

8 cyl 4.6 L Engine +320
8 cyl 5.4 L Engine +335
Air Conditioning +406
Aluminum/Alloy Wheels[Opt on XL,XLT] +161
Anti-Lock Brakes +252
Automatic 4-Speed Transmission +488
Camper/Towing Package +149
Captain Chairs (2)[Opt on XLT] +247
Chrome Wheels[Opt on XL] +101
Compact Disc Changer +201
Limited Slip Differential +131
Power Drivers Seat +181
Side Steps +148

F-250 1998

The 1998 F-150 gets a 50th Anniversary decal affixed to the lower left corner of the windshield. Other changes include making the locking tailgate standard on XLT and Lariat trims, optional on XL and Standard models. Fog lights become optional this year on all four-wheel drive models except for the Lariat, which gets them standard. An STX package featuring 17-inch tires, aluminum wheels, and color-keyed grille debuts as an option for the XLT 2WD. The Lariat receives a color-keyed steering column, leather-wrapped steering wheel, and outside power signal mirrors. Silver Metallic paint replaces Silver Frost paint, and Light Denim Blue replaces Portofino Blue.

Category K

Model Description	Trade-in TMV	Private TMV	Dealer TMV
2 Dr STD 4WD Std Cab LB			
	10941	12215	13595
2 Dr STD Std Cab LB	8987	10034	11168
2 Dr STD 4WD Ext Cab SB			
	11669	13028	14500
2 Dr STD Ext Cab SB	10003	11168	12430
2 Dr Lariat 4WD Std Cab LB			
	13285	14832	16508
2 Dr Lariat Std Cab LB			
	11775	13146	14632
2 Dr Lariat 4WD Ext Cab SB			
	14614	16315	18159
2 Dr Lariat Ext Cab SB			
	12973	14483	16120
2 Dr XL 4WD Std Cab LB			
	11232	12540	13957
2 Dr XL Std Cab LB	9222	10296	11459
2 Dr XL 4WD Ext Cab SB			
	12149	13564	15097
2 Dr XL Ext Cab SB	10982	12261	13647
2 Dr XLT 4WD Std Cab LB			
	12425	13872	15440
2 Dr XLT Std Cab LB	11077	12367	13764
2 Dr XLT 4WD Ext Cab SB			

Model Description	Trade-in TMV	Private TMV	Dealer TMV
	13910	15530	17285
2 Dr XLT Ext Cab SB	12077	13483	15007

OPTIONS FOR F-250

8 cyl 5.4 L Engine +335
AM/FM Stereo Tape +113
Air Conditioning +406
Anti-Lock Brakes +252
Automatic 4-Speed Transmission +488
Automatic Load Leveling +247
Camper/Towing Package +227
Captain Chairs (2) +247
Chrome Wheels +101
Compact Disc Changer +201
Cruise Control +101
Limited Slip Differential +131
Power Drivers Seat +181
Side Steps +148

MUSTANG   1998

The Mustang gains standard equipment, such as power windows and door locks, air conditioning, and premium sound. Options are shuffled as well, making it easier to choose the car you want. GT models get a slight boost in power.

Category E

Model Description	Trade-in TMV	Private TMV	Dealer TMV
2 Dr STD Conv	11260	12577	14004
2 Dr STD Cpe	8189	9146	10184
2 Dr Cobra Conv	15544	17362	19331
2 Dr Cobra Cpe	13648	15244	16973
2 Dr GT Conv	12511	13974	15559
2 Dr GT Cpe	10387	11602	12918

OPTIONS FOR MUSTANG

AM/FM Stereo Tape +199
Anti-Lock Brakes[Std on Cobra] +252
Automatic 4-Speed Transmission +411
Power Drivers Seat[Opt on STD] +121
Sport Seats[Opt on GT Conv] +101

RANGER   1998

The Ranger gets new sheetmetal, a new grille and revised headlamps. The wheelbase on regular cab models has been stretched to provide more cabin room and the displacement of the base engine has been increased. A short- and long-arm (SLA) suspension replaces the Twin-I-Beam suspension found on last year's models. A four-door Ranger join the lineup mid-year.

Category J

Model Description	Trade-in TMV	Private TMV	Dealer TMV
2 Dr Splash 4WD Ext Cab Stepside SB			
	9245	10645	12162
2 Dr Splash 4WD Std Cab Stepside SB			
	8811	10146	11592
2 Dr Splash Ext Cab Stepside SB			
	7800	8982	10262
2 Dr Splash Std Cab Stepside SB			
	7039	8105	9260
2 Dr XL 4WD Std Cab LB			
	7583	8732	9976
2 Dr XL Std Cab LB	5633	6487	7411
2 Dr XL 4WD Ext Cab SB			
	8125	9356	10689
2 Dr XL 4WD Std Cab SB			
	7294	8399	9596
2 Dr XL Ext Cab SB	6933	7983	9121
2 Dr XL Std Cab SB	5295	6097	6966
2 Dr XL 4WD Ext Cab Stepside SB			
	8228	9474	10824
2 Dr XL 4WD Std Cab Stepside SB			
	7439	8565	9786
2 Dr XL Ext Cab Stepside SB			
	7117	8195	9363
2 Dr XL Std Cab Stepside SB			
	5394	6211	7096
2 Dr XLT 4WD Std Cab LB			
	8450	9730	11117
2 Dr XLT Std Cab LB	6428	7401	8456
2 Dr XLT 4WD Ext Cab SB			
	8956	10312	11782
2 Dr XLT 4WD Std Cab SB			
	8131	9363	10697
2 Dr XLT Ext Cab SB	7150	8233	9406
2 Dr XLT Std Cab SB	6139	7069	8076
2 Dr XLT 4WD Ext Cab Stepside SB			
	9100	10479	11972
2 Dr XLT 4WD Std Cab Stepside SB			
	8306	9564	10927
2 Dr XLT Ext Cab Stepside SB			
	7366	8482	9691
2 Dr XLT Std Cab Stepside SB			
	6211	7152	8171

OPTIONS FOR RANGER

6 cyl 3.0 L Engine[Std on 4WD, Splash 2WD Ext Cab] +227
6 cyl 4.0 L Engine +340
AM/FM Compact Disc Player +146
AM/FM Stereo Tape +109
AM/FM Stereo/CD/Tape +146
Air Conditioning +406
Aluminum/Alloy Wheels[Opt on XL,XLT,Ext Cab] +126
Anti-Lock Brakes +252
Automatic 4-Speed Transmission +551
Automatic 5-Speed Transmission +557
Bed Liner +119
Bucket Seats +181
Compact Disc Changer +252
Limited Slip Differential +136
Power Door Locks +121
Power Windows +139

Don't forget to refer to the Mileage Adjustment Table at the back of this book!

Model Description	Trade-in TMV	Private TMV	Dealer TMV	Model Description	Trade-in TMV	Private TMV	Dealer TMV

TAURUS 1998

A mild facelift, revised trim levels and fewer options are the only changes to Ford's mid-size sedan.

Category D

	Trade-in	Private	Dealer
4 Dr LX Sdn	6570	7445	8392
4 Dr SE Sdn	6651	7536	8495
4 Dr SE Wgn	7316	8290	9345
4 Dr SHO Sdn	10642	12058	13592

OPTIONS FOR TAURUS

6 cyl 3.0 L DOHC Engine[Opt on LX,SE] +249
6 cyl 3.0 L EFF Engine +586
6 cyl 3.0 L MFF Engine +586
Aluminum/Alloy Wheels +159
Anti-Lock Brakes[Std on SHO] +302
Chrome Wheels[Opt on SE] +249
Compact Disc Changer[Opt on SE] +177
Dual Power Seats[Opt on SE] +177
Power Door Locks[Opt on LX] +133
Power Drivers Seat +177
Power Moonroof[Opt on SE] +373
Rear Spoiler[Opt on SE] +126

WINDSTAR 1998

Ford widens the driver's door as a stop-gap measure until the 1999 Windstar arrives with a fourth door. Subtle styling revisions and a new Limited model round out the changes for 1998.

Category P

	Trade-in	Private	Dealer
2 Dr STD Cargo Van	6448	7273	8167
2 Dr STD Pass. Van	6892	7774	8730
2 Dr GL Pass. Van	7559	8527	9575
2 Dr LX Pass. Van	8152	9196	10326
2 Dr Limited Pass. Van			
	10450	11787	13236

OPTIONS FOR WINDSTAR

6 cyl 3.8 L Engine[Std on Limited,LX] +345
AM/FM Stereo/CD/Tape[Opt on Limited] +151
Air Conditioning[Std on LX] +431
Aluminum/Alloy Wheels[Opt on GL] +209
Automatic Load Leveling +146
Bucket Seats +247
Camper/Towing Package +206
Captain Chairs (4)[Opt on GL] +360
Child Seats (2) +113
Dual Air Conditioning[Opt on GL,LX] +239
JBL Sound System +257
Leather Seats[Opt on LX] +435
Power Drivers Seat[Opt on GL] +163
Power Windows[Opt on GL,STD] +142
Privacy Glass +209
Traction Control System +199

1997 FORD

AEROSTAR 1997

Ford's aging minivan gets a 5-speed automatic transmission this year. The sound systems are upgraded and the seats are restyled as well.

Category P

	Trade-in	Private	Dealer
2 Dr STD Cargo Van	4333	4945	5693
2 Dr XLT AWD Pass. Van Ext			
	5895	6728	7746
2 Dr XLT Pass. Van	4546	5188	5973
2 Dr XLT Pass. Van Ext			
	5328	6080	7000

OPTIONS FOR AEROSTAR

6 cyl 4.0 L Engine[Opt on 2WD] +134
AM/FM Compact Disc Player +119
AM/FM Stereo Tape +181
Air Conditioning[Opt on STD] +390
Aluminum/Alloy Wheels +163
Camper/Towing Package +125
Captain Chairs (4) +301
Child Seat (1)[Opt on XLT] +101
Dual Air Conditioning +389
Limited Slip Differential +113
Power Windows +119
Privacy Glass +186

ASPIRE 1997

This Kia-built entry-level Ford gets a higher final drive ratio on models equipped with an automatic transmission. New wheel covers, paint choices and interior trim are the only other changes.

Category A

	Trade-in	Private	Dealer
2 Dr STD Hbk	2190	2677	3272
4 Dr STD Hbk	2315	2830	3459

OPTIONS FOR ASPIRE

AM/FM Stereo Tape +231
Air Conditioning +370
Anti-Lock Brakes +255
Automatic 3-Speed Transmission +295
Power Steering +121

CONTOUR 1997

The addition of a Sport Package for the GL and LX models and the inclusion of a standard trunk light are the only changes for the 1997 Contour.

Category C

	Trade-in	Private	Dealer
4 Dr GL Sdn	3649	4277	5046
4 Dr LX Sdn	3784	4436	5233
4 Dr SE Sdn	4257	4990	5887

OPTIONS FOR CONTOUR

6 cyl 2.5 L Engine[Std on SE] +874
AM/FM Compact Disc Player +121
Air Conditioning +357

Model Description	Trade-in TMV	Private TMV	Dealer TMV		Model Description	Trade-in TMV	Private TMV	Dealer TMV

Aluminum/Alloy Wheels[Std on SE] +190
Anti-Lock Brakes +269
Automatic 4-Speed Transmission +366
Leather Seats +401
Power Drivers Seat +157
Power Moonroof +266
Power Windows +152
Rear Spoiler[Opt on GL] +110
Traction Control System +106

CROWN VICTORIA — 1997

After a mild facelift last year, the Crown Vic soldiers on with a few color changes, improved power steering, and the addition of rear air suspension to the handling package.

Category G

Model	Trade-in	Private	Dealer
4 Dr STD Sdn	5864	6764	7864
4 Dr LX Sdn	6430	7416	8622

OPTIONS FOR CROWN VICTORIA
Aluminum/Alloy Wheels +190
Anti-Lock Brakes +222
Dual Power Seats +323
Handling & Performance Package +149
Keyless Entry System +107
Leather Seats +330
Power Door Locks +106
Power Drivers Seat[Opt on STD] +161

E-150 — 1997

Category Q

Model	Trade-in	Private	Dealer
2 Dr STD Econoline	6354	7156	8136
2 Dr Chateau Club Wagon	8373	9430	10721
2 Dr XL Club Wagon	7101	7998	9093
2 Dr XLT Club Wagon	8074	9093	10338

OPTIONS FOR E-150
8 cyl 4.6 L Engine +377
8 cyl 5.4 L Engine +507
AM/FM Stereo Tape[Std on Chateau] +134
Air Conditioning[Opt on STD,XL] +370
Aluminum/Alloy Wheels[Opt on XLT] +139
Anti-Lock Brakes[Opt on STD] +273
Dual Air Conditioning +370
Limited Slip Differential +113
Power Door Locks[Opt on STD,XL] +113
Power Drivers Seat +161
Power Windows[Opt on STD,XL] +145
Privacy Glass +121

E-250 — 1997

Category Q

Model	Trade-in	Private	Dealer
2 Dr STD Cargo Van	7176	8082	9189
2 Dr STD Cargo Van Ext	7476	8419	9572
2 Dr STD Econoline	7027	7914	8998
2 Dr STD Econoline Ext	7326	8251	9381

OPTIONS FOR E-250
8 cyl 5.4 L Engine +507
Air Conditioning +437
Aluminum/Alloy Wheels +139
Anti-Lock Brakes +273
Dual Air Bag Restraints +113
Dual Air Conditioning +437
Limited Slip Differential +113
Power Door Locks +113
Power Windows +145
Privacy Glass +121

E-350 — 1997

Category Q

Model	Trade-in	Private	Dealer
2 Dr STD Econoline	7625	8587	9763
2 Dr STD Econoline Ext	7999	9008	10242
2 Dr Chateau Club Wagon	9419	10608	12061
2 Dr XL Club Wagon	8298	9345	10625
2 Dr XL Club Wagon Ext	8896	10019	11391
2 Dr XLT Club Wagon	8970	10102	11486
2 Dr XLT Club Wagon Ext	9344	10524	11965

OPTIONS FOR E-350
10 cyl 6.8 L Engine +186
8 cyl 7.3 L Turbodiesel Engine +2110
Air Conditioning[Opt on STD,XL] +437
Aluminum/Alloy Wheels +139
Anti-Lock Brakes[Opt on STD] +273
Dual Air Bag Restraints[Opt on STD] +113
Dual Air Conditioning +437
Limited Slip Differential +113
Power Door Locks[Opt on STD,XL] +113
Power Drivers Seat +175
Power Windows[Opt on STD,XL] +145
Privacy Glass +121

ESCORT — 1997

The Ford Escort is totally redesigned this year with improvements across the board. The most noticeable improvements are in the powertrain and ride quality. New sheetmetal gives the Escort a rounder, more aerodynamic appearance as well. To the chagrin of bargain-basement enthusiasts, the GT hatchback version is dropped.

Category B

Model	Trade-in	Private	Dealer
4 Dr STD Sdn	3229	3837	4581
4 Dr LX Sdn	3492	4151	4955
4 Dr LX Wgn	3690	4385	5235

Model Description	Trade-in TMV	Private TMV	Dealer TMV	Model Description	Trade-in TMV	Private TMV	Dealer TMV

OPTIONS FOR ESCORT

Air Conditioning +357
Aluminum/Alloy Wheels +119
Anti-Lock Brakes +255
Automatic 4-Speed Transmission +366
Compact Disc Changer +133

EXPEDITION   1997

Ford's replacement for the aging Bronco is the all-new Expedition. Based on the hugely successful 1997 F-150 platform, this full-size sport-utility vehicle is poised to do battle with the wildly popular Chevrolet Tahoe and GMC Yukon. Ford has priced the Expedition aggressively and stands to steal some sales from GM customers who have been told that they'll have to wait four months for their full-size SUV.

Category N

4 Dr Eddie Bauer 4WD Utility			
	12181	13718	15598
4 Dr Eddie Bauer Utility			
	11876	13375	15208
4 Dr XLT 4WD Utility	11419	12861	14623
4 Dr XLT Utility	9973	11232	12771

OPTIONS FOR EXPEDITION

8 cyl 5.4 L Engine +253
AM/FM Stereo/CD/Tape +159
Automatic Load Leveling +366
Camper/Towing Package +246
Captain Chairs (2) +125
Compact Disc Changer +213
Cruise Control[Opt on XLT] +106
Dual Air Conditioning +316
Leather Seats[Opt on XLT] +448
Limited Slip Differential +141
Power Drivers Seat[Opt on XLT] +134
Power Moonroof +348
Running Boards +195
Third Seat +269

EXPLORER   1997

Ford's best-selling Explorer receives a few appreciated improvements this year. A new SOHC V6 engine is now available, providing nearly as much power as the 5.0-liter V8. Also new is a five-speed automatic transmission, the first ever offered by an American auto manufacturer, which is standard on V6 models equipped with automatic.

Category M

4 Dr Eddie Bauer 4WD Utility			
	10273	11613	13250
4 Dr Eddie Bauer Utility			
	9522	10764	12282
4 Dr Eddie Bauer AWD Utility			
	9748	11019	12573

4 Dr Limited 4WD Utility			
	10947	12375	14120
4 Dr Limited Utility	10762	12166	13881
4 Dr Limited AWD Utility			
	10872	12290	14023
2 Dr Sport 4WD Utility			
	7648	8646	9865
2 Dr Sport Utility	6956	7863	8972
2 Dr XL 4WD Utility	7198	8137	9284
2 Dr XL Utility	6523	7374	8414
4 Dr XL 4WD Utility	7723	8730	9961
4 Dr XL Utility	6990	7902	9016
4 Dr XLT 4WD Utility	8623	9748	11122
4 Dr XLT Utility	7873	8900	10155
4 Dr XLT AWD Utility	8248	9323	10638

OPTIONS FOR EXPLORER

6 cyl 4.0 L SOHC Engine[Opt on Sport,XL,XLT] +190
8 cyl 5.0 L Engine +354
AM/FM Compact Disc Player +124
AM/FM Stereo/CD/Tape[Opt on XLT] +143
Alarm System[Std on Limited] +113
Automatic 4-Speed Transmission +423
Automatic 5-Speed Transmission[Opt on Sport,XL,XLT] +477
Bucket Seats +125
Camper/Towing Package +152
Captain Chairs (2)[Opt on Sport,XL] +125
Compact Disc Changer +166
Dual Power Seats[Opt on Sport,XLT] +224
JBL Sound System[Std on Limited] +246
Leather Seats[Std on Limited] +294
Limited Slip Differential +139
Overhead Console[Std on Limited] +170
Power Drivers Seat +117
Power Moonroof +359
Power Windows[Opt on XL] +119
Running Boards[Std on Limited] +177
Side Steps[Opt on Sport] +133

F-150   1997

Everything is new. New engines, new sheetmetal, and a new suspension compliment dual airbags and class-leading side impact protection in this user-friendly heavy hauler. All SuperCab models get a third door for easy access to the rear compartment. Styling is slightly different depending on what drive system is selected.

Category K

2 Dr STD 4WD Ext Cab LB			
	9107	10279	11711
2 Dr STD 4WD Std Cab LB			
	8121	9166	10443
2 Dr STD Ext Cab LB	7451	8409	9581
2 Dr STD Std Cab LB	6407	7231	8239
2 Dr STD 4WD Ext Cab SB			
	8941	10091	11497

Model Description	Trade-in TMV	Private TMV	Dealer TMV
2 Dr STD 4WD Std Cab SB			
	8026	9059	10321
2 Dr STD Ext Cab SB	7301	8241	9389
2 Dr STD Std Cab SB	6258	7064	8048
2 Dr Lariat 4WD Ext Cab LB			
	11920	13454	15329
2 Dr Lariat 4WD Std Cab LB			
	10416	11756	13394
2 Dr Lariat Ext Cab LB			
	10339	11670	13296
2 Dr Lariat Std Cab LB			
	9164	10343	11784
2 Dr Lariat 4WD Ext Cab SB			
	11846	13370	15233
2 Dr Lariat 4WD Std Cab SB			
	10372	11707	13338
2 Dr Lariat Ext Cab SB			
	10319	11647	13270
2 Dr Lariat Std Cab SB			
	9052	10216	11640
2 Dr Lariat 4WD Ext Cab Stepside SB			
	12218	13790	15712
2 Dr Lariat 4WD Std Cab Stepside SB			
	10654	12025	13700
2 Dr Lariat Ext Cab Stepside SB			
	10445	11789	13432
2 Dr Lariat Std Cab Stepside SB			
	9897	11170	12727
2 Dr XL 4WD Ext Cab LB			
	10098	11397	12985
2 Dr XL 4WD Std Cab LB			
	8589	9694	11045
2 Dr XL Ext Cab LB	8080	9120	10391
2 Dr XL Std Cab LB	6705	7568	8622
2 Dr XL 4WD Ext Cab SB			
	10018	11307	12882
2 Dr XL 4WD Std Cab SB			
	8546	9646	10990
2 Dr XL Ext Cab SB	7972	8997	10251
2 Dr XL Std Cab SB	6631	7484	8527
2 Dr XL 4WD Ext Cab Stepside SB			
	10281	11604	13221
2 Dr XL 4WD Std Cab Stepside SB			
	8791	9922	11305
2 Dr XL Ext Cab Stepside SB			
	8493	9586	10922
2 Dr XL Std Cab Stepside SB			
	7077	7988	9101
2 Dr XLT 4WD Ext Cab LB			
	11399	12865	14658
2 Dr XLT 4WD Std Cab LB			
	9759	11015	12550
2 Dr XLT Ext Cab LB	9387	10595	12071
2 Dr XLT Std Cab LB	8196	9250	10539
2 Dr XLT 4WD Ext Cab SB			
	11250	12698	14467
2 Dr XLT 4WD Std Cab SB			
	9611	10848	12359
2 Dr XLT Ext Cab SB	9109	10281	11714
2 Dr XLT Std Cab SB	8066	9104	10373
2 Dr XLT 4WD Ext Cab Stepside SB			
	11548	13034	14850
2 Dr XLT 4WD Std Cab Stepside SB			
	9920	11197	12757
2 Dr XLT Ext Cab Stepside SB			
	9834	11099	12646
2 Dr XLT Std Cab Stepside SB			
	8717	9838	11209

OPTIONS FOR F-150
8 cyl 4.6 L Engine +285
8 cyl 5.4 L Engine +253
AM/FM Stereo Tape +117
AM/FM Stereo/CD/Tape +134
Air Conditioning +360
Aluminum/Alloy Wheels +143
Anti-Lock Brakes +224
Automatic 4-Speed Transmission +435
Camper/Towing Package +133
Captain Chairs (2) +220
Compact Disc Changer +180
Limited Slip Differential +113
Off-Road Equipment Group +309
Power Drivers Seat +130

F-250 1997

Ford's F-250 joins the F-150 this year in a dramatic redesign. The new model has swoopy styling, a greatly improved interior, a much more rigid chassis, and car-like handling. Do you have to give up that legendary Ford truck toughness? Heck no, this model is more durable than last year's.

Category K

Model Description	Trade-in TMV	Private TMV	Dealer TMV
2 Dr STD 4WD Std Cab LB			
	8654	9768	11129
2 Dr STD Std Cab LB	7077	7988	9101
2 Dr STD 4WD Ext Cab SB			
	9528	10754	12252
2 Dr STD Ext Cab SB	8196	9250	10539
2 Dr Lariat 4WD Std Cab LB			
	10878	12277	13988
2 Dr Lariat Std Cab LB			
	9611	10848	12359
2 Dr Lariat 4WD Ext Cab SB			

Model Description	Trade-in TMV	Private TMV	Dealer TMV
	12144	13706	15616
2 Dr Lariat Ext Cab SB			
	10505	11857	13509
2 Dr XL 4WD Std Cab LB			
	9164	10343	11784
2 Dr XL Std Cab LB	7451	8409	9581
2 Dr XL 4WD Ext Cab SB			
	10133	11436	13030
2 Dr XL Ext Cab SB	8638	9750	11108
2 Dr XL 4WD Ext Cab LB HD			
	10035	11327	12905
2 Dr XL 4WD Std Cab LB HD			
	9105	10276	11708
2 Dr XL Ext Cab LB HD	8635	9746	11104
2 Dr XL Std Cab LB HD	7823	8830	10060
2 Dr XL 4WD Ext Cab SB HD			
	10049	11342	12922
2 Dr XL Ext Cab SB HD	8717	9838	11209
4 Dr XL 4WD Crew Cab SB HD			
	10818	12210	13911
4 Dr XL Crew Cab SB HD			
	9546	10774	12275
2 Dr XLT 4WD Std Cab LB			
	10067	11362	12945
2 Dr XLT Std Cab LB	8866	10007	11401
2 Dr XLT 4WD Ext Cab SB			
	11846	13370	15233
2 Dr XLT Ext Cab SB	9983	11268	12838
2 Dr XLT 4WD Ext Cab LB HD			
	11101	12529	14275
2 Dr XLT 4WD Std Cab LB HD			
	10356	11688	13317
2 Dr XLT Ext Cab LB HD			
	9666	10910	12430
2 Dr XLT Std Cab LB HD			
	8941	10091	11497
2 Dr XLT 4WD Ext Cab SB HD			
	11175	12613	14371
2 Dr XLT Ext Cab SB HD			
	9705	10954	12480
4 Dr XLT 4WD Crew Cab SB HD			
	12293	13875	15808
4 Dr XLT Crew Cab SB HD			
	10803	12193	13892

OPTIONS FOR F-250
8 cyl 5.4 L Engine[Std on HD] +253
8 cyl 7.3 L Turbodiesel Engine +1703
8 cyl 7.5 L Engine +172
AM/FM Compact Disc Player[Opt on XLT] +134
AM/FM Stereo Tape +101
Air Conditioning +360
Anti-Lock Brakes[Std on Lariat] +224

Automatic 4-Speed Transmission +435
Automatic Load Leveling +220
Camper/Towing Package +133
Captain Chairs (2)[Opt on XLT] +277
Compact Disc Changer +180
Limited Slip Differential +113
Power Drivers Seat +161
Side Steps +133

F-350 1997

Category K

Model Description	Trade-in TMV	Private TMV	Dealer TMV
2 Dr XL 4WD Std Cab LB			
	10367	11701	13331
2 Dr XL Ext Cab LB	10281	11604	13221
2 Dr XL Std Cab LB	8642	9754	11113
4 Dr XL 4WD Crew Cab LB			
	12069	13622	15520
4 Dr XL Crew Cab LB	10505	11857	13509
2 Dr XLT 4WD Std Cab LB			
	11473	12950	14754
2 Dr XLT Ext Cab LB	11250	12698	14467
2 Dr XLT Std Cab LB	9983	11268	12838
4 Dr XLT 4WD Crew Cab LB			
	13560	15304	17437
4 Dr XLT Crew Cab LB	11846	13370	15233

OPTIONS FOR F-350
8 cyl 7.3 L Turbodiesel Engine +1703
8 cyl 7.5 L Engine +172
AM/FM Compact Disc Player[Opt on XLT] +134
AM/FM Stereo Tape[Opt on XL] +101
Air Conditioning[Opt on XL] +360
Automatic 4-Speed Transmission +435
Camper/Towing Package +133
Dual Rear Wheels +352
Limited Slip Differential +113
Power Drivers Seat +161
Side Steps +133

MUSTANG 1997

While messing around with the rest of their models, Ford decided to take it easy with changes to the Mustang. GT models and base convertibles get new interior color options, and Stangs equipped with an automatic transmission (what fun) get a thicker shift lever. New 17-inch aluminum wheels are optional on the GT. Lastly, the Passive Anti-Theft System has been introduced to all Mustangs in an attempt decrease this vehicle's extremely high theft rating.

Category E

Model Description	Trade-in TMV	Private TMV	Dealer TMV
2 Dr STD Conv	8799	10044	11565
2 Dr STD Cpe	6812	7776	8954
2 Dr Cobra Conv	13483	15390	17721
2 Dr Cobra Cpe	12064	13770	15856
2 Dr GT Conv	10999	12555	14457

Model Description	Trade-in TMV	Private TMV	Dealer TMV
2 Dr GT Cpe	8161	9315	10726

OPTIONS FOR MUSTANG
AM/FM Compact Disc Player +133
AM/FM Stereo/CD/Tape +177
Air Conditioning +401
Aluminum/Alloy Wheels[Opt on STD] +119
Anti-Lock Brakes[Std on Cobra] +255
Automatic 4-Speed Transmission +366
Bucket Seats +224
Cruise Control +96
Leather Seats +224
Limited Slip Differential[Std on Cobra] +124
Power Drivers Seat[Std on Cobra] +107
Power Windows[Std on Cobra,Conv] +113

PROBE　　　　　　　　1997

Ford adds a GTS Sport Appearance Package to the GT's option sheet. The package includes a rear spoiler, racing stripes and 16-inch chrome wheels.

Category E

Model Description	Trade-in TMV	Private TMV	Dealer TMV
2 Dr STD Hbk	4684	5346	6156
2 Dr GT Hbk	5464	6237	7182

OPTIONS FOR PROBE
AM/FM Compact Disc Player +192
Air Conditioning +401
Aluminum/Alloy Wheels[Std on GT] +210
Anti-Lock Brakes +280
Automatic 4-Speed Transmission +401
Chrome Wheels +175
Leather Seats +224
Power Drivers Seat +130
Power Sunroof +276
Power Windows +117
Rear Spoiler +106

RANGER　　　　　　　　1997

Ford introduces its brand-new five-speed automatic transmission to the Ranger lineup. Available with the V6 engines, the five-speed automatic is designed to improve the Ranger's acceleration, towing, and hill climbing ability.

Category J

Model Description	Trade-in TMV	Private TMV	Dealer TMV
2 Dr STX 4WD Std Cab LB	7251	8416	9839
2 Dr STX 4WD Ext Cab SB	7523	8731	10208
2 Dr STX 4WD Std Cab SB	7112	8254	9650
2 Dr Splash 4WD Ext Cab Stepside SB	7879	9145	10691
2 Dr Splash 4WD Std Cab Stepside SB	7537	8748	10227
2 Dr Splash Ext Cab Stepside SB	6345	7364	8609
2 Dr Splash Std Cab Stepside SB	5710	6626	7747
2 Dr XL 4WD Std Cab LB	6485	7526	8799
2 Dr XL Std Cab LB	4323	5018	5866
2 Dr XL 4WD Ext Cab SB	6979	8100	9470
2 Dr XL 4WD Std Cab SB	6276	7283	8515
2 Dr XL Ext Cab SB	5508	6393	7474
2 Dr XL Std Cab SB	4114	4775	5582
2 Dr XL 4WD Ext Cab Stepside SB	7185	8339	9749
2 Dr XL 4WD Std Cab Stepside SB	6485	7526	8799
2 Dr XL Ext Cab Stepside SB	5721	6640	7763
2 Dr XL Std Cab Stepside SB	4393	5098	5960
2 Dr XLT 4WD Std Cab LB	7193	8348	9760
2 Dr XLT Std Cab LB	5027	5834	6821
2 Dr XLT 4WD Ext Cab SB	7600	8820	10312
2 Dr XLT 4WD Std Cab SB	6965	8084	9451
2 Dr XLT Ext Cab SB	5723	6642	7765
2 Dr XLT Std Cab SB	4881	5665	6623
2 Dr XLT 4WD Ext Cab Stepside SB	7670	8902	10407
2 Dr XLT 4WD Std Cab Stepside SB	7168	8319	9726
2 Dr XLT Ext Cab Stepside SB	5927	6879	8042
2 Dr XLT Std Cab Stepside SB	5013	5818	6802

OPTIONS FOR RANGER
6 cyl 3.0 L Engine +301
AM/FM Compact Disc Player +130
AM/FM Stereo Tape +96
Air Conditioning +360
Aluminum/Alloy Wheels[Std on Splash] +113
Anti-Lock Brakes +273
Automatic 4-Speed Transmission +480
Automatic 5-Speed Transmission +527
Bed Liner +106
Bucket Seats +161
Compact Disc Changer +202
Dual Air Bag Restraints +180
Limited Slip Differential +121
Power Door Locks +107
Power Steering[Std on Splash,STX,Ext Cab,4WD] +124
Power Windows +113

Don't forget to refer to the Mileage Adjustment Table at the back of this book!

Model Description	Trade-in TMV	Private TMV	Dealer TMV	Model Description	Trade-in TMV	Private TMV	Dealer TMV

TAURUS 1997

After totally redesigning the Taurus for 1996, Ford is taking it slow with changes for 97. A few new exterior color choices are added and there are minor changes to a couple of optional equipment packages.

Category D

4 Dr G Sdn	4158	4852	5701
4 Dr GL Sdn	4430	5170	6075
4 Dr GL Wgn	4772	5569	6543
4 Dr LX Sdn	5044	5887	6917
4 Dr LX Wgn	5316	6205	7290
4 Dr SHO Sdn	7907	9228	10842

OPTIONS FOR TAURUS

6 cyl 3.0 L EFF Engine +522
6 cyl 3.0 L MFF Engine +522
AM/FM Compact Disc Player +157
Aluminum/Alloy Wheels +141
Anti-Lock Brakes +269
Chrome Wheels +222
Compact Disc Changer +266
Leather Seats +444
Power Door Locks[Opt on G,GL] +115
Power Drivers Seat[Opt on GL] +152
Power Moonroof +332
Rear Window Wiper +115

THUNDERBIRD 1997

The Thunderbird receives few updates this year. A revised center console, a few new colors, and standard four-wheel disc brakes are the big news for 1997.

Category D

2 Dr LX Cpe	5112	5966	7010

OPTIONS FOR THUNDERBIRD

8 cyl 4.6 L Engine +507
AM/FM Stereo/CD/Tape +169
Aluminum/Alloy Wheels +124
Anti-Lock Brakes +255
Chrome Wheels +260
Leather Seats +220
Limited Slip Differential +113
Power Drivers Seat +130
Power Moonroof +332
Premium Sound System +192
Rear Spoiler +113
Special Factory Paint +101

WINDSTAR 1997

Nothing is new for the 1997 Ford Windsar.

Category P

2 Dr STD Cargo Van	5115	5837	6720
2 Dr GL Pass. Van	5895	6728	7746
2 Dr LX Pass. Van	6606	7539	8680

OPTIONS FOR WINDSTAR

6 cyl 3.8 L Engine[Std on LX] +307
AM/FM Compact Disc Player +145
Air Conditioning +383
Aluminum/Alloy Wheels +186
Automatic Load Leveling +100
Bucket Seats[Opt on Cargo] +244
Camper/Towing Package +157
Captain Chairs (4) +312
Dual Air Conditioning +213
JBL Sound System +228
Leather Seats +387
Power Windows[Std on LX] +124
Privacy Glass +186
Traction Control System +163

1996 FORD

AEROSTAR 1996

Smoother shifting transmission debuts, along with revised A/C controls and a new radio with visible controls. Solar tinted glass is standard.

Category P

2 Dr STD Cargo Van	3345	3892	4648
2 Dr XLT AWD Pass. Van Ext			
	4482	5215	6228
2 Dr XLT Pass. Van	3545	4126	4927
2 Dr XLT Pass. Van Ext			
	4214	4904	5856

OPTIONS FOR AEROSTAR

6 cyl 4.0 L Engine[Opt on 2WD] +130
AM/FM Stereo Tape +148
Air Conditioning[Opt on STD] +376
Aluminum/Alloy Wheels +158
Camper/Towing Package +123
Captain Chairs (2) +203
Captain Chairs (4) +290
Dual Air Conditioning +376
Limited Slip Differential +109
Power Windows +115
Privacy Glass[Opt on Pass. Van,4WD] +179

ASPIRE 1996

Korean-built minicompact loses the SE trim level and several items of standard and optional equipment. Four new colors debut.

Category A

2 Dr STD Hbk	1527	1914	2449
4 Dr STD Hbk	1644	2061	2637

OPTIONS FOR ASPIRE

AM/FM Stereo Tape +202
Air Conditioning +357
Anti-Lock Brakes +247
Automatic 3-Speed Transmission +286

BRONCO 1996

Model Description	Trade-in TMV	Private TMV	Dealer TMV	Model Description	Trade-in TMV	Private TMV	Dealer TMV

Trick new turn signal system is embedded in side view mirrors. Otherwise, minor trim changes mark the passing of the last Bronco.

Category N

2 Dr Eddie Bauer 4WD Utility

	Trade-in	Private	Dealer
	10713	12200	14254
2 Dr XL 4WD Utility	8818	10042	11733
2 Dr XLT 4WD Utility	9547	10872	12702

OPTIONS FOR BRONCO

AM/FM Compact Disc Player +189
AM/FM Stereo/CD/Tape +189
Air Conditioning[Opt on XL,XLT] +340
Alarm System +108
Automatic 4-Speed Transmission[Opt on XL,XLT] +400
Camper/Towing Package +156
Chrome Wheels +173
Leather Seats +301
Limited Slip Differential +108
Power Windows +113
Styled Steel Wheels[Opt on XL] +134

CONTOUR   1996

Designers sculpt and adjust interior seating to make more leg and head room in the back seat. Five new colors are available and improvements to shift effort on manual transmission models make the 1996 Contour more competitive.

Category C

	Trade-in	Private	Dealer
4 Dr GL Sdn	2582	3098	3811
4 Dr LX Sdn	2708	3249	3997
4 Dr SE Sdn	3086	3702	4554

OPTIONS FOR CONTOUR

6 cyl 2.5 L Engine[Std on SE] +468
AM/FM Compact Disc Player +117
Air Conditioning +338
Aluminum/Alloy Wheels +183
Anti-Lock Brakes +247
Automatic 4-Speed Transmission +354
Leather Seats +280
Power Drivers Seat +142
Power Moonroof +257
Power Windows +147

CROWN VICTORIA   1996

A new steering wheel and gas cap are standard, and some equipment has been dropped from the roster, including the JBL sound system and trailer towing package.

Category G

	Trade-in	Private	Dealer
4 Dr STD Sdn	4504	5248	6275
4 Dr LX Sdn	4975	5796	6930

OPTIONS FOR CROWN VICTORIA

Aluminum/Alloy Wheels +183
Anti-Lock Brakes +290
Dual Power Seats +312

Handling & Performance Package +294
Keyless Entry System +132
Leather Seats +280
Power Drivers Seat[Std on LX] +156
Preferred Equipment Package 2 +431

E-150   1996

Category Q

	Trade-in	Private	Dealer
2 Dr STD Econoline	4990	5711	6707
2 Dr Chateau Club Wagon			
	7199	8240	9677
2 Dr XL Club Wagon	5631	6445	7569
2 Dr XL Econoline	5418	6201	7282
2 Dr XLT Club Wagon	6558	7506	8815

OPTIONS FOR E-150

7 Passenger Seating[Opt on XLT] +289
8 cyl 5.0 L Engine[Std on Chateau] +276
8 cyl 5.8 L Engine +371
8 cyl 7.5 L Engine +581
AM/FM Compact Disc Player +129
AM/FM Stereo Tape[Std on Chateau] +130
Air Conditioning[Opt on STD,XL] +357
Aluminum/Alloy Wheels[Opt on XL,XLT] +134
Anti-Lock Brakes[Opt on STD,XL] +264
Automatic 4-Speed Transmission[Opt on STD,XL] +129
Dual Air Conditioning[Std on Chateau] +357
Limited Slip Differential +108
Power Door Locks[Opt on STD,XL] +108
Power Drivers Seat +156
Power Windows[Opt on STD,XL] +141
Privacy Glass[Std on Chateau] +128

E-250   1996

Category Q

	Trade-in	Private	Dealer
2 Dr STD Econoline	5560	6364	7474
2 Dr STD Econoline Ext			
	5774	6608	7761
2 Dr XL Econoline	5987	6853	8048
2 Dr XL Econoline Ext	6202	7098	8336

OPTIONS FOR E-250

8 cyl 5.8 L Engine +371
AM/FM Compact Disc Player +129
Air Conditioning +422
Anti-Lock Brakes +264
Automatic 4-Speed Transmission +129
Dual Air Conditioning +357
Limited Slip Differential +108
Power Door Locks +108
Power Drivers Seat +108
Power Windows +141
Privacy Glass +126

E-350   1996

Category Q

	Trade-in	Private	Dealer
2 Dr STD Econoline	6202	7098	8336
2 Dr STD Econoline Ext			

Don't forget to refer to the Mileage Adjustment Table at the back of this book!

Model Description	Trade-in TMV	Private TMV	Dealer TMV	Model Description	Trade-in TMV	Private TMV	Dealer TMV
	6558	7506	8815				
2 Dr Chateau Club Wagon							
	8198	9383	11019				
2 Dr XL Club Wagon	6772	7750	9102				
2 Dr XL Club Wagon Ext							
	7092	8117	9533				
2 Dr XL Econoline	6701	7669	9007				
2 Dr XL Econoline Ext	6879	7874	9247				
2 Dr XLT Club Wagon	7128	8158	9581				
2 Dr XLT Club Wagon Ext							
	7485	8567	10061				

OPTIONS FOR E-350

7 Passenger Seating[Opt on XLT] +368
8 cyl 5.0 L Engine +310
8 cyl 5.8 L Engine +414
8 cyl 7.3 L Turbodiesel Engine +2039
8 cyl 7.5 L Engine +581
AM/FM Compact Disc Player +129
Air Conditioning[Std on Chateau] +422
Aluminum/Alloy Wheels[Std on Chateau] +134
Anti-Lock Brakes[Std on Chateau] +264
Automatic 4-Speed Transmission +129
Dual Air Conditioning[Std on Chateau] +357
Limited Slip Differential +108
Power Door Locks[Opt on STD,XL] +108
Power Drivers Seat +168
Power Windows[Opt on STD,XL] +141
Privacy Glass[Std on Chateau] +130

ESCORT   1996

Last year for the second-generation Escort. The 1.9-liter engine gets 100,000-mile tune-up interval. Automatic transmissions have lower final drive ratio when coupled with 1.9-liter engine to improve acceleration. Sport/Appearance Group available on four-door models. Ultra Violet decor no longer offered on GT. Integrated child safety seat, added during 1995 model year, continues for 1996 on sedan and wagon.

Category B

Model Description	Trade-in TMV	Private TMV	Dealer TMV
2 Dr STD Hbk	2231	2797	3579
2 Dr GT Hbk	2767	3469	4439
2 Dr LX Hbk	2385	2990	3826
4 Dr LX Hbk	2429	3046	3897
4 Dr LX Sdn	2496	3129	4004
4 Dr LX Wgn	2634	3303	4226

OPTIONS FOR ESCORT

AM/FM Stereo Tape[Std on LX] +202
Air Conditioning +340
Anti-Lock Brakes +247
Automatic 4-Speed Transmission +354
Power Moonroof +183

EXPLORER   1996

The long-awaited V8 AWD Explorers are available in XLT, Eddie Bauer or Limited Edition flavors. An integrated child safety seat is optional, and the Expedition model has been replaced by a Premium trim package for the Sport.

Category M

Model Description	Trade-in TMV	Private TMV	Dealer TMV
4 Dr Eddie Bauer 4WD Utility			
	8055	9261	10926
4 Dr Eddie Bauer AWD Utility			
	8212	9441	11139
4 Dr Eddie Bauer Utility			
	7484	8605	10152
4 Dr Limited 4WD Utility			
	8589	9875	11651
4 Dr Limited AWD Utility			
	8419	9679	11420
4 Dr Limited Utility	8361	9612	11341
2 Dr Sport 4WD Utility			
	5988	6884	8122
2 Dr Sport Utility	5560	6392	7542
2 Dr XL 4WD Utility	5631	6474	7638
2 Dr XL Utility	5203	5982	7058
4 Dr XL 4WD Utility	6130	7048	8315
4 Dr XL Utility	5596	6434	7591
4 Dr XLT 4WD Utility	6843	7867	9282
4 Dr XLT AWD Utility	6975	8019	9461
4 Dr XLT Utility	6273	7212	8509

OPTIONS FOR EXPLORER

8 cyl 5.0 L Engine +416
AM/FM Stereo/CD/Tape +139
Automatic 4-Speed Transmission[Opt on Sport,XL,XLT] +409
Bucket Seats +122
Camper/Towing Package +147
Captain Chairs (2)[Opt on Sport,XL] +122
Compact Disc Changer +161
Dual Power Seats[Opt on XLT] +217
JBL Sound System[Std on Limited] +239
Leather Seats[Std on Limited] +271
Limited Slip Differential +152
Overhead Console[Std on Limited] +165
Power Drivers Seat[Opt on Sport] +113
Power Moonroof +347
Power Windows[Opt on XL] +115
Premium Sport Package +1203
Running Boards[Std on Limited] +171
Side Steps[Opt on Sport] +128

F-150   1996

Category K

Model Description	Trade-in TMV	Private TMV	Dealer TMV
2 Dr Eddie Bauer 4WD Ext Cab LB			
	9903	11241	13089
2 Dr Eddie Bauer 4WD Std Cab LB			
	8675	9848	11467

Model Description	Trade-in TMV	Private TMV	Dealer TMV
2 Dr Eddie Bauer Ext Cab LB	8531	9684	11276
2 Dr Eddie Bauer Std Cab LB	7253	8233	9587
2 Dr Eddie Bauer 4WD Ext Cab SB	9906	11244	13093
2 Dr Eddie Bauer 4WD Std Cab SB	8458	9601	11180
2 Dr Eddie Bauer Ext Cab SB	8390	9523	11089
2 Dr Eddie Bauer Std Cab SB	7210	8184	9530
2 Dr Eddie Bauer 4WD Ext Cab Stepside SB	10049	11407	13282
2 Dr Eddie Bauer 4WD Std Cab Stepside SB	8892	10094	11753
2 Dr Eddie Bauer Ext Cab Stepside SB	8821	10014	11660
2 Dr Eddie Bauer Std Cab Stepside SB	7808	8863	10320
2 Dr Special 4WD Std Cab LB	6863	7790	9071
2 Dr Special Ext Cab LB	6145	6975	8122
2 Dr Special Std Cab LB	5446	6183	7199
2 Dr Special 4WD Std Cab SB	6727	7636	8892
2 Dr Special Ext Cab SB	6073	6894	8027
2 Dr Special Std Cab SB	5397	6127	7134
2 Dr XL 4WD Ext Cab LB	8025	9109	10607
2 Dr XL 4WD Std Cab LB	7084	8042	9364
2 Dr XL Ext Cab LB	6844	7769	9046
2 Dr XL Std Cab LB	5790	6572	7653
2 Dr XL 4WD Ext Cab SB	7952	9027	10511
2 Dr XL 4WD Std Cab SB	6896	7828	9115
2 Dr XL Ext Cab SB	6725	7634	8889
2 Dr XL Std Cab SB	5777	6558	7636
2 Dr XL 4WD Ext Cab Stepside SB	8314	9437	10989
2 Dr XL 4WD Std Cab Stepside SB	7225	8202	9550
2 Dr XL Ext Cab Stepside SB	7013	7960	9269
2 Dr XL Std Cab Stepside SB	6362	7222	8409
2 Dr XLT 4WD Ext Cab LB	9182	10422	12136
2 Dr XLT 4WD Std Cab LB	7730	8774	10217
2 Dr XLT Ext Cab LB	7845	8905	10369
2 Dr XLT Std Cab LB	6795	7714	8982
2 Dr XLT 4WD Ext Cab SB	8818	10010	11656
2 Dr XLT 4WD Std Cab SB	8383	9516	11080
2 Dr XLT Ext Cab SB	7741	8787	10232
2 Dr XLT Std Cab SB	6718	7625	8879
2 Dr XLT 4WD Ext Cab Stepside SB	9398	10668	12422
2 Dr XLT 4WD Std Cab Stepside SB	7880	8945	10416
2 Dr XLT Ext Cab Stepside SB	8169	9273	10798
2 Dr XLT Std Cab Stepside SB	7157	8124	9460

OPTIONS FOR F-150
8 cyl 5.0 L Engine +276
8 cyl 5.8 L Engine +475
AM/FM Compact Disc Player +108
AM/FM Stereo Tape[Opt on Special,XL] +113
Air Conditioning[Opt on Special,XL] +349
Aluminum/Alloy Wheels[Opt on XL,XLT] +139
Anti-Lock Brakes[Opt on XL Std Cab] +217
Automatic 4-Speed Transmission +420
Camper/Towing Package +128
Captain Chairs (2) +211
Limited Slip Differential +108
Power Drivers Seat +126
Side Steps +128

F-250 1996

Category K

Model Description	Trade-in TMV	Private TMV	Dealer TMV
2 Dr XL 4WD Ext Cab LB	9904	11243	13091
2 Dr XL 4WD Std Cab LB	9037	10258	11945
2 Dr XL Ext Cab LB	8458	9601	11180
2 Dr XL Std Cab LB	6795	7714	8982
4 Dr XL 4WD Crew Cab LB	10699	12145	14142
4 Dr XL Crew Cab LB	9253	10504	12231
2 Dr XL 4WD Ext Cab SB	10338	11736	13665
2 Dr XL Ext Cab SB	8531	9684	11276
2 Dr XLT 4WD Ext Cab LB	10989	12474	14525

Model Description	Trade-in TMV	Private TMV	Dealer TMV
2 Dr XLT 4WD Std Cab LB			
	10418	11826	13770
2 Dr XLT Ext Cab LB	9471	10751	12518
2 Dr XLT Std Cab LB	8241	9355	10893
4 Dr XLT 4WD Crew Cab LB			
	11567	13130	15289
4 Dr XLT Crew Cab LB	10483	11900	13856
2 Dr XLT 4WD Ext Cab SB			
	11134	12638	14716
2 Dr XLT Ext Cab SB	9760	11079	12901

OPTIONS FOR F-250
8 cyl 5.0 L Engine[Opt on XL 2WD Std Cab,XLT 2WD Std Cab] +276
8 cyl 5.8 L Engine[Opt on XL 2WD Std Cab,XLT 2WD Std Cab] +475
8 cyl 7.3 L Turbodiesel Engine +1646
8 cyl 7.5 L Engine +166
AM/FM Compact Disc Player[Opt on XLT] +130
Air Conditioning[Opt on XL] +349
Automatic 4-Speed Transmission +431
Camper/Towing Package +128
Captain Chairs (2) +212
Limited Slip Differential +108
Power Drivers Seat +156
Side Steps +128

F-250 HEAVY DUTY　　1996
Category K

Model Description	Trade-in TMV	Private TMV	Dealer TMV
2 Dr XL Std Cab LB	6434	7303	8504
2 Dr XLT Std Cab LB	7446	8452	9842

OPTIONS FOR F-250 HEAVY DUTY
8 cyl 7.3 L Turbodiesel Engine +1468
8 cyl 7.5 L Engine +151
AM/FM Compact Disc Player +130
AM/FM Stereo Tape +108
Air Conditioning[Opt on XL] +349
Automatic 3-Speed Transmission +322
Automatic 4-Speed Transmission +428
Camper/Towing Package +108
Limited Slip Differential +113
Side Steps +128

F-350　　1996
Category K

Model Description	Trade-in TMV	Private TMV	Dealer TMV
2 Dr XL 4WD Std Cab LB			
	9608	10906	12699
2 Dr XL Ext Cab LB	9623	10923	12719
2 Dr XL Std Cab LB	8241	9355	10893
4 Dr XL 4WD Crew Cab LB			
	11278	12802	14907
4 Dr XL Crew Cab LB	9760	11079	12900
2 Dr XLT 4WD Std Cab LB			
	10844	12309	14333
2 Dr XLT Ext Cab LB	10627	12064	14047

Model Description	Trade-in TMV	Private TMV	Dealer TMV
2 Dr XLT Std Cab LB	9182	10422	12136
4 Dr XLT 4WD Crew Cab LB			
	12507	14197	16531
4 Dr XLT Crew Cab LB	11061	12556	14620

OPTIONS FOR F-350
8 cyl 7.3 L Turbodiesel Engine +1702
8 cyl 7.5 L Engine +166
AM/FM Compact Disc Player[Opt on XLT] +130
Air Conditioning[Opt on XL] +349
Automatic 4-Speed Transmission +431
Camper/Towing Package +128
Captain Chairs (2) +108
Dual Rear Wheels +251
Limited Slip Differential +117
Side Steps +128

MUSTANG　　1996

After much anticipation among enthusiasts, Ford plugs a 4.6-liter modular V8 into its pony car. Too bad it doesn't make any more power than the old 5.0-liter motor it replaces. Suspension and steering upgrades compliment the new engine, which does live up to its promise in the limited-edition 305-horsepower Cobra. Base cars also get engine improvements, and all Mustangs get minor styling revisions. Collectors tip: The GTS model, a midyear 1995 V8 base Mustang, has been dropped. Buy one if you can find one.

Category E

Model Description	Trade-in TMV	Private TMV	Dealer TMV
2 Dr STD Conv	6796	7976	9605
2 Dr STD Cpe	5542	6504	7833
2 Dr Cobra Conv	10887	12777	15387
2 Dr Cobra Cpe	9502	11151	13429
2 Dr GT Conv	8512	9990	12030
2 Dr GT Cpe	6466	7589	9139

OPTIONS FOR MUSTANG
AM/FM Compact Disc Player +128
AM/FM Stereo/CD/Tape +171
Air Conditioning[Std on Cobra] +388
Aluminum/Alloy Wheels[Opt on STD] +115
Anti-Lock Brakes[Std on Cobra] +247
Automatic 4-Speed Transmission +354
Bucket Seats +217
Metallic Paint +354
Special Wheels +173

PROBE　　1996

Ford concentrates on the SE and GT trim levels this year, revising and simplifying options lists and making minor cosmetic and trim revisions.

Category E

Model Description	Trade-in TMV	Private TMV	Dealer TMV
2 Dr STD Hbk	3167	3717	4476
2 Dr GT Hbk	3893	4569	5502
2 Dr SE Hbk	3365	3949	4756

Don't forget to refer to the Mileage Adjustment Table at the back of this book!

Model Description	Trade-in TMV	Private TMV	Dealer TMV

OPTIONS FOR PROBE

AM/FM Compact Disc Player +186
Air Conditioning +388
Aluminum/Alloy Wheels +230
Anti-Lock Brakes +247
Automatic 4-Speed Transmission +354
Chrome Wheels +169
Leather Seats +217
Power Drivers Seat +126
Power Sunroof +267
Power Windows +113

RANGER 1996

An optional passenger-side airbag is available, and it comes with a switch that will disable the system if a child seat is installed in the truck. Cool, huh? Super Cab models get standard privacy glass, Splash models lose that putrid green tape stripe, and the Flareside box from the Splash is now available on two-wheel drive, four-cylinder XL and XLT models.

Category J

Model Description	Trade-in TMV	Private TMV	Dealer TMV
2 Dr STX 4WD Std Cab LB			
	6101	7154	8608
2 Dr STX 4WD Ext Cab SB			
	6429	7538	9070
2 Dr STX 4WD Std Cab SB			
	5894	6911	8316
2 Dr Splash 4WD Ext Cab Stepside SB			
	6772	7940	9554
2 Dr Splash 4WD Std Cab Stepside SB			
	6436	7547	9081
2 Dr Splash Ext Cab Stepside SB			
	5162	6053	7283
2 Dr Splash Std Cab Stepside SB			
	4625	5424	6526
2 Dr XL 4WD Std Cab LB			
	5431	6368	7662
2 Dr XL Std Cab LB	3553	4166	5013
2 Dr XL 4WD Ext Cab SB			
	5861	6872	8269
2 Dr XL 4WD Std Cab SB			
	5229	6132	7378
2 Dr XL Ext Cab SB	4425	5189	6243
2 Dr XL Std Cab SB	3419	4009	4824
2 Dr XL 4WD Ext Cab Stepside SB			
	6034	7075	8513
2 Dr XL 4WD Std Cab Stepside SB			
	5431	6368	7662
2 Dr XL Ext Cab Stepside SB			
	4693	5503	6621
2 Dr XL Std Cab Stepside SB			
	3620	4245	5108
2 Dr XLT 4WD Std Cab LB			
	5913	6934	8343
2 Dr XLT Std Cab LB	4157	4874	5865
2 Dr XLT 4WD Ext Cab SB			
	6443	7555	9090
2 Dr XLT 4WD Std Cab SB			
	5805	6807	8190
2 Dr XLT Ext Cab SB	4627	5425	6528
2 Dr XLT Std Cab SB	3956	4638	5581
2 Dr XLT 4WD Ext Cab Stepside SB			
	6570	7704	9270
2 Dr XLT 4WD Std Cab Stepside SB			
	5892	6909	8313
2 Dr XLT Ext Cab Stepside SB			
	4760	5582	6716
2 Dr XLT Std Cab Stepside SB			
	4090	4795	5770

OPTIONS FOR RANGER

6 cyl 3.0 L Engine +289
AM/FM Compact Disc Player +126
Air Conditioning +349
Aluminum/Alloy Wheels +108
Anti-Lock Brakes[Opt on 2WD] +264
Automatic 4-Speed Transmission +452
Bucket Seats +157
Compact Disc Changer +195
Dual Air Bag Restraints +173
Limited Slip Differential +115
Power Steering[Std on Splash,STX,Ext Cab,4WD] +119
Power Windows +108
Sport Seats +157

TAURUS 1996

All-new Taurus debuts in sedan and wagon format, available in GL, LX and SHO trim levels. New or substantially revised engines and suspensions improve the performance of the Taurus, while several functional innovations make the car easier and more enjoyable to drive.

Category D

Model Description	Trade-in TMV	Private TMV	Dealer TMV
4 Dr GL Sdn	3361	3984	4845
4 Dr GL Wgn	3619	4290	5217
4 Dr LX Sdn	3878	4597	5590
4 Dr LX Wgn	4072	4827	5869
4 Dr SHO Sdn	6269	7432	9037

OPTIONS FOR TAURUS

6 cyl 3.0 L EFF Engine +505
6 cyl 3.0 L MFF Engine +505
AM/FM Compact Disc Player +152
Aluminum/Alloy Wheels +137
Anti-Lock Brakes[Std on SHO] +247
Chrome Wheels +215
Compact Disc Changer +257
JBL Sound System +217
Leather Seats[Opt on LX] +429

Don't forget to refer to the Mileage Adjustment Table at the back of this book!

Model Description	Trade-in TMV	Private TMV	Dealer TMV	Model Description	Trade-in TMV	Private TMV	Dealer TMV

Power Door Locks[Opt on GL] +110
Power Drivers Seat[Opt on GL] +147
Power Moonroof +320
Rear Window Wiper +110

THUNDERBIRD 1996

Revised styling greatly improves the look of the Thunderbird for 1996. The Super Coupe is deleted, replaced by a Sport Package for the V8 model. Base V6 engines have been upgraded, and go 100,000 miles between tune-ups. Equipment rosters have been shuffled.

Category D

Model	Trade-in	Private	Dealer
2 Dr LX Cpe	3814	4521	5497

OPTIONS FOR THUNDERBIRD
8 cyl 4.6 L Engine +489
AM/FM Compact Disc Player +186
Aluminum/Alloy Wheels +120
Anti-Lock Brakes +247
Chrome Wheels +251
Leather Seats +212
Limited Slip Differential +108
Power Drivers Seat +126
Power Moonroof +320
Rear Spoiler +108

WINDSTAR 1996

Holy Smokes! That's just what the front tires will be doing, unless you find one with the optional traction control system. Ford boosted output on the 3.8-liter V6 from 155 to 200 horsepower. Trim and equipment have been revised, and four-wheel disc brakes come with traction control or the tow package. A new integrated child safety seat has been added to the options list. Tune-ups happen every 100,000 miles.

Category P

Model	Trade-in	Private	Dealer
2 Dr STD Cargo Van	3947	4593	5485
2 Dr GL Pass. Van	4281	4981	5949
2 Dr LX Pass. Van	5218	6072	7251

OPTIONS FOR WINDSTAR
6 cyl 3.8 L Engine[Std on LX] +296
AM/FM Compact Disc Player +141
Air Conditioning[Std on LX] +371
Aluminum/Alloy Wheels +179
Automatic Load Leveling +126
Bucket Seats +212
Camper/Towing Package[Opt on GL] +152
Captain Chairs (4) +259
Dual Air Conditioning +206
JBL Sound System +220
Leather Seats[Opt on LX] +374
Power Windows[Std on LX] +120
Privacy Glass +179
Traction Control System +158

1995 FORD

AEROSTAR 1995

The XL and Eddie Bauer trim levels are dropped; only the XLT remains. The AWD system is available only in extended-length versions. Antilock brakes become standard for the Aerostar.

Category P

Model	Trade-in	Private	Dealer
2 Dr STD Cargo Van	2651	3082	3800
2 Dr XLT AWD Pass. Van Ext			
	3363	3909	4820
2 Dr XLT Pass. Van	2781	3233	3986
2 Dr XLT Pass. Van Ext			
	3104	3608	4449

OPTIONS FOR AEROSTAR
6 cyl 4.0 L Engine[Opt on XLT Ext] +111
AM/FM Stereo Tape[Std on 4WD] +126
Air Conditioning[Opt on STD] +320
Aluminum/Alloy Wheels +135
Camper/Towing Package +103
Captain Chairs (4) +247
Child Seat (1) +83
Dual Air Conditioning +320
Limited Slip Differential +92
Power Windows +98
Privacy Glass +152

ASPIRE 1995

Commonly referred to as the Expire, the latest runabout from Ford has little to offer but economy. Available as a two- or four-door hatchback, the Aspire comes with dual airbags and available antilock brakes.

Category A

Model	Trade-in	Private	Dealer
2 Dr STD Hbk	1246	1575	2122
4 Dr STD Hbk	1288	1627	2193
2 Dr SE Hbk	1322	1670	2251

OPTIONS FOR ASPIRE
AM/FM Compact Disc Player +129
AM/FM Stereo Tape +172
Air Conditioning +305
Anti-Lock Brakes +210
Automatic 3-Speed Transmission +244
Power Steering[Opt on STD] +92

BRONCO 1995

An available Sport Package and new exterior styling for the Eddie Bauer model are the sole changes for 1995.

Category N

Model	Trade-in	Private	Dealer
2 Dr Eddie Bauer 4WD Utility			
	8541	9792	11878
2 Dr XL 4WD Utility	6874	7881	9560
2 Dr XLT 4WD Utility	7499	8598	10429

Don't forget to refer to the Mileage Adjustment Table at the back of this book!

FORD 95

Model Description	Trade-in TMV	Private TMV	Dealer TMV	Model Description	Trade-in TMV	Private TMV	Dealer TMV

OPTIONS FOR BRONCO

8 cyl 5.8 L Engine +81
AM/FM Compact Disc Player +161
AM/FM Stereo Tape +92
Air Conditioning[Opt on XL,XLT] +290
Alarm System +92
Aluminum/Alloy Wheels[Opt on XLT] +87
Automatic 4-Speed Transmission[Opt on XL,XLT] +342
Camper/Towing Package +133
Chrome Wheels +148
Leather Seats +257
Limited Slip Differential +92
Power Windows +96
Styled Steel Wheels[Opt on XL] +114

CONTOUR 1995

The Contour replaces the much-maligned Tempo in an attempt to compete with European and Japanese compacts. Based on the European Mondeo, the Contour has front-wheel drive and dual airbags. Traction control and antilock brakes are available on all models, as is a V6 engine that produces an impressive 170 horsepower.

Category C

Model	Trade-in	Private	Dealer
4 Dr GL Sdn	2128	2589	3358
4 Dr LX Sdn	2246	2733	3544
4 Dr SE Sdn	2423	2949	3824

OPTIONS FOR CONTOUR

6 cyl 2.5 L Engine[Std on SE] +183
AM/FM Compact Disc Player +129
AM/FM Stereo/CD/Tape[Opt on GL] +92
Air Conditioning +288
Aluminum/Alloy Wheels +157
Anti-Lock Brakes +185
Automatic 4-Speed Transmission +301
Cruise Control +80
Leather Seats +238
Power Drivers Seat +122
Power Moonroof +220
Power Windows +125

CROWN VICTORIA 1995

New grille, trunk lid, wheels, and bumpers freshen the Crown Victoria's styling. Rear window defroster and heated outside mirrors move from the options list to the standard equipment roster. A new interior includes a revised stereo, backlit door switches, restyled instrument panel, and a fresh climate control system.

Category G

Model	Trade-in	Private	Dealer
4 Dr STD Sdn	3401	3949	4862
4 Dr LX Sdn	3728	4328	5329

OPTIONS FOR CROWN VICTORIA

Aluminum/Alloy Wheels +157
Anti-Lock Brakes +183
Dual Power Seats +218

Handling & Performance Package +251
JBL Sound System +203
Leather Seats +238
Power Drivers Seat[Std on LX] +133

E-150 1995

Category Q

Model	Trade-in	Private	Dealer
2 Dr STD Econoline	4311	4963	6050
2 Dr Chateau Club Wagon	6227	7169	8738
2 Dr XL Club Wagon	4790	5515	6722
2 Dr XL Econoline	4654	5357	6530
2 Dr XLT Club Wagon	5611	6460	7874

OPTIONS FOR E-150

8 cyl 5.0 L Engine +235
8 cyl 5.8 L Engine +317
AM/FM Compact Disc Player +111
AM/FM Stereo Tape[Std on Chateau] +111
Air Conditioning[Opt on STD,XL] +305
Aluminum/Alloy Wheels[Opt on XL,XLT] +114
Anti-Lock Brakes[Opt on STD,XL] +225
Automatic 4-Speed Transmission[Opt on STD,XL] +111
Captain Chairs (4)[Opt on XLT] +199
Dual Air Conditioning +305
Limited Slip Differential +92
Power Door Locks[Opt on STD,XL] +92
Power Drivers Seat +133
Power Windows[Opt on STD,XL] +120
Privacy Glass[Std on Chateau] +100

E-250 1995

Category Q

Model	Trade-in	Private	Dealer
2 Dr STD Econoline	4380	5042	6146
2 Dr STD Econoline Ext	4654	5357	6530
2 Dr XL Econoline	4722	5436	6626
2 Dr XL Econoline Ext	4927	5672	6914

OPTIONS FOR E-250

8 cyl 5.8 L Engine +317
AM/FM Compact Disc Player +111
Air Conditioning +359
Anti-Lock Brakes +225
Automatic 4-Speed Transmission +111
Dual Air Conditioning +305
Limited Slip Differential +92
Power Door Locks +92
Power Drivers Seat +143
Power Windows +120
Privacy Glass +100

E-350 1995

Category Q

Model	Trade-in	Private	Dealer
2 Dr STD Econoline	4859	5593	6818
2 Dr STD Econoline Ext	5201	5987	7298

FORD 95

Model Description	Trade-in TMV	Private TMV	Dealer TMV	Model Description	Trade-in TMV	Private TMV	Dealer TMV

Model Description	Trade-in TMV	Private TMV	Dealer TMV
2 Dr Chateau Club Wagon	6638	7641	9314
2 Dr XL Club Wagon	5342	6150	7496
2 Dr XL Club Wagon Ext	5611	6460	7874
2 Dr XL Econoline	5333	6140	7484
2 Dr XL Econoline Ext	5543	6381	7778
2 Dr XLT Club Wagon	5817	6696	8162
2 Dr XLT Club Wagon Ext	6022	6932	8450

OPTIONS FOR E-350

8 cyl 5.0 L Engine +264
8 cyl 5.8 L Engine +353
8 cyl 7.3 L Turbodiesel Engine +1737
8 cyl 7.5 L Engine +494
AM/FM Compact Disc Player +111
Air Conditioning[Std on Chateau] +359
Aluminum/Alloy Wheels[Opt on XLT] +114
Anti-Lock Brakes[Opt on STD,XL] +225
Automatic 4-Speed Transmission +111
Dual Air Conditioning +305
Limited Slip Differential +92
Power Door Locks[Opt on STD,XL] +92
Power Drivers Seat +143
Power Windows[Opt on STD,XL] +120
Privacy Glass[Std on Chateau] +100

ESCORT   1995

A passenger airbag is now available but the motorized seatbelts mysteriously remain. A more powerful, optional air conditioner appears in the revised instrument panel. An integrated child seat is available on sedans and wagons.

Category B

Model Description	Trade-in TMV	Private TMV	Dealer TMV
2 Dr STD Hbk	1653	2088	2814
2 Dr GT Hbk	2094	2645	3564
2 Dr LX Hbk	1801	2275	3065
4 Dr LX Hbk	1836	2319	3125
4 Dr LX Sdn	1902	2402	3237
4 Dr LX Wgn	1983	2506	3376

OPTIONS FOR ESCORT

Air Conditioning +290
Anti-Lock Brakes +148
Automatic 4-Speed Transmission +301
Power Moonroof +157

EXPLORER   1995

Dual airbags top the changes for the redesigned Explorer. Integrated child safety seats are optional on four-door models. Exterior changes include new sheetmetal, headlights, grille, taillights, and side moldings. The Control-Trac four-wheel-drive system automatically sends power to front wheels if it senses rear-wheel slippage. This feature can be locked in for full-time four-wheeling.

Category M

Model Description	Trade-in TMV	Private TMV	Dealer TMV
4 Dr Eddie Bauer 4WD Utility	6710	7741	9460
4 Dr Eddie Bauer Utility	6231	7188	8784
2 Dr Expedition 4WD Utility	5889	6794	8302
4 Dr Limited 4WD Utility	7093	8183	10000
4 Dr Limited Utility	6833	7883	9633
2 Dr Sport 4WD Utility	4862	5609	6854
2 Dr Sport Utility	4439	5121	6258
2 Dr XL 4WD Utility	4793	5529	6757
2 Dr XL Utility	3901	4501	5500
4 Dr XL 4WD Utility	5067	5845	7143
4 Dr XL Utility	4462	5148	6291
4 Dr XLT 4WD Utility	5683	6556	8012
4 Dr XLT Utility	5135	5925	7240

OPTIONS FOR EXPLORER

AM/FM Stereo/CD/Tape +118
Automatic 4-Speed Transmission[Opt on Sport,XL,XLT] +349
Camper/Towing Package +125
Compact Disc Changer +137
Dual Power Seats[Opt on Sport,XLT] +185
JBL Sound System[Std on Limited] +203
Leather Seats[Std on Limited] +231
Limited Slip Differential +114
Overhead Console[Std on Expedition,Limited] +140
Power Drivers Seat[Opt on Sport,XLT] +96
Power Moonroof +295
Power Windows[Opt on XL] +98
Preferred Equipment Package +572
Running Boards[Std on Limited] +146
Side Steps[Opt on Sport,XLT] +109

F-150   1995

Category K

Model Description	Trade-in TMV	Private TMV	Dealer TMV
2 Dr Eddie Bauer 4WD Ext Cab LB	7514	8614	10448
2 Dr Eddie Bauer 4WD Std Cab LB	6750	7738	9386
2 Dr Eddie Bauer Ext Cab LB	6739	7726	9371
2 Dr Eddie Bauer Std Cab LB	5840	6695	8121
2 Dr Eddie Bauer 4WD Ext Cab SB	7490	8587	10415
2 Dr Eddie Bauer 4WD Std Cab SB	6674	7651	9280
2 Dr Eddie Bauer Ext Cab SB			

Model Description	Trade-in TMV	Private TMV	Dealer TMV
	6682	7661	9292
2 Dr Eddie Bauer Std Cab SB	5781	6628	8039
2 Dr Eddie Bauer 4WD Ext Cab Stepside SB	7708	8837	10718
2 Dr Eddie Bauer 4WD Std Cab Stepside SB	7092	8131	9862
2 Dr Eddie Bauer Ext Cab Stepside SB	6945	7963	9658
2 Dr Eddie Bauer Std Cab Stepside SB	5919	6785	8230
2 Dr Lightning Std Cab SB	7639	8758	10623
2 Dr Special 4WD Std Cab LB	5478	6281	7618
2 Dr Special Ext Cab LB	5101	5848	7093
2 Dr Special Std Cab LB	4474	5129	6221
2 Dr Special 4WD Std Cab SB	5426	6221	7545
2 Dr Special Ext Cab SB	4955	5681	6890
2 Dr Special Std Cab SB	4405	5050	6125
2 Dr XL 4WD Ext Cab LB	6331	7259	8804
2 Dr XL 4WD Std Cab LB	5719	6557	7953
2 Dr XL Ext Cab LB	5506	6312	7656
2 Dr XL Std Cab LB	4818	5523	6699
2 Dr XL 4WD Ext Cab SB	6263	7180	8709
2 Dr XL 4WD Std Cab SB	5643	6470	7847
2 Dr XL Ext Cab SB	5368	6155	7465
2 Dr XL Std Cab SB	4749	5444	6603
2 Dr XL 4WD Ext Cab Stepside SB	6538	7496	9092
2 Dr XL 4WD Std Cab Stepside SB	5860	6718	8148
2 Dr XL Ext Cab Stepside SB	5706	6542	7935
2 Dr XL Std Cab Stepside SB	5084	5829	7070
2 Dr XLT 4WD Ext Cab LB	6956	7975	9673
2 Dr XLT 4WD Std Cab LB	6400	7338	8900
2 Dr XLT Ext Cab LB	6194	7101	8613
2 Dr XLT Std Cab LB	5420	6214	7537

Model Description	Trade-in TMV	Private TMV	Dealer TMV
2 Dr XLT 4WD Ext Cab SB	6869	7874	9551
2 Dr XLT 4WD Std Cab SB	6369	7302	8857
2 Dr XLT Ext Cab SB	6125	7022	8517
2 Dr XLT Std Cab SB	5423	6217	7541
2 Dr XLT 4WD Ext Cab Stepside SB	7158	8206	9953
2 Dr XLT 4WD Std Cab Stepside SB	6672	7649	9277
2 Dr XLT Ext Cab Stepside SB	6469	7417	8996
2 Dr XLT Std Cab Stepside SB	5710	6546	7940

OPTIONS FOR F-150
8 cyl 5.0 L Engine +235
8 cyl 5.8 L Engine +405
AM/FM Compact Disc Player +92
AM/FM Stereo Tape[Opt on Special,XL] +96
Air Conditioning[Opt on Special,XL] +297
Aluminum/Alloy Wheels[Opt on XL,XLT] +118
Automatic 4-Speed Transmission +358
Camper/Towing Package +110
Captain Chairs (2) +180
Limited Slip Differential +92
Power Drivers Seat +107
Side Steps +109

F-250 1995

Category K

Model Description	Trade-in TMV	Private TMV	Dealer TMV
2 Dr Special Ext Cab LB	5781	6628	8039
2 Dr XL 4WD Ext Cab LB	7295	8363	10144
2 Dr XL 4WD Std Cab LB	6745	7733	9379
2 Dr XL Ext Cab LB	6331	7259	8804
2 Dr XL Std Cab LB	5093	5839	7082
2 Dr XLT 4WD Ext Cab LB	8328	9547	11580
2 Dr XLT 4WD Std Cab LB	7708	8837	10718
2 Dr XLT Ext Cab LB	7227	8285	10049
2 Dr XLT Std Cab LB	5919	6785	8230

OPTIONS FOR F-250
8 cyl 5.0 L Engine[Opt on XL 2WD Std Cab,XLT 2WD Std Cab] +235
8 cyl 5.8 L Engine[Opt on XL 2WD Std Cab,XLT 2WD Std Cab] +405
8 cyl 7.3 L Turbodiesel Engine +1402
8 cyl 7.5 L Engine +142
AM/FM Compact Disc Player[Opt on XLT] +111
AM/FM Stereo Tape[Opt on Special,XL] +83

Don't forget to refer to the Mileage Adjustment Table at the back of this book!

Model Description	Trade-in TMV	Private TMV	Dealer TMV	Model Description	Trade-in TMV	Private TMV	Dealer TMV
Air Conditioning[Opt on Special,XL] +297				2 Dr GT Cpe	5769	6708	8272
Aluminum/Alloy Wheels[Opt on XL] +141				2 Dr GTS Cpe	5187	6031	7437
Automatic 4-Speed Transmission[Opt on XL,XLT] +358							
Camper/Towing Package +110							
Captain Chairs (2) +181							
Limited Slip Differential +92							
Power Drivers Seat +107							
Side Steps +109							

OPTIONS FOR MUSTANG
AM/FM Compact Disc Player +109
AM/FM Stereo/CD/Tape +146
Air Conditioning +330
Aluminum/Alloy Wheels[Opt on STD] +98
Anti-Lock Brakes[Std on Cobra] +185
Automatic 4-Speed Transmission +301
Compact Disc Changer +166
Leather Seats[Opt on GT] +221

F-350   1995

Category K

Model Description	Trade-in TMV	Private TMV	Dealer TMV
2 Dr XL 4WD Std Cab LB	7295	8363	10144
2 Dr XL Ext Cab LB	7386	8467	10270
2 Dr XL Std Cab LB	6538	7496	9092
4 Dr XL 4WD Crew Cab LB	8603	9863	11963
4 Dr XL Crew Cab LB	7355	8432	10227
2 Dr XLT 4WD Std Cab LB	8328	9547	11580
2 Dr XLT Ext Cab LB	8190	9389	11388
2 Dr XLT Std Cab LB	7353	8429	10224
4 Dr XLT 4WD Crew Cab LB	9635	11046	13398
4 Dr XLT Crew Cab LB	8396	9626	11675

OPTIONS FOR F-350
8 cyl 7.3 L Turbodiesel Engine +1402
8 cyl 7.5 L Engine +142
AM/FM Compact Disc Player[Opt on XLT] +111
AM/FM Stereo Tape[Opt on XL] +83
Air Conditioning[Opt on XL] +295
Automatic 4-Speed Transmission +358
Camper/Towing Package +109
Captain Chairs (2) +92
Dual Rear Wheels +214
Electric Sunroof +295
Limited Slip Differential +92
Power Drivers Seat +107
Side Steps +109

MUSTANG   1995

A power driver's seat moves from the standard equipment list to the options list. A powerful new stereo with a CD changer also debuts on the options list.

Category E

Model Description	Trade-in TMV	Private TMV	Dealer TMV
2 Dr STD Conv	6756	7855	9687
2 Dr STD Cpe	4472	5200	6413
2 Dr Cobra Conv	9334	10853	13384
2 Dr Cobra Cpe	7131	8291	10225
2 Dr Cobra R Cpe	10890	12662	15615
2 Dr GT Conv	7325	8517	10503

PROBE   1995

The SE Package becomes a trim level. Base and GT models receive new taillights. GTs receive 16-inch directional wheels. The rear-window wiper washer, four-way seat height adjuster and graphic equalizer have been deleted from the option list.

Category E

Model Description	Trade-in TMV	Private TMV	Dealer TMV
2 Dr STD Hbk	2658	3090	3811
2 Dr GT Hbk	2909	3382	4171
2 Dr SE Hbk	3047	3543	4369

OPTIONS FOR PROBE
AM/FM Compact Disc Player +159
AM/FM Stereo/CD/Tape +203
Air Conditioning[Std on SE] +330
Aluminum/Alloy Wheels +173
Anti-Lock Brakes +210
Automatic 4-Speed Transmission +301
Chrome Wheels +144
Leather Seats +185
Power Drivers Seat +107
Power Sunroof +227

RANGER   1995

A driver airbag and optional four-wheel antilock brakes are two of the features added to the safety equipment roster of the capable Ford Ranger. SuperCab models can now be had with a power driver's seat.

Category J

Model Description	Trade-in TMV	Private TMV	Dealer TMV
2 Dr STX 4WD Std Cab LB	5411	6260	7677
2 Dr STX 4WD Ext Cab SB	5478	6338	7772
2 Dr STX 4WD Std Cab SB	5210	6029	7393
2 Dr Splash 4WD Ext Cab Stepside SB	5812	6725	8246
2 Dr Splash 4WD Std Cab Stepside SB	5541	6411	7862
2 Dr Splash Ext Cab Stepside SB	4408	5101	6255
2 Dr Splash Std Cab Stepside SB			

Don't forget to refer to the Mileage Adjustment Table at the back of this book!

Model Description	Trade-in TMV	Private TMV	Dealer TMV		Model Description	Trade-in TMV	Private TMV	Dealer TMV
	3881	4490	5506		Power Drivers Seat[Opt on GL] +125			
2 Dr XL 4WD Std Cab LB					Power Moonroof +273			
	4742	5487	6729		Power Passenger Seat +102			
2 Dr XL Std Cab LB	3006	3478	4265		Power Windows[Opt on GL] +98			
2 Dr XL 4WD Ext Cab SB					Rear Window Wiper +94			

Model Description	Trade-in TMV	Private TMV	Dealer TMV
	5103	5904	7240
2 Dr XL 4WD Std Cab SB			
	4475	5178	6350
2 Dr XL Ext Cab SB	3674	4251	5213
2 Dr XL Std Cab SB	2939	3401	4170
2 Dr XLT 4WD Std Cab LB			
	5277	6106	7487
2 Dr XLT Std Cab LB	3607	4174	5118
2 Dr XLT 4WD Ext Cab SB			
	5547	6419	7871
2 Dr XLT 4WD Std Cab SB			
	5050	5844	7166
2 Dr XLT Ext Cab SB	3868	4475	5488
2 Dr XLT Std Cab SB	3407	3942	4834
2 Dr XLT Std Cab Stepside SB			
	3540	4096	5023

OPTIONS FOR RANGER

6 cyl 3.0 L Engine +166
AM/FM Compact Disc Player +107
Air Conditioning +297
Anti-Lock Brakes[Opt on XL,XLT] +111
Automatic 4-Speed Transmission +386
Bucket Seats +133
Compact Disc Changer +166
Limited Slip Differential +98
Sport Seats +133

TAURUS   1995

Sport edition model is introduced as an SE. The SE includes aluminum wheels, sport bucket seats, air conditioning, and a rear defroster. The base engine has been revised to decrease engine noise.

Category D

	Trade-in	Private	Dealer
4 Dr GL Sdn	2374	2846	3633
4 Dr GL Wgn	2483	2977	3800
4 Dr LX Sdn	2519	3021	3856
4 Dr LX Wgn	2739	3284	4192
4 Dr SE Sdn	2471	2963	3782
4 Dr SHO Sdn	3469	4159	5309

OPTIONS FOR TAURUS

6 cyl 3.0 L Flex Fuel Engine +419
6 cyl 3.8 L Engine +205
AM/FM Stereo/CD/Tape +203
Aluminum/Alloy Wheels[Opt on GL] +116
Anti-Lock Brakes[Std on SHO] +210
Automatic 4-Speed Transmission[Opt on SHO] +240
JBL Sound System +185
Leather Seats +221

THUNDERBIRD   1995

The trunk-mounted CD changer is deleted in favor of an in-dash CD-player. Variable-assist power steering is lost from the standard equipment list.

Category D

	Trade-in	Private	Dealer
2 Dr LX Cpe	2800	3357	4285

Category E

	Trade-in	Private	Dealer
2 Dr SC Sprchgd Cpe	5316	6181	7622

OPTIONS FOR THUNDERBIRD

8 cyl 4.6 L Engine +417
AM/FM Compact Disc Player +159
Anti-Lock Brakes[Opt on LX] +210
Automatic 4-Speed Transmission[Opt on SC] +240
Leather Seats[Opt on LX] +181
Power Moonroof +273

WINDSTAR   1995

This year, Ford introduces its version of the front-wheel-drive minivan. Designed to replace the archaic Aerostar, the Windstar offers a wealth of standard equipment. Dual airbags, antilock brakes, a four-speed automatic transmission and V6 power are just a few of the features included in the base price. The Windstar seats seven and has an integrated child seat: an attractive feature for the family with toddlers.

Category P

	Trade-in	Private	Dealer
2 Dr STD Cargo Van	3298	3834	4727
1995.5 2 Dr STD Cargo Van	3492	4059	5005
2 Dr GL Pass. Van	3622	4210	5191
1995.5 2 Dr GL Pass. Van	3816	4436	5469
2 Dr LX Pass. Van	4139	4811	5932
1995.5 2 Dr LX Pass. Van	4527	5262	6488

OPTIONS FOR WINDSTAR

6 cyl 3.8 L Engine[Opt on Cargo] +253
Air Conditioning[Std on LX] +316
Air Conditioning[Std on LX] +316
Aluminum/Alloy Wheels[Opt on GL] +153
Aluminum/Alloy Wheels[Opt on GL] +153
Automatic Load Leveling[Opt on Cargo,LX] +107
Bucket Seats[Opt on LX,Cargo] +181
Bucket Seats[Opt on Cargo] +181
Camper/Towing Package[Std on LX] +129
Camper/Towing Package[Std on LX] +129
Captain Chairs (4) +221
Captain Chairs (4) +221
Compact Disc Changer +148
Dual Air Conditioning +175
Dual Air Conditioning +175
JBL Sound System +188

Model Description	Trade-in TMV	Private TMV	Dealer TMV	Model Description	Trade-in TMV	Private TMV	Dealer TMV
JBL Sound System +188				2 Dr XLT AWD Pass. Van Ext			
Leather Seats +319					2617	3144	4022
Leather Seats +319				2 Dr XLT Pass. Van	2429	2918	3733
Power Windows +102				2 Dr XLT Pass. Van Ext			
Power Windows +102					2485	2985	3819
Premium Sound System +203							
Privacy Glass +153							
Privacy Glass +153							

OPTIONS FOR AEROSTAR
6 cyl 4.0 L Engine +94
7 Passenger Seating[Opt on XL] +89
AM/FM Stereo Tape +108
Air Conditioning[Std on XLT] +272
Aluminum/Alloy Wheels +114
Automatic 4-Speed Transmission[Std on Eddie Bauer,XLT,4WD] +204
Camper/Towing Package +88
Captain Chairs (4) +210
Child Seats (2) +79
Dual Air Conditioning[Std on Eddie Bauer] +272
Leather Seats +219
Limited Slip Differential +79
Privacy Glass +130

1994 FORD

AEROSTAR 1994

A high-mounted rear brake light is standard. No other changes to Ford's venerable minivan.

Category P

Model Description	Trade-in TMV	Private TMV	Dealer TMV
2 Dr STD AWD Cargo Van			
	2119	2545	3256
2 Dr STD AWD Cargo Van Ext			
	2289	2749	3517
2 Dr STD Cargo Van	1818	2184	2794
2 Dr STD Cargo Van Ext			
	1877	2254	2884
2 Dr Eddie Bauer AWD Pass. Van			
	2846	3418	4373
2 Dr Eddie Bauer AWD Pass. Van Ext			
	3027	3636	4652
2 Dr Eddie Bauer Pass. Van			
	2633	3163	4046
2 Dr Eddie Bauer Pass. Van Ext			
	2725	3273	4187
2 Dr Window AWD Cargo Van			
	2240	2691	3442
2 Dr Window AWD Cargo Van Ext			
	2306	2770	3544
2 Dr Window Cargo Van	1971	2368	3029
2 Dr Window Cargo Van Ext			
	2004	2407	3079
2 Dr XL AWD Pass. Van	2307	2772	3546
2 Dr XL AWD Pass. Van Ext			
	2378	2856	3654
2 Dr XL Pass. Van	1814	2179	2788
2 Dr XL Pass. Van Ext	2019	2426	3103
2 Dr XL Plus AWD Pass. Van			
	2412	2898	3707
2 Dr XL Plus AWD Pass. Van Ext			
	2482	2981	3814
2 Dr XL Plus Pass. Van			
	2058	2473	3163
2 Dr XL Plus Pass. Van Ext			
	2179	2618	3349
2 Dr XLT AWD Pass. Van			
	2559	3074	3933

ASPIRE 1994

Ford introduces the Aspire as a replacement for the aging Festiva. This little econobox has a 1.3-liter inline-four that produces a measly 63 horsepower. The Aspire is available with a five-speed manual or a three-speed automatic transmission.

Category A

Model Description	Trade-in TMV	Private TMV	Dealer TMV
2 Dr STD Hbk	865	1141	1601
4 Dr STD Hbk	966	1274	1788
2 Dr SE Hbk	968	1276	1791

OPTIONS FOR ASPIRE
AM/FM Stereo Tape +146
Air Conditioning +258
Anti-Lock Brakes +179
Automatic 3-Speed Transmission +207

BRONCO 1994

The 1994 Bronco receives a driver airbag and door guard beams. ABS now works in two-wheel drive and four-wheel drive.

Category N

Model Description	Trade-in TMV	Private TMV	Dealer TMV
2 Dr Eddie Bauer 4WD Utility			
	6770	7897	9774
2 Dr XL 4WD Utility	5697	6645	8225
2 Dr XLT 4WD Utility	6033	7036	8709

OPTIONS FOR BRONCO
AM/FM Compact Disc Player +137
Air Conditioning[Opt on XL,XLT] +246
Automatic 4-Speed Transmission[Opt on XL,XLT] +290
Camper/Towing Package +113
Chrome Wheels +125
Leather Seats +219

Model Description	Trade-in TMV	Private TMV	Dealer TMV

CROWN VICTORIA 1994

A passenger airbag is now standard. Air conditioning gets CFC-free refrigerant.

Category G

Model	Trade-in	Private	Dealer
4 Dr STD Sdn	2535	3067	3953
4 Dr LX Sdn	2654	3210	4138
4 Dr S Sdn	2531	3061	3946

OPTIONS FOR CROWN VICTORIA
Aluminum/Alloy Wheels +133
Anti-Lock Brakes +155
JBL Sound System +172
Leather Seats +202
Power Drivers Seat[Std on LX] +113
Preferred Equipment Package +486

E-150 1994

Category Q

Model	Trade-in	Private	Dealer
2 Dr STD Econoline	3465	4081	5106
2 Dr Chateau Club Wagon	5100	6006	7515
2 Dr XL Club Wagon	3923	4620	5781
2 Dr XL Econoline	3727	4389	5492
2 Dr XLT Club Wagon	4642	5466	6840

OPTIONS FOR E-150
8 cyl 5.0 L Engine +199
8 cyl 5.8 L Engine +268
AM/FM Compact Disc Player +93
AM/FM Stereo Tape[Std on Chateau] +94
Air Conditioning[Opt on STD,XL] +258
Aluminum/Alloy Wheels[Opt on STD,XL] +97
Anti-Lock Brakes[Opt on STD,XL] +191
Automatic 4-Speed Transmission[Opt on STD,XL] +93
Captain Chairs (4)[Opt on XLT] +169
Dual Air Conditioning[Std on Chateau] +258
Limited Slip Differential +79
Power Door Locks[Opt on STD,XL] +79
Power Drivers Seat +113
Power Windows[Opt on STD,XL] +103

E-250 1994

Category Q

Model	Trade-in	Private	Dealer
2 Dr STD Econoline	3661	4311	5395
2 Dr STD Econoline Ext	3792	4466	5588
2 Dr XL Econoline	3857	4542	5684

OPTIONS FOR E-250
8 cyl 5.8 L Engine +268
AM/FM Compact Disc Player +93
Air Conditioning +305
Aluminum/Alloy Wheels +97
Anti-Lock Brakes +191
Automatic 4-Speed Transmission +93
Dual Air Conditioning +259
Power Drivers Seat +121

Power Windows +103
Privacy Glass +84

E-350 1994

Category Q

Model	Trade-in	Private	Dealer
2 Dr STD Econoline	3923	4620	5781
2 Dr STD Econoline Ext	4119	4851	6070
2 Dr Chateau Club Wagon	5492	6468	8093
2 Dr XL Club Wagon	4773	5620	7033
2 Dr XL Club Wagon Ext	4773	5620	7033
2 Dr XL Econoline	4250	5004	6262
2 Dr XLT Club Wagon	4969	5851	7322
2 Dr XLT Club Wagon Ext	4969	5851	7322

OPTIONS FOR E-350
8 cyl 5.0 L Engine[Opt on XL] +225
8 cyl 5.8 L Engine +300
8 cyl 7.3 L Diesel Engine +1035
8 cyl 7.5 L Engine +421
AM/FM Compact Disc Player +93
Air Conditioning[Opt on STD,XL] +305
Aluminum/Alloy Wheels[Opt on STD,XL] +97
Anti-Lock Brakes[Opt on STD,XL] +191
Automatic 4-Speed Transmission[Std on Chateau] +93
Dual Air Conditioning[Std on Chateau] +258

ESCORT 1994

A driver airbag debuts on all models. Antilock brakes are now available on the GT. The LX-E sedan is dropped from the lineup.

Category B

Model	Trade-in	Private	Dealer
2 Dr STD Hbk	1384	1783	2449
2 Dr GT Hbk	1863	2400	3296
2 Dr LX Hbk	1528	1968	2703
4 Dr LX Hbk	1559	2009	2759
4 Dr LX Sdn	1596	2057	2825
4 Dr LX Wgn	1650	2126	2920

OPTIONS FOR ESCORT
Air Conditioning +246
Anti-Lock Brakes +125
Automatic 4-Speed Transmission +256
Power Moonroof +133

EXPLORER 1994

New wheels and a power equipment group for the Eddie Bauer model are the only changes to this year's Explorer.

Category M

Model	Trade-in	Private	Dealer
2 Dr Eddie Bauer 4WD Utility	4263	5038	6328
2 Dr Eddie Bauer Utility			

Don't forget to refer to the Mileage Adjustment Table at the back of this book!

Model Description	Trade-in TMV	Private TMV	Dealer TMV
	4005	4732	5944
4 Dr Eddie Bauer 4WD Utility	4715	5572	6999
4 Dr Eddie Bauer Utility	4392	5190	6519
4 Dr Limited 4WD Utility	5390	6369	8000
4 Dr Limited Utility	4716	5573	7000
2 Dr Sport 4WD Utility	3811	4503	5656
2 Dr Sport Utility	3431	4054	5092
2 Dr XL 4WD Utility	3553	4198	5273
2 Dr XL Utility	2695	3184	4000
4 Dr XL 4WD Utility	3747	4427	5561
4 Dr XL Utility	3416	4037	5071
4 Dr XLT 4WD Utility	4199	4961	6232
4 Dr XLT Utility	3940	4655	5848

OPTIONS FOR EXPLORER
AM/FM Stereo/CD/Tape[Opt on Limited] +101
Air Conditioning[Std on Limited] +236
Automatic 4-Speed Transmission[Std on Limited] +296
Camper/Towing Package +107
Compact Disc Changer +116
Dual Power Seats[Opt on XLT] +157
JBL Sound System +172
JBL Sound System w/CD +172
Leather Seats[Std on Limited] +196
Running Boards +124
Sunroof +125

F-150   1994

Category K

Model Description	Trade-in TMV	Private TMV	Dealer TMV
2 Dr Lightning Std Cab SB	6064	7074	8757
2 Dr S 4WD Std Cab LB	4478	5224	6467
2 Dr S Ext Cab LB	4021	4690	5806
2 Dr S Std Cab LB	3494	4075	5045
2 Dr S 4WD Std Cab SB	4401	5134	6355
2 Dr S Ext Cab SB	3962	4622	5722
2 Dr S Std Cab SB	3361	3921	4854
2 Dr XL 4WD Ext Cab LB	5075	5920	7329
2 Dr XL 4WD Std Cab LB	4746	5536	6853
2 Dr XL Ext Cab LB	4431	5169	6399
2 Dr XL Std Cab LB	3947	4604	5699
2 Dr XL 4WD Ext Cab SB	5007	5840	7230
2 Dr XL 4WD Std Cab SB	4614	5382	6663
2 Dr XL Ext Cab SB	4350	5075	6282
2 Dr XL Std Cab SB	3823	4459	5520
2 Dr XL 4WD Ext Cab Stepside SB	5207	6074	7519
2 Dr XL 4WD Std Cab Stepside SB	4877	5689	7043
2 Dr XL Ext Cab Stepside SB	4547	5304	6566
2 Dr XL Std Cab Stepside SB	4086	4767	5901
2 Dr XLT 4WD Ext Cab LB	5681	6627	8204
2 Dr XLT 4WD Std Cab LB	5661	6604	8175
2 Dr XLT Ext Cab LB	5012	5846	7237
2 Dr XLT Std Cab LB	4548	5306	6568
2 Dr XLT 4WD Ext Cab SB	5663	6605	8177
2 Dr XLT 4WD Std Cab SB	5138	5994	7420
2 Dr XLT Ext Cab SB	4943	5766	7138
2 Dr XLT Std Cab SB	4485	5232	6477
2 Dr XLT 4WD Ext Cab Stepside SB	5866	6843	8471
2 Dr XLT 4WD Std Cab Stepside SB	5405	6305	7805
2 Dr XLT Ext Cab Stepside SB	5144	6000	7428
2 Dr XLT Std Cab Stepside SB	4811	5613	6948

OPTIONS FOR F-150
8 cyl 5.0 L Engine +199
8 cyl 5.8 L Engine +344
Air Conditioning[Opt on S,XL] +252
Aluminum/Alloy Wheels +101
Automatic 4-Speed Transmission +305
Camper/Towing Package +93
Captain Chairs (2) +153
Limited Slip Differential +79
Power Drivers Seat +91

F-250   1994

Category K

Model Description	Trade-in TMV	Private TMV	Dealer TMV
2 Dr S Ext Cab LB	4943	5766	7138
2 Dr XL 4WD Ext Cab LB	5933	6921	8567
2 Dr XL 4WD Std Cab LB	5537	6458	7995
2 Dr XL Ext Cab LB	5207	6074	7519
2 Dr XL Std Cab LB	4284	4998	6187
2 Dr XLT 4WD Ext Cab LB	6657	7765	9613
2 Dr XLT 4WD Std Cab LB	6196	7227	8947
2 Dr XLT Ext Cab LB	5998	6996	8661
2 Dr XLT Std Cab LB	5141	5997	7424

Don't forget to refer to the Mileage Adjustment Table at the back of this book!

OPTIONS FOR F-250

8 cyl 5.0 L Engine[Opt on XL 2WD Std Cab,XLT 2WD Std Cab] +199
8 cyl 5.8 L Engine[Opt on XL 2WD Std Cab,XLT 2WD Std Cab] +344
8 cyl 7.3 L Diesel Engine +864
8 cyl 7.3 L Turbodiesel Engine +1192
8 cyl 7.5 L Engine +121
AM/FM Compact Disc Player +94
Air Conditioning[Opt on S,XL] +252
Automatic 4-Speed Transmission +305
Camper/Towing Package +93
Captain Chairs (2) +154
Limited Slip Differential +79
Power Drivers Seat +91

F-350   1994

Category K

Model Description	Trade-in TMV	Private TMV	Dealer TMV
2 Dr XL 4WD Std Cab LB	6130	7151	8852
2 Dr XL Ext Cab LB	6262	7304	9042
2 Dr XL Std Cab LB	5537	6458	7995
4 Dr XL 4WD Crew Cab LB	7117	8302	10277
4 Dr XL Crew Cab LB	6064	7074	8757
2 Dr XLT 4WD Std Cab LB	6855	7997	9899
2 Dr XLT Ext Cab LB	7120	8305	10281
2 Dr XLT Std Cab LB	6327	7381	9137
4 Dr XLT 4WD Crew Cab LB	7910	9227	11422
4 Dr XLT Crew Cab LB	6921	8073	9994

OPTIONS FOR F-350

8 cyl 7.3 L Diesel Engine +891
8 cyl 7.3 L Turbodiesel Engine +1192
8 cyl 7.5 L Engine +121
AM/FM Compact Disc Player +93
Air Conditioning[Opt on XL] +251
Automatic 4-Speed Transmission +305
Camper/Towing Package +92
Captain Chairs (2) +79
Dual Rear Wheels +182
Limited Slip Differential +79
Power Drivers Seat +91

MUSTANG   1994

New sheetmetal for the venerable pony. The LX model and hatchback are dropped. The base Mustang gets a 3.8-liter V6, and GT models receive a boost in horsepower. Four-wheel disc brakes are standard on both Mustangs and ABS finally becomes an available option. A passenger airbag, power driver's seat, and tilt steering wheel become standard in 1994. Convertibles are available with a removable hardtop.

Category E

Model Description	Trade-in TMV	Private TMV	Dealer TMV
2 Dr STD Conv	4774	5772	7435
2 Dr STD Cpe	3342	4041	5205
2 Dr Cobra Conv	7520	9092	11711
2 Dr Cobra Cpe	5908	7143	9201
2 Dr GT Conv	6088	7360	9480
2 Dr GT Cpe	4417	5340	6878

OPTIONS FOR MUSTANG

AM/FM Stereo/CD/Tape +124
Air Conditioning +281
Anti-Lock Brakes[Std on Cobra] +157
Automatic 4-Speed Transmission +256
Compact Disc Changer +142
Leather Seats[Opt on GT,STD,Cpe] +189
Special Wheels +125

PROBE   1994

Dual airbags are now standard on all Probes. A Sport Appearance Package is available for base models.

Category E

Model Description	Trade-in TMV	Private TMV	Dealer TMV
2 Dr STD Hbk	2029	2453	3160
2 Dr GT Hbk	2626	3174	4089
2 Dr SE Hbk	2149	2598	3346

OPTIONS FOR PROBE

AM/FM Compact Disc Player +135
Air Conditioning +281
Aluminum/Alloy Wheels +148
Anti-Lock Brakes +179
Automatic 4-Speed Transmission +256
Leather Seats +157
Power Sunroof +193

RANGER   1994

Side-impact door beams are installed on the Ranger to protect occupants. The Splash model is now available as a SuperCab. Look out, the Splash 2WD holds the road better than most sport coupes.

Category J

Model Description	Trade-in TMV	Private TMV	Dealer TMV
2 Dr STX 4WD Std Cab LB	4592	5477	6953
2 Dr STX Std Cab LB	3322	3962	5030
2 Dr STX 4WD Ext Cab SB	4667	5567	7067
2 Dr STX 4WD Std Cab SB	4340	5177	6572
2 Dr STX Ext Cab SB	3525	4205	5338
2 Dr STX Std Cab SB	3145	3751	4762
2 Dr Splash 4WD Ext Cab Stepside SB	4969	5927	7524
2 Dr Splash 4WD Std Cab Stepside SB	4642	5537	7029
2 Dr Splash Ext Cab Stepside SB	3781	4511	5726

Don't forget to refer to the Mileage Adjustment Table at the back of this book!

Model Description	Trade-in TMV	Private TMV	Dealer TMV
2 Dr Splash Std Cab Stepside SB			
	3345	3991	5066
2 Dr XL 4WD Std Cab LB			
	3766	4492	5703
2 Dr XL Std Cab LB	2641	3151	4000
2 Dr XL 4WD Ext Cab SB			
	4087	4875	6189
2 Dr XL 4WD Std Cab SB			
	3520	4199	5330
2 Dr XL Ext Cab SB	3082	3676	4667
2 Dr XL Std Cab SB	2579	3076	3905
2 Dr XLT 4WD Std Cab LB			
	4277	5102	6477
2 Dr XLT Std Cab LB	3019	3601	4572
2 Dr XLT 4WD Ext Cab SB			
	4465	5327	6762
2 Dr XLT 4WD Std Cab SB			
	4090	4878	6193
2 Dr XLT Ext Cab SB	3208	3827	4858
2 Dr XLT Std Cab SB	2893	3451	4381

OPTIONS FOR RANGER
6 cyl 3.0 L Engine +142
60/40 Bench Seat +210
Air Conditioning +252
Automatic 4-Speed Transmission +327
Bucket Seats +113
Sport Seats +113

TAURUS   1994

The passenger airbag is finally a standard equipment item. GL models receive 15-inch wheels and all Tauruses get a new steering wheel. Cellular phones are a new option.

Category D

Model Description	Trade-in TMV	Private TMV	Dealer TMV
4 Dr GL Sdn	1704	2114	2798
4 Dr GL Wgn	1874	2326	3078
4 Dr LX Sdn	2045	2537	3358
4 Dr LX Wgn	2102	2608	3451
4 Dr SHO Sdn	2499	3101	4104

OPTIONS FOR TAURUS
6 cyl 3.8 L Engine[Opt on GL,LX] +174
AM/FM Stereo/CD/Tape +172
Air Conditioning[Std on LX,SHO] +236
Anti-Lock Brakes[Std on SHO] +179
Automatic 4-Speed Transmission[Opt on SHO] +204
JBL Sound System +157
Leather Seats[Std on SHO] +189
Power Drivers Seat[Opt on GL,LX] +107
Power Moonroof +232

TEMPO   1994

CFC-free air conditioning refrigerant and redesigned seatbelts are the only changes this year. The Tempo is mercifully retired after this model year in favor of the new Contour.

Category B

Model Description	Trade-in TMV	Private TMV	Dealer TMV
2 Dr GL Sdn	1224	1577	2166
4 Dr GL Sdn	1224	1577	2166
4 Dr LX Sdn	1330	1714	2354

OPTIONS FOR TEMPO
6 cyl 3.0 L Engine +215
Air Bag Restraint +125
Air Conditioning +219
Automatic 3-Speed Transmission +172

THUNDERBIRD   1994

Dual airbags make their first appearance on the Thunderbird. An optional 4.6-liter V8 replaces last year's 5.0-liter V8. Dual cupholders complement the center console and the airbags are housed in a restyled dashboard.

Category D

Model Description	Trade-in TMV	Private TMV	Dealer TMV
2 Dr LX Cpe	2158	2678	3544
Category E			
2 Dr SC Sprchgd Cpe	4238	5123	6599

OPTIONS FOR THUNDERBIRD
8 cyl 4.6 L Engine +355
Anti-Lock Brakes[Opt on LX] +179
Automatic 4-Speed Transmission[Opt on SC] +204
Compact Disc Changer +189
JBL Sound System +172
Leather Seats +154
Power Moonroof +232

1993 FORD

AEROSTAR   1993

An integrated child seat is introduced as an option.

Category P

Model Description	Trade-in TMV	Private TMV	Dealer TMV
2 Dr STD AWD Cargo Van			
	1605	2012	2690
2 Dr STD AWD Cargo Van Ext			
	1667	2090	2794
2 Dr STD Cargo Van	1390	1742	2329
2 Dr STD Cargo Van Ext			
	1537	1927	2576
2 Dr Eddie Bauer AWD Pass. Van			
	2168	2717	3633
2 Dr Eddie Bauer AWD Pass. Van Ext			
	2279	2856	3819
2 Dr Eddie Bauer Pass. Van			
	2056	2577	3446
2 Dr Eddie Bauer Pass. Van Ext			
	2112	2647	3539

Don't forget to refer to the Mileage Adjustment Table at the back of this book!

Model Description	Trade-in TMV	Private TMV	Dealer TMV
2 Dr Window AWD Cargo Van			
	1619	2029	2713
2 Dr Window Cargo Van	1501	1881	2515
2 Dr XL AWD Pass. Van	1723	2159	2887
2 Dr XL AWD Pass. Van Ext			
	1770	2218	2966
2 Dr XL Pass. Van	1430	1793	2397
2 Dr XL Pass. Van Ext	1554	1948	2604
2 Dr XL Plus AWD Pass. Van			
	1787	2240	2995
2 Dr XL Plus Pass. Van			
	1559	1954	2612
2 Dr XL Plus Pass. Van Ext			
	1611	2020	2700
2 Dr XLT AWD Pass. Van Ext			
	1988	2491	3331
2 Dr XLT Pass. Van	1908	2392	3198
2 Dr XLT Pass. Van Ext			
	1930	2420	3235
2 Dr XLT Plus AWD Pass. Van			
	1955	2450	3276
2 Dr XLT Plus Pass. Van			
	1890	2369	3167

OPTIONS FOR AEROSTAR

Air Conditioning[Std on XLT,XLT Plus,Eddie Bauer] +246
Automatic 4-Speed Transmission[Std on Eddie Bauer,XLT,XLT Plus,4WD] +185
Captain Chairs (4)[Opt on XL,XL Plus,XLT,XLT Plus,Pass. Van Ext] +190
Dual Air Conditioning[Std on Eddie Bauer] +246
Leather Seats +198
Privacy Glass[Std on Eddie Bauer] +117

BRONCO　　　　　　　　1993

Four-wheel antilock brakes introduced on the 1993 Bronco.

Category N

Model Description	Trade-in TMV	Private TMV	Dealer TMV
2 Dr STD 4WD Utility	4198	5016	6380
2 Dr Eddie Bauer 4WD Utility			
	4962	5929	7540
2 Dr XLT 4WD Utility	4453	5321	6767

OPTIONS FOR BRONCO

Air Conditioning[Opt on STD,XLT] +222
Automatic 4-Speed Transmission[Opt on STD,XLT] +262
Leather Seats +197
Styled Steel Wheels +88

CROWN VICTORIA　　　1993

The touring sedan is no longer available. Front-end styling changes include the addition of a grille. Cupholders finally appear in the dashboard. An express-down feature shows up for the driver's side window. An electronic overdrive lock-out debuts on the automatic transmission and a traction control system is available with the antilock brakes option. A 10-disc CD changer and an auto-dimming mirror are new options.

Category G

Model Description	Trade-in TMV	Private TMV	Dealer TMV
4 Dr STD Sdn	1934	2411	3207
4 Dr LX Sdn	2104	2624	3490

OPTIONS FOR CROWN VICTORIA

Aluminum/Alloy Wheels +120
Anti-Lock Brakes +140
Compact Disc Changer +99
Dual Air Bag Restraints +135
Dual Power Seats +167
JBL Sound System +156
Leather Seats +183
Power Drivers Seat +102
Premium Sound System +102

E-150　　　　　　　　　1993

Category Q

Model Description	Trade-in TMV	Private TMV	Dealer TMV
2 Dr STD Econoline	2846	3442	4436
2 Dr Chateau Club Wagon			
	4517	5463	7040
2 Dr Custom Club Wagon			
	3218	3892	5015
2 Dr XL Econoline	3094	3742	4822
2 Dr XLT Club Wagon	3775	4565	5883
2 Dr XLT Super Club Wagon Ext			
	3898	4715	6076

OPTIONS FOR E-150

7 Passenger Seating[Opt on XLT] +189
8 cyl 5.0 L Engine +181
8 cyl 5.8 L Engine +243
8 cyl 7.3 L Diesel Engine +934
8 cyl 7.5 L Engine +380
Air Conditioning[Std on Chateau] +234
Captain Chairs (4)[Opt on XLT] +153
Dual Air Conditioning[Std on Chateau] +234

E-250　　　　　　　　　1993

Category Q

Model Description	Trade-in TMV	Private TMV	Dealer TMV
2 Dr STD Econoline	2846	3442	4436
2 Dr STD Econoline Ext			
	2846	3442	4436
2 Dr XL Econoline	3155	3816	4918
2 Dr XL Econoline Ext	3279	3966	5111

OPTIONS FOR E-250

8 cyl 5.8 L Engine +243
Air Conditioning +276
Dual Air Conditioning +234
Power Drivers Seat +110

E-350　　　　　　　　　1993

Category Q

Model Description	Trade-in TMV	Private TMV	Dealer TMV
2 Dr STD Econoline	3155	3816	4918

Model Description	Trade-in TMV	Private TMV	Dealer TMV
2 Dr STD Econoline Ext			
	3094	3742	4822
2 Dr Custom Club Wagon			
	3338	4038	5203
2 Dr Custom Super Club Wagon Ext			
	3775	4565	5883
2 Dr XL Econoline	3347	4048	5217
2 Dr XL Econoline Ext	3338	4038	5203
2 Dr XLT Super Club Wagon Ext			
	3898	4715	6076

OPTIONS FOR E-350

8 cyl 5.8 L Engine +271
8 cyl 7.3 L Diesel Engine +934
8 cyl 7.5 L Engine +380
Air Conditioning +276
Automatic 4-Speed Transmission +84
Dual Air Conditioning +234
Power Drivers Seat +110
Power Windows +93

ESCORT   1993

Minor styling changes to all trim-levels include new taillights and grille. GT models receive a new spoiler and wheels. The LX models receive body-color spoilers.

Category B

Model Description	Trade-in TMV	Private TMV	Dealer TMV
2 Dr STD Hbk	994	1366	1986
2 Dr GT Hbk	1371	1884	2739
2 Dr LX Hbk	1137	1562	2270
4 Dr LX Hbk	1177	1617	2351
4 Dr LX Sdn	1191	1637	2379
4 Dr LX Wgn	1231	1692	2459
4 Dr LX-E Sdn	1375	1890	2747

OPTIONS FOR ESCORT

Air Conditioning +222
Automatic 4-Speed Transmission +231
Power Moonroof +120

EXPLORER   1993

A new steering wheel and instrument panel freshen the Explorer's interior. New wheels are the only exterior changes. Explorers gain four-wheel antilock brakes that work in both two- and four-wheel-drive modes.

Category M

Model Description	Trade-in TMV	Private TMV	Dealer TMV
2 Dr Eddie Bauer 4WD Utility			
	3394	4169	5461
2 Dr Eddie Bauer Utility			
	3096	3803	4982
4 Dr Eddie Bauer 4WD Utility			
	3573	4389	5749
4 Dr Eddie Bauer Utility			
	3275	4023	5270

Model Description	Trade-in TMV	Private TMV	Dealer TMV
4 Dr Limited 4WD Utility			
	3729	4581	6000
4 Dr Limited Utility	3646	4478	5866
2 Dr Sport 4WD Utility			
	2859	3513	4601
2 Dr Sport Utility	2664	3273	4287
2 Dr XL 4WD Utility	2721	3343	4379
2 Dr XL Utility	2441	2999	3928
4 Dr XL 4WD Utility	2741	3367	4411
4 Dr XL Utility	2654	3260	4270
4 Dr XLT 4WD Utility	3216	3950	5174
4 Dr XLT Utility	2918	3584	4695

OPTIONS FOR EXPLORER

Air Conditioning[Std on Limited] +213
Automatic 4-Speed Transmission[Std on Limited] +268
Camper/Towing Package +96
Dual Power Seats[Opt on XLT] +141
JBL Sound System +156
Leather Seats[Std on Limited] +177
Limited Slip Differential +88
Running Boards +112
Sunroof +114

F-150   1993

Category K

Model Description	Trade-in TMV	Private TMV	Dealer TMV
2 Dr Lightning Std Cab SB			
	4518	5399	6868
2 Dr S 4WD Std Cab LB	3514	4200	5342
2 Dr S Std Cab LB	2698	3225	4102
2 Dr S 4WD Std Cab SB	3437	4108	5225
2 Dr S Std Cab SB	2635	3149	4006
2 Dr XL 4WD Ext Cab LB			
	4150	4960	6309
2 Dr XL 4WD Std Cab LB			
	3771	4506	5732
2 Dr XL Ext Cab LB	3586	4286	5452
2 Dr XL Std Cab LB	3200	3825	4865
2 Dr XL 4WD Ext Cab SB			
	4016	4799	6105
2 Dr XL 4WD Std Cab SB			
	3655	4368	5556
2 Dr XL Ext Cab SB	3465	4141	5267
2 Dr XL Std Cab SB	3137	3749	4769
2 Dr XL 4WD Ext Cab Stepside SB			
	4254	5084	6467
2 Dr XL 4WD Std Cab Stepside SB			
	3890	4649	5914
2 Dr XL Ext Cab Stepside SB			
	3648	4359	5545
2 Dr XL Std Cab Stepside SB			
	3326	3975	5056
2 Dr XLT 4WD Ext Cab LB			

Model Description	Trade-in TMV	Private TMV	Dealer TMV
	4392	5249	6677
2 Dr XLT 4WD Std Cab LB			
	4158	4969	6321
2 Dr XLT Ext Cab LB	3953	4724	6009
2 Dr XLT Std Cab LB	3615	4320	5495
2 Dr XLT 4WD Ext Cab SB			
	4455	5324	6772
2 Dr XLT 4WD Std Cab SB			
	4123	4927	6268
2 Dr XLT Ext Cab SB	3828	4575	5819
2 Dr XLT Std Cab SB	3567	4262	5422
2 Dr XLT 4WD Ext Cab Stepside SB			
	4644	5549	7059
2 Dr XLT 4WD Std Cab Stepside SB			
	4279	5114	6505
2 Dr XLT Ext Cab Stepside SB			
	4133	4939	6283
2 Dr XLT Std Cab Stepside SB			
	3759	4493	5715

OPTIONS FOR F-150

8 cyl 5.0 L Engine +181
8 cyl 5.8 L Engine +311
Air Conditioning +228
Aluminum/Alloy Wheels +91
Automatic 4-Speed Transmission +275
Camper/Towing Package +84
Captain Chairs (2) +139

F-250   1993

Category K

Model Description	Trade-in TMV	Private TMV	Dealer TMV
2 Dr XL 4WD Ext Cab LB			
	5020	5999	7631
2 Dr XL 4WD Std Cab LB			
	4644	5549	7059
2 Dr XL Ext Cab LB	4580	5474	6963
2 Dr XL Std Cab LB	3765	4499	5723
2 Dr XLT 4WD Ext Cab LB			
	5584	6673	8489
2 Dr XLT 4WD Std Cab LB			
	5271	6299	8013
2 Dr XLT Ext Cab LB	5082	6074	7726
2 Dr XLT Std Cab LB	4330	5174	6582

OPTIONS FOR F-250

8 cyl 5.0 L Engine[Opt on XL 2WD Std Cab,XLT 2WD Std Cab] +181
8 cyl 5.8 L Engine[Opt on XL 2WD Std Cab,XLT 2WD Std Cab] +311
8 cyl 7.3 L Diesel Engine +780
8 cyl 7.3 L Turbodiesel Engine +1076
8 cyl 7.5 L Engine +109
Air Conditioning[Opt on XL] +228
Automatic 4-Speed Transmission +275
Camper/Towing Package +84

F-350   1993

Category K

Model Description	Trade-in TMV	Private TMV	Dealer TMV
2 Dr XL 4WD Std Cab LB			
	5271	6299	8013
2 Dr XL Ext Cab LB	5334	6374	8108
2 Dr XL Std Cab LB	4832	5774	7345
4 Dr XL 4WD Crew Cab LB			
	6087	7274	9253
4 Dr XL Crew Cab LB	5201	6215	7906
2 Dr XL 4WD Std Cab SB			
	5216	6233	7929
2 Dr XLT 4WD Std Cab LB			
	5958	7121	9058
2 Dr XLT Ext Cab LB	6149	7349	9348
2 Dr XLT Std Cab LB	5459	6524	8299
4 Dr XLT 4WD Crew Cab LB			
	6777	8099	10302
4 Dr XLT Crew Cab LB	5964	7127	9066

OPTIONS FOR F-350

8 cyl 7.3 L Diesel Engine +804
8 cyl 7.3 L Turbodiesel Engine +1076
8 cyl 7.5 L Engine +109
Air Conditioning[Opt on XL] +227
Automatic 4-Speed Transmission +275
Camper/Towing Package +83
Dual Rear Wheels +164

FESTIVA   1993

No changes to the 1993 Festiva.

Category A

Model Description	Trade-in TMV	Private TMV	Dealer TMV
2 Dr GL Hbk	702	971	1419
2 Dr L Hbk	609	842	1230

OPTIONS FOR FESTIVA

Air Conditioning +198
Automatic 3-Speed Transmission +156

MUSTANG   1993

The Cobra is introduced to the lineup. Two hundred forty-five horsepower, a beefy suspension, and four-wheel disc brakes distinguish it from other Mustangs. Improved stereos grace all Mustangs this year.

Category E

Model Description	Trade-in TMV	Private TMV	Dealer TMV
2 Dr Cobra Hbk	3820	4845	6552
2 Dr GT Conv	4143	5254	7105
2 Dr GT Hbk	3208	4068	5502
2 Dr LX Conv	3605	4571	6182
2 Dr LX Cpe	1883	2388	3230
2 Dr LX Hbk	1937	2456	3322
2 Dr LX 5.0 Conv	3981	5049	6828
2 Dr LX 5.0 Cpe	2690	3412	4614
2 Dr LX 5.0 Hbk	3167	4016	5431

OPTIONS FOR MUSTANG

Don't forget to refer to the Mileage Adjustment Table at the back of this book!

FORD 93

Model Description	Trade-in TMV	Private TMV	Dealer TMV
Air Conditioning +254			
Automatic 4-Speed Transmission +231			
Leather Seats +170			
Sunroof +114			

PROBE 1993

A driver airbag becomes standard on the restyled Probe. The Probe's wheelbase stretches four inches and its curb weight jumps 100 pounds. The slow-selling LX model is dropped. Four-cylinder engines in the base model are good for 115 horsepower; GT models get a twin-cam 2.5-liter V6 engine that makes 164. Antilock brakes become optional for all Probes.

Category E			
2 Dr STD Hbk	1560	1979	2676
2 Dr GT Hbk	2206	2797	3783

OPTIONS FOR PROBE
AM/FM Compact Disc Player +122
Air Conditioning +254
Aluminum/Alloy Wheels[Std on GT] +133
Anti-Lock Brakes +162
Automatic 4-Speed Transmission +231
Leather Seats +141
Power Sunroof +174

RANGER 1993

The classy-looking Ranger Splash is introduced in 1993, offering the first flareside cargo box in the small pickup class. The rest of the Ranger lineup gets new sheetmetal.

Category J			
2 Dr STX 4WD Std Cab LB			
	3376	4146	5429
2 Dr STX Std Cab LB	2430	2984	3907
2 Dr STX 4WD Ext Cab SB			
	3622	4448	5824
2 Dr STX 4WD Std Cab SB			
	3261	4005	5244
2 Dr STX Ext Cab SB	2893	3553	4652
2 Dr STX Std Cab SB	2372	2913	3815
2 Dr Splash 4WD Std Cab Stepside SB			
	3611	4435	5807
2 Dr Splash Std Cab Stepside SB			
	2668	3276	4290
2 Dr Sport 4WD Std Cab LB			
	2964	3640	4767
2 Dr Sport Std Cab LB	2426	2979	3901
2 Dr Sport 4WD Std Cab SB			
	2918	3583	4692
2 Dr Sport Std Cab SB	2369	2910	3810
2 Dr XL 4WD Std Cab LB			
	2846	3494	4576
2 Dr XL Std Cab LB	2329	2860	3745
2 Dr XL 4WD Ext Cab SB			
	3383	4154	5440
2 Dr XL 4WD Std Cab SB			
	2786	3422	4481
2 Dr XL Ext Cab SB	2550	3131	4100
2 Dr XL Std Cab SB	2296	2819	3692
2 Dr XLT 4WD Std Cab LB			
	3201	3931	5148
2 Dr XLT Std Cab LB	2436	2992	3918
2 Dr XLT 4WD Ext Cab SB			
	3557	4368	5720
2 Dr XLT 4WD Std Cab SB			
	3083	3786	4958
2 Dr XLT Ext Cab SB	2615	3212	4206
2 Dr XLT Std Cab SB	2372	2913	3815

OPTIONS FOR RANGER
6 cyl 3.0 L Engine +128
Air Conditioning +228
Automatic 4-Speed Transmission +296

TAURUS 1993

SHOs finally receive an optional automatic transmission. The base L model is dropped in favor of the new entry-level Taurus GL. Body-color bumpers and side moldings are now standard.

Category D			
4 Dr GL Sdn	1296	1732	2460
4 Dr GL Wgn	1395	1865	2649
4 Dr LX Sdn	1495	1999	2838
4 Dr LX Wgn	1644	2199	3122
4 Dr SHO Sdn	1894	2532	3595

OPTIONS FOR TAURUS
6 cyl 3.0 L Flex Fuel Engine +322
6 cyl 3.8 L Engine +158
AM/FM Stereo/CD/Tape[Opt on LX Wgn] +156
Air Conditioning[Opt on GL] +213
Anti-Lock Brakes[Std on SHO] +162
Automatic 4-Speed Transmission[Opt on SHO] +185
Dual Air Bag Restraints +135
JBL Sound System +141
Leather Seats +170
Power Moonroof +210

TEMPO 1993

Say goodbye to the GLS. GL and LX Tempos have removable cupholders and a leather-wrapped shift knob. A driver airbag is optional on both models.

Category B			
2 Dr GL Sdn	853	1172	1703
4 Dr GL Sdn	853	1172	1703
4 Dr LX Sdn	1042	1432	2081

OPTIONS FOR TEMPO
6 cyl 3.0 L Engine +194

Don't forget to refer to the Mileage Adjustment Table at the back of this book!

Model Description	Trade-in TMV	Private TMV	Dealer TMV
Air Bag Restraint +114			
Air Conditioning +198			
Automatic 3-Speed Transmission +156			

THUNDERBIRD 1993

Base and Sport models are discontinued. Restyled alloy wheels and a new steering wheel complete the changes to the 1993 Thunderbird.

Category D

2 Dr LX Cpe	1545	2065	2933

Category E

2 Dr SC Sprchgd Cpe	2959	3753	5075

OPTIONS FOR THUNDERBIRD

8 cyl 5.0 L Engine +307
AM/FM Compact Disc Player +122
AM/FM Stereo/CD/Tape[Opt on SC] +106
Anti-Lock Brakes +162
Automatic 4-Speed Transmission[Opt on SC] +185
Leather Seats +139
Power Moonroof +210

1992 FORD

AEROSTAR 1992

A driver airbag becomes standard on passenger and cargo models. A new dashboard includes redesigned climate controls. On automatics, the shift lever moves from the floor to the column. High-back front bucket seats are now standard for all trim levels. Leather seats are available for the Eddie Bauer model. Outboard rear-seat passengers get a shoulder belt. A new grille and headlights appear on the exterior.

Category P

Model Description	Trade-in TMV	Private TMV	Dealer TMV
2 Dr STD AWD Cargo Van			
	1239	1608	2222
2 Dr STD AWD Cargo Van Ext			
	1306	1695	2342
2 Dr STD Cargo Van	1098	1424	1968
2 Dr STD Cargo Van Ext			
	1150	1491	2061
2 Dr Eddie Bauer AWD Pass. Van			
	1777	2305	3185
2 Dr Eddie Bauer AWD Pass. Van Ext			
	1933	2508	3466
2 Dr Eddie Bauer Pass. Van			
	1578	2046	2828
2 Dr Eddie Bauer Pass. Van Ext			
	1672	2169	2997
2 Dr XL AWD Pass. Van	1269	1646	2274
2 Dr XL AWD Pass. Van Ext			
	1411	1830	2529
2 Dr XL Pass. Van	1098	1424	1968
2 Dr XL Pass. Van Ext	1096	1422	1965
2 Dr XLT AWD Pass. Van			
	1515	1965	2716
2 Dr XLT AWD Pass. Van Ext			
	1557	2020	2792
2 Dr XLT Pass. Van	1358	1762	2435
2 Dr XLT Pass. Van Ext			
	1463	1898	2623

OPTIONS FOR AEROSTAR

Air Conditioning[Std on XLT] +216
Automatic 4-Speed Transmission[Opt on 2WD] +162
Captain Chairs (4) +167
Dual Air Conditioning[Opt on XL,XLT] +216
Leather Seats +175
Plus Package +183

BRONCO 1992

Freshened front-end styling and the addition of the XLT and Eddie Bauer models are the main changes for 1992.

Category N

2 Dr Custom 4WD Utility			
	3530	4422	5908
2 Dr Eddie Bauer 4WD Utility			
	4109	5147	6877
2 Dr XLT 4WD Utility	3877	4857	6489

OPTIONS FOR BRONCO

8 cyl 5.0 L Engine[Opt on Custom,XLT] +159
Air Conditioning[Opt on Custom,XLT] +196
Automatic 4-Speed Transmission +230
Camper/Towing Package +90
Leather Seats +174

CROWN VICTORIA 1992

After a total redesign, the corny LTD moniker is dropped from name and the station wagon body style is deleted from the Crown Vic's lineup. Suspension improvements include gas-charged shock absorbers and rear stabilizer bars. Antilock brakes are optional but four-wheel disc brakes are standard.

Category G

4 Dr STD Sdn	1566	2001	2726
4 Dr LX Sdn	1674	2139	2914
4 Dr Touring Sdn	1890	2416	3291

OPTIONS FOR CROWN VICTORIA

Anti-Lock Brakes +124
Dual Air Bag Restraints +118
JBL Sound System +137
Leather Seats +161

E-150 1992

Category Q

2 Dr STD Club Wagon	2400	3065	4172
2 Dr STD Econoline	2220	2835	3859
2 Dr Chateau Club Wagon			

Don't forget to refer to the Mileage Adjustment Table at the back of this book!

Model Description	Trade-in TMV	Private TMV	Dealer TMV
	3441	4394	5981
2 Dr XL Econoline	2373	3029	4124
2 Dr XLT Club Wagon	2997	3827	5209

OPTIONS FOR E-150
7 Passenger Seating[Opt on XLT] +166
8 cyl 5.0 L Engine +159
8 cyl 5.8 L Engine +213
Captain Chairs (4)[Opt on STD,XL] +135
Dual Air Conditioning[Opt on STD,XL] +205

E-250 — 1992

Category Q

Model Description	Trade-in TMV	Private TMV	Dealer TMV
2 Dr STD Econoline	2331	2977	4052
2 Dr STD Econoline Ext			
	2331	2977	4052
2 Dr XL Econoline	2553	3260	4438
2 Dr XL Econoline Ext	2553	3260	4438

OPTIONS FOR E-250
8 cyl 5.8 L Engine +213
Dual Air Conditioning +206

E-350 — 1992

Category Q

Model Description	Trade-in TMV	Private TMV	Dealer TMV
2 Dr STD Club Wagon	2775	3543	4823
2 Dr STD Econoline	3053	3898	5306
2 Dr STD Econoline Ext			
	2498	3189	4341
2 Dr Chateau Club Wagon Ext			
	3941	5031	6849
2 Dr Super Club Wagon Ext			
	2942	3756	5113
2 Dr XL Econoline Ext	2609	3331	4534
2 Dr XLT Club Wagon Ext			
	3497	4465	6078
2 Dr XLT Pass. Van	3386	4323	5885

OPTIONS FOR E-350
8 cyl 5.8 L Engine +238
8 cyl 7.3 L Diesel Engine +821
8 cyl 7.5 L Engine +334
Dual Air Conditioning +205

ESCORT — 1992

A notchback sedan is introduced as an LX-E trim-level; it offers four-wheel disc brakes, the GT engine, and GT interior touches. The Pony Comfort Group option makes air conditioning and power steering available on the base model.

Category B

Model Description	Trade-in TMV	Private TMV	Dealer TMV
2 Dr GT Hbk	1120	1623	2461
2 Dr LX Hbk	853	1236	1874
4 Dr LX Hbk	872	1263	1916
4 Dr LX Sdn	943	1366	2072
4 Dr LX Wgn	955	1383	2098
4 Dr LX-E Sdn	1123	1627	2467
2 Dr Pony Hbk	776	1125	1706

OPTIONS FOR ESCORT
Air Conditioning +196
Automatic 4-Speed Transmission +203
Power Sunroof +187

EXPLORER — 1992

A 3.55 axle replaces last year's 3.27 on four-wheel drive models. A one-touch-down driver's window becomes standard on all Explorers equipped with power windows. Eddie Bauer models receive color-keyed alloy wheels. A tilt-open sunroof is now available without an option package.

Category M

Model Description	Trade-in TMV	Private TMV	Dealer TMV
2 Dr Eddie Bauer 4WD Utility			
	2764	3530	4806
2 Dr Eddie Bauer Utility			
	2543	3247	4421
4 Dr Eddie Bauer 4WD Utility			
	2930	3741	5094
4 Dr Eddie Bauer Utility			
	2735	3492	4755
2 Dr Sport 4WD Utility			
	2316	2957	4026
2 Dr Sport Utility	2223	2839	3865
2 Dr XL 4WD Utility	2262	2889	3933
2 Dr XL Utility	2100	2682	3652
4 Dr XL 4WD Utility	2281	2913	3966
4 Dr XL Utility	2211	2823	3844
4 Dr XLT 4WD Utility	2339	2986	4066
4 Dr XLT Utility	2310	2950	4017

OPTIONS FOR EXPLORER
Air Conditioning +187
Automatic 4-Speed Transmission +236
Camper/Towing Package +85
Dual Power Seats[Opt on Sport,XLT] +125
JBL Sound System +137
Leather Seats +155
Sunroof +100

F-150 — 1992

Category K

Model Description	Trade-in TMV	Private TMV	Dealer TMV
2 Dr STD 4WD Ext Cab LB			
	3177	3994	5356
2 Dr STD 4WD Std Cab LB			
	2902	3648	4892
2 Dr STD Ext Cab LB	2733	3436	4607
2 Dr STD Std Cab LB	2447	3076	4124
2 Dr STD 4WD Ext Cab SB			
	3074	3865	5182

Model Description	Trade-in TMV	Private TMV	Dealer TMV
2 Dr STD 4WD Std Cab SB			
	2875	3614	4846
2 Dr STD Ext Cab SB	2676	3364	4511
2 Dr STD Std Cab SB	2390	3005	4029
2 Dr STD 4WD Ext Cab Stepside SB			
	3312	4163	5582
2 Dr STD 4WD Std Cab Stepside SB			
	3065	3853	5167
2 Dr STD Ext Cab Stepside SB			
	2890	3633	4871
2 Dr STD Std Cab Stepside SB			
	2671	3358	4503
2 Dr S 4WD Std Cab LB	2614	3287	4407
2 Dr S Ext Cab LB	2441	3069	4115
2 Dr S Std Cab LB	2175	2734	3666
2 Dr S 4WD Std Cab SB	2562	3221	4319
2 Dr S Ext Cab SB	2384	2997	4019
2 Dr S Std Cab SB	2145	2697	3616
2 Dr XL 4WD Ext Cab LB			
	3282	4126	5532
2 Dr XL 4WD Std Cab LB			
	2960	3721	4989
2 Dr XL Ext Cab LB	2842	3572	4790
2 Dr XL Std Cab LB	2565	3224	4323
2 Dr XL 4WD Ext Cab SB			
	3186	4005	5370
2 Dr XL 4WD Std Cab SB			
	2905	3652	4897
2 Dr XL Ext Cab SB	2783	3498	4691
2 Dr XL Std Cab SB	2546	3201	4292
2 Dr XL 4WD Ext Cab Stepside SB			
	3414	4291	5754
2 Dr XL 4WD Std Cab Stepside SB			
	3185	4004	5369
2 Dr XL Ext Cab Stepside SB			
	2951	3710	4975
2 Dr XL Std Cab Stepside SB			
	2787	3504	4698
2 Dr XLT Lariat 4WD Ext Cab LB			
	3418	4296	5761
2 Dr XLT Lariat 4WD Std Cab LB			
	3133	3938	5281
2 Dr XLT Lariat Ext Cab LB			
	2901	3647	4890
2 Dr XLT Lariat Std Cab LB			
	2723	3423	4590
2 Dr XLT Lariat 4WD Ext Cab SB			
	3354	4216	5653
2 Dr XLT Lariat 4WD Std Cab SB			
	3068	3857	5172
2 Dr XLT Lariat Ext Cab SB			
	2912	3660	4908
2 Dr XLT Lariat Std Cab SB			
	2666	3352	4494
2 Dr XLT Lariat 4WD Ext Cab Stepside SB			
	3524	4430	5940
2 Dr XLT Lariat 4WD Std Cab Stepside SB			
	3399	4273	5730
2 Dr XLT Lariat Ext Cab Stepside SB			
	3119	3921	5258
2 Dr XLT Lariat Std Cab Stepside SB			
	2906	3654	4899

OPTIONS FOR F-150
8 cyl 5.0 L Engine +159
8 cyl 5.8 L Engine +274
Air Conditioning[Opt on STD,XL] +200
Automatic 4-Speed Transmission +242
Captain Chairs (2) +122
Nite Trim Package +137

F-250 — 1992

Category K

Model Description	Trade-in TMV	Private TMV	Dealer TMV
2 Dr STD 4WD Ext Cab LB			
	3694	4644	6227
2 Dr STD 4WD Std Cab LB			
	3410	4287	5748
2 Dr STD Ext Cab LB	3013	3787	5078
2 Dr STD Std Cab LB	2614	3287	4407
2 Dr XLT Lariat 4WD Ext Cab LB			
	3922	4930	6611
2 Dr XLT Lariat 4WD Std Cab LB			
	3638	4573	6132
2 Dr XLT Lariat Ext Cab LB			
	3240	4073	5461
2 Dr XLT Lariat Std Cab LB			
	2842	3572	4790

OPTIONS FOR F-250
8 cyl 5.0 L Engine +159
8 cyl 5.8 L Engine +274
8 cyl 7.3 L Diesel Engine +686
8 cyl 7.5 L Engine +96
Air Conditioning[Opt on STD] +200
Aluminum/Alloy Wheels +95
Automatic 4-Speed Transmission +242
Captain Chairs (2) +122

F-350 — 1992

Category K

Model Description	Trade-in TMV	Private TMV	Dealer TMV
2 Dr STD 4WD Std Cab LB			
	3462	4352	5835
2 Dr STD Ext Cab LB	3473	4366	5854
2 Dr STD Std Cab LB	3183	4001	5365
4 Dr STD 4WD Crew Cab LB			
	3922	4930	6611

Don't forget to refer to the Mileage Adjustment Table at the back of this book!

Model Description	Trade-in TMV	Private TMV	Dealer TMV
4 Dr STD Crew Cab LB	3410	4287	5748
2 Dr XLT Lariat 4WD Std Cab LB	3682	4628	6206
2 Dr XLT Lariat Ext Cab LB	3707	4660	6248
2 Dr XLT Lariat Std Cab LB	3332	4189	5617
4 Dr XLT Lariat 4WD Crew Cab LB	4092	5144	6898
4 Dr XLT Lariat Crew Cab LB	3638	4573	6132

OPTIONS FOR F-350
8 cyl 7.3 L Diesel Engine +707
8 cyl 7.5 L Engine +96
Air Conditioning[Opt on STD] +200
Automatic 4-Speed Transmission +242
Captain Chairs (2) +87
Dual Rear Wheels +144

FESTIVA 1992

The GL gets alloy wheels. Sport trim and a spoiler are part of the GL's optional Sport Package.
Category A

Model Description	Trade-in TMV	Private TMV	Dealer TMV
2 Dr GL Hbk	557	810	1232
2 Dr L Hbk	471	685	1042

OPTIONS FOR FESTIVA
Air Conditioning +175
Automatic 3-Speed Transmission +137

MUSTANG 1992

LX models receive color-keyed body side moldings and bumper rub strips. All models get a new dome lamp.
Category E

Model Description	Trade-in TMV	Private TMV	Dealer TMV
2 Dr GT Conv	3280	4397	6257
2 Dr GT Hbk	2399	3215	4576
2 Dr LX Conv	2546	3412	4856
2 Dr LX Cpe	1420	1903	2708
2 Dr LX Hbk	1469	1968	2801
2 Dr LX 5.0 Conv	3182	4265	6070
2 Dr LX 5.0 Cpe	2105	2821	4015
2 Dr LX 5.0 Hbk	2252	3019	4296

OPTIONS FOR MUSTANG
Air Conditioning +223
Automatic 4-Speed Transmission +203
Leather Seats +149

PROBE 1992

The Sport Option Package becomes available for the LX model. A rear window defroster, interval wipers, power mirrors, tinted glass, and a tilt steering wheel are no longer standard on the GT or LX.
Category E

Model Description	Trade-in TMV	Private TMV	Dealer TMV
2 Dr GL Hbk	1175	1575	2241
2 Dr GT Turbo Hbk	1713	2296	3268
2 Dr LX Hbk	1224	1641	2335

OPTIONS FOR PROBE
Air Conditioning +223
Aluminum/Alloy Wheels[Std on GT] +117
Anti-Lock Brakes +142
Automatic 4-Speed Transmission +203
Leather Seats +125

RANGER 1992

No changes to the 1992 Ford Ranger.
Category J

Model Description	Trade-in TMV	Private TMV	Dealer TMV
2 Dr STD 4WD Ext Cab SB	2361	3051	4201
2 Dr STD Ext Cab SB	2039	2635	3628
2 Dr Custom 4WD Std Cab LB	2294	2965	4082
2 Dr Custom Std Cab LB	1892	2445	3366
2 Dr Custom 4WD Std Cab SB	2254	2912	4010
2 Dr Custom Std Cab SB	1864	2409	3317
2 Dr S Std Cab SB	1556	2011	2769
2 Dr STX 4WD Std Cab LB	2415	3120	4296
2 Dr STX Std Cab LB	1992	2574	3544
2 Dr STX 4WD Std Cab SB	2320	2998	4128
2 Dr STX 4WD Ext Cab SB	2575	3328	4582
2 Dr STX Ext Cab SB	2189	2829	3895
2 Dr STX Std Cab SB	1938	2504	3448
2 Dr Sport 4WD Std Cab LB	2220	2869	3950
2 Dr Sport Std Cab LB	1617	2090	2877
2 Dr Sport 4WD Std Cab SB	2205	2849	3922
2 Dr Sport Std Cab SB	1603	2071	2852
2 Dr XLT 4WD Std Cab LB	2522	3259	4487
2 Dr XLT Std Cab LB	1979	2557	3521
2 Dr XLT 4WD Ext Cab SB	2577	3329	4584
2 Dr XLT 4WD Std Cab SB	2469	3190	4392
2 Dr XLT Ext Cab SB	2191	2831	3898
2 Dr XLT Std Cab SB	1926	2488	3426

OPTIONS FOR RANGER
6 cyl 2.9 L Engine +125

Don't forget to refer to the Mileage Adjustment Table at the back of this book!

Model Description	Trade-in TMV	Private TMV	Dealer TMV

6 cyl 3.0 L Engine +112
Air Conditioning +200
Automatic 4-Speed Transmission +261

TAURUS 1992

A passenger airbag is now optional. Interior changes include a new dash. Restyled sheetmetal replaces everything but the doors. Antilock brakes are standard on the SHO and optional on other models. The SHO receives distinctive front-end styling. Wagons get an optional remote lift gate release.

Category D

Model Description	Trade-in TMV	Private TMV	Dealer TMV
4 Dr GL Sdn	999	1411	2098
4 Dr GL Wgn	1084	1532	2278
4 Dr L Sdn	989	1397	2077
4 Dr L Wgn	1039	1468	2183
4 Dr LX Sdn	1174	1659	2467
4 Dr LX Wgn	1200	1695	2520
4 Dr SHO Sdn	1310	1851	2752

OPTIONS FOR TAURUS
6 cyl 3.8 L Engine[Opt on GL] +138
Air Conditioning[Std on LX,SHO] +187
Anti-Lock Brakes[Std on SHO] +142
Dual Air Bag Restraints +118
JBL Sound System +125
Leather Seats +149
Power Moonroof +185

TEMPO 1992

V6 power becomes available but the four-wheel drive option departs. Rear stabilizer bars are added to V6 models and sequential-port fuel injection appears on all Tempos. The GLS model receives fog lamps, alloy wheels and 15-inch tires.

Category B

Model Description	Trade-in TMV	Private TMV	Dealer TMV
2 Dr GL Sdn	688	996	1511
4 Dr GL Sdn	693	1004	1522
2 Dr GLS Sdn	903	1308	1984
4 Dr GLS Sdn	908	1316	1996
4 Dr LX Sdn	776	1125	1706

OPTIONS FOR TEMPO
6 cyl 3.0 L Engine[Std on GLS] +171
Air Conditioning[Std on GLS] +175
Automatic 3-Speed Transmission +137

THUNDERBIRD 1992

A V8 engine is available on the Base and LX Thunderbird; standard on the new Sport. The Sport has alloy wheels and V8 fender badges.

Category D

Model Description	Trade-in TMV	Private TMV	Dealer TMV
2 Dr STD Cpe	1265	1787	2657
2 Dr LX Cpe	1404	1983	2949

Category E

Model Description	Trade-in TMV	Private TMV	Dealer TMV
2 Dr SC Sprchgd Cpe	2497	3347	4763

Category D

Model Description	Trade-in TMV	Private TMV	Dealer TMV
2 Dr Sport Cpe	1397	1974	2935

OPTIONS FOR THUNDERBIRD
8 cyl 5.0 L Engine[Std on Sport] +271
AM/FM Compact Disc Player +107
Anti-Lock Brakes[Std on SC] +142
Automatic 4-Speed Transmission[Opt on SC] +162
JBL Sound System +137
Leather Seats +122
Power Moonroof +185

Don't forget to refer to the Mileage Adjustment Table at the back of this book!

GEO 97-96

Model Description	Trade-in TMV	Private TMV	Dealer TMV	Model Description	Trade-in TMV	Private TMV	Dealer TMV

GEO

Japan

1994 Geo Prizm

1997 GEO

METRO 1997

Geo drops the base sedan variant of the Metro for 1997. A new convenience package is available on LSi models, and the LSi hatchback comes with the larger 1.3-liter engine standard. Two new colors debut.

Category A

	Trade-in	Private	Dealer
2 Dr STD Hbk	1901	2306	2800
2 Dr LSi Hbk	2037	2470	3000
4 Dr LSi Sdn	2173	2635	3200

OPTIONS FOR METRO
AM/FM Stereo/CD/Tape +190
Air Conditioning +258
Anti-Lock Brakes +185
Automatic 3-Speed Transmission +196

PRIZM 1997

The Prizm is essentially carried over for 1997, sporting new door trim panels, standard power steering, new exterior colors, and strengthened side-impact protection.

Category B

	Trade-in	Private	Dealer
4 Dr STD Sdn	3680	4364	5200
4 Dr LSi Sdn	3892	4616	5500

OPTIONS FOR PRIZM
4 cyl 1.8 L Engine +116
AM/FM Stereo/CD/Tape +171
Air Conditioning +262
Aluminum/Alloy Wheels +110
Anti-Lock Brakes +212
Automatic 3-Speed Transmission +163
Automatic 4-Speed Transmission +263

Leather Seats +196
Power Sunroof +222

TRACKER 1997

After a heavy makeover for 1996, changes for 1997 are limited. Convertibles get a standard fold-and-stow rear bench seat along with an enhanced evaporative emissions system. All Trackers can be painted Sunset Red Metallic or Azurite Blue Metallic for the first time. Prices have been at or near 1996 levels in an effort to make the Tracker more attractive to folks shopping Kia Sportage, Toyota RAV4 and Honda CR-V.

Category L

	Trade-in	Private	Dealer
2 Dr STD 4WD Conv	3961	4694	5589
2 Dr STD Conv	3756	4451	5300
4 Dr STD 4WD Wgn	4253	5039	6000
4 Dr STD Wgn	3977	4712	5611
4 Dr LSi 4WD Wgn	4394	5207	6200
4 Dr LSi Wgn	4182	4955	5900

OPTIONS FOR TRACKER
AM/FM Stereo/CD/Tape +190
Air Conditioning +275
Aluminum/Alloy Wheels +120
Anti-Lock Brakes +196
Automatic 3-Speed Transmission +205
Automatic 4-Speed Transmission +312

1996 GEO

METRO 1996

A zoned rear window defroster clears the center of the Metro's tiny rear backlight first, base coupes get dual exterior mirrors, and LSi coupes get cool hubcaps and body-color bumpers that keep it from looking like a refugee from some third-world country.

Category A

	Trade-in	Private	Dealer
2 Dr STD Hbk	1375	1753	2274
4 Dr STD Sdn	1512	1927	2500
2 Dr LSi Hbk	1407	1793	2326
4 Dr LSi Sdn	1633	2081	2700

OPTIONS FOR METRO
AM/FM Stereo/CD/Tape +172
Air Conditioning +179
Anti-Lock Brakes +169
Automatic 3-Speed Transmission +149

PRIZM 1996

An integrated child safety seat is optional on the LSi, and daytime running lights debut, making the Prizm more visible to other motorists, and radar-toting police officers. Three new exterior colors and added equipment to the base model round out the changes to this excellent compact.

Don't forget to refer to the Mileage Adjustment Table at the back of this book!

Model Description	Trade-in TMV	Private TMV	Dealer TMV
Category B			
4 Dr STD Sdn	2719	3341	4200
4 Dr LSi Sdn	2913	3580	4500

OPTIONS FOR PRIZM
AM/FM Stereo/CD/Tape +155
Air Conditioning +238
Anti-Lock Brakes +177
Automatic 3-Speed Transmission +148
Automatic 4-Speed Transmission +239
Leather Seats +177
Power Sunroof +202

TRACKER   1996

A new four-door model joins the lineup, and dual airbags are standard on all Trackers. Four-wheel antilock brakes are optional. Revised styling freshens the new exterior, and daytime running lights make the Tracker more conspicuous to motorists. In a switch from tradition, tasteful exterior colors are newly available. Cruise control is a new convenience option.

Category L			
2 Dr STD 4WD Conv	3346	4064	5056
2 Dr STD Conv	2912	3537	4400
4 Dr STD 4WD Wgn	3508	4260	5300
4 Dr STD Wgn	3390	4117	5122
2 Dr LSi 4WD Conv	3441	4180	5200
2 Dr LSi Conv	3111	3778	4700
4 Dr LSi 4WD Wgn	3706	4502	5600
4 Dr LSi Wgn	3465	4209	5236

OPTIONS FOR TRACKER
AM/FM Stereo/CD/Tape +172
Air Conditioning +222
Anti-Lock Brakes +169
Automatic 3-Speed Transmission +177
Automatic 4-Speed Transmission +239

1995 GEO

METRO   1995

All-new car is larger than previous model, and comes as a two-door hatchback or four-door sedan in base or LSi trim. Dual airbags are standard. ABS is optional on all models. Hatchbacks get the carryover 1.0-liter three-cylinder motor. Optional on LSi hatchback and standard on sedans is a 70-horsepower, 1.3-liter four-cylinder engine. Daytime running lights are standard.

Category A			
2 Dr STD Hbk	1088	1374	1850
4 Dr STD Sdn	1198	1513	2038
2 Dr LSi Hbk	1153	1457	1962
4 Dr LSi Sdn	1293	1633	2200

OPTIONS FOR METRO
AM/FM Stereo/CD/Tape +146
Air Conditioning +152
Anti-Lock Brakes +143
Automatic 3-Speed Transmission +126

PRIZM   1995

Base 1.6-liter engine loses horsepower. All models get new wheelcovers, and leather is newly optional on LSi.

Category B			
4 Dr STD Sdn	1880	2375	3200
4 Dr LSi Sdn	2057	2598	3500

OPTIONS FOR PRIZM
4 cyl 1.8 L Engine[Opt on STD] +89
AM/FM Stereo/CD/Tape +132
Air Conditioning +201
Anti-Lock Brakes +151
Automatic 3-Speed Transmission +125
Automatic 4-Speed Transmission +203
Leather Seats +151
Power Sunroof +171

TRACKER   1995

All 4WD models and Massachusetts-bound Trackers get 95-horsepower engine. Convertible top has been redesigned for easier operation. Expressions Packages offer color-coordinated tops and wheels.

Category L			
2 Dr STD 4WD Conv	2591	3120	4000
2 Dr STD 4WD Utility	2526	3042	3900
2 Dr STD Conv	2267	2730	3500
2 Dr LSi 4WD Conv	2850	3431	4400
2 Dr LSi 4WD Utility	2958	3561	4566

OPTIONS FOR TRACKER
AM/FM Stereo/CD/Tape +146
Air Conditioning +188
Automatic 3-Speed Transmission +151
Hardtop Roof +189

1994 GEO

METRO   1994

Convertible is dropped as is LSi trim level. CFC-free refrigerant is added to air conditioning systems.

Category A			
2 Dr STD Hbk	704	937	1325
4 Dr STD Hbk	717	955	1350
2 Dr XFi Hbk	691	919	1300

OPTIONS FOR METRO
Air Conditioning +135
Automatic 3-Speed Transmission +112

Don't forget to refer to the Mileage Adjustment Table at the back of this book!

GEO 94-92

242   www.edmunds.com

Model Description	Trade-in TMV	Private TMV	Dealer TMV

PRIZM   1994

Passenger airbag is added. Air conditioners get CFC-free coolant.

Category B

	Trade-in	Private	Dealer
4 Dr STD Sdn	1472	1933	2700
4 Dr LSi Sdn	1636	2147	3000

OPTIONS FOR PRIZM
AM/FM Stereo/CD/Tape +117
Air Conditioning +178
Anti-Lock Brakes +134
Automatic 4-Speed Transmission +179
Leather Seats +134
Power Sunroof +152

TRACKER   1994

Trackers sold in California and New York get 95-horsepower version of 1.6-liter engine to clear emissions hurdles. Four-wheel-drive models trade on-/off-road tires for better riding all-season type rubber. Alloy wheels have been restyled. Center console gets cupholders. Interior fabrics are new. Optional is a CD/cassette player.

Category L

	Trade-in	Private	Dealer
2 Dr STD 4WD Conv	1989	2443	3200
2 Dr STD 4WD Utility	2051	2520	3300
2 Dr STD Conv	1741	2138	2800
2 Dr LSi 4WD Conv	2290	2812	3683
2 Dr LSi 4WD Utility	2311	2838	3717

OPTIONS FOR TRACKER
AM/FM Stereo/CD/Tape +129
Air Conditioning +167
Automatic 3-Speed Transmission +134

1993 GEO

METRO   1993

Automatic door locks are added. Convertibles can have an optional CD player.

Category A

	Trade-in	Private	Dealer
2 Dr STD Hbk	481	671	989
4 Dr STD Hbk	497	694	1022
2 Dr LSi Conv	875	1222	1800
2 Dr LSi Hbk	632	882	1300
4 Dr LSi Hbk	658	920	1355
2 Dr XFi Hbk	481	671	989

OPTIONS FOR METRO
Air Conditioning +111

PRIZM   1993

Totally redesigned and available in base or LSi trim in sedan configuration. A driver airbag is standard. ABS is available. Still based on Toyota Corolla design.

Standard engine is a 108-horsepower, DOHC 1.6-liter engine. Available on LSi models is a twin-cam 1.8-liter engine making 115 horsepower.

Category B

	Trade-in	Private	Dealer
4 Dr STD Sdn	1108	1555	2300
4 Dr LSi Sdn	1204	1690	2500

OPTIONS FOR PRIZM
AM/FM Compact Disc Player +83
Air Conditioning +147
Anti-Lock Brakes +110
Automatic 4-Speed Transmission +148
Power Sunroof +124

STORM   1993

Hatchback model is dropped. Base engine loses five horsepower, but peak torque is made at lower rpm. Base models can be equipped with alloys. A CD player is optional.

Category E

	Trade-in	Private	Dealer
2 Dr STD Cpe	935	1297	1900
2 Dr GSi Cpe	1082	1501	2200

OPTIONS FOR STORM
Air Conditioning +129
Automatic 4-Speed Transmission +138

TRACKER   1993

Radios get revised controls.

Category L

	Trade-in	Private	Dealer
2 Dr STD 4WD Conv	1616	2060	2800
2 Dr STD 4WD Utility	1731	2207	3000
2 Dr STD Conv	1443	1839	2500
2 Dr LSi 4WD Conv	1847	2354	3200
2 Dr LSi 4WD Utility	1904	2428	3300

OPTIONS FOR TRACKER
Air Conditioning +138
Automatic 3-Speed Transmission +110
Hardtop Roof +138

1992 GEO

METRO   1992

Styling is revised front and rear. A new instrument panel is installed. New wheelcovers are installed on base and LSi models. Four-door hatchbacks get child safety rear-door locks.

Category A

	Trade-in	Private	Dealer
2 Dr STD Hbk	410	613	950
4 Dr STD Hbk	386	576	894
2 Dr LSi Conv	604	903	1400
2 Dr LSi Hbk	469	701	1087
4 Dr LSi Hbk	480	718	1113
2 Dr XFi Hbk	391	584	906

Don't forget to refer to the Mileage Adjustment Table at the back of this book!

Model Description	Trade-in TMV	Private TMV	Dealer TMV

OPTIONS FOR METRO
Air Conditioning +96

PRIZM 1992

Four-door hatchback is dropped.
Category B

Model	Trade-in	Private	Dealer
4 Dr STD Sdn	764	1153	1800
4 Dr GSi Sdn	1019	1537	2400
4 Dr LSi Sdn	977	1473	2300

OPTIONS FOR PRIZM
Air Conditioning[Opt on STD] +128
Automatic 4-Speed Transmission +128
Power Sunroof +108

STORM 1992

Styling is revised front and rear. GSi models get new 1.8-liter engine making 140 horsepower.
Category E

Model	Trade-in	Private	Dealer
2 Dr 2+2 Cpe	701	1038	1600
2 Dr STD Hbk	744	1103	1700
2 Dr GSi Cpe	832	1232	1900

OPTIONS FOR STORM
Air Conditioning +112
Automatic 4-Speed Transmission +119

TRACKER 1992

Dashboard is slightly revised and a tilt steering column is a new option. Center console includes cupholders. New seat fabrics and cloth bolsters are added.
Category L

Model	Trade-in	Private	Dealer
2 Dr STD 4WD Conv	1398	1811	2500
2 Dr STD 4WD Utility	1541	1997	2757
2 Dr STD Conv	1230	1594	2200
2 Dr LSi 4WD Conv	1590	2060	2843
2 Dr LSi 4WD Utility	1677	2173	3000

OPTIONS FOR TRACKER
Air Conditioning +119
Automatic 3-Speed Transmission +96

Don't forget to refer to the Mileage Adjustment Table at the back of this book!

GMC 01

Model Description	Trade-in TMV	Private TMV	Dealer TMV	Model Description	Trade-in TMV	Private TMV	Dealer TMV

GMC   USA

1995 GMC Suburban

2001 GMC

JIMMY   2001

The Vortec 4300 V6 enjoys another round of improvements, plus the Jimmy adds programmable door locks and a new cargo management system to its long list of features for 2001. A floor-shift option is now available on two-door models with automatic transmission, and the four-wheel-drive SLE version touts restyled alloy wheels. The tarted-up Envoy has been redesigned for 2002, but the glitzy Diamond Edition, introduced last year to mark the 30th anniversary of the Jimmy nameplate, is back — packing more pizzazz.

Category M

Model	Trade-in	Private	Dealer
4 Dr Diamond Edition 4WD Wgn			
	18445	19666	21700
4 Dr Diamond Edition Wgn			
	17255	18397	20300
4 Dr Diamond Edition Special 4WD Wgn			
	20740	22113	24400
4 Dr SLE 4WD Wgn	16235	17309	19100
4 Dr SLE Wgn	14960	15950	17600
2 Dr SLS 4WD Utility	12325	13141	14500
2 Dr SLS Utility	10540	11238	12400
2 Dr SLS Convenience 4WD Utility			
	13940	14863	16400
2 Dr SLS Convenience Utility			
	12240	13050	14400
4 Dr SLT 4WD Wgn	17340	18488	20400
4 Dr SLT Wgn	15555	16584	18300

OPTIONS FOR JIMMY
Automatic 4-Speed Transmission[Opt on SLS] +683

Automatic Dimming Mirror +119
Bose Sound System +338
Camper/Towing Package +143
Climate Control for AC +123
Compact Disc Changer +270
Cruise Control[Opt on SLS] +126
Dual Power Seats +328
Heated Front Seats +171
Locking Differential +184
OnStar Telematic System +356
Power Door Locks[Opt on SLS] +154
Power Drivers Seat +164
Power Sunroof +546
Power Windows[Opt on SLS] +164
Tilt Steering Wheel[Opt on SLS] +119
Tutone Paint +154

SAFARI   2001

Safari gets still more engineering enhancements for its 4.3-liter V6, and higher-output alternators. Door locks have been improved for increased security and remote keyless entry has been made standard on Passenger Van models. To reduce build complexity, preferred equipment groups have been revised and trim levels cut from three to two.

Category P

Model	Trade-in	Private	Dealer
2 Dr SLE AWD Pass. Van Ext			
	15548	16618	18400
2 Dr SLE Pass. Van Ext			
	14534	15534	17200

OPTIONS FOR SAFARI
AM/FM Stereo/CD/Tape +345
Leather Seats +648
Locking Differential +172
Power Drivers Seat +164
Rear Air Conditioning w/Rear Heater +546
Rear Heater +140
Running Boards +273
Trailer Hitch +211

SAVANA   2001

GMC's full-size van gets a bigger, more powerful Big Block V8 engine, the Vortec 8100. There are also more advanced powertrain control modules for the other gas engines in the Savana line, and an improved torque converter for the 4L80-E four-speed automatic transmission. Other changes for 2001 include more robust door and ignition locks, upgraded audio systems, quieter alternators and longer-lasting brake pads. A luxury-lined SLT, complete with leather upholstery and on-board entertainment system, debuted midway through the model year.

Category Q

Model	Trade-in	Private	Dealer
2 Dr G1500 SLT Pass. Van			
	22446	23816	26100

Don't forget to refer to the Mileage Adjustment Table at the back of this book!

Model Description	Trade-in TMV	Private TMV	Dealer TMV	Model Description	Trade-in TMV	Private TMV	Dealer TMV
2 Dr G1500 Pass. Van	14706	15604	17100	2 Dr SLE Std Cab LB	16262	17214	18800
2 Dr G2500 Pass. Van	16168	17155	18800	4 Dr SLE 4WD Ext Cab LB			
2 Dr G3500 Pass. Van	16856	17885	19600		20674	21883	23900
2 Dr G2500 Pass. Van Ext				4 Dr SLE Ext Cab LB	18694	19788	21612
	17114	18159	19900	2 Dr SLE 4WD Std Cab SB			
2 Dr G3500 Pass. Van Ext					17646	18679	20400
	17631	18707	20501	2 Dr SLE Std Cab SB	16166	17112	18689
				4 Dr SLE 4WD Ext Cab SB			
					20328	21517	23500
				4 Dr SLE Ext Cab SB	18079	19137	20900
				4 Dr SLT 4WD Ext Cab LB			
					22404	23715	25900
				4 Dr SLT Ext Cab LB	19895	21059	23000
				4 Dr SLT 4WD Ext Cab SB			
					22058	23348	25500
				4 Dr SLT Ext Cab SB	19636	20785	22700

OPTIONS FOR SAVANA
15 Passenger Seating +253
8 cyl 5.0 L Engine[Opt on 1500] +338
8 cyl 5.7 L Engine[Opt on 1500] +816
8 cyl 6.5 L Turbodiesel Engine +1952
AM/FM Compact Disc Player +370
AM/FM Stereo/CD/Tape[Std on SLT] +438
Aluminum/Alloy Wheels +171
Compact Disc Changer +201
Cruise Control[Std on SLT] +119
Leather Seats[Std on SLT] +887
Locking Differential[Std on SLT] +172
Power Door Locks[Std on SLT] +150
Power Drivers Seat[Std on SLT] +164
Power Passenger Seat[Std on SLT] +164
Power Windows[Std on SLT] +171
Privacy Glass +266
Rear Air Conditioning w/Rear Heater[Std on SLT] +549
Rear Heater +164
Tilt Steering Wheel[Std on SLT] +119

SIERRA 1500   2001

Reliability improvements for all Vortec V6 and V8 engines top the list of changes this year. Consequently, oil-change intervals have been extended to 7,500 miles (sorry, Jiffy Lube). A traction assist feature is now available on two-wheel-drive V8 automatics, thanks to a new electronic throttle control system. Factory-installed OnStar, GM's mobile communications and security system, has been made standard with the SLT trim level. New this year is a 325-horse, all-wheel-drive performance version called the C3.

Category K

Model Description	Trade-in TMV	Private TMV	Dealer TMV
2 Dr SL 4WD Std Cab LB			
	16012	16949	18511
2 Dr SL Std Cab LB	11505	12178	13300
4 Dr SL 4WD Ext Cab LB			
	19030	20144	22000
4 Dr SL Ext Cab LB	16434	17396	18999
2 Dr SL 4WD Std Cab SB			
	15484	16390	17900
2 Dr SL Std Cab SB	11332	11995	13100
4 Dr SL 4WD Ext Cab SB			
	18896	20002	21845
4 Dr SL Ext Cab SB	16359	17316	18912
2 Dr SLE 4WD Std Cab LB			
	18598	19686	21500

OPTIONS FOR SIERRA 1500
8 cyl 4.8 L Engine[Opt on SL Std Cab 2WD] +474
8 cyl 5.3 L Engine +546
AM/FM Stereo/CD/Tape +123
Air Conditioning[Opt on SL] +549
Automatic 4-Speed Transmission[Opt on SL] +747
Automatic Dimming Mirror[Opt on SLE] +119
Bucket Seats +171
Chrome Wheels[Opt on SL] +212
Cruise Control[Opt on SL] +137
Dual Power Seats +328
Electronic Ride Selection +222
Heated Front Seats +171
Locking Differential +195
Off-Road Package +270
Tonneau Cover +164
Traction Control System[Opt on 2WD] +154
Trailer Hitch +195
Tutone Paint +171

SIERRA 1500HD   2001

The extended-cab C3 is an entirely new truck based on the Sierra 1500 half-ton full-size pickup. Its 6.0-liter V8 makes it the only GM half-ton truck available with this engine. Sharing styling cues and feature content with luxury GMC SUVs, think of the C3 as a Denali pickup.

Category K

Model Description	Trade-in TMV	Private TMV	Dealer TMV
4 Dr SLE 4WD Crew Cab SB HD			
	22750	24081	26300
4 Dr SLE Crew Cab SB HD			
	20328	21517	23500
4 Dr SLT 4WD Crew Cab SB HD			
	24047	25454	27800
4 Dr SLT Crew Cab SB HD			
	21625	22891	25000

OPTIONS FOR SIERRA 1500HD

GMC 01

Model Description	Trade-in TMV	Private TMV	Dealer TMV

AM/FM Stereo/CD/Tape +123
Automatic Dimming Mirror[Std on SLT] +119
Bucket Seats[Std on SLT] +171
Dual Power Seats +328
Heated Front Seats +171
Leather Seats[Std on SLT] +874
Locking Differential +195
Privacy Glass +123
Tonneau Cover +164
Trailer Hitch +130

SIERRA 2500   2001

Both light- and heavy-duty 2500s sport new torsion bar front suspensions. Light-duty models now offer optional traction control and standard child safety-seat tethers. Heavy-duty Sierras are completely redesigned for 2001 offering two new engines and transmissions, bigger interiors, and numerous other improvements aimed at buyers looking for a "professional grade" truck from GM.

Category K

Model Description	Trade-in TMV	Private TMV	Dealer TMV
2 Dr SL Std Cab LB	14792	15657	17100
4 Dr SL 4WD Ext Cab SB			
	20068	21243	23200
2 Dr SLE Std Cab LB	16349	17305	18900
4 Dr SLE 4WD Ext Cab SB			
	21798	23074	25200
4 Dr SLT 4WD Ext Cab SB			
	23442	24813	27100

OPTIONS FOR SIERRA 2500

AM/FM Stereo/CD/Tape +123
Air Conditioning[Opt on SL] +549
Automatic 4-Speed Transmission[Opt on SL,SLE] +747
Automatic Dimming Mirror[Opt on SLE] +119
Bucket Seats +171
Cruise Control[Opt on SL] +137
Dual Power Seats[Opt on SLE] +328
Heated Front Seats +171
Locking Differential +195
Tonneau Cover +164
Traction Control System[Opt on Std Cab] +154
Trailer Hitch +130
Tutone Paint +171

SIERRA 2500HD   2001

Both light- and heavy-duty 2500s sport new torsion bar front suspensions. Light-duty models now offer optional traction control and standard child safety-seat tethers. Heavy-duty Sierras are completely redesigned for 2001 offering two new engines and transmissions, bigger interiors, and numerous other improvements aimed at buyers looking for a "professional grade" truck from GM.

Category K

Model Description	Trade-in TMV	Private TMV	Dealer TMV
2 Dr SL 4WD Std Cab LB HD			
	16003	16939	18500
2 Dr SL Std Cab LB HD	14705	15566	17000
4 Dr SL 4WD Crew Cab LB HD			
	20328	21517	23500
4 Dr SL 4WD Ext Cab LB HD			
	19030	20144	22000
4 Dr SL Crew Cab LB HD			
	18731	19827	21654
4 Dr SL Ext Cab LB HD	16954	17946	19600
4 Dr SL 4WD Crew Cab SB HD			
	20155	21334	23300
4 Dr SL 4WD Ext Cab SB HD			
	19020	20134	21989
4 Dr SL Crew Cab SB HD			
	17819	18862	20600
4 Dr SL Ext Cab SB HD	16695	17672	19300
2 Dr SLE 4WD Std Cab LB HD			
	18501	19584	21389
2 Dr SLE Std Cab LB HD			
	15657	16573	18100
4 Dr SLE 4WD Crew Cab LB HD			
	22317	23623	25800
4 Dr SLE 4WD Ext Cab LB HD			
	20760	21975	24000
4 Dr SLE Crew Cab LB HD			
	19895	21059	23000
4 Dr SLE Ext Cab LB HD			
	18867	19971	21811
4 Dr SLE 4WD Crew Cab SB HD			
	22058	23348	25500
4 Dr SLE 4WD Ext Cab SB HD			
	20674	21883	23900
4 Dr SLE Crew Cab SB HD			
	19722	20876	22800
4 Dr SLE Ext Cab SB HD			
	18425	19503	21300
4 Dr SLT 4WD Crew Cab LB HD			
	23788	25180	27500
4 Dr SLT 4WD Ext Cab LB HD			
	23269	24630	26900
4 Dr SLT Crew Cab LB HD			
	21279	22524	24600
4 Dr SLT Ext Cab LB HD			
	20068	21243	23200
4 Dr SLT 4WD Crew Cab SB HD			
	23528	24905	27200
4 Dr SLT 4WD Ext Cab SB HD			
	22144	23440	25600
4 Dr SLT Crew Cab SB HD			
	21020	22250	24300

Model Description	Trade-in TMV	Private TMV	Dealer TMV
4 Dr SLT Ext Cab SB HD			
	19809	20968	22900

OPTIONS FOR SIERRA 2500HD
AM/FM Stereo/CD/Tape +123
Air Conditioning[Opt on SL] +563
Automatic 5-Speed Transmission +819
Automatic Dimming Mirror[Opt on SLE] +119
Bucket Seats[Opt on SLE] +171
Chrome Wheels[Opt on SL] +212
Cruise Control[Opt on SL] +164
Dual Power Seats[Opt on SLE] +328
Heated Front Seats +171
Locking Differential +195
Tonneau Cover +164
Trailer Hitch +130

SIERRA 3500   2001

The General's brand-new HD truck lineup debuts stronger frames; beefed-up suspensions, axles, brakes and cooling systems; new sheetmetal; bigger interiors; and a trio of powerful new V8s - a 6.6-liter Duramax turbodiesel and two gas engines, a hefty 8.1-liter and an improved 6.0-liter. One of the four transmissions, a new Allison five-speed automatic, is designed especially for towing and hauling with GM's helpful "tow-haul" mode and a new "grade-braking" feature.

Category K

Model Description	Trade-in TMV	Private TMV	Dealer TMV
2 Dr SL 4WD Std Cab LB			
	17214	18221	19900
2 Dr SL Std Cab LB	14619	15474	16900
2 Dr SL Ext Cab LB	17906	18953	20700
4 Dr SL 4WD Crew Cab LB			
	21203	22444	24512
4 Dr SL 4WD Ext Cab LB			
	20241	21426	23400
4 Dr SL Crew Cab LB	19895	21059	23000
2 Dr SLE 4WD Std Cab LB			
	18684	19778	21600
2 Dr SLE Std Cab LB	16176	17122	18700
4 Dr SLE 4WD Crew Cab LB			
	23009	24356	26600
4 Dr SLE 4WD Ext Cab LB			
	21798	23074	25200
4 Dr SLE Crew Cab LB	20674	21883	23900
4 Dr SLE Ext Cab LB	20086	21262	23221
4 Dr SLT 4WD Crew Cab LB			
	24566	26004	28400
4 Dr SLT 4WD Ext Cab LB			
	23269	24630	26900
4 Dr SLT Crew Cab LB	22188	23487	25651
4 Dr SLT Ext Cab LB	20760	21975	24000

OPTIONS FOR SIERRA 3500

Model Description	Trade-in TMV	Private TMV	Dealer TMV
AM/FM Stereo/CD/Tape +123			
Air Conditioning[Opt on SL] +563			
Automatic 5-Speed Transmission +819			
Automatic Dimming Mirror[Opt on SLE] +119			
Bucket Seats[Opt on SLE] +171			
Chrome Wheels[Opt on SL] +212			
Cruise Control[Opt on SL] +164			
Dual Power Seats[Opt on SLE] +328			
Heated Front Seats +171			
Locking Differential +195			
Tonneau Cover +164			
Trailer Hitch +130			

SIERRA C3   2001

The extended-cab C3 is a new truck based on the Sierra 1500 half-ton full-size pickup. It's powered by a specially-tuned version of the 6.0-liter Vortec V8. It also gets full-time all-wheel drive, 3/4-ton brakes, and a standard heavy-duty suspension. With styling cues and feature content similar to GMC's SUVs, think of the C3 as the Denali version of the Sierra.

Category K

Model Description	Trade-in TMV	Private TMV	Dealer TMV
4 Dr STD AWD Ext Cab SB			
	29670	31406	34300

SONOMA   2001

An all-new model has been added to the Sonoma lineup for 2001, a four-door Crew Cab, complete with Vortec 4300 V6, automatic transmission, InstaTrac four-wheel-drive system and SLS trim. Powertrain improvements incorporate an advanced control module for the V6 and flex-fuel capability for the four-cylinder. There are also new aluminum wheels with the sport suspension, and programmable automatic power door locks.

Category J

Model Description	Trade-in TMV	Private TMV	Dealer TMV
2 Dr SL Std Cab LB	8083	8652	9600
2 Dr SL 4WD Ext Cab SB			
	12967	13879	15400
2 Dr SL Ext Cab SB	9851	10545	11700
2 Dr SL Std Cab SB	7746	8292	9200
2 Dr SLS Sport Std Cab LB			
	9346	10004	11100
2 Dr SLS Sport 4WD Ext Cab SB			
	13472	14420	16000
2 Dr SLS Sport Ext Cab SB			
	10272	10995	12200
2 Dr SLS Sport Std Cab SB			
	8252	8832	9800
4 Dr SLS 4WD Crew Cab SB			
	16840	18025	20000

OPTIONS FOR SONOMA
6 cyl 4.3 L Vortec Engine[Std on 4WD] +884
AM/FM Compact Disc Player +206

Don't forget to refer to the Mileage Adjustment Table at the back of this book!

Model Description	Trade-in TMV	Private TMV	Dealer TMV
Air Conditioning +549			
Aluminum/Alloy Wheels +191			
Automatic 4-Speed Transmission +747			
Bed Extender +123			
Cruise Control +123			
Highrider Suspension Package +1293			
Locking Differential +184			
Power Door Locks +137			
Power Windows +164			
Sport Suspension +502			
Tilt Steering Wheel +119			
Tonneau Cover +280			

YUKON   2001

The recently redesigned Yukon is virtually unchanged from last year. The high-level Yukon Denali is now based on the revamped Yukon. The Denali gets a 6.0-liter V8 engine along with standard all-wheel drive and a host of other new features designed to elevate the top-of-the-line GMC above and beyond its more basic Yukon cousin.

Model Description	Trade-in TMV	Private TMV	Dealer TMV
Category O			
4 Dr Denali AWD Wgn	29145	30778	33500
Category N			
4 Dr SLE 4WD Wgn	24763	26089	28300
4 Dr SLE Wgn	22400	23600	25600
4 Dr SLT 4WD Wgn	25988	27380	29700
4 Dr SLT Wgn	23625	24891	27000

OPTIONS FOR YUKON
8 cyl 5.3 L Engine +478
Autoride Suspension Package +478
Bucket Seats +256
Camper/Towing Package +145
Dual Air Conditioning +444
Locking Differential[Opt on 2WD] +172
Off-Road Package +116
OnStar Telematic System +356
Power Sunroof +640
Running Boards +270
Third Seat +444
Traction Control System +133

YUKON XL   2001

The Yukon XL gets a new top-of-the-line engine in addition to more horsepower for the 6.0-liter V8. Debuting this year is the Yukon Denali XL featuring standard all-wheel drive and a host of other new features designed to elevate the top-of-the-line GMC above and beyond its more basic Yukon XL stablemate.

Model Description	Trade-in TMV	Private TMV	Dealer TMV
Category O			
4 Dr Denali AWD Wgn	32190	33994	37000
Category N			
4 Dr C1500 SLE Wgn	23625	24891	27000
4 Dr C2500 SLE Wgn	24500	25813	28000
4 Dr K1500 SLE 4WD Wgn			

Model Description	Trade-in TMV	Private TMV	Dealer TMV
	25437	26800	29071
4 Dr K2500 SLE 4WD Wgn			
	26325	27736	30086
4 Dr C1500 SLT Wgn	25313	26669	28929
4 Dr C2500 SLT Wgn	26175	27577	29914
4 Dr K1500 SLT 4WD Wgn			
	27051	28500	30915
4 Dr K2500 SLT 4WD Wgn			
	27199	28656	31085

OPTIONS FOR YUKON XL
Autoride Suspension Package +411
Bucket Seats +256
Heated Front Seats +171
OnStar Telematic System +356
Power Sunroof +683
Running Boards +270

2000 GMC

C/K 2500   2000

GM has refined the Sierra Classic lineup, dropping all 1500 series (half-ton) trucks in favor of workhorse 2500 (three-quarter-ton) and 3500 (one-ton) series models. The only other news is the addition of a new paint color, as this old truck platform (based on the previous-generation C/K pickup) soldiers on for a final year.

Model Description	Trade-in TMV	Private TMV	Dealer TMV
Category K			
2 Dr SL 4WD Ext Cab LB HD			
	16549	18032	19400
2 Dr SL 4WD Std Cab LB HD			
	15014	16359	17600
2 Dr SL Ext Cab LB HD	14331	15615	16800
2 Dr SL Std Cab LB HD	13137	14314	15400
2 Dr SL 4WD Ext Cab SB HD			
	16464	17939	19300
4 Dr SL 4WD Crew Cab SB			
	18000	19612	21100
4 Dr SL Crew Cab SB	16208	17660	19000
2 Dr SLE 4WD Ext Cab LB HD			
	17914	19519	21000
2 Dr SLE 4WD Std Cab LB HD			
	16720	18218	19600
2 Dr SLE Ext Cab LB HD			
	15952	17381	18700
2 Dr SLE Std Cab LB HD			
	14758	16080	17300
2 Dr SLE 4WD Ext Cab SB HD			
	17658	19240	20700
4 Dr SLE 4WD Crew Cab SB			
	19962	21750	23400
4 Dr SLE Crew Cab SB	18255	19891	21400
2 Dr SLT 4WD Ext Cab LB HD			

Model Description	Trade-in TMV	Private TMV	Dealer TMV
	19023	20727	22300
2 Dr SLT 4WD Std Cab LB HD			
	17232	18775	20200
2 Dr SLT Ext Cab LB HD			
	17061	18589	20000
2 Dr SLT Std Cab LB HD			
	15782	17195	18500
2 Dr SLT 4WD Ext Cab SB HD			
	18938	20634	22200
4 Dr SLT 4WD Crew Cab SB			
	21241	23144	24900
4 Dr SLT Crew Cab SB	19109	20820	22400

OPTIONS FOR C/K 2500
8 cyl 6.5 L Turbodiesel Engine +1854
8 cyl 7.4 L Engine +410
AM/FM Compact Disc Player +130
AM/FM Stereo/CD/Tape +198
Air Conditioning[Opt on SL] +549
Automatic 4-Speed Transmission +747
Bed Liner +154
Bucket Seats +256
Cruise Control[Opt on SL] +140
Limited Slip Differential +195
Power Door Locks[Opt on SL] +111
Power Drivers Seat[Std on SLT] +164
Tilt Steering Wheel[Opt on SL] +133

C/K 3500   2000

GM has refined the Sierra Classic's lineup, dropping all 1500 series (half-ton) trucks in favor of workhorse 2500 (three-quarter-ton) and 3500 (one-ton) series models. The only other news is the addition of a new paint color, as this old truck platform (based on the previous-generation C/K pickup) soldiers on into its second decade.

Category K

Model Description	Trade-in TMV	Private TMV	Dealer TMV
2 Dr SL 4WD Ext Cab LB			
	18085	19705	21200
2 Dr SL 4WD Std Cab LB			
	15952	17381	18700
2 Dr SL Ext Cab LB	16293	17753	19100
2 Dr SL Std Cab LB	13820	15057	16200
4 Dr SL 4WD Crew Cab LB			
	18255	19891	21400
4 Dr SL Crew Cab LB	16123	17567	18900
4 Dr SL 4WD Crew Cab SB			
	19279	21006	22600
4 Dr SL Crew Cab SB	17232	18775	20200
2 Dr SLE 4WD Ext Cab LB			
	19706	21471	23100
2 Dr SLE 4WD Std Cab LB			
	17573	19147	20600
2 Dr SLE Ext Cab LB	17744	19333	20800
2 Dr SLE Std Cab LB	15440	16823	18100
4 Dr SLE 4WD Crew Cab LB			
	20817	22682	24403
4 Dr SLE Crew Cab LB	18511	20169	21700
4 Dr SLE 4WD Crew Cab SB			
	23459	25560	27500
4 Dr SLE Crew Cab SB	19620	21378	23000
2 Dr SLT 4WD Ext Cab LB			
	20729	22586	24300
2 Dr SLT 4WD Std Cab LB			
	18341	19984	21500
2 Dr SLT Ext Cab LB	18853	20541	22100
2 Dr SLT Std Cab LB	16635	18125	19500
4 Dr SLT 4WD Crew Cab LB			
	22094	24073	25900
4 Dr SLT Crew Cab LB	19791	21564	23200
4 Dr SLT 4WD Crew Cab SB			
	23033	25096	27000
4 Dr SLT Crew Cab SB	20812	22676	24397

OPTIONS FOR C/K 3500
8 cyl 6.5 L Turbodiesel Engine +1854
8 cyl 7.4 L Engine[Std on Crew Cab] +410
AM/FM Compact Disc Player +130
AM/FM Stereo/CD/Tape +198
Air Conditioning[Opt on SL] +549
Automatic 4-Speed Transmission +747
Bed Liner +154
Bucket Seats +184
Camper/Towing Package +112
Chrome Step Bumper[Opt on SL] +156
Cruise Control[Opt on SL] +140
Dual Rear Wheels[Std on SLE,SLT] +679
Limited Slip Differential +172
Power Door Locks[Opt on SL] +106
Power Drivers Seat[Opt on SLE] +164
Tilt Steering Wheel[Opt on SL] +133
Trailer Hitch +112

ENVOY   2000

Upgraded seats and V6 engine improvements headline changes to GM's high-end compact SUV. There's also a new metallic paint color, and a heavy-duty battery is now standard.

Category O

Model Description	Trade-in TMV	Private TMV	Dealer TMV
4 Dr STD 4WD Wgn	16827	18477	20000

OPTIONS FOR ENVOY
Limited Slip Differential +184
Power Moonroof +512

JIMMY   2000

For 2000, GMC is celebrating the 30th anniversary of its Jimmy nameplate with a dolled-up Diamond Edition model. Other changes center on new equipment and suspension packaging. A heavy-duty battery is now

Model Description	Trade-in TMV	Private TMV	Dealer TMV	Model Description	Trade-in TMV	Private TMV	Dealer TMV

standard, and Jimmy's V6 has been upgraded with a roller timing chain, sprocket and rocker arms for improved durability and reduced noise. There are also two new exterior colors, while the SLE gets a revised cloth interior.

Category M

	Trade-in	Private	Dealer
4 Dr Diamond Edition 4WD Wgn			
	14939	16531	18000
4 Dr Diamond Edition Wgn			
	13860	15337	16700
4 Dr SLE 4WD Wgn	12864	14235	15500
4 Dr SLE Wgn	11785	13041	14200
2 Dr SLS 4WD Utility	9461	10469	11400
2 Dr SLS Utility	7967	8816	9600
2 Dr SLS Convenience 4WD Utility			
	10789	11939	13000
2 Dr SLS Convenience Utility			
	9378	10378	11300
4 Dr SLT 4WD Wgn	13943	15429	16800
4 Dr SLT Wgn	12034	13316	14500

OPTIONS FOR JIMMY
AM/FM Stereo/CD/Tape +233
Automatic 4-Speed Transmission[Opt on SLS] +682
Automatic Load Leveling +171
Camper/Towing Package[Std on Diamond Edition] +143
Climate Control for AC +123
Compact Disc Changer +270
Cruise Control[Opt on SLS] +140
Delco/Bose Stereo System +337
Dual Power Seats +328
Heated Front Seats +171
Limited Slip Differential[Std on SLS,Base 2WD 2DR] +184
Luxury Package +1362
Power Door Locks[Opt on SLS] +119
Power Drivers Seat[Std on Diamond Edition,SLE,SLT] +164
Power Moonroof +512
Power Windows[Opt on SLS] +171
Tilt Steering Wheel[Opt on SLS] +123

SAFARI   2000

The 2000 Safari gets engineering enhancements for its 4.3-liter V6 and ABS components, a tow/haul mode for its four-speed automatic transmission, revised lighting and power locking functions, a larger (27-gallon) composite fuel tank, and a third-row seat as standard equipment.

Category P

	Trade-in	Private	Dealer
2 Dr SL AWD Pass. Van Ext			
	12646	13974	15200
2 Dr SL Pass. Van Ext	11731	12963	14100
2 Dr SLE AWD Pass. Van Ext			
	12895	14250	15500
2 Dr SLE Pass. Van Ext			
	12063	13330	14500

	Trade-in	Private	Dealer
2 Dr SLT AWD Pass. Van Ext			
	15641	17284	18800
2 Dr SLT Pass. Van Ext			
	14559	16088	17500

OPTIONS FOR SAFARI
7 Passenger Seating +270
AM/FM Compact Disc Player +278
AM/FM Stereo/CD/Tape[Std on SLT] +345
Aluminum/Alloy Wheels[Std on SLT] +208
Camper/Towing Package +239
Chrome Wheels[Std on SLE] +233
Cruise Control[Opt on SL] +127
Dual Air Conditioning[Std on SLT] +358
Dual Power Seats +328
Keyless Entry System[Opt on SL] +116
Leather Seats +648
Limited Slip Differential +172
Overhead Console[Opt on SL] +152
Power Door Locks[Opt on SL] +152
Power Drivers Seat[Std on SLT] +164
Power Windows[Opt on SL] +324
Privacy Glass[Opt on SL] +198
Rear Heater[Std on SLT] +140
Running Boards +273
Tilt Steering Wheel[Opt on SL] +119
Trailer Hitch +211

SAVANA   2000

GMC's full-size passenger van gets improved powertrains, increased trailer ratings, seat-mounted tether anchors for installing child safety seats and an optional rear-window defogger.

Category Q

	Trade-in	Private	Dealer
2 Dr G2500 Pass. Van	13641	14972	16200
2 Dr G2500 Pass. Van Ext			
	14651	16081	17400
2 Dr G3500 Pass. Van	14483	15896	17200
2 Dr G3500 Pass. Van Ext			
	14735	16173	17500
2 Dr Pass. Van	12378	13585	14700
2 Dr G1500 SLE Pass. Van			
	13220	14509	15700
2 Dr G2500 SLE Pass. Van			
	14904	16358	17700
2 Dr G2500 SLE Pass. Van Ext			
	16335	17929	19400
2 Dr G3500 SLE Pass. Van			
	15998	17559	19000
2 Dr G3500 SLE Pass. Van Ext			
	16419	18021	19500

OPTIONS FOR SAVANA
15 Passenger Seating +253
8 cyl 5.0 L Engine[Opt on 1500] +337
8 cyl 5.7 L Engine[Opt on 1500] +816

Model Description	Trade-in TMV	Private TMV	Dealer TMV
8 cyl 6.5 L Turbodiesel Engine +1854			
8 cyl 7.4 L Engine +410			
AM/FM Compact Disc Player +370			
AM/FM Stereo/CD/Tape +438			
Aluminum/Alloy Wheels +171			
Camper/Towing Package +212			
Chrome Wheels +171			
Cruise Control[Std on SLE] +140			
Dual Air Conditioning +587			
Dual Power Seats +328			
Limited Slip Differential +172			
Power Door Locks[Opt on STD] +154			
Power Drivers Seat +164			
Power Windows[Std on SLE] +173			
Privacy Glass +266			
Rear Heater +164			
Tilt Steering Wheel[Std on SLE] +123			

SIERRA 1500 — 2000

After a complete redesign last year, GMC's Silverado-based pickup finally gets a fourth door on the extended cab. There's also more power on tap from the 4.8- and 5.3-liter engines, increased trailer ratings and standard programmable automatic door locks. New factory appearance items, such as wheel-lip flares and a soft tonneau cover, are now available on some models.

Category K

Model Description	Trade-in TMV	Private TMV	Dealer TMV
2 Dr SL 4WD Ext Cab LB			
	17829	19426	20900
2 Dr SL 4WD Std Cab LB			
	13564	14779	15900
2 Dr SL Ext Cab LB	14502	15801	17000
2 Dr SL Std Cab LB	9725	10596	11400
2 Dr SL 4WD Ext Cab SB			
	16976	18496	19900
2 Dr SL 4WD Std Cab SB			
	12796	13942	15000
2 Dr SL Ext Cab SB	13990	15243	16400
2 Dr SL Std Cab SB	9554	10410	11200
2 Dr SL 4WD Ext Cab Stepside SB			
	18000	19612	21100
2 Dr SL 4WD Std Cab Stepside SB			
	13820	15057	16200
2 Dr SL Ext Cab Stepside SB			
	15440	16823	18100
2 Dr SL Std Cab Stepside SB			
	11858	12920	13900
2 Dr SLE 4WD Ext Cab LB			
	19109	20820	22400
2 Dr SLE 4WD Std Cab LB			
	16208	17660	19000
2 Dr SLE Ext Cab LB	16805	18311	19700
2 Dr SLE Std Cab LB	13825	15063	16206
2 Dr SLE 4WD Ext Cab SB			
	18853	20542	22101
2 Dr SLE 4WD Std Cab SB			
	14758	16080	17300
2 Dr SLE Ext Cab SB	16635	18125	19500
2 Dr SLE Std Cab SB	13734	14964	16100
2 Dr SLE 4WD Ext Cab Stepside SB			
	19706	21471	23100
2 Dr SLE 4WD Std Cab Stepside SB			
	16549	18032	19400
2 Dr SLE Ext Cab Stepside SB			
	17658	19240	20700
2 Dr SLE Std Cab Stepside SB			
	13985	15238	16394
2 Dr SLT 4WD Ext Cab LB			
	20900	22772	24500
2 Dr SLT Ext Cab LB	18426	20077	21600
2 Dr SLT 4WD Ext Cab SB			
	20473	22307	24000
2 Dr SLT Ext Cab SB	18085	19705	21200
2 Dr SLT 4WD Ext Cab Stepside SB			
	21156	23051	24800
2 Dr SLT Ext Cab Stepside SB			
	18681	20354	21899

OPTIONS FOR SIERRA 1500

8 cyl 4.8 L Engine[Opt on SL,SLE] +474			
8 cyl 5.3 L Engine[Opt on SLE,SLT] +547			
AM/FM Stereo/CD/Tape +198			
Air Conditioning[Opt on SL] +549			
Aluminum/Alloy Wheels +212			
Automatic 4-Speed Transmission[Opt on SL,SLE] +747			
Bucket Seats +171			
Chrome Step Bumper[Opt on SL] +137			
Cruise Control[Opt on SL] +137			
Dual Power Seats +328			
Heated Front Seats +171			
Hinged Fourth Door +225			
Limited Slip Differential +184			
Power Door Locks[Opt on SL] +111			
Tonneau Cover +164			
Trailer Hitch +195			

SIERRA 2500 — 2000

After a complete redesign last year, GMC's Silverado-based pickup finally gets a fourth door on the extended cab. There's also more power on tap in the 4.8- and 5.3-liter engines, increased trailer ratings and standard programmable automatic door locks. New factory appearance items, such as wheel-lip flares and a soft tonneau cover, are now available on some models.

Category K

Model Description	Trade-in TMV	Private TMV	Dealer TMV
2 Dr SL 4WD Ext Cab LB			
	17061	18589	20000
2 Dr SL 4WD Std Cab LB HD			

Don't forget to refer to the Mileage Adjustment Table at the back of this book!

GMC 00

Model Description	Trade-in TMV	Private TMV	Dealer TMV
	14843	16173	17400
2 Dr SL Ext Cab LB	15184	16545	17800
2 Dr SL Std Cab LB	12881	14035	15100
2 Dr SL 4WD Std Cab LB	12966	14128	15200
2 Dr SL 4WD Ext Cab SB HD			
	16891	18403	19800
2 Dr SL Ext Cab SB	13649	14871	16000
2 Dr SLE 4WD Ext Cab LB HD			
	18511	20169	21700
2 Dr SLE 4WD Std Cab LB HD			
	16293	17753	19100
2 Dr SLE Ext Cab LB	16635	18125	19500
2 Dr SLE Std Cab LB	13222	14407	15500
2 Dr SLE Std Cab LB	14246	15522	16700
2 Dr SLE 4WD Ext Cab SB HD			
	18341	19984	21500
2 Dr SLE Ext Cab SB	16038	17474	18800
2 Dr SLT 4WD Ext Cab LB HD			
	19876	21657	23300
2 Dr SLT Ext Cab LB HD			
	18170	19798	21300
2 Dr SLT 4WD Ext Cab SB HD			
	19706	21471	23100
2 Dr SLT Ext Cab SB	17914	19519	21000

OPTIONS FOR SIERRA 2500
8 cyl 6.0 L Engine +242
AM/FM Stereo/CD/Tape +198
Air Conditioning[Opt on SL] +549
Automatic 4-Speed Transmission[Opt on SL,SLE] +747
Bucket Seats +171
Chrome Step Bumper[Opt on SL] +137
Cruise Control[Opt on SL] +137
Dual Power Seats[Opt on SLE] +328
Heated Front Seats +171
Hinged Fourth Door +225
Limited Slip Differential +184
Power Door Locks[Opt on SL] +111
Tonneau Cover +164
Trailer Hitch +222

SONOMA 2000

Four-wheel-drive Sonomas get a higher-output V6 and a handling/trailering suspension standard. GMC drops the 4WD long-bed and High-Rider regular-cab models and adds a new, lower-priced base-trim extended-cab model. All versions get a boost in trailer ratings and a new paint color.

Category J

Model Description	Trade-in TMV	Private TMV	Dealer TMV
2 Dr SL Std Cab LB	7388	8174	8900
2 Dr SL 4WD Ext Cab SB			
	10874	12032	13100
2 Dr SL 4WD Std Cab SB			
	10376	11481	12500

Model Description	Trade-in TMV	Private TMV	Dealer TMV
2 Dr SL Ext Cab SB	8799	9736	10600
2 Dr SL Std Cab SB	7305	8082	8800
2 Dr SLE 4WD Ext Cab SB 4WD Ext Cab SB			
	12285	13593	14800
2 Dr SLE 4WD Std Cab SB 4WD Std Cab SB			
	10957	12123	13200
2 Dr SLE Ext Cab SB Ext Cab SB			
	10293	11389	12400
2 Dr SLE Std Cab SB	8135	9001	9800
2 Dr SLS Sport Std Cab LB			
	8035	8891	9680
2 Dr SLS Sport 4WD Std Cab SB			
	10708	11848	12900
2 Dr SLS Sport Std Cab SB			
	7969	8817	9600
2 Dr SLS Sport 4WD Std Cab Stepside SB			
	10791	11940	13000
2 Dr SLS Sport Std Cab Stepside SB			
	8069	8927	9720
2 Dr SLS Sport 4WD Ext Cab SB			
	11621	12858	14000
2 Dr SLS Sport Ext Cab SB			
	9214	10195	11100
2 Dr SLS Sport 4WD Ext Cab Stepside SB			
	11953	13226	14400
2 Dr SLS Sport Ext Cab Stepside SB			
	9546	10562	11500

OPTIONS FOR SONOMA
6 cyl 4.3 L Engine +884
AM/FM Compact Disc Player +206
AM/FM Stereo/CD/Tape +274
Air Conditioning +549
Aluminum/Alloy Wheels +191
Automatic 4-Speed Transmission +747
Bucket Seats +199
Cruise Control +127
Hinged Third Door +202
Limited Slip Differential +184
Power Door Locks +137
Power Windows +164
Sport Suspension +502
Tilt Steering Wheel +127
ZR2 Highrider Suspension +1225

YUKON 2000

Completely redesigned, Yukon is based on the new Sierra pickup platform with zippy V8 engines and a stouter chassis for a better, more isolated ride.

Category N

Model Description	Trade-in TMV	Private TMV	Dealer TMV
4 Dr SLE 4WD Wgn	21877	23813	25600
4 Dr SLE Wgn	19997	21766	23400
4 Dr SLT 4WD Wgn	22987	25022	26900
4 Dr SLT Wgn	21022	22883	24600

Model Description	Trade-in TMV	Private TMV	Dealer TMV

Model Description	Trade-in TMV	Private TMV	Dealer TMV

OPTIONS FOR YUKON

8 cyl 5.3 L Engine +478
AM/FM Stereo/CD/Tape +137
Bucket Seats +162
Camper/Towing Package +145
Compact Disc Changer +375
Heated Front Seats +239
Limited Slip Differential +172
Power Moonroof +511
Rear Heater +140
Running Boards +222
Third Seat +651
Traction Control System +133
Tutone Paint +137

YUKON DENALI   2000

For the 2000 model year, GMC's Yukon Denali gets a new exterior color and adds GM's OnStar communications system to its already impressive standard equipment list.

Category O

	Trade-in	Private	Dealer
4 Dr Denali 4WD Wgn	24062	26422	28600

YUKON XL   2000

The 2000 GMC Yukon XL is a complete redesign of last year's Suburban model, adding a whole lot of mechanical and comfort upgrades.

Category N

	Trade-in	Private	Dealer
4 Dr C1500 SLE Wgn	21620	23534	25300
4 Dr C2500 SLE Wgn	22646	24650	26500
4 Dr K1500 SLE 4WD Wgn	23757	25859	27800
4 Dr K2500 SLE 4WD Wgn	24782	26975	29000
4 Dr C1500 SLT Wgn	23500	25580	27500
4 Dr C2500 SLT Wgn	24184	26324	28300
4 Dr K1500 SLT 4WD Wgn	25209	27440	29500
4 Dr K2500 SLT 4WD Wgn	26320	28650	30800

OPTIONS FOR YUKON XL

Autoride Suspension Package +411
Bucket Seats +256
Camper/Towing Package +177
Heated Front Seats +171
Limited Slip Differential +172
Power Moonroof +679
Running Boards +222
Traction Control System +133
Trailer Hitch +177
Tutone Paint +137

1999 GMC

CLASSIC C/K 1500   1999

With an all-new Sierra just months away, changes are limited to a few new colors.

Category K

	Trade-in	Private	Dealer
2 Dr C1500 SLE Ext Cab SB	14361	15680	17000
2 Dr K1500 SLE 4WD Ext Cab SB	16302	17800	19298

OPTIONS FOR CLASSIC C/K 1500

8 cyl 5.7 L Engine +402
AM/FM Compact Disc Player +109
AM/FM Stereo/CD/Tape +167
Aluminum/Alloy Wheels +178
Bed Liner +128
Bucket Seats +173
Locking Differential +154
Power Drivers Seat +152

CLASSIC C/K 2500   1999

Mechanical upgrades include new internal components and seals for automatic transmissions, improved cooling system and starter motor durability, and three new exterior paint colors. With an all-new Sierra just months away, changes are limited to a few new colors.

Category K

	Trade-in	Private	Dealer
4 Dr K2500 STD 4WD Crew Cab SB	17402	19001	20600
2 Dr C2500 HD SL Ext Cab LB	13600	14850	16100
2 Dr C2500 HD SL Std Cab LB	12587	13743	14900
2 Dr K2500 HD SL 4WD Ext Cab LB	15543	16972	18400
2 Dr K2500 HD SL 4WD Std Cab LB	14192	15496	16800
2 Dr K2500 HD SL 4WD Ext Cab SB	15459	16879	18300
4 Dr C2500 SL Crew Cab SB	15206	16603	18000
2 Dr C2500 HD SLE Ext Cab LB	15121	16511	17900
2 Dr C2500 HD SLE Std Cab LB	13854	15127	16400
2 Dr K2500 HD SLE 4WD Ext Cab LB	17148	18724	20300
2 Dr K2500 HD SLE 4WD Std Cab LB	16050	17525	19000
2 Dr K2500 HD SLE 4WD Ext Cab SB	17064	18632	20200

Don't forget to refer to the Mileage Adjustment Table at the back of this book!

Model Description	Trade-in TMV	Private TMV	Dealer TMV	Model Description	Trade-in TMV	Private TMV	Dealer TMV
4 Dr C2500 SLE Crew Cab SB				4 Dr K3500 SL 4WD Crew Cab SB			
	16135	17617	19100		17993	19647	21300
4 Dr K2500 SLE 4WD Crew Cab SB				2 Dr C3500 SLE Ext Cab LB			
	18247	19923	21600		16557	18079	19600
2 Dr C2500 HD SLT Ext Cab LB				2 Dr C3500 SLE Std Cab LB			
	16219	17710	19200		14276	15588	16900
2 Dr C2500 HD SLT Std Cab LB				2 Dr K3500 SLE 4WD Ext Cab LB			
	14783	16142	17500		18500	20200	21900
2 Dr K2500 HD SLT 4WD Ext Cab LB				2 Dr K3500 SLE 4WD Std Cab LB			
	18331	20016	21700		16304	17802	19300
2 Dr K2500 HD SLT 4WD Std Cab LB				4 Dr C3500 SLE Crew Cab LB			
	16642	18171	19700		17317	18909	20500
2 Dr K2500 HD SLT 4WD Ext Cab SB				4 Dr K3500 SLE 4WD Crew Cab LB			
	17993	19647	21300		19347	21125	22903
4 Dr C2500 SLT Crew Cab SB				4 Dr C3500 SLE Crew Cab SB			
	17655	19278	20900		18247	19923	21600
4 Dr K2500 SLT 4WD Crew Cab SB				4 Dr K3500 SLE 4WD Crew Cab SB			
	19852	21676	23500		20443	22321	24200
				2 Dr C3500 SLT Ext Cab LB			
					17571	19185	20800
				2 Dr C3500 SLT Std Cab LB			
					15206	16603	18000
				2 Dr K3500 SLT 4WD Ext Cab LB			
					19429	21215	23000
				2 Dr K3500 SLT 4WD Std Cab LB			
					17233	18816	20400
				4 Dr C3500 SLT Crew Cab LB			
					18416	20108	21800
				4 Dr K3500 SLT 4WD Crew Cab LB			
					20527	22414	24300
				4 Dr C3500 SLT Crew Cab SB			
					19342	21120	22897
				4 Dr K3500 SLT 4WD Crew Cab SB			
					21541	23521	25500

OPTIONS FOR CLASSIC C/K 2500
8 cyl 6.5 L Turbodiesel Engine +1561
8 cyl 7.4 L Engine +345
Air Conditioning[Opt on SL] +462
Automatic 4-Speed Transmission +572
Bed Liner +128
Bucket Seats +173
Cruise Control[Opt on SL] +118
Heated Front Seats +129
Locking Differential +163
Power Drivers Seat +138
Tilt Steering Wheel[Opt on SL] +112

CLASSIC C/K 3500   1999

Mechanical upgrades include new internal components and seals for automatic transmissions, improved cooling system and starter motor durability, and three new exterior paint colors. With an all-new Sierra just months away, changes are limited to a few new colors.

Category K

Model Description	Trade-in TMV	Private TMV	Dealer TMV
2 Dr C3500 SL Ext Cab LB			
	15037	16418	17800
2 Dr C3500 SL Std Cab LB			
	12756	13928	15100
2 Dr K3500 SL 4WD Ext Cab LB			
	16895	18448	20000
2 Dr K3500 SL 4WD Std Cab LB			
	14783	16142	17500
4 Dr C3500 SL Crew Cab LB			
	14868	16234	17600
4 Dr K3500 SL 4WD Crew Cab LB			
	16979	18540	20100
4 Dr C3500 SL Crew Cab SB			
	15881	17341	18800

OPTIONS FOR CLASSIC C/K 3500
8 cyl 6.5 L Turbodiesel Engine +1561
8 cyl 7.4 L Engine +345
AM/FM Compact Disc Player +109
AM/FM Stereo/CD/Tape +167
Air Conditioning[Opt on SL] +462
Automatic 4-Speed Transmission +572
Bed Liner +128
Bucket Seats +154
Chrome Step Bumper[Opt on SL] +131
Cruise Control[Opt on SL] +118
Dual Rear Wheels +492
Locking Differential +145
Power Drivers Seat +138
Tilt Steering Wheel[Opt on SL] +112

ENVOY   1999

After its debut as General Motors' high-end compact SUV last year, the GMC Envoy gets equipment

Don't forget to refer to the Mileage Adjustment Table at the back of this book!

Model Description	Trade-in TMV	Private TMV	Dealer TMV	Model Description	Trade-in TMV	Private TMV	Dealer TMV

upgrades for '99. A new mini-module for the driver's airbag allows for steering-wheel radio controls, and the turn-signal stalk now incorporates a flash-to-pass headlamp feature. Heated, eight-way power front seating is improved, thanks to available two-position memory for the driver and power recliners. A liftgate ajar telltale resides in the instrument cluster, and the outside rearview mirrors have been redesigned, featuring electrochromic dimming and power folding capability. GM's advanced AutoTrac active transfer case is now standard, while a new, shift lever-mounted button selects a Tow/Haul mode to optimize transmission shift points. There are three new metallic exterior paint colors: Topaz gold, Meadow green and Indigo blue.

Category O

Model Description	Trade-in	Private	Dealer
4 Dr STD 4WD Wgn	14697	16198	17700

OPTIONS FOR ENVOY
Dual Power Seats +351
Locking Differential +154
Power Moonroof +431

JIMMY 1999

There are three new colors and revised outside mirrors, but most changes to the '99 Jimmy are inside. You'll find new power-seating features, redundant radio controls and a mini-module depowered airbag in the steering wheel, as well as a new Bose premium sound system and six-disc CD changer. A vehicle content theft alarm, flash-to-pass headlamp feature, and liftgate ajar warning lamp have also been added. Four-wheel-drive versions get the new AutoTrac active transfer case and four-door models gain a Tow/Haul mode for the transmission. Finally, the optional Z85 Euro-Ride suspension has been retuned.

Category M

Model Description	Trade-in	Private	Dealer
2 Dr SL 4WD Utility	8737	9719	10700
2 Dr SL Utility	7186	7993	8800
4 Dr SL 4WD Wgn	10697	11898	13100
4 Dr SL Wgn	10044	11172	12300
4 Dr SLE 4WD Wgn	11840	13170	14500
4 Dr SLE Wgn	11105	12353	13600
2 Dr SLS Sport 4WD Utility	10288	11444	12600
2 Dr SLS Sport Utility	7839	8719	9600
4 Dr SLT 4WD Wgn	12901	14351	15800
4 Dr SLT Wgn	11758	13079	14400

OPTIONS FOR JIMMY
AM/FM Stereo/CD/Tape +195
Aluminum/Alloy Wheels[Opt on SL] +161
Automatic 4-Speed Transmission[Std on SLE,SLS Sport,SLT,Wgn] +574
Camper/Towing Package +121

Compact Disc Changer +227
Cruise Control[Opt on SLS Sport] +118
Delco/Bose Stereo System +285
Dual Power Seats +276
Heated Front Seats +144
Locking Differential +154
Power Drivers Seat +138
Power Moonroof +431
Power Windows[Std on SLE,SLT] +144

SAFARI PASSENGER 1999

There are two new exterior paint and body-cladding colors, restyled wheels and outside mirrors, an overhead console and new optional integrated running boards. Additionally, all-wheel-drive Safari models get the new AutoTrac transfer case, and GM's OnStar communications system is now available.

Category P

Model Description	Trade-in	Private	Dealer
2 Dr SL AWD Pass. Van Ext	10853	12126	13400
2 Dr SL Pass. Van Ext	9719	10859	12000
2 Dr SLE AWD Pass. Van Ext	11096	12398	13700
2 Dr SLE Pass. Van Ext	10367	11583	12800
2 Dr SLT AWD Pass. Van Ext	12878	14389	15900
2 Dr SLT Pass. Van Ext	11906	13303	14700

OPTIONS FOR SAFARI PASSENGER
7 Passenger Seating +227
AM/FM Compact Disc Player[Std on SLT] +234
AM/FM Stereo/CD/Tape +292
Aluminum/Alloy Wheels[Std on SLT] +174
Camper/Towing Package +177
Chrome Wheels +152
Dual Air Conditioning +301
Dual Power Seats +276
Leather Seats[Opt on SLT] +546
Locking Differential +145
Power Door Locks[Opt on SL] +128
Power Drivers Seat[Std on SLT] +138
Power Windows[Opt on SL] +152
Privacy Glass[Opt on SL] +167
Rear Heater +118
Rear Window Wiper +118

SAVANA 1999

GMC's full-size van gets two new exterior colors, one new interior color and automatic transmission enhancements.

Category Q

Model Description	Trade-in	Private	Dealer
2 Dr G1500 Cargo Van	8930	9815	10700
2 Dr G1500 Pass. Van	10287	11306	12325
2 Dr G2500 Cargo Van	9181	10090	11000

Don't forget to refer to the Mileage Adjustment Table at the back of this book!

GMC 99

Model Description	Trade-in TMV	Private TMV	Dealer TMV
2 Dr G2500 Cargo Van Ext			
	9348	10274	11200
2 Dr G2500 Pass. Van	11267	12384	13500
2 Dr G2500 Pass. Van Ext			
	11685	12842	14000
2 Dr G3500 Cargo Van	9849	10824	11800
2 Dr G3500 Cargo Van Ext			
	10245	11260	12275
2 Dr G3500 Pass. Van	11434	12567	13700
2 Dr G3500 Pass. Van Ext			
	11852	13026	14200
2 Dr G1500 SLE Pass. Van			
	11101	12200	13300
2 Dr G2500 SLE Pass. Van			
	12019	13209	14400
2 Dr G2500 SLE Pass. Van Ext			
	12519	13760	15000
2 Dr G3500 SLE Pass. Van			
	12102	13301	14500
2 Dr G3500 SLE Pass. Van Ext			
	12603	13851	15100

OPTIONS FOR SAVANA

15 Passenger Seating +213
8 cyl 5.0 L Engine +285
8 cyl 5.7 L Engine[Std on G2500, G3500] +687
8 cyl 6.5 L Turbodiesel Engine +1561
8 cyl 7.4 L Engine +345
AM/FM Compact Disc Player +311
AM/FM Stereo Tape +253
AM/FM Stereo/CD/Tape +369
Air Conditioning[Opt on Cargo, Cargo EXT] +460
Aluminum/Alloy Wheels +144
Camper/Towing Package +178
Chrome Wheels +144
Cruise Control[Opt on STD] +118
Dual Air Conditioning +494
Dual Power Seats +276
Locking Differential +145
Power Door Locks[Opt on STD] +128
Power Drivers Seat +138
Power Windows[Opt on STD] +147
Privacy Glass +224
Rear Heater +138

SIERRA 1500   1999

Finally, the decade-old, full-size GMC pickup based on the C/K gets a complete redesign from the ground-up. Major structural, power, braking and interior enhancements characterize the all-new Sierra. Styling is evolutionary rather than revolutionary, both inside and out.

Category K

Model Description	Trade-in TMV	Private TMV	Dealer TMV
2 Dr SL 4WD Ext Cab LB			
	14445	15773	17100

Model Description	Trade-in TMV	Private TMV	Dealer TMV
2 Dr SL 4WD Std Cab LB			
	11827	12913	14000
2 Dr SL Ext Cab LB	12458	13603	14748
2 Dr SL Std Cab LB	8785	9593	10400
2 Dr SL 4WD Ext Cab SB			
	14361	15680	17000
2 Dr SL 4WD Std Cab SB			
	11658	12729	13800
2 Dr SL Ext Cab SB	12377	13515	14652
2 Dr SL Std Cab SB	8616	9408	10200
2 Dr SL 4WD Ext Cab Stepside SB			
	16050	17525	19000
2 Dr SL 4WD Std Cab Stepside SB			
	12418	13559	14700
2 Dr SL Ext Cab Stepside SB			
	14276	15588	16900
2 Dr SL Std Cab Stepside SB			
	10390	11345	12300
2 Dr SLE 4WD Ext Cab LB			
	15290	16695	18100
2 Dr SLE 4WD Std Cab LB			
	14023	15311	16600
2 Dr SLE Ext Cab LB	14276	15588	16900
2 Dr SLE Std Cab LB	12333	13467	14600
2 Dr SLE 4WD Ext Cab SB			
	15121	16511	17900
2 Dr SLE 4WD Std Cab SB			
	13938	15219	16500
2 Dr SLE Ext Cab SB	14192	15496	16800
2 Dr SLE Std Cab SB	11911	13005	14100
2 Dr SLE 4WD Ext Cab Stepside SB			
	17402	19001	20600
2 Dr SLE 4WD Std Cab Stepside SB			
	14699	16049	17400
2 Dr SLE Ext Cab Stepside SB			
	15628	17064	18500
2 Dr SLE Std Cab Stepside SB			
	12840	14020	15200
2 Dr SLT 4WD Ext Cab LB			
	18585	20292	22000
2 Dr SLT Ext Cab LB	16473	17986	19500
2 Dr SLT 4WD Ext Cab SB			
	18416	20108	21800
2 Dr SLT Ext Cab SB	16305	17804	19302
2 Dr SLT 4WD Ext Cab Stepside SB			
	18753	20477	22200
2 Dr SLT Ext Cab Stepside SB			
	16642	18171	19700

OPTIONS FOR SIERRA 1500

8 cyl 4.8 L Engine[Std on SLT] +341
8 cyl 5.3 L Engine +402

Don't forget to refer to the Mileage Adjustment Table at the back of this book!

GMC 99

Model Description	Trade-in TMV	Private TMV	Dealer TMV	Model Description	Trade-in TMV	Private TMV	Dealer TMV

AM/FM Stereo/CD/Tape +167
Air Conditioning[Opt on SL] +462
Aluminum/Alloy Wheels[Std on SLT] +178
Automatic 4-Speed Transmission[Std on SLT] +572
Bucket Seats +144
Chrome Wheels[Opt on SL] +178
Cruise Control[Opt on SL] +115
Dual Power Seats +276
Locking Differential +154

SIERRA 2500 — 1999

Finally, the decade-old, full-size GMC pickup based on the C/K gets a complete redesign from the ground-up. Major structural, power, braking and interior enhancements characterize the all-new Sierra. Styling is evolutionary rather than revolutionary, both inside and out.

Category K

Model Description	Trade-in TMV	Private TMV	Dealer TMV
2 Dr SL 4WD Ext Cab LB	16304	17802	19300
2 Dr SL 4WD Std Cab LB	13854	15127	16400
2 Dr SL Ext Cab LB	14361	15680	17000
2 Dr SL Std Cab LB	12080	13190	14300
2 Dr SL Std Cab LB	12418	13559	14700
2 Dr SL 4WD Ext Cab SB	16050	17525	19000
2 Dr SL Ext Cab SB	13685	14942	16200
2 Dr SLE 4WD Ext Cab LB	17655	19278	20900
2 Dr SLE 4WD Std Cab LB	15290	16695	18100
2 Dr SLE Ext Cab LB	15797	17248	18700
2 Dr SLE Std Cab LB	13600	14850	16100
2 Dr SLE Std Cab LB	13432	14666	15900
2 Dr SLE 4WD Ext Cab SB	17486	19093	20700
2 Dr SLE Ext Cab SB	15037	16418	17800
2 Dr SLT 4WD Ext Cab LB HD	20781	22690	24600
2 Dr SLT Ext Cab LB HD	18500	20200	21900
2 Dr SLT 4WD Ext Cab SB HD	20527	22414	24300
2 Dr SLT Ext Cab SB	17740	19370	21000

OPTIONS FOR SIERRA 2500
8 cyl 6.0 L Engine[Std on SLT] +287
AM/FM Stereo/CD/Tape +167
Air Conditioning[Opt on SL] +462
Automatic 4-Speed Transmission[Std on SLT] +572
Bucket Seats +144
Chrome Step Bumper[Opt on SL] +115
Cruise Control[Opt on SL] +115

Dual Power Seats +276
Locking Differential +154

SONOMA — 1999

The '99 Sonoma touts four new exterior colors, a new steering wheel with mini-module depowered airbag, and larger, more robust outside rearview mirrors, with the uplevel power mirror gaining a heated feature. AutoTrac, GM's electronic push-button two-speed transfer case, is now standard on four-wheel-drive models, and all Sonomas get a content theft alarm with remote keyless entry as well as a flash-to-pass headlamp feature for the smart stalk. Serious four-wheelers can now order composite skid plates.

Category J

Model Description	Trade-in TMV	Private TMV	Dealer TMV
2 Dr SL 4WD Std Cab LB	8696	9748	10800
2 Dr SL Std Cab LB	6603	7401	8200
2 Dr SL 4WD Std Cab SB	8670	9719	10768
2 Dr SL Std Cab SB	6281	7040	7800
2 Dr SLE 4WD Ext Cab SB	10951	12275	13600
2 Dr SLE 4WD Std Cab SB	9985	11192	12400
2 Dr SLE Ext Cab SB	8561	9596	10632
2 Dr SLE Std Cab SB	7408	8304	9200
2 Dr SLS Sport 4WD Ext Cab Stepside SB	10790	12095	13400
2 Dr SLS Sport 4WD Std Cab Stepside SB	9904	11102	12300
2 Dr SLS Sport Ext Cab Stepside SB	8455	9477	10500
2 Dr SLS Sport Std Cab Stepside SB	7327	8214	9100
2 Dr SLS Sport 4WD Std Cab LB	9501	10651	11800
2 Dr SLS Sport Std Cab LB	7005	7853	8700
2 Dr SLS Sport 4WD Ext Cab SB	10468	11734	13000
2 Dr SLS Sport 4WD Std Cab SB	9179	10290	11400
2 Dr SLS Sport Ext Cab SB	7891	8846	9800
2 Dr SLS Sport Std Cab SB	6925	7762	8600

OPTIONS FOR SONOMA
6 cyl 4.3 L Vortec Engine[Opt on 2WD] +148
AM/FM Compact Disc Player +174
AM/FM Stereo/CD/Tape +231

Don't forget to refer to the Mileage Adjustment Table at the back of this book!

Model Description	Trade-in TMV	Private TMV	Dealer TMV

Air Conditioning +462
Aluminum/Alloy Wheels +161
Automatic 4-Speed Transmission +614
Bucket Seats +167
Cruise Control +106
Hinged Third Door +170
Locking Differential +154
Power Door Locks +115
Power Windows +138
Sport Suspension +423
Tilt Steering Wheel +106
ZR2 Highrider Suspension +1031

SUBURBAN 1999

A couple of new colors are the only modifications to the Suburban.

Category N

Model Description	Trade-in TMV	Private TMV	Dealer TMV
4 Dr C1500 Wgn	14518	15859	17200
4 Dr C2500 Wgn	15109	16504	17900
4 Dr K1500 4WD Wgn	15953	17426	18900
4 Dr K2500 4WD Wgn	16881	18441	20000

OPTIONS FOR SUBURBAN

8 cyl 6.5 L Turbodiesel Engine[Opt on 2500] +1561
8 cyl 7.4 L Engine[Opt on 2500] +327
AM/FM Stereo/CD/Tape +109
Air Conditioning +460
Aluminum/Alloy Wheels +169
Bucket Seats +147
Camper/Towing Package +117
Center & Rear Bench Seat +598
Center Bench Seat +345
Cruise Control +107
Dual Air Conditioning +761
Dual Power Seats +262
Heated Front Seats +191
Leather Seats +682
Locking Differential +138
Power Drivers Seat +131
Power Windows +144
Privacy Glass +165
Rear Heater +112
Running Boards +177
SLE Package +2092
SLT Package +2533
Skid Plates +128

YUKON 1999

More new colors are added as Yukon cruises into 1999.

Category N

Model Description	Trade-in TMV	Private TMV	Dealer TMV
4 Dr SLE 4WD Wgn	16037	17519	19000
4 Dr SLE Wgn	14518	15859	17200
4 Dr SLT 4WD Wgn	17135	18717	20300
4 Dr SLT Wgn	15615	17058	18500

OPTIONS FOR YUKON

AM/FM Stereo/CD/Tape[Std on SLT] +115

Bucket Seats +136
Camper/Towing Package +123
Compact Disc Changer +316
Dual Air Conditioning +316
Dual Power Seats +276
Heated Front Seats +202
Locking Differential +145
Running Boards +186

YUKON DENALI 1999

General Motors brand managers came up with an idea to dress up the GMC Yukon, fill it full of luxury touches and give it a special name to toss their hat into the luxury SUV arena. Enter the 1999 GMC Yukon Denali, with loads of unique features and exclusive exterior paint colors- until, that is, GM decided to spin-off a clone for Cadillac called the Escalade.

Category O

Model Description	Trade-in TMV	Private TMV	Dealer TMV
4 Dr Denali 4WD Wgn	20426	22513	24600

OPTIONS FOR YUKON DENALI

Tutone Paint +115

1998 GMC

ENVOY 1998

GMC is introduces its finest luxury compact SUV to date: the Envoy.

Category O

Model Description	Trade-in TMV	Private TMV	Dealer TMV
4 Dr STD 4WD Wgn	13210	14789	16500

OPTIONS FOR ENVOY

Power Moonroof +378

JIMMY 1998

A revised interior contains dual second-generation airbags, improved climate controls and available premium sound systems. Outside, the front bumper, grille and headlights are new. Side cladding is restyled and SLT models have new alloy wheels. Fresh colors inside and out sum up the changes.

Category M

Model Description	Trade-in TMV	Private TMV	Dealer TMV
2 Dr SL 4WD Utility	8488	9502	10600
2 Dr SL Utility	7687	8605	9600
4 Dr SL 4WD Wgn	9449	10577	11800
4 Dr SL Wgn	8568	9591	10700
4 Dr SLE 4WD Wgn	10249	11474	12800
4 Dr SLE Wgn	9609	10757	12000
2 Dr SLS Sport 4WD Utility			
	9048	10129	11300
2 Dr SLS Sport Utility			
	8328	9322	10400
4 Dr SLS Sport 4WD Wgn			
	9849	11026	12300
4 Dr SLS Sport Wgn	8888	9950	11100

Don't forget to refer to the Mileage Adjustment Table at the back of this book!

Model Description	Trade-in TMV	Private TMV	Dealer TMV
4 Dr SLT 4WD Wgn	10890	12191	13600
4 Dr SLT Wgn	9929	11115	12400

OPTIONS FOR JIMMY

AM/FM Stereo/CD/Tape +172
Air Bag Restraint +113
Aluminum/Alloy Wheels[Opt on SL] +141
Camper/Towing Package +106
Compact Disc Changer +200
Heated Front Seats +126
Locking Differential +127
Power Drivers Seat[Std on SLT,SLE] +126
Power Moonroof +378
Power Windows[Opt on SL] +126

SAFARI 1998

New colors, a theft deterrent system and automatic transmission refinements are the changes to the Safari. This van is one of the few GM models that retains full-power airbags for 1998.

Category P

Model Description	Trade-in	Private	Dealer
2 Dr SL AWD Cargo Van Ext	8867	9987	11200
2 Dr SL Cargo Van Ext	7679	8649	9700
2 Dr SLE AWD Pass. Van Ext	10213	11503	12900
2 Dr SLE Pass. Van Ext	9104	10254	11500
2 Dr SLT AWD Pass. Van Ext	11242	12662	14200
2 Dr SLT Pass. Van Ext	10292	11592	13000
2 Dr SLX AWD Pass. Van Ext	9025	10165	11400
2 Dr SLX Pass. Van Ext	8075	9095	10200

OPTIONS FOR SAFARI

7 Passenger Seating +373
8 Passenger Seating[Opt on SLX] +200
AM/FM Compact Disc Player[Std on SLT] +206
AM/FM Stereo Tape[Std on SLE] +126
AM/FM Stereo/CD/Tape +256
Aluminum/Alloy Wheels[Std on SLT] +138
Camper/Towing Package +156
Child Seats (2) +121
Chrome Wheels +149
Cruise Control[Opt on SL,SLX] +113
Dual Air Conditioning +265
Dual Power Seats +242
Leather Seats +479
Locking Differential +127
Power Door Locks[Opt on SL,SLX] +113
Power Drivers Seat[Std on SLT] +121
Power Windows[Opt on SL,SLX] +126
Privacy Glass[Opt on SL,SLX] +147

SAVANA 1998

New colors, transmission enhancements, more power for the diesel engine, revised uplevel stereos and the addition of a PassLock theft deterrent system mark the changes for 1998. A mini-module driver's airbag is new, but it and the passenger airbag still deploy at full-force levels.

Category Q

Model Description	Trade-in	Private	Dealer
2 Dr G1500 Cargo Van	7689	8558	9500
2 Dr G1500 Pass. Van	9065	10090	11200
2 Dr G2500 Cargo Van	7851	8739	9700
2 Dr G2500 Cargo Van Ext	8256	9189	10200
2 Dr G2500 Pass. Van	9794	10901	12100
2 Dr G2500 Pass. Van Ext	10198	11351	12600
2 Dr G3500 Cargo Van	8580	9549	10600
2 Dr G3500 Cargo Van Ext	8903	9910	11000
2 Dr G3500 Pass. Van	9956	11081	12300
2 Dr G3500 Pass. Van Ext	10279	11441	12700
2 Dr G1500 SLE Pass. Van	9551	10630	11800
2 Dr G2500 SLE Pass. Van	10522	11712	13000
2 Dr G2500 SLE Pass. Van Ext	10846	12072	13400
2 Dr G3500 SLE Pass. Van	10603	11802	13100
2 Dr G3500 SLE Pass. Van Ext	10927	12162	13500

OPTIONS FOR SAVANA

15 Passenger Seating +188
8 cyl 5.0 L Engine +250
8 cyl 5.7 L Engine[Std on G2500,Pass Van,G2500 Pass Van EXT.] +487
8 cyl 6.5 L Turbodiesel Engine +1371
8 cyl 7.4 L Engine +303
AM/FM Compact Disc Player +274
AM/FM Stereo/CD/Tape +324
Air Conditioning[Opt on Cargo,Cargo EXT] +492
Aluminum/Alloy Wheels +126
Camper/Towing Package +156
Chrome Bumpers +126
Chrome Wheels +126
Dual Air Conditioning +434
Dual Power Seats +242
Locking Differential +127
Power Door Locks[Opt on STD] +113
Power Drivers Seat +121
Power Windows[Opt on STD] +129
Privacy Glass +144

Don't forget to refer to the Mileage Adjustment Table at the back of this book!

Rear Heater +121

SIERRA 1500　　　　　1998

With an all-new Sierra just one year away, changes are minimal. Diesel engines make more power and torque, extended cab models get rear heater ducts, a PassLock theft deterrent system is standard, 1500-series trucks get reduced rolling resistance tires and three new colors debut. Second generation airbags are standard.

Category K

Model Description	Trade-in TMV	Private TMV	Dealer TMV
2 Dr C1500 SL Ext Cab LB	9993	11052	12200
2 Dr C1500 SL Std Cab LB	8072	8928	9855
2 Dr K1500 SL 4WD Ext Cab LB	11713	12955	14300
2 Dr K1500 SL 4WD Std Cab LB	10321	11415	12600
2 Dr C1500 SL Ext Cab SB	9584	10599	11700
2 Dr C1500 SL Std Cab SB	7977	8823	9739
2 Dr K1500 SL 4WD Ext Cab SB	11222	12411	13700
2 Dr K1500 SL 4WD Std Cab SB	10157	11234	12400
2 Dr C1500 SL Std Cab Stepside SB	8846	9784	10800
2 Dr K1500 SL 4WD Std Cab Stepside SB	10485	11596	12800
2 Dr C1500 SLE Ext Cab LB	10976	12140	13400
2 Dr C1500 SLE Std Cab LB	9665	10690	11800
2 Dr K1500 SLE 4WD Ext Cab LB	12614	13951	15400
2 Dr K1500 SLE 4WD Std Cab LB	11304	12502	13800
2 Dr C1500 SLE Ext Cab SB	10566	11687	12900
2 Dr C1500 SLE Std Cab SB	9502	10509	11600
2 Dr K1500 SLE 4WD Ext Cab SB	12205	13498	14900
2 Dr K1500 SLE 4WD Std Cab SB	11140	12321	13600
2 Dr C1500 SLE Ext Cab Stepside SB	12123	13408	14800
2 Dr C1500 SLE Std Cab Stepside SB	9829	10871	12000
2 Dr K1500 SLE 4WD Ext Cab Stepside SB	13843	15310	16900
2 Dr K1500 SLE 4WD Std Cab Stepside SB	11468	12683	14000
2 Dr C1500 SLT Ext Cab LB	12287	13589	15000
2 Dr C1500 SLT Std Cab LB	10894	12049	13300
2 Dr K1500 SLT 4WD Ext Cab LB	13925	15401	17000
2 Dr K1500 SLT 4WD Std Cab LB	12532	13861	15300
2 Dr C1500 SLT Ext Cab SB	11877	13136	14500
2 Dr C1500 SLT Std Cab SB	10730	11868	13100
2 Dr K1500 SLT 4WD Ext Cab SB	13433	14857	16400
2 Dr K1500 SLT 4WD Std Cab SB	12369	13680	15100
2 Dr C1500 SLT Ext Cab Stepside SB	13188	14586	16100
2 Dr C1500 SLT Std Cab Stepside SB	11058	12230	13500
2 Dr K1500 SLT 4WD Ext Cab Stepside SB	14744	16307	18000
2 Dr K1500 SLT 4WD Std Cab Stepside SB	12696	14042	15500
2 Dr C1500 Special Std Cab LB	7721	8539	9426
2 Dr K1500 Special 4WD Std Cab LB	9911	10962	12100
2 Dr C1500 Special Std Cab SB	7646	8457	9335
2 Dr K1500 Special 4WD Std Cab SB	9747	10781	11900

OPTIONS FOR SIERRA 1500
8 cyl 5.0 L Engine +250
8 cyl 5.7 L Engine +353
8 cyl 6.5 L Turbodiesel Engine +1706
AM/FM Stereo/CD/Tape +147
Air Conditioning[Opt on SL, Special] +406
Aluminum/Alloy Wheels +172
Automatic 4-Speed Transmission +489
Bed Liner +113
Bucket Seats[Opt on SLE] +126
Chrome Wheels +126
Hinged Third Door +212
Locking Differential +127
Power Drivers Seat[Opt on SLE] +121

GMC 98

Model Description	Trade-in TMV	Private TMV	Dealer TMV	Model Description	Trade-in TMV	Private TMV	Dealer TMV

SIERRA 2500   1998

With an all-new Sierra just one year away, changes are minimal. Diesel engines make more power and torque, extended cab models get rear heater ducts, a PassLock theft deterrent system is standard, 1500-series trucks get reduced rolling resistance tires, and three new colors debut. Second generation airbags are standard.

Category K

Model Description	Trade-in TMV	Private TMV	Dealer TMV
2 Dr C2500 HD SL Ext Cab LB	10894	12049	13300
2 Dr C2500 HD SL Std Cab LB	9993	11052	12200
2 Dr C2500 SL Std Cab LB	9420	10418	11500
2 Dr K2500 HD SL 4WD Ext Cab LB	12696	14042	15500
2 Dr K2500 HD SL 4WD Std Cab LB	11468	12683	14000
2 Dr C2500 SL Ext Cab SB	10812	11958	13200
2 Dr K2500 HD SL 4WD Ext Cab SB	12614	13951	15400
2 Dr C2500 HD SLE Ext Cab LB	12123	13408	14800
2 Dr C2500 HD SLE Std Cab LB	11222	12411	13700
2 Dr C2500 SLE Std Cab LB	10648	11777	13000
2 Dr K2500 HD SLE 4WD Ext Cab LB	13925	15401	17000
2 Dr K2500 HD SLE 4WD Std Cab LB	12778	14133	15600
2 Dr C2500 SLE Ext Cab SB	12061	13339	14724
2 Dr K2500 HD SLE 4WD Ext Cab SB	13843	15310	16900
2 Dr C2500 HD SLT Ext Cab LB	12942	14314	15800
2 Dr C2500 HD SLT Std Cab LB	12021	13296	14676
2 Dr C2500 SLT Std Cab LB	11386	12593	13900
2 Dr K2500 HD SLT 4WD Ext Cab LB	14662	16216	17900
2 Dr K2500 HD SLT 4WD Std Cab LB	13597	15039	16600
2 Dr C2500 SLT Ext Cab SB	12860	14223	15700
2 Dr K2500 HD SLT 4WD Ext Cab SB	14580	16126	17800

OPTIONS FOR SIERRA 2500
8 cyl 5.7 L Engine[Std on HD] +353
8 cyl 6.5 L Turbodiesel Engine +1371
8 cyl 7.4 L Engine +303
AM/FM Stereo/CD/Tape +147
Air Conditioning[Opt on SL] +406
Automatic 4-Speed Transmission +489
Bed Liner +113
Bucket Seats +126
Hinged Third Door +212
Locking Differential +127
Power Drivers Seat[Opt on SLE] +121

SIERRA 3500   1998

With an all-new Sierra just one year away, changes are minimal. Diesel engines make more power and torque, extended cab models get rear heater ducts, a PassLock theft deterrent system is standard, 1500-series trucks get reduced rolling resistance tires, and three new colors debut. Second generation airbags are standard.

Category K

Model Description	Trade-in TMV	Private TMV	Dealer TMV
2 Dr C3500 HD Cab & Chassis Std Cab	12369	13680	15100
2 Dr C3500 SL Ext Cab LB	12287	13589	15000
2 Dr C3500 SL Std Cab LB	10321	11415	12600
2 Dr K3500 SL 4WD Ext Cab LB	13925	15401	17000
2 Dr K3500 SL 4WD Std Cab LB	12041	13317	14700
2 Dr C3500 SL Crew Cab LB	12123	13408	14800
4 Dr K3500 SL 4WD Crew Cab LB	14007	15492	17100
2 Dr C3500 SLE Ext Cab LB	13679	15129	16700
2 Dr C3500 SLE Std Cab LB	11631	12864	14200
2 Dr K3500 SLE 4WD Ext Cab LB	15154	16760	18500
2 Dr K3500 SLE 4WD Std Cab LB	13433	14857	16400
4 Dr C3500 SLE Crew Cab LB	14252	15763	17400
4 Dr K3500 SLE 4WD Crew Cab LB	15891	17575	19400
2 Dr C3500 SLT Ext Cab LB	14416	15944	17600
2 Dr C3500 SLT Std Cab LB	12450	13770	15200

Don't forget to refer to the Mileage Adjustment Table at the back of this book!

GMC 98

Model Description	Trade-in TMV	Private TMV	Dealer TMV
2 Dr K3500 SLT 4WD Ext Cab LB	15973	17666	19500
2 Dr K3500 SLT 4WD Std Cab LB	14171	15673	17300
4 Dr C3500 SLT Crew Cab LB	15072	16669	18400
4 Dr K3500 SLT 4WD Crew Cab LB	16956	18753	20700

OPTIONS FOR SIERRA 3500

8 cyl 6.5 L Turbodiesel Engine +1371
8 cyl 7.4 L Engine +303
AM/FM Stereo/CD/Tape +147
Air Conditioning[Opt on SL] +406
Automatic 4-Speed Transmission +489
Bed Liner +113
Bucket Seats +126
Dual Rear Wheels +432
Locking Differential +127
Power Drivers Seat[Opt on SLE] +121
Power Windows[Opt on SL] +121

SONOMA 1998

Styling is re-tuned inside and out, resulting in a sleeker look and better interior ergonomics. Dual second-generation airbags are standard, and seats are upgraded for improved comfort and appearance. Four-wheel disc brakes are standard on 4WD models and uplevel stereos are new for 1998. New colors inside and out round out the changes.

Category J

Model Description	Trade-in TMV	Private TMV	Dealer TMV
2 Dr SL 4WD Std Cab LB	7613	8615	9700
2 Dr SL Std Cab LB	5729	6483	7300
2 Dr SL 4WD Std Cab SB	7534	8526	9600
2 Dr SL Std Cab SB	5572	6306	7100
2 Dr SLE 4WD Ext Cab SB	9967	11279	12700
2 Dr SLE 4WD Std Cab SB	9383	10617	11955
2 Dr SLE Ext Cab SB	7377	8348	9400
2 Dr SLE Std Cab SB	6593	7460	8400
2 Dr SLS Sport 4WD Std Cab LB	8524	9646	10861
2 Dr SLS Sport Std Cab LB	6476	7328	8251
2 Dr SLS Sport 4WD Ext Cab SB	9889	11190	12600
2 Dr SLS Sport 4WD Std Cab SB	8428	9537	10739
2 Dr SLS Sport Ext Cab SB	7142	8082	9100
2 Dr SLS Sport Std Cab SB			

Model Description	Trade-in TMV	Private TMV	Dealer TMV
	6396	7237	8149
2 Dr SLS Sport 4WD Ext Cab Stepside SB	10595	11989	13500
2 Dr SLS Sport 4WD Std Cab Stepside SB	9339	10568	11900
2 Dr SLS Sport Ext Cab Stepside SB	7299	8259	9300
2 Dr SLS Sport Std Cab Stepside SB	6514	7371	8300

OPTIONS FOR SONOMA

6 cyl 4.3 L Engine[Opt on 2WD] +500
6 cyl 4.3 L Vortec Engine +131
AM/FM Compact Disc Player +152
AM/FM Stereo/CD/Tape +172
Air Conditioning +406
Aluminum/Alloy Wheels[Std on SLE] +141
Automatic 4-Speed Transmission +540
Bucket Seats +122
Highrider Suspension Package +905
Hinged Third Door +190
Locking Differential +127
Power Windows +121
Sport Suspension +230

SUBURBAN 1998

De-powered second-generation airbags protect front seat occupants for 1998. A new innovation called carpeted floor mats finally appears inside the big 'Burban. Standard equipment now includes PassLock theft deterrent system, electrochromic rearview mirror, and automatic four-wheel drive on K-series models.

Category N

Model Description	Trade-in TMV	Private TMV	Dealer TMV
4 Dr C1500 Wgn	12770	14081	15500
4 Dr C2500 Wgn	13677	15080	16600
4 Dr K1500 4WD Wgn	14418	15897	17500
4 Dr K2500 4WD Wgn	15160	16715	18400

OPTIONS FOR SUBURBAN

8 cyl 6.5 L Turbodiesel Engine[Opt on 2500] +1371
8 cyl 7.4 L Engine[Opt on 2500] +288
Air Conditioning +405
Aluminum/Alloy Wheels +148
Bucket Seats +130
Center & Rear Bench Seat +525
Center Bench Seat +303
Dual Air Conditioning +669
Dual Power Seats +115
Heated Front Seats +168
Leather Seats +600
Locking Differential +121
Power Drivers Seat +115
Power Windows +126
Privacy Glass +146
Rear Window Wiper +133
Running Boards +155
SLE Package +1838

Don't forget to refer to the Mileage Adjustment Table at the back of this book!

Model Description	Trade-in TMV	Private TMV	Dealer TMV	Model Description	Trade-in TMV	Private TMV	Dealer TMV

SLT Package +2225
Skid Plates +112

YUKON   1998

The two-door model gets the ax this year. Rear seat passengers are cooled by a newly optional rear air conditioning system. A host of new standard features has been added, including carpeted floor mats. Three new colors spruce up the outside a bit, and second-generation airbags are standard inside.

Category N

Model	Trade-in	Private	Dealer
4 Dr SLE 4WD Wgn	14336	15807	17400
4 Dr SLE Wgn	12935	14262	15700
4 Dr SLT 4WD Wgn	15242	16806	18500
4 Dr SLT Wgn	13924	15352	16900

OPTIONS FOR YUKON

Bucket Seats +197
Camper/Towing Package +124
Compact Disc Changer +277
Dual Air Conditioning[Opt on SLE] +277
Heated Front Seats +177
Locking Differential +127
Running Boards +139

1997 GMC

JIMMY   1997

Highrider off-road package deleted as GMC realigns Jimmy as luxury sport-ute. Instead, buyers can opt for a Gold Edition in one of four colors. New options include a power sunroof and HomeLink universal transmitter. In a fit of good taste, Radar Purple and Bright Teal paint colors are replaced by Fairway Green and Smoky Caramel.

Category M

Model	Trade-in	Private	Dealer
2 Dr SL 4WD Utility	6196	6963	7900
2 Dr SL Utility	5647	6346	7200
4 Dr SL 4WD Wgn	6825	7670	8702
4 Dr SL Wgn	6118	6875	7800
4 Dr SLE 4WD Wgn	8079	9078	10300
4 Dr SLE Wgn	7137	8021	9100
2 Dr SLS Sport 4WD Utility			
	6822	7666	8698
2 Dr SLS Sport Utility			
	6275	7051	8000
4 Dr SLS Sport 4WD Wgn			
	7529	8461	9600
4 Dr SLS Sport Wgn	6902	7756	8800
4 Dr SLT 4WD Wgn	8314	9343	10600
4 Dr SLT Wgn	7608	8549	9700

OPTIONS FOR JIMMY

AM/FM Compact Disc Player +150

Aluminum/Alloy Wheels[Opt on SL] +112
Locking Differential +115
Power Drivers Seat[Std on SLT] +109
Power Moonroof +317
Power Windows[Std on SLE,SLS Sport,SLT] +114

SAFARI   1997

Illuminated entry and daytime running lights debut this year, along with a couple of new colors and automatic transmission improvements. SLT models can be equipped with leather seating, and a HomeLink three-channel transmitter is optional. Speed-sensitive power steering makes parking easier.

Category P

Model	Trade-in	Private	Dealer
2 Dr SL AWD Cargo Van Ext			
	7361	8324	9500
2 Dr SL Cargo Van Ext	6509	7360	8400
2 Dr SLE AWD Pass. Van Ext			
	8291	9375	10700
2 Dr SLE Pass. Van Ext			
	7439	8411	9600
2 Dr SLT AWD Pass. Van Ext			
	9221	10426	11900
2 Dr SLT Pass. Van Ext			
	8368	9463	10800
2 Dr SLX AWD Pass. Van Ext			
	7593	8586	9800
2 Dr SLX Pass. Van Ext			
	6741	7623	8700

OPTIONS FOR SAFARI

7 Passenger Seating +337
8 Passenger Seating[Opt on SLX,SLE Pass Van EX] +180
AM/FM Compact Disc Player +185
AM/FM Stereo/CD/Tape +231
Aluminum/Alloy Wheels[Std on SLT] +155
Camper/Towing Package +141
Chrome Wheels +112
Cruise Control[Opt on SL,SLX] +103
Dual Air Conditioning +238
Dual Power Seats +219
Leather Seats +432
Locking Differential +115
Power Door Locks[Opt on SL,SLX] +102
Power Drivers Seat[Std on SLT] +109
Power Windows[Opt on SL,SLX] +114
Privacy Glass[Opt on SL,SLX] +133

SAVANA   1997

G3500 models get dual airbags, while daytime running lights are a new standard feature. Speed-sensitive steering reduces effort at low speeds. Chrome-plated wheels are a new option. Remote keyless entry key fobs are redesigned, and automatic transmissions provide better fuel economy and smoother shifts.

Model Description	Trade-in TMV	Private TMV	Dealer TMV
Category Q			
2 Dr G1500 Cargo Van	6473	7295	8300
2 Dr G1500 Pass. Van	7643	8614	9800
2 Dr G2500 Cargo Van	6629	7471	8500
2 Dr G2500 Cargo Van Ext			
	6941	7823	8900
2 Dr G2500 Pass. Van	8423	9493	10800
2 Dr G2500 Pass. Van Ext			
	8735	9844	11200
2 Dr G3500 Cargo Van	7175	8086	9200
2 Dr G3500 Cargo Van Ext			
	7487	8438	9600
2 Dr G3500 Pass. Van	8501	9580	10900
2 Dr G3500 Pass. Van Ext			
	8813	9932	11300
2 Dr G1500 SLE Pass. Van			
	8033	9053	10300
2 Dr G3500 SLE Pass. Van			
	8969	10108	11500
2 Dr G3500 SLE Pass. Van Ext			
	9281	10459	11900

OPTIONS FOR SAVANA
15 Passenger Seating +169
8 cyl 5.0 L Engine +226
8 cyl 5.7 L Engine[Std on G3500] +439
8 cyl 6.5 L Turbodiesel Engine +1237
8 cyl 7.4 L Engine +273
AM/FM Compact Disc Player +246
AM/FM Stereo/CD/Tape +292
Air Conditioning[Opt on Cargo] +366
Aluminum/Alloy Wheels +114
Camper/Towing Package +142
Chrome Bumpers[Std on SLE] +114
Chrome Wheels +114
Dual Air Conditioning[Opt on G1500] +391
Dual Power Seats +219
Locking Differential +115
Power Door Locks[Std on SLE] +103
Power Drivers Seat +109
Power Windows[Std on SLE] +117
Privacy Glass +130

SIERRA 1500   1997

A passenger airbag is added to models with a GVWR under 8,600 pounds, and all models get speed-sensitive steering that reduces low-speed effort. K1500 models have a tighter turning radius for better maneuverability. Automatic transmissions are refined to provide smoother shifts and improved efficiency. Three new paint colors debut.

Category K

Model Description	Trade-in TMV	Private TMV	Dealer TMV
2 Dr C1500 GT Std Cab SB			
	8205	9197	10408
2 Dr C1500 SL Ext Cab LB			
	8514	9543	10800
2 Dr C1500 SL Std Cab LB			
	6938	7776	8800
2 Dr K1500 SL 4WD Ext Cab LB			
	9855	11045	12500
2 Dr K1500 SL 4WD Std Cab LB			
	8593	9631	10900
2 Dr C1500 SL Ext Cab SB			
	8041	9013	10200
2 Dr C1500 SL Std Cab SB			
	6780	7599	8600
2 Dr K1500 SL 4WD Ext Cab SB			
	8987	10073	11400
2 Dr K1500 SL 4WD Std Cab SB			
	8436	9455	10700
2 Dr C1500 SL Ext Cab Stepside SB			
	8357	9366	10600
2 Dr C1500 SL Std Cab Stepside SB			
	7805	8748	9900
2 Dr K1500 SL 4WD Ext Cab Stepside SB			
	9618	10780	12200
2 Dr K1500 SL 4WD Std Cab Stepside SB			
	8719	9773	11060
2 Dr C1500 SLE Ext Cab LB			
	9224	10338	11700
2 Dr C1500 SLE Std Cab LB			
	8112	9092	10290
2 Dr K1500 SLE 4WD Ext Cab LB			
	10407	11664	13200
2 Dr K1500 SLE 4WD Std Cab LB			
	9539	10692	12100
2 Dr C1500 SLE Ext Cab SB			
	8830	9896	11200
2 Dr C1500 SLE Std Cab SB			
	7884	8836	10000
2 Dr K1500 SLE 4WD Ext Cab SB			
	10013	11223	12701
2 Dr K1500 SLE 4WD Std Cab SB			
	9145	10250	11600
2 Dr C1500 SLE Ext Cab Stepside SB			
	9461	10603	12000
2 Dr C1500 SLE Std Cab Stepside SB			
	8193	9182	10392
2 Dr K1500 SLE 4WD Ext Cab Stepside SB			
	10485	11752	13300
2 Dr K1500 SLE 4WD Std Cab Stepside SB			
	9697	10868	12300
2 Dr C1500 SLT Ext Cab LB			
	9949	11150	12619
2 Dr C1500 SLT Std Cab LB			

Model Description	Trade-in TMV	Private TMV	Dealer TMV
8783	9843	11140	
2 Dr K1500 SLT 4WD Ext Cab LB			
11274	12636	14300	
2 Dr K1500 SLT 4WD Std Cab LB			
10091	11310	12800	
2 Dr C1500 SLT Ext Cab SB			
9776	10957	12400	
2 Dr C1500 SLT Std Cab SB			
8672	9720	11000	
2 Dr K1500 SLT 4WD Ext Cab SB			
10801	12105	13700	
2 Dr K1500 SLT 4WD Std Cab SB			
9919	11117	12581	
2 Dr C1500 SLT Ext Cab Stepside SB			
10012	11221	12699	
2 Dr C1500 SLT Std Cab Stepside SB			
8909	9985	11300	
2 Dr K1500 SLT 4WD Ext Cab Stepside SB			
11037	12371	14000	
2 Dr K1500 SLT 4WD Std Cab Stepside SB			
10170	11399	12900	
2 Dr C1500 Special Std Cab LB			
6622	7422	8400	
2 Dr K1500 Special 4WD Std Cab LB			
8278	9278	10500	
2 Dr C1500 Special Std Cab SB			
6465	7246	8200	
2 Dr K1500 Special 4WD Std Cab SB			
8128	9110	10310	

OPTIONS FOR SIERRA 1500
8 cyl 5.0 L Engine +226
8 cyl 5.7 L Engine +319
8 cyl 6.5 L Turbodiesel Engine +1540
AM/FM Stereo/CD/Tape +133
Air Conditioning[Opt on SL,Special] +366
Aluminum/Alloy Wheels +114
Automatic 4-Speed Transmission +442
Bed Liner +103
Bucket Seats +114
Chrome Bumpers[Opt on SL] +104
Chrome Wheels[Opt on SL] +114
Hinged Third Door +191
Locking Differential +115
Power Drivers Seat[Opt on SLE] +109

SIERRA 2500   1997

A passenger airbag is added to models with a GVWR under 8,600 pounds, and all models get speed-sensitive steering that reduces low-speed effort. K1500 models have a tighter turning radius for better maneuverability. Automatic transmissions are refined to provide smoother shifts and improved efficiency.

Three new paint colors debut.
Category K

Model Description	Trade-in TMV	Private TMV	Dealer TMV
2 Dr C2500 HD SL Ext Cab LB			
9145	10250	11600	
2 Dr C2500 HD SL Std Cab LB			
8357	9366	10600	
2 Dr C2500 SL Std Cab LB			
7963	8924	10100	
2 Dr K2500 HD SL 4WD Ext Cab LB			
10722	12017	13600	
2 Dr K2500 HD SL 4WD Std Cab LB			
9697	10868	12300	
2 Dr C2500 SL Ext Cab SB			
9461	10603	12000	
2 Dr K2500 HD SL 4WD Ext Cab SB			
10643	11929	13500	
2 Dr C2500 HD SLE Ext Cab LB			
10249	11487	13000	
2 Dr C2500 HD SLE Std Cab LB			
9539	10692	12100	
2 Dr C2500 SLE Std Cab LB			
9066	10161	11500	
2 Dr K2500 HD SLE 4WD Ext Cab LB			
11826	13254	15000	
2 Dr K2500 HD SLE 4WD Std Cab LB			
10880	12194	13800	
2 Dr C2500 SLE Ext Cab SB			
10328	11575	13100	
2 Dr K2500 HD SLE 4WD Ext Cab SB			
11747	13166	14900	
2 Dr C2500 HD SLT Ext Cab LB			
10958	12282	13900	
2 Dr C2500 HD SLT Std Cab LB			
10170	11399	12900	
2 Dr C2500 SLT Std Cab LB			
9776	10957	12400	
2 Dr K2500 HD SLT 4WD Ext Cab LB			
12535	14049	15900	
2 Dr K2500 HD SLT 4WD Std Cab LB			
11510	12901	14600	
2 Dr C2500 SLT Ext Cab SB			
11037	12371	14000	
2 Dr K2500 HD SLT 4WD Ext Cab SB			
12456	13961	15800	

OPTIONS FOR SIERRA 2500
8 cyl 5.7 L Engine[Std on HD] +319
8 cyl 6.5 L Turbodiesel Engine +1540
8 cyl 7.4 L Engine +273
AM/FM Stereo/CD/Tape +133
Air Conditioning[Opt on SL] +366
Automatic 4-Speed Transmission +442

Don't forget to refer to the Mileage Adjustment Table at the back of this book!

Model Description	Trade-in TMV	Private TMV	Dealer TMV

Bed Liner +103
Bucket Seats +114
Hinged Third Door +191
Locking Differential +115
Power Drivers Seat[Opt on SLE] +109
Rear Step Bumper[Opt on SL] +104

SIERRA 3500 — 1997

A passenger airbag is added to models with a GVWR under 8,600 pounds, and all models get speed-sensitive steering that reduces low-speed effort. K1500 models have a tighter turning radius for better maneuverability. Automatic transmissions are refined to provide smoother shifts and improved efficiency. Three new paint colors debut.

Category K

Model	Trade-in	Private	Dealer
2 Dr C3500 SL Ext Cab LB	10643	11929	13500
2 Dr C3500 SL Std Cab LB	8909	9985	11300
2 Dr K3500 SL 4WD Ext Cab LB	12220	13696	15500
2 Dr K3500 SL 4WD Std Cab LB	10407	11664	13200
4 Dr C3500 SL Crew Cab LB	10485	11752	13300
4 Dr K3500 SL 4WD Crew Cab LB	12299	13784	15600
2 Dr C3500 SLE Ext Cab LB	11510	12901	14600
2 Dr C3500 SLE Std Cab LB	9776	10957	12400
2 Dr K3500 SLE 4WD Ext Cab LB	12851	14403	16300
2 Dr K3500 SLE 4WD Std Cab LB	11274	12636	14300
4 Dr C3500 SLE Crew Cab LB	12456	13961	15800
4 Dr K3500 SLE 4WD Crew Cab LB	13481	15110	17100
2 Dr C3500 SLT Ext Cab LB	12693	14226	16100
2 Dr C3500 SLT Std Cab LB	10880	12194	13800
2 Dr K3500 SLT 4WD Ext Cab LB	13560	15198	17200
2 Dr K3500 SLT 4WD Std Cab LB	12378	13873	15700
4 Dr C3500 SLT Crew Cab LB	12772	14314	16200
4 Dr K3500 SLT 4WD Crew Cab LB	14348	16082	18200

OPTIONS FOR SIERRA 3500
8 cyl 6.5 L Turbodiesel Engine +1237
8 cyl 7.4 L Engine +273
AM/FM Stereo/CD/Tape +133
Air Conditioning[Opt on SL] +366
Automatic 4-Speed Transmission +442
Bed Liner +103
Bucket Seats +114
Dual Rear Wheels +389
Locking Differential +115
Power Drivers Seat[Opt on SLE] +109

SONOMA — 1997

Nothing much. Changes are limited to new colors, availability of the Sport Suspension on extended cab models, engine and transmission improvements, lighter-weight plug-in half shafts for 4WD Sonomas, and console-mounted shifter for trucks equipped with a center console and bucket seats.

Category J

Model	Trade-in	Private	Dealer
2 Dr SL 4WD Std Cab LB	6989	7894	9000
2 Dr SL Std Cab LB	5047	5701	6500
2 Dr SL 4WD Std Cab SB	6911	7806	8900
2 Dr SL Std Cab SB	4970	5613	6400
2 Dr SLE 4WD Ext Cab SB	8930	10086	11500
2 Dr SLE 4WD Std Cab SB	7765	8771	10000
2 Dr SLE Ext Cab SB	6445	7280	8300
2 Dr SLE Std Cab SB	5669	6403	7300
2 Dr SLE 4WD Ext Cab Stepside SB	9241	10437	11900
2 Dr SLE 4WD Std Cab Stepside SB	7920	8946	10200
2 Dr SLE Ext Cab Stepside SB	6756	7631	8700
2 Dr SLE Std Cab Stepside SB	5824	6578	7500
2 Dr SLS Sport 4WD Std Cab LB	7455	8420	9600
2 Dr SLS Sport Std Cab LB	5436	6140	7000
2 Dr SLS Sport 4WD Ext Cab SB	8231	9297	10600
2 Dr SLS Sport 4WD Std Cab SB	7222	8157	9300
2 Dr SLS Sport Ext Cab SB	6134	6929	7900
2 Dr SLS Sport Std Cab SB	5203	5876	6700

Don't forget to refer to the Mileage Adjustment Table at the back of this book!

Model Description	Trade-in TMV	Private TMV	Dealer TMV
2 Dr SLS Sport 4WD Ext Cab Stepside SB	8619	9736	11100
2 Dr SLS Sport 4WD Std Cab Stepside SB	7532	8508	9700
2 Dr SLS Sport Ext Cab Stepside SB	6367	7192	8200
2 Dr SLS Sport Std Cab Stepside SB	5591	6315	7200

OPTIONS FOR SONOMA
6 cyl 4.3 L Engine +451
6 cyl 4.3 L Vortec Engine +117
AM/FM Compact Disc Player +185
Air Conditioning +366
Aluminum/Alloy Wheels[Std on SLE] +112
Automatic 4-Speed Transmission +487
Highrider Suspension Package +607
Hinged Third Door +171
Locking Differential +115
Power Windows +108
Sport Suspension +320

SUBURBAN 1997

GMC has added a passenger side airbag and a power lock switch in the cargo compartment. SLE and SLT trim now includes rear heat and air conditioning, as well as remote keyless entry. Uplevel SLT trim also includes a combination CD and cassette player stereo system. All Suburbans receive speed-sensitive power steering, and 4WD models have a tighter turning circle. Two new colors freshen the dated exterior design this year.

Category N

Model Description	Trade-in TMV	Private TMV	Dealer TMV
4 Dr C1500 Wgn	11013	12267	13800
4 Dr C2500 Wgn	11572	12889	14500
4 Dr K1500 4WD Wgn	12210	13601	15300
4 Dr K2500 4WD Wgn	12769	14223	16000

OPTIONS FOR SUBURBAN
8 cyl 6.5 L Turbodiesel Engine +1237
8 cyl 7.4 L Engine +259
Air Conditioning +365
Aluminum/Alloy Wheels +109
Bucket Seats +112
Center Bench Seat +274
Dual Air Conditioning +603
Leather Seats +486
Locking Differential +109
Power Drivers Seat +104
Power Windows +115
Privacy Glass +132
Rear Window Wiper +120
Running Boards +120
SLE Package +1658
SLT Package +2007

YUKON 1997

Dual airbags, speed-sensitive steering and a tighter turning circle for 4WD models. A power lock switch is added to the cargo compartment, and SLT models have a standard CD/cassette combo stereo. Remote keyless entry is standard on four-door models, and on SLE and SLT two-door models. Newly optional on four-door models is a rear air conditioning unit.

Category N

Model Description	Trade-in TMV	Private TMV	Dealer TMV
2 Dr SL 4WD Utility	9577	10667	12000
2 Dr SL Utility	8699	9689	10900
2 Dr SLE 4WD Utility	11332	12623	14200
2 Dr SLE Utility	10215	11378	12800
4 Dr SLE 4WD Wgn	11811	13156	14800
4 Dr SLE Wgn	10774	12000	13500
2 Dr SLT 4WD Utility	12050	13423	15100
2 Dr SLT Utility	10933	12178	13700
4 Dr SLT 4WD Wgn	12370	13778	15500
4 Dr SLT Wgn	11572	12889	14500

OPTIONS FOR YUKON
8 cyl 6.5 L Turbodiesel Engine +1237
Air Conditioning[Opt on SL] +384
Aluminum/Alloy Wheels[Opt on SL] +142
Bucket Seats +108
Dual Air Conditioning +384
Locking Differential +115
Power Drivers Seat[Std on SLT] +109
Running Boards +126

1996 GMC

JIMMY 1996

GMC's popular compact sport utility gets a super-duper optional off-road package called Highrider, as well as an available five-speed transmission. Either of these are available on two-door models only. All Jimmys receive glow-in-the-day headlights and long-life engine coolant. Spark plugs last 100,000 miles. All-wheel drive, which became optional in mid-1995, continues. Conspicuously absent is a passenger airbag.

Category M

Model Description	Trade-in TMV	Private TMV	Dealer TMV
2 Dr STD 4WD Utility	5533	6233	7200
2 Dr STD Utility	4841	5454	6300
4 Dr STD 4WD Wgn	5994	6752	7800
4 Dr STD Wgn	5379	6060	7000
2 Dr SL 4WD Utility	5917	6666	7700
2 Dr SL Utility	5456	6146	7100
4 Dr SL 4WD Wgn	6609	7445	8600
4 Dr SL Wgn	5763	6493	7500
4 Dr SLE 4WD Wgn	6839	7705	8900
4 Dr SLE Wgn	6301	7099	8200
2 Dr SLS 4WD Utility	6224	7012	8100

Don't forget to refer to the Mileage Adjustment Table at the back of this book!

Model Description	Trade-in TMV	Private TMV	Dealer TMV	Model Description	Trade-in TMV	Private TMV	Dealer TMV
2 Dr SLS Utility	5687	6406	7400	2 Dr SLE Pass. Van Ext			
4 Dr SLS 4WD Wgn	6686	7532	8700		5852	6628	7700
4 Dr SLS Wgn	6148	6926	8000	2 Dr SLT AWD Pass. Van Ext			
4 Dr SLT 4WD Wgn	7377	8311	9600		7220	8177	9500
4 Dr SLT Wgn	6762	7618	8800	2 Dr SLT Pass. Van Ext			
					6612	7489	8700

OPTIONS FOR JIMMY
AM/FM Compact Disc Player +142
AM/FM Stereo/CD/Tape +147
Limited Slip Differential +110
Locking Differential +110
Power Windows[Opt on STD] +108

RALLY WAGON   1996

Category Q

Model Description	Trade-in TMV	Private TMV	Dealer TMV
2 Dr G35 Rally Wagon	6805	7727	9000
2 Dr G35 Rally Wagon Ext			
	7032	7985	9300
2 Dr G35 STX Rally Wagon			
	7184	8156	9500
2 Dr G35 STX Rally Wagon Ext			
	7486	8500	9900

OPTIONS FOR RALLY WAGON
15 Passenger Seating +160
8 cyl 6.5 L Diesel Engine +1153
8 cyl 7.4 L Engine +263
AM/FM Compact Disc Player +171
Air Conditioning[Std on STX] +423
Bucket Seats +175
Camper/Towing Package +134
Dual Air Conditioning +542
Locking Differential +110
Privacy Glass +165

SAFARI   1996

An all-new interior debuts with dual airbags, more leg and foot room, and a host of other features. Important among them are the availability of dual integrated child seats and a child-proof lock on the right side sliding door. Under seat heat ducts help warm the rear passengers, and new audio systems include a radio that can be tuned independently by rear seat passengers without disturbing the listening pleasure, or program, that the front occupants are enjoying.

Category P

Model Description	Trade-in TMV	Private TMV	Dealer TMV
2 Dr STD AWD Pass. Van Ext			
	6080	6886	8000
2 Dr STD Pass. Van Ext			
	5396	6112	7100
2 Dr SL AWD Cargo Van Ext			
	5776	6542	7600
2 Dr SL Cargo Van Ext	5244	5939	6900
2 Dr SLE AWD Pass. Van Ext			
	6536	7403	8600

Model Description	Trade-in TMV	Private TMV	Dealer TMV
2 Dr SLX AWD Pass. Van Ext			
	6308	7144	8300
2 Dr SLX Pass. Van Ext			
	5700	6456	7500

OPTIONS FOR SAFARI
7 Passenger Seating +320
8 Passenger Seating[Opt on SLX,STD] +171
AM/FM Compact Disc Player +176
AM/FM Stereo Tape +108
AM/FM Stereo/CD/Tape +176
Camper/Towing Package +134
Dual Air Conditioning +226
Locking Differential +110
Power Windows[Opt on SL] +108

SAVANA   1996

Category Q

Model Description	Trade-in TMV	Private TMV	Dealer TMV
2 Dr G1500 Cargo Van	5444	6182	7200
2 Dr G1500 Pass. Van	6503	7384	8600
2 Dr G2500 Cargo Van	5671	6439	7500
2 Dr G2500 Cargo Van Ext			
	5822	6611	7700
2 Dr G2500 Pass. Van	7184	8156	9500
2 Dr G2500 Pass. Van Ext			
	7713	8757	10200
2 Dr G3500 Cargo Van	6049	6869	8000
2 Dr G3500 Cargo Van Ext			
	6352	7212	8400
2 Dr G3500 Pass. Van	7259	8242	9600
2 Dr G3500 Pass. Van Ext			
	7788	8843	10300

OPTIONS FOR SAVANA
15 Passenger Seating +160
8 cyl 5.0 L Engine +215
8 cyl 5.7 L Engine[Std on G2500,G3500] +418
8 cyl 6.5 L Turbodiesel Engine +1178
8 cyl 7.4 L Engine +260
AM/FM Compact Disc Player +235
AM/FM Stereo/CD/Tape +278
Air Conditioning[Opt on Cargo] +348
Aluminum/Alloy Wheels +108
Camper/Towing Package +134
Chrome Bumpers +108
Dual Air Conditioning +348
Locking Differential +110
Power Windows +111
Privacy Glass +123

Don't forget to refer to the Mileage Adjustment Table at the back of this book!

Model Description	Trade-in TMV	Private TMV	Dealer TMV
SIERRA 1500			**1996**
Category K			
2 Dr C1500 SL Ext Cab LB	7248	8115	9312
2 Dr C1500 SL Std Cab LB	6149	6884	7900
2 Dr K1500 SL 4WD Ext Cab LB	8343	9341	10719
2 Dr K1500 SL 4WD Std Cab LB	7316	8191	9400
2 Dr C1500 SL Ext Cab SB	6927	7756	8900
2 Dr C1500 SL Std Cab SB	6305	7059	8100
2 Dr K1500 SL 4WD Ext Cab SB	8017	8976	10300
2 Dr K1500 SL 4WD Std Cab SB	7229	8094	9288
2 Dr C1500 SL Ext Cab Stepside SB	7062	7907	9073
2 Dr C1500 SL Std Cab Stepside SB	5993	6710	7700
2 Dr K1500 SL 4WD Ext Cab Stepside SB	8215	9198	10555
2 Dr K1500 SL 4WD Std Cab Stepside SB	7550	8453	9700
2 Dr C1500 SLE Ext Cab LB	8313	9308	10681
2 Dr C1500 SLE Std Cab LB	7104	7954	9127
2 Dr K1500 SLE 4WD Ext Cab LB	9262	10370	11900
2 Dr K1500 SLE 4WD Std Cab LB	8406	9412	10800
2 Dr C1500 SLE Ext Cab SB	7861	8801	10100
2 Dr C1500 SLE Std Cab SB	7020	7859	9019
2 Dr K1500 SLE 4WD Ext Cab SB	8882	9944	11411
2 Dr K1500 SLE 4WD Std Cab SB	8250	9237	10600
2 Dr C1500 SLE Ext Cab Stepside SB	8173	9150	10500
2 Dr C1500 SLE Std Cab Stepside SB	7394	8279	9500
2 Dr K1500 SLE 4WD Ext Cab Stepside SB	9107	10196	11700
2 Dr K1500 SLE 4WD Std Cab Stepside SB	8484	9499	10900
2 Dr C1500 SLT Ext Cab LB			
2 Dr C1500 SLT Std Cab LB	8864	9925	11389
2 Dr K1500 SLT 4WD Ext Cab LB	7783	8714	10000
2 Dr K1500 SLT 4WD Std Cab LB	9963	11154	12800
2 Dr C1500 SLT Ext Cab SB	8951	10022	11500
2 Dr C1500 SLT Std Cab SB	8562	9586	11000
2 Dr K1500 SLT 4WD Ext Cab SB	7706	8627	9900
2 Dr K1500 SLT 4WD Std Cab SB	9651	10806	12400
2 Dr C1500 SLT Ext Cab Stepside SB	8795	9847	11300
2 Dr C1500 SLT Std Cab Stepside SB	8717	9760	11200
2 Dr K1500 SLT 4WD Ext Cab Stepside SB	8095	9063	10400
2 Dr K1500 SLT 4WD Std Cab Stepside SB	9807	10980	12600
2 Dr C1500 Special Std Cab LB	9029	10109	11600
2 Dr K1500 Special 4WD Std Cab LB	5604	6274	7200
2 Dr C1500 Special Std Cab SB	7017	7856	9015
2 Dr K1500 Special 4WD Std Cab SB	5448	6100	7000
	6979	7813	8966

OPTIONS FOR SIERRA 1500
8 cyl 5.0 L Engine +215
8 cyl 5.7 L Engine +304
8 cyl 6.5 L Turbodiesel Engine +1466
AM/FM Stereo Tape +111
AM/FM Stereo/CD/Tape +126
Air Conditioning[Opt on SL, Special] +348
Aluminum/Alloy Wheels +108
Automatic 4-Speed Transmission +421
Bucket Seats +108
Chrome Wheels[Opt on SL] +108
Hinged Third Door +182
Locking Differential +110

Model Description	Trade-in TMV	Private TMV	Dealer TMV
SIERRA 2500			**1996**
Category K			
2 Dr C2500 SL Ext Cab LB	7706	8627	9900
2 Dr C2500 SL Std Cab LB	6694	7494	8600
2 Dr K2500 SL 4WD Ext Cab LB	9107	10196	11700

Don't forget to refer to the Mileage Adjustment Table at the back of this book!

Model Description	Trade-in TMV	Private TMV	Dealer TMV
2 Dr K2500 SL 4WD Std Cab LB	8328	9324	10700
2 Dr C2500 SL Ext Cab SB	7647	8562	9825
2 Dr K2500 SL 4WD Ext Cab SB	9107	10196	11700
2 Dr C2500 SLE Ext Cab LB	9184	10283	11800
2 Dr C2500 SLE Std Cab LB	7608	8518	9775
2 Dr K2500 SLE 4WD Ext Cab LB	10118	11329	13000
2 Dr K2500 SLE 4WD Std Cab LB	9262	10370	11900
2 Dr C2500 SLE Ext Cab SD	8640	9673	11100
2 Dr K2500 SLE 4WD Ext Cab SB	10041	11242	12900
2 Dr C2500 SLT Std Cab LB	8173	9150	10500
2 Dr K2500 SLT 4WD Ext Cab LB	10741	12026	13800
2 Dr K2500 SLT 4WD Std Cab LB	9885	11067	12700
2 Dr C2500 SLT Ext Cab SB	9418	10544	12100

OPTIONS FOR SIERRA 2500
8 cyl 5.7 L Engine[Std on HD] +304
8 cyl 6.5 L Turbodiesel Engine +1178
8 cyl 7.4 L Engine +260
AM/FM Stereo/CD/Tape +126
Air Conditioning[Opt on SL] +348
Aluminum/Alloy Wheels +108
Automatic 4-Speed Transmission +421
Bucket Seats +108
Chrome Wheels[Opt on SL] +108
Hinged Third Door +182
Locking Differential +110

SIERRA 3500   1996
Category K

Model Description	Trade-in TMV	Private TMV	Dealer TMV
2 Dr C3500 SL Ext Cab LB	9107	10196	11700
2 Dr C3500 SL Std Cab LB	7706	8627	9900
2 Dr K3500 SL 4WD Ext Cab LB	10430	11677	13400
2 Dr K3500 SL 4WD Std Cab LB	8951	10022	11500
4 Dr C3500 SL Crew Cab LB	9029	10109	11600
4 Dr K3500 SL 4WD Crew Cab LB	10508	11764	13500

Model Description	Trade-in TMV	Private TMV	Dealer TMV
2 Dr C3500 SLE Ext Cab LB	9885	11067	12700
2 Dr K3500 SLE 4WD Ext Cab LB	10975	12287	14100
2 Dr K3500 SLE 4WD Std Cab LB	10585	11852	13600
4 Dr C3500 SLE Crew Cab LB	10663	11939	13700
4 Dr K3500 SLE 4WD Crew Cab LB	11597	12984	14900
2 Dr C3500 SLT Ext Cab LB	10819	12113	13900
2 Dr C3500 SLT Std Cab LB	9262	10370	11900
2 Dr K3500 SLT 4WD Ext Cab LB	11675	13072	15000
2 Dr K3500 SLT 4WD Std Cab LB	10585	11852	13600
4 Dr C3500 SLT Crew Cab LB	11052	12374	14200
4 Dr K3500 SLT 4WD Crew Cab LB	12376	13856	15900

OPTIONS FOR SIERRA 3500
8 cyl 6.5 L Turbodiesel Engine +1178
8 cyl 7.4 L Engine +260
AM/FM Stereo/CD/Tape +126
Air Conditioning[Opt on SL] +348
Automatic 4-Speed Transmission +421
Bucket Seats +108
Dual Rear Wheels +371
Locking Differential +110

SONOMA   1996
Extended-cab models get an optional driver's side rear access panel. All Sonomas are now equipped with four-wheel ABS. A new sport suspension provides sporty handling, and a snazzy Sportside box ends Ford's reign as lord of compact stepsides. A new five-speed transmission improves shifter location and operation when equipped with the base four-cylinder. Still missing is the availability of a passenger airbag.
Category J

Model Description	Trade-in TMV	Private TMV	Dealer TMV
2 Dr SL 4WD Std Cab LB	5916	6749	7900
2 Dr SL Std Cab LB	4119	4699	5500
2 Dr SL 4WD Std Cab SB	5766	6578	7700
2 Dr SL Std Cab SB	3969	4528	5300
2 Dr SLE 4WD Ext Cab SB	7638	8714	10200
2 Dr SLE 4WD Std Cab SB	6066	6920	8100

Model Description	Trade-in TMV	Private TMV	Dealer TMV
2 Dr SLE Ext Cab SB	5655	6451	7551
2 Dr SLE Std Cab SB	4418	5041	5900
2 Dr SLE 4WD Ext Cab Stepside SB			
	7788	8885	10400
2 Dr SLE Ext Cab Stepside SB			
	5691	6493	7600
2 Dr SLS Sport 4WD Std Cab LB			
	6365	7262	8500
2 Dr SLS Sport Std Cab LB			
	4793	5468	6400
2 Dr SLS Sport 4WD Ext Cab SB			
	6890	7860	9200
2 Dr SLS Sport 4WD Std Cab SB			
	6216	7091	8300
2 Dr SLS Sport Ext Cab SB			
	5542	6322	7400
2 Dr SLS Sport Std Cab SB			
	4718	5382	6300
2 Dr SLS Sport 4WD Ext Cab Stepside SB			
	7039	8031	9400
2 Dr SLS Sport 4WD Std Cab Stepside SB			
	6290	7176	8400
2 Dr SLS Sport Ext Cab Stepside SB			
	5578	6364	7449
2 Dr SLS Sport Std Cab Stepside SB			
	4868	5553	6500

OPTIONS FOR SONOMA
6 cyl 4.3 L Engine +429
6 cyl 4.3 L Vortec Engine +112
AM/FM Compact Disc Player +175
Air Conditioning +348
Automatic 4-Speed Transmission +463
Highrider Suspension Package +748
Hinged Third Door +149
Limited Slip Differential +110
Locking Differential +110

SUBURBAN   1996

Giant SUV gets daytime running lights to make it more visible to other drivers. This is akin to installing field lighting on the bow of the Queen Mary. New V8s, quieter tires, and long-life spark plugs and coolant make the Suburban more satisfying to skipper. Rear passengers get warmer faster, thanks to new rear-seat heat ducting. Illuminated entry is newly standard, and electronic 4WD controls are a new option.

Category N

4 Dr C1500 Wgn	9495	10631	12200
4 Dr C2500 Wgn	9962	11154	12800
4 Dr K1500 4WD Wgn	10429	11677	13400
4 Dr K2500 4WD Wgn	10896	12200	14000

OPTIONS FOR SUBURBAN

8 cyl 6.5 L Turbodiesel Engine +1178
8 cyl 7.4 L Engine +247
Air Conditioning +348
Center Bench Seat +261
Compact Disc Changer +247
Dual Air Conditioning +534
Leather Seats +463
Power Windows +109
Privacy Glass +125
Rear Window Wiper +115
SLE Package +1462
SLT Package +1795

VANDURA   1996

Category Q

2 Dr G35 Vandura	6654	7555	8800
2 Dr G35 Vandura Ext	6957	7899	9200

OPTIONS FOR VANDURA
8 cyl 6.5 L Diesel Engine +718
8 cyl 7.4 L Engine +263
Air Conditioning +423
Camper/Towing Package +134
Dual Air Conditioning +683
Locking Differential +110
Power Windows +111
Premium Sound System +108

YUKON   1996

Just what we need: a two-wheel-drive two-door Yukon. A new 5700 Vortec V8 gets long-life coolant and spark plugs, as well as a hefty bump in power and torque. Passenger car tires on less stout Yukons result in a softer, quieter ride. Rear heat ducts, illuminated entry, and height-adjustable seat belts debut. Four-wheel-drive models get a newly optional electronic shift mechanism.

Category N

2 Dr SL 4WD Utility	8016	8976	10300
2 Dr SL Utility	7316	8191	9400
2 Dr SLE 4WD Utility	9417	10544	12100
2 Dr SLE Utility	8639	9673	11100
4 Dr SLE 4WD Wgn	9884	11067	12700
4 Dr SLE Wgn	9184	10283	11800
2 Dr SLT 4WD Utility	9962	11154	12800
2 Dr SLT Utility	9262	10370	11900
4 Dr SLT 4WD Wgn	10429	11677	13400
4 Dr SLT Wgn	9729	10893	12500

OPTIONS FOR YUKON
8 cyl 6.5 L Turbodiesel Engine +1178
Air Conditioning[Opt on SL] +366
Aluminum/Alloy Wheels[Opt on SL] +134
Locking Differential +110

Don't forget to refer to the Mileage Adjustment Table at the back of this book!

GMC 95

Model Description	Trade-in TMV	Private TMV	Dealer TMV	Model Description	Trade-in TMV	Private TMV	Dealer TMV

1995 GMC

JIMMY 1995

All-new SUV appears based on revamped Sonoma. Four-wheel-drive models have electronic transfer case as standard equipment. Spare tire on four-door model is mounted beneath cargo bay instead of in it. Five different suspension packages are available. One engine, a 195-horsepower 4.3-liter V6, is available. All-wheel drive is optional. Driver airbag and air conditioning are standard equipment.

Category M

Model	Trade-in	Private	Dealer
2 Dr STD 4WD Utility	3718	4199	5000
2 Dr STD Utility	3198	3611	4300
4 Dr STD 4WD Wgn	5057	5711	6800
4 Dr STD Wgn	3644	4115	4900
2 Dr SL 4WD Utility	4090	4619	5500
2 Dr SL Utility	3570	4031	4800
4 Dr SLE 4WD Wgn	5354	6046	7200
4 Dr SLE Wgn	5121	5783	6886
2 Dr SLS 4WD Utility	5142	5806	6914
2 Dr SLS Utility	3793	4283	5100
4 Dr SLS 4WD Wgn	5726	6466	7700
4 Dr SLS Wgn	5206	5879	7000
4 Dr SLT 4WD Wgn	6172	6970	8300
4 Dr SLT Wgn	5726	6466	7700

OPTIONS FOR JIMMY

AM/FM Compact Disc Player +132
AM/FM Stereo/CD/Tape[Opt on SLS] +137
Aluminum/Alloy Wheels[Opt on SL,STD] +98
Camper/Towing Package +85
Limited Slip Differential +102
Power Drivers Seat[Opt on SLE,SLS] +96
Power Windows[Opt on STD] +101

RALLY WAGON 1995

Category Q

Model	Trade-in	Private	Dealer
2 Dr G25 Rally Wagon	5788	6580	7900
2 Dr G35 Rally Wagon	5935	6747	8100
2 Dr G35 Rally Wagon Ext	6349	7218	8666
2 Dr G25 STX Rally Wagon	6253	7108	8534
2 Dr G35 STX Rally Wagon	6374	7246	8700
2 Dr G35 STX Rally Wagon Ext	6448	7330	8800

OPTIONS FOR RALLY WAGON

15 Passenger Seating +149
8 cyl 5.0 L Engine[Opt on G25,G35 STX] +231
8 cyl 5.7 L Engine[Opt on G25,G35 STX] +329
8 cyl 6.5 L Diesel Engine +1068

8 cyl 7.4 L Engine +242
AM/FM Compact Disc Player[Opt on STX] +159
Air Conditioning[Std on STX] +391
Bucket Seats[Opt on G35,STX] +162
Camper/Towing Package +125
Dual Air Conditioning +391
Locking Differential +102
Power Door Locks[Std on STX] +90
Privacy Glass +153
Rear Heater +82

SAFARI 1995

Front sheetmetal is restyled. Regular-length versions are dropped from the lineup, leaving only the extended model. Multileaf steel springs replace single-leaf plastic springs. One engine is available, the 190-horsepower, 4.3-liter V6. Air conditioning is newly standard, and remote keyless entry is a new option.

Category P

Model	Trade-in	Private	Dealer
2 Dr STD AWD Pass. Van Ext	4890	5532	6600
2 Dr STD Pass. Van Ext	4298	4861	5800
2 Dr SL AWD Cargo Van Ext	4742	5364	6400
2 Dr SL Cargo Van Ext	4149	4693	5600
2 Dr SLE AWD Pass. Van Ext	5409	6118	7300
2 Dr SLE Pass. Van Ext	4668	5280	6300
2 Dr SLT AWD Pass. Van Ext	5780	6537	7800
2 Dr SLT Pass. Van Ext	5483	6202	7400
2 Dr SLX AWD Pass. Van Ext	4965	5615	6700
2 Dr SLX Pass. Van Ext	4446	5029	6000

OPTIONS FOR SAFARI

7 Passenger Seating +297
8 Passenger Seating[Opt on SLX,STD] +159
AM/FM Compact Disc Player +163
AM/FM Stereo Tape +101
Aluminum/Alloy Wheels +100
Camper/Towing Package +124
Captain Chairs (4) +181
Cruise Control[Opt on SL] +90
Dual Air Conditioning +211
Limited Slip Differential +101
Power Door Locks +90
Power Drivers Seat +96
Power Windows +101
Rear Heater +82
Rear Window Wiper +82
Tinted Glass +80

Don't forget to refer to the Mileage Adjustment Table at the back of this book!

Model Description	Trade-in TMV	Private TMV	Dealer TMV
SIERRA 1500			**1995**
Category K			
2 Dr C1500 SL Ext Cab LB	6364	7128	8400
2 Dr C1500 SL Std Cab LB	5556	6222	7333
2 Dr K1500 SL 4WD Ext Cab LB	6986	7824	9221
2 Dr K1500 SL 4WD Std Cab LB	6288	7043	8300
2 Dr C1500 SL Ext Cab SB	5849	6551	7720
2 Dr C1500 SL Std Cab SB	5506	6166	7267
2 Dr K1500 SL 4WD Ext Cab SB	6672	7472	8806
2 Dr K1500 SL 4WD Std Cab SB	6137	6873	8100
2 Dr C1500 SL Ext Cab Stepside SB	6208	6953	8194
2 Dr C1500 SL Std Cab Stepside SB	5606	6279	7400
2 Dr K1500 SL 4WD Ext Cab Stepside SB	6894	7721	9100
2 Dr K1500 SL 4WD Std Cab Stepside SB	6516	7297	8600
2 Dr C1500 SLE Ext Cab LB	6954	7789	9179
2 Dr C1500 SLE Std Cab LB	6061	6788	8000
2 Dr K1500 SLE 4WD Ext Cab LB	7804	8740	10300
2 Dr K1500 SLE 4WD Std Cab LB	6819	7637	9000
2 Dr C1500 SLE Ext Cab SB	6591	7382	8700
2 Dr C1500 SLE Std Cab SB	5758	6449	7600
2 Dr K1500 SLE 4WD Ext Cab SB	7349	8231	9700
2 Dr K1500 SLE 4WD Std Cab SB	6658	7457	8788
2 Dr C1500 SLE Ext Cab Stepside SB	6743	7552	8900
2 Dr C1500 SLE Std Cab Stepside SB	6217	6963	8206
2 Dr K1500 SLE 4WD Ext Cab Stepside SB	7500	8400	9900
2 Dr K1500 SLE 4WD Std Cab Stepside SB	7046	7891	9300
2 Dr K1500 SLS 4WD Ext Cab SB	6672	7472	8806
2 Dr K1500 SLS 4WD Ext Cab Stepside SB	6894	7721	9100
2 Dr C1500 SLT Ext Cab LB	7576	8485	10000
2 Dr K1500 SLT 4WD Ext Cab LB	8410	9419	11100
2 Dr C1500 SLT Ext Cab SB	7197	8061	9500
2 Dr K1500 SLT 4WD Ext Cab SB	8107	9079	10700
2 Dr C1500 SLT Ext Cab Stepside SB	7425	8315	9800
2 Dr K1500 SLT 4WD Ext Cab Stepside SB	8258	9249	10900
2 Dr C1500 Special Std Cab LB	4925	5515	6500
2 Dr K1500 Special 4WD Std Cab LB	5909	6618	7800
2 Dr C1500 Special Std Cab SB	4773	5346	6300
2 Dr K1500 Special 4WD Std Cab SB	5819	6517	7680

OPTIONS FOR SIERRA 1500

8 cyl 5.0 L Engine +199
8 cyl 5.7 L Engine +281
8 cyl 6.5 L Turbodiesel Engine +1359
AM/FM Stereo Tape[Opt on SL,SLS,Special] +103
AM/FM Stereo/CD/Tape +117
Air Conditioning[Opt on SL,SLS,Special] +323
Aluminum/Alloy Wheels +101
Automatic 4-Speed Transmission +390
Bed Liner +90
Bucket Seats +101
Chrome Bumpers[Opt on SL] +92
Chrome Wheels[Opt on SL] +101
Compact Disc Changer +221
Limited Slip Differential +101
Power Drivers Seat[Opt on SLE] +96

Model Description	Trade-in TMV	Private TMV	Dealer TMV
SIERRA 2500			**1995**
Category K			
2 Dr C2500 SL Ext Cab LB	6894	7721	9100
2 Dr C2500 SL Std Cab LB	5531	6194	7300
2 Dr K2500 SL 4WD Ext Cab LB	7951	8905	10495
2 Dr K2500 SL 4WD Std Cab LB	6516	7297	8600
2 Dr C2500 SL Ext Cab SB	6819	7637	9000

Model Description	Trade-in TMV	Private TMV	Dealer TMV	Model Description	Trade-in TMV	Private TMV	Dealer TMV
2 Dr K2500 SL 4WD Ext Cab SB				4 Dr K3500 SL 4WD Crew Cab LB			
	7728	8655	10200		8788	9843	11600
2 Dr C2500 SLE Ext Cab LB				2 Dr C3500 SLE Ext Cab LB			
	7879	8825	10400		8334	9334	11000
2 Dr C2500 SLE Std Cab LB				2 Dr C3500 SLE Std Cab LB			
	6213	6958	8200		7197	8061	9500
2 Dr K2500 SLE 4WD Ext Cab LB				2 Dr K3500 SLE 4WD Ext Cab LB			
	9016	10097	11900		9319	10437	12300
2 Dr K2500 SLE 4WD Std Cab LB				2 Dr K3500 SLE 4WD Std Cab LB			
	7576	8485	10000		8031	8994	10600
2 Dr C2500 SLE Ext Cab SB				4 Dr C3500 SLE Crew Cab LB			
	7804	8740	10300		8940	10012	11800
2 Dr K2500 SLE 4WD Ext Cab SB				4 Dr K3500 SLE 4WD Crew Cab LB			
	8561	9588	11300		9773	10946	12900
2 Dr C2500 SLT Ext Cab LB				2 Dr C3500 SLT Ext Cab LB			
	8194	9177	10815		9092	10182	12000
2 Dr K2500 SLT 4WD Ext Cab LB				2 Dr K3500 SLT 4WD Ext Cab LB			
	10379	11625	13700		9849	11031	13000
2 Dr C2500 SLT Ext Cab SB							
	8110	9083	10705				
2 Dr K2500 SLT 4WD Ext Cab SB							
	9470	10606	12500				

OPTIONS FOR SIERRA 3500

8 cyl 6.5 L Turbodiesel Engine +1091
8 cyl 7.4 L Engine +241
AM/FM Stereo/CD/Tape +117
Air Conditioning[Opt on SL] +323
Automatic 4-Speed Transmission +390
Bed Liner +90
Bucket Seats +101
Chrome Step Bumper[Opt on SL] +80
Dual Rear Wheels +344
Locking Differential +102
Power Drivers Seat[Opt on SLE] +96

OPTIONS FOR SIERRA 2500

8 cyl 5.0 L Engine[Opt on SL Std Cab,SLE Std Cab 2WD/4WD] +231
8 cyl 5.7 L Engine +281
8 cyl 6.5 L Turbodiesel Engine +1091
8 cyl 7.4 L Engine +241
AM/FM Stereo/CD/Tape +117
Air Conditioning[Opt on SL] +323
Automatic 4-Speed Transmission +390
Bed Liner +90
Bucket Seats +101
Chrome Step Bumper[Opt on SL] +80
Locking Differential +102
Power Drivers Seat[Opt on SLE] +96

SIERRA 3500   1995

Category K

Model Description	Trade-in TMV	Private TMV	Dealer TMV
2 Dr C3500 HD Cab&Chassis SLE Std Cab			
	8864	9928	11700
2 Dr C3500 HD Cab&Chassis Std Cab			
	7804	8740	10300
2 Dr C3500 SL Ext Cab LB			
	7728	8655	10200
2 Dr C3500 SL Std Cab LB			
	6364	7128	8400
2 Dr K3500 SL 4WD Ext Cab LB			
	8713	9758	11500
2 Dr K3500 SL 4WD Std Cab LB			
	7425	8315	9800
4 Dr C3500 SL Crew Cab LB			
	7500	8400	9900

SONOMA   1995

Driver airbag is added, and daytime running lights are standard. Highrider off-road package can be ordered on the Club Coupe. Power window and lock buttons are illuminated at night. Remote keyless entry is a new option. A single key operates both the door locks and the ignition. A manual transmission can now be ordered with the 191-horsepower, 4.3-liter V6.

Category J

Model Description	Trade-in TMV	Private TMV	Dealer TMV
2 Dr SL 4WD Std Cab LB			
	4637	5298	6400
2 Dr SL Std Cab LB	3188	3643	4400
2 Dr SL 4WD Std Cab SB			
	4492	5133	6200
2 Dr SL Std Cab SB	3116	3560	4300
2 Dr SLE 4WD Ext Cab SB			
	6738	7699	9300
2 Dr SLE 4WD Std Cab SB			
	4927	5629	6800
2 Dr SLE Ext Cab SB	4347	4967	6000
2 Dr SLE Std Cab SB	3768	4305	5200
2 Dr SLS 4WD Std Cab LB			

Model Description	Trade-in TMV	Private TMV	Dealer TMV
	5072	5795	7000
2 Dr SLS Std Cab LB	3985	4553	5500
2 Dr SLS 4WD Ext Cab SB			
	6231	7119	8600
2 Dr SLS 4WD Std Cab SB			
	4927	5629	6800
2 Dr SLS Ext Cab SB	4275	4884	5900
2 Dr SLS Std Cab SB	3550	4056	4900

OPTIONS FOR SONOMA
6 cyl 4.3 L CPI Engine +225
6 cyl 4.3 L Engine +398
AM/FM Compact Disc Player +96
Air Conditioning +323
Aluminum/Alloy Wheels +100
Anti-Lock Brakes[Opt on 2WD] +261
Automatic 4-Speed Transmission +430
Highrider Suspension Package +623
Limited Slip Differential +102
Power Windows +95

SUBURBAN 1995

New interior with driver airbag debuts. New dashboard features modular design with controls that are much easier to read and use. 1500 models can now be ordered with turbodiesel engine. Brake/transmission shift interlock is added to automatic transmission. Seats and door panels are revised. New console on models with bucket seats features pivoting writing surface, along with rear cupholders and storage drawer. Uplevel radios come with automatic volume controls that raise or lower the volume depending on vehicle speed.
Category N

Model	Trade-in	Private	Dealer
4 Dr C1500 Wgn	7398	8261	9700
4 Dr C2500 Wgn	7932	8857	10400
4 Dr K1500 4WD Wgn	8237	9198	10800
4 Dr K2500 4WD Wgn	8771	9794	11500

OPTIONS FOR SUBURBAN
8 cyl 6.5 L Turbodiesel Engine +1091
8 cyl 7.4 L Engine +228
Air Conditioning +322
Aluminum/Alloy Wheels[Opt on C1500,K1500] +96
Bucket Seats +99
Captain Chairs (2) +96
Compact Disc Changer +228
Dual Air Conditioning +495
Folding Center/Rear Seats +418
Leather Seats +428
Locking Differential +97
Power Door Locks +86
Power Drivers Seat +91
Power Windows +101
Privacy Glass +116
SLE Package +1354
SLT Package +1663
Skid Plates +86

VANDURA 1995
Category Q

Model	Trade-in	Private	Dealer
2 Dr G15 Vandura	4746	5396	6478
2 Dr G15 Vandura Ext	4771	5424	6512
2 Dr G25 Vandura	4689	5331	6400
2 Dr G25 Vandura Ext	4770	5422	6510
2 Dr G35 Vandura	4836	5497	6600
2 Dr G35 Vandura Ext	5568	6330	7600

OPTIONS FOR VANDURA
8 cyl 5.0 L Engine[Opt on G15,G25] +231
8 cyl 5.7 L Engine[Opt on G25 Ext] +329
8 cyl 6.5 L Diesel Engine +665
8 cyl 7.4 L Engine +242
Air Conditioning +391
Camper/Towing Package +125
Dual Air Conditioning +632
Limited Slip Differential +101
Power Door Locks +90
Power Windows +103
Rear Heater +82

YUKON 1995

New interior with driver airbag debuts. New dashboard features modular design with controls that are much easier to read and use. New four-door model is added midyear, nicely sized between Jimmy and Suburban. New model is offered only in SLE or SLT trim with a 5.7-liter V8 and an automatic transmission in either 2WD or 4WD. Brake/transmission shift interlock is added to automatic transmission. New console on models with bucket seats features pivoting writing surface, along with rear cupholders and storage drawer.
Category N

Model	Trade-in	Private	Dealer
2 Dr STD 4WD Utility	6788	7580	8900
2 Dr SLE 4WD Utility	7627	8517	10000
4 Dr SLE 4WD Wgn	8466	9454	11100
4 Dr SLE Wgn	7932	8857	10400
2 Dr SLT 4WD Utility	8161	9113	10700
4 Dr SLT 4WD Wgn	9000	10050	11800
4 Dr SLT Wgn	8313	9283	10900

OPTIONS FOR YUKON
8 cyl 6.5 L Turbodiesel Engine +1091
AM/FM Stereo/CD/Tape +80
Air Conditioning[Opt on STD] +339
Aluminum/Alloy Wheels +125
Automatic 4-Speed Transmission[Std on Wgn] +351
Bucket Seats +91
Locking Differential +102
Power Door Locks[Opt on STD] +85
Power Drivers Seat[Opt on SLE] +96
Privacy Glass[Opt on STD] +87

Don't forget to refer to the Mileage Adjustment Table at the back of this book!

Model Description	Trade-in TMV	Private TMV	Dealer TMV

1994 GMC

JIMMY 1994

Side-door guard beams and a high-mounted center brake light are added. Front bench seat is now standard on four-door models.

Category M

Model Description	Trade-in TMV	Private TMV	Dealer TMV
2 Dr STD 4WD Utility	3243	3752	4600
2 Dr STD Utility	2538	2936	3600
4 Dr STD 4WD Wgn	3947	4567	5600
4 Dr STD Wgn	3031	3507	4300
2 Dr SLE 4WD Utility	3454	3996	4900
2 Dr SLE Utility	2679	3099	3800
4 Dr SLE 4WD Wgn	4229	4893	6000
4 Dr SLE Wgn	4018	4649	5700
2 Dr SLS 4WD Utility	3525	4078	5000
2 Dr SLS Utility	2890	3344	4100
4 Dr SLS 4WD Wgn	3880	4489	5504
4 Dr SLS Wgn	2820	3262	4000
2 Dr SLT 4WD Utility	4159	4812	5900
2 Dr SLT Utility	3666	4241	5200
4 Dr SLT 4WD Wgn	4300	4975	6100
4 Dr SLT Wgn	3874	4482	5496

OPTIONS FOR JIMMY

6 cyl 4.3 L CPI Engine +166
AM/FM Compact Disc Player +129
AM/FM Stereo/CD/Tape +203
Air Conditioning[Opt on SLS,STD] +257
Automatic 4-Speed Transmission +295
Compact Disc Changer +203
Limited Slip Differential +92
Power Drivers Seat[Std on SLT] +96
Power Windows[Std on SLT] +96

RALLY WAGON 1994

Category Q

Model Description	Trade-in TMV	Private TMV	Dealer TMV
2 Dr G25 Rally Wagon	4483	5202	6400
2 Dr G35 Rally Wagon	4763	5527	6800
2 Dr G35 Rally Wagon Ext	5114	5933	7300
2 Dr G25 STX Rally Wagon	4973	5771	7100

OPTIONS FOR RALLY WAGON

15 Passenger Seating[Opt on G35] +137
8 cyl 5.0 L Engine[Opt on G25,G25 STX] +212
8 cyl 5.7 L Engine[Opt on G25,G25 STX] +302
8 cyl 6.5 L Diesel Engine +980
8 cyl 7.4 L Engine +223
AM/FM Compact Disc Player +146
Air Conditioning[Std on STX] +360
Camper/Towing Package +114

Dual Air Conditioning +360
Limited Slip Differential +92
Power Door Locks[Std on STX] +82
Power Windows[Std on STX] +96
Privacy Glass[Std on STX] +140

SAFARI 1994

Driver airbag is made standard. Side-door guard beams are stronger, and air conditioners use CFC-free refrigerant. A high-mount center brake light is added. Analog gauges get new graphics, and carpet is treated with Scotchgard.

Category P

Model Description	Trade-in TMV	Private TMV	Dealer TMV
2 Dr STD AWD Cargo Van	3365	3968	4973
2 Dr STD AWD Cargo Van Ext	3423	4037	5059
2 Dr STD AWD Pass. Van	3479	4102	5141
2 Dr STD AWD Pass. Van Ext	3519	4149	5200
2 Dr STD Cargo Van	2774	3271	4100
2 Dr STD Cargo Van Ext	2842	3351	4200
2 Dr STD Pass. Van	3045	3591	4500
2 Dr STD Pass. Van Ext	3105	3662	4589
2 Dr SLE AWD Pass. Van Ext	4128	4867	6100
2 Dr SLE Pass. Van	3316	3910	4900
2 Dr SLE Pass. Van Ext	3402	4011	5027
2 Dr SLT AWD Pass. Van Ext	4263	5027	6300
2 Dr SLT Pass. Van	4195	4947	6200
2 Dr SLT Pass. Van Ext	3925	4628	5800
2 Dr SLX AWD Pass. Van Ext	4060	4787	6000
2 Dr SLX Pass. Van	3120	3679	4611
2 Dr SLX Pass. Van Ext	3248	3830	4800

OPTIONS FOR SAFARI

6 cyl 4.3 L CPI Engine[Std on 4WD] +166
7 Passenger Seating +273
8 Passenger Seating +146
AM/FM Compact Disc Player +150
AM/FM Stereo Tape +92
Air Conditioning +257
Aluminum/Alloy Wheels +91
Camper/Towing Package +114
Cruise Control +83

Don't forget to refer to the Mileage Adjustment Table at the back of this book!

Model Description	Trade-in TMV	Private TMV	Dealer TMV
Dual Air Conditioning +192			
Limited Slip Differential +92			
Power Door Locks +82			
Power Drivers Seat +88			
Power Windows +92			

SIERRA 1500   1994

Model Description	Trade-in TMV	Private TMV	Dealer TMV
Category K			
2 Dr K1500 4WD Ext Cab LB	6013	6833	8200
2 Dr K1500 4WD Ext Cab SB	5812	6605	7926
2 Dr K1500 4WD Ext Cab Stepside SB	5866	6666	8000
2 Dr C1500 SL Ext Cab LB	5353	6083	7300
2 Dr C1500 SL Std Cab LB	4548	5168	6202
2 Dr K1500 SL 4WD Std Cab LB	5280	6000	7200
2 Dr C1500 SL Ext Cab SB	4986	5666	6800
2 Dr C1500 SL Std Cab SB	4400	5000	6000
2 Dr K1500 SL 4WD Std Cab SB	5060	5750	6900
2 Dr C1500 SL Ext Cab Stepside SB	5104	5801	6961
2 Dr C1500 SL Std Cab Stepside SB	4545	5165	6198
2 Dr K1500 SL 4WD Std Cab Stepside SB	5162	5866	7039
2 Dr C1500 SLE Ext Cab LB	5606	6371	7645
2 Dr C1500 SLE Std Cab LB	4693	5333	6400
2 Dr K1500 SLE 4WD Ext Cab LB	6233	7083	8500
2 Dr K1500 SLE 4WD Std Cab LB	5720	6500	7800
2 Dr C1500 SLE Ext Cab SB	5206	5916	7100
2 Dr C1500 SLE Std Cab SB	4620	5250	6300
2 Dr K1500 SLE 4WD Ext Cab SB	6086	6916	8300
2 Dr K1500 SLE 4WD Std Cab SB	5646	6416	7700
2 Dr C1500 SLE Ext Cab Stepside SB	5540	6296	7555
2 Dr C1500 SLE Std Cab Stepside SB	4840	5500	6600
2 Dr K1500 SLE 4WD Ext Cab Stepside SB	6160	7000	8400
2 Dr K1500 SLE 4WD Std Cab Stepside SB	5774	6561	7874
2 Dr C1500 SLT Ext Cab SB	6306	7166	8600
2 Dr K1500 SLT 4WD Ext Cab SB	7113	8083	9700
2 Dr C1500 SLT Ext Cab Stepside SB	6453	7333	8800
2 Dr K1500 SLT 4WD Ext Cab Stepside SB	7260	8250	9900
2 Dr C1500 Special Std Cab LB	3886	4417	5300
2 Dr K1500 Special 4WD Std Cab LB	4913	5583	6700
2 Dr C1500 Special Std Cab SB	3813	4333	5200
2 Dr K1500 Special 4WD Std Cab SB	4766	5416	6500

OPTIONS FOR SIERRA 1500
8 cyl 5.0 L Engine +183
8 cyl 5.7 L Engine +258
8 cyl 6.5 L Diesel Engine +976
8 cyl 6.5 L Turbodiesel Engine +1246
AM/FM Stereo Tape +95
Air Conditioning +297
Aluminum/Alloy Wheels +92
Automatic 4-Speed Transmission +357
Bed Liner +83
Bucket Seats +92
Chrome Wheels +92
Limited Slip Differential +92
Power Drivers Seat +88
Power Windows +92

SIERRA 2500   1994

Model Description	Trade-in TMV	Private TMV	Dealer TMV
Category K			
2 Dr K2500 4WD Ext Cab LB	6820	7750	9300
2 Dr K2500 4WD Ext Cab SB	6453	7333	8800
2 Dr C2500 SL Ext Cab LB	6086	6916	8300
2 Dr C2500 SL Std Cab LB	5646	6416	7700
2 Dr K2500 SL 4WD Std Cab LB	5940	6750	8100
2 Dr C2500 SL Ext Cab SB	6086	6916	8300
2 Dr C2500 SLE Ext Cab LB	6526	7416	8900

Model Description	Trade-in TMV	Private TMV	Dealer TMV
2 Dr C2500 SLE Std Cab LB			
	5793	6583	7900
2 Dr K2500 SLE 4WD Ext Cab LB			
	7773	8833	10600
2 Dr K2500 SLE 4WD Std Cab LB			
	6306	7166	8600
2 Dr C2500 SLE Ext Cab SB			
	6380	7250	8700
2 Dr K2500 SLE 4WD Ext Cab SB			
	7553	8583	10300

OPTIONS FOR SIERRA 2500

8 cyl 5.0 L Engine[Opt on SL Std Cab,SLE Std Cab 2WD/4WD] +212
8 cyl 5.7 L Engine +258
8 cyl 6.5 L Diesel Engine +997
8 cyl 6.5 L Turbodiesel Engine +1001
8 cyl 7.4 L Engine +221
Air Conditioning[Opt on SL,STD] +297
Automatic 4-Speed Transmission +357
Bed Liner +83
Bucket Seats +92
Limited Slip Differential +92
Power Drivers Seat +88
Power Windows +92
Premium Sound System +203

SIERRA 3500   1994

Category K

Model Description	Trade-in TMV	Private TMV	Dealer TMV
2 Dr C3500 Std Cab LB	5573	6333	7600
2 Dr K3500 4WD Ext Cab LB			
	7406	8416	10100
4 Dr C3500 Crew Cab LB			
	6380	7250	8700
4 Dr K3500 4WD Crew Cab LB			
	7846	8916	10700
2 Dr C3500 SL Ext Cab LB			
	6526	7416	8900
2 Dr K3500 SL 4WD Std Cab LB			
	6453	7333	8800
2 Dr C3500 SLE Ext Cab LB			
	7295	8291	9949
2 Dr C3500 SLE Std Cab LB			
	5866	6666	8000
2 Dr K3500 SLE 4WD Ext Cab LB			
	8066	9166	11000
2 Dr K3500 SLE 4WD Std Cab LB			
	7224	8209	9851
4 Dr C3500 SLE Crew Cab LB			
	7333	8333	10000
4 Dr K3500 SLE 4WD Crew Cab LB			
	8359	9500	11400

OPTIONS FOR SIERRA 3500

8 cyl 6.5 L Turbodiesel Engine +1001

SONOMA   1994

All-new truck debuts with more powerful engines and available four-wheel ABS. Side-door guard beams are standard. Rear ABS is standard on four-cylinder models; V6 trucks get the new four-wheel ABS system that works in both two- and four-wheel drive. Highrider package is for serious off-roaders. Available only on regular-cab shortbed models, the Highrider includes four-inch wider track, three-inch height increase, off-road suspension and tires, wheel flares, and thick skid plates. Base engine is 118-horse, 2.2-liter four cylinder. Standard on 4WD models is a 165-horsepower, 4.3-liter V6. Optional on all models is a 195-horsepower, high-output 4.3-liter V6.

Category J

Model Description	Trade-in TMV	Private TMV	Dealer TMV
2 Dr SL 4WD Std Cab LB			
	3974	4583	5600
2 Dr SL Std Cab LB	2625	3028	3700
2 Dr SL 4WD Std Cab SB			
	3903	4502	5500
2 Dr SL Std Cab SB	2554	2947	3600
2 Dr SLE 4WD Std Cab LB			
	4683	5402	6600
2 Dr SLE Std Cab LB	3264	3765	4600
2 Dr SLE 4WD Ext Cab SB			
	5606	6466	7900
2 Dr SLE Ext Cab SB	3761	4338	5300
2 Dr SLE Std Cab SB	3051	3519	4300
2 Dr SLS 4WD Ext Cab SB			
	5322	6139	7500
2 Dr SLS 4WD Std Cab SB			
	4257	4911	6000
2 Dr SLS Ext Cab SB	3690	4256	5200
2 Dr SLS Std Cab SB	2838	3274	4000

OPTIONS FOR SONOMA

6 cyl 4.3 L CPI Engine +206
6 cyl 4.3 L Engine +365
AM/FM Compact Disc Player +150
Air Conditioning +297
Aluminum/Alloy Wheels +91
Automatic 4-Speed Transmission +394
Limited Slip Differential +92

SUBURBAN   1994

Model Description	Trade-in TMV	Private TMV	Dealer TMV

Side-door guard beams are added, as well as a high-mounted center brake light. A turbocharged diesel is newly optional on 2500 models. A new grille appears.

Category N

Model	Trade-in	Private	Dealer
4 Dr C1500 Wgn	6427	7242	8600
4 Dr C2500 Wgn	6502	7326	8700
4 Dr K1500 4WD Wgn	7025	7916	9400
4 Dr K2500 4WD Wgn	7249	8168	9700

OPTIONS FOR SUBURBAN
8 cyl 6.5 L Turbodiesel Engine +1001
8 cyl 7.4 L Engine +210
Air Conditioning +295
Aluminum/Alloy Wheels +87
Bucket Seats +91
Captain Chairs (2) +87
Center & Rear Bench Seat +383
Dual Air Conditioning +453
Leather Seats +393
Limited Slip Differential +87
Locking Differential +88
Power Drivers Seat +83
Power Windows +92
Premium Sound System +193
Privacy Glass +106
SLE Decor Group +908

VANDURA 1994

Category Q

Model	Trade-in	Private	Dealer
2 Dr G15 Vandura	3769	4374	5381
2 Dr G15 Vandura Ext	3790	4397	5410
2 Dr G25 Vandura	3713	4308	5300
2 Dr G25 Vandura Ext	3789	4396	5409
2 Dr G35 Vandura	3853	4470	5500
2 Dr G35 Vandura Ext	4413	5121	6300

OPTIONS FOR VANDURA
8 cyl 5.0 L Engine[Opt on G15,G25] +212
8 cyl 5.7 L Engine[Opt on G25] +302
8 cyl 6.5 L Diesel Engine +610
8 cyl 7.4 L Engine +223
AM/FM Compact Disc Player +110
Air Conditioning +360
Camper/Towing Package +114
Dual Air Conditioning +579
Limited Slip Differential +92
Power Door Locks +82
Power Windows +95

YUKON 1994

Air conditioning receives CFC-free coolant. Side-door guard beams are added. A new grille appears, and models equipped with a decor package get composite headlamps. A turbocharged diesel is newly optional. Third brake light is added.

Category N

Model	Trade-in	Private	Dealer
2 Dr STD 4WD Utility	5979	6737	8000
2 Dr SLE 4WD Utility	6801	7663	9100
2 Dr Sport 4WD Utility	6353	7158	8500

OPTIONS FOR YUKON
8 cyl 6.5 L Turbodiesel Engine +1001
Air Conditioning[Std on Sport] +311
Aluminum/Alloy Wheels +114
Automatic 4-Speed Transmission +322
Bucket Seats +84
Locking Differential +92
Luggage Rack +92
Power Drivers Seat +88
Power Windows +97

1993 GMC

JIMMY 1993

Two-door model available in SLT trim. Four-door models get monochromatic paint scheme in SLS trim. V6 engines get internal balance shaft designed to reduce vibration. Automatic transmission receives electronic shift controls and second-gear start feature. Manual lumbar adjusters are newly standard on front seats. Typhoon can be ordered in white as well as black.

Category M

Model	Trade-in	Private	Dealer
2 Dr STD 4WD Utility	2435	2872	3600
2 Dr STD Utility	2134	2517	3155
2 Dr SLE 4WD Utility	3111	3669	4600
2 Dr SLE Utility	2195	2588	3245
4 Dr SLE 4WD Wgn	3314	3909	4900
4 Dr SLE Wgn	2359	2782	3488
2 Dr SLS 4WD Utility	3179	3749	4700
2 Dr SLS Utility	2375	2801	3512
4 Dr SLS 4WD Wgn	3517	4148	5200
2 Dr SLT 4WD Utility	3584	4228	5300
2 Dr SLT Utility	3449	4068	5100
4 Dr SLT 4WD Wgn	3787	4467	5600
4 Dr SLT Wgn	3652	4307	5400

OPTIONS FOR JIMMY
6 cyl 4.3 L CPI Engine +150
AM/FM Compact Disc Player +116
AM/FM Stereo Tape[Std on SLT] +87
Air Conditioning[Std on SLT Wgn] +233
Aluminum/Alloy Wheels[Std on SLT] +83
Automatic 4-Speed Transmission +267
Leather Seats[Std on SLT] +267
Limited Slip Differential +83
Power Drivers Seat +87
Power Windows +87

RALLY WAGON 1993

Category Q

Model	Trade-in	Private	Dealer
2 Dr G15 Rally Wagon	3367	3980	5000

Don't forget to refer to the Mileage Adjustment Table at the back of this book!

Model Description	Trade-in TMV	Private TMV	Dealer TMV
2 Dr G15 Rally Wagon Ext			
	3502	4139	5200
2 Dr G25 Rally Wagon Ext			
	3572	4222	5304
2 Dr G35 Dsl Rally Wagon			
	4310	5094	6400
2 Dr G35 Rally Wagon Ext			
	4243	5014	6300
2 Dr G15 STX Rally Wagon			
	3567	4215	5296
2 Dr G25 STX Rally Wagon Ext			
	3771	4457	5600
2 Dr G35 STX Rally Wagon			
	4041	4776	6000

OPTIONS FOR RALLY WAGON
12 Passenger Seating +255
15 Passenger Seating +124
8 Passenger Seating +124
8 cyl 5.0 L Engine[Opt on G15,G15 STX,G25,G25 STX] +192
8 cyl 5.7 L Engine[Opt on G15,G15 STX,G25,G25 STX] +273
8 cyl 6.2 L Diesel Engine +800
8 cyl 7.4 L Engine +202
AM/FM Compact Disc Player +132
Air Conditioning +325
Bucket Seats +135
Camper/Towing Package +103
Dual Air Conditioning +325
Locking Differential +84
Power Windows +87
Privacy Glass +126

SAFARI   1993

Base 4.3-liter V6 gets 15 additional horsepower. Automatic transmission gets electronic shift controls and second-gear start feature. New speedometer reads to 100 mph. Driver airbag is offered as an option midyear.

Category P

Model Description	Trade-in TMV	Private TMV	Dealer TMV
2 Dr STD AWD Cargo Van Ext			
	2859	3437	4400
2 Dr STD AWD Pass. Van			
	2924	3515	4500
2 Dr STD AWD Pass. Van Ext			
	2989	3593	4600
2 Dr STD Cargo Van	2209	2656	3400
2 Dr STD Cargo Van Ext			
	2339	2812	3600
2 Dr STD Pass. Van	2404	2890	3700
2 Dr STD Pass. Van Ext			
	2448	2943	3768
2 Dr GT Sport Pass. Van Ext			
	2490	2993	3832
2 Dr SLE AWD Pass. Van			
	3184	3827	4900
2 Dr SLE AWD Pass. Van Ext			
	3249	3906	5000
2 Dr SLE Pass. Van	2534	3046	3900
2 Dr SLE Pass. Van Ext			
	2599	3124	4000
2 Dr SLT AWD Pass. Van			
	3314	3984	5100
2 Dr SLT AWD Pass. Van Ext			
	3444	4140	5300
2 Dr SLT Pass. Van	3054	3671	4700
2 Dr SLT Pass. Van Ext			
	3119	3749	4800

OPTIONS FOR SAFARI
6 cyl 4.3 L CPI Engine[Std on 4WD] +150
7 Passenger Seating +246
8 Passenger Seating +132
AM/FM Compact Disc Player +135
AM/FM Stereo Tape +83
Air Bag Restraint[Std on Cargo EXT] +133
Air Conditioning +233
Aluminum/Alloy Wheels +82
Camper/Towing Package +103
Dual Air Conditioning +175
Limited Slip Differential +83
Power Windows +83
Sport Suspension +250

SIERRA 1500   1993

Category K

Model Description	Trade-in TMV	Private TMV	Dealer TMV
2 Dr C1500 Ext Cab LB	4203	4849	5927
2 Dr C1500 Std Cab LB	3706	4277	5227
2 Dr K1500 4WD Ext Cab LB			
	4822	5564	6800
2 Dr K1500 4WD Std Cab LB			
	4405	5082	6212
2 Dr C1500 Ext Cab SB	4164	4805	5873
2 Dr C1500 Std Cab SB	3668	4232	5173
2 Dr K1500 4WD Ext Cab SB			
	4751	5482	6700
2 Dr K1500 4WD Std Cab SB			
	4271	4929	6024
2 Dr C1500 Ext Cab Stepside SB			
	4232	4884	5969
2 Dr C1500 Std Cab Stepside SB			
	3747	4324	5285
2 Dr STD 4WD Std Cab Stepside SB			
	4271	4929	6024
2 Dr C1500 SLE Ext Cab LB			
	4461	5147	6291
2 Dr C1500 SLE Std Cab LB			
	3900	4500	5500
2 Dr K1500 SLE 4WD Ext Cab LB			

Model Description	Trade-in TMV	Private TMV	Dealer TMV
	4983	5749	7027
2 Dr K1500 SLE 4WD Std Cab LB	4628	5340	6527
2 Dr C1500 SLE Ext Cab SB	4327	4993	6103
2 Dr C1500 SLE Std Cab SB	3829	4418	5400
2 Dr K1500 SLE 4WD Ext Cab SB	4944	5705	6973
2 Dr K1500 SLE 4WD Std Cab SB	4590	5296	6473
2 Dr C1500 SLE Ext Cab Stepside SB	4474	5162	6309
2 Dr C1500 SLE Std Cab Stepside SB	3971	4582	5600
2 Dr K1500 SLE 4WD Ext Cab Stepside SB	5034	5809	7100
2 Dr K1500 SLE 4WD Std Cab Stepside SB	4680	5400	6600
2 Dr C1500 SLX Ext Cab LB	4323	4988	6097
2 Dr K1500 SLX 4WD Ext Cab LB	4912	5667	6927
2 Dr C1500 SLX Ext Cab SB	4242	4894	5982
2 Dr C1500 SLX Std Cab SB	3747	4323	5284
2 Dr K1500 SLX 4WD Ext Cab SB	4873	5623	6873
2 Dr C1500 SLX Ext Cab Stepside SB	4388	5063	6188
2 Dr C1500 Special Std Cab LB	2907	3355	4100
2 Dr K1500 Special 4WD Std Cab LB	3780	4362	5331
2 Dr K1500 Sport 4WD Std Cab SB	4538	5236	6400

OPTIONS FOR SIERRA 1500
8 cyl 5.0 L Engine +165
8 cyl 5.7 L Engine +234
8 cyl 6.2 L Diesel Engine +800
AM/FM Stereo Tape +85
Air Conditioning +268
Aluminum/Alloy Wheels +83
Automatic 4-Speed Transmission +324
Bucket Seats +83
Locking Differential +84
Power Windows +83

SIERRA 2500　　1993

Category K

Model Description	Trade-in TMV	Private TMV	Dealer TMV
2 Dr C2500 Ext Cab LB	4467	5154	6300
2 Dr C2500 Std Cab LB	4042	4664	5700
2 Dr K2500 4WD Ext Cab LB	4861	5609	6855
2 Dr K2500 4WD Std Cab LB	4538	5236	6400
2 Dr C2500 Ext Cab SB	4467	5154	6300
2 Dr K2500 4WD Ext Cab SB	4893	5645	6900
2 Dr C2500 SLE Ext Cab LB	5176	5973	7300
2 Dr C2500 SLE Std Cab LB	4349	5018	6133
2 Dr K2500 SLE 4WD Ext Cab LB	5034	5809	7100
2 Dr K2500 SLE 4WD Std Cab LB	5247	6054	7400
2 Dr C2500 SLE Ext Cab SB	4822	5564	6800
2 Dr K2500 SLE 4WD Ext Cab SB	5034	5809	7100
2 Dr C2500 SLX Ext Cab LB	4680	5400	6600
2 Dr C2500 SLX Std Cab LB	4302	4964	6067
2 Dr K2500 SLX 4WD Ext Cab LB	4964	5727	7000
2 Dr C2500 SLX 4WD Ext Cab LB	4751	5482	6700
2 Dr C2500 SLX Ext Cab SB	4609	5318	6500
2 Dr K2500 SLX 4WD Ext Cab SB	4964	5727	7000

OPTIONS FOR SIERRA 2500
8 cyl 5.0 L Engine +192
8 cyl 5.7 L Engine +234
8 cyl 6.2 L Diesel Engine +800
8 cyl 6.5 L Turbodiesel Engine +982
8 cyl 7.4 L Engine +200
Air Conditioning +268
Automatic 4-Speed Transmission +324
Bucket Seats +83
Locking Differential +84
Power Windows +83

SIERRA 3500　　1993

Category K

Model Description	Trade-in TMV	Private TMV	Dealer TMV
2 Dr C3500 Ext Cab LB	5034	5809	7100
2 Dr C3500 Std Cab LB	4609	5318	6500
2 Dr K3500 4WD Ext Cab LB	6007	6932	8472
2 Dr K3500 4WD Std Cab LB	5247	6054	7400

Don't forget to refer to the Mileage Adjustment Table at the back of this book!

Model Description	Trade-in TMV	Private TMV	Dealer TMV	Model Description	Trade-in TMV	Private TMV	Dealer TMV
4 Dr C3500 Crew Cab LB				2 Dr SLE 4WD Std Cab LB			
	5105	5891	7200		2933	3445	4300
4 Dr K3500 4WD Crew Cab LB				2 Dr SLE 4WD Ext Cab SB			
	6169	7118	8700		3410	4006	5000
2 Dr K3500 SL Turbodsl 4WD Ext Cab LB				2 Dr SLE 4WD Std Cab SB			
	7800	9000	11000		2933	3445	4300
2 Dr C3500 SLE Ext Cab LB				2 Dr SLE Ext Cab SB	2523	2965	3700
	5317	6135	7499	2 Dr SLE Std Cab SB	2251	2644	3300
2 Dr C3500 SLE Std Cab LB				2 Dr SLS Std Cab LB	2251	2644	3300
	4822	5564	6800	2 Dr SLS 4WD Std Cab LB			
2 Dr K3500 SLE 4WD Ext Cab LB					2880	3384	4223
	6311	7282	8900	2 Dr SLS 4WD Ext Cab SB			
2 Dr K3500 SLE 4WD Std Cab LB					3342	3926	4900
	5388	6217	7599	2 Dr SLS 4WD Std Cab SB			
4 Dr C3500 SLE Crew Cab LB					2880	3384	4223
	5390	6219	7601	2 Dr SLS Ext Cab SB	2504	2941	3671
4 Dr K3500 SLE 4WD Crew Cab LB				2 Dr SLS Std Cab SB	2227	2617	3266
	6382	7364	9000	2 Dr Special 4WD Std Cab SB			
2 Dr C3500 SLX Ext Cab LB					2592	3045	3800
	5176	5973	7300	2 Dr Special Std Cab SB			
2 Dr C3500 SLX Std Cab LB					2037	2393	2987
	4680	5400	6600				
2 Dr K3500 SLX 4WD Ext Cab LB							
	6047	6977	8528				
2 Dr K3500 SLX 4WD Std Cab LB							
	5319	6137	7501				

OPTIONS FOR SIERRA 3500

8 cyl 6.2 L Diesel Engine +800
8 cyl 6.5 L Turbodiesel Engine +906
8 cyl 7.4 L Engine +200
Air Conditioning +268
Automatic 4-Speed Transmission +324
Bucket Seats +83
Dual Rear Wheels +286
Limited Slip Differential +83

SONOMA   1993

V6 engines get internal balance shaft designed to reduce vibration. Automatic transmission gets electronic shift controls. Syclone dropped.

Category J

Model Description	Trade-in TMV	Private TMV	Dealer TMV
2 Dr STD Std Cab LB	2046	2404	3000
2 Dr STD 4WD Std Cab LB			
	2849	3347	4177
2 Dr STD 4WD Ext Cab SB			
	3205	3766	4700
2 Dr STD 4WD Std Cab SB			
	2849	3347	4177
2 Dr STD Ext Cab SB	2458	2888	3604
2 Dr STD Std Cab SB	2191	2574	3213
2 Dr SLE Std Cab LB	2405	2825	3526

OPTIONS FOR SONOMA

6 cyl 2.8 L Engine +130
6 cyl 4.3 L CPI Engine +186
6 cyl 4.3 L Engine +330
AM/FM Compact Disc Player +135
AM/FM Stereo/CD/Tape +114
Air Conditioning +268
Aluminum/Alloy Wheels +82
Automatic 4-Speed Transmission +356
Locking Differential +84
Sport Suspension +152

SUBURBAN   1993

No changes.
Category N

Model Description	Trade-in TMV	Private TMV	Dealer TMV
4 Dr C1500 Wgn	5123	5865	7100
4 Dr C2500 Wgn	5484	6278	7600
4 Dr K1500 4WD Wgn	5773	6608	8000
4 Dr K2500 4WD Wgn	6133	7021	8500

OPTIONS FOR SUBURBAN

8 cyl 7.4 L Engine +190
Air Conditioning +267
Bucket Seats +83
Center & Rear Bench Seat +348
Center Bench Seat +200
Dual Air Conditioning +411
Locking Differential +80
Power Windows +83
Privacy Glass +96
SLE Package +740

TYPHOON   1993

Model Description	Trade-in TMV	Private TMV	Dealer TMV
Typhoon can be ordered in white as well as black.			
Category F			
2 Dr STD Turbo 4WD Utility			
	7152	8220	10000

OPTIONS FOR TYPHOON
AM/FM Compact Disc Player +150

VANDURA   1993

Category Q

Model Description	Trade-in TMV	Private TMV	Dealer TMV
2 Dr G15 Vandura	2954	3491	4386
2 Dr G15 Vandura Ext	2971	3511	4411
2 Dr G25 Vandura	2965	3504	4403
2 Dr G25 Vandura Ext	3031	3582	4500
2 Dr G35 Vandura	3098	3661	4600
2 Dr G35 Vandura Ext	3637	4298	5400

OPTIONS FOR VANDURA
8 cyl 5.0 L Engine[Opt on G15,G25] +192
8 cyl 5.7 L Engine[Opt on G25,G35] +273
8 cyl 6.2 L Diesel Engine +800
8 cyl 7.4 L Engine +202
AM/FM Compact Disc Player +100
Air Conditioning +325
Camper/Towing Package +103
Dual Air Conditioning +525
Locking Differential +84
Power Windows +85

YUKON   1993

No changes.
Category N

Model Description	Trade-in TMV	Private TMV	Dealer TMV
2 Dr STD 4WD Utility	5051	5782	7000
2 Dr SLE 4WD Utility	5773	6608	8000
2 Dr Sport GT 4WD Utility			
	5989	6856	8300

OPTIONS FOR YUKON
Air Conditioning[Opt on STD] +281
Aluminum/Alloy Wheels +103
Automatic 4-Speed Transmission +292
Locking Differential +84
Luggage Rack +83
Power Windows +88

1992 GMC

JIMMY   1992

Four-wheel ABS is standard on all models. Electronic-shift transfer case is added to options list; comes standard with SLT trim. A high-performance, 4.3-liter V6 debuts with 40 additional horsepower, bringing total output to 200 ponies. Bucket seats are redesigned, a new speedometer is installed, and a four-spoke steering wheel is added.
Category M

Model Description	Trade-in TMV	Private TMV	Dealer TMV
2 Dr STD 4WD Utility	2333	2808	3600
2 Dr STD Utility	1815	2184	2800
4 Dr STD 4WD Wgn	2787	3354	4300
4 Dr STD Wgn	2139	2574	3300
2 Dr SLE 4WD Utility	2657	3198	4100
2 Dr SLE Utility	1944	2340	3000
4 Dr SLE 4WD Wgn	3046	3666	4700
4 Dr SLE Wgn	2204	2652	3400
4 Dr SLT 4WD Wgn	3305	3978	5100
4 Dr SLT Wgn	2268	2730	3500

OPTIONS FOR JIMMY
6 cyl 4.3 L CPI Engine[Opt on SLE] +130
AM/FM Compact Disc Player +101
Air Conditioning +202
Automatic 4-Speed Transmission +231
Leather Seats +231

RALLY WAGON   1992

Category Q

Model Description	Trade-in TMV	Private TMV	Dealer TMV
2 Dr G15 Rally Wagon	2603	3146	4052
2 Dr G15 Rally Wagon Ext			
	2698	3261	4200
2 Dr G25 Rally Wagon Ext			
	2762	3339	4300
2 Dr G35 Dsl Rally Wagon			
	3340	4038	5200
2 Dr G35 Rally Wagon Ext			
	3212	3882	5000
2 Dr G15 STX Rally Wagon			
	2665	3221	4148
2 Dr G25 STX Rally Wagon Ext			
	2955	3572	4600
2 Dr G35 STX Dsl Rally Wagon			
	3597	4348	5600
2 Dr G35 STX Rally Wagon Ext			
	3276	3960	5100

OPTIONS FOR RALLY WAGON
12 Passenger Seating +221
15 Passenger Seating +107
8 Passenger Seating +107
8 cyl 5.0 L Engine[Opt on G15,G25] +166
8 cyl 5.7 L Engine[Opt on G15,G25] +238
8 cyl 6.2 L Diesel Engine +695
8 cyl 7.4 L Engine +175
Air Conditioning +283
Camper/Towing Package +90
Dual Air Conditioning +283
Privacy Glass +110

SAFARI   1992

Dutch rear door treatment is available. With Dutch doors, a rear washer/wiper and rear defogger can be ordered. All-wheel-drive models get high-output, 200-

horsepower V6 standard. Engine is optional on 2WD models.

Category P

Model Description	Trade-in TMV	Private TMV	Dealer TMV
2 Dr STD AWD Cargo Van Ext	2245	2753	3600
2 Dr STD AWD Pass. Van	2257	2768	3620
2 Dr STD AWD Pass. Van Ext	2369	2906	3800
2 Dr STD Cargo Van	1871	2294	3000
2 Dr STD Cargo Van Ext	1995	2447	3200
2 Dr STD Pass. Van	1933	2371	3100
2 Dr STD Pass. Van Ext	2058	2523	3300
2 Dr SLE AWD Pass. Van	2432	2982	3900
2 Dr SLE Pass. Van	2182	2676	3499
2 Dr SLE Pass. Van Ext	2238	2745	3590
2 Dr SLT AWD Pass. Van	2494	3059	4000
2 Dr SLT AWD Pass. Van Ext	3055	3747	4900
2 Dr SLT Pass. Van	2183	2677	3501
2 Dr SLT Pass. Van Ext	2238	2745	3590

OPTIONS FOR SAFARI

6 cyl 4.3 L CPI Engine[Std on 4WD] +130
7 Passenger Seating +214
8 Passenger Seating +115
AM/FM Compact Disc Player +117
Air Conditioning +202
Camper/Towing Package +90
Dual Air Conditioning +152
Sport Suspension[Std on 4WD,STD Pass Van EXT] +217

SIERRA 1500   1992

Category K

Model Description	Trade-in TMV	Private TMV	Dealer TMV
2 Dr C1500 Ext Cab LB	2871	3445	4400
2 Dr C1500 Std Cab LB	2088	2504	3199
2 Dr K1500 4WD Ext Cab LB	3266	3918	5005
2 Dr K1500 4WD Std Cab LB	3145	3773	4819
2 Dr C1500 Ext Cab SB	2737	3283	4194
2 Dr C1500 Std Cab SB	2051	2461	3143
2 Dr K1500 4WD Ext Cab SB	3206	3845	4912
2 Dr K1500 4WD Std Cab SB	3116	3738	4775
2 Dr C1500 Ext Cab Stepside SB	2941	3528	4507
2 Dr K1500 4WD Ext Cab Stepside SB	3275	3929	5019
2 Dr K1500 4WD Std Cab Stepside SB	3155	3784	4834
2 Dr C1500 SLE Ext Cab LB	3072	3685	4707
2 Dr C1500 SLE Std Cab LB	2806	3366	4300
2 Dr K1500 SLE 4WD Ext Cab LB	3529	4233	5407
2 Dr K1500 SLE 4WD Std Cab LB	3256	3907	4990
2 Dr C1500 SLE Ext Cab SB	3012	3614	4616
2 Dr C1500 SLE Std Cab SB	2684	3219	4112
2 Dr K1500 SLE 4WD Ext Cab SB	3454	4143	5292
2 Dr K1500 SLE 4WD Std Cab SB	3196	3835	4898
2 Dr C1500 SLE Ext Cab Stepside SB	3115	3737	4773
2 Dr C1500 SLE Std Cab Stepside SB	2932	3517	4493
2 Dr K1500 SLE 4WD Ext Cab Stepside SB	3589	4306	5500
2 Dr K1500 SLE 4WD Std Cab Stepside SB	3266	3918	5005
2 Dr C1500 SLX Ext Cab LB	3060	3671	4689
2 Dr C1500 SLX Std Cab LB	2736	3283	4193
2 Dr K1500 SLX 4WD Ext Cab LB	3464	4156	5308
2 Dr K1500 SLX 4WD Std Cab LB	3209	3849	4917
2 Dr C1500 SLX Ext Cab SB	2992	3589	4584
2 Dr C1500 SLX Std Cab SB	2668	3200	4088
2 Dr K1500 SLX 4WD Ext Cab SB	3328	3993	5100
2 Dr K1500 SLX 4WD Std Cab SB	3180	3815	4873
2 Dr C1500 SLX Ext Cab Stepside SB	3070	3683	4704
2 Dr C1500 SLX Std Cab Stepside SB	2749	3298	4213
2 Dr K1500 SLX 4WD Ext Cab Stepside SB	3519	4222	5393

Model Description	Trade-in TMV	Private TMV	Dealer TMV	Model Description	Trade-in TMV	Private TMV	Dealer TMV
2 Dr K1500 SLX 4WD Std Cab Stepside SB				8 cyl 6.5 L Turbodiesel Engine +787			
	3250	3899	4980	8 cyl 7.4 L Engine +174			
2 Dr C1500 Special Std Cab LB				Air Conditioning +233			
	1864	2237	2857	Automatic 4-Speed Transmission +281			
2 Dr K1500 Special 4WD Std Cab LB							
	2610	3132	4000				

SIERRA 2500 — *continued options reference*

OPTIONS FOR SIERRA 1500
8 cyl 5.0 L Engine +143
8 cyl 5.7 L Engine +202
8 cyl 6.2 L Diesel Engine +695
Air Conditioning +233
Automatic 4-Speed Transmission +281

SIERRA 2500   1992

Category K

Model Description	Trade-in TMV	Private TMV	Dealer TMV
2 Dr C2500 Ext Cab LB	3408	4088	5222
2 Dr C2500 Std Cab LB	3002	3601	4600
2 Dr K2500 4WD Ext Cab LB			
	3593	4310	5505
2 Dr K2500 4WD Std Cab LB			
	3456	4145	5295
2 Dr C2500 Ext Cab SB	3379	4054	5178
2 Dr K2500 4WD Ext Cab SB			
	3593	4310	5505
2 Dr C2500 SLE Ext Cab LB			
	3515	4217	5386
2 Dr C2500 SLE Std Cab LB			
	3263	3914	5000
2 Dr K2500 SLE 4WD Ext Cab LB			
	3850	4619	5900
2 Dr K2500 SLE 4WD Std Cab LB			
	3583	4299	5491
2 Dr C2500 SLE Ext Cab SB			
	3515	4217	5386
2 Dr K2500 SLE 4WD Ext Cab SB			
	3850	4619	5900
2 Dr C2500 SLX Ext Cab LB			
	3516	4217	5387
2 Dr C2500 SLX Std Cab LB			
	3133	3758	4800
2 Dr K2500 SLX 4WD Ext Cab LB			
	3785	4541	5800
2 Dr K2500 SLX 4WD Std Cab LB			
	3551	4260	5441
2 Dr C2500 SLX Ext Cab SB			
	3462	4153	5305
2 Dr K2500 SLX 4WD Ext Cab SB			
	3785	4541	5800

OPTIONS FOR SIERRA 2500
8 cyl 5.0 L Engine +166
8 cyl 5.7 L Engine +202
8 cyl 6.2 L Diesel Engine +695

SIERRA 3500   1992

Category K

Model Description	Trade-in TMV	Private TMV	Dealer TMV
2 Dr C3500 Ext Cab LB	3459	4149	5300
2 Dr C3500 Std Cab LB	3299	3957	5055
2 Dr K3500 4WD Ext Cab LB			
	4000	4799	6130
2 Dr K3500 4WD Std Cab LB			
	3785	4541	5800
4 Dr C3500 Crew Cab LB			
	3655	4384	5600
4 Dr K3500 4WD Crew Cab LB			
	4307	5167	6600
2 Dr C3500 SLE Ext Cab LB			
	3720	4462	5700
2 Dr C3500 SLE Std Cab LB			
	3394	4071	5200
2 Dr K3500 SLE 4WD Ext Cab LB			
	4111	4932	6300
2 Dr K3500 SLE 4WD Std Cab LB			
	4021	4823	6161
4 Dr K3500 SLE 4WD Crew Cab LB			
	4438	5324	6800
2 Dr C3500 SLX Ext Cab LB			
	3524	4228	5400
2 Dr C3500 SLX Std Cab LB			
	3358	4028	5145
2 Dr K3500 SLX 4WD Ext Cab LB			
	4072	4884	6239
2 Dr K3500 SLX 4WD Std Cab LB			
	3961	4752	6070

OPTIONS FOR SIERRA 3500
8 cyl 6.2 L Diesel Engine +695
8 cyl 6.5 L Turbodiesel Engine +787
8 cyl 7.4 L Engine +174
Air Conditioning +233
Automatic 4-Speed Transmission +281
Dual Rear Wheels +249

SONOMA   1992

New GT model debuts, available on regular-cab shorted 2WD models and including many Syclone styling cues along with high-output, 4.3-liter V6. Front bucket seats are redesigned, integral head restraints are added, and Club Coupes can be equipped with leather seats. New speedometer and four-spoke steering wheel are installed. Premium sound system with CD player is added to options list. Four-wheel-drive models can be equipped with an electronic-shift

Model Description	Trade-in TMV	Private TMV	Dealer TMV	Model Description	Trade-in TMV	Private TMV	Dealer TMV
transfer case.				Air Conditioning +232			
Category J				Center & Rear Bench Seat +302			
2 Dr STD 4WD Std Cab LB				Center Bench Seat +174			
	2219	2699	3500	Dual Air Conditioning +357			
2 Dr STD Std Cab LB	1838	2237	2900	SLE Package +643			

TYPHOON   1992

Typhoon blows into town, featuring Syclone powertrain wrapped in two-door Jimmy body.

Model Description	Trade-in TMV	Private TMV	Dealer TMV
2 Dr STD 4WD Ext Cab SB			
	2409	2931	3800
2 Dr STD 4WD Std Cab SB			
	2219	2699	3500
2 Dr STD Ext Cab SB	2029	2468	3200
2 Dr STD Std Cab SB	1838	2237	2900
2 Dr GT Std Cab SB	2726	3316	4300
2 Dr SLE 4WD Std Cab LB			
	2282	2776	3600
2 Dr SLE Std Cab LB	1902	2314	3000
2 Dr SLE 4WD Ext Cab SB			
	2599	3162	4100
2 Dr SLE 4WD Std Cab SB			
	2346	2853	3700
2 Dr SLE Ext Cab SB	2169	2639	3422
2 Dr SLE Std Cab SB	1902	2314	3000
2 Dr Special 4WD Std Cab SB			
	2141	2605	3378
2 Dr Special Std Cab SB			
	1712	2082	2700

Category F

Model Description	Trade-in TMV	Private TMV	Dealer TMV
2 Dr STD Turbo 4WD Utility			
	5705	6753	8500

OPTIONS FOR TYPHOON
AM/FM Compact Disc Player +130

VANDURA   1992

Category Q

Model Description	Trade-in TMV	Private TMV	Dealer TMV
2 Dr G15 Vandura	2300	2780	3580
2 Dr G15 Vandura Ext	2377	2873	3700
2 Dr G25 Vandura	2316	2800	3606
2 Dr G25 Vandura Ext	2441	2951	3800
2 Dr G35 Vandura	2322	2806	3614
2 Dr G35 Vandura Ext	2698	3261	4200

OPTIONS FOR VANDURA
8 cyl 5.0 L Engine +166
8 cyl 5.7 L Engine +238
8 cyl 6.2 L Diesel Engine +695
8 cyl 7.4 L Engine +175
Air Conditioning +283
Camper/Towing Package +90
Dual Air Conditioning +456

Category F

Model Description	Trade-in TMV	Private TMV	Dealer TMV
2 Dr Syclone Turbo 4WD Std Cab SB			
	4363	5164	6500

OPTIONS FOR SONOMA
6 cyl 2.8 L Engine +113
6 cyl 4.3 L CPI Engine +162
6 cyl 4.3 L Engine +287
AM/FM Compact Disc Player +117
Air Conditioning[Std on GT] +233
Automatic 4-Speed Transmission[Std on GT, Syclone] +310
Leather Seats +231
Sport Suspension +132

SUBURBAN   1992

All-new design debuts based on platform and styling of Sierra. Cargo space and towing capacity are up. ABS works on all four wheels even in 4WD. Tailgate glass is lifted up instead of powered down. No diesel is offered. GM's Instatrac 4WD system is standard on K models.

Category N

Model Description	Trade-in TMV	Private TMV	Dealer TMV
4 Dr C1500 Wgn	3519	4112	5100
4 Dr C2500 Wgn	3657	4273	5300
4 Dr K1500 4WD Wgn	4899	5724	7100
4 Dr K2500 4WD Wgn	5037	5885	7300

OPTIONS FOR SUBURBAN
8 cyl 7.4 L Engine +165

YUKON   1992

Totally redesigned and based on same platform and sheetmetal as Sierra pickup, the old Jimmy becomes the Yukon to differentiate it from the Sonoma-based Jimmy. Six-passenger seating is standard. Cargo area gets fixed metal roof rather than fiberglass shell. Four-wheel ABS is standard and works in 4WD. New Sport appearance package includes two-tone paint and wheelwell flares. Diesel option is dropped. Five-speed manual is standard transmission. An automatic is optional. Shift-on-the-fly 4WD is standard.

Category N

Model Description	Trade-in TMV	Private TMV	Dealer TMV
2 Dr STD 4WD Utility	3795	4434	5500
2 Dr SLE 4WD Utility	4002	4676	5800
2 Dr Sport 4WD Utility			
	4071	4757	5900

OPTIONS FOR YUKON
Air Conditioning +245
Aluminum/Alloy Wheels +90
Automatic 4-Speed Transmission +253

HONDA 01

Model Description	Trade-in TMV	Private TMV	Dealer TMV	Model Description	Trade-in TMV	Private TMV	Dealer TMV

HONDA   *Japan*

1993 Honda Civic

2001 HONDA

ACCORD   2001

Freshened exterior styling debuts for 2001, with a more aggressive-looking front fascia and hood, and an all-new taillight and rear decklid design. Honda also ups the safety features list, making dual-stage, dual-threshold front airbags standard and side airbags available on all models. All Accords now either meet or exceed California's low-emission vehicle (LEV) standards (some Accords meet ULEV standards, and one model sold in California is rated SULEV — see your dealer for details). Improvements aimed at reducing road and wind noise have been made, while EX models get a standard six-disc in-dash CD changer, and all V6 models come with traction control. Mid-year, a DX four-banger equipped with a special value package debuted, adding an automatic transmission, air conditioning, a CD player, floor mats, fake wood interior accents and special exterior trim.

Category D

	Trade-in	Private	Dealer
4 Dr DX Sdn	10435	11153	12349
2 Dr EX Cpe	14600	15604	17278
2 Dr EX V6 Cpe	17183	18365	20335
4 Dr EX Sdn	14627	15633	17310
4 Dr EX V6 Sdn	17184	18366	20336
2 Dr LX Cpe	12778	13657	15122
2 Dr LX V6 Cpe	15317	16371	18127
4 Dr LX Sdn	12779	13658	15123
4 Dr LX V6 Sdn	15317	16371	18127
4 Dr Value Sdn	11486	12276	13593

OPTIONS FOR ACCORD
Anti-Lock Brakes[Opt on LX] +368
Automatic 4-Speed Transmission[Opt on DX,LX,EX] +589
Side Air Bag Restraints[Opt on EX] +184

CIVIC   2001

Honda redesigns its cars and trucks every four to five years, whether they need it or not. For 2001, it's the Civic's turn. Larger inside and out, with more powerful engines but a less sophisticated suspension, coupes and sedans return in familiar DX, LX and EX trims, while HX models come with two doors only. The GX Sedan is powered by natural gas. Unfortunately, the hatchback dies just when Americans are once again figuring out how useful they can be, and the sporty Si goes on hiatus for a year or two.

Category B

	Trade-in	Private	Dealer
2 Dr DX Cpe	8606	9291	10432
4 Dr DX Sdn	8744	9440	10599
2 Dr EX Cpe	11379	12284	13793
4 Dr EX Sdn	11400	12307	13818
2 Dr HX Cpe	9136	9863	11074
2 Dr LX Cpe	9973	10766	12088
4 Dr LX Sdn	10638	11484	12894

OPTIONS FOR CIVIC
Automatic 4-Speed Transmission[Std on VP Sdn] +589
Side Air Bag Restraints +184

CR-V   2001

A darker shade of silver debuts, and child seat-tether anchors are standard. EX and SE models have standard floor mats.

Category L

	Trade-in	Private	Dealer
4 Dr EX AWD Wgn	14496	15455	17054
4 Dr LX AWD Wgn	13326	14208	15678
4 Dr LX Wgn	13029	13891	15328
4 Dr SE 4WD Wgn	15704	16743	18475

OPTIONS FOR CR-V
Automatic 4-Speed Transmission[Opt on EX,LX AWD] +589

INSIGHT   2001

A continuously variable transmission (CVT) is available for 2001, and Monte Carlo Blue Pearl replaces Citrus Yellow on the color chart.

Category B

	Trade-in	Private	Dealer
2 Dr STD Hbk	13328	14388	16155

OPTIONS FOR INSIGHT
Air Conditioning +589

ODYSSEY   2001

Second- and third-row seats get new child seat-tether anchors, stereo speakers are upgraded, an intermittent feature for the rear window wiper is added and floor mats are made standard. LX models get a driver seat

---

Don't forget to refer to the Mileage Adjustment Table at the back of this book!

HONDA 01-00

Model Description	Trade-in TMV	Private TMV	Dealer TMV	Model Description	Trade-in TMV	Private TMV	Dealer TMV

height adjuster and traction control, while EX models benefits from a new alarm feature for the remote control. A brighter Starlight Silver paint color replaces Canyon Stone Silver.

Category P

4 Dr EX Pass. Van	22035	23270	25328
4 Dr LX Pass. Van	20116	21243	23122

OPTIONS FOR ODYSSEY
Navigation System +1472

PASSPORT   2001

Honda adds a LATCH child seat-tether anchor system to the Passport, and all models get a new eight-speaker audio system.

Category M

4 Dr EX 4WD Wgn	18606	19742	21635
4 Dr EX Wgn	17062	18104	19840
4 Dr LX 4WD Wgn	16654	17671	19365
4 Dr LX Wgn	14673	15569	17062

OPTIONS FOR PASSPORT
Automatic 4-Speed Transmission[Std on EX] +847
Compact Disc Changer +294
Leather Seats +515

PRELUDE   2001

Floor mats, rear child seat-tether anchors and an emergency trunk opener are added to the '01 Prelude. Two new colors, Electron Blue and Satin Silver, are also available.

Category E

2 Dr Type SH Cpe	18434	19578	21485
2 Dr STD Cpe	16663	17697	19421

OPTIONS FOR PRELUDE
Automatic 4-Speed Transmission +847

S2000   2001

Indy Yellow is a new color for 2001, good for those folks who wish to attract the attention of local gendarmes as they scream to the S2000's ridiculously high redline. Floor mats, a rear wind deflector, a clock and an emergency trunk release are also new standard items. But Honda has failed to add a passenger airbag shut-off switch, much to our chagrin. Mid-year, a removable aluminum hardtop became available and can be retrofitted to all S2000s.

Category F

2 Dr STD Conv	28667	30064	32392

2000 HONDA

ACCORD   2000

The four-cylinder engines now have a 100,000-mile no-tuneup service life. Side airbags are standard for all V6 models and EX four-cylinders with the leather interior. The feature-laden Accord SE sedan makes its debut this year. In the paint department, Nighthawk Black replaces Starlight Black, and Náples Gold Metallic replaces Heather Mist Metallic; Raisin and Currant have been dropped.

Category D

4 Dr DX Sdn	9705	10813	11835
2 Dr EX Cpe	13655	15213	16651
4 Dr EX Sdn	13819	15396	16851
2 Dr EX V6 Cpe	15808	17612	19277
4 Dr EX V6 Sdn	15809	17613	19278
2 Dr LX Cpe	11752	13093	14331
4 Dr LX Sdn	12053	13428	14698
2 Dr LX V6 Cpe	14107	15717	17203
4 Dr LX V6 Sdn	14107	15717	17203
4 Dr SE Sdn	13560	15107	16535

OPTIONS FOR ACCORD
AM/FM Stereo/CD/Tape +202
Air Conditioning[Opt on DX] +368
Aluminum/Alloy Wheels[Opt on LX,LX V6] +130
Anti-Lock Brakes[Opt on LX] +442
Automatic 4-Speed Transmission[Opt on DX,LX,EX] +589
Compact Disc Changer +332
Gold Package +184
Keyless Entry System[Std on EX] +110
Leather Seats[Opt on EX] +680
Power Drivers Seat[Opt on EX] +162
Rear Spoiler[Std on Cpe] +258
Side Air Bag Restraints[Opt on EX] +166

CIVIC   2000

No styling, content or trim changes for this year. The performance-oriented Si returns for 2000, and there have been paint comings and goings: Taffeta White has been added to the CX and DX Hatchback, and Dark Amethyst has been dropped; Titanium Metallic comes to the DX, LX and EX Sedan, and Vogue Silver is gone. Vintage Plum is now available to the LX and EX Sedan, and Inza Red has been eliminated.

Category B

2 Dr CX Hbk	7403	8336	9198
2 Dr DX Cpe	7931	8932	9855
2 Dr DX Hbk	7878	8872	9789
4 Dr DX Sdn	8033	9047	9982
2 Dr EX Cpe	10169	11452	12636
4 Dr EX Sdn	10482	11804	13024
2 Dr HX Cpe	8401	9461	10439
4 Dr LX Sdn	10091	11364	12539

Category E

2 Dr Si Cpe	13804	15139	16371

Category B

4 Dr VP Sdn Sdn	9959	11215	12375

Don't forget to refer to the Mileage Adjustment Table at the back of this book!

Model Description	Trade-in TMV	Private TMV	Dealer TMV

OPTIONS FOR CIVIC
AM/FM Compact Disc Player[Opt on DX,LX] +184
AM/FM Stereo Tape +147
AM/FM Stereo/CD/Tape +213
Air Conditioning[Opt on CX,DX,HX] +626
Alarm System[Std on EX Cpe] +147
Aluminum/Alloy Wheels[Opt on LX,EX Cpe] +130
Anti-Lock Brakes[Std on Sdn] +442
Automatic 4-Speed Transmission[Std on VP Sdn] +589
Compact Disc Changer +364
Fog Lights[Opt on EX] +110
Keyless Entry System +110
Power Steering[Opt on CX] +184
Rear Spoiler[Std on CX,Hatchback] +202

CR-V   2000

The 2000 Honda CR-V gets a new SE (Special Edition) package.
Category L

Model Description	Trade-in TMV	Private TMV	Dealer TMV
4 Dr EX AWD Wgn	13533	14847	16059
4 Dr LX AWD Wgn	12449	13657	14772
4 Dr LX Wgn	12165	13345	14435
4 Dr Special Edition AWD Wgn			
	16538	18143	19625

OPTIONS FOR CR-V
AM/FM Compact Disc Player[Std on EX] +202
Alarm System[Opt on LX] +147
Automatic 4-Speed Transmission[Opt on EX,LX AWD] +589
Luggage Rack +110

ODYSSEY   2000

Since it was redesigned last year, the only new feature is an optional navigation system on the EX.
Category P

Model Description	Trade-in TMV	Private TMV	Dealer TMV
4 Dr EX Pass. Van	20397	22390	24229
4 Dr LX Pass. Van	18544	20356	22028

OPTIONS FOR ODYSSEY
AM/FM Stereo/CD/Tape +258
Aluminum/Alloy Wheels[Std on EX] +202
Captain Chairs (4)[Std on EX] +147
Compact Disc Changer +405
Fog Lights +110
Leather Seats +589
Navigation System +1472
Trailer Hitch +147

PASSPORT   2000

The Passport receives new front and rear fascias, a modified grille, redesigned front combination lamps and a host of fresh features for a new, top-of-the-line EX-L trim level.
Category M

Model Description	Trade-in TMV	Private TMV	Dealer TMV
4 Dr EX 4WD Wgn	16549	18159	19645
4 Dr EX Wgn	15173	16649	18011
4 Dr LX 4WD Wgn	14808	16248	17578
4 Dr LX Wgn	13052	14322	15494

OPTIONS FOR PASSPORT
AM/FM Stereo/CD/Tape +294
Automatic 4-Speed Transmission[Std on EX] +847
Compact Disc Changer +405
Leather Seats +737

PRELUDE   2000

The 2000 Prelude is a carry-over from 1999 and remains unchanged.
Category E

Model Description	Trade-in TMV	Private TMV	Dealer TMV
2 Dr STD Cpe	14719	16142	17456
2 Dr Type SH Cpe	16751	18371	19866

OPTIONS FOR PRELUDE
AM/FM Stereo Tape +166
Automatic 4-Speed Transmission +737
Compact Disc Changer +368
Fog Lights +110
Gold Package +110
Rear Spoiler[Opt on STD] +258

S2000   2000

Honda brings out the high-revving, high horsepower S2000 for 2000.
Category F

Model Description	Trade-in TMV	Private TMV	Dealer TMV
2 Dr STD Conv	25344	27530	29547

1999 HONDA

ACCORD   1999

The coupes remain unchanged after their recent overhaul, but the sedans receive new seat fabric, and the LX and EX sedans now feature foldaway side mirrors.
Category D

Model Description	Trade-in TMV	Private TMV	Dealer TMV
4 Dr DX Sdn	8843	9879	10916
2 Dr EX Cpe	12526	13995	15463
4 Dr EX Sdn	12759	14255	15751
2 Dr EX V6 Cpe	14692	16415	18137
4 Dr EX V6 Sdn	14692	16415	18137
2 Dr LX Cpe	10981	12269	13556
4 Dr LX Sdn	10982	12270	13557
2 Dr LX V6 Cpe	13111	14648	16185
4 Dr LX V6 Sdn	12411	13866	15321

OPTIONS FOR ACCORD
AM/FM Compact Disc Player +155
AM/FM Stereo/CD/Tape +170
Air Conditioning[Opt on DX] +309
Alarm System[Opt on LX] +124
Aluminum/Alloy Wheels[Opt on LX,LX V6] +109
Anti-Lock Brakes[Opt on LX] +371
Automatic 4-Speed Transmission[Std on EX V6,LX V6] +495
Compact Disc Changer +278

Don't forget to refer to the Mileage Adjustment Table at the back of this book!

Model Description	Trade-in TMV	Private TMV	Dealer TMV

Gold Package +155
Leather Seats[Std on EX V6] +571
Power Drivers Seat[Opt on EX] +137
Rear Spoiler +216

CIVIC 1999

The Civic gets new front and rear styling as well as an improved instrument panel. The DX trim gets a rear wiper and washer, a cargo cover and a low-fuel warning light. A hotrod Si model is introduced mid-year with a 160-hp VTEC engine.

Category B

Model Description	Trade-in TMV	Private TMV	Dealer TMV
2 Dr CX Hbk	6923	7836	8748
2 Dr DX Cpe	7138	8079	9020
2 Dr DX Hbk	7059	7990	8920
4 Dr DX Sdn	7286	8247	9207
2 Dr EX Cpe	9224	10439	11655
4 Dr EX Sdn	9508	10761	12014
2 Dr HX Cpe	7620	8625	9629
4 Dr LX Sdn	9129	10332	11535
Category E			
2 Dr SI Cpe	12444	13718	14993
Category B			
4 Dr VP Sdn	8781	9939	11096

OPTIONS FOR CIVIC
AM/FM Compact Disc Player[Opt on DX,LX] +155
AM/FM Stereo Tape +124
AM/FM Stereo/CD/Tape[Opt on DX,LX] +179
Air Conditioning[Opt on CX,DX,HX] +525
Alarm System +124
Aluminum/Alloy Wheels +109
Anti-Lock Brakes[Std on SI,Sdn] +371
Automatic 4-Speed Transmission[Std on VP] +495
Leather Seats +309
Power Steering[Opt on CX] +155
Rear Spoiler[Std on CX,Hatchback] +170

CR-V 1999

The CR-V gains 20 horsepower, bringing the total output to 146. Automatic transmission models have a revised column shifter with an overdrive switch. The power window buttons are illuminated, the spare tire cover has been upgraded, and the front passenger seat is equipped with an armrest. Since Honda has effectively addressed all of our previous gripes with this year's changes, we'll have to get more creative with our complaints.

Category L

Model Description	Trade-in TMV	Private TMV	Dealer TMV
4 Dr EX AWD Wgn	12188	13461	14734
4 Dr LX AWD Wgn	11212	12383	13554
4 Dr LX Wgn	10949	12093	13237

OPTIONS FOR CR-V
AM/FM Compact Disc Player +170

Alarm System[Opt on LX] +124
Automatic 4-Speed Transmission[Std on 2WD] +495

ODYSSEY 1999

Honda's latest masterpiece, the totally redesigned Odyssey, will finally give Chrysler's minivans a run for their money.

Category P

Model Description	Trade-in TMV	Private TMV	Dealer TMV
4 Dr EX Pass. Van	18538	20443	22348
4 Dr LX Pass. Van	16854	18586	20318

OPTIONS FOR ODYSSEY
Captain Chairs (4)[Std on EX] +124
Leather Seats +495

PASSPORT 1999

Last year, the Passport and the identical Isuzu Rodeo were completely redesigned, so there are no new changes this year.

Category M

Model Description	Trade-in TMV	Private TMV	Dealer TMV
4 Dr EX 4WD Wgn	14507	16025	17543
4 Dr EX Wgn	13296	14687	16079
4 Dr LX 4WD Wgn	12777	14115	15452
4 Dr LX Wgn	11503	12707	13911

OPTIONS FOR PASSPORT
AM/FM Stereo/CD/Tape +247
Automatic 4-Speed Transmission[Std on VP] +711
Leather Seats +618
Limited Slip Differential[Opt on LX] +155

PRELUDE 1999

Prelude gets another five horsepower, bringing it up to 200 horsepower with the manual transmission and 195 horsepower with the automatic. A remote keyless entry system is added, as is an air filtration system, mesh-style grille and new interior color choices.

Category E

Model Description	Trade-in TMV	Private TMV	Dealer TMV
2 Dr STD Cpe	13829	15246	16662
2 Dr Type SH Cpe	15118	16667	18215

OPTIONS FOR PRELUDE
AM/FM Stereo Tape +139
Automatic 4-Speed Transmission +618
Compact Disc Changer +309
Rear Spoiler[Opt on STD] +216

1998 HONDA

ACCORD 1998

Honda redesigns its best-seller for 1998. A 3.0-liter V6 engine makes its debut in LX V6 and EX V6 models, marking the first six-cylinder VTEC in the Honda lineup. The standard 2.3-liter four-banger is also re-engineered, as is the chassis. The new Accord is also larger, and the interior boasts more room inside than

Model Description	Trade-in TMV	Private TMV	Dealer TMV

any of Accord's competitors.

Category D

Model Description	Trade-in TMV	Private TMV	Dealer TMV
4 Dr DX Sdn	7972	8985	10083
2 Dr EX Cpe	11293	12728	14283
4 Dr EX Sdn	10663	12019	13487
2 Dr EX V6 Cpe	13244	14927	16751
4 Dr EX V6 Sdn	13245	14928	16752
2 Dr LX Cpe	9900	11158	12521
4 Dr LX Sdn	9900	11159	12522
2 Dr LX V6 Cpe	11819	13322	14949
4 Dr LX V6 Sdn	11819	13322	14949

OPTIONS FOR ACCORD
AM/FM Compact Disc Player +141
AM/FM Stereo Tape +112
AM/FM Stereo/CD/Tape +155
Air Conditioning[Opt on DX] +281
Alarm System +112
Aluminum/Alloy Wheels[Opt on LX] +99
Anti-Lock Brakes[Std on EX,EX V6,LX V6] +337
Automatic 4-Speed Transmission[Std on EX V6,LX V6] +450
Leather Seats[Std on EX V6] +520
Power Drivers Seat[Std on EX V6,LX V6] +123
Rear Spoiler[Opt on Sdn] +197

CIVIC   1998

Last year's best-selling small car gets minor revisions: select models get new wheelcovers, a rear hatch handle, and map lights.

Category B

Model Description	Trade-in TMV	Private TMV	Dealer TMV
2 Dr CX Hbk	6094	6918	7810
2 Dr DX Cpe	6529	7411	8367
2 Dr DX Hbk	6344	7201	8130
4 Dr DX Sdn	6636	7532	8504
2 Dr EX Cpe	8400	9535	10765
4 Dr EX Sdn	8658	9828	11096
2 Dr HX Cpe	6939	7877	8893
4 Dr LX Sdn	7671	8708	9831

OPTIONS FOR CIVIC
AM/FM Compact Disc Player +141
AM/FM Stereo Tape +112
AM/FM Stereo/CD/Tape +163
Air Conditioning[Std on EX,LX] +478
Alarm System +112
Aluminum/Alloy Wheels +99
Anti-Lock Brakes[Opt on Cpe] +337
Automatic 4-Speed Transmission +450
Compact Disc Changer +335
Power Steering[Opt on CX] +141
Rear Spoiler[Opt on EX, Cpe] +155

CR-V   1998

A manual transmission lowers the ante, making the CR-V a more attractive value than before. Also available is a front-wheel drive LX model, and the EX trim level now includes a CD player, anti-lock brakes, and remote keyless entry.

Category L

Model Description	Trade-in TMV	Private TMV	Dealer TMV
4 Dr EX 4WD Wgn	10892	12160	13534
4 Dr LX 4WD Wgn	10014	11180	12443
4 Dr LX Wgn	9777	10915	12148

OPTIONS FOR CR-V
AM/FM Stereo Tape +112
Automatic 4-Speed Transmission[Std on 2WD] +450

ODYSSEY   1998

The engine is upgraded to a more sophisticated 2.3-liter, good for an extra 10 horsepower and seven foot-pounds of torque. New looks up front come from a revised bumper and grille, and the interior gets dressed in new fabric.

Category P

Model Description	Trade-in TMV	Private TMV	Dealer TMV
4 Dr EX Pass. Van	14378	15988	17733
4 Dr LX Pass. Van	13485	14996	16632

OPTIONS FOR ODYSSEY
Alarm System[Opt on LX] +159
Captain Chairs (4)[Opt on LX] +112
Compact Disc Changer +337

PASSPORT   1998

Like its Isuzu Rodeo counterpart, the Passport has been completely revised from top to bottom. The Passport gets modernized styling, a user-friendly interior, more powerful V6 and added room for passengers and cargo.

Category M

Model Description	Trade-in TMV	Private TMV	Dealer TMV
4 Dr EX 4WD Wgn	12743	14168	15712
4 Dr EX Wgn	11680	12987	14402
4 Dr LX 4WD Wgn	11224	12479	13839
4 Dr LX Wgn	10121	11253	12479

OPTIONS FOR PASSPORT
AM/FM Compact Disc Player +169
AM/FM Stereo/CD/Tape +225
Automatic 4-Speed Transmission[Opt on LX] +647
Leather Seats +562
Limited Slip Differential[Opt on LX] +141

PRELUDE   1998

The Prelude doesn't change for 1998, because you don't mess with success. (Pssst, buy this car!)

Category E

Model Description	Trade-in TMV	Private TMV	Dealer TMV
2 Dr STD Cpe	12389	13680	15079
2 Dr Type SH Cpe	13533	14943	16471

OPTIONS FOR PRELUDE
AM/FM Stereo Tape +126
Automatic 4-Speed Transmission +562

Don't forget to refer to the Mileage Adjustment Table at the back of this book!

Model Description	Trade-in TMV	Private TMV	Dealer TMV
Compact Disc Changer +281			
Rear Spoiler[Opt on STD] +197			

1997 HONDA

ACCORD 1997

Changes to the ever-popular Accord include the deletion of antilock brakes on the LX five-speed models and the discontinuation of the EX coupes with leather. No other changes for the 1997 Accord.

Category D

Model Description	Trade-in TMV	Private TMV	Dealer TMV
4 Dr DX Sdn	7085	8028	9181
2 Dr EX Cpe	10427	11815	13512
4 Dr EX Sdn	10504	11903	13612
4 Dr EX Wgn	11191	12681	14502
4 Dr EX V6 Sdn	11895	13478	15414
2 Dr LX Cpe	8935	10124	11578
4 Dr LX Sdn	9031	10233	11703
4 Dr LX Wgn	10251	11616	13284
4 Dr LX V6 Sdn	10642	12059	13791
2 Dr Special Edition Cpe			
	10298	11669	13345
4 Dr Special Edition Sdn			
	10380	11762	13451
4 Dr Value Sdn	8469	9597	10975

OPTIONS FOR ACCORD
AM/FM Compact Disc Player[Opt on EX,LX] +122
AM/FM Stereo/CD/Tape +134
Air Conditioning[Opt on DX] +244
Alarm System[Opt on EX,EX V6,LX] +97
Anti-Lock Brakes[Opt on LX] +414
Automatic 4-Speed Transmission[Opt on DX,LX,EX] +390
Compact Disc Changer +220
Gold Package +122
Leather Seats[Opt on EX] +451
Power Drivers Seat[Opt on EX] +108
Rear Spoiler +170

CIVIC 1997

For some reason, Honda deletes the Civic EX Coupe five-speed with ABS model. Maybe they think that people who like to row their own gears don't worry about whether they can stop or not. DX models receive new wheel covers, all Civics get 14-inch wheels, and the LX sedan gets air conditioning.

Category B

Model Description	Trade-in TMV	Private TMV	Dealer TMV
2 Dr CX Hbk	5284	6034	6950
2 Dr DX Cpe	5912	6752	7777
2 Dr DX Hbk	5545	6331	7293
4 Dr DX Sdn	6009	6862	7904
2 Dr EX Cpe	7606	8686	10005
4 Dr EX Sdn	7841	8953	10313
2 Dr HX Cpe	6284	7176	8266

Model Description	Trade-in TMV	Private TMV	Dealer TMV
4 Dr LX Sdn	6946	7932	9137

OPTIONS FOR CIVIC
AM/FM Compact Disc Player +122
AM/FM Stereo/CD/Tape +141
Air Conditioning[Std on EX,LX] +414
Alarm System +97
Anti-Lock Brakes[Opt on Cpe] +292
Automatic 4-Speed Transmission +390
Compact Disc Changer +290
Leather Seats +244
Power Steering[Std on EX,HX,LX,DX,Sdn] +122
Rear Spoiler +134

CIVIC DEL SOL 1997

No changes to Honda's two-seater.

Category E

Model Description	Trade-in TMV	Private TMV	Dealer TMV
2 Dr S Cpe	9176	10263	11591
2 Dr Si Cpe	10703	11971	13520
2 Dr VTEC Cpe	12094	13526	15277

OPTIONS FOR CIVIC DEL SOL
AM/FM Stereo Tape +109
Air Conditioning +414
Alarm System +97
Automatic 4-Speed Transmission +487
Power Steering +122

CR-V 1997

Priced competitively with mini-utes, the CR-V offers more passenger room and cargo capacity than its peers. The CR-V is available with antilock brakes.

Category L

Model Description	Trade-in TMV	Private TMV	Dealer TMV
4 Dr STD AWD Wgn	9062	10157	11496

OPTIONS FOR CR-V
AM/FM Compact Disc Player +134
AM/FM Stereo Tape +97
Alarm System +97
Anti-Lock Brakes +292

ODYSSEY 1997

No changes for the 1997 Honda Odyssey.

Category P

Model Description	Trade-in TMV	Private TMV	Dealer TMV
4 Dr EX Pass. Van	12443	13929	15746
4 Dr LX Pass. Van	11340	12694	14350

OPTIONS FOR ODYSSEY
AM/FM Compact Disc Player +134
Captain Chairs (4)[Opt on LX] +97
Luggage Rack +122

PASSPORT 1997

Honda drops the slow-selling DX four-cylinder Passport.

Category M

Model Description	Trade-in TMV	Private TMV	Dealer TMV
4 Dr EX 4WD Wgn	9889	11040	12447
4 Dr EX Wgn	9295	10377	11699

Don't forget to refer to the Mileage Adjustment Table at the back of this book!

Model Description	Trade-in TMV	Private TMV	Dealer TMV
4 Dr LX 4WD Wgn	8654	9662	10893
4 Dr LX Wgn	7806	8714	9825

OPTIONS FOR PASSPORT
AM/FM Compact Disc Player +146
AM/FM Stereo/CD/Tape +195
Air Conditioning[Std on EX,4WD] +292
Automatic 4-Speed Transmission[Opt on LX,4WD] +473
Compact Disc Changer +268
Leather Seats +487
Limited Slip Differential[Opt on LX] +122

PRELUDE   1997

The Prelude is totally redesigned for 1997. A base model is available with a five-speed manual or four-speed automatic gearbox, but the top-of-the-line Type SH model, featuring Honda's new Active Torque Transfer System, can only be had as a manual. Both the base and Type SH Preludes feature last year's VTEC engine which produces 195-horsepower for 1997.

Category E

Model Description	Trade-in TMV	Private TMV	Dealer TMV
2 Dr STD Cpe	10986	12288	13878
2 Dr Type SH Cpe	11864	13269	14987

OPTIONS FOR PRELUDE
AM/FM Stereo Tape +109
Alarm System +97
Automatic 4-Speed Transmission +487
Compact Disc Changer +244
Leather Seats +317
Rear Spoiler +170

1996 HONDA

ACCORD   1996

All Accords get revised styling, featuring new taillights and bumper covers. Wagons have a new roof rack, while sedans boast a new pass-through ski sack.

Category D

Model Description	Trade-in TMV	Private TMV	Dealer TMV
4 Dr 25th Anniversary Sdn			
	7379	8483	10007
4 Dr DX Sdn	6101	7013	8273
2 Dr EX Cpe	8342	9589	11312
4 Dr EX Sdn	8590	9875	11649
4 Dr EX Wgn	9622	11062	13049
4 Dr EX V6 Sdn	10794	12409	14638
2 Dr LX Cpe	7721	8875	10470
4 Dr LX Sdn	7805	8973	10585
4 Dr LX Wgn	8268	9504	11212
4 Dr LX V6 Sdn	10184	11708	13811

OPTIONS FOR ACCORD
AM/FM Compact Disc Player +116
AM/FM Stereo/CD/Tape +128
Air Conditioning[Opt on DX] +232
Anti-Lock Brakes[Opt on LX] +440
Automatic 4-Speed Transmission[Opt on DX,LX,EX,] +371
Compact Disc Changer +209
Gold Package +116
Leather Seats[Opt on EX] +428
Rear Spoiler +162

CIVIC   1996

Keeping to their legendary four-year redesign schedule, Honda engineers have created a more powerful, and more contemporary Civic for 1996. This is a great car for those concerned about reliability and value, but who don't want to sacrifice style.

Category B

Model Description	Trade-in TMV	Private TMV	Dealer TMV
2 Dr CX Hbk	4335	5041	6017
2 Dr DX Cpe	5056	5880	7018
2 Dr DX Hbk	4583	5330	6362
4 Dr DX Sdn	5198	6045	7215
2 Dr EX Cpe	6228	7243	8645
4 Dr EX Sdn	6769	7872	9396
2 Dr HX Cpe	5436	6322	7545
4 Dr LX Sdn	6078	7068	8436

OPTIONS FOR CIVIC
AM/FM Compact Disc Player +116
AM/FM Stereo/CD/Tape +134
Air Conditioning[Std on EX] +393
Anti-Lock Brakes[Opt on LX,Cpe] +279
Automatic 4-Speed Transmission +371
Compact Disc Changer +277
Power Steering[Opt on CX,DX] +116
Rear Spoiler +128

CIVIC DEL SOL   1996

No changes to the 1996 del Sol.

Category E

Model Description	Trade-in TMV	Private TMV	Dealer TMV
2 Dr S Cpe	8172	9153	10506
2 Dr Si Cpe	9398	10526	12082
2 Dr VTEC Cpe	10559	11825	13574

OPTIONS FOR CIVIC DEL SOL
Air Conditioning +393
Automatic 4-Speed Transmission +464
Power Steering[Opt on S] +116

ODYSSEY   1996

Minivan-wagon hybrid carries into 1996 sans changes.

Category P

Model Description	Trade-in TMV	Private TMV	Dealer TMV
4 Dr EX Pass. Van	10397	11777	13682
4 Dr LX Pass. Van	8911	10093	11726

PASSPORT   1996

New wheels, dual airbags, available ABS, and a stronger V6 engine are the changes for the 1996 Isuzu Rodeo, er, we mean Passport.

Category M

Model Description	Trade-in TMV	Private TMV	Dealer TMV
4 Dr DX Wgn	5923	6672	7707
4 Dr EX 4WD Wgn	9143	10300	11898
4 Dr EX Wgn	8594	9681	11183
4 Dr LX 4WD Wgn	8001	9014	10412
4 Dr LX Wgn	7233	8148	9412

OPTIONS FOR PASSPORT
Air Conditioning[Std on EX,4WD] +279
Automatic 4-Speed Transmission[Opt on LX,4WD] +371
Luggage Rack +116

PRELUDE   1996

This is the last year for the current-generation Prelude. All of the really exciting stuff happens in 1997.

Category E

	Trade-in	Private	Dealer
2 Dr S Cpe	8297	9292	10666
2 Dr Si Cpe	9397	10524	12080
2 Dr VTEC Cpe	10560	11826	13575

OPTIONS FOR PRELUDE
AM/FM Stereo/CD/Tape +162
Automatic 4-Speed Transmission +371
Rear Spoiler +162

1995 HONDA

ACCORD   1995

Finally, a V6 is offered in the midsized Honda! Unfortunately, it fails to improve performance figures because of the mandatory automatic transmission. V6 Accords gain different front styling as a result of the increased size of the engine bay. All V6 Accords come with standard antilock brakes.

Category D

	Trade-in	Private	Dealer
4 Dr DX Sdn	5262	6047	7355
2 Dr EX Cpe	7173	8243	10027
4 Dr EX Sdn	7244	8325	10126
4 Dr EX Wgn	7948	9134	11110
4 Dr EX V6 Sdn	9134	10497	12768
2 Dr LX Cpe	6276	7212	8773
4 Dr LX Sdn	6348	7295	8873
4 Dr LX Wgn	6937	7972	9697
4 Dr LX V6 Sdn	8039	9238	11237

OPTIONS FOR ACCORD
AM/FM Stereo/CD/Tape +108
Air Conditioning[Opt on DX] +198
Anti-Lock Brakes[Opt on LX] +237
Automatic 4-Speed Transmission[Opt on DX,LX,EX] +316
Compact Disc Changer +177
Gold Package +98
Leather Seats[Std on EX V6] +365
Power Drivers Seat +87

CIVIC   1995

No changes for the last year of the current Civic.

Category B

	Trade-in	Private	Dealer
2 Dr CX Hbk	3379	3961	4931
2 Dr DX Cpe	3939	4618	5749
2 Dr DX Hbk	3558	4171	5193
4 Dr DX Sdn	4146	4860	6051
2 Dr EX Cpe	4604	5397	6719
4 Dr EX Sdn	5296	6209	7730
4 Dr LX Sdn	4400	5158	6422
2 Dr Si Hbk	4446	5212	6489
2 Dr VX Hbk	4079	4782	5954

OPTIONS FOR CIVIC
AM/FM Compact Disc Player +98
Air Conditioning[Std on EX Sdn] +335
Anti-Lock Brakes[Opt on LX,Cpe] +237
Automatic 4-Speed Transmission +316
Leather Seats +198
Rear Spoiler +108

CIVIC DEL SOL   1995

Antilock brakes are now standard on VTEC models. Power door locks are also new to the standard equipment lists of Si and VTEC models. All del Sols get a remote trunk release.

Category E

	Trade-in	Private	Dealer
2 Dr S Cpe	6931	7818	9296
2 Dr Si Cpe	7750	8741	10394
2 Dr VTEC Cpe	9439	10646	12659

OPTIONS FOR CIVIC DEL SOL
AM/FM Stereo/CD/Tape +138
Air Conditioning +335
Automatic 4-Speed Transmission +395

ODYSSEY   1995

Honda finally gets its minivan in the form of the Odyssey. Unique to the Odyssey is five-door design that includes four passenger car-like swing-out doors. LX and EX models come standard with antilock brakes and dual airbags.

Category P

	Trade-in	Private	Dealer
4 Dr EX Pass. Van	9073	10318	12392
4 Dr LX Pass. Van	7891	8974	10778

OPTIONS FOR ODYSSEY
Alarm System +86
Captain Chairs (4) +79
Luggage Rack +98

PASSPORT   1995

Midyear change gives the Passport driver and passenger airbags in a redesigned dashboard.

Category M

Model Description	Trade-in TMV	Private TMV	Dealer TMV	Model Description	Trade-in TMV	Private TMV	Dealer TMV
4 Dr DX Wgn	5216	5890	7014	2 Dr EX Cpe	6115	7144	8860
1995.5 4 Dr DX Wgn	5655	6386	7604	4 Dr EX Sdn	6178	7218	8951
4 Dr EX 4WD Wgn	7884	8903	10601	4 Dr EX Wgn	6924	8089	10032
1995.5 4 Dr EX 4WD Wgn	8268	9336	11117	2 Dr LX Cpe	5342	6241	7740
1995.5 4 Dr EX Wgn	7946	8973	10685	4 Dr LX Sdn	5400	6310	7825
4 Dr LX 4WD Wgn	7122	8043	9577	4 Dr LX Wgn	5779	6752	8373
4 Dr LX Wgn	6283	7096	8449				
1995.5 4 Dr LX 4WD Wgn	7310	8254	9829				
1995.5 4 Dr LX Wgn	6662	7523	8958				

OPTIONS FOR PASSPORT
AM/FM Stereo Tape +98
AM/FM Stereo Tape +98
Air Conditioning[Opt on DX,2WD] +237
Air Conditioning[Opt on DX,2WD] +237
Alarm System +79
Automatic 4-Speed Transmission +316
Automatic 4-Speed Transmission +316
Gold Package +77
Leather Seats +395
Limited Slip Differential +98
Luggage Rack +98
Running Boards +79

OPTIONS FOR ACCORD
AM/FM Compact Disc Player[Opt on EX Sdn,LX Sdn] +91
AM/FM Stereo/CD/Tape[Opt on EX Sdn,LX Sdn] +101
Air Conditioning[Opt on DX] +183
Anti-Lock Brakes[Std on EX] +220
Automatic 4-Speed Transmission +293
Compact Disc Changer +164
Gold Package +91
Leather Seats +338
Rear Spoiler +128

PRELUDE   1995

The ill-conceived Si 4WS is mercifully dropped from the Prelude lineup. The fourth-generation Prelude is nearing the end of its life. Few changes for 1995, except the addition of air conditioning to the standard equipment list of S models.

Category E

	Trade-in	Private	Dealer
2 Dr S Cpe	7344	8284	9850
2 Dr SE Cpe	8522	9612	11429
2 Dr Si Cpe	8233	9286	11042
2 Dr VTEC Cpe	9220	10400	12366

OPTIONS FOR PRELUDE
Alarm System +79
Automatic 4-Speed Transmission +316
Leather Seats +256

CIVIC   1994

The passenger airbag is now standard on all Civics. Antilock brakes are optional on the LX sedan, EX coupe and Si hatchback.

Category B

	Trade-in	Private	Dealer
2 Dr CX Hbk	2782	3270	4083
2 Dr DX Cpe	3300	3879	4844
2 Dr DX Hbk	2996	3521	4397
4 Dr DX Sdn	3518	4135	5164
2 Dr EX Cpe	4231	4973	6210
4 Dr EX Sdn	4456	5237	6540
4 Dr LX Sdn	3942	4634	5786
2 Dr Si Hbk	4035	4743	5923
2 Dr VX Hbk	3317	3899	4869

OPTIONS FOR CIVIC
AM/FM Compact Disc Player +91
Air Conditioning[Std on EX Sdn] +311
Anti-Lock Brakes[Opt on LX,Si,Cpe] +220
Automatic 4-Speed Transmission +293
Leather Seats +183

1994 HONDA

ACCORD   1994

Once again, Honda's best-selling model is redesigned. Changes for 1994 make the vehicle more competitive with its midsize rival, the Ford Taurus. Shorter and wider than the previous generation Accord, the 1994 model is available in three trim levels. Antilock brakes are standard on the EX and are finally available on the LX and DX. New engines across the board improve horsepower figures for all Accords.

Category D

	Trade-in	Private	Dealer
2 Dr DX Cpe	4449	5198	6447
4 Dr DX Sdn	4646	5428	6732

CIVIC DEL SOL   1994

VTEC technology makes its way to the del Sol, giving buyers a choice of three models. VTEC del Sols offer 35 more horsepower than the Si. A passenger airbag joins the standard equipment list for all models. VTEC del Sols gain performance-oriented upgrades that include a beefier suspension, larger tires and bigger brakes.

Category E

	Trade-in	Private	Dealer
2 Dr S Cpe	5478	6261	7567
2 Dr Si Cpe	6236	7128	8615
2 Dr VTEC Cpe	6768	7736	9349

OPTIONS FOR CIVIC DEL SOL
AM/FM Stereo Tape[Opt on S] +83
Air Conditioning +311

Don't forget to refer to the Mileage Adjustment Table at the back of this book!

Model Description	Trade-in TMV	Private TMV	Dealer TMV	Model Description	Trade-in TMV	Private TMV	Dealer TMV
Automatic 4-Speed Transmission +366				2 Dr EX Cpe	5022	5885	7322
Compact Disc Changer +183				4 Dr EX Sdn	5074	5946	7398
Leather Seats +220				4 Dr EX Wgn	5751	6739	8385
				2 Dr LX Cpe	4385	5138	6393

PASSPORT   1994

Honda loyalists waiting for the launch of a Honda sport utility should be thrilled with the Passport, until they discover that it's an Isuzu. Based on the highly successful Rodeo, the Honda Passport has very little to distinguish it from its less expensive twin. Two- and four-wheel-drive models are available in three trim levels ranging from the budget-minded DX to the top-end EX.

Category M			
4 Dr DX Wgn	4550	5264	6454
4 Dr EX 4WD Wgn	6803	7870	9650
4 Dr LX 4WD Wgn	6165	7132	8745
4 Dr LX Wgn	5515	6381	7824

OPTIONS FOR PASSPORT

AM/FM Stereo Tape[Std on EX] +91
Air Conditioning[Opt on DX, 2WD] +220
Automatic 4-Speed Transmission +293
Luggage Rack +91

PRELUDE   1994

Dual airbags are standard on all Preludes this year. Improved interior ergonomics, freshened front-end styling, and environmentally conscious CFC-free air conditioning are also welcome changes to this car.

Category E			
2 Dr S Cpe	6081	6950	8400
2 Dr Si Cpe	7168	8193	9902
2 Dr Si 4WS Cpe	7942	9078	10971
2 Dr VTEC Cpe	7989	9132	11037

OPTIONS FOR PRELUDE

AM/FM Stereo/CD/Tape +128
Air Conditioning[Opt on S] +201
Aluminum/Alloy Wheels[Opt on S] +91
Automatic 4-Speed Transmission +293
Rear Spoiler[Opt on S] +128

1993 HONDA

ACCORD   1993

The SE model is re-introduced as the top-of-the-line Accord. A passenger airbag is added.

Category D			
4 Dr 10th Anniversary Sdn			
	4939	5787	7200
2 Dr DX Cpe	3703	4338	5398
4 Dr DX Sdn	3868	4532	5639

Model Description	Trade-in TMV	Private TMV	Dealer TMV
2 Dr EX Cpe	5022	5885	7322
4 Dr EX Sdn	5074	5946	7398
4 Dr EX Wgn	5751	6739	8385
2 Dr LX Cpe	4385	5138	6393
4 Dr LX Sdn	4439	5201	6471
4 Dr LX Wgn	4771	5591	6956
2 Dr SE Cpe	5978	7004	8715
4 Dr SE Sdn	6164	7223	8987

OPTIONS FOR ACCORD

AM/FM Stereo/CD/Tape +90
Air Conditioning[Opt on DX] +164
Anti-Lock Brakes[Opt on LX] +197
Automatic 4-Speed Transmission[Opt on DX,LX,EX] +262
Gold Package +82
Leather Seats[Std on SE] +303
Rear Spoiler +114

CIVIC   1993

A coupe body style is added to the Civic stable. EX models get standard power steering and a sunroof. A passenger airbag is available on the EX coupe.

Category B			
2 Dr CX Hbk	2068	2467	3132
2 Dr DX Cpe	2562	3056	3879
2 Dr DX Hbk	2323	2771	3518
4 Dr DX Sdn	2743	3272	4153
2 Dr EX Cpe	3393	4047	5138
4 Dr EX Sdn	3533	4214	5350
4 Dr LX Sdn	2997	3575	4538
2 Dr Si Hbk	3069	3661	4647
2 Dr VX Hbk	2572	3068	3895

OPTIONS FOR CIVIC

AM/FM Compact Disc Player +82
Air Conditioning +279
Automatic 4-Speed Transmission +262
Dual Air Bag Restraints +131
Rear Spoiler +90

CIVIC DEL SOL   1993

The sun, that's what Honda wants you to think of when you picture this open-air replacement for the CRX. Poised to recapture some of the two-seater market from the Mazda Miata, the del Sol offers solid performance and value. Usable trunk space and improved body rigidity are the benefits the del Sol has over its rivals. We think, however, that the Miata's superior horsepower and rear-wheel drive will prove to be more fun in the long run.

Category E			
2 Dr S Cpe	4618	5395	6692
2 Dr Si Cpe	5225	6105	7572

OPTIONS FOR CIVIC DEL SOL

Don't forget to refer to the Mileage Adjustment Table at the back of this book!

Model Description	Trade-in TMV	Private TMV	Dealer TMV

AM/FM Compact Disc Player +97
Air Conditioning +279
Automatic 4-Speed Transmission +328
Leather Seats +197

PRELUDE   1993

More power, in the form of Honda's exclusive VTEC system, is available to the Prelude. A boost of 30 horsepower for top-end Preludes means that this car won't be the laughingstock of stoplight drags anymore.

Category E

Model Description	Trade-in	Private	Dealer
2 Dr S Cpe	5038	5886	7301
2 Dr Si Cpe	5910	6906	8565
2 Dr Si 4WS Cpe	6447	7533	9343
2 Dr VTEC Cpe	6552	7656	9496

OPTIONS FOR PRELUDE

AM/FM Compact Disc Player +99
Air Conditioning[Opt on S] +180
Automatic 4-Speed Transmission +262
Leather Seats +213

1992 HONDA

ACCORD   1992

The SE model is dropped. The EX model gains antilock brakes with rear discs instead of drums. Horsepower is up in the EX sedans, 10 more than last year's 130. A driver airbag is added to the standard equipment list.

Category D

Model Description	Trade-in	Private	Dealer
2 Dr DX Cpe	3078	3668	4651
4 Dr DX Sdn	3219	3836	4864
2 Dr EX Cpe	4239	5052	6406
4 Dr EX Sdn	4286	5107	6476
4 Dr EX Wgn	5135	6119	7759
2 Dr LX Cpe	3679	4384	5559
4 Dr LX Sdn	3726	4440	5630
4 Dr LX Wgn	4057	4835	6131

OPTIONS FOR ACCORD

Air Conditioning[Opt on DX] +143
Automatic 4-Speed Transmission +230
Leather Seats +266
Rear Spoiler +100

CIVIC   1992

A driver airbag is standard on all new Civics. Unfortunately, the wagon body style is dropped from the lineup. VTEC power is available by way of the top-end EX model. All sedans now have power steering added to their standard equipment list.

Category B

Model Description	Trade-in	Private	Dealer
2 Dr CX Hbk	1564	1902	2467
2 Dr DX Hbk	1780	2165	2808
4 Dr DX Sdn	2057	2502	3245
4 Dr EX Sdn	2505	3048	3952
4 Dr LX Sdn	2300	2798	3628
2 Dr Si Hbk	2340	2846	3691
2 Dr VX Hbk	2156	2624	3402

OPTIONS FOR CIVIC

Air Conditioning +244
Automatic 4-Speed Transmission +230

PRELUDE   1992

Totally redesigned for 1992, the fourth generation Prelude sports a driver airbag in all models and a standard passenger airbag on the Si 4WS. Antilock brakes are still available only on Si models.

Category E

Model Description	Trade-in	Private	Dealer
2 Dr S Cpe	4542	5309	6588
2 Dr Si Cpe	5366	6272	7783

OPTIONS FOR PRELUDE

AM/FM Stereo/CD/Tape +100
Air Conditioning[Opt on S] +158
Automatic 4-Speed Transmission +230
Compact Disc Changer +143
Dual Air Bag Restraints +115
Leather Seats +187
Rear Spoiler[Opt on Si] +100

HYUNDAI 01

Model Description	Trade-in TMV	Private TMV	Dealer TMV	Model Description	Trade-in TMV	Private TMV	Dealer TMV

HYUNDAI   S. Korea

1995 Hyundai Sonata

2001 HYUNDAI

ACCENT   2001

For 2001, Accent GL and GS get a more powerful and fuel efficient 1.6-liter, DOHC inline four-cylinder engine.

Category A

Model	Trade-in	Private	Dealer
4 Dr GL Sdn	6509	7119	8136
2 Dr GS Hbk	5891	6444	7364
2 Dr L Hbk	5694	6228	7118

OPTIONS FOR ACCENT
AM/FM Compact Disc Player +233
Air Conditioning +497
Automatic 4-Speed Transmission +398
Power Windows +162
Rear Spoiler +262

ELANTRA   2001

Bigger inside and out, the redesigned 2001 Elantra boasts stylish sheet metal, a refined 140-horsepower engine and improved noise, vibration and harshness characteristics. Poised to tackle the best in the class, the Elantra comes well equipped for less than $13,000. Though the useful station wagon model has been stricken from the lineup, a five-door hatchback is set to debut later this year.

Category B

Model	Trade-in	Private	Dealer
4 Dr GLS Sdn	7934	8749	10107
4 Dr GT Hbk	8197	9039	10442

OPTIONS FOR ELANTRA
AM/FM Compact Disc Player +216
Alarm System +126
Anti-Lock Brakes +571
Automatic 4-Speed Transmission +398
Cruise Control +166

Power Moonroof +497

SANTA FE   2001

For 2001, Hyundai brings to market its very own sport-utility. The Santa Fe is based on a modified Sonata midsize car platform and is available with either front-wheel drive or full-time four-wheel drive with either a four-cylinder or V6 engine.

Category M

Model	Trade-in	Private	Dealer
4 Dr GL 4WD Wgn	13610	14731	16598
4 Dr GL Wgn	11478	12423	13998
4 Dr GLS 4WD Wgn	14257	15430	17386
4 Dr GLS Wgn	13287	14381	16204
4 Dr LX 4WD Wgn	15031	16269	18331
4 Dr LX Wgn	14064	15222	17151

OPTIONS FOR SANTA FE
6 cyl 2.7 L Engine[Opt on GL] +796
Alarm System[Opt on GL] +123
Anti-Lock Brakes +332
Automatic 4-Speed Transmission[Opt on GL] +398
Heated Front Seats +172
Keyless Entry System[Opt on GL] +116
Limited Slip Differential[Std on LX] +166
Traction Control System +133

SONATA   2001

The Sonata gets only minor trim changes for 2001, such as a new grille design and some tweaks to the rear deck lid. Additional features are ladled onto the standard equipment list.

Category C

Model	Trade-in	Private	Dealer
4 Dr GLS Sdn	10334	11296	12901
4 Dr STD Sdn	9034	9876	11279

OPTIONS FOR SONATA
AM/FM Compact Disc Player[Std on GLS] +199
Automatic 4-Speed Transmission +332
Keyless Entry System +119
Leather Seats +879
Power Moonroof +431
Rear Spoiler +292

TIBURON   2001

Following last year's freshening, the Tiburon sees only minor trim changes for 2001, such as redesigned wheels and the addition of a rear spoiler as standard equipment.

Category E

Model	Trade-in	Private	Dealer
2 Dr STD Cpe	9464	10297	11684

OPTIONS FOR TIBURON
AM/FM Stereo/CD/Tape +266
Anti-Lock Brakes +497
Automatic 4-Speed Transmission +531
Leather Seats +497
Power Sunroof +464

HYUNDAI 01-99

Model Description	Trade-in TMV	Private TMV	Dealer TMV

XG300 — 2001

Hyundai goes after the Honda Accord V6 and Toyota Camry V6 by offering more for less. Fully loaded with equipment, the new XG300 undercuts both competitors on price. But, as we all know, there's more to the value equation than an attractive MSRP, especially in the meat of the sedan marketplace.

Category D

Model	Trade-in	Private	Dealer
4 Dr L Sdn	14899	16126	18170
4 Dr STD Sdn	14017	15171	17094

OPTIONS FOR XG300
Compact Disc Changer +332
Power Moonroof[Std on L] +497

2000 HYUNDAI

ACCENT — 2000

The Accent has been completely redesigned for the 2000 model year.

Category A

Model	Trade-in	Private	Dealer
4 Dr GL Sdn	6054	6997	7867
2 Dr GS Hbk	5545	6408	7205
2 Dr L Hbk	5213	6025	6774

OPTIONS FOR ACCENT
AM/FM Compact Disc Player +233
Air Conditioning +659
Alarm System +165
Automatic 4-Speed Transmission +531
Luggage Rack +119
Power Door Locks +113
Power Windows +162
Rear Spoiler +262

ELANTRA — 2000

In an effort to mold its image into that of a serious, first-rate automobile manufacturer, Hyundai has recently added standard equipment and enhanced the performance of several of its cars. The redesigned Accent and new Sonata are proving that this South Korean automaker has finally learned how to build a good car. The current Elantra provides even more proof, and the company offers an industry-leading warranty program to back it up.

Category B

Model	Trade-in	Private	Dealer
4 Dr GLS Sdn	7029	8249	9375
4 Dr GLS Wgn	7358	8636	9815

OPTIONS FOR ELANTRA
AM/FM Compact Disc Player +216
Alarm System +126
Aluminum/Alloy Wheels +133
Anti-Lock Brakes +571
Automatic 4-Speed Transmission +531

Cruise Control +166
Luggage Rack[Std on Wgn] +119
Power Moonroof +497
Rear Spoiler +262

SONATA — 2000

With new standard 15-inch alloy wheels, standard side airbags, and some option changes, Hyundai's 2000 Sonata maintains the same base MSRP as last year.

Category C

Model	Trade-in	Private	Dealer
4 Dr STD Sdn	7689	8752	9732
4 Dr GLS Sdn	9036	10284	11436

OPTIONS FOR SONATA
AM/FM Compact Disc Player[Std on GLS] +199
AM/FM Stereo Tape[Std on STD] +166
AM/FM Stereo/CD/Tape +299
Alarm System +133
Anti-Lock Brakes +497
Automatic 4-Speed Transmission +531
Leather Seats +531
Power Drivers Seat +176
Power Moonroof +431
Rear Spoiler +275
Traction Control System +182

TIBURON — 2000

Hyundai's Tiburon is now offered in just one trim level. It receives new interior and exterior styling as well as alloy wheels, a power package and four-wheel disc brakes standard.

Category E

Model	Trade-in	Private	Dealer
2 Dr STD Hbk	8366	9738	11005

OPTIONS FOR TIBURON
AM/FM Stereo/CD/Tape +266
Alarm System +189
Anti-Lock Brakes +497
Automatic 4-Speed Transmission +531
Leather Seats +497
Power Moonroof +464
Rear Spoiler +331

1999 HYUNDAI

ACCENT — 1999

The L model has power steering standard, the GS and GL models have standard alloy wheels and a couple of new paint options are available. Hyundai's new, industry leading buyer assurance program is also worth taking note of.

Category A

Model	Trade-in	Private	Dealer
4 Dr GL Sdn	4899	5802	6705
2 Dr GS Hbk	4551	5389	6228
2 Dr L Hbk	3678	4356	5034

Don't forget to refer to the Mileage Adjustment Table at the back of this book!

HYUNDAI 99-98

Model Description	Trade-in TMV	Private TMV	Dealer TMV	Model Description	Trade-in TMV	Private TMV	Dealer TMV

OPTIONS FOR ACCENT
AM/FM Compact Disc Player +179
Air Conditioning +511
Alarm System +128
Automatic 4-Speed Transmission +411
Flip-Up Sunroof +228
Power Windows +126
Rear Spoiler +203

ELANTRA 1999

The 1999 Elantra boasts a more powerful engine, styling changes and the best buyer assurance program of any car in this class.
Category B

Model	Trade-in	Private	Dealer
4 Dr GL Sdn	5675	6747	7818
4 Dr GL Wgn	5754	6841	7927
4 Dr GLS Sdn	6015	7150	8286
4 Dr GLS Wgn	6385	7590	8796

OPTIONS FOR ELANTRA
AM/FM Compact Disc Player +167
Aluminum/Alloy Wheels +103
Anti-Lock Brakes +442
Automatic 4-Speed Transmission[Std on GLS Wgn] +411
Cruise Control +129
Power Door Locks[Std on GLS] +115
Power Mirrors[Std on GLS] +103
Power Moonroof +385
Power Windows[Std on GLS] +141
Rear Spoiler +203

SONATA 1999

Hyundai's Sonata is completely new and much-improved for 1999.
Category C

Model	Trade-in	Private	Dealer
4 Dr STD Sdn	6751	7787	8824
4 Dr GLS Sdn	7812	9011	10211

OPTIONS FOR SONATA
AM/FM Compact Disc Player[Std on GLS] +155
AM/FM Stereo/CD/Tape +231
Alarm System +103
Anti-Lock Brakes +385
Automatic 4-Speed Transmission +411
Cruise Control[Std on GLS] +132
Leather Seats[Opt on GLS] +411
Power Drivers Seat +135
Power Moonroof +334
Rear Spoiler +213
Traction Control System +141

TIBURON 1999

Nothing changes on the Tiburon for 1999, but the company's all-new, industry leading buyer assurance program is worth investigation.
Category E

Model	Trade-in	Private	Dealer
2 Dr STD Hbk	6992	8281	9570

Model	Trade-in	Private	Dealer
2 Dr FX Hbk	7672	9086	10500

OPTIONS FOR TIBURON
AM/FM Compact Disc Player +179
AM/FM Stereo/CD/Tape +205
Air Conditioning +462
Alarm System +146
Aluminum/Alloy Wheels[Std on FX] +257
Anti-Lock Brakes +385
Automatic 4-Speed Transmission +411
Cruise Control +111
Leather Seats +385
Power Sunroof +360
Rear Spoiler[Std on FX] +257

1998 HYUNDAI

ACCENT 1998

The Accent GSi replaces the Accent GT this year. New front and rear fascias, and new engine mounts, which reduce engine vibration and harshness, are the only other changes to Hyundai's smallest car.
Category A

Model	Trade-in	Private	Dealer
4 Dr GL Sdn	3756	4543	5395
2 Dr GS Hbk	3604	4358	5176
2 Dr GSi Hbk	3970	4802	5703
2 Dr L Hbk	2731	3302	3922

OPTIONS FOR ACCENT
AM/FM Compact Disc Player +143
Air Conditioning +401
Alarm System +102
Anti-Lock Brakes +249
Automatic 4-Speed Transmission +308
Flip-Up Sunroof +181
Rear Spoiler +162

ELANTRA 1998

No changes to the Elantra for 1998.
Category B

Model	Trade-in	Private	Dealer
4 Dr STD Sdn	4167	5101	6113
4 Dr STD Wgn	4481	5486	6574
4 Dr GLS Sdn	4534	5550	6651
4 Dr GLS Wgn	5039	6169	7393

OPTIONS FOR ELANTRA
AM/FM Compact Disc Player +133
Air Conditioning +405
Anti-Lock Brakes +351
Automatic 4-Speed Transmission[Std on GLS Wgn] +325
Power Moonroof +305
Rear Spoiler +162

SONATA 1998

No changes to the Sonata for 1998.
Category C

Model	Trade-in	Private	Dealer
4 Dr STD Sdn	4867	5668	6536

Don't forget to refer to the Mileage Adjustment Table at the back of this book!

Model Description	Trade-in TMV	Private TMV	Dealer TMV	Model Description	Trade-in TMV	Private TMV	Dealer TMV
4 Dr GL Sdn	5381	6267	7227	4 Dr GLS Sdn	3457	4386	5522
4 Dr GL V6 Sdn	5700	6639	7656	4 Dr GLS Wgn	3845	4879	6142
4 Dr GLS Sdn	6085	7087	8172				

OPTIONS FOR SONATA
AM/FM Stereo/CD/Tape +183
Anti-Lock Brakes +305
Automatic 4-Speed Transmission[Opt on STD] +325
Cruise Control[Opt on GL, GL V6] +105
Leather Seats +325
Power Moonroof +271
Rear Spoiler +169

OPTIONS FOR ELANTRA
AM/FM Compact Disc Player +109
Air Conditioning +301
Anti-Lock Brakes +184
Automatic 4-Speed Transmission[Opt on STD] +268
Power Moonroof +251
Rear Spoiler +132

TIBURON   1998

Base Tiburons get the 2.0-liter 140-horsepower engine as standard equipment.
Category E

	Trade-in	Private	Dealer
2 Dr STD Hbk	5440	6607	7871
2 Dr FX Hbk	6119	7432	8854

OPTIONS FOR TIBURON
AM/FM Stereo/CD/Tape +163
Air Conditioning +366
Alarm System +116
Aluminum/Alloy Wheels[Std on FX] +203
Anti-Lock Brakes +305
Automatic 4-Speed Transmission +325
Leather Seats +305
Power Sunroof +285
Rear Spoiler[Std on FX] +183

SONATA   1997

Sheetmetal is all-new, and gives Sonata a more substantial look despite somewhat controversial retro-style front fascia and grille. Flush-fitting doors and restyled exterior mirrors help quiet the ride, while horn activation switches from spoke button to center steering wheel pad.
Category C

	Trade-in	Private	Dealer
4 Dr STD Sdn	3645	4514	5575
4 Dr GL Sdn	4030	4991	6164
4 Dr GLS Sdn	4559	5646	6973

OPTIONS FOR SONATA
6 cyl 3.0 L Engine[Opt on GL] +335
AM/FM Stereo/CD/Tape +150
Anti-Lock Brakes +251
Automatic 4-Speed Transmission[Opt on STD] +268
Leather Seats +268
Power Moonroof +235
Rear Spoiler +134

1997 HYUNDAI

ACCENT   1997

In the absence of truly ground-breaking improvement, Hyundai revises trim levels, adding GS hatchback and GL sedan mid-range models.
Category A

	Trade-in	Private	Dealer
4 Dr GL Sdn	2449	3088	3870
2 Dr GS Hbk	2353	2968	3719
2 Dr GT Hbk	2673	3371	4224
2 Dr L Hbk	2161	2726	3416

OPTIONS FOR ACCENT
AM/FM Compact Disc Player +117
Air Conditioning +329
Anti-Lock Brakes +194
Automatic 4-Speed Transmission +252
Flip-Up Sunroof +146
Rear Spoiler[Std on GT] +132

TIBURON   1997

Loosely based on the 1993 HCD-II concept car, the Tiburon (Spanish for shark) debuts as a budget sport coupe that promises to gobble competitors such as the Toyota Paseo like so much chum.
Category E

	Trade-in	Private	Dealer
2 Dr STD Hbk	3924	4956	6217
2 Dr FX Hbk	4352	5496	6895

OPTIONS FOR TIBURON
AM/FM Stereo/CD/Tape +134
Air Conditioning +293
Aluminum/Alloy Wheels[Std on FX] +150
Anti-Lock Brakes +251
Automatic 4-Speed Transmission +268
Leather Seats +251
Power Sunroof +235
Rear Spoiler[Std on FX] +150

ELANTRA   1997

Elantra rolls into 1997 with zero changes, save for a slight price increase.
Category B

	Trade-in	Private	Dealer
4 Dr STD Sdn	3071	3897	4906
4 Dr STD Wgn	3259	4134	5205

1996 HYUNDAI

ACCENT   1996

Hyundai is painting the Accent in some new colors this year, and height-adjustable seatbelt anchors are standard. Front and rear center consoles with

---

Don't forget to refer to the Mileage Adjustment Table at the back of this book!

Model Description	Trade-in TMV	Private TMV	Dealer TMV

cupholders debut, and optional air conditioning is now CFC-free. A new, 105-horsepower GT hatch debuted midyear.

Category A

Model Description	Trade-in TMV	Private TMV	Dealer TMV
2 Dr STD Hbk	1538	2046	2747
4 Dr STD Sdn	1621	2157	2896
2 Dr GT Hbk	1811	2409	3235
2 Dr L Hbk	1453	1933	2596

OPTIONS FOR ACCENT

Air Conditioning +241
Anti-Lock Brakes +148
Automatic 4-Speed Transmission +199
Flip-Up Sunroof +117
Sunroof +134

ELANTRA   1996

All-new Elantra is a slickly styled sedan or wagon featuring dual airbags, side-impact protection, and a more powerful engine. Pricing is up as well, pushing this Hyundai squarely into Dodge Neon and Honda Civic territory.

Category B

Model Description	Trade-in TMV	Private TMV	Dealer TMV
4 Dr STD Sdn	2028	2731	3703
4 Dr STD Wgn	2190	2950	4000
4 Dr GLS Sdn	2288	3082	4178
4 Dr GLS Wgn	2547	3431	4651

OPTIONS FOR ELANTRA

Air Conditioning +241
Anti-Lock Brakes +148
Automatic 4-Speed Transmission[Opt on STD,Sdn] +214
Rear Spoiler +106

SONATA   1996

Noise, vibration and harshness are quelled with the addition of insulation to the floor and cowl, and liquid-filled V6 engine mounts. ABS is available as a stand-alone option on the GLS, and Steel Gray joins the color chart. Upgraded seat fabric comes in the base and GL models, while all Sonatas get CFC-free A/C.

Category C

Model Description	Trade-in TMV	Private TMV	Dealer TMV
4 Dr STD Sdn	2438	3127	4079
4 Dr GL Sdn	2726	3497	4561
4 Dr GL V6 Sdn	2896	3714	4844
4 Dr GLS Sdn	3115	3995	5211

OPTIONS FOR SONATA

AM/FM Stereo/CD/Tape +121
Anti-Lock Brakes +201
Automatic 4-Speed Transmission[Opt on STD] +181
Leather Seats +214
Power Moonroof +179

1995 HYUNDAI

ACCENT   1995

Dramatically improved car replaces Excel in lineup. Dual airbags are standard, and ABS is optional. Power comes from the 1.5-liter Alpha engine which debuted in 1993 Scoupe.

Category A

Model Description	Trade-in TMV	Private TMV	Dealer TMV
2 Dr STD Hbk	1151	1545	2203
4 Dr STD Sdn	1215	1632	2326
2 Dr L Hbk	1087	1460	2082

OPTIONS FOR ACCENT

Air Conditioning +195
Anti-Lock Brakes +119
Automatic 4-Speed Transmission +161
Power Sunroof +119

ELANTRA   1995

No changes.

Category B

Model Description	Trade-in TMV	Private TMV	Dealer TMV
4 Dr STD Sdn	1299	1761	2533
4 Dr GLS Sdn	1471	1995	2869
4 Dr SE Sdn	1319	1789	2573

OPTIONS FOR ELANTRA

4 cyl 1.8 L Engine[Std on GLS] +212
Air Conditioning +195
Anti-Lock Brakes +119
Automatic 4-Speed Transmission +173
Power Moonroof +162

SCOUPE   1995

No changes.

Category E

Model Description	Trade-in TMV	Private TMV	Dealer TMV
2 Dr STD Cpe	1326	1782	2540
2 Dr STD Turbo Cpe	1671	2244	3199
2 Dr LS Cpe	1510	2028	2892

OPTIONS FOR SCOUPE

Air Conditioning +173
Automatic 4-Speed Transmission +140

SONATA   1995

Brand-new Sonata debuted in mid-1994. Dual airbags are standard. A 137-horsepower engine powers base and GL models while a 142-horsepower V6 is optional on midlevel GL and standard on GLS. Both engines are Mitsubishi-based designs. New car meets 1997 side-impact standards. Air conditioning and cassette stereo are standard on all models.

Category C

Model Description	Trade-in TMV	Private TMV	Dealer TMV
4 Dr STD Sdn	1799	2426	3469

Don't forget to refer to the Mileage Adjustment Table at the back of this book!

Model Description	Trade-in TMV	Private TMV	Dealer TMV
4 Dr GL Sdn	1999	2694	3853
4 Dr GL V6 Sdn	2127	2867	4101
4 Dr GLS Sdn	2320	3128	4473

OPTIONS FOR SONATA
AM/FM Stereo/CD/Tape +97
Anti-Lock Brakes +162
Automatic 4-Speed Transmission[Opt on STD] +146
Leather Seats +173
Power Moonroof +140
Power Sunroof +130
Rear Spoiler +87

1994 HYUNDAI

ELANTRA   1994

Styling is updated, and a driver airbag is standard. ABS is optional on GLS models. CFC-free refrigerant replaces freon in Elantra's air conditioning system.
Category B

Model Description	Trade-in TMV	Private TMV	Dealer TMV
4 Dr STD Sdn	934	1364	2081
4 Dr GLS Sdn	1046	1527	2330

OPTIONS FOR ELANTRA
4 cyl 1.8 L Engine[Opt on STD] +172
Air Conditioning +158
Anti-Lock Brakes +97
Automatic 4-Speed Transmission +141
Power Sunroof +97

EXCEL   1994

Four-speed manual dropped from base car in favor of five-speed unit. Base sedan is discontinued. New interior fabrics and wheel covers spruce up the Excel. Air conditioners get CFC-free coolant.
Category A

Model Description	Trade-in TMV	Private TMV	Dealer TMV
2 Dr STD Hbk	643	928	1402
4 Dr GL Sdn	786	1135	1715
2 Dr GS Hbk	786	1135	1715

OPTIONS FOR EXCEL
Air Conditioning +141
Automatic 4-Speed Transmission +114
Power Sunroof +97

SCOUPE   1994

Base and LS models receive new interior fabrics, wheel covers and revised trim molding. CFC-free refrigerant is added to the air conditioner.
Category E

Model Description	Trade-in TMV	Private TMV	Dealer TMV
2 Dr STD Cpe	832	1222	1872
2 Dr STD Turbo Cpe	1059	1556	2383
2 Dr LS Cpe	938	1377	2110

OPTIONS FOR SCOUPE
Air Conditioning +141
Automatic 4-Speed Transmission +114

Power Sunroof +114

SONATA   1994

No changes.
Category C

Model Description	Trade-in TMV	Private TMV	Dealer TMV
4 Dr STD Sdn	1256	1787	2671
4 Dr GLS Sdn	1389	1976	2954
4 Dr GLS V6 Sdn	1539	2189	3272
4 Dr V6 Sdn	1406	2000	2990

OPTIONS FOR SONATA
AM/FM Stereo/CD/Tape +79
Anti-Lock Brakes +132
Automatic 4-Speed Transmission +118
Leather Seats +141
Power Sunroof +105

1993 HYUNDAI

ELANTRA   1993

Base model gets a black grille, while GLS features a body-color piece. GLS also gets new wheelcovers and steering wheel. All automatic models and the five-speed GLS get a new 1.8-liter engine good for 124 horsepower.
Category B

Model Description	Trade-in TMV	Private TMV	Dealer TMV
4 Dr STD Sdn	653	1033	1667
4 Dr GLS Sdn	743	1175	1896

OPTIONS FOR ELANTRA
4 cyl 1.8 L Engine[Opt on STD] +149
Air Conditioning +137
Automatic 4-Speed Transmission +122

EXCEL   1993

Slight styling revisions update Excel.
Category A

Model Description	Trade-in TMV	Private TMV	Dealer TMV
2 Dr STD Hbk	500	776	1235
4 Dr STD Sdn	684	1061	1688
4 Dr GL Sdn	626	970	1544
2 Dr GS Hbk	576	893	1421

OPTIONS FOR EXCEL
Air Conditioning +122
Automatic 4-Speed Transmission +99

SCOUPE   1993

Styling updates, a new engine, and a new Turbo model summarize the big news for 1993. The new motor is a 1.5-liter SOHC four-cylinder designed and built by Hyundai. Called Alpha, the new engine makes 92 horsepower in base and LS Scoupes; 115 horsepower in Turbo format. Turbos are available only with a manual transmission. Dashboard is slightly revised and features rotary climate controls.
Category E

Don't forget to refer to the Mileage Adjustment Table at the back of this book!

HYUNDAI 93-92

Model Description	Trade-in TMV	Private TMV	Dealer TMV
2 Dr STD Cpe	638	965	1509
2 Dr STD Turbo Cpe	844	1276	1996
2 Dr LS Cpe	714	1079	1688

OPTIONS FOR SCOUPE
Air Conditioning +122
Automatic 4-Speed Transmission +99

SONATA 1993

Front air intake is now body-color, and new wheelcovers debut.
Category C

Model Description	Trade-in TMV	Private TMV	Dealer TMV
4 Dr STD Sdn	972	1426	2183
4 Dr GLS Sdn	1079	1583	2422

OPTIONS FOR SONATA
6 cyl 3.0 L Engine +152
Anti-Lock Brakes +114
Automatic 4-Speed Transmission +102
Leather Seats +122
Power Sunroof +91

1992 HYUNDAI

ELANTRA 1992

Brand-new compact is slotted between Excel and Sonata. All models come standard with a 113-horsepower, 1.6-liter, twin-cam four-cylinder engine. Horsepower drops to 105 with the automatic transmission.
Category B

Model Description	Trade-in TMV	Private TMV	Dealer TMV
4 Dr STD Sdn	465	809	1382
4 Dr GLS Sdn	515	895	1529

OPTIONS FOR ELANTRA
Air Conditioning +118
Automatic 4-Speed Transmission +105

EXCEL 1992

GLS sedan dropped from lineup.
Category A

Model Description	Trade-in TMV	Private TMV	Dealer TMV
2 Dr STD Hbk	382	643	1079
4 Dr STD Sdn	452	761	1277
4 Dr GL Sdn	487	819	1374
2 Dr GS Hbk	437	736	1235

OPTIONS FOR EXCEL
Air Conditioning +105
Automatic 4-Speed Transmission +85

SCOUPE 1992

No changes.
Category E

Model Description	Trade-in TMV	Private TMV	Dealer TMV
2 Dr STD Cpe	460	775	1301
2 Dr LS Cpe	521	878	1473

OPTIONS FOR SCOUPE
Air Conditioning +105
Automatic 4-Speed Transmission +85

SONATA 1992

Styling is tweaked, ABS is optional on GLS V6 models, and a new 2.0-liter, twin-cam engine replaces the less-powerful, 2.4-liter base unit.
Category C

Model Description	Trade-in TMV	Private TMV	Dealer TMV
4 Dr STD Sdn	552	949	1611
4 Dr GLS Sdn	688	1183	2008

OPTIONS FOR SONATA
6 cyl 3.0 L Engine +131
Air Conditioning[Std on GLS] +85
Anti-Lock Brakes +98
Automatic 4-Speed Transmission +89
Leather Seats +105
Power Sunroof +79

Don't forget to refer to the Mileage Adjustment Table at the back of this book!

INFINITI 01-00

Model Description	Trade-in TMV	Private TMV	Dealer TMV	Model Description	Trade-in TMV	Private TMV	Dealer TMV

INFINITI — Japan

1993 Infiniti J30

2001 INFINITI

G20 — 2001

G20t comes with standard leather and a power sunroof this year. Luxury models can be equipped with leather and a manual transmission simultaneously. And hold on to your hat — the side marker lights switch from amber lenses to clear.

Category H

	Trade-in	Private	Dealer
4 Dr Touring Sdn	16281	17185	18692
4 Dr Luxury Sdn	14574	15384	16733

OPTIONS FOR G20
Automatic 4-Speed Transmission +505
Compact Disc Changer +290
Heated Front Seats +158
Heated Power Mirrors +142
Infiniti Communicator +1009
Leather Seats +536
Power Moonroof +599

I30 — 2001

This year, two new colors are added along with steering wheel-mounted controls, an anti-glare rearview mirror with integrated compass and an emergency inside trunk release. The brilliant blue xenon headlights previously available only on Touring models can now be ordered on base Luxury trim cars, as well.

Category H

	Trade-in	Private	Dealer
4 Dr Touring Sdn	21122	22295	24250
4 Dr STD Sdn	20033	21146	23000

OPTIONS FOR I30
Compact Disc Changer +379
Heated Front Seats +237
Infiniti Communicator +1009
Navigation System +1262
Rear Spoiler +158
Traction Control System +189
Xenon Headlamps +315

Q45 — 2001

Few changes accompany the current Q45 as it gasps a few final breaths before a welcome, and long overdue, redesign debuts in spring of 2001. A new Luxury model replaces last year's Anniversary Edition. All Qs get body-colored door handles and license plate surrounds, revised taillights, real bird's eye maple wood interior trim and a leather-wrapped steering wheel rim trimmed in ersatz timber. The Touring model has standard bright-finish 17-inch wheels.

Category I

	Trade-in	Private	Dealer
4 Dr STD Sdn	31707	33102	35427
4 Dr Touring Sdn	32553	33985	36372

OPTIONS FOR Q45
Compact Disc Changer +379
Heated Front Seats +265
Infiniti Communicator +1009
Navigation System +1262
Rear Spoiler +334
Tutone Paint +315

QX4 — 2001

For 2001, the QX4 gets a substantial power boost from a brand-new V6 engine. Cosmetic updates include the addition of standard xenon high-intensity headlights, revised exterior styling, new alloy wheels and a more upscale interior. A navigation system is available, as is an on-board entertainment system. A less costly 2WD model is offered for the first time, and Infiniti's signature analog clock has been added to the dash, along with electro-fluorescent gauge illumination.

Category O

	Trade-in	Private	Dealer
4 Dr STD 4WD Wgn	24471	25722	27808
4 Dr STD Wgn	23482	24683	26684

OPTIONS FOR QX4
Camper/Towing Package +205
Entertainment System +819
Heated Seats +284
Limited Slip Differential +189
Navigation System +1262
Power Moonroof +599
Tutone Paint +315

2000 INFINITI

G20 — 2000

The G20 entry-level compact receives numerous mechanical improvements, exterior and interior enhancements and safety additions for 2000, including

---

Don't forget to refer to the Mileage Adjustment Table at the back of this book!

Model Description	Trade-in TMV	Private TMV	Dealer TMV

more horsepower, revised transmissions, and a new muffler.

Category H

4 Dr Luxury Sdn	13093	14273	15361
4 Dr Touring Sdn	13941	15196	16355

OPTIONS FOR G20

Automatic 4-Speed Transmission +505
Compact Disc Changer +452
Heated Front Seats +158
Heated Power Mirrors +142
Infiniti Communicator +505
Leather Seats +536
Power Drivers Seat +173
Power Moonroof +599

I30   2000

2000 marks the introduction of the all-new Infiniti I30.

Category H

4 Dr STD Sdn	18576	20249	21793
4 Dr Touring Sdn	19047	20763	22346

OPTIONS FOR I30

Compact Disc Changer +379
Heated Front Seats +237
Infiniti Communicator +511
Rear Spoiler +158
Traction Control System +161

Q45   2000

For 2000 the Q45 celebrates a decade of production with a special 10th Anniversary model. All Qs receive a new 100,000-mile tune-up interval and special child seat tethers.

Category I

4 Dr Anniversary Sdn	27736	29536	31197
4 Dr STD Sdn	27165	28928	30555
4 Dr Touring Sdn	27819	29624	31290

OPTIONS FOR Q45

Compact Disc Changer +379
Gold Package +158
Heated Front Seats +221
Infiniti Communicator +511
Rear Spoiler +221

QX4   2000

Infiniti's luxury SUV gets minor improvements to its emissions system but is otherwise a carryover from the 1999 model year. A more powerful QX4 will be available soon as a 2001 model.

Category O

4 Dr STD 4WD Wgn	21607	23518	25282

OPTIONS FOR QX4

Camper/Towing Package +205
Compact Disc Changer +379
Heated Front Seats +221

Infiniti Communicator +511
Limited Slip Differential +189
Power Moonroof +599
Trailer Hitch +173

1999 INFINITI

G20   1999

The G20 returns to the Infiniti lineup after a two-year hiatus. This entry-level compact is based on the European- and Japanese- market Primera, which has garnered a great deal of acclaim from the foreign automotive press.

Category H

4 Dr STD Sdn	11569	12805	14042
4 Dr Touring Sdn	12591	13937	15283

OPTIONS FOR G20

Automatic 4-Speed Transmission +408
Heated Front Seats +128
Heated Power Mirrors +114
Leather Seats +434
Power Drivers Seat +141
Power Moonroof +485

I30   1999

Traction control is available as an option, the audio faceplate has been updated and an ignition immobilizer is offered on the I30.

Category H

4 Dr STD Sdn	14443	15986	17530
4 Dr Touring Sdn	14998	16601	18204

OPTIONS FOR I30

Automatic 4-Speed Transmission[Opt on Touring] +510
Compact Disc Changer +340
Heated Front Seats +213
Infiniti Communicator +459
Leather Seats[Opt on STD] +510
Limited Slip Differential[Opt on STD] +170
Power Moonroof[Opt on STD] +485
Traction Control System[Opt on STD] +145

Q45   1999

Several small exterior and interior enhancements have been added to the Q for 1999, including a new sunroof, revised front styling and the return of the analog clock.

Category I

4 Dr STD Sdn	22153	23894	25635
4 Dr Touring Sdn	22698	24481	26265

OPTIONS FOR Q45

Compact Disc Changer +340
Heated Front Seats +199
Infiniti Communicator +459
Rear Spoiler +199

Model Description	Trade-in TMV	Private TMV	Dealer TMV

QX4 — 1999

Infiniti's luxury sport-ute enters its third year with no major changes.

Category O

4 Dr STD 4WD Wgn	18556	20293	22029

OPTIONS FOR QX4

Camper/Towing Package +184
Compact Disc Changer +340
Heated Front Seats +199
Infiniti Communicator +459
Limited Slip Differential +170
Power Moonroof +485
Running Boards +184
Trailer Hitch +156

1998 INFINITI

I30 — 1998

Side-impact airbags make their way into the Infiniti I30, as do new headlamps, taillamps, center console and wheels.

Category H

4 Dr STD Sdn	12214	13666	15239
4 Dr Touring Sdn	12790	14310	15957

OPTIONS FOR I30

Automatic 4-Speed Transmission[Opt on Touring] +426
Compact Disc Changer +283
Heated Front Seats[Opt on STD] +177
Infiniti Communicator +383
Leather Seats[Opt on STD] +425
Limited Slip Differential[Opt on STD] +142
Power Moonroof[Opt on STD] +404
Traction Control System +120

Q45 — 1998

The Q45 gets front seatbelt pretensioners. No other changes for Infiniti's flagship.

Category I

4 Dr STD Sdn	18577	20138	21828
4 Dr Touring Sdn	19108	20712	22451

OPTIONS FOR Q45

Compact Disc Changer[Opt on STD] +283
Heated Front Seats[Opt on STD] +165
Infiniti Communicator +383

QX4 — 1998

No changes to the QX4.

Category O

4 Dr STD 4WD Wgn	16595	18212	19963

OPTIONS FOR QX4

Compact Disc Changer +283
Heated Front Seats +165
Limited Slip Differential +142

Power Moonroof +404
Trailer Hitch +130

1997 INFINITI

I30 — 1997

A few new paint colors are the only changes to the 1997 I30.

Category H

4 Dr STD Sdn	10710	11921	13401
4 Dr Touring Sdn	11175	12438	13982

OPTIONS FOR I30

Automatic 4-Speed Transmission +362
Heated Front Seats[Opt on STD] +151
Leather Seats[Opt on STD] +362
Limited Slip Differential[Opt on STD] +121
Power Moonroof[Opt on STD] +343
Traction Control System +102

J30 — 1997

Last year for the J30.

Category H

4 Dr STD Sdn	11429	12721	14300
1997.5 4 Dr STD Sdn	11109	12365	13900
4 Dr Touring Sdn	10726	11939	13421
1997.5 4 Dr Touring Sdn	10726	11939	13421

Q45 — 1997

This totally redesigned car has almost nothing in common with its predecessor. Power now comes via a 4.1-liter V8 engine and is still delivered through the rear wheels. The Q45 no longer has aspirations to be a sports sedan, its prime duties now are interstate cruising.

Category I

4 Dr STD Sdn	14832	16270	18028
1997.5 4 Dr STD Sdn	14832	16270	18028
4 Dr Touring Sdn	15194	16667	18468
1997.5 4 Dr Touring Sdn	15194	16667	18468

OPTIONS FOR Q45

Heated Front Seats +141
Heated Front Seats[Opt on STD] +141

QX4 — 1997

A version of Nissan's wonderful four-wheeler is introduced by Infiniti, aiming to compete with the Mercury Mountaineer, Acura SLX and Land Rover Discovery. Differences between the QX4 and the Pathfinder include the Q's full-time four-wheel drive system, a more luxurious interior, and some different sheetmetal.

Category O

4 Dr STD AWD Wgn	13860	15355	17183

Don't forget to refer to the Mileage Adjustment Table at the back of this book!

Model Description	Trade-in TMV	Private TMV	Dealer TMV

Model Description	Trade-in TMV	Private TMV	Dealer TMV

OPTIONS FOR QX4
Heated Front Seats +141
Limited Slip Differential +121
Power Moonroof +343

1996 INFINITI

G20 1996

Emergency locking front and rear seatbelts have been installed, and fake wood is applied on models equipped with the Leather Appointment Package. This is the last year for the entry-level Infiniti.

Category H

Model	Trade-in	Private	Dealer
4 Dr STD Sdn	6147	6937	8028
4 Dr Touring Sdn	6664	7521	8704

OPTIONS FOR G20
Automatic 4-Speed Transmission +307
Dual Power Seats[Opt on STD] +168
Leather Seats[Opt on STD] +261
Power Moonroof[Opt on STD] +307

I30 1996

New luxo-sport sedan based on the Nissan Maxima arrived during 1995. Slotted between the G20 and the J30, the I30 competes with the Lexus ES 300, BMW 3-Series, and the new Acura TL-Series. If you like big chrome grilles, this is the car to buy.

Category H

Model	Trade-in	Private	Dealer
4 Dr STD Sdn	9080	10247	11859
4 Dr Touring Sdn	9516	10739	12428

OPTIONS FOR I30
Automatic 4-Speed Transmission +307
Heated Front Seats[Opt on STD] +128
Leather Seats[Opt on STD] +306
Limited Slip Differential[Opt on STD] +102
Power Moonroof[Opt on STD] +291

J30 1996

Three new colors join the paint palette.

Category H

Model	Trade-in	Private	Dealer
4 Dr STD Sdn	9073	10239	11850
4 Dr Touring Sdn	9115	10287	11905

Q45 1996

Active suspension model is canceled, but two new exterior colors are available.

Category I

Model	Trade-in	Private	Dealer
4 Dr STD Sdn	11543	12876	14717
4 Dr Touring Sdn	11715	13068	14937

OPTIONS FOR Q45
AM/FM Compact Disc Player +119
AM/FM Stereo/CD/Tape +168

Heated Front Seats +119
Traction Control System +204

1995 INFINITI

G20 1995

All-season tires are added to the G20. No other changes are made to the entry-level Infiniti.

Category H

Model	Trade-in	Private	Dealer
4 Dr STD Sdn	4832	5476	6550
4 Dr Touring Sdn	5184	5876	7028

OPTIONS FOR G20
Automatic 4-Speed Transmission +189
Dual Power Seats +131
Leather Seats[Opt on STD] +201
Power Moonroof[Opt on STD] +225

J30 1995

Redesigned taillights, power lumbar support for the driver's seat, and an anti-glare mirror mark the changes for the 1995 J30.

Category H

Model	Trade-in	Private	Dealer
4 Dr STD Sdn	7725	8755	10472

OPTIONS FOR J30
Rear Spoiler +71
Touring Package +224

Q45 1995

Alloy wheels for the base model are about the only changes for the Q45.

Category I

Model	Trade-in	Private	Dealer
4 Dr A Sdn	9954	11159	13167
4 Dr STD Sdn	9623	10787	12728

OPTIONS FOR Q45
AM/FM Compact Disc Player +92
Compact Disc Changer[Std on A] +158
Heated Front Seats[Std on A] +92
Rear Spoiler +92
Touring Package +329
Traction Control System[Std on A] +158

1994 INFINITI

G20 1994

No changes to the G20.

Category H

Model	Trade-in	Private	Dealer
4 Dr STD Sdn	3902	4512	5527

OPTIONS FOR G20
Automatic 4-Speed Transmission +172
Dual Power Seats +119
Leather Seats +183
Power Moonroof +204

Don't forget to refer to the Mileage Adjustment Table at the back of this book!

Model Description	Trade-in TMV	Private TMV	Dealer TMV

J30 1994

Heated front seats and the addition of two speakers further pamper passengers in the J30.

Category H

4 Dr STD Sdn	6529	7548	9247

OPTIONS FOR J30
Touring Package +203

Q45 1994

A passenger airbag appears on the restyled 1994 Infiniti. Changes to the grille, bumpers and fog lights will distinguish this car from previous models.

Category I

4 Dr A Sdn	8547	9712	11652
4 Dr STD Sdn	8064	9162	10993

OPTIONS FOR Q45
Heated Front Seats[Std on A] +84
Rear Spoiler +84
Touring Package +299
Traction Control System[Std on A] +143

1993 INFINITI

G20 1993

Driver and passenger airbags are introduced as a midyear change to the G20.

Category H

4 Dr STD Sdn	2869	3452	4424

OPTIONS FOR G20
Automatic 4-Speed Transmission +143
Leather Seats +152
Power Sunroof +161

J30 1993

A new introduction to the Infiniti lineup, the J30 really shakes things up. Love it or hate it, this car certainly turns heads. Powered by a 210-horsepower V6 gleaned from the Nissan 300ZX, the J30 is shifted by a four-speed automatic transmission. Dual airbags are standard on the J30, as are antilock brakes.

Category H

4 Dr STD Sdn	4766	5735	7350

OPTIONS FOR J30
Touring Package +169

Q45 1993

Interior designers get a hold of the Q, sprucing, coloring and covering everything in beautiful new materials; even the clock on this car masquerades as a hand-crafted timepiece. Additional touches include map pockets to the front seat backs.

Category I

4 Dr A Sdn	6097	7108	8793
4 Dr STD Sdn	5498	6409	7928

OPTIONS FOR Q45
Rear Spoiler +70
Touring Package +248
Traction Control System +119

1992 INFINITI

G20 1992

New tires and an automatic transmission are introduced on Infiniti junior.

Category H

4 Dr STD Sdn	2160	2658	3487

OPTIONS FOR G20
Automatic 4-Speed Transmission +130
Leather Seats +138
Power Sunroof +147

M30 1992

Last year for the M30.

Category H

2 Dr STD Conv	3995	4915	6448
2 Dr STD Cpe	2973	3658	4799

Q45 1992

High-performance tires and new exterior colors are available on the 1992 Q45.

Category I

4 Dr A Sdn	5098	6067	7682
4 Dr STD Sdn	4629	5509	6975

OPTIONS FOR Q45
Touring Package +226
Traction Control System +108

Don't forget to refer to the Mileage Adjustment Table at the back of this book!

ISUZU 01-00

Model Description	Trade-in TMV	Private TMV	Dealer TMV	Model Description	Trade-in TMV	Private TMV	Dealer TMV

ISUZU   Japan

1996 Isuzu Oasis

2001 ISUZU

RODEO   2001

An Anniversary Edition trim package that includes two-tone paint, leather seating, and special chrome wheels is the only addition to 2001 Rodeos.

Category M

Model Description	Trade-in	Private	Dealer
4 Dr LS 4WD Wgn	15563	16609	18353
4 Dr LS Wgn	14051	14995	16569
4 Dr LSE 4WD Wgn	17934	19140	21149
4 Dr LSE Wgn	16858	17991	19880
4 Dr S V6 4WD Wgn	14145	15095	16680
4 Dr S V6 Wgn	12512	13353	14755
4 Dr S Wgn	11013	11753	12987

OPTIONS FOR RODEO
Air Conditioning[Std on LS,LSE] +559
Aluminum/Alloy Wheels[Std on LS,LSE] +235
Automatic 4-Speed Transmission[Std on LSE] +587
Dual Power Seats[Opt on LS] +264
Gold Package +344
Leather Seats[Opt on LS] +587
Luggage Rack[Std on LS,LSE] +115
Nakamichi Sound System[Opt on LS] +529
Power Door Locks[Opt on S] +126
Power Drivers Seat[Opt on LS] +129
Power Moonroof[Opt on LS] +411
Power Windows[Opt on S] +176
Privacy Glass[Opt on LS] +162
Running Boards +211
Tutone Paint[Opt on LS] +176

RODEO SPORT   2001

Formerly the Amigo, Isuzu's two door sport-ute gets a name change and two new colors. A wheezing four-cylinder automatic with either a hard or soft top is also new for 2001.

Category L

Model Description	Trade-in	Private	Dealer
2 Dr STD Conv	9614	10316	11486
2 Dr STD Utility	9450	10140	11290
2 Dr V6 4WD Conv	11906	12776	14225
2 Dr V6 4WD Utility	12119	13004	14479
2 Dr V6 Conv	11268	12091	13462
2 Dr V6 Utility	10974	11775	13111

OPTIONS FOR RODEO SPORT
Air Conditioning +558
Aluminum/Alloy Wheels +235
Automatic 4-Speed Transmission[Std on V6] +587
Limited Slip Differential +147
Power Door Locks +126
Power Windows +176
Running Boards +209

TROOPER   2001

An Anniversary package commemorating Isuzu's 85th year is the only new option for 2001 Troopers.

Category M

Model Description	Trade-in	Private	Dealer
4 Dr LS 4WD Wgn	17062	18209	20120
4 Dr LS Wgn	16036	17114	18910
4 Dr Limited 4WD Wgn	19080	20363	22500
4 Dr Limited Wgn	18146	19366	21399
4 Dr S 4WD Wgn	15819	16882	18654
4 Dr S Wgn	15262	16288	17998

OPTIONS FOR TROOPER
Automatic 4-Speed Transmission[Opt on S] +911
Gold Package +235
Leather Seats[Opt on LS] +720
Nakamichi Sound System[Opt on LS] +529
Pearlescent White Paint +264
Power Moonroof[Opt on LS] +646
Running Boards +199

VEHICROSS   2001

Rear child seat-tether anchors are the only new additions for 2001.

Category M

Model Description	Trade-in	Private	Dealer
2 Dr STD 4WD Utility	18953	20227	22350

OPTIONS FOR VEHICROSS
Luggage Rack +172

2000 ISUZU

AMIGO   2000

Redesigned front styling and several new colors are available for the new year. The Ironman package offers the Rodeo's Intelligent Suspension Control system.

Model Description	Trade-in TMV	Private TMV	Dealer TMV
Category L			
2 Dr S Conv	9593	10618	11564
2 Dr S Utility	9593	10618	11564
2 Dr S V6 4WD Conv	12007	13290	14474
2 Dr S V6 4WD Utility	12256	13566	14775
2 Dr S V6 Conv	11350	12562	13682
2 Dr S V6 Utility	11155	12348	13448

OPTIONS FOR AMIGO

AM/FM Compact Disc Player +206
Air Conditioning +558
Alarm System +109
Aluminum/Alloy Wheels +235
Automatic 4-Speed Transmission[Opt on V6 4WD Conv] +470
Compact Disc Changer +294
Ironman Package +565
Limited Slip Differential[Std on S] +147
Luggage Rack +97
Power Door Locks +117
Power Windows +132
Side Steps +209
Trailer Hitch +149

HOMBRE 2000

Hombres receive an upgraded standard suspension package and V6 engines get a horsepower boost. The three-door Space Cab gets a bare bones S trim model.

Model Description	Trade-in TMV	Private TMV	Dealer TMV
Category J			
2 Dr S 4WD Std Cab SB	11053	12360	13566
2 Dr S Ext Cab SB	8331	9317	10226
2 Dr S Std Cab SB	7680	8589	9427
2 Dr S V6 4WD Ext Cab SB	11376	12721	13963
2 Dr S V6 Ext Cab SB	10198	11404	12517
2 Dr XS 4WD Ext Cab SB	12976	14511	15927
2 Dr XS Ext Cab SB	9993	11175	12266
2 Dr XS Std Cab SB	8119	9079	9965
2 Dr XS V6 Ext Cab SB	10799	12076	13255

OPTIONS FOR HOMBRE

AM/FM Compact Disc Player +323
AM/FM Stereo Tape[Opt on S,S V6,Std Cab] +224
Air Conditioning[Opt on S,S V6] +559
Aluminum/Alloy Wheels[Opt on XS V6,2WD] +294
Automatic 4-Speed Transmission[Opt on S,XS,4WD] +629
Cruise Control +140
Heated Power Mirrors[Opt on XS Ext Cab] +103
Hinged Third Door +220
Power Door Locks +117
Power Windows +138

RODEO 2000

The Rodeo marches into the 2000 model year with an aggressive exterior restyle, a collection of ergonomic and quality improvements, and interior upgrades.

Model Description	Trade-in TMV	Private TMV	Dealer TMV
Category M			
4 Dr LS 4WD Wgn	13908	15293	16571
4 Dr LS Wgn	12567	13818	14973
4 Dr LSE 4WD Wgn	15555	17103	18533
4 Dr LSE Wgn	14714	16179	17531
4 Dr S Wgn	9693	10658	11549
4 Dr S V6 4WD Wgn	12634	13892	15053
4 Dr S V6 Wgn	11091	12195	13214

OPTIONS FOR RODEO

AM/FM Compact Disc Player +217
AM/FM Stereo/CD/Tape +250
Air Conditioning[Std on LS,LSE] +559
Alarm System[Opt on S V6] +117
Aluminum/Alloy Wheels[Std on LS,LSE] +117
Automatic 4-Speed Transmission[Std on LSE] +588
Brush Guard +175
Compact Disc Changer[Std on LSE] +381
Gold Package +136
Ironman Package +618
Luggage Rack[Std on LS,LSE] +115
Power Moonroof[Opt on LS] +411
Running Boards +211
Side Steps +209
Trailer Hitch +149

TROOPER 2000

A two-wheel drive model is available in the S trim, as well as the new mid-level LS and top-level Limited guises; all receive slight exterior restyling. The 10 year/120,000-mile powertrain warranty, the longest in America, ensures longevity.

Model Description	Trade-in TMV	Private TMV	Dealer TMV
Category M			
4 Dr LS 4WD Wgn	15970	17560	19028
4 Dr LS Wgn	15035	16532	17914
4 Dr Limited 4WD Wgn	17880	19660	21303
4 Dr Limited Wgn	17066	18766	20334
4 Dr S 4WD Wgn	14954	16443	17817
4 Dr S Wgn	14222	15638	16945

OPTIONS FOR TROOPER

AM/FM Compact Disc Player +323
AM/FM Stereo/CD/Tape +367
Automatic 4-Speed Transmission[Opt on S] +881
Brush Guard +230
Compact Disc Changer[Opt on S] +381
Gold Package +117
Power Moonroof[Opt on LS] +646
Running Boards +199
Side Steps +199
Trailer Hitch +149

VEHICROSS 2000

Fat 18-inch wheels replace the previous 16-inchers. The new year also brings standard A/C, new exterior colors and a 10-year/120,000-mile powertrain warranty, the longest in America.

Model Description	Trade-in TMV	Private TMV	Dealer TMV	Model Description	Trade-in TMV	Private TMV	Dealer TMV

Category M
2 Dr STD 4WD Utility — 17223 · 18938 · 20521

OPTIONS FOR VEHICROSS
Ironman Package +585
Luggage Rack +172

1999 ISUZU

AMIGO — 1999

Two body styles are available, hardtop or softtop, and an automatic transmission is now offered with the V6 engine.

Category L

Model Description	Trade-in	Private	Dealer
2 Dr S 4WD Conv	10737	11997	13257
2 Dr S Conv	9010	10068	11125
2 Dr S Utility	9010	10068	11125
2 Dr S V6 4WD Conv	11423	12763	14104
2 Dr S V6 4WD Utility	11566	12924	14281
2 Dr S V6 Conv	10598	11842	13086
2 Dr S V6 Utility	11583	12942	14301

OPTIONS FOR AMIGO
AM/FM Compact Disc Player +245
Air Conditioning +466
Alarm System +105
Aluminum/Alloy Wheels +295
Automatic 4-Speed Transmission +383
Compact Disc Changer +319
Power Door Locks +105
Power Windows +148
Side Steps +175
Trailer Hitch +124

HOMBRE — 1999

Hombres receive additional exterior colors and a new bumper fascia. A three-door spacecab model is now available.

Category J

Model Description	Trade-in	Private	Dealer
2 Dr S 4WD Std Cab SB	8729	9923	11118
2 Dr S Std Cab SB	6354	7223	8093
2 Dr XS 4WD Ext Cab SB	11282	12826	14370
2 Dr XS Ext Cab SB	8715	9907	11100
2 Dr XS Std Cab SB	6969	7922	8876
2 Dr XS V6 Ext Cab SB	10377	11797	13217

OPTIONS FOR HOMBRE
AM/FM Compact Disc Player +270
AM/FM Stereo Tape +187
Air Conditioning +466
Aluminum/Alloy Wheels[Std on 4WD] +245
Automatic 4-Speed Transmission[Std on XS V6] +525
Cruise Control +118
Hinged Third Door +184
Power Door Locks[Opt on XS Ext Cab] +99
Power Windows +116

OASIS — 1999

Only one trim level is available for 1999. Oasis has a new seating arrangement, interior and exterior refinements, and a couple of new colors.

Category P
4 Dr S Pass. Van — 13786 · 15342 · 16898

OPTIONS FOR OASIS
AM/FM Compact Disc Player +230
Compact Disc Changer +277
Luggage Rack +112
Power Sunroof +466

RODEO — 1999

Isuzu juggles minor standard and optional equipment for 1999, making items from last year's S V6 preferred equipment package standard on the LS, and last year's LS equipment standard on a new trim level called LSE.

Category M

Model Description	Trade-in	Private	Dealer
4 Dr LS 4WD Wgn	12038	13395	14752
4 Dr LS Wgn	10904	12133	13362
4 Dr LSE 4WD Wgn	13587	15119	16651
4 Dr LSE Wgn	12412	13812	15211
4 Dr S Wgn	8135	9052	9969
4 Dr S V6 4WD Wgn	10954	12189	13424
4 Dr S V6 Wgn	9446	10511	11576

OPTIONS FOR RODEO
AM/FM Compact Disc Player +182
AM/FM Stereo/CD/Tape +208
Air Conditioning[Std on LS,LSE] +466
Alarm System[Opt on S V6] +99
Aluminum/Alloy Wheels[Std on LSE] +99
Automatic 4-Speed Transmission[Std on LSE 4WD] +490
Brush Guard +146
Compact Disc Changer +319
Power Moonroof[Opt on LS] +344
Running Boards +177
Trailer Hitch +124

TROOPER — 1999

A gold trim package is added to the Trooper's option list and Torque on Demand is now standard with the automatic transmission.

Category M
4 Dr S 4WD Wgn — 12083 · 13445 · 14807

OPTIONS FOR TROOPER
AM/FM Compact Disc Player +270
AM/FM Stereo/CD/Tape +307
Automatic 4-Speed Transmission +687
Compact Disc Changer +319
Dual Power Seats +221
Fog Lights +99
Gold Package +99
Heated Front Seats +148

Don't forget to refer to the Mileage Adjustment Table at the back of this book!

Model Description	Trade-in TMV	Private TMV	Dealer TMV
Heated Power Mirrors +99			
Leather Seats +614			
Limited Slip Differential +142			
Luxury Package +2005			
Power Moonroof +540			
Privacy Glass +110			
Running Boards +167			
Trailer Hitch +124			

VEHICROSS 1999

Isuzu imports its unique-looking, award-winning SUV to the U.S. in 1999.

Category M

	Trade-in TMV	Private TMV	Dealer TMV
2 Dr STD 4WD Utility	14444	16073	17701

OPTIONS FOR VEHICROSS

Ironman Package +489

1998 ISUZU

AMIGO 1998

Isuzu reintroduces its convertible sport utility after a three-year hiatus. This model comes with a modest four-cylinder engine, but the powerful V6 from the Rodeo is available and turns this 4WD droptop into a screamer.

Category L

	Trade-in TMV	Private TMV	Dealer TMV
2 Dr S 4WD Utility	8395	9435	10563
2 Dr S Utility	7171	8060	9023
2 Dr S V6 4WD Utility	9545	10728	12010

OPTIONS FOR AMIGO

AM/FM Compact Disc Player +216
AM/FM Stereo Tape +141
Air Conditioning +412
Aluminum/Alloy Wheels +216
Compact Disc Changer +282
Limited Slip Differential +108
Power Windows +129
Trailer Hitch +110

HOMBRE 1998

Four-wheel drive arrives, finally. Also new are a theft deterrent system and dual airbags housed in a revised instrument panel, with a passenger-side airbag cutoff switch so the kiddies can ride up front.

Category J

	Trade-in TMV	Private TMV	Dealer TMV
2 Dr S 4WD Std Cab SB	8092	9098	10188
2 Dr S Std Cab SB	5930	6667	7466
2 Dr XS 4WD Ext Cab SB			
	10393	11685	13085
2 Dr XS Ext Cab SB	7777	8744	9791
2 Dr XS Std Cab SB	6099	6857	7678
2 Dr XS V6 Ext Cab SB	9454	10630	11903

OPTIONS FOR HOMBRE

AM/FM Compact Disc Player +129
AM/FM Stereo Tape +165

Model Description	Trade-in TMV	Private TMV	Dealer TMV
Air Conditioning +362			
Aluminum/Alloy Wheels[Std on S,4WD] +121			
Automatic 4-Speed Transmission[Std on XS V6] +464			
Cruise Control[Opt on XS] +104			
Power Windows[Opt on XS] +102			

OASIS 1998

The engine is upgraded to a more sophisticated 2.3-liter, good for an extra 10 horsepower and 7 foot-ponds of torque, and the transmission is revised. A tachometer is now standard, so you can better measure all that extra power.

Category P

	Trade-in TMV	Private TMV	Dealer TMV
4 Dr LS Pass. Van	12482	13983	15608
4 Dr S Pass. Van	11852	13277	14820

OPTIONS FOR OASIS

AM/FM Compact Disc Player +203
Compact Disc Changer +245
Luggage Rack[Opt on S] +100

RODEO 1998

Though it may not look like it, Isuzu has completely revised the Rodeo from top to bottom, giving it more modern styling, a user-friendly interior, more V6 power, and added room for passengers and cargo.

Category M

	Trade-in TMV	Private TMV	Dealer TMV
4 Dr LS 4WD Wgn	10925	12235	13655
4 Dr LS Wgn	10419	11668	13022
4 Dr S Wgn	7027	7870	8783
4 Dr S V6 4WD Wgn	8969	10045	11210
4 Dr S V6 Wgn	8126	9100	10156

OPTIONS FOR RODEO

AM/FM Compact Disc Player +160
AM/FM Stereo/CD/Tape +183
Air Conditioning[Std on LS] +412
Automatic 4-Speed Transmission[Std on LS] +433
Brush Guard +129
Compact Disc Changer +282
Leather Seats +432
Power Moonroof +303
Power Windows[Std on LS] +128
Running Boards +156
Trailer Hitch +110

TROOPER 1998

A bigger and lighter engine provides huge improvements in horsepower and torque (up 13 and 22 percent, respectively). And the new Torque On Demand (TOD) drive system replaces conventional four-high mode for better performance on paved or slippery roads.

Category M

	Trade-in TMV	Private TMV	Dealer TMV
4 Dr Luxury 4WD Wgn	11395	12761	14242
4 Dr S 4WD Wgn	10551	11817	13188

Don't forget to refer to the Mileage Adjustment Table at the back of this book!

Model Description	Trade-in TMV	Private TMV	Dealer TMV

OPTIONS FOR TROOPER

AM/FM Compact Disc Player +239
AM/FM Stereo/CD/Tape +270
Automatic 4-Speed Transmission[Opt on S] +542
Compact Disc Changer[Opt on S] +282
Dual Power Seats[Opt on S] +195
Heated Front Seats[Opt on S] +129
Leather Seating Package +649
Leather Seats[Opt on S] +542
Limited Slip Differential +125
Performance Package +481
Privacy Glass +97
Running Boards +148

1997 ISUZU

HOMBRE   1997

A Spacecab model debuts, with seating for five passengers and your choice of four-cylinder or V6 power. Other news includes two fresh paint colors and revised graphics.

Category J

Model Description	Trade-in TMV	Private TMV	Dealer TMV
2 Dr S Std Cab SB	4846	5586	6491
2 Dr XS Ext Cab SB	6183	7128	8282
2 Dr XS Std Cab SB	4939	5693	6615
2 Dr XS V6 Ext Cab SB	6716	7742	8996

OPTIONS FOR HOMBRE

AM/FM Compact Disc Player +108
Air Conditioning +303
Automatic 4-Speed Transmission[Opt on S,XS] +354

OASIS   1997

Cruise control is added to the S model's standard equipment list, and four new colors are available.

Category P

Model Description	Trade-in TMV	Private TMV	Dealer TMV
4 Dr LS Pass. Van	10724	12278	14178
4 Dr S Pass. Van	9861	11291	13038

OPTIONS FOR OASIS

AM/FM Compact Disc Player +171

RODEO   1997

All 4WD models get a standard shift-on-the-fly transfer case, and improvements have been made to reduce noise, vibration and harshness.

Category M

Model Description	Trade-in TMV	Private TMV	Dealer TMV
4 Dr LS 4WD Wgn	8425	9585	11002
4 Dr LS Wgn	8172	9296	10671
4 Dr S Wgn	5448	6198	7114
4 Dr S V6 4WD Wgn	7050	8021	9207
4 Dr S V6 Wgn	6377	7255	8328

OPTIONS FOR RODEO

AM/FM Compact Disc Player +134
AM/FM Stereo/CD/Tape +154

Air Conditioning[Std on LS] +345
Aluminum/Alloy Wheels[Std on LS] +145
Anti-Lock Brakes +290
Automatic 4-Speed Transmission[Opt on S V6,4WD] +352
Brush Guard +110
Compact Disc Changer +236
Leather Seats +433
Limited Slip Differential +102
Moonroof +127
Power Windows[Std on LS] +104
Running Boards +122

TROOPER   1997

Antilock brakes are now standard on all models, and dealers get a wider profit margin to help increase sales. Despite delirious requests by a certain consumer group, Isuzu will not equip the Trooper with training wheels for 1997.

Category M

Model Description	Trade-in TMV	Private TMV	Dealer TMV
4 Dr LS 4WD Wgn	9520	10830	12432
4 Dr Limited 4WD Wgn	11183	12723	14604
4 Dr S 4WD Wgn	8064	9173	10530

OPTIONS FOR TROOPER

AM/FM Compact Disc Player +199
AM/FM Stereo Tape[Opt on S] +134
Air Conditioning[Opt on S] +290
Aluminum/Alloy Wheels[Opt on S] +166
Automatic 4-Speed Transmission[Opt on S] +453
Compact Disc Changer[Opt on S] +236
Dual Power Seats[Opt on S] +163
Heated Front Seats[Opt on LS] +108
Leather Seats[Opt on LS] +453
Limited Slip Differential[Opt on LS,S] +105
Power Moonroof[Opt on LS] +399
Power Windows[Opt on S] +100
Running Boards +124

1996 ISUZU

HOMBRE   1996

In a switch from history, Isuzu clones a Chevy S-10 and dumps its Japanese-built compact truck. Sheetmetal is unique to Isuzu, but everything else is pure General Motors.

Category J

Model Description	Trade-in TMV	Private TMV	Dealer TMV
2 Dr S Std Cab SB	3911	4526	5375
2 Dr XS Std Cab SB	4251	4920	5843

OPTIONS FOR HOMBRE

Air Conditioning +274

OASIS   1996

New Isuzu minivan is a clone of the Honda Odyssey, except for the grille, badging and wheels. The Isuzu offers a better warranty, too.

Category P

Don't forget to refer to the Mileage Adjustment Table at the back of this book!

Model Description	Trade-in TMV	Private TMV	Dealer TMV
4 Dr LS Pass. Van	9441	10779	12628
4 Dr S Pass. Van	8337	9519	11151

OPTIONS FOR OASIS
AM/FM Compact Disc Player +154

RODEO 1996

Finally, Isuzu's Rodeo can be equipped with four-wheel antilock brakes, and 4WD models get a standard shift-on-the-fly system. New style wheels debut, and the engine now makes 190 horsepower. Increased wheel track improves ride quality, and spare tire covers are redesigned.

Category M

Model	Trade-in	Private	Dealer
4 Dr LS 4WD Wgn	7803	8915	10451
4 Dr LS Wgn	7649	8739	10245
4 Dr S Wgn	4739	5415	6348
4 Dr S V6 4WD Wgn	6114	6985	8189
4 Dr S V6 Wgn	5593	6390	7491

OPTIONS FOR RODEO
AM/FM Compact Disc Player +121
Air Conditioning[Std on LS] +311
Aluminum/Alloy Wheels[Std on LS] +262
Anti-Lock Brakes +262
Automatic 4-Speed Transmission[Opt on S V6,4WD] +318
Compact Disc Changer +214
Leather Seats +392
Moonroof +115
Running Boards +110

TROOPER 1996

More standard equipment, a horsepower boost for the SOHC V6 engine, and standard shift-on-the-fly debut for 1996.

Category M

Model	Trade-in	Private	Dealer
4 Dr LS 4WD Wgn	7844	8962	10506
4 Dr Limited 4WD Wgn	9014	10299	12074
4 Dr S 4WD Wgn	7841	8959	10502
4 Dr SE 4WD Wgn	9171	10479	12284

OPTIONS FOR TROOPER
AM/FM Compact Disc Player +180
AM/FM Stereo Tape[Opt on S] +121
Air Conditioning[Opt on S] +262
Aluminum/Alloy Wheels[Opt on S] +151
Anti-Lock Brakes[Opt on LS,S] +393
Automatic 4-Speed Transmission[Opt on S] +410
Compact Disc Changer[Opt on LS,S] +214
Dual Power Seats[Opt on LS] +147
Leather Seats[Opt on LS] +410
Power Moonroof[Opt on LS] +361
Running Boards +112

1995 ISUZU

HALF TON PICKUP 1995

Spacecab, V6 power and automatic transmission are canceled for 1995. All that's left are four-cylinder regular-cab trucks in 2WD or 4WD. California didn't get any 1995 Pickups, thanks to strict emissions regulations.

Category J

Model	Trade-in	Private	Dealer
2 Dr S Std Cab LB	3181	3703	4574
2 Dr S 4WD Std Cab SB	4072	4741	5855
2 Dr S Std Cab SB	2929	3410	4212

OPTIONS FOR HALF TON PICKUP
Air Conditioning +231
Wheel Package +144

RODEO 1995

Midyear change gives the Rodeo driver and passenger airbags in a redesigned dashboard. S V6 models can be equipped with a Bright Package that includes lots of chrome trim and aluminum wheels.

Category M

Model	Trade-in	Private	Dealer
4 Dr LS 4WD Wgn	6189	7097	8611
4 Dr LS Wgn	6116	7014	8510
4 Dr S 4WD Wgn	5387	6178	7496
4 Dr S Wgn	4055	4650	5642
4 Dr S V6 Wgn	4699	5388	6538

OPTIONS FOR RODEO
AM/FM Compact Disc Player +107
AM/FM Stereo Tape +72
AM/FM Stereo/CD/Tape +122
Air Conditioning[Std on LS] +274
Anti-Lock Brakes +231
Automatic 4-Speed Transmission[Opt on S,S V6,4WD] +280
Bright Package +360
Compact Disc Changer +188
Dual Air Bag Restraints[Opt on S,S V6,2WD] +115
Running Boards +97

TROOPER 1995

Dual airbags are standard. Styling is revised. A new top-of-the-line trim level debuts. The Limited has a power sunroof, leather upholstery, heated seats, and wood grain trim. Suspensions have been reworked to provide a better ride.

Category M

Model	Trade-in	Private	Dealer
4 Dr LS 4WD Wgn	6388	7325	8888
4 Dr Limited 4WD Wgn	7755	8894	10791
2 Dr RS 4WD Utility	6324	7252	8799
4 Dr S 4WD Wgn	6292	7216	8755
4 Dr SE 4WD Wgn	7525	8630	10471

OPTIONS FOR TROOPER
AM/FM Compact Disc Player +159
Air Conditioning[Opt on S] +231
Aluminum/Alloy Wheels[Opt on S] +132
Anti-Lock Brakes[Opt on S] +347
Automatic 4-Speed Transmission[Opt on LS,S,RS] +360

Don't forget to refer to the Mileage Adjustment Table at the back of this book!

Model Description	Trade-in TMV	Private TMV	Dealer TMV	Model Description	Trade-in TMV	Private TMV	Dealer TMV
Compact Disc Changer[Opt on S,SE] +188				AM/FM Stereo/CD/Tape +112			
Keyless Entry System[Opt on LS,S] +72				Air Bag Restraint[Opt on S V6] +106			
Limited Slip Differential[Opt on LS, S] +84				Air Conditioning[Std on LS] +252			
Power Door Locks[Opt on S] +72				Automatic 4-Speed Transmission[Opt on S,S V6,4WD] +257			
Power Windows[Opt on S] +80							

1994 ISUZU

AMIGO — 1994

Automatic transmission disappears from options list, and base 2.3-liter, four-cylinder engine is no longer available. Power steering, power outside mirrors, a center floor console, and 16-inch tires are all newly standard.

Category L

	Trade-in	Private	Dealer
2 Dr S 4WD Utility	4176	4926	6175
2 Dr S Utility	3701	4366	5473
2 Dr XS 4WD Utility	4274	5041	6320
2 Dr XS Utility	3860	4552	5707

OPTIONS FOR AMIGO

AM/FM Stereo Tape +86
Air Conditioning +252
Sunroof +79

HALF TON PICKUP — 1994

Vent windows are dropped. Models with 2.6-liter engine get standard power steering. Outside mirrors are revised.

Category J

	Trade-in	Private	Dealer
2 Dr STD Std Cab SB	2156	2572	3265
2 Dr S Std Cab LB	2467	2944	3737
2 Dr S 4WD Std Cab SB	3264	3893	4943
2 Dr S Ext Cab SB	2888	3445	4374
2 Dr S 2.6 Ext Cab SB	2888	3445	4374
2 Dr S 2.6 Std Cab SB	2730	3257	4135

OPTIONS FOR HALF TON PICKUP

6 cyl 3.1 L Engine +227
Air Conditioning +212
Tire/Wheel Package +133

RODEO — 1994

S model gets standard power steering. LS models are equipped with standard air conditioning. Front vent windows are dropped. All V6 models come with standard rear wiper/washer and tailgate spare tire carrier.

Category M

	Trade-in	Private	Dealer
4 Dr LS 4WD Wgn	5080	5996	7522
4 Dr LS Wgn	4729	5581	7002
4 Dr S 4WD Wgn	4101	4840	6072
4 Dr S Wgn	3171	3743	4696
4 Dr S V6 Wgn	3644	4301	5396

OPTIONS FOR RODEO

TROOPER — 1994

Four-wheel ABS filters down to the Trooper S options sheet. Gray leather upholstery is a new options for the LS model, and it includes heated front seats with power adjustments. RS gets new alloys.

Category M

	Trade-in	Private	Dealer
4 Dr LS 4WD Wgn	5210	6149	7714
2 Dr RS 4WD Utility	4681	5525	6931
4 Dr S 4WD Wgn	4006	4728	5931
4 Dr SE 4WD Wgn	6186	7301	9159

OPTIONS FOR TROOPER

AM/FM Compact Disc Player +146
AM/FM Stereo/CD/Tape +165
Air Conditioning[Opt on S] +212
Aluminum/Alloy Wheels +121
Anti-Lock Brakes[Opt on S] +318
Automatic 4-Speed Transmission[Std on SE] +331
Dual Power Seats[Opt on LS] +119
Heated Front Seats[Opt on LS] +79
Leather Seats[Opt on LS] +331
Limited Slip Differential[Opt on S] +77
Power Sunroof[Opt on LS] +152
Power Windows[Opt on S] +73

1993 ISUZU

AMIGO — 1993

Amigo gets a new grille.

Category L

	Trade-in	Private	Dealer
2 Dr S 4WD Utility	2903	3501	4498
2 Dr S Utility	2313	2790	3584
2 Dr XS 4WD Utility	3165	3817	4904
2 Dr XS Utility	2612	3151	4048

OPTIONS FOR AMIGO

4 cyl 2.6 L Engine[Opt on S Utility] +92
AM/FM Stereo Tape +74
Air Conditioning +218
Aluminum/Alloy Wheels[Opt on S,2WD] +115
Amigo Tire/Wheel Package +178
Automatic 4-Speed Transmission +178

HALF TON PICKUP — 1993

LS trim level dropped. Two models discontinued: one-ton Longbed and 4WD Spacecab. A new grille graces the front of the Pickup.

Category J

	Trade-in	Private	Dealer
2 Dr S Std Cab LB	1959	2389	3105
2 Dr S 4WD Std Cab SB	2438	2973	3864
2 Dr S Ext Cab SB	2232	2722	3538
2 Dr S Std Cab SB	1818	2217	2882

Don't forget to refer to the Mileage Adjustment Table at the back of this book!

Model Description	Trade-in TMV	Private TMV	Dealer TMV
2 Dr S 2.6 Std Cab SB	2101	2562	3330

OPTIONS FOR HALF TON PICKUP
6 cyl 3.1 L Engine +197
Air Conditioning +184
Pickup 4WD Bright Package +286

RODEO 1993

More potent V6 engine filters into Rodeo from big brother Trooper for a horsepower boost of 55 ponies. A new grille is installed up front.

Category M

Model Description	Trade-in TMV	Private TMV	Dealer TMV
4 Dr LS 4WD Wgn	3350	4101	5352
4 Dr LS Wgn	3329	4075	5318
4 Dr S 4WD Wgn	3062	3748	4892
4 Dr S Wgn	2342	2866	3741
4 Dr S V6 Wgn	2739	3352	4375

OPTIONS FOR RODEO
Air Conditioning +218
Automatic 4-Speed Transmission +222
Rodeo Tire/Wheel Package +184

STYLUS 1993

Sporty XS model is dropped, along with its twin-cam engine.

Category B

Model Description	Trade-in TMV	Private TMV	Dealer TMV
4 Dr S Sdn	981	1317	1877

OPTIONS FOR STYLUS
Air Conditioning +172
Automatic 3-Speed Transmission +126

TROOPER 1993

A short-wheelbase two-door model joins the lineup in RS trim. Four-wheel ABS is optional on this stubby new model.

Category M

Model Description	Trade-in TMV	Private TMV	Dealer TMV
4 Dr LS 4WD Wgn	4138	5065	6610
2 Dr RS 4WD Utility	3624	4436	5790
4 Dr S 4WD Wgn	3234	3959	5167

OPTIONS FOR TROOPER
AM/FM Compact Disc Player +126
AM/FM Stereo/CD/Tape +143
Air Conditioning[Opt on S] +184
Aluminum/Alloy Wheels[Opt on S] +105
Anti-Lock Brakes +275
Automatic 4-Speed Transmission +286
Leather Seats +286
Power Sunroof +132

1992 ISUZU

AMIGO 1992

Those who hate shifting their own gears are in luck; an automatic is newly optional.

Category L

Model Description	Trade-in TMV	Private TMV	Dealer TMV
2 Dr S 4WD Utility	2421	3032	4050
2 Dr S Utility	1932	2420	3232
2 Dr XS 4WD Utility	2650	3318	4432
2 Dr XS Utility	2166	2712	3623

OPTIONS FOR AMIGO
4 cyl 2.6 L Engine[Opt on S Utility] +83
Air Conditioning +197
Aluminum/Alloy Wheels +104
Automatic 4-Speed Transmission +162

HALF TON PICKUP 1992

No changes.

Category J

Model Description	Trade-in TMV	Private TMV	Dealer TMV
2 Dr LS 4WD Ext Cab SB	2750	3510	4778
2 Dr LS Ext Cab SB	2126	2714	3694
2 Dr S Std Cab LB	1489	1901	2587
2 Dr S 4WD Std Cab SB	1994	2546	3465
2 Dr S Ext Cab SB	1703	2174	2959
2 Dr S Std Cab SB	1398	1785	2429

OPTIONS FOR HALF TON PICKUP
4 cyl 2.6 L Engine +83
6 cyl 3.1 L Engine[Opt on S] +178
Air Conditioning +165
Automatic 4-Speed Transmission +165

IMPULSE 1992

XS gets ten more horsepower, thanks to a larger 1.8-liter twin-cam engine.

Category E

Model Description	Trade-in TMV	Private TMV	Dealer TMV
2 Dr RS Turbo AWD Cpe	1566	2186	3219
2 Dr XS Cpe	1255	1751	2579
2 Dr XS Hbk	1313	1833	2700

OPTIONS FOR IMPULSE
Air Conditioning[Std on RS] +155
Automatic 4-Speed Transmission[Std on RS] +155
Impulse RS Package +155
Power Sunroof +119

ONE TON 1992

Category J

Model Description	Trade-in TMV	Private TMV	Dealer TMV
2 Dr S Std Cab LB	1859	2374	3231

OPTIONS FOR ONE TON
Air Conditioning +165

RODEO 1992

No changes.

Category M

Model Description	Trade-in TMV	Private TMV	Dealer TMV
4 Dr LS 4WD Wgn	2761	3459	4622
4 Dr LS Wgn	2649	3319	4435
4 Dr S 4WD Wgn	2496	3126	4178

Don't forget to refer to the Mileage Adjustment Table at the back of this book!

Model Description	Trade-in TMV	Private TMV	Dealer TMV		Model Description	Trade-in TMV	Private TMV	Dealer TMV
4 Dr S Wgn	2014	2523	3372					
4 Dr S V6 Wgn	2173	2722	3638					
4 Dr XS 4WD Wgn	2898	3631	4852					
4 Dr XS Wgn	2315	2900	3876					

OPTIONS FOR RODEO
Air Conditioning +197
Automatic 3-Speed Transmission +114
Automatic 4-Speed Transmission +201

STYLUS   1992

RS gets 10 more horsepower, thanks to a larger 1.8-liter twin-cam engine.
Category B

Model Description	Trade-in TMV	Private TMV	Dealer TMV
4 Dr RS Sdn	885	1247	1851
4 Dr S Sdn	761	1073	1592

OPTIONS FOR STYLUS
Air Conditioning +155
Automatic 3-Speed Transmission +114

TROOPER   1992

Beefy SUV moves upscale with total redesign that renders it longer, wider, taller and heavier. Four-wheel ABS is optional on LS models. A new Isuzu-designed 3.2-liter V6 powers Trooper; base models have an SOHC unit, while LS models get a DOHC engine good for 190 horsepower.
Category M

Model Description	Trade-in TMV	Private TMV	Dealer TMV
4 Dr LS 4WD Wgn	3612	4525	6047
4 Dr S 4WD Wgn	2601	3258	4354

OPTIONS FOR TROOPER
AM/FM Compact Disc Player +114
Air Conditioning[Opt on S] +165
Anti-Lock Brakes[Std on S] +249
Automatic 4-Speed Transmission +259
Power Sunroof +119

Don't forget to refer to the Mileage Adjustment Table at the back of this book!

JAGUAR 01

Model Description	Trade-in TMV	Private TMV	Dealer TMV	Model Description	Trade-in TMV	Private TMV	Dealer TMV

JAGUAR   *Britain*

1995 Jaguar XJ12

2001 JAGUAR

S-TYPE   2001

The S-Type gets new 10-spoke alloy wheels for 2001, along with exterior color options Onyx White and Roman Bronze. The folks at Jaguar have decided to move the six-disc CD changer from the glove box to the trunk. ISOFIX is added to the rear for securing child seats and Reverse Park Control now comes standard. An electronically controlled, speed-proportional power steering system is new this year and the software for the Voice Activation Control system has been upgraded. A Deluxe Communications Package featuring a Motorola Timeport digital phone system is a new option.

Category I

	Trade-in	Private	Dealer
4 Dr 3.0L Sdn	32472	33795	36000
4 Dr 4.0L Sdn	35813	37272	39704

OPTIONS FOR S-TYPE
Automatic Stability Control[Opt on 3.0] +348
Compact Disc Changer +556
Electronic Suspension +313
Heated Front Seats +198
Navigation System +1321
Premium Sound System[Opt on 3.0] +1043
Rain Sensing Windshield Wipers[Opt on 3.0] +139
Sport Package +765
Sport Wheels +209

XJ-SERIES   2001

Jaguar's premium sedan receives only minor content changes for 2001. The XJ8 and XJ8 L both receive a six-disc CD changer as standard equipment. The Vanden Plas gets a premium sound system with the CD changer as standard, as well as heated front and rear

seats. Heated rear seats are standard on the XJR, and the navigation system is standard on the Vanden Plas Supercharged. For all models, Jaguar has added a new reverse parking control system and strengthened the chassis with new crush tubes, doors, hinges and steering columns. There are also new exterior colors, a new style of wheel for Vanden Plas models and an optional dealer-installed Motorola Timeport digital phone. Topping things off is a new, no-cost scheduled maintenance program that covers four regular service visits under the four-year/50,000-mile limited warranty.

Category F

	Trade-in	Private	Dealer
4 Dr Vanden Plas Sprchgd Sdn	56730	58706	62000

Category I

	Trade-in	Private	Dealer
4 Dr Vanden Plas Sdn	46384	48274	51424
4 Dr XJ8 Sdn	37659	39193	41750
4 Dr XJ8L Sdn	43171	44930	47861

Category F

	Trade-in	Private	Dealer
4 Dr XJR Sprchgd Sdn	52613	54445	57500

OPTIONS FOR XJ-SERIES
Heated Seats[Std on S/C] +348
Navigation System +1182
Premium Sound System[Opt on XJ8,XJ8L] +695

XK-SERIES   2001

For 2001, a limited edition XKR "Silverstone" model will be offered, equipped with 20-inch BBS wheels, Brembo brakes and unique interior treatments. The Silverstone, as well as the regular XKR Coupe and Convertible, have additional safety equipment in the form of seat-mounted side airbags and an Adaptive Restraint Technology System (ARTS) that ultrasonically detects occupants. There are also standard child seat-anchor points for the rear seats and a reverse parking-control system. The premium audio system with a six-disc CD changer and the GPS navigation system are now standard equipment on XK8s. Topping things off are minor exterior styling changes and a new, no-cost scheduled maintenance program that covers four regular service visits under the four-year/50,000-mile limited warranty.

Category F

	Trade-in	Private	Dealer
2 Dr XK8 Conv	57188	59180	62500
2 Dr XK8 Cpe	50325	52078	55000
2 Dr XKR Sprchgd Conv	68168	70542	74500
2 Dr XKR Sprchgd Cpe	74984	77596	81950
2 Dr XKR Silverstone Sprchgd Conv			
	86925	89953	95000
2 Dr XKR Silverstone Sprchgd Cpe			
	81893	84745	89500

Don't forget to refer to the Mileage Adjustment Table at the back of this book!

Model Description	Trade-in TMV	Private TMV	Dealer TMV	Model Description	Trade-in TMV	Private TMV	Dealer TMV

OPTIONS FOR XK-SERIES
Navigation System +1668
Sport Wheels[Std on XKR] +348

2000 JAGUAR

S-TYPE — 2000

From the ground up, this is a completely new sport sedan based on the new Ford midsize platform. Lincoln worked with Jaguar to develop this platform, which is also used for Lincoln's LS sedan.

Category I

Model Description	Trade-in TMV	Private TMV	Dealer TMV
4 Dr 3.0L Sdn	29935	31789	33500
4 Dr 4.0L Sdn	31722	33687	35500

OPTIONS FOR S-TYPE
Automatic Dimming Mirror[Opt on 3.0] +99
Compact Disc Changer +529
Heated Front Seats +198
Navigation System +1321
Power Moonroof[Std on 4.0 L] +660
Sport Package +726

XJ-SERIES — 2000

A fifth model — the supercharged Vanden Plas — has been added. All XJ8 Sedans gain all-speed traction control, improved ABS, rain-sensing windshield wipers, and child seat-anchor brackets as standard equipment. A new navigation system is being offered as optional equipment, as is an upgraded 320-watt Alpine system. The anti-theft system now has an encrypted key transponder. There are two new exterior colors and one new interior color.

Category I

Model Description	Trade-in TMV	Private TMV	Dealer TMV
4 Dr Vanden Plas Sdn	37685	40019	42173
4 Dr XJ8 Sdn	31838	33809	35629
4 Dr XJ8L Sedan	36696	38968	41066
Category F			
4 Dr Vanden Plas Sprchgd Sdn	49201	52087	54750

OPTIONS FOR XJ-SERIES
Compact Disc Changer[Std on S/C] +348
Harman Kardon Sound System[Std on S/C] +799
Heated Seats[Std on S/C] +281
Navigation System +991

XJR — 2000

The XJR gains all-speed traction control, improved ABS, rain-sensing windshield wipers, child seat-anchor brackets, and an upgraded 320-watt Alpine system as standard equipment. A new navigation system is being offered as optional equipment. The anti-theft system now has an encrypted key transponder. The XJR also gets new 18-inch wheels and a different sew style for the seats.

Category F

Model Description	Trade-in TMV	Private TMV	Dealer TMV
4 Dr XJR Sprchgd Sdn	45733	48415	50891

XK-SERIES — 2000

The XK8 Coupe and Convertible gain all-speed traction control, improved ABS, bigger front brakes, rain-sensing windshield wipers, and child seat-anchor brackets as standard equipment. A new navigation system is being offered as optional equipment, as is an upgraded 320-watt Alpine system. The standard audio system gets two more speakers, for a total of six. The anti-theft system has been upgraded with an encrypted key transponder. Both the standard 17-inch wheels and the optional 18-inch wheels have been restyled. The front seatbelt pre-tensioners are now electronically controlled.

Category F

Model Description	Trade-in TMV	Private TMV	Dealer TMV
2 Dr XK8 Conv	47680	50476	53057
2 Dr XK8 Cpe	42478	44969	47269

OPTIONS FOR XK-SERIES
Compact Disc Changer +417
Harman Kardon Sound System +869
Heated Front Seats +268
Navigation System +991

XKR — 2000

The performance-minded, supercharged V8 powered, XKR is new for 2000.

Category F

Model Description	Trade-in TMV	Private TMV	Dealer TMV
2 Dr STD Sprchgd Conv	59760	63265	66500
2 Dr STD Sprchgd Cpe	55716	58984	62000

OPTIONS FOR XKR
Navigation System +991

1999 JAGUAR

XJ-SERIES — 1999

Jaguar's venerable XJ sedans enter '99 largely unchanged after a major workover in '98.

Category F

Model Description	Trade-in TMV	Private TMV	Dealer TMV
4 Dr XJR Sprchgd Sdn	36892	39326	41759
Category I			
4 Dr Vanden Plas Sdn	30934	33144	35353
4 Dr XJ8 Sdn	26935	28859	30783
4 Dr XJ8L Sedan	28198	30212	32226

OPTIONS FOR XJ-SERIES
Chrome Wheels[Opt on XJR] +460
Compact Disc Changer[Std on S/C] +288
Harman Kardon Sound System[Std on S/C] +662
Heated Seats[Std on S/C] +208
Traction Control System[Std on S/C] +288

Model Description	Trade-in TMV	Private TMV	Dealer TMV

XK-SERIES 1999

The stunning XK returns for '99 with no significant changes.

Category F

2 Dr XK8 Conv	41132	43845	46558
2 Dr XK8 Cpe	36044	38422	40799

OPTIONS FOR XK-SERIES
Chrome Wheels +492
Compact Disc Changer +345
Harman Kardon Sound System +719
Heated Front Seats +222
Traction Control System +345

1998 JAGUAR

XJ-SERIES 1998

A new V8 engine, taken from the XK8 coupe and convertible, makes its way into the engine bay. A revised instrument panel greatly improves interior ergonomics. Cruise and satellite stereo controls are located on the steering wheel.

Category I

4 Dr Vanden Plas Sdn	25154	27166	29346
4 Dr XJ8 Sdn	21882	23633	25529
4 Dr XJ8L Sdn	22700	24516	26483

Category F

4 Dr XJR Sprchgd Sdn	30252	32534	35007

OPTIONS FOR XJ-SERIES
Chrome Wheels[Opt on XJR] +391
Compact Disc Changer +244
Harman Kardon Sound System +562
Heated Seats +177
Traction Control System +244

XK-SERIES 1998

The 1998 XK8 gets automatic on/off headlamps, an engine immobilizer feature as part of the security system, and a cellular phone keypad integrated into the stereo controls. Other changes include the addition of two new exterior colors.

Category F

2 Dr XK8 Conv	35112	37761	40631
2 Dr XK8 Cpe	27766	29860	32130

OPTIONS FOR XK-SERIES
Chrome Wheels +418
Compact Disc Changer +293
Harman Kardon Sound System +611
Heated Front Seats +188
Traction Control System +293

1997 JAGUAR

XJ-SERIES 1997

The 1997 XJ-Series loses the V12 model that has been a mainstay of the Jaguar lineup for so many years. A long-wheelbase model becomes available this year, filling a niche between the XJ6 and the Vanden Plas. All models receive a contoured bench seat and three-point seatbelts for rear occupants. The XJ6 replaces last year's chrome-vane grille with a black-vane grille, and the convenience group becomes optional on this model. The XJR loses its rear passenger heater ducts.

Category I

4 Dr Vanden Plas Sdn	18578	20343	22500
4 Dr XJ6 Sdn	16539	18110	20031
4 Dr XJ6L Sdn	17123	18750	20738

Category F

4 Dr XJR Sprchgd Sdn	21298	23354	25867

OPTIONS FOR XJ-SERIES
Chrome Wheels +318
Compact Disc Changer +199
Harman Kardon Sound System +458
Heated Seats +145
Special Factory Paint +199
Traction Control System +199

XK8 1997

An all-new Jaguar debuts this year, replacing the stodgy XJ-S. This new sports car boasts the first V-8 engine ever found in a Jag, as well as an all-new 5-speed manual transmission that features normal and sport modes. The XK8 is available in coupe and convertible forms, but Jaguar insiders expect a full 70% of sales to be of the convertible.

Category F

2 Dr XK8 Conv	28402	31144	34495
2 Dr XK8 Cpe	22087	24219	26825

OPTIONS FOR XK8
Chrome Wheels +340
Compact Disc Changer +239
Harman Kardon Sound System +478
Heated Front Seats +139
Special Factory Paint +199
Traction Control System +239

1996 JAGUAR

XJ-SERIES 1996

On the XJ6, thicker side window glass insulates passengers from annoying wind noise and outside distractions. After a 20-year reign, the XJS coupe is put out to pasture. The only model offered for 1996 is the

Don't forget to refer to the Mileage Adjustment Table at the back of this book!

JAGUAR 96-93

Model Description	Trade-in TMV	Private TMV	Dealer TMV	Model Description	Trade-in TMV	Private TMV	Dealer TMV

six-cylinder convertible; the most popular XJS in its unremarkable history. The changes for 1996 include new wheels, new bucket seats, additional chrome exterior trim, and an adjustable, wood-trimmed steering wheel.

Category I

4 Dr Vanden Plas Sdn	14936	16538	18750
4 Dr XJ12 Sdn	19353	21429	24295
4 Dr XJ6 Sdn	13753	15228	17265

Category F

4 Dr XJR Sprchgd Sdn	17499	19275	21727
2 Dr XJS Conv	14613	16096	18144

OPTIONS FOR XJ-SERIES

Chrome Wheels +263
Compact Disc Changer +164
Heated Front Seats +126
Heated Seats +126
Special Factory Paint +164
Sport Suspension +148
Traction Control System +164

1995 JAGUAR

XJ-SERIES   1995

Horsepower is upped for naturally aspirated 4.0-liter engine, and inline-six and V12 engines. New sheetmetal showcases a more traditional Jaguar, ironic considering the amount of input Ford had into the creation of this car. XJS V12 models get new wheels and a plethora of standard equipment such as heated seats and a multi-disc CD changer. A supercharged XJR model is introduced.

Category I

4 Dr XJ12 Sdn	15339	16954	19647
4 Dr XJ6 Sdn	11609	12831	14869
4 Dr XJ6 Vanden Plas Sdn			
	12882	14239	16500

Category F

4 Dr XJR Sprchgd Sdn	13476	14895	17260
2 Dr XJS Conv	12518	13836	16033
2 Dr XJS Cpe	10659	11781	13652
2 Dr XJS V12 Conv	16193	17898	20740
2 Dr XJS V12 Cpe	14400	15916	18443

OPTIONS FOR XJ-SERIES

AM/FM Compact Disc Player +98
Chrome Wheels +223
Compact Disc Changer +140
Heated Front Seats +106
Heated Seats +106
Limited Slip Differential[Opt on Vanden Plas,XJ6] +88
Luxury Package +453
Power Sunroof +252

Rear Spoiler[Opt on XJS Conv] +88
Special Factory Paint +140
Traction Control System +140

1994 JAGUAR

XJ-SERIES   1994

A passenger airbag joins the safety equipment roster. CFC-free air conditioning is added to the standard equipment list. For the XJS, a five-speed manual transmission is available as a new option for the 4.0-liter inline-six engine. An XJR-S derived XJ-S 6.0-liter V12 is available, they are differentiated by a rear spoiler, mirrors, grille, and alloy wheels. The XJ-12 is available with a 301-horsepower engine and a four-speed automatic transmission.

Category F

2 Dr XJS Cpe	8077	9099	10801

Category I

4 Dr XJ12 Sdn	11103	12614	15132
4 Dr XJ6 Sdn	7121	8090	9705
4 Dr XJ6 Vanden Plas Sdn			
	7991	9079	10891

Category F

2 Dr XJS Conv	10271	11570	13734
2 Dr XJS V12 Conv	12161	13699	16262
2 Dr XJS V12 Cpe	10515	11845	14061

OPTIONS FOR XJ-SERIES

Compact Disc Changer +106
Dual Air Bag Restraints +106
Heated Front Seats +81
Power Sunroof +190
Special Factory Paint +106
Sport Handling Package +171

1993 JAGUAR

XJ-SERIES   1993

The XJ6 loses the Sovereign model. Comfy power seats, integrated fog lights and new wheels mark the changes for Britain's most popular luxury sedan. ON the XJS, the V12 engine is dropped in favor of a 4.0-liter inline-six. Mercifully, a four-speed automatic transmission replaces the previous three-speed. A traction control system starts the car in second gear to limit wheel-spin on slippery surfaces.

Category I

4 Dr XJ12 Sdn	7735	8933	10930
4 Dr XJ6 Sdn	5717	6603	8079
4 Dr XJ6 Vanden Plas Sdn			
	6334	7315	8950

Category F

2 Dr XJS Conv	6658	7667	9348

Don't forget to refer to the Mileage Adjustment Table at the back of this book!

Model Description	Trade-in TMV	Private TMV	Dealer TMV	Model Description	Trade-in TMV	Private TMV	Dealer TMV
2 Dr XJS Cpe	5711	6577	8019				

OPTIONS FOR XJ-SERIES
Compact Disc Changer +93
Power Sunroof +167
Special Factory Paint +93

1992 JAGUAR

XJ-SERIES   1992

The XJS gets a new grille and headlights. Two-driver memory is also available for the mirrors and driver's seat.

Category I

Model Description	Trade-in TMV	Private TMV	Dealer TMV
4 Dr XJ6 Sdn	4349	5143	6467
4 Dr XJ6 Majestic Sdn	6076	7185	9034
4 Dr XJ6 Sovereign Sdn			
	5057	5980	7519
4 Dr XJ6 Vanden Plas Sdn			
	5336	6311	7935

Category F

Model Description	Trade-in TMV	Private TMV	Dealer TMV
2 Dr XJS Conv	7545	8920	11212
2 Dr XJS Cpe	6196	7325	9207

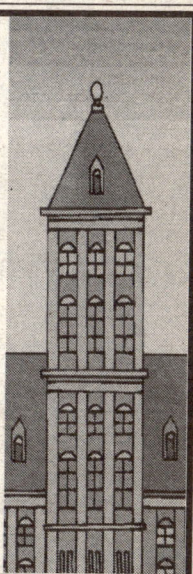

Don't forget to refer to the Mileage Adjustment Table at the back of this book!

Model Description	Trade-in TMV	Private TMV	Dealer TMV	Model Description	Trade-in TMV	Private TMV	Dealer TMV

JEEP   USA

1997 Jeep Wrangler

2001 JEEP

CHEROKEE   2001

The 4.0-liter PowerTech inline-six engine, which now meets LEV requirements in all 50 states, is standard equipment in all 2001 Cherokees. The 2.5-liter inline four, along with the SE trim, is dropped. The previous Limited trim is also dropped, with the former Classic trim is now labeled Limited. All 2001 Cherokees offer child seat-tether anchors as standard equipment, and Steel Blue replaces Desert Sand as an exterior color choice.

Category M

	Trade-in	Private	Dealer
4 Dr Classic 4WD Wgn	13733	14641	16156
4 Dr Classic Wgn	12885	13738	15159
4 Dr Limited 4WD Wgn	13869	14786	16316
4 Dr Limited Wgn	12960	13818	15247
2 Dr SE 4WD Utility	11628	12398	13680
2 Dr SE Utility	10751	11462	12648
4 Dr SE 4WD Wgn	12255	13066	14418
4 Dr SE Wgn	11359	12110	13363
2 Dr Sport 4WD Utility	12357	13175	14538
2 Dr Sport Utility	11565	12330	13606
4 Dr Sport 4WD Wgn	13025	13887	15324
4 Dr Sport Wgn	12080	12880	14212

OPTIONS FOR CHEROKEE
AM/FM Stereo/CD/Tape +257
Air Conditioning[Std on Limited] +533
Aluminum/Alloy Wheels[Opt on SE, Sport] +154
Anti-Lock Brakes +376
Automatic 4-Speed Transmission[Opt on SE, Sport] +592
Camper/Towing Package +154
Cruise Control +156

Dual Power Seats[Opt on Limited] +282
Heated Front Seats +345
Infinity Sound System +219
Leather Seats[Opt on Limited] +439
Locking Differential +179
Overhead Console[Std on Limited] +147
Power Drivers Seat[Opt on Classic 4] +188
Power Windows[Std on Limited 2WD] +156
Privacy Glass[Std on Limited] +169
Up Country Suspension Group +454

GRAND CHEROKEE   2001

A new five-speed automatic tranny provides a second overdrive ratio, resulting in greater fuel economy and reduced noise, vibration and harshness in models equipped with the 4.7-liter V8. Chrome front tow hooks are now included if you get the skid plate group on the Limited model, while the Laredo model offers a Special Appearance Group package with 17-inch, five-spoke aluminum wheels, colored metallic front fascia and body cladding, body color license brow and liftgate handle, fog lamps, body side stripe, and leather seats. A hydraulically driven engine-cooling fan improves fuel economy on the 4.7-liter V8 and a quarter-turn fuel cap improves efficiency at the gas station. Limiteds get an AM/FM stereo with cassette and CD player as standard equipment, along with optional new "Euro-style" gathered leather seats. The Trailer Tow Group now includes an underdash connector to make plugging in aftermarket trailer wiring harnesses a snap. Finally, child seat tether anchors improve the Grand Cherokee's family-friendly nature while a LEV-compliant 4.7-liter V8 makes this Jeep more earth-friendly.

Category M

	Trade-in	Private	Dealer
4 Dr Laredo 4WD Wgn	17808	18986	20950
4 Dr Laredo Wgn	16575	17672	19500
4 Dr Limited 4WD Wgn	22066	23526	25960
4 Dr Limited Wgn	19961	21281	23483

OPTIONS FOR GRAND CHEROKEE
8 cyl 4.7 L Engine +671
AM/FM Stereo/CD/Tape[Opt on Laredo] +219
Camper/Towing Package +154
Compact Disc Changer +188
Dual Power Seats +283
Heated Front Seats +156
Leather Seats[Opt on Laredo] +364
Locking Differential[Opt on 2WD] +179
Power Drivers Seat[Std on Limited] +188
Power Sunroof +501
Skid Plates +125
Up Country Suspension Group +360

WRANGLER   2001

The Wrangler gets a number of improvements for 2001.

Model Description	Trade-in TMV	Private TMV	Dealer TMV
4 Dr SE Wgn	9156	10083	10939
2 Dr Sport 4WD Utility			
	10508	11572	12554
2 Dr Sport Utility	9862	10860	11782
4 Dr Sport 4WD Wgn	11176	12307	13352
4 Dr Sport Wgn	10266	11305	12265

All models benefit from a new four-ply soft top that reduces wind and road noise at speed. Deep tint windows are now standard on the Sahara hardtop and optional on Sport and SE models with the solid-shell roof. Two new center console designs are available on all models, as is a premium subwoofer. The add-a-trunk feature and removable side steps have been redesigned to improve functionality, and a new instrument cluster, low-pivot steering column, rearview mirror, airbag cutoff switch, child seat-tether anchors, and multifunction headlight/wiper stalk are standard across the entire model line. The ABS system is upgraded; intermittent windshield wipers are now standard, and the 4.0-liter inline six now meets LEV requirements in all 50 states. Sienna Pearl Coat, Amber Fire and Steel Blue exterior colors have been added, while Medium Fern Green and Desert Sand have been dropped.

Category L

Model Description	Trade-in TMV	Private TMV	Dealer TMV
2 Dr SE 4WD Utility	10709	11445	12673
2 Dr Sahara 4WD Utility			
	16433	17563	19447
2 Dr Sport 4WD Utility			
	13176	14082	15593

OPTIONS FOR WRANGLER

AM/FM Stereo Tape[Opt on SE] +201
Air Conditioning +561
Aluminum/Alloy Wheels[Std on Sahara] +311
Anti-Lock Brakes +376
Automatic 3-Speed Transmission +392
Cruise Control +157
Hardtop Roof +474
Locking Differential +179
Premium Sound System +125
Tilt Steering Wheel[Std on Sahara] +122

2000 JEEP

CHEROKEE — 2000

The 2000 Cherokee scores the '99 Grand Cherokee's redesigned 4.0-liter PowerTech inline six in addition to a new five-speed manual transmission. The Limited model sports bright chrome accents, including the front grille, the headlamp surrounds, the side graphics, the rear license-plate brow, and the 16-inch wheels.

Category M

Model Description	Trade-in TMV	Private TMV	Dealer TMV
4 Dr Classic 4WD Wgn	11856	13057	14165
4 Dr Classic Wgn	11134	12261	13302
4 Dr Limited 4WD Wgn	13014	14332	15548
4 Dr Limited Wgn	11908	13114	14227
2 Dr SE 4WD Utility	9274	10213	11080
2 Dr SE Utility	8649	9525	10333
4 Dr SE 4WD Wgn	9942	10949	11878

OPTIONS FOR CHEROKEE

6 cyl 4.0 L Engine[Opt on SE] +623
AM/FM Stereo/CD/Tape +298
Air Conditioning[Std on Limited] +533
Aluminum/Alloy Wheels[Opt on SE,Sport] +154
Anti-Lock Brakes +375
Automatic 3-Speed Transmission +392
Automatic 4-Speed Transmission[Opt on SE,Sport] +592
Camper/Towing Package +154
Cruise Control[Std on Limited 2WD] +156
Heated Front Seats +345
Heated Power Mirrors +109
Infinity Sound System +219
Lighted Entry System[Opt on SE,Sport] +101
Limited Slip Differential +179
Overhead Console[Std on Limited] +147
Power Drivers Seat[Opt on Classic 4] +188
Power Windows[Std on Limited 2WD] +156
Privacy Glass[Std on Limited] +169
Tilt Steering Wheel +97
Trailer Hitch +165

GRAND CHEROKEE — 2000

New exterior cladding has been slapped onto the Laredo, and both models have received interior touch-ups. Two-wheel drive is available with the 4.7-liter V8. Shale Green and Silverstone are the new skin tones.

Category M

Model Description	Trade-in TMV	Private TMV	Dealer TMV
4 Dr Laredo 4WD Wgn	15066	16592	18000
4 Dr Laredo Wgn	14104	15532	16850
4 Dr Limited 4WD Wgn	19318	21274	23080
4 Dr Limited Wgn	17217	18961	20570

OPTIONS FOR GRAND CHEROKEE

8 cyl 4.7 L Engine +671
AM/FM Stereo/CD/Tape[Opt on Laredo] +219
Alarm System[Opt on Laredo] +160
Camper/Towing Package +154
Compact Disc Changer +188
Dual Power Seats[Opt on Laredo] +283
Heated Front Seats +156
Infinity Sound System[Opt on Laredo] +319
Keyless Entry System[Opt on Laredo] +107
Leather Seats[Opt on Laredo] +364
Limited Slip Differential +179
Power Sunroof +502
Quadra-Trac Transfer Case[Opt on Laredo] +345
QuadraDrive Transfer Case[Opt on Laredo] +279
Skid Plates +125
Trailer Hitch +160

Don't forget to refer to the Mileage Adjustment Table at the back of this book!

JEEP 00-99

Model Description	Trade-in TMV	Private TMV	Dealer TMV	Model Description	Trade-in TMV	Private TMV	Dealer TMV

WRANGLER — 2000

A reengineered 4.0-liter PowerTech inline six-cylinder that is more refined and quiet, with reduced emissions, is standard for Sport and Sahara for 2000. Shift quality kicks up a notch, thanks to an all-new five-speed manual transmission. A radio/cassette combo with four speakers is now standard for the Sport, and the Sahara gains a radio/CD. Solar Yellow, Patriot Blue and Silverstone are additional exterior colors.

Category L

Model Description	Trade-in TMV	Private TMV	Dealer TMV
2 Dr SE 4WD Utility	9569	10551	11457
2 Dr Sahara 4WD Utility	14434	15915	17282
2 Dr Sport 4WD Utility	11921	13144	14273

OPTIONS FOR WRANGLER

AM/FM Compact Disc Player[Std on Sahara] +527
AM/FM Stereo Tape[Opt on SE] +201
Air Conditioning +561
Aluminum/Alloy Wheels[Std on Sahara] +311
Anti-Lock Brakes +375
Automatic 3-Speed Transmission +392
Color Match Dual Roofs +875
Cruise Control +156
Hardtop Roof +474
Limited Slip Differential +179
Locking Differential +179
Privacy Glass +255
Steel Wheels +144
Tilt Steering Wheel[Std on Sahara] +122

1999 JEEP

CHEROKEE — 1999

The Cherokee Sport gets a revised front fascia including body-colored grille and bumpers. New exterior colors include Forest Green and Desert Sand, to match the most common Cherokee surroundings.

Category M

Model Description	Trade-in TMV	Private TMV	Dealer TMV
4 Dr Classic 4WD Wgn	9990	11126	12263
4 Dr Classic Wgn	9596	10688	11780
4 Dr Limited 4WD Wgn	10934	12178	13422
4 Dr Limited Wgn	10462	11652	12843
2 Dr SE 4WD Utility	8180	9111	10042
2 Dr SE Utility	7394	8236	9077
4 Dr SE 4WD Wgn	8554	9528	10501
4 Dr SE Wgn	7709	8586	9463
2 Dr Sport 4WD Utility	9282	10338	11394
2 Dr Sport Utility	8593	9571	10549
4 Dr Sport 4WD Wgn	9675	10776	11877
4 Dr Sport Wgn	8888	9900	10911

OPTIONS FOR CHEROKEE

6 cyl 4.0 L Engine[Opt on SE] +509
AM/FM Stereo Tape[Opt on SE] +153
AM/FM Stereo/CD/Tape +243
Air Conditioning[Std on Limited] +435
Aluminum/Alloy Wheels[Opt on SE,Sport] +124
Anti-Lock Brakes +306
Automatic 3-Speed Transmission +318
Automatic 4-Speed Transmission[Opt on SE,Sport] +482
Automatic Locking Hubs (4WD)[Opt on Utility] +203
Camper/Towing Package +124
Cruise Control[Std on Limited] +128
Heated Front Seats +281
Infinity Sound System +179
Locking Differential +145
Overhead Console[Std on Limited] +121
Power Drivers Seat[Std on Limited] +153
Power Windows[Std on Limited] +128
Privacy Glass[Std on Limited] +138
Styled Steel Wheels[Std on SE] +124

GRAND CHEROKEE — 1999

A lot. The new-for-99 Grand Cherokee contains only 127 carryover parts from the current model, and gets a new powertrain, rear suspension, braking and steering systems, 4WD system, interior and exterior styling.

Category M

Model Description	Trade-in TMV	Private TMV	Dealer TMV
4 Dr Laredo 4WD Wgn	13441	14971	16500
4 Dr Laredo Wgn	12097	13473	14850
4 Dr Limited 4WD Wgn	16361	18223	20085
4 Dr Limited Wgn	14316	15945	17574

OPTIONS FOR GRAND CHEROKEE

8 cyl 4.7 L Engine +490
AM/FM Compact Disc Player +152
AM/FM Stereo/CD/Tape[Opt on Laredo] +179
Alarm System[Opt on Laredo] +131
Camper/Towing Package +124
Compact Disc Changer +153
Dual Power Seats[Opt on Laredo] +230
Heated Front Seats +128
Infinity Sound System[Opt on Laredo] +261
Leather Seats[Opt on Laredo] +296
Locking Differential +145
Power Sunroof +409
QuadraDrive Transfer Case[Opt on Laredo] +226
Skid Plates +102
Sunscreen Glass[Opt on Laredo] +141

WRANGLER — 1999

The Wrangler's interior finally enters the '90s with rotary HVAC controls, replacing the old slider control system. The hard or soft top is available in Dark Tan, and new colors decorate both the exterior and the interior.

Category L

Model Description	Trade-in TMV	Private TMV	Dealer TMV
2 Dr SE 4WD Utility	8566	9523	10481
2 Dr Sahara 4WD Utility			

Model Description	Trade-in TMV	Private TMV	Dealer TMV
	12611	14021	15431
2 Dr Sport 4WD Utility			
	10549	11729	12908

OPTIONS FOR WRANGLER

AM/FM Stereo Tape[Std on Sahara] +163
Air Conditioning +458
Aluminum/Alloy Wheels[Std on Sahara] +128
Anti-Lock Brakes +306
Automatic 3-Speed Transmission +318
Color Match Dual Roofs +713
Cruise Control +128
Hardtop Roof +386
Locking Differential +145
Privacy Glass +206
Steel Wheels[Opt on SE] +118
Tilt Steering Wheel +100

1998 JEEP

CHEROKEE   1998

Cherokee Classic and Limited replace the Cherokee Country. A new 2.5-liter four-cylinder engine is now the base engine for the SE, available with an optional three-speed automatic. New colors include Chili Pepper Red, Emerald Green and Deep Amethyst.

Category M

Model Description	Trade-in TMV	Private TMV	Dealer TMV
4 Dr Classic 4WD Wgn	9172	10204	11322
4 Dr Classic Wgn	8545	9507	10548
4 Dr Limited 4WD Wgn	10270	11425	12677
4 Dr Limited Wgn	9564	10640	11806
2 Dr SE 4WD Utility	7369	8198	9096
2 Dr SE Utility	6586	7326	8129
4 Dr SE 4WD Wgn	7674	8538	9473
4 Dr SE Wgn	6899	7675	8516
2 Dr Sport 4WD Utility			
	8122	9036	10026
2 Dr Sport Utility	7691	8557	9494
4 Dr Sport 4WD Wgn	8780	9768	10838
4 Dr Sport Wgn	8027	8930	9908

OPTIONS FOR CHEROKEE

6 cyl 4.0 L Engine[Opt on SE] +463
AM/FM Stereo Tape[Opt on SE] +139
AM/FM Stereo/CD/Tape +221
Air Conditioning[Std on Limited] +395
Aluminum/Alloy Wheels +114
Anti-Lock Brakes +279
Automatic 3-Speed Transmission +309
Automatic 4-Speed Transmission[Opt on SE,Sport] +439
Automatic Locking Hubs (4WD)[Opt on Utility] +184
Camper/Towing Package +141
Cruise Control[Std on Limited] +116
Infinity Sound System +163
Locking Differential +132
Overhead Console[Std on Limited] +109
Power Drivers Seat[Std on Limited] +139

Power Windows[Std on Limited] +116
Privacy Glass[Std on Limited] +125
Sunscreen Glass[Opt on Sport] +125

GRAND CHEROKEE   1998

A 5.9-liter V8 making 245 horsepower and 345 foot-pounds torque powers the Grand Cherokee 5.9 Limited, making it the mightiest of all Jeeps. With the addition of the 5.9, the putrid Orvis model dies. Two new colors and "next-generation" airbags round out the changes.

Category M

Model Description	Trade-in TMV	Private TMV	Dealer TMV
4 Dr 5.9 Limited 4WD Wgn			
	15366	17094	18967
4 Dr Laredo 4WD Wgn	10937	12167	13500
4 Dr Laredo Wgn	10329	11491	12750
4 Dr Limited 4WD Wgn	13954	15524	17225
4 Dr Limited Wgn	12230	13606	15096
4 Dr TSi 4WD Wgn	11760	13083	14516
4 Dr TSi Wgn	10976	12210	13548

OPTIONS FOR GRAND CHEROKEE

8 cyl 5.2 L Engine +409
AM/FM Stereo/CD/Tape[Opt on Laredo] +163
Camper/Towing Package +114
Dual Power Seats[Std on Limited,Limited 5.9] +209
Heated Front Seats[Std on Limited 5.9] +116
Infinity Sound System +237
Leather Seats[Opt on Laredo] +269
Locking Differential[Std on Limited 5.9] +132
Power Sunroof[Std on Limited 5.9] +353
Sunscreen Glass[Opt on Laredo] +128

WRANGLER   1998

Jeep has improved off-road capability by increasing the axle ratio offered with the 4.0-liter engine and revising the torsion bar for better steering. Optional this year are a tilting driver's seat, automatic speed control, a combination CD/cassette stereo, a new Smart Key Immobilizer theft deterrent system and two new colors.

Category L

Model Description	Trade-in TMV	Private TMV	Dealer TMV
2 Dr SE 4WD Utility	7620	8507	9468
2 Dr Sahara 4WD Utility			
	11585	12934	14395
2 Dr Sport 4WD Utility			
	10497	11719	13043

OPTIONS FOR WRANGLER

AM/FM Stereo Tape[Std on Sahara] +149
AM/FM Stereo/CD/Tape +139
Air Conditioning +416
Aluminum/Alloy Wheels[Opt on Sport] +123
Anti-Lock Brakes +279
Automatic 3-Speed Transmission +290

Don't forget to refer to the Mileage Adjustment Table at the back of this book!

Color Match Dual Roofs +649
Cruise Control +116
Hardtop Roof +351
Locking Differential +132
Privacy Glass +188

1997 JEEP

CHEROKEE — 1997

A new interior sporting modern instrumentation debuts. Front and rear styling is refined, and the rear liftgate is now stamped from steel. Multi-plex wiring is designed to improve reliability of the electrical system, while a new paint process aims to polish the finish of all Cherokees.

Category M

Model Description	Trade-in TMV	Private TMV	Dealer TMV
4 Dr Country 4WD Wgn	8123	9105	10306
4 Dr Country Wgn	7667	8595	9728
2 Dr SE 4WD Utility	6073	6807	7705
2 Dr SE Utility	5086	5701	6453
4 Dr SE 4WD Wgn	6301	7063	7994
4 Dr SE Wgn	5845	6552	7416
2 Dr Sport 4WD Utility	6681	7489	8476
2 Dr Sport Utility	6376	7148	8090
4 Dr Sport 4WD Wgn	6984	7829	8861
4 Dr Sport Wgn	6604	7403	8379

OPTIONS FOR CHEROKEE

6 cyl 4.0 L Engine[Opt on SE] +417
AM/FM Stereo Tape[Opt on SE] +126
AM/FM Stereo/CD/Tape +200
Air Conditioning +357
Aluminum/Alloy Wheels[Std on Country] +102
Anti-Lock Brakes +251
Automatic 4-Speed Transmission[Std on Country] +396
Automatic Locking Hubs (4WD) +166
Camper/Towing Package +102
Infinity Sound System +146
Leather Seats +351
Locking Differential +120
Overhead Console +98
Power Drivers Seat +126
Power Windows[Opt on Sport] +94
Privacy Glass +113

GRAND CHEROKEE — 1997

Last year's integrated child safety seat has mysteriously disappeared from press kit and dealer order sheet radar. Other big news is the availability of the optional 5.2-liter V8 engine in 2WD models, and a six-cylinder that qualifies the JGC as a Transitional Low Emissions Vehicle (TLEV) in California. Refinements have been made to the ABS system, entry-level cassette stereo,

and floor carpet fit. In January, a sporty TSi model debuted with monotone paint, special aluminum wheels, and other goodies.

Category M

Model Description	Trade-in TMV	Private TMV	Dealer TMV
4 Dr Laredo 4WD Wgn	9655	10823	12250
4 Dr Laredo Wgn	8473	9498	10750
4 Dr Limited 4WD Wgn	12070	13530	15314
4 Dr Limited Wgn	11311	12679	14351
4 Dr TSi 4WD Wgn	10931	12253	13869
4 Dr TSi Wgn	10097	11318	12810

OPTIONS FOR GRAND CHEROKEE

8 cyl 5.2 L Engine +350
AM/FM Stereo/CD/Tape +146
Automatic Locking Hubs (4WD) +120
Compact Disc Changer +126
Dual Power Seats[Std on Limited] +189
Infinity Sound System[Std orl Limited] +214
Leather Seats[Std on Limited] +243
Limited Slip Differential +120
Locking Differential +120
Power Sunroof +319
Sunscreen Glass[Std on Limited] +113

WRANGLER — 1997

Jeep has totally redesigned this American icon. A Quadra-coil suspension improves on and off-road manners; while dual airbags and optional antilock brakes increase the Wrangler's ability to keep occupants safe. Round, retro-style headlights add a nostalgic touch to this venerable ground-pounder. Fortunately, none of these refinements soften the Wrangler's tough exterior. A restyled interior includes integrated air vents, a glovebox, and car-like stereo controls and accessory switches.

Category L

Model Description	Trade-in TMV	Private TMV	Dealer TMV
2 Dr SE 4WD Utility	7004	7849	8882
2 Dr Sahara 4WD Utility	10017	11226	12703
2 Dr Sport 4WD Utility	8963	10044	11366

OPTIONS FOR WRANGLER

AM/FM Stereo Tape[Std on Sahara] +134
Air Conditioning +376
Aluminum/Alloy Wheels[Opt on Sport] +97
Anti-Lock Brakes +251
Automatic 3-Speed Transmission +262
Hardtop Roof +317
Locking Differential +120
Power Steering[Opt on SE] +126

1996 JEEP

CHEROKEE — 1996

Perennial favorite rolls into 1996 with improved

Model Description	Trade-in TMV	Private TMV	Dealer TMV

engines, new colors, upgraded Selec-Trac four-wheel-drive system, more standard equipment, and the same sheetmetal that it wore on introduction day in 1983.

Category M

Model Description	Trade-in TMV	Private TMV	Dealer TMV
4 Dr Country 4WD Wgn	5583	6311	7317
4 Dr Country Wgn	5362	6062	7028
2 Dr SE 4WD Utility	3967	4484	5199
2 Dr SE Utility	3673	4152	4814
4 Dr SE 4WD Wgn	4345	4912	5695
4 Dr SE Wgn	3893	4401	5102
2 Dr Sport 4WD Utility	4701	5314	6161
2 Dr Sport Utility	4323	4886	5665
4 Dr Sport 4WD Wgn	4921	5563	6450
4 Dr Sport Wgn	4628	5231	6065

OPTIONS FOR CHEROKEE
6 cyl 4.0 L Engine[Opt on SE] +269
AM/FM Stereo/CD/Tape +157
Air Conditioning +276
Anti-Lock Brakes +198
Automatic 4-Speed Transmission +297
Infinity Sound System +116
Leather Seats +276
Off-Road Suspension Package +347
Power Drivers Seat +98

GRAND CHEROKEE — 1996

Jeep turns its flagship into an Explorer killer with dual airbags, revised styling, a better V6 engine, improved front suspension, and an upgraded Selec-Trac four-wheel-drive system. Interiors have been restyled, featuring new luxury doodads and an optional integrated child safety seat. Trim levels are two: Laredo and Limited. The gaudy Orvis continues as an option on the Limited. It's almost perfect; if they could just get rid of that pesky spare tire in the cargo hold.

Category M

Model Description	Trade-in TMV	Private TMV	Dealer TMV
4 Dr Laredo 4WD Wgn	8012	9057	10500
4 Dr Laredo Wgn	7249	8194	9500
4 Dr Limited 4WD Wgn	10284	11625	13478
4 Dr Limited Wgn	8595	9716	11264

OPTIONS FOR GRAND CHEROKEE
8 cyl 5.2 L Engine +287
AM/FM Compact Disc Player[Opt on Laredo] +98
AM/FM Stereo/CD/Tape +116
Dual Power Seats +149
Infinity Sound System[Opt on Laredo] +169
Leather Seats[Opt on Laredo] +190
Power Sunroof +252

1995 JEEP

CHEROKEE — 1995

Driver airbag is added on all models. SE model gets reclining bucket seats.

Category M

Model Description	Trade-in TMV	Private TMV	Dealer TMV
4 Dr Country 4WD Wgn	4517	5105	6086
4 Dr Country Wgn	4302	4862	5796
2 Dr SE 4WD Utility	3192	3608	4301
2 Dr SE Utility	3011	3403	4057
4 Dr SE 4WD Wgn	3510	3967	4729
4 Dr SE Wgn	3117	3523	4200
2 Dr Sport 4WD Utility	3800	4295	5120
2 Dr Sport Utility	3517	3975	4739
4 Dr Sport 4WD Wgn	4087	4620	5507
4 Dr Sport Wgn	3729	4215	5024

OPTIONS FOR CHEROKEE
6 cyl 4.0 L Engine[Opt on SE] +279
Air Conditioning +287
Aluminum/Alloy Wheels[Std on Country] +84
Anti-Lock Brakes +205
Automatic 4-Speed Transmission +308
Automatic Locking Hubs (4WD) +98
Camper/Towing Package +83
Cruise Control +79
Infinity Sound System +120
Leather Seats +285
Limited Slip Differential +98
Off-Road Suspension Package +359
Power Drivers Seat +102

GRAND CHEROKEE — 1995

Rear disc brakes are added to all models. An Orvis trim package is added to the Limited 4WD. New options are an integrated child safety seat and a flip-up liftgate window. Optional V8 engine gets a torque increase. A 2WD Limited model is newly available. A power sunroof is added to the options list.

Category M

Model Description	Trade-in TMV	Private TMV	Dealer TMV
4 Dr Laredo 4WD Wgn	7413	8379	9988
4 Dr Laredo Wgn	6086	6879	8200
4 Dr Limited 4WD Wgn	8461	9563	11400
4 Dr Limited Wgn	7457	8428	10047
4 Dr SE 4WD Wgn	7099	8023	9564
4 Dr SE Wgn	5521	6240	7439

OPTIONS FOR GRAND CHEROKEE
8 cyl 5.2 L Engine +297
AM/FM Compact Disc Player +102
Automatic Locking Hubs (4WD) +98
Camper/Towing Package +84
Dual Power Seats +154
Infinity Sound System[Std on Limited] +175
Leather Seats[Std on Limited] +197
Limited Slip Differential +98
Power Drivers Seat +90
Power Passenger Seat +82
Power Sunroof +261

Don't forget to refer to the Mileage Adjustment Table at the back of this book!

Model Description	Trade-in TMV	Private TMV	Dealer TMV	Model Description	Trade-in TMV	Private TMV	Dealer TMV

WRANGLER 1995

S model can be equipped with new Rio Grande package. Renegade is dropped from lineup. An optional dome light can be attached to the optional sound bar.

Category L

	Trade-in TMV	Private TMV	Dealer TMV
2 Dr Rio Grande 4WD Utility			
	5447	6186	7418
2 Dr S 4WD Utility	4952	5624	6744
2 Dr SE 4WD Utility	6155	6990	8382
2 Dr Sahara 4WD Utility			
	6721	7633	9153

OPTIONS FOR WRANGLER
AM/FM Stereo Tape +109
Air Conditioning +308
Aluminum/Alloy Wheels +79
Anti-Lock Brakes +205
Automatic 3-Speed Transmission +214
Hardtop Roof +259
Locking Differential +98
Rear Heater +128

1994 JEEP

CHEROKEE 1994

Side-door guard beams have been added, and center high-mounted brake light is new. Base model gets SE nomenclature.

Category M

	Trade-in TMV	Private TMV	Dealer TMV
2 Dr Country 4WD Utility			
	3423	3948	4824
2 Dr Country Utility	3081	3554	4342
4 Dr Country 4WD Wgn	3629	4186	5114
4 Dr Country Wgn	3355	3870	4728
2 Dr SE 4WD Utility	2807	3238	3956
2 Dr SE Utility	2328	2685	3281
4 Dr SE 4WD Wgn	2891	3334	4074
4 Dr SE Wgn	2670	3080	3763
2 Dr Sport 4WD Utility			
	2965	3420	4178
2 Dr Sport Utility	2860	3299	4031
4 Dr Sport 4WD Wgn	3392	3913	4781
4 Dr Sport Wgn	2923	3372	4120

OPTIONS FOR CHEROKEE
6 cyl 4.0 L Engine[Opt on SE] +256
Air Conditioning +262
Anti-Lock Brakes +188
Automatic 4-Speed Transmission +281
Automatic Locking Hubs (4WD) +90
Leather Seats +262
Limited Slip Differential +90
Power Drivers Seat +93

GRAND CHEROKEE 1994

Side-door guard beams are added for 1994. Grand Wagoneer trim level is dropped. Base model is now called SE. Limited gets rear disc brakes.

Category M

	Trade-in TMV	Private TMV	Dealer TMV
4 Dr Laredo 4WD Wgn	5464	6302	7700
4 Dr Laredo Wgn	5368	6193	7566
4 Dr Limited 4WD Wgn	7188	8292	10131
4 Dr SE 4WD Wgn	5266	6074	7421
4 Dr SE Wgn	4587	5291	6465

OPTIONS FOR GRAND CHEROKEE
8 cyl 5.2 L Engine +272
AM/FM Compact Disc Player +93
AM/FM Stereo/CD/Tape +110
Automatic 4-Speed Transmission[Std on Limited, 2WD] +276
Automatic Locking Hubs (4WD)[Std on Limited 4WD] +90
Dual Power Seats[Std on Limited] +141
Infinity Sound System +160
Leather Seats[Std on Limited] +181
Limited Slip Differential +90
Power Drivers Seat +82
Power Windows[Opt on SE] +83

WRANGLER 1994

The four-cylinder engine can be saddled with an automatic transmission this year. Base trim is now termed SE. Center high-mounted brake light is added.

Category L

	Trade-in TMV	Private TMV	Dealer TMV
2 Dr Renegade 4WD Utility			
	6154	7097	8668
2 Dr S 4WD Utility	3966	4574	5586
2 Dr SE 4WD Utility	4992	5757	7031
2 Dr Sahara 4WD Utility			
	5608	6466	7898
2 Dr Sport 4WD Utility			
	5265	6072	7416

OPTIONS FOR WRANGLER
AM/FM Stereo Tape +100
Air Conditioning +281
Anti-Lock Brakes +189
Automatic 3-Speed Transmission +197
Hardtop Roof +237
Locking Differential +90

1993 JEEP

CHEROKEE 1993

Lineup is shuffled to make room for Grand Cherokee. Country trim replaces Limited. Base prices fall substantially, but models are decontented to achieve lower price.

Category M

	Trade-in TMV	Private TMV	Dealer TMV
2 Dr STD 4WD Utility	2153	2531	3162

Don't forget to refer to the Mileage Adjustment Table at the back of this book!

Model Description	Trade-in TMV	Private TMV	Dealer TMV
2 Dr STD Utility	1696	1994	2491
4 Dr STD 4WD Wgn	2212	2601	3249
4 Dr STD Wgn	2045	2404	3003
2 Dr Country 4WD Utility			
	2674	3145	3928
2 Dr Country Utility	2479	2915	3641
4 Dr Country 4WD Wgn	2936	3452	4312
4 Dr Country Wgn	2551	3000	3747
2 Dr Sport 4WD Utility			
	2235	2627	3282
2 Dr Sport Utility	2205	2593	3239
4 Dr Sport 4WD Wgn	2537	2983	3726
4 Dr Sport Wgn	2221	2611	3262

OPTIONS FOR CHEROKEE

6 cyl 4.0 L Engine[Opt on STD] +218
Air Conditioning +225
Anti-Lock Brakes +161
Automatic 4-Speed Transmission +241
Off-Road Suspension Package +181
Power Drivers Seat +79

GRAND CHEROKEE   1993

Introduced in April, 1992, Grand Cherokee gets a V8-engine option and a Grand Wagoneer model that includes the V8 and fake-wood siding. Late in the year, 2WD models in Base and Laredo trim are introduced. A driver airbag and ABS that works in 2WD or 4WD are standard.

Category M

	Trade-in	Private	Dealer
4 Dr STD 4WD Wgn	3718	4372	5461
4 Dr STD Wgn	3523	4142	5174
4 Dr Laredo 4WD Wgn	4732	5564	6950
4 Dr Laredo Wgn	4153	4883	6100
4 Dr Limited 4WD Wgn	6263	7363	9198

OPTIONS FOR GRAND CHEROKEE

8 cyl 5.2 L Engine +233
AM/FM Compact Disc Player +79
Air Conditioning[Std on Limited] +225
Automatic 4-Speed Transmission[Std on Limited, 2WD] +236
Leather Seats[Opt on Laredo] +155

GRAND WAGONEER   1993

Category N

	Trade-in	Private	Dealer
4 Dr STD 4WD Wgn	4881	5739	7169

WRANGLER   1993

ABS that works in both two- and four-wheel drive is newly optional with six-cylinder engines. Islander model disappears. Other changes include a stainless steel exhaust system, tamper-resistant odometer, and tinted plastic windows for the convertible. Sport package includes new graphics and five-spoke steel wheels.

Model Description	Trade-in TMV	Private TMV	Dealer TMV
Category L			
2 Dr STD 4WD Utility	3811	4479	5593
2 Dr Renegade 4WD Utility			
	4927	5792	7232
2 Dr S 4WD Utility	3154	3707	4629
2 Dr Sahara 4WD Utility			
	4467	5251	6557

OPTIONS FOR WRANGLER

6 cyl 4.0 L Engine[Opt on S, STD] +222
AM/FM Stereo Tape +86
Air Conditioning +241
Anti-Lock Brakes +161
Automatic 3-Speed Transmission +168
Hardtop Roof +203
Option Package +264
Sport Package +336

1992 JEEP

CHEROKEE   1992

Sport models gain a glass sunroof option, while Laredos get vent windows. All radios now have an integral digital clock. Leather upholstery is available on Laredo for the first time. Detachable cupholders are added to the center console.

	Trade-in	Private	Dealer
Category M			
2 Dr STD 4WD Utility	1798	2164	2776
2 Dr STD Utility	1557	1875	2405
4 Dr STD 4WD Wgn	2033	2448	3140
4 Dr STD Wgn	1744	2101	2694
4 Dr Briarwood 4WD Wgn			
	3052	3676	4714
2 Dr Laredo 4WD Utility			
	2093	2520	3232
4 Dr Laredo 4WD Wgn	2242	2700	3463
4 Dr Laredo Wgn	2088	2515	3225
4 Dr Limited 4WD Wgn	3177	3825	4906
2 Dr Sport 4WD Utility			
	1869	2250	2886
4 Dr Sport 4WD Wgn	2169	2611	3349
4 Dr Sport Wgn	1815	2186	2803

OPTIONS FOR CHEROKEE

6 cyl 4.0 L Engine[Opt on Laredo, Sport, STD] +193
Air Conditioning[Opt on Laredo, Sport, STD] +199
Anti-Lock Brakes +142
Automatic 4-Speed Transmission[Opt on Laredo, Sport, STD] +213
Leather Seats[Opt on Laredo, Sport, STD] +197
Off-Road Package +131
Sport Package +226
Sunroof +167

Model Description	Trade-in TMV	Private TMV	Dealer TMV

COMANCHE — 1992

Sport option group debuts. Radios have digital clocks. Detachable cupholders are added to center console.

Category J

Model Description	Trade-in TMV	Private TMV	Dealer TMV
2 Dr STD 4WD Std Cab LB	2077	2528	3279
2 Dr STD Std Cab LB	1503	1829	2372
2 Dr STD 4WD Std Cab SB	1983	2413	3130
2 Dr STD Std Cab SB	1382	1682	2182
2 Dr Eliminator 4WD Std Cab LB	2464	2998	3889
2 Dr Eliminator Std Cab LB	2028	2469	3202
2 Dr Eliminator 4WD Std Cab SB	2464	2998	3889
2 Dr Eliminator Std Cab SB	2028	2469	3202
2 Dr Pioneer 4WD Std Cab LB	2344	2852	3700
2 Dr Pioneer Std Cab LB	1923	2341	3036
2 Dr Pioneer 4WD Std Cab SB	2284	2779	3605
2 Dr Pioneer Std Cab SB	1648	2005	2601
2 Dr Sport 4WD Std Cab LB	2163	2633	3415
2 Dr Sport Std Cab LB	1610	1959	2541
2 Dr Sport 4WD Std Cab SB	2037	2479	3216
2 Dr Sport Std Cab SB	1610	1959	2541

OPTIONS FOR COMANCHE

6 cyl 4.0 L Engine +145
Air Conditioning +190
Automatic 4-Speed Transmission +190
Off-Road Package +131

WRANGLER — 1992

Three-point seatbelts anchored to the roll bar are added. New colors round out the changes.

Category L

Model Description	Trade-in TMV	Private TMV	Dealer TMV
2 Dr STD 4WD Utility	2680	3227	4137
2 Dr Islander 4WD Utility	2805	3377	4330
2 Dr Renegade 4WD Utility	3429	4127	5292
2 Dr S 4WD Utility	2119	2551	3271
2 Dr Sahara 4WD Utility	3241	3902	5003

OPTIONS FOR WRANGLER

6 cyl 4.0 L Engine +196
AM/FM Stereo Tape +77
Air Conditioning +213
Automatic 3-Speed Transmission +148
Hardtop Roof +180

Don't forget to refer to the Mileage Adjustment Table at the back of this book!

KIA
S. Korea

1997 Kia Sephia

2001 KIA

OPTIMA   2001

Kia joins the high-stakes poker game that is the midsize sedan market with the all-new Optima. Available in four- and six-cylinder models and two trim levels, the Optima offers a loaded deck of standard features, including air conditioning, side airbags, four-wheel independent suspension and power windows, locks and mirrors.

Category C

Model Description	Trade-in TMV	Private TMV	Dealer TMV
4 Dr LX Sdn	9246	10107	11543
4 Dr LX V6 Sdn	10843	11853	13537
4 Dr SE Sdn	10453	11427	13050
4 Dr SE V6 Sdn	11681	12769	14583

OPTIONS FOR OPTIMA
AM/FM Stereo/CD/Tape[Opt on LX,LX V6] +337
Anti-Lock Brakes[Opt on V6] +450
Automatic 4-Speed Transmission[Std on V6] +482
Cruise Control[Opt on LX] +142
Leather Seats[Opt on SE,SE V6] +564

RIO   2001

With a base MSRP that makes it the least expensive car in America, the roomy little Rio is a peppy 96-horsepower entry-level sedan. While the design of and materials used on this car are nothing to write home about, build quality is impressively tight. And Kia's new Long Haul Warranty Program offers the added security of a 10-year/100,000-mile limited powertrain warranty, along with impressive levels of bumper-to-bumper and roadside assistance coverage.

Category A

Model Description	Trade-in TMV	Private TMV	Dealer TMV
4 Dr STD Sdn	5561	6115	7039

OPTIONS FOR RIO
AM/FM Compact Disc Player +224
AM/FM Stereo Tape +181
Air Conditioning +425
Aluminum/Alloy Wheels +178
Anti-Lock Brakes +227
Automatic 4-Speed Transmission +496

SEPHIA   2001

The 2001 Sephia features new safety items such as child seat anchors, front seatbelt pre-tensioners and an emergency internal trunk release. Changes for the 2001 model year also include dual visor vanity mirrors, a coin tray and a gas-cap tether.

Category B

Model Description	Trade-in TMV	Private TMV	Dealer TMV
4 Dr LS Sdn	6585	7262	8389
4 Dr STD Sdn	5764	6356	7343

OPTIONS FOR SEPHIA
AM/FM Compact Disc Player +167
Air Conditioning +510
Aluminum/Alloy Wheels +193
Automatic 4-Speed Transmission +552
Compact Disc Changer +190
Cruise Control +142
Keyless Entry System[Opt on LS] +142

SPECTRA   2001

2001 sees few changes to Kia's sporty five-door hatchback, which was introduced last year to attract younger customers to the brand. The top-rung GSX trim level gets a gas-cap tether, coin holder and dual visor vanity mirrors. Kia's Long Haul Warranty Program has also been introduced for this model year.

Category B

Model Description	Trade-in TMV	Private TMV	Dealer TMV
4 Dr GS Hbk	6727	7418	8570
4 Dr GSX Hbk	7993	8814	10182

OPTIONS FOR SPECTRA
AM/FM Compact Disc Player +167
Air Conditioning[Opt on GS] +510
Anti-Lock Brakes +453
Automatic 4-Speed Transmission +552
Compact Disc Changer +190
Cruise Control +142
Keyless Entry System +142

SPORTAGE   2001

Kia's Long-Haul warranty, introduced late in model-year 2000, provides powertrain coverage for 10 years or 100,000 miles, while a new Limited trim level includes lots of standard goodies over the already well-equipped Base and EX versions.

Category L

Model Description	Trade-in TMV	Private TMV	Dealer TMV
4 Dr EX 4WD Wgn	10409	11324	12850
4 Dr EX Wgn	9778	10638	12072

Don't forget to refer to the Mileage Adjustment Table at the back of this book!

KIA 01-99

Model Description	Trade-in TMV	Private TMV	Dealer TMV
2 Dr STD 4WD Conv	8835	9613	10908
2 Dr STD Conv	8461	9206	10446
4 Dr STD 4WD Wgn	9544	10384	11783
4 Dr STD Wgn	8974	9763	11079

OPTIONS FOR SPORTAGE
AM/FM Compact Disc Player[Std on EX] +269
AM/FM Stereo Tape +181
Air Conditioning[Std on EX] +510
Aluminum/Alloy Wheels[Std on EX] +193
Anti-Lock Brakes +278
Automatic 4-Speed Transmission[Std on CONV] +567
Compact Disc Changer +190
Cruise Control[Opt on STD] +142
Leather Seats +482

2000 KIA

SEPHIA — 2000
The Sephia has improved seat fabric, a new audio system and two new colors for 2000.

Category B			
4 Dr STD Sdn	4247	4908	5519
4 Dr LS Sdn	4670	5398	6069

OPTIONS FOR SEPHIA
AM/FM Compact Disc Player +269
AM/FM Stereo Tape +181
Air Conditioning +510
Alarm System +110
Aluminum/Alloy Wheels +193
Anti-Lock Brakes +453
Automatic 4-Speed Transmission +552
Cruise Control +142
Power Door Locks +113
Power Steering[Std on LS] +147
Power Windows +198
Rear Spoiler +99

SPECTRA — 2000
The Spectra is new for 2000. Similar in size to the Sephia, Kia hopes the Spectra will attract younger buyers due to the versatile four-door hatchback design and sportier styling.

Category B			
4 Dr GS Sdn	5214	6026	6776
4 Dr GSX Sdn	5694	6580	7399

OPTIONS FOR SPECTRA
AM/FM Compact Disc Player +167
Air Conditioning[Opt on GS] +510
Anti-Lock Brakes +453
Automatic 4-Speed Transmission +563
Compact Disc Changer +223
Cruise Control +142
Keyless Entry System +104
Power Mirrors +99
Rear Spoiler[Opt on GS] +142

SPORTAGE — 2000
Kia ushers in the 2000 Sportage with a new sound system, dual airbags, new colors and some additional equipment, but keeps last year's MSRP.

Category L			
2 Dr STD 4WD Conv	7431	8459	9408
2 Dr STD Conv	7043	8018	8917
4 Dr STD 4WD Wgn	7876	8966	9972
4 Dr STD Wgn	7590	8640	9609
4 Dr EX 4WD Wgn	8522	9701	10789
4 Dr EX Wgn	7940	9039	10053

OPTIONS FOR SPORTAGE
AM/FM Compact Disc Player[Std on EX] +269
AM/FM Stereo Tape +167
AM/FM Stereo/CD/Tape +269
Air Conditioning[Std on EX] +510
Aluminum/Alloy Wheels[Std on EX] +193
Anti-Lock Brakes +278
Automatic 4-Speed Transmission[Std on CONV] +567
Compact Disc Changer +223
Leather Seats +482
Luggage Rack[Std on EX] +110
Rear Spoiler +107

1999 KIA

SEPHIA — 1999
The Sephia was entirely redesigned in '98 and enters '99 essentially unchanged.

Category B			
4 Dr STD Sdn	3501	4099	4697
4 Dr LS Sdn	3928	4598	5269

OPTIONS FOR SEPHIA
AM/FM Compact Disc Player +219
AM/FM Stereo Tape +148
Air Conditioning +414
Alarm System +90
Aluminum/Alloy Wheels +156
Anti-Lock Brakes +368
Automatic 4-Speed Transmission +449
Cruise Control +115
Leather Seats +253
Power Door Locks +92
Power Steering[Std on LS] +120
Power Windows +160

SPORTAGE — 1999
A new two-door convertible model joins the four-door Sportage in 1999. The convertible comes in either a 4x2 layout with automatic transmission or a 4x4 layout with five-speed manual transmission. It also boasts dual front airbags and a driver's side front knee bag.

Don't forget to refer to the Mileage Adjustment Table at the back of this book!

Model Description	Trade-in TMV	Private TMV	Dealer TMV
Category L			
2 Dr STD 4WD Conv	6638	7603	8569
2 Dr STD Conv	6188	7088	7988
4 Dr STD 4WD Wgn	6827	7821	8814
4 Dr STD Wgn	6724	7702	8680
4 Dr EX 4WD Wgn	7564	8664	9765
4 Dr EX Wgn	6976	7991	9006

OPTIONS FOR SPORTAGE

AM/FM Compact Disc Player[Std on EX] +219
AM/FM Stereo Tape[Opt on STD] +136
Air Conditioning[Std on EX] +414
Aluminum/Alloy Wheels[Std on EX, 4WD] +156
Anti-Lock Brakes +226
Automatic 4-Speed Transmission +459
Leather Seats +391
Luggage Rack[Std on EX] +90

1998 KIA

SEPHIA   1998

The Sephia is totally redesigned for 1998.

Category B			
4 Dr STD Sdn	2642	3207	3819
4 Dr LS Sdn	3041	3691	4396

OPTIONS FOR SEPHIA

AM/FM Compact Disc Player +192
AM/FM Stereo Tape[Std on GS] +129
Air Conditioning +364
Aluminum/Alloy Wheels +137
Anti-Lock Brakes +324
Automatic 4-Speed Transmission +394
Cruise Control +101
Power Steering[Opt on STD] +106
Power Windows[Opt on LS] +142

SPORTAGE   1998

There are lots of improvements this year for the Sportage, including a new grille, new alloy wheels, tilt steering wheel, passenger-side airbag, better brakes, improved air conditioning and four-wheel ABS that replaces last year's rear-wheel ABS.

Category L			
4 Dr STD 4WD Wgn	6331	7296	8341
4 Dr STD Wgn	5766	6645	7597
4 Dr EX 4WD Wgn	7120	8205	9381
4 Dr EX Wgn	6480	7467	8537

OPTIONS FOR SPORTAGE

AM/FM Compact Disc Player +192
Air Conditioning +364
Aluminum/Alloy Wheels[Std on EX, 4WD] +137
Anti-Lock Brakes +199
Automatic 4-Speed Transmission +404
Leather Seats +364

1997 KIA

SEPHIA   1997

RS models get body-color bumpers this year, and a tan interior is newly available with black exterior paint.

Category B			
4 Dr GS Sdn	2105	2660	3337
4 Dr LS Sdn	1925	2432	3051
4 Dr RS Sdn	1738	2195	2754

OPTIONS FOR SEPHIA

AM/FM Compact Disc Player +155
AM/FM Stereo Tape[Std on GS] +104
Air Conditioning +284
Aluminum/Alloy Wheels[Opt on GS] +110
Anti-Lock Brakes +261
Automatic 4-Speed Transmission +285

SPORTAGE   1997

An automatic transmission is offered on 2WD models, and the EX trim level is available in 2WD for the first time. Power door locks, a theft deterrent system, and a spare tire carrier are all standard on all Sportages for 1997. A new option is a CD player. Sportage gets a new grille. A tan interior can be combined with black paint for the first time. Base 2WD models lose their standard alloy wheels.

Category L			
4 Dr STD 4WD Wgn	5128	6002	7070
4 Dr STD Wgn	4659	5453	6423
4 Dr EX 4WD Wgn	5320	6227	7335
4 Dr EX Wgn	4939	5780	6809

OPTIONS FOR SPORTAGE

AM/FM Compact Disc Player +155
AM/FM Stereo Tape +96
Air Conditioning +293
Aluminum/Alloy Wheels[Opt on STD Wgn] +110
Automatic 4-Speed Transmission +326
Leather Seats +326

1996 KIA

SEPHIA   1996

Styling and suspension tweaks, dual airbags, and new twin-cam motors appeared with the introduction of the 1995.5 Sephia. These improvements, along with interior revisions and improved equipment levels, make the Kia more competitive in the compact sedan marketplace. Sephia now meets 1997 side-impact standards, and GS models can be equipped with antilock brakes. Sephia comes with 5 year/60,000 mile powertrain coverage.

Don't forget to refer to the Mileage Adjustment Table at the back of this book!

Model Description	Trade-in TMV	Private TMV	Dealer TMV
Category B			
4 Dr GS Sdn	1661	2194	2931
4 Dr LS Sdn	1536	2030	2712
4 Dr RS Sdn	1370	1810	2418

OPTIONS FOR SEPHIA
AM/FM Stereo Tape[Std on GS] +97
Air Conditioning +263
Aluminum/Alloy Wheels[Opt on GS] +103
Anti-Lock Brakes[Opt on GS] +242
Automatic 4-Speed Transmission +302

SPORTAGE   1996

The world's first knee airbag arrives in conjunction with a driver airbag, and a two-wheel drive edition is available this year. A spirited twin-cam engine arrived late in 1995, and cured Sportage's power ills.

Category L			
4 Dr STD 4WD Wgn	3800	4549	5583
4 Dr STD Wgn	3436	4114	5049
4 Dr EX 4WD Wgn	4084	4889	6000
4 Dr EX Wgn	4807	5755	7063

OPTIONS FOR SPORTAGE
4 cyl 2.0 L DOHC Engine +181
Air Conditioning +272
Automatic 4-Speed Transmission +302
Leather Seats +302

1995 KIA

SEPHIA   1995

Oh no, another Korean manufacturer trying to break into the American market. But wait, this one is actually worth considering; a lot of help from Mazda and Ford mean that this little upstart is actually making fairly reliable little cars. The Sephia has plenty of Mazda parts and Kia has a long history of building durable, cheap cars.

Category B			
4 Dr GS Sdn	1252	1622	2238
1995.5 4 Dr GS Sdn	1276	1653	2281
4 Dr LS Sdn	1146	1485	2049
1995.5 4 Dr LS Sdn	1172	1518	2094
4 Dr RS Sdn	1031	1335	1842
1995.5 4 Dr RS Sdn	1079	1397	1928

OPTIONS FOR SEPHIA
AM/FM Stereo Tape[Opt on GS] +74
AM/FM Stereo Tape[Opt on GS] +74
Air Conditioning +201
Air Conditioning +201
Aluminum/Alloy Wheels[Opt on GS] +79
Aluminum/Alloy Wheels[Opt on GS] +79
Automatic 4-Speed Transmission +203
Automatic 4-Speed Transmission +203
Dual Air Bag Restraints +139

SPORTAGE   1995

Another mini-SUV is introduced, competing with everything from the Jeep Cherokee to the Geo Tracker. The Sportage offers comfortable seating for four, ample storage space, and available four-wheel drive. Designed with Ford and Mazda, with suspension tuning by Lotus, the Sportage should provide a good deal of fun and durability.

Category L			
4 Dr STD 4WD Wgn	2758	3365	4376
4 Dr STD Wgn	2497	3046	3962
4 Dr EX 4WD Wgn	3164	3860	5020

OPTIONS FOR SPORTAGE
4 cyl 2.0 L DOHC Engine +139
Air Conditioning +209
Automatic 4-Speed Transmission +232
Leather Seats +197

1994 KIA

SEPHIA   1994

New subcompact sedan from South Korea based on 1990-1994 Mazda Protege platform and powered by a 1.6-liter, 88-horsepower four-cylinder engine. Sold only in the western and southwestern regions of the U.S.

Category B			
4 Dr GS Sdn	946	1322	1948
4 Dr LS Sdn	865	1209	1781
4 Dr RS Sdn	794	1109	1634

OPTIONS FOR SEPHIA
Air Conditioning +159
Automatic 4-Speed Transmission +161

Don't forget to refer to the Mileage Adjustment Table at the back of this book!

LAND ROVER 01-99

| Model Description | Trade-in TMV | Private TMV | Dealer TMV | Model Description | Trade-in TMV | Private TMV | Dealer TMV |

LAND ROVER Britain

1995 Land Rover Discovery

2001 LAND ROVER

DISCOVERY SERIES II   2001

Land Rover introduces three new trim levels to the Discovery Series II lineup — SD, LE and SE. New paint options are Oslo Blue and Bonatti Gray.

Category O

	Trade-in	Private	Dealer
4 Dr LE 4WD Wgn	24365	25402	27132
4 Dr SD 4WD Wgn	24066	25091	26799
4 Dr SE 4WD Wgn	26236	27353	29216

OPTIONS FOR DISCOVERY SERIES II
Automatic Load Leveling +488
Automatic Stability Control[Opt on SE] +325
Dual Sunroofs +976
Heated Front Seats +325
Rear Air Conditioning w/Rear Heater +488
Special Factory Paint +195
Third Seat +781

RANGE ROVER   2001

Land Rover's venerable Range Rover will now come standard with a 4.6-liter V8 engine. A navigation system is now standard on the 4.6 HSE model and optional on the 4.6 SE, as is a new premium audio system. New exterior colors are Oslo Blue and Bonatti Grey.

Category O

	Trade-in	Private	Dealer
4 Dr 4.6 HSE AWD Wgn	47145	49153	52500
4 Dr 4.0 SE AWD Wgn	41757	43536	46500

OPTIONS FOR RANGE ROVER
Navigation System +1949
Special Factory Paint +195

2000 LAND ROVER

DISCOVERY SERIES II   2000

The Discovery was completely redesigned last year and sees only minor interior trim revisions for the 2000 model year.

Category O

	Trade-in	Private	Dealer
4 Dr Series II AWD Wgn	21610	22940	24169

OPTIONS FOR DISCOVERY SERIES II
Compact Disc Changer +407
Dual Air Conditioning +487
Dual Power Seats +440
Dual Sunroofs +976
Heated Front Seats +325
Leather Seats +635
Luggage Rack +98
Performance Package +1793
Rear Seat Package +879
Special Factory Paint +195

RANGE ROVER   2000

The 2000 Range Rover now qualifies as a low-emissions vehicle. Interior and exterior upgrades improve the vehicle's look and feel, and new trim levels allow buyers to further dress up their Range Rover's appearance

Category O

	Trade-in	Private	Dealer
4 Dr 4.0 SE AWD Wgn	34706	36844	38817
4 Dr 4.6 HSE AWD Wgn	41474	44028	46386
4 Dr 4.6 Vitesse AWD Wgn	41910	44491	46874
4 Dr County AWD Wgn	33616	35686	37597

OPTIONS FOR RANGE ROVER
Luggage Rack[Opt on County] +163
Navigation System +1851
Special Factory Paint +195

1999 LAND ROVER

DISCOVERY   1999

The release of the 1999 Discovery Series II sees the first engineering redesign since the vehicle's European introduction 11 years ago. Traction Control, Active Cornering Enhancement and Hill Descent Control are new standard features.

Category O

	Trade-in	Private	Dealer
4 Dr SD AWD Wgn	18261	19699	21136
4 Dr Series II AWD Wgn	18981	20475	21969

OPTIONS FOR DISCOVERY
Compact Disc Changer +308

Don't forget to refer to the Mileage Adjustment Table at the back of this book!

Model Description	Trade-in TMV	Private TMV	Dealer TMV

Dual Air Conditioning +370
Dual Power Seats[Std on SD] +333
Dual Sunroofs +741
Heated Front Seats +247
Leather Seats[Std on SD] +481
Performance Package +1359
Rear Jump Seats +617
Rear Seat Package +863
Special Factory Paint +148

RANGE ROVER   1999

Engine upgrades, new color schemes, traction control and standard side-mounted airbags are some of the additions to the 1999 Range Rovers, which will be introduced later in the year. For now, interim Range Rover models called the 4.0 and 4.0S are available.

Category O

Model	Trade-in	Private	Dealer
4 Dr 4.0 AWD Wgn	27214	29357	31499
4 Dr 4.0 S AWD Wgn	27214	29357	31499
4 Dr 4.0 SE AWD Wgn	27449	29609	31770
4 Dr 4.6 HSE AWD Wgn	32955	35549	38143

OPTIONS FOR RANGE ROVER
Navigation System +1123
Special Factory Paint +148

1998 LAND ROVER

DISCOVERY   1998

Changes to the Discovery include interior trim enhancements for the LE and LSE. The rearview mirror also features map lights for the first time.

Category O

Model	Trade-in	Private	Dealer
4 Dr 50TH Anniversary AWD Wgn			
	16913	18452	20120
4 Dr LE AWD Wgn	15486	16896	18423
4 Dr LSE AWD Wgn	16098	17564	19151

OPTIONS FOR DISCOVERY
Compact Disc Changer[Opt on LE] +272
Dual Air Conditioning +327
Rear Jump Seats +544
Special Factory Paint +130

RANGE ROVER   1998

Range Rover models get a new Harmon Kardon audio system this year. Other changes include a new upholstery stitch pattern and a leather-wrapped gearshift knob.

Category O

Model	Trade-in	Private	Dealer
4 Dr 4.0 SE AWD Wgn	23293	25413	27710
4 Dr 4.6 HSE AWD Wgn	27509	30013	32726
4 Dr 50TH Anniversary AWD Wgn			
	23876	26050	28404

OPTIONS FOR RANGE ROVER

Special Factory Paint +130

1997 LAND ROVER

DEFENDER 90   1997

After a one-year hiatus, Defender 90 returns in convertible and hardtop bodystyles. A 4.0-liter V8 engine is standard, mated to a ZF four-speed automatic transmission. A redesigned center console includes cupholders, and hardtops have new interior trim. Convertibles get improved top sealing, while all Defender 90s are treated to fresh paint colors.

Category O

Model	Trade-in	Private	Dealer
2 Dr STD 4WD Conv	27791	30543	33907
2 Dr STD 4WD Utility	28177	30968	34378

OPTIONS FOR DEFENDER 90
Air Conditioning +570
Special Factory Paint +142

DISCOVERY   1997

A diversity antenna is added, and all interiors are trimmed with polished burled walnut. The sunroof has darker tinting, the airbag system benefits from simplified operation, and engine management is improved. Three new exterior colors debut: Oxford Blue, Rioja Red and Charleston Green.

Category O

Model	Trade-in	Private	Dealer
4 Dr LSE AWD Wgn	13286	14601	16209
4 Dr SD AWD Wgn	11699	12857	14273
4 Dr SE AWD Wgn	13004	14291	15865
4 Dr SE7 AWD Wgn	14079	15473	17177
4 Dr XD AWD Wgn	12438	13670	15175

OPTIONS FOR DISCOVERY
Compact Disc Changer +297
Dual Power Seats[Opt on SD] +321
Leather Seats[Opt on SD] +463
Rear Jump Seats[Std on SE7] +558
Special Factory Paint +142

RANGE ROVER   1997

4.0 SE gets three new exterior colors (Oxford Blue, Rioja Red and White Gold, all matched to Saddle leather interior), a HomeLink transmitter, and jeweled wheel center caps. The 4.6 HSE gets three new exterior colors (British Racing Green, Monza Red, AA Yellow), one new interior color (Lightstone with contrasting piping), and a leather shift handle.

Category O

Model	Trade-in	Private	Dealer
4 Dr 4.0 SE AWD Wgn	18334	20150	22369
4 Dr 4.6 HSE AWD Wgn	22803	25061	27821

OPTIONS FOR RANGE ROVER
Kensington Interior Package +1352
Special Factory Paint +142

Don't forget to refer to the Mileage Adjustment Table at the back of this book!

Model Description	Trade-in TMV	Private TMV	Dealer TMV

Vitesse Package +332

1996 LAND ROVER

DISCOVERY 1996

Three new trim levels, a revised engine that gets better around-town fuel economy, new colors, increased seat travel, and new power seats sum up the changes for 1996.

Category O

Model	Trade-in	Private	Dealer
4 Dr SD AWD Wgn	10090	11134	12577
4 Dr SE AWD Wgn	10672	11777	13303
4 Dr SE7 AWD Wgn	10865	11990	13544

OPTIONS FOR DISCOVERY
AM/FM Stereo/CD/Tape +119
Automatic 4-Speed Transmission[Std on SE] +393
Compact Disc Changer +214
Leather Seats[Opt on SD] +333
Special Factory Paint[Opt on SD] +102
Third Seat[Std on SE7] +205

RANGE ROVER 1996

Base 4.0 SE model is unchanged for 1996. A new, more powerful 4.6 HSE model debuts, giving buyers extra horsepower, fat wheels and tires, mud flaps, and chrome exhaust for a $7,000 premium over the 4.0 SE.

Category O

Model	Trade-in	Private	Dealer
4 Dr 4.0 SE AWD Wgn	14850	16388	18511
4 Dr 4.6 HSE AWD Wgn	18433	20341	22977

OPTIONS FOR RANGE ROVER
AM/FM Compact Disc Player +171
Special Factory Paint +102

1995 LAND ROVER

DEFENDER 1995

Category O

Model	Trade-in	Private	Dealer
2 Dr STD 4WD Utility	19373	21558	25200

OPTIONS FOR DEFENDER
Air Conditioning +455
Aluminum/Alloy Wheels +587
Special Factory Paint +132

DISCOVERY 1995

Category O

Model	Trade-in	Private	Dealer
4 Dr STD AWD Wgn	8572	9539	11151

OPTIONS FOR DISCOVERY
AM/FM Compact Disc Player +189
Automatic 4-Speed Transmission +341
Dual Air Conditioning +284
Dual Sunroofs +568
Jump Seat +95
Leather Jump Seat +189

Leather Seats +370
Special Factory Paint +114

RANGE ROVER 1995

The new 4.0 SE is introduced as a late '95 model. Styling is an evolution of the classic Range Rover look. A new chassis sports an electronic air suspension and a 4.0-liter V8 that produces 190 horse-power. This top-of-the-line SUV also includes luxuries such as the obligatory leather and wood trimmed cabin and a premium stereo with a 6-disc CD changer.

Category O

Model	Trade-in	Private	Dealer
4 Dr 4.0 SE AWD Wgn	12388	13785	16114
4 Dr County Classic AWD Wgn	10440	11618	13581
4 Dr County LWB AWD Wgn	11032	12276	14350

1994 LAND ROVER

DEFENDER 1994

Category O

Model	Trade-in	Private	Dealer
2 Dr 90 4WD Utility	18578	20987	25000

OPTIONS FOR DEFENDER
Air Conditioning +456
Aluminum/Alloy Wheels +589
Hardtop Roof +570
Premium Soft Top Package +380

DISCOVERY 1994

Category O

Model	Trade-in	Private	Dealer
4 Dr STD AWD Wgn	7568	8549	10184

OPTIONS FOR DISCOVERY
Automatic 4-Speed Transmission +342
Dual Air Conditioning +285
Dual Sunroofs +570
Leather Seats +371
Rear Jump Seats +447
Special Factory Paint +114

RANGE ROVER 1994

Category O

Model	Trade-in	Private	Dealer
4 Dr County LWB AWD Wgn	8918	10074	12000
4 Dr County SWB AWD Wgn	8205	9268	11041

OPTIONS FOR RANGE ROVER
Black Sable Edition +399

1993 LAND ROVER

DEFENDER 1993

Category O

Model	Trade-in	Private	Dealer
4 Dr STD 4WD Wgn	16672	19232	23500

Don't forget to refer to the Mileage Adjustment Table at the back of this book!

Model Description	Trade-in TMV	Private TMV	Dealer TMV	Model Description	Trade-in TMV	Private TMV	Dealer TMV

OPTIONS FOR DEFENDER
AM/FM Stereo Tape +144

RANGE ROVER   1993

Category O

Model Description	Trade-in TMV	Private TMV	Dealer TMV
4 Dr County AWD Wgn	6454	7445	9097
4 Dr LWB AWD Wgn	7008	8084	9878

OPTIONS FOR RANGE ROVER
Chrome Wheels +158
Compact Disc Changer +173
Running Boards +72
Special Factory Paint +86

1992 LAND ROVER

RANGE ROVER   1992

Category O

Model Description	Trade-in TMV	Private TMV	Dealer TMV
4 Dr STD AWD Wgn	4944	5776	7163
4 Dr County AWD Wgn	5387	6294	7806
4 Dr LSE AWD Wgn	5070	5923	7346

Don't forget to refer to the Mileage Adjustment Table at the back of this book!

LEXUS 01

Model Description	Trade-in TMV	Private TMV	Dealer TMV	Model Description	Trade-in TMV	Private TMV	Dealer TMV

LEXUS   Japan

1994 Lexus GS 300

2001 LEXUS

ES 300   2001

A glow-in-the-dark emergency trunk release handle is now located in the cargo compartment, while child seat-tether anchors have been added inside.

Category H

	Trade-in	Private	Dealer
4 Dr STD Sdn	21805	22816	24500

OPTIONS FOR ES 300
Chrome Wheels +1261
Compact Disc Changer +783
Electronic Suspension +449
Heated Front Seats +319
Leather Seats +725
Nakamichi Sound System +1181
Power Moonroof +620
Traction Control System +399
Xenon Headlamps +373

GS 300   2001

GS 430 gets a new ULEV-certified, 4.3-liter V8 good for 300 horsepower and 325 ft-lbs. of torque, resulting in sub-6-second acceleration times to 60 mph. GS 300 has new E-shift buttons on the steering wheel for manual control of the automatic transmission's shift points. On the safety front, standard side curtain airbags debut on both models, and a new sensor detects if the front passenger seat is unoccupied, deactivating the front passenger airbag if nobody is sitting in that seat. Additionally, a new child seat-tether restraint has been added, along with impact-detecting door locks and an emergency trunk release handle that glows in the dark inside the cargo area. Exterior changes include water-repellent front door glass, a new grille with a bigger "L" badge, revised taillights, larger exhaust pipes with stainless steel tips and new six-spoke alloy wheels. HID headlights are optional on GS 300 but standard on GS 430. Inside, steering wheel controls for the audio system come standard, a compass has been added, and a new DVD-based navigation system is optional. Bummer that it's bundled with trip computer, audio and climate control systems. Mark Levinson audio is newly optional, replacing Nakamichi as the premium sound supplier. GS 300 gets more wood trim inside the cabin, while GS 430 dashboards have new metallic-gray trim. A wood and leather steering wheel is optional on the 430. Four new colors round out this long list of updates for 2001.

Category I

	Trade-in	Private	Dealer
4 Dr GS 300 Sdn	28738	30043	32218

OPTIONS FOR GS 300
Chrome Wheels +1232
Compact Disc Changer +783
Heated Front Seats +319
Leather Seats +870
Memory System +333
Navigation System +1450
Power Moonroof +739
Xenon Headlamps +373

GS 430   2001

GS 430 gets a new ULEV-certified, 4.3-liter V8 good for 300 horsepower and 325 ft-lbs. of torque, resulting in sub-6-second acceleration times to 60 mph. GS 300 has new E-shift buttons on the steering wheel for manual control of the automatic transmission's shift points. On the safety front, standard side curtain airbags debut on both models, and a new sensor detects if the front passenger seat is unoccupied, deactivating the front passenger airbag if nobody is sitting in that seat. Additionally, a new child seat-tether restraint has been added, along with impact-detecting door locks and an emergency trunk release handle that glows in the dark inside the cargo area. Exterior changes include water-repellent front door glass, a new grille with a bigger "L" badge, revised taillights, larger exhaust pipes with stainless steel tips and new six-spoke alloy wheels. HID headlights are optional on GS 300 but standard on GS 430. Inside, steering wheel controls for the audio system come standard, a compass has been added, and a new DVD-based navigation system is optional. Bummer that it's bundled with trip computer, audio and climate control systems. Mark Levinson audio is newly optional, replacing Nakamichi as the premium sound supplier. GS 300 gets more wood trim inside the cabin, while GS 430 dashboards have new metallic-gray trim. A wood and leather steering wheel is optional on the

LEXUS 01

Model Description	Trade-in TMV	Private TMV	Dealer TMV	Model Description	Trade-in TMV	Private TMV	Dealer TMV

430. Four new colors round out this long list of updates for 2001.

Category I

4 Dr GS 430 Sdn	35114	36709	39366

OPTIONS FOR GS 430

Chrome Wheels +1232
Compact Disc Changer +783
Heated Front Seats +319
Leather Seats +870
Memory System +333
Navigation System +1450
Power Moonroof +739
Rear Spoiler +319

IS 300   2001

Lexus continues to change gears, moving away from single-minded relentless pursuits of perfection to chase performance. The new IS 300, complete with rear-wheel drive and a 215-horse inline six, chases the BMW 3 Series in the entry luxury sport marketplace, and will continue to do so until a proper manual transmission is available next year.

Category H

4 Dr STD Sdn	21360	22350	24000

OPTIONS FOR IS 300

Dual Power Seats +301
Heated Front Seats +319
Leather Seats +725
Limited Slip Differential +283
Power Moonroof +725

LS 430   2001

The completely redesigned third-generation Lexus flagship features a larger 4.3-liter engine that meets ULEV standards, a freshened aerodynamic shape that allows for a more spacious interior, and a new suspension that offers greater stability and a smoother ride. A richer, more stylish interior with advanced safety and luxury features also debuts.

Category I

4 Dr STD Sdn	39694	41496	44500

OPTIONS FOR LS 430

Automatic Load Leveling +507
Chrome Wheels +1232
Heated Seats +638
Navigation System +1450
Park Distance Control +435
Power Moonroof +812
Power Rear Seat Adjusters +1015
Rear Air Conditioning w/Rear Heater +725

LX 470   2001

The LX 470 finally adds the all-important optional DVD-based navigation system (and if you turn down the nav,

you get a compass on the rearview mirror). The optional Nakamichi audio system is gone in favor of an optional nine-speaker Mark Levinson system. The standard audio system is enhanced with an Automatic Sound Levelizer (ASL). Last year's optional wood and leather trim on the steering wheel and shift knob is now a standard feature. New security features include a key card immobilizer and a free-wheel key cylinder that prevents people from opening the door with anything other than the LX 470 key. Second-row passengers will benefit from child seat anchors and improved cupholders in the rear of the center console. The standard alloy wheels have a new surface treatment, and chrome wheels are optional. The fuel cap now has a tether to appease the absent-minded. Two new exterior colors will be offered - Mystic Sea Opalescent and Blue Vapor Metallic.

Category O

4 Dr STD AWD Wgn	42480	44550	48000

OPTIONS FOR LX 470

Chrome Wheels +942
Compact Disc Changer +783
Navigation System +1450

RX 300   2001

Vehicle Skid Control (VSC), traction control and Brake Assist safety technologies are now standard, as is water-repellant front door and side-view mirror glass. Lights front and rear are revised, and the grille has been changed to a simpler design with chrome accents and a larger Lexus badge. HID headlights and chrome-plated wheels are optional for 2001, the full-size spare is newly mounted to a matching alloy wheel and a larger 19.8-gallon fuel tank increases driving range. Inside, new cloth upholstery debuts and an all-black leather option is available. Chrome door handles and scuff plates emblazoned with the Lexus logo class up the joint, while an additional cupholder is available to rear seat occupants. Optional for 2001 are a wood-rimmed steering wheel and wood trimmed shift knob. Two-level seat heaters are also available. A DVD-based navigation system is optional, with the contiguous U.S. mapped onto a single disc. Child seat-tether anchors and ISO-FIX bars have been added this year. Models with 4WD get pre-wiring for towing and a standard rear bumper protector. Four new colors round out the list of changes for 2001.

Category O

4 Dr STD AWD Wgn	26304	27586	29722
4 Dr STD Wgn	24860	26071	28090

OPTIONS FOR RX 300

Camper/Towing Package +225
Chrome Wheels +1232

Don't forget to refer to the Mileage Adjustment Table at the back of this book!

LEXUS 01-00

Model Description	Trade-in TMV	Private TMV	Dealer TMV	Model Description	Trade-in TMV	Private TMV	Dealer TMV

Compact Disc Changer +783
Heated Front Seats +319
Leather Seats +834
Nakamichi Sound System +1181
Navigation System +1450
Power Moonroof +725
Rear Spoiler +203
Trailer Hitch +225
Xenon Headlamps +373

2000 LEXUS

ES 300   2000

The Lexus ES 300 sports new front-end styling and taillights. The rearview and driver's side mirrors are now electrochromatic for improved nighttime performance. The interior gets new colors and additional wood trim on the audio/heater panel. The mirrors are added to the memory seat function. High-intensity discharge headlights are optional, as are 16-inch wheels. Brake Assist is included in the Vehicle Skid Control option. A particle-and-odor air filter is a new option. The ES 300 also receives child seat-anchor brackets and three new colors.

Category H

| 4 Dr STD Sdn | 20098 | 21608 | 23001 |

OPTIONS FOR ES 300
AM/FM Stereo/CD/Tape +399
Compact Disc Changer +435
Heated Front Seats +254
Leather Seats +725
Nakamichi Sound System +870
Power Moonroof +620

GS   2000

Both the GS 300 and GS 400 get a new brake-assist system and child seat-anchor brackets. The GS 300 is certified as a low-emission vehicle. Crystal White and Millennium Silver Metallic replace Diamond White Pearl and Alpine Silver Metallic.

Category I

| 4 Dr GS 300 Sdn | 25831 | 27753 | 29527 |
| 4 Dr GS 400 Sdn | 31353 | 33686 | 35839 |

OPTIONS FOR GS
Chrome Wheels +580
Compact Disc Changer +435
Heated Front Seats +254
Leather Seats[Std on GS 400] +870
Nakamichi Sound System +942
Navigation System +1450
Platinum Series +2472
Power Moonroof +689
Rear Spoiler +254

LS 400   2000

Only minor changes are scheduled for 2000 LS 400s. Brake assist has been added to the Vehicle Skid Control system. A new onboard refueling vapor recovery system allows the LS 400 to meet transitional low-emission vehicle status. Child seat anchor-brackets are standard.

Category I

| 4 Dr STD Sdn | 32806 | 35247 | 37500 |

OPTIONS FOR LS 400
Automatic Load Leveling +507
Chrome Wheels +580
Compact Disc Changer +435
Heated Front Seats +254
Nakamichi Sound System +870
Navigation System +1450
Power Moonroof +692

LX 470   2000

A Vehicle Stability Control system and a Brake Assist system are now standard, as are last year's optional moonroof and illuminated running boards. The LX 470 also gets an optional wood and leather steering wheel and shift knob.

Category O

| 4 Dr STD AWD Wgn | 38388 | 41176 | 43750 |

OPTIONS FOR LX 470
Luggage Rack +217
Nakamichi Sound System +870
Trailer Hitch +163

RX 300   2000

The RX 300 remains mechanically unchanged. A Mineral Green Opalescent paint replaces Desert Bronze Metallic on the order sheet.

Category O

| 4 Dr STD AWD Wgn | 23853 | 25586 | 27185 |
| 4 Dr STD Wgn | 22577 | 24217 | 25731 |

OPTIONS FOR RX 300
AM/FM Stereo/CD/Tape +417
Automatic Dimming Mirror +98
Compact Disc Changer +435
Gold Package +217
Heated Front Seats +254
Leather Seats +834
Limited Slip Differential +254
Luggage Rack +159
Nakamichi Sound System +942
Power Moonroof +725
Rear Spoiler +181
Traction Control System +217
Trailer Hitch +163

Don't forget to refer to the Mileage Adjustment Table at the back of this book!

Model Description	Trade-in TMV	Private TMV	Dealer TMV

SC — 2000

The 2000 Lexus SC 300 and SC 400 are unchanged except for paint selection; Cinnabar Pearl replaces Baroque Red Metallic.

Category I

Model Description	Trade-in TMV	Private TMV	Dealer TMV
2 Dr SC300 Cpe	29156	31325	33328
2 Dr SC400 Cpe	36226	38922	41410

OPTIONS FOR SC
Automatic Dimming Mirror[Std on SC400] +123
Chrome Wheels +580
Gold Package +181
Heated Front Seats +254
Leather Seats[Std on SC400] +870
Nakamichi Sound System +870
Power Moonroof +725
Rear Spoiler +254
Traction Control System +435

1999 LEXUS

ES 300 — 1999

A new 3.0-liter V6 engine with VVTi (Variable Valve Timing with intelligence) gives the 1999 ES300 more horsepower, lower emissions and improved fuel economy. Optional Vehicle Skid Control (VSC) is available on the new ES as are one-touch open and close front windows and a one touch operated moonroof.

Category H

Model Description	Trade-in TMV	Private TMV	Dealer TMV
4 Dr STD Sdn	18306	19820	21334

OPTIONS FOR ES 300
AM/FM Stereo/CD/Tape +332
Chrome Wheels +536
Compact Disc Changer +402
Heated Front Seats +234
Leather Seats +670
Nakamichi Sound System +804
Power Moonroof +573

GS — 1999

The GS series was totally redesigned last year with improvements in performance and a completely new look. As a result, the 1999 model goes unchanged except for the addition of daytime running lights and standard floor mats.

Category I

Model Description	Trade-in TMV	Private TMV	Dealer TMV
4 Dr GS 300 Sdn	22883	24803	26723
4 Dr GS 400 Sdn	27459	29762	32066

OPTIONS FOR GS
Chrome Wheels +536
Compact Disc Changer +402
Heated Front Seats +234
Leather Seats[Std on GS 400] +804

Nakamichi Sound System +871
Navigation System +1072
Power Moonroof +636
Rear Spoiler +234

LS 400 — 1999

After a number of improvements to the LS400 last year, the 1999 model sees only minor upgrades to interior trim levels. Daytime running lights are now standard equipment and Mystic Gold Metallic replaces Cashmere Beige.

Category I

Model Description	Trade-in TMV	Private TMV	Dealer TMV
4 Dr STD Sdn	28687	31093	33500

OPTIONS FOR LS 400
Automatic Load Leveling +469
Chrome Wheels +536
Compact Disc Changer +402
Heated Front Seats +234
Nakamichi Sound System +804
Navigation System +1072
Power Moonroof +640

LX 470 — 1999

For 1999 the LX470 gets a redesigned roof rack, standard floor mats, and an optional Nakamichi audio system featuring a dash-mounted, single-feed six-disc CD changer.

Category O

Model Description	Trade-in TMV	Private TMV	Dealer TMV
4 Dr STD AWD Wgn	33476	36113	38750

OPTIONS FOR LX 470
Gold Package +234
Luggage Rack +201
Nakamichi Sound System +723
Power Moonroof +766
Trailer Hitch +151

RX 300 — 1999

The RX300 is an all new car-based SUV from Lexus designed to compete in the luxury SUV segment.

Category O

Model Description	Trade-in TMV	Private TMV	Dealer TMV
4 Dr STD Wgn	22190	23938	25686
4 Dr STD AWD Wgn	23236	25067	26897

OPTIONS FOR RX 300
AM/FM Compact Disc Player +211
Compact Disc Changer +402
Heated Front Seats +234
Leather Seats +770
Limited Slip Differential +234
Luggage Rack +147
Metallic Paint +121
Nakamichi Sound System +871
Power Moonroof +670
Special Factory Paint +121
Traction Control System +201
Trailer Hitch +151

Don't forget to refer to the Mileage Adjustment Table at the back of this book!

Model Description	Trade-in TMV	Private TMV	Dealer TMV	Model Description	Trade-in TMV	Private TMV	Dealer TMV

SC — 1999

The SC coupe gets minor enhancements this year including new, perforated leather inserts, larger brakes on the SC300, daytime running lights, and a new three-spoke steering wheel similar to the GS series sport sedans.

Category I

	Trade-in	Private	Dealer
2 Dr SC300 Cpe	25552	27695	29839
2 Dr SC400 Cpe	31247	33868	36490

OPTIONS FOR SC

Automatic Dimming Mirror[Std on SC400] +114
Chrome Wheels +536
Gold Package +167
Heated Front Seats +234
Leather Seats[Std on SC400] +804
Nakamichi Sound System +723
Power Moonroof +670
Rear Spoiler +234
Traction Control System +402

1998 LEXUS

ES 300 — 1998

Side-impact airbags debut on Lexus's entry-level car, as does an engine immobilizer anti-theft system and an optional Nakamichi audio system. Reduced force front airbags are also new on all 1998 Lexus models.

Category H

	Trade-in	Private	Dealer
4 Dr STD Sdn	16442	17979	19645

OPTIONS FOR ES 300

AM/FM Stereo/CD/Tape +285
Chrome Wheels +460
Compact Disc Changer +345
Heated Front Seats +201
Leather Seats +575
Nakamichi Sound System +690
Power Moonroof +491
Traction Control System +158

GS — 1998

A totally redesigned GS appears for 1998. Featuring the familiar inline-six engine of the previous model in the GS300 or an overhead cam V8 with continuously variable valve timing in the GS400, the new cars live up to the promise of providing serious fun in an elegant package.

Category I

	Trade-in	Private	Dealer
4 Dr GS300 Sdn	20004	21845	23840
4 Dr GS400 Sdn	23150	25281	27590

OPTIONS FOR GS

Chrome Wheels +460
Compact Disc Changer +345
Heated Front Seats +201

Leather Seats[Std on GS 400] +690
Nakamichi Sound System +747
Navigation System +920
Power Moonroof +546
Rear Spoiler +201

LS 400 — 1998

Lexus further refines its flagship by introducing a new four-cam V8 engine that features continuously variable valve timing. Also new this year is a five-speed automatic transmission, Vehicle Skid Control (VSC) and a host of interior improvements.

Category I

	Trade-in	Private	Dealer
4 Dr STD Sdn	23075	25199	27500

OPTIONS FOR LS 400

Automatic Load Leveling +402
Chrome Wheels +460
Compact Disc Changer +345
Gold Package +201
Heated Front Seats +201
Nakamichi Sound System +690
Navigation System +920
Power Moonroof +549

LX 470 — 1998

Lexus' new LX470 luxury SUV replaces the LX450, offering a completely new body design, a more powerful engine, a roomier interior and more standard perks.

Category O

	Trade-in	Private	Dealer
4 Dr STD AWD Wgn	32022	34364	36900

OPTIONS FOR LX 470

Power Moonroof +658

SC — 1998

The SC400 gets a new four-liter four-cam aluminum V8 engine this year, while the SC300 continues with the inline-six motor from last year. Both powerplants benefit from continuously variable valve timing technology. An engine immobilizer, depowered airbags and a sophisticated five-speed automatic transmission are standard this year as well. The SC300 loses its five-speed manual transmission.

Category I

	Trade-in	Private	Dealer
2 Dr SC300 Cpe	20529	22419	24466
2 Dr SC400 Cpe	26935	29415	32101

OPTIONS FOR SC

Automatic Dimming Mirror[Std on SC400] +98
Chrome Wheels +460
Compact Disc Changer +345
Gold Package +144
Heated Front Seats +201
Leather Seats +690
Nakamichi Sound System +621
Power Moonroof +575

Don't forget to refer to the Mileage Adjustment Table at the back of this book!

Model Description	Trade-in TMV	Private TMV	Dealer TMV

Rear Spoiler +201
Traction Control System +345

1997 LEXUS

ES 300 — 1997

The entry-level Lexus has been totally redesigned this year, growing in nearly every dimension. Lexus manages to eke out more power from the ES300's 3.0-liter V6 engine. No longer just a dressed-up Camry, the ES300 has finally come into its own.

Category H

Model	Trade-in	Private	Dealer
4 Dr STD Sdn	14423	15796	17475

OPTIONS FOR ES 300
AM/FM Stereo/CD/Tape +233
Chrome Wheels +377
Compact Disc Changer +283
Gold Package +139
Heated Front Seats +165
Leather Seats +471
Power Moonroof +403
Traction Control System +130

GS 300 — 1997

Nothing at all, seriously.

Category I

Model	Trade-in	Private	Dealer
4 Dr GS300 Sdn	17155	18655	20489

OPTIONS FOR GS 300
Chrome Wheels +377
Compact Disc Changer +283
Heated Front Seats +165
Leather Seats +565
Nakamichi Sound System +612
Power Moonroof +447
Traction Control System +236

LS 400 — 1997

Side-impact airbags are standard.

Category I

Model	Trade-in	Private	Dealer
4 Dr STD Sdn	20053	21807	23950
4 Dr Coach Sdn	22764	24755	27188

OPTIONS FOR LS 400
AM/FM Stereo/CD/Tape +283
Automatic Load Leveling +330
Chrome Wheels +377
Compact Disc Changer +283
Driver's Memory System +236
Heated Front Seats +165
Nakamichi Sound System +565
Power Moonroof +445
Traction Control System +283

LX 450 — 1997

There are no changes to the 1997 LX450.

Category O

Model	Trade-in	Private	Dealer
4 Dr STD 4WD Wgn	20406	22322	24663

OPTIONS FOR LX 450
Compact Disc Changer +283
F&R Locking Differential +382
Luggage Rack +106
Power Moonroof +530
Running Boards +127
Trailer Hitch +106

SC — 1997

Minor interior and exterior enhancements update the look of the SC coupes.

Category I

Model	Trade-in	Private	Dealer
2 Dr SC300 Cpe	16811	18281	20078
2 Dr SC400 Cpe	22293	24242	26625

OPTIONS FOR SC
Automatic 4-Speed Transmission[Std on SC400] +325
Chrome Wheels +377
Compact Disc Changer +283
Gold Package +118
Heated Front Seats +165
Leather Seats[Std on SC400] +565
Nakamichi Sound System +509
Power Moonroof +471
Rear Spoiler +165
Traction Control System +283

1996 LEXUS

ES 300 — 1996

Two new colors are available.

Category H

Model	Trade-in	Private	Dealer
4 Dr STD Sdn	11273	12403	13963

OPTIONS FOR ES 300
AM/FM Compact Disc Player +107
AM/FM Stereo/CD/Tape +214
Chrome Wheels +346
Compact Disc Changer +259
Heated Front Seats +151
Leather Seats +432
Power Moonroof +370

GS — 1996

A five-speed automatic transmission makes the GS 300 feel more sporty, while rear styling revisions and five new exterior colors update the suave exterior. 1997 side-impact standards are met this year, and the power moonroof features one-touch operation.

Category I

Model	Trade-in	Private	Dealer
4 Dr GS300 Sdn	15411	16867	18878

OPTIONS FOR GS
Chrome Wheels +346

Don't forget to refer to the Mileage Adjustment Table at the back of this book!

Model Description	Trade-in TMV	Private TMV	Dealer TMV

Compact Disc Changer +259
Leather Seats +519
Nakamichi Sound System +562
Power Moonroof +411
Traction Control System +216

LS 400   1996

Deep Jewel Green Pearl is newly available on the paint palette.

Category I

4 Dr STD Sdn	16735	18317	20500

OPTIONS FOR LS 400

Automatic Load Leveling +303
Chrome Wheels +346
Compact Disc Changer +259
Gold Package +151
Heated Front Seats +151
Nakamichi Sound System +519
Power Moonroof +413
Traction Control System +259

LX 450   1996

Lexus clones a Toyota Land Cruiser, puts some fancy wheels on it, and slathers leather and wood all over the interior to capitalize on the booming sport-ute market.

Category O

4 Dr STD 4WD Wgn	18525	20328	22819

OPTIONS FOR LX 450

Compact Disc Changer +259
F&R Locking Differential +350
Luggage Rack +97
Power Moonroof +487
Running Boards +117
Trailer Hitch +97

SC   1996

SC300 boasts a larger options roster with the addition of a one-touch operation moonroof and electrochromatic rearview mirrors. The buttery V8 from the LS 400 is installed in the SC 400, and chrome wheels are available. Auto-dimming electrochromic inside and outside rearview mirrors are now standard, a new remote keyless entry system debuts, and the optional moonroof now features one-touch operation.

Category I

2 Dr SC300 Cpe	14713	16103	18023
2 Dr SC400 Cpe	18937	20726	23197

OPTIONS FOR SC

Automatic 4-Speed Transmission[Std on SC400] +298
Chrome Wheels +346
Compact Disc Changer +259
Heated Front Seats +151
Leather Seats[Std on SC400] +519
Nakamichi Sound System +467

Power Moonroof +432
Rear Spoiler +151
Traction Control System +259

1995 LEXUS

ES 300   1995

Styling is freshened, and chrome wheels are available. Trunk-mounted CD changer is a new option.

Category H

4 Dr STD Sdn	9948	11001	12755

OPTIONS FOR ES 300

Chrome Wheels +308
Compact Disc Changer +231
Gold Package +114
Heated Front Seats +135
Leather Seats +385
Power Moonroof +329

GS   1995

No changes.

Category I

4 Dr GS300 Sdn	13229	14550	16751

OPTIONS FOR GS

Compact Disc Changer +231
Gold Package +116
Heated Front Seats +135
Leather Seats +462
Nakamichi Sound System +501
Power Moonroof +366
Traction Control System +193

LS 400   1995

All-new car looks pretty much the same as it has for half a decade. The interior and trunk are larger, the engine more powerful, and the car is quicker than before. Six-disc CD changer is dash-mounted.

Category I

4 Dr STD Sdn	13821	15200	17500

OPTIONS FOR LS 400

AM/FM Compact Disc Player +173
Automatic Load Leveling +270
Chrome Wheels +308
Compact Disc Changer +231
Gold Package +135
Heated Front Seats +135
Nakamichi Sound System +462
Power Moonroof +368
Traction Control System +231

SC   1995

Revised styling and new wheels spruce up the look of these coupes. 1997 side-impact standards are met this year. A cupholder is added inside.

LEXUS 95-93

Model Description	Trade-in TMV	Private TMV	Dealer TMV
Category I			
2 Dr SC300 Cpe	12547	13799	15887
2 Dr SC400 Cpe	15202	16720	19249

OPTIONS FOR SC

AM/FM Stereo/CD/Tape +231
Automatic 4-Speed Transmission[Std on SC400] +265
Compact Disc Changer +231
Gold Package +96
Heated Front Seats +135
Leather Seats[Std on SC400] +462
Nakamichi Sound System +416
Power Moonroof +385
Rear Spoiler +135
Traction Control System +231

1994 LEXUS

ES 300   1994

Passenger airbag added. New 3.0-liter engine has aluminum block and a few more horsepower. Several convenience features are now standard, including an outside temperature gauge.

Model Description	Trade-in TMV	Private TMV	Dealer TMV
Category H			
4 Dr STD Sdn	8279	9302	11008

OPTIONS FOR ES 300

Compact Disc Changer +205
Gold Package +101
Heated Front Seats +120
Leather Seats +342
Power Moonroof +292

GS   1994

No changes.

Model Description	Trade-in TMV	Private TMV	Dealer TMV
Category I			
4 Dr GS300 Sdn	10468	11679	13697

OPTIONS FOR GS

AM/FM Stereo/CD/Tape +205
Compact Disc Changer +205
Heated Front Seats +120
Leather Seats +410
Nakamichi Sound System +445
Power Moonroof +325
Traction Control System +171

LS 400   1994

Minor trim revisions.

Model Description	Trade-in TMV	Private TMV	Dealer TMV
Category I			
4 Dr STD Sdn	11273	12577	14750

OPTIONS FOR LS 400

AM/FM Stereo/CD/Tape +205
Compact Disc Changer +205
Electric Air Suspension +274
Gold Package +120
Heated Front Seats +120

Memory System +171
Nakamichi Sound System +410
Power Moonroof +327
Traction Control System +205

SC   1994

Air conditioning is now CFC-free.

Model Description	Trade-in TMV	Private TMV	Dealer TMV
Category I			
2 Dr SC300 Cpe	9580	10688	12535
2 Dr SC400 Cpe	12673	14139	16582

OPTIONS FOR SC

Automatic 4-Speed Transmission[Std on SC400] +236
Compact Disc Changer +205
Heated Front Seats +120
Leather Seats[Std on SC400] +410
Nakamichi Sound System +370
Power Moonroof +342
Rear Spoiler +120
Traction Control System +205

1993 LEXUS

ES 300   1993

A fuel cap tether and automatic-locking safety belt retractors are added.

Model Description	Trade-in TMV	Private TMV	Dealer TMV
Category H			
4 Dr STD Sdn	6751	7651	9150

OPTIONS FOR ES 300

AM/FM Stereo Tape +107
AM/FM Stereo/CD/Tape +156
Automatic 4-Speed Transmission +221
Compact Disc Changer +190
Gold Package +93
Heated Front Seats +111
Leather Seats +316
Power Moonroof +270

GS   1993

New sports sedan looks great, but fails to deliver much performance. Arrived late in 1993 with dual airbags, ABS and CFC-free air conditioning.

Model Description	Trade-in TMV	Private TMV	Dealer TMV
Category I			
4 Dr GS300 Sdn	8199	9261	11031

OPTIONS FOR GS

Chrome Wheels +253
Compact Disc Changer +190
Gold Package +95
Heated Front Seats +111
Leather Seats +380
Nakamichi Sound System +411
Power Moonroof +300
Traction Control System +158

Don't forget to refer to the Mileage Adjustment Table at the back of this book!

LEXUS 93-92

Model Description	Trade-in TMV	Private TMV	Dealer TMV	Model Description	Trade-in TMV	Private TMV	Dealer TMV

LS 400   1993

Passenger airbag added. New alloy wheels debut. Brakes and tires are bigger. Styling is touched up, and interiors receive a host of upgrades. CFC-free air conditioning replaces Freon-based unit.

Category I

4 Dr STD Sdn	10034	11334	13500

OPTIONS FOR LS 400
AM/FM Compact Disc Player +142
Automatic Load Leveling +228
Compact Disc Changer +190
Heated Front Seats +111
Memory System +158
Nakamichi Sound System +380
Power Moonroof +302
Traction Control System +190

SC   1993

Passenger airbag added. Automatic headlamp system debuts, and owners could pre-wire the car for use with a Portable Plus cellular phone.

Category I

2 Dr SC300 Cpe	8133	9187	10943
2 Dr SC400 Cpe	10826	12229	14566

OPTIONS FOR SC
Automatic 4-Speed Transmission[Std on SC400] +218
Compact Disc Changer +190
Gold Package +79
Heated Front Seats +111
Leather Seats[Std on SC400] +380
Nakamichi Sound System +341
Power Moonroof +316
Premium Sound System +380
Rear Spoiler +111
Traction Control System +190

1992 LEXUS

ES 300   1992

Camry-based replacement for ES250. ABS and driver airbag are standard.

Category H

4 Dr STD Sdn	5382	6212	7595

OPTIONS FOR ES 300
AM/FM Compact Disc Player +75
AM/FM Stereo/CD/Tape +150
Automatic 4-Speed Transmission +212
Compact Disc Changer +182
Gold Package +89
Heated Front Seats +106
Leather Seats +303
Power Moonroof +259

LS 400   1992

No changes.

Category I

4 Dr STD Sdn	7965	9098	10987

OPTIONS FOR LS 400
AM/FM Compact Disc Player +136
Automatic Load Leveling +212
Compact Disc Changer +182
Gold Package +106
Heated Front Seats +106
Memory System +152
Power Moonroof +290
Premium Sound System +218
Traction Control System +182

SC   1992

Introduced in June 1991, these sleek coupes feature standard ABS and driver airbag. Traction control is optional with automatic transmission. SC300 is powered by inline six-cylinder engine.

Category I

2 Dr SC300 Cpe	7266	8300	10023
2 Dr SC400 Cpe	9315	10640	12849

OPTIONS FOR SC
AM/FM Compact Disc Player +91
Automatic 4-Speed Transmission[Std on SC400] +209
Compact Disc Changer +182
Heated Front Seats +106
Leather Seats[Std on SC400] +364
Power Moonroof +303
Premium Sound System +364
Rear Spoiler +106
Traction Control System +182

Don't forget to refer to the Mileage Adjustment Table at the back of this book!

LINCOLN 01

Model Description	Trade-in TMV	Private TMV	Dealer TMV	Model Description	Trade-in TMV	Private TMV	Dealer TMV

LINCOLN   USA

1999 Lincoln Town Car

2001 LINCOLN

CONTINENTAL   2001

The Continental remains relatively unchanged for 2001. A universal garage door opener is standard, and the individual bucket seat option (five-passenger) now requires the Driver's Select System. Two new exterior colors have been added. Like all Lincoln products, the Continental now has complimentary maintenance at no additional charge for the first 3 years/36,000 miles in service.

Category I

	Trade-in	Private	Dealer
4 Dr STD Sdn	23814	25329	27853

OPTIONS FOR CONTINENTAL
Alpine Audio System +327
Chrome Wheels +487
Compact Disc Changer +345
Heated Seats +228
Power Moonroof +869

LS   2001

V6 models now come with standard traction control and optional AdvanceTrac. All models receive a glow-in-the-dark manual trunk release and child safety-seat anchor points. The sport package has a new 17-inch chrome wheel design and a mini spare tire and wheel instead of the previous 16-inch non-matching aluminum wheel (both late availability). Inside, there is an additional power point, a revised cupholder design, an optional six-disc in-dash CD changer and an optional mirror-mounted compass. The height adjustable rear-seat head restraints have been deleted from V8 automatics. Four new exterior colors are offered. Lincoln now offers complimentary maintenance at no additional charge for the first 3 years/36,000 miles in service.

Category H

	Trade-in	Private	Dealer
4 Dr V6 Sdn	24078	25524	27933
4 Dr V8 Sdn	25012	26513	29016

OPTIONS FOR LS
17 Inch Chrome Wheels +481
Alpine Audio System +327
Automatic 5-Speed Transmission[Opt on V6] +829
Chrome Wheels +481
Compact Disc Changer +345
Heated Front Seats +228
Power Moonroof +572
Sport Suspension +170
Traction Control System +419

NAVIGATOR   2001

Auxiliary climate control is standard on both two- and four-wheel-drive models. Both the second- and third-row seats get lower child safety-seat anchors. Lincoln now offers complimentary maintenance at no additional charge for the first 3 years/36,000 miles in service.

Category O

	Trade-in	Private	Dealer
4 Dr STD 4WD Wgn	30059	31596	34158
4 Dr STD Wgn	27503	28909	31253

OPTIONS FOR NAVIGATOR
17 Inch Chrome Wheels +339
Alpine Audio System +330
Compact Disc Changer +339
Entertainment System +729
Navigation System +1136
Park Distance Control +145
Power Moonroof +851

TOWN CAR   2001

Horsepower has been increased throughout the model lineup. Inside, the Town Car gains adjustable pedals, seat-belt pretensioners, upgraded map pockets and leather grab handles. Signature models have a wood-trimmed steering wheel as standard and the front seats in Executive models have power lumbar adjustment as standard. Lincoln now offers complimentary maintenance at no additional charge for the first 3 years/36,000 miles in service.

Category I

	Trade-in	Private	Dealer
4 Dr Cartier Sdn	27350	29089	31988
4 Dr Cartier L Sdn	29166	31021	34112
4 Dr Executive Sdn	23840	25356	27883
4 Dr Executive L Sdn	26718	28417	31249
4 Dr Signature Sdn	25475	27095	29795

OPTIONS FOR TOWN CAR
Chrome Wheels[Std on Cartier] +396
Compact Disc Changer +339

Model Description	Trade-in TMV	Private TMV	Dealer TMV
Heated Seats[Opt on Signature] +228			
Power Moonroof +863			
Tutone Paint +148			

2000 LINCOLN

CONTINENTAL 2000

The Continental receives additional safety features, including side airbags, an emergency trunk release, child seat-anchor brackets, and Lincoln's Belt Minder system.

Category I

Model Description	Trade-in TMV	Private TMV	Dealer TMV
4 Dr STD Sdn	21034	23037	24886

OPTIONS FOR CONTINENTAL
Alpine Audio System +322
Chrome Wheels +481
Compact Disc Changer +339
Heated Front Seats +165
Power Moonroof +863
Rescu Package +399
Special Factory Paint +170

LS 2000

From the ground up, this is a completely new sport sedan based on an all-new mid-size platform. Lincoln worked with Jaguar to develop this platform, which is also being used for Jaguar's S-type sedan. It is the first Lincoln in over two decades not classified as a full-size vehicle, and should appeal to buyers looking for something sportier and smaller than the Town Car or Continental.

Category H

Model Description	Trade-in TMV	Private TMV	Dealer TMV
4 Dr V6 Sdn	21607	23377	25010
4 Dr V8 Sdn	22527	24371	26074

OPTIONS FOR LS
Alpine Audio System +328
Compact Disc Changer +345
Heated Front Seats +228
Power Moonroof +573
Rescu System +621
Special Factory Paint +214
Sport Package +404
Sport Suspension +170

NAVIGATOR 2000

The 2000 Navigator is now available with a fully integrated satellite navigation system, as well as a reverse-sensing system. Side airbags are standard, while new climate-controlled seats for the driver and front passenger are optional. The 2000 Navigator also features several exterior and interior styling changes.

Model Description	Trade-in TMV	Private TMV	Dealer TMV
Category O			
4 Dr STD 4WD Wgn	26985	29218	31279
4 Dr STD Wgn	23521	25467	27263

OPTIONS FOR NAVIGATOR
Alpine Audio System +325
Chrome Wheels +199
Compact Disc Changer +339
Dual Air Conditioning +402
Heated Front Seats +165
Navigation System +1137
Power Moonroof +943

TOWN CAR 2000

The Town Car receives additional safety features, including an emergency trunk release, child seat-anchor brackets, and Lincoln's Belt Minder system. A new storage armrest has been placed on the front-passenger door-trim panel. One new exterior color has been added: Autumn Red Clearcoat Metallic.

Category I

Model Description	Trade-in TMV	Private TMV	Dealer TMV
4 Dr Cartier L Sdn	22134	24242	26188
4 Dr Cartier Sdn	21103	23113	24968
4 Dr Executive L Sdn	20627	22592	24405
4 Dr Executive Sdn	17851	19551	21120
4 Dr Signature Sdn	19278	21114	22809

OPTIONS FOR TOWN CAR
Chrome Wheels[Std on Cartier] +396
Compact Disc Changer +327
Heated Front Seats[Std on Cartier] +165
Power Moonroof +863
Special Factory Paint +157
Tutone Paint +214

1999 LINCOLN

CONTINENTAL 1999

Lincoln's luxury liner gets added safety in 1999 with the addition of standard side airbags for the driver and front passenger. There's five new exterior colors, upgraded interior trim options, two new wheel designs and an improved audio system. Otherwise the Lincoln remains unchanged after its major rework in 1998.

Category I

Model Description	Trade-in TMV	Private TMV	Dealer TMV
4 Dr STD Sdn	17813	19715	21618

OPTIONS FOR CONTINENTAL
Alpine Audio System +257
Chrome Wheels +385
Compact Disc Changer +271
Heated Front Seats +132
Power Moonroof +691
Rescu Package +456
Special Factory Paint +137

NAVIGATOR 1999

LINCOLN 99-97

Model Description	Trade-in TMV	Private TMV	Dealer TMV	Model Description	Trade-in TMV	Private TMV	Dealer TMV

Into its second year, Lincoln's Navigator enters 1999 with more power, adjustable pedals, speed-sensitive stereo volume, and a hands-free cellular phone. Also, the optional third row seat is mounted on rollers this year for easy installation and removal.

Category O

4 Dr STD 4WD Wgn	24138	26223	28307
4 Dr STD Wgn	21363	23207	25052

OPTIONS FOR NAVIGATOR
AM/FM Stereo/CD/Tape +114
Alpine Audio System +260
Chrome Wheels +160
Compact Disc Changer +271
Dual Air Conditioning +321
Heated Front Seats +132
Limited Slip Differential[Opt on 2WD] +116
Power Moonroof +754

TOWN CAR   1999

Standard side airbags improve the Town Car's ability to protect occupants and a new JBL audio system makes getting there even more fun.

Category I

4 Dr Cartier Sdn	17782	19682	21581
4 Dr Executive Sdn	15636	17307	18977
4 Dr Signature Sdn	16710	18495	20280

OPTIONS FOR TOWN CAR
Chrome Wheels[Std on Cartier] +317
Compact Disc Changer +271
Heated Front Seats[Std on Cartier] +132
Power Moonroof +691
Special Factory Paint +166

1998 LINCOLN

CONTINENTAL   1998

Lincoln's front-wheel drive luxo-barge gets a bigger grille (just what it needs) and rounded corners. It also gets an interior freshening that replaces the digital clock with an analog timepiece.

Category I

4 Dr STD Sdn	14914	16663	18559

OPTIONS FOR CONTINENTAL
Chrome Wheels +330
Compact Disc Changer +233
Heated Front Seats +113
JBL Sound System +221
Power Moonroof +593
Rescu Package +391
Special Factory Paint +117

MARK VIII   1998

No changes to Lincoln's muscle car.
Category I

2 Dr STD Cpe	16291	18202	20273
2 Dr LSC Cpe	16850	18827	20969

OPTIONS FOR MARK VIII
AM/FM Compact Disc Player +262
Chrome Wheels[Opt on STD] +330
Compact Disc Changer +262
Heated Front Seats +113
Power Moonroof +593
Special Factory Paint +143

NAVIGATOR   1998

This all-new entrant into the luxury SUV market is the first truck ever sold by Lincoln. Based on the highly-acclaimed Ford Expedition, the Navigator is powered by a 5.4-liter SOHC V8 engine and has standard goodies that include illuminated running boards and a load-leveling air suspension. This truck also features one of the largest grilles this side of a Kenworth.

Category O

4 Dr STD 4WD Wgn	20015	21864	23868
4 Dr STD Wgn	18279	19968	21798

OPTIONS FOR NAVIGATOR
Chrome Wheels +137
Compact Disc Changer +233
Dual Air Conditioning +276
Heated Front Seats +113
Limited Slip Differential[Opt on 2WD] +100
Power Moonroof +648

TOWN CAR   1998

Lincoln redesigns its Town Car this year, making it lower, stiffer and faster. The interior is nicely improved as well, with softer seats and better positioned controls.

Category I

4 Dr Cartier Sdn	15769	17620	19624
4 Dr Executive Sdn	13178	14724	16399
4 Dr Signature Sdn	14067	15717	17505

OPTIONS FOR TOWN CAR
Chrome Wheels +273
Compact Disc Changer +233
Heated Front Seats[Std on Cartier] +113
JBL Sound System[Std on Cartier] +221
Leather Seats[Std on Cartier] +223
Power Moonroof +593
Special Factory Paint +143

1997 LINCOLN

CONTINENTAL   1997

The changes to the 1997 Continental are minor this year. The first is the addition of a single-key locking system that locks the doors, glove box, and trunk with a turn of the wrist. The second is the addition of all-speed traction control. Lastly, the Continental

Model Description	Trade-in TMV	Private TMV	Dealer TMV

receives a minor interior and exterior facelift.

Category I

| 4 Dr STD Sdn | 10665 | 12022 | 13680 |

OPTIONS FOR CONTINENTAL
Chrome Wheels +265
Compact Disc Changer +177
JBL Sound System +187
Power Moonroof +477
Rescu Package +314

MARK VIII   1997

Lincoln thoroughly updates this personal coupe, lighting the darn thing up like a Christmas tree in the process. The Mark now has high-intensity discharge front headlamps, cornering lamps, a neon rear applique, and puddle lamps. Wow, you'll see this thing from miles away. The hood, grille and interior have also been slightly redesigned.

Category I

| 2 Dr STD Cpe | 13645 | 15381 | 17503 |
| 2 Dr LSC Cpe | 14274 | 16090 | 18310 |

OPTIONS FOR MARK VIII
AM/FM Compact Disc Player +210
Chrome Wheels[Opt on STD] +265
Compact Disc Changer +210
Power Moonroof +477

TOWN CAR   1997

The Town Car's power steering has been improved. Watch out, Mario!

Category I

4 Dr Cartier Sdn	12623	14229	16192
4 Dr Executive Sdn	10930	12320	14020
4 Dr Signature Sdn	11494	12957	14744

OPTIONS FOR TOWN CAR
Chrome Wheels +218
Compact Disc Changer +187
JBL Sound System[Std on Cartier] +257
Leather Seats[Std on Cartier] +179
Power Moonroof +477

1996 LINCOLN

CONTINENTAL   1996

The big news for Continental is an optional gee-whiz rescue unit that uses a Global Positioning Satellite to pinpoint your location for roadside assistance, medical, and law enforcement personnel in the event of an emergency. Likely the greatest safety advance since airbags and antilock brakes. Also new are run-flat Michelin tires, a 75th Diamond Anniversary Edition, and a standard anti-theft system. It's getting there.

Category I

| 4 Dr STD Sdn | 8113 | 9183 | 10662 |

OPTIONS FOR CONTINENTAL
Chrome Wheels +219
Compact Disc Changer +155
JBL Sound System +147
Personal Security Package +518
Power Moonroof +394

MARK VIII   1996

Last year's limited-edition LSC model goes full-time for 1996. Eight new colors are available, and borderless floor mats debut. A Touring Package and 75th Diamond Anniversary model are offered.

Category I

| 2 Dr STD Cpe | 10501 | 11887 | 13801 |
| 2 Dr LSC Cpe | 10939 | 12382 | 14376 |

OPTIONS FOR MARK VIII
Chrome Wheels[Opt on STD] +219
Compact Disc Changer +212
JBL Sound System +147
Power Moonroof +394

TOWN CAR   1996

Engine upgrades, new automatic climate controls, and real wood on the dashboard in Cartier models sum up the changes to the Town Car.

Category I

4 Dr Cartier Sdn	10073	11402	13238
4 Dr Executive Sdn	8693	9840	11424
4 Dr Signature Sdn	9176	10387	12059

OPTIONS FOR TOWN CAR
Compact Disc Changer +155
JBL Sound System[Std on Cartier] +147
Leather Seats[Std on Cartier] +148
Power Moonroof +394

1995 LINCOLN

CONTINENTAL   1995

An all-new Continental is released with a V8 DOHC engine. A new suspension system that adjusts the shock absorbers to the prevailing driving conditions debuts, as does a memory seat system that will retain the seating preferences for two people. The new Continental has swoopier styling which is geared towards attracting a more youthful audience.

Category I

| 4 Dr STD Sdn | 5974 | 6915 | 8482 |

OPTIONS FOR CONTINENTAL
Chrome Wheels +171
Compact Disc Changer +114
JBL Sound System +114

Don't forget to refer to the Mileage Adjustment Table at the back of this book!

LINCOLN 95-93

Model Description	Trade-in TMV	Private TMV	Dealer TMV	Model Description	Trade-in TMV	Private TMV	Dealer TMV

Power Moonroof +307

MARK VIII — 1995

Lincoln's premium touring coupe receives significant changes across the board. A new instrument panel houses a new stereo with larger buttons. A feature called retained accessory power makes an appearance on the Mark VIII, allowing passengers 10 seconds to close the window after the car is turned off.

Category I

Model	Trade-in	Private	Dealer
2 Dr STD Cpe	7488	8667	10631
2 Dr LSC Cpe	7852	9088	11148

OPTIONS FOR MARK VIII
Chrome Wheels +171
Compact Disc Changer +136
JBL Sound System +114
Power Moonroof +307

TOWN CAR — 1995

Exterior changes on the Town Car include new headlights, grille, taillights, bumpers, and bodyside molding. The outside mirrors have been moved forward slightly to increase visibility. An electronic steering switch selector allows the driver to select the type of steering effort they want. The instrument panel includes a redesigned two-spoke steering wheel, illuminated switches, and improved stereos with larger controls. Signature and Cartier models get steering wheel-mounted stereo and climate controls. A gate access unit integrated into the driver's side visor allows up to three frequencies to be programmed into its memory.

Category I

Model	Trade-in	Private	Dealer
4 Dr Cartier Sdn	7006	8109	9947
4 Dr Executive Sdn	5860	6782	8319
4 Dr Signature Sdn	6337	7335	8997

OPTIONS FOR TOWN CAR
Compact Disc Changer +120
JBL Sound System[Std on Cartier] +114
Leather Seats[Std on Cartier] +115
Power Moonroof +307

1994 LINCOLN

CONTINENTAL — 1994

Suspension changes improve the Continental's ride. A memory feature on the remote keyless entry automatically adjusts the driver's seat to a pre-set position each time it's activated. Exterior changes include revised taillamps, grille and rocker moldings. A retractable trunk cord is standard on all Continentals; it is designed to keep the trunk from bouncing around when it has to be left open for large loads.

Category I

Model	Trade-in	Private	Dealer
4 Dr Executive Sdn	3269	3874	4882
4 Dr Signature Sdn	3478	4121	5194

OPTIONS FOR CONTINENTAL
JBL Sound System +82
Power Moonroof +220

MARK VIII — 1994

Chrome wheels are now an available option on the Mark VIII. There is a memory feature for the seats and outside mirrors.

Category I

Model	Trade-in	Private	Dealer
2 Dr STD Cpe	5409	6410	8078

OPTIONS FOR MARK VIII
AM/FM Compact Disc Player[Opt on STD] +97
Chrome Wheels +123
Compact Disc Changer +97
JBL Sound System[Opt on STD] +82
Power Moonroof +220

TOWN CAR — 1994

A dual exhaust system on the Town Car is made standard this year, upping horsepower to 210. All models receive solar tinted glass. The Jack Nicklaus Special Edition has been dropped.

Category I

Model	Trade-in	Private	Dealer
4 Dr Cartier Sdn	4970	5889	7422
4 Dr Executive Sdn	3811	4517	5692
4 Dr Signature Sdn	4207	4986	6283

OPTIONS FOR TOWN CAR
Compact Disc Changer +82
JBL Sound System[Std on Cartier] +82
Leather Seats[Std on Cartier] +83
Power Moonroof +220

1993 LINCOLN

CONTINENTAL — 1993

Bucket seats are available this year with a handy center console. The Signature series gets remote keyless entry, aluminum wheels, and the Comfort and Convenience Group added to its standard features list. Both models receive adjustable seatbelt anchor points.

Category I

Model	Trade-in	Private	Dealer
4 Dr Executive Sdn	2598	3146	4060
4 Dr Signature Sdn	2798	3389	4373

OPTIONS FOR CONTINENTAL
Power Sunroof +166

MARK VIII — 1993

The Mark VIII debuts replacing the dated Mark VII.

Model Description	Trade-in TMV	Private TMV	Dealer TMV

Based on the Thunderbird platform, the new Mark has a sportier feel than previous models. A twin-cam, 4.6-liter V8 produces 280 horsepower in the Mark VIII, and the transmission is an electronically controlled four-speed automatic.

Category I

2 Dr STD Cpe	4257	5155	6652

OPTIONS FOR MARK VIII
Chrome Wheels +101
Compact Disc Changer +80
Power Sunroof +166

TOWN CAR   1993

Styling changes and an optional Handling Package mark the differences in this year's Town Car. The formerly optional geometric aluminum wheels are made standard and the grille and headlights are slightly altered. The Handling Package consists of a firmer suspension and larger tires. The Executive series gains some features that were standard on the other models.

Category I

4 Dr Cartier Sdn	3694	4473	5772
4 Dr Executive Sdn	3049	3693	4765
4 Dr Signature Sdn	3342	4048	5223

OPTIONS FOR TOWN CAR
Full Vinyl Top +121
Power Sunroof +166

1992 LINCOLN

CONTINENTAL   1992

The passenger airbag is revived this year and two trim-levels are available, the Signature and the Executive. Several optional safety features debut this year, such as an electrochromatic rearview mirror and a remote keyless entry system with a panic button.

Model Description	Trade-in TMV	Private TMV	Dealer TMV

Category I

4 Dr Executive Sdn	1946	2466	3332
4 Dr Signature Sdn	2067	2620	3540

OPTIONS FOR CONTINENTAL
Power Moonroof +155

MARK VII   1992

The final year for the Mark VII, changes are limited to minor alterations of the interior.

Category H

2 Dr Bill Blass Cpe	2891	3634	4874
2 Dr LSC Cpe	2776	3490	4681

OPTIONS FOR MARK VII
Power Moonroof +138

TOWN CAR   1992

Transmission adaptations include electronic shift controls, overdrive lockout, and a feature that won't allow the car to be shifted out of "Park" unless the brake is on.

Category I

4 Dr Cartier Sdn	2838	3596	4859
4 Dr Executive Sdn	2195	2782	3759
4 Dr Signature Sdn	2410	3053	4126

OPTIONS FOR TOWN CAR
Full Vinyl Top +103
Power Moonroof +155

Don't forget to refer to the Mileage Adjustment Table at the back of this book!

MAZDA 01

Model Description	Trade-in TMV	Private TMV	Dealer TMV	Model Description	Trade-in TMV	Private TMV	Dealer TMV

MAZDA

Japan

1995 Mazda Millenia

2001 MAZDA

626 — 2001

The 626's interior gains a new modular audio system, a new rear deck with child safety-seat anchors, and an internal emergency trunk release. Mazda has also made EZ-Kool glass standard on all models and side airbags a stand-alone option on models with a V6 and automatic transmissions. All 626s are now 50-state emission compliant.

Category B

Model	Trade-in	Private	Dealer
4 Dr ES Sdn	13407	14617	16634
4 Dr ES V6 Sdn	14733	16063	18279
4 Dr LX Sdn	11992	13074	14878
4 Dr LX V6 Sdn	12956	14126	16075

OPTIONS FOR 626

AM/FM Stereo/CD/Tape[Std on ES V6] +210
Alarm System[Std on ES V6] +150
Aluminum/Alloy Wheels[Std on ES,ES V6] +269
Anti-Lock Brakes +299
Automatic 4-Speed Transmission[Std on ES] +479
Bose Sound System[Std on ES V6] +210
Compact Disc Changer +135
Fog Lights +150
Power Drivers Seat[Std on ES V6] +150
Power Moonroof[Std on ES V6] +539
Rear Spoiler +236
Side Air Bag Restraints +150
Traction Control System +150

B-SERIES — 2001

More power is the big news for the '01 B-Series. The B4000 boasts a new 4.0-liter SOHC V6, while the B2300 has a new 2.3-liter four-cylinder engine. The flexible-fuel feature on the 3.0-liter V6 has been dropped. Mazda has also made ABS standard on all models. A new 4x2 Dual Sport trim level gives a two-wheeler the raised-suspension look of a four-by. While they were at it, Mazda product planners also modified the exterior and interior styling. To the chagrin of Troy Lee but probably nobody else, the B-Series Troy Lee edition has been dropped.

Category J

Model	Trade-in	Private	Dealer
2 Dr B2300 SE Std Cab SB	9714	10508	11832
2 Dr B2300 SX Std Cab SB	8544	9243	10407
2 Dr B2500 SE Std Cab SB	8751	9467	10659
2 Dr B2500 SX Std Cab SB	7497	8109	9131
2 Dr B3000 DS Ext Cab SB	11539	12483	14055
2 Dr B3000 DS Std Cab SB	9875	10682	12028
2 Dr B3000 SE 4WD Ext Cab SB	13066	14135	15915
2 Dr B3000 SE 4WD Std Cab SB	11593	12541	14121
2 Dr B3000 SE Ext Cab SB	10786	11668	13138
2 Dr B3000 SE Std Cab SB	9852	10658	12000
4 Dr B3000 SE Ext Cab SB	11914	12888	14512
4 Dr B4000 DS Ext Cab SB	12776	13821	15562
4 Dr B4000 SE 4WD Ext Cab SB	13865	14999	16888

OPTIONS FOR B-SERIES

Air Conditioning[Opt on B2500 SX,B3000 SX] +482
Automatic 4-Speed Transmission +599
Bed Extender +126
Bed Liner +119
Power Windows[Std on B4000 SE,B4000TL] +144
Running Boards +221
Tonneau Cover +198

MILLENIA — 2001

Mazda has strengthened the Millenia's body structure to improve torsional rigidity by 30 percent. Combined with a new rear stabilizer bar and a larger front stabilizer bar, improved handling is the result. Visually, the car should be more appealing thanks to new front and rear styling. The interior has been updated significantly,

Don't forget to refer to the Mileage Adjustment Table at the back of this book!

MAZDA 01

Model Description	Trade-in TMV	Private TMV	Dealer TMV	Model Description	Trade-in TMV	Private TMV	Dealer TMV

as well. Hardware changes include larger disc brakes, a revised ABS system and standard side airbags for both models.

Category H

| 4 Dr Premium Sdn | 18385 | 19498 | 21353 |
| 4 Dr S Sprchrgd Sdn | 19010 | 20161 | 22079 |

OPTIONS FOR MILLENIA
17 Inch Chrome Wheels +359
Bose Sound System[Opt on STD] +479
Compact Disc Changer +299
Heated Front Seats +180
Heated Power Mirrors +123
Pearlescent White Paint +227
Traction Control System[Opt on STD] +180
Tutone Paint +227

MPV 2001

Not much changes on Mazda's minivan. Keyless entry is standard on MPV LX, and the AM/FM/CD/cassette audio system is standard on LX and ES models. Child safety-seat anchors have been added to all MPV models, as have new exterior color choices. The 2.5-liter V6 engine now complies with NLEV emissions standards.

Category P

4 Dr DX Pass. Van	13599	14534	16093
4 Dr ES Pass. Van	17037	18209	20162
4 Dr LX Pass. Van	15110	16150	17882

OPTIONS FOR MPV
Aluminum/Alloy Wheels[Std on ES] +150
Compact Disc Changer[Std on ES] +269
Entertainment System +955
Fog Lights +150
Luggage Rack +120
Power Moonroof +419
Power Windows[Opt on DX] +153
Rear Air Conditioning w/Rear Heater[Std on ES] +356
Rear Heater +117
Side Air Bag Restraints[Std on ES] +159

MX-5 MIATA 2001

For 2001, the Miata receives a host of minor changes. Horsepower has been increased, and a six-speed manual transmission is now optional on Miata LS. Both the exterior and interior have been updated and there are four new exterior colors. Regular Miatas now have 15-inch wheels as standard equipment, while both the Miata LS and cars equipped with the optional suspension package get 16-inch wheels. Safety and security is improved via seatbelt pre-tensioners, improved ABS, an engine immobilizer, an internal trunk release, and optional keyless remote (standard on Miata LS).

Category E

2 Dr MX-5 LS Conv	15682	16680	18342
2 Dr MX-5 Special Edition Conv			
	16873	17947	19735
2 Dr MX-5 Conv	13860	14741	16210

OPTIONS FOR MX-5 MIATA
6-Speed Transmission +389
Anti-Lock Brakes +329
Automatic 4-Speed Transmission +539
Hardtop Roof +898
Limited Slip Differential[Opt on MX-5] +150
Rear Spoiler +177

PROTEGE 2001

Already one of the best-looking economy sedans on the market, the Protege receives freshened exterior styling for 2001. ES models now have standard 16-inch wheels, and 15-inch wheels are optional on LX models. A larger 2.0-liter engine replaces the previous 1.8-liter engine. All Proteges get a revised interior and improvements to ride comfort, braking effort and steering feel. Front seatbelt pre-tensioners are standard.

Category B

4 Dr DX Sdn	8048	8774	9985
4 Dr ES Sdn	11267	12284	13979
4 Dr LX Sdn	9772	10654	12124
4 Dr MP3 Sdn	13557	14781	16820

OPTIONS FOR PROTEGE
4 cyl 2.0 L Engine[Opt on LX] +239
Air Conditioning[Std on ES] +658
Anti-Lock Brakes +299
Automatic 4-Speed Transmission +479
Compact Disc Changer +299
Power Moonroof +419
Rear Spoiler +198
Side Air Bag Restraints +150

TRIBUTE 2001

Mazda's first sport-utility vehicle since the departure of the Navajo half a decade ago, the Tribute combines car-like ride and handling with the ability to go in the snow and tote up to five passengers and a healthy amount of their luggage. With the most powerful V6 in its class, in addition to handsome looks and a spacious cabin, the Tribute should find huge success despite an increasingly crowded small-SUV marketplace.

Category L

4 Dr DX 4WD Wgn	14131	15066	16625
4 Dr DX V6 4WD Wgn	15742	16784	18520
4 Dr DX V6 Wgn	14746	15722	17348
4 Dr DX Wgn	12922	13777	15202
4 Dr ES V6 4WD Wgn	17649	18817	20764
4 Dr ES V6 Wgn	16751	17859	19707
4 Dr LX V6 4WD Wgn	16890	18007	19870

Don't forget to refer to the Mileage Adjustment Table at the back of this book!

Model Description	Trade-in TMV	Private TMV	Dealer TMV
4 Dr LX V6 Wgn	15994	17052	18816

OPTIONS FOR TRIBUTE
AM/FM Stereo Tape +120
Aluminum/Alloy Wheels[Opt on DX] +224
Anti-Lock Brakes +180
Camper/Towing Package +210
Power Moonroof +359
Premium Sound System +302
Side Air Bag Restraints +150

2000 MAZDA

626   2000

Improvements in styling, handling, steering, interior content, and options are the highlights of the 2000 626.
Category D

Model Description	Trade-in TMV	Private TMV	Dealer TMV
4 Dr ES Sdn	11161	12520	13774
4 Dr ES V6 Sdn	12294	13791	15173
4 Dr LX Sdn	9941	11151	12268
4 Dr LX V6 Sdn	10899	12226	13451

OPTIONS FOR 626
AM/FM Stereo Tape +150
AM/FM Stereo/CD/Tape[Std on ES V6] +210
Alarm System[Std on ES V6] +150
Aluminum/Alloy Wheels[Std on ES,ES V6] +299
Anti-Lock Brakes +330
Automatic 4-Speed Transmission[Std on ES] +479
Bose Sound System[Std on ES V6] +210
Compact Disc Changer +134
Fog Lights +150
Heated Power Mirrors[Std on ES V6] +93
Power Drivers Seat[Std on ES V6] +150
Power Moonroof[Std on ES V6] +539
Rear Spoiler +236
Side Air Bag Restraints +150
Traction Control System +119

B-SERIES   2000

Two B3000 regular-cab models are added—SX and SE. The B2500 Troy Lee edition has been discontinued. Fog lights are standard on all 4x4 models. A CD-equipped audio system is standard on all B4000 models. P225/70R15 tires are standard on SX models, and air conditioning is standard on SE and Troy Lee edition models. A 6,000-pound trailer hitch is standard on B4000 4x4s and optional on B4000 4x2 models. Troy Lee editions get standard leather-wrapped steering wheels.
Category J

Model Description	Trade-in TMV	Private TMV	Dealer TMV
2 Dr B2500 SE Ext Cab SB	8495	9510	10448
2 Dr B2500 SE Std Cab SB	6861	7682	8439
2 Dr B2500 SX Std Cab SB	5636	6310	6932
2 Dr B3000 SE 4WD Std Cab SB	9311	10424	11452
2 Dr B3000 SE Ext Cab SB	8821	9875	10849
2 Dr B3000 SE Std Cab SB	7106	7956	8740
4 Dr B3000 SE 4WD Ext Cab SB	10781	12070	13260
4 Dr B3000 SE Ext Cab SB	9148	10242	11252
2 Dr B3000 SX Std Cab SB	5881	6584	7233
4 Dr B3000 TL Ext Cab SB	9965	11156	12256
4 Dr B4000 SE 4WD Ext Cab SB	12088	13534	14868
4 Dr B4000 SE Ext Cab SB	11598	12985	14265
4 Dr B4000 TL 4WD Ext Cab SB	12660	14174	15571

OPTIONS FOR B-SERIES
AM/FM Stereo Tape +119
Air Conditioning[Opt on B2500 SX,B3000 SX] +481
Anti-Lock Brakes +299
Automatic 4-Speed Transmission +655
Automatic 5-Speed Transmission[Opt on B4000 4WD] +685
Bed Liner[Std on B4000 SE,B4000TL] +119
Cruise Control[Std on B4000] +99
Power Door Locks[Std on B4000 SE,B4000TL] +111
Power Windows[Std on B4000 SE,B4000TL] +144
Tilt Steering Wheel[Std on B4000 SE,B4000TL] +111

MILLENIA   2000

Millenia models receive considerable price reductions to make them more competitive in the market. Mazda is also offering a special 2000 Millenium edition of the Millenia. This version comes with 17-inch chrome wheels, an in-dash six-disc CD changer, suede seat and door trim, and a choice of either Highlight Silver Mica or Millennium Red Mica paint.
Category H

Model Description	Trade-in TMV	Private TMV	Dealer TMV
4 Dr STD Sdn	13413	14715	15917
4 Dr Millennium Supercharged Sdn	15940	17487	18915
4 Dr S Supercharged Sdn	15750	17279	18690

OPTIONS FOR MILLENIA
Bose Sound System[Opt on STD] +419
Chrome Wheels[Opt on S] +299

Don't forget to refer to the Mileage Adjustment Table at the back of this book!

MAZDA 00-99

Model Description	Trade-in TMV	Private TMV	Dealer TMV	Model Description	Trade-in TMV	Private TMV	Dealer TMV

Dual Power Seats[Opt on STD] +383
Heated Front Seats +180
Heated Power Mirrors +123
Leather Seats[Opt on STD] +658
Power Moonroof[Opt on STD] +553
Special Factory Paint +228
Traction Control System[Opt on STD] +180

MPV   2000

The MPV has been completely redesigned from top to bottom. Several unique features, like hinged rear doors and all-wheel drive, have disappeared. At the same time, items like roll-down windows in the sliding doors and tailgate seating in the third-row seats certify the MPV as a standout vehicle.

Category P

Model Description	Trade-in	Private	Dealer
4 Dr DX Pass. Van	11327	12604	13784
4 Dr ES Pass. Van	14178	15778	17254
4 Dr LX Pass. Van	12752	14191	15519

OPTIONS FOR MPV

Alarm System[Std on ES] +105
Aluminum/Alloy Wheels[Std on ES] +150
Compact Disc Changer[Std on ES] +359
Cruise Control[Opt on DX] +105
Dual Air Conditioning[Std on ES] +356
Fog Lights +150
GFX Package +539
Lighted Entry System[Opt on LX] +102
Luggage Rack[Opt on DX] +105
Power Door Locks[Opt on DX] +134
Power Moonroof +419
Power Windows[Opt on DX] +153
Rear Heater +117
Rear Spoiler +159
Side Air Bag Restraints[Std on ES] +159

MX-5 MIATA   2000

The Miata's option packages have been simplified. There are now two models — Miata and Miata LS — and three option packages. A six-speed Miata Special-Edition will also be available by spring 2000.

Category E

Model Description	Trade-in	Private	Dealer
2 Dr MX-5 Conv	12200	13339	14391
2 Dr MX-5 LS Conv	13826	15117	16309
2 Dr MX-5 Special ED. Conv			
	14477	15829	17077

OPTIONS FOR MX-5 MIATA

AM/FM Stereo Tape +119
Air Conditioning[Opt on MX-5,MX-5 LS] +539
Anti-Lock Brakes +330
Automatic 4-Speed Transmission +509
Cruise Control[Opt on MX-5] +108
Fog Lights[Opt on MX-5,MX-5 LS] +150
Hardtop Roof +718
Limited Slip Differential[Opt on MX-5] +150

Power Door Locks[Opt on MX-5] +114
Rear Spoiler +180

PROTEGE   2000

Front-seat side airbags and an improved ABS system are new to the LX premium and ES premium packages. The LX and ES also get illuminated power window switches. Chrome plating has been added to the inner door handles, and a Mazda symbol now appears on the steering wheel, the parking brake button, and the automatic transmission shift-lever button. The Twilight Blue Mica exterior color has been discontinued and replaced with Midnight Blue Mica.

Category B

Model Description	Trade-in	Private	Dealer
4 Dr DX Sdn	7038	8185	9244
4 Dr ES Sdn	9098	10581	11950
4 Dr LX Sdn	7983	9284	10485

OPTIONS FOR PROTEGE

AM/FM Compact Disc Player[Opt on DX] +299
AM/FM Stereo Tape +150
AM/FM Stereo/CD/Tape +210
Air Conditioning[Std on ES] +658
Alarm System[Std on ES] +111
Anti-Lock Brakes +479
Automatic 4-Speed Transmission +479
Power Moonroof +479
Rear Spoiler +119
Side Air Bag Restraints +150

1999 MAZDA

626   1999

After a major makeover in '98, the 626 slides into '99 with only one major change: a new height-adjustable seat for the driver.

Category D

Model Description	Trade-in	Private	Dealer
4 Dr ES Sdn	9268	10462	11656
4 Dr ES V6 Sdn	10532	11889	13246
4 Dr LX Sdn	8341	9416	10491
4 Dr LX V6 Sdn	9184	10368	11551

OPTIONS FOR 626

AM/FM Stereo Tape +120
AM/FM Stereo/CD/Tape +168
Alarm System[Std on ES V6] +120
Aluminum/Alloy Wheels[Std on ES V6] +240
Anti-Lock Brakes +264
Automatic 4-Speed Transmission[Std on ES] +384
Bose Sound System[Std on ES V6] +168
Power Drivers Seat[Std on ES,ES V6] +120
Power Moonroof[Std on ES V6] +432
Traction Control System[Opt on ES V6,LX V6] +96

B-SERIES   1999

The B-Series now comes with a four-door option called

MAZDA 99

Model Description	Trade-in TMV	Private TMV	Dealer TMV	Model Description	Trade-in TMV	Private TMV	Dealer TMV

the Cab Plus 4. Option packages have been consolidated and simplified this year to reduce buyer confusion. A class III frame mounted hitch receiver is available with V6 applications.

Category J

Model Description	Trade-in TMV	Private TMV	Dealer TMV
2 Dr B2500 SE Ext Cab SB	7209	8109	9010
2 Dr B2500 SE Std Cab SB	5927	6667	7408
4 Dr B2500 SE Ext Cab SB	7458	8390	9322
2 Dr B2500 SX Std Cab SB	4725	5316	5906
2 Dr B2500 TL Std Cab SB	6327	7117	7908
2 Dr B3000 SE 4WD Ext Cab SB	8993	10116	11240
2 Dr B3000 SE 4WD Std Cab SB	8330	9370	10411
2 Dr B3000 SE Ext Cab SB	7439	8369	9298
4 Dr B3000 SE 4WD Ext Cab SB	8948	10066	11184
4 Dr B3000 SE Ext Cab SB	7849	8829	9810
4 Dr B3000 TL Ext Cab SB	8570	9640	10711
2 Dr B4000 SE 4WD Ext Cab SB	10252	11533	12814
2 Dr B4000 SE Ext Cab SB	9019	10146	11273
2 Dr B4000 SE Std Cab SB	7529	8469	9410
4 Dr B4000 SE 4WD Ext Cab SB	10372	11668	12964
4 Dr B4000 SE Ext Cab SB	9050	10181	11312
4 Dr B4000 TL 4WD Ext Cab SB	11052	12433	13814

OPTIONS FOR B-SERIES
Air Conditioning[Opt on B2500 SX] +387
Anti-Lock Brakes +240
Automatic 4-Speed Transmission +526
Automatic 5-Speed Transmission[Std on B4000 SE 2WD CAB PLUS/ CAB PLUS4] +526
Bed Liner +95
Power Windows +115

MIATA   1999

Mazda cautiously redesigns the Miata, improving the car in every way without bumping up the price or diluting the car's personality. Very nice job.

Category E

Model Description	Trade-in TMV	Private TMV	Dealer TMV
2 Dr MX-5 Conv	11424	12640	13856
2 Dr MX-5 10TH Anniv. Conv	15577	17236	18894

OPTIONS FOR MIATA
AM/FM Stereo Tape[Opt on MX-5] +96
AM/FM Stereo/CD/Tape[Opt on MX-5] +168
Air Conditioning +432
Anti-Lock Brakes +264
Automatic 4-Speed Transmission +409
Bose Sound System[Opt on MX-5] +264
Fog Lights[Opt on MX-5] +120
Hardtop Roof +640
Leather Seats[Opt on MX-5] +430
Limited Slip Differential[Opt on MX-5] +120
Popular Equipment Package +932
Power Door Locks[Opt on MX-5] +91
Power Steering[Opt on MX-5] +144
Power Windows[Opt on MX-5] +104
Rear Spoiler[Opt on MX-5] +144

MILLENIA   1999

Revised front- and rear-end styling, plus an optional two-tone color scheme, separate the '99 Millenia from past models.

Category H

Model Description	Trade-in TMV	Private TMV	Dealer TMV
4 Dr STD Sdn	12057	13363	14669
4 Dr S Supercharged Sdn	13575	15046	16516

OPTIONS FOR MILLENIA
Bose Sound System[Std on S] +336
Chrome Wheels +240
Dual Power Seats[Std on S] +307
Heated Front Seats +144
Heated Power Mirrors +99
Leather Seats[Std on S] +528
Power Moonroof[Std on S] +444
Special Factory Paint +182
Traction Control System[Std on S] +144

PROTEGE   1999

The Protege gets an extensive makeover for '99 that includes new exterior and interior styling, a more powerful engine lineup, additional luxury options, and five new colors.

Category B

Model Description	Trade-in TMV	Private TMV	Dealer TMV
4 Dr DX Sdn	5776	6700	7623
4 Dr ES Sdn	7786	9030	10275
4 Dr LX Sdn	6614	7672	8729

OPTIONS FOR PROTEGE
AM/FM Compact Disc Player[Opt on DX] +240
AM/FM Stereo Tape +120
AM/FM Stereo/CD/Tape +168
Air Conditioning[Std on ES] +528

Don't forget to refer to the Mileage Adjustment Table at the back of this book!

Model Description	Trade-in TMV	Private TMV	Dealer TMV
Aluminum/Alloy Wheels +192			
Anti-Lock Brakes +384			
Automatic 4-Speed Transmission +384			
Power Moonroof +384			
Rear Spoiler +96			

1998 MAZDA

626 — 1998

Mazda redesigns the 626, giving it more upscale styling, more powerful engines, a tighter body and increased cargo and people space while retaining the sedan's distinctive sporting nature.

Category D

Model Description	Trade-in TMV	Private TMV	Dealer TMV
4 Dr DX Sdn	6644	7518	8465
4 Dr ES Sdn	9550	10806	12168
4 Dr LX Sdn	7557	8552	9629
4 Dr LX V6 Sdn	8387	9491	10687

OPTIONS FOR 626

AM/FM Compact Disc Player[Opt on DX] +145
AM/FM Stereo Tape +104
Air Conditioning[Opt on DX] +409
Alarm System[Opt on LX] +104
Aluminum/Alloy Wheels[Std on ES] +208
Anti-Lock Brakes[Opt on LX] +228
Automatic 4-Speed Transmission +332
Bose Sound System[Std on ES] +145
Keyless Entry System[Opt on LX] +125
Leather Seats[Opt on LX] +289
Power Drivers Seat[Std on ES] +104
Power Moonroof[Std on ES] +374

B-SERIES PICKUP — 1998

Fresh styling, a revised front suspension, a larger regular cab, a more powerful 2.5-liter four-cylinder engine, a stiffer frame and a new 4WD system ensure that Mazda's compact truck will remain competitive through the end of the century.

Category J

Model Description	Trade-in TMV	Private TMV	Dealer TMV
2 Dr B2500 SE Ext Cab SB			
	5803	6577	7416
2 Dr B2500 SE Std Cab SB			
	4797	5437	6131
4 Dr B2500 SE Ext Cab SB			
	5969	6765	7628
2 Dr B2500 SX Std Cab SB			
	4023	4560	5142
2 Dr B3000 SE 4WD Ext Cab SB			
	7196	8156	9196
2 Dr B3000 SE 4WD Std Cab SB			
	6886	7805	8800
2 Dr B3000 SE Ext Cab SB			
	6112	6927	7811
2 Dr B3000 SX 4WD Std Cab SB			
	5946	6739	7599
2 Dr B4000 SE 4WD Ext Cab SB			
	8511	9647	10877
2 Dr B4000 SE Ext Cab SB			
	6732	7630	8603

OPTIONS FOR B-SERIES PICKUP

AM/FM Stereo/CD/Tape +116
Air Conditioning +334
Alarm System +104
Aluminum/Alloy Wheels +110
Anti-Lock Brakes +293
Automatic 4-Speed Transmission +455
Automatic 5-Speed Transmission[Opt on B4000] +470
Bed Liner +115
Limited Slip Differential +115
Power Windows +100

MILLENIA — 1998

Millenia carries over into 1998 with no changes.

Category H

Model Description	Trade-in TMV	Private TMV	Dealer TMV
4 Dr STD Sdn	10510	11762	13118
4 Dr S Supercharged Sdn			
	11577	12956	14450

OPTIONS FOR MILLENIA

Bose Sound System[Std on S] +291
Compact Disc Changer[Opt on STD] +228
Dual Power Seats[Std on S] +208
Heated Front Seats +125
Leather Seats[Std on S] +457
Power Moonroof[Std on S] +413
Premium Package +416
Special Factory Paint +145
Traction Control System[Std on S] +125

MPV — 1998

A CD player is now standard.

Category P

Model Description	Trade-in TMV	Private TMV	Dealer TMV
2 Dr ES 4WD Pass. Van	11039	12448	13975
2 Dr ES Pass. Van	9981	11255	12635
2 Dr LX 4WD Pass. Van	10132	11425	12826
2 Dr LX Pass. Van	8620	9720	10912

OPTIONS FOR MPV

AM/FM Stereo Tape +104
AM/FM Stereo/CD/Tape[Opt on LX 4WD] +104
Air Conditioning +249
Aluminum/Alloy Wheels[Std on ES 4WD] +205
Automatic Load Leveling[Opt on LX] +205
Captain Chairs (4)[Opt on LX 4WD] +167
Dual Air Conditioning +499
Leather Seats[Opt on LX] +457
Luggage Rack[Opt on LX] +118
Power Moonroof +499
Privacy Glass +104

Don't forget to refer to the Mileage Adjustment Table at the back of this book!

Model Description	Trade-in TMV	Private TMV	Dealer TMV

PROTEGE   1998

A CD player is standard on ES and LX. It also comes on DX models equipped with an option package.

Category B

Model Description	Trade-in TMV	Private TMV	Dealer TMV
4 Dr DX Sdn	4657	5369	6140
4 Dr ES Sdn	6321	7287	8333
4 Dr LX Sdn	5240	6040	6908

OPTIONS FOR PROTEGE

AM/FM Compact Disc Player[Opt on DX] +208
AM/FM Stereo Tape +104
AM/FM Stereo/CD/Tape +145
Air Conditioning[Std on ES] +416
Aluminum/Alloy Wheels +167
Anti-Lock Brakes +332
Automatic 4-Speed Transmission +332
Compact Disc Changer +228
Power Moonroof +291

1997 MAZDA

626   1997

LX V6 and ES models gain power and torque, while the four-cylinder LX gets a Lexus-like trim package that includes two-tone paint, chrome wheel covers, leather interior, and other creature comforts. Audio systems are revised and two new colors debut.

Category D

Model Description	Trade-in TMV	Private TMV	Dealer TMV
4 Dr DX Sdn	5265	5960	6810
4 Dr ES Sdn	7856	8894	10162
4 Dr LX Sdn	6075	6877	7858
4 Dr LX V6 Sdn	6803	7702	8800

OPTIONS FOR 626

AM/FM Compact Disc Player +131
AM/FM Stereo Tape[Opt on DX] +90
Air Conditioning[Opt on DX] +369
Alarm System[Opt on LX,LX V6] +93
Aluminum/Alloy Wheels[Opt on LX] +188
Anti-Lock Brakes[Std on ES] +300
Automatic 4-Speed Transmission +300
Chrome Wheels[Opt on LX] +93
Keyless Entry System[Std on ES] +113
Leather Seats[Std on ES] +260
Power Drivers Seat[Opt on LX V6] +93
Power Moonroof +328

B-SERIES PICKUP   1997

The lineup is trimmed, leaving just B2300 and B4000 models available. SE-5 designation returns to bolster marketing efforts. B4000 pickups can be equipped with a new five-speed automatic transmission.

Category J

Model Description	Trade-in TMV	Private TMV	Dealer TMV
2 Dr B2300 Std Cab SB	3033	3478	4022
2 Dr B2300 SE Ext Cab SB	4882	5599	6474
2 Dr B2300 SE Std Cab SB	3699	4242	4905
2 Dr B4000 4WD Ext Cab SB	6731	7718	8925
2 Dr B4000 4WD Std Cab SB	5473	6276	7258
2 Dr B4000 SE 4WD Ext Cab SB	7470	8566	9906
2 Dr B4000 SE Ext Cab SB	5400	6192	7160

OPTIONS FOR B-SERIES PICKUP

Air Conditioning +301
Anti-Lock Brakes +253
Automatic 4-Speed Transmission +401
Automatic 5-Speed Transmission +414
Bed Liner +103
Camper/Towing Package +124
Compact Disc Changer +166
Dual Air Bag Restraints +93
Limited Slip Differential +103
Sport Seats +135

MIATA   1997

Mazda adds a Touring Package to the options list, consisting of alloy wheels, power steering, leather-wrapped steering wheel, power mirrors, power windows, and door map pockets. Midyear a new M-Edition debuts, sporting Marina Green paint and chromed alloy wheels. Summertime brings the limited-production STO-Edition, of which 1,500 were produced.

Category E

Model Description	Trade-in TMV	Private TMV	Dealer TMV
2 Dr MX-5 Conv	8112	9174	10472
2 Dr MX-5 M-Edition Conv	10242	11584	13223
2 Dr MX-5 STO Conv	9586	10842	12376

OPTIONS FOR MIATA

AM/FM Stereo/CD/Tape[Opt on MX-5] +131
Air Conditioning[Opt on MX-5] +337
Anti-Lock Brakes +337
Automatic 4-Speed Transmission +319
Hardtop Roof +499
Leather Seats[Opt on MX-5] +335
Power Steering[Opt on MX-5] +113
Rear Spoiler +113

MILLENIA   1997

Models equipped with leather are upgraded this year with an eight-way power passenger seat, 16-inch alloy wheels, and revised final drive ratio for better low-end response. S models also get the power passenger

Model Description	Trade-in TMV	Private TMV	Dealer TMV	Model Description	Trade-in TMV	Private TMV	Dealer TMV

seat. All Millenias have a new rear-window-mounted diversity antenna, a new sound system with in-dash CD player, revised center console design, and Michelin tires.

Category H

Model Description	Trade-in	Private	Dealer
4 Dr STD Sdn	9181	10311	11692
4 Dr L Sdn	9340	10490	11895
4 Dr S Supercharged Sdn			
	10219	11477	13014

OPTIONS FOR MILLENIA
Bose Sound System +262
Heated Front Seats +113
Special Factory Paint +131
Traction Control System[Std on S] +113

MPV 1997

Four-wheel ABS is standard across the board, and all but the LX 2WD model are dressed in dorky All-Sport exterior trim.

Category P

Model Description	Trade-in	Private	Dealer
2 Dr ES 4WD Pass. Van	9478	10753	12311
2 Dr ES Pass. Van	8522	9669	11070
2 Dr LX 4WD Pass. Van	8816	10002	11452
2 Dr LX Pass. Van	7274	8252	9448

OPTIONS FOR MPV
7 Passenger Seating[Opt on LX] +150
AM/FM Compact Disc Player +131
AM/FM Stereo/CD/Tape +93
Air Conditioning +224
Aluminum/Alloy Wheels[Std on ES,4WD] +185
Automatic Load Leveling[Opt on LX] +185
Dual Air Conditioning +412
Luggage Rack[Std on ES,4WD] +106
Power Moonroof +449
Privacy Glass +93

MX6 1997

All LS models get a rear spoiler.

Category E

Model Description	Trade-in	Private	Dealer
2 Dr STD Cpe	7277	8229	9394
2 Dr LS Cpe	8682	9819	11208

OPTIONS FOR MX6
Air Conditioning[Std on LS] +337
Alarm System[Opt on STD] +93
Anti-Lock Brakes +300
Automatic 4-Speed Transmission +300
Leather Seats +260
Power Drivers Seat +116
Power Sunroof[Std on LS] +281
Rear Spoiler[Std on LS] +141

PROTEGE 1997

Styling revisions inside and out update this roomy compact nicely.

Category B

Model Description	Trade-in	Private	Dealer
4 Dr DX Sdn	4162	4855	5702
4 Dr ES Sdn	5602	6535	7675
4 Dr LX Sdn	4721	5508	6469

OPTIONS FOR PROTEGE
AM/FM Compact Disc Player[Opt on LX] +131
AM/FM Stereo Tape[Opt on DX] +93
AM/FM Stereo/CD/Tape[Opt on LX] +131
Air Conditioning[Std on ES] +374
Aluminum/Alloy Wheels +150
Anti-Lock Brakes +300
Automatic 4-Speed Transmission +300
Power Moonroof +262

1996 MAZDA

626 1996

Chrome is tacked on front and rear, and the hood is raised a bit to give the 626 a more substantial look. ABS is available as a stand alone option on LX and LX V6 models for the first time (formerly, you had to buy an option package), and side-impact protection meets 1997 standards.

Category D

Model Description	Trade-in	Private	Dealer
4 Dr DX Sdn	3825	4452	5319
4 Dr ES Sdn	5626	6549	7823
4 Dr LX Sdn	4275	4976	5945
4 Dr LX V6 Sdn	4876	5675	6780

OPTIONS FOR 626
AM/FM Stereo/CD/Tape +124
Air Conditioning[Opt on DX] +342
Aluminum/Alloy Wheels +177
Anti-Lock Brakes[Std on ES] +283
Automatic 4-Speed Transmission +283
Keyless Entry System[Opt on LX,LX V6] +100
Leather Seats +247
Power Moonroof[Std on ES] +310

B-SERIES PICKUP 1996

A passenger side airbag comes with SE Plus and LE trim levels, and it can be deactivated in the event that a rear facing child safety seat is installed. SE models also get new chrome bumpers.

Category J

Model Description	Trade-in	Private	Dealer
2 Dr B2300 Std Cab LB	3199	3710	4416
2 Dr B2300 4WD Std Cab SB			
	4551	5277	6281
2 Dr B2300 Ext Cab SB	3911	4535	5398
2 Dr B2300 Std Cab SB	2986	3463	4122
2 Dr B2300 SE Ext Cab SB			
	4337	5030	5986

Model Description	Trade-in TMV	Private TMV	Dealer TMV
2 Dr B2300 SE Std Cab SB	3697	4288	5103
2 Dr B3000 4WD Ext Cab SB	5332	6184	7360
2 Dr B3000 SE Ext Cab SB	4480	5195	6183
2 Dr B4000 LE 4WD Ext Cab SB	7892	9152	10893
2 Dr B4000 LE Ext Cab SB	5190	6019	7164
2 Dr B4000 SE 4WD Ext Cab SB	6755	7833	9323
2 Dr B4000 SE 4WD Std Cab SB	5475	6349	7557

OPTIONS FOR B-SERIES PICKUP
Air Conditioning[Std on B4000 LE] +285
Anti-Lock Brakes +240
Automatic 4-Speed Transmission +370
Bed Liner +98
Camper/Towing Package +108
Compact Disc Changer +157

MIATA   1996

Side-impact standards for 1997 are met a year early, and to offset the added weight, Mazda boosts power and torque.
Category E

2 Dr MX-5 Conv	6307	7149	8312
2 Dr MX-5 M-Edition Conv	8302	9411	10942

OPTIONS FOR MIATA
AM/FM Compact Disc Player +168
AM/FM Stereo/CD/Tape +124
Air Conditioning[Opt on MX-5] +320
Anti-Lock Brakes[Opt on MX-5] +320
Automatic 4-Speed Transmission +301
Hardtop Roof +473
Leather Seats[Opt on MX-5] +318
Power Steering[Opt on MX-5] +106
Rear Spoiler +106

MILLENIA   1996

The Millenia S gets revised bright-finish alloy wheels.
Category H

4 Dr STD Sdn	7362	8347	9706
4 Dr L Sdn	7746	8782	10212
4 Dr S Supercharged Sdn	8437	9565	11123

OPTIONS FOR MILLENIA
Bose Sound System +425

Compact Disc Changer +195
Heated Front Seats +106
Traction Control System[Std on S] +106

MPV   1996

New styling up front, a fourth door on the driver's side, and a revised instrument panel with dual airbags sum up the changes to Mazda's attempt at a minivan.
Category P

2 Dr DX Pass. Van	5125	5878	6919
2 Dr ES 4WD Pass. Van	7020	8052	9478
2 Dr ES Pass. Van	6037	6925	8151
2 Dr LX 4WD Pass. Van	6388	7328	8625
2 Dr LX Pass. Van	5405	6200	7298

OPTIONS FOR MPV
7 Passenger Seating[Opt on LX] +142
AM/FM Compact Disc Player +124
Air Conditioning +320
Aluminum/Alloy Wheels[Opt on 2WD] +176
Automatic Load Leveling[Opt on LX] +176
Dual Air Conditioning +390
Power Moonroof +425

MX6   1996

No changes for 1995.
Category E

2 Dr STD Cpe	6041	6848	7962
2 Dr LS Cpe	7169	8126	9448
2 Dr M-Edition Cpe	8619	9771	11360

OPTIONS FOR MX6
Air Conditioning[Std on STD] +320
Anti-Lock Brakes[Opt on LS,STD] +283
Automatic 4-Speed Transmission +283
Leather Seats[Opt on LS] +247
Power Drivers Seat[Opt on LS] +110
Power Sunroof[Opt on STD] +266
Rear Spoiler[Opt on LS,STD] +133

PROTEGE   1996

No changes for 1996.
Category B

4 Dr DX Sdn	3191	3809	4663
4 Dr ES Sdn	4305	5139	6291
4 Dr LX Sdn	3340	3987	4881

OPTIONS FOR PROTEGE
Air Conditioning[Std on ES] +355
Aluminum/Alloy Wheels +142
Anti-Lock Brakes +283
Automatic 4-Speed Transmission +283
Power Moonroof +248

1995 MAZDA

626   1995

Don't forget to refer to the Mileage Adjustment Table at the back of this book!

Model Description	Trade-in TMV	Private TMV	Dealer TMV

ES gets remote keyless entry, which is available on LX and LX-V6 models. New wheels and wheelcovers are added across the board.

Category D

Model	Trade-in TMV	Private TMV	Dealer TMV
4 Dr DX Sdn	3085	3569	4376
4 Dr ES Sdn	4553	5268	6459
4 Dr LX Sdn	3379	3909	4793
4 Dr LX V6 Sdn	3893	4504	5522

OPTIONS FOR 626

Air Conditioning[Opt on DX] +298
Aluminum/Alloy Wheels[Opt on LX] +155
Anti-Lock Brakes[Std on ES] +170
Automatic 4-Speed Transmission +248
Power Moonroof[Std on ES] +272

929 1995

Leather seats, wood trim and remote keyless entry are standard. Final year for sleek executive sedan.

Category H

Model	Trade-in TMV	Private TMV	Dealer TMV
4 Dr STD Sdn	5997	6853	8280

OPTIONS FOR 929

Limited Slip Differential +78

B-SERIES PICKUP 1995

Redesigned dashboard with driver airbag debuts. Four-wheel ABS is standard on 4WD and 2WD B4000 models.

Category J

Model	Trade-in TMV	Private TMV	Dealer TMV
2 Dr B2300 Std Cab LB	2862	3301	4033
2 Dr B2300 4WD Std Cab SB	4048	4670	5705
2 Dr B2300 Ext Cab SB	3484	4019	4910
2 Dr B2300 Std Cab SB	2792	3221	3935
2 Dr B2300 SE Ext Cab SB	3700	4268	5214
2 Dr B2300 SE Std Cab SB	3357	3872	4731
2 Dr B3000 SE 4WD Ext Cab SB	4608	5315	6493
2 Dr B3000 SE Ext Cab SB	3770	4348	5312
2 Dr B3000 SE Std Cab SB	3429	3955	4832
2 Dr B4000 LE 4WD Ext Cab SB	7051	8133	9936
2 Dr B4000 LE Ext Cab SB	4468	5153	6296
2 Dr B4000 SE 4WD Ext Cab SB	5934	6844	8362
2 Dr B4000 SE 4WD Std Cab SB	4817	5556	6788
2 Dr B4000 SE Ext Cab SB	3839	4428	5410

OPTIONS FOR B-SERIES PICKUP

Air Conditioning[Std on B4000 LE] +250
Automatic 4-Speed Transmission +324
Compact Disc Changer +138
Sport Seats +112

MIATA 1995

Option packages are revised, and a gorgeous M-Edition with Merlot Mica paint, tan top, tan leather interior, and 15-inch BBS rims is available.

Category E

Model	Trade-in TMV	Private TMV	Dealer TMV
2 Dr MX-5 Conv	4986	5678	6830
2 Dr MX-5 M-Edition Conv	6521	7425	8932

OPTIONS FOR MIATA

AM/FM Stereo/CD/Tape +108
Air Conditioning[Opt on MX-5] +278
Anti-Lock Brakes[Opt on MX-5] +170
Automatic 4-Speed Transmission +264
Hardtop Roof +413
Leather Seats[Opt on MX-5] +277
Limited Slip Differential +78
Sensory Sound System +272
Sport Seats +108

MILLENIA 1995

Luxury-oriented model that was to be in Mazda's aborted upscale Amati luxury division. Positioned to do battle with entry-level Lexus, Infiniti and BMW models. S models have 2.3-liter V6 with Miller-cycle technology and 210 horsepower. Dual airbags and ABS are standard on all models. The Millenia S adds traction control.

Category H

Model	Trade-in TMV	Private TMV	Dealer TMV
4 Dr STD Sdn	5557	6351	7673
4 Dr S Supercharged Sdn	6435	7354	8885

OPTIONS FOR MILLENIA

Bose Sound System +216
Compact Disc Changer +170
Heated Front Seats +93
Leather Seats[Std on S] +340
Power Moonroof[Std on S] +286
Power Passenger Seat[Std on S] +108
Traction Control System[Opt on STD] +93

MPV 1995

New lineup includes L, LX and LXE trim levels. All come with seven-passenger seating. Four-cylinder engine has been dropped.

Category P

Model	Trade-in TMV	Private TMV	Dealer TMV
2 Dr L Pass. Van	3951	4521	5470
2 Dr LX 4WD Pass. Van	5178	5924	7168

Don't forget to refer to the Mileage Adjustment Table at the back of this book!

Model Description	Trade-in TMV	Private TMV	Dealer TMV
2 Dr LX Pass. Van	4088	4677	5659
2 Dr LXE 4WD Pass. Van			
	5723	6547	7922
2 Dr LXE Pass. Van	4701	5378	6507

OPTIONS FOR MPV
Air Conditioning +186
Aluminum/Alloy Wheels +153
Automatic Load Leveling[Opt on LX] +153
Camper/Towing Package[Opt on LX,LX 4WD] +93
Dual Air Conditioning +340
Power Moonroof +372

MX3 **1995**

GS model, and its cool 1.8-liter, V6 engine, vanishes. ABS is available only with manual transmission.

Category E

2 Dr STD Hbk	3251	3702	4453

OPTIONS FOR MX3
Air Conditioning +232
Aluminum/Alloy Wheels +100
Anti-Lock Brakes +248
Automatic 4-Speed Transmission +248
Power Sunroof +216
Power Windows +74
Rear Spoiler +78

MX6 **1995**

No changes for 1995.

Category E

2 Dr STD Cpe	4412	5024	6044
2 Dr LS Cpe	5186	5905	7104

OPTIONS FOR MX6
Air Conditioning[Std on LS] +278
Anti-Lock Brakes +248
Automatic 4-Speed Transmission +248
Leather Seats +215
Power Sunroof[Std on LS] +232
Rear Spoiler +116

PROTEGE **1995**

Totally redesigned, the Protege grows substantially in interior volume. Has 10 more cubic feet of volume than Honda Civic. Dual airbags are finally added. ABS is standard on ES trim level; optional on LX.

Category B

4 Dr DX Sdn	2785	3285	4118
4 Dr ES Sdn	3371	3976	4985
4 Dr LX Sdn	2932	3459	4336

OPTIONS FOR PROTEGE
AM/FM Stereo Tape[Opt on DX] +78
Air Conditioning[Std on ES] +310
Aluminum/Alloy Wheels +124
Anti-Lock Brakes[Opt on LX] +248
Automatic 4-Speed Transmission +248

Power Moonroof +216

RX-7 **1995**

CFC-free refrigerant is added to air conditioner. Touring package ousted. Red leather option dumped. Last year for RX-7.

Category F

2 Dr STD Turbo Rotary Cpe			
	15411	17306	20464

OPTIONS FOR RX-7
Air Dam +78
Automatic 4-Speed Transmission +232
Leather Seats +248
Power Sunroof +216
Rear Spoiler +93
Sport Suspension +232

1994 MAZDA

323 **1994**

No changes. Final year for homely, slow-selling hatchback.

Category B

2 Dr STD Hbk	1424	1770	2347

OPTIONS FOR 323
AM/FM Stereo Tape +113
Air Conditioning +211
Automatic 4-Speed Transmission +197

626 **1994**

Passenger airbag added. LX-V6 debuts. Four-cylinder models get new Ford transmission for smoother shifting than previous Mazda unit. ABS becomes standard on ES trim level, as well as leather seats and power sunroof.

Category D

4 Dr DX Sdn	2500	2959	3723
4 Dr ES Sdn	3571	4226	5317
4 Dr LX Sdn	2681	3173	3992
4 Dr LX V6 Sdn	2941	3480	4379

OPTIONS FOR 626
AM/FM Stereo/CD/Tape[Opt on LX V6] +98
Air Conditioning[Opt on DX] +270
Aluminum/Alloy Wheels +140
Anti-Lock Brakes +154
Automatic 4-Speed Transmission +224
Leather Seats +195
Power Moonroof[Std on ES] +246

929 **1994**

Trimmed to one model. Console cupholder added, height-adjustable seatbelts debut, and a limited-slip differential is included with the Cold Package. Premium Package adds remote keyless entry. New alloy wheels are standard.

Don't forget to refer to the Mileage Adjustment Table at the back of this book!

EDMUNDS® USED CARS & TRUCKS

Model Description	Trade-in TMV	Private TMV	Dealer TMV	Model Description	Trade-in TMV	Private TMV	Dealer TMV
Category H				replaced by Montego Blue. M-Edition is painted			
4 Dr STD Sdn	4600	5350	6600	Montego Blue with chromed alloys.			

OPTIONS FOR 929
Compact Disc Changer +176
Leather Seats +253
Power Passenger Seat +91
Premium Package +854

B-SERIES PICKUP 1994

Mazda revises the styling of Ford's Ranger, slaps its name on the tailgate, and has a new compact pickup to sell. Base, SE and LE trim levels are offered in two- or four-wheel drive and two bodystyles.

	Trade-in	Private	Dealer
Category J			
2 Dr B2300 Ext Cab SB	2880	3343	4116
2 Dr B2300 Std Cab SB	2338	2715	3342
2 Dr B2300 SE Std Cab SB	2751	3194	3932
2 Dr B3000 4WD Ext Cab SB	3919	4550	5601
2 Dr B3000 4WD Std Cab SB	3438	3992	4914
2 Dr B3000 Ext Cab SB	3025	3512	4324
2 Dr B3000 SE Std Cab LB	2952	3428	4220
2 Dr B3000 SE Ext Cab SB	3094	3592	4422
2 Dr B3000 SE Std Cab SB	2822	3277	4034
2 Dr B4000 LE 4WD Ext Cab SB	5638	6546	8059
2 Dr B4000 LE Ext Cab SB	3851	4471	5504
2 Dr B4000 SE Std Cab LB	2957	3433	4226
2 Dr B4000 SE 4WD Ext Cab SB	5019	5827	7174
2 Dr B4000 SE 4WD Std Cab SB	4194	4870	5995

OPTIONS FOR B-SERIES PICKUP
Air Conditioning +226
Automatic 4-Speed Transmission[Std on B4000 LE] +294
Bed Liner +77

MIATA 1994

Dual airbags arrive, and a 1.8-liter four cylinder making 128 horsepower replaces the original 1.6-liter engine. Sharp new alloy wheels debut. Optional automatic gets electronic shift controls. Larger diameter disc brakes are standard. Bigger gas tank added. New R package debuts with sportier suspension. Superman Blue

	Trade-in	Private	Dealer
Category E			
2 Dr MX-5 Conv	4047	4771	5977
2 Dr MX-5 M-Edition Conv	4758	5609	7027

OPTIONS FOR MIATA
AM/FM Stereo/CD/Tape[Opt on MX-5] +98
Air Conditioning[Opt on MX-5] +253
Anti-Lock Brakes +154
Automatic 4-Speed Transmission +238
Hardtop Roof +374
Leather Seats[Opt on MX-5] +252

MPV 1994

Side-door impact beams are added. Four-wheel disc brakes are new. Standard tire size increases.

	Trade-in	Private	Dealer
Category P			
2 Dr STD 4WD Pass. Van	3827	4449	5486
2 Dr STD Pass. Van	3101	3606	4446

OPTIONS FOR MPV
6 cyl 3.0 L Engine[Opt on STD] +211
7 Passenger Seating[Opt on STD] +113
8 Passenger Seating[Opt on STD] +105
AM/FM Compact Disc Player +98
Air Conditioning +168
Aluminum/Alloy Wheels +139
Automatic Load Leveling[Opt on STD] +139
Camper/Towing Package +84
Dual Air Conditioning +309
Leather Seats +309
Luxury Package +632
Power Moonroof +337

MX3 1994

Base model gets more power, and a passenger airbag is added. ABS can be ordered on base models for the first time. Can't get ABS on GS with automatic transmission. Base cars can be equipped with power sunroof. Both models get new wheels.

	Trade-in	Private	Dealer
Category E			
2 Dr STD Hbk	2795	3294	4127
2 Dr GS Hbk	3082	3633	4551

OPTIONS FOR MX3
Air Conditioning +211
Aluminum/Alloy Wheels[Opt on STD] +91
Anti-Lock Brakes +224
Automatic 4-Speed Transmission +224
Power Sunroof +197

MX6 1994

Passenger airbag debuts. Air conditioning and power sunroof become standard on LS.

MAZDA 94-93

Model Description	Trade-in TMV	Private TMV	Dealer TMV	Model Description	Trade-in TMV	Private TMV	Dealer TMV
Category E				*Leather Seats +224*			
2 Dr STD Cpe	3368	3970	4974	*Power Moonroof +238*			
2 Dr LS Cpe	4228	4984	6244	*Power Sunroof +197*			
				R-2 Package +519			
OPTIONS FOR MX6				*Rear Spoiler +84*			
Air Conditioning[Std on LS] +253				*Sport Suspension +211*			
Anti-Lock Brakes +224				*Touring Package +744*			
Automatic 4-Speed Transmission +224							

1993 MAZDA

Leather Seats +195
Power Drivers Seat[Opt on LS] +87
Power Sunroof[Std on LS] +211
Rear Spoiler +105

323 — 1993

No changes.

Model Description	Trade-in TMV	Private TMV	Dealer TMV
Category B			
2 Dr STD Hbk	941	1226	1700
2 Dr SE Hbk	1150	1498	2077

NAVAJO — 1994

Restyled alloy wheels are new. Since Ford won't give Mazda a four-door version of Explorer to sell, this is final year for Navajo as Mazda picks up its toys and goes home to pout.

Model Description	Trade-in TMV	Private TMV	Dealer TMV
Category M			
2 Dr DX 4WD Utility	4504	5187	6325
2 Dr DX Utility	3521	4055	4945
2 Dr LX 4WD Utility	4995	5752	7015
2 Dr LX Utility	3848	4432	5405

OPTIONS FOR NAVAJO
AM/FM Compact Disc Player +105
Air Conditioning +211
Automatic 4-Speed Transmission +224
Leather Seats +224
Moonroof +238

OPTIONS FOR 323
AM/FM Stereo Tape +97
Air Conditioning +182
Automatic 4-Speed Transmission +170

626 — 1993

Completely redesigned for 1993. First import-badged car to be classified domestic by EPA. Driver airbag is standard, and ABS is optional. Top-end ES model gets 2.5-liter V6 engine. DX and LX powered by four-cylinder motor.

Model Description	Trade-in TMV	Private TMV	Dealer TMV
Category D			
4 Dr DX Sdn	2074	2514	3248
4 Dr ES Sdn	2676	3244	4191
4 Dr LX Sdn	2408	2920	3772

PROTEGE — 1994

Minor styling revisions include new grille, headlamps, hood and front fascia.

Model Description	Trade-in TMV	Private TMV	Dealer TMV
Category B			
4 Dr DX Sdn	1899	2361	3131
4 Dr LX Sdn	2227	2768	3671
4 Dr Special Sdn	1572	1954	2591

OPTIONS FOR PROTEGE
Air Conditioning +281
Aluminum/Alloy Wheels +113
Automatic 4-Speed Transmission +224
Power Sunroof +197

OPTIONS FOR 626
AM/FM Compact Disc Player +85
AM/FM Stereo/CD/Tape +85
Air Conditioning[Opt on DX] +233
Aluminum/Alloy Wheels[Opt on LX] +121
Anti-Lock Brakes +134
Automatic 4-Speed Transmission +194
Leather Seats +169
Power Moonroof +212

929 — 1993

Glass moonroof replaces steel offering. Revised alloy wheels, optional wood trim and optional power passenger's seat are new for 1993.

Model Description	Trade-in TMV	Private TMV	Dealer TMV
Category H			
4 Dr STD Sdn	3631	4295	5400

RX-7 — 1994

Dual airbags appear, and softer suspension settings are available. Seatbacks get map pockets, and power windows have a driver express-down feature.

Model Description	Trade-in TMV	Private TMV	Dealer TMV
Category F			
2 Dr STD Turbo Rotary Cpe	11246	12972	15848

OPTIONS FOR 929
AM/FM Compact Disc Player +78
Compact Disc Changer +152
Leather Seats +218
Power Passenger Seat +78
Premium Package +737
Premium Sound System +109

OPTIONS FOR RX-7
AM/FM Compact Disc Player +105
Automatic 4-Speed Transmission +211
Bose Sound System +224

Don't forget to refer to the Mileage Adjustment Table at the back of this book!

Model Description	Trade-in TMV	Private TMV	Dealer TMV

B-SERIES PICKUP 1993

No changes.

Category J

Model Description	Trade-in TMV	Private TMV	Dealer TMV
2 Dr B2200 Std Cab LB	1981	2352	2972
2 Dr B2200 Ext Cab SB	2299	2731	3450
2 Dr B2200 Std Cab SB	1960	2328	2941
2 Dr B2600i 4WD Ext Cab SB	3153	3745	4731
2 Dr B2600i 4WD Std Cab SB	2956	3511	4436
2 Dr B2600i Ext Cab SB	2364	2808	3548

OPTIONS FOR B-SERIES PICKUP

Air Conditioning +195
Automatic 4-Speed Transmission +253

MIATA 1993

Limited Edition available with black paint and red leather interior; just 1,500 were produced. Yellow dropped from paint roster. Tan roof and leather interior optional on red and white cars. A 130-watt Sensory Sound System is newly optional.

Category E

Model Description	Trade-in TMV	Private TMV	Dealer TMV
2 Dr MX-5 Conv	3115	3792	4919
2 Dr MX-5 Limited Conv	3977	4841	6280

OPTIONS FOR MIATA

AM/FM Compact Disc Player +115
AM/FM Stereo/CD/Tape[Opt on MX-5] +85
Air Conditioning[Opt on MX-5] +218
Anti-Lock Brakes[Opt on MX-5] +134
Automatic 4-Speed Transmission +206
Hardtop Roof +323
Leather Seats[Opt on MX-5] +217

MPV 1993

Keyless entry system added to options list. Driver airbag added midyear.

Category P

Model Description	Trade-in TMV	Private TMV	Dealer TMV
2 Dr STD 4WD Pass. Van	3083	3705	4743
2 Dr STD Pass. Van	2651	3187	4079

OPTIONS FOR MPV

6 cyl 3.0 L Engine[Opt on STD] +182
8 Passenger Seating[Opt on STD] +91
AM/FM Compact Disc Player[Opt on STD 4WD] +85
Air Bag Restraint[Opt on STD] +97
Air Conditioning +145
Aluminum/Alloy Wheels[Opt on STD] +120
Automatic Load Leveling +120
Camper/Towing Package[Opt on STD] +72
Dual Air Conditioning +267
Leather Seats +267

MPV Option Package D +545
Option Package D +618
Power Moonroof +291
Power Sunroof +170

MX3 1993

A cassette stereo is made standard, and Laguna Blue Metallic is a new color.

Category E

Model Description	Trade-in TMV	Private TMV	Dealer TMV
2 Dr STD Hbk	1939	2360	3062
2 Dr GS Hbk	2408	2931	3802
2 Dr Special Hbk	2676	3257	4225

OPTIONS FOR MX3

AM/FM Compact Disc Player +78
Air Conditioning +182
Aluminum/Alloy Wheels[Opt on STD] +78
Anti-Lock Brakes +194
Automatic 4-Speed Transmission +194
Power Sunroof[Opt on GS] +170

MX6 1993

All-new this year, sporting dramatically swept bodywork and a speedy LS model with 2.5-liter V6 engine. EPA says MX-6 is a domestic car. Driver airbag standard, while ABS is optional.

Category E

Model Description	Trade-in TMV	Private TMV	Dealer TMV
2 Dr STD Cpe	2810	3419	4436
2 Dr LS Cpe	3010	3664	4753

OPTIONS FOR MX6

AM/FM Compact Disc Player +78
AM/FM Stereo/CD/Tape +158
Air Conditioning +218
Anti-Lock Brakes +194
Automatic 4-Speed Transmission +194
Leather Seats +169
Power Drivers Seat +75
Power Sunroof +182
Rear Spoiler +91

NAVAJO 1993

Four-wheel ABS is newly standard.

Category M

Model Description	Trade-in TMV	Private TMV	Dealer TMV
2 Dr DX 4WD Utility	3681	4371	5520
2 Dr DX Utility	3067	3642	4600
2 Dr LX 4WD Utility	4064	4826	6095
2 Dr LX Utility	3297	3915	4945

OPTIONS FOR NAVAJO

AM/FM Compact Disc Player +91
Air Conditioning +182
Automatic 4-Speed Transmission +194
Leather Seats +194
Navajo LX Leather Package +404
Sunroof +97

Don't forget to refer to the Mileage Adjustment Table at the back of this book!

MAZDA 93-92

Model Description	Trade-in TMV	Private TMV	Dealer TMV

PROTEGE 1993

Trim and equipment revisions.

Category B

Model Description	Trade-in TMV	Private TMV	Dealer TMV
4 Dr DX Sdn	1443	1879	2606
4 Dr LX Sdn	1684	2193	3041

OPTIONS FOR PROTEGE

Air Conditioning +242
Aluminum/Alloy Wheels[Opt on LX] +97
Automatic 4-Speed Transmission +194
Power Sunroof +170

RX-7 1993

All-new supercar designed with a singular purpose: speed. Convertible dropped. 2+2 version canceled. Twin-turbo rotary engine is standard. Driver airbag and ABS are standard.

Category F

Model Description	Trade-in TMV	Private TMV	Dealer TMV
2 Dr STD Turbo Rotary Cpe			
	8546	9984	12380

OPTIONS FOR RX-7

AM/FM Compact Disc Player +91
AM/FM Stereo/CD/Tape +134
Automatic 4-Speed Transmission +182
Bose Sound System +194
Leather Seats +194
Power Sunroof +170
Premium Sound System +109
R-1 Package +242
Rear Spoiler +72
Touring Package +642

1992 MAZDA

323 1992

New taillights debut.

Category B

Model Description	Trade-in TMV	Private TMV	Dealer TMV
2 Dr STD Hbk	769	1014	1423
2 Dr SE Hbk	922	1217	1707

OPTIONS FOR 323

AM/FM Stereo Tape +87
Air Conditioning +163
Automatic 4-Speed Transmission +153

626 1992

Touring Sedan is dropped.

Category D

Model Description	Trade-in TMV	Private TMV	Dealer TMV
4 Dr DX Sdn	1422	1797	2422
4 Dr LX Sdn	1607	2031	2738

OPTIONS FOR 626

Air Conditioning +211
Aluminum/Alloy Wheels +110
Anti-Lock Brakes +120

Automatic 4-Speed Transmission +175
Power Moonroof +191

929 1992

Completely redesigned. Dual airbags and antilock brakes are standard.

Category H

Model Description	Trade-in TMV	Private TMV	Dealer TMV
4 Dr STD Sdn	2763	3437	4560

OPTIONS FOR 929

AM/FM Stereo/CD/Tape +142
Compact Disc Changer +136
Leather Seats +197
Power Moonroof +186
Premium Package +663
Premium Sound System +98

B-SERIES PICKUP 1992

New steering wheel and minor trim changes. Extended-cab models get new rear lap/shoulder seatbelts.

Category J

Model Description	Trade-in TMV	Private TMV	Dealer TMV
2 Dr B2200 Std Cab LB	1698	2060	2663
2 Dr B2200 Ext Cab SB	2075	2518	3255
2 Dr B2200 Std Cab SB	1635	1984	2565
2 Dr B2600i 4WD Ext Cab SB			
	2704	3281	4242
2 Dr B2600i 4WD Std Cab SB			
	2579	3129	4045
2 Dr B2600i Ext Cab SB			
	2150	2608	3372
2 Dr B2600i Std Cab SB			
	1761	2136	2762

OPTIONS FOR B-SERIES PICKUP

Air Conditioning +175
Automatic 4-Speed Transmission +228

MIATA 1992

Silver paint dropped in favor of yellow and black. Remote trunk release added. Optional hardtop gets rear window defogger. Brilliant Black special edition available.

Category E

Model Description	Trade-in TMV	Private TMV	Dealer TMV
2 Dr MX-5 Conv	2472	3117	4191

OPTIONS FOR MIATA

AM/FM Compact Disc Player +104
Air Conditioning +197
Anti-Lock Brakes +120
Automatic 4-Speed Transmission +186
Hardtop Roof +291
Leather Seats +195
Package C +425
Premium Sound System +98

MPV 1992

Don't forget to refer to the Mileage Adjustment Table at the back of this book!

MAZDA 92

Model Description	Trade-in Value	Market Value	Model Description	Trade-in Value	Market Value

Eight-passenger seating and power moonroof added to options list. Five-speed manual transmission dropped. V6 engine gets five additional horsepower. New alloy wheels debut.

Category P

2 Dr STD 4WD Pass. Van			
	2528	3113	4087
2 Dr STD Pass. Van	2293	2823	3707

OPTIONS FOR MPV
6 cyl 3.0 L Engine[Opt on STD] +163
8 Passenger Seating[Opt on STD] +82
AM/FM Compact Disc Player +76
Air Conditioning +131
Aluminum/Alloy Wheels[Opt on STD] +108
Automatic Load Leveling +108
Dual Air Conditioning +240
Leather Seats +240
Luxury Package +491
Power Moonroof +262

MX3   1992

All-new sport coupe takes over where Honda CRX left off. A 1.8-liter V6 engine, the industry's smallest, is standard on GS models. ABS optional on GS.

Category E

2 Dr STD Hbk	1371	1729	2325
2 Dr GS Hbk	1746	2201	2960

OPTIONS FOR MX3
AM/FM Stereo Tape +87
AM/FM Stereo/CD/Tape +126
Air Conditioning +163
Anti-Lock Brakes +175
Automatic 4-Speed Transmission +175
Power Sunroof +153

MX6   1992

No changes.
Category E

2 Dr DX Cpe	1870	2358	3171
2 Dr GT Turbo Cpe	2369	2987	4017
2 Dr LX Cpe	2058	2595	3489

OPTIONS FOR MX6
Air Conditioning +197
Anti-Lock Brakes +175
Automatic 4-Speed Transmission +175
Power Sunroof +163
Rear Spoiler +82

NAVAJO   1992

A base model joins the lineup, called DX. Upper trim level becomes LX. Two-wheel drive is now available in either trim level.

Category M

2 Dr DX 4WD Utility	3081	3737	4830
2 Dr DX Utility	2567	3114	4025
2 Dr LX 4WD Utility	3374	4093	5290
2 Dr LX Utility	2934	3559	4600

OPTIONS FOR NAVAJO
Air Conditioning +163
Automatic 4-Speed Transmission +175
Leather Seats +175
Moonroof +186

PROTEGE   1992

New taillights are added, and the all-wheel-drive model is dropped.

Category B

4 Dr DX Sdn	1149	1515	2126
4 Dr LX Sdn	1355	1788	2508

OPTIONS FOR PROTEGE
Air Conditioning +218
Aluminum/Alloy Wheels[Opt on LX] +87
Automatic 4-Speed Transmission +175
Power Sunroof +153

Don't forget to refer to the Mileage Adjustment Table at the back of this book!

MERCEDES-BENZ 01

Model Description	Trade-in TMV	Private TMV	Dealer TMV	Model Description	Trade-in TMV	Private TMV	Dealer TMV

MERCEDES   Germany

1997 Mercedes-Benz C230

2001 MERCEDES-BENZ

C-CLASS   2001

Ever expanding and improving its brood of stately vehicles, Mercedes gives the C-Class a complete overhaul for 2001. A choice of two new engines, increased safety features and sleeker sheetmetal tempt those who seek to gain a foothold into the exalted realms of Mercedes ownership.

Category H

Model	Trade-in	Private	Dealer
4 Dr C240 Sdn	26042	27151	29000
4 Dr C320 Sdn	31430	32769	35000

OPTIONS FOR C-CLASS
Automatic 5-Speed Transmission[Std on C320] +1021
Bose Sound System[Std on C320] +467
COMAND System +1598
Compact Disc Changer +448
Heated Front Seats +487
Metallic Paint +491
Power Moonroof +785
Rain Sensing Windshield Wipers +118
Ski Sack +157
Sport Seats +314
Xenon Headlamps +668

CL-CLASS   2001

The CL600 makes its debut with a 362-horsepower V12 and the CL55 arrives with a 354-horsepower 5.5-liter V8. Distronic cruise control, a high-tech system using radar, braking and acceleration to maintain a specified distance from other vehicles, is standard on the CL600 and optional on other CL models. Web-based services, such as e-mail and stock quotes, will also be on board for the 2001 model year.

Category I

Model	Trade-in	Private	Dealer
2 Dr CL500 Cpe	80520	83325	88000
2 Dr CL55 Cpe	91500	94688	100000
2 Dr CL600 Cpe	105225	108891	115000

OPTIONS FOR CL-CLASS
Park Distance Control +781

CLK-CLASS   2001

TeleAid comes standard on every CLK model this year, and the front windows lower slightly when you open the doors and seal (foop!) tight when you close them. The AMG-produced CLK55 arrives this year, offering power and handling a cut above the CLK430.

Category F

Model	Trade-in	Private	Dealer
2 Dr CLK320 Conv	44504	45935	48321
2 Dr CLK320 Cpe	36840	38025	40000
2 Dr CLK430 Conv	50988	52629	55362
2 Dr CLK430 Cpe	44719	46158	48555
2 Dr CLK55 Cpe	62189	64189	67523

OPTIONS FOR CLK-CLASS
COMAND System +1598
Compact Disc Changer +448
Heated Front Seats +487
Power Moonroof +829
Rain Sensing Windshield Wipers +118
Ski Sack +157
Xenon Headlamps +471

E-CLASS   2001

E320 Sedans can now be ordered with the sport package, which includes AMG aerodynamic enhancements, specific foglights and 17-inch wheels and tires. E-Class sunroofs now feature one-touch opening.

Category I

Model	Trade-in	Private	Dealer
4 Dr E320 AWD Sdn	41175	42609	45000
4 Dr E320 AWD Wgn	41955	43416	45852
4 Dr E320 Sdn	40260	41663	44000
4 Dr E320 Wgn	40837	42260	44631
4 Dr E430 AWD Sdn	46858	48490	51211
4 Dr E430 Sdn	43920	45450	48000

Category F

Model	Trade-in	Private	Dealer
4 Dr E55 Sdn	60786	62741	66000

OPTIONS FOR E-CLASS
Bose Sound System[Std on E430] +336
COMAND System +1598
Compact Disc Changer +448
Heated Front Seats +487
Leather Seats[Opt on E320 Wgn] +1080
Power Moonroof +829
Rain Sensing Windshield Wipers +118
Xenon Headlamps +471

Don't forget to refer to the Mileage Adjustment Table at the back of this book!

MERCEDES-BENZ 01-00

Model Description	Trade-in TMV	Private TMV	Dealer TMV	Model Description	Trade-in TMV	Private TMV	Dealer TMV

M-CLASS 2001

The TeleAid emergency calling system is now standard on every M-Class model, and smart dual-stage front airbags know when to deploy with partial force or full force. All models also feature expanded off-road capabilities with new downhill traction control and a new crawling mode for very slow and steep off-roading. Finally, a new M-Class sport package debuts this year.

Category O

4 Dr ML320 AWD Wgn	27642	28884	30954
4 Dr ML430 AWD Wgn	33844	35365	37899
4 Dr ML55 AWD Wgn	51870	54201	58085

OPTIONS FOR M-CLASS

Automatic Dimming Mirror[Opt on ML320] +130
Bose Sound System +844
Dual Power Seats[Opt on ML320] +485
Heated Front Seats[Opt on ML320] +487
Leather Seats[Opt on ML320] +1157
Metallic Paint +381
Power Skyview Roof +1924
Power Sunroof +860
Privacy Glass[Opt on ML320] +187
Rain Sensing Windshield Wipers +118
Third Seat +1060
Xenon Headlamps[Std on ML55] +668

S-CLASS 2001

Two new models debut this year with the S600 and S55. The S-Class gets a powerful 12-cylinder engine along with standard Active Body Control and Internet access to keep up with life in the techno-savvy 21st century. The AMG-massaged S55 has a powerful V8, 18-inch wheels and suspension upgrades for improved handling.

Category I

4 Dr S430 Sdn	60390	62494	66000
4 Dr S500 Sdn	65880	68175	72000
4 Dr S55 Sdn	85573	88554	93522
4 Dr S600 Sdn	100650	104156	110000

OPTIONS FOR S-CLASS

Compact Disc Changer +448
Four Place Seating +3040
Heated Seats +487
Park Distance Control +781
Power Rear Seat Adjusters +1402
Rear Air Conditioning w/Rear Heater[Std on S600] +785
Xenon Headlamps +457

SL-CLASS 2001

Twenty of you will get a special Formula 1 SL500 to commemorate the U.S. Grand Prix at Indianapolis and Mercedes Formula 1 world championship ... that they lost this year to Ferrari. Any-hoo, these 20 SLs get 18-inch AMG Monoblock alloy wheels, cross-drilled brake rotors, xenon headlights, machined aluminum interior pieces, racing pedals, a chromed windblocker and special napa leather interior accents. Another 1,500 lucky dogs will get their hands on the Silver Arrow edition, a — you guessed it — silver-colored SL (available with either the V8 or the V12 engine) littered both inside and out with polished aluminum trim. The rest of the SL line gets some minor aerodynamic enhancements for 2001.

Category F

2 Dr SL500 Conv	66965	69119	72709
2 Dr SL600 Conv	91179	94112	99000

OPTIONS FOR SL-CLASS

Compact Disc Changer[Std on SL600] +511
Heated Seats[Std on SL600] +487
Panorama Removable Roof +3102
Xenon Headlamps[Std on SL600] +471

SLK-CLASS 2001

A new, V6-powered SLK320 joins the line-up while the SLK230 gets more power and a $2,100 price reduction. Both versions get a new six-speed manual tranny in addition to the five-speed automatic that's been available since the car's introduction, and all models benefit from a revised interior and exterior.

Category F

2 Dr SLK230 Kompressor Sprchgd Conv

	32235	33272	35000
2 Dr SLK320 Conv	37761	38976	41000

OPTIONS FOR SLK-CLASS

Automatic 5-Speed Transmission +746
Compact Disc Changer +448
Designo Copper Edition +3770
Dual Power Seats[Opt on SLK230] +485
Heated Seats +487
Metallic Paint +491
Tilt and Telescopic Steering Wheel[Opt on SLK230] +236
Xenon Headlamps +471

2000 MERCEDES-BENZ

C-CLASS 2000

TeleAid, which can assist in summoning help if you're ill or involved in a crash, is a brilliant new standard feature. A Touch Shift automanual transmission is added to all C-Class models, and stability control is standard this year. C-Class now comes with free scheduled service for the duration of the warranty period.

Category H

4 Dr C230 Komp Sdn	25510	27325	29000
4 Dr C280 Sdn	27269	29209	31000

OPTIONS FOR C-CLASS

Don't forget to refer to the Mileage Adjustment Table at the back of this book!

MERCEDES-BENZ 00

Model Description	Trade-in TMV	Private TMV	Dealer TMV	Model Description	Trade-in TMV	Private TMV	Dealer TMV

Bose Sound System[Std on C280] +425
Compact Disc Changer +403
Dual Power Seats[Std on C280] +503
Full Leather Seat Trim +1004
Heated Front Seats +314
Leather Seats[Std on C280] +864
Metallic Paint +448
Option Package K2 +1339
Power Moonroof +829
Ski Sack +112
Sport Seats +522
Sport Suspension +664
Xenon Headlamps +471

C43 — 2000

TeleAid, which can assist in summoning help if you're ill or involved in a crash, is a new standard feature. A Touch Shift automanual transmission is added to simulate the thrill of shifting gears manually. Free scheduled service for the duration of the warranty period has been added to the lengthy standard equipment list.

Category F

4 Dr C43 Sdn	39718	41916	43946

OPTIONS FOR C43
Compact Disc Changer +448
Metallic Paint +448
Option Package K2 +1339
Ski Sack +130
Xenon Headlamps +471

CL-CLASS — 2000

2000 marks the introduction of an all-new CL500 that is lighter, less expensive, and more advanced than the previous version.

Category I

2 Dr CL500 Cpe	66461	70130	73516

OPTIONS FOR CL-CLASS
CL1 Package +1157
Parktronic System +728

CLK-CLASS — 2000

The CLK430 Convertible debuts, reminding us, for a premium price, what a drop-top muscle car from the '70s was like. Turn-signal indicators have been added to exterior mirrors, stability control is standard on all models, automatics get Touch Shift manual gear selection, and TeleAid emergency cellular service is standard. A new instrument cluster and multi-function steering wheel are added, and buyers can opt for the confusing COMAND navigation/phone/trip computer/ sound system. CLK320s benefit from exterior cosmetic changes including new wheels, while 430s are enhanced inside with new black birdseye maple wood trim. Free maintenance for the duration of the warranty

is now included.

Category F

2 Dr CLK320 Conv	41574	43876	46000
2 Dr CLK320 Cpe	31101	32823	34412
2 Dr CLK430 Conv	45641	48168	50500
2 Dr CLK430 Cpe	42977	45356	47552

OPTIONS FOR CLK-CLASS
AM/FM Compact Disc Player +205
COMAND System +1489
Compact Disc Changer +448
Heated Front Seats +196
Metallic Paint +448
Power Moonroof +829
Ski Sack +112
Steering Wheel Radio Controls[Opt on CLK320] +93
Xenon Headlamps +471

E-CLASS — 2000

Though it might not look different, the E-Class receives a substantial freshening for 2000, with an entirely new front end and a revised interior. Stability control, a Touch Shift automanual transmission, and side airbags for all outboard seating positions are now standard. A multi-function steering wheel debuts, and E430 models can be equipped with 4matic all-wheel drive. TeleAid, a cellular emergency service, is standard and the confounding COMAND system is optional. For 2000, free maintenance is provided for the duration of the warranty period. The E300 turbodiesel model has been dropped. Other changes are limited to minor cosmetic and functional upgrades.

Category I

4 Dr E320 AWD Sdn	38339	40455	42409
4 Dr E320 AWD Wgn	39457	41635	43645
4 Dr E320 Sdn	36161	38157	40000
4 Dr E320 Wgn	37600	39675	41591
4 Dr E430 4WD Sdn	41586	43881	46000
4 Dr E430 Sdn	40098	42312	44355

OPTIONS FOR E-CLASS
Air Dam +130
Bose Sound System[Std on E430] +336
COMAND System +1489
Compact Disc Changer +448
Full Leather Seat Trim +854
Heated Front Seats +314
Metallic Paint +448
Nappa Leather Seat Trim +1268
Option Package K2 +1190
Option Package K2a +1341
Package K2 +1190
Parktronic System +728
Power Moonroof +829
Rear Spoiler +298
Spoke Wheels +336
Sport Package E3 +2842

Don't forget to refer to the Mileage Adjustment Table at the back of this book!

Model Description	Trade-in TMV	Private TMV	Dealer TMV	Model Description	Trade-in TMV	Private TMV	Dealer TMV

MERCEDES-BENZ 00

Xenon Headlamps +471

E55 2000

Though it might not look different, the E55 receives the same substantial freshening for 2000 that other E-Class models get, which includes an entirely new front end and a revised interior. A Touch Shift automanual transmission and side airbags for all outboard seating positions are now standard. A multi-function steering wheel debuts, and TeleAid, a cellular emergency service, comes with the package for 2000. Thankfully, the confounding COMAND system is optional. Hard-charging drivers will be happy to learn that free maintenance is provided for the duration of the warranty period.

Category F

4 Dr E55 Sdn	52860	55786	58487

OPTIONS FOR E55
AM/FM Stereo/CD/Tape +314
Compact Disc Changer +448
Metallic Paint +448

M-CLASS 2000

All M-Class models get an interior facelift available in one of three new colors, optional third-row seating and a Touch Shift automanual transmission. ML320 buyers get body-color bumpers and trim, real walnut inside, leather-wrapped steering wheel and gearshift knob, revised interior fabric, seatback map pockets and footwell lamps. In addition to these items, a standard navigation system, high-grade leather, and heated seats come on all ML430s.

Category O

4 Dr ML320 AWD Wgn	25053	26795	28403

OPTIONS FOR M-CLASS
Automatic Dimming Mirror[Std on ML430] +130
Bose Sound System +302
Compact Disc Changer +404
Dual Power Seats[Std on ML430] +485
Heated Front Seats[Std on ML430] +354
Leather Seats[Std on ML430] +1157
M7 Third Row Seat Package +864
Metallic Paint +404
Power Moonroof +736
Power Skyview Roof +1335
Privacy Glass[Std on ML430] +187
Running Boards +224

ML55 2000

Mercedes goes overboard on power and performance with the new ML55. Correct us if we're wrong, but weren't SUVs originally designed for rugged off-road travel?

Category O

4 Dr ML55 AWD Wgn	47531	50836	53887

OPTIONS FOR ML55
Metallic Paint +354

S-CLASS 2000

An all-new S-Class debuts for the millennium with enhanced performance and a snazzy COMAND system.

Category I

4 Dr S430 Sdn	56050	59144	62000
4 Dr S500 Sdn	58762	62006	65000

OPTIONS FOR S-CLASS
AM/FM Compact Disc Player +229
Automatic Load Leveling[Std on S500] +609
Climate Comfort Rear Seat +1085
Compact Disc Changer +434
Dual Air Conditioning +914
Four Place Seating Package +2554
Heated Seats +430
Parktronic System +695
Power Rear Seat Adjusters +647
S1 Audio Package +941
S2 Lighting Package +647
S3 Comfort Package +1160
S4 Convenience Package +1941
Special Factory Paint +343
Xenon Headlamps +457

SL-CLASS 2000

Designo editions debut in Slate Blue and Black Diamond with special color-coordinated interior trim. Non-designo versions can be painted in Desert Silver. TeleAid is standard, as is a StarTAC digital phone with voice-recognition technology on the SL600. Free maintenance now covers you during the warranty period. For more than 80 grand, it oughta cover you for the life of the car.

Category F

2 Dr SL500 STD Conv	59008	62275	65290
2 Dr SL600 STD Conv	79005	83379	87416

OPTIONS FOR SL-CLASS
Adaptive Damping System[Std on SL600] +1335
Compact Disc Changer[Std on SL600] +511
Heated Front Seats[Std on SL600] +444
Removable Panorama Roof +2232
SL1 Sport Option Package +2578
Xenon Headlamps[Std on SL600] +471

SLK 2000

Designo editions debut and include special paint and trim in either Copper or Electric Green hues.

Category F

2 Dr Kompressor Sprchgd Conv	27272	28781	30175

Don't forget to refer to the Mileage Adjustment Table at the back of this book!

Model Description	Trade-in TMV	Private TMV	Dealer TMV	Model Description	Trade-in TMV	Private TMV	Dealer TMV

OPTIONS FOR SLK
Automatic 5-Speed Transmission +708
Compact Disc Changer +448
Designo Copper Edition +3331
Heated Front Seats +444
Metallic Paint +467
Option Package K2 +1199
Option Package K2a +1434

1999 MERCEDES-BENZ

C-CLASS 1999

The SLK's 2.3-liter supercharged engine gets dropped into the C-Class, replacing the normally-aspirated engine of the last C230. Performance has been turned up a notch. In addition, leather seating surfaces are now standard across the C-Class line.

Category F
4 Dr C43 Sdn	32333	34166	36000

Category H
4 Dr C230 Komp Sdn	22471	24236	26000
4 Dr C280 Sdn	23336	25168	27000

OPTIONS FOR C-CLASS
Bose Sound System[Opt on Kompressor] +322
Compact Disc Changer +338
Dual Power Seats[Opt on Kompressor] +381
Full Leather Seat Trim +747
Heated Front Seats[Std on C43] +264
Leather Seats[Opt on Kompressor] +726
Metallic Paint +338
Option Package C1 +672
Power Moonroof[Std on C43] +626
Sport Seats +395
Sport Suspension[Std on C43] +502
Traction Control System[Std on C43] +396
Xenon Headlamps +396

CL-CLASS 1999

The CL coupes are carryover models for 1999 with no changes.

Category I
2 Dr CL500 Cpe	54730	57929	61127
2 Dr CL600 Cpe	66543	70432	74321

OPTIONS FOR CL-CLASS
Adaptive Damping System[Std on CL600] +858
Metallic Paint +338
Traction Control System[Std on CL600] +396

CLK320 1999

These guys are still on a roll. Last year, Mercedes introduced an all-new sport coupe that is an amalgamation of C- and SLK-Class technologies, available this year with a larger engine in the CLK 430 model, and now they're rolling out the CLK 320 Cabriolet, a convertible version of the fabulous little car.

Category F
2 Dr CLK320 Conv	34948	36930	38912
2 Dr CLK320 Cpe	28310	29915	31521

OPTIONS FOR CLK320
Compact Disc Changer +338
Heated Front Seats +336
Metallic Paint +338
Power Moonroof +626
Traction Control System +564
Xenon Headlamps +396

CLK430 1999

These guys are still on a roll. Last year, Mercedes introduced an all-new sport coupe that is an amalgamation of C- and SLK-Class technologies, available this year with a larger engine in the CLK 430 model, and now they're rolling out the CLK 320 Cabriolet, a convertible version of the fabulous little car.

Category F
2 Dr CLK430 Cpe	36896	38989	41081

OPTIONS FOR CLK430
Compact Disc Changer +338
Heated Front Seats +99
Metallic Paint +338
Option Package K4 +844
Power Moonroof +626
Xenon Headlamps +396

E-CLASS 1999

More airbags find room in the E-Class, which now features a full curtain side airbag protection system. The E300 Turbodiesel and E320 wagon are enhanced with leather seat inserts, and all E-Class cars get fiber-optic technology in their sound system/optional telephone unit. A performance-oriented E55 model is also available, bringing with it a fire-breathing V8.

Category I
4 Dr E300TD Turbodsl Sdn	31472	33312	35151
4 Dr E320 AWD Sdn	35814	37907	40000
4 Dr E320 AWD Wgn	36709	38855	41000
4 Dr E320 Sdn	33844	35822	37800
4 Dr E320 Wgn	34202	36201	38200
4 Dr E430 Sdn	37206	39381	41555

Category F
4 Dr E55 Sdn	49397	52199	55000

OPTIONS FOR E-CLASS
AM/FM Stereo/CD/Tape +617
Air Dam +99
Bose Sound System[Std on E430,E55] +254
Compact Disc Changer +338
Electronic Stability Program +564
Heated Front Seats[Std on E55] +264

Don't forget to refer to the Mileage Adjustment Table at the back of this book!

MERCEDES-BENZ 99-98

Model Description	Trade-in TMV	Private TMV	Dealer TMV	Model Description	Trade-in TMV	Private TMV	Dealer TMV

Leather Seats[Opt on Wgn, Turbodsl] +747
Metallic Paint +338
Option Package E1 +429
Parktronic System +550
Power Moonroof[Std on E55] +626
Rear Spoiler[Std on E55] +225
Spoke Wheels +254
Sport Package E3 +660
Traction Control System[Opt on Turbodsl,Wgn] +564
Xenon Headlamps[Std on E55] +396

M-CLASS 1999

Mercedes expands its M-Class with the addition of the more powerful and luxurious ML430 and gives the 320 more standard equipment.

Category O

Model			
4 Dr ML320 AWD Wgn	22194	24050	25906
4 Dr ML430 AWD Wgn	27313	29597	31881

OPTIONS FOR M-CLASS

Automatic Dimming Mirror[Std on ML430] +99
Bose Sound System +254
Compact Disc Changer +338
Dual Power Seats[Std on ML430] +366
Heated Front Seats +268
Leather Seats[Std on ML430] +874
M4 Option Package +660
Metallic Paint +338
Power Moonroof +617
Power Skyview Roof +1121
Privacy Glass +141
Running Boards +169
Third Seat +172
Trailer Hitch +102
Trip Computer +99

S-CLASS 1999

The folks at the three-pointed star unleash an S-Class Mercedes that offers freshened styling, unstoppable engines and a host of luxuries. A limited-production Grand Edition S500 also debuts.

Category I

Model			
4 Dr S320 LWB Sdn	34760	36792	38823
4 Dr S320 SWB Sdn	33064	34997	36929
4 Dr S420 Sdn	38152	40381	42611
4 Dr S500 Sdn	44368	46961	49554
4 Dr S600 Sdn	61858	65473	69088

OPTIONS FOR S-CLASS

Adaptive Damping System[Std on S600] +832
Automatic Load Leveling[Std on S500,S600] +512
Compact Disc Changer[Std on S600] +329
Dual Air Conditioning[Std on S600] +768
Four Place Power Seating +1656
Grand Edition Package +1030
Heated Front Seats[Std on S500,S600] +327
Parktronic System +524
Power Rear Seat Adjusters +544

Traction Control System[Std on S600] +384
Xenon Headlamps[Std on S500,S600] +384

SL-CLASS 1999

The SL500 gets a brand-spankin'-new 5.0-liter V8 that delivers better performance than ever before. Both SL models get side view mirrors from the SLK, body-colored door handles and new side molding, new taillights, new exterior colors, a new instrument panel, new shifter and shift gate, and a new four-spoke steering wheel.

Category F

Model			
2 Dr SL500 STD Conv	50397	53255	56113
2 Dr SL600STD Conv	60067	63473	66880

OPTIONS FOR SL-CLASS

Compact Disc Changer[Std on SL600] +429
Removable Panorama Roof +1875
SL1 Sport Option Package +2165
Xenon Headlamps[Std on SL600] +396

SLK230 1999

This year, Mercedes gives the SLK a standard five-speed manual transmission, optional Sport Package, a new-generation stereo with cassette that uses fiber-optic technology, and integrated controls for a cellular phone.

Category F

Model			
2 Dr STD Sprchgd Conv	24756	26160	27564
2 Dr Sport Sprchgd Conv	26525	28030	29534

OPTIONS FOR SLK230

AM/FM Compact Disc Player +231
Automatic 5-Speed Transmission +507
Compact Disc Changer +396
Heated Front Seats +336
Metallic Paint +338

1998 MERCEDES-BENZ

C-CLASS 1998

The C280 is the lucky recipient of Mercedes' new V-type engine technology, receiving a 2.8-liter unit for the engine bay. BabySmart car seats, Brake Assist and side airbags also debut on the C-Class this year. For the C43, think BMW M3 without all the fun of a stick shift. The C43 is fast and stylish, but the automatic transmission robs plenty of the fun.

Category F

Model			
4 Dr C43 Sdn	29282	31067	33000

Category H

Model			
4 Dr C230 Sdn	17826	19349	21000
4 Dr C280 Sdn	20882	22666	24600

OPTIONS FOR C-CLASS

Bose Sound System[Opt on C230] +273

Don't forget to refer to the Mileage Adjustment Table at the back of this book!

Model Description	Trade-in TMV	Private TMV	Dealer TMV	Model Description	Trade-in TMV	Private TMV	Dealer TMV
Compact Disc Changer +287				4 Dr E300TD Turbodsl Sdn			
Dual Power Seats[Opt on C230] +323					27932	29880	31991
Heated Front Seats +224				4 Dr E320 AWD Sdn	31869	34092	36500
Leather Seats +610				4 Dr E320 AWD Wgn	32305	34559	37000
Limited Slip Differential[Opt on C230] +167				4 Dr E320 Sdn	30123	32224	34500
Metallic Paint +287				4 Dr E320 Wgn	31432	33625	36000
Power Moonroof +531				4 Dr E430 Sdn	34536	36945	39555
Sport Seats +335							
Sport Suspension +426							
Traction Control System +336							
Xenon Headlamps +336							

CL-CLASS 1998

In keeping with Mercedes' somewhat odd habit of changing their cars' names just as people are getting the hang of them, the former S-Class coupes are now dubbed the CL-Class. Other than that confusing switch, the only changes to these big coupes are the addition of BabySmart airbag technology and Brake Assist to the standard equipment lists.

Category I

2 Dr CL500 Cpe	43281	46299	49570
2 Dr CL600 Cpe	52737	56416	60401

OPTIONS FOR CL-CLASS
Adaptive Damping System[Std on CL600] +727
Metallic Paint +287
Traction Control System[Std on CL600] +336

CLK320 1998

Mercedes rolls out an all-new sport coupe that is an amalgamation of C- and SLK-Class technologies, with E-Class style up front. The CLK is infused with the same 3.2-liter V6 that has made its way into the ML320 and E320.

Category F

2 Dr STD Cpe	27612	29295	31118

OPTIONS FOR CLK320
Compact Disc Changer +287
Heated Front Seats +285
Metallic Paint +287
Power Moonroof +531

E-CLASS 1998

All-wheel drive comes to the Mercedes' E-Class lineup via the E320 sedan and all-new E320 wagon. Like the rest of Mercedes' model lineup, E-Class cars formerly powered by an inline-six engine now receive a more fuel efficient V6 unit that is also supposed to improve the cars' low-end torque. The 1998 E-Class cars receive the benefit of BabySmart airbags which are able to detect the presence of a Mercedes' car seat in the front passenger seat and disable the front passenger airbag. Brake Assist is also a new feature, which aids drivers' stopping distance in a panic stop situation.

Category I

OPTIONS FOR E-CLASS
Bose Sound System[Std on E430] +273
Compact Disc Changer +287
Heated Front Seats +224
Leather Seats[Opt on E300TD,Wgn] +633
Option Package E1 +364
Parktronic System +467
Power Moonroof +531
Rear Spoiler +191
Spoke Wheels +215
Sport Package E3 +559
Traction Control System +478
Xenon Headlamps +336

M-CLASS 1998

Mercedes enters the sport-ute fray with the introduction of the ML320. Designed from a clean sheet of paper, the ML320 offers the best of the car and truck worlds.

Category O

4 Dr ML320 AWD Wgn	20205	22100	24152

OPTIONS FOR M-CLASS
Bose Sound System +502
Compact Disc Changer +287
Dual Power Seats +311
Heated Front Seats +227
Leather Seats +742
M4 Option Package +559
Metallic Paint +227
Power Moonroof +524
Privacy Glass +120
Running Boards +144

S-CLASS 1998

The uber-Mercedes are not changed much in anticipation of the cars' imminent replacement. Brake Assist and BabySmart appear in the lineup, but the S320s don't receive the V6 engines that have empowered lesser Mercedes, like the C280 and E320.

Category I

4 Dr S320 LWB Sdn	29576	31639	33874
4 Dr S320 SWB Sdn	28847	30859	33039
4 Dr S420 Sdn	34238	36627	39214
4 Dr S500 Sdn	39949	42735	45754
4 Dr S600 Sdn	48427	51805	55464

OPTIONS FOR S-CLASS
Adaptive Damping System[Std on S600] +706
Automatic Load Leveling[Std on S500,S600] +434
Compact Disc Changer[Std on S600] +279

Don't forget to refer to the Mileage Adjustment Table at the back of this book!

Model Description	Trade-in TMV	Private TMV	Dealer TMV

Dual Air Conditioning[Std on S600] +651
Four Place Power Seating +1404
Heated Front Seats[Std on S500,S600] +276
Parktronic System +445
Power Rear Seat Adjusters +461
Traction Control System[Std on S600] +326
Xenon Headlamps[Std on S500,S600] +326

SL-CLASS 1998

The bargain basement, ha ha, SL320 has been discontinued this year, leaving only the wallet busting SL500 and SL600. The big news is the $10,000 price reduction of the SL500; this car cost only $79,900 when new.

Category F

Model Description	Trade-in TMV	Private TMV	Dealer TMV
2 Dr SL500 Conv	42557	45151	47961
2 Dr SL500 SL1 Sport Conv	44223	46918	49838
2 Dr SL600 Conv	45389	48155	51152
2 Dr SL600 SL1 Sport Conv	47888	50806	53968

OPTIONS FOR SL-CLASS

AM/FM Compact Disc Player[Opt on SL500] +239
Adaptive Damping System[Opt on SL500] +951
Compact Disc Changer +364
Heated Front Seats[Opt on SL500] +285
Removable Panorama Roof +1590
Traction Control System +335
Xenon Headlamps[Opt on SL500] +336

SLK230 1998

Mercedes-Benz releases an all-new retractable-hardtop roadster. Powered by a supercharged 2.3-liter engine, which is hooked to a five-speed automatic transmission, the SLK races to 60 mph in just over seven seconds.

Category F

Model Description	Trade-in TMV	Private TMV	Dealer TMV
2 Dr STD Sprchgd Conv	23611	25050	26609

OPTIONS FOR SLK230

Compact Disc Changer +336
Heated Front Seats +285
Metallic Paint +287

1997 MERCEDES-BENZ

C-CLASS 1997

The C220 is replaced by a more powerful C230. The C36 gains more horsepower. All C-Class models have redesigned headlamps.

Category F

Model Description	Trade-in TMV	Private TMV	Dealer TMV
4 Dr C36 Sdn	23347	24991	27000

Category H

4 Dr C230 Sdn	14737	15980	17500
4 Dr C280 Sdn	17987	19504	21359

OPTIONS FOR C-CLASS

Alarm System +165
Bose Sound System[Opt on C230] +242
Compact Disc Changer +242
Dual Power Seats[Opt on C230] +272
Heated Front Seats +189
Leather Seats[Std on C36] +482
Limited Slip Differential +141
Metallic Paint +242
Power Moonroof[Std on C36] +440
Sport Suspension +358
Traction Control System +283

E-CLASS 1997

The Mercedes-Benz E300D and E320 receive the driver-adaptable five-speed automatic transmission. The E-Class also has a smart sensor to determine if anyone is sitting in the passenger seat and to determine whether or not to deploy the air bag. The E420 can be had with a Sport Package.

Category I

Model Description	Trade-in TMV	Private TMV	Dealer TMV
4 Dr E300D Dsl Sdn	23777	25714	28082
4 Dr E320 Sdn	25401	27470	30000
4 Dr E420 Sdn	27941	30218	33000

OPTIONS FOR E-CLASS

AM/FM Stereo/CD/Tape +354
Bose Sound System[Std on E420] +226
Chrome Wheels +222
Compact Disc Changer +242
Heated Front Seats +189
Leather Seats[Opt on E300D] +534
Limited Slip Differential[Opt on E320] +201
Option Package E4 +250
Power Moonroof +440
Rear Spoiler +161
Sport Package E6 +873
Xenon Headlamps +283

S-CLASS 1997

It's a big year for the big Benz. After a few years of relatively minor changes, the S-Class gets its share of the fun that has been flying around the Stuttgart design studios. Side impact air bags debut in all S-Class cars this year. S-Class coupes get new front bumpers. All cars get new alloy wheels. A Parktronic system is available for those who aren't comfortable parking their $100,000 car in a narrow space. Mercedes' outstanding Automatic Slip Reduction (ASR) traction control system is finally available on the S320s. Lastly, a rain sensor system is now standard on all models. (It adjusts the speed of the wipers to the intensity of the rain.)

Category I

4 Dr S320 LWB Sdn	25935	28048	30631
4 Dr S320 SWB Sdn	24738	26753	29217
4 Dr S420 Sdn	27731	29990	32752

Don't forget to refer to the Mileage Adjustment Table at the back of this book!

Model Description	Trade-in TMV	Private TMV	Dealer TMV
2 Dr S500 Cpe	33916	36679	40057
4 Dr S500 Sdn	32186	34809	38014
2 Dr S600 Cpe	44255	47861	52268
4 Dr S600 Sdn	41075	44422	48512

OPTIONS FOR S-CLASS
Adaptive Damping System +595
Automatic Load Leveling[Opt on S320,S420] +366
Dual Air Conditioning[Std on S600] +549
Four Place Power Seating +1184
Heated Front Seats[Opt on S320,S420] +233
Parktronic System +375
Power Rear Seat Adjusters +389
Traction Control System[Opt on S420,S500] +274
Xenon Headlamps[Std on S500,S600] +274

SL-CLASS 1997

A Panorama hardtop is now available, and it helps improve top-up visibility. ASR traction control is now standard on the SL320. A rain sensor is now standard on all models as well.

Category F

Model Description	Trade-in TMV	Private TMV	Dealer TMV
2 Dr SL320 Conv	38483	41193	44505
2 Dr SL500 Conv	39402	42176	45567
2 Dr SL500 SL1 Sport Conv	40252	43086	46550
2 Dr SL600 Conv	42248	45223	48859

OPTIONS FOR SL-CLASS
Adaptive Damping System +802
Air Dam +121
Compact Disc Changer +307
Heated Front Seats[Std on SL600] +240
Panorama Removable Roof +1341
Rear Spoiler +201
SL1 Sport Package +1548
Traction Control System[Opt on SL500] +283
Xenon Headlamps[Std on SL600] +283

1996 MERCEDES-BENZ

C-CLASS 1996

An infrared remote security system, dual cupholders in the console, a delayed headlamp dousing system, and reconfigured option packages mark the changes to the baby Benz.

Category F

Model Description	Trade-in TMV	Private TMV	Dealer TMV
4 Dr C36 Sdn	21069	22720	25000

Category H

Model Description	Trade-in TMV	Private TMV	Dealer TMV
4 Dr C220 Sdn	11791	12906	14446
4 Dr C280 Sdn	14531	15905	17803

OPTIONS FOR C-CLASS
Alarm System +149
Bose Sound System[Opt on C220] +211
Compact Disc Changer +218
Heated Front Seats +170

Leather Seats[Std on C36] +458
Limited Slip Differential +134
Metallic Paint +228
Power Moonroof[Std on C36] +410
Power Passenger Seat +167
Power Sunroof +410
Sport Suspension +341
Traction Control System +255

E-CLASS 1996

All-new and sporting a face anybody's mother could love, the E-Class comes in three flavors: E300 Diesel, E320 and E420. A new front suspension and larger wheels and tires provide better handling response, while optional gas-discharge headlamps mark new technology. Side-impact airbags are included in the doors of all E-Class models. E420's can be had with ESP, which is a new safety system that makes sure the E420 is under control at all times. The E420 also gets a new five-speed transmission.

Category I

Model Description	Trade-in TMV	Private TMV	Dealer TMV
4 Dr E300D Dsl Sdn	20064	21720	24006
4 Dr E320 Sdn	21146	22891	25300

OPTIONS FOR E-CLASS
Bose Sound System +211
Compact Disc Changer +218
Heated Front Seats +170
Leather Seats[Std on E320] +507
Limited Slip Differential +191
Metallic Paint +262
Power Moonroof +410
Xenon Headlamps[Opt on E300D] +255

S-CLASS 1996

No cosmetic improvements to the S-Class this year; everything new is under the skin. ESP is standard on the S600 and optional on V8 models. ESP is a stability control system designed to help the driver keep the S-Class under control at all times. V8 and V12 versions get a new five-speed automatic, and all models get a standard power glass sunroof and smog-sensing climate control system. The S350 Turbodiesel is history.

Category I

Model Description	Trade-in TMV	Private TMV	Dealer TMV
4 Dr S320 LWB Sdn	22645	24514	27094
4 Dr S320 SWB Sdn	21958	23770	26272
4 Dr S420 Sdn	23958	25934	28664
2 Dr S500 Cpe	28852	31233	34520
4 Dr S500 Sdn	24926	26983	29823
2 Dr S600 Cpe	36437	39443	43595
4 Dr S600 Sdn	33924	36724	40589

OPTIONS FOR S-CLASS
AM/FM Compact Disc Player[Opt on S500] +124
AM/FM Stereo/CD/Tape[Std on S600] +165
Adaptive Damping System +536

Don't forget to refer to the Mileage Adjustment Table at the back of this book!

MERCEDES-BENZ 96-95

Model Description	Trade-in TMV	Private TMV	Dealer TMV	Model Description	Trade-in TMV	Private TMV	Dealer TMV

Compact Disc Changer +223
Dual Air Conditioning[Std on S600] +495
Electronic Stability Program[Opt on S420] +653
Four Place Power Seating +1068
Heated Front Seats[Opt on S320,S420] +221
Power Moonroof +446

SL-CLASS   1996

Tweaked styling and new alloys freshen the exterior of the SL roadster. Underneath, ESP keeps drivers on track in lousy driving conditions. It comes standard on the SL600; can be ordered for the SL320 and SL500. Side airbags are standard across the board. A five-speed automatic is included with SL500 and SL600. Cool gas-discharge headlamps are not available on the SL320.

Category F

	Trade-in	Private	Dealer
2 Dr SL320 Conv	29614	31935	35140
2 Dr SL500 Conv	33336	35948	39556
2 Dr SL600 Conv	35857	38667	42548

OPTIONS FOR SL-CLASS

Adaptive Damping System +723
Hardtop Roof +1182
Heated Front Seats +228
Slip Control +421
Xenon Headlamps +255

1995 MERCEDES-BENZ

C-CLASS   1995

The AMG-prepared C36 is introduced to the C-Class family. This little mighty mouse runs circles around its lesser siblings and gives BMW M3 owners something to think about. Only 300 copies of the C36 are available in 1995; get one if you can.

Category F

	Trade-in	Private	Dealer
4 Dr C36 Sdn	19074	20546	23000

Category H

	Trade-in	Private	Dealer
4 Dr C220 Sdn	9911	10893	12530
4 Dr C280 Sdn	12302	13521	15552

OPTIONS FOR C-CLASS

AM/FM Compact Disc Player[Opt on C280] +113
Alarm System +132
Bose Sound System[Opt on C220] +187
Chrome Wheels[Opt on C280] +136
Compact Disc Changer[Opt on C220] +194
Gold Package +119
Heated Front Seats +151
Heated Seats +151
Leather Seats[Std on C36] +407
Limited Slip Differential +119
Metallic Paint +202
Option Package C1 +405
Power Moonroof +364
Power Passenger Seat[Opt on C220] +148

Traction Control System +227

E-CLASS   1995

No changes for the last year of this rendition of the E-Class.

Category I

	Trade-in	Private	Dealer
4 Dr E300D Dsl Sdn	14251	15349	17180
2 Dr E320 Conv	30871	33250	37216
2 Dr E320 Cpe	19468	20969	23470
4 Dr E320 Sdn	15529	16726	18721
4 Dr E320 Wgn	16956	18263	20441
4 Dr E420 Sdn	18245	19651	21995

OPTIONS FOR E-CLASS

Compact Disc Changer +194
Heated Front Seats[Std on E420,Conv] +151
Leather Seats[Opt on E300D,Wgn] +451
Limited Slip Differential +170
Metallic Paint +102
Option Package E1 +246
Premium Sound System +153
Sportline Package +306
Telescopic Steering Wheel[Std on E420] +102
Traction Control System[Opt on E320 Sdn] +340

S-CLASS   1995

Minuscule exterior changes and a drop in price are about the only changes to the S-Class.

Category I

	Trade-in	Private	Dealer
4 Dr S320 LWB Sdn	20397	21969	24589
4 Dr S320 SWB Sdn	19096	20568	23021
4 Dr S350D Turbodsl Sdn	20402	21974	24595
4 Dr S420 Sdn	22042	23740	26572
2 Dr S500 Cpe	25623	27597	30889
4 Dr S500 Sdn	22767	24521	27446
2 Dr S600 Cpe	29905	32210	36052
4 Dr S600 Sdn	26691	28748	32177

OPTIONS FOR S-CLASS

AM/FM Compact Disc Player +110
Adaptive Damping System +477
Compact Disc Changer +198
Dual Air Conditioning[Std on S600] +440
Four Place Power Seating +949
Heated Front Seats[Std on S500,S600] +196
Power Moonroof +397

SL-CLASS   1995

Traction control is now standard on the SL320. Price cuts are the only other change for the Mercedes roadster.

Category F

	Trade-in	Private	Dealer
2 Dr SL320 Conv	25584	27558	30849
2 Dr SL500 Conv	29078	31323	35063
2 Dr SL600 Conv	31073	33471	37468

Don't forget to refer to the Mileage Adjustment Table at the back of this book!

MERCEDES-BENZ 95-93

Model Description	Trade-in TMV	Private TMV	Dealer TMV

OPTIONS FOR SL-CLASS
Adaptive Damping System[Std on SL600] +643
Hardtop Roof +1051
Heated Front Seats[Std on SL600] +202

1994 MERCEDES-BENZ

C-CLASS   1994

This peppy replacement for the 190 is long-awaited. Longer and wider than the 190, the C-Class gives rear seat passengers more room. Standard on the C-Class are dual airbags, a wood-trimmed interior, four-wheel antilock brakes and a power sunroof. The C-Class cars are available in four- or six-cylinder flavors with a standard automatic transmission.

Category H
4 Dr C220 Sdn	8787	9792	11467
4 Dr C280 Sdn	10099	11253	13178

OPTIONS FOR C-CLASS
Alarm System +112
Bose Sound System +158
Heated Front Seats +128
Leather Seats +345
Metallic Paint +171
Power Moonroof +308
Power Passenger Seat[Opt on C220] +126
Traction Control System +192

E-CLASS   1994

In an effort at simplification, Mercedes renames its 300-Class, now calling it the E-Class. Like the new C-Class, the numeral after the E indicates the engine's size. Pretty cool, huh? Coupe, convertible, sedan and wagon body styles are still offered.

Category I
2 Dr E320 Conv	24162	26236	29692
2 Dr E320 Cpe	17204	18681	21142
4 Dr E320 Sdn	12607	13689	15492
4 Dr E320 Wgn	13392	14541	16457
4 Dr E420 Sdn	14100	15310	17327

Category F
4 Dr E500 Sdn	25027	26914	30058

OPTIONS FOR E-CLASS
Heated Front Seats[Std on E500] +128
Leather Seats[Opt on Wgn] +381
Sport Suspension +187
Sportline Package +259
Traction Control System[Std on E500] +288

S-CLASS   1994

The big Benz gains Mercedes's new alphanumeric nomenclature that makes it easier to identify the vehicle family and engine size. Fuel economy is improved for the S-Class, and all but the S600 switch to H-rated tires for increased traction in inclement weather.

Category I
4 Dr S320 Sdn	16925	18378	20799
4 Dr S350D Turbodsl Sdn	18760	20370	23053
4 Dr S420 Sdn	20191	21924	24812
2 Dr S500 Cpe	22595	24534	27766
4 Dr S500 Sdn	20764	22546	25516
2 Dr S600 Cpe	24718	26839	30375
4 Dr S600 Sdn	22727	24678	27929

OPTIONS FOR S-CLASS
Adaptive Damping System +403
Dual Air Conditioning[Std on S600] +372
Four Place Seating +577
Heated Front Seats[Std on S500,S600] +166
Limited Slip Differential +139
Power Moonroof +335
Power Sunroof +279
Rear Power Seatback +168
Traction Control System[Opt on S320,S420] +186

SL-CLASS   1994

The 300SL becomes the SL320 as a new powerplant slips into the engine bay. Offering the same horsepower as the previous engine, the SL320 throws out considerably more torque than last year's model. A Bose stereo is added to the standard equipment lists of the entire SL-Class.

Category F
2 Dr SL320 Conv	22388	24075	26888
2 Dr SL500 Conv	24952	26832	29967
2 Dr SL600 Conv	26767	28784	32147

OPTIONS FOR SL-CLASS
Adaptive Damping System[Std on SL600] +544
Heated Front Seats[Std on SL600] +171
Metallic Paint +87
Traction Control System[Opt on SL320] +202

1993 MERCEDES-BENZ

190   1993

No changes for the little Mercedes that could; still a good car at a relatively good price. A new model replaces the 190 for 1994.

Category H
4 Dr 190E Sdn	5814	6573	7837
4 Dr 190E 2.6 Sdn	6673	7544	8995

OPTIONS FOR 190
190E 2.6 Sportline Package +562
AM/FM Stereo/CD/Tape +138
Automatic 4-Speed Transmission +225
Compact Disc Changer +150
Dual Power Seats[Opt on STD] +145
Heated Front Seats +81

Don't forget to refer to the Mileage Adjustment Table at the back of this book!

Model Description	Trade-in TMV	Private TMV	Dealer TMV

Leather Seats +249
Limited Slip Differential +97
Power Sunroof +244
Traction Control System +150

300 — 1993

All but the turbo models receive a larger engine. A driver airbag is finally standard on the 300-Class Mercedes. A 300 CE cabriolet model is brought into the fold; it has a power top and a pop-up roll bar similar to the one found on the SL-roadsters.

Category I

Model Description	Trade-in TMV	Private TMV	Dealer TMV
2 Dr 300CE Conv	22280	24425	28000
2 Dr 300CE Cpe	13199	14470	16588
4 Dr 300D Turbodsl Sdn	8764	9608	11014
4 Dr 300E Sdn	11469	12574	14414
4 Dr 300E 2.8 Sdn	10344	11340	13000
4 Dr 300E 4matic 4WD Sdn	12398	13592	15581
4 Dr 300SD Turbodsl Sdn	18067	19806	22705
4 Dr 300SE Sdn	17329	18997	21778

Category F

Model Description	Trade-in TMV	Private TMV	Dealer TMV
2 Dr 300SL Conv	23309	25443	28999

Category I

Model Description	Trade-in TMV	Private TMV	Dealer TMV
4 Dr 300TE Wgn	12314	13499	15475
4 Dr 300TE 4matic 4WD Wgn	13642	14955	17144

OPTIONS FOR 300
300E Sportline Package +231
AM/FM Compact Disc Player[Opt on 300E] +100
Adaptive Damping System +389
Automatic 5-Speed Transmission[Opt on 300SL] +275
CE Sportline Package +200
Compact Disc Changer +150
Dual Air Conditioning +333
Four Place Seating +625
Hardtop Roof +500
Heated Front Seats +81
Leather Seats[Opt on 300D,300TE,2.8] +287
Locking Differential +97
Power Moonroof +250
Power Rear Seat Back +150
Power Sunroof +250
Third Seat +213
Traction Control System +150

400 — 1993

The 400SE becomes the 400SEL in order to compete with the longer wheelbase sedans from BMW.

Category I

Model Description	Trade-in TMV	Private TMV	Dealer TMV
4 Dr 400E Sdn	12893	14134	16203
4 Dr 400SEL Sdn	17791	19504	22359

OPTIONS FOR 400
Adaptive Damping System +361
Compact Disc Changer +150
Dual Air Conditioning +388
Four Place Seating +625
Heated Front Seats +81
Power Moonroof +250
Power Rear Seat Back +150
Power Sunroof[Std on 400E] +250
Traction Control System +150

500 — 1993

No changes to 500-Series models.

Category F

Model Description	Trade-in TMV	Private TMV	Dealer TMV
4 Dr 500E Sdn	19692	21494	24499

Category I

Model Description	Trade-in TMV	Private TMV	Dealer TMV
2 Dr 500SEC Cpe	22126	24257	27807
4 Dr 500SEL Sdn	20420	22386	25663

Category F

Model Description	Trade-in TMV	Private TMV	Dealer TMV
2 Dr 500SL Conv	22183	24213	27598

OPTIONS FOR 500
Adaptive Damping System +361
Dual Air Conditioning +388
Four Place Seating +712
Hardtop Roof +500
Heated Front Seats[Opt on 500SL] +81
Power Moonroof +250
Power Sunroof +250

600SEC — 1993

Category I

Model Description	Trade-in TMV	Private TMV	Dealer TMV
2 Dr STD Cpe	24630	27002	30954

OPTIONS FOR 600SEC
Four Place Seating +712
Power Moonroof +250
Power Sunroof +250

600SEL — 1993

Category I

Model Description	Trade-in TMV	Private TMV	Dealer TMV
4 Dr STD Sdn	22290	24436	28013

OPTIONS FOR 600SEL
Four Place Seating +712
Power Moonroof +250
Power Sunroof +250

600SL — 1993

Category F

Model Description	Trade-in TMV	Private TMV	Dealer TMV
2 Dr STD Conv	24235	26454	30152

OPTIONS FOR 600SL
Hardtop Roof +500

1992 MERCEDES-BENZ

190 — 1992

Model Description	Trade-in TMV	Private TMV	Dealer TMV	Model Description	Trade-in TMV	Private TMV	Dealer TMV

A sportline package is now available on the six-cylinder 190E 2.6. The package consists of go-fast goodies like V-rated tires, a sport-tuned suspension and quicker steering.

Category H

Model Description	Trade-in TMV	Private TMV	Dealer TMV
4 Dr 190E Sdn	5066	5746	6879
4 Dr 190E 2.6 Sdn	5902	6694	8014

OPTIONS FOR 190
Automatic 4-Speed Transmission +204
Automatic Load Leveling +113
Dual Power Seats +131
Leather Seats +225
Limited Slip Differential +88
Locking Differential +88
Power Sunroof +220
Sportline Package +204

300   1992

Mercedes brings out a new S-Class lineup. The 300SE and 300SD are more powerful and sleeker than their forebears. Safety and comfort have also been improved in these big sedans. The rest of the 300 numbered cars are unchanged.

Category I

Model Description	Trade-in TMV	Private TMV	Dealer TMV
2 Dr 300CE Cpe	10861	12110	14190
4 Dr 300D Turbodsl Sdn	7807	8705	10200
4 Dr 300E Sdn	9492	10583	12401
4 Dr 300E 2.6 Sdn	8420	9387	11000
4 Dr 300E 4matic 4WD Sdn	10137	11301	13243
4 Dr 300SD Turbodsl Sdn	15230	16981	19898
4 Dr 300SE Sdn	13459	15006	17584
Category F			
2 Dr 300SL Conv	18466	20600	24157
Category I			
4 Dr 300TE Wgn	9918	11057	12957
4 Dr 300TE 4matic 4WD Wgn	10923	12179	14271

OPTIONS FOR 300
Adaptive Damping System +351
Automatic 4-Speed Transmission[Opt on 300SL] +204
Automatic Load Leveling[Std on 300TE] +113
Dual Air Bag Restraints[Std on 300SD,300SL] +88
Four Place Seating +565
Leather Seats[Opt on 300D,300TE,300E STD Sdn] +260
Limited Slip Differential +88
Locking Differential +88
Power Sunroof +226
Rear Power Seats +136
Sportline Package +204
Third Seat +192

400   1992

A new model is introduced to the lineup of midsize Mercedes: the 400E. It offers V8 power, a first in this line of cars, and comes standard with an automatic transmission. Dual airbags are now standard on these pricey sedans, as are neat features like traction control, a five-speed automatic transmission, heated front seats, double paned side-windows, and a self-leveling system.

Category I

Model Description	Trade-in TMV	Private TMV	Dealer TMV
4 Dr 400E Sdn	10673	11900	13944
4 Dr 400SE Sdn	14949	16667	19530

OPTIONS FOR 400
Adaptive Damping System +326
Automatic Load Leveling +113
Dual Air Conditioning +350
Four Place Seating +565
Power Seatback Recliner +136
Power Sunroof +226
Traction Control System +136

500   1992

A new 500E model is introduced to the Mercedes top-drawer lineup.

Category F

Model Description	Trade-in TMV	Private TMV	Dealer TMV
4 Dr 500E Sdn	16611	18531	21731
Category I			
4 Dr 500SEL Sdn	17795	19840	23249
Category F			
2 Dr 500SL Conv	19367	21605	25336

OPTIONS FOR 500
Adaptive Damping System +326
Air Bag Restraint[Std on 500E] +91
Dual Air Conditioning +350
Four Place Seating +643
Power Moonroof +226

600SEL   1992

Category I

Model Description	Trade-in TMV	Private TMV	Dealer TMV
4 Dr STD Sdn	18767	20923	24518

OPTIONS FOR 600SEL
Four Place Seating +643

Don't forget to refer to the Mileage Adjustment Table at the back of this book!

MERCURY 01

Model Description	Trade-in TMV	Private TMV	Dealer TMV	Model Description	Trade-in TMV	Private TMV	Dealer TMV

MERCURY   USA

1995 Mercury Sable

2001 MERCURY

COUGAR   2001

Exterior and interior changes are extensive for the Cougar. At first glance outside, you'll notice new front and rear fascias, new headlights with a projector and reflector system, a new grille, a new spoiler, new fog lights, and 16-inch painted or 17-inch machined aluminum wheels. New clearcoat metallic colors include Dark Shadow Grey, Tropic Green, French Blue and Sunburst Gold. Later in the year, two special editions — the Cougar Zn and C2— will be offered.

Category E

2 Dr I4 Cpe	10250	11094	12500
2 Dr V6 Cpe	11070	11981	13500

OPTIONS FOR COUGAR
Anti-Lock Brakes +305
Compact Disc Changer +213
Keyless Entry System +115
Leather Seats +366
Power Sunroof +375
Rear Spoiler +143
Side Air Bag Restraints +238
Traction Control System +143

GRAND MARQUIS   2001

Power from the V8 engine is improved. The interior gets minor improvements and an optional adjustable pedal assembly. Safety has been improved via a crash severity sensor, safety belt pretensioners, dual-stage airbags and seat position sensors.

Category G

4 Dr GS Sdn	14930	15781	17200
4 Dr LS Sdn	16492	17433	19000

OPTIONS FOR GRAND MARQUIS
Air Suspension System[Opt on LS] +165
Aluminum/Alloy Wheels +195
Anti-Lock Brakes +305
Automatic Dimming Mirror +115
Automatic Load Leveling +244
Compact Disc Changer +213
Keyless Entry System[Std on LS] +146
Leather Seats +448
Power Passenger Seat[Opt on LS] +213

MOUNTAINEER   2001

Not much changes for 2001, as Mercury's Explorer clone has a new child safety-seat tether anchor system. The rest of the vehicle is all carryover.

Category M

4 Dr STD 4WD Wgn	18275	19484	21500
4 Dr STD AWD Wgn	18530	19756	21800
4 Dr STD Wgn	16660	17763	19600

OPTIONS FOR MOUNTAINEER
8 cyl 5.0 L Engine[Opt on 2WD] +283
AM/FM Stereo/CD/Tape +268
Automatic Load Leveling +241
Chrome Wheels +302
Climate Control for AC +152
Dual Power Seats +372
Keyless Entry System +125
Leather Seats +488
Limited Slip Differential[Std on AWD] +216
Park Distance Control +155
Power Drivers Seat +186
Power Moonroof +488
Premium Sound System +268
Side Air Bag Restraints +241

SABLE   2001

A new child safety-seat restraint system is in place as well as a larger 18-gallon fuel tank. There's also a clearcoat metallic paint swap, trading Tropic Green for Spruce Green. Otherwise, no changes for the recently freshened Sable.

Category D

4 Dr GS Sdn	12726	13766	15500
4 Dr GS Wgn	13218	14299	16100
4 Dr LS Sdn	12972	14032	15800
4 Dr LS Premium Sdn	13629	14743	16600
4 Dr LS Premium Wgn	14450	15631	17600

OPTIONS FOR SABLE
6 cyl 3.0 L 24V Engine[Opt on LS] +424
Aluminum/Alloy Wheels[Opt on GS Sdn] +241
Anti-Lock Brakes +366
Chrome Wheels +180
Compact Disc Changer +213
Power Drivers Seat[Opt on GS] +241
Power Moonroof +543
Power Passenger Seat[Opt on LS Premium] +213

Don't forget to refer to the Mileage Adjustment Table at the back of this book!

MERCURY 01-00

Model Description	Trade-in TMV	Private TMV	Dealer TMV	Model Description	Trade-in TMV	Private TMV	Dealer TMV

Premium Sound System +408
Side Air Bag Restraints +238

VILLAGER   2001

Numerous exterior and interior revisions are on tap for 2001. Also new are optional 16-inch wheels and tires, drivetrain changes for better engine smoothness, new seatbelt pre-tensioners to improve safety, and the addition of an anchorage point for attaching a child seat.

Category P

	Trade-in	Private	Dealer
4 Dr Estate Pass. Van	18383	19552	21500
4 Dr Sport Pass. Van	17528	18642	20500
4 Dr STD Pass. Van	15390	16369	18000

OPTIONS FOR VILLAGER

AM/FM Stereo/CD/Tape +527
Anti-Lock Brakes +360
Camper/Towing Package +152
Climate Control for AC +149
Entertainment System +789
Leather Seats[Opt on Sport] +485
Power Drivers Seat[Opt on STD] +186
Power Moonroof +472
Premium Sound System[Opt on STD] +189
Rear Air Conditioning w/Rear Heater[Opt on Sport] +213
Tutone Paint +180

2000 MERCURY

COUGAR   2000

All Cougars receive an emergency trunk release as standard equipment, as well as a redesigned floor console. Citrus Gold, Light Blue, and Light Sapphire are the three new clearcoat metallic paints available.

Category E

	Trade-in	Private	Dealer
2 Dr I4 Cpe	9146	10266	11300
2 Dr V6 Cpe	9874	11084	12200

OPTIONS FOR COUGAR

AM/FM Stereo/CD/Tape +134
Anti-Lock Brakes +305
Automatic 4-Speed Transmission +497
Compact Disc Changer +213
Cruise Control +104
Keyless Entry System +115
Leather Seats +546
Lighted Entry System +109
Power Drivers Seat +143
Power Sunroof +375
Rear Spoiler +143
Side Air Bag Restraints +229
Traction Control System +143

GRAND MARQUIS   2000

The Marquis receives additional safety features, including an emergency trunk release, child seat anchor brackets, and Mercury's Belt Minder system. The interior gets a new trim color, Dark Charcoal. One new exterior color will be offered, Tropic Green. The handling package's rear-axle ratio changes from 3.27 to 3.55. The Grand Marquis Limited will be offered later in the 2000 model year.

Category G

	Trade-in	Private	Dealer
4 Dr GS Sdn	12779	13934	15000
4 Dr LS Sdn	13972	15234	16400

OPTIONS FOR GRAND MARQUIS

Aluminum/Alloy Wheels +196
Anti-Lock Brakes +366
Automatic Dimming Mirror +115
Climate Control for AC +107
Compact Disc Changer +213
Dual Power Seats +372
Gold Package +280
Keyless Entry System[Std on LS] +146
Leather Seats +448
Traction Control System +107

MOUNTAINEER   2000

Mountaineer is uprated with new Premier and Monterey trim packages, which include tan leather upholstery, special paint, upgraded alloy wheels and wood-grain dash trim.

Category M

	Trade-in	Private	Dealer
4 Dr STD 4WD Wgn	16030	17626	19100
4 Dr STD AWD Wgn	16366	17996	19500
4 Dr STD Wgn	14687	16150	17500

OPTIONS FOR MOUNTAINEER

8 cyl 5.0 L Engine[Opt on 2WD] +283
AM/FM Stereo/CD/Tape +268
Alarm System +152
Automatic Dimming Mirror +113
Automatic Load Leveling +241
Camper/Towing Package +152
Chrome Wheels +301
Climate Control for AC +152
Compact Disc Changer +226
Dual Power Seats +372
Keyless Entry System +125
Leather Seats +579
Limited Slip Differential[Std on AWD] +216
Overhead Console +107
Power Drivers Seat +186
Power Moonroof +488
Side Air Bag Restraints +238
Sport Seats +366

MYSTIQUE   2000

The Mystique comes standard with an emergency glow-in-the-dark trunk release, designed to allow a child or adult trapped in the trunk to open it from the inside. Two new exterior colors debut.

Don't forget to refer to the Mileage Adjustment Table at the back of this book!

Model Description	Trade-in TMV	Private TMV	Dealer TMV
Category C			
4 Dr GS Sdn	8778	9830	10800
4 Dr LS Sdn	9754	10922	12000

OPTIONS FOR MYSTIQUE
AM/FM Compact Disc Player +168
Aluminum/Alloy Wheels[Std on LS] +259
Anti-Lock Brakes +305
Automatic 4-Speed Transmission +497
Fog Lights[Std on LS] +125
Keyless Entry System[Std on LS] +115
Power Drivers Seat[Std on LS] +213
Power Moonroof +363
Rear Spoiler +149
Traction Control System +107

SABLE 2000

The 2000 Mercury Sable gains new sheetmetal and additional refinements. The freshened styling includes a raised hood and decklid, a larger grille, improved headlamps and taillights, and new mirrors. The instrument panel has been updated, and the new integrated control panel provides better functionality. The Sable also gains significant improvements to its safety and powertrain components.

Category D			
4 Dr GS Sdn	10118	11305	12400
4 Dr GS Wgn	11097	12399	13600
4 Dr LS Sdn	10771	12034	13200
4 Dr LS Premium Sdn	11505	12854	14100
4 Dr LS Premium Wgn	12076	13493	14800

OPTIONS FOR SABLE
6 cyl 3.0 L DOHC Engine[Opt on LS,Wgn] +424
Aluminum/Alloy Wheels[Opt on GS Sdn] +241
Anti-Lock Brakes +366
Chrome Wheels +354
Compact Disc Changer +213
Dual Power Seats +457
Power Drivers Seat[Opt on GS] +241
Power Moonroof +451
Side Air Bag Restraints +238
Traction Control System +107

VILLAGER 2000

The convenience, comfort, and luxury option packages have been simplified. All 2000 Villagers meet federal low-emission vehicle status and come standard with a child seat-anchor system. A new rear-seat video entertainment system is now optional.

Category P			
4 Dr STD Pass. Van	12845	14122	15300
4 Dr Estate Pass. Van	15868	17445	18900
4 Dr Sport Pass. Van	14692	16152	17500

OPTIONS FOR VILLAGER
AM/FM Stereo/CD/Tape +418

Aluminum/Alloy Wheels[Opt on STD] +180
Anti-Lock Brakes +360
Camper/Towing Package +152
Climate Control for AC +109
Compact Disc Changer +226
Dual Air Conditioning[Opt on STD] +283
Entertainment System +606
Leather Seats[Opt on Sport] +381
Power Drivers Seat[Opt on STD] +186
Power Moonroof +472
Premium Sound System[Opt on STD] +430
Privacy Glass +253
Trip Computer +121
Video Cassette Recorder +152

COUGAR 1999

Mercury reintroduces the Cougar this year after a one-year hiatus that saw the departure of most of Ford Motor Co.'s personal coupes. The new model is built on the Mondeo global platform that is also the basis for the Ford Contour and Mercury Mystique. This new coupe is powered by the same engine choices as the Contour/Mystique, which means that buyers can choose between a zippy Zetec four-cylinder and a high-revving Duratec V6.

Category E			
2 Dr I4 Cpe	8430	9515	10600
2 Dr V6 Cpe	8986	10143	11300

OPTIONS FOR COUGAR
Anti-Lock Brakes +248
Automatic 4-Speed Transmission +405
Compact Disc Changer +174
Keyless Entry System +94
Leather Seats +445
Power Drivers Seat +117
Power Sunroof +306
Rear Spoiler +117
Side Air Bag Restraints +186
Traction Control System +117

GRAND MARQUIS 1999

Not much. This traditional American sedan got a revised rear suspension and exterior styling last year. This year all it gets are some new color options.

Category G			
4 Dr GS Sdn	11159	12229	13300
4 Dr LS Sdn	12166	13333	14500

OPTIONS FOR GRAND MARQUIS
Aluminum/Alloy Wheels +159
Anti-Lock Brakes +298
Automatic Dimming Mirror[Opt on LS] +94
Compact Disc Changer +174
Dual Power Seats +302
Gold Package +228

Don't forget to refer to the Mileage Adjustment Table at the back of this book!

MERCURY 99

Model Description	Trade-in TMV	Private TMV	Dealer TMV	Model Description	Trade-in TMV	Private TMV	Dealer TMV

Keyless Entry System[Opt on GS] +119
Leather Seats[Opt on LS] +365

MOUNTAINEER 1999

For '99 the Mountaineer gets optional rear load leveling and a reverse parking aid. It also receives a new seat design.

Category M

Model Description	Trade-in TMV	Private TMV	Dealer TMV
4 Dr STD 4WD Wgn	13519	15010	16500
4 Dr STD AWD Wgn	14093	15647	17200
4 Dr STD Wgn	12782	14191	15600

OPTIONS FOR MOUNTAINEER

8 cyl 5.0 L Engine[Opt on 2WD] +231
AM/FM Compact Disc Player +161
AM/FM Stereo/CD/Tape +218
Alarm System +124
Chrome Wheels +245
Climate Control for AC +124
Compact Disc Changer +184
Dual Power Seats +302
Keyless Entry System +101
Leather Seats +472
Limited Slip Differential +177
Power Drivers Seat +151
Power Moonroof +397
Rear Heater +100
Side Air Bag Restraints +194
Sport Seats +298

MYSTIQUE 1999

The Mystique gets a revised instrument panel and redesigned front seats this year. A six-way power adjustable seat is now standard on the LS model and all Mystiques benefit from a revised suspension and larger fuel tank. Medium Steel Blue replaces Light Denim Blue as an exterior color. A final note to family-oriented shoppers: the optional integrated child safety seat is no longer available.

Category C

Model Description	Trade-in TMV	Private TMV	Dealer TMV
4 Dr GS Sdn	7804	8752	9700
4 Dr LS Sdn	8608	9654	10700

OPTIONS FOR MYSTIQUE

AM/FM Compact Disc Player +137
Aluminum/Alloy Wheels[Std on LS] +211
Anti-Lock Brakes +248
Automatic 4-Speed Transmission +405
Fog Lights[Opt on GS] +101
Keyless Entry System[Opt on GS] +94
Power Drivers Seat[Std on LS] +174
Power Moonroof +296
Rear Spoiler +121

SABLE 1999

Still smarting from that 1996 "redesign" that had many longtime Sable fans running to the competition, Mercury performed some minor cosmetic surgery in '98 to help soften the Sable's front end. This year's changes are limited to new wheel designs, a revised gauge cluster and interior console, as well as suspension alterations designed to improve overall ride quality. The particulate filtration system has been deleted from this year's models.

Category D

Model Description	Trade-in TMV	Private TMV	Dealer TMV
4 Dr GS Sdn	8232	9266	10300
4 Dr LS Sdn	8712	9806	10900
4 Dr LS Wgn	9271	10436	11600

OPTIONS FOR SABLE

6 cyl 3.0 L DOHC Engine +276
Alarm System +124
Aluminum/Alloy Wheels[Std on LS] +197
Anti-Lock Brakes +298
Chrome Wheels +287
Compact Disc Changer +174
Dual Power Seats +372
Keyless Entry System[Std on LS] +94
Leather Seats +445
Power Drivers Seat[Std on LS] +197
Power Moonroof +367
Third Seat +100

TRACER 1999

The Tracer gets a new sport wagon model to help extend its appeal to young buyers. The LS Sport Wagon model comes standard with leather seating surfaces and 15-inch wheels. Other changes include a standard interior trunk release on all sedans. A remote, keyless entry and AM/FM cassette player is standard on LS models.

Category B

Model Description	Trade-in TMV	Private TMV	Dealer TMV
4 Dr GS Sdn	5583	6391	7200
4 Dr LS Sdn	5970	6835	7700
4 Dr LS Wgn	6513	7457	8400

OPTIONS FOR TRACER

Air Conditioning[Std on LS] +395
Aluminum/Alloy Wheels +131
Anti-Lock Brakes +199
Automatic 4-Speed Transmission +405
Compact Disc Changer +147
Cruise Control[Opt on LS] +94
Leather Seats +199
Power Windows +119

VILLAGER 1999

The Mercury Villager is completely redesigned for '99. Improvements range from a more powerful engine to a larger interior to a second sliding door on the driver's side. New styling features include larger headlights and a distinctive front grille. Inside, ergonomics have been addressed with easier to reach controls and an

Model Description	Trade-in TMV	Private TMV	Dealer TMV	Model Description	Trade-in TMV	Private TMV	Dealer TMV

innovative storage shelf located behind the third seat.

Category P

4 Dr STD Pass. Van	10961	12130	13300
4 Dr Estate Pass. Van	13021	14411	15800
4 Dr Sport Pass. Van	12609	13955	15300

OPTIONS FOR VILLAGER

AM/FM Stereo/CD/Tape +340
Aluminum/Alloy Wheels[Opt on STD] +147
Anti-Lock Brakes +293
Camper/Towing Package +124
Child Seats (2) +119
Compact Disc Changer +184
Dual Air Conditioning +231
Dual Power Seats +302
Leather Seats +311
Power Drivers Seat +151
Power Moonroof +386
Premium Sound System[Opt on STD] +350
Privacy Glass +206

1998 MERCURY

GRAND MARQUIS 1998

Vive le Grand Marquis! The last of the American rear-drive sedans gets substantial improvements this year, including a new instrument panel, new steering gear and an improved ride, thanks to a Watt's linkage suspension. All-speed traction control debuts this year as well.

Category G

4 Dr GS Sdn	9605	10659	11800
4 Dr LS Sdn	10419	11562	12800

OPTIONS FOR GRAND MARQUIS

Aluminum/Alloy Wheels +139
Anti-Lock Brakes +337
Compact Disc Changer +152
Dual Power Seats +264
Keyless Entry System[Opt on GS] +104
Leather Seats +318

MOUNTAINEER 1998

The Mountaineer gets minor front and rear styling tweaks as it enters its second year of production. In addition, a new model, with full-time four-wheel drive, receives the SOHC V6 and five-speed automatic transmission that became available on the Explorer last year.

Category M

4 Dr STD 4WD Wgn	11506	12895	14400
4 Dr STD AWD Wgn	11746	13164	14700
4 Dr STD Wgn	10787	12089	13500

OPTIONS FOR MOUNTAINEER

8 cyl 5.0 L Engine[Opt on 2WD] +202
AM/FM Stereo/CD/Tape +141

Alarm System +108
Bucket Seats +238
Chrome Wheels +215
Climate Control for AC +108
Compact Disc Changer +160
Dual Power Seats +264
Leather Seats +284
Limited Slip Differential[Opt on 2WD] +155
Power Drivers Seat +132
Power Moonroof +347
Running Boards +171

MYSTIQUE 1998

The 1998 Mystique receives a freshened interior and exterior that includes new wheels and a new front end. Mechanical enhancements include 100,000-mile maintenance intervals for the 2.0-liter Zetec engine, improved manual transmission shifter feel, improved NVH and improved air conditioning performance. New interior pieces are intended to distinguish the Mystique from its otherwise-identical twin, the Ford Contour.

Category C

4 Dr GS Sdn	6312	7218	8200
4 Dr LS Sdn	7082	8098	9200

OPTIONS FOR MYSTIQUE

AM/FM Compact Disc Player +119
Aluminum/Alloy Wheels[Opt on GS] +183
Anti-Lock Brakes +216
Automatic 4-Speed Transmission +353
Leather Seats +388
Power Drivers Seat[Opt on GS] +152
Power Moonroof +258
Rear Spoiler +105

SABLE 1998

A mild facelift and fewer options are the only change to Mercury's mid-size sedan.

Category D

4 Dr GS Sdn	7323	8320	9400
4 Dr LS Sdn	7712	8762	9900
4 Dr LS Wgn	8413	9559	10800

OPTIONS FOR SABLE

6 cyl 3.0 L DOHC Engine +215
Alarm System +108
Aluminum/Alloy Wheels[Opt on GS] +171
Anti-Lock Brakes +260
Chrome Wheels +251
Compact Disc Changer +152
Dual Power Seats +303
Leather Seats +388
Power Drivers Seat[Opt on GS] +152
Power Moonroof +321

TRACER 1998

No changes to Mercury's recently redesigned entry-level car.

Don't forget to refer to the Mileage Adjustment Table at the back of this book!

Model Description	Trade-in TMV	Private TMV	Dealer TMV
Category B			
4 Dr GS Sdn	4737	5535	6400
4 Dr LS Sdn	5034	5881	6800
4 Dr LS Wgn	5330	6227	7200

OPTIONS FOR TRACER
Air Conditioning[Opt on GS] +345
Aluminum/Alloy Wheels +115
Anti-Lock Brakes +173
Automatic 4-Speed Transmission +353
Compact Disc Changer +223
Power Windows[Opt on LS] +104

VILLAGER   1998

No changes to the 1998 Villager as Mercury readies a replacement.

Model Description	Trade-in TMV	Private TMV	Dealer TMV
Category P			
2 Dr GS Cargo Van	8759	9787	10900
2 Dr GS Pass. Van	8884	9926	11055
2 Dr LS Pass. Van	10447	11673	13001
2 Dr Nautica Pass. Van	10688	11942	13300

OPTIONS FOR VILLAGER
7 Passenger Seating[Opt on GS] +144
AM/FM Stereo/CD/Tape +297
Air Conditioning[Opt on GS] +371
Aluminum/Alloy Wheels[Opt on GS] +128
Anti-Lock Brakes +256
Camper/Towing Package +108
Child Seats (2)[Std on Nautica] +104
Compact Disc Changer +294
Cruise Control +97
Dual Air Conditioning +371
Dual Power Seats +256
Leather Seats[Opt on LS] +270
Power Door Locks[Opt on GS] +124
Power Drivers Seat +171
Power Moonroof +337
Power Windows[Opt on GS] +115
Premium Sound System[Opt on GS] +305
Privacy Glass[Opt on GS] +180

1997 MERCURY

COUGAR XR7   1997

Mercury gives you the chance to buy a special anniversary edition replete with plenty of badges, a special interior and a few luxury doo-dads.

Model Description	Trade-in TMV	Private TMV	Dealer TMV
Category D			
2 Dr XR7 Cpe	5630	6562	7700

OPTIONS FOR COUGAR XR7
8 cyl 4.6 L Engine +419
AM/FM Compact Disc Player +159
Alarm System +93
Aluminum/Alloy Wheels +167
Anti-Lock Brakes +211

Dual Power Seats +107
Power Drivers Seat +107
Power Moonroof +274
Premium Sound System +107
Rear Spoiler +93
Sport Suspension +167

GRAND MARQUIS   1997

After a mild facelift last year, the Grand Marquis soldiers on with a few color changes, improved power steering and the addition of rear air suspension to the handling package.

Model Description	Trade-in TMV	Private TMV	Dealer TMV
Category G			
4 Dr GS Sdn	7513	8497	9700
4 Dr LS Sdn	9605	10863	12400

OPTIONS FOR GRAND MARQUIS
Aluminum/Alloy Wheels +118
Anti-Lock Brakes +258
Dual Power Seats +134
Leather Seats +273
Premium Sound System[Opt on LS] +134

MOUNTAINEER   1997

The all-new Mercury Mountaineer is yet another entrant into the booming luxury sport-utility market. Based on the wildly successful Ford Explorer, the Mountaineer is intended to appeal to outdoor sophisticates rather than true roughnecks. Distinguishing characteristics of the Mountaineer include four-wheel antilock brakes, a pushrod V8 engine and optional all-wheel drive.

Model Description	Trade-in TMV	Private TMV	Dealer TMV
Category M			
4 Dr STD AWD Wgn	10100	11360	12900
4 Dr STD Wgn	9396	10568	12000

OPTIONS FOR MOUNTAINEER
AM/FM Stereo/CD/Tape +120
Alarm System +93
Bucket Seats +203
Compact Disc Changer +137
Dual Power Seats +227
JBL Sound System +307
Leather Seats +243
Power Drivers Seat +113
Power Moonroof +296
Running Boards +147

MYSTIQUE   1997

The addition of a Spree Package for the GS model and the inclusion of a tilt steering wheel and standard trunk light are the only changes for the 1997 Mystique.

Model Description	Trade-in TMV	Private TMV	Dealer TMV
Category C			
4 Dr STD Sdn	4730	5527	6500
4 Dr GS Sdn	4803	5612	6600
4 Dr LS Sdn	5385	6292	7400

Don't forget to refer to the Mileage Adjustment Table at the back of this book!

MERCURY 97-96

Model Description	Trade-in TMV	Private TMV	Dealer TMV	Model Description	Trade-in TMV	Private TMV	Dealer TMV

OPTIONS FOR MYSTIQUE

6 cyl 2.5 L Engine +367
AM/FM Compact Disc Player +102
Air Conditioning +294
Aluminum/Alloy Wheels[Opt on GS] +157
Anti-Lock Brakes +211
Automatic 4-Speed Transmission +302
Leather Seats +332
Power Drivers Seat[Opt on GS] +129
Power Moonroof +220
Power Windows +100
Premium Sound System +100

SABLE   1997

The 1997 Sable LS can now be had with Ford's outstanding Mach audio system. Other changes, occurring at the end of the 1996 model year, include the addition of a mass airflow sensor to the Vulcan V6, and improvements to the Duratec V6 to improve responsiveness.

Category D

Model	Trade-in	Private	Dealer
4 Dr GS Sdn	5850	6817	8000
4 Dr GS Wgn	5996	6988	8200
4 Dr LS Sdn	6508	7584	8900
4 Dr LS Wgn	6508	7584	8900

OPTIONS FOR SABLE

Alarm System[Opt on LS] +93
Aluminum/Alloy Wheels[Opt on GS] +117
Anti-Lock Brakes +222
Chrome Wheels +215
Compact Disc Changer +220
Leather Seats[Opt on GS] +367
Power Door Locks[Opt on GS] +96
Power Drivers Seat[Opt on GS] +126
Power Moonroof +274
Rear Window Wiper +94

TRACER   1997

The Mercury Tracer is totally redesigned this year with enhancements across the board. The most noticeable improvements are in the powertrain and in the ride quality. New sheetmetal gives the Tracer a rounder, more aerodynamic appearance as well. The speedy LTS sedan is discontinued.

Category B

Model	Trade-in	Private	Dealer
4 Dr GS Sdn	3619	4286	5100
4 Dr LS Sdn	3761	4454	5300
4 Dr LS Wgn	3903	4622	5500

OPTIONS FOR TRACER

Air Conditioning +294
Aluminum/Alloy Wheels[Opt on LS] +98
Anti-Lock Brakes +211
Automatic 4-Speed Transmission +302
Compact Disc Changer +129

VILLAGER   1997

For 1997, the Villager offers a few more luxury items to distinguish it from the Nissan Quest. Quad captain's chairs are a nice alternative to the middle-row bench, and the addition of rear radio controls and rear air conditioning should also make rear seat passengers happy.

Category P

Model	Trade-in	Private	Dealer
2 Dr GS Cargo Van	6545	7470	8600
2 Dr GS Pass. Van	6926	7904	9100
2 Dr LS Pass. Van	8144	9294	10700
2 Dr Nautica Pass. Van	8220	9381	10800

OPTIONS FOR VILLAGER

7 Passenger Seating[Opt on GS] +123
AM/FM Stereo/CD/Tape +254
Air Conditioning[Opt on GS Cargo] +317
Aluminum/Alloy Wheels[Opt on GS] +110
Anti-Lock Brakes[Opt on GS] +219
Camper/Towing Package +93
Captain Chairs (4)[Opt on LS] +231
Dual Air Conditioning +317
Dual Power Seats +219
Leather Seats[Opt on LS] +231
Power Door Locks[Opt on GS Cargo] +105
Power Drivers Seat +147
Power Moonroof +288
Power Windows[Opt on GS Cargo, GS Pass] +98
Premium Sound System[Opt on GS Pass Van] +262
Privacy Glass +154

1996 MERCURY

COUGAR   1996

New styling and powertrain improvements highlight the 1996 Cougar. Some formerly standard equipment is now optional. New options include a revamped cruise control system and a Total Anti-theft System. Four new colors debut.

Category D

Model	Trade-in	Private	Dealer
2 Dr XR7 Cpe	4341	5164	6300

OPTIONS FOR COUGAR

8 cyl 4.6 L Engine +372
AM/FM Compact Disc Player +141
Anti-Lock Brakes +165
Chrome Wheels +190
Leather Seats +161
Power Moonroof +244
Premium Sound System +141

GRAND MARQUIS   1996

This distant descendant of the Turnpike Cruiser gets engine and transmission upgrades, a new steering

MERCURY 96

Model Description	Trade-in TMV	Private TMV	Dealer TMV	Model Description	Trade-in TMV	Private TMV	Dealer TMV

wheel and a new gas cap design. Passenger power lumbar support has been deleted.

Category G

4 Dr GS Sdn	6045	6866	8000
4 Dr LS Sdn	6422	7295	8500

OPTIONS FOR GRAND MARQUIS

Aluminum/Alloy Wheels[Opt on LS] +105
Anti-Lock Brakes +221
Camper/Towing Package +296
Leather Seats +212
Power Passenger Seat +118
Premium Sound System +118

MYSTIQUE — 1996

More rear seat room is the big story for Mystique in 1996. Gearshift effort has been improved on manual transmissions, a new Sport Appearance Package is available, and five new colors are on the palette. Alloy wheels have been restyled on LS models.

Category C

4 Dr GS Sdn	3479	4160	5100
4 Dr LS Sdn	3820	4568	5600

OPTIONS FOR MYSTIQUE

6 cyl 2.5 L Engine +325
Air Conditioning +257
Aluminum/Alloy Wheels +139
Anti-Lock Brakes +188
Automatic 4-Speed Transmission +268
Leather Seats +196
Power Drivers Seat[Opt on GS] +108
Power Moonroof +196
Rear Spoiler +114

SABLE — 1996

Fresh off the drawing boards for 1996, and it seems the drawing boards were poorly lit. Styling is heavy-handed and homely, but definitely not dull. Otherwise, the new Sable is an excellent car, powered by new engines, suspended by new components, and innovative in nearly every way. Longer and wider sedan and wagon bodystyles are offered in GS and LS trim.

Category D

4 Dr G Sdn	4134	4918	6000
4 Dr GS Sdn	4341	5164	6300
4 Dr GS Wgn	4685	5573	6800
4 Dr LS Sdn	4823	5737	7000
4 Dr LS Wgn	5236	6229	7600

OPTIONS FOR SABLE

Aluminum/Alloy Wheels[Opt on GS] +103
Anti-Lock Brakes +188
Chrome Wheels +190
Compact Disc Changer +196
JBL Sound System +165
Leather Seats +325

Power Drivers Seat[Opt on GS] +112
Power Moonroof +244
Preferred Equipment Package +411

TRACER — 1996

Automatic transmission modifications make base Tracers more responsive, and the standard 1.9-liter engine now goes 100,000 miles between tune-ups. Last year's integrated child seat continues, and Trio models are now available in all colors, including a new one called Toreador Red.

Category B

4 Dr STD Sdn	2570	3171	4000
4 Dr STD Wgn	2699	3329	4200
4 Dr LTS Sdn	2956	3646	4600

OPTIONS FOR TRACER

Air Conditioning +258
Anti-Lock Brakes +188
Automatic 4-Speed Transmission +268
Power Moonroof +172

VILLAGER — 1996

A passenger-side airbag is installed in a redesigned dashboard for 1996, and fresh front and rear styling updates this versatile van. Villager also gets an optional integrated child seat, automatic climate control system, and remote keyless entry system. Substantial trim and functional changes make Villager competitive once again.

Category P

2 Dr GS Cargo Van	5571	6381	7500
2 Dr GS Pass. Van	5869	6722	7900
2 Dr LS Pass. Van	6611	7573	8900
2 Dr Nautica Pass. Van			
	6909	7913	9300

OPTIONS FOR VILLAGER

AM/FM Stereo/CD/Tape +226
Air Conditioning[Opt on GS Cargo] +282
Captain Chairs (4)[Opt on LS] +201
Dual Air Conditioning +282
Leather Seats[Opt on LS] +205
Power Drivers Seat +130
Power Moonroof +255
Premium Sound System[Opt on GS] +232
Privacy Glass[Opt on GS] +136

1995 MERCURY

COUGAR — 1995

A Sport Appearance Package is offered to spruce up the Cougar with BBS wheels and a luggage rack. Unfortunately, the trunk-mounted CD-changer is

---

Don't forget to refer to the Mileage Adjustment Table at the back of this book!

MERCURY 95

Model Description	Trade-in TMV	Private TMV	Dealer TMV	Model Description	Trade-in TMV	Private TMV	Dealer TMV

deleted from the option list. Antilock brakes and a traction-lock axle are available as separate options for the first time this year.

Category D

2 Dr XR7 Cpe	3262	3914	5000

OPTIONS FOR COUGAR

8 cyl 4.6 L Engine +313
Anti-Lock Brakes +139
Leather Seats +136
Power Moonroof +205
Power Passenger Seat +80
Premium Sound System +119

GRAND MARQUIS   1995

Updated styling and an increased number of convenience features improve upon last year's model. A battery saver shuts off power to accessories or lights 10 minutes after the ignition is switched off. The mast antenna has been replaced by an integrated rear window antenna. Interior updates include a 12-volt outlet in a redesigned dashboard. Enlarged stereo controls improve ease of operation and bigger gauges improve the instrument panel.

Category G

4 Dr GS Sdn	4197	4873	6000
4 Dr LS Sdn	4827	5604	6900

OPTIONS FOR GRAND MARQUIS

Aluminum/Alloy Wheels[Opt on LS] +88
Anti-Lock Brakes +166
Camper/Towing Package +249
Leather Seats +178
Power Passenger Seat[Opt on LS] +100
Power Sunroof +194
Premium Sound System +100

MYSTIQUE   1995

Introduced to replace the aging Topaz, the Mystique is a virtual twin to the Ford Contour. Euro-styling combined with German engineering results in a $20,000 American car that can compete with import sedans that cost nearly twice as much. You may choose between two trim levels, the base GS or the more luxurious LS. A 170-horsepower V6 engine is optional.

Category C

4 Dr GS Sdn	2699	3262	4200
4 Dr LS Sdn	2956	3572	4600

OPTIONS FOR MYSTIQUE

6 cyl 2.5 L Engine +274
AM/FM Compact Disc Player +76
Air Conditioning +216
Aluminum/Alloy Wheels +118
Anti-Lock Brakes +158
Automatic 4-Speed Transmission +226

Leather Seats +165
Power Drivers Seat[Opt on GS] +91
Power Moonroof +165

SABLE   1995

Last year for the Sable in its current form. New cylinder heads and crankshafts are intended to decrease engine noise by reducing vibration. Solar control window glass makes a brief appearance on the sedan and wagon.

Category D

4 Dr GS Sdn	3197	3835	4900
4 Dr GS Wgn	3392	4070	5200
4 Dr LS Sdn	3523	4227	5400
4 Dr LS Wgn	3849	4618	5900

OPTIONS FOR SABLE

6 cyl 3.8 L Engine +147
AM/FM Compact Disc Player[Opt on LS] +97
Aluminum/Alloy Wheels[Opt on GS] +87
Anti-Lock Brakes[Opt on GS] +158
Chrome Wheels +161
Dual Power Seats +194
Leather Seats +248
Power Drivers Seat[Opt on GS] +94
Power Moonroof +205

TRACER   1995

A passenger airbag is finally available for the Tracer. Unfortunately, some engineering genius decided to retain the annoying motorized shoulder belts. An integrated child seat is introduced as an optional safety feature. The Trio package is introduced, designed to give budget shoppers the option of purchasing some of the more popular LTS features such as the spoiler, aluminum wheels and leather-wrapped steering wheel.

Category B

4 Dr STD Sdn	2007	2516	3363
4 Dr STD Wgn	2051	2571	3437
4 Dr LTS Sdn	2208	2768	3700

OPTIONS FOR TRACER

AM/FM Compact Disc Player +90
Air Conditioning +217
Anti-Lock Brakes +111
Automatic 4-Speed Transmission +226
Power Moonroof +145

VILLAGER   1995

No changes for the Villager.

Category P

2 Dr GS Cargo Van	3933	4558	5600
2 Dr GS Pass. Van	4284	4965	6100
2 Dr LS Pass. Van	5127	5942	7300

Don't forget to refer to the Mileage Adjustment Table at the back of this book!

MERCURY 95-94

Model Description	Trade-in TMV	Private TMV	Dealer TMV
2 Dr Nautica Pass. Van	5548	6430	7900

OPTIONS FOR VILLAGER
7 Passenger Seating[Opt on GS] +91
AM/FM Stereo/CD/Tape +189
Air Conditioning +237
Aluminum/Alloy Wheels +82
Captain Chairs (4)[Opt on LS] +169
Dual Air Conditioning +129
Leather Seats[Opt on LS] +173
Power Moonroof +215
Premium Sound System +195
Privacy Glass[Opt on GS Pass Van] +115

1994 MERCURY

CAPRI   1994

A passenger airbag is added. A new suspension on the XR2 improves handling. Both trim levels get a freshened exterior. Slow sales make this the final year for this car.
Category E

Model Description	Trade-in TMV	Private TMV	Dealer TMV
2 Dr STD Conv	2334	2883	3800
2 Dr XR2 Turbo Conv	2702	3339	4400

OPTIONS FOR CAPRI
Air Conditioning +194
Automatic 4-Speed Transmission +169
Hardtop Roof[Opt on STD] +303
Leather Seats +133

COUGAR   1994

Dual airbags are finally available on the Cougar. The standard four-speed automatic transmission gains electronic shift controls and an overdrive lockout switch. Optional traction control joins the lineup of safety features. Updated front and rear fascias, taillamps and headlights round out the changes.
Category D

Model Description	Trade-in TMV	Private TMV	Dealer TMV
2 Dr XR7 Cpe	2538	3161	4200

OPTIONS FOR COUGAR
8 cyl 4.6 L Engine +274
Anti-Lock Brakes +121
Compact Disc Changer +85
JBL Sound System +140
Leather Seats +119
Power Moonroof +180
Premium Sound System +104

GRAND MARQUIS   1994

The Grand Marquis passes the stringent 1997 side-impact standards this year. Wire-spoke wheelcovers are now part of the standard equipment package.
Category G

Model Description	Trade-in TMV	Private TMV	Dealer TMV
4 Dr GS Sdn	3232	3858	4900
4 Dr LS Sdn	3826	4566	5800

OPTIONS FOR GRAND MARQUIS
Aluminum/Alloy Wheels +78
Anti-Lock Brakes +146
Camper/Towing Package +218
Leather Seats +156
Power Passenger Seat[Opt on LS] +87
Premium Sound System[Opt on LS] +87

SABLE   1994

Rear window defroster becomes standard equipment on the sedan and wagon. The wagon gets a standard rear window wiper as well. CFC-free air conditioning is introduced to the Sable.
Category D

Model Description	Trade-in TMV	Private TMV	Dealer TMV
4 Dr GS Sdn	2357	2936	3900
4 Dr GS Wgn	2478	3086	4100
4 Dr LS Sdn	2599	3237	4300
4 Dr LS Wgn	2780	3462	4600

OPTIONS FOR SABLE
6 cyl 3.8 L Engine +128
AM/FM Compact Disc Player[Opt on LS] +85
Anti-Lock Brakes +138
Leather Seats +217
Power Drivers Seat[Opt on GS] +82
Power Moonroof +180

TOPAZ   1994

The Topaz receives CFC-free air conditioning. This will be the last year for the Topaz; Mercury is replacing it with an all-new compact called the Mystique.
Category B

Model Description	Trade-in TMV	Private TMV	Dealer TMV
2 Dr GS Sdn	1307	1679	2300
4 Dr GS Sdn	1363	1752	2400

OPTIONS FOR TOPAZ
6 cyl 3.0 L Engine +165
Air Bag Restraint[Opt on GS] +97
Air Conditioning +194
Automatic 3-Speed Transmission +133

TRACER   1994

A driver's side airbag is introduced on all models. New alloy wheels and optional antilock brakes show up on the LTS.
Category B

Model Description	Trade-in TMV	Private TMV	Dealer TMV
4 Dr STD Sdn	1468	1886	2584
4 Dr STD Wgn	1486	1910	2616
4 Dr LTS Sdn	1818	2336	3200

OPTIONS FOR TRACER
AM/FM Compact Disc Player +78
Air Conditioning +190
Anti-Lock Brakes +97
Automatic 4-Speed Transmission +198
Power Moonroof +127

Don't forget to refer to the Mileage Adjustment Table at the back of this book!

Model Description	Trade-in TMV	Private TMV	Dealer TMV

VILLAGER · 1994

A driver airbag is installed in the Villager and a special edition luxury model debuts. Borrowing the name of an upscale men's clothier, the Nautica edition of the Villager includes such niceties as two-tone paint, alloy wheels and leather upholstery; all tastefully done in blue and white befitting a nautical theme.

Category P

Model Description	Trade-in TMV	Private TMV	Dealer TMV
2 Dr GS Cargo Van	3321	3951	5000
2 Dr GS Pass. Van	3520	4188	5300
2 Dr LS Pass. Van	4384	5215	6600
2 Dr Nautica Pass. Van	4583	5452	6900

OPTIONS FOR VILLAGER
AM/FM Stereo/CD/Tape +165
Air Conditioning[Opt on GS Cargo] +207
Captain Chairs (4)[Opt on LS] +148
Compact Disc Changer +90
Dual Air Conditioning +113
Leather Seats[Opt on LS] +151
Power Moonroof +188
Premium Sound System[Opt on GS] +171
Privacy Glass +101

1993 MERCURY

CAPRI · 1993

A new radio is introduced as the only change on the 1993 Capri.

Category E

Model Description	Trade-in TMV	Private TMV	Dealer TMV
2 Dr STD Conv	1871	2369	3200
2 Dr XR2 Turbo Conv	2163	2740	3700

OPTIONS FOR CAPRI
Air Conditioning[Opt on STD] +164
Automatic 4-Speed Transmission +143
Hardtop Roof +256
Leather Seats +113
Premium Sound System +92

COUGAR · 1993

The LS trim level is dropped in favor of the XR7. The XR7 is decontented for 1993, losing the V8 engine, limited-slip axle and antilock brakes from the standard equipment lists. Split-fold rear seats are no longer available.

Category D

Model Description	Trade-in TMV	Private TMV	Dealer TMV
2 Dr XR7 Cpe	1714	2271	3200

OPTIONS FOR COUGAR
8 cyl 5.0 L Engine +243
Anti-Lock Brakes +102
Dual Power Seats +106

JBL Sound System +117
Leather Seats +100
Power Moonroof +151
Premium Sound System +88

GRAND MARQUIS · 1993

A passenger airbag, an overdrive-lockout selector on the automatic gearshift, a stainless steel exhaust system, an express-down driver's window, and dual front cupholders appear on the Grand Marquis's extensive standard equipment list this year.

Category G

Model Description	Trade-in TMV	Private TMV	Dealer TMV
4 Dr GS Sdn	2429	2981	3900
4 Dr LS Sdn	2990	3669	4800

OPTIONS FOR GRAND MARQUIS
Anti-Lock Brakes +123
Camper/Towing Package +185
Full Vinyl Top +215
Leather Seats +132

SABLE · 1993

The lower body-side cladding and bumpers become body colored for 1993. Bucket seats become an option on both body styles.

Category D

Model Description	Trade-in TMV	Private TMV	Dealer TMV
4 Dr GS Sdn	1714	2271	3200
4 Dr GS Wgn	1822	2414	3401
4 Dr LS Sdn	1821	2412	3399
4 Dr LS Wgn	1928	2555	3600

OPTIONS FOR SABLE
6 cyl 3.8 L Engine +109
Anti-Lock Brakes +116
JBL Sound System +102
Leather Seats +184
Power Sunroof +143

TOPAZ · 1993

Mercury offers only one trim level for the Topaz this year: the lowly GS.

Category B

Model Description	Trade-in TMV	Private TMV	Dealer TMV
2 Dr GS Sdn	966	1316	1900
4 Dr GS Sdn	1017	1386	2000

OPTIONS FOR TOPAZ
6 cyl 3.0 L Engine +140
Air Bag Restraint[Opt on GS] +81
Air Conditioning +164
Automatic 3-Speed Transmission[Opt on GS] +113

TRACER · 1993

Beefy stabilizer arms on all trim levels improve handling. Base models receive a new fascia and the LTS receives a one-piece spoiler. All models get new interior fabrics and tail lamps.

Category B

Don't forget to refer to the Mileage Adjustment Table at the back of this book!

Model Description	Trade-in TMV	Private TMV	Dealer TMV
4 Dr STD Sdn	1119	1524	2200
4 Dr STD Wgn	1170	1594	2300
4 Dr LTS Sdn	1272	1732	2500

OPTIONS FOR TRACER

Air Conditioning +161
Automatic 4-Speed Transmission +167
Power Moonroof[Opt on LTS,STD] +107

VILLAGER   1993

Mercury joins the minivan fray by introducing a vehicle designed jointly with Nissan. Attractive styling and standard features such as antilock brakes are certainly commendable, but the absence of airbags would lead us toward another model.

Category P

Model Description	Trade-in TMV	Private TMV	Dealer TMV
2 Dr GS Cargo Van	2519	3112	4100
2 Dr GS Pass. Van	2703	3339	4400
2 Dr LS Pass. Van	3563	4402	5800

OPTIONS FOR VILLAGER

AM/FM Stereo/CD/Tape +140
Air Conditioning[Opt on GS Cargo] +175
Captain Chairs (4) +125
Leather Seats +128
Power Sunroof +143

1992 MERCURY

CAPRI   1992

The XR2 receives 15-inch wheels, new tires and updated cabin trim. Power door locks are no longer available but cruise control is added to the options list.

Category E

Model Description	Trade-in TMV	Private TMV	Dealer TMV
2 Dr STD Conv	1403	1852	2600
2 Dr XR2 Turbo Conv	1889	2493	3500

OPTIONS FOR CAPRI

Air Conditioning[Opt on STD] +136
Automatic 4-Speed Transmission +119
Hardtop Roof +211
Leather Seats +93

COUGAR   1992

The 25th anniversary edition debuts. A unique LS model becomes available this year equipped with 5.0-liter V8 engine, monochromatic colors, BBS aluminum wheels, and special trim. White sidewall tires and the anti-theft system are no longer available.

Category D

Model Description	Trade-in TMV	Private TMV	Dealer TMV
2 Dr LS Cpe	1183	1677	2500
2 Dr XR7 Cpe	1420	2012	3000

OPTIONS FOR COUGAR

8 cyl 5.0 L Engine[Opt on LS] +202
Anti-Lock Brakes[Opt on LS] +85

JBL Sound System +97
Leather Seats +83
Power Moonroof +126

GRAND MARQUIS   1992

New sheetmetal debuts on the Grand Marquis. Rounded styling and two additional inches in length give the car a sleeker appearance. The old V8 engine is replaced with a 4.6-liter V8 that makes between 40 and 60 more horsepower, depending on the exhaust system. A new passenger airbag is added to the options list. Antilock brakes are available in the performance and handling package. The wagon is discontinued.

Category G

Model Description	Trade-in TMV	Private TMV	Dealer TMV
4 Dr GS Sdn	2010	2569	3500
4 Dr LS Sdn	2240	2863	3900

OPTIONS FOR GRAND MARQUIS

Anti-Lock Brakes +102
Camper/Towing Package +153
Full Vinyl Top +177
JBL Sound System +97
Leather Seats[Opt on LS] +110

SABLE   1992

Sable gets dual airbags for front seat occupants. New sheetmetal does little to change the looks of the car. Fifteen-inch wheels replace last year's 14-inchers. Additional radio controls have been placed near the steering wheel and the power window buttons have been moved to the armrest. Variable-assist power steering becomes standard and the heated windshield is dropped from the options list.

Category D

Model Description	Trade-in TMV	Private TMV	Dealer TMV
4 Dr GS Sdn	1306	1852	2761
4 Dr GS Wgn	1424	2019	3010
4 Dr LS Sdn	1420	2012	3000
4 Dr LS Wgn	1467	2079	3100

OPTIONS FOR SABLE

6 cyl 3.8 L Engine +90
Anti-Lock Brakes +96
JBL Sound System +85
Leather Seats +152
Power Moonroof +126

TOPAZ   1992

V6 is available for those who need a little more horsepower. Unfortunately the all-wheel-drive system is dropped from the option list.

Category B

Model Description	Trade-in TMV	Private TMV	Dealer TMV
2 Dr GS Sdn	858	1211	1800

Don't forget to refer to the Mileage Adjustment Table at the back of this book!

Model Description	Trade-in TMV	Private TMV	Dealer TMV	Model Description	Trade-in TMV	Private TMV	Dealer TMV
4 Dr GS Sdn	905	1278	1900				
4 Dr LS Sdn	953	1346	2000				
4 Dr LTS Sdn	1048	1480	2200				
2 Dr XR5 Sdn	1008	1423	2115				

OPTIONS FOR TOPAZ
6 cyl 3.0 L Engine[Opt on GS,LS] +116
Air Conditioning[Opt on GS,LS] +136
Automatic 3-Speed Transmission +93

TRACER   1992

No changes.
Category B

4 Dr STD Sdn	1080	1525	2266
4 Dr STD Wgn	1090	1540	2288
4 Dr LTS Sdn	1096	1548	2300

OPTIONS FOR TRACER
Air Conditioning +133
Automatic 4-Speed Transmission +138

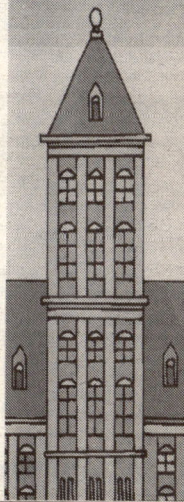

Don't forget to refer to the Mileage Adjustment Table at the back of this book!

MITSUBISHI 01

Model Description	Trade-in TMV	Private TMV	Dealer TMV	Model Description	Trade-in TMV	Private TMV	Dealer TMV

MITSUBISHI   Japan

1994 Mitsubishi Diamante

2001 MITSUBISHI

DIAMANTE   2001

This Mitsubishi model doesn't change much from last year, but product planners add tether anchors for child seats, fog lights on the LS, and new seat fabric and wheel cover for the ES. Greenies can rest easy knowing that it meets LEV standards for all states.

Category H

Model Description	Trade-in	Private	Dealer
4 Dr ES Sdn	17860	18950	20767
4 Dr LS Sdn	19974	21193	23225

OPTIONS FOR DIAMANTE
Heated Front Seats +129
Traction Control System +158

ECLIPSE   2001

The new year for the Eclipse sees a standard spoiler, tether anchors for child seats and engines that meet LEV emissions standards.

Category E

Model Description	Trade-in	Private	Dealer
2 Dr GS Hbk	12910	13818	15332
2 Dr GT Hbk	14338	15346	17028
2 Dr RS Hbk	12314	13181	14625

OPTIONS FOR ECLIPSE
Anti-Lock Brakes +410
Automatic 4-Speed Transmission +458
Infinity Sound System +172
Leather Seats +261
Power Drivers Seat +143
Power Moonroof[Std on GS] +419
Side Air Bag Restraints +143

ECLIPSE SPYDER   2001

Mitsubishi's 2001 Eclipse Spyder is all-new inside and

out and based on the recently redesigned Eclipse Coupe, embodying a youthful image and providing a sporty drive. But the turbocharged engine is no longer on the menu.

Category E

Model Description	Trade-in	Private	Dealer
2 Dr GS Conv	16361	17512	19431
2 Dr GT Conv	17831	19086	21177

OPTIONS FOR ECLIPSE SPYDER
Anti-Lock Brakes +410
Automatic 4-Speed Transmission +573
Leather Seats +344
Power Drivers Seat +143
Side Air Bag Restraints +143

GALANT   2001

Mitsubishi's fourth-generation Galant features some new standard and optional equipment, like a LATCH system for child seats and traction control and heated mirrors for cold-weather dwellers who purchase the all-weather package. It now meets LEV standards.

Category D

Model Description	Trade-in	Private	Dealer
4 Dr DE Sdn	11748	12713	14321
4 Dr ES Sdn	12095	13089	14745
4 Dr ES V6 Sdn	13793	14926	16815
4 Dr GTZ Sdn	16013	17329	19521
4 Dr LS Sdn	15759	17053	19211

OPTIONS FOR GALANT
Anti-Lock Brakes[Opt on ES] +552
Power Moonroof[Std on GTZ,LS] +487
Side Air Bag Restraints[Std on GTZ,LS] +172
Traction Control System[Opt on ES V6] +115

MIRAGE   2001

All 2001 Mirages now have tether anchors for child seats and meet LEV standards. A power sunroof is now available with the coupe's sport package. Sedan buyers can choose from the LS or the new base ES trim model that replaces the DE model. Nothing else has changed but the designation - John Mellencamp? John Cougar? John Cougar Mellencamp?

Category B

Model Description	Trade-in	Private	Dealer
2 Dr DE Cpe	7402	8096	9253
4 Dr ES Sdn	8681	9495	10851
2 Dr LS Cpe	8971	9812	11214
4 Dr LS Sdn	8801	9626	11001

OPTIONS FOR MIRAGE
AM/FM Compact Disc Player[Std on LS,Sdn] +229
Air Conditioning[Std on LS] +504
Aluminum/Alloy Wheels[Opt on DE,Cpe] +230
Automatic 4-Speed Transmission +458
Power Door Locks[Opt on DE Cpe] +117
Power Moonroof[Opt on LS] +458
Power Windows[Std on LS,Sdn] +149

Don't forget to refer to the Mileage Adjustment Table at the back of this book!

MITSUBISHI 01-00

Model Description	Trade-in TMV	Private TMV	Dealer TMV

MONTERO 2001

The Montero is redesigned for 2001 and features a sculpted body, stiffer frame, improved suspension and more interior room.

Category M

	Trade-in	Private	Dealer
4 Dr Limited 4WD Wgn	22868	24322	26746
4 Dr XLS 4WD Wgn	20112	21391	23523

OPTIONS FOR MONTERO
Climate Control for AC +143
Dual Air Conditioning +372
Limited Slip Differential +143
Power Moonroof +544

MONTERO SPORT 2001

Because the Montero Sport underwent an update last year, this midsize SUV pretty much remains static for 2001. You can now get the base level ES trim in a 4WD configuration, and the XS trim level debuts with the 3.5-liter V6 from the pricey Limited model. A Lower Anchor Tether Child (LATCH) restraint system comes standard, and the light trucks meet LEV standards.

Category M

	Trade-in	Private	Dealer
4 Dr 3.5XS 4WD Wgn	18288	19451	21389
4 Dr 3.5XS Wgn	16998	18079	19881
4 Dr ES 4WD Wgn	15920	16933	18620
4 Dr ES Wgn	14139	15038	16537
4 Dr LS 4WD Wgn	17253	18350	20179
4 Dr LS Wgn	16047	17068	18769
4 Dr LTD 4WD Wgn	20522	21827	24002
4 Dr LTD Wgn	19696	20948	23036
4 Dr XLS 4WD Wgn	18357	19524	21470
4 Dr XLS Wgn	17106	18194	20007

OPTIONS FOR MONTERO SPORT
Infinity Sound System[Opt on XLS] +201
Leather Seats +573
Limited Slip Differential[Opt on XLS] +143
Power Moonroof[Opt on XLS] +487

2000 MITSUBISHI

DIAMANTE 2000

This Mitsubishi model doesn't change much from last year, but product planners add a couple of standard features, replace four colors, and offer a new all-weather package for the LS buyer.

Category H

	Trade-in	Private	Dealer
4 Dr ES Sdn	15326	16764	18091
4 Dr LS Sdn	17059	18660	20137

OPTIONS FOR DIAMANTE
AM/FM Stereo/CD/Tape +229
Aluminum/Alloy Wheels[Std on LS] +481

Compact Disc Changer +343
Fog Lights +92
Heated Front Seats +129
Heated Power Mirrors +100
Traction Control System +158

ECLIPSE 2000

Mitsubishi's 2000 Eclipse is redesigned inside and out and based on the Galant sedan platform, embodying a youthful image and providing a sporty drive. V6 power is now available, but the spunky turbocharged engine is gone as is the all-wheel drive model.

Category E

	Trade-in	Private	Dealer
2 Dr GS Hbk	11538	12775	13917
2 Dr GT Hbk	12250	13563	14775
2 Dr RS Hbk	10670	11813	12869

OPTIONS FOR ECLIPSE
AM/FM Stereo/CD/Tape +229
Anti-Lock Brakes +410
Automatic 4-Speed Transmission +458
Compact Disc Changer +343
Infinity Sound System +172
Leather Seats +261
Power Drivers Seat +143
Power Moonroof[Std on GS] +419
Rear Spoiler[Std on GT] +183
Side Air Bag Restraints +143
Traction Control System +143

GALANT 2000

After a '99 redesign, Mitsubishi's fourth-generation Galant features some new standard and optional equipment, like cruise-control memory function, an in-dash CD player, larger tires and four new colors.

Category D

	Trade-in	Private	Dealer
4 Dr DE Sdn	9696	10806	11830
4 Dr ES Sdn	10371	11558	12654
4 Dr ES V6 Sdn	11467	12779	13991
4 Dr GTZ Sdn	13322	14847	16255
4 Dr LS Sdn	12817	14284	15638

OPTIONS FOR GALANT
AM/FM Stereo Tape +129
Alarm System[Std on GTZ,LS] +143
Aluminum/Alloy Wheels[Opt on ES,ES V6] +100
Anti-Lock Brakes[Opt on ES] +552
Compact Disc Changer +386
Heated Power Mirrors[Opt on ES] +100
Infinity Sound System[Std on GTZ,LS] +172
Leather Seats[Std on GTZ,LS] +487
Power Moonroof[Std on GTZ,LS] +487
Side Air Bag Restraints[Std on GTZ,LS] +172

MIRAGE 2000

The DE Sedan now comes with the more powerful 1.8-liter engine in place of last year's base 1.5-liter

MITSUBISHI 00-99

Model Description	Trade-in TMV	Private TMV	Dealer TMV	Model Description	Trade-in TMV	Private TMV	Dealer TMV

powerplant. All DE models (sedans and coupes) get a host of luxury items and larger brakes as standard equipment. The LS Sedan also gets a few more standard goodies for 2000.

Category B

Model Description	Trade-in TMV	Private TMV	Dealer TMV
2 Dr DE Cpe	5753	6550	7285
4 Dr DE Sdn	6786	7726	8593
2 Dr LS Cpe	7081	8061	8966
4 Dr LS Sdn	8168	9298	10342

OPTIONS FOR MIRAGE
AM/FM Compact Disc Player[Std on LS,Sdn] +229
AM/FM Stereo Tape +202
Air Conditioning[Std on LS] +504
Aluminum/Alloy Wheels[Opt on DE,Cpe] +230
Automatic 4-Speed Transmission[Std on LS Sdn] +435
Cruise Control[Opt on DE Sdn] +100
Power Door Locks[Opt on DE Cpe] +117
Power Mirrors[Std on LS] +106
Power Windows[Std on LS,Sdn] +149
Rear Spoiler[Opt on LS Cpe] +100

MONTERO 2000

The Montero's list of standard features has been lengthened, and a new Endeavor package adds even more luxury items to Mitsubishi's largest SUV.

Category M

Model Description	Trade-in TMV	Private TMV	Dealer TMV
4 Dr STD 4WD Wgn	16802	18333	19747

OPTIONS FOR MONTERO
Compact Disc Changer +387
Endeavor Package +859
Heated Front Seats +129
Heated Power Mirrors +100
Infinity Sound System +143
Leather Seats +687
Power Drivers Seat +175
Power Moonroof +544

MONTERO SPORT 2000

The 2000 Montero Sport receives significant interior and exterior styling updates like a new grille, revised headlights, body-colored bumpers and new center console design, as well as several technical improvements, including a limited-slip differential on XLS and Limited models, and 16-inch alloy wheels.

Category M

Model Description	Trade-in TMV	Private TMV	Dealer TMV
4 Dr ES Wgn	12288	13408	14442
4 Dr LS 4WD Wgn	14710	16051	17289
4 Dr LS Wgn	13671	14918	16068
4 Dr Limited 4WD Wgn	17307	18885	20341
4 Dr Limited Wgn	16614	18128	19526
4 Dr XLS 4WD Wgn	16181	17656	19017
4 Dr XLS Wgn	15057	16429	17696

OPTIONS FOR MONTERO SPORT
Alarm System[Std on Limited] +86

Compact Disc Changer +343
Fog Lights[Opt on LS] +115
Heated Front Seats +143
Infinity Sound System[Opt on XLS] +201
Keyless Entry System[Opt on LS] +143
Leather Seats +573
Limited Slip Differential[Opt on XLS] +143
Luggage Rack[Opt on ES,LS] +158
Power Moonroof[Opt on XLS] +487
Side Steps[Opt on LS] +143
Trailer Hitch +144

1999 MITSUBISHI

3000GT 1999

The 1999 3000GT sees some styling changes and a few choice pieces of standard equipment, including antilock brakes and a power sunroof for the SL.

Category F

Model Description	Trade-in TMV	Private TMV	Dealer TMV
2 Dr STD Cpe	14378	15911	17444
2 Dr SL Cpe	19029	21058	23087
2 Dr VR-4 Turbo AWD Cpe	25457	28172	30886

OPTIONS FOR 3000GT
AM/FM Compact Disc Player +192
AM/FM Stereo/CD/Tape[Opt on STD] +350
Automatic 4-Speed Transmission +429
Compact Disc Changer +289
Leather Seats[Opt on STD] +398

DIAMANTE 1999

Only one Diamante model is available, replacing the ES and LS models. Mitsubishi also adds some new standard features, options and exterior colors to this top-level model.

Category H

Model Description	Trade-in TMV	Private TMV	Dealer TMV
4 Dr STD Sdn	13965	15559	17154

OPTIONS FOR DIAMANTE
AM/FM Compact Disc Player +192
AM/FM Stereo/CD/Tape +192
Aluminum/Alloy Wheels +405
Chrome Wheels +405
Compact Disc Changer +289
Dual Power Seats +254
Heated Front Seats +108
Infinity Sound System +121
Leather Seats +434
Power Drivers Seat +121
Power Moonroof +465
Traction Control System +133

ECLIPSE 1999

For 1999, the Eclipse gets a host of new standard equipment, and there is a new Sports Value Option

Model Description	Trade-in TMV	Private TMV	Dealer TMV
Package for buyers of the GS.			
Category E			
2 Dr GS Hbk	9905	10957	12010
2 Dr GS-T Turbo Hbk	12939	14314	15689
2 Dr GSX Turbo AWD Hbk			
	15016	16612	18208
2 Dr RS Hbk	8786	9720	10654

OPTIONS FOR ECLIPSE
AM/FM Compact Disc Player[Opt on GS,RS] +192
AM/FM Stereo/CD/Tape[Opt on GS] +192
Air Conditioning[Opt on GS,RS] +415
Alarm System[Opt on GS,RS] +162
Aluminum/Alloy Wheels[Std on GSX] +167
Anti-Lock Brakes[Std on GSX] +345
Automatic 4-Speed Transmission +352
Compact Disc Changer +289
Cruise Control[Opt on GS,RS] +96
Leather Seats[Std on GSX] +220
Power Door Locks[Opt on GS,RS] +96
Power Moonroof[Opt on GS,RS] +352
Power Windows[Opt on GS,RS] +133
Rear Spoiler[Opt on RS] +154

ECLIPSE SPYDER   1999

Sundance Plum Pearl exterior paint replaces Magenta Gray Pearl, black leather interior replaces the gray, and the GS-T model gets white-faced instrumentation.

Category E

Model Description	Trade-in TMV	Private TMV	Dealer TMV
2 Dr Spyder GS Conv	11229	12423	13616
2 Dr Spyder GS-T Turbo Conv			
	14075	15571	17067

OPTIONS FOR ECLIPSE SPYDER
Alarm System[Opt on GS] +162
Anti-Lock Brakes +345
Automatic 4-Speed Transmission +352
Compact Disc Changer +289
Cruise Control[Opt on GS] +96
Infinity Sound System[Opt on GS] +211
Leather Seats[Opt on GS] +273
Rear Spoiler[Opt on GS] +154

GALANT   1999

The all-new '99 Galant lineup features a new V6 engine option, more standard equipment and a GTZ model with a sport-tuned suspension.

Category D

Model Description	Trade-in TMV	Private TMV	Dealer TMV
4 Dr DE Sdn	8058	9087	10115
4 Dr ES Sdn	8623	9724	10824
4 Dr ES V6 Sdn	9670	10904	12138
4 Dr GTZ Sdn	11766	13268	14769
4 Dr LS Sdn	11202	12632	14061

OPTIONS FOR GALANT
AM/FM Compact Disc Player +192
Alarm System +121

Anti-Lock Brakes[Std on LS] +465
Compact Disc Changer +325
Leather Seats[Std on GTZ,LS] +410
Power Moonroof[Std on GTZ,LS] +410
Side Air Bag Restraints[Std on GTZ,LS] +144

MIRAGE   1999

A new rear deck lid and taillamps, new seat fabric and some different exterior colors premier on the Mirage. The LS trim level also gets a few interior enhancements.

Category B

Model Description	Trade-in TMV	Private TMV	Dealer TMV
2 Dr DE Cpe	4636	5406	6175
4 Dr DE Sdn	5128	5979	6830
2 Dr LS Cpe	6041	7043	8046
4 Dr LS Sdn	5620	6552	7485

OPTIONS FOR MIRAGE
AM/FM Compact Disc Player[Std on LS Cpe] +192
AM/FM Stereo Tape +170
Air Conditioning[Std on LS Cpe] +425
Aluminum/Alloy Wheels[Std on Cpe] +193
Anti-Lock Brakes +353
Automatic 4-Speed Transmission +366
Keyless Entry System +120
Power Door Locks +99
Power Mirrors +89
Power Moonroof +383
Power Windows +125
Tilt Steering Wheel[Opt on DE] +89

MONTERO   1999

Nothing changes on the Montero this year, but one less paint color is available.

Category M

Model Description	Trade-in TMV	Private TMV	Dealer TMV
4 Dr STD 4WD Wgn	14783	16358	17934

OPTIONS FOR MONTERO
AM/FM Compact Disc Player +192
Chrome Wheels +447
Compact Disc Changer +326
Heated Front Seats +108
Infinity Sound System +121
Keyless Entry System +104
Leather Seats +580
Locking Differential +137
Luggage Rack +119
Power Drivers Seat +147
Power Moonroof +458
Premium Package +531
Trailer Hitch +121

MONTERO SPORT   1999

A new Limited model joins the Montero Sport lineup and with it comes a powerful new V6 engine.

Category M

Model Description	Trade-in TMV	Private TMV	Dealer TMV
4 Dr ES Wgn	8530	9440	10349

MITSUBISHI 99-98

Model Description	Trade-in TMV	Private TMV	Dealer TMV
4 Dr LS 4WD Wgn	12545	13882	15219
4 Dr LS Wgn	11875	13140	14406
4 Dr Limited 4WD Wgn	15890	17583	19277
4 Dr Limited Wgn	14802	16380	17958
4 Dr XLS 4WD Wgn	14216	15732	17247
4 Dr XLS Wgn	13213	14622	16030

OPTIONS FOR MONTERO SPORT
AM/FM Compact Disc Player[Opt on LS,XLS] +192
Air Conditioning[Opt on ES] +442
Automatic 4-Speed Transmission[Opt on LS] +415
Compact Disc Changer +289
Fog Lights[Opt on LS,XLS] +96
Infinity Sound System[Opt on XLS] +169
Keyless Entry System[Std on Limited,XLS] +121
Luggage Rack +133
Power Moonroof[Std on Limited] +410
Trailer Hitch +121

1998 MITSUBISHI

3000GT — 1998
SL and VR-4 models get a standard power sunroof this year.
Category F

Model	Trade-in	Private	Dealer
2 Dr STD Cpe	13375	14798	16340
2 Dr SL Cpe	17305	19146	21141
2 Dr VR-4 Turbo AWD Cpe	22405	24789	27371

OPTIONS FOR 3000GT
AM/FM Compact Disc Player +170
AM/FM Stereo/CD/Tape[Opt on STD] +308
Anti-Lock Brakes[Opt on SL] +362
Automatic 4-Speed Transmission[Opt on STD,SL] +379
Compact Disc Changer +255
Leather Seats[Opt on STD] +351

DIAMANTE — 1998
All Diamantes get standard ABS and remote keyless entry for 1998.
Category H

Model	Trade-in	Private	Dealer
4 Dr ES Sdn	10855	12153	13560
4 Dr LS Sdn	13629	15259	17025

OPTIONS FOR DIAMANTE
AM/FM Compact Disc Player +170
Aluminum/Alloy Wheels[Opt on ES] +357
Chrome Wheels +357
Compact Disc Changer +255
Dual Power Seats +223
Infinity Sound System +106
Leather Seats[Opt on ES] +383
Luxury Group +319
Power Drivers Seat[Opt on ES] +106
Power Moonroof[Opt on ES] +410

ECLIPSE — 1998
The GSX gets a standard sunroof, power driver's seat and remote keyless entry.
Category E

Model	Trade-in	Private	Dealer
2 Dr GS Hbk	8214	9205	10278
2 Dr GS-T Turbo Hbk	9948	11148	12448
2 Dr GSX Turbo AWD Hbk	11606	13006	14522
2 Dr RS Hbk	7160	8023	8959

OPTIONS FOR ECLIPSE
AM/FM Compact Disc Player[Opt on GS,RS] +170
Air Conditioning[Opt on GS,RS] +367
Alarm System[Std on GSX,Spyder GS-T] +142
Aluminum/Alloy Wheels[Opt on GS,RS] +149
Anti-Lock Brakes +305
Automatic 4-Speed Transmission +293
Compact Disc Changer +255
Infinity Sound System +182
Leather Seats[Std on GSX] +195
Limited Slip Differential +113
Power Moonroof[Std on GSX] +312
Power Windows[Opt on GS,RS] +118
Rear Spoiler[Opt on RS,Spyder GS] +136

ECLIPSE SPYDER — 1998
Eclipse Spyder GS gets air conditioning, AM/FM stereo with CD player and wheel locks. The Spyder GS-T is now flashier than ever before thanks to standard 16-inch chrome-plated alloy wheels. All models have a fresh black interior appearance with gray cloth.
Category E

Model	Trade-in	Private	Dealer
2 Dr Spyder GS Conv	9252	10368	11577
2 Dr Spyder GS-T Turbo Conv	11490	12876	14377

OPTIONS FOR ECLIPSE SPYDER
Alarm System[Opt on Spyder GS] +142
Anti-Lock Brakes +305
Automatic 4-Speed Transmission +341
Compact Disc Changer +255
Infinity Sound System[Opt on Spyder GS] +186
Leather Seats[Opt on Spyder GS] +241
Rear Spoiler[Opt on Spyder GS] +136

GALANT — 1998
Solar tinted glass makes it harder to tan in the new Galant. The ES gets a standard manual transmission, and the ES and LS have a new black grille with chrome accents. The LS also benefits from standard antilock brakes. All models have a new heavy-duty starter and battery.
Category G

Model	Trade-in	Private	Dealer
4 Dr DE Sdn	6201	7045	7960
4 Dr ES Sdn	6889	7827	8843

Don't forget to refer to the Mileage Adjustment Table at the back of this book!

Model Description	Trade-in TMV	Private TMV	Dealer TMV
4 Dr LS Sdn	8267	9393	10612

OPTIONS FOR GALANT
AM/FM Compact Disc Player +170
AM/FM Stereo Tape[Opt on DE] +149
Air Conditioning[Opt on DE] +384
Alarm System[Opt on ES] +106
Anti-Lock Brakes[Opt on ES] +410
Automatic 4-Speed Transmission[Std on LS] +333
Compact Disc Changer +288
Leather Seats[Opt on ES] +362
Power Moonroof[Opt on ES] +362

MIRAGE   1998

Some new colors to choose from and a new heavy duty starter and battery make the Mirage more reliable.

Category B

Model Description	Trade-in TMV	Private TMV	Dealer TMV
2 Dr DE Cpe	3776	4457	5194
4 Dr DE Sdn	4306	5082	5923
2 Dr LS Cpe	4968	5863	6833
4 Dr LS Sdn	4769	5629	6560

OPTIONS FOR MIRAGE
AM/FM Compact Disc Player[Opt on Sdn] +170
AM/FM Stereo Tape +150
Air Conditioning[Opt on DE,Sdn] +375
Anti-Lock Brakes +312
Automatic 4-Speed Transmission +290
Fog Lights +88
Keyless Entry System +106
Power Moonroof +337
Power Windows +111

MONTERO   1998

A revised front bumper and grille, new fenders and new rear quarter panels mark the exterior changes. Inside is a new steering wheel, while the standard equipment list now includes ABS, air conditioning, third row seats and alloy wheels.

Category M

Model Description	Trade-in TMV	Private TMV	Dealer TMV
4 Dr STD 4WD Wgn	13242	14745	16373

OPTIONS FOR MONTERO
AM/FM Compact Disc Player +170
Chrome Wheels +260
Compact Disc Changer +288
Heated Front Seats +96
Infinity Sound System +106
Keyless Entry System +92
Leather Seats +510
Locking Differential +121
Luggage Rack +105
Power Drivers Seat +129
Power Moonroof +405
Premium Package +213
Sport Suspension +119
Trailer Hitch +108

MONTERO SPORT   1998

Montero Sports get lots of features added to their option packages, and 4WD models now come with standard ABS.

Category M

Model Description	Trade-in TMV	Private TMV	Dealer TMV
4 Dr ES Wgn	7878	8772	9741
4 Dr LS 4WD Wgn	10478	11668	12956
4 Dr LS Wgn	9666	10763	11952
4 Dr XLS 4WD Wgn	14459	16100	17878
4 Dr XLS Wgn	12509	13929	15467

OPTIONS FOR MONTERO SPORT
AM/FM Compact Disc Player +170
Air Conditioning[Std on XLS] +390
Aluminum/Alloy Wheels[Opt on LS] +182
Appearance Package +322
Automatic 4-Speed Transmission[Std on XLS, 2WD] +367
Compact Disc Changer +288
Keyless Entry System +106
Limited Slip Differential[Opt on LS, 2WD] +121
Luggage Rack +118
Power Door Locks[Opt on LS] +100
Power Mirrors[Opt on LS] +92
Power Moonroof[Opt on LS] +362
Power Windows[Opt on LS] +121
Side Steps[Opt on ES,LS] +149
Trailer Hitch +108

1997 MITSUBISHI

3000GT   1997

A value-leader base model is introduced. It has less than stellar performance and we think that it's embarrassing that this car is in the same lineup as the earth-scorching VR-4.

Category F

Model Description	Trade-in TMV	Private TMV	Dealer TMV
2 Dr STD Cpe	11971	13530	15436
2 Dr SL Cpe	14666	16577	18912
2 Dr VR-4 Turbo AWD Cpe			
	19819	22401	25557

OPTIONS FOR 3000GT
AM/FM Compact Disc Player +154
AM/FM Stereo/CD/Tape[Opt on STD] +280
Anti-Lock Brakes[Opt on SL] +328
Automatic 4-Speed Transmission +337
Compact Disc Changer +232
Infinity Sound System +151
Keyless Entry System[Opt on SL] +99
Leather Seats[Opt on STD] +320
Power Sunroof +339

DIAMANTE   1997

After a one-year hiatus, the Diamante returns to the Mitsubishi lineup sporting clean, crisp styling, a full-

MITSUBISHI 97

Model Description	Trade-in TMV	Private TMV	Dealer TMV

load of luxury features, and a lower price. The old car barely registered on near-luxury car buyers' radar; this new one deserves consideration and a close inspection.

Category H

4 Dr ES Sdn	8693	9800	11153
4 Dr LS Sdn	10512	11851	13487

OPTIONS FOR DIAMANTE

AM/FM Compact Disc Player +154
Aluminum/Alloy Wheels[Opt on ES] +325
Anti-Lock Brakes +283
Compact Disc Changer +232
Dual Power Seats[Opt on LS] +203
Infinity Sound System +97
Leather Seats[Opt on ES] +348
Luxury Group +289
Power Drivers Seat[Opt on ES] +97
Power Moonroof +372

ECLIPSE   1997

Revised styling makes the attractive Eclipse drop-dead gorgeous. New interior fabrics and paint colors debut as well. Antilock brakes are now available on the GS model, and a CD player joins its standard equipment list. Two new exterior colors, new seat fabrics and a new interior color combination round out the changes.

Category E

2 Dr STD Hbk	5574	6344	7285
2 Dr GS Hbk	7004	7971	9153
2 Dr GS-T Turbo Hbk	8433	9598	11021
2 Dr GSX Turbo AWD Hbk			
	9291	10574	12142
2 Dr RS Hbk	6074	6913	7938

OPTIONS FOR ECLIPSE

AM/FM Compact Disc Player +154
AM/FM Stereo Tape[Opt on GS-T,RS,STD] +125
AM/FM Stereo/CD/Tape[Opt on GS] +154
Air Conditioning[Opt on GS,RS,STD] +332
Alarm System[Std on Spyder GS-T] +130
Aluminum/Alloy Wheels[Opt on GS,RS] +134
Anti-Lock Brakes +276
Automatic 4-Speed Transmission +266
Compact Disc Changer +232
Infinity Sound System +165
Leather Seats +176
Limited Slip Differential +102
Power Drivers Seat[Opt on GSX,RS] +97
Power Moonroof +283
Power Windows[Opt on GS,RS] +106
Rear Spoiler[Opt on RS,Spyder GS] +124

ECLIPSE SPYDER   1997

The 1997 Spyder gets revised front and rear styling. Anti-lock brakes are now available on the GS model.

Two new exterior colors, new seat fabrics, and a new interior color combination round out the changes.

Category E

2 Dr Spyder GS Conv	7712	8777	10079
2 Dr Spyder GS-T Turbo Conv			
	9975	11352	13036

OPTIONS FOR ECLIPSE SPYDER

AM/FM Stereo/CD/Tape[Opt on Spyder GS] +154
Air Conditioning[Opt on Spyder GS] +345
Alarm System[Opt on Spyder GS] +130
Anti-Lock Brakes +276
Automatic 4-Speed Transmission +328
Compact Disc Changer +232
Infinity Sound System +168
Leather Seats[Opt on Spyder GS] +176
Rear Spoiler[Opt on Spyder GS] +124

GALANT   1997

Mitsubishi shuffles the Galant lineup, replacing the S sedan with a base model called the DE. Front and rear fascias have been redesigned, and the interiors of all models have been upgraded by the addition of more ergonomically correct center armrests, upgraded upholstery, additional sound deadening material, and a new steering wheel.

Category D

4 Dr DE Sdn	4815	5612	6586
4 Dr ES Sdn	5665	6603	7749
4 Dr LS Sdn	6869	8006	9395

OPTIONS FOR GALANT

AM/FM Compact Disc Player +154
AM/FM Stereo Tape[Opt on DE] +135
AM/FM Stereo/CD/Tape +116
Air Conditioning[Opt on DE] +349
Anti-Lock Brakes +373
Automatic 4-Speed Transmission[Opt on DE] +337
Compact Disc Changer +255
Leather Seats[Opt on ES] +328
Power Moonroof[Opt on ES] +307
Rear Spoiler +118

MIRAGE   1997

The Mirage is totally redesigned for 1997, sharing little with the model it replaces. Mitsubishi claims that interior size has been increased and that NVH have been reduced.

Category B

2 Dr DE Cpe	3002	3560	4242
4 Dr DE Sdn	3514	4167	4965
2 Dr LS Cpe	3903	4629	5515
4 Dr LS Sdn	3845	4560	5433

OPTIONS FOR MIRAGE

AM/FM Compact Disc Player +154
AM/FM Stereo Tape[Opt on DE,Sdn] +136

Don't forget to refer to the Mileage Adjustment Table at the back of this book!

Model Description	Trade-in TMV	Private TMV	Dealer TMV

AM/FM Stereo/CD/Tape +97
Air Conditioning +340
Aluminum/Alloy Wheels[Opt on Sdn] +154
Anti-Lock Brakes +283
Automatic 4-Speed Transmission +275
Keyless Entry System +96
Power Moonroof +283
Power Windows +100

MONTERO 1997

This all-new entry from Mitsubishi is poised to steal sales in the ever-growing midsized sport-utility segment. Based on the same floorpan as the full-sized Montero, the Montero Sport is shorter in length, lighter in weight, and generally more nimble than its big brother.

Category M

	Trade-in	Private	Dealer
4 Dr LS 4WD Wgn	10544	11852	13451
4 Dr SR 4WD Wgn	13199	14837	16838

OPTIONS FOR MONTERO

AM/FM Compact Disc Player +154
Air Conditioning[Opt on LS] +348
Aluminum/Alloy Wheels[Opt on LS] +135
Anti-Lock Brakes +236
Chrome Wheels +358
Compact Disc Changer +261
Fog Lights +89
Infinity Sound System[Opt on LS] +97
Leather Seats[Opt on LS] +464
Luggage Rack +95
Power Drivers Seat[Opt on LS] +118
Power Moonroof[Opt on LS] +367
Privacy Glass[Opt on LS] +97
Side Steps[Opt on LS] +142
Third Seat +118
Trailer Hitch +97

MONTERO SPORT 1997

This all-new entry from Mitsubishi is poised to steal sales in the ever-growing midsized sport-utility segment. Based on the same floorpan as the full-sized Montero, the Montero Sport is shorter in length, lighter in weight, and generally more nimble than its big brother.

Category M

	Trade-in	Private	Dealer
4 Dr ES Wgn	6963	7827	8883
4 Dr LS 4WD Wgn	8684	9761	11078
4 Dr LS Wgn	8372	9411	10680
4 Dr XLS 4WD Wgn	12049	13544	15371

OPTIONS FOR MONTERO SPORT

AM/FM Compact Disc Player +154
AM/FM Stereo/CD/Tape[Opt on LS 4WD] +97
Air Conditioning[Std on XLS] +354
Aluminum/Alloy Wheels[Opt on LS] +165
Anti-Lock Brakes +236
Appearance Package +300

Automatic 4-Speed Transmission[Std on XLS,2WD] +309
Compact Disc Changer +261
Infinity Sound System[Opt on LS] +135
LS Appearance Package +693
Leather Seats[Opt on LS] +425
Limited Slip Differential +109
Luggage Rack +100
Power Door Locks[Opt on LS] +91
Power Moonroof[Opt on LS] +307
Power Windows[Opt on LS] +109
Premium Package +365
Side Steps[Opt on ES,LS] +135
Trailer Hitch[Opt on ES,LS] +97

1996 MITSUBISHI

3000GT 1996

Base model gets new cloth interior, while upper trim levels receive a choice of black or tan leather. Remote keyless entry gets panic feature, and several new colors are available.

Category F

	Trade-in	Private	Dealer
2 Dr STD Cpe	11784	13298	15389
2 Dr SL Cpe	13749	15515	17954
2 Dr Spyder SL Conv	22416	25295	29272
2 Dr Spyder VR-4 Turbo AWD Conv			
	25561	28844	33379
2 Dr VR-4 Turbo AWD Cpe			
	17440	19681	22775

OPTIONS FOR 3000GT

Automatic 4-Speed Transmission +342
Chrome Wheels[Opt on SL] +215
Compact Disc Changer +220
Power Sunroof +323
Special Factory Paint +73

DIAMANTE 1996

The only Diamantes sold this year were for fleet sales. So unless you see one at a rental car auction, chances are not good that you'll find a used 1996 model.

Category H

	Trade-in	Private	Dealer
4 Dr ES Sdn	7237	8268	9691

ECLIPSE 1996

The "Spyder" (convertible) version debuts, as do three new colors.

Audio systems are revised, and RS models can be ordered with a rear spoiler. Remote keyless entry systems get a new panic feature.

Category E

	Trade-in	Private	Dealer
2 Dr STD Hbk	4421	5085	6001
2 Dr GS Hbk	5712	6570	7754
2 Dr GS-T Turbo Hbk	6665	7665	9047

Don't forget to refer to the Mileage Adjustment Table at the back of this book!

Model Description	Trade-in TMV	Private TMV	Dealer TMV
2 Dr GSX Turbo AWD Hbk			
	7617	8760	10339
2 Dr RS Hbk	4897	5632	6647
2 Dr Spyder GS Conv	6377	7334	8656
2 Dr Spyder GS-T Turbo Conv			
	8045	9252	10920

OPTIONS FOR ECLIPSE

AM/FM Compact Disc Player +146
AM/FM Stereo Tape[Opt on RS,STD] +118
Air Conditioning[Opt on GS-T,GSX] +316
Alarm System[Opt on GS,GSX,Spyder GS,Hbk] +123
Aluminum/Alloy Wheels[Std on GS-T,GSX] +128
Anti-Lock Brakes +263
Automatic 4-Speed Transmission +258
Compact Disc Changer +220
Infinity Sound System +156
Leather Seats[Std on GSX,GS-T Turbo Conv] +168
Power Sunroof +269
Power Windows[Opt on GS] +101
Rear Spoiler[Opt on GS Conv,RS] +118

GALANT   1996

A Homelink transmitter is available, and a panic feature debuts on keyless entry systems. New two-tone interiors debut, and four fresh exterior colors join the palette. Other changes include new wheelcovers, expanded availability of alloy wheels, and a heavy duty defroster with timer. LS models have standard leather seating and antilock brakes are available across the line.

Category D

Model Description	Trade-in TMV	Private TMV	Dealer TMV
4 Dr ES Sdn	4958	5857	7099
4 Dr LS Sdn	5628	6649	8058
4 Dr S Sdn	3819	4512	5468

OPTIONS FOR GALANT

AM/FM Compact Disc Player +146
AM/FM Stereo Tape[Opt on S] +129
Air Conditioning[Opt on S] +332
Anti-Lock Brakes +355
Automatic 4-Speed Transmission[Opt on S] +327
Compact Disc Changer +243
Power Moonroof[Opt on ES] +293
Power Windows[Opt on S] +101

MIGHTY MAX PICKUP   1996

No changes this year, the Mighty Max's last.

Category J

Model Description	Trade-in TMV	Private TMV	Dealer TMV
2 Dr STD Std Cab SB	3317	3863	4617

OPTIONS FOR MIGHTY MAX PICKUP

AM/FM Compact Disc Player +211
AM/FM Stereo Tape +180
Air Conditioning +278
Automatic 4-Speed Transmission +474

Power Steering +112

MIRAGE   1996

Four colors debut, and the Preferred Equipment Packages are revised a bit.

Category B

Model Description	Trade-in TMV	Private TMV	Dealer TMV
2 Dr LS Cpe	3137	3811	4743
2 Dr S Cpe	2469	3000	3733
4 Dr S Sdn	3126	3798	4726

OPTIONS FOR MIRAGE

AM/FM Compact Disc Player +146
AM/FM Stereo Tape +130
Air Conditioning +323
Automatic 3-Speed Transmission[Opt on LS] +198
Automatic 4-Speed Transmission +243

MONTERO   1996

Refinements result in a better SUV this year. A passenger airbag has been installed, optional side steps make it easier to clamber aboard, and split-fold second row seats increase versatility. New colors, new seat fabrics and better audio systems round out the package.

Category M

Model Description	Trade-in TMV	Private TMV	Dealer TMV
4 Dr LS 4WD Wgn	8137	9356	11038
4 Dr SR 4WD Wgn	11044	12698	14981

OPTIONS FOR MONTERO

AM/FM Compact Disc Player +146
Air Conditioning[Opt on LS] +331
Aluminum/Alloy Wheels[Opt on LS] +129
Anti-Lock Brakes[Opt on LS] +426
Automatic 4-Speed Transmission[Opt on LS] +327
Chrome Wheels +341
Compact Disc Changer +318
Leather Seats +441
Leather/Wood Package +610
Power Moonroof[Opt on LS] +323
Power Sunroof +323
Side Steps[Opt on SR] +130

1995 MITSUBISHI

3000GT   1995

The VR-4 gains chrome-plated alloy wheels as standard equipment.

Category F

Model Description	Trade-in TMV	Private TMV	Dealer TMV
2 Dr STD Cpe	9279	10456	12418
2 Dr SL Cpe	10965	12356	14675
2 Dr Spyder SL Conv	19387	21847	25947
2 Dr Spyder VR-4 Turbo AWD Conv			
	22469	25320	30071
2 Dr VR-4 Turbo AWD Cpe			
	13803	15554	18473

Don't forget to refer to the Mileage Adjustment Table at the back of this book!

Model Description	Trade-in TMV	Private TMV	Dealer TMV
4 Dr STD 4WD Hbk	2999	3701	4872
4 Dr STD Hbk	2768	3417	4498

OPTIONS FOR EXPO
Air Conditioning +207
Anti-Lock Brakes +192
Power Windows +78

GALANT 1995

The much anticipated V6 engine never transpired in the 1995 Galant due to the increased costs and complexity involved in making the model. The 1995 Galants are available in three trim-levels, all with the 141-horsepower four-cylinder.
Category D

Model Description	Trade-in TMV	Private TMV	Dealer TMV
4 Dr ES Sdn	3587	4304	5498
4 Dr LS Sdn	3649	4378	5593
4 Dr S Sdn	2721	3265	4171

OPTIONS FOR GALANT
AM/FM Compact Disc Player +118
AM/FM Stereo Tape[Opt on S] +104
Air Conditioning[Opt on S] +266
Anti-Lock Brakes +284
Automatic 4-Speed Transmission[Opt on S] +214
Leather Seats +251
Power Drivers Seat +82
Power Windows[Opt on S] +82

MIGHTY MAX PICKUP 1995

The Mighty Max line is drastically reduced. Remaining is a four-cylinder two-wheel-drive regular-cab model.
Category J

Model Description	Trade-in TMV	Private TMV	Dealer TMV
2 Dr STD Std Cab SB	2837	3302	4078

OPTIONS FOR MIGHTY MAX PICKUP
AM/FM Compact Disc Player +170
AM/FM Stereo Tape +145
Air Conditioning +223
Automatic 4-Speed Transmission +381
Power Steering +90

MIRAGE 1995

The often changing Mitsubishi Mirage is once again revised, this time with dual airbags. LS versions get bigger alloy wheels.
Category B

Model Description	Trade-in TMV	Private TMV	Dealer TMV
2 Dr ES Cpe	2147	2651	3489
4 Dr ES Sdn	2367	2922	3846
2 Dr LS Cpe	2203	2720	3580
2 Dr S Cpe	1817	2243	2952
4 Dr S Sdn	2201	2717	3576

OPTIONS FOR MIRAGE
AM/FM Compact Disc Player +118
AM/FM Stereo Tape[Opt on ES Sdn,S Cpe] +104

OPTIONS FOR 3000GT
AM/FM Stereo/CD/Tape +214
Automatic 4-Speed Transmission[Std on VR-4] +257
Chrome Wheels[Opt on SL] +172
Compact Disc Changer +177
Power Sunroof +260
Sunroof +260

DIAMANTE 1995

The base Diamante sedan is sent out to pasture, available only to fleet purchasers such as rental car agencies. No other changes for the Mitsubishi flagship.
Category H

Model Description	Trade-in TMV	Private TMV	Dealer TMV
4 Dr STD Wgn	5823	6757	8315
4 Dr ES Sdn	5538	6427	7909
4 Dr LS Sdn	7101	8240	10140

OPTIONS FOR DIAMANTE
Compact Disc Changer +177
Power Moonroof +284
Power Passenger Seat +89
Traction Control System +82

ECLIPSE 1995

Radically redesigned, the new Eclipse sports bulging shoulders and no-nonsense looks, particularly in GSX guise. Engine ratings are improved for all models, while the turbocharged GS-T and GSX produce a mighty 210 horsepower at 6,000 rpm. Antilock brakes are optional on all models. Dual airbags are finally standard on the Eclipse.
Category E

Model Description	Trade-in TMV	Private TMV	Dealer TMV
2 Dr GS Hbk	4374	5049	6174
2 Dr GS-T Turbo Hbk	5223	6029	7372
2 Dr GSX Turbo AWD Hbk	6725	7763	9492
2 Dr RS Hbk	3787	4371	5345

OPTIONS FOR ECLIPSE
AM/FM Compact Disc Player +118
AM/FM Stereo Tape[Opt on RS] +95
Air Conditioning[Opt on GS,RS] +254
Alarm System +99
Aluminum/Alloy Wheels[Std on GSX] +103
Anti-Lock Brakes +211
Automatic 4-Speed Transmission +204
Compact Disc Changer +177
Infinity Sound System[Opt on GS] +126
Leather Seats[Opt on GS,RS] +135
Power Sunroof +216
Power Windows[Opt on GS] +82
Rear Spoiler[Opt on RS] +94

EXPO 1995

This is the last year for the Expo.
Category B

Model Description	Trade-in TMV	Private TMV	Dealer TMV	Model Description	Trade-in TMV	Private TMV	Dealer TMV

Air Bag Restraint +118
Air Conditioning +260
Automatic 3-Speed Transmission[Opt on Cpe] +159
Automatic 4-Speed Transmission +195
Power Windows[Opt on ES Sdn] +77

MONTERO   1995

The Montero LS gets a more powerful V6 that offers a 26-horsepower boost over last year's marginal 151-horsepower rating. Towing capacity increases to 5,000 pounds for all models. Tricky, electronic shock absorbers return to the Montero SR's standard equipment list, letting drivers choose between soft, medium or hard setting depending on their preferences.

Category M

	Trade-in	Private	Dealer
4 Dr LS 4WD Wgn	6480	7499	9197
4 Dr SR 4WD Wgn	8133	9412	11544

OPTIONS FOR MONTERO
AM/FM Compact Disc Player +118
AM/FM Stereo/CD/Tape +162
Anti-Lock Brakes[Opt on LS] +180
Automatic 4-Speed Transmission[Opt on LS] +263
Chrome Wheels +273
Compact Disc Changer +199
Leather Seats +354
Leather/Wood Package +490
Power Drivers Seat +90
Power Sunroof[Opt on LS] +260

1994 MITSUBISHI

3000GT   1994

The 3000GT gets a passenger airbag. The 3000GT VR-4 gets a totally unnecessary 20 extra horsepower. But, hey, you won't find us complaining. To harness the extra power, the VR-4 switches to a six-speed manual gearbox. Freshened styling and CFC-free air conditioning round out the changes for all models.

Category F

	Trade-in	Private	Dealer
2 Dr STD Cpe	7184	8405	10440
2 Dr SL Cpe	8452	9888	12282
2 Dr VR-4 Turbo AWD Cpe	10564	12359	15351

OPTIONS FOR 3000GT
Automatic 4-Speed Transmission +216
Chrome Wheels +145
Compact Disc Changer +149
Leather Seats[Opt on SL] +205
Sunroof +219

DIAMANTE   1994

A passenger airbag and CFC-free air conditioning make the Diamante much friendlier to its passengers and the environment. A five-door wagon model introduced late last year comes with the 175-horsepower engine that is standard in the ES sedan. New wood trim and an upgraded Infinity stereo debut on the 1994 Diamante.

Category H

	Trade-in	Private	Dealer
4 Dr STD Wgn	4435	5239	6579
4 Dr ES Sdn	4368	5160	6479
4 Dr LS Sdn	5459	6448	8097

OPTIONS FOR DIAMANTE
AM/FM Compact Disc Player[Opt on STD Wgn] +99
Anti-Lock Brakes[Std on LS] +182
Compact Disc Changer +149
Leather Seats[Std on LS] +223
Power Passenger Seat[Opt on ES] +74
Power Sunroof +199

ECLIPSE   1994

Last year for the current edition of the Diamond Star sport coupe. Turbo engines gain a minimal boost in horsepower. Several of the models get more standard equipment in an attempt to increase sales in this edition's final year.

Category E

	Trade-in	Private	Dealer
2 Dr GS Turbo Hbk	4032	4764	5984
2 Dr GS 1.8 Hbk	2915	3445	4327
2 Dr GS 2.0 Hbk	3350	3958	4972
2 Dr GSX Turbo AWD Hbk	4466	5277	6629

OPTIONS FOR ECLIPSE
AM/FM Compact Disc Player[Opt on GS 1.8, GS 2.0] +99
AM/FM Stereo/CD/Tape[Opt on GS 2.0] +99
Air Conditioning[Opt on GS 1.8] +214
Anti-Lock Brakes[Opt on GS] +178
Automatic 4-Speed Transmission +171
Leather Seats +114
Sunroof +88

EXPO   1994

The Expo and LRV receive a driver airbag this year. Unfortunately, the Expo loses its up-level SP model, but base models do receive better standard equipment as a result. LRVs are available only as two-wheel-drive models in 1994; the AWD has been axed. This is the last year for the Expo LRV, although it will live on as the Eagle Summit wagon.

Category B

	Trade-in	Private	Dealer
4 Dr STD 4WD Hbk	2556	3182	4226
4 Dr STD Hbk	2329	2900	3851
2 Dr LRV 1.8 Hbk	1932	2405	3194
2 Dr LRV 2.4 Hbk	1988	2476	3288
2 Dr LRV Sport Hbk	2499	3112	4133

Don't forget to refer to the Mileage Adjustment Table at the back of this book!

Model Description	Trade-in TMV	Private TMV	Dealer TMV	Model Description	Trade-in TMV	Private TMV	Dealer TMV

OPTIONS FOR EXPO
AM/FM Compact Disc Player +93
Air Conditioning +174
Anti-Lock Brakes +162
Automatic 4-Speed Transmission +199
Power Sunroof +162

GALANT 1994

Dual airbags debut on this totally redesigned sedan. Four trim-levels are offered, ranging from the low-level S to the luxury ES and sporty GS models. An automatic transmission is standard on the ES and LS models. GS Galants come with a twin-cam engine rated at 160 horsepower.

Category D

4 Dr ES Sdn	2717	3335	4364
4 Dr GS Sdn	3248	3987	5217
4 Dr LS Sdn	2953	3624	4743
4 Dr S Sdn	2126	2610	3415

OPTIONS FOR GALANT
AM/FM Compact Disc Player[Opt on LS] +99
AM/FM Stereo/CD/Tape[Opt on ES,S] +74
Air Conditioning[Opt on S] +224
Anti-Lock Brakes +240
Automatic 4-Speed Transmission[Opt on GS,S] +223
Leather Seats[Opt on LS] +211

MIGHTY MAX PICKUP 1994

The Mighty Max gains a few safety features such as a high-mounted rear stop light and side-impact door guard beams. The vehicle is otherwise unchanged.

Category J

2 Dr STD 4WD Std Cab SB	3304	3941	5003
2 Dr STD Ext Cab SB	2569	3065	3891
2 Dr STD Std Cab SB	2141	2554	3242

OPTIONS FOR MIGHTY MAX PICKUP
AM/FM Stereo Tape +122
Air Conditioning +188
Automatic 4-Speed Transmission +321

MIRAGE 1994

The Mirage finally gains a standard driver airbag, but the LS loses its optional antilock brakes. The LS coupe gets the 1.8-liter engine that was formerly available only on the LS and ES sedans. S and ES coupes get power steering added to their standard equipment lists, and LS sedans get alloy wheels.

Category B

2 Dr ES Cpe	1681	2092	2779
4 Dr ES Sdn	1979	2464	3273
2 Dr LS Cpe	1952	2431	3228
4 Dr LS Sdn	2386	2970	3945

2 Dr S Cpe	1464	1823	2421
4 Dr S Sdn	1844	2296	3049

OPTIONS FOR MIRAGE
AM/FM Compact Disc Player +99
AM/FM Stereo Tape[Opt on ES,S] +88
Air Conditioning +219
Automatic 3-Speed Transmission +134
Automatic 4-Speed Transmission[Opt on ES,Cpe] +164
Compact Disc Changer +149

MONTERO 1994

Deciding to go the luxury sport-ute route, Mitsubishi drops its entry-level Monteros. The remaining models are the luxury-oriented LS and sporty SR. A driver airbag is standard on the 1994 Montero. Antilock brakes move from the standard equipment list to the option list of both trucks. CFC-free air conditioning, a third-row bench seat, heated outside mirrors, and a leather-wrapped steering wheel become standard equipment. SR models finally receive a gutsier engine to move this scale-tipping SUV around; a 215-horsepower V6 engine is now standard on that model.

Category M

4 Dr LS 4WD Wgn	4809	5627	6990
4 Dr SR 4WD Wgn	6478	7580	9417

OPTIONS FOR MONTERO
AM/FM Stereo/CD/Tape +137
Air Conditioning[Opt on LS] +223
Aluminum/Alloy Wheels[Opt on LS] +88
Anti-Lock Brakes[Opt on LS] +152
Automatic 4-Speed Transmission[Opt on LS] +222
Chrome Wheels +231
Compact Disc Changer +169
Leather Seats +299
Power Drivers Seat +75
Power Sunroof +219

PRECIS 1994

Category A

2 Dr STD Hbk	726	948	1318

OPTIONS FOR PRECIS
Air Conditioning +174
Automatic 4-Speed Transmission +199

1993 MITSUBISHI

3000GT 1993

Leather makes its way into the top-of-the-line VR-4. Base models get bigger and better standard equipment lists that include air conditioning, power windows, power door locks, and cruise control (to name a few).

Category F

2 Dr STD Cpe	5019	6078	7843
2 Dr SL Cpe	6127	7420	9574

Don't forget to refer to the Mileage Adjustment Table at the back of this book!

Model Description	Trade-in TMV	Private TMV	Dealer TMV
2 Dr VR-4 Turbo AWD Cpe			
	7822	9472	12222

OPTIONS FOR 3000GT
Automatic 4-Speed Transmission +188
Chrome Wheels +127
Compact Disc Changer +129
Leather Seats[Opt on SL] +178
Sunroof +190

DIAMANTE   1993

Base models are now called ES and gain cruise control, a power trunk opener and steering wheel mounted stereo controls.
Category H

Model Description	Trade-in TMV	Private TMV	Dealer TMV
4 Dr ES Sdn	2659	3331	4451
4 Dr ES Wgn	2719	3406	4551
4 Dr LS Sdn	3868	4845	6474

OPTIONS FOR DIAMANTE
AM/FM Compact Disc Player +87
Aluminum/Alloy Wheels[Opt on ES] +182
Anti-Lock Brakes[Opt on ES] +158
Compact Disc Changer +129
Diamante Euro Handling Package +335
Diamante Leather Seat Package +357
Leather Seats[Std on ES] +195
Power Sunroof +173
Premium Sound System[Opt on ES] +97

ECLIPSE   1993

The GS model gets a rear spoiler. GSX Eclipses now have standard antilock brakes. Some interior changes include new seat stitching and a new manual shift knob. Exterior changes are limited to new wheels and optional graphics.
Category E

Model Description	Trade-in TMV	Private TMV	Dealer TMV
2 Dr GS 2.0 Hbk	2334	2932	3930
2 Dr GSX Turbo AWD Hbk			
	3310	4159	5574

OPTIONS FOR ECLIPSE
AM/FM Compact Disc Player[Opt on GS 2.0,GSX] +87
Air Conditioning +186
Aluminum/Alloy Wheels[Opt on GS 2.0] +75
Automatic 4-Speed Transmission +149
Leather Seats[Opt on GSX] +99
Premium Sound System[Opt on GS 2.0] +87
Sunroof[Opt on GS 2.0,GSX] +75

EXPO   1993

Mitsubishi increases the number of valves on the Expo's 2.4-liter engine, improving horsepower by 12 percent. Sport and AWD Sport Expo LRVs get the larger 2.4-liter engine found on the Expo. More equipment is now standard on the LRV Sport models.
Category B

Model Description	Trade-in TMV	Private TMV	Dealer TMV
4 Dr STD 4WD Hbk	1748	2327	3291
4 Dr STD Hbk	1505	2004	2834
2 Dr LRV 4WD Hbk	1454	1936	2738
2 Dr LRV Hbk	1350	1797	2542
2 Dr LRV Sport Hbk	1650	2197	3107
4 Dr SP 4WD Hbk	2100	2795	3954
4 Dr SP Hbk	1934	2573	3640

OPTIONS FOR EXPO
AM/FM Compact Disc Player +81
Air Conditioning +151
Anti-Lock Brakes +140
Automatic 4-Speed Transmission +173
Power Sunroof +140

GALANT   1993

Sporty VR-4 model goes the way of the buffalo. GS and GSR models are combined into the previously named luxury LS. The former LS model is now the ES model. Base Galants are now called S models. Confused? So are we. All 1993 Galants use the SOHC 2.0-liter engine, which makes 121-horsepower this year with the addition of an extra two valves per cylinder.
Category D

Model Description	Trade-in TMV	Private TMV	Dealer TMV
4 Dr ES Sdn	1698	2221	3093
4 Dr LS Sdn	1805	2361	3288
4 Dr S Sdn	1380	1805	2514

OPTIONS FOR GALANT
AM/FM Compact Disc Player[Opt on LS] +87
AM/FM Stereo Tape +75
Air Conditioning +195
Automatic 4-Speed Transmission[Opt on S] +151
Power Sunroof +151
Premium Sound System[Opt on ES] +97

MIGHTY MAX PICKUP   1993

The Mighty Max is unchanged for 1993.
Category J

Model Description	Trade-in TMV	Private TMV	Dealer TMV
2 Dr STD 4WD Std Cab SB			
	2574	3139	4081
2 Dr STD Ext Cab SB	1990	2426	3154
2 Dr STD Std Cab SB	1697	2069	2690

OPTIONS FOR MIGHTY MAX PICKUP
AM/FM Stereo Tape +106
Air Conditioning +164
Automatic 4-Speed Transmission +280

MIRAGE   1993

The Mirage is totally redesigned this year, gaining size but losing weight. A coupe and sedan are offered in Base, S, ES and LS trim-levels. A five-speed manual transmission is standard on all vehicles, although an automatic is available on all Mirages except the S coupe. Antilock brakes make their first appearance on

MITSUBISHI 93-92

Model Description	Trade-in TMV	Private TMV	Dealer TMV	Model Description	Trade-in TMV	Private TMV	Dealer TMV

the Mirage, becoming an available option on the LS sedan.

Category B

Model Description	Trade-in TMV	Private TMV	Dealer TMV
2 Dr ES Cpe	1098	1461	2067
4 Dr ES Sdn	1297	1726	2442
2 Dr LS Cpe	1280	1704	2410
4 Dr LS Sdn	1528	2033	2876
2 Dr S Cpe	955	1270	1797
4 Dr S Sdn	1194	1589	2247

OPTIONS FOR MIRAGE
AM/FM Compact Disc Player +87
AM/FM Stereo Tape[Opt on ES,S] +76
Air Conditioning +190
Aluminum/Alloy Wheels +87
Anti-Lock Brakes +158
Automatic 3-Speed Transmission +117
Automatic 4-Speed Transmission +143

MONTERO   1993

Shift-on-the-fly four-wheel drive is introduced to the 1993 Montero. Antilock brakes become standard equipment for the SR and optional for the RS; they were formerly standard only on the LS. Top-of-the-line Monteros may now be ordered with a leather and wood package, for those who really want to get down and dirty.

Category M

Model Description	Trade-in TMV	Private TMV	Dealer TMV
4 Dr STD 4WD Wgn	3269	3988	5185
4 Dr LS 4WD Wgn	4485	5470	7113
4 Dr RS 4WD Wgn	3932	4796	6236
4 Dr SR 4WD Wgn	4607	5620	7307

OPTIONS FOR MONTERO
AM/FM Compact Disc Player +87
Air Conditioning +195
Anti-Lock Brakes +132
Automatic 4-Speed Transmission[Std on LS,SR] +192
Leather Seats +260
Montero Leather & Wood Package +487
Power Sunroof +190

PRECIS   1993

No changes for the last year of this little hatchback.

Category A

Model Description	Trade-in TMV	Private TMV	Dealer TMV
2 Dr STD Hbk	629	853	1226

OPTIONS FOR PRECIS
Air Conditioning +151
Automatic 4-Speed Transmission +173

1992 MITSUBISHI

3000GT   1992

New paint. That's the only change for the highly touted 3000GT.

Category F

Model Description	Trade-in TMV	Private TMV	Dealer TMV
2 Dr STD Cpe	3642	4578	6138
2 Dr SL Cpe	4796	6028	8083
2 Dr VR-4 Turbo AWD Cpe			
	5949	7478	10027

OPTIONS FOR 3000GT
AM/FM Compact Disc Player[Opt on STD] +78
AM/FM Stereo/CD/Tape +142
Air Conditioning[Opt on STD] +127
Anti-Lock Brakes[Opt on STD] +166
Automatic 4-Speed Transmission +170
Leather Seats +161
Premium Sound System[Opt on STD] +107
Sunroof +171

DIAMANTE   1992

As a replacement for the low-tech Sigma, the Diamante offers V6 power delivering 175-horsepower in the base model, 202-horsepower in the LS. Antilock brakes are standard on the LS and optional on the base, and a driver airbag is standard on both models. A Euro Handling Package and an electronically controlled suspension that includes traction control is an available option on the LS.

Category H

Model Description	Trade-in TMV	Private TMV	Dealer TMV
4 Dr STD Sdn	2107	2725	3757
4 Dr LS Sdn	2846	3682	5076

OPTIONS FOR DIAMANTE
AM/FM Stereo/CD/Tape +78
Aluminum/Alloy Wheels[Std on LS] +164
Anti-Lock Brakes[Std on LS] +144
Euro Handling Package +303
Leather Seats +176
Luxury Package +244
Power Sunroof +156
Premium Sound System[Opt on STD] +88

ECLIPSE   1992

Freshened front-end styling includes aero headlights and a new air dam. The GS-X model loses leather trim from its options list.

Category E

Model Description	Trade-in TMV	Private TMV	Dealer TMV
2 Dr STD Hbk	1534	2008	2798
2 Dr GS Hbk	1687	2208	3077
2 Dr GS Turbo Hbk	2045	2677	3730
2 Dr GSX Turbo AWD Hbk			
	2557	3347	4663

OPTIONS FOR ECLIPSE
4 cyl 2.0 L 16V Engine[Opt on GS] +98
AM/FM Compact Disc Player[Opt on GS,GS Turbo] +78
AM/FM Stereo/CD/Tape +78
Air Conditioning[Std on GSX] +169
Anti-Lock Brakes +140

Don't forget to refer to the Mileage Adjustment Table at the back of this book!

MITSUBISHI 92

Model Description	Trade-in TMV	Private TMV	Dealer TMV	Model Description	Trade-in TMV	Private TMV	Dealer TMV

Automatic 4-Speed Transmission +135
Leather Seats +89
Premium Sound System +78

EXPO   1992

Mitsubishi creates a van/station wagon hybrid. Designed to compete with everything from the Dodge Caravan to the Subaru Legacy wagon, the Expo seats seven while the Expo LRV seats five. Three models are available including a Sport all-wheel drive, a logical choice for residents of bad-weather states.

Category B

Model	Trade-in	Private	Dealer
2 Dr LRV Hbk	985	1360	1984
2 Dr LRV Sport 4WD Hbk			
	1336	1844	2691
2 Dr LRV Sport Hbk	1032	1424	2078
4 Dr SP 4WD Hbk	1500	2071	3022
4 Dr SP Hbk	1406	1941	2833

OPTIONS FOR EXPO
Air Conditioning +137
Anti-Lock Brakes +127
Automatic 4-Speed Transmission +156
Power Sunroof +127

GALANT   1992

The GS-X model is discontinued in favor of ultra-high performance VR-4. A 195-horsepower engine lurks under its sedate exterior. Standard antilock brakes, four-wheel steering, and leather seating surfaces are a few of the standard equipment items found on this very competent sedan. A Euro Handling Package and an Electronically Controlled Suspension are available options on the LS model.

Category D

Model	Trade-in	Private	Dealer
4 Dr STD Sdn	1003	1360	1955
4 Dr GS Sdn	1311	1778	2557
4 Dr GSR Sdn	1428	1937	2785
4 Dr GSX AWD Sdn	1504	2039	2932
4 Dr LS Sdn	1295	1756	2525
4 Dr VR-4 Turbo AWD Sdn			
	1954	2651	3811

OPTIONS FOR GALANT
AM/FM Compact Disc Player[Opt on GSR, VR-4] +78
Air Conditioning[Std on VR-4] +176
Anti-Lock Brakes[Std on VR-4] +189
Automatic 4-Speed Transmission[Opt on GS, STD] +137
Leather Seats +166
Power Sunroof +137
Premium Sound System +88

MIGHTY MAX PICKUP   1992

Safety-interlocks are now standard on manual transmission models, requiring the clutch to be fully depressed before the vehicle will start. The automatic transmission also gets a shift-interlock, requiring the brake to be depressed before the car can be shifted out of park. Two-wheel-drive Mighty Max models lose their rear-wheel antilock brakes.

Category J

Model	Trade-in	Private	Dealer
2 Dr Mighty Max 4WD Std Cab SB			
	2278	2886	3899
2 Dr Mighty Max Std Cab SB			
	1519	1924	2600
2 Dr Mighty Max Macro Ext Cab SB			
	1736	2199	2971

OPTIONS FOR MIGHTY MAX PICKUP
AM/FM Stereo Tape +95
Air Conditioning +148
Automatic 4-Speed Transmission +252

MIRAGE   1992

Base models finally lose the sticky vinyl interior in favor of full-cloth seats. LS models receive minor exterior trim changes.

Category B

Model	Trade-in	Private	Dealer
2 Dr STD Hbk	761	1050	1532
4 Dr STD Sdn	895	1235	1802
4 Dr GS Sdn	1119	1545	2254
4 Dr LS Sdn	940	1297	1893
2 Dr VL Hbk	716	988	1442

OPTIONS FOR MIRAGE
Air Conditioning +172
Aluminum/Alloy Wheels +78
Automatic 3-Speed Transmission[Opt on Hbk] +106
Automatic 4-Speed Transmission +129

MONTERO   1992

An all-new Montero is introduced. The new Montero features new wheels, a new grille, more interesting sheetmetal, more curves around the edges, and a very serious-looking blackout treatment on the formerly chrome accessories. Horsepower is upped but only enough to keep pace with its 125-pound weight gain. Antilock brakes are standard on the LS and optional on the SR model, working in both two- and four-wheel-drive mode.

Category M

Model	Trade-in	Private	Dealer
4 Dr STD 4WD Wgn	2883	3612	4827
4 Dr LS 4WD Wgn	4189	5249	7014
4 Dr RS 4WD Wgn	3434	4302	5749
4 Dr SR 4WD Wgn	4073	5103	6820

OPTIONS FOR MONTERO
AM/FM Compact Disc Player +78
AM/FM Stereo/CD/Tape[Opt on LS] +107
Air Conditioning +176
Anti-Lock Brakes +119
Automatic 4-Speed Transmission +174

Don't forget to refer to the Mileage Adjustment Table at the back of this book!

Model Description	Trade-in TMV	Private TMV	Dealer TMV	Model Description	Trade-in TMV	Private TMV	Dealer TMV

Leather Seats +234
Power Sunroof +171

ONE TON   1992

Category J
2 Dr Mighty Max Std Cab SB

| | 1253 | 1587 | 2144 |

OPTIONS FOR ONE TON
Air Conditioning +137

PRECIS   1992

The bargain-basement Precis gets a nose job.
Category A

| 2 Dr STD Hbk | 444 | 632 | 946 |

OPTIONS FOR PRECIS
Air Conditioning +137
Automatic 4-Speed Transmission +156

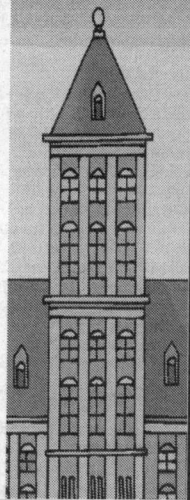

Don't forget to refer to the Mileage Adjustment Table at the back of this book!

NISSAN 01

Model Description	Trade-in TMV	Private TMV	Dealer TMV	Model Description	Trade-in TMV	Private TMV	Dealer TMV

NISSAN   Japan

1996 Nissan 300ZX

2001 NISSAN

ALTIMA   2001

GXE is available with a new Limited Edition package, which includes goodies like an eight-way power driver seat, remote keyless entry, floor mats, special badging and a security system.

Category C

	Trade-in	Private	Dealer
4 Dr GLE Sdn	12955	13964	15646
4 Dr GXE Sdn	10622	11449	12828
4 Dr SE Sdn	11917	12845	14392
4 Dr XE Sdn	9876	10645	11927

OPTIONS FOR ALTIMA

AM/FM Compact Disc Player +180
AM/FM Stereo/CD/Tape[Opt on GXE] +271
Air Conditioning[Std on GLE,SE] +340
Anti-Lock Brakes +339
Automatic 4-Speed Transmission[Std on GLE] +544
Compact Disc Changer +298
Cruise Control[Std on GLE,SE] +169
Keyless Entry System[Opt on GXE] +119
Leather Seats[Opt on SE] +883
Lighted Entry System[Opt on GXE] +115
Power Door Locks[Opt on GXE] +146
Power Drivers Seat[Opt on SE] +180
Power Moonroof +577
Rear Spoiler[Std on SE] +230
Side Air Bag Restraints[Std on GLE] +169

FRONTIER   2001

Fresh new styling with a decidedly industrial theme injects some much-needed personality into the Frontier for 2001. A supercharged V6, making 210 horsepower and 246 foot-pounds of torque (231 ft-lbs with a manual tranny), is available on special Desert Runner, King Cab and Crew Cab models, which get black-chrome headlight surrounds. Supercharged Frontiers come standard with 17-inch wheels and a limited-slip differential and can be equipped with leather upholstery, bundled in a package that includes a premium audio system with in-dash CD changer and steering wheel controls, plus a security system. Interiors get new fabrics, gauges and dash trimmings, as well as a new steering wheel. Tailgate locks are standard across the board, and a number of new colors, with names straight out of a J.Crew catalog, are available, like Khaki, Salsa and Denim.

Category J

	Trade-in	Private	Dealer
2 Dr SC Sprchrgd 4WD Ext Cab SB	14541	15580	17311
2 Dr SC Sprchrgd Ext Cab SB	12995	13923	15470
4 Dr SC Sprchrgd 4WD Crew Cab SB	15835	16966	18851
4 Dr SC Sprchrgd Crew Cab SB	14457	15490	17211
2 Dr Desert Runner SE Ext Cab SB	12599	13499	14999
2 Dr SE 4WD Ext Cab SB	14279	15299	16999
4 Dr SE 4WD Crew Cab SB	15709	16831	18701
4 Dr SE Crew Cab SB	13990	14990	16655
2 Dr Desert Runner XE Ext Cab SB	11131	11926	13251
2 Dr XE 4WD Ext Cab SB	12828	13744	15271
2 Dr XE Ext Cab SB	9537	10218	11353
2 Dr XE Std Cab SB	8305	8898	9887
4 Dr XE 4WD Crew Cab SB	14259	15278	16975
4 Dr XE Crew Cab SB	12562	13460	14955

OPTIONS FOR FRONTIER

AM/FM Compact Disc Player +318
AM/FM Stereo/CD/Tape +204
Air Conditioning[Std on Desert Runner SE,SE,Crew Cab] +645
Alarm System +136
Aluminum/Alloy Wheels[Std on Desert Runner SE,SE] +169
Automatic 4-Speed Transmission +713
Bed Extender +156
Bed Liner +210
Compact Disc Changer +379
Leather Seats +679
Limited Slip Differential +136
Luggage Rack +132
Pop-Up Moonroof +204
Power Door Locks +153
Power Mirrors +136

Don't forget to refer to the Mileage Adjustment Table at the back of this book!

NISSAN 01

Model Description	Trade-in TMV	Private TMV	Dealer TMV	Model Description	Trade-in TMV	Private TMV	Dealer TMV

Power Windows +170
Running Boards[Std on SE] +224
Tilt Steering Wheel[Opt on XE] +126
Tonneau Cover +753
Trailer Hitch +224

MAXIMA   2001

A 20th Anniversary edition includes the 227-horsepower version of the standard 3.0-liter V6 from the Infiniti I30, as well as goodies like bronze-lensed headlight covers, a body kit, ersatz carbon fiber interior trim, drilled metal pedals and a number of features normally optional on the SE. This special model also gets an exclusive color: Majestic Blue. A new Meridian package is optional on all Maximas, bundling side-impact airbags and a low washer fluid indicator with heated front seats and side mirrors, as well as special trunk lid trim. Adding optional traction control to the SE or GLE results in a Z Edition Maxima, for some zany reason.

Category D

	Trade-in	Private	Dealer
4 Dr GLE Sdn	17528	18771	20842
4 Dr GXE Sdn	15071	16139	17920
4 Dr SE Sdn	15815	16936	18805
4 Dr SE 20th Anniversary Sdn	18260	19554	21712

OPTIONS FOR MAXIMA

Automatic 4-Speed Transmission[Std on GLE] +340
Bose Sound System[Std on GLE] +611
Chrome Wheels +842
Compact Disc Changer +312
Heated Front Seats +170
Heated Power Mirrors +139
Leather Seats[Std on GLE] +765
Power Drivers Seat +170
Power Moonroof +611
Power Passenger Seat[Opt on SE] +224
Rear Spoiler[Std on SE] +325
Side Air Bag Restraints +170
Traction Control System +203

PATHFINDER   2001

A long-overdue 250-horsepower V6 engine debuts for 2001, making Pathfinder the most powerful SUV in its class. An interior freshening and more standard goodies, as well as snazzy options like an in-dash navigation system and an entertainment system for rear-seat occupants, are new for 2001. Also added to the LE's option list this fall is the handy All-Mode automatic 4WD system from the Infiniti QX4.

Category M

	Trade-in	Private	Dealer
4 Dr LE 4WD Wgn	21647	23024	25318
4 Dr LE Wgn	19951	21220	23335
4 Dr SE 4WD Wgn	20159	21441	23578
4 Dr SE Wgn	18639	19824	21800
4 Dr XE 4WD Wgn	20177	21460	23599
4 Dr XE Wgn	18662	19849	21827

OPTIONS FOR PATHFINDER

Automatic 4-Speed Transmission[Opt on SE] +679
Compact Disc Changer +488
Dual Power Seats +306
Entertainment System +883
Gold Package +264
Heated Front Seats +136
Leather Seats +611
Limited Slip Differential +169
Navigation System +1358
Power Moonroof +611
Side Air Bag Restraints +204
Trailer Hitch +264

QUEST   2001

Despite the company's decision to kill the Quest after a short 2002 model run, Nissan imbues the 2001 Quest minivan with a raft of minor improvements. Styling front and rear is freshened, and redesigned alloy wheels debut on all models. The entry-level GXE gains a rear stabilizer bar, while the sporty SE receives acceleration-sensitive strut valving and a strut tower brace. New interior gauges and fabrics spice things up, and a 130-watt Super Sound system is standard on SE and GLE. Luxury GLE models also get an in-dash six-CD changer and a wood 'n' leather steering wheel. An optional overhead family entertainment system replaces the former floor-mounted model, though that rather archaic unit can still be specified for SE and GLE Quests equipped with a sunroof. Front seatbelts now have pretensioners for improved occupant protection, and crash test scores are up this year, as well.

Category P

	Trade-in	Private	Dealer
4 Dr GLE Pass. Van	17896	19034	20931
4 Dr GXE Pass. Van	14945	15895	17479
4 Dr SE Pass. Van	16235	17267	18988

OPTIONS FOR QUEST

AM/FM Stereo/CD/Tape[Opt on GXE] +237
Automatic Dimming Mirror +142
Captain Chairs (2)[Opt on GXE] +509
Child Seat (1)[Opt on GXE] +156
Dual Air Conditioning[Opt on GXE] +440
Fog Lights +257
Heated Front Seats[Opt on SE] +135
Leather Seats[Opt on SE] +745
Power Drivers Seat +211
Power Moonroof +577
Power Passenger Seat[Opt on SE] +224
Running Boards +359
Trailer Hitch +196
Tutone Paint +203

SENTRA   2001

Model Description	Trade-in TMV	Private TMV	Dealer TMV	Model Description	Trade-in TMV	Private TMV	Dealer TMV

Redesigned and released late in the 2000 model year, the 2001 Sentra is carrying over unchanged in XE, GXE, SE and super ultra low-emission CA trims.

Category B

4 Dr CA Sdn	9754	10612	12042
4 Dr GXE Sdn	8960	9748	11062
4 Dr SE Sdn	9834	10699	12141
4 Dr XE Sdn	7960	8660	9827

OPTIONS FOR SENTRA

AM/FM Compact Disc Player +135
Air Conditioning[Opt on XE] +544
Alarm System +115
Aluminum/Alloy Wheels[Std on SE] +406
Anti-Lock Brakes +272
Automatic 4-Speed Transmission +544
Compact Disc Changer +271
Power Moonroof +407
Rear Spoiler +230
Side Air Bag Restraints +204

XTERRA   2001

SE models come with titanium interior accents as well as a premium audio system boasting 100 watts of peak power and a six-disc in-dash CD changer. New steering wheel-mounted audio controls can be used to operate this system. New colors, including one called Gold Rush, and restyled 16-inch alloy wheels round out the changes.

Category M

4 Dr SE 4WD Wgn	17782	18913	20798
4 Dr SE Wgn	16119	17144	18853
4 Dr XE V6 4WD Wgn	14853	15798	17372
4 Dr XE V6 Wgn	13960	14848	16328
4 Dr XE Wgn	12596	13397	14732

OPTIONS FOR XTERRA

AM/FM Stereo/CD/Tape +204
Alarm System[Std on SE] +136
Aluminum/Alloy Wheels[Std on SE] +406
Automatic 4-Speed Transmission +679
Automatic Dimming Mirror +149
Compact Disc Changer +298
Cruise Control[Std on SE] +126
Fog Lights[Std on SE] +153
Keyless Entry System[Opt on XE V6] +115
Limited Slip Differential[Std on SE] +170
Power Door Locks[Std on SE] +153
Power Mirrors[Std on SE] +126
Power Windows[Std on SE] +173
Side Steps[Opt on XE, XE V6] +204
Tilt Steering Wheel[Std on SE] +115
Trailer Hitch +237

2000 NISSAN

ALTIMA   2000

2000 Altimas receive fresh sheetmetal, comfort and convenience enhancements, engine refinements, and a revised suspension.

Category C

4 Dr GLE Sdn	10814	12042	13175
4 Dr GXE Sdn	8923	9936	10871
4 Dr SE Sdn	9982	11115	12161
4 Dr XE Sdn	8091	9010	9858

OPTIONS FOR ALTIMA

AM/FM Compact Disc Player +180
AM/FM Stereo Tape +136
AM/FM Stereo/CD/Tape[Opt on GXE] +187
Air Conditioning[Std on GLE, SE] +340
Aluminum/Alloy Wheels[Opt on GXE] +406
Anti-Lock Brakes +338
Automatic 4-Speed Transmission[Std on GLE] +544
Cruise Control[Std on GLE, SE] +169
Fog Lights[Opt on GXE, XE] +102
Gold Package +122
Keyless Entry System[Opt on GXE] +119
Leather Seats[Opt on SE] +675
Lighted Entry System[Opt on GXE] +115
Power Door Locks[Opt on GXE] +146
Power Drivers Seat[Opt on SE] +180
Power Moonroof +577
Rear Spoiler[Std on SE] +278
Side Air Bag Restraints[Std on GLE] +170
XE Option Package +816

FRONTIER   2000

Nissan's pickup line expands to 11 models, including the new Desert Runner and a four-door Frontier Crew Cab.

Category J

2 Dr Desert Runner SE Ext Cab SB			
	11416	12634	13758
2 Dr Desert Runner XE Ext Cab SB			
	10094	11170	12164
2 Dr SE 4WD Ext Cab SB			
	13170	14574	15871
4 Dr SE 4WD Crew Cab SB			
	14195	15708	17106
4 Dr SE Crew Cab SB	11868	13134	14302
2 Dr XE 4WD Ext Cab SB			
	11049	12227	13315
2 Dr XE Ext Cab SB	8674	9599	10453
2 Dr XE Std Cab SB	7564	8370	9115
4 Dr XE 4WD Crew Cab SB			
	12618	13964	15206
4 Dr XE Crew Cab SB	11032	12209	13295
2 Dr XE V6 4WD Ext Cab SB			
	11791	13048	14209

OPTIONS FOR FRONTIER

AM/FM Compact Disc Player +318

Model Description	Trade-in TMV	Private TMV	Dealer TMV

AM/FM Stereo/CD/Tape +204
Air Conditioning[Std on Desert Runner SE,SE,Crew Cab] +645
Alarm System +136
Aluminum/Alloy Wheels[Std on Desert Runner SE,SE] +169
Automatic 4-Speed Transmission +713
Bed Extender +203
Bed Liner +203
Camper/Towing Package +170
Compact Disc Changer +379
Cruise Control[Opt on Desert Runner XE,XE,XE V6,Crew Cab] +112
Flip-Up Sunroof +170
Fog Lights[Opt on XE] +136
Keyless Entry System +102
Limited Slip Differential +136
Luggage Rack +132
Power Door Locks +153
Power Mirrors +136
Power Windows +170
Privacy Glass[Opt on XE] +102
Running Boards[Std on SE] +170
Tilt Steering Wheel[Opt on XE] +126

MAXIMA 2000

The Maxima has been (controversially) redesigned, providing more power, more room and more amenities to the luxury/performance sedan buyer. Key among the improvements is 222 horsepower from the standard V6, a boost in rear-seat legroom and an available 200-watt Bose audio system.

Category D			
4 Dr GLE Sdn	15908	17602	19165
4 Dr GXE Sdn	13043	14432	15714
4 Dr SE Sdn	14346	15873	17283

OPTIONS FOR MAXIMA

AM/FM Stereo/CD/Tape[Opt on GXE] +271
Aluminum/Alloy Wheels[Opt on GXE] +425
Automatic 4-Speed Transmission[Std on GLE] +679
Bose Sound System[Std on GLE] +611
Climate Control for AC[Opt on SE] +101
Compact Disc Changer +406
Dual Power Seats[Opt on SE] +374
Gold Package +264
Heated Front Seats +170
Heated Power Mirrors +139
Leather Seats[Std on GLE] +765
Power Drivers Seat +170
Power Moonroof +611
Rear Spoiler[Std on SE] +325
Side Air Bag Restraints +170
Traction Control System +203

PATHFINDER 2000

After a substantial update in the middle of the 1999 model year, the Pathfinder soldiers into the new millennium without change. However, rumor has it that later in 2000 the Pathfinder will get a massive power upgrade.

Category M			
4 Dr LE 4WD Wgn	18332	20189	21902
4 Dr LE Wgn	17187	18927	20533
4 Dr SE 4WD Wgn	17416	19179	20807
4 Dr SE Wgn	16042	17666	19165
4 Dr XE 4WD Wgn	16576	18255	19804
4 Dr XE Wgn	15277	16824	18252

OPTIONS FOR PATHFINDER

Alarm System[Opt on XE] +153
Automatic 4-Speed Transmission[Opt on SE] +679
Compact Disc Changer +476
Cruise Control[Opt on XE] +115
Gold Package +264
Heated Front Seats +204
Heated Power Mirrors[Opt on XE] +146
Keyless Entry System[Opt on XE] +122
Leather Seats +611
Limited Slip Differential +169
Power Door Locks[Opt on XE] +170
Power Drivers Seat +211
Power Moonroof +611
Power Windows[Opt on XE] +194
Side Air Bag Restraints +204
Trailer Hitch +264

QUEST 2000

A stabilizer bar is now standard on the GLE model while new titanium-colored accents have been added to the 16-inch SE and 15-inch GXE alloy wheels. The SE gets auto on/off headlights and all Quests now come with a video entertainment system at no extra cost.

Category P			
4 Dr GLE	15392	16947	18382
4 Dr GXE	13011	14326	15539
4 Dr SE	14360	15811	17150

OPTIONS FOR QUEST

AM/FM Stereo/CD/Tape[Opt on GXE] +291
Aluminum/Alloy Wheels[Opt on GXE] +132
Camper/Towing Package +126
Child Seats (2) +156
Compact Disc Changer +406
Dual Air Conditioning[Opt on GXE] +440
Dual Power Seats[Opt on SE] +442
Fog Lights +238
Leather Seats[Opt on SE] +745
Power Drivers Seat +211
Power Moonroof +577
Running Boards +338
Trailer Hitch +196
Tutone Paint +102

SENTRA 2000

The Sentra has been completely overhauled for the

Model Description	Trade-in TMV	Private TMV	Dealer TMV	Model Description	Trade-in TMV	Private TMV	Dealer TMV

2000 model year. A better ride, more powerful engines, and a new enviro-friendly version top the bill, and we likes what we sees.

Category B

4 Dr GXE Sdn	7934	9157	10287
4 Dr SE Sdn	8676	10014	11249
4 Dr XE Sdn	7044	8130	9133

OPTIONS FOR SENTRA
AM/FM Stereo Tape +204
Air Conditioning[Opt on XE] +544
Alarm System +115
Aluminum/Alloy Wheels[Std on SE] +406
Anti-Lock Brakes +338
Automatic 4-Speed Transmission +544
Compact Disc Changer +271
Limited Slip Differential +132
Overhead Console +102
Power Sunroof +374
Rear Spoiler +230
Side Air Bag Restraints +170

XTERRA   2000

A truck-based mini-SUV, the athletic new Xterra competes with several smaller vehicles built on car platforms.

Category M

4 Dr SE 4WD Wgn	16458	18125	19663
4 Dr SE Wgn	14804	16303	17687
4 Dr XE V6 4WD Wgn	13623	15003	16276
4 Dr XE V6 Wgn	12994	14310	15524
4 Dr XE Wgn	11419	12575	13642

OPTIONS FOR XTERRA
AM/FM Compact Disc Player[Opt on XE] +170
Alarm System[Std on SE] +136
Aluminum/Alloy Wheels[Std on SE] +406
Automatic 4-Speed Transmission +679
Camper/Towing Package +170
Compact Disc Changer +442
Cruise Control[Std on SE] +126
Fog Lights[Std on SE] +153
Keyless Entry System[Opt on XE V6] +115
Limited Slip Differential[Std on SE] +170
Luggage Rack[Std on SE] +136
Power Door Locks[Std on SE] +153
Power Mirrors[Std on SE] +126
Power Windows[Std on SE] +173
Tilt Steering Wheel[Std on SE] +115

1999 NISSAN

ALTIMA   1999

All 1999 models get two new exterior colors, improved speakers and a new head unit for the three-in-one stereo combo. The GLE trim level gets alloy wheels added to its standard equipment list, and all alloy wheels now have a bright finish instead of a painted finish. All SE trim levels are now called SE Limited (SE-L) models and come with additional equipment.

Category C

4 Dr GLE Sdn	9846	11001	12156
4 Dr GXE Sdn	8209	9171	10134
4 Dr SE Sdn	9392	10493	11595
4 Dr SE Limited Sdn	9677	10812	11947
4 Dr XE Sdn	7247	8097	8947

OPTIONS FOR ALTIMA
AM/FM Stereo Tape +109
AM/FM Stereo/CD/Tape[Opt on GXE] +151
Air Conditioning[Opt on GXE] +273
Alarm System[Opt on GXE] +136
Aluminum/Alloy Wheels[Opt on GXE] +327
Anti-Lock Brakes +271
Automatic 4-Speed Transmission[Std on GLE] +437
Cruise Control[Opt on XE] +135
Gold Package +98
Keyless Entry System[Opt on GXE] +96
Leather Seats[Std on GLE] +544
Power Drivers Seat[Std on GLE] +144
Power Moonroof +463
Rear Spoiler +222

FRONTIER   1999

Two new King Cab models debut with a powerful V6 engine under the hood, and new standard and optional equipment is available.

Category J

2 Dr SE 4WD Ext Cab SB			
	11610	12870	14131
2 Dr SE Ext Cab SB	8514	9438	10363
2 Dr XE 4WD Ext Cab SB			
	9907	10983	12059
2 Dr XE 4WD Std Cab SB			
	9055	10039	11022
2 Dr XE Ext Cab SB	7508	8323	9138
2 Dr XE Std Cab SB	6578	7293	8007
2 Dr XE V6 4WD Ext Cab SB			
	10449	11583	12718

OPTIONS FOR FRONTIER
AM/FM Compact Disc Player +256
AM/FM Stereo/CD/Tape +164
Air Conditioning[Std on SE] +518
Alarm System +109
Aluminum/Alloy Wheels[Std on SE] +135
Automatic 4-Speed Transmission +573
Bed Liner +164
Compact Disc Changer +305
Cruise Control +90
Flip-Up Sunroof +136
Limited Slip Differential +109
Power Door Locks +123
Power Mirrors +109

Don't forget to refer to the Mileage Adjustment Table at the back of this book!

Model Description	Trade-in TMV	Private TMV	Dealer TMV	Model Description	Trade-in TMV	Private TMV	Dealer TMV
Power Windows +136				*Alarm System[Opt on XE] +123*			
Tilt Steering Wheel[Opt on XE] +101				*Alarm System[Opt on XE] +123*			

MAXIMA   1999

Traction Control is now available on models with automatic transmissions and, in addition to minor interior enhancements, four new colors debut. The SE trim level has been renamed SE-Limited (SE-L) and offers new standard features.

Category D

	Trade-in	Private	Dealer
4 Dr GLE Sdn	14144	15739	17335
4 Dr GXE Sdn	11167	12426	13686
4 Dr SE Sdn	12656	14083	15511
4 Dr SE Limited Sdn	12656	14083	15511

OPTIONS FOR MAXIMA

AM/FM Stereo/CD/Tape[Opt on GXE] +218
Alarm System[Std on GLE] +109
Aluminum/Alloy Wheels[Opt on GXE] +340
Anti-Lock Brakes +271
Automatic 4-Speed Transmission[Std on GLE] +545
Bose Sound System[Std on GLE] +490
Compact Disc Changer +327
Dual Power Seats[Std on GLE] +299
Gold Package +213
Heated Front Seats +136
Heated Power Mirrors +111
Keyless Entry System[Std on GLE] +96
Leather Seats[Std on GLE] +614
Power Drivers Seat +136
Power Moonroof +490
Rear Spoiler[Opt on GLE,GXE] +262
Side Air Bag Restraints +136
Traction Control System +164

PATHFINDER   1999

Only the LE trim level sees change in 1999, with new body-color fender flares and SE-style alloy wheels, tires and tubular step rails.

Category M

	Trade-in	Private	Dealer
4 Dr LE 4WD Wgn	17602	19476	21351
4 Dr LE Wgn	15637	17302	18967
1999.5 4 Dr LE 4WD Wgn	16393	18138	19884
1999.5 4 Dr LE Wgn	15478	17127	18775
4 Dr SE 4WD Wgn	15491	17140	18790
1999.5 4 Dr SE Limited 4WD Wgn	15491	17140	18790
1999.5 4 Dr SE Limited Wgn	14731	16300	17869
4 Dr XE 4WD Wgn	13975	15464	16952
4 Dr XE Wgn	12842	14209	15577
1999.5 4 Dr XE 4WD Wgn	15184	16801	18418
1999.5 4 Dr XE Wgn	14126	15631	17135

OPTIONS FOR PATHFINDER

AM/FM Stereo/CD/Tape[Opt on SE Limited] +191
AM/FM Stereo/CD/Tape[Std on LE] +191

Aluminum/Alloy Wheels[Opt on XE] +136
Automatic 4-Speed Transmission[Opt on SE Limited,XE] +545
Automatic 4-Speed Transmission[Opt on SE,XE] +545
Bose Sound System[Std on LE] +245
Bose Sound System[Std on LE] +245
Cruise Control[Opt on XE] +93
Cruise Control[Opt on XE] +93
Dual Power Seats +327
Fog Lights[Opt on SE Limited] +101
Fog Lights[Opt on SE,XE] +101
Gold Package +213
Gold Package +213
Heated Front Seats[Opt on SE Limited] +164
Heated Front Seats[Std on LE 4WD] +164
Heated Power Mirrors[Opt on XE] +118
Heated Power Mirrors[Opt on XE] +118
Keyless Entry System[Opt on XE] +98
Keyless Entry System[Opt on XE] +98
Leather Seats[Opt on SE Limited] +491
Leather Seats[Opt on LE,SE] +491
Limited Slip Differential[Opt on SE Limited] +135
Limited Slip Differential[Std on LE 4WD] +135
Luggage Rack[Opt on XE] +147
Power Door Locks[Opt on XE] +136
Power Door Locks[Opt on XE] +136
Power Drivers Seat[Opt on LE,SE Limited] +169
Power Moonroof +490
Power Moonroof +490
Power Windows[Opt on XE] +155
Power Windows[Opt on XE] +155
Side Air Bag Restraints +164
Trailer Hitch +213

QUEST   1999

Nissan redesigns its minivan for 1999 and adds a new SE trim level, standard driver-side sliding rear door and a more powerful engine.

Category P

	Trade-in	Private	Dealer
4 Dr GLE Pass. Van	13752	15318	16883
4 Dr GXE Pass. Van	11842	13190	14538
4 Dr SE Pass. Van	13370	14892	16414

OPTIONS FOR QUEST

AM/FM Stereo/CD/Tape +233
Aluminum/Alloy Wheels[Opt on GXE] +107
Camper/Towing Package +101
Child Seats (2) +124
Compact Disc Changer[Std on GLE] +327
Dual Air Conditioning[Opt on GXE] +354
Dual Power Seats[Opt on SE] +354
Leather Seats[Std on GLE] +597
Power Drivers Seat +169
Power Moonroof +464

SENTRA   1999

Fresh front-end styling, a Limited Edition Option

Model Description	Trade-in TMV	Private TMV	Dealer TMV	Model Description	Trade-in TMV	Private TMV	Dealer TMV

Package for GXE models, and some new paint colors constitute the changes for 1999.

Category B

4 Dr GXE Sdn	7093	8090	9087
4 Dr SE Sdn	7531	8590	9649
4 Dr SE Limited Sdn	7677	8757	9836
4 Dr XE Sdn	5996	6839	7682

OPTIONS FOR SENTRA

AM/FM Stereo Tape[Opt on XE] +164
AM/FM Stereo/CD/Tape +259
Air Conditioning[Opt on XE] +437
Alarm System[Opt on SE,SE Limited] +93
Aluminum/Alloy Wheels[Opt on GXE] +327
Anti-Lock Brakes +271
Automatic 4-Speed Transmission +437
Fog Lights[Opt on GXE] +135
Power Moonroof +299
Rear Spoiler[Opt on GXE,XE] +184
Sport Seats +136

1998 NISSAN

200SX   1998

Exterior enhancements include new headlights, taillights, front and rear bumpers and revised grille. Three new colors are available for 1998.

Category E

2 Dr STD Cpe	5953	6701	7511
2 Dr SE Cpe	7218	8125	9107
2 Dr SE-R Cpe	7739	8711	9764

OPTIONS FOR 200SX

AM/FM Compact Disc Player +227
AM/FM Stereo/CD/Tape[Opt on SE-R] +169
Air Conditioning[Opt on STD] +483
Alarm System +120
Anti-Lock Brakes +241
Automatic 4-Speed Transmission +387
Power Moonroof[Std on LE] +241

240SX   1998

No changes to Nissan's sporty coupe.

Category E

2 Dr STD Cpe	8557	9632	10796
2 Dr LE Cpe	11215	12624	14150
2 Dr SE Cpe	10215	11498	12888

OPTIONS FOR 240SX

AM/FM Compact Disc Player +227
AM/FM Stereo Tape[Opt on STD] +97
Air Conditioning[Opt on STD] +483
Aluminum/Alloy Wheels[Opt on STD] +189
Anti-Lock Brakes +338
Automatic 4-Speed Transmission +387
Compact Disc Changer +270
Limited Slip Differential +96

Power Moonroof[Std on LE] +435
Tilt Steering Wheel[Opt on STD] +92

ALTIMA   1998

Altima is totally, and unnecessarily, redesigned for 1998. The Altima's new look is more wedge-shaped, with a trunk that looks like it has met the business end of a band saw. Standard equipment is up, including a CD player on every model except the XE.

Category C

4 Dr GLE Sdn	8770	9904	11133
4 Dr GXE Sdn	7691	8685	9763
4 Dr SE Sdn	8410	9498	10676
4 Dr XE Sdn	6829	7712	8669

OPTIONS FOR ALTIMA

AM/FM Stereo Tape[Opt on GXE,XE] +97
AM/FM Stereo/CD/Tape[Opt on GXE] +133
Air Conditioning[Opt on XE] +242
Alarm System[Opt on GXE] +97
Aluminum/Alloy Wheels[Std on SE] +144
Anti-Lock Brakes +241
Automatic 4-Speed Transmission[Std on GLE] +387
Cruise Control[Opt on XE] +120
Leather Seats[Opt on SE] +481
Power Drivers Seat[Std on GLE] +128
Power Moonroof +410
Rear Spoiler[Std on SE] +198

FRONTIER   1998

Nissan introduces an all-new truck for 1998. This model, named the Frontier, is larger than the model it replaces, and has improved interior ergonomics.

Category J

2 Dr STD Std Cab SB	5725	6459	7254
2 Dr SE 4WD Ext Cab SB	9835	11096	12461
2 Dr SE Ext Cab SB	8587	9688	10880
2 Dr XE 4WD Ext Cab SB	8808	9937	11160
2 Dr XE 4WD Std Cab SB	8147	9191	10322
2 Dr XE Ext Cab SB	7046	7949	8927
2 Dr XE Std Cab SB	6312	7121	7997

OPTIONS FOR FRONTIER

AM/FM Compact Disc Player[Opt on XE] +227
AM/FM Stereo/CD/Tape[Opt on XE] +145
Alarm System +97
Aluminum/Alloy Wheels[Std on SE,XE Ext Cab SB] +120
Automatic 4-Speed Transmission[Opt on 2WD] +451
Bed Liner[Opt on STD,XE,2WD] +144
Compact Disc Changer +270
Power Door Locks[Opt on XE] +108
Power Mirrors[Opt on XE] +97
Power Windows[Opt on XE] +120

Model Description	Trade-in TMV	Private TMV	Dealer TMV

MAXIMA 1998

Side-impact airbags are added to the optional equipment lists of the SE and GLE models. Sterling Mist is a new color choice for this sporty sedan.

Category D

Model	Trade-in	Private	Dealer
4 Dr GLE Sdn	12259	13691	15242
4 Dr GXE Sdn	10070	11246	12520
4 Dr SE Sdn	11092	12388	13791

OPTIONS FOR MAXIMA

AM/FM Stereo/CD/Tape[Opt on GXE] +193
Alarm System[Std on GLE] +97
Aluminum/Alloy Wheels[Opt on GXE] +302
Anti-Lock Brakes +241
Automatic 4-Speed Transmission[Std on GLE] +483
Bose Sound System +435
Compact Disc Changer +290
Dual Power Seats[Opt on SE] +265
Heated Front Seats +120
Heated Power Mirrors +98
Leather Seats[Opt on SE] +544
Power Drivers Seat +120
Power Moonroof +435
Rear Spoiler[Std on SE] +207
Side Air Bag Restraints +120

PATHFINDER 1998

The only changes to the 1998 Pathfinder include chrome bumpers for the XE model, the addition of air conditioning to XE and SE standard equipment lists and additions to the XE Sport Package equipment.

Category M

Model	Trade-in	Private	Dealer
4 Dr LE 4WD Wgn	15091	16853	18763
4 Dr LE Wgn	13986	15619	17389
4 Dr SE 4WD Wgn	13250	14797	16474
4 Dr XE 4WD Wgn	11852	13236	14736
4 Dr XE Wgn	10969	12250	13638

OPTIONS FOR PATHFINDER

AM/FM Stereo Tape +189
AM/FM Stereo/CD/Tape[Opt on SE] +169
Alarm System[Opt on XE] +108
Aluminum/Alloy Wheels[Opt on XE] +120
Automatic 4-Speed Transmission[Std on LE] +483
Bose Sound System[Opt on SE] +290
Dual Power Seats +290
Heated Front Seats[Opt on SE] +145
Heated Power Mirrors[Opt on SE] +104
Leather Seats[Opt on SE] +435
Limited Slip Differential[Std on LE] +120
Luggage Rack[Opt on XE] +131
Power Door Locks[Opt on XE] +120
Power Moonroof +435
Power Windows[Opt on XE] +138
Trailer Hitch +189

QUEST 1998

No changes to the 1998 Quest.

Category P

Model	Trade-in	Private	Dealer
2 Dr GXE Pass. Van	11424	12819	14330
2 Dr XE Pass. Van	10386	11653	13027

OPTIONS FOR QUEST

AM/FM Stereo/CD/Tape[Opt on XE] +207
Aluminum/Alloy Wheels[Opt on XE] +94
Anti-Lock Brakes[Opt on XE] +241
Captain Chairs (4)[Opt on XE] +290
Child Seats (2)[Opt on XE] +96
Compact Disc Changer +290
Dual Air Conditioning[Opt on XE] +314
Dual Power Seats +314
Leather Seats +530
Power Moonroof +410

SENTRA 1998

A new Sentra SE debuts, sporting the same 140-horsepower engine and styling cues found in the 200SX SE-R coupe. Other changes include an exterior freshening that features new front and rear fascias.

Category B

Model	Trade-in	Private	Dealer
4 Dr STD Sdn	4854	5549	6303
4 Dr GLE Sdn	6710	7671	8713
4 Dr GXE Sdn	6282	7182	8157
4 Dr SE Sdn	6852	7834	8898
4 Dr XE Sdn	5496	6284	7137

OPTIONS FOR SENTRA

AM/FM Stereo Tape[Opt on STD] +145
AM/FM Stereo/CD/Tape[Std on GLE] +230
Air Conditioning[Opt on STD] +387
Anti-Lock Brakes +241
Automatic 4-Speed Transmission +387
Compact Disc Changer +270
Power Moonroof +265
Rear Spoiler[Std on SE] +164

1997 NISSAN

200SX 1997

A spoiler is now standard on all models. An additional exterior color is the only other change for 1997.

Category E

Model	Trade-in	Private	Dealer
2 Dr STD Cpe	5636	6378	7284
2 Dr SE Cpe	6647	7521	8590
2 Dr SE-R Cpe	7081	8013	9151

OPTIONS FOR 200SX

AM/FM Compact Disc Player +200
AM/FM Stereo Tape[Opt on STD] +193
Air Conditioning[Opt on STD] +428
Alarm System +107
Anti-Lock Brakes +214
Automatic 4-Speed Transmission +343
Compact Disc Changer +287
Power Moonroof +192

Don't forget to refer to the Mileage Adjustment Table at the back of this book!

Model Description	Trade-in TMV	Private TMV	Dealer TMV	Model Description	Trade-in TMV	Private TMV	Dealer TMV

240SX — 1997

Extensive exterior changes update the look of the 240SX. A luxury model is introduced midyear.

Category E

Model	Trade-in	Private	Dealer
2 Dr STD Cpe	7009	7931	9058
2 Dr LE Cpe	8740	9890	11295
2 Dr SE Cpe	7977	9027	10309

OPTIONS FOR 240SX

AM/FM Compact Disc Player +200
Air Conditioning[Opt on STD] +428
Aluminum/Alloy Wheels[Opt on STD] +167
Anti-Lock Brakes +214
Automatic 4-Speed Transmission +343
Compact Disc Changer +287
Leather Seats[Opt on SE] +321
Power Moonroof[Std on LE] +385
Special Factory Paint +171

ALTIMA — 1997

1997 models are virtually identical to 1996 models, except for the addition of new emissions equipment.

Category C

Model	Trade-in	Private	Dealer
4 Dr GLE Sdn	7987	9016	10274
1997.5 4 Dr GLE Sdn	7709	8702	9916
4 Dr GXE Sdn	6111	6899	7861
1997.5 4 Dr GXE Sdn	6251	7057	8041
4 Dr SE Sdn	6945	7840	8934
1997.5 4 Dr SE Sdn	7015	7919	9024
4 Dr XE Sdn	5556	6272	7147
1997.5 4 Dr XE Sdn	5764	6507	7415

OPTIONS FOR ALTIMA

AM/FM Compact Disc Player +200
AM/FM Compact Disc Player +200
AM/FM Stereo/CD/Tape[Std on GLE] +118
Air Conditioning[Opt on GXE,XE] +214
Air Conditioning[Opt on GXE,XE] +214
Alarm System[Opt on GXE] +107
Aluminum/Alloy Wheels[Opt on GXE] +128
Aluminum/Alloy Wheels[Opt on GXE] +128
Anti-Lock Brakes +267
Anti-Lock Brakes +267
Automatic 4-Speed Transmission[Std on GLE] +343
Automatic 4-Speed Transmission +343
Compact Disc Changer +287
Compact Disc Changer +287
Cruise Control[Opt on GXE,XE] +106
Cruise Control[Opt on GXE,XE] +106
Leather Seats +427
Leather Seats[Std on GLE] +427
Power Moonroof[Std on GLE] +363
Power Moonroof +363
Rear Spoiler[Std on SE] +175

HALF TON — 1997

Category J

Model	Trade-in	Private	Dealer
2 Dr STD Std Cab SB	4580	5167	5884
2 Dr XE 4WD Std Cab SB	6584	7428	8459
2 Dr XE Std Cab SB	5367	6055	6895

OPTIONS FOR HALF TON

AM/FM Compact Disc Player +200
AM/FM Stereo Tape +150
Air Conditioning +428
Aluminum/Alloy Wheels +214
Automatic 4-Speed Transmission[Opt on XE Std Cab] +428
Bed Liner +128
Compact Disc Changer +236

KING CAB — 1997

No changes for 1997.

Category J

Model	Trade-in	Private	Dealer
2 Dr SE 4WD Ext Cab SB	8445	9527	10849
2 Dr SE Ext Cab SB	7156	8073	9194
2 Dr XE 4WD Ext Cab SB	7514	8477	9654
2 Dr XE Ext Cab SB	6298	7105	8091

OPTIONS FOR KING CAB

AM/FM Compact Disc Player +200
AM/FM Stereo Tape[Opt on XE] +150
Air Conditioning[Opt on XE] +428
Aluminum/Alloy Wheels[Opt on XE] +214
Automatic 4-Speed Transmission[Opt on 2WD] +428
Bed Liner +128
Compact Disc Changer +236

MAXIMA — 1997

The Nissan Maxima gets a new grille, headlights, bumpers and taillights. New alloy wheels and fog lights on the SE, new wheel covers on the GXE, and new aluminum wheels on the GLE round out the changes.

Category D

Model	Trade-in	Private	Dealer
4 Dr GLE Sdn	10430	11729	13317
4 Dr GXE Sdn	8343	9383	10653
4 Dr SE Sdn	9040	10166	11542

OPTIONS FOR MAXIMA

AM/FM Compact Disc Player +118
AM/FM Stereo/CD/Tape[Opt on GXE] +171
Aluminum/Alloy Wheels[Opt on GXE] +267
Anti-Lock Brakes +214
Automatic 4-Speed Transmission[Opt on GLE] +514
Bose Sound System +385
Compact Disc Changer +256
Dual Power Seats[Opt on SE] +236
Heated Front Seats +107
Leather Seats[Opt on SE] +481
Power Drivers Seat +107
Power Moonroof +385

Don't forget to refer to the Mileage Adjustment Table at the back of this book!

Model Description	Trade-in TMV	Private TMV	Dealer TMV

PATHFINDER 1997

Changes to the 1997 Nissan Pathfinder include storage pockets added at all doors, a new exterior color and an available Bose sound system.

Category M

Model Description	Trade-in TMV	Private TMV	Dealer TMV
4 Dr LE 4WD Wgn	13292	14854	16763
4 Dr LE Wgn	11998	13408	15131
4 Dr SE 4WD Wgn	11136	12445	14044
4 Dr XE 4WD Wgn	9915	11080	12504
4 Dr XE Wgn	9197	10277	11598

OPTIONS FOR PATHFINDER

AM/FM Stereo Tape +167
AM/FM Stereo/CD/Tape[Std on SE] +150
Air Conditioning[Std on LE] +428
Alarm System[Opt on XE] +96
Aluminum/Alloy Wheels[Opt on XE] +107
Automatic 4-Speed Transmission[Std on LE] +428
Bose Sound System[Opt on SE] +257
Dual Power Seats +257
Heated Front Seats[Opt on SE] +128
Heated Power Mirrors[Opt on SE] +93
Leather Seats[Opt on SE] +385
Limited Slip Differential[Std on LE] +106
Luggage Rack[Opt on XE] +116
Power Door Locks[Opt on XE] +107
Power Moonroof +385
Power Windows[Opt on XE] +122
Running Boards +128

QUEST 1997

A few new colors are the only changes to the 1997 Quest.

Category P

Model Description	Trade-in TMV	Private TMV	Dealer TMV
2 Dr GXE Pass. Van	10293	11599	13196
2 Dr XE Pass. Van	8493	9571	10889

OPTIONS FOR QUEST

AM/FM Stereo/CD/Tape +184
Alarm System[Opt on XE] +96
Anti-Lock Brakes[Opt on XE] +214
Captain Chairs (4)[Opt on XE] +256
Compact Disc Changer +256
Dual Air Conditioning[Opt on XE] +278
Dual Power Seats +278
Heated Power Mirrors[Opt on XE] +94
Leather Seats +469
Luggage Rack[Opt on XE] +118
Power Door Locks[Opt on XE] +101
Power Moonroof +364
Power Windows[Opt on XE] +113

SENTRA 1997

The base model is now simply called "Base" instead of S. Nissan works to quiet the Sentra's interior by using a bigger muffler and reducing the number of suspension-mounting points.

Category B

Model Description	Trade-in TMV	Private TMV	Dealer TMV
4 Dr STD Sdn	4382	5075	5923
4 Dr GLE Sdn	5957	6900	8052
4 Dr GXE Sdn	5341	6186	7219
4 Dr XE Sdn	4998	5789	6756

OPTIONS FOR SENTRA

AM/FM Compact Disc Player +200
AM/FM Stereo Tape[Opt on STD] +128
Air Conditioning[Opt on STD] +319
Anti-Lock Brakes +214
Automatic 4-Speed Transmission +343
Compact Disc Changer +239
Power Moonroof +236
Rear Spoiler +145

1996 NISSAN

200SX 1996

Body-color door handles and outside mirrors are newly standard on SE and SE-R models.

Category E

Model Description	Trade-in TMV	Private TMV	Dealer TMV
2 Dr STD Cpe	4299	4844	5596
2 Dr SE Cpe	4872	5489	6342
2 Dr SE-R Cpe	5588	6297	7275

OPTIONS FOR 200SX

AM/FM Stereo Tape[Opt on STD] +178
Air Conditioning[Opt on STD] +396
Anti-Lock Brakes +395
Automatic 4-Speed Transmission +316
Power Moonroof +178

240SX 1996

Sporty new fabrics and a new grille are the only changes to the attractive 240SX.

Category E

Model Description	Trade-in TMV	Private TMV	Dealer TMV
2 Dr STD Cpe	6305	7104	8208
2 Dr SE Cpe	6465	7284	8416

OPTIONS FOR 240SX

Air Conditioning[Std on SE] +395
Alarm System[Opt on SE] +99
Aluminum/Alloy Wheels[Std on SE] +154
Anti-Lock Brakes +395
Automatic 4-Speed Transmission +316
Leather Seats +297
Power Sunroof +356
Special Factory Paint +157

300ZX 1996

It's the end of the world as we know it. The final Z-car is produced for 1996.

Category F

Model Description	Trade-in TMV	Private TMV	Dealer TMV
2 Dr 2+2 Cpe	13886	15645	18074
2 Dr STD Conv	17472	19685	22741
2 Dr STD Cpe	13416	15115	17462

Don't forget to refer to the Mileage Adjustment Table at the back of this book!

Model Description	Trade-in TMV	Private TMV	Dealer TMV
2 Dr STD Turbo Cpe	15448	17404	20106

OPTIONS FOR 300ZX
Automatic 4-Speed Transmission +356
Glass Panel T-tops[Std on 2+2,Turbo] +569
Leather Seats[Std on Conv] +435
Power Drivers Seat[Std on Turbo] +118
Special Factory Paint +157

ALTIMA   1996

New wheelcovers, power lock logic and fresh GXE upholstery update this hot-selling sedan.

Category C

Model Description	Trade-in TMV	Private TMV	Dealer TMV
4 Dr GLE Sdn	5894	6698	7809
4 Dr GXE Sdn	4889	5556	6478
4 Dr SE Sdn	5492	6242	7277
4 Dr XE Sdn	4555	5176	6035

OPTIONS FOR ALTIMA
AM/FM Stereo/CD/Tape +109
Air Conditioning[Opt on GXE,XE] +197
Anti-Lock Brakes +247
Automatic 4-Speed Transmission[Std on GLE] +328
Cruise Control[Opt on GXE,XE] +99
Leather Seats +394
Power Moonroof +336
Power Sunroof[Std on SE] +336

HALF TON   1996

Category J

Model Description	Trade-in TMV	Private TMV	Dealer TMV
2 Dr STD Std Cab SB	3747	4262	4974
2 Dr XE 4WD Std Cab SB			
	5205	5921	6909
2 Dr XE Std Cab SB	4233	4815	5619

OPTIONS FOR HALF TON
AM/FM Stereo Tape +139
Air Conditioning +395
Aluminum/Alloy Wheels +197
Automatic 4-Speed Transmission[Opt on XE Std Cab] +396
Bed Liner +118
Power Steering[Opt on STD] +126

KING CAB   1996

Category J

Model Description	Trade-in TMV	Private TMV	Dealer TMV
2 Dr SE 4WD Ext Cab SB			
	6939	7893	9211
2 Dr SE Ext Cab SB	6037	6868	8014
2 Dr XE 4WD Ext Cab SB			
	6454	7341	8567
2 Dr XE Ext Cab SB	5135	5841	6816

OPTIONS FOR KING CAB
AM/FM Stereo Tape[Std on SE 4WD] +139
Air Conditioning[Opt on XE] +395
Aluminum/Alloy Wheels[Opt on XE] +197
Automatic 4-Speed Transmission[Opt on 2WD] +396
Flip-Up Sunroof[Opt on SE 4WD] +139

Model Description	Trade-in TMV	Private TMV	Dealer TMV
Power Windows[Opt on SE 4WD] +105			

MAXIMA   1996

All new for 1995, the excellent Maxima receives few changes for 1996. A four-way power passenger seat is available, a new center console cupholder will hold a Big Gulp, and two new colors grace the Maxima's decidedly dull flanks. Taillights are as ugly as ever.

Category D

Model Description	Trade-in TMV	Private TMV	Dealer TMV
4 Dr GLE Sdn	8736	9911	11532
4 Dr GXE Sdn	6720	7624	8871
4 Dr SE Sdn	7392	8386	9758

OPTIONS FOR MAXIMA
AM/FM Stereo/CD/Tape[Opt on GXE] +157
Aluminum/Alloy Wheels[Opt on GXE] +247
Anti-Lock Brakes +197
Automatic 4-Speed Transmission[Std on GLE] +396
Bose Sound System +315
Compact Disc Changer +236
Gold Package +154
Heated Front Seats +99
Leather Seats[Opt on SE] +445
Power Drivers Seat[Std on GLE] +99
Power Moonroof +356
Power Passenger Seat +99
Rear Spoiler +170

PATHFINDER   1996

Outstanding new Pathfinder debuts with dual airbags and great interior styling. Engine output is up, but the Pathfinder is still not going to win any drag races. The new interior is open, airy, and much more comfortable than most of its competitors.

Category M

Model Description	Trade-in TMV	Private TMV	Dealer TMV
4 Dr LE 4WD Wgn	11036	12514	14555
4 Dr LE Wgn	10208	11576	13464
4 Dr SE 4WD Wgn	9519	10793	12554
4 Dr XE 4WD Wgn	8346	9463	11007
4 Dr XE Wgn	7518	8525	9915

OPTIONS FOR PATHFINDER
AM/FM Stereo/CD/Tape[Opt on XE 4WD] +139
Air Conditioning[Opt on LE] +395
Automatic 4-Speed Transmission[Std on LE] +396
Dual Power Seats +237
Heated Front Seats[Opt on SE] +118
Leather Seats[Opt on SE] +356
Limited Slip Differential[Opt on SE,XE] +99
Luggage Rack[Opt on XE] +107
Power Door Locks[Opt on XE] +99
Power Moonroof +356
Power Windows[Opt on XE] +112

QUEST   1996

Substantial upgrades include dual airbags, integrated child safety seats, side-impact protection meeting 1997

NISSAN 96-95

Model Description	Trade-in TMV	Private TMV	Dealer TMV	Model Description	Trade-in TMV	Private TMV	Dealer TMV

passenger car standards, revamped fabrics, new colors, freshened styling, and a cool, in-dash six-disc CD changer. The Quest is still in the hunt.

Category P

2 Dr GXE Pass. Van	8524	9717	11363
2 Dr XE Pass. Van	6875	7836	9164

OPTIONS FOR QUEST
Anti-Lock Brakes[Opt on XE] +276
Compact Disc Changer +236
Dual Air Conditioning[Opt on XE] +257
Leather Seats +433
Luggage Rack[Opt on XE] +109
Power Passenger Seat +123
Power Windows[Opt on XE] +105

SENTRA   1996

Prices have crept up, making the Sentra a hard sell against the Neon, Prizm and Cavalier. Still, you may be able to find a good deal on a former rental vehicle. We've seen tons of them at the Alamo rental lots.

Category B

4 Dr STD Sdn	3267	3854	4663
4 Dr GLE Sdn	4357	5139	6218
4 Dr GXE Sdn	4229	4987	6035
4 Dr XE Sdn	3844	4534	5486

OPTIONS FOR SENTRA
AM/FM Compact Disc Player[Opt on XE] +186
AM/FM Stereo Tape[Opt on STD] +118
Air Conditioning[Opt on STD] +294
Anti-Lock Brakes +197
Automatic 4-Speed Transmission +316

1995 NISSAN

200SX   1995

A Sentra derived 200SX is introduced to the sporting public. Basically a two-door version of the redesigned Sentra, the 200SX comes equipped with dual airbags. The 200SX has two available powerplants, a 1.6-liter four-cylinder that produces 115-horsepower or a 2.0-liter four that is good for 140 ponies.

Category E

2 Dr STD Cpe	3720	4202	5005
2 Dr SE Cpe	3995	4513	5375
2 Dr SE-R Cpe	4684	5291	6302

OPTIONS FOR 200SX
AM/FM Stereo Tape[Opt on STD] +159
Air Conditioning[Opt on STD] +355
Anti-Lock Brakes +177
Automatic 4-Speed Transmission +284
Power Moonroof +159

240SX   1995

Totally redesigned, the 240SX loses its hatchback and

convertible body styles. Available as a base or SE model, the 240 uses the same engine as the previous generation model. Dual airbags are standard on the new 240SX as are side door beams that help the car meet federal side-impact standards.

Category E

2 Dr STD Cpe	5235	5913	7043
2 Dr SE Cpe	5555	6275	7474

OPTIONS FOR 240SX
AM/FM Compact Disc Player +166
Air Conditioning[Std on SE] +354
Aluminum/Alloy Wheels[Std on SE] +139
Anti-Lock Brakes +177
Automatic 4-Speed Transmission +284
Leather Seats +266
Power Moonroof +318
Power Sunroof +318
Special Factory Paint +141

300ZX   1995

No changes for the 300ZX.

Category F

2 Dr 2+2 Cpe	11568	12995	15372
2 Dr STD Conv	14511	16300	19282
2 Dr STD Cpe	11156	12531	14824
2 Dr STD Turbo Cpe	12765	14339	16962

OPTIONS FOR 300ZX
AM/FM Compact Disc Player[Opt on Conv] +124
Automatic 4-Speed Transmission +319
Glass Panel T-tops[Std on 2+2, Turbo] +510
Leather Seats[Std on Conv] +389
Power Drivers Seat[Opt on STD Cpe] +107
Special Factory Paint +141

ALTIMA   1995

Minor exterior tweaks to the grille, taillights and wheels are the only changes for this attractive compact from Tennessee.

Category C

4 Dr GLE Sdn	4909	5618	6800
4 Dr GXE Sdn	4017	4597	5564
4 Dr SE Sdn	4655	5328	6448
4 Dr XE Sdn	3507	4014	4858

OPTIONS FOR ALTIMA
AM/FM Compact Disc Player +166
Air Conditioning[Opt on GXE,XE] +177
Anti-Lock Brakes +177
Automatic 4-Speed Transmission[Std on GLE] +284
Compact Disc Changer +238
Leather Seats +353
Power Moonroof[Opt on GXE] +301

HALF TON   1995

Category J

2 Dr STD Std Cab SB	2950	3372	4075

Don't forget to refer to the Mileage Adjustment Table at the back of this book!

Model Description	Trade-in TMV	Private TMV	Dealer TMV	Model Description	Trade-in TMV	Private TMV	Dealer TMV
2 Dr HD Std Cab LB	3754	4291	5186				
2 Dr XE 4WD Std Cab SB							
	4559	5211	6298				
2 Dr XE Std Cab SB	3219	3679	4446				

OPTIONS FOR HALF TON
AM/FM Stereo Tape +124
Air Conditioning +354
Automatic 4-Speed Transmission[Opt on XE] +355
Power Steering[Opt on XE] +113

KING CAB 1995

Category J

Model Description	Trade-in TMV	Private TMV	Dealer TMV
2 Dr SE V6 4WD Ext Cab SB			
	6504	7434	8984
2 Dr XE 4WD Ext Cab SB			
	5231	5978	7225
2 Dr XE Ext Cab SB	3889	4445	5372
2 Dr XE V6 4WD Ext Cab SB			
	5700	6515	7873
2 Dr XE V6 Ext Cab SB	4426	5058	6113

OPTIONS FOR KING CAB
AM/FM Stereo Tape[Opt on XE] +124
Air Conditioning[Opt on XE] +354
Automatic 4-Speed Transmission +355
Flip-Up Sunroof +124
Limited Slip Differential[Opt on XE V6] +89
Power Steering[Opt on XE] +98
Power Windows[Opt on SE V6] +93

MAXIMA 1995

Wow, what a beauty. The redesigned Maxima bows with an aerodynamic shape and a lengthened wheelbase. The new Maxima is available as a budget-minded GXE, sporty SE or luxurious GLE. All Maximas get the 190-horsepower engine previously exclusive to the SE.

Category D

Model Description	Trade-in TMV	Private TMV	Dealer TMV
4 Dr GLE Sdn	6602	7592	9240
4 Dr GXE Sdn	5533	6362	7743
4 Dr SE Sdn	5973	6868	8359

OPTIONS FOR MAXIMA
AM/FM Compact Disc Player[Opt on GXE] +98
AM/FM Stereo/CD/Tape[Std on GLE] +141
Aluminum/Alloy Wheels[Opt on GXE] +221
Anti-Lock Brakes +177
Automatic 4-Speed Transmission[Std on GLE] +355
Bose Sound System[Std on GLE] +284
Gold Package +138
Heated Front Seats +89
Heated Power Mirrors[Std on GLE] +73
Leather Seats[Std on GLE] +398
Power Drivers Seat[Std on GLE] +89
Power Moonroof +318
Rear Spoiler[Std on SE] +152

PATHFINDER 1995

Whoopee. A two-wheel-drive version of Nissan's ancient sport utility is now available in LE flavor.

Category M

Model Description	Trade-in TMV	Private TMV	Dealer TMV
4 Dr LE 4WD Wgn	9088	10237	12151
4 Dr LE Wgn	8250	9292	11030
4 Dr SE 4WD Wgn	7900	8898	10562
4 Dr XE 4WD Wgn	6642	7481	8880
4 Dr XE Wgn	6292	7087	8412

OPTIONS FOR PATHFINDER
AM/FM Stereo/CD/Tape[Opt on SE] +124
Air Conditioning[Std on LE] +354
Automatic 4-Speed Transmission[Std on LE] +355
Heated Front Seats[Opt on XE] +107
Leather Seats[Opt on SE] +319
Power Windows[Opt on XE] +100

QUEST 1995

GXE models get standard captain's chairs for second-row occupants. The Extra Performance Package is renamed the Handling Package. No other significant changes for the Quest.

Category P

Model Description	Trade-in TMV	Private TMV	Dealer TMV
2 Dr GXE Pass. Van	6584	7533	9114
2 Dr XE Pass. Van	5596	6403	7747

OPTIONS FOR QUEST
AM/FM Compact Disc Player +124
AM/FM Stereo/CD/Tape[Opt on GXE] +152
Anti-Lock Brakes[Opt on XE] +177
Dual Air Conditioning[Opt on XE] +230
Leather Seats +388
Luggage Rack[Opt on XE] +98
Power Moonroof +301
Power Passenger Seat +110
Power Sunroof +230

SENTRA 1995

An all-new Sentra is released featuring aero styling and a stubby trunk. The 1995 Sentra is available only as a four-door sedan, the two-door model now being called the 200SX. Increased interior space is the most noticeable feature of the redesign. The engines remain unchanged from previous models.

Category B

Model Description	Trade-in TMV	Private TMV	Dealer TMV
4 Dr STD Sdn	2774	3272	4102
4 Dr GLE Sdn	3514	4145	5196
4 Dr GXE Sdn	3267	3854	4831
4 Dr XE Sdn	3143	3708	4648

OPTIONS FOR SENTRA
Air Conditioning[Opt on STD] +264
Aluminum/Alloy Wheels +212
Anti-Lock Brakes +177
Automatic 4-Speed Transmission +284

Don't forget to refer to the Mileage Adjustment Table at the back of this book!

Model Description	Trade-in TMV	Private TMV	Dealer TMV

1994 NISSAN

240SX — 1994

A convertible body style is the sole offering this year as the coupe is set for a complete redesign.

Category E

Model Description	Trade-in TMV	Private TMV	Dealer TMV
2 Dr SE Conv	4723	5571	6984

OPTIONS FOR 240SX
Air Conditioning +311

300ZX — 1994

A passenger airbag is a new safety feature on the 300ZX, which allows the use of manual seatbelts. Remote keyless entry is another new feature for the 300ZX.

Category F

Model Description	Trade-in TMV	Private TMV	Dealer TMV
2 Dr 2+2 Cpe	9546	10944	13275
2 Dr STD Conv	11855	13592	16486
2 Dr STD Cpe	9184	10530	12772
2 Dr STD Turbo Cpe	10168	11658	14140

OPTIONS FOR 300ZX
AM/FM Compact Disc Player[Opt on STD Cpe] +109
AM/FM Stereo/CD/Tape +155
Automatic 4-Speed Transmission +280
Glass Panel T-tops[Opt on STD] +448
Leather Seats[Std on Conv] +343
Special Factory Paint +124

ALTIMA — 1994

A passenger-side airbag is added to this hot-selling Tennessee-built compact. SE models gain a standard sunroof and GLEs have it as an available option.

Category C

Model Description	Trade-in TMV	Private TMV	Dealer TMV
4 Dr GLE Sdn	4112	4791	5923
4 Dr GXE Sdn	3024	3524	4356
4 Dr SE Sdn	3810	4439	5488
4 Dr XE Sdn	2903	3382	4181

OPTIONS FOR ALTIMA
AM/FM Compact Disc Player[Opt on GXE] +146
AM/FM Stereo/CD/Tape[Opt on GXE, SE] +86
Air Conditioning[Std on GLE, SE] +155
Anti-Lock Brakes +155
Automatic 4-Speed Transmission[Std on GLE] +250
Compact Disc Changer +209
Cruise Control[Opt on GXE, XE] +78
Leather Seats +310
Power Sunroof[Opt on GXE] +265

HALF TON — 1994

Category J

Model Description	Trade-in TMV	Private TMV	Dealer TMV
2 Dr STD Std Cab SB	2670	3090	3790
2 Dr V6 Std Cab LB	3190	3692	4529
2 Dr XE 4WD Std Cab SB	3777	4372	5362
2 Dr XE Std Cab SB	2865	3316	4067

OPTIONS FOR HALF TON
AM/FM Stereo Tape +109
Air Conditioning +311
Automatic 4-Speed Transmission +312
Bed Liner +93
Power Steering[Opt on XE] +99

KING CAB — 1994

Category J

Model Description	Trade-in TMV	Private TMV	Dealer TMV
2 Dr SE V6 4WD Ext Cab SB	4688	5426	6655
2 Dr SE V6 Ext Cab SB	4298	4974	6101
2 Dr XE 4WD Ext Cab SB	4494	5201	6379
2 Dr XE Ext Cab SB	3516	4069	4991
2 Dr XE V6 4WD Ext Cab SB	4623	5351	6563

OPTIONS FOR KING CAB
AM/FM Stereo Tape +109
Air Conditioning +311
Aluminum/Alloy Wheels +155
Automatic 4-Speed Transmission +312
Bed Liner +93
Flip-Up Sunroof +109
Limited Slip Differential +78
Power Steering[Opt on XE] +86

MAXIMA — 1994

No changes for the 1994 Maxima.

Category D

Model Description	Trade-in TMV	Private TMV	Dealer TMV
4 Dr GXE Sdn	4884	5606	6809
4 Dr SE Sdn	5079	5830	7081

OPTIONS FOR MAXIMA
Anti-Lock Brakes +155
Automatic 4-Speed Transmission[Opt on SE] +312
Bose Sound System[Std on SE] +249
Leather Seats +351
Power Sunroof +203

PATHFINDER — 1994

The LE model is introduced for the country-club crowd. Standard equipment on the LE includes leather upholstery, heated seats, a CD player, and a luggage rack. All 1994 Pathfinders sport a redesigned dashboard and instrument panel. SE models get new alloy wheels and a sunroof.

Category M

Model Description	Trade-in TMV	Private TMV	Dealer TMV
4 Dr LE 4WD Wgn	7625	8717	10536
4 Dr SE 4WD Wgn	6411	7329	8858
4 Dr XE 4WD Wgn	5368	6136	7417
4 Dr XE Wgn	5160	5898	7129

Don't forget to refer to the Mileage Adjustment Table at the back of this book!

Model Description	Trade-in TMV	Private TMV	Dealer TMV

Model Description	Trade-in TMV	Private TMV	Dealer TMV

OPTIONS FOR PATHFINDER

Air Conditioning[Std on LE] +311
Automatic 4-Speed Transmission[Std on LE] +312
Heated Front Seats[Opt on SE] +93
Leather Seats[Opt on SE] +280

QUEST   1994

The Quest gets a driver airbag added to its standard equipment list for 1994. GXE models can now be had with a premium audio package that includes a CD player.

Category P

2 Dr GXE Pass. Van	5603	6505	8009
2 Dr XE Pass. Van	4712	5471	6735

OPTIONS FOR QUEST

AM/FM Stereo/CD/Tape +134
Anti-Lock Brakes[Opt on XE] +155
Dual Air Conditioning[Opt on XE] +203
Leather Seats +342
Power Moonroof +265

SENTRA   1994

CFC-free coolant is now standard on vehicles equipped with air conditioning. XE models get more standard equipment that includes air conditioning, cruise control and a stereo with cassette player.

Category B

2 Dr E Sdn	1870	2293	2998
4 Dr E Sdn	1927	2363	3089
4 Dr GXE Sdn	2815	3451	4512
1994.5 2 Dr Limited Sdn	2370	2906	3799
1994.5 4 Dr Limited Sdn	2391	2931	3832
2 Dr SE Sdn	2324	2849	3725

Category E

2 Dr SE-R Sdn	3006	3546	4445

Category B

2 Dr XE Sdn	2210	2710	3543
4 Dr XE Sdn	2266	2779	3633

OPTIONS FOR SENTRA

AM/FM Stereo/CD/Tape[Opt on XE] +148
Air Bag Restraint +101
Air Bag Restraint +101
Air Conditioning[Opt on E,SE,SE-R] +232
Aluminum/Alloy Wheels[Std on GXE,SE-R] +186
Anti-Lock Brakes +155
Automatic 4-Speed Transmission +250
Automatic 4-Speed Transmission +250
Power Sunroof +172

1993 NISSAN

240SX   1993

The luxury-oriented LE is dropped from the 240SX lineup due to poor sales. Don't worry, those with a penchant for leather can still get their kicks in a cowhide-equipped SE model. Half of the 240SXs produced this year have CFC-free air conditioning.

Category E

2 Dr STD Cpe	2705	3258	4179
2 Dr STD Hbk	2818	3394	4353
2 Dr SE Conv	3920	4721	6055
2 Dr SE Cpe	2834	3413	4378
2 Dr SE Hbk	3625	4365	5599

OPTIONS FOR 240SX

Air Conditioning +279
Anti-Lock Brakes +140
Automatic 4-Speed Transmission[Std on Conv] +224
Flip-Up Sunroof +126
Leather Seats +210
Power Sunroof +251
Special Factory Paint +112

300ZX   1993

The first chop-top Z-car debuts this year. A basket handle behind the seats reduces body flex in the 300ZX and gives the seatbelts an anchor point. No changes for the other models.

Category F

2 Dr 2+2 Cpe	7544	8785	10853
2 Dr STD Conv	9874	11498	14205
2 Dr STD Cpe	7093	8260	10204
2 Dr STD Turbo Cpe	9941	11576	14301

OPTIONS FOR 300ZX

Automatic 4-Speed Transmission +252
Bose Sound System +196
Glass Panel T-tops[Std on 2+2,Turbo] +404
Leather Seats +308
Power Drivers Seat[Opt on STD Cpe] +84
Premium Sound System[Opt on STD Cpe] +196
Special Factory Paint +112

ALTIMA   1993

The Infiniti-inspired Altima replaces the aging Stanza. Swooping sheetmetal, a longer wheelbase, and increased cabin size distinguish the Altima from its lackluster predecessor. The Altima is powered by a twin-cam four-cylinder that produces 150 horsepower. A driver airbag is standard on the Altima, as are motorized seatbelts.

Category C

4 Dr GLE Sdn	3527	4113	5090
4 Dr GXE Sdn	2554	2978	3685
4 Dr SE Sdn	3101	3616	4475
4 Dr XE Sdn	2493	2908	3598

OPTIONS FOR ALTIMA

AM/FM Compact Disc Player +132
Air Conditioning[Opt on GXE,XE] +140
Aluminum/Alloy Wheels[Opt on GXE] +84

Don't forget to refer to the Mileage Adjustment Table at the back of this book!

Model Description	Trade-in TMV	Private TMV	Dealer TMV

Anti-Lock Brakes +140
Automatic 4-Speed Transmission[Std on GLE] +224
Leather Seats +278
Power Moonroof +238
Rear Spoiler +114

HALF TON 1993

Category J

Model Description	Trade-in TMV	Private TMV	Dealer TMV
2 Dr STD Std Cab LB	2548	3016	3797
2 Dr STD 4WD Std Cab SB			
	3045	3605	4538
2 Dr STD Std Cab SB	2113	2501	3148

OPTIONS FOR HALF TON
6 cyl 3.0 L Engine[Opt on STD 4WD] +154
AM/FM Stereo Tape[Opt on STD] +98
Air Conditioning +279
Automatic 4-Speed Transmission +280

KING CAB 1993

Category J

Model Description	Trade-in TMV	Private TMV	Dealer TMV
2 Dr STD 4WD Ext Cab SB			
	3791	4488	5649
2 Dr STD Ext Cab SB	3108	3679	4631
2 Dr SE 4WD Ext Cab SB			
	4288	5076	6390
2 Dr SE Ext Cab SB	3667	4341	5464

OPTIONS FOR KING CAB
AM/FM Stereo Tape[Opt on STD 2WD] +98
Air Conditioning +279
Aluminum/Alloy Wheels[Opt on SE] +140
Automatic 4-Speed Transmission +280
Sunroof +140

MAXIMA 1993

The driver airbag is now standard on Nissan's front-wheel drive midsize sedan. Both cars have CFC-free air conditioning and SE models get a trick new stereo, compliments of Bose.

Category D

Model Description	Trade-in TMV	Private TMV	Dealer TMV
4 Dr GXE Sdn	4025	4718	5873
4 Dr SE Sdn	4151	4866	6057

OPTIONS FOR MAXIMA
AM/FM Stereo/CD/Tape +112
Anti-Lock Brakes +140
Automatic 4-Speed Transmission[Opt on SE] +280
Bose Sound System[Std on SE] +223
Dual Power Seats +154
Leather Seats +315
Luxury Package +434
Power Sunroof +182

NX 1993

The 2000 gets a standard T-top. New interior fabrics mark the only other changes for the NX line.

Category E

Model Description	Trade-in TMV	Private TMV	Dealer TMV
2 Dr 1600 Cpe	2097	2525	3239
2 Dr 2000 Cpe	2606	3138	4025

OPTIONS FOR NX
Air Conditioning[Opt on XE] +210
Anti-Lock Brakes +168
Automatic 4-Speed Transmission +182
T-Bar Roof[Opt on 1600] +252

PATHFINDER 1993

CFC-free air conditioning is standard and side-impact door beams are introduced to protect occupants. The Pathfinder's standard stereo gets its wattage increased and the SE's leather seats are now heated. How cozy.

Category M

Model Description	Trade-in TMV	Private TMV	Dealer TMV
4 Dr SE 4WD Wgn	5446	6424	8055
4 Dr XE 4WD Wgn	4695	5538	6944
4 Dr XE Wgn	4257	5022	6296

OPTIONS FOR PATHFINDER
Air Conditioning[Opt on XE] +279
Automatic 4-Speed Transmission +280
Heated Front Seats[Opt on SE] +84
Leather Seats +252
Luggage Rack[Opt on SE,XE 4WD] +76
Power Windows[Opt on XE] +79
Sport Package +210
Sunroof +238

QUEST 1993

After messing around with the Axxess and Nissan Van, Nissan finally gets it right on this joint project with Mercury. The Quest is a front-engine, front-wheel-drive minivan that is built alongside the Villager at the Ford plant in Avon Lake, Ohio. The Quest is powered by a 3.0-liter V6 engine that produces 150-horsepower. The Quest seats seven and has standard air conditioning, a tilt steering wheel, and a stereo with cassette. Antilock brakes are optional on the Quest.

Category P

Model Description	Trade-in TMV	Private TMV	Dealer TMV
2 Dr STD Cargo Van	3468	4155	5299
2 Dr GXE Pass. Van	4605	5516	7036
2 Dr XE Pass. Van	3648	4370	5574

OPTIONS FOR QUEST
7 Passenger Seating[Opt on XE] +98
AM/FM Compact Disc Player[Opt on GXE] +98
AM/FM Stereo Tape[Opt on GXE,Cargo] +91
Anti-Lock Brakes +140
Dual Air Conditioning[Opt on XE] +182
Leather Seats +306
Luggage Rack[Opt on XE] +77
Power Passenger Seat[Opt on GXE] +86
Power Sunroof +182
Power Windows[Opt on XE] +74

SENTRA 1993

A driver airbag is now standard on the GXE model. Base

Don't forget to refer to the Mileage Adjustment Table at the back of this book!

Model Description	Trade-in TMV	Private TMV	Dealer TMV

models ditch the Flintstone transmissions, gaining a standard five-speed manual or optional four-speed automatic in place of the archaic four-speed manual and three-speed automatic that was formerly available. All Sentras receive minor nose work that includes a redesigned grille, headlights and front fascia.

Model Description	Trade-in TMV	Private TMV	Dealer TMV
Category B			
2 Dr E Sdn	1411	1806	2465
4 Dr E Sdn	1621	2074	2831
4 Dr GXE Sdn	2175	2784	3799
2 Dr SE Sdn	1688	2161	2949
Category E			
2 Dr SE-R Sdn	2459	2961	3798
Category B			
2 Dr XE Sdn	1658	2122	2896
4 Dr XE Sdn	1725	2209	3014

OPTIONS FOR SENTRA
AM/FM Stereo Tape +84
Air Bag Restraint +91
Air Conditioning[Std on GXE] +208
Anti-Lock Brakes +140
Automatic 4-Speed Transmission +224
Power Steering[Opt on E] +77
Power Sunroof +154

1992 NISSAN

240SX — 1992

Nissan chops the top off the 240SX, adding a convertible to this versatile line of cars. Antilock brakes are made available on the LE model.

Model Description	Trade-in TMV	Private TMV	Dealer TMV
Category E			
2 Dr STD Cpe	2352	2860	3706
2 Dr STD Hbk	2372	2884	3738
2 Dr LE Hbk	3076	3741	4848
2 Dr SE Conv	3304	4017	5206
2 Dr SE Cpe	2373	2886	3740
2 Dr SE Hbk	2747	3340	4329

OPTIONS FOR 240SX
Air Conditioning[Std on LE] +249
Anti-Lock Brakes +125
Automatic 4-Speed Transmission[Std on Conv] +199
Flip-Up Sunroof +112
Leather Seats[Opt on SE] +186
Power Sunroof +224

300ZX — 1992

The driver airbag is moved to the standard equipment list this year. No other changes to this fine car.

Model Description	Trade-in TMV	Private TMV	Dealer TMV
Category F			
2 Dr 2+2 Cpe	6149	7327	9291
2 Dr STD Cpe	5903	7034	8919
2 Dr STD Turbo Cpe	7010	8353	10592

OPTIONS FOR 300ZX
Automatic 4-Speed Transmission[Opt on SE] +224
Bose Sound System[Std on 2+2, Turbo] +175
Glass Panel T-tops[Std on Turbo] +358
Leather Seats +274
Power Drivers Seat[Opt on STD Cpe] +75
Special Factory Paint +99

HALF TON — 1992

Model Description	Trade-in TMV	Private TMV	Dealer TMV
Category J			
2 Dr STD Std Cab LB	2203	2661	3426
2 Dr STD 4WD Std Cab SB	2500	3021	3889
2 Dr STD Std Cab SB	1905	2302	2963

OPTIONS FOR HALF TON
6 cyl 3.0 L Engine +137
AM/FM Stereo Tape +87
Air Conditioning +249
Automatic 4-Speed Transmission +249

KING CAB — 1992

Model Description	Trade-in TMV	Private TMV	Dealer TMV
Category J			
2 Dr STD 4WD Ext Cab SB	3036	3668	4722
2 Dr STD Ext Cab SB	2322	2805	3611
2 Dr SE 4WD Ext Cab SB	3512	4244	5463
2 Dr SE Ext Cab SB	2976	3596	4629

OPTIONS FOR KING CAB
AM/FM Stereo Tape +87
AM/FM Stereo/CD/Tape +116
Air Conditioning +249
Aluminum/Alloy Wheels +124
Automatic 4-Speed Transmission +249
Flip-Up Sunroof +87

MAXIMA — 1992

The Maxima gets an available driver airbag and a bigger engine for the SE. The SE's new engine is a DOHC, 190-horsepower V6. Unfortunately, the SE loses its standard sunroof. All Maximas receive a new grille and taillights for 1992.

Model Description	Trade-in TMV	Private TMV	Dealer TMV
Category D			
4 Dr GXE Sdn	3433	4062	5111
4 Dr SE Sdn	3466	4101	5160

OPTIONS FOR MAXIMA
Air Bag Restraint +94
Anti-Lock Brakes +124
Automatic 4-Speed Transmission[Opt on SE] +249
Bose Sound System[Std on SE] +199
Dual Power Seats +137
Leather Seats +280
Luxury Package +386
Power Sunroof +162

Don't forget to refer to the Mileage Adjustment Table at the back of this book!

NISSAN 92

Model Description	Trade-in TMV	Private TMV	Dealer TMV
NX			**1992**

The optional T-tops are now available on the 1600. The NX 2000 is available this year with a power package that adds power windows, power door locks and cruise control.

Model Description	Trade-in TMV	Private TMV	Dealer TMV
Category E			
2 Dr 1600 Cpe	1795	2183	2829
2 Dr 2000 Cpe	2042	2483	3218

OPTIONS FOR NX
Air Conditioning +186
Anti-Lock Brakes +150
Automatic 4-Speed Transmission +162
T-Tops (Solid/Colored) +224

Model Description	Trade-in TMV	Private TMV	Dealer TMV
PATHFINDER			**1992**

Safari Green paint is a new exterior color choice for this aging veteran of the sport-ute wars. No other changes are made.

Model Description	Trade-in TMV	Private TMV	Dealer TMV
Category M			
4 Dr SE 4WD Wgn	4559	5470	6988
4 Dr XE 4WD Wgn	3830	4595	5870
4 Dr XE Wgn	3526	4230	5404

OPTIONS FOR PATHFINDER
AM/FM Compact Disc Player[Opt on SE] +87
Air Conditioning[Opt on XE] +249
Automatic 4-Speed Transmission +249
Flip-Up Sunroof +112
Leather Seats +224
Premium Sound System[Opt on SE] +150

Model Description	Trade-in TMV	Private TMV	Dealer TMV
SENTRA			**1992**

A passenger's side vanity mirror and black body-side moldings are now standard on the two-door Sentra. The Value Option Package (includes air conditioning, cruise control, and a stereo) is extended to the SE Sentras this year.

Model Description	Trade-in TMV	Private TMV	Dealer TMV
Category B			
2 Dr E Sdn	1139	1502	2108
4 Dr E Sdn	1238	1633	2291
4 Dr GXE Sdn	1684	2221	3116
2 Dr SE Sdn	1436	1894	2658
Category E			
2 Dr SE-R Sdn	2073	2520	3266
Category B			
2 Dr XE Sdn	1337	1763	2474
4 Dr XE Sdn	1435	1893	2656

OPTIONS FOR SENTRA
AM/FM Stereo Tape +75
Air Conditioning[Std on GXE] +185
Anti-Lock Brakes +124
Automatic 4-Speed Transmission +199
Power Sunroof +137

Model Description	Trade-in TMV	Private TMV	Dealer TMV
STANZA			**1992**

A sporty SE model joins the roster of available Stanzas this year. Distinguished by a blacked-out grille, fog lights, rear spoiler, and leather-wrapped steering wheel and shift knob, the SE is attempting to draw in customers who want more from their compact family sedan.

Model Description	Trade-in TMV	Private TMV	Dealer TMV
Category C			
4 Dr GXE Sdn	1986	2662	3789
4 Dr SE Sdn	1938	2599	3699
4 Dr XE Sdn	1465	1964	2796

OPTIONS FOR STANZA
Air Conditioning[Opt on XE] +186
Anti-Lock Brakes +150
Automatic 4-Speed Transmission[Std on GXE] +162
Power Sunroof +175

Don't forget to refer to the Mileage Adjustment Table at the back of this book!

OLDSMOBILE 01

| Model Description | Trade-in TMV | Private TMV | Dealer TMV | Model Description | | Trade-in TMV | Private TMV | Dealer TMV |

OLDSMOBILE USA

1996 Oldsmobile Achieva

2001 OLDSMOBILE

ALERO 2001

A five-speed manual transmission is now available with the four-cylinder engine, an eight-speaker premium sound system is now standard on the GLS (optional on GL), a refined ABS system and 16-inch wheels are now standard on the GLS.

Category C

	Trade-in	Private	Dealer
2 Dr GL Cpe	11220	12150	13700
4 Dr GL Sdn	11220	12150	13700
2 Dr GLS Cpe	13268	14367	16200
4 Dr GLS Sdn	13104	14190	16000
2 Dr GX Cpe	10401	11263	12700
4 Dr GX Sdn	10483	11352	12800

OPTIONS FOR ALERO

6 cyl 3.4 L Engine[Opt on GL] +388
AM/FM Stereo/CD/Tape[Std on GLS] +118
Aluminum/Alloy Wheels[Std on GLS] +133
Power Moonroof +385
Rear Spoiler +133

AURORA 2001

Oldsmobile has redesigned the Aurora, plopping its flagship sedan onto a more rigid but still front-drive platform. Remaining stylish and contemporary, Aurora is more conventional in appearance but overall, remains an enticing package. 3.5 V6 and 4.0 V8 versions are available, each equipped with a full load of luxury accoutrements.

Category H

	Trade-in	Private	Dealer
4 Dr 3.5 Sdn	19290	20418	22300
4 Dr 4.0 Sdn	21885	23165	25300

OPTIONS FOR AURORA

Bose Sound System +296
Chrome Wheels +473
Compact Disc Changer +272
Heated Front Seats +204
Power Moonroof +648
Special Factory Paint +234

BRAVADA 2001

In the last model year before the long-awaited redesign, Oldsmobile adds a few goodies to distract us. Once a dealer-installed option, the OnStar communications system is now a factory-installed option. The Bravada's already comfortable seating is enhanced by new standard equipment such as an eight-way power passenger seat and memory control for the driver seat. A new option group includes the towing package, OnStar and white-letter tires. Previously available only with a package, the Platinum Edition (two-tone paint treatment) is now a stand-alone option. Those longing for a more understated green can now select Sage Green as an exterior color.

Category M

	Trade-in	Private	Dealer
4 Dr STD AWD Wgn	16699	17787	19600

OPTIONS FOR BRAVADA

Bose Sound System +293
Camper/Towing Package +124
Compact Disc Changer +234
Heated Front Seats +148
Power Moonroof +473

INTRIGUE 2001

The Intrigue receives only minor changes for 2001, including two new exterior colors and a standard air filtration system. The OnStar driver assistance system is now standard on GLS models while Precision Control System equipped models receive exterior "PCS" badging.

Category D

	Trade-in	Private	Dealer
4 Dr GL Sdn	14112	15157	16900
4 Dr GLS Sdn	15448	16592	18500
4 Dr GX Sdn	12943	13902	15500

OPTIONS FOR INTRIGUE

AM/FM Stereo/CD/Tape[Std on GLS] +266
Bose Sound System +296
Chrome Wheels +355
Compact Disc Changer +272
Heated Front Seats[Opt on GL] +175
Leather Seats[Opt on GL] +589
Power Drivers Seat[Std on GL] +180
Power Moonroof +443
Power Passenger Seat[Opt on GL] +148
Rear Spoiler +133

Don't forget to refer to the Mileage Adjustment Table at the back of this book!

Model Description	Trade-in TMV	Private TMV	Dealer TMV	Model Description	Trade-in TMV	Private TMV	Dealer TMV

SILHOUETTE 2001

Oldsmobile is giving minivan buyers good reason to shop the Silhouette for 2001, even if General Motors has issues a death sentence for the brand. All models get freshened styling, a touring suspension package with self-leveling suspension and an air inflation kit, fold-flat second-row captain's chairs, improved sound-deadening insulation and standard OnStar communications. Upscale GLS and Premiere models have two-tone leather seating, a rear parking aid, an integrated universal garage door opener, 16-inch wheels with an available chrome finish, power sliding driver door, in-dash CD changer, third-row captain's chairs, stowable third-row seat, wood-grain accents, eight-way power front seats, and dual-zone A/C as either optional or standard. The Premiere also gets an updated onboard entertainment system with a larger video screen.

Category P

4 Dr GL Pass. Van Ext	16684	17703	19400
4 Dr GLS Pass. Van Ext			
	18834	19984	21900
4 Dr Premiere Pass. Van Ext			
	20984	22265	24400

OPTIONS FOR SILHOUETTE

Aluminum/Alloy Wheels[Opt on GL] +175
Camper/Towing Package +133
Chrome Wheels +411
Compact Disc Changer +175
Heated Front Seats +115
Park Distance Control +115
Power Sliding Door[Opt on GL] +266
Rear Air Conditioning w/Rear Heater[Opt on GL] +266
Traction Control System[Opt on GL] +115

2000 OLDSMOBILE

ALERO 2000

A performance suspension is newly optional on GL models. The four-cylinder gets a composite intake manifold, while all models benefit from the addition of three rear-shelf anchors for child safety-seat restraints. If glitz is your thing, you can now opt for a new gold package on GL and GLS versions.

Category C

2 Dr GL Cpe	9362	10578	11700
4 Dr GL Sdn	9362	10578	11700
2 Dr GLS Cpe	11522	13019	14400
4 Dr GLS Sdn	11442	12928	14300
2 Dr GX Cpe	8482	9583	10600
4 Dr GX Sdn	8562	9674	10700

OPTIONS FOR ALERO

6 cyl 3.4 L Engine[Opt on GL] +452
AM/FM Stereo Tape[Std on GL] +131
AM/FM Stereo/CD/Tape[Std on GLS] +118
Aluminum/Alloy Wheels[Std on GLS] +236
Automatic 4-Speed Transmission[Std on GLS] +266
Cruise Control[Opt on GX] +133
Leather Seats[Opt on GL] +533
Power Drivers Seat[Opt on GL] +180
Power Moonroof +385
Rear Spoiler +133

BRAVADA 2000

GM's OnStar communications system is now available as a dealer-installed option, and a new cargo management system is expected sometime this year. Special color treatments include a new Jewelcoat Red option that features a deep red base color finished with a red-tinted final top coat in place of the usual clearcoat. There's also a Platinum Edition option that adds pewter-colored lower body cladding.

Category M

| 4 Dr STD AWD Wgn | 14181 | 15491 | 16700 |

OPTIONS FOR BRAVADA

Bose Sound System +293
Camper/Towing Package +124
Compact Disc Changer +234
Dual Power Seats +296
Gold Package +103
Heated Front Seats +148
Power Moonroof +443

INTRIGUE 2000

All Intrigues get restyled six-spoke 16-inch alloy wheels in either silver argent paint or chrome, and the option of adding Oldsmobile's Precision Control System (PCS). The full-function traction-control unit that's standard on the GL and GLS is now available on the GX. Retained accessory power becomes standard, and GL buyers can opt for the revised heated seats on the GLS.

Category D

4 Dr GL Sdn	11728	13014	14200
4 Dr GLS Sdn	12720	14113	15400
4 Dr GX Sdn	10737	11914	13000

OPTIONS FOR INTRIGUE

AM/FM Stereo/CD/Tape[Std on GLS] +266
Bose Sound System +251
Chrome Wheels +355
Compact Disc Changer +272
Dual Power Seats[Opt on GL] +360
Heated Front Seats[Opt on GL] +175
Leather Seats[Opt on GL] +589
Power Drivers Seat[Std on GL] +180
Power Moonroof +443
Rear Spoiler +133

Don't forget to refer to the Mileage Adjustment Table at the back of this book!

Model Description	Trade-in TMV	Private TMV	Dealer TMV

SILHOUETTE 2000

Olds has canned its 112-inch wheelbase GS, meaning all 2000 Silhouettes (GL, GLS and Premiere) are now extended-length (120-inch wheelbase), seven-passenger models. The traction-control system has been improved, and heated front seats are available in leather. There's also a redesigned instrument cluster with dual trip odometers, as well as upgraded radios, interior lighting and electrical system functions.

Category P

Model Description	Trade-in TMV	Private TMV	Dealer TMV
4 Dr GL Pass. Van Ext	13433	14768	16000
4 Dr GLS Pass. Van Ext			
	15112	16614	18000
4 Dr Premiere Pass. Van Ext			
	17211	18921	20500

OPTIONS FOR SILHOUETTE
AM/FM Stereo/CD/Tape[Opt on GL,GLS] +118
Aluminum/Alloy Wheels[Opt on GL] +175
Automatic Load Leveling[Opt on GL,GLS] +160
Camper/Towing Package +133
Captain Chairs (4)[Opt on GL] +175
Dual Air Conditioning[Opt on GL] +266
Dual Power Seats[Opt on GL] +340
Heated Front Seats +115
Keyless Entry System[Opt on GL] +139
Overhead Console[Opt on GL] +103
Power Sliding Door[Opt on GL] +266
Traction Control System[Opt on GL] +115

1999 OLDSMOBILE

ALERO 1999

Oldsmobile has dropped the slow-selling Achieva in favor of this new clean-sheet design patterned after the successful Intrigue midsize sedan. Available in both two- and four-door configurations with three well-equipped trim levels the Alero represents a quantum leap forward over previous small Olds models.

Category C

Model Description	Trade-in TMV	Private TMV	Dealer TMV
2 Dr GL Cpe	8183	9292	10400
4 Dr GL Sdn	8026	9113	10200
2 Dr GLS Cpe	9285	10542	11800
4 Dr GLS Sdn	9285	10542	11800
2 Dr GX Cpe	7239	8219	9200
4 Dr GX Sdn	7318	8309	9300

OPTIONS FOR ALERO
6 cyl 3.4 L Engine[Opt on GL] +351
AM/FM Stereo Tape[Opt on GX] +101
Aluminum/Alloy Wheels[Opt on GL] +183
Cruise Control[Opt on GX] +103
Leather Seats[Opt on GL] +413
Power Drivers Seat[Opt on GL] +140
Power Moonroof +298

Rear Spoiler +103

AURORA 1999

It's the status quo again in Auroraville, except this year Olds has added two more hydraulic engine mounts (for a total of three to better isolate engine vibrations. Other than that, a few new colors have been added (Galaxy Silver, Copper Nightmist and Dark Bronzemist).

Category H

Model Description	Trade-in TMV	Private TMV	Dealer TMV
4 Dr STD Sdn	15196	16798	18400

OPTIONS FOR AURORA
Chrome Wheels +367
Compact Disc Changer +211
Delco/Bose Stereo System +382
Heated Front Seats +135
Metallic Paint +182
Power Moonroof +503

BRAVADA 1999

In the wake of last year's restyle, Bravada sees feature refinements for '99. The driver-side airbag has been redesigned into a mini-module to permit a clearer view of the instruments, while the turn signal stalk now provides a flash-to-pass feature. A telltale warning lamp has been added to alert the driver when the tailgate lift glass is ajar. And an anti-theft alarm system is now standard. There's also an option package that combines a driver-side memory seat and a power passenger-side seat, as well as sound system upgrades across the board.

Category M

Model Description	Trade-in TMV	Private TMV	Dealer TMV
4 Dr STD AWD Wgn	11869	13135	14400

OPTIONS FOR BRAVADA
Bose Sound System +228
Camper/Towing Package +96
Compact Disc Changer +182
Dual Power Seats +230
Heated Front Seats +114
Power Moonroof +344

CUTLASS 1999

No changes to Oldsmobile's fresh-in-'97 bread-and-butter sedan, except for two new colors, Bronze Mist and Dark Cherry, and the addition of a Gold Package.

Category C

Model Description	Trade-in TMV	Private TMV	Dealer TMV
4 Dr GL Sdn	7711	8755	9800
4 Dr GLS Sdn	8419	9560	10700

OPTIONS FOR CUTLASS
Aluminum/Alloy Wheels[Opt on GL] +145
Power Drivers Seat[Opt on GL] +140
Power Moonroof +298
Power Windows[Opt on GL] +117

OLDSMOBILE 99

Model Description	Trade-in TMV	Private TMV	Dealer TMV

EIGHTY EIGHT 1999

Nothing, unless you count the fact the Eighty-Eight gets two new exterior colors, Champagne and Evergreen, and the LS model gets the option of white-stripe 16-inch tires. Oh, wait. Oldsmobile is celebrating the nameplate's golden anniversary with a special 50th Anniversary Edition Eighty Eight. It has 16-inch aluminum wheels fitted with 215/65SR blackwalls, a highly contented leather interior package and special badging finished in, what else? gold.

Category G

Model	Trade-in	Private	Dealer
4 Dr 50TH Anniversary Sdn	11450	12675	13900
4 Dr STD Sdn	9720	10760	11800
4 Dr LS Sdn	10544	11672	12800

OPTIONS FOR EIGHTY EIGHT
Aluminum/Alloy Wheels[Opt on STD] +158
Automatic Load Leveling[Std on LS] +114
Dual Power Seats[Std on LS] +168
Keyless Entry System[Opt on STD] +108
Leather Seats[Std on 50th Anniversary] +379
Power Moonroof +476

INTRIGUE 1999

Last year, Oldsmobile dumped the stodgy Cutlass Supreme for the Intrigue; a suave, sophisticated sporty sedan designed to take on the best of the imports. For '99 Olds is dumping the 3800 Series II V6 that powers the Intrigue for an all-new, 24-valve 3.5-liter twin cam V6. Until production of the 3.5 liter (a design based on the Aurora V8) can be ramped up to meet the Intrigue build schedule, the new 215-horsepower engine will come standard only in the new top-line GLS model, and optional in the base GX and mid-line GL series. Full function traction control is now available in models equipped with the new powerplant. Minor feature revisions, one new color and new badging rounds out the changes this year.

Category D

Model	Trade-in	Private	Dealer
4 Dr GL Sdn	9248	10374	11500
4 Dr GLS Sdn	10455	11727	13000
4 Dr GX Sdn	8766	9833	10900

OPTIONS FOR INTRIGUE
6 cyl 3.5 L Engine[Std on GLS] +182
AM/FM Stereo/CD/Tape[Std on GLS] +207
Bose Sound System +195
Chrome Wheels +276
Compact Disc Changer +211
Leather Seats[Std on GLS] +458
Power Drivers Seat[Opt on GX] +140
Power Moonroof +344
Rear Spoiler +103

LSS 1999

The LSS gets two new exterior colors (Champagne and Evergreen) for '99. Olds has also upgraded the standard radio to an AM/FM stereo cassette with CD player and seek-scan, auto tone control, digital clock and power antenna.

Category G

Model	Trade-in	Private	Dealer
4 Dr STD Sdn	9637	10669	11700
4 Dr STD Sprchgd Sedan	12768	14134	15500

OPTIONS FOR LSS
Chrome Wheels +276
Power Moonroof +476

SILHOUETTE 1999

Olds is headlining its Premiere Edition, a loaded-up model that debuted in mid-'98 with a standard integrated video entertainment system in back. But other news for 1999 includes a horsepower and torque increase for Silhouette's 3.4-liter V6, plus the addition of a theft-deterrent system and heated outside rearview mirrors as standard equipment. And if four new exterior colors (Sky, Ruby, Silvermist and Cypress) weren't enough, then consider the availability of a new Gold Package (but only if you must).

Category P

Model	Trade-in	Private	Dealer
4 Dr GL Pass. Van Ext	11938	13169	14400
4 Dr GLS Pass. Van Ext	13182	14541	15900
4 Dr GS Pass. Van	12353	13626	14900
4 Dr Premiere Pass. Van Ext	14342	15821	17300

OPTIONS FOR SILHOUETTE
8 Passenger Seating +129
Aluminum/Alloy Wheels[Opt on GL,GS] +135
Automatic Load Leveling[Std on Premiere] +124
Camper/Towing Package +103
Captain Chairs (4)[Opt on GL,GS] +135
Child Seats (2) +103
Dual Air Conditioning[Opt on GL] +207
Dual Power Seats[Opt on GL] +264
Keyless Entry System[Opt on GL] +108
Leather Seats[Std on GLS,Premiere] +437
Power Sliding Door[Opt on GL] +207

1998 OLDSMOBILE

ACHIEVA 1998

Oldsmobile limited sales of the Achieva to fleets for 1998, so if you're considering one, it's probably a former rental car.

Model Description	Trade-in TMV	Private TMV	Dealer TMV
Category C			
4 Dr SL Sdn	5168	5951	6800

AURORA 1998

Status quo in Auroraville, but second-generation airbags have been added.

Category H			
4 Dr STD Sdn	12464	13970	15600

OPTIONS FOR AURORA
Chrome Wheels +329
Compact Disc Changer +189
Delco/Bose Stereo System +341
Heated Front Seats +121
Metallic Paint +162
Power Moonroof +409

BRAVADA 1998

Front styling is revised, and new body-side cladding alters the Bravada's profile. Inside, dual second generation airbags are housed in a new dashboard. A heated driver's side exterior mirror is newly standard, while heated front seats have been added to the options roster. Battery rundown protection and a theft deterrent system are new standard features.

Category M			
4 Dr STD AWD Wgn	10515	11708	13000

OPTIONS FOR BRAVADA
Power Moonroof +308

CUTLASS 1998

No changes to Oldsmobile's fresh bread-and-butter sedan, except for the addition of second-generation airbags.

Category C			
4 Dr GL Sdn	6384	7351	8400
4 Dr GLS Sdn	6916	7964	9100

OPTIONS FOR CUTLASS
Aluminum/Alloy Wheels[Opt on GL] +130
Power Drivers Seat[Opt on GL] +124
Power Moonroof +244
Power Windows +104

EIGHTY EIGHT 1998

Virtually nothing, unless you find a new fuel cap, better access to rear seat belts, new ABS wheel-speed sensors and a couple of new colors intriguing. Second-generation airbags are standard.

Category G			
4 Dr STD Sdn	7937	8927	10000
4 Dr LS Sdn	8652	9731	10900

OPTIONS FOR EIGHTY EIGHT
Aluminum/Alloy Wheels[Std on LS] +135
Dual Power Seats +144

Leather Seats +409

INTRIGUE 1998

Oldsmobile dumps the stodgy Cutlass Supreme for the Intrigue: a suave, sophisticated, sporty sedan designed to take on the best of the imports. Too bad refinement issues exist. Second-generation airbags are standard equipment.

Category D			
4 Dr STD Sdn	7922	8919	10000
4 Dr GL Sdn	8318	9365	10500
4 Dr GLS Sdn	9110	10257	11500

OPTIONS FOR INTRIGUE
AM/FM Stereo/CD/Tape[Std on GLS] +185
Bose Sound System +174
Chrome Wheels +246
Compact Disc Changer +189
Leather Seats[Opt on GL] +409
Power Drivers Seat[Std on GL] +124
Power Moonroof +285

LSS 1998

New colors, improved ABS, a revised electrochromic rearview mirror, second-generation airbags and a redesigned fuel cap are the major changes for 1998.

Category G			
4 Dr STD Sdn	9525	10713	12000
4 Dr STD Sprchgd Sdn	10319	11606	13000

OPTIONS FOR LSS
Chrome Wheels +246
Power Moonroof +409

REGENCY 1998

Minor changes to this retirement village special for '98. The ABS is upgraded, it's easier to get at the rear seat belts, colors are revised and the "unleaded fuel only" label is removed from the inside of the fuel door.

Category H			
4 Dr STD Sdn	11106	12447	13900

OPTIONS FOR REGENCY
Power Moonroof +409

SILHOUETTE 1998

Side-impact airbags are standard for front seat passengers, and Oldsmobile is building more short-wheelbase vans with dual sliding doors. Front airbags get second generation technology, which results in slower deployment speeds. Midyear, a Premiere Edition debuted, loaded with standard features including a TV/VCP setup in back.

Category P			
4 Dr GL Pass. Van Ext	10329	11467	12700
4 Dr GLS Pass. Van Ext			

Don't forget to refer to the Mileage Adjustment Table at the back of this book!

Model Description	Trade-in TMV	Private TMV	Dealer TMV
	11549	12822	14200
4 Dr GS Pass. Van	10411	11557	12800
4 Dr Premiere Pass. Van Ext			
	13176	14627	16200

OPTIONS FOR SILHOUETTE
8 Passenger Seating[Opt on GL,GS] +97
Aluminum/Alloy Wheels[Opt on GL,GS] +117
Automatic Load Leveling[Opt on GL,GS] +103
Dual Air Conditioning[Opt on GL,GLS] +185
Dual Power Seats[Opt on GL] +236
Leather Seats +358
Power Sliding Door +162
Privacy Glass[Opt on GL] +100

1997 OLDSMOBILE

ACHIEVA 1997
Side-impact standards are met, and standard equipment lists are enhanced. Series II Coupe gets new alloy wheels, and the lineup has been simplified.
Category C

2 Dr SC Series II Cpe	4297	5018	5900
4 Dr SL Series II Sdn	4151	4848	5700

OPTIONS FOR ACHIEVA
5-Speed Transmission +191
6 cyl 3.1 L Engine +159
Power Drivers Seat +94
Power Moonroof +216
Power Windows +94

AURORA 1997
Larger front brakes, an in-dash CD player for the Bose sound system, a tilt-down right-hand exterior mirror for backing assistance, an integrated rearview mirror compass, and a three-channel garage door opener are added this year.
Category H

4 Dr STD Sdn	9640	11017	12700

OPTIONS FOR AURORA
Chrome Wheels +278
Compact Disc Changer +160
Delco/Bose Stereo System +289
Heated Front Seats +108
Metallic Paint +138
Power Moonroof +347

BRAVADA 1997
Bravada drops the split-tailgate arrangement at the rear in favor of a top-hinged liftgate with separately lifting glass. So, tailgate parties aren't as convenient, but loading cargo sure is easier. Also new to the options list is a power tilt and slide sunroof. Included with the hole in the roof are a mini-overhead console, a pop-up wind deflector, and a sun shade. Rear disc brakes replace the former drums, combining with the front discs to provide better stopping ability.
Category M

4 Dr STD AWD Wgn	8472	9565	10900

OPTIONS FOR BRAVADA
Power Moonroof +261

CUTLASS 1997
Oldsmobile retires the Ciera and introduces the Cutlass, based on the same platform as Chevy's new Malibu. Cutlass is more upscale that its Chevrolet counterpart, offering a slightly more powerful V-6 engine on all models, and a sunroof option, standard leather interior, and larger wheels on the GLS.
Category C

4 Dr STD Sdn	5098	5954	7000
4 Dr GLS Sdn	5753	6719	7900

OPTIONS FOR CUTLASS
Aluminum/Alloy Wheels[Opt on STD] +110
Power Drivers Seat[Opt on STD] +106
Power Moonroof +207

CUTLASS SUPREME 1997
Alloy wheels and a power trunk release are added to the standard equipment list, while coupes gain side-impact protection that meets federal safety standards. The 3.4-liter DOHC V-6 engine is dropped from the options list.
Category D

2 Dr SL Series III Cpe			
	5268	6183	7300
4 Dr SL Series III Sdn			
	5990	7030	8300

OPTIONS FOR CUTLASS SUPREME
Leather Seats +277
Power Drivers Seat +94
Power Moonroof +242

EIGHTY EIGHT 1997
Side-impact protection is upgraded to federal safety standards, interiors are improved, and new Oldsmobile logos adorn the body.
Category G

4 Dr STD Sdn	5968	6837	7900
4 Dr LS Sdn	6497	7443	8600

OPTIONS FOR EIGHTY EIGHT
Aluminum/Alloy Wheels[Std on LS] +113
Dual Power Seats +122
Leather Seats +179

Don't forget to refer to the Mileage Adjustment Table at the back of this book!

Model Description	Trade-in TMV	Private TMV	Dealer TMV

LSS 1997

Minor changes accompany Oldsmobile's euro-flavored sedan into 1997. The center console and shifter are new, and other interior upgrades have been made. New, more prominent badging has been added to the exterior. Finally, the final-drive ratio has been changed to 2.93:1 from 2.97:1.

Category G

Model	Trade-in	Private	Dealer
4 Dr STD Sdn	7479	8568	9900
4 Dr STD Sprchgd Sdn	7856	9001	10400

OPTIONS FOR LSS

Chrome Wheels +209
Power Moonroof +347

REGENCY 1997

New name for an old concept. Look closely...see the old Eighty Eight before 1996's restyle? Regency takes over where the Ninety Eight left off, satisfying traditional Oldsmobile buyers.

Category H

Model	Trade-in	Private	Dealer
4 Dr STD Sdn	8729	9976	11500

OPTIONS FOR REGENCY

Power Moonroof +347

SILHOUETTE 1997

Completely redesigned, the new Silhouette comes in several trim levels and two sizes, each with a healthy load of standard equipment.

Category P

Model	Trade-in	Private	Dealer
2 Dr STD Pass. Van	7003	7992	9200
2 Dr STD Pass. Van Ext	7536	8600	9900
2 Dr GL Pass. Van Ext	7992	9121	10500
2 Dr GLS Pass. Van Ext	8677	9903	11400

OPTIONS FOR SILHOUETTE

Aluminum/Alloy Wheels[Opt on GL] +99
Automatic Load Leveling[Opt on GL] +94
Dual Air Conditioning[Opt on GL] +156
Leather Seats +303
Power Moonroof +242

1996 OLDSMOBILE

ACHIEVA 1996

Substantial upgrades make the Achieva palatable for 1996. A new interior with dual airbags, standard air conditioning, a new base engine, daytime running lights, a theft-deterrent system and optional traction control make this Oldsmobile an excellent value in the compact class.

Category C

Model	Trade-in	Private	Dealer
2 Dr SC Series III Cpe	3205	3833	4700
4 Dr SL Series III Sdn	3137	3751	4600

OPTIONS FOR ACHIEVA

6 cyl 3.1 L Engine +143
Automatic 4-Speed Transmission +305
Power Moonroof +194

AURORA 1996

Daytime running lights are added, and looking through the backlight won't make your eyes water from distortions anymore. We knew it was only a matter of time before some goofball decided chrome wheels and a gold package would look great on the otherwise classy Aurora. The new Oldsmobile? What's that? When do we get the fake convertible roof, guys?

Category H

Model	Trade-in	Private	Dealer
4 Dr STD Sdn	7520	8646	10200

OPTIONS FOR AURORA

Chrome Wheels +250
Compact Disc Changer +144
Delco/Bose Stereo System +260
Metallic Paint +124
Power Moonroof +312
Special Factory Paint +124

BRAVADA 1996

Nice truck, but how many luxury SUV's do we really need? The only thing different about the Bravada to differentiate it from the Chevy Blazer and GMC Jimmy are the seats, front styling, trim — and the price tag.

Category M

Model	Trade-in	Private	Dealer
4 Dr STD AWD Wgn	7150	8221	9700

CIERA 1996

Bestseller prepares for retirement at the end of the year, receiving badge revisions, some additional standard equipment and an improved, optional V6 engine.

Category D

Model	Trade-in	Private	Dealer
4 Dr SL Wgn	3721	4426	5400
4 Dr SL Series II Sdn	3445	4098	5000

OPTIONS FOR CIERA

6 cyl 3.1 L Engine[Opt on Sdn] +254
Power Windows +106

CUTLASS SUPREME 1996

The convertible has been retired. The sedan and coupe enjoy their last year in production, receiving engine upgrades for 1996.

Category D

Model	Trade-in	Private	Dealer
2 Dr SL Series IV Cpe	4755	5656	6900

Don't forget to refer to the Mileage Adjustment Table at the back of this book!

Model Description	Trade-in TMV	Private TMV	Dealer TMV
4 Dr SL Series IV Sdn	4617	5492	6700

OPTIONS FOR CUTLASS SUPREME
6 cyl 3.4 L Engine +227
AM/FM Compact Disc Player +110
Leather Seats +249
Power Moonroof +218

EIGHTY EIGHT   1996

Royale designation dropped, and the Eighty Eight gets fresh Aurora-inspired styling front and rear. Standard equipment levels go up, and daytime running lights are added.
Category G

Model Description	Trade-in TMV	Private TMV	Dealer TMV
4 Dr STD Sdn	4849	5543	6500
4 Dr LS Sdn	5446	6225	7300
4 Dr LSS Sdn	6416	7333	8600
4 Dr LSS Sprchgd Sdn	6640	7589	8900

OPTIONS FOR EIGHTY EIGHT
AM/FM Stereo Tape[Opt on STD] +118
Aluminum/Alloy Wheels[Opt on STD] +104
Chrome Wheels +188
Leather Seats[Std on LSS] +162
Power Drivers Seat[Opt on STD] +110
Power Moonroof +324

NINETY-EIGHT   1996

Supercharged engine dropped from this model, and daytime running lamps have been added. Don't expect a 1997 Ninety Eight.
Category H

Model Description	Trade-in TMV	Private TMV	Dealer TMV
4 Dr Series II Sdn	7299	8392	9900

OPTIONS FOR NINETY-EIGHT
Power Moonroof +312

SILHOUETTE   1996

New 180-horsepower 3.4-liter V6 makes the Silhouette even better able to imitate Japan's bullet train.
Category P

Model Description	Trade-in TMV	Private TMV	Dealer TMV
2 Dr Series II Pass. Van	5757	6657	7900

OPTIONS FOR SILHOUETTE
Dual Air Conditioning +141
Leather Seats +272
Power Sliding Door +110

1995 OLDSMOBILE

ACHIEVA   1995

Fewer options and powertrains are available; SOHC and high-output Quad 4 engines are gone. Standard engine makes 150 horsepower this year, up from 115 in 1994. A V6 is optional. Air conditioning is standard.

Model Description	Trade-in TMV	Private TMV	Dealer TMV
Category C			
4 Dr S Sdn	2072	2495	3200
2 Dr S Series II Cpe	2201	2651	3400

OPTIONS FOR ACHIEVA
6 cyl 3.1 L Engine +120
Air Conditioning +185
Aluminum/Alloy Wheels +75
Automatic 3-Speed Transmission +145
Automatic 4-Speed Transmission +257
Power Moonroof +163

AURORA   1995

World-class V8 front-drive luxury sedan features cutting-edge styling, dual airbags, ABS and traction control.
Category H

Model Description	Trade-in TMV	Private TMV	Dealer TMV
4 Dr STD Sdn	5216	6035	7400

OPTIONS FOR AURORA
Compact Disc Changer +122
Delco/Bose Stereo System +219
Heated Front Seats +78
Power Moonroof +262

CIERA   1995

Offered in a single trim level this year. Rear defroster and cassette player are standard. Brake/transmission shift interlock is new.
Category D

Model Description	Trade-in TMV	Private TMV	Dealer TMV
4 Dr SL Sdn	2628	3142	4000
4 Dr SL Wgn	3022	3614	4600

OPTIONS FOR CIERA
6 cyl 3.1 L Engine[Opt on Sdn] +213
Aluminum/Alloy Wheels[Opt on Sdn] +78
Automatic 4-Speed Transmission[Opt on Sdn] +237
Power Drivers Seat +81
Power Windows +90

CUTLASS SUPREME   1995

Redesigned dashboard equipped with dual airbags debuts. Single trim level offered this year. Front bench seat is no longer available. Front seatbelts are mounted to door pillars instead of doors. Air conditioning, power windows, power locks, tilt steering, and cassette player are standard on all models.
Category D

Model Description	Trade-in TMV	Private TMV	Dealer TMV
2 Dr STD Conv	4664	5578	7100
2 Dr S Cpe	3088	3692	4700
4 Dr S Sdn	3088	3692	4700

OPTIONS FOR CUTLASS SUPREME
6 cyl 3.4 L Engine +191
AM/FM Compact Disc Player +93
Aluminum/Alloy Wheels[Std on Conv] +75
Leather Seats[Opt on S] +209
Power Moonroof +184

Don't forget to refer to the Mileage Adjustment Table at the back of this book!

Model Description	Trade-in TMV	Private TMV	Dealer TMV	Model Description	Trade-in TMV	Private TMV	Dealer TMV

EIGHTY-EIGHT ROYALE 1995

Engine upgraded to 3800 Series II status, and supercharged 3.8-liter V6 is a new option on LSS models. New on-board navigation system called Guidestar was a $1,995 option, originally available only in California.

Category G

Model Description	Trade-in TMV	Private TMV	Dealer TMV
4 Dr STD Sdn	3427	3980	4900
4 Dr LS Sdn	3847	4467	5500
4 Dr LSS Sdn	4197	4873	6000
4 Dr LSS Sprchgd Sdn	4546	5279	6500

OPTIONS FOR EIGHTY-EIGHT ROYALE
AM/FM Stereo/CD/Tape +152
Compact Disc Changer +172
Leather Seats[Std on LSS] +210
Traction Control System[Opt on LS,STD] +85

NINETY-EIGHT 1995

Engine upgraded to 3800 Series II status. Alloy wheels are standard. Flash-to-pass is new standard feature.

Category H

Model Description	Trade-in TMV	Private TMV	Dealer TMV
4 Dr STD Sdn	5287	6117	7500
4 Dr STD Sprchgd Sdn	5639	6524	8000

OPTIONS FOR NINETY-EIGHT
Power Moonroof +262

SILHOUETTE 1995

3.1-liter V6 engine dropped in favor of more powerful 3.8-liter V6.

Category P

Model Description	Trade-in TMV	Private TMV	Dealer TMV
2 Dr STD Pass. Van	4255	4947	6100

OPTIONS FOR SILHOUETTE
Dual Air Conditioning +119
Leather Seats +229
Power Sliding Door +93

1994 OLDSMOBILE

ACHIEVA 1994

Driver airbag debuts. 3.1-liter V6 replaces 3.3-liter V6 on options sheet. Hot-rod SCX gone from lineup.

Category C

Model Description	Trade-in TMV	Private TMV	Dealer TMV
2 Dr S Cpe	1436	1835	2500
4 Dr S Sdn	1494	1909	2600
2 Dr SC Cpe	1781	2276	3100
4 Dr SL Sdn	1839	2349	3200

OPTIONS FOR ACHIEVA
6 cyl 3.1 L Engine +97
Air Conditioning[Opt on S] +149
Astro Roof +181
Automatic 3-Speed Transmission +118

Automatic 4-Speed Transmission +208
Leather Seats +118
Power Moonroof +133
Power Sunroof +133

BRAVADA 1994

New Special Edition model has gold trim. Doors get guard beams. Shock absorbers are softened for a better ride.

Category M

Model Description	Trade-in TMV	Private TMV	Dealer TMV
4 Dr STD AWD Wgn	4748	5592	7000
4 Dr Special Edition AWD Wgn	4408	5193	6500

OPTIONS FOR BRAVADA
Leather Seats +144

CUTLASS CIERA 1994

Driver airbag and ABS standard for all models. Four-cylinder engine back in base models, producing 120 horsepower. A 3.1-liter V6 replaces last year's 3.3-liter V6. Variable-assist steering is a new option on sedans. SL replaced by Special Edition models.

Category D

Model Description	Trade-in TMV	Private TMV	Dealer TMV
4 Dr S Sdn	1820	2275	3034
4 Dr S Wgn	1944	2430	3241
4 Dr Special Edition Sdn	1620	2025	2700
4 Dr Special Edition Wgn	1919	2400	3200

OPTIONS FOR CUTLASS CIERA
6 cyl 3.1 L Engine[Opt on Sdn] +102
Automatic 4-Speed Transmission[Std on S Sdn] +171
Leather Seats +144
Option Package 2 +224
Third Seat +74

CUTLASS SUPREME 1994

Driver airbag added and ABS is made standard on all models. International Series dropped. Special Editions are on sale, carrying one-price stickers and a healthy load of standard equipment. 3.1-liter V6 makes 20 more horsepower. 3.4-liter V6 makes 15 more horsepower. New standard features include tilt steering, intermittent wipers, Pass-Key theft deterrent system, and rear defogger.

Category D

Model Description	Trade-in TMV	Private TMV	Dealer TMV
2 Dr STD Conv	3359	4199	5600
2 Dr S Cpe	2126	2658	3544
4 Dr S Sdn	2159	2700	3600
2 Dr Special Edition Cpe	2017	2522	3363
4 Dr Special Edition Sdn	2073	2592	3456

Model Description	Trade-in TMV	Private TMV	Dealer TMV

OPTIONS FOR CUTLASS SUPREME
6 cyl 3.4 L Engine +155
AM/FM Compact Disc Player +75
Leather Seats[Std on STD] +170
Power Moonroof +148
Power Sunroof +149

EIGHTY-EIGHT ROYALE 1994

Passenger airbag is housed in a new dashboard featuring more compact layout and new four-spoke steering wheel. Grille is body-color. Headlamps and turn signals are restyled. Traction control system can now reduce engine power as well as apply brakes to slipping wheel. New Special Edition model is available.
Category G

Model Description	Trade-in TMV	Private TMV	Dealer TMV
4 Dr STD Sdn	2640	3150	4000
4 Dr LS Sdn	3035	3622	4600
4 Dr LSS Sdn	2969	3543	4500
4 Dr Special Edition Sdn	2442	2913	3700

OPTIONS FOR EIGHTY-EIGHT ROYALE
AM/FM Stereo/CD/Tape +123
Dual Power Seats +111
Leather Seats[Std on LS Special Edit.] +171

NINETY-EIGHT 1994

Passenger airbag is housed in a new dashboard featuring more compact layout. Touring Sedan is dropped, and a Special Edition is added. Supercharged engine is now available on the Elite, and it gains horsepower and torque. Traction control system can now reduce engine power as well as apply brakes to slipping wheel. There is an additional inch of seat travel. The grille and headlamps are restyled.
Category H

Model Description	Trade-in TMV	Private TMV	Dealer TMV
4 Dr STD Sdn	3461	4075	5100
4 Dr Elite Sdn	3936	4635	5800
4 Dr Elite Sprchgd Sdn	4139	4874	6100
4 Dr Special Edition Sdn	3325	3916	4900

OPTIONS FOR NINETY-EIGHT
Astro Roof +272
Leather Seats[Opt on Elite,STD] +170
Power Moonroof +212

SILHOUETTE 1994

Driver airbag added to standard equipment list. Traction control and integrated child seats are new options. Power sliding side door debuts. New Special Edition model is available.
Category P

Model Description	Trade-in TMV	Private TMV	Dealer TMV
2 Dr STD Pass. Van	3187	3792	4800
2 Dr Special Edition Pass. Van	3121	3713	4700

OPTIONS FOR SILHOUETTE
6 cyl 3.8 L Engine[Opt on STD] +171
Automatic 4-Speed Transmission[Opt on STD] +171
Dual Air Conditioning +96
Leather Seats +186
Option Package 2 +159

1993 OLDSMOBILE

ACHIEVA 1993

All four-cylinder engines lose five horsepower, thanks to emissions regulations. They also get new engine mounts and other revisions aimed at making them smoother and quieter. Battery rundown protection is new standard feature.
Category C

Model Description	Trade-in TMV	Private TMV	Dealer TMV
2 Dr S Cpe	865	1178	1700
4 Dr S Sdn	916	1248	1800
2 Dr SL Cpe	1170	1593	2298
4 Dr SL Sdn	1172	1596	2302

OPTIONS FOR ACHIEVA
4 cyl 2.3 L Quad 4 Engine +104
6 cyl 3.3 L Engine +83
Air Conditioning +122
Automatic 3-Speed Transmission[Opt on S] +95

BRAVADA 1993

Electronic shift controls added to transmission. Gold Package is new option. Driver's seat gets six-way power adjustment. Both front seats gain power lumbar adjusters. Sun visors get extender panels, and a new overhead console with compass is added.
Category M

Model Description	Trade-in TMV	Private TMV	Dealer TMV
4 Dr STD AWD Wgn	3070	3719	4800

OPTIONS FOR BRAVADA
Leather Seats +117

CUTLASS CIERA 1993

Driver airbag is standard on SL; optional on S. Four-cylinder engine dropped in favor of standard V6 power. Air conditioning also makes the standard equipment list. SL sedans get a trunk cargo net; SL wagons get a cargo cover. Leather is new option on base model.
Category D

Model Description	Trade-in TMV	Private TMV	Dealer TMV
4 Dr S Sdn	1228	1592	2200
4 Dr S Cruiser Wgn	1340	1737	2400
4 Dr SL Sdn	1619	2099	2900
4 Dr SL Cruiser Wgn	1674	2171	3000

OPTIONS FOR CUTLASS CIERA
6 cyl 3.3 L Engine[Opt on S] +117

Don't forget to refer to the Mileage Adjustment Table at the back of this book!

OLDSMOBILE 93-92

Model Description	Trade-in TMV	Private TMV	Dealer TMV

Air Bag Restraint[Opt on S] +87
Automatic 4-Speed Transmission[Std on SL Cruiser] +139
Leather Seats +117

CUTLASS SUPREME 1993

3.4-liter, twin-cam engine now available in convertible, but can't be ordered with five-speed transmission anymore. International Series gets new alloys, and all models are equipped with automatic power door locks.

Category D

	Trade-in	Private	Dealer
2 Dr STD Conv	2063	2675	3696
2 Dr International Cpe			
	2067	2681	3704
4 Dr International Sdn			
	2121	2751	3800
2 Dr S Cpe	1505	1951	2696
4 Dr S Sdn	1509	1957	2704
2 Dr Special Cpe	1449	1879	2596
4 Dr Special Sdn	1453	1885	2604

OPTIONS FOR CUTLASS SUPREME
6 cyl 3.4 L Engine[Opt on Conv,S] +126
Anti-Lock Brakes[Opt on S,STD] +122
Automatic 4-Speed Transmission[Opt on S] +139
Leather Seats +139
Option Package 3 +183
Power Sunroof +122

EIGHTY-EIGHT ROYALE 1993

ABS is standard on all models. Engine makes more torque. LSS gets new alloy wheels and variable-assist power steering.

Category G

	Trade-in	Private	Dealer
4 Dr STD Sdn	1926	2366	3100
4 Dr LS Sdn	2174	2671	3500

OPTIONS FOR EIGHTY-EIGHT ROYALE
LSS Package +329
Leather Seats +139
Option Package C1 +239

NINETY-EIGHT 1993

Base V6 makes more torque. Touring Sedan gets body-color grille and headlight trim. Base model loses standard cassette player.

Category H

	Trade-in	Private	Dealer
4 Dr Regency Sdn	2396	2922	3800
4 Dr Regency Elite Sdn			
	2774	3384	4400
4 Dr Regency Touring Sdn			
	3026	3692	4800
4 Dr Regency Touring Sprchgd Sdn			
	3216	3922	5100
4 Dr Special Sdn	2207	2692	3500

OPTIONS FOR NINETY-EIGHT
Leather Seats[Opt on Regency,Regency Elite] +139
Power Sunroof +122

SILHOUETTE 1993

Subtle restyle includes front and rear fascias, as well as alloy wheels. Optional V6 makes more power.

Category P

	Trade-in	Private	Dealer
2 Dr STD Pass. Van	2556	3135	4100

OPTIONS FOR SILHOUETTE
6 cyl 3.8 L Engine +139
Automatic 4-Speed Transmission +139
Dual Air Conditioning +79
Leather Seats +151
Sunroof +113

1992 OLDSMOBILE

ACHIEVA 1992

Cutlass Calais replacement. SCX coupe is hot-rod of the bunch, featuring a 190-horsepower Quad 4 engine. ABS is standard. Computer Command Ride is optional on SL and SC, and allows driver to select one of three suspension settings.

Category C

	Trade-in	Private	Dealer
2 Dr S Cpe	535	784	1200
4 Dr S Sdn	580	850	1300
2 Dr SCX Cpe	847	1242	1900
2 Dr SL Cpe	713	1046	1600
4 Dr SL Sdn	803	1177	1800

OPTIONS FOR ACHIEVA
4 cyl 2.3 L Quad 4 Engine[Opt on S] +92
Air Conditioning +107
Automatic 3-Speed Transmission[Opt on S] +84

BRAVADA 1992

CD player and outside spare tire carrier are new options. New speedometer placed in dashboard. Midyear, a 200-horsepower V6 is added.

Category M

	Trade-in	Private	Dealer
4 Dr STD AWD Wgn	2747	3442	4600

OPTIONS FOR BRAVADA
Leather Seats +103

CUSTOM CRUISER 1992

A more powerful 5.7-liter V8 is newly optional.

Category G

	Trade-in	Private	Dealer
4 Dr STD Wgn	1720	2275	3200

OPTIONS FOR CUSTOM CRUISER
Dual Power Seats +76
Leather Seats +103

Don't forget to refer to the Mileage Adjustment Table at the back of this book!

EDMUNDS® USED CARS & TRUCKS

Model Description	Trade-in TMV	Private TMV	Dealer TMV

CUTLASS CIERA 1992

Coupe and base sedan are given the axe. Automatic door locks made standard.

Category D

Model	Trade-in	Private	Dealer
4 Dr S Sdn	842	1164	1700
4 Dr S Cruiser Wgn	941	1301	1900
4 Dr SL Sdn	1238	1711	2500
4 Dr SL Cruiser Wgn	1288	1780	2600

OPTIONS FOR CUTLASS CIERA
6 cyl 3.3 L Engine[Opt on S] +103
Air Conditioning[Opt on S] +107
Automatic 4-Speed Transmission[Std on SL Cruiser] +122
Leather Seats[Opt on SL Sdn] +103

CUTLASS SUPREME 1992

Styling is updated front and rear. Four-cylinder engine dropped. International Series models get 3.4-liter twin-cam engine, heads-up instrument display and ABS standard. Sedans get folding rear seatback. Alloys are standard on SL models.

Category D

Model	Trade-in	Private	Dealer
2 Dr STD Conv	1882	2601	3800
2 Dr International Cpe	1733	2396	3500
4 Dr International Sdn	1832	2533	3700
2 Dr S Cpe	1088	1504	2197
4 Dr S Sdn	1091	1508	2203

OPTIONS FOR CUTLASS SUPREME
6 cyl 3.4 L Engine +110
Anti-Lock Brakes[Opt on S, STD] +107
Astro Roof +149
Automatic 4-Speed Transmission[Std on STD] +122
Leather Seats +121

EIGHTY-EIGHT ROYALE 1992

Redesigned and based on Ninety-Eight platform. Available only as a sedan; coupe dropped from lineup. Driver airbag is standard. LS models have standard ABS; this feature is optional on base models. 3.8-liter V6 makes 170 horsepower. Passenger and cargo volume are both up. Traction control is optional on LS models. Midyear, an LSS model debuted with FE3 suspension, alloy wheels and bucket seats.

Category G

Model	Trade-in	Private	Dealer
4 Dr STD Sdn	1397	1848	2600
4 Dr LS Sdn	1558	2062	2900

OPTIONS FOR EIGHTY-EIGHT ROYALE
AM/FM Stereo/CD/Tape[Opt on LS] +88
Anti-Lock Brakes[Opt on STD] +107
Leather Seats +122
Option Package 2 +191

NINETY-EIGHT 1992

Supercharged engine is optional on Touring Sedan. Traction control is optional on any model.

Category H

Model	Trade-in	Private	Dealer
4 Dr Regency Sdn	2117	2636	3500
4 Dr Regency Elite Sdn	2238	2786	3700
4 Dr Regency Touring Sdn	2722	3389	4500
4 Dr Regency Touring Sprchgd Sdn	2843	3539	4700

OPTIONS FOR NINETY-EIGHT
Astro Roof +195
Leather Seats[Std on Regency Touring] +121

SILHOUETTE 1992

Newly optional 165-horsepower, 3.8-liter V6 is highly recommended. ABS is made standard. Larger wheels and tires are standard. New options include sunroof, remote keyless entry and rear climate controls.

Category P

Model	Trade-in	Private	Dealer
2 Dr STD Pass. Van	1926	2479	3400

OPTIONS FOR SILHOUETTE
6 cyl 3.8 L Engine +122
Automatic 4-Speed Transmission +122
Leather Seats +133

TORONADO 1992

Trofeo gets firmer suspension and bigger wheels and tires.

Category H

Model	Trade-in	Private	Dealer
2 Dr STD Cpe	2238	2786	3700
2 Dr Trofeo Cpe	2480	3088	4100

OPTIONS FOR TORONADO
Astro Roof +195
Leather Seats[Opt on STD] +130

PLYMOUTH 01-00

Model Description	Trade-in TMV	Private TMV	Dealer TMV	Model Description	Trade-in TMV	Private TMV	Dealer TMV

PLYMOUTH   USA

1995 Plymouth Neon

2001 PLYMOUTH

NEON   2001

Side-impact airbags and leather seats are now available in Plymouth's economy car. A center shoulder belt for the rear seat and an internal emergency trunk release further improve this Plymouth's safety consciousness. Both a Sun and Sound or a Value/Fun option group is available this year, each of which includes a sunroof. New interior and exterior options for the Neon pump some life into this fading brand, but if you've got a hankering for the Plymouth nameplate, act fast; as of 2002 Plymouth will be closing shop and subsuming its identity to the gods of DaimlerChrysler.

Category B

	Trade-in	Private	Dealer
4 Dr LX Highline Sdn	8855	9659	11000
4 Dr Highline Sdn	8453	9220	10500

OPTIONS FOR NEON
Air Conditioning +613
Aluminum/Alloy Wheels +218
Anti-Lock Brakes +365
Automatic 3-Speed Transmission +368
Compact Disc Changer +230
Cruise Control +138
Leather Seats +405
Power Moonroof +364
Power Windows +157
Side Air Bag Restraints +215

PROWLER   2001

Get your Plymouth Prowler while you can. After 2001 it goes away and becomes the Chrysler Prowler. Sure, it will be the identical car, but that powerful Plymouth Prowler alliteration will be gone forever! Oh, yeah, you can get these in copper metallic and a silver/black combination this year. New adjustable damper shocks are offered as standard equipment.

Category F

	Trade-in	Private	Dealer
2 Dr STD Conv	36941	38463	41000

2000 PLYMOUTH

BREEZE   2000

New colors and child-seat tether anchorages update the Breeze for 2000.

Category C

	Trade-in	Private	Dealer
4 Dr STD Sdn	8000	9040	10000

OPTIONS FOR BREEZE
4 cyl 2.4 L Engine +276
AM/FM Compact Disc Player +215
AM/FM Stereo Tape +110
Aluminum/Alloy Wheels +420
Anti-Lock Brakes +346
Automatic 4-Speed Transmission +644
Compact Disc Changer +230
Cruise Control +107
Heated Power Mirrors +107
Keyless Entry System +104
Power Door Locks +113
Power Drivers Seat +147
Power Sunroof +426
Power Windows +153
Special Factory Paint +123

NEON   2000

Side-impact airbags and leather seats are now available in Plymouth's economy car. If you've got a hankering for the Plymouth nameplate, act fast; as of 2002 Plymouth will be closing shop and subsuming its identity to the gods of DaimlerChrysler.

Category B

	Trade-in	Private	Dealer
4 Dr Highline Sdn	6397	7231	8000
4 Dr LX Sedan Sdn	7197	8134	9000

OPTIONS FOR NEON
AM/FM Compact Disc Player +242
Air Conditioning[Std on LX Sdn] +613
Alarm System[Std on LX Sdn] +107
Aluminum/Alloy Wheels +251
Anti-Lock Brakes +515
Automatic 3-Speed Transmission +368
Compact Disc Changer +306
Cruise Control +132
Keyless Entry System[Opt on Highline] +101
Power Door Locks[Opt on Highline] +101
Power Moonroof +364
Power Windows[Std on LX Sdn] +157
Traction Control System +123

Model Description	Trade-in TMV	Private TMV	Dealer TMV

PROWLER 2000

Prowler Purple is discontinued, replaced by Prowler Silver for 2000. Chrome wheels are standard, as is a new leather shift boot and speed-sensitive volume for the stereo.

Category F

2 Dr STD Conv	32522	34851	37000

OPTIONS FOR PROWLER
Tutone Paint +215
Woodward Edition Group +919

VOYAGER 2000

Four new colors and a new T-Plus option package that includes a V6 and power goodies for about $20,000 are new this year.

Category P

2 Dr STD Pass. Van	9237	10258	11200
4 Dr Grand Pass. Van	11217	12456	13600
4 Dr Grand SE Pass. Van	11959	13280	14500
4 Dr SE Pass. Van	11794	13097	14300

OPTIONS FOR VOYAGER
6 cyl 3.0 L Engine[Opt on STD] +491
6 cyl 3.3 L Engine +595
6 cyl 3.3 L Flex Fuel Engine[Opt on STD] +595
7 Passenger Seating[Opt on STD] +230
AM/FM Stereo/CD/Tape +383
Air Conditioning[Opt on STD] +257
Alarm System +107
Aluminum/Alloy Wheels +254
Anti-Lock Brakes[Std on SE] +346
Automatic 4-Speed Transmission[Opt on STD] +123
Automatic Load Leveling +177
Camper/Towing Package +257
Captain Chairs (4) +411
Child Seats (2) +137
Cruise Control[Std on SE] +110
Dual Air Conditioning +521
Heated Power Mirrors[Std on SE] +110
Infinity Sound System +441
Lighted Entry System +104
Luggage Rack +120
Power Door Locks[Std on SE] +137
Power Drivers Seat +187
Power Windows[Std on SE] +162
Sliding Driver Side Door[Opt on STD] +364
Sunscreen Glass[Std on SE] +276
Tilt Steering Wheel[Std on SE] +107

1999 PLYMOUTH

BREEZE 1999

Power windows, locks and mirrors, along with floor mats and a driver's seat height adjuster are now standard on the Breeze. In addition, the suspension has been revised for a more pleasant ride. What more could you ask? Oh yeah: the Noise, Vibration and Harshness levels have also been reduced.

Category C

4 Dr STD Sdn	6675	7538	8400
4 Dr Expresso Sdn	6755	7627	8500

OPTIONS FOR BREEZE
4 cyl 2.4 L Engine +231
AM/FM Compact Disc Player +115
Aluminum/Alloy Wheels +352
Anti-Lock Brakes +291
Automatic 4-Speed Transmission +539
Compact Disc Changer +193
Power Drivers Seat[Opt on STD] +123
Power Sunroof +357
Power Windows +129
Special Factory Paint +103

NEON 1999

The Neon is now based on the same platform as the Viper. No, just kidding. Nothing's changed for '99.

Category B

2 Dr Competition Cpe	5282	6091	6900
4 Dr Competition Sdn	5435	6267	7100
2 Dr Expresso Cpe	5817	6709	7600
4 Dr Expresso Sdn	5971	6885	7800
2 Dr Highline Cpe	5511	6356	7200
4 Dr Highline Sdn	5588	6444	7300

OPTIONS FOR NEON
AM/FM Compact Disc Player +203
AM/FM Stereo Tape +133
Air Conditioning[Std on Expresso] +513
Aluminum/Alloy Wheels +211
Anti-Lock Brakes +432
Automatic 3-Speed Transmission +308
Compact Disc Changer +257
Competition Package +513
Cruise Control +111
Power Moonroof +307
Power Windows +131

PROWLER 1999

A brand-new 3.5-liter engine under the hood creates performance more fitting a hot rod. Also new for '99 is one more color option: Prowler Yellow.

Category F

2 Dr STD Conv	28786	30893	33000

OPTIONS FOR PROWLER
Chrome Wheels +513
Special Factory Paint +513

VOYAGER 1999

SE trim levels get body-colored door and liftgate

Don't forget to refer to the Mileage Adjustment Table at the back of this book!

Model Description	Trade-in TMV	Private TMV	Dealer TMV

handles, as well as a body-colored front grille. All models add a cargo net between the front seats, and the new exterior color this year is Light Cypress Green.

Category P

Model Description	Trade-in TMV	Private TMV	Dealer TMV
2 Dr STD Pass. Van	7994	8847	9700
4 Dr Grand Pass. Van	9725	10762	11800
4 Dr Expresso Pass. Van			
	10549	11675	12800
4 Dr Grand Expresso Pass. Van			
	11044	12222	13400
4 Dr Grand SE Pass. Van			
	10496	11615	12735
4 Dr SE Pass. Van	10273	11369	12465

OPTIONS FOR VOYAGER

6 cyl 3.0 L Engine[Opt on STD] +411
6 cyl 3.3 L Engine +498
6 cyl 3.8 L Engine +172
7 Passenger Seating[Opt on STD] +193
AM/FM Compact Disc Player +167
AM/FM Stereo/CD/Tape[Opt on SE] +321
Air Conditioning[Opt on Grand,STD] +216
Aluminum/Alloy Wheels +136
Anti-Lock Brakes[Opt on Grand,STD] +291
Automatic 4-Speed Transmission[Opt on STD] +103
Automatic Load Leveling +149
Camper/Towing Package +216
Captain Chairs (4) +345
Child Seats (2) +115
Dual Air Conditioning +437
Infinity Sound System +371
Luggage Rack +100
Power Door Locks +115
Power Drivers Seat +156
Power Windows +109
Sliding Driver Side Door[Opt on STD] +307
Special Factory Paint +103
Sunscreen Glass[Std on Expresso,Grand Expresso] +231

1998 PLYMOUTH

BREEZE   1998

Availability of a 2.4-liter engine brings150 horsepower and 167 foot-pounds of torque, and that's just what the Breeze needs to live up to its name. Both engines can meet California emissions regulations, and new engine mounts helps make them quieter. An Expresso package adds some aesthetic changes, a power sunroof is now optional and there are six new colors to choose from.

Category C

Model Description	Trade-in TMV	Private TMV	Dealer TMV
4 Dr STD Sdn	5773	6602	7500
4 Dr Expresso Sdn	5892	6738	7655

OPTIONS FOR BREEZE

4 cyl 2.4 L Engine +196

AM/FM Compact Disc Player +98
Aluminum/Alloy Wheels +299
Anti-Lock Brakes +246
Automatic 4-Speed Transmission +458
Compact Disc Changer +164
Power Sunroof +304
Power Windows +109

NEON   1998

California and other emission-regulating states get an LEV (Low Emission Vehicle) engine calibration. Also changed this year are ABS, a new ignition key lock and the addition of four new colors.

Category B

Model Description	Trade-in TMV	Private TMV	Dealer TMV
2 Dr Competition Cpe	4163	4901	5700
4 Dr Competition Sdn	4363	5137	5974
2 Dr Expresso Cpe	4675	5503	6400
4 Dr Expresso Sdn	4529	5331	6200
2 Dr Highline Cpe	4374	5149	5988
4 Dr Highline Sdn	4410	5192	6038
4 Dr Style Sdn	5186	6105	7100

OPTIONS FOR NEON

AM/FM Compact Disc Player +162
AM/FM Stereo Tape +114
Air Conditioning[Std on Expresso, Style] +437
Aluminum/Alloy Wheels[Std on Style] +155
Anti-Lock Brakes +261
Automatic 3-Speed Transmission +262
Compact Disc Changer +218
Competition Package +437
Power Moonroof +261
Power Windows +112

VOYAGER   1998

Expresso Decor Package, four new exterior colors, and "next generation" depowered airbags sum up the changes this year.

Category P

Model Description	Trade-in TMV	Private TMV	Dealer TMV
2 Dr STD Pass. Van	6549	7389	8300
4 Dr Grand Pass. Van	7338	8280	9300
4 Dr Expresso Pass. Van			
	8127	9170	10300
4 Dr Grand Expresso Pass. Van			
	8600	9704	10900
4 Dr Grand SE Pass. Van			
	8364	9437	10600
4 Dr SE Pass. Van	7811	8814	9900

OPTIONS FOR VOYAGER

6 cyl 3.0 L Engine[Opt on STD] +336
7 Passenger Seating[Opt on STD] +124
AM/FM Compact Disc Player +142
AM/FM Stereo/CD/Tape[Opt on Grand SE,SE] +273
Air Conditioning[Opt on Grand,Grand SE,SE,STD] +183
Aluminum/Alloy Wheels +115

Don't forget to refer to the Mileage Adjustment Table at the back of this book!

Model Description	Trade-in TMV	Private TMV	Dealer TMV
Anti-Lock Brakes[Opt on Grand,STD] +246			
Automatic 4-Speed Transmission[Opt on Grand,STD] +109			
Automatic Load Leveling +127			
Captain Chairs (4) +293			
Child Seats (2) +98			
Dual Air Conditioning +372			
Dual Power Seats +264			
Infinity Sound System +173			
Power Door Locks +98			
Power Windows +115			
Sliding Driver Side Door[Opt on STD] +261			
Sunscreen Glass[Opt on Grand,Grand SE,SE,STD] +196			

1997 PLYMOUTH

BREEZE — 1997

Plymouth is inching the Breeze up-market in both price and content. This year sees a fairly sizable price hike and the addition of luxury options such as an in-dash CD changer. Changes to the standard equipment list bring a nicer center console, improved basic stereos, and increased flow rear seat heater ducts.

Category C

	Trade-in	Private	Dealer
4 Dr STD Sdn	4735	5529	6500

OPTIONS FOR BREEZE

4 cyl 2.4 L Engine +183
AM/FM Compact Disc Player +142
Aluminum/Alloy Wheels +279
Anti-Lock Brakes +230
Automatic 4-Speed Transmission +347
Compact Disc Changer +153
Power Windows +102

NEON — 1997

1997 Neons are made quieter with the addition of a structural oil pan. Other changes include new optional radios, a new seat fabric, new wheels and wheel covers, and a few new paint colors.

Category B

	Trade-in	Private	Dealer
2 Dr STD Cpe	3051	3613	4300
4 Dr STD Sdn	3264	3865	4600
2 Dr Expresso Cpe	3768	4462	5310
4 Dr Expresso Sdn	3903	4622	5500
2 Dr Highline Cpe	3477	4117	4900
4 Dr Highline Sdn	3754	4445	5290

OPTIONS FOR NEON

AM/FM Compact Disc Player +116
AM/FM Stereo Tape +106
Air Conditioning[Opt on STD] +408
Aluminum/Alloy Wheels +145
Anti-Lock Brakes +230
Automatic 3-Speed Transmission +244
Compact Disc Changer +204
Competition Package +230
Power Moonroof +243

Power Windows +104

PROWLER — 1997

Plymouth brings a Hot Rod style show car to market. Although the Prowler's V6 kicks out a respectable 214 horsepower, it comes only with a 4-speed automatic transmission. More show than go, some enthusiasts will lament the Prowler's lack of a V8 and a 4-speed manual gearbox.

Category F

	Trade-in	Private	Dealer
2 Dr STD Conv	25526	27989	31000

VOYAGER — 1997

For 1997, the Plymouth minivans receive a cornucopia of changes. This year brings new wheel covers, improved antilock braking systems, an accident response system that unlocks the doors and turns on the interior lights if the air bags deploy, better radios, a quieter interior, and more optional equipment for Base and SE models.

Category P

	Trade-in	Private	Dealer
2 Dr Grand Pass. Van	6127	7015	8100
2 Dr STD Pass. Van	5370	6149	7100
2 Dr Grand SE Pass. Van	6656	7621	8800
2 Dr SE Pass. Van	6278	7188	8300

OPTIONS FOR VOYAGER

6 cyl 3.0 L Engine +106
6 cyl 3.3 L Engine +515
7 Passenger Seating +116
AM/FM Stereo/CD/Tape +255
Air Conditioning +172
Aluminum/Alloy Wheels +169
Anti-Lock Brakes[Std on SE] +230
Automatic 3-Speed Transmission[Opt on SE] +213
Automatic 4-Speed Transmission[Opt on Grand,STD] +102
Automatic Load Leveling +119
Captain Chairs (4) +255
Dual Air Conditioning +347
Power Drivers Seat +124
Power Windows[Opt on SE] +108
Premium Sound System[Opt on SE] +294
Sliding Driver Side Door +243
Sunscreen Glass +183

1996 PLYMOUTH

BREEZE — 1996

The Breeze is introduced this year as Chrysler Corporation's bargain-basement midsize sedan. Nicely equipped with air conditioning and a decent stereo, the Breeze has a surprising amount of interior room.

Don't forget to refer to the Mileage Adjustment Table at the back of this book!

EDMUNDS® USED CARS & TRUCKS   www.edmunds.com   447

Model Description	Trade-in TMV	Private TMV	Dealer TMV
Category C			
4 Dr STD Sdn	3069	3670	4500

OPTIONS FOR BREEZE

AM/FM Compact Disc Player +123
AM/FM Stereo/CD/Tape +104
Air Conditioning +176
Anti-Lock Brakes +199
Automatic 4-Speed Transmission +299
Compact Disc Changer +132
Power Sunroof +245

NEON   1996

Antilock brakes are optional across the line, and base models get more standard equipment for 1996. A value-packed Expresso package is aimed at twenty-something first-time buyers. A base coupe is newly available, and all Neons are supposedly quieter than last year. A power moonroof joins the options list, and a remote keyless entry system with panic alarm is available.

Category B			
2 Dr STD Cpe	2447	2973	3700
4 Dr STD Sdn	2513	3053	3800
2 Dr Highline Cpe	2579	3134	3900
4 Dr Highline Sdn	2788	3388	4216
2 Dr Sport Cpe	2899	3523	4384
4 Dr Sport Sdn	2910	3536	4400

OPTIONS FOR NEON

AM/FM Compact Disc Player +169
Air Conditioning +352
Aluminum/Alloy Wheels +125
Anti-Lock Brakes +199
Automatic 3-Speed Transmission +212
Competition Package +199
Power Moonroof +210

VOYAGER   1996

Chrysler's stylists and engineers have achieved what many thought was impossible: they substantially improved upon their original formula in every way. Interior comfort is top-notch, and the left-hand passenger door is an industry first.

Category P			
2 Dr Grand Pass. Van	4461	5192	6200
2 Dr STD Pass. Van	4317	5024	6000
2 Dr Grand SE Pass. Van			
	5109	5945	7100
2 Dr SE Pass. Van	4821	5610	6700

OPTIONS FOR VOYAGER

6 cyl 3.0 L Engine[Std on Grand] +271
6 cyl 3.3 L Engine +314
7 Passenger Seating[Opt on STD] +123
AM/FM Stereo/CD/Tape +220
Air Conditioning +148

Aluminum/Alloy Wheels +146
Anti-Lock Brakes[Opt on Grand, STD] +199
Captain Chairs (4) +263
Dual Air Conditioning +299
Premium Sound System[Opt on SE] +254
Sliding Driver Side Door +176
Sunscreen Glass +158

1995 PLYMOUTH

ACCLAIM   1995

The Acclaim is into the home stretch of its career.

Category C			
4 Dr STD Sdn	1992	2407	3100

OPTIONS FOR ACCLAIM

6 cyl 3.0 L Engine +183

NEON   1995

The all-new Neon is introduced as Plymouth's entry in the compact car class. Roomy, cute and quick are three of the best adjectives we can find for this car. Unfortunately, Chrysler Corporation is still grappling with reliability and noise issues. The Neon is available in coupe and sedan bodystyles in three trim-levels. Safety equipment includes standard dual airbags, optional antilock brakes and an optional integrated child seat.

Category B			
4 Dr STD Sdn	1723	2127	2800
2 Dr Highline Cpe	1908	2355	3100
4 Dr Highline Sdn	2154	2659	3500
2 Dr Sport Cpe	2339	2887	3800
4 Dr Sport Sdn	2277	2811	3700

OPTIONS FOR NEON

AM/FM Compact Disc Player +113
Air Conditioning +270
Aluminum/Alloy Wheels[Opt on Highline Cpe] +96
Anti-Lock Brakes[Std on Sport] +152
Automatic 3-Speed Transmission +162
Leather Seats +121

VOYAGER   1995

A 3.3-liter V6 natural gas engine is available this year. Plymouth introduces a snazzy Rallye package for those trying to disguise the fact that they are driving a minivan.

Category P			
2 Dr Grand Pass. Van	3432	4014	4984
2 Dr STD Pass. Van	3030	3544	4400
2 Dr Grand LE AWD Pass. Van			
	4545	5316	6600
2 Dr Grand LE Pass. Van			
	4132	4832	6000
2 Dr LE Pass. Van	4041	4726	5868

Don't forget to refer to the Mileage Adjustment Table at the back of this book!

PLYMOUTH 95-94

Model Description	Trade-in TMV	Private TMV	Dealer TMV
2 Dr Grand SE AWD Pass. Van	3947	4617	5732
2 Dr Grand SE Pass. Van	3650	4269	5300
2 Dr SE Pass. Van	3454	4040	5016

OPTIONS FOR VOYAGER
6 cyl 3.8 L Engine[Opt on LE] +90
7 Passenger Seating[Opt on STD] +77
AM/FM Compact Disc Player +88
AM/FM Stereo/CD/Tape +168
Air Conditioning[Std on LE] +113
Anti-Lock Brakes[Std on LE,4WD] +152
Captain Chairs (4) +168
Dual Air Conditioning +229
Infinity Sound System +106
Leather Seats +214
Power Drivers Seat +82
Sunscreen Glass +121

1994 PLYMOUTH

ACCLAIM　1994

The Acclaim gains a motorized passenger seatbelt. The flexible-fuel model is now available to retail customers.
Category C

Model	Trade-in	Private	Dealer
4 Dr STD Sdn	1084	1390	1900

OPTIONS FOR ACCLAIM
6 cyl 3.0 L Engine +164
Air Conditioning +171
Anti-Lock Brakes +158
Automatic 3-Speed Transmission +134
Automatic 4-Speed Transmission +194

COLT　1994

A driver's airbag is now standard on the Colt. CFC-free air conditioning optional.
Category B

Model	Trade-in	Private	Dealer
2 Dr STD Sdn	1147	1500	2087
4 Dr STD 4WD Wgn	2112	2761	3842
4 Dr STD Sdn	1381	1805	2512
4 Dr STD Wgn	1869	2443	3400
2 Dr GL Sdn	1319	1725	2400
4 Dr GL Sdn	1429	1868	2600
4 Dr SE Wgn	2066	2700	3758

OPTIONS FOR COLT
4 cyl 1.8 L Engine[Opt on GL] +84
Air Conditioning +171
Anti-Lock Brakes +146
Automatic 3-Speed Transmission +134
Automatic 4-Speed Transmission +194

LASER　1994

The final year for the Laser brings automatic-locking retractors for rear seats, making them more compatible for child seats.
Category E

Model	Trade-in	Private	Dealer
2 Dr STD Hbk	1572	1995	2700
2 Dr RS Hbk	1689	2143	2900
2 Dr RS Turbo AWD Hbk	2154	2734	3700
2 Dr RS Turbo Hbk	1980	2512	3400

OPTIONS FOR LASER
AM/FM Compact Disc Player +85
Air Conditioning +171
Anti-Lock Brakes +146
Automatic 4-Speed Transmission +183
Sunroof +122

SUNDANCE　1994

The Sundance gets a motorized passenger shoulder belt and CFC-free air conditioning.
Category B

Model	Trade-in	Private	Dealer
2 Dr STD Hbk	1209	1581	2200
4 Dr STD Hbk	1264	1653	2300
2 Dr Duster Hbk	1319	1725	2400
4 Dr Duster Hbk	1539	2012	2800

OPTIONS FOR SUNDANCE
6 cyl 3.0 L Engine +164
Air Conditioning +171
Anti-Lock Brakes +146
Automatic 3-Speed Transmission +134
Automatic 4-Speed Transmission +183
Premium Sound System +85
Sunroof +122

VOYAGER　1994

New safety features include a passenger airbag and side-impact door beams that meet federal 1997 passenger car standards. Other changes include a new dashboard, optional integrated child seats and new body moldings.
Category P

Model	Trade-in	Private	Dealer
2 Dr Grand Pass. Van	2811	3388	4350
2 Dr STD Pass. Van	2262	2726	3500
2 Dr Grand LE AWD Pass. Van	3813	4595	5900
2 Dr Grand LE Pass. Van	3296	3972	5100
2 Dr LE Pass. Van	3102	3739	4800
2 Dr Grand SE AWD Pass. Van	3167	3817	4900
2 Dr Grand SE Pass. Van	2973	3583	4600
2 Dr SE Pass. Van	2650	3193	4100

OPTIONS FOR VOYAGER
Air Conditioning[Opt on Grand,SE,STD] +102

Don't forget to refer to the Mileage Adjustment Table at the back of this book!

Model Description	Trade-in TMV	Private TMV	Dealer TMV	Model Description	Trade-in TMV	Private TMV	Dealer TMV

Anti-Lock Brakes[Std on 4WD] +138
Captain Chairs (4) +152
Dual Air Bag Restraints +134
Dual Air Conditioning +206
Infinity Sound System +96
Leather Seats +193
Sunscreen Glass +109

1993 PLYMOUTH

ACCLAIM — 1993

The Acclaim is now available to fleet purchasers as a flexible-fuel vehicle, able to run on a fuel mix that is 85 percent methanol.

Category C

4 Dr STD Sdn	909	1243	1800

OPTIONS FOR ACCLAIM
6 cyl 3.0 L Engine +138
AM/FM Compact Disc Player +87
Air Conditioning +143
Anti-Lock Brakes +133
Automatic 3-Speed Transmission +113
Automatic 4-Speed Transmission +164

COLT — 1993

The Colt is redesigned for 1993. The hatchback is dropped in favor of two- and four-door notchback styles and the GL model is equipped with a 113-horsepower engine that is optional on the base.

Category B

2 Dr STD Sdn	848	1139	1624
4 Dr STD 4WD Wgn	1410	1894	2700
4 Dr STD Sdn	969	1301	1855
4 Dr STD Wgn	1149	1543	2200
2 Dr GL Sdn	954	1281	1827
4 Dr GL Sdn	1030	1384	1973
4 Dr SE Wgn	1201	1613	2300

OPTIONS FOR COLT
Air Conditioning +143
Anti-Lock Brakes +123
Automatic 3-Speed Transmission[Opt on GL] +113
Automatic 4-Speed Transmission +164

LASER — 1993

The all-wheel drive Laser is now available with an automatic transmission. New alloy wheels are introduced to all but the base Laser. A gold package is available for those of you wanting the ever-popular midlife crisis look.

Category E

2 Dr STD Hbk	1049	1409	2010
2 Dr RS Hbk	1143	1535	2190
2 Dr RS Turbo AWD Hbk	1774	2384	3400
2 Dr RS Turbo Hbk	1565	2103	3000

OPTIONS FOR LASER
AM/FM Stereo/CD/Tape +118
Air Conditioning +143
Anti-Lock Brakes +123
Automatic 4-Speed Transmission +153

SUNDANCE — 1993

The Sundance is available with antilock brakes in 1993.

Category B

2 Dr STD Hbk	914	1227	1750
4 Dr STD Hbk	992	1333	1900
2 Dr Duster Hbk	1097	1473	2100
4 Dr Duster Hbk	1149	1543	2200

OPTIONS FOR SUNDANCE
6 cyl 3.0 L Engine +138
Air Conditioning +143
Anti-Lock Brakes +123
Automatic 3-Speed Transmission +113
Automatic 4-Speed Transmission +153

VOYAGER — 1993

Front shoulder belts are now height adjustable on the Voyager. All-wheel drive models gain new exterior and interior options.

Category P

2 Dr Grand Pass. Van	1969	2468	3300
2 Dr STD Pass. Van	1790	2244	3000
2 Dr Grand LE AWD Pass. Van			
	2745	3440	4600
2 Dr Grand LE Pass. Van			
	2506	3141	4200
2 Dr LE AWD Pass. Van	2625	3291	4400
2 Dr LE Pass. Van	2458	3081	4120
2 Dr Grand SE AWD Pass. Van			
	2208	2767	3700
2 Dr Grand SE Pass. Van			
	2029	2543	3400
2 Dr SE AWD Pass. Van	2434	3052	4080
2 Dr SE Pass. Van	1850	2319	3100

OPTIONS FOR VOYAGER
Anti-Lock Brakes +116
Captain Chairs (4) +128
Dual Air Conditioning +174
Leather Seats[Opt on LE] +163

1992 PLYMOUTH

ACCLAIM — 1992

Plymouth trims the fat, offering the Acclaim in only one trim level for 1992. The remaining Acclaim can be had with four-cylinder or V6 power.

Don't forget to refer to the Mileage Adjustment Table at the back of this book!

PLYMOUTH 92

Model Description	Trade-in TMV	Private TMV	Dealer TMV
Category C			
4 Dr STD Sdn	721	1051	1600

OPTIONS FOR ACCLAIM
6 cyl 3.0 L Engine +123
Air Conditioning +128
Anti-Lock Brakes +119
Automatic 3-Speed Transmission +101
Automatic 4-Speed Transmission +146
Premium Sound System +91

COLT   1992

Factory options list is pared in a cost-savings measure. A 113-horsepower engine is standard and a 118-horsepower engine is optional.

Model Description	Trade-in TMV	Private TMV	Dealer TMV
Category B			
2 Dr STD Hbk	730	1019	1500
4 Dr STD 4WD Wgn	1070	1494	2200
4 Dr STD Wgn	876	1222	1800
2 Dr GL Hbk	779	1087	1600
4 Dr SE Wgn	973	1358	2000

OPTIONS FOR COLT
Air Conditioning +128
Anti-Lock Brakes +109
Automatic 3-Speed Transmission +101
Automatic 4-Speed Transmission +146

LASER   1992

The Laser gains all-wheel drive as an option that greatly improves handling. Front and rear styling changes include headlights, taillamps, and a new rear spoiler on turbo models.

Model Description	Trade-in TMV	Private TMV	Dealer TMV
Category E			
2 Dr STD Hbk	811	1145	1700
2 Dr RS Hbk	955	1347	2000
2 Dr RS Turbo AWD Hbk	1241	1751	2600
2 Dr RS Turbo Hbk	1098	1549	2300

OPTIONS FOR LASER
Air Conditioning +128
Anti-Lock Brakes +109
Automatic 4-Speed Transmission +137

SUNDANCE   1992

The RS trim level is dropped due to poor sales. No other changes to the Sundance.

Model Description	Trade-in TMV	Private TMV	Dealer TMV
Category B			
2 Dr America Hbk	770	1074	1582
4 Dr America Hbk	787	1099	1618
2 Dr Duster Hbk	859	1199	1766
4 Dr Duster Hbk	924	1290	1900
2 Dr Highline Hbk	828	1155	1701
4 Dr Highline Hbk	832	1161	1710

OPTIONS FOR SUNDANCE
6 cyl 3.0 L Engine +123
Air Conditioning +128
Automatic 3-Speed Transmission +101
Automatic 4-Speed Transmission +137
Sunroof +91

VOYAGER   1992

The driver airbag first seen on the 1991 model becomes standard in 1992. An integrated child seat is available for those with toddlers.

Model Description	Trade-in TMV	Private TMV	Dealer TMV
Category P			
2 Dr Grand Pass. Van	1538	2011	2800
2 Dr STD Pass. Van	1167	1526	2125
2 Dr Grand LE AWD Pass. Van			
	2142	2801	3900
2 Dr Grand LE Pass. Van			
	1945	2544	3542
2 Dr LE AWD Pass. Van	1977	2586	3600
2 Dr LE Pass. Van	1897	2481	3455
2 Dr LX AWD Pass. Van	2032	2657	3700
2 Dr LX Pass. Van	1940	2537	3532
2 Dr Grand SE AWD Pass. Van			
	1881	2461	3426
2 Dr Grand SE Pass. Van			
	1732	2265	3154
2 Dr SE AWD Pass. Van	1783	2331	3246
2 Dr SE Pass. Van	1249	1634	2275

OPTIONS FOR VOYAGER
Anti-Lock Brakes +103
Dual Air Conditioning +155
Leather Seats +145
Premium Sound System +131
Sunscreen Glass +82

Don't forget to refer to the Mileage Adjustment Table at the back of this book!

PONTIAC 01

Model Description	Trade-in TMV	Private TMV	Dealer TMV	Model Description	Trade-in TMV	Private TMV	Dealer TMV

PONTIAC USA

1996 Pontiac Firebird Coupe

2001 PONTIAC

AZTEK 2001

Pontiac brings forth a new so-called Sport Recreation Vehicle, blending attributes of a station wagon, minivan, SUV and Pumbaa the talking pig (from "The Lion King") into an interesting, if not different, offering.

Category L

	Trade-in	Private	Dealer
4 Dr GT AWD Wgn	15427	16504	18300
4 Dr GT Wgn	13994	14971	16600
4 Dr STD AWD Wgn	13825	14791	16400
4 Dr STD Wgn	12308	13167	14600

OPTIONS FOR AZTEK

AM/FM Stereo/CD/Tape +208
Camper/Towing Package +233
Captain Chairs (4) +192
Compact Disc Changer +189
Heated Front Seats +157
Power Drivers Seat +154
Power Moonroof +416
Privacy Glass +160

BONNEVILLE 2001

Because Pontiac's flagship sedan, built on the Cadillac Seville's platform with rakish styling and high-tech goodies such as an integrated chassis control system, was all-new last year, 2001 sees little change. Heated seats are available on the SE and SLE, and Ivory White is a new color for the year. OnStar telematics with a 1-year membership is optional on the SE but comes standard with the SLE and SSEi.

Category G

	Trade-in	Private	Dealer
4 Dr SE Sdn	15743	16664	18200
4 Dr SLE Sdn	17041	18038	19700
4 Dr SSEi Sprchgd Sdn	20760	21975	24000

OPTIONS FOR BONNEVILLE

17 Inch Chrome Wheels +381
AM/FM Stereo/CD/Tape[Std on SSEi] +127
Compact Disc Changer +381
Dual Air Conditioning[Opt on SE] +320
Heated Front Seats +189
Leather Seats[Std on SSEi] +544
OnStar Telematic System +304
Power Moonroof +691
Power Passenger Seat[Std on SSEi] +211

FIREBIRD 2001

For 2001, V8-equipped Formula and Trans Am receive five more horsepower and five more ft-lb of torque, new exterior and interior colors join the palette, and the Ram Air Formula is dropped from the lineup.

Category E

	Trade-in	Private	Dealer
2 Dr Formula Cpe	15390	16369	18000
2 Dr Trans Am Conv	21033	22371	24600
2 Dr Trans Am Cpe	17357	18460	20300
2 Dr STD Conv	16331	17369	19100
2 Dr STD Cpe	11714	12458	13700

OPTIONS FOR FIREBIRD

Automatic 4-Speed Transmission[Opt on STD] +521
Chrome Wheels +381
Compact Disc Changer +381
Glass Panel i-Tops[Std on Trans Am] +637
Leather Seats[Std on Trans Am] +368
Limited Slip Differential +192
Monsoon Sound System[Opt on STD Cpe] +211
Power Drivers Seat[Std on Trans Am,Conv] +173
Power Windows[Opt on Base Cpe] +189
Ram Air Performance Package +2015
T-Tops (Solid/Colored) +636
Traction Control System +160

GRAND AM 2001

For 2001, the Grand Am gets audio improvements, a wheel upgrade and revised paint choices.

Category C

	Trade-in	Private	Dealer
2 Dr GT Cpe	12890	13944	15700
4 Dr GT Sdn	13054	14121	15900
2 Dr GT1 Cpe	13547	14654	16500
4 Dr GT1 Sdn	13711	14832	16700
2 Dr SE Cpe	9524	10302	11600
4 Dr SE Sdn	9606	10391	11700
2 Dr SE1 Cpe	10673	11546	13000
4 Dr SE1 Sdn	11001	11901	13400

OPTIONS FOR GRAND AM

6 cyl 3.4 L Engine +419
AM/FM Stereo/CD/Tape +125
Aluminum/Alloy Wheels[Opt on SE,SE1 Cpe] +313
Automatic 4-Speed Transmission[Opt on SE,SE1] +528

Don't forget to refer to the Mileage Adjustment Table at the back of this book!

Model Description	Trade-in TMV	Private TMV	Dealer TMV
Chrome Wheels +413			
Cruise Control[Opt on SE] +150			
Leather Seats +304			
Monsoon Sound System[Opt on SE1] +217			
Power Moonroof[Std on GT1] +381			
Rear Spoiler[Std on GT,GT1] +125			

GRAND PRIX   2001

The Grand Prix receives only minor changes for 2001 including a Special Edition appearance package on GT and GTP models and optional 16-inch, three-spoke aluminum wheels. The OnStar system is now available on GTP models while SE models receive a slight front-end revision.

Category D

Model Description	Trade-in TMV	Private TMV	Dealer TMV
2 Dr GT Cpe	13360	14350	16000
4 Dr GT Sdn	13611	14619	16300
2 Dr GTP Sprchgd Cpe	14921	16026	17869
4 Dr GTP Sprchgd Sdn	14972	16082	17931
4 Dr SE Sdn	12191	13094	14600

OPTIONS FOR GRAND PRIX

Aluminum/Alloy Wheels[Opt on SE] +189
Automatic Dimming Mirror +119
Bose Sound System +237
Chrome Wheels +413
Cruise Control[Opt on SE] +150
Leather Seats +304
OnStar Telematic System +304
Power Drivers Seat[Std on GTP] +195
Power Moonroof +365
Rear Spoiler[Opt on SE] +125
Trip Computer[Opt on GT] +127

MONTANA   2001

Updated styling and more feature content top the list of changes to the Montana for 2001, but perhaps most importantly, GM has figured out how to provide buyers with a third-row seat that flips and folds to create a flat load floor in extended-length models. New standard features include OnStar communications, power windows, a CD player and remote keyless entry. A rear parking aid sensor, power driver's side sliding door and a six-disc in-dash CD changer are new options. When you buy the available TV/VCP setup, you get a larger screen for 2001.

Category P

Model Description	Trade-in TMV	Private TMV	Dealer TMV
4 Dr Convenience Pass. Van Ext			
	18318	19511	21500
4 Dr Vision Pass. Van Ext			
	20192	21508	23700
4 Dr Sport Pass. Van	17466	18604	20500
4 Dr Sport Pass. Van Ext			
	18659	19874	21900
4 Dr Value Pass. Van	15166	16154	17800

Model Description	Trade-in TMV	Private TMV	Dealer TMV
4 Dr STD Pass. Van	16188	17243	19000
4 Dr STD Pass. Van Ext			
	17040	18150	20000

OPTIONS FOR MONTANA

Aluminum/Alloy Wheels +179
Automatic Load Leveling +127
Compact Disc Changer +189
Heated Front Seats +125
Leather Seats +752
Park Distance Control +125
Rear Air Conditioning w/Rear Heater +288

SUNFIRE   2001

A standard rear spoiler and a new exterior color are the only new additions to the Sunfire for 2001. The GT convertible is no longer available, leaving the sedan and coupe versions as the only available body styles.

Category B

Model Description	Trade-in TMV	Private TMV	Dealer TMV
2 Dr GT Cpe	10063	10977	12500
2 Dr SE Cpe	8292	9045	10300
4 Dr SE Sdn	8533	9308	10600

OPTIONS FOR SUNFIRE

4 cyl 2.4 L Engine[Std on GT] +288
AM/FM Compact Disc Player +205
Aluminum/Alloy Wheels[Opt on SE] +189
Automatic 3-Speed Transmission +384
Automatic 4-Speed Transmission +134
Cruise Control +150
Monsoon Sound System +125
Power Door Locks +141
Power Moonroof +381
Power Windows +185
Traction Control System +125

2000 PONTIAC

BONNEVILLE   2000

Brand-new from the ground up, Pontiac's flagship sedan moves onto a stiffer platform with rakish styling and high-tech goodies such as an integrated chassis control system.

Category G

Model Description	Trade-in TMV	Private TMV	Dealer TMV
4 Dr SE Sdn	13059	14224	15300
4 Dr SLE Sdn	14339	15619	16800
4 Dr SSEi Sprchgd Sdn	18095	19709	21200

OPTIONS FOR BONNEVILLE

AM/FM Compact Disc Player +205
AM/FM Stereo/CD/Tape[Std on SSEi] +127
Alarm System[Opt on SE] +122
Aluminum/Alloy Wheels[Opt on SE] +208
Chrome Wheels +381
Compact Disc Changer +381
Dual Power Seats[Std on SSEi] +391
Heated Front Seats +96

Don't forget to refer to the Mileage Adjustment Table at the back of this book!

Model Description	Trade-in TMV	Private TMV	Dealer TMV
Keyless Entry System[Opt on SE] +96			
Leather Seats[Std on SSEi] +544			
Power Drivers Seat[Opt on SE] +195			
Power Moonroof +627			
Traction Control System[Std on SSEi] +111			

FIREBIRD 2000

New wheels, exterior and interior colors, and engine revisions for improved emissions and better throttle response on manual-transmission-equipped cars top the list of Firebird changes for 2000.

Category E	Trade-in TMV	Private TMV	Dealer TMV
2 Dr STD Conv	14768	16189	17500
2 Dr STD Cpe	10802	11841	12800
2 Dr Formula Cpe	13924	15263	16500
2 Dr SLP Firehawk Cpe	20084	22016	23800
2 Dr Trans Am Conv	19747	21646	23400
2 Dr Trans Am Cpe	15780	17299	18700

OPTIONS FOR FIREBIRD

17 Inch Chrome Wheels[Opt on Trans Am] +511
8 cyl 5.7 L w/Ram Air Engine +959
AM/FM Stereo Tape[Opt on Trans Am] +161
AM/FM Stereo/CD/Tape +211
Alarm System[Std on Trans Am,Conv] +111
Automatic 4-Speed Transmission[Opt on STD] +522
Bilstein Suspension System +161
Bucket Seats[Opt on Trans Am] +99
Chrome Wheels +381
Compact Disc Changer +381
Glass Panel T-tops[Std on Trans Am] +637
High Torque Differential +192
Keyless Entry System[Opt on Cpe] +96
Leather Seats[Std on Trans Am] +368
Lighted Entry System[Std on Trans Am,Conv] +109
Limited Slip Differential +192
Monsoon Sound System[Opt on STD Cpe] +211
Performance Differential +313
Power Door Locks[Opt on Base Cpe] +143
Power Drivers Seat[Std on Trans Am,Conv] +173
Power Windows[Opt on Base Cpe] +189
Ram Air Performance Package +959
Rear Spoiler[Opt on SLP Firehawk Cpe] +127
Sport Appearance Package +665
Traction Control System +161

GRAND AM 2000

In the wake of its 1999 redesign, Grand Am gets engine improvements, interior upgrades (including a revamped center console), new exterior appearance packages and revised paint choices.

Category C	Trade-in TMV	Private TMV	Dealer TMV
2 Dr GT Cpe	11600	12952	14200
4 Dr GT Sdn	11764	13135	14400
2 Dr GT1 Cpe	12254	13682	15000
4 Dr GT1 Sdn	12499	13955	15300

Model Description	Trade-in TMV	Private TMV	Dealer TMV
2 Dr SE Cpe	8333	9304	10200
4 Dr SE Sdn	8414	9395	10300
2 Dr SE1 Cpe	9231	10307	11300
4 Dr SE1 Sdn	9558	10672	11700
2 Dr SE2 Cpe	10947	12222	13400
4 Dr SE2 Sdn	11682	13043	14300

OPTIONS FOR GRAND AM

6 cyl 3.4 L Engine +419
AM/FM Compact Disc Player[Std on GT1,SE2] +134
AM/FM Stereo/CD/Tape +125
Aluminum/Alloy Wheels[Opt on SE,SE1 Cpe] +192
Automatic 4-Speed Transmission[Opt on SE,SE1] +502
Chrome Wheels +413
Cruise Control[Opt on SE] +150
Keyless Entry System +96
Leather Seats +304
Power Drivers Seat[Opt on GT,SE2] +169
Power Moonroof[Std on GT1] +381
Rear Spoiler[Std on GT,GT1] +125

GRAND PRIX 2000

Improvements to the base 3.1-liter V6 net a gain of 15 horsepower, as well as improved durability, reduced noise and lower emissions. A limited run (2000 coupes) of Daytona Pace Car replicas will be built, featuring unique exterior and interior details. Also new are a revised antitheft system, five-spoke silver-painted wheels, three new exterior colors and Cyclone cloth upholstery.

Category D	Trade-in TMV	Private TMV	Dealer TMV
2 Dr GT Cpe	11311	12605	13800
4 Dr GT Sdn	11720	13062	14300
2 Dr GTP Sprchgd Cpe	12130	13519	14800
4 Dr GTP Sprchgd Sdn	12048	13427	14700
4 Dr SE Sdn	10081	11235	12300

OPTIONS FOR GRAND PRIX

6 cyl 3.8 L Engine[Std on GT] +265
AM/FM Stereo/CD/Tape +192
Alarm System[Std on GTP] +161
Aluminum/Alloy Wheels[Opt on SE] +189
Automatic Dimming Mirror +119
Bose Sound System +253
Cast Alloy Wheels +189
Climate Control for AC[Opt on GT] +125
Compact Disc Changer +294
Cruise Control[Opt on SE] +150
Gold Package +381
Keyless Entry System[Std on GTP] +96
Leather Seats +304
Power Drivers Seat[Std on GTP] +195
Power Moonroof +365
Rear Spoiler[Opt on SE] +111
Spoke Wheels +189
Trip Computer[Opt on GT] +127

Don't forget to refer to the Mileage Adjustment Table at the back of this book!

Model Description	Trade-in TMV	Private TMV	Dealer TMV

MONTANA 2000

The 2000 Montana boasts improvements to its V6 and antilock brakes, an upgraded electrical system, a revised instrument cluster and radios, a quieter climate-control blower motor, the option of heated leather seats, reading lamps and oil-life monitoring as well as new paint schemes.

Category P

Model Description	Trade-in TMV	Private TMV	Dealer TMV
4 Dr STD Pass. Van	12475	13788	15000
4 Dr STD Pass. Van Ext	14221	15718	17100
4 Dr Vision Pass. Van Ext	14970	16546	18000

OPTIONS FOR MONTANA
8 Passenger Seating +179
AM/FM Compact Disc Player +169
AM/FM Stereo/CD/Tape +234
Alarm System +122
Aluminum/Alloy Wheels +179
Automatic Load Leveling +127
Camper/Towing Package +96
Captain Chairs (4) +189
Dual Air Conditioning +288
Dual Power Seats +368
Heated Front Seats +189
Keyless Entry System +111
Leather Seats +637
Luggage Rack +111
Overhead Console +111
Power Drivers Seat +173
Power Sliding Door +288
Power Windows +208
Privacy Glass +177
Sport Suspension +596
Steering Wheel Radio Controls +119
Traction Control System +125
Tutone Paint +96

SUNFIRE 2000

Redesigned front and rear fascias for a sportier appearance, a new five-speed manual transmission and the availability of the premium Monsoon audio system lead Sunfire's upgrade list for 2000. There are also restyled rocker-panel moldings, new wheels and exterior colors, as well as a revised instrument panel cluster, floor console and upholstery.

Category B

Model Description	Trade-in TMV	Private TMV	Dealer TMV
2 Dr GT Conv	10966	12440	13800
2 Dr GT Cpe	8820	10006	11100
2 Dr SE Cpe	7072	8023	8900
4 Dr SE Sdn	7152	8113	9000

OPTIONS FOR SUNFIRE
4 cyl 2.4 L Engine[Std on GT] +288
AM/FM Compact Disc Player +205

AM/FM Stereo Tape[Opt on SE] +106
AM/FM Stereo/CD/Tape +205
Alarm System[Std on Conv] +115
Aluminum/Alloy Wheels[Opt on SE] +189
Automatic 3-Speed Transmission +384
Automatic 4-Speed Transmission[Std on Conv] +134
Cruise Control[Std on Conv] +150
Keyless Entry System +96
Monsoon Sound System +125
Power Door Locks[Std on Conv] +141
Power Moonroof +381
Power Windows[Std on Conv] +185
Rear Spoiler[Opt on SE Sdn] +96
Tilt Steering Wheel[Opt on SE] +106
Traction Control[Std on Conv] +125

1999 PONTIAC

BONNEVILLE 1999

All the '99 model year has to offer the rapidly aging Bonneville is a couple of new exterior colors and the availability of GM's dealer-installed OnStar mobile communications system.

Category G

Model Description	Trade-in TMV	Private TMV	Dealer TMV
4 Dr SE Sdn	10132	11216	12300
4 Dr SLE Sdn	11450	12675	13900
4 Dr SSE Sdn	13015	14408	15800
4 Dr SSEi Sprchgd Sdn	13674	15137	16600

OPTIONS FOR BONNEVILLE
AM/FM Compact Disc Player[Opt on SE,SLE] +168
Alarm System[Std on SSEi] +100
Aluminum/Alloy Wheels[Opt on SE] +170
Bucket Seats +168
Chrome Wheels +312
Dual Power Seats[Opt on SE,SLE] +320
Leather Seats +445
Power Drivers Seat[Opt on SE] +160
Power Moonroof +513
Premium Sound System[Opt on SE] +168

FIREBIRD 1999

After last year's freshening, Firebird gets minor revisions and a few new standard items. Electronic traction control is now available on all models, with a bigger gas tank and an oil life monitor standard. A Torsen limited-slip rear axle comes with V8 models (and V6 cars with the performance package), while an eight-speaker Delco/Monsoon sound system goes into the convertible. A power-steering cooler is now available for V8s, and a Hurst shifter is optional on the six-speed manual transmission. The Ram Air WS6 package now sports dual outlet exhaust, and two new exterior colors debut, Pewter and Medium Blue metallic.

Category E

Model Description	Trade-in TMV	Private TMV	Dealer TMV
2 Dr STD Conv	13030	14415	15800

Don't forget to refer to the Mileage Adjustment Table at the back of this book!

Model Description	Trade-in TMV	Private TMV	Dealer TMV
2 Dr STD Cpe	10061	11131	12200
2 Dr Formula Cpe	12535	13868	15200
2 Dr Trans Am Conv	17896	19798	21700
2 Dr Trans Am Cpe	14020	15510	17000

OPTIONS FOR FIREBIRD

30th Anniversary Package +826
8 cyl 5.7 L w/Ram Air Engine +786
AM/FM Stereo/CD/Tape +173
Automatic 4-Speed Transmission[Opt on STD] +428
Chrome Wheels +312
Compact Disc Changer +312
Glass Panel T-tops[Std on Trans Am] +521
Leather Seats[Std on Trans Am] +301
Limited Slip Differential[Opt on STD] +157
Power Door Locks[Opt on STD Cpe] +118
Power Drivers Seat[Std on Trans Am, Conv] +141
Power Windows[Opt on STD Cpe] +155
Ram Air Performance Package +786
Sport Appearance Package +545
Traction Control System +131

GRAND AM   1999

New for 1999, the Grand Am offers a host of standard and optional equipment as well as a completely redesigned exterior.

Category C

Model Description	Trade-in TMV	Private TMV	Dealer TMV
2 Dr GT Cpe	9639	10846	12054
4 Dr GT Sdn	9755	10978	12200
2 Dr GT1 Cpe	10235	11518	12800
4 Dr GT1 Sdn	10555	11878	13200
2 Dr SE Cpe	7357	8278	9200
4 Dr SE Sdn	7676	8638	9600
2 Dr SE1 Cpe	8476	9538	10600
4 Dr SE1 Sdn	8956	10078	11200
2 Dr SE2 Cpe	9036	10168	11300
4 Dr SE2 Sdn	9712	10929	12146

OPTIONS FOR GRAND AM

6 cyl 3.4 L Engine[Opt on SE1] +344
AM/FM Compact Disc Player[Std on GT1,SE2] +109
Alarm System[Opt on GT Cpe] +131
Aluminum/Alloy Wheels +157
Cruise Control[Opt on SE] +124
Leather Seats +250
Power Drivers Seat +139
Power Moonroof[Std on GT1] +312

GRAND PRIX   1999

The Grand Prix gets more muscle for '99 with low-restriction air-induction components giving the naturally aspirated 3.8-liter V6 five more horsepower, to 200. This engine is standard on the GT (sedan and coupe) and optional on the SE sedan. A traction control indicator and on/off button are now standard on GTP models. Minor revisions are in order inside, with front-door courtesy lamps and a six-speaker sound system now standard, with an eight-speaker Bose audio unit and OnStar mobile communications system optional. Outside, a rear deck spoiler is standard on the GT model, and two colors have been added to the 1999 exterior paint chart.

Category D

Model Description	Trade-in TMV	Private TMV	Dealer TMV
2 Dr GT Cpe	9871	11035	12200
4 Dr GT Sdn	10356	11578	12800
2 Dr GTP Sprchgd Cpe	10761	12030	13300
4 Dr GTP Sprchgd Sdn	11570	12935	14300
4 Dr SE Sdn	9062	10131	11200

OPTIONS FOR GRAND PRIX

6 cyl 3.8 L Engine[Std on GT] +217
AM/FM Stereo/CD/Tape[Opt on GT Cpe] +157
Alarm System[Std on GTP] +131
Aluminum/Alloy Wheels +155
Bose Sound System +208
Compact Disc Changer +242
Cruise Control[Opt on SE] +124
Leather Seats +250
Power Drivers Seat[Std on GTP] +160
Power Moonroof +299
Spoke Wheels +155

MONTANA   1999

After a ground-up redesign in 1997, the entire line gets a name change this year, from Trans Sport to Montana (the name pulled from 98's sporty trim package). Regular-wheelbase models come with one or two sliding doors, while extended wheelbase vans get two only with a right-side power sliding door option. Side-impact airbags are standard, as are 15-inch 215-70R white-letter puncture sealant tires. New two-tone paint jobs are available and four new exterior colors are offered, as are options for front-row leather seats and an overhead video system. Better still, a special sport performance package adds cast aluminum wheels, traction control and a specially tuned sport suspension for soccer dads (and moms) who are sport sedan wannabees.

Category P

Model Description	Trade-in TMV	Private TMV	Dealer TMV
2 Dr STD Pass. Van	10667	11884	13100
4 Dr STD Pass. Van	11970	13335	14700
4 Dr STD Pass. Van Ext	12296	13698	15100

OPTIONS FOR MONTANA

8 Passenger Seating +147
AM/FM Compact Disc Player +139
AM/FM Stereo/CD/Tape +191
Aluminum/Alloy Wheels +147
Captain Chairs (4) +155
Dual Air Conditioning +236
Dual Power Seats +301

Model Description	Trade-in TMV	Private TMV	Dealer TMV
Leather Seats +521			
Power Drivers Seat +141			
Power Sliding Door +236			
Power Windows +170			
Privacy Glass +144			
Sport Suspension[Std on 3-Door Passenger Van] +487			

SUNFIRE 1999

After Sunfire coupes got a rear spoiler last year, this year it's the sedan's turn, only as an option. The top-line 2.4-liter twin-cam engine is revised to improve breathing, including new fuel injectors, injection rails, exhaust manifold and catalytic converter. Fern Green Metallic is added to the paint color chart.

Category B

Model Description	Trade-in TMV	Private TMV	Dealer TMV
2 Dr GT Conv	9691	11096	12500
2 Dr GT Cpe	7365	8433	9500
2 Dr SE Cpe	5892	6746	7600
4 Dr SE Sdn	5970	6835	7700

OPTIONS FOR SUNFIRE

4 cyl 2.4 L Engine[Std on GT] +236
AM/FM Compact Disc Player[Std on GT] +168
Air Conditioning[Std on GT] +435
Aluminum/Alloy Wheels[Std on GT] +155
Automatic 3-Speed Transmission +314
Automatic 4-Speed Transmission[Std on Conv] +109
Cruise Control[Std on Conv] +124
Power Door Locks[Std on Conv] +115
Power Moonroof +312
Power Windows[Std on Conv] +153

1998 PONTIAC

BONNEVILLE 1998

Second-generation airbags are standard, the SE comes with a standard decklid spoiler, and the SSE gets more standard equipment. New colors freshen the rapidly aging Bonneville.

Category G

Model Description	Trade-in TMV	Private TMV	Dealer TMV
4 Dr SE Sdn	8295	9210	10200
4 Dr SLE Sdn	9597	10654	11800
4 Dr SSE Sdn	10898	12099	13400
4 Dr SSEi Sprchgd Sdn	12118	13453	14900

OPTIONS FOR BONNEVILLE

AM/FM Compact Disc Player[Opt on SE,SLE] +154
Aluminum/Alloy Wheels[Opt on SE] +155
Chrome Wheels +286
Dual Power Seats[Opt on SE,SLE] +293
Leather Seats +408
Power Drivers Seat[Opt on SE] +147
Power Moonroof +471
Premium Sound System[Opt on SE] +154

FIREBIRD 1998

Firebirds get a minor restyle that is most evident from the front end. Also on tap for Formula and Trans Am models is a de-tuned Corvette engine making 305 horsepower without Ram Air induction. Base models can be equipped with a new Sport Appearance Package, and two new exterior colors debut. Second-generation airbags are standard.

Category E

Model Description	Trade-in TMV	Private TMV	Dealer TMV
2 Dr STD Conv	11801	13097	14500
2 Dr STD Cpe	8464	9393	10400
2 Dr Formula Cpe	11231	12464	13800
2 Dr Trans Am Conv	15626	17342	19200
2 Dr Trans Am Cpe	12452	13819	15300

OPTIONS FOR FIREBIRD

8 cyl 5.7 L w/Ram Air Engine +720
Automatic 4-Speed Transmission[Opt on STD] +391
Chrome Wheels +286
Compact Disc Changer +286
Glass Panel T-tops[Std on Trans Am] +478
Leather Seats[Std on Trans Am] +312
Performance/Handling Package +565
Power Drivers Seat[Std on Trans Am] +147
Power Windows[Opt on STD Cpe] +142
Premium Sound System[Opt on Trans Am Cpe] +206
Sport Appearance Package +499
Traction Control System +216

GRAND AM 1998

Second generation airbags are newly standard, and option groups are simplified.

Category C

Model Description	Trade-in TMV	Private TMV	Dealer TMV
2 Dr GT Cpe	6951	7838	8800
4 Dr GT Sdn	7266	8195	9200
2 Dr SE Cpe	6240	7037	7900
4 Dr SE Sdn	6319	7126	8000

OPTIONS FOR GRAND AM

6 cyl 3.1 L Engine +216
Aluminum/Alloy Wheels[Opt on SE] +144
Automatic 4-Speed Transmission +389
Cruise Control +114
Leather Seats +229
Power Drivers Seat +164
Power Moonroof +286
Power Windows +125
Premium Sound System[Opt on GT,SE] +194
Sport Wheels +155

GRAND PRIX 1998

Supercharged GTP models get traction control, and new colors are available inside and out. Second-generation airbags debut as standard equipment.

Category D

Model Description	Trade-in TMV	Private TMV	Dealer TMV
2 Dr GT Cpe	8796	9902	11100
4 Dr GT Sdn	8955	10080	11300
2 Dr GTP Sprchgd Cpe	9589	10794	12100

Model Description	Trade-in TMV	Private TMV	Dealer TMV
4 Dr GTP Sprchgd Sdn	10064	11329	12700
4 Dr SE Sdn	8004	9010	10100

OPTIONS FOR GRAND PRIX

6 cyl 3.8 L Engine[Opt on SE] +199
AM/FM Compact Disc Player +139
Aluminum/Alloy Wheels[Opt on SE] +125
Compact Disc Changer +286
Cruise Control[Opt on SE] +114
Leather Seats +229
Power Drivers Seat +147
Power Moonroof +273
Spoke Wheels +142

SUNFIRE 1998

All coupes have a rear spoiler, a new six-speaker sound system is available, the base four-cylinder gets some additional low-end punch, and Topaz Gold Metallic is added to the paint color chart. Second-generation airbags are added as standard equipment.

Category B

Model Description	Trade-in TMV	Private TMV	Dealer TMV
2 Dr GT Cpe	6374	7394	8500
2 Dr SE Conv	7724	8960	10300
2 Dr SE Cpe	4799	5568	6400
4 Dr SE Sdn	4874	5655	6500

OPTIONS FOR SUNFIRE

4 cyl 2.4 L Engine[Opt on SE] +216
AM/FM Compact Disc Player[Std on GT,Conv] +154
Air Conditioning[Std on GT,Conv] +398
Aluminum/Alloy Wheels[Opt on SE] +142
Automatic 3-Speed Transmission +287
Automatic 4-Speed Transmission[Opt on GT,SE] +101
Cruise Control[Std on Conv] +114
Power Moonroof +286
Power Windows +139

TRANS SPORT 1998

Short-wheelbase models get the dual sliding doors and power sliding door options. Side-impact airbags are standard, and a white two-tone paint job is new. Second generation airbags are standard for front seat occupants.

Category P

Model Description	Trade-in TMV	Private TMV	Dealer TMV
2 Dr STD Pass. Van	8916	10060	11300
4 Dr STD Pass. Van Ext	9626	10861	12200
4 Dr Montana Pass. Van	10415	11752	13200
4 Dr Montana Pass. Van Ext	10888	12286	13800

OPTIONS FOR TRANS SPORT

8 Passenger Seating +127
AM/FM Compact Disc Player +127
AM/FM Stereo/CD/Tape +127
Aluminum/Alloy Wheels[Opt on STD] +134
Captain Chairs (4) +252
Dual Air Conditioning +216
Dual Power Seats +130
Leather Seats +633
Power Drivers Seat +130
Power Sliding Door +185
Power Windows +132
Premium Sound System +264
Privacy Glass +132
Sliding Driver Side Door[Std on Montana,Pass. Van Ext] +209

1997 PONTIAC

BONNEVILLE 1997

Changes for 1997 are few. Supercharged Bonnevilles get a new transmission, a new Delco/Bose premium sound system is optional on the SSE, and the EYE CUE head-up display has a new motorized adjustment feature. Two new exterior colors, a new interior color and a new interior fabric liven the aging Bonneville visually.

Category G

Model Description	Trade-in TMV	Private TMV	Dealer TMV
4 Dr SE Sdn	6665	7491	8500
4 Dr SE Sprchgd Sdn	7998	8989	10200
4 Dr SSE Sdn	8860	9958	11300
4 Dr SSEi Sprchgd Sdn	9644	10839	12300

OPTIONS FOR BONNEVILLE

AM/FM Compact Disc Player +129
AM/FM Stereo/CD/Tape +190
Aluminum/Alloy Wheels[Opt on SE] +141
Automatic Load Leveling[Opt on SE] +166
Chrome Wheels +259
Computer Command Ride Package +196
Dual Power Seats +266
Leather Seats +338
Power Drivers Seat[Opt on SE] +133
Power Moonroof +426
Premium Sound System[Opt on SE] +139

FIREBIRD 1997

Pontiac upgrades the Firebird in several ways for 1997. Performance freaks will appreciate the addition of Ram Air induction to the options list of the Formula and Trans Am convertibles. Audiophiles will be blown away by the newly optional 500-watt Monsoon sound system. Luxury intenders can get power seats swathed in leather this year. Safety-conscious buyers will find daytime running lights. Additional cosmetic and comfort items keep the fourth-generation Firebird fresh for its fifth year.

Category E

Model Description	Trade-in TMV	Private TMV	Dealer TMV
2 Dr STD Conv	10150	11477	13100
2 Dr STD Cpe	6818	7710	8800
2 Dr Formula Conv	11854	13405	15300

Don't forget to refer to the Mileage Adjustment Table at the back of this book!

Model Description	Trade-in TMV	Private TMV	Dealer TMV
2 Dr Formula Cpe	9142	10338	11800
2 Dr Trans Am Conv	13016	14719	16800
2 Dr Trans Am Cpe	10072	11390	13000

OPTIONS FOR FIREBIRD
8 cyl 5.7 L w/Ram Air Engine +653
AM/FM Compact Disc Player +100
Automatic 4-Speed Transmission[Opt on STD] +354
Chrome Wheels +259
Compact Disc Changer +259
Glass Panel T-tops +433
Leather Seats +350
Performance Package +239
Performance/Handling Package +511
Power Drivers Seat +118
Power Windows[Std on Trans Am,Conv] +126
Sport Appearance Package +459
Traction Control System +196

GRAND AM   1997

Very minimal changes this year as Pontiac concentrates on Grand Prix and Trans Sport launches. Air conditioning is now standard. Also, three new colors are added.
Category C

Model Description	Trade-in TMV	Private TMV	Dealer TMV
2 Dr GT Cpe	5377	6197	7200
4 Dr GT Sdn	5526	6369	7400
2 Dr SE Cpe	5153	5939	6900
4 Dr SE Sdn	5153	5939	6900

OPTIONS FOR GRAND AM
6 cyl 3.1 L Engine +196
AM/FM Stereo/CD/Tape +176
Aluminum/Alloy Wheels[Opt on SE] +130
Automatic 4-Speed Transmission +352
Leather Seats +303
Power Drivers Seat +259
Power Moonroof +259
Power Windows +114
Premium Sound System[Opt on GT,SE] +176

GRAND PRIX   1997

Pontiac redesigns the Grand Prix for 1997, giving buyers slick new styling, a longer and wider wheelbase, and available supercharged V6 power on GT models. Traction control, antilock brakes, dual airbags and side-impact protection are standard. Optional is a built-in child safety seat.
Category D

Model Description	Trade-in TMV	Private TMV	Dealer TMV
2 Dr GT Cpe	6561	7568	8800
4 Dr GT Sdn	7530	8686	10100
2 Dr GTP Sprchgd Cpe	7604	8772	10200
4 Dr GTP Sprchgd Sdn	8052	9288	10800
4 Dr SE Sdn	5890	6794	7900

OPTIONS FOR GRAND PRIX
6 cyl 3.8 L Engine[Opt on SE] +181

AM/FM Compact Disc Player +109
AM/FM Stereo/CD/Tape +130
Aluminum/Alloy Wheels[Opt on SE] +113
Compact Disc Changer +259
Leather Seats +207
Power Drivers Seat +118
Power Moonroof +281
Spoke Wheels +124

SUNFIRE   1997

SE Convertible gets a higher level of standard equipment, including an automatic transmission. Coupes get a new front seatbelt guide loop, and a new Sports Interior trim debuts called Patina/Redondo cloth.
Category B

Model Description	Trade-in TMV	Private TMV	Dealer TMV
2 Dr GT Cpe	4790	5605	6600
2 Dr SE Conv	6387	7473	8800
2 Dr SE Cpe	3702	4331	5100
4 Dr SE Sdn	3919	4586	5400

OPTIONS FOR SUNFIRE
4 cyl 2.4 L Engine[Opt on SE] +196
5-Speed Transmission +352
AM/FM Compact Disc Player +144
Air Conditioning[Std on Conv] +362
Aluminum/Alloy Wheels[Opt on SE] +121
Automatic 3-Speed Transmission +239
Automatic 4-Speed Transmission[Std on Conv] +352
Power Moonroof +259
Power Sunroof +259
Power Windows +126

TRANS SPORT   1997

After years of taking it on the chin, Pontiac redesigns the Trans Sport and lands one squarely in Chrysler's face. This van is good-looking, loaded with features and fun to drive. Wait. Did we say fun to drive?
Category P

Model Description	Trade-in TMV	Private TMV	Dealer TMV
2 Dr SE Pass. Van	7487	8573	9900
2 Dr SE Pass. Van Ext	7714	8833	10200

OPTIONS FOR TRANS SPORT
7 Passenger Seating[Opt on Pass. Van] +115
8 Passenger Seating +115
AM/FM Compact Disc Player +109
AM/FM Stereo/CD/Tape +152
Aluminum/Alloy Wheels +113
Captain Chairs (4) +229
Dual Air Conditioning +200
Dual Power Seats +251
Leather Seats +459
Power Drivers Seat +118
Power Moonroof +303
Power Windows +119
Sliding Driver Side Door +152
Sport Suspension +109

PONTIAC 96

Model Description	Trade-in TMV	Private TMV	Dealer TMV	Model Description	Trade-in TMV	Private TMV	Dealer TMV

1996 PONTIAC

BONNEVILLE 1996

The Series II V6 has been supercharged for 1996, pumping out 240 horsepower. Styling front and rear has been tweaked, and daytime running lights debut.

Category G

4 Dr SE Sdn	5169	5854	6800
4 Dr SE Sprchgd Sdn	5853	6629	7700
4 Dr SLE Sdn	6537	7404	8600
4 Dr SSE Sdn	7070	8006	9300
4 Dr SSE Sprchgd Sdn	7374	8351	9700

OPTIONS FOR BONNEVILLE

AM/FM Stereo/CD/Tape +171
Aluminum/Alloy Wheels +128
Automatic Load Leveling[Opt on SE] +150
Bucket Seats +124
Chrome Wheels +234
Computer Command Ride Package +177
Leather Seats +306
Power Drivers Seat[Opt on SE] +120
Power Moonroof +386
Power Passenger Seat +120
Premium Sound System +125
SSEI Supercharger Package +529

FIREBIRD 1996

A new standard V6 makes 40 more horsepower than the old one. The LT1 V8 also makes more power, particularly when equipped with Ram Air induction. A new color livens up the exterior, as if it needed it.

Category E

2 Dr STD Conv	9151	10394	12111
2 Dr STD Cpe	5667	6437	7500
2 Dr Formula Conv	9596	10900	12700
2 Dr Formula Cpe	7103	8068	9400
2 Dr Trans Am Conv	10352	11758	13700
2 Dr Trans Am Cpe	9067	10299	12000

OPTIONS FOR FIREBIRD

8 cyl 5.7 L w/Ram Air Engine +590
Air Conditioning[Opt on STD Cpe] +197
Automatic 4-Speed Transmission[Opt on STD] +310
Bucket Seats[Opt on Trans Am Cpe] +129
Chrome Wheels +197
Compact Disc Changer +234
Glass Panel T-tops +382
Leather Seats +316
Performance/Handling Package +210
Power Drivers Seat +120
Power Windows[Std on Trans Am,Conv] +114
Premium Sound System[Opt on Cpe] +170
Traction Control System +177

GRAND AM 1996

New styling, a new base engine, and ... what's this? Dual airbags and body-mounted seatbelts? Will wonders never cease?

Category C

2 Dr GT Cpe	3887	4649	5700
4 Dr GT Sdn	4092	4893	6000
2 Dr SE Cpe	3478	4159	5100
4 Dr SE Sdn	3410	4078	5000

OPTIONS FOR GRAND AM

6 cyl 3.1 L Engine +155
AM/FM Compact Disc Player +159
AM/FM Stereo Tape +120
AM/FM Stereo/CD/Tape +236
Air Conditioning[Opt on SE] +327
Aluminum/Alloy Wheels +118
Automatic 4-Speed Transmission +313
Leather Seats +273
Power Drivers Seat +133
Power Moonroof +234
Premium Sound System[Opt on GT] +159

GRAND PRIX 1996

Minor trim and powertrain improvements to the only car in GM's stable that still has those stupid door-mounted seatbelts. Do yourself a favor. Buy the 1997 GP.

Category D

4 Dr GT Sdn	4823	5737	7000
2 Dr GTP Cpe	4892	5819	7100
2 Dr SE Cpe	4479	5328	6500
4 Dr SE Sdn	4134	4918	6000

OPTIONS FOR GRAND PRIX

Anti-Lock Brakes[Opt on SE] +177
GT Performance Package +895
Leather Seats +273
Power Moonroof +254

SUNFIRE 1996

Traction control, remote keyless entry and steering wheel radio controls are newly available. Old Quad 4 engine dumped in favor of new 2.4-liter twin-cam engine. Two new paint choices spiff up the exterior.

Category B

2 Dr GT Cpe	3765	4452	5400
2 Dr SE Conv	4810	5688	6900
2 Dr SE Cpe	2998	3545	4300
4 Dr SE Sdn	3067	3627	4400

OPTIONS FOR SUNFIRE

4 cyl 2.4 L Engine[Opt on SE] +155
AM/FM Compact Disc Player +129
Air Conditioning[Std on Conv] +313
Automatic 3-Speed Transmission[Std on Conv] +216

Don't forget to refer to the Mileage Adjustment Table at the back of this book!

Model Description	Trade-in TMV	Private TMV	Dealer TMV	Model Description	Trade-in TMV	Private TMV	Dealer TMV
Power Sunroof +234				2 Dr STD Cpe	4272	4845	5800
				2 Dr Formula Conv	7880	8938	10700
				2 Dr Formula Cpe	5524	6265	7500
				2 Dr Trans Am Conv	8396	9522	11400
				2 Dr Trans Am Cpe	6555	7434	8900

TRANS SPORT 1996

A 180-horsepower 3.4-liter V6 replaces last year's pathetic base engine as well as the optional 3.8-liter V6. Front air conditioning is standard equipment for 1996.

Category P

2 Dr SE Pass. Van	5469	6406	7700

OPTIONS FOR TRANS SPORT
7 Passenger Seating +277
AM/FM Compact Disc Player +213
Air Conditioning +177
Dual Air Conditioning +181
Flip-Up Sunroof +118
Leather Seats +343
Power Drivers Seat +107
Power Sliding Door +138
Power Windows +108

1995 PONTIAC

BONNEVILLE 1995

Base engine is upgraded to 3800 Series II status, gaining 35 horsepower in the process. SE models with the SLE package can be ordered with the supercharged 3.8-liter V6. Computer Command Ride is made available on SE models.

Category G

4 Dr SE Sdn	3970	4581	5600
4 Dr SE Sprchgd Sdn	4466	5154	6300
4 Dr SSE Sdn	5175	5972	7300
4 Dr SSEi Sprchgd Sdn	5600	6462	7900

OPTIONS FOR BONNEVILLE
AM/FM Compact Disc Player +101
Aluminum/Alloy Wheels[Opt on SE] +110
Automatic Load Leveling[Opt on SE] +129
Dual Power Seats +208
Leather Seats +265
Power Drivers Seat[Opt on SE] +104
Power Moonroof +333
Power Passenger Seat +104
Premium Sound System[Opt on SE] +109

FIREBIRD 1995

Traction control is added as an option on Formula and Trans Am. Trans Am GT is dropped from lineup. Californians get a 3.8-liter V6 equipped with an automatic transmission on base models instead of the 3.4-liter V6. The new engine meets strict emissions standards in that state, and makes 40 additional horsepower.

Category E

2 Dr STD Conv	6702	7601	9100

OPTIONS FOR FIREBIRD
AM/FM Compact Disc Player +79
Air Conditioning[Std on Trans Am,Conv] +171
Automatic 4-Speed Transmission +269
Glass Panel T-tops +330
Leather Seats[Opt on Formula,STD] +195
T-Tops (Solid/Colored) +221

GRAND AM 1995

Base engine upgraded to a 150-horsepower version of the Quad 4. High-output Quad 4 motor is dropped from the GT, which now uses the same standard and optional powerplants as the SE. Variable-effort power steering is a new option on GT models, rear suspensions are redesigned, and SE models get restyled wheelcovers and alloy wheels.

Category C

2 Dr GT Cpe	2764	3340	4300
4 Dr GT Sdn	2828	3418	4400
2 Dr SE Cpe	2378	2874	3700
4 Dr SE Sdn	2507	3029	3900

OPTIONS FOR GRAND AM
6 cyl 3.1 L Engine +134
Air Conditioning[Opt on SE] +283
Aluminum/Alloy Wheels[Opt on SE] +102
Automatic 3-Speed Transmission +153
Automatic 4-Speed Transmission +271
Leather Seats +162
Power Moonroof +203
Premium Sound System[Opt on GT Cpe,SE] +138

GRAND PRIX 1995

Brake/transmission shift interlock is added. GT coupe dropped in favor of GTP Package. GT sedan continues. Variable-effort steering is added to GTP and GT. New alloys debut on GT and GTP. Coupes can be equipped with a White Appearance Package, which includes color-keyed alloys and special pinstriping. Floor consoles are redesigned on models with bucket seats.

Category D

4 Dr GT Sdn	3816	4560	5800
2 Dr GTP Cpe	3948	4717	6000
2 Dr SE Cpe	3619	4324	5500
4 Dr SE Sdn	3158	3774	4800

OPTIONS FOR GRAND PRIX
AM/FM Stereo/CD/Tape[Opt on GTP Cpe] +102
Anti-Lock Brakes[Opt on SE] +153
Compact Disc Changer +156
Leather Seats +237

Don't forget to refer to the Mileage Adjustment Table at the back of this book!

Model Description	Trade-in TMV	Private TMV	Dealer TMV	Model Description	Trade-in TMV	Private TMV	Dealer TMV

Power Moonroof +194

SUNFIRE 1995

All-new replacement for aged Sunbird comes in SE coupe or sedan, and GT coupe trim levels. An SE convertible debuted midyear. Dual airbags, ABS, tilt steering and tachometer are standard. Base engine is a 2.2-liter four cylinder good for 120 horsepower. GT models get a 150-horsepower Quad 4 engine, which is optional on SE. Order the four-speed automatic transmission, and you'll get traction control.

Category B

2 Dr GT Cpe	2749	3368	4400
2 Dr SE Conv	3437	4210	5500
2 Dr SE Cpe	2124	2603	3400
4 Dr SE Sdn	2187	2679	3500

OPTIONS FOR SUNFIRE
4 cyl 2.3 L Quad 4 Engine[Opt on SE] +153
AM/FM Compact Disc Player +109
Air Conditioning +271
Automatic 3-Speed Transmission[Std on Conv] +187
Power Sunroof +203

TRANS SPORT 1995

A brake/transmission shift interlock is added. New overhead console includes outside temperature gauge, compass and storage bin.

Category P

2 Dr SE Pass. Van	4063	4752	5900

OPTIONS FOR TRANS SPORT
6 cyl 3.8 L Engine +271
7 Passenger Seating +90
AM/FM Compact Disc Player +90
Air Conditioning +153
Automatic 4-Speed Transmission +237
Dual Air Conditioning +153
Flip-Up Sunroof +102
Leather Seats +296
Power Door Locks +88
Power Drivers Seat +92
Power Sliding Door +119
Power Windows +94
Premium Sound System +85
Privacy Glass +83

1994 PONTIAC

BONNEVILLE 1994

Dual airbags are standard. SE and SSE trim levels are available. Californians get SLE model. SSEi is an option package on SSE. Supercharged engine in SSEi package gets 20 more horsepower. Automatic transmission gains Normal and Performance shift modes when hooked to supercharged engine. Traction control gains ability to retard engine power as well as apply brakes to slow spinning wheel(s). Get traction control on the SSE, and you can opt for Computer Command Ride, a suspension package that automatically adjusts the suspension to meet the demands of the driver.

Category G

4 Dr SE Sdn	3211	3807	4800
4 Dr SSE Sdn	4214	4996	6300
4 Dr SSEi Sprchgd Sdn	4549	5393	6800

OPTIONS FOR BONNEVILLE
AM/FM Compact Disc Player +90
AM/FM Stereo/CD/Tape +133
Aluminum/Alloy Wheels[Opt on SE] +99
Leather Seats +237
Power Drivers Seat[Opt on SE] +93
Power Moonroof +299
Power Passenger Seat +93
Power Sunroof +211
Premium Sound System[Opt on SE] +98
Sport Suspension +152

FIREBIRD 1994

Trans Am GT debuts. Six-speed transmission is saddled with a first-to-fourth skip shift feature designed to improve fuel economy. Automatic is new electronically controlled unit with the V8 engine, and it features Normal and Performance modes. Remote keyless entry, cassette player, and leather-wrapped steering wheel move from the Trans Am standard equipment list to the options sheet. T/A also loses Batwing rear spoiler to GT, taking Formula's more subdued rear treatment. Convertible debuts at midyear.

Category E

2 Dr STD Conv	5373	6321	7900
2 Dr STD Cpe	3401	4000	5000
2 Dr Formula Conv	5849	6881	8600
2 Dr Formula Cpe	4421	5201	6500
2 Dr Trans Am Cpe	5033	5921	7400
2 Dr Trans Am 25th Anniv. Cpe	5781	6801	8500
2 Dr Trans Am GT Conv	6597	7761	9700
2 Dr Trans Am GT Cpe	5305	6241	7800

OPTIONS FOR FIREBIRD
AM/FM Stereo/CD/Tape[Opt on Trans Am] +101
Air Conditioning +152
Automatic 4-Speed Transmission +241
Glass Panel T-tops +296
Leather Seats[Std on Trans Am GT Conv] +176
Power Windows[Opt on Formula,STD] +88
Premium Sound System +132

Model Description	Trade-in TMV	Private TMV	Dealer TMV

GRAND AM 1994

Driver airbag added. A 3.1-liter V6 replaces last year's optional 3.3-liter V6. Four-speed automatic debuts; standard with V6 and optional on four-cylinder models.

Category C

Model Description	Trade-in TMV	Private TMV	Dealer TMV
2 Dr GT Cpe	2234	2821	3800
4 Dr GT Sdn	2352	2970	4000
2 Dr SE Cpe	2054	2593	3493
4 Dr SE Sdn	2062	2604	3507

OPTIONS FOR GRAND AM

6 cyl 3.1 L Engine +121
Air Conditioning[Opt on SE] +253
Aluminum/Alloy Wheels[Opt on SE] +92
Automatic 3-Speed Transmission +138
Automatic 4-Speed Transmission +242
Leather Seats +145
Power Sunroof +182
Premium Sound System +124

GRAND PRIX 1994

Interior is redesigned to accommodate dual airbags. LE and STE sedans are dropped; GT and GTP become option packages on SE coupe. A GT package is available on SE sedan, and includes 3.4-liter V6, alloys, low-profile tires, ABS, and sport suspension. Front seatbelts are anchored to pillars instead of doors on sedan; coupe retains door-mounted belts. 3.1-liter V6 is up 20 horsepower. Twin-cam 3.4-liter V6 is up ten horsepower. Five-speed manual and three-speed automatic transmissions are dropped in favor of four-speed automatic. Coupes gain standard equipment, including 16-inch alloys, cruise, and leather-wrapped steering wheel with integral radio controls.

Category D

Model Description	Trade-in TMV	Private TMV	Dealer TMV
2 Dr SE Cpe	2396	3008	4027
4 Dr SE Sdn	2364	2968	3973

OPTIONS FOR GRAND PRIX

6 cyl 3.4 L Engine +304
Anti-Lock Brakes +138
Leather Seats +213
Power Sunroof +211

SUNBIRD 1994

GT coupe, SE convertible and SE sedan vanish. Surviving are LE models and an SE coupe that comes standard with the GT's old body work. Convertibles get alloys and rear spoiler standard. SE comes with a 3.1-liter V6 standard.

Category B

Model Description	Trade-in TMV	Private TMV	Dealer TMV
2 Dr LE Conv	2068	2680	3700
2 Dr LE Cpe	1450	1879	2594
4 Dr LE Sdn	1457	1888	2606
2 Dr SE Cpe	1677	2173	3000

OPTIONS FOR SUNBIRD

6 cyl 3.1 L Engine[Opt on LE] +182
AM/FM Compact Disc Player[Opt on LE,SE] +107
Air Conditioning +214
Automatic 3-Speed Transmission +168
Sunroof +138

TRANS SPORT 1994

Driver airbag debuts and new front styling improves doorstop looks. Dashboard gets styling tweak to shorten visual acreage on top. A power sliding side door and integrated child seats are newly optional. Automatic power door locks are added, and rear seats gain a fold-and-stow feature. Traction control is made available at midyear; requires 3.8-liter engine.

Category P

Model Description	Trade-in TMV	Private TMV	Dealer TMV
2 Dr SE Pass. Van	3272	3958	5100

OPTIONS FOR TRANS SPORT

6 cyl 3.8 L Engine +242
7 Passenger Seating +81
AM/FM Compact Disc Player +81
Air Conditioning +138
Automatic 4-Speed Transmission +213
Dual Air Conditioning +138
Flip-Up Sunroof +92
Leather Seats +265
Power Drivers Seat +82
Power Sliding Door +107
Power Windows +84

1993 PONTIAC

BONNEVILLE 1993

SSE gets supercharged engine option. ABS is standard on all models. Sport Luxury Edition (SLE) for SE includes chrome grille, decklid spoiler, cross-lace alloy wheels, bigger tires, leather seats, and performance-oriented transaxle ratio.

Category G

Model Description	Trade-in TMV	Private TMV	Dealer TMV
4 Dr SE Sdn	2722	3276	4200
4 Dr SSE Sdn	3565	4290	5500
4 Dr SSEi Sprchgd Sdn	3759	4524	5800

OPTIONS FOR BONNEVILLE

Dual Air Bag Restraints[Opt on SSE] +118
Leather Seats[Std on SSEi] +184
Power Sunroof +162

FIREBIRD 1993

Brand new car debuts, marking first redesign since 1982. Base, Formula and Trans Am trim levels are available. Base car powered by 160-horsepower 3.4-liter V6. Formula and T/A get 5.7-liter V8 worth 275 horsepower. Formula and T/A get a standard six-speed manual transmission. Dual airbags and ABS

PONTIAC 93-92

Model Description	Trade-in TMV	Private TMV	Dealer TMV	Model Description	Trade-in TMV	Private TMV	Dealer TMV

are standard.

Category E

2 Dr STD Cpe	2693	3220	4100
2 Dr Formula Cpe	3743	4477	5700
2 Dr Trans Am Cpe	4466	5341	6800

OPTIONS FOR FIREBIRD

Air Conditioning[Opt on STD Cpe] +118
Automatic 4-Speed Transmission +187
Leather Seats[Std on Trans Am] +136
Premium Sound System[Opt on STD Cpe] +102
Sunroof +106
T-Tops (Solid/Colored) +154

GRAND AM　　　　　　　1993

Four-cylinder engines lose five horsepower, but gain modifications designed to reduce engine noise. Climate controls are revised, instrument panel graphics are revised on the SE, and battery-saver protection is added.

Category C

2 Dr GT Cpe	1574	2109	3000
4 Dr GT Sdn	1627	2179	3100
2 Dr SE Cpe	1417	1898	2700
4 Dr SE Sdn	1522	2039	2900

OPTIONS FOR GRAND AM

4 cyl 2.3 L Quad 4 Engine[Opt on SE] +151
6 cyl 3.3 L Engine +108
Air Conditioning +196
Automatic 3-Speed Transmission +106
Premium Sound System +96

GRAND PRIX　　　　　　1993

An electronically-controlled four-speed automatic is optional on LE sedan and SE coupe. A Sport Appearance Package for the LE sedan includes aero body panels, heads-up display, and bucket seats with console. Automatic door locks are standard. Chime added to warn driver if turn signal has been left on.

Category D

2 Dr GT Cpe	2268	2918	4000
4 Dr LE Sdn	1588	2042	2800
2 Dr SE Cpe	1701	2188	3000
4 Dr SE Sdn	1758	2261	3100
4 Dr STE Sdn	2438	3136	4300

OPTIONS FOR GRAND PRIX

6 cyl 3.4 L Engine +235
Aero Performance Package +390
Anti-Lock Brakes[Opt on LE,SE] +106
Automatic 4-Speed Transmission[Opt on LE,SE] +165
Leather Seats +165
Power Sunroof +162

LE MANS　　　　　　　1993

New front styling and revised taillights debut. New moldings and wheelcovers complete the minor makeover.

Category A

2 Dr SE Cpe	716	1010	1500
4 Dr SE Sdn	764	1078	1600
2 Dr Value Leader Cpe	430	606	900

OPTIONS FOR LE MANS

Air Conditioning +165
Automatic 3-Speed Transmission +130
Sunroof +106

SUNBIRD　　　　　　　1993

Base models can be equipped with a V6, and midline coupe gets Sport Appearance Package, which includes GT styling.

Category B

2 Dr GT Cpe	1514	2034	2900
2 Dr LE Cpe	1129	1516	2162
4 Dr LE Sdn	1134	1523	2172
2 Dr SE Conv	1776	2385	3400
2 Dr SE Cpe	1183	1589	2266
4 Dr SE Sdn	1201	1613	2300

OPTIONS FOR SUNBIRD

6 cyl 3.1 L Engine[Std on GT] +140
AM/FM Compact Disc Player +82
Air Conditioning +165
Automatic 3-Speed Transmission +130
Sunroof +106

TRANS SPORT　　　　　1993

GT model canceled. SE is only trim level. Leather seats and steering wheel controls for the radio have been added to the options sheet. Climate controls are bigger. Sunroof becomes optional midyear.

Category P

2 Dr SE Pass. Van	2395	2997	4000

OPTIONS FOR TRANS SPORT

6 cyl 3.8 L Engine +188
Air Conditioning +106
Automatic 4-Speed Transmission +165
Dual Air Conditioning +106
Leather Seats +205

1992 PONTIAC

BONNEVILLE　　　　　　1992

Earns restyle that swaps stodgy, three-box design theme for flowing lines reminiscent of the Jaguar XJ6. LE trim level dies. 3.8-liter V6 gets five additional horsepower. SSEi has a supercharged V6 worth 205

Model Description	Trade-in TMV	Private TMV	Dealer TMV

horsepower and standard traction control. Traction control is optional on other Bonnevilles. ABS is standard on SSE and SSEi; optional on SE with Sport Appearance Package. A passenger airbag is standard on SSEi, optional on SSE. A heads-up display is standard on SSEi and optional on SSE.

Category G

Model Description	Trade-in TMV	Private TMV	Dealer TMV
4 Dr SE Sdn	1781	2275	3100
4 Dr SSE Sdn	2470	3156	4300
4 Dr SSE Sprchgd Sdn	2700	3450	4700
4 Dr SSEi Sprchgd Sdn	2987	3817	5200

OPTIONS FOR BONNEVILLE

Anti-Lock Brakes[Opt on SE] +122
Dual Air Bag Restraints[Opt on SSE] +106
Leather Seats +165
Option Package +209
Power Moonroof +208
Power Sunroof +146
Premium Equipment Package +249

FIREBIRD 1992

Pontiac takes great pains to reduce the number of squeaks and rattles in the Firebird. Body has been stiffened for a tighter feel. Performance Equipment Group is available on Formula and Trans Am coupes, and boosts tuned-port 5.0-liter to 230 horsepower.

Category E

2 Dr STD Conv	3112	3857	5100
2 Dr STD Cpe	1953	2420	3200
2 Dr Formula Cpe	2624	3252	4300
2 Dr Trans Am Conv	3966	4916	6500
2 Dr Trans Am Cpe	2868	3555	4700
2 Dr Trans Am GTA Cpe	4210	5219	6900

OPTIONS FOR FIREBIRD

8 cyl 5.7 L Engine[Opt on Formula, Trans Am] +106
Air Conditioning[Opt on STD] +106
Automatic 4-Speed Transmission +168
Glass Panel T-tops +206
Leather Seats +122
Premium Sound System +91
T-Tops (Solid/Colored) +138

GRAND AM 1992

Redesign nets Grand Am swoopy look, standard ABS and optional V6 power. Car is now based on same platform as Chevy Corsica/Beretta. SE and GT models are available. Standard engine is a 120-horsepower SOHC engine. GT gets 180-horsepower Quad 4. Optional on both is a 3.3-liter V6. Hook an automatic to the Quad 4 engine and horsepower drops to 160.

Category C

2 Dr GT Cpe	1274	1809	2700
4 Dr GT Sdn	1321	1876	2800
2 Dr SE Cpe	1085	1541	2300
4 Dr SE Sdn	1132	1608	2400

OPTIONS FOR GRAND AM

4 cyl 2.3 L Quad 4 Engine[Opt on Sdn] +136
6 cyl 3.3 L Engine +97
Air Conditioning +176
Automatic 3-Speed Transmission +95

GRAND PRIX 1992

All sedans get STE light-bar front styling treatment. Base 160-horsepower Quad 4 motor replaced by 140-horsepower 3.1-liter V6. GTP coupe still has 210-horsepower twin-cam V6 standard. ABS is standard on GT, GTP, and STE; optional on LE and SE. Base SE coupes can be dressed in GT lower-body extensions.

Category D

2 Dr GT Cpe	1634	2259	3300
4 Dr LE Sdn	1337	1848	2700
2 Dr SE Cpe	1387	1917	2800
4 Dr SE Sdn	1535	2122	3100
4 Dr STE Sdn	1783	2464	3600

OPTIONS FOR GRAND PRIX

6 cyl 3.4 L Engine +212
Aero Performance Package +350
Anti-Lock Brakes[Opt on LE, SE] +95
Automatic 4-Speed Transmission[Opt on LE, SE] +148
Leather Seats +148
Power Sunroof +146

LE MANS 1992

LE designation swapped for SE nomenclature. Coupe gets amber turn signals.

Category A

2 Dr SE Cpe	552	833	1300
4 Dr SE Sdn	637	961	1500
2 Dr Value Leader Cpe	297	448	700

OPTIONS FOR LE MANS

Air Conditioning +148
Automatic 3-Speed Transmission +116
Sunroof +95

SUNBIRD 1992

ABS is standard. LE designation extended to base coupe and sedan. 2.0-liter four-cylinder engine gets 15 more horsepower. Brake/transmission shift interlock is added. Fuel capacity jumps to 15.2 gallons. Automatic door locks lock doors when automatic is shifted from "Park" or manually shifted car begins moving forward. Convertible gets glass rear window at midyear.

Category B

2 Dr GT Cpe	1247	1754	2600
2 Dr LE Cpe	815	1147	1700

Don't forget to refer to the Mileage Adjustment Table at the back of this book!

PONTIAC 92

Model Description	Trade-in TMV	Private TMV	Dealer TMV	Model Description	Trade-in TMV	Private TMV	Dealer TMV
4 Dr LE Sdn	850	1196	1772				
2 Dr SE Conv	1391	1957	2900				
2 Dr SE Cpe	877	1233	1828				
4 Dr SE Sdn	911	1282	1900				

OPTIONS FOR SUNBIRD
6 cyl 3.1 L Engine[Opt on SE] +126
Air Conditioning +148
Automatic 3-Speed Transmission +116
Sunroof +95

TRANS SPORT   1992

ABS is standard. SE becomes base model; new top-of-the-line is the GT. GT gets a standard 3.8-liter V6 good for 165 horsepower. SE retains old 3.1-liter, but offers the bigger motor as an option. 15-inch wheels replace 14-inch wheels on both models. Remote keyless entry and rear climate controls are added to the options list.

Category P

Model Description	Trade-in TMV	Private TMV	Dealer TMV
2 Dr GT Pass. Van	2197	2873	4000
2 Dr SE Pass. Van	1867	2442	3400

OPTIONS FOR TRANS SPORT
6 cyl 3.8 L Engine[Opt on SE] +169
Air Conditioning[Opt on SE] +95
Automatic 4-Speed Transmission[Opt on SE] +148
Dual Air Conditioning +95

Don't forget to refer to the Mileage Adjustment Table at the back of this book!

PORSCHE 01-00

Model Description	Trade-in TMV	Private TMV	Dealer TMV	Model Description	Trade-in TMV	Private TMV	Dealer TMV

PORSCHE Germany

1997 Porsche 911

2001 PORSCHE

911   2001

After a one-year hiatus, the 911 Turbo model makes its much-anticipated return and brings with it 415 tire-shredding horsepower. All 911s get electric engine cover and trunk releases, improved interior lighting, and improved trunk carpet. A new optional audio system includes a bass box, there are optional "Turbo Look 1" wheels, a self dimming day/night rear view mirror, and a new three-spoke steering wheel with colored Porsche crests.

Category F

Model	Trade-in	Private	Dealer
2 Dr Carrera Conv	62956	64981	68356
2 Dr Carrera Cpe	55090	56862	59815
2 Dr Carrera 4 AWD Conv			
	67511	69683	73302
2 Dr Carrera 4 AWD Cpe			
	59645	61563	64761
Category R			
2 Dr Turbo AWD Cpe	91581	94166	98474

OPTIONS FOR 911

AM/FM Compact Disc Player +256
Aero Kit +7000
Automatic 5-Speed Transmission +2923
Automatic Dimming Mirror +590
Compact Disc Changer +603
Dual Power Seats +1234
Heated Front Seats +325
Leather Seat Package +2992
Leather Seats[Std on Turbo] +2748
Luggage Rack +333
Metallic Paint +1885
Metallic Paint To Sample +2927

Navigation System +3026
Park Distance Control +444
Rear Window Wiper +286
Special Factory Paint +1885
Sport Classic Wheels[Opt on Cpe] +2274
Sport Design Wheels +2274
Sport Suspension +590
Traction Control System[Opt on Carrera] +1038

BOXSTER   2001

Minor interior changes are in store for 2001. The Boxster S' thicker roof lining has migrated to the regular Boxster. Both cars now feature a hidden cell phone antenna, a gauge cluster design similar to the 911's, improved interior lighting and better dashboard material quality. Porsche has also added a new button to the ignition key to control the driver's seat and outside memory function. In terms of optional equipment, the sophisticated Porsche Stability Management system is now available for the Boxster and Boxster S.

Category F

Model	Trade-in	Private	Dealer
2 Dr S Conv	41395	42727	44946
2 Dr STD Conv	34918	36041	37913

OPTIONS FOR BOXSTER

AM/FM Compact Disc Player +256
Aero Kit +5321
Automatic 5-Speed Transmission +2744
Automatic Dimming Mirror +590
Compact Disc Changer +675
Cruise Control +456
Dual Power Seats +1299
Hardtop Roof +1962
Heated Front Seats +325
Leather Seat Package +2026
Luggage Rack +393
Metallic Paint +2573
Navigation System +3026
Painted Rims +145
Park Distance Control +444
Special Factory Paint +688
Sport Classic Wheels +1090
Sport Design Wheels +2274
Sport Suspension +590
Traction Control System +1038
Trip Computer +365

2000 PORSCHE

911   2000

A new exhaust system bumps horsepower from 296 to 300. Already featured on Carrera 4 models, two-wheel-drive Carreras now get an electronic drive-by-wire throttle and optional PSM stability control. All models receive an upgraded interior console and materials. The formerly optional charcoal odor filter is now standard. There are two new standard and one new optional exterior colors.

Category F

Model Description	Trade-in TMV	Private TMV	Dealer TMV
2 Dr Carrera Conv	56713	59676	62412
2 Dr Carrera Cpe	49623	52216	54610
2 Dr Carrera 4 AWD Conv			
	60817	63995	66929
2 Dr Carrera 4 AWD Cpe			
	53728	56535	59127

OPTIONS FOR 911

AM/FM Compact Disc Player +256
Aluminum & Chrome Package[Opt on Carrera Cpe] +609
Auto-Manual Transmission +2639
Automatic Dimming Mirror +461
Compact Disc Changer +573
Dual Power Seats +1234
Full Leather Interior[Opt on Carrera Conv] +1210
Heated Front Seats +325
Leather Dashboard Package[Opt on Carrera Cpe] +2252
Leather Interior Trim[Opt on Carrera Cpe] +1616
Limited Slip Differential[Opt on Carrera] +986
Luggage Rack +121
Metallic Paint +653
Navigation System +2731
Onboard Computer +223
Rear Window Wiper +273
Special Factory Paint +1260
Special Interior Trim[Opt on Carrera Conv] +316
Sport Classic Wheels[Opt on Cpe] +2049
Sport Design Radial Wheels[Opt on Carrera Cpe] +2049
Sport Seats +605
Traction Control System[Opt on Carrera] +707

BOXSTER   2000

The big news for 2000 is the Boxster S. This more powerful version of the Boxster features a bigger engine that generates 250 horsepower. The regular Boxster (if you can call it that) also gets a horsepower boost in 2000, going from 201 to 217. Both models feature upgraded interior materials and new exterior colors.

Category F

Model Description	Trade-in TMV	Private TMV	Dealer TMV
2 Dr STD Conv	31416	33058	34573
2 Dr S Conv	37460	39417	41224

OPTIONS FOR BOXSTER

18 Inch Sport Classic Wheels +3216
AM/FM Compact Disc Player +256
AM/FM Stereo/CD/Tape +489
Auto-Manual Transmission +2479
Automatic Dimming Mirror +458
Boxster Design Wheels +986
Compact Disc Changer +675
Cruise Control +456
Dyno Wheels +902
Hardtop Roof +1863
Heated Front Seats +325
Leather Seat/Interior Trim +1616

Luggage Rack +203
Metallic Paint +653
Navigation System +2731
Onboard Computer +365
Power Seats w/Memory +1234
Roll/Light Bar +418
Special Factory Paint +653
Special Leather Seat Trim +383
Sport Classic Wheels +902
Sport Design Radial Wheels +3216
Sport Package +1714
Technic Sport Package +1575
Tonneau Cover +1025
Traction Control System +707

1999 PORSCHE

911   1999

Everything just got better with the totally redesigned 911, internally named the 996. The 911 Coupe, Cabriolet and Carrera 4 (available as either a coupe or cabrio) are all available for the 1999 model year.

Category F

Model Description	Trade-in TMV	Private TMV	Dealer TMV
2 Dr Carrera Conv	51483	54255	57027
2 Dr Carrera Cpe	45048	47473	49899
2 Dr Carrera 4 AWD Conv			
	55209	58181	61154
2 Dr Carrera 4 AWD Cpe			
	48773	51399	54025

OPTIONS FOR 911

AM/FM Compact Disc Player +210
AM/FM Stereo/CD/Tape +399
Aluminum & Chrome Package[Opt on Carrera Cpe] +498
Auto-Manual Transmission +2160
Automatic Dimming Mirror +377
Compact Disc Changer +469
Dual Power Seats +1011
Hardtop Roof +8088
Heated Front Seats +266
Leather Dashboard Package +1711
Leather Interior Trim[Opt on Carrera Cpe] +1323
Limited Slip Differential[Opt on Carrera] +809
Luggage Rack +100
Metallic Paint +535
Onboard Computer +183
PCM Info/Navigation System +1788
Power Drivers Seat +250
Premium Sound System +399
Rear Window Wiper +223
Special Factory Paint +1032
Sport Classic Wheels[Opt on Cpe] +1765
Sport Design Radial Wheels[Opt on Carrera Cpe] +1765
Sport Seats +495
Targa Wheels[Opt on Carrera 4 Cpe] +619
Technology Alloy Wheels +2039
Traction Control System[Opt on Carrera] +579

Don't forget to refer to the Mileage Adjustment Table at the back of this book!

Model Description	Trade-in TMV	Private TMV	Dealer TMV

BOXSTER 1999

The Boxster is slowly adding features and options. This year, a Classic Package includes metallic paint and all-leather seats, and adds special highlights to the interior. The gas tank is increased from a 12.5- to a 14.1- gallon capacity, and gas-discharge Litronic headlights are optional. All the features in the Sport Package are individually optional this year, and 18-inch wheels are now available.

Category F

2 Dr STD Conv	28519	30054	31590

OPTIONS FOR BOXSTER
AM/FM Compact Disc Player +210
AM/FM Stereo/CD/Tape +400
Auto-Manual Transmission +2029
Automatic Dimming Mirror +376
Boxster Design Wheels +983
Compact Disc Changer +553
Cruise Control +373
Hardtop Roof +1526
Heated Front Seats +266
Leather Seat/Interior Trim +1323
Light Alloy Turbo Wheels +998
Metallic Paint +535
Onboard Computer +299
Roll/Light Bar +342
Special Factory Paint +535
Special Leather Seat Trim +1575
Sport Classic Wheels +1655
Sport Design Wheels +983
Sport Package +2082
Technic Sport Package +1290
Traction Control System +579

1998 PORSCHE

911 1998

The current-generation 911 goes the way of the dodo at year's end, when it will be replaced by the next evolutionary step toward the perfect driving machine.

Category F

2 Dr Carrera AWD Conv	59800	63197	66877
2 Dr Carrera Conv	53202	56224	59498
2 Dr Carrera 4S AWD Cpe			
	53202	56224	59498
2 Dr Carrera S Cpe	47427	50121	53040
2 Dr Targa Cpe	49489	52300	55346

OPTIONS FOR 911
5-Spoke Cast Alloy Wheels[Opt on Conv] +927
AM/FM Compact Disc Player +203
Aero Kit[Opt on S Cpe] +3492
Auto-Manual Transmission +1990
Automatic Dimming Mirror +288
Compact Disc Changer +522

Dual Power Seats +645
Hardtop Roof[Opt on Cabriolet] +7809
Heated Front Seats +371
Hi-Fi Sound Stereo Equipment[Opt on S Cpe] +598
Leather Interior Trim[Opt on S Cpe] +1847
Leather Seats +991
Leather/Vinyl Interior Trim[Opt on S Cpe] +373
Limited Slip Differential[Std on Carrera 4S, 4WD] +804
Metallic Paint +2531
Onboard Computer +282
Power Drivers Seat +363
Rear Window Wiper +229
Special Chassis[Opt on S Cpe] +432
Special Factory Paint +996
Special Leather Interior Trim[Opt on S Cpe] +1823
Sport Chassis w/18 Inch Wheels[Opt on S Cpe] +2379
Sport Classic Wheels +1704
Targa Wheels +598
Technology Alloy Wheels +1969
Traction Control System[Opt on 2WD] +804

BOXSTER 1998

Side air bags are standard for 1998.

Category F

2 Dr STD Conv	26179	27666	29277

OPTIONS FOR BOXSTER
AM/FM Compact Disc Player +203
AM/FM Stereo/CD/Tape +387
Alarm System +393
Auto-Manual Transmission +1958
Boxster Design Wheels +949
Compact Disc Changer +533
Cruise Control +360
Hardtop Roof +1089
Heated Front Seats +257
Leather Seat/Interior Trim +1252
Metallic Paint +517
Onboard Computer +288
Roll/Light Bar +330
Special Leather Seat Trim +1492
Sport Classic Wheels +1598
Sport Package +2010
Technic Sport Package +1245
Theft Deterrent System +393
Traction Control System +559

1997 PORSCHE

911 1997

The only change to this year's Porsche 911 is the availability of a Porsche-engineered child seat that will deactivate the passenger airbag when it is in place.

Category F

2 Dr Carrera AWD Conv	52142	55633	59899
2 Dr Carrera Conv	47366	50537	54412
2 Dr Carrera Cpe	42191	45015	48467

Don't forget to refer to the Mileage Adjustment Table at the back of this book!

Model Description	Trade-in TMV	Private TMV	Dealer TMV
2 Dr Carrera 4S AWD Cpe			
	48957	52234	56240
2 Dr Targa Cpe	43783	46714	50296
Category R			
2 Dr Turbo AWD Cpe	66005	69631	74064
2 Dr Turbo S AWD Cpe	96405	101702	108176

OPTIONS FOR 911

17 Inch Cup Design Wheels[Opt on Carrera Cpe] +861
17 Inch Targa Wheels[Opt on Carrera Cpe] +555
5 Spoke Light Alloy Wheels[Opt on Carrera Cpe] +861
AM/FM Compact Disc Player +188
Aero Kit[Opt on Carrera 4S Cpe, Carrera Cpe] +3244
Aluminum & Chrome Package +1237
Auto-Manual Transmission +1849
Automatic Dimming Mirror[Std on Turbo S] +267
Compact Disc Changer +485
Dual Power Seats[Std on Turbo, Turbo S] +599
Hardtop Roof +7254
Heated Front Seats[Std on Turbo S] +345
Hi-Fi Sound System[Opt on Carrera 4S Cpe, Carrera Cpe] +555
Leather Interior Trim[Opt on Carrera 4S Cpe] +930
Leather Seats[Std on Turbo, Turbo S] +921
Limited Slip Differential[Opt on Targa, 2WD] +748
Metallic Paint[Std on Turbo, Turbo S] +2351
Onboard Computer[Std on Turbo, Turbo S] +262
Pearlescent White Paint[Opt on Carrera 4S Cpe, Carrera Cpe] +6203
Power Drivers Seat +337
Rear Window Wiper[Std on Turbo, Turbo S] +213
Special Factory Paint +925

BOXSTER 1997

This all-new roadster is introduced to compete in the revitalized midpriced sports car category. The Boxster features a 2.5-liter six-cylinder engine, a five-speed manual or five-speed Tiptronic transmission, and a power top that closes in an impressive 12 seconds.
Category F

Model Description	Trade-in TMV	Private TMV	Dealer TMV
2 Dr STD Conv	24324	25952	27942

OPTIONS FOR BOXSTER

AM/FM Compact Disc Player +188
AM/FM Stereo/CD/Tape +358
Aero Kit +894
Alarm System +365
Auto-Manual Transmission +1818
Automatic Dimming Mirror +337
Boxster Design Wheels +882
Compact Disc Changer +496
Cruise Control +334
Hardtop Roof +1011
Heated Front Seats +505
Leather Seat Trim +1145
Metallic Paint +479
Onboard Computer +267
Rain Sensing Windshield Wipers +236

Roll/Light Bar +169
Special Factory Paint +479
Special Leather Seat Trim +1368
Sport Classic Wheels +1485
Sport Package +1799
Tonneau Cover +506
Traction Control System +492

1996 PORSCHE

911 1996

Trick Targa model joins the lineup, and power is up in midrange revs. New Carrera 4S model provides Turbo looks without Turbo price or performance. Bigger wheels are standard across the line, as well as Litronic headlights. New stereos and exterior colors compliment one new interior color this year. Remote keyless entry system gets an immobilizer feature.
Category R

Model Description	Trade-in TMV	Private TMV	Dealer TMV
2 Dr Turbo AWD Cpe	60640	64602	70073
Category F			
2 Dr Carrera AWD Conv	46688	49765	54015
2 Dr Carrera AWD Cpe	39962	42596	46233
2 Dr Carrera Conv	42336	45127	48980
2 Dr Carrera Cpe	36402	38801	42114
2 Dr Carrera 4S AWD Cpe			
	43920	46814	50812
2 Dr Targa Cpe	41149	43862	47607

OPTIONS FOR 911

5 Spoke Light Alloy Wheels[Opt on Carrera, Targa] +883
AM/FM Compact Disc Player +193
AM/FM Stereo/CD/Tape +336
Auto-Manual Transmission +2410
Compact Disc Changer +497
Dual Power Seats[Std on STD] +614
Heated Front Seats +353
Hi-Fi Sound System[Opt on Carrera 4S] +568
Leather Seats[Std on Turbo] +944
Limited Slip Differential[Opt on 2WD] +766
Metallic Paint +633
Onboard Computer +268
Pearlescent White Paint +6360
Power Drivers Seat +223
Rear Window Wiper[Std on STD] +218
Seat Package +1247
Spoke Wheels +883
Steering Wheel Package +740

1995 PORSCHE

911 1995

Category F

Model Description	Trade-in TMV	Private TMV	Dealer TMV
2 Dr Carrera AWD Conv	39421	42156	46715
2 Dr Carrera AWD Cpe	34783	37197	41219

Don't forget to refer to the Mileage Adjustment Table at the back of this book!

Model Description	Trade-in TMV	Private TMV	Dealer TMV
2 Dr Carrera Conv	37103	39677	43968
2 Dr Carrera Cpe	30919	33064	36640

OPTIONS FOR 911
5 Spoke Light Alloy Wheels[Opt on Carrera Cpe] +733
AM/FM Compact Disc Player +160
AM/FM Stereo/CD/Tape +278
Active Brake Differential[Opt on Conv] +507
Auto-Manual Transmission +1573
Chrome Wheels[Opt on Carrera Conv] +609
Compact Disc Changer +357
Dual Power Seats +509
Heated Front Seats +203
Hi-Fi Sound System w/Amplifier[Opt on Conv] +405
Leather Seats +783
Limited Slip Differential[Opt on 2WD] +617
Metallic Paint +408
Onboard Computer +140
Pearlescent White Paint +5278
Power Drivers Seat +185
Pressure Cast Alloy Wheels[Opt on Conv] +761
Rear Window Wiper +170
Seat Package +1035
Steering Wheel Package +615
Telephone Handset Kit +634

928   1995
Category F

Model Description	Trade-in TMV	Private TMV	Dealer TMV
2 Dr GTS Cpe	33067	35362	39186

OPTIONS FOR 928
Auto-Manual Transmission +1395
Heated Front Seats +254
Leather Seat Package +837
Package 1 +634
Package 2 +532
Package 3 +888
Package 4 +532

968   1995
Category F

Model Description	Trade-in TMV	Private TMV	Dealer TMV
2 Dr STD Conv	20870	22318	24732
2 Dr STD Cpe	17005	18185	20152

OPTIONS FOR 968
17 Inch 5-Spoke Wheels[Opt on Conv] +583
AM/FM Compact Disc Player +254
AM/FM Stereo/CD/Tape +330
Auto-Manual Transmission +1395
Compact Disc Changer +356
Heated Front Seats +254
Leather Seats +786
Limited Slip Differential +254
Metallic Paint +381
Power Drivers Seat +229
Power Passenger Seat +229
Special Factory Paint +330

1994 PORSCHE

911   1994

Porsche modernizes the 911, updating and improving the car without killing its character. A more aerodynamic body and various tweaks to the engine and suspension make this old favorite even better.

Category F
2 Dr America Roadster Conv

Model Description	Trade-in TMV	Private TMV	Dealer TMV
	42054	45218	50491
2 Dr Cabriolet Conv	32496	34941	39016
2 Dr Carrera AWD Cpe	35448	38115	42560
2 Dr Carrera Cpe	26762	28775	32131
Category R			
2 Dr Carrera Turbo Cpe			
	42819	46020	51355
Category F			
2 Dr RS America Cpe	19115	20553	22950
2 Dr Speedster Conv	27825	29918	33407
2 Dr Targa Cpe	28291	30420	33967
2 Dr Wide Body AWD Cpe			
	34974	37606	41991
2 Dr Wide Body Cpe	29056	31242	34885

OPTIONS FOR 911
5 Spoke 17-Inch Wheels +499
AM/FM Compact Disc Player +137
AM/FM Stereo Tape[Std on Cabriolet Conv,Carrera 4WD Cpe] +239
Air Conditioning[Std on Cabriolet Conv,Carrera 4WD Cpe] +390
Auto-Manual Transmission +1346
Climate Control for AC[Opt on RS America] +260
Compact Disc Changer +305
Hardtop Roof +5278
Heated Front Seats +174
Limited Slip Differential +528
Metallic Paint +349
Power Drivers Seat +158
Power Passenger Seat +195
Power Sunroof[Std on Carrera] +521
Rear Window Wiper +146

911S   1994
Category R

Model Description	Trade-in TMV	Private TMV	Dealer TMV
2 Dr STD Turbo Cpe	42919	46127	51474

OPTIONS FOR 911S
AM/FM Compact Disc Player +217
Air Dam +217
Aluminum/Alloy Wheels +369
Compact Disc Changer +304
Heated Front Seats +217

928   1994
Category F

Model Description	Trade-in TMV	Private TMV	Dealer TMV
2 Dr GTS Cpe	26028	27986	31250

Don't forget to refer to the Mileage Adjustment Table at the back of this book!

PORSCHE 94-92

Model Description	Trade-in TMV	Private TMV	Dealer TMV

OPTIONS FOR 928
Heated Front Seats +217
Leather Seat Package +716
Metallic Paint +325
Package 1 +542
Package 2 +455
Package 3 +760
Package 4 +455
Sport Suspension +386

968 — 1994

Category F

Model Description	Trade-in TMV	Private TMV	Dealer TMV
2 Dr STD Cpe	14528	15621	17443
2 Dr Cabriolet Conv	17586	18909	21114

OPTIONS FOR 968
5-Spoke 17-Inch Wheels +499
AM/FM Compact Disc Player +217
Auto-Manual Transmission +1193
Compact Disc Changer +304
Heated Front Seats +217
Leather Seats +672
Limited Slip Differential +217
Metallic Paint +325
Power Drivers Seat +195
Power Passenger Seat +195
Premium Sound System +369
Rear Spoiler +195
Sport Chassis +803

1993 PORSCHE

911 — 1993

Category F

Model Description	Trade-in TMV	Private TMV	Dealer TMV
2 Dr America Roadster Conv	36460	39712	45133
2 Dr Cabriolet AWD Conv	28542	31088	35331
2 Dr Cabriolet Conv	25172	27418	31160
2 Dr Carrera AWD Cpe	25650	27939	31752
2 Dr Carrera Cpe	22464	24468	27808
2 Dr RS America Cpe	17677	19254	21882
2 Dr Targa AWD Cpe	26868	29265	33259
2 Dr Targa Cpe	22998	25050	28469

OPTIONS FOR 911
AM/FM Compact Disc Player +115
AM/FM Stereo Tape[Std on Cabriolet Conv,Carrera 4WD Cpe] +201
AM/FM Stereo/CD/Tape +201
Air Conditioning[Std on Cabriolet Conv,Carrera 4WD Cpe] +328
Auto-Manual Transmission +1132
Climate Control for AC[Opt on RS America] +218
Compact Disc Changer +257

Dual Power Seats +366
Hardtop Roof +4438
Heated Front Seats +146
Leather Seats[Opt on Cabriolet] +564
Limited Slip Differential +444
Metallic Paint +293
Power Drivers Seat +133
Power Passenger Seat +164
Power Sunroof[Std on Carrera] +438
Rear Window Wiper +122
Spoke Wheels +527

928 — 1993

Category F

Model Description	Trade-in TMV	Private TMV	Dealer TMV
2 Dr GTS Cpe	20668	22511	25584

OPTIONS FOR 928
AM/FM Stereo Tape +201
Auto-Manual Transmission +1003

968 — 1993

Category F

Model Description	Trade-in TMV	Private TMV	Dealer TMV
2 Dr STD Conv	15836	17249	19603
2 Dr STD Cpe	12337	13438	15272

OPTIONS FOR 968
5 Spoke 17-Inch Wheels[Opt on Cpe] +419
968 Special Chassis[Opt on Cpe] +730
AM/FM Stereo Tape +201
Auto-Manual Transmission +1003
Compact Disc Changer +255
Dual Power Seats[Opt on Conv] +218
Heated Front Seats +183
Leather Interior w/Black Belt[Opt on Cpe] +438
Leather Seats +565
Limited Slip Differential +183
Metallic Paint +274
Metallic Paint To Sample +875
Painted Rims[Opt on Conv] +365
Power Drivers Seat[Opt on Conv] +164
Rear Spoiler +164
Special Factory Paint +237
Special Leather Upholstry[Opt on Cpe] +529
Sport Seats +274

1992 PORSCHE

911 — 1992

Category F

Model Description	Trade-in TMV	Private TMV	Dealer TMV
2 Dr America Roadster Conv	30228	33197	38146

Category R

Model Description	Trade-in TMV	Private TMV	Dealer TMV
2 Dr STD Turbo Cpe	30947	34013	39123

Category F

Model Description	Trade-in TMV	Private TMV	Dealer TMV
2 Dr Cabriolet Conv	23524	25835	29686
2 Dr Carrera Cpe	19432	21341	24522
2 Dr Carrera 4 AWD Conv			

Don't forget to refer to the Mileage Adjustment Table at the back of this book!

Model Description	Trade-in TMV	Private TMV	Dealer TMV
	26449	29047	33377
2 Dr Carrera 4 AWD Cpe			
	23976	26331	30257
2 Dr Carrera 4 Targa AWD Cpe			
	24663	27086	31124
2 Dr Targa Cpe	19791	21736	24976

OPTIONS FOR 911
Auto-Manual Transmission +1096
Climate Control for AC[Opt on America Roadster] +212
Compact Disc Changer +249
Dual Power Seats[Std on STD] +355
Hardtop Roof +4300
Heated Front Seats +142
Leather Seats[Opt on America Roadster] +546
Limited Slip Differential +430
Metallic Paint +284
Onboard Computer +98
Power Drivers Seat +128
Power Passenger Seat +159
Rear Window Wiper[Opt on Carrera] +118
Special Factory Paint +548
Special Leather Seat Trim[Opt on Turbo] +512
Tonneau Cover[Opt on Conv] +318

968 — 1992

944 replacement arrives, sporting 928-inspired front end and the most powerful (naturally aspirated) 4-cylinder engine available anywhere.

Model Description	Trade-in TMV	Private TMV	Dealer TMV
Category F			
2 Dr STD Cpe	11155	12251	14077
2 Dr Cabriolet Conv	14322	15729	18074

OPTIONS FOR 968
Auto-Manual Transmission +971
Compact Disc Changer +248
Heated Front Seats +176
Leather Seats +548
Metallic Paint +265
Power Drivers Seat +159
Power Passenger Seat +159
Special Factory Paint +230

Don't forget to refer to the Mileage Adjustment Table at the back of this book!

Model Description	Trade-in TMV	Private TMV	Dealer TMV

SAAB   Sweden

1997 Saab 900 Convertible

Model Description	Trade-in TMV	Private TMV	Dealer TMV
4 Dr Aero Turbo Sdn	29789	31371	34006
4 Dr Aero Turbo Wgn	30005	31597	34252
4 Dr SE V6t Turbo Sdn	28461	29972	32490
4 Dr SE V6t Turbo Wgn	28972	30510	33073
4 Dr 2.3t Turbo Sdn	24574	25878	28052
4 Dr 2.3t Turbo Wgn	25289	26632	28869

OPTIONS FOR 9-5
Automatic 4-Speed Transmission[Std on SE V6t] +731
Harman Kardon Sound System[Opt on 2.3t] +396
Heated Seats +363
Leather Seats[Opt on 2.3t] +488
Metallic Paint +274

2001 SAAB

9-3   2001

The base convertible has been dropped for this year while all other models get two new colors. The OnStar telematics system and traction control are now standard.
Category H

	Trade-in	Private	Dealer
4 Dr SE Turbo Hbk	21736	22848	24700

Category F
2 Dr Viggen Turbo Conv

	Trade-in	Private	Dealer
	33167	34863	37690
2 Dr Viggen Turbo Hbk	26440	27793	30046
4 Dr Viggen Turbo Hbk	26745	28113	30392

Category H

	Trade-in	Private	Dealer
2 Dr SE Turbo Conv	27005	28386	30688
2 Dr STD Turbo Hbk	17835	18747	20267
4 Dr STD Turbo Hbk	18576	19526	21109

OPTIONS FOR 9-3
Automatic 4-Speed Transmission +731
Climate Control for AC[Opt on SE Conv] +122
Dual Air Conditioning +305
Heated Front Seats +274
Leather Seats[Std on SE,Viggen,Conv] +823
Metallic Paint +274
Power Moonroof[Opt on STD] +701
Power Passenger Seat[Opt on SE Conv] +213

9-5   2001

Entry-level models get more horsepower from the turbo four-cylinder while all models get the OnStar telematics system, turbo gauges, and two new colors.
Category I

2000 SAAB

9-3   2000

The base model gets restyled 15-inch alloy wheels, while the SE version gains performance enhancements and increased horsepower. The sporty 9-3 Viggen offers even more power, and is available as a five-door or convertible in addition to the coupe. All engines are now LEV compliant and GM's OnStar "Telematics" System becomes optional across the model lineup.
Category H

	Trade-in	Private	Dealer
2 Dr STD Turbo Conv	21453	23135	24687
2 Dr STD Turbo Hbk	13332	14377	15342
4 Dr STD Turbo Hbk	14221	15336	16365
2 Dr SE HO Turbo Conv	22418	24175	25797
4 Dr SE HO Turbo Hbk	16294	17571	18750

Category F
2 Dr Viggen Turbo Conv

	Trade-in	Private	Dealer
	27232	29384	31370
2 Dr Viggen Turbo Hbk	20875	22524	24047
4 Dr Viggen Turbo Hbk	21300	22983	24537

OPTIONS FOR 9-3
AM/FM Compact Disc Player +152
Automatic 4-Speed Transmission +731
Compact Disc Changer +274
Heated Front Seats +225
Heated Seats +317
Leather Seats[Std on SE HO,Viggen,Conv] +670
Metallic Paint +213
OnStar Telematic System +545
Power Moonroof[Opt on STD] +701

9-5   2000

Intended to do for the 9-5 line what the Viggen does for the 9-3, Saab debuts the high-performance 9-5 Aero Sedan and Wagon with 230 horsepower. Entry-level sedans and wagons sport new 16-inch 10-spoke alloy wheels, and all SE versions offer a turbo V6 and auto-dimming rearview mirror. The 9-5 Wagon Gary Fisher Edition offers a sportier exterior design and a Saab

Don't forget to refer to the Mileage Adjustment Table at the back of this book!

SAAB 00-98

Model Description	Trade-in TMV	Private TMV	Dealer TMV	Model Description	Trade-in TMV	Private TMV	Dealer TMV

Limited Edition Gary Fisher mountain bike. A sunroof and traction-control system (TCS) have been added to the standard equipment list.

Category I

	Trade-in	Private	Dealer
4 Dr 2.3t Turbo Sdn	18667	20127	21474
4 Dr 2.3t Turbo Wgn	18963	20446	21814
4 Dr Aero Turbo Sdn	23808	25670	27388
4 Dr Aero Turbo Wgn	23388	25216	26904
4 Dr Gary Fisher ED. Turbo Wgn	22123	23852	25449
4 Dr SE V6t Turbo Sdn	22334	24080	25692
4 Dr SE V6t Turbo Wgn	22334	24080	25692

OPTIONS FOR 9-5

Automatic 4-Speed Transmission[Std on SE V6t] +731
BBS Wheel Upgrade +1005
Harman Kardon Sound System[Opt on 2.3t] +396
Heated Seats +317
Leather Seats[Opt on 2.3t] +823
Metallic Paint +213
OnStar Telematic System +545
Wheel and Tire Package +1189

1999 SAAB

9-3   1999

Saab changed about 1,000 suspension, steering and interior pieces on the 900 and decided to change the car's name to the 9-3, giving it a mild exterior freshening to boot. Around mid-year, a high-output version of its 2.0-liter turbo four-cylinder (making an amazing 200 horsepower) becomes the standard engine in the uplevel SE five-door and SE Convertible models equipped with a manual transmission. All SE's also get new five-spoke 16-inch alloy wheels. All five-speed manual 9-3s get revised gearbox ratios and a numerically higher (4.05:1) final drive ratio for better off-the-line feel. A revised 9-3 interior headliner provides more padding for increased protection in the event of a crash. And five-door SE variants add an integrated driver-seat armrest and a centrally located cupholder that swings out from the instrument panel.

Category H

	Trade-in	Private	Dealer
2 Dr STD Turbo Conv	16230	17700	19170
2 Dr STD Turbo Hbk	11255	12275	13294
4 Dr STD Turbo Hbk	11769	12835	13901
2 Dr SE Turbo Conv	21542	23493	25444
4 Dr SE Turbo Hbk	14015	15285	16554
2 Dr SE HO Turbo Conv	22203	24214	26225
4 Dr SE HO Turbo Hbk	14123	15402	16681

Category F

	Trade-in	Private	Dealer
2 Dr Viggen Turbo Hbk	18899	20779	22659

OPTIONS FOR 9-3

Automatic 4-Speed Transmission +570

Child Seat (1) +149
Compact Disc Changer +222
Heated Front Seats +183
Heated Seats +258
Leather Seats[Std on SE,SE HO,Viggen,Conv] +668
Power Moonroof[Opt on STD] +570
Styling Value Package +661

9-5   1999

Saab's 9-5 model replaces the 9000 line for 1999. Available as a sedan or a station wagon with turbocharged four-cylinder or V6 engines, the new 9-5 is designed to showcase three Saab "world-first" technologies: an active head-restraint system, ventilated seats, and an "asymmetrically turbocharged" V6. Saab has added two-stage head- and chest-protecting side airbags and its new force-reducing front seatbelt pre-tensioners as standard equipment. Also available on all 9-5 models is GM's dealer-installed OnStar mobile communications system.

Category I

	Trade-in	Private	Dealer
4 Dr SE V6 Turbo Sdn	18434	20208	21981
4 Dr SE Turbo Sdn	16843	18463	20083
4 Dr STD Turbo Sdn	15439	16924	18409
4 Dr STD Turbo Wgn	16201	17760	19318
4 Dr V6 Turbo Wgn	18459	20234	22010

OPTIONS FOR 9-5

Automatic 4-Speed Transmission[Std on SE V6,V6 Turbo Wgn] +570
Child Seat (1) +149
Heated Seats +258
Leather Seats[Opt on STD,STD Turbo Wgn] +668
Power Moonroof[Opt on STD] +570
Power Ventilated Seats +458
Rear Spoiler +146
Spoke Wheels +173

1998 SAAB

900   1998

The Saab 900 three-door hatchback gets the same turbocharged engine as the SE models this year. Other changes include the addition of body-color front and rear bumpers.

Category H

	Trade-in	Private	Dealer
2 Dr S Conv	13268	14588	16019
2 Dr S Turbo Hbk	10733	11801	12958
4 Dr S Hbk	10879	11962	13135
2 Dr SE Turbo Conv	15353	16881	18536
2 Dr SE Turbo Hbk	11516	12662	13904
4 Dr SE Turbo Hbk	11762	12933	14201

OPTIONS FOR 900

Don't forget to refer to the Mileage Adjustment Table at the back of this book!

Model Description	Trade-in TMV	Private TMV	Dealer TMV	Model Description	Trade-in TMV	Private TMV	Dealer TMV

Automatic 4-Speed Transmission +395
Child Seats (2) +105
Leather Seats[Std on SE,Conv] +456
Power Moonroof[Opt on S] +395

9000 — 1998

No changes to the aging 9000.
Category I

Model	Trade-in	Private	Dealer
4 Dr CSE Turbo Hbk	12632	13978	15437

OPTIONS FOR 9000
Automatic 4-Speed Transmission +366

1997 SAAB

900 — 1997

No changes to this aging model.
Category H

Model	Trade-in	Private	Dealer
2 Dr S Conv	10881	12075	13534
2 Dr S Hbk	8849	9820	11006
4 Dr S Hbk	9085	10082	11300
2 Dr SE Turbo Conv	12625	14009	15702
2 Dr SE Turbo Hbk	9318	10340	11589
4 Dr SE Turbo Hbk	10292	11421	12801
2 Dr SE Talladega Turbo Conv	12783	14185	15899
2 Dr SE Talladega Turbo Hbk	10114	11223	12579
4 Dr SE Talladega Turbo Hbk	10434	11578	12977
2 Dr SE V6 Conv	13076	14510	16263
4 Dr SE V6 Hbk	10672	11843	13274

OPTIONS FOR 900
Automatic 4-Speed Transmission[Std on SE V6] +330
Leather Seats[Opt on S Hbk] +385
Power Moonroof[Opt on S] +330

9000 — 1997

No changes to this aging model.
Category I

Model	Trade-in	Private	Dealer
4 Dr Aero Turbo Hbk	12009	13424	15154
4 Dr CS Turbo Hbk	8434	9428	10643
4 Dr CSE Turbo Hbk	10136	11331	12791
4 Dr CSE Anniversary Turbo Hbk	10548	11791	13311
4 Dr CSE V6 Hbk	10956	12248	13826

OPTIONS FOR 9000
Automatic 4-Speed Transmission[Std on CSE V6] +342
Dual Power Seats[Opt on CS] +180
Leather Seats[Opt on CS] +507
Power Moonroof[Opt on CS] +365

1996 SAAB

900 — 1996

The popular Saab 900 SE five-door is available this year with the amazing turbocharged four-cylinder engine. An automatic transmission is now optional on turbos. V6 models come only with an automatic. Adjustable driver's lumbar support is now standard on all 900 models.
Category H

Model	Trade-in	Private	Dealer
2 Dr S Conv	9137	10267	11827
2 Dr S Hbk	7188	8077	9305
4 Dr S Hbk	7338	8246	9499
2 Dr SE Turbo Conv	11038	12404	14289
2 Dr SE Turbo Hbk	8149	9157	10549
4 Dr SE Turbo Hbk	8507	9559	11012
2 Dr SE V6 Conv	11957	13436	15478
4 Dr SE V6 Hbk	8964	10073	11604

OPTIONS FOR 900
Automatic 4-Speed Transmission[Opt on S,SE] +289
Compact Disc Changer +130
Leather Seats[Std on SE,SEV6,Conv] +341
Power Moonroof[Opt on S] +289

9000 — 1996

The 9000 sedans are dropped, leaving only the hatchback bodystyle. Cupholders for rear seat passengers, new upholstery for the CS, and new three-spoke alloy wheels for the CS and CSE round out the major developments for this year's model.
Category I

Model	Trade-in	Private	Dealer
4 Dr Aero Turbo Hbk	10052	11330	13096
4 Dr CS Turbo Hbk	6741	7599	8783
4 Dr CSE Turbo Hbk	7904	8909	10298
4 Dr CSE V6 Hbk	9439	10640	12298

OPTIONS FOR 9000
Automatic 4-Speed Transmission[Opt on CS,CSE] +303
Dual Power Seats[Opt on CS] +159
Leather Seats[Opt on CS] +450
Power Moonroof[Opt on CS] +323

1995 SAAB

900 — 1995

Daytime Running Lights (DRLs) are now standard on the 900. A convertible 900 appeared in 1995, and all 900 models get a new three-spoke steering wheel and an anti-theft alarm.
Category H

Model	Trade-in	Private	Dealer
2 Dr S Conv	6722	7594	9046
2 Dr S Hbk	5569	6291	7494
4 Dr S Hbk	5454	6161	7339
2 Dr SE Conv	8405	9494	11310

Don't forget to refer to the Mileage Adjustment Table at the back of this book!

Model Description	Trade-in TMV	Private TMV	Dealer TMV
2 Dr SE Turbo Conv	7378	8335	9929
2 Dr SE Turbo Hbk	6705	7574	9023
4 Dr SE Hbk	6651	7513	8950

OPTIONS FOR 900

AM/FM Compact Disc Player[Opt on S Conv] +87
Automatic 4-Speed Transmission +237
Compact Disc Changer[Opt on Hbk] +107
Leather Seats[Std on SE,SE,Conv] +279
Power Moonroof[Opt on S] +237

9000   1995

Saab adds a light-pressure turbo and a V6 to their large-car engine roster. V6 cars come only with an automatic transmission. Daytime running lights (DRLs) become standard on all 9000s this year.

Category I

Model Description	Trade-in TMV	Private TMV	Dealer TMV
4 Dr Aero Turbo Hbk	7688	8665	10293
4 Dr CDE Sdn	6709	7561	8982
4 Dr CS Turbo Hbk	5030	5669	6734
4 Dr CSE Hbk	6687	7537	8953
4 Dr CSE Turbo Hbk	6600	7438	8836

OPTIONS FOR 9000

Automatic 4-Speed Transmission[Opt on S,SE] +225
Dual Power Seats[Opt on CS Turbo] +131
Leather Seats[Std on SE,SE V6,Conv] +369
Power Moonroof[Opt on S] +265

1994 SAAB

900   1994

A totally new Saab is introduced with a little help from GM. The new 900 is available as two-door and two-door hatchbacks or a two-door convertible. The 900SE four-door features a V6 engine that was developed by GM for use in its Opels. Saab gets a new optional automatic transmission as well that offers three types of driving modes: sport, winter and economy. Saab's very cool black panel instrument cluster and dual airbags debut on this vehicle as well.

Category H

Model Description	Trade-in TMV	Private TMV	Dealer TMV
2 Dr STD Turbo Conv	6292	7225	8782
2 Dr Commemorative Turbo Conv			
	7406	8506	10338
2 Dr S Conv	5357	6153	7478
2 Dr S Hbk	3720	4273	5193
4 Dr S Hbk	3672	4217	5125
2 Dr SE Turbo Hbk	5330	6121	7440
4 Dr SE Hbk	5281	6065	7372

OPTIONS FOR 900

6 cyl 2.5 L Engine[Opt on S] +380
AM/FM Stereo/CD/Tape[Opt on S] +126
Automatic 3-Speed Transmission +136

Automatic 4-Speed Transmission +194
Leather Seats[Opt on S] +229
Power Moonroof[Opt on S] +194
Power Sunroof +185

9000   1994

Dual airbags for the 9000! CS models get front and rear fog lights. Unfortunately, traction control is dropped for all models.

Category I

Model Description	Trade-in TMV	Private TMV	Dealer TMV
4 Dr Aero Turbo Hbk	6083	6986	8491
4 Dr CD Turbo Sdn	4474	5138	6245
4 Dr CDE Sdn	4720	5420	6588
4 Dr CDE Turbo Sdn	5796	6657	8091
4 Dr CS Hbk	3801	4366	5306
4 Dr CS Turbo Hbk	4591	5272	6408
4 Dr CSE Hbk	4771	5480	6660
4 Dr CSE Turbo Hbk	5595	6426	7810

OPTIONS FOR 9000

AM/FM Stereo/CD/Tape +126
Automatic 4-Speed Transmission +184
Leather Seats[Opt on CD,CS] +302
Power Moonroof[Opt on CD] +217

1993 SAAB

900   1993

New nomenclature reflects Saab's current identity crisis. Base models are now called the CS and CD; luxury models are called CSE and CDE. Hatchbacks get more sedan-like styling that increases their length by four inches. A new Aero hatchback enters the lineup. The Aero is the fastest vehicle in the large-car class. It is powered by a 225-horsepower version of the inline-four found in the other turbo models, and it offers exceptional handling.

Category H

Model Description	Trade-in TMV	Private TMV	Dealer TMV
2 Dr STD Turbo Conv	4974	5777	7115
2 Dr STD Turbo Hbk	4735	5500	6774
2 Dr Commemorative Turbo Hbk			
	4899	5690	7008
2 Dr S Conv	4838	5619	6921
2 Dr S Hbk	2679	3111	3832
4 Dr S Sdn	3047	3539	4359
2 Dr S Luxury Hbk	3394	3942	4855
4 Dr S Luxury Sdn	3556	4130	5087

OPTIONS FOR 900

Automatic 3-Speed Transmission +112

9000   1993

New nomenclature reflects Saab's current identity crisis. Base models are now called the CS and CD; luxury

Don't forget to refer to the Mileage Adjustment Table at the back of this book!

Model Description	Trade-in TMV	Private TMV	Dealer TMV
Category I			
4 Dr Aero Turbo Hbk	4925	5789	7229
4 Dr CD Sdn	3212	3776	4715
4 Dr CD Turbo Sdn	3683	4329	5406
4 Dr CDE Sdn	3825	4496	5614
4 Dr CDE Turbo Sdn	4733	5563	6947
4 Dr CS Hbk	3271	3845	4801
4 Dr CS Turbo Hbk	3745	4402	5497
4 Dr CSE Hbk	3926	4614	5762
4 Dr CSE Turbo Hbk	4831	5679	7091

models are called CSE and CDE. Hatchbacks get more sedan-like styling that increases their length by four inches. A new Aero hatchback enters the lineup. The Aero is the fastest vehicle in the large-car class. It is powered by a 225-horsepower version of the inline-four found in the other turbo models, and it offers exceptional handling.

OPTIONS FOR 9000
Automatic 4-Speed Transmission[Std on CD Sdn] +152
Dual Power Seats +88
Leather Seats[Opt on CD,CS] +250
Power Sunroof[Opt on CD,CS] +153

1992 SAAB

900   1992

A limited-edition Griffin Edition is introduced as the "crhme de la crhme" 9000 for 1992. It is available only as a four-door turbo sedan. All turbo models get traction control for 1992. All Saab 9000s get a sunroof as well.

Model Description	Trade-in TMV	Private TMV	Dealer TMV
Category H			
2 Dr STD Hbk	1978	2374	3034
2 Dr STD Turbo Conv	3918	4701	6008
2 Dr STD Turbo Hbk	2948	3538	4521
4 Dr STD Sdn	2011	2413	3084
2 Dr S Conv	3314	3978	5083
2 Dr S Hbk	2345	2815	3597
4 Dr S Sdn	2455	2946	3765

OPTIONS FOR 900
Automatic 3-Speed Transmission +89
Automatic 4-Speed Transmission +128

9000   1992

A limited-edition Griffin Edition is introduced as the "crhme de la crhme" 9000 for 1992. It is available only as a four-door turbo sedan. All turbo models get traction control for 1992. All Saab 9000s get a sunroof as well.

Model Description	Trade-in TMV	Private TMV	Dealer TMV
Category I			
4 Dr STD Hbk	2601	3097	3925
4 Dr STD Turbo Hbk	3563	4243	5377
4 Dr CD Sdn	2830	3371	4272
4 Dr CD Turbo Sdn	3778	4499	5702
4 Dr CD Griffin Turbo Sdn			
	4026	4795	6077
4 Dr S Hbk	2722	3242	4109

OPTIONS FOR 9000
AM/FM Stereo/CD/Tape[Opt on S Hbk] +83
Automatic 4-Speed Transmission[Std on CD] +121

Don't forget to refer to the Mileage Adjustment Table at the back of this book!

Model Description	Trade-in TMV	Private TMV	Dealer TMV	Model Description	Trade-in TMV	Private TMV	Dealer TMV

SATURN 01-00

SATURN USA

1998 Saturn SL2

2001 SATURN

L-SERIES 2001

The Saturn L-Series sedans and wagons didn't exactly set the world on fire when they were introduced in 2000, but they return for 2001 virtually unchanged. Saturn has addressed safety concerns by making front and rear head curtain airbags optional on all trim levels. All sedans are now equipped with a three-point seatbelt in the rear center seat, but this feature is still not available in wagons. Sedans also will get an emergency trunk release handle. New colors include Cream White, Bright Silver, Silver Blue and Straight Shade Black. Bright White, Silver, Silver Plum and Blackberry have been discontinued.

Category D

4 Dr L100 Sdn	9442	10213	11500
4 Dr L200 Sdn	11166	12079	13600
4 Dr L300 Sdn	12643	13677	15400
4 Dr LW200 Wgn	12397	13411	15100
4 Dr LW300 Wgn	13793	14921	16800

OPTIONS FOR L-SERIES
AM/FM Compact Disc Player +195
AM/FM Stereo/CD/Tape +148
Aluminum/Alloy Wheels[Std on L300,LW300] +235
Anti-Lock Brakes +235
Automatic 4-Speed Transmission[Std on L300,LW] +579
Fog Lights[Std on L300,LW300] +151
Head Protection Air Bag +266
Leather Seats +871
Power Drivers Seat +219
Power Sunroof +488
Traction Control System +168

S-SERIES 2001

GM is giving Saturns a major redesign in 2003. As such, the S-Series sees no change from last year, save for optional head-curtain airbags.

Category B

3 Dr SC1 Cpe	7889	8606	9800
3 Dr SC2 Cpe	10224	11152	12700
4 Dr SL Sdn	6682	7288	8300
4 Dr SL1 Sdn	7245	7903	9000
4 Dr SL2 Sdn	8050	8781	10000
4 Dr SW2 Wgn	9177	10011	11400

OPTIONS FOR S-SERIES
AM/FM Compact Disc Player +195
AM/FM Stereo/CD/Tape +148
Air Conditioning[Std on Wgn,SC2 Cpe,SL2 Sdn] +646
Aluminum/Alloy Wheels +235
Anti-Lock Brakes +202
Automatic 4-Speed Transmission +579
Cruise Control +175
Head Protection Air Bag +219
Leather Seats +471
Power Door Locks +168
Power Sunroof +488
Power Windows[Std on Wgn] +178
Rear Spoiler[Std on SC2] +151
Traction Control System +135

2000 SATURN

L-SERIES 2000

The L-Series is a new midsize line of sedans and wagons that was developed for Saturn customers moving up from the smaller cars. Offered in three trim levels, with two engines and manual or automatic transmissions (depending on model), the L-Series is based on the European-market Opel Vectra platform, and consequently carries a distinct import feel.

Category D

4 Dr LS Sdn	8259	9268	10200
4 Dr LS1 Sdn	9150	10268	11300
4 Dr LS2 Sdn	10203	11449	12600
4 Dr LW1 Wgn	10122	11358	12500
4 Dr LW2 Wgn	11417	12812	14100

OPTIONS FOR L-SERIES
AM/FM Compact Disc Player +195
AM/FM Stereo/CD/Tape +148
Aluminum/Alloy Wheels[Std on LS2 Sdn,LW2 Wgn] +235
Anti-Lock Brakes +468
Automatic 4-Speed Transmission[Std on Wgn,LS2 Sdn] +578
Fog Lights[Std on LS2 Sdn,LW2 Wgn] +114
Heated Front Seats +168
Leather Seats +603
Power Drivers Seat +219

SATURN 00-99

Model Description	Trade-in TMV	Private TMV	Dealer TMV	Model Description	Trade-in TMV	Private TMV	Dealer TMV

Power Sunroof +505
Rear Spoiler[Std on Wgn (???)] +151
Traction Control System +135

S-SERIES 2000

Saturn has redesigned the body panels and cockpit of its S-Series SL Sedan and SW Wagon this year. GM's OnStar communications system will now be available as a dealer-installed option across the Saturn line.

Category B

Model	Trade-in	Private	Dealer
3 Dr SC1 Cpe	7231	8203	9100
3 Dr SC2 Cpe	8661	9825	10900
4 Dr SL Sdn	5721	6490	7200
4 Dr SL1 Sdn	6436	7302	8100
4 Dr SL2 Sdn	7390	8383	9300
4 Dr SW2 Wgn	8423	9555	10600

OPTIONS FOR S-SERIES
AM/FM Compact Disc Player +342
AM/FM Stereo Tape +195
AM/FM Stereo/CD/Tape +342
Air Conditioning[Std on Wgn,SC2 Cpe,SL2 Sdn] +646
Alarm System +114
Aluminum/Alloy Wheels +235
Anti-Lock Brakes +333
Automatic 4-Speed Transmission +578
Cruise Control +175
Fog Lights[Std on Cpe] +107
Keyless Entry System +100
Leather Seats +464
Power Door Locks +168
Power Mirrors +114
Power Sunroof +468
Power Windows[Std on Wgn] +178
Premium Sound System[Opt on Cpe] +235
Rear Spoiler[Std on SC2] +139
Traction Control System +135

1999 SATURN

SC 1999

Saturn continues on its refinement theme for 1999. Refined powertrain performance, interior upgrades and new wheel selections top the list of changes for SC1 and SC2 models. New later this year on all coupes is a standard driver's-side third door to improve access to the rear seats. Improvements to both the single- and dual-overhead cam engines (including new pistons, connecting rods and crankshafts) are designed to reduce noise, vibration and harshness while improving fuel economy about one mpg across the board. The SC2 gets redesigned standard wheel covers and new optional 15-inch aluminum wheels. Interior cloth fabrics have been revised, the capacity of the windshield washer solvent bottle has been increased to one gallon, and there's a new Green exterior paint. In a move

backward, all Coupes will revert to rear drum brakes, replacing the once-available rear discs on SC2 with ABS.

Category B

Model	Trade-in	Private	Dealer
2 Dr SC1 Cpe	5616	6358	7100
3 Dr SC1 Cpe	6091	6895	7700
2 Dr SC2 Cpe	6825	7727	8629
3 Dr SC2 Cpe	6938	7854	8771

OPTIONS FOR SC
AM/FM Compact Disc Player +272
AM/FM Stereo Tape +143
Air Conditioning[Std on SC2] +526
Alarm System +96
Aluminum/Alloy Wheels +192
Anti-Lock Brakes +272
Automatic 4-Speed Transmission +472
Cruise Control +143
Leather Seats +384
Power Door Locks +137
Power Mirrors +96
Power Sunroof +382
Power Windows +145
Premium Sound System +192
Rear Spoiler[Std on SC2] +134
Traction Control System +110

SL 1999

Powertrain components in both the single- and dual-overhead cam engines (such as pistons, connecting rods, crankshaft and timing chain) have been revised to reduce noise, vibration and harshness, while returning an increase of about one mpg across the board. Three new exterior colors debut: Dark Blue on SL, Green and Blackberry on SL1 and SL2. Front seatbelts have been repositioned, and the windshield washer solvent bottle's capacity has been upped to one full gallon. Sadly, Saturn has moved to rear drum brakes on all models, replacing the rear discs that had been available on SL2s with ABS.

Category B

Model	Trade-in	Private	Dealer
4 Dr SL Sdn	4983	5642	6300
4 Dr SL1 Sdn	5932	6716	7500
4 Dr SL2 Sdn	6565	7433	8300

OPTIONS FOR SL
AM/FM Compact Disc Player +280
AM/FM Stereo Tape +143
Air Conditioning[Std on SL2] +526
Alarm System +93
Aluminum/Alloy Wheels +192
Anti-Lock Brakes +272
Automatic 4-Speed Transmission +472
Cruise Control +143
Leather Seats +379
Power Door Locks +137
Power Mirrors +93

Don't forget to refer to the Mileage Adjustment Table at the back of this book!

SATURN 99-98

Model Description	Trade-in TMV	Private TMV	Dealer TMV	Model Description	Trade-in TMV	Private TMV	Dealer TMV

Power Sunroof +382
Power Windows +140
Premium Sound System +192
Rear Spoiler +113
Traction Control System +110

SW 1999

As with the rest of the 1999 Saturn line, SW models are sure to benefit from revised powertrain components in both the single- and dual-overhead cam engines. The pistons, connecting rods, crankshaft and timing chain in these motors have been redesigned to reduce noise, vibration and harshness, while returning an increase of about one mpg across the board. Wagons have a new Green exterior color. The only other changes are repositioned front seatbelts for easier access and increased windshield washer solvent bottle capacity, which is now one full gallon.

Category B

Model	Trade-in	Private	Dealer
4 Dr SW1 Wgn	6170	6985	7800
4 Dr SW2 Wgn	6961	7880	8800

OPTIONS FOR SW

AM/FM Compact Disc Player +230
AM/FM Stereo Tape +143
Air Conditioning[Std on SW2] +526
Aluminum/Alloy Wheels +192
Anti-Lock Brakes +272
Automatic 4-Speed Transmission +472
Cruise Control +160
Leather Seats +384
Power Door Locks +137
Power Mirrors +113
Power Windows +145
Premium Sound System +192
Traction Control System +110

1998 SATURN

SC 1998

Refinement is the name of the game for 1998. Improvements to the suspension, transmission and engine blocks are designed to smooth the ride, reduce noise, increase durability and provide slick shifts. Second-generation airbags deploy with less force than the old ones. A child seatbelt comfort guide has been added in the back seat, and SC1 models have a new wheel design. Dark Blue is the single new color.

Category B

Model	Trade-in	Private	Dealer
2 Dr SC1 Cpe	4861	5600	6400
2 Dr SC2 Cpe	5849	6737	7700

OPTIONS FOR SC

AM/FM Compact Disc Player +244
AM/FM Stereo Tape +127
Air Conditioning[Opt on SC1] +472
Aluminum/Alloy Wheels +172

Anti-Lock Brakes +342
Automatic 4-Speed Transmission +423
Cruise Control +127
Leather Seats +345
Power Door Locks +123
Power Sunroof +342
Power Windows +130
Premium Sound System +172
Rear Spoiler[Std on SC2] +100
Traction Control System +98

SL 1998

Minor trim modifications, reduced force airbags, and hardware improvements to stifle unwanted noise, vibration and harshness are on tap for 1998.

Category B

Model	Trade-in	Private	Dealer
4 Dr STD Sdn	4406	5075	5800
4 Dr SL1 Sdn	4785	5512	6300
4 Dr SL2 Sdn	5545	6387	7300

OPTIONS FOR SL

AM/FM Compact Disc Player +251
AM/FM Stereo Tape +127
Air Conditioning[Std on SL2] +472
Aluminum/Alloy Wheels +172
Anti-Lock Brakes +342
Automatic 4-Speed Transmission +423
Cruise Control +127
Leather Seats +339
Power Door Locks +123
Power Sunroof +342
Power Windows +126
Premium Sound System +172
Rear Spoiler +100
Traction Control System +98

SW 1998

1998 brings fresh colors, revised fabrics, redesigned wheels, reduced force airbags and more attempts at reducing noise and vibration levels.

Category B

Model	Trade-in	Private	Dealer
4 Dr SW1 Wgn	4785	5512	6300
4 Dr SW2 Wgn	6001	6912	7900

OPTIONS FOR SW

AM/FM Compact Disc Player +206
AM/FM Stereo Tape +127
Air Conditioning[Opt on SW1] +472
Aluminum/Alloy Wheels +172
Anti-Lock Brakes +342
Automatic 4-Speed Transmission +423
Cruise Control +143
Leather Seats +345
Power Door Locks +123
Power Mirrors +100
Power Windows +130
Premium Sound System +172
Traction Control System +98

Don't forget to refer to the Mileage Adjustment Table at the back of this book!

SATURN 97-96

Model Description	Trade-in TMV	Private TMV	Dealer TMV	Model Description	Trade-in TMV	Private TMV	Dealer TMV

1997 SATURN

SC 1997

Saturn restyles its sport coupe, moving it to the SL/SW platform in the process. The result is a larger, roomier and heavier car. Dashboard is carried over, but interior trim is new. Newly optional is an in-dash CD player. More steps are taken to reduce noise, vibration and harshness.

Category B

Model	Trade-in	Private	Dealer
2 Dr SC1 Cpe	4024	4688	5500
2 Dr SC2 Cpe	4755	5540	6500

OPTIONS FOR SC
AM/FM Compact Disc Player +220
AM/FM Stereo Tape +220
Air Conditioning +413
Aluminum/Alloy Wheels +131
Anti-Lock Brakes +309
Automatic 4-Speed Transmission +373
Cruise Control +116
Leather Seats +309
Power Door Locks +111
Power Sunroof +309
Power Windows +118
Premium Sound System +155
Rear Spoiler[Std on SC2] +91

SL 1997

Once again, Saturn attempts to quell noise, vibration, and harshness (NVH) with improved engine mounts, revised torque struts, thicker dash mat, and non-asbestos organic front brake pads. Other changes are limited to new colors, an optional in-dash CD player, a panic mode for the security system, and a low-fuel indicator.

Category B

Model	Trade-in	Private	Dealer
4 Dr STD Sdn	3731	4347	5100
4 Dr SL1 Sdn	4024	4688	5500
4 Dr SL2 Sdn	4463	5199	6100

OPTIONS FOR SL
AM/FM Compact Disc Player +234
AM/FM Stereo Tape +123
Air Conditioning +413
Aluminum/Alloy Wheels +138
Anti-Lock Brakes +309
Automatic 4-Speed Transmission +373
Cruise Control +116
Leather Seats +306
Power Door Locks +111
Power Sunroof +309
Power Windows +111
Premium Sound System +155
Rear Spoiler +91

SW 1997

Once again, Saturn attempts to quell noise, vibration, and harshness (NVH) with improved engine mounts, revised torque struts, thicker dash mat, and non-asbestos organic front brake pads. Other changes are limited to a new color, an optional in-dash CD player, a panic mode for the security system, and a low-fuel indicator.

Category B

Model	Trade-in	Private	Dealer
4 Dr SW1 Wgn	4170	4859	5700
4 Dr SW2 Wgn	4828	5626	6600

OPTIONS FOR SW
AM/FM Compact Disc Player +186
AM/FM Stereo Tape +116
Air Conditioning +413
Aluminum/Alloy Wheels +155
Anti-Lock Brakes +309
Automatic 4-Speed Transmission +373
Cruise Control +120
Leather Seats +309
Power Door Locks +111
Power Windows +116
Premium Sound System +155

1996 SATURN

SC 1996

Coupe carries over in anticipation of all-new styling to arrive for 1997. Traction control can now be ordered with the manual transmission and antilock brake system.

Category B

Model	Trade-in	Private	Dealer
2 Dr SC1 Cpe	3228	3846	4700
2 Dr SC2 Cpe	3571	4255	5200

OPTIONS FOR SC
Air Conditioning +384
Aluminum/Alloy Wheels +123
Anti-Lock Brakes +332
Automatic 4-Speed Transmission +347
Compact Disc Changer +261
Cruise Control +109
Leather Seats +288
Power Door Locks +104
Power Sunroof +288
Power Windows +110
Premium Sound System +146

SL 1996

New bodywork and interior improvements make the SL an excellent value in the compact sedan class. SL's meet 1997 side-impact standards for the first time. A five-speed and traction control are no longer mutually exclusive items. The back seat is actually livable this year. Daytime running lights are standard, and rain

Model Description	Trade-in TMV	Private TMV	Dealer TMV

water won't leak all over your stuff anymore when you open the trunk.

Category B

Model Description	Trade-in TMV	Private TMV	Dealer TMV
4 Dr STD Sdn	2679	3192	3900
4 Dr SL1 Sdn	2816	3355	4100
4 Dr SL2 Sdn	3297	3928	4800

OPTIONS FOR SL

AM/FM Compact Disc Player +213
Air Conditioning +384
Aluminum/Alloy Wheels +130
Anti-Lock Brakes +332
Automatic 4-Speed Transmission +347
Cruise Control +109
Leather Seats +288
Power Door Locks +104
Power Sunroof +288
Power Windows +104
Premium Sound System +146

SW   1996

Sporty wagon gets more conventional, but more attractive, plastic panels for 1996. Wagon meets 1997 side-impact standards this year, and five-speed models can be equipped with traction control. The rear seat is more comfortable, and head room is improved. Daytime running lights debut. Avoid new purple color, unless you want the kids calling your car the Barneymobile in front of friends and relatives.

Category B

Model Description	Trade-in TMV	Private TMV	Dealer TMV
4 Dr SW1 Wgn	3159	3764	4600
4 Dr SW2 Wgn	5220	6219	7600

OPTIONS FOR SW

Air Conditioning +384
Aluminum/Alloy Wheels +130
Anti-Lock Brakes +332
Automatic 4-Speed Transmission +347
Cruise Control +109
Leather Seats +288
Power Door Locks +104
Power Windows +109
Premium Sound System +146

1995 SATURN

SC   1995

Dashboard is redesigned and now contains two airbags. Base engine is rated at 100 horsepower, up 15 from last year. With the automatic transmission, traction control is included with optional ABS. Styling is cleaned up front and rear. Manual three-point front seatbelts replace automatic type. SC1 gets new bucket seats.

Category B

Model Description	Trade-in TMV	Private TMV	Dealer TMV
2 Dr SC1 Cpe	2346	2854	3700

Model Description	Trade-in TMV	Private TMV	Dealer TMV
2 Dr SC2 Cpe	2600	3162	4100

OPTIONS FOR SC

Air Conditioning +301
Aluminum/Alloy Wheels +97
Anti-Lock Brakes +162
Automatic 4-Speed Transmission +272
Cruise Control +85
Leather Seats +226
Power Door Locks +81
Power Sunroof +226
Power Windows +87
Premium Sound System +114

SL   1995

Dashboard is redesigned and now contains two airbags. Base engine is rated at 100 horsepower, up 15 from last year. With the automatic transmission, traction control is included with optional ABS. Styling is cleaned up front and rear. Manual three-point front seatbelts replace automatic type.

Category B

Model Description	Trade-in TMV	Private TMV	Dealer TMV
4 Dr STD Sdn	2029	2468	3200
4 Dr SL1 Sdn	2219	2700	3500
4 Dr SL2 Sdn	2410	2931	3800

OPTIONS FOR SL

Air Conditioning +301
Aluminum/Alloy Wheels +102
Anti-Lock Brakes +162
Automatic 4-Speed Transmission +272
Compact Disc Changer +180
Cruise Control +85
Leather Seats +226
Power Door Locks +81
Power Sunroof +226
Power Windows +81
Premium Sound System +114

SW   1995

Dashboard is redesigned and now contains two airbags. Base engine is rated at 100 horsepower, up 15 from last year. With the automatic transmission, traction control is included with optional ABS. Styling is cleaned up front and rear. Manual three-point front seatbelts replace automatic type.

Category B

Model Description	Trade-in TMV	Private TMV	Dealer TMV
4 Dr SW1 Wgn	2346	2854	3700
4 Dr SW2 Wgn	2473	3008	3900

OPTIONS FOR SW

Air Conditioning +301
Aluminum/Alloy Wheels +102
Anti-Lock Brakes +162
Automatic 4-Speed Transmission +272
Cruise Control +85
Leather Seats +226
Power Door Locks +81

Don't forget to refer to the Mileage Adjustment Table at the back of this book!

SATURN 95-93

Model Description	Trade-in TMV	Private TMV	Dealer TMV	Model Description	Trade-in TMV	Private TMV	Dealer TMV

Power Windows +85
Premium Sound System +114

1994 SATURN

SC · 1994

CFC-free refrigerant is added to air conditioning system. Automatic transmission's Performance mode is recalibrated to give smoother shifts. New central unlocking feature on power door locks allows all doors to be unlocked with a twist of the key. New alloy wheels are optional on SC1.

Category B

	Trade-in	Private	Dealer
2 Dr SC1 Cpe	1978	2482	3321
2 Dr SC2 Cpe	2072	2600	3479

OPTIONS FOR SC

AM/FM Compact Disc Player +138
Air Conditioning +257
Aluminum/Alloy Wheels +82
Anti-Lock Brakes +138
Automatic 4-Speed Transmission +232
Cruise Control +72
Leather Seats +192
Power Sunroof +192
Power Windows +74
Premium Sound System +97

SL · 1994

CFC-free refrigerant is added to air conditioning system. Automatic transmission's Performance mode is recalibrated to give smoother shifts. New central unlocking feature on power door locks allows all doors to be unlocked with a twist of the key. New alloy wheels are optional on SL2.

Category B

	Trade-in	Private	Dealer
4 Dr STD Sdn	1548	1943	2600
4 Dr SL1 Sdn	1906	2391	3200
4 Dr SL2 Sdn	2025	2541	3400

OPTIONS FOR SL

AM/FM Compact Disc Player +143
Air Conditioning +257
Aluminum/Alloy Wheels +87
Anti-Lock Brakes +138
Automatic 4-Speed Transmission +232
Cruise Control +72
Leather Seats +192
Power Steering +79
Power Sunroof +192
Premium Sound System +97

SW · 1994

CFC-free refrigerant is added to air conditioning system. Automatic transmission's Performance mode is recalibrated to give smoother shifts. New central unlocking feature on power door locks allows all doors to be unlocked with a twist of the key. New alloy wheels are optional on SW2.

Category B

	Trade-in	Private	Dealer
4 Dr SW1 Wgn	1989	2496	3340
4 Dr SW2 Wgn	2061	2585	3460

OPTIONS FOR SW

AM/FM Compact Disc Player +117
Air Conditioning +257
Aluminum/Alloy Wheels +87
Anti-Lock Brakes +138
Automatic 4-Speed Transmission +232
Cruise Control +72
Leather Seats +192
Power Windows +72
Premium Sound System +97

1993 SATURN

SC · 1993

Driver airbag added. Cars with ABS and automatic transmission can be ordered with traction control. SC coupe equipped with same 85-horsepower 1.9-liter engine as in SL.

Category B

	Trade-in	Private	Dealer
2 Dr SC1 Cpe	1416	1860	2600
2 Dr SC2 Cpe	1743	2290	3200

OPTIONS FOR SC

AM/FM Compact Disc Player +119
Air Conditioning +220
Aluminum/Alloy Wheels +71
Anti-Lock Brakes +119
Automatic 4-Speed Transmission +198
Leather Seats +165
Power Sunroof +165
Premium Sound System +84

SL · 1993

Driver airbag added. SL2 gets new front fascia and optional fog lights. Cars with ABS and automatic transmission can be ordered with traction control. SL2 suspension provides softer ride.

Category B

	Trade-in	Private	Dealer
4 Dr STD Sdn	1144	1503	2100
4 Dr SL1 Sdn	1416	1860	2600
4 Dr SL2 Sdn	1580	2075	2900

OPTIONS FOR SL

AM/FM Compact Disc Player +122
AM/FM Stereo/CD/Tape +132
Air Conditioning +220
Aluminum/Alloy Wheels +74
Anti-Lock Brakes +119
Automatic 4-Speed Transmission +198
Leather Seats +165

Don't forget to refer to the Mileage Adjustment Table at the back of this book!

Model Description	Trade-in TMV	Private TMV	Dealer TMV
Power Moonroof +156			
Power Sunroof +165			
Premium Sound System +84			

SW   1993

Driver airbag added, and is standard on SW. Cars with ABS and automatic transmission can be ordered with traction control. New station wagon model comes in SW1 and SW2 trim, and rear wiper/washer and defogger are standard. SW1 equipped with same 85-horsepower 1.9-liter engine as in SL. SW2 gets twin-cam 124-horsepower engine and SL2's sport suspension.

Category B

Model Description	Trade-in TMV	Private TMV	Dealer TMV
4 Dr SW1 Wgn	1525	2003	2800
4 Dr SW2 Wgn	1580	2075	2900

OPTIONS FOR SW

AM/FM Compact Disc Player +101
Air Conditioning +220
Aluminum/Alloy Wheels +74
Anti-Lock Brakes +119
Automatic 4-Speed Transmission +198
Premium Sound System +84

1992 SATURN

SC   1992

New engine and transmission mounting system supposedly cuts down on noise and vibration. Passenger compartment gets added acoustic insulation. Alloy wheels are redesigned.

Category B

Model Description	Trade-in TMV	Private TMV	Dealer TMV
2 Dr SC2 Cpe	1230	1706	2500

OPTIONS FOR SC

AM/FM Compact Disc Player +104
Air Bag Restraint +95
Air Conditioning +193
Anti-Lock Brakes +104
Automatic 4-Speed Transmission +174
Leather Seats +145
Power Sunroof +145
Premium Sound System +74

SL   1992

New engine and transmission mounting system supposedly cuts down on noise and vibration. Passenger compartment gets added acoustic insulation. Leather and a rear deck spoiler are new for SL2 models. Alloy wheels are redesigned.

Category B

Model Description	Trade-in TMV	Private TMV	Dealer TMV
4 Dr STD Sdn	886	1229	1800
4 Dr SL1 Sdn	984	1365	2000
4 Dr SL2 Sdn	1132	1570	2300

OPTIONS FOR SL

AM/FM Compact Disc Player +107
Air Bag Restraint +95
Air Conditioning +193
Anti-Lock Brakes +104
Automatic 4-Speed Transmission +174
Leather Seats +145
Power Sunroof +145
Premium Sound System +74

Don't forget to refer to the Mileage Adjustment Table at the back of this book!

Model Description	Trade-in TMV	Private TMV	Dealer TMV	Model Description	Trade-in TMV	Private TMV	Dealer TMV

SUBARU — Japan

1997 Subaru Legacy

2001 SUBARU

FORESTER — 2001

The 2001 Forester receives slight alterations to the front and rear fascias, a new Premium Package, and upgrades to the interior.

Category L

Model	Trade-in	Private	Dealer
4 Dr L AWD Wgn	15019	16036	17732
4 Dr S AWD Wgn	15924	17002	18800

OPTIONS FOR FORESTER
AM/FM Compact Disc Player +282
Alarm System +118
Aluminum/Alloy Wheels +400
Automatic 4-Speed Transmission +538
Automatic Dimming Mirror +123
Brush Guard +252
Compact Disc Changer +463
Keyless Entry System +151
Leather Seats +870
Power Moonroof[Opt on S] +437
Premium Sound System +672
Rear Spoiler +198
Side Air Bag Restraints[Opt on S] +168
Trailer Hitch +198

IMPREZA — 2001

RS models get carbon fiber patterned interior trim, a CD player, and embroidered floor mats.

Category B

Model	Trade-in	Private	Dealer
2 Dr L AWD Cpe	11264	12267	13940
4 Dr L AWD Sdn	11264	12267	13940
4 Dr L AWD Wgn	11553	12582	14298
4 Dr Outback Sport AWD Wgn	12614	13739	15612
2 Dr RS AWD Cpe	12686	13817	15701
4 Dr RS AWD Sdn	12686	13817	15701

OPTIONS FOR IMPREZA
AM/FM Compact Disc Player +225
Alarm System +118
Aluminum/Alloy Wheels[Opt on L] +353
Automatic 4-Speed Transmission +538
Fog Lights[Opt on L] +159
Keyless Entry System +151
Leather Seats +870
Luggage Rack +161
Premium Sound System +550

LEGACY — 2001

The Brighton model is stricken from the Legacy lineup. All 2001 Legacys comply with low-emission vehicle (LEV) standards and come with standard 24-hour roadside assistance. Legacy L models now include an ambient temperature gauge, a dual mode digital trip odometer, and a fixed intermittent rear wiper with washer on the wagons. GT models feature a power moonroof, six-way power driver's seat, limited-slip rear differential and multi-reflector halogen fog lights.

Category D

Model	Trade-in	Private	Dealer
4 Dr GT AWD Sdn	16284	17439	19363
4 Dr GT AWD Wgn	16969	18172	20177
4 Dr GT Limited AWD Sdn	17420	18656	20714
4 Dr L AWD Sdn	13559	14520	16122
4 Dr L AWD Wgn	14090	15089	16754

OPTIONS FOR LEGACY
AM/FM Compact Disc Player +282
Alarm System +118
Aluminum/Alloy Wheels[Opt on Brighton,L] +353
Automatic 4-Speed Transmission +538
Automatic Dimming Mirror +123
Compact Disc Changer +334
Fog Lights[Opt on Brighton,L] +174
Keyless Entry System[Opt on L] +118
Painted Rims +353
Premium Sound System +672
Rear Spoiler +198

OUTBACK — 2001

Two new models, the H6-3.0 L.L.Bean Edition and the H6-3.0 VDC, both featuring a more-powerful 3.0-liter engine, join the happy Outback family. Braking is upgraded this year via larger front rotors with twin piston calipers.

Category D

Model	Trade-in	Private	Dealer
4 Dr L.L. Bean Edition AWD Wgn	21874	23425	26010
4 Dr Limited AWD Sdn	19131	20487	22748

Model Description	Trade-in TMV	Private TMV	Dealer TMV
4 Dr Limited AWD Wgn	19363	20736	23024
4 Dr VDC AWD Wgn	22810	24427	27122
4 Dr STD AWD Wgn	15559	16662	18501

OPTIONS FOR OUTBACK
AM/FM Compact Disc Player[Opt on STD Wgn] +243
Alarm System +118
Automatic 4-Speed Transmission[Opt on Wgn] +538
Automatic Dimming Mirror +123
Compact Disc Changer +350
Heated Front Seats +168
Premium Sound System +672
Rear Spoiler +198
Trailer Hitch +198

2000 SUBARU

FORESTER   2000

This year, Forester L gets standard cruise control and Forester S receives a viscous limited-slip rear differential at base price increases of $100.
Category L

Model Description	Trade-in TMV	Private TMV	Dealer TMV
4 Dr L AWD Wgn	12396	13611	14732
4 Dr S AWD Wgn	13871	15230	16485

OPTIONS FOR FORESTER
AM/FM Compact Disc Player +282
AM/FM Stereo/CD/Tape +282
Aluminum/Alloy Wheels +400
Automatic 4-Speed Transmission +538
Brush Guard +252
Compact Disc Changer +463
Keyless Entry System +151
Leather Seats +602
Skid Plates +107
Trailer Hitch +198

IMPREZA   2000

For 2000, Subaru introduces the new Impreza 2.5 RS Sedan, a cross between an aggressive driver's car and a sedan. More standard equipment comes on the 2.5 Coupe and Sedan while the L model remains unchanged. All Impreza models now come with 24-hour roadside assistance.
Category B

Model Description	Trade-in TMV	Private TMV	Dealer TMV
2 Dr L AWD Cpe	9204	10404	11511
4 Dr L AWD Sdn	9383	10606	11735
4 Dr L AWD Wgn	9797	11074	12253
2 Dr RS AWD Cpe	11216	12678	14027
4 Dr RS AWD Sdn	11591	13101	14496

OPTIONS FOR IMPREZA
AM/FM Compact Disc Player +282
AM/FM Stereo/CD/Tape +282
Aluminum/Alloy Wheels[Opt on L] +393
Automatic 4-Speed Transmission +538
Cruise Control[Opt on L] +134
Fog Lights[Opt on L] +118
Keyless Entry System +151
Luggage Rack +161
Rear Spoiler[Std on RS,Cpe] +235
Skid Plates[Opt on RS Sdn] +107

IMPREZA OUTBACK   2000

For 2000, Subaru's Impreza Outback Sport receives some exterior design changes and 24-hour roadside assistance.
Category B

Model Description	Trade-in TMV	Private TMV	Dealer TMV
4 Dr Outback Sport AWD Wgn			
	10919	12342	13656

OPTIONS FOR IMPREZA OUTBACK
AM/FM Compact Disc Player +282
Aluminum/Alloy Wheels +369
Automatic 4-Speed Transmission +538
Fog Lights +165
Keyless Entry System +151

LEGACY   2000

Subaru's Legacy is completely redesigned for the millennium.
Category D

Model Description	Trade-in TMV	Private TMV	Dealer TMV
4 Dr Brighton AWD Wgn	10587	11719	12764
4 Dr GT AWD Sdn	13004	14395	15678
4 Dr GT AWD Wgn	13930	15419	16794
4 Dr GT Limited AWD Sdn			
	14319	15850	17263
4 Dr L AWD Sdn	10683	11826	12880
4 Dr L AWD Wgn	11401	12620	13745

OPTIONS FOR LEGACY
AM/FM Compact Disc Player +282
AM/FM Stereo/CD/Tape[Opt on L Wgn] +282
Aluminum/Alloy Wheels[Opt on Brighton,L] +400
Automatic 4-Speed Transmission +538
Compact Disc Changer +334
Cruise Control[Opt on Brighton] +134
Fog Lights[Opt on Brighton,L] +187
Keyless Entry System[Opt on L] +118
Leather Seats[Std on GT Limited] +622
Luggage Rack[Opt on Wgn] +186
Power Moonroof[Opt on L] +606
Rear Spoiler[Opt on GT Sdn,L Sdn] +198

OUTBACK   2000

As with the Legacy platform it's based on, Subaru's hot-selling Outback is completely redesigned for the millennium.
Category D

Model Description	Trade-in TMV	Private TMV	Dealer TMV
4 Dr STD AWD Wgn	14313	15843	17256
4 Dr Limited AWD Sdn	16206	17939	19538
4 Dr Limited AWD Wgn	16396	18149	19767

OPTIONS FOR OUTBACK

Don't forget to refer to the Mileage Adjustment Table at the back of this book!

Model Description	Trade-in TMV	Private TMV	Dealer TMV

AM/FM Compact Disc Player[Opt on STD Wgn] +282
AM/FM Stereo/CD/Tape +282
Alarm System +118
Automatic 4-Speed Transmission[Opt on Wgn] +538
Child Seat (1) +134
Compact Disc Changer +334
Gold Package +118
Heated Front Seats +169
Heated Power Mirrors +130
Limited Slip Differential +134
Trailer Hitch +198

1999 SUBARU

FORESTER   1999

This year, Forester's engine makes more torque and the automatic transmission has been improved. L and S models have longer lists of standard equipment and two new colors are available.

Category L

Model	Trade-in	Private	Dealer
4 Dr STD AWD Wgn	11425	12579	13734
4 Dr L AWD Wgn	11670	12850	14029
4 Dr S AWD Wgn	13104	14428	15752

OPTIONS FOR FORESTER

AM/FM Compact Disc Player +232
AM/FM Stereo/CD/Tape +232
Aluminum/Alloy Wheels[Std on S] +328
Automatic 4-Speed Transmission +441
Compact Disc Changer +380
Cruise Control[Std on S] +110
Keyless Entry System +124
Leather Seats +603
Trailer Hitch +163

IMPREZA   1999

More horsepower, more torque and a more efficient automatic transmission is the big news this year. Multi-reflector halogen headlights are new and Outback Sport gets a revised grille. The 2.5 RS gets silver alloy wheels, a new front bumper, white gauge faces and more torque, as well as an upgraded leather-wrapped steering wheel and shift knob. Two new colors are available for 1999.

Category B

Model	Trade-in	Private	Dealer
2 Dr L AWD Cpe	8315	9453	10591
4 Dr L AWD Sdn	8545	9715	10884
4 Dr L AWD Wgn	8774	9974	11175
4 Dr Outback Sport AWD Wgn	9927	11286	12644
2 Dr RS AWD Cpe	10439	11868	13296

OPTIONS FOR IMPREZA

AM/FM Compact Disc Player +232
Aluminum/Alloy Wheels[Std on RS] +322
Automatic 4-Speed Transmission +441

Cruise Control +110
Keyless Entry System +124
Luggage Rack[Opt on LJ +132
Rear Spoiler[Opt on Sdn] +193

LEGACY   1999

Subaru celebrates 30 years of selling cars in the United States by adding special editions to the Legacy lineup. The L sedan and wagon are available with a package of goodies that includes power moonroof, alloy wheels, rear spoiler or roof rack, body-color trim, power antenna, and seat height adjuster. New colors include Sandstone Metallic and Winestone Pearl. The 2.5GT Limited is newly available with a manual transmission, while all 2.5GT, Limited and Outback models receive standard remote keyless entry.

Category D

Model	Trade-in	Private	Dealer
4 Dr 30th Anniversary AWD Sdn	11512	12828	14143
4 Dr Brighton AWD Wgn	8850	9861	10872
4 Dr GT AWD Sdn	11227	12510	13793
4 Dr GT AWD Wgn	11974	13342	14710
4 Dr GT Ltd. 30th Ann AWD Sdn	12457	13881	15304
4 Dr L AWD Sdn	9759	10874	11989
4 Dr L AWD Wgn	10133	11291	12449
4 Dr Limited 30TH ANN AWD Sdn	13271	14788	16304
4 Dr Outback AWD Wgn	11061	12324	13588
4 Dr Outback Ltd 30th AWD Wgn	12806	14269	15732

OPTIONS FOR LEGACY

30th Anniversary Edition L Package +551
AM/FM Compact Disc Player[Std on GT Lim 30th An,Outback Lim 30th An,SUS Lim 30th An] +232
AM/FM Stereo/CD/Tape[Opt on Outback] +232
Aluminum/Alloy Wheels[Opt on Brighton,L] +328
Automatic 4-Speed Transmission +441
Compact Disc Changer +274
Cruise Control[Opt on Brighton] +110
Dual Sunroofs +496
Fog Lights[Opt on Brighton,L] +153
Heated Front Seats[Opt on Outback] +138
Heated Power Mirrors[Opt on Outback] +108
Keyless Entry System[Opt on Brighton,L] +124
Leather Seats[Opt on 30th Anniversary,GT,Outback] +620
Luggage Rack[Opt on Brighton,L] +153
Power Moonroof[Opt on L] +496
Rear Spoiler[Opt on Brighton,L,Outback,Outback Ltd 30th] +163
Trailer Hitch +163

Model Description	Trade-in TMV	Private TMV	Dealer TMV	Model Description	Trade-in TMV	Private TMV	Dealer TMV

1998 SUBARU

FORESTER 1998

Subaru attacks the mini-SUV market head-on with the Forester, which actually constitutes an SUV body on an Impreza platform with a Legacy engine under the hood. The most car-like of the mini-utes, Forester is also the most powerful. Airbags remain the full power variety, despite new rules allowing lower deployment speeds.

Category L

4 Dr STD AWD Wgn	9820	10896	12061
4 Dr L AWD Wgn	10530	11684	12933
4 Dr S AWD Wgn	11516	12777	14143

OPTIONS FOR FORESTER
AM/FM Compact Disc Player +200
Aluminum/Alloy Wheels[Std on S] +283
Automatic 4-Speed Transmission +380
Compact Disc Changer +327
Heated Front Seats +107
Keyless Entry System +107
Leather Seats +521
Trailer Hitch +141

IMPREZA 1998

Impreza gets a new dashboard and revised door panels. The entry-level Brighton coupe is dropped, and the high-end 2.5RS coupe is added. No depowered airbags here.

Category B

2 Dr L AWD Cpe	6563	7534	8585
4 Dr L AWD Sdn	6868	7884	8984
4 Dr L AWD Wgn	6907	7928	9034
4 Dr Outback Sport AWD Wgn			
	7941	9115	10387
2 Dr RS AWD Cpe	8060	9251	10542

OPTIONS FOR IMPREZA
AM/FM Compact Disc Player +200
AM/FM Stereo/CD/Tape +154
Aluminum/Alloy Wheels[Std on RS] +278
Automatic 4-Speed Transmission +380
Keyless Entry System +107
Leather Seats +547
Luggage Rack[Opt on L] +114
Rear Spoiler[Opt on Sdn] +166

LEGACY 1998

Prices remain stable while equipment is shuffled and the LSi model is dropped. All Legacy sedans and wagons except the Outback sport the grille and multi-reflector halogen lights found on the 2.5GT. A new Limited model joins the 2.5GT lineup, and a dual power moonroof package is available for the Outback Limited wagon. Outbacks get new alloy wheels, an overhead console and longer splash guards, while mid-year Outback Limiteds with revised trim and added content were dubbed 30th Anniversary models. The cold weather package has heated windshield wiper nozzles this year instead of an engine block heater. The Brighton wagon's stereo loses half its wattage, Limited models have a standard CD player and the base Outback comes with a Weatherband radio. Full power airbags continue, despite new government rules allowing automakers to install reduced force bags to better protect small adults.

Category D

4 Dr Brighton AWD Wgn	7217	8089	9033
4 Dr GT AWD Sdn	9398	10533	11763
4 Dr GT AWD Wgn	10090	11309	12629
4 Dr GT Limited AWD Sdn			
	10536	11808	13187
4 Dr L AWD Sdn	7684	8612	9617
4 Dr L AWD Wgn	8833	9899	11055
4 Dr Outback AWD Wgn	9136	10240	11435
4 Dr Outback Limited AWD Wgn			
	10434	11694	13059

OPTIONS FOR LEGACY
AM/FM Compact Disc Player[Std on Limited] +200
AM/FM Stereo/CD/Tape +200
Aluminum/Alloy Wheels[Opt on Brighton,L] +283
Automatic 4-Speed Transmission[Std on GT Limited] +380
Compact Disc Changer +236
Dual Sunroofs +428
Fog Lights[Opt on Brighton,L] +132
Heated Front Seats[Opt on Outback] +119
Keyless Entry System +107
Leather Seats[Opt on GT,Outback] +535
Luggage Rack[Opt on Brighton] +132
Rear Spoiler[Std on GT,GT Limited] +141
Spoke Wheels +302
Trailer Hitch +141

1997 SUBARU

IMPREZA 1997

Imprezas receive a facelifted front end that includes a Hemi-sized hood scoop. A new Outback Sport Wagon debuts, with nearly six-inches of additional ground clearance, fog lights, and a slightly raised roof. LX model disappears, which means only the Outback is equipped with ABS. Power and torque for both Impreza engines is up for 1997, and some new colors are available. HVAC controls are revised.

Category B

2 Dr Brighton AWD Cpe	4089	4781	5626
2 Dr L AWD Cpe	5222	6105	7185
4 Dr L AWD Sdn	5417	6333	7453
4 Dr L AWD Wgn	5530	6465	7609

Don't forget to refer to the Mileage Adjustment Table at the back of this book!

Model Description	Trade-in TMV	Private TMV	Dealer TMV
4 Dr Outback Sport AWD Wgn			
	6327	7398	8706

OPTIONS FOR IMPREZA
4 cyl 2.2 L Engine[Opt on Brighton] +117
AM/FM Compact Disc Player +165
Aluminum/Alloy Wheels +229
Automatic 4-Speed Transmission +274
Compact Disc Changer +165
Rear Spoiler[Opt on Brighton,Sdn] +138
Special Wheels +249

LEGACY   1997

Front-wheel drive models are given the ax as Subaru returns to its all-wheel drive roots. Power and torque are up marginally with the base 2.2-liter engine. The 2.5-liter motor (also stronger this year and now available with a manual transmission) is now the only engine mated to the Outback . L models gain cruise control, anti-lock brakes, and power door locks as standard equipment. GT's get a manual transmission, larger tires, and revised styling. The Outback lineup is expanded with the introduction of a Limited model, which includes a leather interior, new alloy wheels, fresh exterior colors, and woodgrain interior trim.

Category D

Model Description	Trade-in TMV	Private TMV	Dealer TMV
4 Dr Brighton AWD Wgn	5327	6085	7011
4 Dr GT AWD Sdn	8345	9532	10982
4 Dr GT AWD Wgn	8561	9779	11267
4 Dr L AWD Sdn	6104	6972	8033
4 Dr L AWD Wgn	7414	8468	9757
4 Dr LSi AWD Sdn	8735	9978	11496
4 Dr LSi AWD Wgn	9242	10557	12163
4 Dr Outback AWD Sdn	8349	9536	10987
4 Dr Outback AWD Wgn	8195	9361	10785
4 Dr Outback Limited AWD Wgn			
	8692	9928	11439

OPTIONS FOR LEGACY
AM/FM Compact Disc Player +165
AM/FM Stereo/CD/Tape +165
Aluminum/Alloy Wheels[Opt on Brighton,L] +234
Automatic 4-Speed Transmission[Std on LSi] +314
Compact Disc Changer[Std on LSi] +195
Fog Lights[Opt on Brighton,L,LSi] +109
Leather Seats +441
Luggage Rack[Opt on Brighton,L,LSi] +108
Rear Spoiler[Std on GT] +115
Spoke Wheels +234
Trailer Hitch +115

SVX   1997

A body-color grille debuts, along with P215/55VR16 tires. You wanted an SVX in Laguna Blue? Tough rocks, pal. That color vanishes this year.

Category E

Model Description	Trade-in TMV	Private TMV	Dealer TMV
2 Dr L AWD Cpe	9044	10227	11673
2 Dr LSi AWD Cpe	10561	11943	13632

OPTIONS FOR SVX
AM/FM Compact Disc Player +255

1996 SUBARU

IMPREZA   1996

The formerly optional 2.2-liter engine is standard across the board, except in the new budget-minded Brighton AWD Coupe. A new grille accompanies the bigger engine, and a five-speed is available as well.

Category B

Model Description	Trade-in TMV	Private TMV	Dealer TMV
2 Dr Brighton AWD Cpe	3567	4226	5137
2 Dr L AWD Cpe	4239	5023	6105
4 Dr L AWD Sdn	4356	5162	6274
4 Dr L AWD Wgn	4390	5202	6323
2 Dr LX AWD Cpe	5102	6045	7348
4 Dr LX AWD Sdn	5161	6116	7434
4 Dr LX AWD Wgn	5401	6400	7779
4 Dr Outback AWD Wgn	5158	6112	7429

OPTIONS FOR IMPREZA
AM/FM Compact Disc Player +156
Aluminum/Alloy Wheels[Std on LX 4WD Cpe] +217
Anti-Lock Brakes[Opt on L] +260
Automatic 4-Speed Transmission[Opt on L ,Outback,Cpe] +297
Compact Disc Changer +204
Rear Spoiler[Std on L,LX] +133
Special Wheels +236

LEGACY   1996

A new sport model debuts, with a larger, more powerful engine. The 2.5GT is available in sedan or wagon format. The luxury-oriented LSi model also gets the new motor. A knobby-tired, raised-roof Outback wagon appears, offering 7.3 inches of ground clearance and an optional 2.5-liter engine. Designed specifically for American consumers, the Outback provides a car-like ride with light-duty off-road ability.

Category D

Model Description	Trade-in TMV	Private TMV	Dealer TMV
4 Dr Brighton AWD Wgn	4753	5504	6540
4 Dr GT AWD Sdn	6657	7708	9160
4 Dr GT AWD Wgn	7187	8321	9888
4 Dr L AWD Sdn	5315	6154	7313
4 Dr L AWD Wgn	6190	7167	8517
4 Dr L Sdn	4949	5731	6810
4 Dr L Wgn	5146	5958	7080
4 Dr LS AWD Sdn	6604	7647	9087
4 Dr LS AWD Wgn	7096	8217	9764
4 Dr LSi AWD Sdn	7749	8972	10662

Don't forget to refer to the Mileage Adjustment Table at the back of this book!

Model Description	Trade-in TMV	Private TMV	Dealer TMV
4 Dr LSi AWD Wgn	8368	9689	11513
4 Dr Outback AWD Wgn	6594	7635	9073

OPTIONS FOR LEGACY
4 cyl 2.5 L DOHC Engine[Std on GT,LSi] +371
AM/FM Compact Disc Player[Opt on Outback] +156
AM/FM Stereo/CD/Tape +156
Aluminum/Alloy Wheels[Opt on L] +217
Anti-Lock Brakes[Opt on L] +260
Automatic 4-Speed Transmission[Std on GT,LS,LSi] +297
Fog Lights[Opt on LSi] +103
Luggage Rack[Opt on Brighton] +103
Rear Spoiler[Std on GT] +139

SVX   1996

Umm ... the L model gets standard solar-reduction glass this year. Whoopee.
Category E

2 Dr L AWD Cpe	6510	7440	8724
2 Dr LSi AWD Cpe	8072	9225	10818

OPTIONS FOR SVX
AM/FM Compact Disc Player +241

1995 SUBARU

IMPREZA   1995

An Impreza coupe and an Outback Wagon are added to Subaru's subcompact line of cars in an attempt to broaden their appeal with sporting and outdoor enthusiasts. Top-of-the-line LX model is introduced, replacing the LS trim-level, with an available 2.2-liter engine taken from the Legacy. Unfortunately it is available only with an automatic transmission.
Category B

2 Dr STD Cpe	2631	3172	4074
4 Dr STD Sdn	2631	3172	4074
2 Dr L AWD Cpe	3524	4249	5457
2 Dr L Cpe	3030	3654	4693
4 Dr L AWD Sdn	3524	4249	5457
4 Dr L AWD Wgn	3551	4282	5500
4 Dr L Sdn	3030	3654	4693
4 Dr L Spec. Edition Sdn			
	3165	3816	4901
4 Dr L Special Edit. AWD Sdn			
	3578	4314	5541
4 Dr L Special Edit. AWD Wgn			
	3623	4369	5611
2 Dr LX AWD Cpe	4140	4991	6411
4 Dr LX AWD Sdn	4113	4959	6369
4 Dr LX AWD Wgn	4149	5002	6425
4 Dr Outback AWD Wgn	4063	4899	6292
4 Dr Outback Spec. Ed. AWD Wgn			
	3623	4369	5611

OPTIONS FOR IMPREZA
4 cyl 2.2 L Engine +95
4WD Active Safety Group +247
AM/FM Compact Disc Player +133
Air Conditioning[Opt on STD,L 4WD Cpe] +254
Aluminum/Alloy Wheels[Std on LX 4WD Sdn] +186
Anti-Lock Brakes[Opt on L] +222
Automatic 4-Speed Transmission[Std on L Spec. Edition,LX,L Special Edit. 4WD Sdn] +222

LEGACY   1995

New sheetmetal freshens the flanks of one of our favorite compact sedans and wagons. Unfortunately the turbocharged engine has been dropped, leaving the Legacy with a rather anemic 2.2-liter four-cylinder that produces a meager 135 horsepower. The value leader Brighton wagon is introduced for budding naturalists. It includes all-wheel drive, air conditioning and a stereo with cassette. The Outback Wagon is also introduced as an alternative to the burgeoning SUV market.
Category D

4 Dr STD Sdn	3398	3971	4926
4 Dr Brighton AWD Wgn	3772	4409	5469
4 Dr L AWD Sdn	4230	4944	6133
4 Dr L AWD Wgn	4581	5354	6642
4 Dr L Sdn	3914	4574	5674
4 Dr L Wgn	4074	4762	5907
4 Dr LS AWD Sdn	4945	5779	7169
4 Dr LS AWD Wgn	5105	5966	7401
4 Dr LSi AWD Sdn	5985	6994	8677
4 Dr LSi AWD Wgn	6209	7256	9002
4 Dr Outback AWD Wgn	4672	5460	6774

OPTIONS FOR LEGACY
AM/FM Stereo/CD/Tape[Opt on L,LSi] +133
Air Conditioning[Opt on STD] +254
Aluminum/Alloy Wheels[Opt on Brighton,L,LSi] +186
Anti-Lock Brakes[Opt on L] +222
Automatic 4-Speed Transmission[Std on LS,LSi] +254
Compact Disc Changer +158
Leather Seats +357
Option Package 1 +492
Power Moonroof[Opt on L] +285
Rear Spoiler[Opt on L,LS] +94

SVX   1995

Dual airbags are extended to the base model.
Category E

2 Dr L AWD Cpe	4440	5125	6267
2 Dr L AWD Cpe	5841	6742	8244
2 Dr LS AWD Cpe	4440	5125	6267
2 Dr LSi AWD Cpe	7335	8467	10353

OPTIONS FOR SVX
AM/FM Compact Disc Player +206

Don't forget to refer to the Mileage Adjustment Table at the back of this book!

SUBARU® 94-93

Model Description	Trade-in TMV	Private TMV	Dealer TMV	Model Description	Trade-in TMV	Private TMV	Dealer TMV

1994 SUBARU

IMPREZA — 1994

A passenger airbag joins the driver's airbag on all models. LS Imprezas have standard antilock brakes, automatic transmission and sunroof.

Category B

	Trade-in	Private	Dealer
4 Dr STD Sdn	2104	2661	3588
4 Dr L AWD Sdn	2583	3266	4404
4 Dr L AWD Wgn	2678	3387	4567
4 Dr L Sdn	2250	2845	3836
4 Dr L Wgn	2321	2934	3957
4 Dr LS AWD Sdn	3602	4554	6142
4 Dr LS AWD Wgn	4025	5090	6864

OPTIONS FOR IMPREZA
Air Conditioning[Std on LS] +225
Anti-Lock Brakes[Std on LS] +197
Automatic 4-Speed Transmission[Std on LS] +197
Dual Air Bag Restraints[Std on LS] +169
Power Sunroof[Std on LS] +197

JUSTY — 1994

Continuously variable transmission is no longer available. Base models gain a standard rear-window defroster. Last year for the Justy runabout.

Category A

	Trade-in	Private	Dealer
2 Dr DL Hbk	1151	1455	1963
4 Dr GL 4WD Hbk	1411	1785	2407

OPTIONS FOR JUSTY
Air Conditioning +197

LEGACY — 1994

Antilock brakes become optional on the L sedan.

Category D

	Trade-in	Private	Dealer
4 Dr L AWD Sdn	3126	3720	4709
4 Dr L AWD Wgn	3916	4660	5899
4 Dr L Sdn	2820	3356	4248
4 Dr L Wgn	3015	3587	4541
4 Dr LS AWD Sdn	4246	5052	6395
4 Dr LS AWD Wgn	4382	5214	6601
4 Dr LS Sdn	3933	4680	5924
4 Dr LS Wgn	4069	4842	6129
4 Dr LSi AWD Sdn	4345	5170	6545
4 Dr LSi AWD Wgn	4712	5606	7097
4 Dr Sport Turbo AWD Sdn	4265	5075	6424
4 Dr Touring Turbo AWD Wgn	4833	5751	7280

OPTIONS FOR LEGACY
AM/FM Compact Disc Player[Opt on L] +118
Air Conditioning[Opt on L] +225

Aluminum/Alloy Wheels[Opt on L] +165
Anti-Lock Brakes[Opt on L] +197
Automatic 4-Speed Transmission[Opt on L] +225
Power Moonroof[Opt on L,LS 4WD Sdn] +253

LOYALE — 1994

The Loyale is available only in the wagon bodystyle and is seeing its last year as the Impreza is set to take over the duties of all-wheel drive subcompact in Subaru's lineup.

Category C

	Trade-in	Private	Dealer
4 Dr STD 4WD Wgn	2629	3181	4101

OPTIONS FOR LOYALE
Automatic 3-Speed Transmission +155

SVX — 1994

Subaru introduces two-wheel drive "value leaders" to the SVX lineup called the L and LS. These new SVXs offer the same 3.3-liter Flat-6 found in the LSi, and antilock brakes are standard on the LS . A passenger airbag becomes standard on the uplevel LS and LSi models.

Category E

	Trade-in	Private	Dealer
2 Dr L AWD Cpe	3436	4127	5279
2 Dr LS AWD Cpe	4092	4915	6287
2 Dr LSi AWD Cpe	6150	7388	9450

OPTIONS FOR SVX
AM/FM Compact Disc Player +183
Dual Air Bag Restraints[Opt on L] +141

1993 SUBARU

IMPREZA — 1993

Designed as a replacement for the aging Loyale, the Impreza is a subcompact available as a sedan or wagon. A driver airbag and available antilock brakes are important safety features included on the Impreza that never found their way to the Loyale. The Impreza is powered by a 1.8-liter 118-horsepower engine. Front-wheel drive and full-time all-wheel drive models are offered.

Category B

	Trade-in	Private	Dealer
4 Dr STD Sdn	1700	2214	3070
4 Dr L AWD Sdn	2071	2697	3740
4 Dr L AWD Wgn	2098	2732	3788
4 Dr L Sdn	1997	2601	3607
4 Dr L Wgn	2057	2678	3714
4 Dr LS AWD Sdn	2621	3413	4733
4 Dr LS AWD Wgn	3042	3961	5493
4 Dr LS Sdn	2398	3123	4331
4 Dr LS Wgn	2457	3199	4436

OPTIONS FOR IMPREZA

Don't forget to refer to the Mileage Adjustment Table at the back of this book!

Model Description	Trade-in TMV	Private TMV	Dealer TMV
Air Conditioning[Std on STD] +189			
Aluminum/Alloy Wheels +138			
Automatic 4-Speed Transmission[Opt on L] +166			

JUSTY — 1993

The base Justy gets a larger engine that increases horsepower to GL standards.

Category A

Model Description	Trade-in TMV	Private TMV	Dealer TMV
2 Dr STD Hbk	1081	1401	1936
2 Dr GL Hbk	1328	1722	2379
4 Dr GL 4WD Hbk	1379	1788	2470
4 Dr GL Hbk	1439	1866	2578

OPTIONS FOR JUSTY
Air Conditioning +165
Automatic 3-Speed Transmission[Opt on 4WD] +118

LEGACY — 1993

A driver airbag is now standard on all Legacys. Touring wagons and LSi wagons were introduced in 1992 as upscale versions of the Legacy. Commendably, antilock brakes are now standard on all Legacys except the L models. Several new trim-levels of the Legacy are available for 1993. Based on the L wagon, these models are geared to appeal to different groups of outdoor enthusiasts such as skiers, beach combers and campers. The standard equipment lists of these models reflects the differences in their target market, such as heated seats and a ski rack on the Alpine model.

Category D

Model Description	Trade-in TMV	Private TMV	Dealer TMV
4 Dr L AWD Sdn	2721	3367	4445
4 Dr L AWD Wgn	3069	3798	5014
4 Dr L Sdn	2533	3135	4139
4 Dr L Wgn	2640	3268	4314
4 Dr LS AWD Sdn	3217	3982	5256
4 Dr LS AWD Wgn	3324	4114	5431
4 Dr LS Sdn	3076	3807	5026
4 Dr LS Wgn	3081	3813	5034
4 Dr LSi AWD Sdn	3411	4222	5573
4 Dr LSi AWD Wgn	3874	4795	6330
4 Dr Sport Turbo AWD Sdn	3232	4001	5281
4 Dr Touring Turbo AWD Wgn	3529	4368	5766

OPTIONS FOR LEGACY
AM/FM Stereo/CD/Tape[Opt on LS 4WD Wgn] +99
Aluminum/Alloy Wheels +138
Anti-Lock Brakes[Opt on L Wgn] +166
Automatic 4-Speed Transmission[Opt on L,Sport] +189

LOYALE — 1993

New colors are the only changes to the Loyale.

Category C

Model Description	Trade-in TMV	Private TMV	Dealer TMV
4 Dr STD 4WD Sdn	1551	2005	2761
4 Dr STD 4WD Wgn	1677	2168	2986
4 Dr FWD Sdn	1381	1785	2459
4 Dr FWD Wgn	1487	1923	2648

OPTIONS FOR LOYALE
Automatic 3-Speed Transmission +130

SVX — 1993

No changes for Subaru's quirky sports car.

Category E

Model Description	Trade-in TMV	Private TMV	Dealer TMV
2 Dr 25th Anniversary AWD Cpe	5575	6689	8547
2 Dr LS AWD Cpe	3433	4119	5263
2 Dr LS-L AWD Cpe	3852	4622	5906
2 Dr XR AWD Cpe	3898	4678	5977

1992 SUBARU

JUSTY — 1992

The Subaru Justy is unchanged.

Category A

Model Description	Trade-in TMV	Private TMV	Dealer TMV
2 Dr STD Hbk	837	1135	1632
2 Dr GL 4WD Hbk	1214	1646	2367
2 Dr GL Hbk	1002	1359	1954
4 Dr GL 4WD Hbk	1282	1738	2499

OPTIONS FOR JUSTY
Air Conditioning +142
Automatic 3-Speed Transmission +101

LEGACY — 1992

A driver airbag is now standard on the Legacy LS and LSi; it is optional on L model. A trunk pass-through opening in the rear seats, rear heater ducts, and cupholders integrated into the dashboard give more utility to the passengers.

Category D

Model Description	Trade-in TMV	Private TMV	Dealer TMV
4 Dr L 4WD Sdn	1800	2356	3283
4 Dr L 4WD Wgn	2230	2919	4067
4 Dr L Sdn	1561	2043	2847
4 Dr L Wgn	1616	2116	2948
4 Dr LE Turbo 4WD Wgn	2472	3236	4509
4 Dr LS 4WD Sdn	2377	3112	4336
4 Dr LS 4WD Wgn	2472	3236	4509
4 Dr LS Sdn	2248	2943	4101
4 Dr LS Wgn	2236	2927	4079
4 Dr LSi 4WD Sdn	2534	3316	4621
4 Dr LSi Sdn	2366	3097	4316
4 Dr Sport Turbo 4WD Sdn	2305	3018	4205

OPTIONS FOR LEGACY
Air Conditioning[Opt on L] +161
Anti-Lock Brakes[Opt on L] +142

Don't forget to refer to the Mileage Adjustment Table at the back of this book!

Model Description	Trade-in TMV	Private TMV	Dealer TMV	Model Description	Trade-in TMV	Private TMV	Dealer TMV

Automatic 4-Speed Transmission[Opt on L,Sport] +161

LOYALE   1992

Still no changes for the Loyale.

Category C

Model Description	Trade-in TMV	Private TMV	Dealer TMV
4 Dr STD 4WD Sdn	1147	1574	2287
4 Dr STD 4WD Wgn	1245	1709	2483
4 Dr STD Sdn	1013	1391	2021
4 Dr STD Wgn	1097	1506	2188

OPTIONS FOR LOYALE
Automatic 3-Speed Transmission +111

SVX   1992

Subaru replaces the odd XT6 with the equally unusual SVX. Performance numbers are quite good with the standard 3.3-liter Flat-6 engine and standard all-wheel drive. The strange two-piece side windows, designed to decrease interior turbulence when the window is opened, leave something to be desired. Antilock brakes and a driver airbag are standard.

Category E

Model Description	Trade-in TMV	Private TMV	Dealer TMV
2 Dr STD AWD Cpe	2920	3645	4854

OPTIONS FOR SVX
AM/FM Stereo/CD/Tape +111
Leather Seats +182
Power Sunroof +172

Don't forget to refer to the Mileage Adjustment Table at the back of this book!

Model Description	Trade-in TMV	Private TMV	Dealer TMV

SUZUKI
Japan

1998 Suzuki Esteem

2001 SUZUKI

ESTEEM 2001

In an effort to ply prospective Esteem buyers, Suzuki has equipped every model with an in-dash CD player. Stereo head units also get larger controls. Elsewhere, you will find gentle cosmetic changes: The front grille has been restyled, the seats are wrapped in a new fabric and floor mats are standard. Sky Blue Metallic is no longer available as an exterior color.

Category B

Model Description	Trade-in TMV	Private TMV	Dealer TMV
4 Dr GL Sdn	7275	7953	9083
4 Dr GL Wgn	7581	8287	9464
4 Dr GLX Sdn	7758	8481	9686
4 Dr GLX Wgn	8046	8796	10045
4 Dr GLX Plus Sdn	9868	10788	12320
4 Dr GLX Plus Wgn	10305	11265	12865
4 Dr GLX Sport Sdn	9212	10070	11500

OPTIONS FOR ESTEEM
Automatic 4-Speed Transmission +542

GRAND VITARA 2001

Standard Grand Vitaras get redesigned front and rear bumpers and a restyled grille. New interior features include a redesigned AM/FM stereo with an in-dash CD player, adjustable front seat armrests, redesigned head restraints, child seat-tether hooks, and a new seat fabric. Top-of-the-line Grand Vitara Limiteds also get the improved stereo along with a tilt-and-slide power sunroof and new aluminum wheels.

Category L

Model Description	Trade-in TMV	Private TMV	Dealer TMV
4 Dr JLS Hardtop	11834	12743	14258
4 Dr JLS Plus Hardtop	13279	14299	15999
4 Dr JLS Plus SE 4WD Hardtop	15574	16770	18764
4 Dr JLS Plus SE Hardtop	14762	15895	17785
4 Dr JLX 4WD Hardtop	12589	13556	15167
4 Dr JLX Plus 4WD Hardtop	14091	15173	16977
4 Dr Limited 4WD Hardtop	15697	16903	18912
4 Dr Limited Hardtop	14820	15958	17855

SWIFT 2001

The 2001 Suzuki Swift remains mechanically unchanged. Suzuki has changed the exterior color options slightly: Bright White and Platinum Silver Metallic replace Polar White and Mercury Silver Metallic.

Category A

Model Description	Trade-in TMV	Private TMV	Dealer TMV
2 Dr GA Hbk	4946	5469	6341
2 Dr GL Hbk	5548	6135	7113

OPTIONS FOR SWIFT
Automatic 3-Speed Transmission +352

VITARA 2001

All Vitara models get a restyled front grille, new seat fabric, a larger audio unit with an in-dash CD player, and new exterior colors.

Category L

Model Description	Trade-in TMV	Private TMV	Dealer TMV
2 Dr JLS Conv	10285	11074	12391
4 Dr JLS Wgn	11422	12300	13762
2 Dr JLX 4WD Conv	11797	12703	14213
4 Dr JLX 4WD Wgn	12480	13438	15036
2 Dr JS Conv	8815	9492	10620
4 Dr JS Wgn	10646	11464	12827
2 Dr JX 4WD Conv	10604	11419	12776
4 Dr JX 4WD Wgn	11998	12919	14455

OPTIONS FOR VITARA
Aluminum/Alloy Wheels +271
Automatic 4-Speed Transmission +542

XL-7 2001

The Suzuki XL-7 is an all-new midsize SUV based on a stretched Grand Vitara. It is the first in this class to offer third-row seating and a starting price of under $20,000.

Category M

Model Description	Trade-in TMV	Private TMV	Dealer TMV
4 Dr Plus 4WD Wgn	14793	15787	17444
4 Dr Plus Wgn	14330	15294	16899
4 Dr Touring 4WD Wgn	15451	16489	18220
4 Dr Touring Wgn	15319	16349	18065
4 Dr STD 4WD Wgn	14107	15056	16636
4 Dr STD Wgn	13300	14194	15684

Don't forget to refer to the Mileage Adjustment Table at the back of this book!

SUZUKI 01-99

Model Description	Trade-in TMV	Private TMV	Dealer TMV	Model Description	Trade-in TMV	Private TMV	Dealer TMV

OPTIONS FOR XL-7
Automatic 4-Speed Transmission[Opt on Plus, Touring] +542

2000 SUZUKI

ESTEEM   2000

All Esteems get the 1.8-liter engine starting with the September 1999 production run. GLX and GLX+ models receive 15-inch wheels and tires as standard equipment. Two new paint colors, Bluish Black Pearl and Cassis Red Pearl, replace Mars Red and Midnight Black.

Category B

	Trade-in	Private	Dealer
4 Dr GL Sdn	5382	6150	6858
4 Dr GL Wgn	5850	6684	7454
4 Dr GLX Sdn	6083	6950	7751
4 Dr GLX Wgn	6317	7218	8050

OPTIONS FOR ESTEEM
4 cyl 1.8 L Engine[Opt on GL] +271
Anti-Lock Brakes +309
Automatic 4-Speed Transmission +541
Cruise Control +108
Power Moonroof +352

GRAND VITARA   2000

The 2000 Limited Edition Grand Vitara comes with leather seats, privacy glass, fog lamps, a hard spare tire cover, an armrest, gold emblems, and a special black-and-white paint scheme. The spare tire cover on regular Grand Vitaras features a new design. The '99 model's base trim levels JS and JS+ have been renamed JLS and JLS+. A CD changer is standard equipment on JLS+ and JLX+ models.

Category L

	Trade-in	Private	Dealer
4 Dr JLS Hardtop	9866	11063	12168
4 Dr JLX 4WD Hardtop	10386	11646	12809
4 Dr Limited 4WD Hardtop	12270	13759	15133
4 Dr Limited Hardtop	11734	13158	14472

OPTIONS FOR GRAND VITARA
Aluminum/Alloy Wheels[Std on Limited] +95
Anti-Lock Brakes[Std on Limited] +433
Automatic 4-Speed Transmission[Std on Limited] +541
Compact Disc Changer[Std on Limited] +298

SWIFT   2000

The 2000 Suzuki Swift remains mechanically unchanged. Two new exterior colors - Brilliant Blue Metallic and Catseye Blue Metallic - are offered.

Category A

	Trade-in	Private	Dealer
2 Dr GA Hbk	3886	4489	5046
2 Dr GL Hbk	4411	5097	5729

OPTIONS FOR SWIFT
AM/FM Stereo Tape[Std on GL] +122
Air Conditioning[Std on GL] +433
Automatic 3-Speed Transmission +352

VITARA   2000

Four-door models receive a new luggage cover for 2000. The Vitara two-door JLS/JLX is equipped with air conditioning as standard equipment. There are three new paint colors, and four-wheel-drive models have a "4x4" sticker in the rear-quarter windows.

Category L

	Trade-in	Private	Dealer
2 Dr JLS Conv	8375	9391	10329
4 Dr JLS Wgn	9635	10804	11883
2 Dr JLX 4WD Conv	10055	11275	12401
4 Dr JLX 4WD Wgn	10727	12029	13230
2 Dr JS Conv	6946	7789	8567
4 Dr JS Wgn	9044	10141	11154
2 Dr JX 4WD Conv	8963	10050	11054
4 Dr JX 4WD Wgn	10222	11462	12607

OPTIONS FOR VITARA
Aluminum/Alloy Wheels +148
Automatic 4-Speed Transmission +541

1999 SUZUKI

ESTEEM   1999

A restyled front end with multi-reflector headlights and an overall smoother body distinguishes the 1999 Esteem line from its predecessors. Base GL models now come with the 14-inch wheels that were standard on GLX models. Interior surfaces have been upgraded and a Clarion AM/FM cassette is now available. But the exciting news comes in the form of an all-new, 1.8-liter inline four that makes 122 horsepower.

Category B

	Trade-in	Private	Dealer
4 Dr GL Sdn	4709	5454	6198
4 Dr GL Wgn	4920	5697	6475
4 Dr GLX Sdn	5172	5990	6807
4 Dr GLX Wgn	5383	6233	7084

OPTIONS FOR ESTEEM
4 cyl 1.8 L Engine +218
Anti-Lock Brakes +248
Automatic 4-Speed Transmission +435
Power Sunroof +283

GRAND VITARA   1999

The Grand Vitara is a completely new design from Suzuki and offers plenty of passenger room along with a standard V6 engine.

Category L

Don't forget to refer to the Mileage Adjustment Table at the back of this book!

Model Description	Trade-in TMV	Private TMV	Dealer TMV
4 Dr JLX 4WD Hardtop	9152	10439	11726
4 Dr JS Hardtop	8328	9499	10670

OPTIONS FOR GRAND VITARA
Anti-Lock Brakes +349
Automatic 4-Speed Transmission +435

SWIFT   1999

With the exception of some color changes, the Suzuki Swift remains unchanged for '99.
Category A

2 Dr STD Hbk	3597	4210	4822

OPTIONS FOR SWIFT
AM/FM Stereo Tape +98
Air Conditioning +349
Automatic 3-Speed Transmission +283

VITARA   1999

The Vitara is an all-new model that replaces the Sidekick as Suzuki's entry into the mini SUV class.
Category L

4 Dr JS Wgn	7597	8666	9734
2 Dr JS 1.6 Conv	5962	6801	7639
2 Dr JS 2.0 Conv	6616	7547	8477
4 Dr JX 4WD Wgn	8415	9599	10782
2 Dr JX 1.6 4WD Conv	7352	8385	9419
2 Dr JX 2.0 4WD Conv	7843	8946	10049

OPTIONS FOR VITARA
Air Conditioning +349
Aluminum/Alloy Wheels +120
Automatic 4-Speed Transmission +435
Power Door Locks[Opt on JS, JX] +105
Power Windows[Opt on JS, JX] +109

1998 SUZUKI

ESTEEM   1998

A wagon adds diversity to the Esteem lineup.
Category B

4 Dr GL Sdn	3599	4233	4920
4 Dr GL Wgn	3768	4431	5150
4 Dr GL SE Wgn	4305	5064	5885
4 Dr GLX Sdn	3970	4669	5426
4 Dr GLX Wgn	4138	4867	5656
4 Dr GLX SE Wgn	4676	5499	6391

OPTIONS FOR ESTEEM
Anti-Lock Brakes +205
Automatic 4-Speed Transmission[Opt on GL,GLX] +360
Power Sunroof +234

SIDEKICK   1998

A couple of new colors debut.
Category L

Model Description	Trade-in TMV	Private TMV	Dealer TMV
2 Dr JS Conv	4797	5485	6231
4 Dr JS Wgn	5842	6681	7589
2 Dr JX 4WD Conv	5953	6807	7733
4 Dr JX 4WD Wgn	6476	7406	8413
4 Dr JX FLT 4WD Wgn	7508	8586	9754
2 Dr JX SE 4WD Conv	6540	7479	8496
4 Dr Sport JLX 4WD Wgn			
	7817	8939	10155
4 Dr Sport JS Wgn	6831	7812	8874
4 Dr Sport JX 4WD Wgn	7226	8263	9387
4 Dr Sport JX SE 4WD Wgn			
	7621	8715	9900

OPTIONS FOR SIDEKICK
Air Conditioning[Opt on JS, JX] +276
Anti-Lock Brakes[Std on Sport JLX] +216
Automatic 3-Speed Transmission +216
Automatic 4-Speed Transmission +342

SWIFT   1998

Swift's engine makes nine more horsepower this year, and one more pound of torque.
Category A

2 Dr STD Hbk	2691	3192	3734

OPTIONS FOR SWIFT
Air Conditioning +288
Anti-Lock Brakes +202
Automatic 3-Speed Transmission +216

X-90   1998

The VIN number is new for 1998.
Category L

2 Dr STD 4WD Utility	4476	5118	5814
2 Dr STD Utility	3972	4542	5160
2 Dr SE 4WD Utility	4764	5448	6189

OPTIONS FOR X-90
AM/FM Stereo Tape[Opt on 2WD] +117
Air Conditioning[Std on SE] +288
Automatic 4-Speed Transmission +342

1997 SUZUKI

ESTEEM   1997

No changes to the economical Esteem.
Category B

4 Dr GL Sdn	2908	3424	4054
4 Dr GLX Sdn	3142	3699	4380

OPTIONS FOR ESTEEM
Anti-Lock Brakes +173
Automatic 4-Speed Transmission +303

SIDEKICK   1997

A JS Sport 2WD model is added to the Sidekick lineup.

Don't forget to refer to the Mileage Adjustment Table at the back of this book!

SUZUKI 97-95

Model Description	Trade-in TMV	Private TMV	Dealer TMV

It has a DOHC engine that makes 120 horsepower at 6500 rpm. There are no changes to the rest of the Sidekick line.

Category L

Model Description	Trade-in TMV	Private TMV	Dealer TMV
2 Dr JS Conv	3897	4522	5285
4 Dr JS Wgn	4827	5601	6546
2 Dr JX 4WD Conv	5006	5808	6789
4 Dr JX 4WD Wgn	5348	6205	7252
4 Dr Sport JLX 4WD Wgn	6389	7413	8664
4 Dr Sport JS Wgn	5575	6468	7560
4 Dr Sport JX 4WD Wgn	5901	6847	8003

OPTIONS FOR SIDEKICK
Air Conditioning[Opt on JS,JX] +232
Anti-Lock Brakes[Opt on Sport JLX] +182
Automatic 3-Speed Transmission +182
Automatic 4-Speed Transmission +288

SWIFT 1997

New paint colors (Victory Red and Bright Teal Metallic) and new seat coverings are the only changes to the 1996 Swift.

Category A

Model Description	Trade-in TMV	Private TMV	Dealer TMV
2 Dr STD Hbk	2131	2554	3072

OPTIONS FOR SWIFT
Air Conditioning +243
Anti-Lock Brakes +170
Automatic 3-Speed Transmission +166

X-90 1997

No changes to Suzuki's interesting alternative to AWD vehicles.

Category L

Model Description	Trade-in TMV	Private TMV	Dealer TMV
2 Dr STD 4WD Utility	3629	4210	4921
2 Dr STD Utility	2599	3016	3525

OPTIONS FOR X-90
AM/FM Stereo Tape +98
Air Conditioning +243
Anti-Lock Brakes +182
Automatic 4-Speed Transmission +288

1996 SUZUKI

ESTEEM 1996

New for 1996 are daytime running lights, standard air conditioning and body-color bumpers on the GL.

Category B

Model Description	Trade-in TMV	Private TMV	Dealer TMV
4 Dr GL Sdn	2387	2945	3715
4 Dr GLX Sdn	2492	3075	3879

OPTIONS FOR ESTEEM
Anti-Lock Brakes +164
Automatic 4-Speed Transmission +286

SIDEKICK 1996

Lots of changes to this mini SUV: the 16-valve, 95-horsepower engine is available across the board (except in the Sport), and dual airbags are housed in a revised instrument panel. New fabrics, colors and styling revisions update the Sidekick nicely. All-new for 1996 is a Sport variant, equipped with lots of exclusive standard equipment, a 120-horsepower twin-cam motor, a wider track, two-tone paint and a dorky chrome grille.

Category L

Model Description	Trade-in TMV	Private TMV	Dealer TMV
2 Dr JS Conv	3511	4129	4984
4 Dr JS Wgn	4021	4730	5709
2 Dr JX 4WD Conv	4328	5090	6144
4 Dr JX 4WD Wgn	4817	5666	6839
4 Dr Sport JLX 4WD Wgn	5698	6702	8089
4 Dr Sport JX 4WD Wgn	5405	6357	7673

OPTIONS FOR SIDEKICK
Air Conditioning[Opt on JS,JX] +219
Anti-Lock Brakes[Opt on JS,JX] +172
Automatic 3-Speed Transmission +172
Automatic 4-Speed Transmission +286

SWIFT 1996

Oh boy. Two new colors and new seat fabrics. Whoopee.

Category A

Model Description	Trade-in TMV	Private TMV	Dealer TMV
2 Dr STD Hbk	1731	2135	2694

OPTIONS FOR SWIFT
Air Conditioning +229
Anti-Lock Brakes +169
Automatic 3-Speed Transmission +186

X-90 1996

Based on Sidekick platform, this new concept features a two-seat cockpit, T-top roof, conventional trunk, and available four-wheel drive. Loaded with standard equipment, the X-90 is an interesting vehicle indeed.

Category L

Model Description	Trade-in TMV	Private TMV	Dealer TMV
2 Dr STD 4WD Utility	2986	3512	4239
2 Dr STD Utility	2366	2783	3359

OPTIONS FOR X-90
Air Conditioning +229
Automatic 4-Speed Transmission +272

1995 SUZUKI

ESTEEM 1995

The 1995 Esteem is Suzuki's latest entry in the hotly contested subcompact car market. The Esteem has standard antilock brakes and dual airbags but is

Model Description	Trade-in TMV	Private TMV	Dealer TMV

saddled with a 1.6-liter engine. Competition from Toyota, Geo and Honda is stiff, but low resale values may make this car worthwhile.

Category B

Model Description	Trade-in TMV	Private TMV	Dealer TMV
4 Dr GL Sdn	1591	1939	2521
4 Dr GLX Sdn	1671	2037	2648

OPTIONS FOR ESTEEM
Air Conditioning +158
Anti-Lock Brakes +136
Automatic 4-Speed Transmission +238

SAMURAI 1995

The Samurai is retired this year with no changes.

Category L

Model Description	Trade-in TMV	Private TMV	Dealer TMV
2 Dr JL 4WD Conv	1530	1821	2307

OPTIONS FOR SAMURAI
AM/FM Stereo Tape +72
Air Conditioning +155

SIDEKICK 1995

The convertible model gets a new top.

Category L

Model Description	Trade-in TMV	Private TMV	Dealer TMV
4 Dr JLX 4WD Wgn	3853	4588	5812
2 Dr JS Conv	2782	3312	4196
4 Dr JS Wgn	3204	3814	4832
2 Dr JX 4WD Conv	3196	3806	4821
4 Dr JX 4WD Wgn	3505	4173	5286

OPTIONS FOR SIDEKICK
Air Conditioning +182
Automatic 3-Speed Transmission +143
Automatic 4-Speed Transmission +226

SWIFT 1995

The sedan is dropped and dual airbags are added. Antilock brakes become a much appreciated option. The two-door GT hatchback has also been dropped.

Category A

Model Description	Trade-in TMV	Private TMV	Dealer TMV
2 Dr STD Hbk	1337	1668	2219

OPTIONS FOR SWIFT
Air Conditioning +191
Anti-Lock Brakes +133
Automatic 3-Speed Transmission +131

1994 SUZUKI

SAMURAI 1994

Another Samurai commits Hari-Kari; the two-wheel drive model is no longer available. Other changes are limited to the addition of a high-mounted rear brake light.

Category L

Model Description	Trade-in TMV	Private TMV	Dealer TMV
2 Dr JL 4WD Conv	1310	1590	2055

OPTIONS FOR SAMURAI
Air Conditioning +138

SIDEKICK 1994

All Sidekicks get an alarm and a tilt steering wheel as standard equipment this year. A high-mounted rear brake light is a new safety item found on all Sidekicks.

Category L

Model Description	Trade-in TMV	Private TMV	Dealer TMV
4 Dr JLX 4WD Wgn	2955	3584	4634
2 Dr JS Conv	2325	2821	3647
4 Dr JS Wgn	2656	3222	4166
2 Dr JX 4WD Conv	2603	3157	4082
4 Dr JX 4WD Wgn	2844	3451	4461

OPTIONS FOR SIDEKICK
Air Conditioning +162
Automatic 3-Speed Transmission +128
Automatic 4-Speed Transmission +202
Flip-Up Sunroof[Opt on JX 4WD Wgn] +85

SWIFT 1994

The GA hatchback gets a cargo cover and both GA models get a right sideview mirror. Will wonders never cease?

Category A

Model Description	Trade-in TMV	Private TMV	Dealer TMV
2 Dr GA Hbk	870	1128	1558
4 Dr GA Sdn	968	1255	1733
4 Dr GS Sdn	1130	1465	2023
2 Dr GT Hbk	1256	1628	2248

OPTIONS FOR SWIFT
Air Conditioning +170
Automatic 3-Speed Transmission +117

1993 SUZUKI

SAMURAI 1993

When are they going to retire this thing? The Samurai continues unchanged.

Category L

Model Description	Trade-in TMV	Private TMV	Dealer TMV
2 Dr JA Conv	760	951	1271
2 Dr JL 4WD Conv	957	1199	1602

OPTIONS FOR SAMURAI
Air Conditioning +124

SIDEKICK 1993

No changes for the Sidekick.

Category L

Model Description	Trade-in TMV	Private TMV	Dealer TMV
4 Dr JLX 4WD Wgn	2540	3181	4250
2 Dr JS Conv	1911	2393	3197
4 Dr JS Wgn	2125	2662	3556
2 Dr JX 4WD Conv	2147	2689	3592
4 Dr JX 4WD Wgn	2323	2910	3887

Don't forget to refer to the Mileage Adjustment Table at the back of this book!

Model Description	Trade-in TMV	Private TMV	Dealer TMV	Model Description	Trade-in TMV	Private TMV	Dealer TMV

OPTIONS FOR SIDEKICK
Air Conditioning +145
Automatic 3-Speed Transmission +114
Automatic 4-Speed Transmission +180

SWIFT   1993

The doors lock when the Swift reaches speeds of 8 mph or more; apparently Suzuki thinks that anyone crazy enough to buy this car won't be able to figure out how to do this on their own.

Category A

Model	Trade-in	Private	Dealer
2 Dr GA Hbk	676	925	1340
4 Dr GA Sdn	739	1011	1465
4 Dr GS Sdn	864	1182	1713
2 Dr GT Hbk	962	1316	1907

OPTIONS FOR SWIFT
Air Conditioning +152
Automatic 3-Speed Transmission +104

1992 SUZUKI

SAMURAI   1992

The Samurai loses a trim-level, making it available only as a two-wheel drive JA or four-wheel drive JL. The JL model loses its back seat.

Category L

Model	Trade-in	Private	Dealer
2 Dr JA Conv	609	793	1100
2 Dr JL 4WD Conv	801	1043	1446

OPTIONS FOR SAMURAI
Air Conditioning +114

SIDEKICK   1992

Four-door models receive an increase of 15 horsepower and a four-speed automatic transmission. All Sidekicks get a redesigned instrument panel.

Category L

Model	Trade-in	Private	Dealer
4 Dr JLX 4WD Wgn	2015	2624	3640
2 Dr JS Conv	1567	2040	2830
4 Dr JS Wgn	1719	2239	3106
2 Dr JX 4WD Conv	1769	2304	3195
4 Dr JX 4WD Wgn	1840	2396	3323

OPTIONS FOR SIDEKICK
Air Conditioning +134
Automatic 3-Speed Transmission +105
Automatic 4-Speed Transmission +167
Hardtop Roof +140
Leather Seats +105

SWIFT   1992

All Swifts get a redesigned front and rear fascia as well as a new dashboard. GS sedans receive power steering and new hub caps.

Category A

Model	Trade-in	Private	Dealer
2 Dr GA Hbk	563	793	1175
4 Dr GA Sdn	627	882	1307
4 Dr GS Sdn	735	1035	1534
2 Dr GT Hbk	812	1142	1693

OPTIONS FOR SWIFT
Air Conditioning +140
Automatic 3-Speed Transmission +97

Don't forget to refer to the Mileage Adjustment Table at the back of this book!

TOYOTA 01

Model Description	Trade-in TMV	Private TMV	Dealer TMV	Model Description	Trade-in TMV	Private TMV	Dealer TMV

TOYOTA   *Japan*

1994 Toyota Corolla

2001 TOYOTA

4RUNNER   2001

Base models have been killed, leaving Limited and SR5 trim levels equipped with a standard automatic transmission, Vehicle Skid Control (VSC), traction control and ABS with electronic brake force distribution and brake assist. All 4Runners have power door locks this year, as well as a pre-wired trailer hitch harness, a modified grille design and freshened taillights. New wheels for Limited and Sport debut, and a new premium 3-in-1 audio system with a CD changer is available. Revised sun visors with extensions and a HomeLink programmable transmitter come standard on Limited and can be ordered on SR5. Limited also gets a new color of wood trim, and standard front seat heaters. There's bad news for hardcore off-roaders — the optional differential lock has been discontinued with the demise of the manual transmission. Three new colors replace two old ones on the color chart.

Category M

	Trade-in	Private	Dealer
4 Dr Limited 4WD Wgn	25200	26675	29133
4 Dr Limited Wgn	22916	24258	26493
4 Dr SR5 4WD Wgn	19671	20822	22741
4 Dr SR5 Wgn	17469	18491	20195

OPTIONS FOR 4RUNNER
Aluminum/Alloy Wheels[Std on Limited] +302
Fog Lights[Opt on SR5] +120
Leather Seats[Opt on SR5] +910
Power Sunroof +593
Premium Sound System +146
Rear Heater +124
Sport Seats +302

AVALON   2001

Two colors, Cognac Brown and Constellation Blue Pearl, are dumped for 2001, and an emergency trunk release has been added. No other changes have been made to this imitation Buick, which was completely redesigned last year.

Category G

	Trade-in	Private	Dealer
4 Dr XL Sdn	20148	21218	23000
4 Dr XLS Sdn	20546	21636	23454

OPTIONS FOR AVALON
Aluminum/Alloy Wheels[Opt on XL] +280
Dual Power Seats +302
Heated Front Seats +229
JBL Sound System[Opt on XL] +262
Keyless Entry System[Opt on XL] +127
Leather Seats +618
Pearlescent White Paint +160
Power Moonroof +662
Traction Control System +618

CAMRY   2001

Want air conditioning, power windows/locks/mirrors and variable intermittent wipers on the CE? Buy the Value Package. To get remote keyless entry or a power driver's seat on the LE, you must buy a Value Package. A power moonroof and six-disc in-dash CD changer requires the Leather Value Package on XLE models. LE V6 models get daytime running lights standard, while JBL audio is newly optional on all LEs. The anti-theft system with engine immobilizer is restricted to XLE V6 models.

Category D

	Trade-in	Private	Dealer
4 Dr CE Sdn	11492	12307	13665
4 Dr LE Sdn	12962	13881	15413
4 Dr LE V6 Sdn	14066	15063	16725
4 Dr XLE V6 Sdn	17032	18239	20252
4 Dr XLE Sdn	15361	16450	18265

OPTIONS FOR CAMRY
Air Conditioning[Opt on CE] +731
Aluminum/Alloy Wheels[Std on XLE,XLE V6] +280
Anti-Lock Brakes[Opt on CE,LE] +444
Automatic 4-Speed Transmission[Opt on CE,LE V6] +582
Cruise Control[Opt on CE] +182
JBL Sound System[Opt on LE,LE V6] +211
Keyless Entry System[Opt on LE,LE V6] +127
Leather Seats +672
Power Door Locks[Opt on CE] +172
Power Drivers Seat +226
Power Moonroof +727
Power Windows[Opt on CE] +193
Side Air Bag Restraints +182
Traction Control System +218
Tutone Paint +146

Model Description	Trade-in TMV	Private TMV	Dealer TMV	Model Description	Trade-in TMV	Private TMV	Dealer TMV

CAMRY SOLARA 2001

Top-level SLE models can be equipped with a new JBL audio system, so long as you order leather upholstery. Option package fiddling makes it easier to equip a Solara the way you like. The anti-theft and engine immobilizer system is restricted to SLEs, while SEs now come standard with a six-speaker cassette stereo. Twilight Blue Pearl is replaced by Indigo Ink as an exterior color.

Category D

2 Dr SE Conv	18082	19363	21500
2 Dr SE Cpe	12550	13440	14923
2 Dr SE V6 Conv	20689	22155	24600
2 Dr SE V6 Cpe	14393	15413	17114
2 Dr SLE Conv	22539	24137	26800
2 Dr SLE Cpe	18176	19464	21612

OPTIONS FOR CAMRY SOLARA
Aluminum/Alloy Wheels[Std on SLE] +317
Automatic 4-Speed Transmission[Std on SLE,Conv] +582
JBL Sound System[Std on SLE] +146
Leather Seats[Std on SLE] +655
Pearlescent White Paint +160
Power Drivers Seat[Std on SLE] +284
Power Moonroof +655
Rear Spoiler[Std on SLE,Conv] +156
Side Air Bag Restraints +182
Traction Control System +218

CELICA 2001

Brand new last year, the hot Celica motors into 2001 with no changes.

Category E

2 Dr GT Hbk	13299	14124	15500
2 Dr GT-S Hbk	15444	16403	18000

OPTIONS FOR CELICA
Aluminum/Alloy Wheels[Opt on GT] +280
Anti-Lock Brakes +400
Automatic 4-Speed Transmission +509
Cruise Control[Opt on GT] +146
Leather Seats +789
Power Door Locks[Opt on GT] +164
Power Moonroof +640
Power Windows[Opt on GT] +178
Premium Sound System[Opt on GT] +240
Rear Spoiler +317
Side Air Bag Restraints +182

COROLLA 2001

Mid-grade CE trim replaces entry-level VE, top-line LE replaces mid-grade CE, and a sporty new CE-based S model debuts. Front and rear lighting is restyled, and the fascia up front is tweaked and now includes a chrome-ringed grille. An internal trunk release has been added, along with a push-button fresh/ recirculate control for the ventilation system. Two new colors replace an equal number of shades that are fading away.

Category B

4 Dr CE Sdn	7966	8617	9703
4 Dr LE Sdn	8734	9448	10638
4 Dr S Sdn	8493	9188	10345

OPTIONS FOR COROLLA
AM/FM Stereo Tape[Opt on VE] +153
Air Conditioning +691
Aluminum/Alloy Wheels +266
Anti-Lock Brakes +400
Automatic 3-Speed Transmission +302
Automatic 4-Speed Transmission +593
Cruise Control +182
Power Door Locks +196
Power Moonroof +520
Power Windows[Std on LE] +208
Side Air Bag Restraints +182

ECHO 2001

In an effort to protect occupants of this lightweight economy car better, Toyota makes side airbags optional for 2001. Brilliant Blue Pearl is a new color.

Category A

4 Dr STD Sdn	7380	7988	9000
2 Dr STD Cpe	6767	7324	8252

OPTIONS FOR ECHO
AM/FM Stereo/CD/Tape +196
Air Conditioning +672
Anti-Lock Brakes +429
Automatic 4-Speed Transmission +582
Keyless Entry System +127
Power Door Locks +164
Power Mirrors +131
Power Windows +193
Side Air Bag Restraints +182

HIGHLANDER 2001

Based on the same platform as the Lexus RX 300, Toyota's new Highlander SUV represents the best blend of a station wagon, a minivan and a sport utility available on the market today. Available only with a V6 and an automatic transmission driving power to the front or all the wheels, Highlander will be sold in one trim level with a Limited package listed on the option sheet.

Category M

4 Dr V6 4WD Wgn	20621	21828	23839
4 Dr V6 Wgn	19480	20620	22520
4 Dr STD 4WD Wgn	19228	20353	22229
4 Dr STD Wgn	18136	19197	20966

OPTIONS FOR HIGHLANDER
AM/FM/Stereo/CD/Tape +287

Model Description	Trade-in TMV	Private TMV	Dealer TMV	Model Description	Trade-in TMV	Private TMV	Dealer TMV

TOYOTA 01

Alarm System +156
Aluminum/Alloy Wheels +364
Camper/Towing Package +211
Climate Control for AC +182
Heated Front Seats +320
Keyless Entry System +160
Leather Seats +739
Limited Slip Differential +284
Luggage Rack +160
Power Drivers Seat +284
Power Sunroof +593
Privacy Glass +226
Side Air Bag Restraints +182
Traction Control System +618
Trailer Hitch +211

LAND CRUISER 2001

A navigation system is newly optional (and plays DVD movies when the vehicle is not in motion). Standard equipment now includes an electrochromic rearview mirror with compass and JBL audio with a 6-disc, in-dash CD changer. Each of the power windows now features one-touch up and down control. Three new colors replace Desert Bronze on the color chart, and the alloy wheels have a new chrome-like finish. So, uh, why is it that you wanted that more expensive Lexus LX 470?

Category O
4 Dr STD 4WD Wgn	38399	40124	43000

OPTIONS FOR LAND CRUISER
Navigation System +2183
Third Seat +1648

MR2 SPYDER 2001

Brand new last year, the spunky but not spacious MR2 Spyder rolls into 2001 without changes.
Category E
2 Dr Spyder Conv	18876	20048	22000

OPTIONS FOR MR2 SPYDER
Leather Seats +451

PRIUS 2001

Toyota's Prius, a gas/electric hybrid that follows in the more-expensive Honda Insight's footsteps, offers space for five adults coupled with class-leading fuel economy.
Category B
4 Dr STD Sdn	14679	15880	17880

RAV4 2001

Completely redesigned, RAV4 grows in size and gets a more powerful engine, along with edgy new styling.
Category L
4 Dr STD AWD Wgn	13436	14360	15900

4 Dr STD Wgn	12675	13547	15000

OPTIONS FOR RAV4
AM/FM Stereo/CD/Tape +364
Air Conditioning +717
Aluminum/Alloy Wheels +291
Anti-Lock Brakes +429
Automatic 4-Speed Transmission +691
Cruise Control +182
Fog Lights +120
Keyless Entry System +160
Leather Seats +546
Limited Slip Differential +284
Luggage Rack +160
Power Door Locks +175
Power Sunroof +593
Power Windows +200
Privacy Glass +226
Rear Spoiler +146

SEQUOIA 2001

In a bid to take over the world, Toyota releases the Tundra pickup-based Sequoia, a full-size SUV that represents the first serious challenge to the Chevrolet Tahoe/Suburban, Ford Expedition, and GMC Yukon from across either ocean. Is nothing sacred?
Category N
4 Dr Limited 4WD Wgn	33957	35661	38500
4 Dr Limited Wgn	30164	31678	34200
4 Dr SR5 4WD Wgn	28224	29640	32000
4 Dr SR5 Wgn	24167	25379	27400

OPTIONS FOR SEQUOIA
AM/FM Stereo/CD/Tape[Std on Limited] +375
Aluminum/Alloy Wheels[Std on Limited] +364
Dual Air Conditioning[Std on Limited] +415
Dual Power Seats[Opt on SR5 2WD] +477
Head Protection Air Bag +182
Keyless Entry System[Std on Limited] +160
Leather Seats[Std on Limited] +910
Luggage Rack[Std on Limited] +160
Power Sunroof +731
Rear Spoiler +146
Running Boards[Std on Limited] +291
Side Air Bag Restraints +182

SIENNA 2001

Like other minivans on the market, the 2001 Sienna can be equipped with an on-board entertainment system. Dual power sliding doors are newly optional, and the safety-conscious will like the fact that side airbags and a stability control system are available. Sienna's smooth V6 makes more power and torque this year. A rear defroster is now standard on all Siennas, while JBL audio, heated front seats and an electrochromic rearview mirror with integrated compass are optional on XLE models. Styling has been

Model Description	Trade-in TMV	Private TMV	Dealer TMV

tweaked front and rear, four new colors replace four old colors, and all Siennas come with a driver's side sliding door.

Category P

Model Description	Trade-in TMV	Private TMV	Dealer TMV
4 Dr CE Pass. Van	17598	18584	20228
4 Dr LE Pass. Van	18956	20018	21788
4 Dr XLE Pass. Van	21116	22299	24271

OPTIONS FOR SIENNA
Aluminum/Alloy Wheels[Std on XLE] +346
Camper/Towing Package +502
Captain Chairs (4)[Opt on LE] +648
Child Seat (1) +182
Cruise Control[Opt on CE] +131
Heated Front Seats +320
Keyless Entry System[Std on XLE] +160
Leather Seats +1026
Luggage Rack[Std on XLE] +160
Power Door Locks[Opt on CE] +175
Power Dual Sliding Doors +655
Power Moonroof +640
Power Sliding Door +287
Power Windows[Opt on CE] +193
Side Air Bag Restraints +182
Traction Control System +400

TACOMA   2001

Jumping on the crew-cab truck bandwagon, Toyota releases the attractive Double Cab. Also, in an effort to broaden the Tacoma's appeal, a new StepSide version is available, and the S-Runner sport truck debuts. Revised front styling and new alloy wheels give Tacoma a more rugged look. New exterior colors and option package content shuffling sum up the obvious changes for 2001.

Category J

Model Description	Trade-in TMV	Private TMV	Dealer TMV
2 Dr Prerunner Ext Cab SB			
	11858	12643	13951
2 Dr Prerunner Std Cab SB			
	9815	10464	11547
2 Dr Prerunner V6 Ext Cab SB			
	13312	14193	15661
4 Dr Prerunner Crew Cab SB			
	13146	14016	15466
4 Dr Prerunner V6 Crew Cab SB			
	13809	14723	16246
2 Dr S-Runner V6 Ext Cab SB			
	13082	13948	15391
2 Dr STD 4WD Ext Cab SB			
	13342	14225	15697
2 Dr STD 4WD Std Cab SB			
	11692	12465	13755
2 Dr STD Ext Cab SB	10396	11083	12230
2 Dr STD Std Cab SB	8392	8947	9873
2 Dr V6 4WD Ext Cab SB			
	14192	15132	16697
4 Dr V6 4WD Crew Cab SB			
	16142	17210	18990

OPTIONS FOR TACOMA
AM/FM Stereo/CD/Tape[Std on Limited] +240
Air Conditioning[Opt on Limited V6,V6,Std Cab] +364
Aluminum/Alloy Wheels[Std on Limited] +269
Anti-Lock Brakes +429
Automatic 4-Speed Transmission[Opt on SR5 V6,STD] +524
Chrome Wheels +342
Locking Differential[Opt on Prerunner] +247
Pop-Up Moonroof +284
Power Door Locks[Std on Limited] +167
Power Windows[Std on Limited] +193
Privacy Glass +131
Running Boards +229
TRD Off-Road Package +582

TUNDRA   2001

Newly optional on Limited is a package that matches the bumpers and tailgate handle to the body color. The TRD Off-Road package is now available on Access Cabs with a V8 engine, while models equipped with a V6 receive an upgraded alternator. A note-pad holder is now optional on SR5 and Limited, while Base regular cab trucks lose their standard cassette player. Two new colors are available, filling slots left vacant by three old colors that have been discontinued.

Category K

Model Description	Trade-in TMV	Private TMV	Dealer TMV
4 Dr Limited V8 4WD Ext Cab SB			
	22215	23515	25682
4 Dr Limited V8 Ext Cab SB			
	19457	20596	22494
2 Dr SR5 V6 4WD Std Cab LB			
	17536	18562	20273
4 Dr SR5 V6 4WD Ext Cab SB			
	18081	19139	20903
4 Dr SR5 V6 Ext Cab SB			
	15551	16461	17978
4 Dr SR5 V8 4WD Ext Cab SB			
	19938	21105	23050
4 Dr SR5 V8 Ext Cab SB			
	17194	18201	19878
2 Dr STD Std Cab LB	11370	12035	13144

OPTIONS FOR TUNDRA
Air Conditioning[Opt on STD] +717
Aluminum/Alloy Wheels[Std on Limited] +276
Anti-Lock Brakes +458
Automatic 4-Speed Transmission[Opt on SR5 V6,STD] +560
Leather Seats +1033
Power Door Locks[Std on Limited] +160
Power Drivers Seat +156
Power Mirrors[Std on Limited] +131
Power Windows[Std on Limited] +182

Don't forget to refer to the Mileage Adjustment Table at the back of this book!

Model Description	Trade-in TMV	Private TMV	Dealer TMV	Model Description	Trade-in TMV	Private TMV	Dealer TMV

Privacy Glass +131
Sliding Rear Window +116
Styled Steel Wheels[Std on SR5 V8,Ext Cab] +160
Tilt Steering Wheel[Opt on STD] +146
Tutone Paint +266

2000 TOYOTA

4RUNNER 2000

Optional color-coordinated fender flares are available on the SR5. An AM/FM/Cassette/CD is now available on base models, and is standard on SR5 and Limited models. Daytime running lights are now included with the antilock brake package.

Category M

Model Description	Trade-in TMV	Private TMV	Dealer TMV
4 Dr STD 4WD Wgn	15413	16854	18184
4 Dr STD Wgn	14410	15757	17000
4 Dr Limited 4WD Wgn	24076	26326	28404
4 Dr Limited Wgn	21834	23875	25759
4 Dr SR5 4WD Wgn	17351	18973	20470
4 Dr SR5 Wgn	15967	17460	18838

OPTIONS FOR 4RUNNER
AM/FM Compact Disc Player +291
AM/FM Stereo/CD/Tape[Opt on STD,SR5 V6 2WD] +509
Air Conditioning[Std on Limited] +717
Alarm System[Std on Limited] +233
Aluminum/Alloy Wheels[Std on Limited] +302
Anti-Lock Brakes[Opt on STD] +429
Automatic 4-Speed Transmission[Opt on STD,SR5 V6 4WD] +654
Black Elite Package +378
Camper/Towing Package +127
Climate Control for AC[Opt on SR5] +131
Compact Disc Changer +482
Cruise Control[Opt on STD] +182
Exterior Package +615
Fog Lights[Opt on SR5] +120
Gold Elite Package +184
Gold Package +184
Keyless Entry System[Opt on SR5] +164
Leather Seats[Opt on SR5] +910
Limited Slip Differential +247
Luggage Rack +109
Metallic Paint +146
Power Door Locks[Opt on STD,SR5 V6 2WD] +178
Power Mirrors[Std on Limited] +146
Power Moonroof +593
Power Windows[Std on Limited] +193
Privacy Glass[Opt on STD] +226
Rear Heater +124
Running Boards[Std on Limited] +251
Sport Package +1014
Sport Seats +302
Steel Wheels +437
Tilt Steering Wheel[Opt on STD] +178
Trailer Hitch +127

AVALON 2000

Entering its second generation, the 2000 Avalon is roomier, more powerful and more technically advanced. The Kentucky-built Avalon features new styling inside and out, enhanced safety features, increased engine performance, and more comfort and convenience than its predecessor.

Category G

Model Description	Trade-in TMV	Private TMV	Dealer TMV
4 Dr XL Sdn	18473	20047	21500
4 Dr XLS Sdn	18626	20214	21679

OPTIONS FOR AVALON
Alarm System[Opt on XL] +290
Aluminum/Alloy Wheels[Opt on XL] +280
Automatic Dimming Mirror[Opt on XL] +109
Compact Disc Changer +400
Dual Power Seats[Opt on XL] +302
Gold Package +119
Heated Front Seats +229
JBL Sound System[Opt on XL] +263
Keyless Entry System[Opt on XL] +127
Leather Seats +618
Power Moonroof +640
Special Factory Paint +160
Traction Control System +218

CAMRY 2000

The Camry sedan receives minor updates for the 2000 model year. The exterior benefits from new front and rear styling. Camry LE models get 15-inch tires with new wheel covers while the XLE gets standard 16-inch tires. Four-cylinder models make three more horsepower than last year. Interior upgrades include an available JBL premium audio system, automatic climate control, larger buttons on the audio faceplate, imitation wood trim on XLE models, optional leather seats with driver-side power on LE models, and new LE model seat fabric. The hood is now supported with struts and dampers.

Category D

Model Description	Trade-in TMV	Private TMV	Dealer TMV
4 Dr CE Sdn	10193	11279	12281
4 Dr LE Sdn	11476	12699	13828
4 Dr LE V6 Sdn	12360	13676	14892
4 Dr XLE Sdn	13643	15097	16439
4 Dr XLE V6 Sdn	15329	16962	18470

OPTIONS FOR CAMRY
AM/FM Stereo Tape[Std on CE] +172
AM/FM Stereo/CD/Tape[Opt on CE] +509
Air Conditioning[Opt on CE] +731
Alarm System[Opt on CE] +290
Aluminum/Alloy Wheels[Std on XLE,XLE V6] +266
Anti-Lock Brakes[Opt on CE,LE] +444
Automatic 4-Speed Transmission[Opt on CE,LE V6] +582
Automatic Dimming Mirror +109
Black Elite Package +597

Don't forget to refer to the Mileage Adjustment Table at the back of this book!

Model Description	Trade-in TMV	Private TMV	Dealer TMV
Compact Disc Changer +400			
Cruise Control[Opt on CE] +146			
Fog Lights +290			
Gold Package +142			
JBL Sound System[Opt on LE,LE V6] +211			
Keyless Entry System[Opt on LE,LE V6] +127			
Leather Seats +672			
Power Door Locks[Opt on CE] +172			
Power Drivers Seat +226			
Power Mirrors[Opt on CE] +164			
Power Moonroof +727			
Power Windows[Opt on CE] +193			
Rear Spoiler +255			
Side Air Bag Restraints +182			
Traction Control System +218			

CAMRY SOLARA   2000

Solara four-cylinder models will achieve ultra-low-emission vehicle (ULEV) status. A convertible version is now offered for topless fun. SLE models get a JBL premium audio system as standard equipment, and a six-disc in-dash CD changer is optional. Two new exterior colors are offered.

Category D

Model Description	Trade-in TMV	Private TMV	Dealer TMV
2 Dr SE Conv	15971	17672	19243
2 Dr SE Cpe	11155	12344	13441
2 Dr SE V6 Conv	19089	21123	23000
2 Dr SE V6 Cpe	12841	14209	15472
2 Dr SLE Conv	20666	22867	24900
2 Dr SLE Cpe	16050	17760	19339

OPTIONS FOR CAMRY SOLARA

Alarm System[Std on SLE] +280			
Aluminum/Alloy Wheels[Std on SLE] +317			
Anti-Lock Brakes[Opt on SE] +400			
Automatic 4-Speed Transmission[Std on SLE,Conv] +582			
Automatic Dimming Mirror[Std on SLE] +124			
Compact Disc Changer +364			
Gold Package +135			
JBL Sound System[Std on SLE] +364			
Keyless Entry System[Std on SLE] +127			
Leather Seats[Std on SLE] +655			
Power Drivers Seat[Std on SLE] +284			
Power Moonroof +654			
Rear Spoiler[Std on SLE,Conv] +156			
Side Air Bag Restraints +182			
Special Factory Paint +160			
Traction Control System +218			

CELICA   2000

The all-new 2000 Celica is considerably more performance-oriented than the previous model. Highlights include an exciting exterior, a 180-horsepower engine and six-speed gearbox for the GT-S, and sharp handling.

Category E

Model Description	Trade-in TMV	Private TMV	Dealer TMV
2 Dr GT Hbk	12578	13786	14900
2 Dr GT-S Hbk	13457	14749	15941

OPTIONS FOR CELICA

AM/FM Stereo Tape +146			
Alarm System +309			
Aluminum/Alloy Wheels[Opt on GT] +317			
Anti-Lock Brakes +400			
Automatic 4-Speed Transmission +509			
Compact Disc Changer +400			
Cruise Control[Opt on GT] +146			
Gold Package +142			
Leather Seats +789			
Power Door Locks[Opt on GT] +164			
Power Moonroof +640			
Power Windows[Opt on GT] +178			
Rear Spoiler +317			
Side Air Bag Restraints +182			

COROLLA   2000

The Corolla receives increased performance from VVT-i engine technology. Horsepower jumps from 120 to 125. The Corolla also achieves low-emission vehicle status this year.

Category B

Model Description	Trade-in TMV	Private TMV	Dealer TMV
4 Dr CE Sdn	8329	9474	10531
4 Dr LE Sdn	8738	9940	11049
4 Dr VE Sdn	7909	8996	10000

OPTIONS FOR COROLLA

AM/FM Compact Disc Player +218			
AM/FM Stereo Tape[Opt on VE] +146			
Air Conditioning[Std on LE] +691			
Alarm System +290			
Aluminum/Alloy Wheels +302			
Anti-Lock Brakes +400			
Automatic 3-Speed Transmission +437			
Automatic 4-Speed Transmission +582			
Compact Disc Changer +400			
Cruise Control +156			
Gold Package +130			
Keyless Entry System +134			
Power Door Locks[Std on LE] +164			
Power Moonroof +535			
Power Windows[Std on LE] +208			
Rear Spoiler +215			
Side Air Bag Restraints +182			

ECHO   2000

The 2000 Toyota Echo brings a new name and a fresh concept to the Toyota lineup. Designed to attract youthful buyers, the Echo features a roomy and comfortable interior, superb gas mileage, and an affordable price.

Category A

Model Description	Trade-in TMV	Private TMV	Dealer TMV
2 Dr STD Cpe	6033	6811	7529
4 Dr STD Sdn	6731	7599	8400

OPTIONS FOR ECHO

AM/FM Compact Disc Player +164			

Don't forget to refer to the Mileage Adjustment Table at the back of this book!

TOYOTA 00

Model Description	Trade-in TMV	Private TMV	Dealer TMV	Model Description	Trade-in TMV	Private TMV	Dealer TMV

AM/FM Stereo Tape +124
AM/FM Stereo/CD/Tape +196
Air Conditioning +672
Alarm System +146
Aluminum/Alloy Wheels +182
Anti-Lock Brakes +429
Automatic 4-Speed Transmission +582
Compact Disc Changer +418
Power Door Locks +164
Power Steering +196

LAND CRUISER 2000

The Land Cruiser receives new standard equipment features, such as vehicle skid control and an Active TRAC electronic four-wheel-drive system with torque transfer capability. Additional newly standard equipment includes illuminated entry for the remote keyless-entry system, power tilt/slide moonroof and a leather interior. The optional third-row seat now includes rear air conditioning.

Category O

Model	Trade-in	Private	Dealer
4 Dr STD 4WD Wgn	33127	35489	37669

OPTIONS FOR LAND CRUISER
Dual Air Conditioning +415
Gold Package +250
Luggage Rack +236
Running Boards +564
Third Seat +222

MR2 SPYDER 2000

Toyota revives the MR2 nameplate on a minimalist two-seat roadster, set to compete directly with the ever-popular Mazda Miata. Only 5,000 are being built and sold, so if you want one, be prepared for some hair-grabbing at the dealer.

Category E

Model	Trade-in	Private	Dealer
2 Dr Spyder Conv	16329	17896	19343

RAV4 2000

The RAV4 SUV remains largely unchanged for 2000. A new cupholder design and the extinction of the two-door RAV4 convertible are the big news for '00.

Category L

Model	Trade-in	Private	Dealer
4 Dr STD AWD Wgn	11728	12871	13926
4 Dr STD Wgn	10908	11971	12952
4 Dr L Special Edit. AWD Wgn	13531	14850	16067
4 Dr L Special Edit. Wgn	13081	14356	15533

OPTIONS FOR RAV4
AM/FM Compact Disc Player[Opt on STD] +327
AM/FM Stereo Tape[Opt on STD] +255
AM/FM Stereo/CD/Tape +364
Air Conditioning[Opt on STD] +717

Alarm System +255
Aluminum/Alloy Wheels[Opt on STD] +357
Anti-Lock Brakes +458
Automatic 4-Speed Transmission +763
Compact Disc Changer +437
Cruise Control[Opt on STD] +182
Leather Seats +546
Limited Slip Differential +284
Luggage Rack +182
Power Door Locks[Opt on STD] +175
Power Mirrors[Opt on STD] +149
Power Moonroof +593
Power Windows[Opt on STD] +200
Privacy Glass[Opt on STD] +226
Side Steps +172
Trailer Hitch +109

SIENNA 2000

New for Sienna are two exterior colors and various audio enhancements. All grades feature a standard AM/FM/cassette audio system. XLE models add a CD deck and offer an optional in-dash six-disc changer.

Category P

Model	Trade-in	Private	Dealer
2 Dr CE Pass. Van	15758	17298	18719
4 Dr LE Pass. Van	16668	18297	19800
4 Dr XLE Pass. Van	18689	20515	22200

OPTIONS FOR SIENNA
Alarm System[Std on XLE] +233
Aluminum/Alloy Wheels[Std on XLE] +346
Automatic Dimming Mirror[Std on XLE] +109
Camper/Towing Package +502
Captain Chairs (2) +182
Captain Chairs (4)[Opt on LE] +648
Child Seat (1) +182
Compact Disc Changer +400
Cruise Control[Opt on CE] +131
Dual Air Conditioning[Opt on CE] +429
Gold Package +119
Keyless Entry System[Std on XLE] +160
Leather Seats +1026
Luggage Rack[Std on XLE] +160
Power Door Locks[Opt on CE] +175
Power Moonroof +640
Power Sliding Door +287
Power Windows[Opt on CE] +193
Privacy Glass[Opt on CE] +263
Rear Spoiler +207
Running Boards +433
Sliding Driver Side Door[Opt on CE] +287
Trailer Hitch +211

TACOMA 2000

Tacomas with four-cylinder engines and four-wheel drive achieve improved performance from an enhanced gear ratio. Base-grade Tacomas feature new designs for the interior fabric and exterior mirrors.

Don't forget to refer to the Mileage Adjustment Table at the back of this book!

TOYOTA 00-99

Model Description	Trade-in TMV	Private TMV	Dealer TMV	Model Description	Trade-in TMV	Private TMV	Dealer TMV

Daytime running lights are now included with the antilock brake package. There are also two new colors as well as a color-keyed package for those who like the monochrome look.

Category J

Model Description	Trade-in TMV	Private TMV	Dealer TMV
2 Dr STD 4WD Ext Cab SB	11861	13036	14120
2 Dr STD 4WD Std Cab SB	11434	12567	13612
2 Dr STD Ext Cab SB	8902	9784	10598
2 Dr STD Std Cab SB	7270	7989	8654
2 Dr Limited 4WD Ext Cab SB	17220	18926	20500
2 Dr Prerunner Ext Cab SB	11698	12857	13926
2 Dr Prerunner Std Cab SB	8331	9156	9918
2 Dr Prerunner V6 Ext Cab SB	11952	13135	14228
2 Dr SR5 4WD Ext Cab SB	12252	13465	14585
2 Dr SR5 Ext Cab SB	11353	12477	13515
2 Dr SR5 V6 4WD Ext Cab SB	13313	14632	15849
2 Dr SR5 V6 Ext Cab SB	11598	12747	13807
2 Dr V6 4WD Ext Cab SB	12006	13195	14293
2 Dr V6 Ext Cab SB	10945	12028	13029

OPTIONS FOR TACOMA
AM/FM Compact Disc Player +496
AM/FM Stereo/CD/Tape[Std on Limited] +421
Air Conditioning[Opt on Limited V6,V6,Std Cab] +717
Alarm System +182
Aluminum/Alloy Wheels[Std on Limited] +269
Anti-Lock Brakes +429
Automatic 4-Speed Transmission[Opt on SR5 V6,STD] +528
Automatic Locking Hubs (4WD) +175
Bed Liner +218
Chrome Bumpers +291
Compact Disc Changer +437
Cruise Control[Opt on SR5 V6] +182
Keyless Entry System +109
Limited Slip Differential +247
Off-Road Package +960
Power Door Locks[Std on Limited] +167
Power Windows[Std on Limited] +193
Running Boards +208
Styled Steel Wheels[Std on Base 4WD Std Cab] +342
Tilt Steering Wheel[Std on Limited] +178
Tonneau Cover +255
Trailer Hitch +204

TUNDRA   2000

This is an all-new, full-size pickup truck designed to compete with the Ford F-150, Chevrolet Silverado 1500, GMC Sierra 1500 and Dodge Ram 1500. It features an optional V8 engine and can be ordered in a two or four-door, regular- or extended-cab configuration.

Category K

Model Description	Trade-in TMV	Private TMV	Dealer TMV
2 Dr STD Std Cab LB	9502	10407	11243
4 Dr Limited 4WD Ext Cab SB	18342	20090	21703
4 Dr Limited Ext Cab SB	16111	17647	19064
2 Dr SR5 V6 4WD Std Cab LB	13302	14570	15740
4 Dr SR5 V6 4WD Ext Cab SB	15483	16959	18321
4 Dr SR5 V6 Ext Cab SB	13512	14799	15988
2 Dr SR5 V8 4WD Std Cab LB	15128	16569	17900
4 Dr SR5 V8 4WD Ext Cab SB	16442	18009	19455
4 Dr SR5 V8 Ext Cab SB	14211	15565	16815

OPTIONS FOR TUNDRA
AM/FM Stereo/CD/Tape[Std on Limited] +182
Air Conditioning[Opt on STD] +717
Aluminum/Alloy Wheels[Std on Limited] +160
Anti-Lock Brakes +400
Automatic 4-Speed Transmission[Opt on SR5 V6,STD] +611
Bed Liner +218
Compact Disc Changer +182
Cruise Control[Opt on SR5 V6] +164
Keyless Entry System +124
Leather Seats +654
Power Door Locks[Std on Limited] +160
Power Drivers Seat +156
Power Mirrors[Std on Limited] +131
Power Windows[Std on Limited] +182
Rear Step Bumper[Std on Limited,SR5 V8] +109
Running Boards +146
Spoke Wheels +276
Styled Steel Wheels[Std on SR5 V8,Ext Cab] +255
Tonneau Cover +255
Trailer Hitch +164
Tutone Paint +236

1999 TOYOTA

4RUNNER   1999

The 4Runner receives a number of upgrades this year, starting with a new and improved four-wheel drive system equipped with a center differential and featuring

TOYOTA 99

Model Description	Trade-in TMV	Private TMV	Dealer TMV	Model Description	Trade-in TMV	Private TMV	Dealer TMV

a full-time 4WD mode in addition to the current two-high, four-high and four-low modes. New exterior features include a front bumper redesign, multi-reflector headlamps, and an enhanced sport package with fender flares and a hood scoop on the SR5 model. Inside, a new center console/cupholder design will improve beverage-carrying capacity of the 4Runner and an automatic climate control system will be featured on the Limited models.

Category M

Model Description	Trade-in TMV	Private TMV	Dealer TMV
4 Dr STD 4WD Wgn	12547	13790	15033
4 Dr STD Wgn	12159	13363	14568
4 Dr Limited 4WD Wgn	20042	22028	24013
4 Dr Limited Wgn	18331	20147	21963
4 Dr SR5 4WD Wgn	17109	18804	20499
4 Dr SR5 Wgn	14176	15581	16985

OPTIONS FOR 4RUNNER

AM/FM Compact Disc Player[Std on Limited] +231
AM/FM Stereo/CD/Tape +405
Air Conditioning[Std on Limited] +569
Alarm System[Std on Limited] +185
Aluminum/Alloy Wheels[Std on Limited] +240
Anti-Lock Brakes[Std on Limited, SR5] +342
Automatic 4-Speed Transmission[Opt on STD, SR5 V6 4WD] +521
Black Elite Package +300
Camper/Towing Package +101
Compact Disc Changer +381
Cruise Control[Opt on STD] +145
Fog Lights +95
Gold Package +147
Keyless Entry System[Std on Limited] +130
Leather Seats[Opt on SR5] +723
Locking Differential +197
Metallic Paint +115
Power Door Locks[Opt on STD] +141
Power Mirrors[Opt on STD] +115
Power Moonroof +472
Power Windows[Std on Limited] +275
Privacy Glass[Opt on STD] +179
Rear Heater +98
Rear Window Wiper[Opt on STD] +104
Running Boards[Std on Limited] +199
Sport Package +807
Sport Seats +240
Steel Wheels +346
Tilt Steering Wheel[Opt on STD] +141
Trailer Hitch +101

AVALON 1999

After a body makeover and safety improvements (side airbags) last year, the Avalon heads into '99 with only minor updates. Daytime running lights with auto-off color-keyed foglamp covers and dual heated color keyed power mirrors are new this year. A new three-in-one ETR/cassette/CD sound system is optional on the XL model and Lunar Mist metallic replaces Golden Sand metallic.

Category G

Model Description	Trade-in TMV	Private TMV	Dealer TMV
4 Dr XL Sdn	14094	15647	17200
4 Dr XLS Sdn	15607	17327	19047

OPTIONS FOR AVALON

AM/FM Compact Disc Player +194
AM/FM Stereo/CD/Tape[Opt on XL] +110
Alarm System[Opt on XL] +231
Aluminum/Alloy Wheels[Opt on XL] +222
Compact Disc Changer +318
Dual Power Seats[Opt on XL] +240
Gold Package +95
Heated Front Seats +183
Leather Seats +491
Power Moonroof +521
Special Factory Paint +127
Traction Control System +193

CAMRY 1999

If it ain't broken, don't fix (or change) it. The Camry is already Toyota's best-selling car so changes to the '99 are minimal. Two new audio systems are available and both include three-in-one ETR/cassette/CD features. Also available are daytime running lights with auto-off. Vintage Red Pearl, Sable Pearl, and Woodland Pearl replace Sunfire Red Pearl, Ruby Red and Classic Green Pearl.

Category D

Model Description	Trade-in TMV	Private TMV	Dealer TMV
4 Dr CE Sdn	8758	9796	10835
4 Dr LE Sdn	10244	11458	12673
4 Dr LE V6 Sdn	10869	12158	13447
4 Dr XLE Sdn	11808	13208	14608
4 Dr XLE V6 Sdn	12980	14520	16059

OPTIONS FOR CAMRY

AM/FM Compact Disc Player[Std on XLE, XLE V6] +194
AM/FM Stereo/CD/Tape +405
Air Conditioning[Opt on CE] +580
Alarm System[Std on XLE, XLE V6] +231
Aluminum/Alloy Wheels[Std on XLE, XLE V6] +210
Anti-Lock Brakes[Opt on CE, LE] +353
Automatic 4-Speed Transmission[Opt on CE] +462
Black Elite Package +474
Compact Disc Changer +318
Cruise Control[Opt on CE] +115
Fog Lights +231
Gold Package +112
Leather Seats +534
Power Door Locks[Opt on CE] +136
Power Drivers Seat +179
Power Mirrors[Opt on CE] +130
Power Moonroof +578
Power Windows[Opt on CE] +153
Rear Spoiler +203
Side Air Bag Restraints +145

Don't forget to refer to the Mileage Adjustment Table at the back of this book!

TOYOTA 99

Model Description	Trade-in TMV	Private TMV	Dealer TMV	Model Description	Trade-in TMV	Private TMV	Dealer TMV

Traction Control System +173

CAMRY SOLARA   1999

Everything. This all-new coupe is based on the Camry platform. Designed jointly by the Toyota Motor Corporation in Japan and the Toyota Technical Center in Ann Arbor, Michigan, the Solara is targeted at consumers who want the style of a sports car but the room and comfort of a larger, more practical vehicle.

Category D

	Trade-in	Private	Dealer
2 Dr SE Cpe	10009	11196	12383
2 Dr SE V6 Cpe	11495	12858	14221
2 Dr SLE Cpe	13606	15220	16833

OPTIONS FOR CAMRY SOLARA

AM/FM Stereo/CD/Tape[Std on SLE] +161
Alarm System[Std on SLE] +247
Aluminum/Alloy Wheels[Std on SLE] +252
Anti-Lock Brakes[Opt on SE] +353
Automatic 4-Speed Transmission[Std on SLE] +514
Gold Package +119
JBL Sound System[Std on SLE] +321
Keyless Entry System[Std on SLE] +112
Leather Seats[Std on SLE] +578
Power Drivers Seat[Std on SLE] +250
Power Moonroof +577
Rear Spoiler +138
Side Air Bag Restraints +161
Special Factory Paint +128
Traction Control System +193

CELICA   1999

The Celica GT Sport Coupe has been discontinued along with the color Galaxy Blue Metallic.

Category E

	Trade-in	Private	Dealer
2 Dr GT Conv	14389	15856	17324
2 Dr GT Hbk	11545	12722	13900

OPTIONS FOR CELICA

AM/FM Stereo/CD/Tape[Std on Conv] +318
Alarm System +245
Aluminum/Alloy Wheels[Std on Conv] +252
Anti-Lock Brakes +318
Automatic 4-Speed Transmission +462
Compact Disc Changer +318
Gold Package +112
Leather Seats +626
Power Moonroof +509
Sport Suspension +303

COROLLA   1999

A major makeover in '98 means only minor updates to the Corolla in '99. The VE model will feature a Deluxe AM/FM ETR four-speaker audio system as standard equipment. A Touring Package will be standard equipment on the Corolla LE model. Five new exterior colors include Silver Stream Opal, Venetian Red Pearl, Dark Emerald Pearl, Aqua Blue Metallic and Twilight Blue Pearl.

Category B

	Trade-in	Private	Dealer
4 Dr CE Sdn	7253	8202	9152
4 Dr LE Sdn	7568	8559	9550
4 Dr VE Sdn	6736	7618	8500

OPTIONS FOR COROLLA

AM/FM Compact Disc Player +173
AM/FM Stereo Tape[Opt on VE] +115
AM/FM Stereo/CD/Tape +260
Air Conditioning[Std on LE] +549
Alarm System +231
Aluminum/Alloy Wheels +240
Anti-Lock Brakes +318
Automatic 3-Speed Transmission +346
Automatic 4-Speed Transmission +462
Compact Disc Changer +318
Cruise Control +125
Gold Package +103
Keyless Entry System +107
Power Door Locks[Std on LE] +130
Power Moonroof +426
Power Windows[Std on LE] +165
Rear Spoiler +171
Side Air Bag Restraints +145

LAND CRUISER   1999

The Land Cruiser was reintroduced in '98 with major upgrades. As such, it enters '99 completely unchanged.

Category O

	Trade-in	Private	Dealer
4 Dr STD 4WD Wgn	31963	34482	37000

OPTIONS FOR LAND CRUISER

Camper/Towing Package +101
Dual Air Conditioning +329
Gold Package +198
Leather Seats +1052
Locking Differential +203
Luggage Rack +188
Power Moonroof +611
Running Boards +448
Third Seat +176
Third Seat Package +657

RAV4   1999

Toyota promises minor upgrades for it's mini-SUV in '99. Leather seats and color-keyed body cladding are now available as part of the "L Special Edition" package. Color-keyed mirrors and door handles can also be had this year and the spare tire is now a full-size steel wheel with a soft cover.

Category L

	Trade-in	Private	Dealer
2 Dr STD AWD Conv	10111	11183	12254
2 Dr STD Conv	8827	9763	10698
4 Dr STD AWD Wgn	10272	11361	12449

Don't forget to refer to the Mileage Adjustment Table at the back of this book!

Model Description	Trade-in TMV	Private TMV	Dealer TMV	Model Description	Trade-in TMV	Private TMV	Dealer TMV
4 Dr STD Wgn	9819	10860	11900	Privacy Glass[Opt on CE] +207			
4 Dr Special Edition AWD Wgn				Rear Spoiler +165			
	11235	12426	13616	Running Boards +344			
				Sliding Driver Side Door[Opt on CE] +229			
				Trailer Hitch +168			

OPTIONS FOR RAV4

AM/FM Compact Disc Player +260
AM/FM Stereo Tape[Opt on STD] +203
AM/FM Stereo/CD/Tape +289
Air Conditioning[Opt on STD] +569
Alarm System +203
Aluminum/Alloy Wheels +283
Anti-Lock Brakes +364
Automatic 4-Speed Transmission +607
Compact Disc Changer +346
Cruise Control[Opt on STD] +145
Leather Seats +434
Limited Slip Differential +225
Luggage Rack +145
Power Door Locks[Opt on STD] +139
Power Mirrors[Opt on STD] +119
Power Moonroof +472
Power Windows[Opt on STD] +159
Privacy Glass[Opt on STD] +179

SIENNA 1999

Entering its second full model year of production at Toyota's Kentucky plant, the Sienna minivan gets a right side power sliding door. An engine immobilizer system has been added to the keyless-entry security system and all Siennas will be equipped with daytime running lights. Selected models have a full size spare tire and Woodland Pearl replaces Classic Green Pearl as an exterior color option.

Category P

Model Description	Trade-in TMV	Private TMV	Dealer TMV
2 Dr CE Pass. Van	15210	16805	18400
4 Dr LE Pass. Van	16165	17860	19555
4 Dr XLE Pass. Van	16699	18451	20202

OPTIONS FOR SIENNA

AM/FM Compact Disc Player[Std on XLE] +185
Alarm System[Std on XLE] +185
Aluminum/Alloy Wheels[Std on XLE] +275
Camper/Towing Package +399
Captain Chairs (4) +514
Child Seat (1) +145
Compact Disc Changer +318
Cruise Control[Opt on CE] +104
Dual Air Conditioning[Opt on CE] +342
Gold Package +95
Keyless Entry System[Std on XLE] +127
Leather Seats +815
Luggage Rack[Std on XLE] +127
Power Door Locks[Opt on CE] +139
Power Mirrors[Opt on CE] +110
Power Moonroof +509
Power Sliding Door +229
Power Windows[Opt on CE] +153

TACOMA 1999

Toyota adds new front seat belt pretensioners and force limiters. Newly optional on Xtra Cab models is an AM/FM four-speaker CD audio system while 4x4s get 15"x7" inch steel wheels. The PreRunner adds a regular cab option to its model mix. Natural White, Imperial Jade Mica and Horizon Blue Metallic replace White, Copper Canyon Mica, Evergreen Pearl, and Cool Steel Metallic as color options.

Category J

Model Description	Trade-in TMV	Private TMV	Dealer TMV
2 Dr STD 4WD Ext Cab SB			
	10699	11759	12819
2 Dr STD 4WD Std Cab SB			
	10308	11329	12350
2 Dr STD Ext Cab SB	9049	9946	10842
2 Dr STD Std Cab SB	6377	7008	7640
2 Dr Limited 4WD Ext Cab SB			
	15858	17429	19000
2 Dr Prerunner Ext Cab SB			
	10494	11533	12573
2 Dr Prerunner Std Cab SB			
	8960	9847	10735
2 Dr Prerunner V6 Ext Cab SB			
	10594	11644	12693
2 Dr SR5 4WD Ext Cab SB			
	10840	11914	12988
2 Dr SR5 Ext Cab SB	9202	10113	11025
2 Dr SR5 V6 4WD Ext Cab SB			
	11623	12775	13926
2 Dr SR5 V6 Ext Cab SB			
	9928	10911	11895
2 Dr V6 4WD Ext Cab SB			
	10977	12065	13152
2 Dr V6 Ext Cab SB	9605	10556	11508

OPTIONS FOR TACOMA

AM/FM Compact Disc Player[Std on Limited] +392
AM/FM Stereo/CD/Tape +335
Air Conditioning[Opt on Limited,STD,V6] +569
Alarm System +145
Aluminum/Alloy Wheels[Std on Limited] +214
Anti-Lock Brakes[Opt on STD] +342
Automatic 4-Speed Transmission[Std on Limited,SR5 2WD] +419
Automatic Locking Hubs (4WD) +139
Bed Liner +172
Chrome Bumpers[Std on Limited] +231

Model Description	Trade-in TMV	Private TMV	Dealer TMV	Model Description	Trade-in TMV	Private TMV	Dealer TMV
Compact Disc Changer +346				Category G			
Cruise Control[Std on Limited] +145				4 Dr XL Sdn	12309	13601	15000
Locking Differential +197				4 Dr XLS Sdn	13297	14692	16204
Power Door Locks[Std on Limited] +133							
Power Steering[Opt on STD 4 cyl] +173				**OPTIONS FOR AVALON**			
Power Windows[Std on Limited] +153				AM/FM Compact Disc Player +100			
Styled Steel Wheels +272				Alarm System[Opt on XL] +168			
TRD Off-Road Package +514				Aluminum/Alloy Wheels[Opt on XL] +229			
Tilt Steering Wheel[Std on Limted] +141				Compact Disc Changer +288			
Tonneau Cover +203				Dual Power Seats[Opt on XL] +446			
Trailer Hitch +161				Heated Front Seats +166			

1998 TOYOTA

4RUNNER   1998

For 1998, the Toyota 4Runner gets rotary HVAC controls, a new four-spoke steering wheel and revised audio control head units.

Category M			
4 Dr STD 4WD Wgn	10205	11285	12456
4 Dr STD Wgn	9908	10957	12094
4 Dr Limited 4WD Wgn	18097	20014	22090
4 Dr Limited Wgn	16104	17809	19657
4 Dr SR5 4WD Wgn	14510	16046	17711
4 Dr SR5 Wgn	12756	14107	15570

OPTIONS FOR 4RUNNER
AM/FM Compact Disc Player[Std on Limited] +210
AM/FM Stereo/CD/Tape +368
Air Conditioning[Std on Limited] +517
Aluminum/Alloy Wheels[Std on Limited] +218
Anti-Lock Brakes[Opt on STD] +310
Automatic 4-Speed Transmission[Std on Limited,SR5 2WD] +472
Black Elite Package +273
Compact Disc Changer +347
Cruise Control[Std on Limited] +131
Elite Package +263
Gold Package +134
Keyless Entry System +118
Leather Seats[Opt on SR5] +657
Locking Differential +171
Power Door Locks[Opt on STD] +128
Power Mirrors[Opt on STD] +106
Power Moonroof +480
Power Windows[Std on Limited] +243
Privacy Glass[Opt on STD] +155
Running Boards[Opt on SR5,STD] +181
Sport Seats +218
Steel Wheels +316
Theft Deterrent System +210
Tilt Steering Wheel[Opt on STD] +123

AVALON   1998

The Avalon gets side-impact airbags, new headlights and taillamps, a new grille, a new trunk lid and pretensioner seatbelts with force limiters.

Leather Bucket Seat Package +528
Power Moonroof +515
Special Factory Paint +110
Traction Control System +158

CAMRY   1998

Side-impact airbags debut on the recently redesigned Camry. Depowered front airbags further enhance this car's ability to protect its occupant in a crash. An engine immobilizer feature is now part of the theft-deterrent package.

Category D			
4 Dr CE Sdn	7154	8066	9054
4 Dr CE V6 Sdn	8447	9524	10691
4 Dr LE Sdn	8752	9867	11076
4 Dr LE V6 Sdn	9133	10297	11558
4 Dr XLE Sdn	10730	12098	13580
4 Dr XLE V6 Sdn	11796	13300	14929

OPTIONS FOR CAMRY
AM/FM Compact Disc Player[Std on XLE,XLE V6] +176
AM/FM Stereo Tape[Opt on CE] +122
AM/FM Stereo/CD/Tape +368
Air Conditioning[Std on XLE,XLE V6] +528
Alarm System[Std on XLE,XLE V6] +208
Aluminum/Alloy Wheels[Std on XLE,XLE V6] +218
Anti-Lock Brakes[Opt on CE 4 cyl] +288
Automatic 4-Speed Transmission[Opt on CE,CE V6] +420
Black Elite Package +439
Compact Disc Changer +288
Fog Lights +210
Gold Package +103
Leather Seats +486
Power Door Locks[Opt on CE,CE V6] +123
Power Drivers Seat +163
Power Mirrors[Opt on CE,CE V6] +118
Power Moonroof +525
Power Windows[Opt on CE,CE V6] +139
Rear Spoiler +184
Side Air Bag Restraints +131
Traction Control System +131

CELICA   1998

Celica ST is eliminated. GT's get more standard features and one new color: Caribbean Green Metallic.

Model Description	Trade-in TMV	Private TMV	Dealer TMV
Category E			
2 Dr GT Conv	13798	15257	16837
2 Dr GT Cpe	10229	11311	12482
2 Dr GT Hbk	10388	11486	12676

OPTIONS FOR CELICA

AM/FM Compact Disc Player +226
AM/FM Stereo/CD/Tape[Opt on Hbk] +288
Alarm System +223
Aluminum/Alloy Wheels[Std on Conv] +229
Anti-Lock Brakes +288
Automatic 4-Speed Transmission +472
Compact Disc Changer +288
Gold Package +103
Keyless Entry System +208
Leather Seats +570
Power Moonroof +399
Rear Spoiler[Opt on Cpe] +229
Sport Suspension +275

COROLLA 1998

The Toyota Corolla is completely redesigned this year with a new engine, new sheetmetal and a new standard for safety in compact cars: optional front passenger side-impact airbags.

Category B			
4 Dr CE Sdn	6130	6959	7856
4 Dr LE Sdn	6579	7468	8431
4 Dr VE Sdn	5931	6732	7600

OPTIONS FOR COROLLA

AM/FM Compact Disc Player +158
AM/FM Stereo Tape[Opt on VE] +106
AM/FM Stereo/CD/Tape +236
Air Conditioning[Opt on VE] +500
Alarm System +210
Aluminum/Alloy Wheels +218
Anti-Lock Brakes +288
Automatic 3-Speed Transmission +263
Automatic 4-Speed Transmission +420
Compact Disc Changer +288
Cruise Control[Opt on CE,LE] +114
Gold Package +94
Keyless Entry System[Opt on CE,LE] +97
Power Door Locks[Opt on CE] +118
Power Moonroof +386
Power Windows[Opt on CE] +149
Rear Spoiler +155
Side Air Bag Restraints +131

LAND CRUISER 1998

For 1998, Land Cruiser gets a more powerful V8 engine, standard ABS, an increase in structural rigidity, an improved suspension system, increased passenger and cargo room and a slew of new colors.

Category O

Model Description	Trade-in TMV	Private TMV	Dealer TMV
4 Dr STD 4WD Wgn	29267	31779	34500

OPTIONS FOR LAND CRUISER

Gold Package +181
Leather Seats +956
Locking Differential +184
Luggage Rack +158
Power Moonroof +622
Running Boards +407
Third Seat +160
Third Seat Package +596

RAV4 1998

Toyota's jellybean enters its third year of production with minor changes to the grille, headlights, taillamps and interior. Four-door RAV4s get new seat fabric. A late-year introduction of the new RAV4 convertible makes this sport-ute more appealing for those who live in the sunbelt.

Category L			
2 Dr STD AWD Conv	9587	10702	11911
2 Dr STD AWD Utility	9237	10312	11476
2 Dr STD Conv	9119	10180	11330
2 Dr STD Utility	7716	8614	9587
4 Dr STD AWD Wgn	9307	10391	11564
4 Dr STD Wgn	8989	10035	11168
4 Dr L Special Edition Wgn			
	10463	11681	13000

OPTIONS FOR RAV4

AM/FM Compact Disc Player +236
AM/FM Stereo Tape +184
AM/FM Stereo/CD/Tape +263
Air Conditioning +517
Alarm System +210
Aluminum/Alloy Wheels +257
Anti-Lock Brakes +310
Automatic 4-Speed Transmission +578
Compact Disc Changer +316
Cruise Control +131
Keyless Entry System +97
Leather Seats +394
Limited Slip Differential +197
Luggage Rack +131
Luxury Package +1206
Power Door Locks +126
Power Mirrors +107
Power Moonroof +480
Power Windows +145
Privacy Glass +155
Rear Heater +103
Side Steps +123
Spoke Wheels +359

SIENNA 1998

A new minivan from Toyota brings some innovation to

TOYOTA 98

Model Description	Trade-in TMV	Private TMV	Dealer TMV		Model Description	Trade-in TMV	Private TMV	Dealer TMV

the family truckster market. A powerful 194-horsepower V6 engine rests under the hood of all models. Safety equipment includes standard anti-lock brakes, low tire pressure warning systems and five mph front and rear bumpers. Sienna boasts outstanding crash test scores.

Category P

Model Description	Trade-in TMV	Private TMV	Dealer TMV
2 Dr CE Pass. Van	13707	15191	16800
2 Dr LE Pass. Van	13874	15377	17005
4 Dr XLE Pass. Van	14470	16038	17736

OPTIONS FOR SIENNA

AM/FM Compact Disc Player[Std on XLE] +168
Alarm System +208
Aluminum/Alloy Wheels[Opt on LE] +320
Captain Chairs (4)[Opt on LE] +131
Child Seat (1) +131
Compact Disc Changer +288
Dual Air Conditioning[Opt on CE] +236
Keyless Entry System[Std on XLE] +115
Leather Seats +741
Luggage Rack[Std on XLE] +110
Power Door Locks[Opt on CE] +126
Power Moonroof +515
Power Windows[Opt on CE] +139
Privacy Glass[Opt on CE] +189
Rear Spoiler +149
Running Boards +313
Sliding Driver Side Door +197
Trailer Hitch +152

SUPRA   1998

Variable Valve Timing with Intelligence appears on the new Supra. No other changes to Toyota's bargain basement exotic.

Category F

Model Description	Trade-in TMV	Private TMV	Dealer TMV
2 Dr STD Hbk	16675	18385	20237
2 Dr STD Turbo Hbk	21417	23613	25992

OPTIONS FOR SUPRA

AM/FM Stereo Tape +126
AM/FM Stereo/CD/Tape +533
Compact Disc Changer +341
Gold Package +157
Leather Seats[Std on Turbo] +525
Power Drivers Seat[Std on Turbo] +131
Sport Roof[Opt on STD] +1314

T100   1998

No changes to Toyota's full-size truck.

Category K

Model Description	Trade-in TMV	Private TMV	Dealer TMV
2 Dr STD Std Cab LB	6266	6975	7742
2 Dr DX 4WD Ext Cab SB	11476	12773	14179
2 Dr DX Ext Cab SB	9948	11073	12291
2 Dr SR5 4WD Ext Cab SB	11984	13339	14807
2 Dr SR5 Ext Cab SB	10340	11509	12775

OPTIONS FOR T100

AM/FM Compact Disc Player +137
AM/FM Stereo Tape[Std on SR5] +200
Air Conditioning +316
Alarm System +155
Aluminum/Alloy Wheels +281
Anti-Lock Brakes +310
Automatic 4-Speed Transmission +472
Bed Liner +157
Bucket Seats +173
Cruise Control +131
Power Door Locks +115
Power Mirrors +106
Power Windows +128
Privacy Glass[Opt on DX] +106
Rear Step Bumper +106
Running Boards +243
Tilt Steering Wheel[Std on SR5] +123
Tonneau Cover +197
Trailer Hitch +103

TACOMA   1998

The 1998 four-wheel drive Tacomas receive fresh front-end styling that makes them more closely resemble their two-wheel drive brothers. A new option package appears for 1998 as well; the TRD (no, not short for "turd") Off-Road Package for extended cab models is designed to make the Tacoma appeal to would-be Baja 1000 racers. On the safety front, Toyota introduces a passenger's side airbag that can be deactivated with a cut-off switch, making the Tacoma somewhat safer for children and short adults. Toyota also offers a new Tacoma PreRunner for 1998, billing it as a two-wheel drive truck with four-wheel drive performance.

Category J

Model Description	Trade-in TMV	Private TMV	Dealer TMV
2 Dr STD 4WD Ext Cab SB	9285	10290	11380
2 Dr STD 4WD Std Cab SB	8936	9904	10953
2 Dr STD Ext Cab SB	6308	6992	7732
2 Dr STD Std Cab SB	5529	6128	6777
2 Dr Limited 4WD Ext Cab SB	12227	13551	14986
2 Dr Prerunner Ext Cab SB	8878	9839	10881
2 Dr Prerunner V6 Ext Cab SB	9114	10101	11171
2 Dr SR5 4WD Ext Cab SB	9345	10357	11454
2 Dr SR5 Ext Cab SB	7554	8373	9259
2 Dr SR5 V6 4WD Ext Cab SB	10358	11480	12695
2 Dr SR5 V6 Ext Cab SB	8722	9667	10690

Model Description	Trade-in TMV	Private TMV	Dealer TMV	Model Description	Trade-in TMV	Private TMV	Dealer TMV
2 Dr V6 4WD Ext Cab SB				4 Dr Limited 4WD Wgn	16128	17906	20080
	9578	10616	11740	4 Dr Limited Wgn	14258	15830	17752
2 Dr V6 Ext Cab SB	7943	8804	9736	4 Dr SR5 4WD Wgn	12544	13927	15618
				4 Dr SR5 Wgn	11687	12976	14551

OPTIONS FOR TACOMA
AM/FM Compact Disc Player +357
AM/FM Stereo Tape[Opt on STD, V6] +194
AM/FM Stereo/CD/Tape +305
Air Conditioning[Opt on Limited, STD, V6] +517
Alarm System +131
Aluminum/Alloy Wheels[Std on Limited] +194
Anti-Lock Brakes +310
Automatic 4-Speed Transmission[Std on Prerunner, Prerunner V6] +394
Automatic Locking Hubs (4WD)[Std on Limited] +121
Bed Liner +157
Chrome Bumpers[Opt on SR5, SR5 V6, STD, V6] +123
Compact Disc Changer +288
Cruise Control[Std on Limited] +131
Flip-Up Sunroof +205
Locking Differential +171
Power Door Locks[Std on Limited] +121
Power Steering[Opt on STD 4 cyl] +158
Power Windows[Std on Limited] +139
Running Boards +149
TRD Off-Road Package +467
Tilt Steering Wheel[Std on Limited] +123
Tonneau Cover +184

TERCEL — 1998

For 1998, the Tercel is available exclusively as a two-door CE model with additional standard features like color-keyed grille and bumpers, rear seat headrests, AM/FM stereo with cassette, air conditioning, digital clock and power steering.

Category A

	Trade-in	Private	Dealer
2 Dr CE Sdn	5862	6677	7559

OPTIONS FOR TERCEL
AM/FM Compact Disc Player +239
Alarm System +155
Anti-Lock Brakes +288
Automatic 3-Speed Transmission +263
Compact Disc Changer +316
Power Door Locks +126
Power Windows +137

1997 TOYOTA

4RUNNER — 1997

Toyota's hot-selling redesign receives minor changes. The most noticeable is the addition of the 2WD Limited to the model lineup. SR5 models receive new interior fabrics.

Category M

	Trade-in	Private	Dealer
4 Dr STD 4WD Wgn	9505	10553	11834
4 Dr STD Wgn	9139	10147	11379

OPTIONS FOR 4RUNNER
AM/FM Compact Disc Player +185
AM/FM Stereo/CD/Tape +323
Air Conditioning[Opt on SR5, STD] +453
Alarm System[Std on Limited] +148
Aluminum/Alloy Wheels[Opt on SR5, STD] +192
Anti-Lock Brakes[Opt on STD] +272
Automatic 4-Speed Transmission[Opt on STD, SR5 4WD] +415
Compact Disc Changer +300
Cruise Control[Opt on SR5, STD] +134
Elite Package +230
Gold Package +111
Keyless Entry System +104
Leather Seats[Opt on SR5, STD] +576
Locking Differential +150
Power Door Locks[Opt on STD] +112
Power Moonroof +422
Power Windows[Opt on SR5, STD] +203
Privacy Glass[Opt on STD] +136
Running Boards[Opt on SR5, STD] +153
Sport Seats +315
Steel Wheels +277
Theft Deterrent System +184
Tilt Steering Wheel[Opt on STD] +109

AVALON — 1997

More power, more torque, and added standard features make the Avalon one of the most appealing full-sized sedans.

Category G

	Trade-in	Private	Dealer
4 Dr XL Sdn	10455	11600	13000
4 Dr XLS Sdn	10668	11837	13265

OPTIONS FOR AVALON
AM/FM Stereo/CD/Tape +346
Alarm System[Opt on XL] +101
Aluminum/Alloy Wheels[Opt on XL] +200
Compact Disc Changer +254
Dual Power Seats[Opt on XL] +392
Leather Seats +463
Power Bench Seat[Opt on XL] +392
Power Moonroof +452
Special Factory Paint +97
Traction Control System +138

CAMRY — 1997

Toyota plays the market conservatively with the all-new Camry, giving consumers exactly what they want; a roomy, attractive, feature-laden car with available V6 performance and the promise of excellent reliability as well as resale value. The Camry is the new standard

Model Description	Trade-in TMV	Private TMV	Dealer TMV	Model Description	Trade-in TMV	Private TMV	Dealer TMV

for midsized sedans.

Category D

4 Dr CE Sdn	6362	7220	8269
4 Dr CE V6 Sdn	7472	8480	9711
4 Dr LE Sdn	7768	8816	10096
4 Dr LE V6 Sdn	8804	9991	11442
4 Dr XLE Sdn	8508	9655	11057
4 Dr XLE V6 Sdn	9396	10663	12211

OPTIONS FOR CAMRY

6 Disc CD Autochanger +277
AM/FM Compact Disc Player +155
AM/FM Stereo/CD/Tape +323
Air Conditioning[Std on CE,CE V6] +463
Alarm System[Std on XLE,XLE V6] +166
Aluminum/Alloy Wheels[Std on XLE,XLE V6] +192
Anti-Lock Brakes[Opt on CE] +254
Automatic 4-Speed Transmission[Opt on CE] +369
Compact Disc Changer +254
Elite Package +230
Leather Seats +426
Power Door Locks[Opt on CE,CE V6] +109
Power Drivers Seat +116
Power Mirrors[Opt on CE,CE V6] +104
Power Moonroof +462
Power Windows[Opt on CE,CE V6] +122
Rear Spoiler +161
Theft Deterrent System +148
Traction Control System +138

CELICA   1997

GT Coupe is gone, and Fiesta Blue Metallic can be specified for cars equipped with black sport cloth interior.

Category E

2 Dr GT Conv	11799	13213	14941
2 Dr GT Hbk	8754	9803	11085
2 Dr GT Limited Edit. Conv			
	11850	13270	15005
2 Dr ST Cpe	7917	8866	10025
2 Dr ST Hbk	8069	9036	10218
2 Dr ST Limited Edit. Hbk			
	8603	9633	10893

OPTIONS FOR CELICA

AM/FM Compact Disc Player +198
AM/FM Stereo/CD/Tape[Opt on GT] +346
Air Conditioning[Opt on GT,ST] +463
Alarm System +196
Aluminum/Alloy Wheels[Opt on GT,ST] +200
Anti-Lock Brakes +254
Automatic 4-Speed Transmission +369
Compact Disc Changer +254
Keyless Entry System +182
Leather Seats +500
Power Door Locks[Opt on ST] +116

Power Moonroof +350
Power Windows[Opt on ST] +131
Rear Spoiler[Opt on GT,ST] +192
Sport Seats +447
Sport Suspension +230

COROLLA   1997

The Classic Edition (CE) debuts and the slow-selling DX Wagon gets the ax.

Category B

4 Dr STD Sdn	5218	5942	6827
4 Dr CE Sdn	5589	6364	7312
4 Dr DX Sdn	5582	6356	7303

OPTIONS FOR COROLLA

AM/FM Compact Disc Player +138
AM/FM Stereo/CD/Tape +207
Air Conditioning[Std on CE] +438
Alarm System +136
Aluminum/Alloy Wheels +192
Anti-Lock Brakes +254
Automatic 3-Speed Transmission +230
Automatic 4-Speed Transmission +369
Compact Disc Changer +254
Cruise Control +99
Power Door Locks[Opt on DX] +104
Power Steering[Opt on STD] +124
Power Sunroof +274
Power Windows[Opt on DX] +131
Rear Spoiler +136

LAND CRUISER   1997

The Black Package is discontinued, but black paint becomes an available color choice. A 40th-Anniversary Package lets buyers slather their Cruiser in leather and choose one of two unique paint schemes.

Category O

4 Dr 40th Anniv. Ltd. 4WD Wgn			
	21917	24045	26645
4 Dr STD 4WD Wgn	21387	23463	26000

OPTIONS FOR LAND CRUISER

AM/FM Compact Disc Player +207
AM/FM Stereo/CD/Tape +435
Aluminum/Alloy Wheels +242
Compact Disc Changer +369
Dual Power Seats[Opt on STD] +300
Gold Package +158
Keyless Entry System +182
Leather Seats[Opt on STD] +691
Locking Differential +161
Luggage Rack +138
Power Moonroof +437
Privacy Glass[Opt on STD] +116
Running Boards +321
Theft Deterrent System +178
Third Seat Package +487

Don't forget to refer to the Mileage Adjustment Table at the back of this book!

TOYOTA 97

Model Description	Trade-in TMV	Private TMV	Dealer TMV	Model Description	Trade-in TMV	Private TMV	Dealer TMV

PASEO 1997

For some reason, Toyota product planners took a look at the cheap convertible market and thought, "Hmmm...a convertible Tercel with fancy styling will just kill the Sunfire SE Convertible's sales and make us rich." Coupes get dual-visor vanity mirrors, fresh door trim and rotary-heater controls.

Category E

	Trade-in	Private	Dealer
2 Dr STD Conv	7080	7928	8965
2 Dr STD Cpe	4719	5285	5976

OPTIONS FOR PASEO
AM/FM Compact Disc Player +211
AM/FM Stereo Tape +104
AM/FM Stereo/CD/Tape +116
Air Conditioning +426
Alarm System +136
Aluminum/Alloy Wheels +192
Anti-Lock Brakes +254
Automatic 4-Speed Transmission +369
Compact Disc Changer +322
Cruise Control +134
Flip-Up Sunroof +188
Power Door Locks +122
Power Windows +128
Rear Spoiler +192

PREVIA 1997

Category P

	Trade-in	Private	Dealer
2 Dr DX Sprchgd AWD Pass. Van	10587	11813	13312
2 Dr DX Sprchgd Pass. Van	9216	10284	11588
2 Dr LE Sprchgd AWD Pass. Van	12339	13768	15514
2 Dr LE Sprchgd Pass. Van	10968	12238	13790

OPTIONS FOR PREVIA
AM/FM Compact Disc Player +211
AM/FM Stereo/CD/Tape +346
Alarm System +101
Aluminum/Alloy Wheels +200
Anti-Lock Brakes +272
Captain Chairs (4) +401
Compact Disc Changer +322
Cruise Control[Opt on DX] +104
Dual Air Conditioning[Opt on DX] +516
Gold Package +138
Keyless Entry System +182
Leather Seats +553
Luggage Rack +123
Power Door Locks[Opt on DX] +116
Power Moonroof +507
Power Windows[Opt on DX] +131
Privacy Glass +196
Running Boards +155

RAV4 1997

New fabric debuts on the two-door RAV, and a sunroof is finally available on the four-door. Improvements have also been made by using sound deadening material in the dash area, reducing engine noise in the passenger compartment.

Category L

	Trade-in	Private	Dealer
2 Dr STD AWD Utility	7767	8705	9852
2 Dr STD Utility	6473	7254	8210
4 Dr STD AWD Wgn	7979	8942	10120
4 Dr STD Wgn	7562	8476	9592

OPTIONS FOR RAV4
AM/FM Compact Disc Player +192
AM/FM Stereo Tape +161
AM/FM Stereo/CD/Tape +230
Air Conditioning +453
Alarm System +178
Aluminum/Alloy Wheels +225
Anti-Lock Brakes +272
Automatic 4-Speed Transmission +484
Compact Disc Changer +250
Cruise Control +134
Leather Seats +346
Limited Slip Differential +173
Luggage Rack +116
Power Door Locks +111
Power Mirrors +94
Power Moonroof +422
Power Windows +128
Spoke Wheels +315
T-Tops (Solid/Colored) +207

SUPRA 1997

Turbo models get the six-speed manual transmission back, but the bigger news details massive price cuts. Turbos with automatics are $12,000 dollars less expensive than last year! All Supras commemorate the nameplate's 15th anniversary with a rear spoiler, premium sound and special badging. Despite price cuts, equipment levels are enhanced across the board.

Category F

	Trade-in	Private	Dealer
2 Dr STD Hbk	14909	16608	18684
2 Dr STD Turbo Hbk	20667	23022	25900

OPTIONS FOR SUPRA
AM/FM Compact Disc Player +182
AM/FM Stereo/CD/Tape[Std on Turbo] +468
Automatic 4-Speed Transmission[Std on Turbo] +415
Compact Disc Changer +300
Gold Package +138
Leather Seats[Std on Turbo] +462
Power Drivers Seat[Std on Turbo] +116
Sport Roof +1152

T100 1997

TOYOTA 97-96

Model Description	Trade-in TMV	Private TMV	Dealer TMV	Model Description	Trade-in TMV	Private TMV	Dealer TMV

Two new colors debut and the optional wheel and tire packages are larger this year. Standard models get radio pre-wiring, midlevel models get fabric door trim panels, and SR5 models get chrome wheel arches.

Category K

Model Description	Trade-in TMV	Private TMV	Dealer TMV
2 Dr STD Std Cab LB	5321	5957	6734
2 Dr DX 4WD Ext Cab SB	9653	10807	12217
2 Dr DX Ext Cab SB	7981	8935	10101
2 Dr SR5 4WD Ext Cab SB	10337	11573	13083
2 Dr SR5 Ext Cab SB	8285	9276	10486

OPTIONS FOR T100

AM/FM Compact Disc Player +211
AM/FM Stereo Tape +175
AM/FM Stereo/CD/Tape +230
Air Conditioning +277
Alarm System +136
Aluminum/Alloy Wheels +247
Anti-Lock Brakes +272
Automatic 4-Speed Transmission +415
Bed Liner +138
Cruise Control +116
Flip-Up Sunroof +134
Power Door Locks +101
Power Windows +112
Premium Sound System +193
Running Boards +214
Sport Seats +153
Tilt Steering Wheel +109
Tonneau Cover +173

TACOMA   1997

The 1997 Tacoma receives several new value packages that make optioning the truck easier. A locking rear-wheel differential is now available on all 4WD models. Bucket seats can be had on all Xtracab Tacomas this year; not just the SR5. Two-wheel drive models have new headlamps and a new grille that make the vehicle look more like the T100.

Category J

Model Description	Trade-in TMV	Private TMV	Dealer TMV
2 Dr STD 4WD Ext Cab SB	7415	8286	9351
2 Dr STD 4WD Std Cab SB	7084	7916	8933
2 Dr STD Ext Cab SB	6280	7017	7919
2 Dr STD Std Cab SB	4388	4904	5534
2 Dr SR5 4WD Ext Cab SB	9382	10484	11831
2 Dr V6 4WD Ext Cab SB	8323	9301	10496
2 Dr V6 4WD Std Cab SB	7112	7948	8969
2 Dr V6 Ext Cab SB	6859	7665	8650

OPTIONS FOR TACOMA

AM/FM Compact Disc Player +211
AM/FM Stereo/CD/Tape +267
Air Conditioning +453
Alarm System +111
Aluminum/Alloy Wheels[Std on SR5] +161
Anti-Lock Brakes +272
Automatic 4-Speed Transmission +369
Automatic Locking Hubs (4WD)[Std on SR5] +106
Bed Liner +138
Chrome Step Bumper[Std on SR5] +109
Compact Disc Changer +322
Electric Sunroof +180
Locking Differential +150
Power Windows +120
Running Boards +124
Tonneau Cover +138

TERCEL   1997

Standard and DX trim levels are shelved in favor of CE trim for all Tercels. All models have upgraded cloth trim, new rotary heater controls, a trip odometer, and a storage console. New wheelcovers adorn standard 14-inch wheels.

Category A

Model Description	Trade-in TMV	Private TMV	Dealer TMV
2 Dr CE Sdn	4514	5209	6058
4 Dr CE Sdn	4728	5456	6346
2 Dr Limited Edition Sdn	4585	5291	6154

OPTIONS FOR TERCEL

AM/FM Compact Disc Player +211
AM/FM Stereo Tape +161
Air Conditioning +426
Alarm System +136
Anti-Lock Brakes +254
Automatic 3-Speed Transmission +230
Automatic 4-Speed Transmission +323
Compact Disc Changer +277
Power Door Locks +111
Power Steering +124
Power Windows +120
Rear Spoiler +230

1996 TOYOTA

4RUNNER   1996

A cool new 4Runner with a potent V6, big bruiser styling, and lots more interior room debuts. This thing annihilates most compact off-road vehicles.

Category M

Model Description	Trade-in TMV	Private TMV	Dealer TMV
4 Dr STD 4WD Wgn	9578	10721	12301
4 Dr STD Wgn	9074	10158	11654
4 Dr Limited 4WD Wgn	13574	15195	17434
4 Dr SR5 4WD Wgn	11765	13170	15110
4 Dr SR5 Wgn	10030	11228	12882

Don't forget to refer to the Mileage Adjustment Table at the back of this book!

Model Description	Trade-in TMV	Private TMV	Dealer TMV

OPTIONS FOR 4RUNNER

AM/FM Compact Disc Player +169
AM/FM Stereo/CD/Tape +295
Air Conditioning[Opt on SR5,STD] +415
Aluminum/Alloy Wheels[Opt on SR5,STD] +176
Anti-Lock Brakes[Opt on STD] +249
Automatic 4-Speed Transmission[Opt on STD,SR5 4WD] +380
Compact Disc Changer +275
Cruise Control[Opt on SR5,STD] +106
Gold Package +101
Keyless Entry System +95
Leather Seats[Opt on SR5] +528
Locking Differential +137
Power Door Locks[Opt on STD] +103
Power Moonroof +387
Power Windows[Opt on 2WD] +162
Privacy Glass[Opt on STD] +125
Running Boards +139
Sport Seats +302
Steel Wheels +253
Theft Deterrent System +168

AVALON   1996

No changes as cloud car floats into its second year.

Category G

Model Description	Trade-in TMV	Private TMV	Dealer TMV
4 Dr XL Sdn	8670	9649	11000
4 Dr XLS Sdn	9093	10119	11536

OPTIONS FOR AVALON

AM/FM Stereo/CD/Tape +317
Aluminum/Alloy Wheels[Opt on XL] +184
Anti-Lock Brakes[Opt on XL] +414
Compact Disc Changer +232
Dual Power Seats[Opt on XL] +359
Leather Seats +424
Power Bench Seat +359
Power Moonroof +414

CAMRY   1996

The 1996 Camry remains virtually unchanged from last year's model. Minor engine adjustments mean that the four-cylinder is fully compliant with all On-Board Diagnostic standards, and is now certified as a Transitional Low Emission Vehicle powerplant. Additionally, the interior of the DX line gets a new seat fabric, the LE Sedan is available with a leather package, and the Wagon can now be ordered with a power-operated driver seat.

Category D

Model Description	Trade-in TMV	Private TMV	Dealer TMV
4 Dr Collector Sdn	8752	10083	11921
2 Dr DX Cpe	5041	5808	6867
4 Dr DX Sdn	5181	5969	7057
2 Dr LE Cpe	6161	7098	8392
4 Dr LE Sdn	6372	7341	8679
4 Dr LE Wgn	6651	7663	9060
2 Dr LE V6 Cpe	6861	7905	9346
4 Dr LE V6 Sdn	7002	8066	9537
4 Dr LE V6 Wgn	7421	8550	10109
2 Dr SE Cpe	7352	8470	10014
4 Dr SE Sdn	7491	8631	10204
4 Dr XLE Sdn	6931	7985	9441
4 Dr XLE V6 Sdn	7912	9115	10777

OPTIONS FOR CAMRY

AM/FM Compact Disc Player +193
AM/FM Stereo/CD/Tape[Std on Collector] +295
Air Conditioning[Opt on DX] +424
Aluminum/Alloy Wheels +176
Anti-Lock Brakes[Std on XLE,XLE V6] +401
Automatic 4-Speed Transmission[Opt on DX] +337
Compact Disc Changer +232
Gold Package +106
Leather Seats[Std on Collector] +390
Luggage Rack +108
Power Drivers Seat[Opt on LE,LE V6] +106
Power Moonroof +422
Power Passenger Seat +116
Power Windows[Opt on DX] +111
Rear Spoiler +148
Theft Deterrent System +135
Third Seat +145

CELICA   1996

Minor front end freshening doesn't help much. A new spoiler, new wheelcovers, two new colors, and revised fabrics debut this year.

Category E

Model Description	Trade-in TMV	Private TMV	Dealer TMV
2 Dr GT Conv	9532	10739	12407
2 Dr GT Cpe	6819	7683	8876
2 Dr GT Hbk	6892	7765	8971
2 Dr GT 25th Anniv. Conv	10602	11945	13800
2 Dr ST Cpe	6201	6986	8071
2 Dr ST Hbk	6264	7057	8153
2 Dr ST 25th Anniv. Hbk	7112	8013	9257

OPTIONS FOR CELICA

AM/FM Compact Disc Player[Opt on GT,ST] +181
AM/FM Stereo/CD/Tape[Opt on GT] +317
Air Conditioning[Opt on GT,ST] +424
Alarm System[Opt on GT,ST] +179
Aluminum/Alloy Wheels +184
Anti-Lock Brakes +359
Automatic 4-Speed Transmission +337
Compact Disc Changer +232
Keyless Entry System +166
Leather Seats +458
Power Door Locks[Opt on ST] +106
Power Moonroof[Opt on GT,ST] +321
Power Windows[Opt on ST] +116
Rear Spoiler[Opt on GT,ST] +176

TOYOTA 96

Model Description	Trade-in TMV	Private TMV	Dealer TMV	Model Description	Trade-in TMV	Private TMV	Dealer TMV

Sport Seats +409
Sport Suspension +211

COROLLA 1996

The Toyota Corolla heads into 1996 with a redesigned front and rear fascia, three new colors, new wheel covers, an optional integrated child seat, and a revised interior. Additionally, the five-speed manual transmission has been revised for a better feel and more positive gear engagement.

Category B

	Trade-in	Private	Dealer
4 Dr STD Sdn	4366	5077	6059
4 Dr DX Sdn	4504	5238	6251
4 Dr DX Wgn	4781	5560	6636

OPTIONS FOR COROLLA
AM/FM Compact Disc Player +127
Air Conditioning +401
Alarm System +125
Aluminum/Alloy Wheels +176
Anti-Lock Brakes +348
Automatic 3-Speed Transmission +211
Automatic 4-Speed Transmission +337
Compact Disc Changer +232
Power Door Locks +95
Power Steering[Std on DX] +114
Power Sunroof +251
Power Windows +116
Rear Spoiler +125

LAND CRUISER 1996

The Black Paint Package debuts, for those who enjoy spending long hours maintaining the finish on their truck.

Category O

	Trade-in	Private	Dealer
4 Dr STD 4WD Wgn	15452	17200	19615

OPTIONS FOR LAND CRUISER
AM/FM Compact Disc Player +189
AM/FM Stereo/CD/Tape +398
Aluminum/Alloy Wheels +221
Compact Disc Changer +337
Dual Power Seats +275
Gold Package +145
Keyless Entry System +166
Leather Seats +634
Leather Trim Package +469
Luggage Rack +127
Power Moonroof +500
Privacy Glass +106
Running Boards +294
Third Seat Package +446

PASEO 1996

All new Paseo looks like last year's car, but is much improved. It now meets 1997 passenger car safety standards, and has a split-fold rear seat.

Category E

	Trade-in	Private	Dealer
2 Dr STD Cpe	4106	4626	5344

OPTIONS FOR PASEO
AM/FM Compact Disc Player +193
Air Conditioning +390
Alarm System +125
Aluminum/Alloy Wheels +176
Anti-Lock Brakes +359
Automatic 4-Speed Transmission +337
Compact Disc Changer +295
Cruise Control +122
Electric Sunroof +275
Keyless Entry System +166
Power Door Locks +106
Power Windows +116
Rear Spoiler +176

PREVIA 1996

Supercharged engines for everyone!

Category P

	Trade-in	Private	Dealer
2 Dr DX Sprchgd AWD Pass. Van	8331	9408	10895
2 Dr DX Sprchgd Pass. Van	7245	8181	9474
2 Dr LE Sprchgd AWD Pass. Van	9708	10962	12695
2 Dr LE Sprchgd Pass. Van	8694	9817	11369

OPTIONS FOR PREVIA
AM/FM Compact Disc Player +193
AM/FM Stereo/CD/Tape +317
Aluminum/Alloy Wheels +184
Anti-Lock Brakes +249
Captain Chairs (4) +367
Compact Disc Changer +295
Dual Air Conditioning[Opt on DX] +473
Dual Sunroofs +623
Gold Package +126
Keyless Entry System +166
Leather Seats +801
Luggage Rack +113
Power Door Locks[Opt on DX] +106
Power Moonroof +464
Power Windows[Opt on DX] +121
Privacy Glass +179
Running Boards +142

RAV4 1996

A cool new mini-ute based on passenger car mechanicals debuts this year. Available as a two-door or four-door, the RAV4 has a gutsy powerplant and cute-as-can-be styling. We like the RAV, but think that the Jeep Cherokee offers more bang-for-the-buck.

Category L

	Trade-in	Private	Dealer
2 Dr STD AWD Utility	7011	7899	9125
2 Dr STD Utility	5863	6605	7631

Don't forget to refer to the Mileage Adjustment Table at the back of this book!

Model Description	Trade-in TMV	Private TMV	Dealer TMV
4 Dr STD AWD Wgn	7182	8092	9348
4 Dr STD Wgn	6851	7719	8917

OPTIONS FOR RAV4

AM/FM Compact Disc Player +176
AM/FM Stereo Tape +148
Air Conditioning +415
Alarm System +162
Aluminum/Alloy Wheels +207
Anti-Lock Brakes +249
Automatic 4-Speed Transmission +443
Compact Disc Changer +230
Cruise Control +122
Flip-Up Sunroof +253
Limited Slip Differential +159
Luggage Rack +106
Power Door Locks +101
Power Windows +116
Spoke Wheels +289
T-Tops (Solid/Colored) +189

SUPRA   1996

Manual transmission Turbo models are history, thanks to stringent emission regulations. Don't worry, they're back for 1997.

Category F

Model Description	Trade-in TMV	Private TMV	Dealer TMV
2 Dr STD Hbk	13336	14971	17229
2 Dr STD Turbo Hbk	17804	19986	23000

OPTIONS FOR SUPRA

AM/FM Compact Disc Player +166
AM/FM Stereo/CD/Tape +429
Automatic 4-Speed Transmission[Std on Turbo] +380
Compact Disc Changer +275
Dual Power Seats +177
Gold Package +126
Leather Seats +422
Limited Slip Differential[Std on Turbo] +213
Rear Spoiler +194
Sport Roof +1055

T100   1996

Essentially a carryover, but DX models are scrapped. Strangely, regular cabs can't be equipped with cruise control anymore. A new shade of red is offered, and tan interiors are offered in a wider variety of trucks.

Category K

Model Description	Trade-in TMV	Private TMV	Dealer TMV
2 Dr STD Std Cab LB	4672	5248	6042
2 Dr DX 4WD Ext Cab SB	8751	9829	11317
2 Dr DX Ext Cab SB	7194	8080	9303
2 Dr SR5 4WD Ext Cab SB	9494	10663	12277
2 Dr SR5 Ext Cab SB	7417	8330	9591

OPTIONS FOR T100

AM/FM Compact Disc Player +193
AM/FM Stereo/CD/Tape +211

Model Description	Trade-in TMV	Private TMV	Dealer TMV
Air Conditioning +380			
Alarm System +125			
Aluminum/Alloy Wheels +255			
Anti-Lock Brakes +414			
Automatic 4-Speed Transmission +380			
Bed Liner +126			
Chrome Wheels +260			
Cruise Control +106			
Electric Sunroof +210			
Power Windows +103			
Running Boards +196			

TACOMA   1996

Regular Cab 4WD models can be equipped with a new Off-Road Package.

Category J

Model Description	Trade-in TMV	Private TMV	Dealer TMV
2 Dr STD 4WD Ext Cab SB	5696	6418	7416
2 Dr STD 4WD Std Cab SB	5331	6007	6941
2 Dr STD Ext Cab SB	4601	5184	5990
2 Dr STD Std Cab SB	3432	3868	4469
2 Dr SR5 4WD Ext Cab SB	8106	9134	10554
2 Dr V6 4WD Ext Cab SB	6207	6995	8082
2 Dr V6 4WD Std Cab SB	5550	6254	7226
2 Dr V6 Ext Cab SB	5111	5760	6655

OPTIONS FOR TACOMA

AM/FM Compact Disc Player +193
AM/FM Stereo Tape[Std on SR5] +238
Air Conditioning +415
Alarm System +101
Aluminum/Alloy Wheels +148
Anti-Lock Brakes +414
Automatic 4-Speed Transmission +380
Automatic Locking Hubs (4WD) +98
Bed Liner +126
Compact Disc Changer +295
Cruise Control +106
Flip-Up Sunroof +165
Off-Road Package +811
Power Steering[Std on SR5,V6,4WD] +127
Power Windows +110
Running Boards +114
Tonneau Cover +127
Wheel Package +159

TERCEL   1996

Base cars can be equipped with fabric seats, and a ... ha,ha,ha ... "Sports" package is available.

Category A

Model Description	Trade-in TMV	Private TMV	Dealer TMV
2 Dr STD Sdn	3187	3707	4424
2 Dr DX Sdn	3880	4513	5386

Don't forget to refer to the Mileage Adjustment Table at the back of this book!

Model Description	Trade-in TMV	Private TMV	Dealer TMV
4 Dr DX Sdn	4019	4674	5578

OPTIONS FOR TERCEL
AM/FM Compact Disc Player +193
AM/FM Stereo Tape +148
Air Conditioning +390
Alarm System +125
Anti-Lock Brakes +359
Automatic 3-Speed Transmission +295
Automatic 4-Speed Transmission +299
Compact Disc Changer +295
Electric Sunroof +210
Power Door Locks +101
Power Steering +114
Power Windows +110
Rear Spoiler +210

1995 TOYOTA

4RUNNER — 1995

V6 models get new tape stripes. Whoo-hoo!
Category M

Model Description	Trade-in TMV	Private TMV	Dealer TMV
4 Dr Limited 4WD Wgn	8820	9904	11709
4 Dr SR5 4WD Wgn	7800	8758	10354
4 Dr SR5 Wgn	8091	9085	10741
4 Dr SR5 V6 4WD Wgn	8639	9700	11468

OPTIONS FOR 4RUNNER
AM/FM Compact Disc Player +155
AM/FM Stereo/CD/Tape +272
Air Conditioning[Std on Limited] +382
Aluminum/Alloy Wheels[Opt on SR5] +161
Anti-Lock Brakes +229
Automatic 4-Speed Transmission[Std on 2WD] +349
Compact Disc Changer +252
Gold Package +93
Leather Seats[Opt on SR5 V6] +485
Power Moonroof +317
Power Windows[Opt on SR5 V6,2WD] +149
Running Boards +128
Sport Seats +161
Tilt Steering Wheel[Opt on SR5 4WD] +91
Tinted Glass +115

AVALON — 1995

Marginally larger than the Camry, the Avalon is a true six-passenger sedan set to conquer Buick LeSabre and Ford Crown Victoria. Dual airbags, power windows, power mirrors, and power locks are standard. ABS is optional. Mechanicals are mostly Camry-based.
Category G

Model Description	Trade-in TMV	Private TMV	Dealer TMV
4 Dr XL Sdn	6864	7665	9000
4 Dr XLS Sdn	7491	8365	9822

OPTIONS FOR AVALON
Alarm System[Opt on XL] +115
Aluminum/Alloy Wheels[Opt on XL] +149

Anti-Lock Brakes[Opt on XL] +380
Compact Disc Changer +213
Dual Power Seats +161
Leather Seats +330
Power Moonroof +342

CAMRY — 1995

Front and rear styling is updated, ABS is standard on XLE model, and Camry now meets 1997 side-impact protection standards. DX wagon dumped from lineup.
Category D

Model Description	Trade-in TMV	Private TMV	Dealer TMV
2 Dr DX Cpe	4266	4902	5963
4 Dr DX Sdn	4335	4981	6059
2 Dr LE Cpe	5160	5930	7213
4 Dr LE Sdn	5229	6009	7309
4 Dr LE Wgn	5642	6483	7886
2 Dr LE V6 Cpe	5778	6639	8076
4 Dr LE V6 Sdn	5848	6721	8175
4 Dr LE V6 Wgn	6261	7195	8752
2 Dr SE Cpe	6330	7274	8848
4 Dr SE Sdn	6399	7353	8944
4 Dr XLE Sdn	5782	6644	8082
4 Dr XLE V6 Sdn	6537	7512	9137

OPTIONS FOR CAMRY
AM/FM Compact Disc Player +130
AM/FM Stereo/CD/Tape +272
Air Conditioning[Opt on DX] +389
Alarm System +115
Aluminum/Alloy Wheels +141
Anti-Lock Brakes[Std on XLE,XLE V6] +213
Automatic 4-Speed Transmission[Opt on DX] +311
Compact Disc Changer +213
Elite Package +193
Gold Package +76
Leather Seats +359
Luggage Rack +99
Power Drivers Seat[Std on XLE,XLE V6] +97
Power Moonroof +388
Power Passenger Seat +107
Rear Spoiler +136
Third Seat +133

CELICA — 1995

GT convertible returns to lineup, available in red, white, blue or black.
Category E

Model Description	Trade-in TMV	Private TMV	Dealer TMV
2 Dr GT Conv	7938	8914	10540
2 Dr GT Cpe	5845	6564	7761
2 Dr GT Hbk	5917	6645	7857
2 Dr ST Cpe	5340	5996	7090
2 Dr ST Hbk	5484	6159	7282

OPTIONS FOR CELICA

Don't forget to refer to the Mileage Adjustment Table at the back of this book!

TOYOTA 95

Model Description	Trade-in TMV	Private TMV	Dealer TMV	Model Description	Trade-in TMV	Private TMV	Dealer TMV

Model Description	Trade-in TMV	Private TMV	Dealer TMV
AM/FM Compact Disc Player +167			
AM/FM Stereo/CD/Tape +213			
Air Conditioning +389			
Alarm System +164			
Aluminum/Alloy Wheels +168			
Anti-Lock Brakes +213			
Automatic 4-Speed Transmission +311			
Compact Disc Changer +213			
Leather Seats +420			
Power Moonroof +295			
Rear Spoiler +161			
Sport Seats +376			
Sport Suspension +193			

COROLLA — 1995

1.8-liter engine loses ten horsepower to meet stricter emissions regulations. Torque is up, though. DX models get new interior fabric.

Category B

Model Description	Trade-in	Private	Dealer
4 Dr STD Sdn	3439	4028	5009
4 Dr DX Sdn	3637	4260	5298
4 Dr DX Wgn	3835	4492	5587
4 Dr LE Sdn	4100	4802	5972

OPTIONS FOR COROLLA

AM/FM Compact Disc Player +116	
Air Conditioning[Std on LE] +368	
Alarm System +115	
Aluminum/Alloy Wheels +161	
Anti-Lock Brakes +213	
Automatic 3-Speed Transmission +193	
Automatic 4-Speed Transmission +311	
Compact Disc Changer +213	
Power Door Locks[Opt on DX] +87	
Power Sunroof +230	
Power Windows[Opt on DX] +107	

HALF TON — 1995

Category J

Model Description	Trade-in	Private	Dealer
2 Dr STD Std Cab SB	3306	3712	4389
2 Dr DX 4WD Ext Cab SB			
	6037	6779	8015
2 Dr DX 4WD Std Cab SB			
	5462	6133	7252
2 Dr DX Ext Cab SB	4671	5245	6202
2 Dr DX Std Cab SB	3665	4115	4866
2 Dr DX V6 4WD Ext Cab SB			
	6540	7343	8683
2 Dr DX V6 4WD Std Cab SB			
	5965	6698	7920
2 Dr DX V6 Ext Cab SB	5103	5730	6775
2 Dr SR5 4WD Ext Cab SB			
	7402	8312	9828
2 Dr SR5 Ext Cab SB	5821	6537	7729

OPTIONS FOR HALF TON

AM/FM Compact Disc Player +174

Model Description	Trade-in	Private	Dealer
AM/FM Stereo Tape +110			
Air Conditioning +311			
Aluminum/Alloy Wheels +97			
Anti-Lock Brakes +136			
Anti-Lock Rear Brakes +97			
Automatic 4-Speed Transmission +330			
Automatic Locking Hubs (4WD) +78			
Bed Liner +97			
Compact Disc Changer +213			
Flip-Up Sunroof +139			
Power Steering[Opt on DX] +109			
Power Windows[Opt on SR5] +97			
Tonneau Cover +97			

LAND CRUISER — 1995

Redesigned dashboard carries dual airbags, and ABS is now standard. Revised grille carries Toyota logo rather than nameplate.

Category O

Model Description	Trade-in	Private	Dealer
4 Dr STD 4WD Wgn	13710	15225	17750

OPTIONS FOR LAND CRUISER

AM/FM Compact Disc Player +174	
AM/FM Stereo/CD/Tape +366	
Aluminum/Alloy Wheels +203	
Compact Disc Changer +310	
Dual Power Seats +252	
Gold Package +133	
Leather Seats +582	
Leather Trim Package +431	
Locking Differential +136	
Luggage Rack +116	
Power Moonroof +367	
Privacy Glass +97	
Rear Spoiler +97	
Running Boards +270	
Third Seat Package +409	

MR2 — 1995

Final year for Mister Two. Several states lose Turbo model, which wouldn't pass emissions regulations. Base models with T-bar roof get power windows and locks standard.

Category E

Model Description	Trade-in	Private	Dealer
2 Dr STD Cpe	5990	6726	7953
2 Dr STD Turbo Cpe	6927	7779	9198

OPTIONS FOR MR2

AM/FM Compact Disc Player +155	
AM/FM Stereo/CD/Tape +232	
Air Conditioning +232	
Alarm System +97	
Anti-Lock Brakes +252	
Automatic 4-Speed Transmission +311	
Compact Disc Changer +252	
Flip-Up Sunroof +147	
Leather Seats +388	
Limited Slip Differential +155	
Power Door Locks +79	

Don't forget to refer to the Mileage Adjustment Table at the back of this book!

TOYOTA 95

Model Description	Trade-in TMV	Private TMV	Dealer TMV	Model Description	Trade-in TMV	Private TMV	Dealer TMV

Power Drivers Seat +116
Power Mirrors +78
Power Steering +115
Power Windows +103
T-Bar Roof Package +458

PASEO 1995

Several states with strict emissions laws get detuned Paseo for 1995.

Category E

Model Description	Trade-in TMV	Private TMV	Dealer TMV
2 Dr STD Cpe	3464	3889	4599

OPTIONS FOR PASEO

AM/FM Compact Disc Player +177
AM/FM Stereo Tape +87
Air Conditioning +359
Alarm System +115
Aluminum/Alloy Wheels +161
Anti-Lock Brakes +213
Automatic 4-Speed Transmission +311
Compact Disc Changer +271
Cruise Control +113
Electric Sunroof +252
Rear Spoiler +161

PREVIA 1995

Seatback map pockets and an illuminated driver's visor vanity mirror are standard on all models.

Category P

Model Description	Trade-in TMV	Private TMV	Dealer TMV
2 Dr DX AWD Pass. Van	6778	7686	9199
2 Dr DX Pass. Van	5870	6656	7966
2 Dr DX Sprchgd AWD Pass. Van	6918	7845	9389
2 Dr DX Sprchgd Pass. Van	6010	6814	8156
2 Dr LE AWD Pass. Van	7827	8875	10622
2 Dr LE Pass. Van	7058	8003	9579
2 Dr LE Sprchgd AWD Pass. Van	8106	9192	11001
2 Dr LE Sprchgd Pass. Van	7197	8161	9768

OPTIONS FOR PREVIA

AM/FM Compact Disc Player +177
AM/FM Stereo/CD/Tape +291
Alarm System +85
Aluminum/Alloy Wheels +168
Anti-Lock Brakes +229
Captain Chairs (2) +201
Compact Disc Changer +271
Dual Air Conditioning[Opt on DX] +434
Dual Moonroofs +572
Gold Package +116
Leather Seats +465
Luggage Rack +104
Moonroof +155
Power Moonroof +427

Power Windows[Opt on DX] +110
Privacy Glass +164
Running Boards +130

SUPRA 1995

No changes.

Category F

Model Description	Trade-in TMV	Private TMV	Dealer TMV
2 Dr STD Hbk	11193	12498	14673
2 Dr STD Turbo Hbk	15257	17036	20000

OPTIONS FOR SUPRA

AM/FM Compact Disc Player +153
AM/FM Stereo/CD/Tape +394
Automatic 4-Speed Transmission +349
Compact Disc Changer +252
Leather Seats +388
Limited Slip Differential[Std on Turbo] +195
Power Drivers Seat +97
Rear Spoiler +178
Sport Roof +969

T100 1995

The 1995 T100 adds an extended-cab body style to fill out this midsized truck's lineup. A much more powerful DOHC V6 engine is introduced this year as are four-wheel antilock brakes. The antilock brakes are available only on DX and Xtracab models equipped V6 engine.

Category K

Model Description	Trade-in TMV	Private TMV	Dealer TMV
2 Dr STD Std Cab LB	5265	5947	7083
2 Dr DX 4WD Std Cab LB	7400	8358	9955
2 Dr DX Std Cab LB	6119	6911	8232
2 Dr DX 4WD Ext Cab SB	8111	9161	10912
2 Dr DX Ext Cab SB	6688	7554	8998
2 Dr DX 1 Ton Std Cab LB	6190	6992	8328
2 Dr SR5 4WD Ext Cab SB	8751	9884	11773
2 Dr SR5 Ext Cab SB	7186	8117	9668
2 Dr V6 Std Cab LB	5621	6349	7562

OPTIONS FOR T100

AM/FM Compact Disc Player +101
AM/FM Stereo/CD/Tape +193
Air Conditioning +232
Alarm System +115
Aluminum/Alloy Wheels +207
Anti-Lock Brakes +229
Automatic 4-Speed Transmission +349
Bed Liner +116
Running Boards +180
Tonneau Cover +145

Don't forget to refer to the Mileage Adjustment Table at the back of this book!

TOYOTA 95-94

Model Description	Trade-in TMV	Private TMV	Dealer TMV	Model Description	Trade-in TMV	Private TMV	Dealer TMV

TACOMA 1995

Toyota puts a city on wheels. No. New compact pickup with a real name debuted in March, 1995. Optional four-wheel ABS, a driver airbag, and potent new engines are highlights of the new design. Rack and pinion steering replaces the old recirculating ball-type on the old truck. Front seatbelts are height adjustable.

Category J

Model Description	Trade-in TMV	Private TMV	Dealer TMV
2 Dr STD 4WD Ext Cab SB			
	4887	5487	6488
2 Dr STD 4WD Std Cab SB			
	4600	5165	6107
2 Dr STD Ext Cab SB	3737	4197	4962
2 Dr STD Std Cab SB	2946	3308	3912
2 Dr SR5 4WD Ext Cab SB			
	7330	8231	9732
2 Dr V6 4WD Ext Cab SB			
	5677	6375	7538
2 Dr V6 4WD Std Cab SB			
	4561	5122	6056
2 Dr V6 Ext Cab SB	4493	5046	5966

OPTIONS FOR TACOMA
AM/FM Compact Disc Player +177
AM/FM Stereo Tape +143
Air Conditioning +382
Aluminum/Alloy Wheels +136
Anti-Lock Brakes +229
Automatic 4-Speed Transmission +281
Automatic Locking Hubs (4WD) +90
Bed Liner +116
Flip-Up Sunroof +151
Power Steering[Opt on 2WD] +116
Wheel Package +145

TERCEL 1995

Redesigned, but based on 1991-1994 generation. Coupe and sedan body styles. Coupe available in Standard and DX trim; sedan comes in DX flavor only. Dual airbags are standard. Height-adjustable seat belts are new. Car now meets 1997 side-impact standards. Engine is more powerful than before.

Category A

Model Description	Trade-in TMV	Private TMV	Dealer TMV
2 Dr STD Sdn	2597	3032	3757
2 Dr DX Sdn	2930	3421	4239
4 Dr DX Sdn	3063	3576	4431

OPTIONS FOR TERCEL
AM/FM Compact Disc Player +177
AM/FM Stereo Tape +136
Air Conditioning +359
Alarm System +115
Anti-Lock Brakes +213
Automatic 3-Speed Transmission +193
Automatic 4-Speed Transmission +272

Compact Disc Changer +232
Power Door Locks +93
Power Steering +105
Power Windows +101

1994 TOYOTA

4RUNNER 1994

Four-wheel ABS available on models with V6 engine. Side-door guard beams added. Air conditioners get CFC-free refrigerant. Optional leather can be had in new Oak color.

Category M

Model Description	Trade-in TMV	Private TMV	Dealer TMV
4 Dr SR5 4WD Wgn	7163	8117	9707
4 Dr SR5 V6 4WD Wgn	7944	9002	10765
4 Dr SR5 V6 Wgn	7589	8599	10284

OPTIONS FOR 4RUNNER
AM/FM Compact Disc Player +137
AM/FM Stereo/CD/Tape +240
Air Conditioning +338
Alarm System +110
Aluminum/Alloy Wheels +142
Anti-Lock Brakes +203
Automatic 4-Speed Transmission[Std on 2WD] +308
Compact Disc Changer +222
Leather Seats +428
Power Moonroof +280
Power Windows +132
Privacy Glass +101
Running Boards +113
Sport Seats +142

CAMRY 1994

Coupe body style debuts in DX, LE and SE form. All Camrys get passenger airbag. V6 engine is tweaked for more power. New fuzzy logic controls govern automatic transmission. SE models get standard power windows, locks, mirrors and cruise control.

Category D

Model Description	Trade-in TMV	Private TMV	Dealer TMV
2 Dr DX Cpe	3715	4344	5391
4 Dr DX Sdn	3782	4422	5488
4 Dr DX Wgn	4381	5122	6357
2 Dr LE Cpe	4377	5117	6351
4 Dr LE Sdn	4445	5197	6450
4 Dr LE Wgn	4777	5585	6932
2 Dr LE V6 Cpe	4844	5663	7028
4 Dr LE V6 Sdn	4977	5818	7221
4 Dr LE V6 Wgn	5374	6283	7798
2 Dr SE Cpe	5175	6050	7509
4 Dr SE Sdn	5308	6206	7702
4 Dr XLE Sdn	4910	5740	7124
4 Dr XLE V6 Sdn	5441	6361	7895

OPTIONS FOR CAMRY

Don't forget to refer to the Mileage Adjustment Table at the back of this book!

Model Description	Trade-in TMV	Private TMV	Dealer TMV

AM/FM Compact Disc Player +115
AM/FM Stereo/CD/Tape +240
Air Conditioning[Opt on DX] +345
Aluminum/Alloy Wheels[Std on XLE V6] +125
Anti-Lock Brakes +189
Automatic 4-Speed Transmission[Opt on DX Sdn,DX Cpe] +275
Compact Disc Changer +189
Elite Package +171
Leather Seats +317
Power Drivers Seat +86
Power Moonroof[Std on XLE,XLE V6] +343
Power Sunroof +275
Rear Spoiler +120
Third Seat +118

CELICA   1994

Redesigned coupe and liftback debut. Turbocharged All-Trac is gone. ST and GT are only trim levels. Dual airbags are standard; ABS is optional. Power mirrors and driver's seat height adjuster are standard.

Category E

Model Description	Trade-in	Private	Dealer
2 Dr GT Cpe	4736	5429	6585
2 Dr GT Hbk	4804	5508	6680
2 Dr ST Cpe	4256	4879	5917
2 Dr ST Hbk	4393	5036	6108

OPTIONS FOR CELICA

AM/FM Stereo/CD/Tape +189
Air Conditioning +345
Aluminum/Alloy Wheels +149
Anti-Lock Brakes +189
Automatic 4-Speed Transmission +275
Leather Seats +371
Power Sunroof +257
Rear Spoiler +142
Sport Seats +332
Sport Suspension +171

COROLLA   1994

Passenger airbag added. Passenger seatbelts have automatic locking retractors. CFC-free refrigerant is added to air conditioning system.

Category B

Model Description	Trade-in	Private	Dealer
4 Dr STD Sdn	2884	3401	4262
4 Dr DX Sdn	3014	3555	4455
4 Dr DX Wgn	3277	3864	4843
4 Dr LE Sdn	3408	4018	5036

OPTIONS FOR COROLLA

AM/FM Compact Disc Player +103
Air Conditioning[Std on LE] +326
Aluminum/Alloy Wheels +142
Anti-Lock Brakes +189
Automatic 3-Speed Transmission +171
Automatic 4-Speed Transmission +275
Compact Disc Changer +189
Power Sunroof +205

HALF TON   1994

Category J

Model Description	Trade-in	Private	Dealer
2 Dr STD Std Cab SB	2694	3044	3628
2 Dr DX 4WD Ext Cab SB	5105	5768	6874
2 Dr DX 4WD Std Cab SB	4396	4967	5919
2 Dr DX Ext Cab SB	3687	4166	4965
2 Dr DX Std Cab SB	3120	3525	4201
2 Dr DX V6 4WD Ext Cab SB	5601	6329	7542
2 Dr DX V6 4WD Std Cab SB	5034	5689	6779
2 Dr DX V6 Ext Cab SB	4112	4646	5537
2 Dr SR5 V6 4WD Ext Cab SB	6664	7531	8974
2 Dr SR5 V6 Ext Cab SB	4679	5287	6301

OPTIONS FOR HALF TON

AM/FM Compact Disc Player +154
AM/FM Stereo/CD/Tape +214
Air Conditioning +275
Aluminum/Alloy Wheels[Opt on SR5] +86
Anti-Lock Rear Brakes[Std on SR5] +86
Automatic 4-Speed Transmission +291
Bed Liner +86
Compact Disc Changer +189
Flip-Up Sunroof +124
Pop-Up Moonroof +124

LAND CRUISER   1994

Standard sound system has nine speakers instead of five. Passenger seatbelts have automatic locking retractors.

Category O

Model Description	Trade-in	Private	Dealer
4 Dr STD 4WD Wgn	10750	12137	14448

OPTIONS FOR LAND CRUISER

AM/FM Stereo/CD/Tape +324
Aluminum/Alloy Wheels +180
Anti-Lock Brakes +240
Leather Seats +623
Leather Trim Package +623
Limited Slip Differential +171
Luggage Rack +103
Power Drivers Seat +120
Power Moonroof +325
Power Passenger Seat +120
Privacy Glass +86
Running Boards +238
Third Rear Seat Package +308

MR2   1994

Passenger airbag debuts. ABS made standard. Taillights are revised, and the suspension gets further

Model Description	Trade-in TMV	Private TMV	Dealer TMV

fine-tuning. Base models get standard air conditioning (made standard last year on turbo), which is CFC-free on both models.

Category E

Model Description	Trade-in TMV	Private TMV	Dealer TMV
2 Dr STD Cpe	5079	5823	7062
2 Dr STD Turbo Cpe	6383	7318	8875

OPTIONS FOR MR2

AM/FM Compact Disc Player +137
AM/FM Stereo/CD/Tape +206
Alarm System +86
Anti-Lock Brakes +222
Automatic 4-Speed Transmission +275
Compact Disc Changer +222
Flip-Up Sunroof +130
Leather Seats +343
Limited Slip Differential +137
Power Steering +101
Power Windows +91
Premium Sound System +206
T-Bar Roof +404

PASEO   1994

CFC-free A/C added. Passenger seatbelts get automatic locking retractors.

Category E

Model Description	Trade-in TMV	Private TMV	Dealer TMV
2 Dr STD Cpe	2540	2911	3531

OPTIONS FOR PASEO

AM/FM Stereo Tape +77
Air Conditioning +317
Aluminum/Alloy Wheels +142
Anti-Lock Brakes +189
Automatic 4-Speed Transmission +275
Cruise Control +99
Pop-Up Moonroof +130
Rear Spoiler +142

PREVIA   1994

Passenger airbag added. Supercharged engine included on S/C models. Manual transmission is dropped. CFC-free air conditioning is new. Leather is available on LE models. New front bucket seats are installed.

Category P

Model Description	Trade-in TMV	Private TMV	Dealer TMV
2 Dr DX AWD Pass. Van	5598	6440	7843
2 Dr DX Pass. Van	4923	5664	6898
2 Dr LE AWD Pass. Van	6407	7371	8977
2 Dr LE Pass. Van	5732	6595	8032
2 Dr LE Sprchgd AWD Pass. Van			
	6947	7991	9733
2 Dr LE Sprchgd Pass. Van			
	6272	7216	8788

OPTIONS FOR PREVIA

AM/FM Compact Disc Player +157
AM/FM Stereo/CD/Tape +257

Alarm System +75
Aluminum/Alloy Wheels +149
Anti-Lock Brakes +203
Captain Chairs (2) +178
Compact Disc Changer +240
Cruise Control +77
Dual Air Conditioning[Opt on DX] +384
Dual Moonroofs +506
Leather Seats +411
Luggage Rack +92
Power Moonroof +377
Power Windows +98
Premium Sound System +291
Privacy Glass +145
Running Boards +115

SUPRA   1994

Base model gets revised final-drive ratio for improved launch.

Category F

Model Description	Trade-in TMV	Private TMV	Dealer TMV
2 Dr STD Hbk	9184	10528	12768
2 Dr STD Turbo Hbk	12228	14018	17000

OPTIONS FOR SUPRA

AM/FM Compact Disc Player +136
AM/FM Stereo/CD/Tape +348
Automatic 4-Speed Transmission +308
Leather Seats +343
Limited Slip Differential[Std on Turbo] +173
Rear Spoiler +158
Sport Roof +857

T100   1994

Driver airbag is added, and base models get four-cylinder engine. Side-door guard beams are installed, and beds get cargo tie-down hooks. Formerly standard rear ABS is now optional on base and DX trucks.

Category K

Model Description	Trade-in TMV	Private TMV	Dealer TMV
2 Dr STD Std Cab LB	2975	3411	4137
2 Dr DX 4WD Std Cab LB			
	5326	6106	7407
2 Dr DX Std Cab LB	4288	4917	5964
2 Dr DX 1 Ton Std Cab LB			
	4565	5234	6349
2 Dr SR5 4WD Std Cab LB			
	6502	7455	9043
2 Dr SR5 Std Cab LB	5188	5948	7215

OPTIONS FOR T100

AM/FM Compact Disc Player +89
AM/FM Stereo/CD/Tape +171
Air Conditioning +206
Alarm System +101
Aluminum/Alloy Wheels +184
Anti-Lock Rear Brakes[Std on SR5] +111
Automatic 4-Speed Transmission +308
Bed Liner +102

Model Description	Trade-in TMV	Private TMV	Dealer TMV
TERCEL			**1994**

CFC-free refrigerant added to optional A/C. Passenger seatbelts get automatic locking retractors. LE sedan is dropped.

Category A

Model Description	Trade-in TMV	Private TMV	Dealer TMV
2 Dr STD Sdn	2003	2378	3003
2 Dr DX Sdn	2196	2608	3293
4 Dr DX Sdn	2649	3144	3971

OPTIONS FOR TERCEL

4-Speed Transmission +214
AM/FM Stereo Tape +120
Air Conditioning +317
Alarm System +101
Anti-Lock Brakes +189
Automatic 3-Speed Transmission +171
Power Steering +93

1993 TOYOTA

Model Description	Trade-in TMV	Private TMV	Dealer TMV
4RUNNER			**1993**

Two-door model is dropped from lineup, a victim of import tariffs. Four-wheel drive models come standard with 4WDemand system. Alloy wheels available only on V6 models, and now include chrome package.

Category M

Model Description	Trade-in TMV	Private TMV	Dealer TMV
4 Dr SR5 4WD Wgn	5684	6519	7910
4 Dr SR5 V6 4WD Wgn	6862	7870	9550
4 Dr SR5 V6 Wgn	5753	6598	8007

OPTIONS FOR 4RUNNER

AM/FM Compact Disc Player +126
AM/FM Stereo/CD/Tape +220
Air Conditioning +311
Aluminum/Alloy Wheels +131
Anti-Lock Rear Brakes +79
Automatic 4-Speed Transmission[Opt on 4WD] +283
Compact Disc Changer +205
Leather Seats +394
Power Moonroof +257
Power Windows +121
Running Boards +104
Sport Seats +131

Model Description	Trade-in TMV	Private TMV	Dealer TMV
CAMRY			**1993**

DX models get color-keyed bodyside moldings. Oak is a new interior color.

Category D

Model Description	Trade-in TMV	Private TMV	Dealer TMV
4 Dr DX Sdn	3235	3790	4716
4 Dr DX Wgn	3697	4332	5390
4 Dr DX V6 Sdn	3961	4641	5774
4 Dr LE Sdn	3829	4486	5582
4 Dr LE Wgn	4098	4801	5974
4 Dr LE V6 Sdn	4224	4949	6158
4 Dr LE V6 Wgn	4555	5337	6641
4 Dr SE Sdn	4088	4790	5960
4 Dr XLE Sdn	4225	4951	6160
4 Dr XLE V6 Sdn	4687	5492	6833

OPTIONS FOR CAMRY

AM/FM Compact Disc Player +105
AM/FM Stereo/CD/Tape +220
Air Conditioning[Opt on DX,DX V6] +316
Aluminum/Alloy Wheels[Opt on LE,LE V6] +115
Anti-Lock Brakes +174
Automatic 4-Speed Transmission[Opt on SE,DX Sdn] +252
Compact Disc Changer +174
Leather Seats +292
Power Moonroof +315
Third Seat +109

Model Description	Trade-in TMV	Private TMV	Dealer TMV
CELICA			**1993**

ABS is standard on All-Trac model; optional for first time on GT convertible.

Category E

Model Description	Trade-in TMV	Private TMV	Dealer TMV
2 Dr STD Turbo AWD Hbk	5531	6451	7984
2 Dr GT Conv	4872	5683	7033
2 Dr GT Cpe	3877	4522	5596
2 Dr GT Hbk	3893	4540	5619
2 Dr GT-S Hbk	4148	4838	5988
2 Dr ST Cpe	3226	3763	4657

OPTIONS FOR CELICA

AM/FM Compact Disc Player +135
AM/FM Stereo/CD/Tape +174
Air Conditioning[Std on STD] +316
Alarm System +133
Aluminum/Alloy Wheels[Opt on GT] +137
Anti-Lock Brakes[Std on STD] +174
Automatic 4-Speed Transmission +252
Compact Disc Changer +174
Keyless Entry System +125
Leather Seats +342
Power Sunroof[Std on STD] +236

Model Description	Trade-in TMV	Private TMV	Dealer TMV
COROLLA			**1993**

All-new Corolla arrives with driver airbag. Sedan and wagon body styles available. All-Trac wagon dies. Interior volume increases enough to move Corolla out of subcompact classification. Height-adjustable seat belts are standard. ABS optional on all models.

Category B

Model Description	Trade-in TMV	Private TMV	Dealer TMV
4 Dr STD Sdn	2418	2890	3678
4 Dr DX Sdn	2481	2966	3774
4 Dr DX Wgn	2608	3118	3968
4 Dr LE Sdn	2799	3346	4258

OPTIONS FOR COROLLA

Air Conditioning[Std on LE] +299

Don't forget to refer to the Mileage Adjustment Table at the back of this book!

Model Description	Trade-in TMV	Private TMV	Dealer TMV
Aluminum/Alloy Wheels +131			
Anti-Lock Brakes +174			
Automatic 3-Speed Transmission +157			
Automatic 4-Speed Transmission +252			
Power Sunroof +188			

HALF TON — 1993

Category J

Model Description	Trade-in TMV	Private TMV	Dealer TMV
2 Dr STD Std Cab SB	2401	2754	3343
2 Dr Deluxe Std Cab LB	3293	3777	4584
2 Dr Deluxe 4WD Ext Cab SB	4254	4879	5922
2 Dr Deluxe 4WD Std Cab SB	3773	4328	5253
2 Dr Deluxe Ext Cab SB	3224	3699	4489
2 Dr Deluxe Std Cab SB	2813	3227	3916
2 Dr Deluxe V6 4WD Ext Cab SB	4528	5194	6304
2 Dr Deluxe V6 Ext Cab SB	3568	4093	4967
2 Dr SR5 V6 4WD Ext Cab SB	5763	6611	8023
2 Dr SR5 V6 Ext Cab SB	3910	4486	5444

OPTIONS FOR HALF TON
6 cyl 3.0 L Engine[Opt on Deluxe] +252
AM/FM Compact Disc Player +142
AM/FM Stereo Tape +89
Air Conditioning +252
Aluminum/Alloy Wheels +79
Anti-Lock Rear Brakes[Opt on Deluxe] +79
Automatic 4-Speed Transmission +268
Sunroof +120

LAND CRUISER — 1993

New 4.5-liter inline six pumps out 57 more horsepower than last year's engine; output is up to 212. Air conditioning and cruise control are added to the standard equipment list. Front and rear differential locks are newly optional. New leather package is available. Side-door guard beams added.

Category O

Model Description	Trade-in TMV	Private TMV	Dealer TMV
4 Dr STD 4WD Wgn	9133	10473	12706

OPTIONS FOR LAND CRUISER
AM/FM Compact Disc Player +142
AM/FM Stereo/CD/Tape +298
Aluminum/Alloy Wheels +165
Anti-Lock Brakes +220
Compact Disc Changer +252
Dual Power Seats +205
Leather Seats +473

Leather Trim Package +350
Locking Differential +111
Luggage Rack +95
Power Moonroof +299
Privacy Glass +79
Running Boards +220
Third Seat +140

MR2 — 1993

Suspension revisions aim to cure quirky cornering characteristics. All Turbos come with a standard T-bar roof. Base MR2s get V-rated tires, and alloy wheels have been redesigned. An eight-speaker stereo, air conditioning, cruise, power windows, and power door locks are all newly standard on Turbo.

Category E

Model Description	Trade-in TMV	Private TMV	Dealer TMV
2 Dr STD Cpe	3951	4608	5703
2 Dr STD Turbo Cpe	5136	5990	7413

OPTIONS FOR MR2
AM/FM Compact Disc Player +126
AM/FM Stereo/CD/Tape +189
Air Conditioning +189
Alarm System +79
Anti-Lock Brakes +205
Automatic 4-Speed Transmission +252
Compact Disc Changer +205
Leather Seats +315
Limited Slip Differential +126
Power Steering +93
Power Windows +83
Premium Sound System +189
Rear Spoiler +79
Sunroof +120
T-Tops (Solid/Colored)[Std on Turbo] +520

PASEO — 1993

Driver airbag added, and ABS is now optional. Interior fabrics are revised. Two new colors.

Category E

Model Description	Trade-in TMV	Private TMV	Dealer TMV
2 Dr STD Cpe	1975	2304	2851

OPTIONS FOR PASEO
Air Conditioning +292
Alarm System +93
Aluminum/Alloy Wheels +131
Anti-Lock Brakes +174
Automatic 4-Speed Transmission +252
Cruise Control +91
Moonroof +126
Rear Spoiler +131

PREVIA — 1993

All Previas seat seven instead of five. Only 2WD DX can be equipped with manual transmission. All-Tracs and 2WD LE get rear disc brakes.

Category P
2 Dr Deluxe AWD Pass. Van

Model Description	Trade-in TMV	Private TMV	Dealer TMV
	4366	5067	6236
2 Dr Deluxe Pass. Van	3572	4146	5102
2 Dr LE AWD Pass. Van	5159	5988	7370
2 Dr LE Pass. Van	4564	5298	6520

OPTIONS FOR PREVIA
AM/FM Compact Disc Player +144
AM/FM Stereo/CD/Tape +236
Aluminum/Alloy Wheels +137
Anti-Lock Brakes +186
Automatic 4-Speed Transmission[Std on LE, 4WD] +252
Captain Chairs (2) +164
Compact Disc Changer +220
Dual Air Conditioning[Std on LE] +353
Dual Sunroofs +465
Power Sunroof +252
Privacy Glass +133

SUPRA   1993

Debuted in summer 1993. All-new car features dual airbags and ABS. Twin Turbo model has 320 horsepower and traction control.

Category F

Model Description	Trade-in TMV	Private TMV	Dealer TMV
2 Dr STD Hbk	8391	9772	12073
2 Dr STD Turbo Hbk	10356	12060	14900

OPTIONS FOR SUPRA
AM/FM Compact Disc Player +125
Automatic 4-Speed Transmission +283
Leather Seats +315
Limited Slip Differential[Std on Turbo] +159
Power Sunroof +220
Rear Spoiler +145
Solid Targa Top +315
T-Tops (Solid/Colored) +315

T100   1993

New full-size Toyota pickup designed to battle Chevy C/K, Ford F-Series and Dodge Ram. 150-horsepower V6 is only powerplant. One-ton model handles 2,570 lbs.

Category K

Model Description	Trade-in TMV	Private TMV	Dealer TMV
2 Dr 1 Ton Std Cab LB	3656	4271	5296
2 Dr STD 4WD Std Cab LB			
	4320	5047	6259
2 Dr STD Std Cab LB	3456	4038	5007
2 Dr SR5 4WD Std Cab LB			
	4984	5823	7221
2 Dr SR5 Std Cab LB	3855	4504	5585

OPTIONS FOR T100
AM/FM Compact Disc Player +82
AM/FM Stereo/CD/Tape +157
Air Conditioning +189
Aluminum/Alloy Wheels +168
Automatic 4-Speed Transmission +283
Bed Liner +95

TERCEL   1993

Driver airbag added, and ABS is optional for first time. Sedans get height-adjustable seatbelts. Exteriors get a new grille. DX models get body-color bumpers and moldings. Airbag is housed in new steering wheel. LE gets standard power steering.

Category A

Model Description	Trade-in TMV	Private TMV	Dealer TMV
2 Dr STD Sdn	1644	2007	2613
2 Dr DX Sdn	1766	2156	2807
4 Dr DX Sdn	1949	2379	3097
4 Dr LE Sdn	2131	2602	3387

OPTIONS FOR TERCEL
AM/FM Compact Disc Player +144
AM/FM Stereo Tape +111
Air Conditioning +292
Anti-Lock Brakes +174
Automatic 3-Speed Transmission +157
Compact Disc Changer +189

1992 TOYOTA

4RUNNER   1992

New grille, front bumper and aero headlights debut. Power steering and a rear wiper/washer are standard on all models. Spare tire is moved underneath body of truck. Leather seats are newly optional on four-door models with a V6 engine.

Category M

Model Description	Trade-in TMV	Private TMV	Dealer TMV
2 Dr SR5 4WD Utility	6111	7118	8796
4 Dr SR5 4WD Wgn	4634	5397	6670
4 Dr SR5 Wgn	4902	5710	7056

OPTIONS FOR 4RUNNER
6 cyl 3.0 L Engine[Std on Utility, 2WD] +279
AM/FM Compact Disc Player +117
AM/FM Stereo/CD/Tape +205
Air Conditioning +289
Aluminum/Alloy Wheels +122
Automatic 4-Speed Transmission[Opt on 4WD] +264
Leather Seats +367
Power Moonroof +239
Power Windows +113
Running Boards +97
Sport Seats +122

CAMRY   1992

Redesign nets a driver airbag, larger engines, more interior volume and a sporty SE model. All-Trac has been dropped. ABS is optional across all trim levels and body styles.

Category D

Model Description	Trade-in TMV	Private TMV	Dealer TMV
4 Dr Deluxe Sdn	2843	3389	4297
4 Dr Deluxe Wgn	3349	3991	5061
4 Dr LE Sdn	3412	4066	5156

Don't forget to refer to the Mileage Adjustment Table at the back of this book!

Model Description	Trade-in TMV	Private TMV	Dealer TMV
4 Dr LE Wgn	3599	4289	5439
4 Dr SE Sdn	3538	4217	5347
4 Dr XLE Sdn	3604	4295	5447

OPTIONS FOR CAMRY
6 cyl 3.0 L Engine[Std on SE] +381
AM/FM Compact Disc Player +98
AM/FM Stereo/CD/Tape +205
Air Conditioning[Opt on Deluxe] +294
Aluminum/Alloy Wheels[Std on SE] +107
Anti-Lock Brakes +161
Automatic 4-Speed Transmission[Std on LE,XLE,Wgn] +235
Bicentennial Package +353
Leather Seats +272
Power Moonroof[Std on XLE] +293
Rear Spoiler[Opt on LE] +102
Third Seat +101

CELICA 1992

Subtle restyling, larger wheels and tires, and wider availability of ABS.
Category E

Model Description	Trade-in TMV	Private TMV	Dealer TMV
2 Dr STD Turbo AWD Hbk	4187	4955	6234
2 Dr GT Conv	4124	4880	6140
2 Dr GT Cpe	3172	3754	4723
2 Dr GT Hbk	3235	3828	4817
2 Dr GT-S Hbk	3426	4054	5101
2 Dr ST Cpe	2728	3228	4062

OPTIONS FOR CELICA
AM/FM Compact Disc Player +126
AM/FM Stereo/CD/Tape +161
Air Conditioning +294
Aluminum/Alloy Wheels[Opt on GT] +128
Anti-Lock Brakes +161
Automatic 4-Speed Transmission +235
Leather Seats +318
Power Sunroof +220
Rear Spoiler +122

COROLLA 1992

LE sedan comes with an automatic only. Coupe body style is dropped.
Category B

Model Description	Trade-in TMV	Private TMV	Dealer TMV
4 Dr STD Sdn	1519	1904	2546
4 Dr Deluxe AWD Wgn	2075	2601	3477
4 Dr Deluxe Sdn	1593	1997	2670
4 Dr Deluxe Wgn	1729	2167	2898
4 Dr LE Sdn	2017	2528	3380

OPTIONS FOR COROLLA
AM/FM Compact Disc Player +88
Air Conditioning +279
Alarm System +87
Aluminum/Alloy Wheels +122

Automatic 3-Speed Transmission +146
Automatic 4-Speed Transmission +235
Power Sunroof +174

CRESSIDA 1992

No changes.
Category H

Model Description	Trade-in TMV	Private TMV	Dealer TMV
4 Dr STD Sdn	3608	4223	5249

OPTIONS FOR CRESSIDA
AM/FM Compact Disc Player +98
Anti-Lock Brakes +196
Dual Power Seats +130
Leather Seats +261
Power Moonroof +279

HALF TON 1992

Category J

Model Description	Trade-in TMV	Private TMV	Dealer TMV
2 Dr STD Std Cab SB	2038	2387	2967
2 Dr Deluxe 4WD Std Cab LB	3641	4263	5300
2 Dr Deluxe Std Cab LB	2827	3310	4115
2 Dr Deluxe 4WD Ext Cab SB	3879	4542	5646
2 Dr Deluxe 4WD Std Cab SB	3485	4080	5072
2 Dr Deluxe Ext Cab SB	3024	3541	4402
2 Dr Deluxe Std Cab SB	2696	3156	3924
2 Dr SR5 4WD Ext Cab SB	5129	6005	7465
2 Dr SR5 Ext Cab SB	3723	4359	5419

OPTIONS FOR HALF TON
6 cyl 3.0 L Engine[Opt on Deluxe] +235
AM/FM Stereo/CD/Tape +183
Air Conditioning +235
Anti-Lock Brakes +102
Automatic 4-Speed Transmission +250
Sunroof +111

LAND CRUISER 1992

Power windows, locks and outside mirrors are standard this year.
Category O

Model Description	Trade-in TMV	Private TMV	Dealer TMV
4 Dr STD 4WD Wgn	6996	8123	10001

OPTIONS FOR LAND CRUISER
AM/FM Stereo/CD/Tape +277
Air Conditioning +235
Aluminum/Alloy Wheels +154
Leather Seats +440
Luggage Rack +88
Power Sunroof +293

Don't forget to refer to the Mileage Adjustment Table at the back of this book!

Model Description	Trade-in TMV	Private TMV	Dealer TMV	Model Description	Trade-in TMV	Private TMV	Dealer TMV
Premium Sound System +235				*Category P*			
Third Seat +130				2 Dr Deluxe AWD Pass. Van			
					3290	3901	4919

MR2 — 1992

ABS is optional.
Category E

Model Description	Trade-in TMV	Private TMV	Dealer TMV
2 Dr STD Cpe	3045	3604	4534
2 Dr STD Turbo Cpe	3743	4429	5573

OPTIONS FOR MR2

AM/FM Compact Disc Player +117
AM/FM Stereo Tape +78
AM/FM Stereo/CD/Tape +176
Air Conditioning +176
Aluminum/Alloy Wheels +88
Anti-Lock Brakes +191
Automatic 4-Speed Transmission +235
Glass Panel T-tops +346
Leather Seats +293
Power Steering +87
Power Windows +78
Premium Sound System +176
Sunroof +111
T-Tops (Solid/Colored) +484

ONE TON — 1992

Category J

Model Description	Trade-in TMV	Private TMV	Dealer TMV
2 Dr STD Std Cab LB	2827	3310	4115

OPTIONS FOR ONE TON

AM/FM Stereo Tape +78
Air Conditioning +176
Anti-Lock Brakes +191
Automatic 4-Speed Transmission +235

PASEO — 1992

Sporty version of the Tercel offers more horsepower, stiffer suspension, and racier bodywork than its more pedestrian counterpart.
Category E

Model Description	Trade-in TMV	Private TMV	Dealer TMV
2 Dr STD Cpe	1586	1876	2361

OPTIONS FOR PASEO

Air Conditioning +272
Aluminum/Alloy Wheels +122
Automatic 4-Speed Transmission +235
Cruise Control +85
Moonroof +117
Rear Spoiler +122

PREVIA — 1992

Driver airbag is added, and with new knee bolsters under the dash and a third brake light, the 1992 Previa becomes the first minivan to meet passenger car safety requirements, including standards for roof crush and side-impact protection. ABS is newly optional on DX models. LE models get standard power windows, locks and mirrors.

Category P

Model Description	Trade-in TMV	Private TMV	Dealer TMV
2 Dr Deluxe AWD Pass. Van			
	3290	3901	4919
2 Dr Deluxe Pass. Van	2847	3376	4257
2 Dr LE AWD Pass. Van	4175	4951	6243
2 Dr LE Pass. Van	3732	4426	5581

OPTIONS FOR PREVIA

AM/FM Compact Disc Player +134
AM/FM Stereo/CD/Tape +220
Aluminum/Alloy Wheels +128
Anti-Lock Brakes +173
Automatic 4-Speed Transmission[Std on LE] +235
Captain Chairs (2) +153
Dual Air Conditioning[Std on LE] +329
Dual Sunroofs +433
Privacy Glass +125

SUPRA — 1992

Automatic transmission gets revised shift points.
Category F

Model Description	Trade-in TMV	Private TMV	Dealer TMV
2 Dr STD Hbk	4111	4867	6126
2 Dr STD Turbo Hbk	4753	5627	7083

OPTIONS FOR SUPRA

AM/FM Compact Disc Player +116
Anti-Lock Brakes[Std on Turbo] +235
Automatic 4-Speed Transmission +264
Leather Seats +293
Limited Slip Differential[Std on Turbo] +148
Solid Targa Top +293

TERCEL — 1992

No changes.
Category A

Model Description	Trade-in TMV	Private TMV	Dealer TMV
2 Dr STD Sdn	1229	1529	2028
2 Dr DX Sdn	1346	1674	2221
4 Dr DX Sdn	1464	1820	2415
4 Dr LE Sdn	1639	2038	2704

OPTIONS FOR TERCEL

AM/FM Stereo Tape +102
Air Conditioning +272
Automatic 3-Speed Transmission +146
Power Steering +79

VOLKSWAGEN 01

Model Description	Trade-in TMV	Private TMV	Dealer TMV	Model Description	Trade-in TMV	Private TMV	Dealer TMV

VOLKSWAGEN Germany

1996 Volkswagen Cabrio

2001 VOLKSWAGEN

CABRIO 2001

A top-of-the-line GLX trim level has been added to the existing lineup for 2001. All models get an anti "trunk entrapment" button to keep people from getting stuck in the cargo hold.

Category E

Model Description	Trade-in TMV	Private TMV	Dealer TMV
2 Dr GL Conv	14020	14985	16592
2 Dr GLS Conv	14811	15830	17528
2 Dr GLX Conv	16128	17237	19086

OPTIONS FOR CABRIO
Automatic 4-Speed Transmission +673

EUROVAN 2001

The EuroVan sees many upgrades for the 2001 model year; chief among them is a more powerful 201-horsepower V6 engine. Refinements have also been made to the electronic stability control system. Other changes include a new premium stereo, single seats for second-row seating and standard integrated foglights.

Category P

Model Description	Trade-in TMV	Private TMV	Dealer TMV
2 Dr GLS Pass. Van	19610	20787	22749
2 Dr MV Pass. Van	21185	22457	24577

OPTIONS FOR EUROVAN
Heated Front Seats +308
Pearlescent White Paint +211
Power Sunroof +769
Weekender Package +2552

GOLF 2001

All Golf models get clear side marker lights, trunk entrapment buttons, new cupholders and head protection airbags. Golf GL and GLS get higher-quality interior fabrics and the GTI benefits from a new 16-inch wheel design, optional 17-inch wheels, and multi-function steering wheel controls.

Category B

Model Description	Trade-in TMV	Private TMV	Dealer TMV
2 Dr GL Hbk	10565	11423	12853
2 Dr GL TDI Turbodsl Hbk	11441	12370	13918
4 Dr GLS Hbk	11545	12482	14045
4 Dr GLS TDI Turbodsl Hbk	12254	13249	14908
4 Dr GLS Turbo Hbk	12591	13613	15317

OPTIONS FOR GOLF
Aluminum/Alloy Wheels[Opt on GLS] +211
Automatic 4-Speed Transmission +673
Heated Front Seats +192
Monsoon Sound System +250
Power Moonroof +454

GTI 2001

All Golf models get clear side marker lights, trunk entrapment buttons, new cupholders and head protection airbags. Golf GL and GLS get higher-quality interior fabrics and the GTI benefits from a new 16-inch wheel design, optional 17-inch wheels, and multi-function steering wheel controls.

Category E

Model Description	Trade-in TMV	Private TMV	Dealer TMV
2 Dr GLS Turbo Hbk	13761	14707	16285
2 Dr GLX VR6 Hbk	16551	17690	19587

OPTIONS FOR GTI
Automatic 4-Speed Transmission[Opt on GLS] +673
Heated Front Seats[Opt on GLS] +115
Leather Seats[Opt on GLS] +692
Monsoon Sound System[Opt on GLS] +250
Steering Wheel Radio Controls[Opt on GLS] +115

JETTA 2001

For 2001, improved cloth and velour interior materials come standard in the GL and GLS trim. Side curtain airbags that offer head protection for front and rear passengers are introduced this year, and steering wheel controls for the audio and cruise systems are available on GLS/GLX trim models. Optional 17-inch wheels and a sport suspension can be had on GLX models and GLS models with the 1.8T or VR6 engine. The Wolfsburg Edition returns as a limited-edition model in early 2001 — standard features include sport suspension, bolstered sport seats and 16-inch BBS wheels. All models get redesigned cupholders and a trunk entrapment release button. Finally, for those seeking more utility in the Jetta lineup, a wagon arrives in the spring of 2001.

Model Description	Trade-in TMV	Private TMV	Dealer TMV

Category C

Model Description	Trade-in TMV	Private TMV	Dealer TMV
4 Dr GL Sdn	11440	12209	13491
4 Dr GL TDI Turbodsl Sdn	12600	13447	14859
4 Dr GLS Sdn	12088	12901	14255
4 Dr GLS TDI Turbodsl Sdn	13091	13970	15437
4 Dr GLS Turbo Sdn	13144	14028	15500
4 Dr GLS VR6 Sdn	13658	14576	16106
4 Dr GLS VR6 Wgn	14719	15708	17357
4 Dr GLS Wgn	12911	13779	15225
4 Dr GLS Wolfsburg Edition Sdn	13580	14493	16014
4 Dr GLX VR6 Sdn	17390	18559	20507
4 Dr GLX VR6 Wgn	18255	19482	21527

OPTIONS FOR JETTA
Aluminum/Alloy Wheels[Std on GLX VR6] +219
Automatic 4-Speed Transmission +673
Heated Front Seats[Std on GLX VR6] +115
Leather Seats[Std on GLX VR6] +423
Monsoon Sound System[Std on GLX VR6] +250
Power Moonroof[Std on GLX VR6] +454
Steering Wheel Radio Controls +115

NEW BEETLE   2001

A limited-edition Sport model arrives in 2001 — it's a GLS 1.8T model with leather sport seats, 17-inch alloy wheels, an eight-speaker Monsoon sound system, a sunroof and a cold weather package. You can order 17-inch alloy wheels a la carte for GLS 1.8T and GLX models, while high-intensity discharge headlights are optional on all GLS and GLX models. New standard features for the GLX include the Monsoon sound system (optional for GLS), rain-sensing wipers and a self-dimming rearview mirror. All New Beetles benefit from larger exterior mirrors, redesigned cupholders and a trunk entrapment release button.

Category E

Model Description	Trade-in TMV	Private TMV	Dealer TMV
2 Dr GL Hbk	11503	12294	13613
2 Dr GLS Hbk	11995	12820	14195
2 Dr GLS TDI Turbodsl Hbk	12717	13592	15050
2 Dr GLS Turbo Hbk	13475	14402	15947
2 Dr GLX Turbo Hbk	15250	16299	18047

OPTIONS FOR NEW BEETLE
Aluminum/Alloy Wheels[Std on GLX] +308
Automatic 4-Speed Transmission +673
Heated Front Seats[Std on GLX] +115
Leather Seats[Std on GLX] +654
Monsoon Sound System[Opt on GLS] +250
Power Moonroof[Std on GLX] +603

NEW PASSAT   2001

The 2001.5 Passat arrives this spring with updated exterior styling, minor interior changes and a more powerful four-cylinder engine, but if you liked the "old" styling, a few 2001s should linger on dealership lots for a while. New features for the 2001 model year — standard front and rear side curtain airbags, optional steering wheel controls for the audio and cruise for GLS (standard on the GLX) and a standard trunk entrapment release button — carry over into 2001.5 Passats.

Category D

Model Description	Trade-in TMV	Private TMV	Dealer TMV
4 Dr GLS Turbo Sdn	15395	16347	17933
4 Dr GLS Turbo Wgn	16351	17362	19046
4 Dr GLS V6 AWD Sdn	20050	21290	23355
4 Dr GLS V6 AWD Wgn	20656	21933	24061
4 Dr GLS V6 Sdn	17661	18753	20572
4 Dr GLS V6 Wgn	18223	19350	21227
4 Dr GLX AWD Sdn	23452	24901	27317
4 Dr GLX AWD Wgn	24058	25545	28023
4 Dr GLX Sdn	21024	22323	24489
4 Dr GLX Wgn	21631	22968	25196

OPTIONS FOR NEW PASSAT
Aluminum/Alloy Wheels[Std on GLX] +269
Automatic 5-Speed Transmission[Std on AWD] +826
Heated Front Seats[Std on GLX] +250
Leather Seats[Std on GLX] +654
Monsoon Sound System[Std on GLX] +250
Power Moonroof[Std on GLX] +769
Steering Wheel Radio Controls[Std on GLX] +115

PASSAT   2001

The 2001.5 Passat arrives this spring with updated exterior styling, minor interior changes and a more powerful four-cylinder engine, but if you liked the "old" styling, a few 2001s should linger on dealership lots for a while. New features for the 2001 model year — standard front and rear side curtain airbags, optional steering wheel controls for the audio and cruise for GLS (standard on the GLX) and a standard trunk entrapment release button — carry over into 2001.5 Passats.

Category D

Model Description	Trade-in TMV	Private TMV	Dealer TMV
4 Dr GLS Turbo Sdn	15024	15952	17500
4 Dr GLS Turbo Wgn	15576	16538	18143
4 Dr GLS V6 AWD Sdn	19082	20261	22227
4 Dr GLS V6 AWD Wgn	19634	20847	22870
4 Dr GLS V6 Sdn	16818	17858	19590
4 Dr GLS V6 Wgn	17370	18444	20233
4 Dr GLX AWD Sdn	22089	23455	25730
4 Dr GLX AWD Wgn	22641	24041	26373
4 Dr GLX Sdn	19824	21049	23091

Don't forget to refer to the Mileage Adjustment Table at the back of this book!

Model Description	Trade-in TMV	Private TMV	Dealer TMV	Model Description	Trade-in TMV	Private TMV	Dealer TMV
4 Dr GLX Wgn	20376	21635	23734	2 Dr GTI GLS Turbo Hbk			
					12294	13603	14812

OPTIONS FOR PASSAT
Aluminum/Alloy Wheels[Std on GLX,AWD] +269
Automatic 5-Speed Transmission[Std on AWD] +826
Heated Front Seats[Opt on GLS,GLS V6] +250
Leather Seats[Std on GLX] +730
Monsoon Sound System[Std on GLX] +250
Power Moonroof[Std on GLX] +769
Steering Wheel Radio Controls[Std on GLX] +115

Model Description	Trade-in TMV	Private TMV	Dealer TMV
Category B			
4 Dr GLS TDI Turbodsl Hbk			
	11220	12670	14009
Category E			
2 Dr GTI GLX Hbk	14531	16079	17508

OPTIONS FOR GOLF
AM/FM Compact Disc Player +211
Aluminum/Alloy Wheels[Std on GTI,GLX] +211
Automatic 4-Speed Transmission +673
Compact Disc Changer +381
Heated Front Seats[Std on GLX] +192
Leather Seats[Std on GLX] +423
Metallic Paint +135
Monsoon Sound System[Std on GLX] +227
Power Moonroof[Std on GTI,GLX] +454

2000 VOLKSWAGEN

CABRIO — 2000

Volkswagen's Cabrio gets minor equipment updates for the millennium.

	Trade-in	Private	Dealer
Category E			
2 Dr GL Conv	12501	13833	15062
2 Dr GLS Conv	14722	16290	17738

OPTIONS FOR CABRIO
Aluminum/Alloy Wheels[Opt on GL] +284
Automatic 4-Speed Transmission +673
Compact Disc Changer +381
Cruise Control[Opt on GL] +131
Heated Front Seats[Opt on GL] +192
Heated Power Mirrors[Opt on GL] +135
Keyless Entry System +135
Power Windows[Opt on GL] +195

EUROVAN — 2000

For its second year back in the U.S., Volkswagen's EuroVan receives minor equipment updates.

	Trade-in	Private	Dealer
Category P			
2 Dr GLS Pass. Van	17638	19386	21000
2 Dr MV Pass. Van	18940	20817	22550

OPTIONS FOR EUROVAN
Compact Disc Changer +346
Heated Front Seats +308
Metallic Paint +211
Power Moonroof +769
Weekender Package +2552

GOLF — 2000

VW's Golf arrives for 2000 with several equipment updates. But the big news is that the 150-horsepower, turbocharged engine found in the New Beetle Turbo is standard for the GTI and optional on the Golf GLS.

	Trade-in	Private	Dealer
Category B			
2 Dr GL Hbk	9681	10933	12088
2 Dr GL TDI Turbodsl Hbk			
	10478	11833	13083
4 Dr GLS Hbk	10574	11940	13202
4 Dr GLS Turbo Hbk	11526	13016	14391
Category E			
2 Dr GTI GLS Hbk	11828	13088	14251

JETTA — 2000

VW's 2000 Jetta arrives with an optional turbocharged 1.8T engine on the GLS for that extra zip-a-dee-doo-dah as well as minor equipment updates.

	Trade-in	Private	Dealer
Category C			
4 Dr GL Sdn	10655	11719	12701
4 Dr GL TDI Turbodsl Sdn			
	11731	12903	13984
4 Dr GLS Sdn	11257	12381	13418
4 Dr GLS Turbo Sdn	12236	13457	14585
4 Dr GLS TDI Turbodsl Sdn			
	12185	13402	14525
4 Dr GLS VR6 Sdn	12712	13981	15153
4 Dr GLX VR6 Sdn	15460	17004	18429

OPTIONS FOR JETTA
AM/FM Compact Disc Player +192
AM/FM Stereo/CD/Tape +192
Aluminum/Alloy Wheels[Std on GLX VR6] +219
Automatic 4-Speed Transmission +673
Compact Disc Changer +381
Heated Front Seats[Std on GLX VR6] +192
Leather Seats[Std on GLX VR6] +615
Metallic Paint +135
Monsoon Sound System[Std on GLX VR6] +227
Power Moonroof[Std on GLX VR6] +454
Sport Seats +115

NEW BEETLE — 2000

Several minor equipment upgrades, such as improved theft protection, debut on the 2000 New Beetle.

	Trade-in	Private	Dealer
Category E			
2 Dr GL Hatchback	10531	11653	12688
2 Dr GLS Hbk	10979	12148	13228
2 Dr GLS Turbo Hbk	12327	13640	14852
2 Dr GLS TDI Turbodsl Hbk			
	11637	12877	14021

Don't forget to refer to the Mileage Adjustment Table at the back of this book!

Model Description	Trade-in TMV	Private TMV	Dealer TMV
2 Dr GLX Turbo Hbk	13691	15150	16496

OPTIONS FOR NEW BEETLE

Aluminum/Alloy Wheels[Std on GLX] +238
Automatic 4-Speed Transmission +673
Compact Disc Changer +384
Heated Front Seats[Std on GLX] +231
Leather Seats[Std on GLX] +654
Metallic Paint +115
Power Moonroof[Std on GLX] +603
Rear Spoiler[Std on GLX, Turbo] +173

PASSAT 2000

The radio display and anti-theft system have been updated. A brake-wear indicator is now standard on all models.
Category D

Model Description	Trade-in TMV	Private TMV	Dealer TMV
4 Dr GLS Turbo Sdn	13746	15058	16270
4 Dr GLS Turbo Wgn	14254	15616	16872
4 Dr GLS V6 4WD Sdn	17443	19109	20646
4 Dr GLS V6 4WD Wgn	17952	19667	21249
4 Dr GLS V6 Sdn	15399	16870	18227
4 Dr GLS V6 Wgn	15908	17427	18829
4 Dr GLX 4WD Sdn	20089	22007	23778
4 Dr GLX 4WD Wgn	20598	22564	24380
4 Dr GLX Sdn	18045	19768	21359
4 Dr GLX Wgn	18554	20326	21961

OPTIONS FOR PASSAT

Aluminum/Alloy Wheels[Std on GLX, AWD] +269
Auto-Manual Transmission +827
Compact Disc Changer +381
Heated Front Seats[Opt on GLS, GLS V6] +250
Leather Seats[Std on GLX] +730
Metallic Paint +135
Monsoon Sound System[Std on GLX] +227
Power Moonroof[Std on GLX] +769

1999 VOLKSWAGEN

CABRIO 1999

Volkswagen imparts new Euro-styling on the '99 Cabrios, making them more aerodynamic and adding twin headlights that show interior elements through the lens. Cabrio interiors also receive makeovers.
Category E

Model Description	Trade-in TMV	Private TMV	Dealer TMV
2 Dr GL Conv	10675	11892	13108
2 Dr NEW GL Conv	11158	12429	13700
2 Dr GLS Conv	12191	13580	14969
2 Dr NEW GLS Conv	12569	14001	15433

OPTIONS FOR CABRIO

Air Conditioning[Opt on GL] +529
Aluminum/Alloy Wheels[Opt on GL, NEW GL] +227
Automatic 4-Speed Transmission +538
Compact Disc Changer +305
Cruise Control[Opt on GL, NEW GL] +105

Heated Front Seats[Std on NEW GLS] +153
Heated Power Mirrors[Opt on GL, NEW GL] +108
Keyless Entry System[Opt on GL, NEW GL] +108
Metallic Paint +108
Power Windows[Opt on GL, NEW GL] +157
Side Air Bag Restraints[Opt on GL, GLS] +243
Sport Seats[Opt on GL] +108

EUROVAN 1999

After a five-year hiatus, the funky EuroVan passenger van returns to the U.S. with a six-cylinder engine, structural improvements and new safety features.
Category P

Model Description	Trade-in TMV	Private TMV	Dealer TMV
2 Dr GLS Pass. Van	15062	16666	18270
2 Dr MV Pass. Van	15763	17441	19120

OPTIONS FOR EUROVAN

Compact Disc Changer +277
Heated Front Seats +246
Metallic Paint +169
Power Moonroof +615
Weekender Package +2042

GOLF 1999

The four-cylinder GTI is dropped in favor of a four-door Wolfsburg Edition during the final year for the current Golf.
Category B

Model Description	Trade-in TMV	Private TMV	Dealer TMV
4 Dr GL Hbk	8136	9215	10294
Category E			
2 Dr GTI VR6 Hbk	12479	13900	15322
Category B			
4 Dr Wolfsburg Hbk	9668	10951	12233

OPTIONS FOR GOLF

AM/FM Compact Disc Player +169
AM/FM Stereo Tape[Opt on GL] +298
AM/FM Stereo/CD/Tape[Opt on Wolfsburg] +184
Air Conditioning[Opt on GL] +529
Anti-Lock Brakes[Std on VR6] +477
Automatic 4-Speed Transmission +538
Compact Disc Changer +305
Leather Seats +338
Metallic Paint +108
Power Moonroof[Std on VR6] +363
Side Air Bag Restraints +243

GTI 1999

VW's all-new Golf GTIs arrive in 1999 with new interior and exterior designs and more powerful engines.
Category E

Model Description	Trade-in TMV	Private TMV	Dealer TMV
2 Dr NEW GLS Hbk	10553	11756	12958
2 Dr NEW GLX Hbk	13080	14571	16061

OPTIONS FOR GTI

AM/FM Compact Disc Player +169
Automatic 4-Speed Transmission +538
Compact Disc Changer +307

Don't forget to refer to the Mileage Adjustment Table at the back of this book!

Heated Front Seats[Std on NEW GLX] +138
Leather Seats[Std on NEW GLX] +338
Metallic Paint +108

JETTA 1999

Volkswagen trims model availability, killing the GLS and GT in favor of the Wolfsburg Edition.
Category C

Model	Trade-in	Private	Dealer
4 Dr GL Sdn	9218	10254	11290
4 Dr GLX Sdn	12227	13601	14976
4 Dr TDI Turbodsl Sdn	10048	11177	12307
4 Dr Wolfsburg Sdn	10268	11423	12577

OPTIONS FOR JETTA

AM/FM Stereo Tape[Opt on GL,TDI] +298
Air Conditioning[Opt on GL,TDI] +529
Aluminum/Alloy Wheels[Opt on GL,TDI] +175
Anti-Lock Brakes[Std on GLX] +477
Automatic 4-Speed Transmission +538
Compact Disc Changer[Std on Wolfsburg] +305
Cruise Control[Opt on GL] +138
Heated Front Seats +153
Heated Power Mirrors[Opt on TDI] +108
Leather Seats +492
Metallic Paint +108
Power Moonroof[Std on GLX] +363
Power Windows[Opt on TDI] +175
Side Air Bag Restraints +243

NEW BEETLE 1999

A high-performance turbo model debuts this year. A small spoiler over the rear window is the only exterior telltale that the Slug Bug next to you has the 150-horsepower 1.8-liter turbocharged inline-four from the larger Passat sedan under the hood.
Category E

Model	Trade-in	Private	Dealer
2 Dr GL Hbk	9480	10560	11640
2 Dr GLS Hbk	9883	11009	12135
2 Dr GLS Turbo Hbk	11097	12361	13625
2 Dr GLS TDI Turbodsl Hbk	10476	11669	12863
2 Dr GLX Turbo Hbk	12031	13401	14772

OPTIONS FOR NEW BEETLE

Aluminum/Alloy Wheels[Std on GLX] +191
Automatic 4-Speed Transmission +538
Compact Disc Changer +307
Heated Front Seats[Std on GLX] +184
Leather Seats[Std on GLX] +523
Power Moonroof[Std on GLX] +482

NEW GOLF 1999

VW's all-new Golf arrives in 1999 with new interior and exterior designs and more powerful engines.
Category B

Model	Trade-in	Private	Dealer
2 Dr NEW GL Hbk	8636	9781	10927

Model	Trade-in	Private	Dealer
2 Dr NEW GL TDI Turbodsl Hbk	9347	10587	11827
4 Dr NEW GLS Hbk	9433	10684	11935
4 Dr NEW GLS TDI Turbodsl Hbk	10009	11336	12664

OPTIONS FOR NEW GOLF

Aluminum/Alloy Wheels +162
Automatic 4-Speed Transmission +538
Compact Disc Changer +307
Metallic Paint +108
Power Moonroof +492

NEW JETTA 1999

VW's all-new 1999 Jetta arrives with bigger engines, updated styling and new standard equipment.
Category C

Model	Trade-in	Private	Dealer
4 Dr NEW GL Sdn	9584	10662	11739
4 Dr NEW GL TDI Turbodsl Sdn	10552	11738	12924
4 Dr NEW GLS Sdn	10125	11264	12402
4 Dr NEW GLS TDI Turbodsl Sdn	10961	12193	13425
4 Dr NEW GLS VR6 Sdn	11433	12719	14004
4 Dr NEW GLX VR6 Sdn	13906	15470	17033

OPTIONS FOR NEW JETTA

AM/FM Stereo/CD/Tape[Opt on NEW GLS] +153
Aluminum/Alloy Wheels[Std on NEW GLX] +175
Automatic 4-Speed Transmission +538
Compact Disc Changer +307
Heated Front Seats[Std on NEW GLX] +184
Leather Seats[Std on NEW GLX] +523
Metallic Paint +108
Power Moonroof[Std on NEW GLX] +492

PASSAT 1999

After promising the availability of all-wheel drive this year, Volkswagen, in a last-minute product change, has cancelled the Synchro all-wheel drive option on all Passats for 1999 and will not be offering the GLS wagon with a V6 engine.
Category D

Model	Trade-in	Private	Dealer
4 Dr GLS Turbo Sdn	12039	13408	14777
4 Dr GLS Turbo Wgn	12484	13904	15324
4 Dr GLS V6 Sdn	13487	15021	16555
4 Dr GLX Sdn	15805	17602	19400

OPTIONS FOR PASSAT

AM/FM Compact Disc Player +169
Aluminum/Alloy Wheels +215
Auto-Manual Transmission +661
Compact Disc Changer +305
Heated Front Seats[Std on GLX] +199
Leather Seats[Std on GLX] +584
Metallic Paint +108
Power Moonroof[Std on GLX] +615

VOLKSWAGEN 98

Model Description	Trade-in TMV	Private TMV	Dealer TMV	Model Description	Trade-in TMV	Private TMV	Dealer TMV

1998 VOLKSWAGEN

CABRIO 1998

The Highline trim designation is replaced by more sensible GLS nomenclature, though we'd prefer to see something like GTI grace the rear flanks of this drop-top. New GLS model gets a power top, making the Cabrio easier to live with. Optional are side impact airbags mounted inside the seats. Newly standard on both base and GLS are door pocket liners, a trunk cargo net and sport seats with height adjustment. Still no much-needed power boost.

Category E

2 Dr GL Conv	9968	11167	12466
2 Dr GLS Conv	11075	12408	13851

OPTIONS FOR CABRIO

Air Conditioning[Opt on GL] +483
Aluminum/Alloy Wheels[Opt on GL] +208
Automatic 4-Speed Transmission +492
Compact Disc Changer +278
Cruise Control[Opt on GL] +96
Heated Front Seats +141
Heated Power Mirrors[Opt on GL] +99
Keyless Entry System[Opt on GL] +99
Metallic Paint +99
Power Windows[Opt on GL] +144
Side Air Bag Restraints +223

GOLF 1998

GTI VR6 receives several cosmetic upgrades taken from the 1997 Driver's Edition. Among them are a chrome-tipped exhaust pipe, silver/white-faced instruments, embossed sill covers, leather-wrapped steering wheel, shift boot and handbrake lever (with stitching designed to coordinate with new Sport-Jacquard seat fabric) and the aluminum ball shift knob. Exclusive to the VR6 for 1998 are the Speedline 15-inch alloys from the Driver's Edition and one-touch up power windows with pinch protection. All GTIs get standard remote keyless entry.

Category B

4 Dr GL Hbk	6910	7873	8916

Category E

2 Dr GTI Hbk	8676	9719	10850
2 Dr GTI VR6 Hbk	10706	11994	13389

Category B

4 Dr K2 Hbk	7333	8355	9462
4 Dr Wolfsburg Hbk	7651	8717	9872

OPTIONS FOR GOLF

AM/FM Compact Disc Player +155
AM/FM Stereo Tape[Opt on GL] +272
Air Conditioning[Opt on GL,K2] +483
Anti-Lock Brakes[Std on GTI,GTI VR6] +436

Automatic 4-Speed Transmission +492
Compact Disc Changer +278
Cruise Control[Opt on Wolfsburg] +99
Heated Power Mirrors[Opt on Wolfsburg] +99
Leather Seats +309
Metallic Paint +99
Power Moonroof[Opt on GL,K2] +331
Power Windows[Opt on Wolfsburg] +144
Side Air Bag Restraints +223

JETTA 1998

The TDI has finally arrived. New wheel covers and colors spruce up the exterior for another year, while remote keyless entry makes it easier to lock and unlock the Jetta. GLX models have new one-touch up power windows with pinch protection.

Category C

4 Dr GL Sdn	7730	8655	9657
4 Dr GLS Sdn	10259	11487	12817
4 Dr GLX Sdn	10674	11951	13335
4 Dr GT Sdn	8538	9560	10667
4 Dr K2 Sdn	9128	10221	11404
4 Dr TDI Turbodsl Sdn	8945	10015	11175
4 Dr Wolfsburg Sdn	9149	10244	11430

OPTIONS FOR JETTA

AM/FM Compact Disc Player +155
AM/FM Stereo Tape[Opt on GL,GT,TDI] +272
AM/FM Stereo/CD/Tape +141
Air Conditioning[Opt on GL,GT,TDI] +483
Aluminum/Alloy Wheels[Opt on GL,TDI] +160
Anti-Lock Brakes[Std on GLX] +436
Automatic 4-Speed Transmission +492
Bose Sound System[Opt on GLS] +211
Compact Disc Changer[Std on Wolfsburg] +278
Cruise Control[Std on GLS,GLX,TDI] +126
Heated Front Seats +141
Heated Power Mirrors[Opt on TDI,Wolfsburg] +99
Leather Seats +449
Metallic Paint +99
Power Moonroof[Std on GLX,Wolfsburg] +331
Power Windows[Std on GLS,GLX] +160
Side Air Bag Restraints +223

NEW BEETLE 1998

Volkswagen attempts to revive a legend using retro styling touches wrapped around Golf underpinnings.

Category E

2 Dr STD Hbk	8654	9695	10823
2 Dr TDI Turbodsl Hbk	9293	10411	11622

OPTIONS FOR NEW BEETLE

Aluminum/Alloy Wheels +174
Anti-Lock Brakes +169
Automatic 4-Speed Transmission +492
Compact Disc Changer +281
Cruise Control[Opt on STD] +99

Don't forget to refer to the Mileage Adjustment Table at the back of this book!

Model Description	Trade-in TMV	Private TMV	Dealer TMV

Heated Front Seats +169
Power Moonroof +388
Power Windows +155

PASSAT 1998

An all-new Passat arrives wearing stylish sheetmetal over a stretched Audi A4 platform. Engine choices include a spunky turbocharged four or a silky V6.

Category D

Model Description	Trade-in TMV	Private TMV	Dealer TMV
4 Dr GLS Turbo Sdn	10962	12242	13629
4 Dr GLS Turbo Wgn	11367	12695	14133
4 Dr GLS V6 Sdn	12280	13714	15268
4 Dr GLX Sdn	14141	15793	17582

OPTIONS FOR PASSAT
Auto-Manual Transmission +604
Heated Front Seats[Std on GLX] +182
Leather Seats[Std on GLX] +492
Power Moonroof[Std on GLX] +480
Rear Spoiler +169

1997 VOLKSWAGEN

CABRIO 1997

Cabrio comes in two trim levels for 1997: Base and Highline. Base models are decontented versions of last year's car, priced a couple thousand dollars lower to entice young drivers. Highline models have standard alloy wheels, fog lights and leather seats. Engines have a redesigned cylinder head resulting in quieter operation.

Category E

Model Description	Trade-in TMV	Private TMV	Dealer TMV
2 Dr STD Conv	8429	9538	10894
2 Dr Highline Conv	9045	10235	11689

OPTIONS FOR CABRIO
Air Conditioning[Opt on STD] +399
Aluminum/Alloy Wheels[Opt on STD] +172
Automatic 4-Speed Transmission +406
Compact Disc Changer +230
Heated Front Seats +110
Power Windows[Opt on STD] +119

EUROVAN 1997

Category P

Model Description	Trade-in TMV	Private TMV	Dealer TMV
2 Dr Campmobile Pass. Van			
	13178	14659	16468

OPTIONS FOR EUROVAN
Aluminum/Alloy Wheels +104
Compact Disc Changer +230

GOLF 1997

GTI VR6 gets a lowered suspension for improved handling, and a redesigned cylinder head quiets GL and GTI models. A K2 edition debuted in December, 1996, sporting heated front seats, premium sound, and

a rack with either skis or a snowboard attached. Spring, 1997, brought a slick Trek model with alloys and a bike up top.

Category B

Model Description	Trade-in TMV	Private TMV	Dealer TMV
2 Dr GL Hbk	5583	6423	7449
4 Dr GL Hbk	5955	6851	7946
Category E			
2 Dr GTI Hbk	7215	8164	9324
2 Dr GTI VR6 Hbk	9045	10235	11689
Category B			
4 Dr K2 Hbk	6023	6929	8036
4 Dr Trek Hbk	6101	7018	8140

OPTIONS FOR GOLF
AM/FM Compact Disc Player +128
AM/FM Stereo Tape[Opt on GL, Trek] +225
Air Conditioning[Opt on GL, K2, Trek] +399
Anti-Lock Brakes[Opt on GL] +359
Automatic 4-Speed Transmission +406
Compact Disc Changer +230
Leather Seats +256
Power Moonroof[Opt on GL, K2, Trek] +274

JETTA 1997

Wolfsburg models are gone, and the Jetta GT arrives sporting the look of the GLX without that darn expensive VR6 engine. Trek gets alloy wheels. GL, GLS, Trek and GT run more quietly, thanks to a new cylinder head design.

Category C

Model Description	Trade-in TMV	Private TMV	Dealer TMV
4 Dr GL Sdn	6017	6778	7709
4 Dr GLS Sdn	7584	8544	9717
4 Dr GLX Sdn	8785	9896	11255
4 Dr GT Sdn	6339	7142	8122
4 Dr TDI Turbodsl Sdn	7307	8232	9362
4 Dr Trek Sdn	6351	7155	8137

OPTIONS FOR JETTA
AM/FM Compact Disc Player +128
AM/FM Stereo Tape[Std on GLS] +225
Air Conditioning[Std on GLS, GLX] +399
Aluminum/Alloy Wheels[Opt on GL] +132
Anti-Lock Brakes[Std on GLX] +359
Automatic 4-Speed Transmission +406
Bose Sound System[Opt on GLS] +174
Compact Disc Changer +230
Cruise Control[Std on GLS, GLX] +104
Heated Front Seats +116
Leather Seats +371
Power Moonroof[Opt on GLX] +274
Power Windows[Opt on Trek] +132
Rear Spoiler[Opt on GLS] +139

PASSAT 1997

GLS model vanishes from radar as Volkswagen prepares for launch of all-new Passat in mid-1997.

Category D

Don't forget to refer to the Mileage Adjustment Table at the back of this book!

Model Description	Trade-in TMV	Private TMV	Dealer TMV
4 Dr GLX Sdn	8764	9855	11189
4 Dr GLX Wgn	8898	10006	11360
4 Dr TDI Turbodsl Sdn	8090	9097	10328
4 Dr TDI Turbodsl Wgn	8730	9816	11145

OPTIONS FOR PASSAT
Aluminum/Alloy Wheels +162
Anti-Lock Brakes[Opt on TDI] +359
Automatic 4-Speed Transmission +371
Compact Disc Changer +230
Heated Front Seats +151
Leather Seats +406
Power Moonroof +398

1996 VOLKSWAGEN

CABRIO   1996

Daytime running lights and new body-color side moldings alter the exterior appearance of the 1996 Cabrio. A new color scheme also livens things up. Central locking and unlocking switch is dash mounted.
Category E

Model Description	Trade-in TMV	Private TMV	Dealer TMV
2 Dr STD Conv	7070	8025	9344

OPTIONS FOR CABRIO
Air Conditioning +368
Aluminum/Alloy Wheels +250
Automatic 4-Speed Transmission +376
Compact Disc Changer +212
Leather Seats +546

GOLF   1996

The Golf Sport becomes the GTI, powered by a 2.0-liter four-cylinder with alloys, sport seats, and smoke-tinted taillights. GTI VR6 continues, with firmer front suspension, three new colors, and new "Pininfarina" style alloy wheels. Black leather seats are newly optional on GTI VR6. Automatic transmissions are smoother this year.
Category B

Model Description	Trade-in TMV	Private TMV	Dealer TMV
4 Dr GL Hbk	4474	5206	6216
4 Dr TDI Turbodsl Hbk	5271	6132	7322

OPTIONS FOR GOLF
AM/FM Stereo Tape +208
Air Conditioning +368
Anti-Lock Brakes +332
Automatic 4-Speed Transmission +376
Compact Disc Changer +212
Power Moonroof +253

GTI   1996
Category E

Model Description	Trade-in TMV	Private TMV	Dealer TMV
2 Dr STD Hbk	5941	6743	7851
2 Dr VR6 Hbk	7655	8689	10117

OPTIONS FOR GTI
Automatic 4-Speed Transmission +376

Compact Disc Changer +212
Leather Seats +236

JETTA   1996

A new grille is added up front. GLX models get a firmer front suspension and new "Bugatti" style wheels. New colors sum up the changes.
Category C

Model Description	Trade-in TMV	Private TMV	Dealer TMV
4 Dr City Sdn	4702	5329	6195
4 Dr GL Sdn	4770	5406	6285
4 Dr GLS Sdn	6306	7147	8308
4 Dr GLX Sdn	7106	8054	9363
4 Dr TDI Turbodsl Sdn	5655	6409	7451
4 Dr Trek Limited Ed. Sdn	5330	6041	7023
4 Dr Wolfsburg Sdn	5280	5984	6956

OPTIONS FOR JETTA
AM/FM Compact Disc Player[Opt on Trek] +119
AM/FM Stereo Tape[Std on GLS] +208
Air Conditioning[Std on GLS,GLX] +368
Anti-Lock Brakes[Std on GLX] +332
Automatic 4-Speed Transmission +376
Bose Sound System[Opt on GLS] +160
Compact Disc Changer +212
Heated Front Seats +107
Leather Seats +343
Power Moonroof[Std on GLX,Wolfsburg] +253

PASSAT   1996

Daytime running lights debut, two new colors are added to the palette, and a new price-leader GLS model powered by a 2.0-liter, 115-horsepower, four-cylinder engine is introduced. Midyear, a Turbo Direct Injection (TDI) diesel model appears in sedan and wagon form.
Category D

Model Description	Trade-in TMV	Private TMV	Dealer TMV
4 Dr GLS Sdn	6190	7067	8277
4 Dr GLX Sdn	7484	8544	10007
4 Dr GLX Wgn	7649	8731	10227
4 Dr TDI Turbodsl Sdn	6548	7476	8756
4 Dr TDI Turbodsl Wgn	6731	7684	9000

OPTIONS FOR PASSAT
AM/FM Stereo/CD/Tape[Opt on GLS] +107
Aluminum/Alloy Wheels +150
Anti-Lock Brakes[Std on GLX] +332
Automatic 4-Speed Transmission +343
Compact Disc Changer +212
Heated Front Seats +139
Leather Seats +376
Power Moonroof +367

Don't forget to refer to the Mileage Adjustment Table at the back of this book!

Model Description	Trade-in TMV	Private TMV	Dealer TMV

1995 VOLKSWAGEN

CABRIO 1995

Dual airbags, ABS, and 115-horsepower engine are standard on this Golf derivative. Manual top only.

Category E

2 Dr STD Conv	6098	6849	8101

OPTIONS FOR CABRIO

AM/FM Compact Disc Player +181
Air Conditioning +312
Aluminum/Alloy Wheels +134
Automatic 4-Speed Transmission +318
Compact Disc Changer +180
Leather Seats +463

EUROVAN 1995

Category P

2 Dr Campmobile Pass. Van	9721	10994	13116

OPTIONS FOR EUROVAN

Automatic 4-Speed Transmission +309

GOLF 1995

GTI VR6 debuts, with 2.8-liter V6, ABS, and traction control. Entry-level City trim level introduced for four-door models. Two-door Golf switches from GL to Sport designation, and includes spoked alloy wheels and blacked out taillights. Golf meets 1997 side-impact standards. Front seatbelts have height adjusters and emergency tensioners. Daytime running lights are standard on all Golf models.

Category B

4 Dr STD Hbk	3479	4050	5003
4 Dr Celebration Hbk	3505	4080	5040
4 Dr City Hbk	3086	3593	4438
2 Dr GL Hbk	3598	4189	5174
4 Dr GL Hbk	3838	4468	5519

Category E

2 Dr GTI VR6 Hbk	6017	6758	7993

Category B

2 Dr Sport Hbk	4235	4930	6090

OPTIONS FOR GOLF

AM/FM Stereo Tape[Opt on City,STD] +176
Air Conditioning[Std on GTI VR6,GL,Sport] +312
Aluminum/Alloy Wheels[Opt on GL] +91
Anti-Lock Brakes[Std on GTI VR6] +282
Automatic 4-Speed Transmission +318
Compact Disc Changer +180
Power Moonroof[Std on GTI VR6,Sport] +215
Premium Sound System[Opt on Celebration] +137

JETTA 1995

Entry-level City trim level introduced. Jetta meets 1997 side-impact standards. Front seatbelts have height adjusters and emergency tensioners. Daytime running lights are standard on all Jetta models.

Category C

4 Dr STD Sdn	3916	4512	5504
4 Dr Celebration Sdn	4061	4679	5708
4 Dr City Sdn	3648	4202	5127
4 Dr GL Sdn	4565	5259	6416
4 Dr GLS Sdn	4918	5666	6913
4 Dr GLX Sdn	5631	6487	7914

OPTIONS FOR JETTA

AM/FM Stereo Tape[Std on GL,GLS,GLX] +176
Air Conditioning[Std on GL,GLS,GLX,STD] +312
Aluminum/Alloy Wheels[Opt on GL] +79
Anti-Lock Brakes[Std on GLX] +282
Automatic 4-Speed Transmission +318
Compact Disc Changer +180
Cruise Control[Opt on Celebration] +79
Leather Seats +291
Power Moonroof[Std on GLS,GLX] +215

PASSAT 1995

Reskinned for 1995, VW adds dual airbags, three-point seatbelts, and side-impact protection that meets 1997 safety standards. Climate control system gains dust and pollen filter. GLX is only trim level.

Category D

4 Dr GLS Sdn	4999	5748	6996
4 Dr GLX Sdn	5878	6759	8226
4 Dr GLX Wgn	6010	6910	8410

OPTIONS FOR PASSAT

Anti-Lock Brakes[Opt on GLS] +282
Automatic 4-Speed Transmission +291
Compact Disc Changer +180
Heated Front Seats +118
Leather Seats +318
Power Moonroof +310

1994 VOLKSWAGEN

CORRADO 1994

Adaptive dual-mode automatic transmission debuts. Meets 1997 side-impact standards. Speed-activated spoiler rises at 55 mph instead of 45 mph.

Category E

2 Dr SLC Cpe	5025	5840	7199

OPTIONS FOR CORRADO

Automatic 4-Speed Transmission +239
Compact Disc Changer +179
Heated Front Seats +75
Power Sunroof +224

Don't forget to refer to the Mileage Adjustment Table at the back of this book!

Model Description	Trade-in TMV	Private TMV	Dealer TMV

GOLF — 1994

Two-door GL debuts. ABS is optional. Dual airbags are phased in shortly after 1994 production begins.

Category B

Model Description	Trade-in TMV	Private TMV	Dealer TMV
2 Dr GL Hbk	2827	3369	4273
4 Dr GL Hbk	2713	3234	4101
2 Dr Limited Hbk	3202	3816	4840

OPTIONS FOR GOLF

AM/FM Compact Disc Player[Opt on Limited] +82
AM/FM Stereo Tape +145
Air Conditioning +257
Aluminum/Alloy Wheels +75
Anti-Lock Brakes +231
Automatic 4-Speed Transmission +262
Dual Air Bag Restraints +119
Power Moonroof +176

JETTA — 1994

GLS and GLX models arrive this year. ABS is optional on GL and GLS; standard on GLX. Dual airbags are phased in shortly after 1994 production begins. GLX features 2.8-liter V6 and traction control.

Category C

Model Description	Trade-in TMV	Private TMV	Dealer TMV
4 Dr GL Sdn	2885	3360	4153
4 Dr GLS Sdn	3433	3999	4942
4 Dr GLX Sdn	4232	4930	6093
4 Dr Limited Edition Sdn	3060	3564	4405

OPTIONS FOR JETTA

AM/FM Stereo Tape[Opt on GL] +145
Air Conditioning[Std on GLS,GLX] +257
Anti-Lock Brakes[Std on GLX] +231
Automatic 4-Speed Transmission +262
Compact Disc Changer +148
Dual Air Bag Restraints +119
Leather Seats +239
Power Moonroof +176
Premium Sound System[Opt on Limited] +112
Rear Spoiler[Opt on GLS] +90

PASSAT — 1994

GL dropped, leaving only the V6 GLX. ABS and traction control are standard. Adaptive dual-mode transmission debuts.

Category D

Model Description	Trade-in TMV	Private TMV	Dealer TMV
4 Dr GLX Sdn	5489	6286	7614
4 Dr GLX Wgn	5600	6413	7768

OPTIONS FOR PASSAT

Automatic 4-Speed Transmission +239
Compact Disc Changer +148
Heated Front Seats +97
Leather Seats +262

1993 VOLKSWAGEN

CABRIOLET — 1993

Carat replaced by Classic. Base models get leatherette upholstery option. Audio systems are upgraded, and CD player joins options list.

Category E

Model Description	Trade-in TMV	Private TMV	Dealer TMV
2 Dr STD Conv	4124	4802	5932
2 Dr Classic Conv	4747	5527	6828

OPTIONS FOR CABRIOLET

Air Conditioning[Opt on STD] +184
Automatic 3-Speed Transmission +142
Compact Disc Changer +118

CORRADO — 1993

In mid-1992, supercharged four-cylinder engine was replaced by 2.8-liter V6. V6 model designated SLC. ABS and traction control are standard. BBS wheels dumped in favor of five-spoke VW design. Fuel capacity up four gallons, and front styling is tweaked. A/C is CFC-free. Radio turns off with ignition switch.

Category E

Model Description	Trade-in TMV	Private TMV	Dealer TMV
2 Dr SLC Cpe	4189	4878	6026

OPTIONS FOR CORRADO

Automatic 4-Speed Transmission +190
Leather Seats +190
Power Sunroof +178

EUROVAN — 1993

The EuroVan is introduced as a replacement for the aging Vanagon. Major differences over the previous generation Volkswagen van are the switch to a front-engine/front-wheel drive platform. Antilock brakes are available on the EuroVan, and it has a 2.5-liter four-cylinder engine that produces 109-horsepower. A five-speed manual transmission is standard, a four-speed automatic is optional.

Category P

Model Description	Trade-in TMV	Private TMV	Dealer TMV
2 Dr CL Pass. Van	2897	3437	4336
2 Dr GL Pass. Van	3538	4196	5294
2 Dr MV Pass. Van	3795	4501	5679

OPTIONS FOR EUROVAN

Anti-Lock Brakes +178
Automatic 4-Speed Transmission +202
Dual Air Conditioning[Opt on CL] +296
Weekender Package +787

FOX — 1993

Air conditioning is standard. Five-speed transmission replaces four-speed unit on Base coupe. Base model gets wheelcovers, dual outside mirrors, body-color bumpers and bigger tires. GL model gets upgraded

---

Don't forget to refer to the Mileage Adjustment Table at the back of this book!

VOLKSWAGEN 93-92

Model Description	Trade-in TMV	Private TMV	Dealer TMV
interior trim.			
Category A			
2 Dr Polo Sdn	1065	1353	1831
2 Dr Wolfsburg Sdn	990	1257	1701
4 Dr Wolfsburg GL Sdn	1237	1570	2125

GOLF 1993

All new Golf debuts, but a strike at the assembly plant in Mexico restricts sales to Southern California and parts of New England.

Category B

4 Dr GL Hbk	2004	2544	3444

OPTIONS FOR GOLF
AM/FM Stereo Tape +115
Air Conditioning +204
Automatic 4-Speed Transmission +207
Power Sunroof +178

JETTA 1993

All new Jetta debuts, but a strike at the assembly plant in Mexico restricts sales to Southern California and parts of New England.

Category C

4 Dr GL Sdn	2229	2800	3751

OPTIONS FOR JETTA
AM/FM Stereo Tape +115
Air Conditioning +204
Automatic 4-Speed Transmission +207
Power Sunroof +178

PASSAT 1993

GLX trim level introduced, with 2.8-liter V6, ABS and traction control. Fog lamps and six-spoke alloys indicate GLX model. CL trim dropped. GL gets suspension modifications. All models get trip computer and CFC-free air conditioning.

Category D

4 Dr GL Sdn	2886	3499	4521
4 Dr GL Wgn	2971	3602	4654
4 Dr GLX Sdn	3565	4323	5585
4 Dr GLX Wgn	3648	4423	5714

OPTIONS FOR PASSAT
Automatic 4-Speed Transmission +190
Heated Front Seats +77
Leather Seats +207
Power Sunroof[Opt on GL] +178

1992 VOLKSWAGEN

CABRIOLET 1992

Etienne Aigner edition dropped. Three-point seatbelts are added to the back seat. Base model gets full wheelcovers. Radio turns off with ignition switch.

Category E

2 Dr STD Conv	3529	4295	5573
2 Dr Carat Conv	3871	4712	6114
2 Dr Wolfsburg Class. Conv	3964	4825	6260

OPTIONS FOR CABRIOLET
Air Conditioning[Opt on Carat,STD] +175
Automatic 3-Speed Transmission +134
Automatic 4-Speed Transmission +191
Power Convertible Top[Opt on Carat] +169

CORRADO 1992

No changes.
Category E

2 Dr STD Sprchgd Cpe	3242	3946	5120
2 Dr SLC Cpe	3317	4038	5239

OPTIONS FOR CORRADO
AM/FM Stereo Tape[Opt on STD] +79
Anti-Lock Brakes[Opt on STD] +169
Automatic 4-Speed Transmission +180
Leather Seats +180
Power Sunroof +169

FOX 1992

Radio turns off with ignition switch.
Category A

2 Dr STD Sdn	859	1144	1618
4 Dr GL Sdn	947	1260	1783

OPTIONS FOR FOX
Air Conditioning[Std on GL] +157

GOLF 1992

Radio turns off with ignition switch.
Category B

2 Dr GL Hbk	1406	1839	2559
4 Dr GL Hbk	1457	1905	2651

Category E

2 Dr GTI Hbk	2172	2644	3430
2 Dr GTI 16V Hbk	2701	3288	4266

OPTIONS FOR GOLF
AM/FM Stereo Tape +109
Air Conditioning +194
Automatic 3-Speed Transmission +134
Sunroof +90

JETTA 1992

ECOdiesel debuts, featuring turbocharging and fewer pollutants. Two-door model dropped. GL models get new wheelcovers. Radio turns off with ignition switch.
Category C

4 Dr Carat Sdn	1473	1940	2718
4 Dr GL Sdn	1384	1822	2553
4 Dr GL ECO Dsl Sdn	1418	1867	2616

Don't forget to refer to the Mileage Adjustment Table at the back of this book!

Model Description	Trade-in TMV	Private TMV	Dealer TMV	Model Description	Trade-in TMV	Private TMV	Dealer TMV
4 Dr GLI Sdn	1633	2151	3013				

OPTIONS FOR JETTA
AM/FM Stereo Tape[Std on GLI 16V] +109
Air Conditioning +194
Anti-Lock Brakes +175
Automatic 3-Speed Transmission +134
Sunroof +90

PASSAT   1992

New entry-level CL trim level introduced.

Category D			
4 Dr CL Sdn	1833	2259	2967
4 Dr GL Sdn	2196	2705	3554
4 Dr GL Wgn	2259	2782	3655

OPTIONS FOR PASSAT
AM/FM Stereo Tape[Opt on CL] +79
Air Conditioning[Opt on CL] +157
Aluminum/Alloy Wheels +79
Anti-Lock Brakes +175
Automatic 4-Speed Transmission +180
Compact Disc Changer +112
Leather Seats +197
Power Sunroof +169

Don't forget to refer to the Mileage Adjustment Table at the back of this book!

Model Description	Trade-in TMV	Private TMV	Dealer TMV	Model Description	Trade-in TMV	Private TMV	Dealer TMV

VOLVO 00

VOLVO — Sweden

1997 Volvo 960

2001 VOLVO

C70   2001

Volvo has dropped the C70 Coupe light-pressure turbo (LPT), meaning only the high-pressure turbo coupe (HPT) is offered. A new five-speed automatic transmission is optional equipment. Exterior styling remains the same, but there are new 16-inch wheels for all models, with the 17-inch wheels still being optional. Simulated wood trim replaces the previous car's burled walnut wood trim. The coupe's previously standard equipment of the trip computer, auto-dimming rearview mirror, simulated wood trim, leather upholstery and sunroof are now part of the Grand Touring option package. The premium audio system is optional on the HPT coupe and standard on the HPT convertible.

Category F

Model	Trade-in	Private	Dealer
2 Dr HT Turbo Conv	32021	33326	35500
2 Dr HT Turbo Cpe	24354	25346	27000
2 Dr LT Turbo Conv	30217	31448	33500
2 Dr SE HT Turbo Cpe	25707	26754	28500

OPTIONS FOR C70
Automatic 4-Speed Transmission[Opt on HT] +677
Compact Disc Changer +812
Dolby Pro Logic Stereo[Opt on LT] +406
Heated Front Seats +159
Power Moonroof[Opt on LT Cpe] +812
Traction Control System +365
Trip Computer[Opt on LT] +169

S40   2001

Only a year after debuting them on U.S. shores, Volvo has updated the S40 and V40 for 2001. Both the sedan and wagon gain additional crash protection in the form of standard head-protection airbags, dual-stage front airbags and a new child seat-safety system. Under the hood, engine improvements have been made to increase power and lower emissions. There's also a new five-speed automatic transmission that takes the place of the previous four-speed. Other changes are found in the cabin, with new material colors, a redesigned center stack for better functionality, more durable front-seat materials and improved switchgear. Rounding out the S40 and V40's 2001 changes are restyled headlights, bumpers and fenders.

Category D

Model	Trade-in	Private	Dealer
4 Dr STD Turbo Sdn	15836	16835	18500

OPTIONS FOR S40
AM/FM Stereo/CD/Tape +328
Child Seat (1) +203
Fog Lights +118
Heated Front Seats +169
Leather Seats +609
Metallic Paint +271
Power Drivers Seat +304
Power Moonroof +745
Premium Sound System +474
Rear Spoiler +169
Traction Control System +169

S60   2001

The S60 is Volvo's new sedan that takes the place of the discontinued S70 Sedan. Smaller than the S80 but bigger than the S40, Volvo has designed the S60 to be sporty as well as safe. Like the Audi A4 or BMW 3 Series, it should appeal to drivers who are looking for a sedan that is fun to drive.

Category H

Model	Trade-in	Private	Dealer
4 Dr 2.4 Sdn	19404	20378	22000
4 Dr 2.4T Turbo Sdn	21609	22693	24500
4 Dr T5 Turbo Sdn	23153	24314	26250

OPTIONS FOR S60
AM/FM Stereo/CD/Tape[Std on T5] +328
Automatic 5-Speed Transmission +135
Compact Disc Changer +812
Heated Front Seats +159
Leather Seats +812
Metallic Paint +271
Navigation System +1691
Power Drivers Seat[Opt on 2.4] +335
Power Moonroof +812
Power Passenger Seat[Opt on 2.4T] +237
Traction Control System +372

S80   2001

Volvo has added a new trim level, the S80 T6 Executive. Additional standard content for all trim levels comes in the form of leather seating, a luggage holder, remote retractable rear head restraints, memory position

---

Don't forget to refer to the Mileage Adjustment Table at the back of this book!

VOLVO 01-00

Model Description	Trade-in TMV	Private TMV	Dealer TMV	Model Description	Trade-in TMV	Private TMV	Dealer TMV

mirrors, and Homelink. The 2.9 gets new 16-inch wheels and an auto-dimming rearview mirror as standard. All S80s get dual-stage airbags. The available Security Package for the S80 2.9 and T6 will now include the Interior Air Quality System, or IAQS, which keeps the passenger cabin free from odors and pollutants.

Category I

Model Description	Trade-in TMV	Private TMV	Dealer TMV
4 Dr 2.9 Sdn	27174	28590	30950
4 Dr T-6 Turbo Sdn	30291	31869	34500
4 Dr T-6 Executive Turbo Sdn	34023	35795	38750

OPTIONS FOR S80

Compact Disc Changer +677
Heated Front Seats +304
Metallic Paint +271
Navigation System +1691
Power Moonroof +812
Traction Control System +744

V40   2001

Only a year after debuting them on U.S. shores, Volvo has updated the S40 and V40 for 2001. Both the sedan and wagon gain additional crash protection in the form of standard head-protection airbags, dual-stage front airbags and a new child seat-safety system. Under the hood, engine improvements have been made to increase power and lower emissions. There's also a new five-speed automatic transmission that takes the place of the previous four-speed. Other changes are found in the cabin, with new material colors, a redesigned center stack for better functionality, more durable front-seat materials and improved switchgear. Rounding out the S40 and V40's 2001 changes are restyled headlights, bumpers and fenders.

Category D

Model Description	Trade-in TMV	Private TMV	Dealer TMV
4 Dr STD Turbo Wgn	16692	17745	19500

OPTIONS FOR V40

AM/FM Stereo/CD/Tape +328
Child Seat (1) +203
Fog Lights +118
Heated Front Seats +169
Leather Seats +609
Metallic Paint +271
Power Drivers Seat +304
Power Moonroof +745
Rear Spoiler +135
Traction Control System +169

V70   2001

The Volvo V70 has been redesigned for 2001. Major changes include a new body structure, fresh styling, a revised interior and upgraded feature content. Safety figures prominently with the new V70 (as usual), but it is also more sporting than before, especially in T5 trim.

Category H

Model Description	Trade-in TMV	Private TMV	Dealer TMV
4 Dr 2.4M Wgn	20948	21998	23750
4 Dr 2.4T Turbo Wgn	23594	24777	26750
4 Dr T5 Turbo Wgn	25213	26478	28586
4 Dr XC Turbo AWD Wgn	26901	28251	30500

OPTIONS FOR V70

AM/FM Stereo/CD/Tape[Std on T5] +328
Automatic 5-Speed Transmission[Std on 2.4T,XC] +677
Child Seats (2) +203
Compact Disc Changer +677
Heated Front Seats +159
Leather Seats +812
Navigation System +1691
Power Moonroof +812
Power Passenger Seat[Std on T5] +237
Premium Sound System[Std on T5] +237
Third Seat +677
Traction Control System[Opt on GLT,SE,STD] +372
Trip Computer[Opt on GLT,STD] +169

2000 VOLVO

C70   2000

Volvo introduces an HPT convertible and makes minor equipment changes to all C70s for 2000.

Category F

Model Description	Trade-in TMV	Private TMV	Dealer TMV
2 Dr HT Turbo Conv	27437	29506	31416
2 Dr HT Turbo Cpe	23172	24919	26532
2 Dr LT Turbo Conv	25693	27631	29419
2 Dr LT Turbo Cpe	22051	23713	25248

OPTIONS FOR C70

17 Inch Multi-Spoke Alloys +271
Automatic 4-Speed Transmission[Opt on HT] +660
Dolby Pro Logic Stereo[Opt on LT] +407
Full Soft Leather Seating +1083
Heated Front Seats +159
Leather Seats[Opt on LT Cpe] +727
Power Moonroof[Opt on LT Cpe] +812
Spoke Wheels +271
Traction Control System +365
Trip Computer[Opt on LT] +169

S40   2000

The S40 is Volvo's completely new entry-level sedan. Along with its wagon variant, the V40, this car rounds out Volvo's vehicle lineup. Safety, styling, and comfort are its main attributes.

Category D

Model Description	Trade-in TMV	Private TMV	Dealer TMV
4 Dr STD Turbo Sdn	14573	15965	17250

OPTIONS FOR S40

AM/FM Compact Disc Player +169
Child Seats (2) +135
Compact Disc Changer +335

Model Description	Trade-in TMV	Private TMV	Dealer TMV	Model Description	Trade-in TMV	Private TMV	Dealer TMV

Heated Front Seats +169
Leather Seats +609
Power Drivers Seat +169
Power Moonroof +745
Rear Spoiler +135
Touring Package +1015
Traction Control System +169
Trip Computer +101

S70 — 2000

Engine improvements, a new transmission, and equipment upgrades constitute the changes for the 2000 S70.

Category H

	Trade-in	Private	Dealer
4 Dr STD Sdn	17521	18886	20145
4 Dr STD Turbo AWD Sdn	21388	23054	24591
4 Dr GLT Turbo Sdn	20026	21585	23024
4 Dr GLT SE Turbo Sdn	20410	21999	23466
4 Dr SE Sdn	19254	20753	22137
4 Dr T-5 Turbo Sdn	21181	22830	24352

OPTIONS FOR S70

AM/FM Stereo/CD/Tape[Opt on GLT,STD,STD Turbo] +328
Automatic 4-Speed Transmission[Opt on T-5] +660
Automatic 5-Speed Transmission[Opt on SE,STD] +660
Dual Power Seats[Opt on GLT,STD Turbo] +440
Fog Lights +101
Heated Front Seats +159
Leather Seats +727
Power Drivers Seat[Opt on STD] +335
Power Moonroof +812
Rear Spoiler +200
Traction Control System +365
Trip Computer[Opt on GLT,STD,STD Turbo] +169

S80 — 2000

The 2.9 and T-6 models go unchanged, save a few new colors and options.

Category I

	Trade-in	Private	Dealer
4 Dr 2.9 Sdn	22937	24791	26502
4 Dr T-6 Turbo Sdn	25589	27658	29567

OPTIONS FOR S80

Compact Disc Changer +507
Dynamic Stability Control +745
Heated Front Seats +304
Leather Seats +809
Navigation System +1691
Power Moonroof +812

V40 — 2000

The S40 is Volvo's completely new entry-level sedan. Along with its wagon variant, the V40, this car rounds out Volvo's vehicle lineup. Safety, styling, and comfort are its main attributes.

Category D

	Trade-in	Private	Dealer
4 Dr STD Turbo Wgn	14995	16428	17750

OPTIONS FOR V40

AM/FM Compact Disc Player +169
Child Seats (2) +135
Compact Disc Changer +335
Heated Front Seats +169
Leather Seats +609
Power Drivers Seat +169
Power Moonroof +745
Rear Spoiler +135
Sport Plus Package +1286
Touring Package +1015
Traction Control System +169
Trip Computer +101

V70 — 2000

Engine improvements, a new transmission, and equipment upgrades constitute the changes for these 2000 Volvos. The V70 AWD and V70 T-5 have been discontinued.

Category H

	Trade-in	Private	Dealer
4 Dr STD Wgn	19014	20494	21861
4 Dr GLT Turbo Wgn	20994	22629	24138
4 Dr R Turbo AWD Wgn	25748	27752	29603
4 Dr SE Wgn	20400	21988	23454
4 Dr XC Turbo AWD Wgn	24166	26047	27784
4 Dr XC SE Turbo AWD Wgn	24547	26459	28223

OPTIONS FOR V70

AM/FM Stereo/CD/Tape[Opt on GLT,STD Turbo,XC] +328
Automatic 5-Speed Transmission[Opt on SE,STD] +660
Child Seats (2) +139
Dual Power Seats[Opt on GLT,XC] +440
Fog Lights[Opt on GLT,STD] +101
Heated Front Seats[Opt on GLT,SE,STD] +159
Leather Seats[Opt on GLT,STD,XC] +727
Power Drivers Seat[Opt on STD] +335
Power Moonroof[Std on R,XC SE] +812
Rear Spoiler[Opt on GLT,STD] +200
Traction Control System[Opt on GLT,SE,STD] +365
Trip Computer[Opt on GLT,STD] +169

1999 VOLVO

70-SERIES — 1999

Volvo's first all-wheel drive sedan debuts, vehicle options and color choices have been simplified, and S70/V70 models get new standard equipment.

Category H

	Trade-in	Private	Dealer
4 Dr STD Sdn	15878	17283	18689
4 Dr STD Turbo AWD Sdn	19403	21121	22839
4 Dr STD Turbo AWD Wgn	20244	22036	23828

Don't forget to refer to the Mileage Adjustment Table at the back of this book!

VOLVO 99-98

Model Description	Trade-in TMV	Private TMV	Dealer TMV
4 Dr STD Wgn	17355	18892	20428
4 Dr GLT Turbo Sdn	18144	19750	21356
4 Dr GLT Turbo Wgn	18734	20393	22051
4 Dr R Turbo AWD Wgn	22875	24900	26925
4 Dr T-5 Turbo Sdn	19156	20852	22548
4 Dr T-5 Turbo Wgn	20087	21865	23643
4 Dr XC Turbo AWD Wgn	20705	22538	24371

OPTIONS FOR 70-SERIES
AM/FM Stereo/CD/Tape[Std on R,T-5] +266
Aluminum/Alloy Wheels[Opt on Non Turbo] +164
Automatic 4-Speed Transmission[Std on GLT,R,XC,4WD] +535
Automatic Load Leveling[Std on R,XC] +271
Climate Control for AC[Opt on STD] +137
Dual Power Seats[Std on R,T-5] +356
Heated Front Seats[Opt on GLT,STD,T-5] +130
Leather Seats[Std on R] +590
Power Drivers Seat[Opt on STD] +271
Power Moonroof[Std on R] +658
Rear Spoiler +162
Sport Suspension[Opt on T-5] +96
Traction Control System[Std on R,XC,4WD] +296
Trip Computer[Opt on GLT,STD] +137

C70   1999
Volvo offers a light pressure turbocharged engine in the coupe to entice consumers looking for a lower-priced ticket. Both coupes and convertibles get a bit of new standard and optional equipment.
Category F

	Trade-in	Private	Dealer
2 Dr HT Turbo Cpe	20421	22031	23641
2 Dr LT Turbo Conv	23847	25728	27608
2 Dr LT Turbo Cpe	18964	20460	21955

OPTIONS FOR C70
Automatic 4-Speed Transmission[Std on LT] +535
Dolby Pro Logic Stereo[Opt on LT] +326
Heated Front Seats +130
Spoke Wheels +164
Traction Control System +296
Trip Computer[Std on HT] +137

S80   1999
This long overdue redesign of the S90 counts several firsts to its credit: first with a transverse inline six, first with fully integrated GSM phone, first to carry an environmental specification (Europe only at introduction), and the S80 boasts the world's smallest manual transmission. Whoo-hoo!
Category I

	Trade-in	Private	Dealer
4 Dr 2.9 Sdn	19111	20979	22847
4 Dr T-6 Turbo Sdn	22060	24217	26373

OPTIONS FOR S80
Compact Disc Changer +412
Heated Front Seats[Std on T-6] +247

Leather Seats +655
Navigation System +1095
Power Moonroof +658

1998 VOLVO

C70   1998
Volvo performs a slam-dunk with its first new coupe in years; the convertible is somewhat less thrilling. Modeled on the S70 chassis, the C70 shares sheetmetal with the S70 from the windshield forward, and is powered by the same set of turbocharged powerplants.
Category F

	Trade-in	Private	Dealer
2 Dr STD Turbo Cpe	18008	19879	21907
2 Dr LT Turbo Conv	21249	23458	25850

OPTIONS FOR C70
Automatic 4-Speed Transmission +461
Compact Disc Changer +213
Dolby Pro Logic Stereo +312
Heated Front Seats +114
Premium Leather Seating[Opt on LT] +628
Spoke Wheels +944
Traction Control System +210

S70   1998
Volvo's 850 sedan gets a new name, new nose, body-color trim, stronger side-impact protection, more powerful turbo engines, redesigned interior, and revised suspension. A great car has been made better.
Category H

	Trade-in	Private	Dealer
4 Dr STD Sdn	12387	13611	14936
4 Dr GLT Turbo Sdn	14686	16137	17708
4 Dr GT Sdn	12874	14145	15523
4 Dr T-5 Turbo Sdn	16207	17808	19542

OPTIONS FOR S70
AM/FM Stereo/CD/Tape[Std on T-5] +229
Aluminum/Alloy Wheels[Opt on STD] +213
Automatic 4-Speed Transmission[Std on GLT] +461
Dual Power Seats[Std on T-5] +470
Leather Seats +513
Power Drivers Seat[Opt on STD] +234
Rear Spoiler +166
Traction Control System +370

S90   1998
Absolutely nothing changes on this aged warhorse.
Category I

	Trade-in	Private	Dealer
4 Dr STD Sdn	15461	17018	18704

OPTIONS FOR S90
AM/FM Stereo/CD/Tape +229
Heated Front Seats +163
Locking Differential +141

Don't forget to refer to the Mileage Adjustment Table at the back of this book!

Model Description	Trade-in TMV	Private TMV	Dealer TMV
V70			**1998**

Volvo's 850 wagon gets a new name, new nose, body-color trim, stronger side-impact protection, more powerful turbo engines, redesigned interior and revised suspension. A great car has been made better. All-wheel drive versions arrive to battle luxury SUVs.

Category H

Model	Trade-in	Private	Dealer
4 Dr STD Turbo AWD Wgn			
	16972	18649	20465
4 Dr STD Wgn	13349	14668	16096
4 Dr GLT Turbo Wgn	15480	17009	18665
4 Dr GT Wgn	14358	15777	17313
4 Dr R Turbo AWD Wgn	20553	22583	24782
4 Dr T-5 Turbo Wgn	17663	19408	21298
4 Dr XC Turbo AWD Wgn	18825	20685	22699

OPTIONS FOR V70

AM/FM Stereo/CD/Tape[Std on T-5] +229
Aluminum/Alloy Wheels[Opt on STD] +178
Automatic 4-Speed Transmission[Std on GLT,R,XC,4WD] +461
Automatic Load Leveling[Std on R,XC,4WD] +234
Dual Power Seats[Std on R,T-5,XC] +470
Heated Front Seats[Std on R,XC,4WD] +118
Leather Seats[Std on R,XC] +518
Power Drivers Seat[Std on GLT,GT,4WD] +234
Power Moonroof[Opt on STD,XC] +567
Rear Spoiler +118
Third Seat +118
Traction Control System[Std on R,XC,4WD] +370

V90			**1998**

Absolutely nothing changes on this aged warhorse.

Category I

	Trade-in	Private	Dealer
4 Dr STD Wgn	14939	16443	18073

OPTIONS FOR V90

AM/FM Stereo/CD/Tape +229
Automatic Load Leveling +234
Heated Front Seats +163
Locking Differential +141

1997 VOLVO

850			**1997**

Looking for the Turbo? Inexplicably, Volvo tossed two decades of tradition and the Turbo nameplate out the door. The Turbo is now known as the T-5. GLT models get a new engine that makes 22 more horsepower than last year, and peak torque at a low 1,800 rpm. Base and GLT models meet Transitional Low Emission Vehicle (TLEV) regulations this year.

Category H

	Trade-in	Private	Dealer
4 Dr STD Sdn	10536	11648	13008
4 Dr STD Wgn	11587	12811	14306

	Trade-in	Private	Dealer
4 Dr GLT Turbo Sdn	11783	13027	14547
4 Dr GLT Turbo Wgn	12235	13527	15106
4 Dr R Turbo Sdn	14366	15882	17736
4 Dr R Turbo Wgn	15734	17395	19425
4 Dr T-5 Turbo Sdn	13187	14579	16281
4 Dr T-5 Turbo Wgn	13731	15180	16952

OPTIONS FOR 850

AM/FM Compact Disc Player +189
AM/FM Stereo/CD/Tape[Std on R,T-5] +137
Aluminum/Alloy Wheels[Opt on STD] +156
Automatic 4-Speed Transmission[Opt on STD] +381
Automatic Load Leveling[Std on R] +193
Dual Power Seats[Std on R,T-5] +386
Grand Touring Package +347
Heated Front Seats[Std on R] +98
Leather Seats[Std on R] +420
Power Drivers Seat[Opt on STD] +189
Power Moonroof[Opt on STD] +410
Rear Spoiler[Std on R] +150
Traction Control System[Std on R] +127
Wood Trim Package +316

960			**1997**

Automatic load leveling joins the options list for the wagon, while tailored leather seating is no longer available on the wagon.

Category I

	Trade-in	Private	Dealer
4 Dr STD Sdn	11823	13073	14601
4 Dr STD Wgn	12719	14063	15707

OPTIONS FOR 960

AM/FM Stereo/CD/Tape +189
Automatic Load Leveling +193
Locking Differential +98

S90			**1997**

Midyear, Volvo went and switched names for the 960. The sedan is now known as S90, while the wagon is now the V90.

Category I

	Trade-in	Private	Dealer
4 Dr STD Sdn	14153	15649	17478

OPTIONS FOR S90

AM/FM Stereo/CD/Tape +189
Locking Differential +98

V90			**1997**

Midyear, Volvo went and switched names for the 960. The sedan is now known as S90, while the wagon is now the V90.

Category I

	Trade-in	Private	Dealer
4 Dr STD Wgn	12810	14165	15820

OPTIONS FOR V90

AM/FM Stereo/CD/Tape +189
Automatic Load Leveling +193
Locking Differential +117

Model Description	Trade-in TMV	Private TMV	Dealer TMV	Model Description	Trade-in TMV	Private TMV	Dealer TMV

1996 VOLVO

850 — 1996

This year all Volvo 850s are equipped with front seat side-impact airbags, optional traction control (TRACS), and a life insurance policy that pays $250,000 to the estate of any occupant who loses their life in the 850 as the result of an accident.

Category H

	Trade-in	Private	Dealer
4 Dr STD Sdn	9599	10648	12098
4 Dr STD Turbo Sdn	11940	13246	15049
4 Dr STD Turbo Wgn	12365	13718	15585
4 Dr STD Wgn	9880	10961	12453
4 Dr GLT Sdn	10239	11359	12905
4 Dr GLT Wgn	10602	11761	13362
4 Dr Platinum Ltd. Ed. Turbo Sdn	12902	14313	16261
4 Dr Platinum Ltd. Ed. Turbo Wgn	13742	15245	17320
4 Dr R Turbo Sdn	13487	14962	16999
4 Dr R Turbo Wgn	14107	15650	17780

OPTIONS FOR 850
AM/FM Compact Disc Player[Opt on GLT,STD] +191
AM/FM Stereo/CD/Tape +138
Aluminum/Alloy Wheels[Opt on STD Sdn,STD Wgn] +158
Automatic 4-Speed Transmission[Opt on GLT,Non-Turbo] +384
Automatic Load Leveling[Opt on GLT,STD] +195
Compact Disc Changer +177
Dual Power Seats[Std on R] +317
Grand Touring Package +351
Leather Seats[Opt on GLT,STD] +424
Power Drivers Seat[Opt on STD Sdn,STD Wgn] +195
Power Passenger Seat[Opt on GLT,STD] +195
Third Seat +120
Traction Control System[Opt on GLT,STD] +118

960 — 1996

This year all Volvo 960s are equipped with front seat side-impact airbags, a multi-step power door locking system that increases driver safety when entering the vehicle in parking lots, and a life insurance policy that pays $250,000 to the estate of any occupant who loses their life in the 960 as a result of a car accident.

Category I

	Trade-in	Private	Dealer
4 Dr STD Sdn	10252	11446	13095
4 Dr STD Wgn	10901	12170	13923

OPTIONS FOR 960
AM/FM Compact Disc Player +191
Heated Front Seats +156
Third Seat +120

1995 VOLVO

850 — 1995

Side airbags are standard on all 850 Turbos this year; optional on other 850s. All models get Turbo's rounded front styling.

Category H

	Trade-in	Private	Dealer
4 Dr STD Sdn	7041	7841	9175
4 Dr STD Turbo Sdn	9292	10348	12108
4 Dr STD Turbo Wgn	9615	10708	12529
4 Dr STD Wgn	7516	8370	9794
4 Dr GLT Sdn	7785	8670	10144
4 Dr GLT Wgn	9042	10069	11782
4 Dr T-5R Turbo Sdn	10367	11545	13509
4 Dr T-5R Turbo Wgn	10839	12070	14123

OPTIONS FOR 850
AM/FM Stereo/CD/Tape +120
Aluminum/Alloy Wheels[Std on GLT,T-5R,Turbo] +137
Automatic 4-Speed Transmission[Std on T-5R,Turbo] +334
Compact Disc Changer +153
Grand Luxury Package +304
Grand Touring Package +304
Leather Seats[Std on T-5R,STD Turbo Sdn] +368
Power Drivers Seat[Std on GLT,T-5R,Turbo] +166
Power Passenger Seat[Opt on STD,GLT Wgn] +169
Rear Spoiler[Std on T-5R] +131
Side Air Bag Restraints +103

940 — 1995

Daytime running lights debut. Level I and Level II trim is dropped in favor of less confusing base and Turbo designations.

Category I

	Trade-in	Private	Dealer
4 Dr STD Sdn	7089	7916	9294
4 Dr STD Turbo Sdn	7555	8436	9904
4 Dr STD Turbo Wgn	8110	9056	10632
4 Dr STD Wgn	7754	8658	10165

OPTIONS FOR 940
Aluminum/Alloy Wheels +109
Heated Front Seats +103
Leather Seats +85
Power Drivers Seat +153
Power Moonroof +308

960 — 1995

Substantially revised with new sheetmetal and detuned powertrain. Horsepower is down to 181 from 201, thanks to emissions standards. Daytime running lights are added. The dashboard is softened with more curves and contours. Suspensions are revised, and larger tires are standard. Other new standard equipment includes remote locking, an alarm system, headlight

VOLVO 95-93

wipers and washers, and wood interior trim.

Category I

Model Description	Trade-in TMV	Private TMV	Dealer TMV
4 Dr STD Sdn	7485	8358	9813
4 Dr STD Wgn	7806	8716	10233

OPTIONS FOR 960
Compact Disc Changer +222
Leather Seats +85
Third Seat +104

1994 VOLVO

850 — 1994

Turbo model debuts with 222-horsepower 2.3-liter five-cylinder engine, and a wagon body style is introduced with standard integrated child seat. Turbo is available in either sedan or wagon format. Warranty is upped to 4 years/50,000 miles.

Category H

Model Description	Trade-in TMV	Private TMV	Dealer TMV
4 Dr STD Turbo Sdn	7147	8053	9564
4 Dr STD Turbo Wgn	7402	8341	9905
4 Dr GLT Sdn	5692	6414	7617
4 Dr GLTS Sdn	6304	7104	8436
4 Dr GLTS Wgn	6561	7392	8779

OPTIONS FOR 850
Aluminum/Alloy Wheels[Std on GLTS,Wgn] +112
Automatic 4-Speed Transmission[Opt on GLT,GLTS,Sdn] +273
Automatic Load Leveling +138
Climate Control for AC[Opt on GLTS] +84
Leather Seats[Opt on GLT,GLTS,Sdn] +301
Power Drivers Seat[Std on GLTS,Wgn] +136
Power Passenger Seat +138
Rear Spoiler +108
Spoke Wheels +98

940 — 1994

940 gets passenger airbag. Level I 940s have 114-horsepower 2.3-liter engine; equip a 940 with Level II trim and you get a turbocharged version of this engine.

Category I

Model Description	Trade-in TMV	Private TMV	Dealer TMV
4 Dr STD Sdn	5706	6439	7662
4 Dr STD Turbo Sdn	6344	7160	8519
4 Dr STD Turbo Wgn	6780	7651	9104
4 Dr STD Wgn	5974	6742	8022

OPTIONS FOR 940
Aluminum/Alloy Wheels +90
Compact Disc Changer +182
Heated Front Seats +84
Power Drivers Seat[Std on Turbo] +126
Power Passenger Seat +112
Power Sunroof[Std on Turbo] +224

960 — 1994

Base 960 is heavily decontented, and is available only in sedan format. Level II 960 adds leather, moonroof and other nice stuff.

Category I

Model Description	Trade-in TMV	Private TMV	Dealer TMV
4 Dr STD Sdn	5904	6663	7928
4 Dr Level II Sdn	6808	7683	9142
4 Dr Level II Wgn	7009	7910	9412

OPTIONS FOR 960
AM/FM Stereo/CD/Tape +136
Aluminum/Alloy Wheels +90
Compact Disc Changer +182
Power Passenger Seat[Std on Wgn] +112
Power Sunroof[Opt on STD] +224
Premium Sound System +154
Third Seat +85

1993 VOLVO

240 — 1993

GL model dropped, again. Metallic paint doesn't cost extra this year, air conditioning gets CFC-free refrigerant, and plush floormats are standard.

Category D

Model Description	Trade-in TMV	Private TMV	Dealer TMV
4 Dr STD Sdn	3873	4555	5691
4 Dr STD Wgn	4136	4864	6077

OPTIONS FOR 240
Automatic 4-Speed Transmission +185
Leather Seats +173

850 — 1993

740 replacement arrives with 168-horsepower inline five-cylinder engine. Dual airbags and ABS are standard. Automatic transmission has Economy and Sport shift modes, as well as a winter second-gear start feature. Car meets 1997 side-impact standards, traction control is optional, and sedans have standard integrated child safety seats. Wagon not available.

Category H

Model Description	Trade-in TMV	Private TMV	Dealer TMV
4 Dr GLT Sdn	4677	5348	6467
4 Dr GLTS Sdn	5254	6008	7265

OPTIONS FOR 850
Automatic 4-Speed Transmission +225
Dual Power Seats +186
Leather Seats[Opt on GLT] +249

940 — 1993

Wagons have integrated child seats. All stereos have anti-theft feature, and air conditioning is free of CFCs. Wagons have an extra four gallons of fuel capacity and a revised rear seat. 940 GL dropped, but a base sedan and wagon continue.

Category I

Model Description	Trade-in TMV	Private TMV	Dealer TMV
4 Dr STD Sdn	4621	5285	6391
4 Dr STD Turbo Sdn	5486	6274	7587

Don't forget to refer to the Mileage Adjustment Table at the back of this book!

EDMUNDS® USED CARS & TRUCKS · www.edmunds.com · 551

VOLVO 93-92

Model Description	Trade-in TMV	Private TMV	Dealer TMV
4 Dr STD Turbo Wgn	5975	6834	8264
4 Dr STD Wgn	5068	5796	7009
4 Dr S Sdn	5196	5942	7186
4 Dr S Wgn	5317	6081	7354

OPTIONS FOR 940
Air Bag Restraint +116
Power Passenger Seat +93

960 — 1993

960 gets passenger airbag. Wagons have integrated child seats. All stereos have anti-theft feature, and air conditioning is free of CFCs. Wagons have an extra four gallons of fuel capacity and a revised rear seat.

Category I

	Trade-in	Private	Dealer
4 Dr STD Sdn	5550	6347	7676
4 Dr STD Wgn	5703	6523	7888

1992 VOLVO

240 — 1992

ABS is newly standard. GL model returns as top-of-the-line, and adds a sunroof and heated mirrors, among other items, over the base car. GL grille is chrome rather than matte black.

Category D

	Trade-in	Private	Dealer
4 Dr STD Sdn	3173	3782	4797
4 Dr STD Wgn	3234	3854	4888
4 Dr GL Sdn	3278	3907	4955

OPTIONS FOR 240
Anti-Lock Brakes[Std on Wgn] +160
Automatic 4-Speed Transmission +150
Leather Seats +141

740 — 1992

ABS is standard across the board. A locking differential is newly standard. Turbo sedan and 780 coupe have been dropped. Turbo wagon continues.

Category H

	Trade-in	Private	Dealer
4 Dr STD Sdn	3752	4357	5366
4 Dr STD Turbo Wgn	4370	5075	6250
4 Dr STD Wgn	3872	4496	5537
4 Dr GL Wgn	4055	4709	5799

OPTIONS FOR 740
Leather Seats +178

940 — 1992

940 GLE, and its twin-cam engine, is discontinued for 1992.

Category I

	Trade-in	Private	Dealer
4 Dr STD Turbo Sdn	3598	4158	5092
4 Dr STD Turbo Wgn	3890	4495	5505
4 Dr GL Sdn	3119	3605	4414

OPTIONS FOR 940
Power Drivers Seat +84
Power Passenger Seat +75

960 — 1992

960 model replaces 940 SE in lineup; is powered by 2.9-liter twin-cam inline-six good for 201 horsepower.

Category I

	Trade-in	Private	Dealer
4 Dr STD Sdn	4384	5066	6204
4 Dr STD Wgn	4734	5471	6700

Notes

Notes

Notes

Notes

BUYER'S DECISION GUIDES
SCHEDULED RELEASE DATES
FOR 2001/2002*

VOL. 35/36/37		RELEASE DATE	COVER DATE
C3504	NEW CARS & TRUCKS: Prices & Reviews [American & Import]		
		DEC 01	WINTER/SPRING 02
C3601	NEW CARS & TRUCKS: Prices & Reviews [American & Import]		
		MAY 02	SUMMER/FALL 02
U3602	USED CARS & TRUCKS: Prices	JUL 02	FALL/WINTER 02
C3602	NEW CARS & TRUCKS: Prices & Reviews [American & Import]		
		DEC 02	WINTER/SPRING 03
U3701	USED CARS & TRUCKS: Prices	JAN 03	SPRING/SUMMER 03

*Subject to Change

edmunds.com℠ — SINGLE COPIES / ORDER FORM

Please send me:

☐ **USED CARS & TRUCKS: PRICES** *(includes S&H)* **$14.99**

☐ **NEW CARS & TRUCKS**
    — American & Import *(includes S&H)* **$14.99**

Name _____

Email _____

Address _____

City, State, Zip _____

Phone _____

PAYMENT: ___ MASTERCARD ___ VISA ___ CHECK or MONEY ORDER $ _____

Make check or money order payable to:

Edmunds.com, Inc. *P.O.Box 338, Shrub Oaks, NY 10588*

For more information or to order by phone, call **(914) 962-6297**

Credit Card # _____ Exp. Date: _____

Cardholder Name: _____

Signature _____

Prices above include shipping within the U.S. and Canada only. Other countries, please add $7.00 to the price ($14.99+7.00) per book (via air mail) and $2.00 to the price ($14.99+2.00) per book (surface mail). Please pay through an American Bank or with American Currency. Rates subject to change without notice.

edmunds.com℠ SUBSCRIPTIONS / ORDER FORM

BUYER'S PRICE GUIDES

Please send me a one year subscription for:

☐ **USED CARS & TRUCKS: PRICES**
AMERICAN & IMPORT (package price includes $10.00 S&H) **$18.40**
Canada $21.40/Foreign Countries $25.40 (includes air mail S&H)
2 issues/yr

☐ **NEW CARS & TRUCKS**
AMERICAN & IMPORT (package price includes $10.00 S&H) **$18.40**
Canada $21.40/Foreign Countries $25.40 (includes air mail S&H)
2 issues/yr

Name _____

Email _____

Address _____

City, State, Zip _____

Phone _____

PAYMENT: __ MC __ VISA __ Check or Money Order-Amount $_____ Rates subject to change without notice

Make check or money order payable to:
Edmunds.com, Inc. P.O.Box 338, Shrub Oaks, NY 10588
*For more information or to order by phone, call **(914) 962-6297***

Credit Card # _____ Exp. Date: _____

Cardholder Name: _____

Signature _____

MILEAGE TABLE

Top Two Rows: Average Mileage Range
Bottom Row: Cents per mile to add/subtract if mileage is outside of range

Category	01	00	99	98	97	96	95	94	93	92
A,B,G	8,800-12,000 +/- 7 cents	22,000-26,000 +/- 7 cents	34,900-40,000 +/- 6 cents	47,200-54,000 +/- 6 cents	59,200-67,700 +/- 5 cents	70,400-80,400 +/- 5 cents	80,900-91,900 +/- 4 cents	90,700-102,600 +/- 4 cents	99,500-112,300 +/- 3 cents	107,400-121,200 +/- 3 cents
C,D,E	8,500-11,700 +/- 7 cents	21,500-25,600 +/- 7 cents	34,100-39,300 +/- 6 cents	46,000-52,800 +/- 6 cents	57,600-65,900 +/- 6 cents	68,700-78,100 +/- 5 cents	79,300-89,600 +/- 5 cents	89,000-100,300 +/- 4 cents	97,600-110,200 +/- 3 cents	105,700-119,300 +/- 3 cents
F	5,500-7,500 +/- 9 cents	14,500-17,000 +/- 9 cents	23,500-27,000 +/- 9 cents	32,500-37,000 +/- 8 cents	41,500-47,000 +/- 7 cents	50,500-57,000 +/- 6 cents	59,500-67,000 +/- 6 cents	68,000-76,500 +/- 5 cents	76,000-85,500 +/- 5 cents	83,500-94,000 +/- 4 cents
H	7,500-10,400 +/- 8 cents	19,600-23,000 +/- 8 cents	31,100-35,200 +/- 7 cents	42,200-47,200 +/- 7 cents	54,200-60,400 +/- 6 cents	66,700-74,200 +/- 6 cents	78,300-87,000 +/- 5 cents	89,900-100,200 +/- 4 cents	100,800-112,400 +/- 4 cents	109,400-121,500 +/- 3 cents
I	6,700-9,100 +/- 10 cents	18,200-21,100 +/- 9 cents	30,000-33,700 +/- 9 cents	41,500-45,900 +/- 8 cents	53,000-58,200 +/- 7 cents	64,000-69,800 +/- 7 cents	74,500-81,000 +/- 6 cents	85,200-92,600 +/- 6 cents	96,100-104,600 +/- 5 cents	106,500-115,800 +/- 5 cents
J,L,O,P	8,100-11,300 +/- 8 cents	20,500-24,700 +/- 8 cents	32,700-38,500 +/- 7 cents	44,800-52,400 +/- 7 cents	56,600-65,600 +/- 6 cents	67,700-78,200 +/- 6 cents	78,000-89,600 +/- 5 cents	87,700-100,000 +/- 5 cents	96,700-109,800 +/- 4 cents	105,300-118,900 +/- 4 cents
K,TM,N,Q	8,500-11,900 +/- 7 cents	21,400-25,800 +/- 7 cents	34,100-40,200 +/- 7 cents	46,700-54,600 +/- 6 cents	59,000-68,500 +/- 6 cents	70,600-81,700 +/- 5 cents	81,500-93,700 +/- 5 cents	91,700-104,600 +/- 4 cents	100,700-114,800 +/- 4 cents	109,000-123,900 +/- 3 cents
R	3,400-4,800 +/- 13 cents	8,000-9,400 +/- 12 cents	12,500-14,100 +/- 11 cents	17,500-19,400 +/- 10 cents	22,500-24,800 +/- 10 cents	27,500-30,200 +/- 9 cents	32,500-35,700 +/- 8 cents	37,400-41,100 +/- 8 cents	42,100-46,300 +/- 8 cents	46,700-51,400 +/- 7 cents

* Mileage adjustment is not to exceed 50% of vehicle's adjusted trade-in value!

edmunds.com